Counseling and Psychotherapy Theories in Context and Practice

THIRD EDITION

Counseling and Psychotherapy Theories in Context and Practice
Skills, Strategies, and Techniques

John Sommers-Flanagan
Rita Sommers-Flanagan

WILEY

Library of Congress Cataloging-in-Publication Data

Names: Sommers-Flanagan, John, 1957- author. | Sommers-Flanagan, Rita, 1953-
author.
Title: Counseling and psychotherapy theories in context and practice : skills, strategies, and techniques /
by John Sommers-Flanagan and Rita Sommers-Flanagan.
Description: Third edition. | Hoboken, New Jersey : John Wiley and Sons, Inc., 2018. | Includes bibliographical
references and index. |
Identifiers: LCCN 2017057071 (print) | LCCN 2017059381 (ebook) |
ISBN 9781119279143 (pdf) | ISBN 9781119279136 (enhanced ePub) |
ISBN 9781119473305 (loose-leaf)
Subjects: LCSH: Counseling psychology. | Counseling. | Psychotherapy.
Classification: LCC BF636.6 (ebook) | LCC BF636.6 .S658 2018 (print) |
DDC 158.3—dc23
LC record available at https://lccn.loc.gov/2017057071

Cover image: ©Mike Powell/Getty Images
Cover design by Wiley

Set in 10/12 pt Janson Text LT Std by Aptara, Noida

Printed in the United States of America

SKY10031196_110321

Brief Contents

Contents

Preface

In 2003, around the time when Jack Johnson released his second studio album, titled, *On and On*, we published the first edition of *Counseling and Psychotherapy Theories in Context and Practice*. Fifteen years later, time has continued rolling on and on ... and now we're entering the Third Edition of this theories text.

Since 2003, some things have changed and some have stayed the same. To keep pace with the changes, we've added well over 250 new citations and resources. To stick with (and respect) the past, we're still citing original sources from way back in the late 1800s and early 1900s. We think the best therapists keep one foot in the past, while embracing the future.

The older theories in this text are like fine wines; for the most part, they've aged well. Why? They've aged well because they started with strong foundations and adapted, changed, and incorporated new knowledge and skills along the way. Every chapter in this text combines the old and the new in ways that will enable you to help people change more quickly, overcome their personal problems, and face the turbulent times of the early twenty-first century.

Our biggest goal is to help you build your foundation for becoming a competent professional helper. In our wildest dreams, we hope to inform and inspire you to apply the theories in ways that will allow you to practice, on and on, into the future with wisdom, compassion, and professional integrity.

WHAT'S NEW IN THE THIRD EDITION?

Over the past several years, we gathered feedback to improve this textbook. We received written commentary from over 50 psychology and counselor education faculty, as well as several practicing clinicians. The feedback was positive, but many excellent ideas about how to improve the text were also provided. When possible and practical, we integrated this feedback into the Third Edition. The result: a theories textbook that's better than ever.

Here's a summary of what's new in the Third Edition.

The textbook is more tightly organized. Every chapter leads with refined learner objectives. To help readers immediately grasp the theories, key terms are defined very early in each chapter.

Based on reviewer passion for diversity and spirituality, new sections and content are integrated into all of the 12 major theory chapters. Each chapter now includes sections titled (a) cultural sensitivity, (b) gender and sexuality, and (c) spirituality.

Neuroscience is also a new feature. Although the text continues to focus on nonmedical approaches to counseling and psychotherapy, information on the brain is included throughout, via a feature called the "Brain Box."

New content is distributed throughout the text. Examples include:

- Multicultural humility (Chapters 1 and 13)
- Adlerian play therapy (Chapter 3)
- Motivational interviewing (expanded coverage in Chapter 5)
- Schedules of reinforcement (Chapter 7)
- Shame attacking exercises (Chapter 8)
- Relational cultural therapy (expanded coverage in Chapter 10)
- Intersectionality (Chapters 10 and 13)
- Narrative exposure therapy (Chapter 11)
- Multidimensional family therapy (Chapter 12)
- Multicultural and social justice counseling competencies (Chapter 13)
- Assimilative integration (Chapter 14)
- Mindfulness-based cognitive therapy (Chapter 14)

As noted previously, there are over 250 new, cutting edge citations. These citations address a wide range of issues, including the latest reviews and meta-analyses on the evidence-based status of specific counseling and psychotherapy approaches.

The end of every chapter includes a list of key terms. These key terms are in boldface when initially introduced and defined in the text.

WORDS TO THE WISE

As before, we've used cross-disciplinary terminology and resources when writing about counseling and psychotherapy. What this means is that we relied on citations from across the psychology, counseling, and social work literature. Our focus was on the "best fit" for chapter content and not on emphasizing specific discipline-oriented resources. In keeping with this emphasis, we alternatively refer to counselors, psychotherapists, and therapists throughout the text.

Each theories chapter includes a sample informed consent. These informed consents are not comprehensive; they don't include traditional informed consent content such as potential therapy risks or emergency contact instructions. The samples are written in ways to give a flavor to how practitioners from different theoretical orientations could use theory to personalize an informed consent.

To bring the theories to life, this text includes many specific case examples and extended case material. Across all case examples, client confidentiality has been maintained. Sometimes pseudonyms are used; other times identifying information was changed.

ORGANIZATIONAL FEATURES

This textbook has a foundational introductory chapter, followed by 12 chapters focusing on specific counseling and psychotherapy theories, and a final chapter on psychotherapy and counseling integration. All of the theories chapters follow the same organizational structure:

- *Learner Objectives*: Readers can see the roadmap for their learning at the beginning of their journey.

- *Introduction*: Including a definition of key terms and, when appropriate, a short biographical profile of the person(s) who developed the theory.

- *Historical Context*: Every theory has cultural and historical context. In some cases, when needed, an additional history section may be included, for example, Evolution and Development in Psychoanalytic Theory and Practice.

- *Theoretical Principles*: Core theoretical principles are described and explained. As much as possible, concrete and real-life examples are included to help bring abstract theoretical principles to life.

- *The Practice of ...*: This section describes the distinct assessment and therapy approaches associated with each theory and ends with two case vignettes to help readers apply the material.

- *Case Presentation*: For every theory there's an extended case presentation that includes (a) a problem (or goal) list, (b) problem (or case) formulation, (c) specific interventions, and (d) outcomes assessment.

- *Evaluations and Applications*: This section provides a review of the evidence-based status of each theory-based approach. In addition, an analysis of how well the approach addresses issues related to culture, gender, sexuality, and spirituality is included.

- *Concluding Comments*: Final quotations and commentary are included.

- *Chapter Summary and Review*: A detailed chapter summary and list of key terms are provided.

Additional learning features include *Reflections* boxes to help readers pause and engage in focused reflection. In addition, every chapter includes *Putting It in Practice* boxes. These boxes range from practitioner commentaries to sample informed consents, to specific practice activities. These boxes establish connections between dense or abstract theoretical material and concrete clinical practice.

ACCESS TO ENHANCED FEATURES

This edition comes with access to additional features via the enhanced ebook version, which contains dynamic content to further enrich your understanding of the text. This can be accessed by purchasing the enhanced ebook edition via www.wiley.com or www.vitalsource.com. This interactive e-text features the following interactivities:

Videos

This edition features 15 videos of different therapy approaches in action. These approaches include:

Psychoanalytic

Adlerian

Existential

Gestalt

Person-Centered

Motivational Interviewing

Behavioral

Cognitive Behavioral

Reality Therapy

Feminist

Solution-Focused

Family Systems

Whether you're watching these videos within the context of a Counseling and Psychotherapy course or on your own, you may use the videos in any of several different ways. How you choose to use them will depend on your own individual teaching and learning needs. Here are a few ideas:

> You can watch the clip in its entirety and just focus on absorbing what you see as an example of a particular therapy prototype.

> You can watch the chapter in segments, as each video includes an introduction to the specific approach, followed by a video clip of the therapy session, followed by a brief discussion, followed by a final clip from the therapy session.

> You can also watch these videos or segments with a critical eye. Because the therapy sessions are spontaneous and nonscripted, you may notice points during which the therapist struggles (as John does while trying to illustrate the psychoanalytic approach during a 20 minute clip). These struggles may involve the challenges of adhering to a single theoretical model or, quite simply, the struggle of what to say at any given point in a therapy session. In fact, as we've watched these videos ourselves (and with students), some of our best learning has come when our students (a) notice a missed therapeutic opportunity, (b) notice a theoretical inconsistency, or (c) spontaneously begin discussing how they might have behaved differently (and more effectively!) had they been the therapist in the video.

No matter how you use the videos, we strongly recommend that you be sure to press the pause button (at least occasionally). We recommend this even if you're watching videos in their entirety. This is because, as with all therapy sessions, the interactions are rich and nuanced and therefore deserve thought, reflection, and, whenever possible, a lively discussion (you can even do the discussion with yourself if you're feeling in a Gestalt sort of mood). We hope you learn and enjoy the videos and that you find them helpful in your growth and development as a professional counselor or psychotherapist.

Practice Questions

At the end of each chapter, you will have the option to test your understanding of key concepts by going through the set of practice questions supplied. Each of these are tied back to the Learner Objectives listed at the start of each chapter.

In conclusion, although we're happy with the videos that accompany this textbook, all theory demonstration videos are imperfect. Therefore, we encourage you to not only view our videos but to also view others, and then use whatever fits your teaching style and purpose. To help us to keep improving our video demonstrations, please feel free to email John at john.sf@mso.umt.edu to share your perspective and offer compliments or constructive feedback.

BEYOND THIS TEXTBOOK

This textbook has additional resources available for students and faculty, which can be accessed using the book's product page at www.wiley.com. These include:

A *Student Manual and Study Guide* for students. Including content linked to each chapter, this supplementary resource provides students with more of what they need to learn and master the theories of counseling and psychotherapy. The *Student Manual and Study Guide* offers:

- A **theories beliefs pre- and post-test** in each chapter.

- An **opening professional development essay** written by a student, practitioner, or faculty member who is active within the counseling or psychology professions.

- A **theory review** section that includes a **glossary of key terms, theories crossword puzzle,** and **critical reflections** on each theory.

- A section on **practice activities** designed to help students experience and practice implementation of each theory.

- A section for each chapter titled **Testing Yourself** that includes a **25-item multiple choice practice test** and a comprehensive **short-answer question review**; these materials will help students succeed on even the most difficult examinations.

- **A closing essay** by another student or practitioner who has applied theory-based knowledge in a practice setting.

A revised online *Instructor's Resource Manual* that includes the following teaching aids is also available:

- Sample course syllabi.

- Supplementary lecture outlines and ideas.

- A test bank with 50 multiple choice questions for each chapter.

- Generic PowerPoint slides that can be downloaded and adapted for instructor needs.

ACKNOWLEDGMENTS

Like raising children, writing textbooks requires a small village of support people if you ever hope to get a well-developed child (or book) out of your house. We have many people to thank and will undoubtedly miss a few and then need several years of therapy to get over our guilt. Oh well. We've never let the fear of additional therapy scare us out of trying to do the right thing ... which in this case means thanking as many people as we can think of to thank.

Bunched in a small group at the first of the thank-you line is the Wiley team. In particular, we thank Tisha Rossi, Jenny Ng, Monica Rogers, Leah Michael, Christina Verigan, Veronica Visenti, and Audrey Koh. All of our Wiley support people deserve gold stars for walking us through the publishing process and assisting with last-minute details. Thank you again and again. Thanks also to Joey Moore for his help with key terms and a final editing review.

This next list includes individuals who have contributed to chapters either through helpful reviews or via contribution of written material. These honorees are listed alphabetically by first name.

Alan Tjeltveit, Muhlenberg University

Alyssa Swan, Eastern Illinois University

Amanda Minor, Salve Regina University

Amy Barth, University of Wisconsin—Whitewater

Ana Herrera, Wake Forest University

Angela Touchton, Lindsey Wilson College

Ann McCaughan, University of Illinois—Springfield

Ariel Winston, South University

Bearlyn Ash, Governors State University

Becca Morra, Xavier University

Benjamin Willis, Scranton University

Brenda O'Beirne, University of Wisconsin—Whitewater

Carleton Brown, University of Texas at El Paso

Chad Luke, Tennessee Tech University

Curt Tweedy, Missoula Youth Homes

Cyndi Matthews, University of Louisiana at Monroe

Dana Griffin, Independent Practice

Daniel McManus, Kent State University

Daniel Williamson, University of Mary Hardin-Baylor

David Jones, Cincinnati Christian University

David Julius Ford, James Madison University

David Pfaff, University of Central Oklahoma

Dawn Hudak, Pace University

Diane Shea, Holy Family University

Emily Petkus, Shenandoah University

Everett Painter, University of Tennessee—Knoxville

G. Collerone, National Institute of Education

Isabelle Ong, Wake Forest University

Jane Webber, Kean University

Jennifer Williamson, University of Mary Hardin-Baylor

Joan Vanderschaaf, National Louis University

Joanne Jodry, Monmouth University

JoAnne Sanders, Heidelberg University

Jon Carlson, Adler University

Judith Beck, Beck Institute for Cognitive Therapy and Research

Justin Lauka, Adler University

Jyoti Nanda, Regent's College, United Kingdom

K. Michelle Hunnicutt Hollenbaugh, Texas A&M University, Corpus Christi

Katerine Wix, Governor's State University

Kathleen McClesky, Longwood University

Kirk Schneider, Saybrook Graduate School

Kristen Langellier, Idaho State University

Kurt Kraus, Shippensburg University

Laura M. Schmuldt, Lindsey Wilson College

Lauren Ostrowski, Independent Practice

Leslie Greenberg, York University

Mary Mayorga, Texas A&M University—San Antonio

Megan Caldwell, Walden University

Michelle Johnson, Walden University

Michelle Santiago, Morarian Theological Seminary

Natalie Rogers, California Institute of Integral Studies

Nick Heck, University of Montana

Nicki Nance, Webster University

Olwen Anderson, Independent Practice

Patricia Robey, Governors State University

Quentin Hunter, University of Louisville

Rebecca Milner, East Tennessee State University

Reginald W. Holt, Central Connecticut State University

Reka Farago, University of Northern Colorado

Richard E. Watts, Sam Houston State University

Robert J. Zeglin, University of North Florida

Robert Wubbolding, International Center for Reality Therapy

Rochelle Cade, University of Mary Hardin-Baylor

Sally L. Kuhlenschmidt, Western Kentucky University

Sarah Campbell, Capella University

Susan Henderson, Sam Houston State University

Susan Schwendener, Northeastern Illinois University

Tamara Tribitt, University of Redlands

Thomas Burdenski, Tarleton State University

Tracey Duncan, New Jersey City University

Troyann I. Gentile, Lindsey Wilson College

Veronica I. Johnson, University of Montana

Finally, since authors typically thank their lovely spouses for support and patience, we'd like to finish by thanking each other for being the super-glue that helps everything stick together.

John Sommers-Flanagan
Rita Sommers-Flanagan
Absarokee and Missoula, Montana

About the Authors

John Sommers-Flanagan, PhD, is a clinical psychologist and professor of counselor education at the University of Montana. He is co-host of the "Practically Perfect Parenting Podcast" and is author or coauthor of over 50 professional publications. John is a long-time member of both the American Counseling Association and the American Psychological Association; he regularly presents professional workshops at the annual conferences of both these organizations. John has an active blog at https://johnsommersflanagan.com/.

Rita Sommers-Flanagan, PhD, is professor emeritus of counselor education at the University of Montana, where she taught for 24 years. Among her favorite teaching and research areas are ethics and women's issues. While at UM, she also served as the director of Women's Studies and acting director of the Practical Ethics Center. She is the co-author of quite a few professional articles, book chapters, and books. Probably over 40, maybe even 50, but who's counting? She also publishes essays, poems, and other creative writing endeavors. As a clinical psychologist, she has worked with youth, families, couples, and women for many years.

John and Rita work together and separately training professionals in counseling and psychotherapy, ethics, suicide assessment, and parenting. They have produced and are producing many different professional training videos with Alexander Street Press, Psychotherapy.net, and Microtraining Associates. John and Rita enjoy providing professional workshops, seminars, and professional presentations nationally and internationally.

Together, John and Rita have coauthored nine books, including:

- *How to Listen so Parents Will Talk and Talk so Parents Will Listen* (2011, Wiley)

- *Tough Kids, Cool Counseling* (2nd ed., 2007, American Counseling Association)

- *Clinical Interviewing* (6th ed., 2017, Wiley)

- *Becoming an Ethical Helping Professional* (2007, Wiley)

John and Rita have two daughters, one son-in-law, three grandchildren, and can hardly believe their good fortune. They are deeply rooted in Montana, and in the summers, alternate writing with irrigating and haying on the family ranch. Both John and Rita enjoy exercising, gardening, exploring alternative energy technologies, and restoring old log cabins, old sheds, and any other old thing that crosses their path—which, given the passage of time, is now starting to include each other.

Psychotherapy and Counseling Essentials
An Introduction

LEARNER OBJECTIVES

- Identify key reasons for studying counseling and psychotherapy theories
- Place the development of counseling and psychotherapy in historical context
- Define counseling and psychotherapy
- Review and describe scientific achievements leading to evidence-based psychotherapy and counseling procedures
- List and articulate essential ethical issues within the mental health and helping professions
- Describe the historical context, complexities, and potential of neuroscience for counseling and psychotherapy research and practice
- Discuss issues pertaining to the emergence of your personal theory of counseling and psychotherapy
- Describe the authors' personal and professional biases
- Summarize core content and key terms associated with psychotherapy and counseling essentials

WHY LEARN THEORIES?

About a decade ago, we were flying back from a professional conference when a professor (we'll call him Darrell) from a large Midwestern university spotted an empty seat next to us. He sat down, and initiated the sort of conversation that probably only happens among university professors.

"I think theories are passé. There has to be a better way to teach students how to actually do counseling and psychotherapy."

When confronted like this, I (John) like to pretend I'm Carl Rogers (see Chapter 5), so I paraphrased, "You're thinking there's a better way."

"Yes!" he said. "All the textbooks start with Freud and crawl their way to the present. We waste time reviewing outdated theories that were developed by old white men. What's the point?"

"The old theories seem pointless to you." John felt congruent with his inner Rogers.

"Worse than pointless." He glared. "They're destructive! We live in a diverse culture. I'm a white heterosexual male and they don't even fit for me. We need to teach our students the technical skills to implement empirically supported treatments. That's what our clients want and that's what they deserve. For the next edition of your theories

text, you should put traditional theories of counseling and psychotherapy in the dumpster where they belong."

John's Carl Rogers persona was about to go all Albert Ellis (see Chapter 8) when the plane's intercom crackled to life. The flight attendant asked everyone to return to their seats. Our colleague reluctantly rose and bid us farewell.

****

On the surface, Darrell's argument is compelling. Counseling and psychotherapy theories must address unique issues pertaining to women and racial, ethnic, sexual, and religious minorities. Theories also need to be more practical. Students should be able to read a theories chapter and finish with a clear sense of how to apply that theory in practice.

However, Darrell's argument is also off target. Although he's advocating an evidence-based (scientific) orientation, he doesn't seem to appreciate the central role of theory to science. From early prehistoric writing to the present, theory has been used to guide research and practice. Why? Because theory provides direction and without theory, practitioners would be setting sail without proper resources for navigation. In the end, you might find your way, but you would have had a shorter trip with GPS.

Counseling and psychotherapy theories are well-developed systems for understanding, explaining,

Counseling and Psychotherapy Theories in Context and Practice: Skills, Strategies, and Techniques, Third Edition. John Sommers-Flanagan and Rita Sommers-Flanagan. © 2018 John Wiley & Sons, Inc. Published 2018 by John Wiley & Sons, Inc. Companion website: www.wiley.com/go/sommers-flanagan/theories3e

predicting, and controlling human behavior. When someone on Twitter writes, "I have a theory that autism is caused by biological fathers who played too many computer games when they were children" it's not a theory. More likely, it's a thought or a guess or a goofy statement pertaining to that person's idiosyncratic take on reality; it might be an effort to prove a point or sound clever, but it's not a theory (actually, that particular idea isn't even a good dissertation hypothesis).

Theories are foundations from which we build our understanding of human development, human suffering, self-destructive behavior, and positive change. Without theory, we can't understand why people engage in self-destructive behaviors or why they sometimes stop being self-destructive. If we can't understand why people behave in certain ways, then our ability to identify and apply effective treatments is compromised. In fact, every evidence-based or empirically supported approach rests on the shoulders of counseling and psychotherapy theory.

In life and psychotherapy, there are repeating patterns. I (John) recall making an argument similar to Darrell's while in graduate school. I complained to a professor that I wanted to focus on learning the essentials of becoming a great therapist. Her feedback was direct: I could become a technician who applied specific procedures to people or I could grapple with deeper issues and become a real therapist with a more profound understanding of human problems. If I chose the latter, then I could articulate the benefits and limitations of specific psychological change strategies and modify those strategies to fit unique and diverse clients.

Just like Darrell, my professor was biased, but in the opposite direction. She valued nuance, human mystery, and existential angst. She devalued what she viewed (at the time) as the superficiality of behavior therapies.

Both viewpoints have relevance to counseling and psychotherapy. We need technical skills for implementing research-based treatments, but we also need respect and empathy for idiosyncratic individuals who come to us for compassion and insight. We need the ability to view clients and problems from many perspectives—ranging from the indigenous to the contemporary medical model. To be proficient at applying specific technical skills, we need to understand the nuances and dynamics of psychotherapy and how human change happens. In the end, that means we need to study theories.

Contemporary Theories, Not Pop Psychology

Despite Darrell's argument that traditional theories belong in the dumpster, all the theories in this text—even the old ones—are contemporary and relevant. They're contemporary because they (a) have research support and (b) have been updated or adapted for working with diverse clients. They're relevant because they include specific strategies and techniques that facilitate emotional,

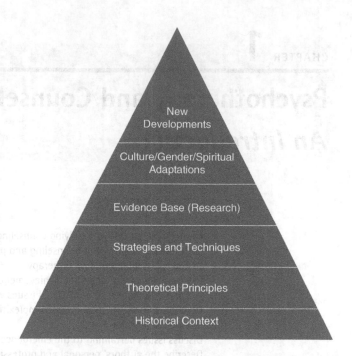

FIGURE 1.1   Counseling and Psychotherapy Theory: Foundations, Principles, and Practice

psychological, and behavioral change (see Figure 1.1). Although some of these theories are more popular than others, they shouldn't be confused with "pop" psychology.

Another reason these theories don't belong in the dumpster is because their development and application include drama and intrigue that rival anything Hollywood has to offer. They include literature, myth, religion, and our dominant and minority political and social systems. They address and attempt to explain big issues, including:

• How we define mental health.

• Whether we believe in mental illness.

• Views on love, meaning, death, and personal responsibility.

• What triggers anger, joy, sadness, and depression.

• Why trauma and tragedy strengthens some people, while weakening others.

There's no single explanation for these and other big issues; often mental health professionals are in profound disagreement. Therefore, it should be no surprise that this book—a book about the major contemporary theories and techniques of psychotherapy and counseling—will contain controversy and conflict. We do our best to bring you more than just the theoretical facts; we also bring you the thrills and disappointments linked to these theories of human motivation, functioning, and change.

Human Suffering and Hope

A young man named Adrian came for counseling. He described these problems:

- Constant worry that he hadn't turned off his kitchen stove.
- Repeated checking to see if he had properly engaged his car's emergency brake … even when parked on level ground.
- Repeated thoughts of contamination. He wondered, "Have I been infected by worms and germs?"
- Hands that were red and chapped from washing 50+ times a day.

Midway through Adrian's second session, he reported intrusive obsessive thoughts. Adrian kept thinking that a woman in the waiting room had placed a foot on his (Adrian's) pop bottle. Adrian wanted to go back to double-check the scene.

The therapist did some reality testing. She gently asked Adrian how likely it was that his pop bottle had been contaminated. Adrian said the bottle had been in his own hands and that the other client had been seated across the room. He admitted that it probably didn't happen.

Then the therapist asked Adrian to engage in response prevention. Instead of giving into his checking impulse, she engaged Adrian in a relaxation activity, including deep breathing. This approach was used to help break the link between Adrian's obsessive thoughts and maladaptive checking behaviors.

After 20 minutes of relaxation and therapeutic conversation, Adrian reported feeling better. A few minutes later, he asked to use the restroom. As he left, the therapist wondered if Adrian might be leaving to perform a checking ritual. She waited a moment and then walked to the waiting room. Adrian was seated about 15 feet away from a pop bottle, leg stretched out as far as possible, trying to reach the bottle with his foot. His foot was still at least 10 feet from the bottle. The therapist interrupted the process and escorted Adrian back to the counseling office.

Although there's a mental disorder diagnosis for Adrian's condition (obsessive-compulsive disorder) and research-based therapies available, there's no guarantee he can successfully change. Psychotherapy is an imperfect science. There's much about human behavior, the brain, emotions, and interpersonal relationships that we don't know. However, hope remains. Many individuals like Adrian seek help, overcome their debilitating behaviors, and go on to lead happy and meaningful lives.

Understanding why people suffer, how they change, and how to help them live satisfying lives is a fascinating and important undertaking. It's also the reason this book exists.

What Is a Theory?

A **theory** involves a gathering together and organizing of knowledge about a particular object or phenomenon. In psychology, theories are used to generate hypotheses about human thinking, emotions, and behavior. A good theory should clearly explain what causes client problems (or psychopathology) and offer specific strategies for alleviating these problems. Think about Adrian: a good theory would (a) explain how he developed his obsessive-compulsive symptoms, (b) provide guidance for what strategies or procedures his therapist should use, and (c) predict how Adrian will respond to various therapy techniques. These predictions should guide Adrian's therapist on what techniques to use, how long therapy will last, and how a particular technique is likely to affect Adrian.

Theories provide therapists with models or foundations from which they provide professional service. To be without a theory or without direction and guidance is something most of us would rather avoid (Prochaska & Norcross, 2014).

Context

Context is defined as the particular set of circumstances surrounding a specific event or situation. Nothing happens without context.

The theories we cover in this book are products of their contextual origins. The socioeconomic status of the theorists and the surrounding politics, culture, wars, scientific discoveries, religions, and many other factors were operating together to create and sustain the theories we write about and the professional activity that we've come to know as counseling and psychotherapy. Even now, as you read this, contextual factors are influencing the way in which the public regards and professionals practice psychotherapy. Context will continue to define and redefine what we mean by counseling and psychotherapy into the future.

HISTORICAL CONTEXT

Contemporary psychology and psychotherapy originated in Western Europe and the United States in the late 1800s. During that time, women and other minorities were usually excluded from higher education. Consequently, much of psychotherapy's history was written from the perspective of educated white men, including Jewish males, advocating a particular theory. This tendency, so dominant in psychology, has inspired book and chapter titles such as, "Even the rats were white and male" (Guthrie, 2004; Mays, 1988).

Recognizing that there are neglected feminist and multicultural voices within the history of psychotherapy, we begin our exploration of contemporary theories and techniques of counseling and psychotherapy with a look back to its origins.

The Father of Psychotherapy?

Sigmund Freud is often considered the father of modern psychotherapy, but of course Freud had professional forebears as well. In fact, around the turn of the century the Frenchman, Pierre Janet, claimed that Freud's early work was not original:

> We are glad to find that several authors, particularly M. M. Breuer and Freud, have recently verified our interpretation *already somewhat old*, of subconscious fixed ideas with hystericals. (Janet, 1901, p. 290, italics added)

Janet believed *he* was developing a new theory about human functioning, a theory that Freud was simply helping to validate. Janet and Freud were competitive rivals. With regard to their relationship, Bowers and Meichenbaum (1984) wrote: "It is clear from their writings that Freud and Janet had a barely concealed mutual animosity" (p. 11).

Questions remain regarding who initially led the psychotherapy and counseling movements in Western Europe and, later, the United States. However, the whole idea of crowning one individual as the first, or greatest, originator of psychotherapy is a masculinized and Western endeavor (Jordan, Walker, & Hartling, 2004; Jordan, 2010). It's also inappropriate to credit white Western European males with the origins of counseling and psychotherapy theory and practice. All theories draw concepts from earlier human practices and beliefs.

Bankart (1997) articulated this point about historic discovery:

> My best friend has a bumper sticker on his truck that reads, "Indians Discovered Columbus." Let's heed the warning. Nineteenth-century European physicians no more discovered the unconscious than John Rogers Clark "discovered" Indiana. Indeed, a stronger argument could be made for the reverse, as the bumper sticker states so elegantly. (p. 21)

Of course, nineteenth century European physicians didn't discover the unconscious (Ellenberger, 1970). Nevertheless, we're intrigued by the implications of Bankart's comment. Could it be that European physicians, Russian feminists, the Senoi Indians, and many other individuals and cultural groups were "discovered" by the human unconscious? Of all the theorists we write about, we think Carl Jung would most appreciate the idea of an active unconscious seeking recognition in the human community (our Jungian chapter is on the companion website www.wiley.com/go/sommers-flanagan/theories3e).

Four Historical–Cultural Perspectives

Early treatments for human distress and disturbance typically consisted of biomedical, spiritual, psychosocial, and indigenous procedures. Often, theorists and practitioners repeatedly discover, rediscover, and recycle explanations and treatments through the ages; this is one reason why a quick historical review is useful.

The Biomedical Perspective

The **biomedical perspective** involves belief that biological, genetic, or physiological factors cause mental and emotional problems and are central to therapeutic strategies. Consistent with the biomedical perspective, archaeological evidence exists for an ancient treatment procedure called **trephining**. Trephining involved using a stone tool to chip away at a human skull to create a circular opening. It's believed, in the absence of written documentation, that this was a shamanic treatment designed to release evil spirits from the afflicted individual's brain, although trephining involved a physical intervention. Apparently some patients survived this crude procedure, living for many years afterward (Selling, 1943).

About a half million years later, a similar procedure, the prefrontal lobotomy, emerged as a popular medical treatment in the United States. This medical procedure was hailed as an important step forward in the treatment of mental disorders. Prefrontal lobotomies were described as an exciting new medical procedure in *Time* magazine in 1942 (from Dawes, 1994).

Although lobotomies and trephining are no longer in vogue, current brain-based physical or biomedical interventions include psychotropic medications, electroconvulsive therapy (ECT), transcranial magnetic stimulation, vagus nerve stimulation, and deep brain stimulation (Blumberger et al., 2016; Brunoni et al., 2016). The biological perspective is an important area for research and treatment. Although responsible counselors and psychotherapists keep abreast of developments from the biomedical perspective, this text focuses on nonbiological or psychosocial explanations and treatments.

The Religious/Spiritual Perspective

Clergy, shamans, mystics, monks, elders, and other religious and spiritual leaders have been sought for advice and counsel over the centuries. It was reported that Hild of Whitby (an abbess of a double monastery in the seventh century) possessed prudence of such magnitude that not only ordinary folk but even kings and princes would come to ask advice for their difficulties (Petroff, 1986). For many Native Americans, spiritual authority and practices still hold more salience for healing than counseling or psychotherapy (Francis & Bance, 2016; King, Trimble, Morse, & Thomas, 2014). The same is true for other indigenous people, as well as Western Europeans who have strongly held religious commitments. Many Asian and African cultures also believe spiritual concerns and practices are intricately related to psychological health (D. W. Sue & D. Sue, 2016).

The **religious/spiritual perspective** emphasizes spiritual explanations for human distress and recovery.

Contemporary psychosocial interventions sometimes incorporate spirituality (Johnson, 2013). Two prominent approaches with scientific support, dialectical behavior therapy (DBT) and acceptance and commitment therapy (ACT), use Buddhist mindfulness approaches to facilitate emotional regulation (Hayes, 2002; Hayes, Strosahl, & Wilson, 1999; Linehan, 2000). Most practitioners readily acknowledge the emotional healing potential of spiritual practices. Matching client spirituality with spiritually oriented treatments tends to improve outcomes (Worthington, Hook, Davis, & McDaniel, 2011).

The Psychosocial Perspective

Humans have probably always understood that verbal and relational interactions—the essence of the **psychosocial perspective**—can change thoughts, mood, and behavior. At a minimum, we know that indigenous healers used psychological and relational techniques similar to current theory-based psychosocial strategies. Typical examples include Siddhartha Gautama (563–483 b.c.), better known as the Buddha, and the Roman philosopher Epictetus (50–138 a.d.), both of whom are forebears to contemporary cognitive theory and therapy.

A less cited example, from the tenth and eleventh centuries, is Avicenna (980–1037 a.d.), a renowned figure in Islamic medicine. The following case description illustrates Avicenna's psychological approach:

> A certain prince … was afflicted with melancholia, and suffered from the delusion that he was a cow … he would low like a cow, causing annoyance to everyone, crying "Kill me so that a good stew may be made of my flesh," [and] … he would eat nothing…. Avicenna was persuaded to take the case…. First of all he sent a message to the patient bidding him to be of good cheer because the butcher was coming to slaughter him. Whereas … the sick man rejoiced. Some time afterwards, Avicenna, holding a knife in his hand, entered the sickroom saying, "Where is this cow that I may kill it?" The patient lowed like a cow to indicate where he was. By Avicenna's orders he was laid on the ground bound hand and foot. Avicenna then felt him all over and said, "He is too lean, and not ready to be killed; he must be fattened." Then they offered him suitable food of which he now partook eagerly, and gradually he gained strength, got rid of his delusion, and was completely cured. (Browne, 1921, pp. 88–89)

Avicenna's treatment approach appears to fit within a strategic or constructive theoretical model (see Chapter 11).

The Feminist/Multicultural Perspective

The **feminist/multicultural perspective** uses social and cultural oppression and liberation from oppression as primary explanations for mental disorders and therapeutic recovery. As an organized, academic discipline, feminist and multicultural pedagogy is relatively young. However, because these perspectives have likely simmered in the background or operated in indigenous cultures, we include them here.

As discussed previously, traditional historical voices have been predominately white and male. The fact that much of what we read and digest as history has the sound and look of whiteness and maleness is an example of context. Human history and knowledge can't help but be influenced by those who write and tell the story. Nevertheless, as human service providers, mental health professionals must be aware of alternative perspectives that include minority voices (Hays, 2013; D. W. Sue & D. Sue, 2016).

Brown (2010) discussed one way in which the feminist mindset differs from traditional male perspectives.

> Feminist therapy, unlike many other theories of therapy, does not have an identifiable founding parent or parents who created it. It is a paradigm developed from the grassroots of many different feminists practicing psychotherapy, and its beginnings occurred in the context of many people's experiences and interactions in personal, political, and professional settings. Because there is no central authority, accrediting body, or founder, those who identify as its practitioners do not always agree on the boundaries of what constitutes feminist therapy. (p. 7)

Feminist influences have quietly (and sometimes less quietly) influenced therapy process. Over the past 40-plus years, many feminist concepts and procedures have been integrated into all counseling and psychotherapy approaches. Mutuality, mutual empathy, client empowerment, and informed consent all give psychotherapy a more feminist look and feel (Brown, 2010; Jordan, 2010; J. Sommers-Flanagan & Sommers-Flanagan, 2017). Similarly, as the United States has become more culturally diverse and the dominant culture has opened itself to alternative cultural paradigms, new therapeutic possibilities have emerged and been woven into therapy. Most notably, we now know that cultural sensitivity and cultural humility (and therefore multicultural training) improve therapy outcomes with diverse client populations (Griner & Smith, 2006; Smith, Rodríguez, & Bernal, 2011). Additionally, Eastern wellness techniques and strategies such as mindfulness have been integrated into contemporary and evidence-based therapy approaches (Linehan, 1993).

Historically, counseling and psychotherapy focused on helping individuals move toward individuation, independence, and rational thinking. Behavior associated with dependence and emotional expression was often viewed as pathological. In contrast, feminist and multicultural perspectives emphasize relationship and community over individuality (Jordan, 2010). Going forward, feminist and multicultural values will continue to influence and be integrated into traditional psychotherapy systems.

DEFINITIONS OF COUNSELING AND PSYCHOTHERAPY

Many students have asked us, "Should I get a PhD in psychology, a master's degree in counseling, or a master's in social work?"

This question usually brings forth a lengthy response, during which we not only explain the differences between these various degrees, but also discuss additional career information pertaining to the PsyD degree, psychiatry, school counseling, school psychology, and psychiatric nursing. This sometimes leads to the confusing topic of the differences between counseling and psychotherapy. As time permits, we also share our thoughts about less-confusing topics, like the meaning of life.

Sorting out differences between mental health disciplines is difficult. Jay Haley (1977) was once asked: "In relation to being a successful therapist, what are the differences between psychiatrists, social workers, and psychologists?" He responded: "Except for ideology, salary, status, and power, the differences are irrelevant" (p. 165). Obviously, many different professional tracks can lead you toward becoming a successful mental health professional—despite a few ideological, salary, status, and power differences.

In this section we explore three confusing questions: What is psychotherapy? What is counseling? And what are the differences between the two?

What Is Psychotherapy?

Anna O., an early psychoanalytic patient of Josef Breuer (a mentor of Sigmund Freud), called her treatment the **talking cure**. This is an elegant, albeit vague, description of psychotherapy. Technically, it tells us very little, but at the intuitive level, it explains psychotherapy very well. Anna was saying something most people readily admit: talking, expressing, verbalizing, or sharing one's pain and life story is potentially healing.

As we write today, heated arguments about how to practice psychotherapy continue (Baker & McFall, 2014; Laska, Gurman, & Wampold, 2014). This debate won't soon end and is directly relevant to how psychotherapy is defined (Wampold & Imel, 2015). We explore dimensions of this debate in the pages to come. For now, keep in mind that although historically Anna O. viewed and experienced *talking as her cure* (an expressive-cathartic process), many contemporary researchers and writers emphasize that the opposite is more important—that a future Anna O. would benefit even more from *listening to and learning from her therapist* (a receptive-educational process). Based on this perspective, some researchers and practitioners believe therapists are more effective when they actively and expertly *teach their clients* cognitive and behavioral principles and skills (aka psychoeducation).

REFLECTIONS

Where do you stand on this issue? What are the advantages of listening to clients? What are the advantages of actively teaching clients skills? Might these perspectives be combined?

We have several favorite psychotherapy definitions:

- A conversation with a therapeutic purpose (Korchin, 1976, p. 281).

- The purchase of friendship (Schofield, 1964, p. 1).

- When one person with an emotional disorder gets help from another person who has a little less of an emotional disorder (J. Watkins, personal communication, October 13, 1983).

What Is Counseling?

Counselors have struggled to define their craft in ways similar to psychotherapists. Here's a sampling:

- Counseling is the artful application of scientifically derived psychological knowledge and techniques for the purpose of changing human behavior (Burke, 1989, p. 12).

- Counseling consists of whatever ethical activities a counselor undertakes in an effort to help the client engage in those types of behavior that will lead to a resolution of the client's problems (Krumboltz, 1965, p. 3).

- [Counseling is] an activity … for working with relatively normal-functioning individuals who are experiencing developmental or adjustment problems (Kottler & Brown, 1996, p. 7).

We now turn to the question of the differences between counseling and psychotherapy.

What Are the Differences Between Psychotherapy and Counseling?

Years ago, Patterson (1973) wrote: "There are no essential differences between counseling and psychotherapy" (p. xiv). We basically agree with Patterson, but we like how Corsini and Wedding (2000) framed it:

> Counseling and psychotherapy are the same qualitatively; they differ only quantitatively; there is nothing that a psychotherapist does that a counselor does not do. (p. 2)

This statement implies that counselors and psychotherapists engage in the same behaviors—listening, questioning, interpreting, explaining, and advising—but may do so in different proportions.

The professional literature mostly implies that psychotherapists are less directive, go a little deeper, work a little longer, and charge a higher fee. In contrast, counselors are slightly more directive, work more on developmentally normal—but troubling—issues, work more overtly on practical client problems, work more briefly, and charge a bit less. In the case of individual counselors and psychotherapists, each of these tendencies may be reversed; some counselors work longer with clients and charge more, whereas some psychotherapists work more briefly with clients and charge less.

> ### REFLECTIONS
>
> How are counseling and psychotherapy viewed in your community or university? Are they equal (or unequal) in status? Why? Who sees a counselor? Who sees a psychotherapist? How do training programs in counseling, social work, psychology, and psychiatry distinguish themselves from one another on your campus or in your community?

A Working Definition of Counseling and Psychotherapy

There are strong similarities between counseling and psychotherapy. Because the similarities vastly outweigh the differences we use the words counseling and psychotherapy interchangeably. Sometimes we use the word therapy as an alternative.

To capture the natural complexity of this thing called psychotherapy, we offer the following 12-part definition. Counseling or psychotherapy is:

(a) a process that involves (b) a trained professional who abides by (c) accepted ethical guidelines and has (d) competencies for working with (e) diverse individuals who are in distress or have life problems that led them to (f) seek help (possibly at the insistence of others) or they may be (g) seeking personal growth, but either way, these parties (h) establish an explicit agreement (informed consent) to (i) work together (more or less collaboratively) toward (j) mutually acceptable goals (k) using theoretically based or evidence-based procedures that, in the broadest sense, have been shown to (l) facilitate human learning or human development or reduce disturbing symptoms.

Although this definition is long and multifaceted, it's still probably insufficient. For example, it wouldn't fit for any self-administered forms of therapy, such as self-analysis or self-hypnosis—although we're quite certain that if you read through this definition several times, you're likely to experience a self-induced hypnotic trance state.

THE SCIENTIFIC CONTEXT OF COUNSELING AND PSYCHOTHERAPY

This section reviews historical and contemporary developments in the evaluation of counseling and psychotherapy.

Eysenck's Review

In 1952, Hans Eysenck published a controversial article titled "The Effects of Psychotherapy: An Evaluation." He concluded that after over 50 years of psychotherapy, research, and practice, no evidence existed attesting to its beneficial effects. He stated that "roughly 2/3 of a group of neurotic patients will recover or improve to a marked extent within about two years of the onset of their illness [in the absence of treatment]" (Eysenck, 1952, p. 322). He compared this natural recovery rate with rates produced by traditional psychotherapy and reported:

> … patients treated by means of psychoanalysis improved to the extent of 44%; patients treated eclectically improved to the extent of 64%; patients treated only custodially or by general practitioners improved to the extent of 72%. There thus appears to be an inverse correlation between recovery and psychotherapy. (p. 322)

Eysenck's article sparked strong reactions among psychotherapy researchers and practitioners. Supporters of psychotherapy complained that Eysenck's conclusions were based on poorly controlled studies; they claimed that he didn't address severity of diagnosis issues, and that the outcome measures used in the studies were generally poor and crude. The critics were correct—Eysenck's review was flawed, primarily because many existing studies of counseling and psychotherapy effectiveness were also flawed. Despite the fact that psychotherapy researchers and practitioners in the 1950s believed psychotherapy was more effective than no treatment, they hadn't gathered scientific evidence to support their beliefs.

A Psychotherapy Research Boom

Eysenck's scathing critique motivated psychotherapy researchers. Outcome studies proliferated, and Eysenck's critique was (mostly) laid to rest in the 1970s and early 1980s after several substantial and positive reviews of psychotherapy efficacy.

Mary Smith and Gene Glass published two highly influential reviews of psychotherapy outcomes. They used a new statistical method (meta-analysis) to combine information across different treatment outcomes studies (Smith & Glass, 1977; Smith, Glass, & Miller, 1980). **Meta-analysis**, now a household name in research and statistics, pools together and obtains an overall average treatment effect size across different therapy research

Table 1.1   A Closer Look at Effect Sizes

Descriptive terms	ES or *d*	Percentile rank magnitude of ES
Extremely large	+2.00	97.7 [The treated group scores two standard deviations better on the outcome measures]
Very large	+1.00	84.0 [The treated group scores one standard deviation better on the outcome measures]
Large	+0.80	79.0
Smith & Miller, 1977	+0.68	75.0
Medium	+0.50	69.0
Small	+0.20	58.0
None	+0.00	50.0 [There is no difference between the treatment and a control group]
Adverse effects	−0.20	42.0

Note: This table places the Smith and Glass (1977) meta-analysis results in context of Cohen's (1977) traditional descriptive terms of small, medium, and large effect sizes. These effect sizes are also listed in terms of their percentile rank. When researchers, like Smith and colleagues, state: "the average client treated with psychotherapy was better off than 75% of clients who received no treatment" they're using percentile rankings. As you can see from the table, if there is no effect size (*d* = +0.00), then "the average person receiving the intervention would be better off than 50% of people not receiving treatment." Although some participants may improve or get worse, on average, there is no effect.

studies. **Effect size** (ES or *d*) is a statistic used to estimate how much change is produced by a particular intervention. ES is reported as the statistic *d* and represents the difference in efficacy between evaluated interventions (e.g., psychoanalytic psychotherapy or cognitive therapy) and no-treatment control groups. Additional information about the meta-analytic effect size (ES or *d*) is given in Table 1.1.

Smith and Glass published their first review in 1977: "Meta-analysis of Psychotherapy Outcome Studies." They evaluated 375 outcome studies and reported that the average study "showed a 0.68 standard deviation superiority [ES or *d*] of the treated group over the control group" (Smith & Glass, 1977, p. 756). They concluded that the average client treated with psychotherapy was better off than 75% of clients who received no treatment (see also Table 1.1). Later, they expanded their study to 475 outcome studies and published the results in a book and concluded that the average treated person was better off than 80% of the untreated sample (Smith, Glass, & Miller, 1980).

Although Smith and colleagues helped settle the issue of whether psychotherapy is generally efficacious, they didn't clear up the big debate over whether one form of therapy was more effective than others. This is because they found that different theory-based techniques didn't produce significantly different outcomes. Their findings, consistent with previous and later research, lent support to the conclusion that "Everybody has won and all must

have prizes" (a quotation from *Alice in Wonderland*'s Dodo bird). The relative equivalent efficacy of various therapy approaches is now commonly referred to as the **Dodo bird effect** (Luborsky, Singer, & Luborsky, 1975; Marcus, O'Connell, Norris, & Sawaqdeh, 2014).

Overall, despite initial outrage over Eysenck's article, he provided the field of psychotherapy with a much-needed reality check. Perhaps the most important and enduring consequence of Eysenck's critique was a stronger emphasis on scientific evidence to support counseling and psychotherapy practice.

The Great Psychotherapy Debate

At the close of the twentieth century, Hubble, Duncan, and Miller (1999) reflected on psychotherapy outcomes research with undaunted optimism:

> The uncertainties loosed on the clinical and counseling disciplines by Eysenck and like-minded critics have now been set aside. Therapy works.... More than 40 years of outcome research make clear that therapists are not witch doctors, snake oil peddlers, or over-achieving do-gooders.... Study after study, meta-analyses, and scholarly reviews have legitimized psychologically based or informed interventions. (1999, pp. 1–2)

Nearly everyone still agrees that psychotherapy is more effective than no treatment (Corey, 2017; Norcross & Lambert, 2011).

Given the celebratory language, you might be thinking: What's left to argue about? Well, as is typically the case with humans, there's plenty to keep arguing about. The biggest of these arguments focuses on the following point and counterpoint:

- *Point*: Research has demonstrated the superiority of specific psychotherapy techniques for specific mental disorders; these techniques should be identified as "empirically supported" or "evidence-based" and should constitute the specific procedures that mental health practitioners employ.

- *Counterpoint*: A broader examination of the research reveals that different therapy approaches include common therapeutic factors. These factors account for most of the positive change that occurs in psychotherapy and so psychotherapists should deliver therapy in ways that emphasize these common factors.

Wampold (Wampold et al., 1997; Wampold & Imel, 2015) labeled the specific techniques versus common factors conflict as: **The Great Psychotherapy Debate**. In this section we dive headlong into the great psychotherapy debate and then step back to examine questions about what constitutes science and whether we can generalize scientific research findings to clinical practice.

Common Therapeutic Factors

Common therapeutic factors (aka common factors) are elements that exist across a wide range of different therapy approaches. Some researchers and practitioners view common factors as the primary reason why therapy is effective (J. Sommers-Flanagan, 2015). Common factors include, but are not limited to:

- A culturally appropriate or sanctioned explanation (or myth) for client distress combined with a similarly sanctioned rationale for the treatment (ritual) procedures.

- A healing setting where the therapy takes place.

- Advice or education.

- An emotionally charged relationship bond between client and therapist.

- Catharsis or emotional expression.

- Exposure to feared stimuli.

- Feedback from the therapist.

- Insight into one's problems.

- Positive expectations (aka hope).

- The working alliance.

- Therapist credibility or expertise.

- Trust in the therapist (this alphabetized list is compiled and adapted from Frank & Frank, 1991; Lambert & Ogles, 2014; Laska, Gurman, & Wampold, 2014).

Common factors were previously called "*nonspecific factors*" (Strupp & Hadley, 1979). More recently researchers and practitioners have begun operationalizing common factors and so the term nonspecific factors has been criticized and, for the most part, discarded.

Many different researchers have proposed theoretical models and empirical analyses focusing on common factors (Frank, 1961; Lambert & Ogles, 2014; Rosenzweig, 1936; Wampold & Imel, 2015). The following discussion focuses on Lambert's (1992) four-factor model. We focus on this model because it is simple, straightforward, and has empirical support (Cuijpers et al., 2012). However, other common factor models exist.

In a narrative review of the literature, Lambert (1992) identified and described four common therapy factors. He then estimated each factor's contribution to positive therapeutic change (see Figure 1.2).

Lambert's estimates weren't perfectly precise predictions for every case (Beutler, 2009). However, his conceptual framework has become a popular way of thinking about how therapy works.

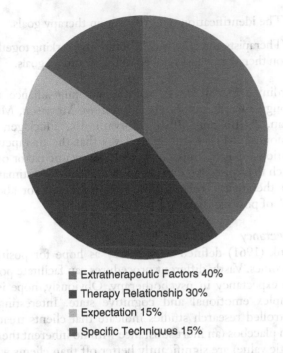

- Extratherapeutic Factors 40%
- Therapy Relationship 30%
- Expectation 15%
- Specific Techniques 15%

FIGURE 1.2   Lambert's Common Factors

Extratherapeutic Factors

Extratherapeutic factors include client factors such as severity of disturbance, motivation, capacity to relate to others, ego strength, psychological-mindedness, the ability to identify a single problem to work on in counseling, and "sources of help and support within [client] environments" (Asay & Lambert, 1999, p. 33). For example, many clients who experience spontaneous remission (sudden improvement without therapy) probably do so because of positive support from important people in their lives. Lambert (1992) linked extratherapeutic change factors to about 40% of client success. In a meta-analysis of 31 studies of nondirective treatment of depression, Cuijpers et al. (2012) estimated that 33.3% of improvement was related to extratherapy factors.

Therapeutic Relationship

Therapeutic relationship is a broad term used to refer to many different factors that contribute to rapport and a positive working relationship between therapist and client. When most practitioners think of the therapeutic relationship, they think of Rogers (1942a, 1957) core conditions of (a) congruence, (b) unconditional positive regard, and (c) empathic understanding. Although Rogers's concepts are complex and sometimes elusive, information is available on how to operationalize these core relationship conditions (see Chapter 6; Norcross, 2011; J. Sommers-Flanagan, 2015).

In addition, Bordin (1979) described three dimensions of the working alliance. The **working alliance** includes:

1. A positive interpersonal bond between therapists and clients.

2. The identification of agreed-upon therapy goals.

3. Therapists and clients collaboratively working together on therapeutic tasks linked to the identified goals.

Bordin's tripartite model of the working alliance has strong research support (Constantino, Morrison, MacEwan, & Boswell, 2013; Horvath, Re, Flückiger, & Symonds, 2011). Lambert believes that the therapeutic relationship is the most powerful therapeutic factor over which therapists can directly exert control. He estimated that therapeutic relationship factors account for about 30% of positive therapy outcomes.

Expectancy

Frank (1961) defined **expectancy** as hope for positive outcomes. Vastly different procedures can facilitate positive expectancy in psychotherapy. Obviously, hope is a complex emotional and cognitive state. Interestingly, controlled research studies indicate that clients treated with placebos (an inert substance with no inherent therapeutic value) are significantly better off than clients who receive no treatment and often do just as well as clients who take antidepressant medications for depressive symptoms (J. Sommers-Flanagan & Campbell, 2009; Turner, Matthews, Linardatos, Tell, & Rosenthal, 2008). Lambert estimated that expectation, hope, and placebo factors account for about 15% of the variation in therapy outcomes. One way in which modern practitioners foster hope is by providing clients with a persuasive rationale for why the specific treatment being provided is likely to effectively remediate the client's specific problems (Laska & Wampold, 2014).

Techniques

In the 1870s, Anton Mesmer, then famous for "mesmerizing" or hypnotizing patients, claimed that his particular technique—using purple robes, rods of iron, and magnetic baths—produced therapeutic change due to shifting magnetic fields. More recently, psychoanalysts believe that helping clients develop insight into repeating destructive relationship patterns is essential; in contrast, behaviorists claim exposure and response prevention techniques are powerful interventions.

Common factor proponents view Mesmer, the psychoanalysts, and the behaviorists as incorrect regarding the mechanisms of change in psychotherapy (Laska et al., 2014; Norcross & Lambert, 2011). Instead, they believe extratherapeutic factors, the therapy relationship, and expectation are more robustly linked to positive outcomes. Duncan and colleagues (2010) wrote:

> To be frank, any assertion for the superiority of special treatments for specific disorders should be regarded, at best, as misplaced enthusiasm, far removed from the best interests of consumers. (p. 422)

This isn't to say that techniques are unimportant to therapy success. In most cases, extratherapeutic factors, the relationship, and expectation are all activated when therapists employ specific therapy techniques. Consequently, although different techniques don't produce superior outcomes, doing counseling or psychotherapy without theory-based techniques is difficult to imagine.

Lambert estimated that 15% of positive treatment outcomes are related to the specific techniques employed. In contrast, Wampold and Imel (2015) reported that it may be as low as 1%. Cuijpers and colleagues (2012) reported that specific therapy approaches accounted for 17.1% of treatment outcomes.

What Constitutes Evidence? Efficacy, Effectiveness, and Other Research Models

Contemporary helping interventions should have at least some supportive scientific evidence. This statement, as bland and general as it seems, would generate substantial controversy among academics, scientists, and people on the street. One person's evidence may or may not meet another person's standards.

It may sound odd, but subjectivity is a palpable problem in scientific research. Humans are inherently subjective and humans design the studies, construct and administer the assessment instruments, and conduct the statistical analyses. Consequently, measuring treatment outcomes inevitably includes error and subjectivity. Despite this, we support and respect the scientific method and appreciate efforts to measure (as objectively as possible) psychotherapy outcomes.

There are two primary approaches to counseling and psychotherapy outcomes research: (1) efficacy research and (2) effectiveness research. These terms flow from the well-known experimental design concepts of internal and external validity (Campbell, Stanley, & Gage, 1963). **Efficacy research** employs experimental designs that emphasize **internal validity**, allowing researchers to comment on causal mechanisms; **effectiveness research** uses experimental designs that emphasize **external validity**, allowing researchers to comment on generalizability of their findings.

Efficacy Research

Efficacy research involves tightly controlled experimental trials with high internal validity. Within medicine, psychology, counseling, and social work, **randomized controlled trials (RCTs)** are the gold standard for determining treatment efficacy. An RCT statistically compares outcomes between randomly assigned treatment and control groups. In medicine and psychiatry, the control group is usually administered an inert placebo (i.e., placebo pill). In the end, treatment is considered efficacious if the active medication relieves symptoms, on average, at a rate significantly higher than the placebo. In psychology, counseling, and social work, treatment groups are generally compared with a waiting list or attention-placebo control group.

To maximize researcher control over independent variables, RCTs require that participants meet specific inclusion and exclusion criteria prior to being randomly assigned to a treatment or comparison group. This allows researchers to statistically determine with a greater degree of certainty whether the treatment itself had a direct or causal effect on treatment outcomes.

In 1986, Gerald Klerman, then head of the National Institute of Mental Health, gave a keynote address to the Society for Psychotherapy Research. During his speech, he emphasized that psychotherapy should be evaluated systematically through RCTs. He claimed:

> We must come to view psychotherapy as we do aspirin. That is, each form of psychotherapy must have known ingredients, we must know what these ingredients are, they must be trainable and replicable across therapists, and they must be administered in a uniform and consistent way within a given study. (Quoted in Beutler, 2009, p. 308)

Klerman's speech advocated for the medicalization of psychotherapy. Klerman's motivation for medicalizing psychotherapy was probably based in part on his awareness of increasing health care costs and heated competition for health care dollars. This is an important contextual factor. The events that ensued were partly an effort to place psychological interventions on par with medical interventions.

The strategy of using science to compete for health care dollars eventually coalesced into a movement within professional psychology. In 1993, Division 12 (the Society of Clinical Psychology) of the American Psychological Association (APA) formed a "Task Force on Promotion and Dissemination of Psychological Procedures." This task force published an initial set of **empirically validated treatments**. To be considered empirically validated, treatments were required to be (a) manualized and (b) shown to be superior to a placebo or other treatment, or equivalent to an already established treatment in at least two "good" group design studies or in a series of single case design experiments conducted by different investigators (Chambless et al., 1998).

Division 12's empirically validated treatments were controversial. Critics protested that the process favored behavioral and cognitive behavioral treatments. Others complained about forgoing clinical sensitivity and intuition in favor of manualized treatment protocols (Silverman, 1996). In response, Division 12 held to their procedures for identifying efficacious treatments, but changed the name from empirically validated treatments to **empirically supported treatments (ESTs)**.

Advocates of the EST perspective often refer to treatment providers as "psychological clinical scientists" and view the need for cost-efficiency in health care delivery as driving EST use (Baker & McFall, 2014, p. 483). Further, they don't view the understanding or implementation of common factors in psychotherapy as an "important personal activity and goal" (p. 483).

Baker, McFall, and Shoham (2008) argued that treatments based on efficacy research (i.e., RCTs) generally remain highly efficacious when directly "exported" to clinical settings. Their position is aligned with the medical model and strongly values efficacy research as the road to developing valid psychological procedures for treating medical conditions. However, other researchers are less optimistic about the ease, utility, and validity of generalizing efficacy research into real-world clinical settings (Santucci, Thomassin, Petrovic, & Weisz, 2015; Singer & Greeno, 2013).

Effectiveness Research

Sternberg, Roediger, and Halpern (2007) described effectiveness studies:

> An effectiveness study is one that considers the outcome of psychological treatment, as it is delivered in real-world settings. Effectiveness studies can be methodologically rigorous …, but they do not include random assignment to treatment conditions or placebo control groups. (p. 208)

Effectiveness research focuses on collecting data with external validity. This usually involves a "real-world" setting, instead of a laboratory. Effectiveness research can be scientifically rigorous, but it doesn't involve random assignment to treatment and control conditions. Similarly, inclusion and exclusion criteria for clients to participate are less rigid and more like actual clinical practice, where clients come to therapy with a mix of different symptoms or diagnoses. The purpose is to evaluate counseling and psychotherapy as it is practiced in the real world.

Other Research Models

Other research models are also used to inform researchers and clinical practitioners about therapy process and outcomes. These models include survey research, single-case designs, and qualitative studies. However, based on current mental health care reimbursement practices and future trends, providers are increasingly expected to provide services consistent with findings from efficacy and effectiveness research—and the medical model (Baker & McFall, 2014).

Techniques or Common Factors? The Wrong Question

Wampold (Wampold, 2001, 2010; Wampold & Imel, 2015) and others claim that common factors provide a better empirical explanation for treatment success than specific treatment models. In contrast, Baker and McFall (2014) and like-minded researchers contend that common or nonspecific factors contribute little to the understanding and application of counseling and psychotherapy interventions (Chambless et al., 2006). Although it would be nice if everyone agreed, when prestigious scientists and practitioners genuinely disagree, it typically means that important lessons can be learned from both sides of the argument. The question shouldn't be, "Techniques or common factors?" but, instead, "How do techniques *and* common factors operate together to produce positive therapy outcomes?" There's nothing wrong with applying principles and techniques from both the common factors and EST perspectives (Constantino & Bernecker, 2014; Hofmann & Barlow, 2014). In fact, we suspect that the best EST providers are also sensitive to common factors and that the best common factors-oriented clinicians are open to using empirically supported techniques.

Empirically Supported Treatments (ESTs)

ESTs are manualized approaches designed to treat specific mental disorders or other client problems. In 2011, Division 12 of APA (the original architect of the EST movement) launched a new website on research-supported psychological treatments. Using the criteria that Chambless et al. (1998) initially outlined, this website includes treatments that are (a) strong (aka well-established), (b) modest (aka probably efficacious), and (c) controversial (when there are conflicting empirical findings or debates over the mechanism of change).

At the time of this writing, 80 ESTs for 17 different psychological disorders and behavior problems were listed on the Division 12 website. For example, relaxation training is listed as having "strong research support" for treating insomnia. Other organizations also maintain empirically supported or evidence-based lists. For example, the Substance Abuse and Mental Health Services Administration (SAMHSA) has a broader list referred to as the National Registry of Evidence-Based Programs and Practices. This registry includes 397 evidence-based programs and practices. Recently, the *Journal of Clinical Child & Adolescent Psychology* published an "Evidence Base Update." The authors wrote:

> Six treatments reached well-established status for child and adolescent anxiety, 8 were identified as probably efficacious, 2 were identified as possibly efficacious, 6 treatments were deemed experimental, and 8 treatments of questionable efficacy emerged. (Higa-McMillan, Francis, Rith-Najarian, & Chorpita, 2016, p. 91)

To become proficient in providing a specific EST requires professional training on how to implement the treatment. In some cases certification is necessary.

It's impossible to obtain training to implement all the ESTs available. Professionals select trainings that reflect their unique interests. In an interview some years ago, Dr. Eliana Gil (Gil, 2010; Gil & Shaw, 2013), a renowned expert in child trauma, indicated that she obtained training in as many different approaches to treating child trauma as possible. Although she valued some approaches over others, she had trained in child-centered play therapy, eye movement desensitization reprocessing (EMDR), trauma informed cognitive behavior therapy, and others. She believed that having expertise in many different approaches for treating childhood trauma made her a better trauma therapist.

With the abundance of ESTs and the fact that many clients have problems outside the scope of ESTs, we sometimes wonder if we should abandon theory and technique and focus instead on how best to employ the common factors. Although a case might be made for doing just that, it's probably impossible to separate common factors from technique (Safran, Muran, & Eubanks-Carter, 2011). Norcross and Lambert (2011) wrote:

> The relationship does not exist apart from what the therapist does in terms of method, and we cannot imagine any treatment methods that would not have some relational impact. Put differently, treatment methods are relational acts. (p. 5)

Each theory-based approach, when practiced well, includes or activates common factors. In fact, when employed sensitively and competently, the specific techniques instill hope, strengthen the therapeutic relationship, and activate extratherapeutic factors. In summary, embracing a reasonable and scientifically supported theoretical perspective and using it faithfully is one of the best ways to:

- Help clients activate their extratherapeutic factors.
- Develop a positive working relationship.
- Create expectancy or placebo effects.
- Know how to use many different techniques that fit within your theoretical frame.

As Baker, McFall, and Shoham (2008) described, even though it's a research-based fact that physicians with a better bedside manner produce better outcomes, medicine involves more than a bedside manner—it also involves specific medical procedures. The EST movement is an effort to establish psychological procedures that are as effective as medical procedures. As we move into the future, we need to embrace both an understanding of psychological procedures and common factors; this can also be framed as the science and art of psychotherapy.

REFLECTIONS

Which common factors do you think are most important? Do you agree that the common factors can be activated by specific techniques?

ETHICAL ESSENTIALS

A good ethics code defines the professional knowledge base, describes the activities sanctioned in the profession, and provides a clear picture of the boundaries of professional activity. Most codes have three discernable dimensions: educational, aspirational, and judicial (Elliott-Boyle, 1985). As you read your professional ethics code, see if you can recognize these three components.

What follows is a bare-bones consideration of basic ethical issues. Graduate training programs usually include a whole class or seminar in applied ethics, and ethical issues should be a common discussion topic in classes and supervision throughout graduate studies.

Competence and Informed Consent

Competence is a central tenet of all professional codes: practitioners must have adequate knowledge and skills to perform specific professional services (R. Sommers-Flanagan & Sommers-Flanagan, 2007). As a student, you're expected to strive toward competency. Your path includes training and supervision from knowledgeable instructors and supervisors. However, competency is an elusive goal (J. Sommers-Flanagan, 2015). The knowledge base for competent counseling and psychotherapy is ever-changing. We think this is one of the best parts of being a mental health professional. There's always more to learn. Most ethics codes and state licensing boards encourage or mandate continuing professional education to maintain your professional license (Welfel, 2016).

Researchers have identified three primary strategies for developing counseling and psychotherapy competence (Hill, 2014; Woodside, Oberman, Cole, & Carruth, 2007).

1. *Working out your own issues*: This involves a journey of improving yourself—a journey that includes self-awareness, personal growth activities, and sometimes personal therapy. Engaging in self-care that helps you live a balanced and healthy lifestyle is recommended—because you're the instrument through which you provide services. Your purpose in providing therapy should be to help others and not as a means of meeting your own personal needs.

2. *Working within a learning community*: A learning community not only increases your access to cutting-edge knowledge and information, it also provides unmatched opportunity to observe practicing therapists through video, audio, and role-plays. Learning communities facilitate critical analysis and critical thinking processes.

3. *Skills practice and feedback*: Allen Ivey once wrote that therapy skill development requires "Practice, practice, practice, feedback, feedback, feedback" (J. Sommers-Flanagan & Heck, 2012, p. 152). Whether learning to ride a bicycle, navigate the Internet, or develop therapy skills, there's nothing quite like practice and feedback to facilitate learning.

Closely related to competence is the important ethical concept of informed consent. **Informed consent** refers to clients' rights to know about and consent to ways you intend to work with them. Clients have the right to know your training status, supervision arrangements, the type of therapy you're offering, your rationale for your particular treatment approach, how long therapy is likely to last, and potential benefits and harm associated with therapy. Informed consent includes a written statement as well as an interactive discussion. Involving your client in a dialogue around the preceding topics can be empowering (Harris & Robinson Kurpius, 2014; Pomerantz & Handelsman, 2004).

Multicultural Sensitivity, Competence, and Humility

From a different cultural perspective, even the most basic therapy components (e.g., the 50-minute hour and the talking cure) can seem odd or unnecessary. D. W. Sue and Sue (2016) noted that all too often traditional counseling and psychotherapy have reinforced cultural stereotypes and forced minority clients to fit into a dominant, white American frame.

Despite historical cultural insensitivity, for the past 30-plus years, the mental health professions (counseling, psychology, social work, and psychiatry) have promoted multicultural knowledge and competence. Each discipline has made commitments to multicultural sensitivity and published multicultural competencies (be sure to peruse your professional association's website for multicultural competencies from the American Counseling Association, American Psychological Association, and the National Association of Social Work). Even further, multicultural competencies have been integrated into professional training programs and in the ethical standards for counselors, psychologists, and social workers. For example, the latest revision of the ACA ethical standards includes "honoring diversity and embracing a multicultural approach" as one of several "core professional values of the counseling profession" (American Counseling Association, 2014, p. 3). When it comes to teaching or training individuals to become professional counselors, ACA Standard F.11.c. reads:

> Counselor educators infuse material related to multiculturalism/diversity into all courses and workshops for the development of professional counselors. (p. 14)

Multicultural competencies across counseling, psychology, and social work are very similar. The focus is on competency within four general areas (these areas are listed below and described in greater detail in Chapter 13):

1. Self-awareness.
2. Multicultural knowledge.
3. Culturally specific techniques.
4. Advocacy.

Confidentiality

Confidentiality means that information clients share with therapists is private and not shared without client permission. Confidentiality helps build trust. When clients come to counseling, they'll wonder if you will keep their words private. You'll be expected to hold what your client says to you in strict confidence.

Many professions include client confidentiality. In fact, honoring confidentiality boundaries is often part of what it means to be a professional. This is true in fields ranging from architecture to law to business (R. Sommers-Flanagan, Elliott, & Sommers-Flanagan, 1998).

Confidentiality is central to psychotherapy. Mental health professionals create safe environments where clients can disclose and work on their deepest issues. Practically speaking, you need to keep the identity of your client confidential, you need to keep therapy notes and videos secure, and you can't discuss the content of therapy sessions in ways that identify your client. You also need to research the limits of confidentiality legally and ethically in your state, province, or region, and in the context of the clinic or lab in which you work. As a part of informed consent, you should provide a written description of confidentiality and its limits to clients and review confidentiality verbally as well. Clients should understand the limits of confidentiality before therapy begins.

Why is confidentiality so important? The theories in this book vary in their explanations of why things go wrong for people and how therapists should intervene. They also vary in how much they value the therapeutic relationship between client and practitioner, but all theoretical perspectives involve an interpersonal enterprise in which the professional relationship is foundational and trust is essential.

Multiple Roles

Because psychotherapy involves a relationship with strict boundaries and expectations, mental health professionals usually restrict their work to people they don't know from other contexts. Consequently, you'll typically avoid holding multiple roles in clients' lives—including roles or relationships characterized as friendship, romance, or business (Barnett, Lazarus, Vasquez, Johnson, & Moorehead-Slaughter, 2007). **Multiple roles** are defined as situations where professionals simultaneously hold more than one role in their clients' lives (Welfel, 2016).

To make matters more complex, ethics codes also include an acknowledgment that sometimes multiple relationships are beneficial to clients. However, sorting out your own best interests from the best interests of your clients can be difficult. Our advice is to seek supervision and consultation when potential multiple roles emerge. This will help you manage these relationships in sensitive and ethical ways.

There are many examples of boundary breaks that lead to inappropriate or unacceptable client–therapist relationships. It's especially hard to find a portrayal of a good therapist in film or on television. If you watch therapists on the screen, you might assume that all therapists are reckless, unprofessional risk-takers who establish multiple roles and violate relationship boundaries. You also might assume that therapists can't resist their sexual impulses, often ending up in bed with their clients (or their client's husband, wife, sibling, or best friend). In truth, therapist–client sexual relations occur among a small minority of therapy cases. Even so, any instance of therapist–client sex is too many (Gottlieb & Younggren, 2009).

As you begin learning about theories and techniques associated with mental health work, it will be natural for you to try out some of the less risky ideas you're learning with friends or family members (e.g., active listening, visual imagery). However, even low-risk activities aren't without potential negative consequences. For example, engaging in nondirective, active listening with someone who's accustomed to having lively, interactive exchanges won't go unnoticed. One of our friends told us that she was very relieved when we finally got over our "Carl Rogers" stage and she could hear a direct, bossy opinion from us again.

Overall, it's best to restrain your impulse to practice therapy techniques on friends, family members, or even innocent bystanders—with the exception of listening respectfully.

Doing No Harm: A Convergence of Ethics and Science

The Latin phrase, **primum non nocere** ("first, do no harm") is an ethical mandate for medical and mental health professionals. Despite this mandate, research shows that psychotherapy can and does produce *negative outcomes* or client deterioration; estimates indicate that approximately 3–10% of psychotherapy cases result in client deterioration (Lambert & Lambert, 2010; Lambert, 2013b). Negative effects may even climb as high as 15% with substance abuse treatments (Moos, 2005, 2012).

PUTTING IT IN PRACTICE

1.1 Beneficence: Helping Not Hurting

Reproduced with permission of Alan C. Tjeltveit, PhD, Professor of Psychology, Muhlenberg College

"I want to help people," many people reply when asked, "Why do you want to go into psychology or counseling?" That desire to benefit others is essential to being a good psychotherapist or counselor. However, that desire to help may also contribute to dangerous unforeseen consequences.

Beneficence, the American Psychological Association (APA, 2010) ethics code notes, means striving "to benefit those with whom [psychologists] work" (Principle A, p. 1062). Similarly, Principle A1a of the American Counseling Association (ACA, 2014) ethics code begins, "The primary responsibility of counselors is to respect the dignity and promote the welfare of clients" (p. 4). This fits with what "profession" has historically meant. The "defining characteristic" of the professional, Pope and Vasquez (2016) note, has been "an ethic of placing the client's well-being foremost and not allowing professional judgment or services to be drawn off course by one's own needs" (p. 64).

So, how can wanting to help people be problematic or even dangerous?

Suppose a 23-year-old client enters counseling because painful, ongoing tension with his parents, with whom he is living, distresses him profoundly. Motivated to help the client, the counselor advises him to move out and become more independent. The client complies, breaking off family ties, but then becomes very depressed because he and his culture deeply value close family relationships. That intervention, though well-intended, harmed that client, in whose culture family relationships are very important.

In addition to a motivation to benefit others, excellent clinical work and optimally ethical practice thus requires:

- Competence. We must possess or obtain relevant knowledge and skills so we can, in fact, help people. This includes reliable scientific knowledge.
- Recognizing diverse ideas about what "benefit" means. Determining what will benefit a particular client is often challenging. "Benefit"—which is tied to the goals of psychotherapy—has to do with ideas about what is a good life for a person, obligations, and what is right and wrong (Tjeltveit, 2006). Deep cultural and philosophical differences exist about such ideas. Ideas about benefit may also be tied to client and therapist religiousness, spirituality, religiousness and spirituality, or neither. It is crucial that psychotherapists don't assume that their ideas about a good life ("benefit") are the only or only correct ideas, in part so they don't impose their views on clients.
- Openness to relevant, reliable empirical evidence. Our intuitions about what will help a person may be mistaken. Obtaining relevant empirical evidence about what actually benefits people in general is thus essential, as is evidence about what harms people (Lilienfeld, 2007). Where relevant, reliable empirical evidence about the benefits and risks of treatment options is not available, or client characteristics indicate that an intervention that is generally effective may not help (or even harm) a particular client, we need to make the best possible judgment. Taking client views and choices very seriously and substantial humility are, however, essential, so we exhibit the respect for clients addressed in the APA (2010) and ACA (2014) ethics codes.

- Cultural sensitivity. Insensitivity and imposing ideas about the good life and well-being that are foreign to the client may result in harm to them, despite our wanting to help them. Sensitivity benefits clients and avoids harming them.
- Avoiding harm. The ethical principle of beneficence is often yoked with the ethical principle of nonmaleficence or harm avoidance (don't harm clients). Expressed in medical ethics as *Primum non nocere*, or "Above all [or first] do no harm" (Beauchamp & Childress, 2013, p. 150), its relevance to psychotherapy and counseling is this: any intervention that has the power to benefit also has the power to harm. Mental health professionals need to be aware of the potential negative consequences of the services they provide and avoid such harm. The goal is to benefit clients in ways that don't harm them. How to do so, of course, is one of the great challenges of clinical practice.
- Self-care. Professionals are not obligated to harm or impoverish themselves in order to benefit others. Neglecting oneself is, however, an occupational hazard of the mental health professions. Care for others thus needs to be matched with self-care. We need to be able to sustain ourselves in order to continue to benefit others. Psychotherapists who don't do so get burned out, provide substandard care, develop their own psychological problems, and/or act unethically. A variety of self-care strategies exist, with each professional needing to develop a repertoire that works, including interpersonal support, the right balance of work and relaxation, and so forth.
- Drawing on ethical and psychological sources that sustain a commitment to help others. Entering a field with a desire to help others is relatively easy. Far more difficult is identifying rich, sustaining sources that enable us to continue to be motivated to help others across the span of a career. Doing so is difficult, but mental health professionals face few more crucial tasks.

Those factors all help structure, channel, and empower professionals' commitment to beneficence, to helping others. Technical knowledge and training is not enough if a professional is not committed to helping those with whom he or she works.

When we draw on sustaining psychological, social, and ethical resources, avoid harming clients, exhibit humility about what we know, attend to relevant empirical evidence, respect client views on the meaning of benefit, and exhibit cultural sensitivity, then we can provide the greatest benefit to our clients. That is what the mental health professions are, at core, all about.

One of three sources usually accounts for client deterioration: (1) therapist factors, (2) client factors, or (3) specific psychological interventions.

1. Therapist Factors

Counselors and psychotherapists can differ dramatically in their therapeutic skills and talents. In a study of 71 therapists who provided counseling services for clients with similar problems, Lambert (2007) reported that "One therapist who saw more than 160 patients had a 19% deterioration rate, whereas another saw more than 300 patients, with less than 1% deteriorating" (p. 11). If you could choose between these two therapists, your choice would be obvious. Unfortunately, the therapists in Lambert's study were anonymous and therefore no conclusions could be made regarding specific qualities associated with high success and failure rates. However, other research suggests that the following four therapist factors or behaviors may be linked with negative outcomes:

1. Therapists who show little empathic attunement or warmth in their interactions with clients (Greenberg, Watson, Elliot, & Bohart, 2001).

2. Therapists who employ overly confrontational or intrusive therapy approaches (Castonguay, Boswell, Constantino, Goldfried, & Hill, 2010; Mohr, 1995).

3. Therapists using poor assessment procedures (including culturally biased assessments; Pieterse & Miller, 2010).

4. Therapists whose personality or approach is a poor fit for a given client (Beutler, 2009).

Therapists may be unaware of their negative behaviors and negative treatment outcomes. Clearly, therapists need to make great efforts to scrutinize themselves and systematically evaluate their outcomes (Meier, 2015).

2. Client Factors

Extratherapeutic factors likely account for the greatest proportion of positive therapy outcomes (Lambert, 1992; Wampold & Imel, 2015). It follows that negative client characteristics (including a lack of personal resources) might contribute to negative treatment outcomes. Client factors that can contribute to adverse outcomes include:

- Low client motivation (Clarkin, Levy, Lenzenweger, & Kernberg, 2004; Dimidjian & Hollon, 2011).
- High client psychopathology (e.g., comorbidity, paranoia, antisocial behavior; Davidson, Perry, & Bell, 2015).
- Limited client personal resources (e.g., limited intelligence, insight, family, or social support; Leibert, Smith, & Agaskar, 2011).

It's difficult to change or modify extratherapeutic factors that clients bring into the therapy office and it's impossible to know what strengths or weaknesses clients have before they arrive for treatment. Given these limitations, developing a strong working alliance is even more important when clients have few extratherapeutic factors (Leibert, Smith, & Agaskar, 2011).

Beutler's (2009) review shows that one of the most significant contributors to positive treatment outcomes is goodness of fit. Beutler wrote: "The fit of the treatment to the particular patient accounted for the strongest effects on outcomes of all variable classes at one year after treatment" (p. 313). Consequently, practicing therapists should modify their approaches based on individual client features.

3. Psychological Intervention Factors

Lilienfeld (Lilienfeld, 2007; Lilienfeld, Lynn, & Lohr, 2003) systematically reviewed psychotherapy outcomes literature and identified specific therapy approaches that produce unacceptable negative effects. He refers to these therapy approaches as **potentially harmful therapies** (PHTs). In developing his PHT list, Lilienfeld (2007) relied on (a) at least one replicated RCT showing potential harm; (b) meta-analytic reviews of multiple RCTs; and (c) research reports linking sudden adverse events to the initiation of therapy (p. 58).

The potential negative psychotherapy effects are not minor. In many situations charismatic therapists can have a powerfully positive or negative influence on clients. As Beutler (2009, p. 307) wrote: "In some cases, such as rebirthing therapy, the result has been death; in others, such as reprogramming therapy, it has been the psychological destruction of lives and families."

The seriousness of PHT effects is a reminder of psychotherapy potency. It's also a reminder of how important it is for ethical therapists to stay attuned not only to efficacy and effectiveness studies but also to research that identifies treatment approaches that have heightened risks. Lilienfeld listed 11 PHTs:

Potentially Harmful Therapies

1. Critical incident stress debriefing.
2. Scared straight interventions.
3. Facilitated communication.
4. Attachment therapies (e.g., rebirthing).
5. Recovered-memory techniques.
6. DID-oriented therapy.
7. Induction of "alter" personalities.
8. Grief counseling for individuals with normal bereavement reactions.
9. Expressive-experiential therapies.
10. Boot-camp interventions for conduct disorder.
11. DARE (Drug Abuse Resistance Education) programs.

We should emphasize that PHTs are not harmful therapies; they're potentially harmful therapies. Although some are dangerous and sometimes lethal, others can be implemented appropriately (for detailed information, see Lilienfeld, 2007).

Going Forward and Getting Positive

After focusing on negative therapy outcomes, negative therapist characteristics, and PHTs, it's time to refocus on the positive. Overall, there are good reasons to be hopeful about achieving positive outcomes. In particular, there are several steps you can take to minimize negative outcomes and maximize positive ones.

A Plan for Maximizing Positive Outcomes

William Glasser and Robert Wubbolding (see Chapter 9) would likely say: there's nothing like a good plan to help with goal attainment. Here are some ideas for maximizing your positive outcomes.

1. The therapy relationship (working alliance) is your best tool for creating positive outcomes. This means you should intentionally try to be genuine, accept clients for who they are, and show empathy (see Chapter 6 for much more on these person-centered therapy conditions). Additionally, consistent with Bordin's (1979) tripartite working alliance, you should: (a) establish an emotional connection with clients; (b) set common goals; and (c) collaborate on therapy tasks linked to therapy goals (J. Sommers-Flanagan, 2015; see Norcross, 2011, for more on "evidence-based relationships").

2. Integrate empirically supported treatments (ESTs) into your therapy practice. Many different ESTs are available, but to use them, you'll need advanced

training and supervision. Also, because there are so many ESTs, you should learn a few for working with specific populations (e.g., if you want to work with individuals suffering from trauma, learning both trauma-focused cognitive behavioral therapy (TF-CBT) and/or eye movement desensitization reprocessing (EMDR) would be useful).

3. Use evidence-based principles (EBPs). There will be situations when clients don't perfectly fit an EST approach. In those cases you should follow EBPs. For example, using Beutler's systematic treatment selection model (see Chapter 14), you can select approaches that are a good fit for specific clients and their particular problems (Beutler, 2011; Beutler, Harwood, Bertoni, & Thomann, 2006).

4. To avoid negative outcomes, you should: (a) continually work on self-awareness using individual supervision, peer supervision, and client feedback or progress monitoring; (b) individualize therapy approaches to fit clients—rather than expecting all clients to benefit from one approach; and (c) avoid using PHTs or use them in ways that reduce potential harm (Lilienfeld, 2007).

5. Use flexible, but systematic and culturally sensitive assessment approaches to tailor the treatment to clients and their problems. Ethical therapists conduct assessment prior to using specific therapy interventions. As you read each chapter, you'll see that each theory includes recommended assessment strategies. However, regardless of theory, therapeutic assessment should be collaborative, empathic, and culturally sensitive (Finn, Fischer, & Handler, 2012).

6. Use **practice-based evidence** or **progress monitoring** (PM) to track therapy process and outcomes. Practice-based evidence (aka PM) involves collecting data, sometimes every session, pertaining to client symptoms and/or client satisfaction (Meier, 2015). Duncan, Miller, and Sparks (2004) refer to this as **client informed therapy**. Regardless of the terminology, it helps to empower clients to directly share their treatment progress (or lack thereof) with their therapists. This allows therapists to make modifications in their approach as needed (Lambert, 2010).

Additional Ethical Issues

You will face many more ethical issues as you provide mental health services. Most ethics experts consider ethical codes as a rudimentary and surface effort to hold practitioners to higher standards of care (R. Sommers-Flanagan & Sommers-Flanagan, 2007; Welfel, 2016). Ethical codes have become increasingly legalistic and sometimes serve protective rather than proactive or aspirational functions. Being an ethical practitioner requires ongoing attention

to the heart of the profession. At a minimum, it includes consultation with colleagues, a good ethical problem-solving model, continuing education, and a willingness to scrutinize your own behaviors.

NEUROSCIENCE IN COUNSELING AND PSYCHOTHERAPY

A recent title search of the PsycInfo database using a combination of "neuroscience" and "counseling" or "psychotherapy" revealed two publications from 1980 to 1999. In contrast, there were 93 published works from 2000 to 2015. This is one indicator of the enthusiasm and excitement surrounding potential integrations of neuroscience and counseling/psychotherapy.

Neuroscientific findings are increasingly recognized as having profound implications for counseling and psychotherapy research and practice. In some cases this recognition comes grudgingly. In others, enthusiasts view neuroscience as transforming everything we know about counseling and psychotherapy. Recently, the new terms "neuropsychotherapy" and "neurocounseling" have been introduced. Given this trend, in chapters where neuroscience research has been applied to specific theories, we've included special coverage in the form of Brain Boxes (see Brain Box 1.1).

Historical Reflections

In 1980, I (John) began my career in mental health as a recreation therapist in a 22-bed psychiatric hospital. The patients were experiencing severe depression, manic episodes, and psychotic symptoms.

There was an intimidating psychiatrist (Dr. M) on the unit who was a fan of biological psychiatry. He would smile as I engaged patients in the "Newlyfriend Game" (like the Newlywed Game, only better), relaxation groups, bowling nights, and ice cream socials. Occasionally Dr. M cornered me, explaining how my recreational programs had no influence on our patients' mental health. He waxed eloquent about brain chemistry. True, the Thorazine and Haldol he prescribed had nasty side effects, but eventually, he claimed, there would be designer drugs that restored neurochemical balance and cured mental disorders. Everything else was irrelevant.

The chemical imbalance theory of mental disorders dominated mental health etiology through the 1980s and 1990s. Etiological explanations focused on too much dopamine (causing schizophrenia) and not enough norepinephrine or serotonin (causing depression). No one knew what caused these so-called imbalances, but biogenetic factors were the prime suspects. Although I kept silent with Dr. M, I held tight to my beliefs that social, psychological, and physical experiences could be therapeutic.

BRAIN BOX

1.1 Three Pounds of Theoretical Elegance

This Brain Box is a brief, oversimplified description of the brain. I apologize, in advance, to you and to brains everywhere for this oversimplification and likely misrepresentation. The problem is that even if I took a whole chapter or a whole book to describe these three pounds of elegance, it would still be an oversimplification. Such is the nature and mystery of the human brain.

You may already be familiar with the concepts described here. If so, it's a review. If you may be less familiar, then it's an introduction. For more information on neuroscience and therapy, we recommend *Neuroscience for Counselors and Therapists: Integrating the Sciences of Mind and Brain* by Chad Luke.

Brain structure: The human brain has indentations, folds, and fissures. It's slick and slimy. Put simply, it's not a pretty sight. However, the brain's form maximizes its function. One example: if you could lay out and spread its surface area onto a table, it would be about the size of two pages of a newspaper. The folds and fissures allow more surface area to fit within the human skull.

Scientists describe the brain as having four lobes: the frontal, parietal, occipital, and temporal (see Figure 1.3). The fissures or sulci of the brain demarcate the four lobes. At the bottom of the brain is the brainstem and cerebellum.

Each lobe is generally associated with different brain functions. I say "generally" because brains are specific and systemic. Although individuals have similar brain structures, individual brains are more unique than a fingerprint on a snowflake.

The **frontal lobe** is primarily associated with complex thought processes such as planning, reasoning, and decision-making (much, but not all, of what psychoanalysts

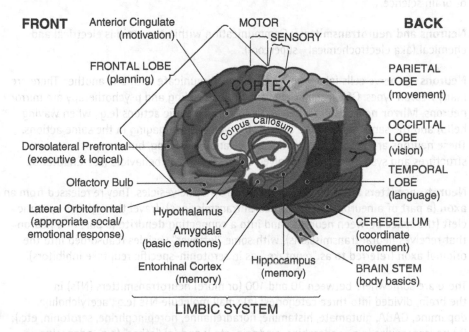

FIGURE 1.3   **A Look at the Brain**
(*Source:* http://www.brainwaves.com/. Reproduced with permission of Brainwaves)

refer to as ego functions). The frontal lobe also appears involved in expressive language and contains the motor cortex.

The **parietal lobe** includes the somatosensory cortex. This surface area involves sensory processing (including pain and touch). It also includes spatial or visual orientation.

The **temporal lobes** are located symmetrically on each side of the brain (just above the ears). They're involved in auditory perception and processing. They contain the hippocampus and are involved in memory formation and storage.

The **occipital lobe** is located in the back of the brain and is the primary visual processing center.

I'm using all four lobes right now to type, read, edit, re-think, re-type, re-read, shift my position, and recall various relevant and irrelevant experiences. The idea that we only use 10% of our brains is a silly myth. They even busted it on the *Mythbusters* television show.

The brain includes two **hemispheres**. They're separated by the longitudinal fissure and communicate with each other primarily via the corpus callosum. The hemispheres are nearly mirror images of each other in size and shape. However, their neurotransmitter quantities and receptor subtypes are quite different. The **right hemisphere** controls the left side of the body and is primarily involved in spatial, musical, and artistic/creative functions. In contrast, the left hemisphere controls the right side of the body and is involved in language, logical thinking, and linear analysis. There are exceptions to these general descriptions and these exceptions are larger in brains of individuals who are left-handed. Woo-hoo for lefties.

The **limbic system** is located deep within the brain. It has several structures involved in memory and emotional experiencing. These include, but are not limited to, the amygdala, basal ganglia, cingulate gyrus, hippocampus, hypothalamus, and thalamus. The limbic system and its structural components are currently very popular; they're like the Beyoncé of brain science.

Neurons and neurotransmitters: Communication within the brain is electrical and chemical (aka electrochemical = supercool).

Neurons are nerve cells (aka brain cells) that communicate with one another. There are many neuron types. Of particular relevance to counseling and psychotherapy are mirror neurons. **Mirror neurons** fire when you engage in specific actions (e.g., when waving hello) and the same neurons fire as you observe others engaging in the same actions. These neurons are central to empathy and vicarious learning, but many other brain structures and systems are also involved in these complex behaviors (see Chapter 5).

Neurotransmitters are chemicals packed into synaptic vesicles. They're released from an **axon** (a part of a neuron that sends neural transmissions), travel through the synaptic cleft (the space between neurons), and into a connecting **dendrite** (a part of a neuron that receives neural transmissions), with some "leftover" vesicles reabsorbed into the original axon (referred to as "reuptake," as in serotonin-specific reuptake inhibitors).

There are somewhere between 30 and 100 (or more) neurotransmitters (NTs) in the brain, divided into three categories: (a) small molecule NTs (e.g., acetylcholine, dopamine, GABA, glutamate, histamine, noradrenaline, norepinephrine, serotonin, etc.); (b) neuropeptides (e.g., endorphins, oxytocin, etc.); and (c) "other" (e.g., adenosine, endocannadinoids, nitric oxide, etc.). Neurotransmitters are classified as excitatory or inhibitory or both. For example, norepinephrine is an excitatory neurotransmitter, dopamine is both excitatory and inhibitory, and serotonin is inhibitory. Although several chemical imbalance hypotheses regarding the etiology of mental disorders have been promoted (e.g., "low" serotonin at the synaptic cleft causes depression), when it comes to the brain, I caution you against enthusiastic acceptance of any simplistic explanations. A significant portion of the scientific community consider the dopamine and serotonin hypotheses to be primarily mythical (see Breggin, 2016; Edwards, Bacanu, Bigdeli, Moscati, & Kendler, 2016; Moncrieff, 2015).

As I pursued graduate studies, I found evidence to support my beliefs including a study showing that testosterone levels vary as a function of winning or losing tennis matches (Booth, Shelley, Mazur, Tharp, & Kittok, 1989). If our testosterone levels changed based on competitive tennis, what other ways might human experiences influence the brain?

In 1998, while perusing research on serotonin and depression, I discovered that treadmill running increased brain serotonin in rats. The researcher described the complexity of the phenomenon:

> Lipolysis-elicited release of free fatty acids displaces the binding of tryptophan to albumin and because exercise increases the ratio of circulating free tryptophan to the sum of the concentrations of the amino acids that compete with tryptophan for uptake at the blood–brain barrier level, tryptophan enters markedly in the brain compartment. (Chaoeloff, 1997, p. 58)

It seemed possible that physical exercise might increase serotonin in human brains and also help alleviate depression.

Then, along came neurogenesis. **Neurogenesis** is the creation of new brain cells. It has been long known that during fetal development, cells are created and migrate to specific places in the brain and body where they engage in their specific role and function. Cells that become rods and cones end up in the eyes, while other cells become bone, and still others end up in the cerebral cortex. In the 1980s and 1990s, everyone agreed that neurogenesis continued during infancy, but most neuroscientists also believed that after early childhood the brain locked down and neurogenesis stopped. In other words, as adults, we only had neuronal pruning (cell death).

In the late 1980s, neuroscientists began conducting research that shook long-held assumptions about neurogenesis. For example, one research team (Jenkins, Merzenich, Ochs, Allard, & Guk-Robles, 1990) housed adult monkeys in cages where the monkeys had to use their middle finger to rotate a disc to get banana pellets. Even after a short time period (1 week), brain autopsies showed that the monkeys had an enlarged region in their motor cortex. The conclusion: in adult monkeys, repeated physical behaviors stimulate neurogenesis in the motor cortex. This seemed like common sense. Not only do our brains shape our experiences, but our experiences shape the brain (literally).

As it turns out, neurogenesis slows with age, but doesn't stop. It continues throughout the lifespan. New learning stimulates cell birth and growth in the hippocampus (and other areas involving memory processing and storage). This "new brain research" left open the possibility that counseling and psychotherapy might stimulate neurochemical changes and cell birth in the human brain.

As brain research continues to accelerate, implications and applications of neuroscience to counseling and psychotherapy have flourished (Satel & Lilienfeld, 2013). Practitioners have created new marketing terminology like "brain-based therapy," "neuropsychotherapy," "neurocounseling," and "interpersonal neurobiology," despite the lack of clear scientific evidence to support these terms. In some cases, birthing of this new terminology has caused lamentation within the neuroscience and academic communities (Bott, Radke, & Kiely, 2016; Lilienfeld, Schwartz, Meca, Sauvigné, & Satel, 2015).

Appreciating Neuroscience Complexities

Where does all this take us? As Dr. M would say, the brain is central to mood and behavior change. We now know that the reverse is also true: mood, behavior, and social interaction are central to brain development and change. The influence goes in both directions. More importantly, we need to acknowledge that relationships between and among brain structures, neurotransmitters, hormones, other chemicals, and human behaviors are extremely complex and still largely unexplained. The brain is functioning as a whole, as regions, as inter- and intracellular processes, while doing all these activities both sequentially and simultaneously.

Here's an example of the complexities we must take into account as we attempt to use neuroscience findings in therapeutic practice. It appears that meditation and interpersonal empathic experiences stimulate the anterior insular cortex (AIC) and perhaps facilitate neurogenesis! So what does this mean exactly? The following excerpt from the neuroscience literature helps illustrate the difficulty of making direct inferences (Mutschler, Reinbold, Wankerl, Seifritz, & Ball, 2013):

> In summary, we argue that the dorsal AIC plays a pivotal role in empathy (similarly as during emotion processing and pain) by integrating sensory stimuli with its salience,

possibly via connections to the cingulate cortex....
As mentioned above we assume that the overall role
of the morphometrically identified area in the dorsal
AIC related to individual differences in empathy which
overlaps the DGR might be involved in integrating
information which is relevant for socio-emotional and
cognitive processing. Thus, we assume that empathy
is not (only) related to a specific "socio-emotional"
interaction area, but to a superordinate "domain-general"
area, in line with concepts of empathy that include not
only social and emotional, but also cognitive aspects....
Whether our findings in the dorsal AIC have also a
relation to the "von Economo neurons" [VENs,...]
remains to be determined. VENs have been hypothesized
to play a role in social-emotional processing including
empathy...." (Reproduced under the Creative Commons
Attribution License, *Source:* Mutschler, Reinbold,
Wankerl, Seifritz, and Ball, 2013, p. 6)

This excerpt should inspire us all to pause with respect
for the complexity of neuroscience; it should also slow
down simplistic conclusions. If we just focus on empathy and the insula, we can see many sources of potential
error: (a) much of the neuroscience empathy research
focuses on empathy for physical pain; (b) empathy is hard
to measure; (c) it's possible for a human brain to "light
up" with empathy, but for the human to not express
empathy; (d) while empathy is generally considered a
positive quality, some people use empathy to manipulate
and hurt others; (e) there is brain structural and functional overlap; and (f) the role of the VENs is unknown.

EMERGENCE OF PERSONAL THEORY

If you want to be an excellent mental health professional,
then it makes sense to closely study the thinking of some
of the greatest minds and models in the field. This text
covers 12 of the most comprehensive and practical theories in existence. We hope you absorb each theory as
thoroughly as possible and try experiencing them from
the inside out. As you proceed through each chapter, suspend doubt and try thinking like a practitioner from each
theoretical orientation.

It's also important for you to discover which theory or
theories are the best fit for you. You'll have opportunities
to reflect on the content of this text and hopefully that will
help you develop your own ideas about human functioning and change. Although we're not recommending that
you develop a 13th theory, we are recommending that you
explore how to integrate your genuine self into these different theoretical perspectives.

Some of you reading this book may already have considerable knowledge and experience about counseling
and psychotherapy theories. However, even if you have
very little knowledge and experience, you undoubtedly
have some preexisting ideas about what helps people
change. Therefore, before reading Chapters 2 through
14, we encourage you to look at your own implicit ideas
about people and how they change.

Your First Client and Your First Theory

Pretend this is the first day of your career as a mental
health professional. You have all the amenities: a taste-
fully decorated office, two comfortable chairs, a graduate
degree, and a client.

You also have everything that any scarecrow, tin man, or
lion might yearn for: a brain full of knowledge about how to
provide therapy, a heart with compassion for a diverse range
of clients, and courage to face the challenge of providing
therapy services. But do you have what it takes to help a fellow human being climb from a pit of despair? Do you have
the judgment to apply your knowledge in an effective way?

You walk to the waiting room. She's there. She's your
first client ever. You greet her. The two of you walk back
to the office.

In the first 20 minutes, you learn quite a lot about
your client: she's a 21-year-old college student experiencing apathy, insomnia, no romantic interests, carbohy-
drate cravings, an absence of hobbies, and extremely poor
grades. She's not using drugs or alcohol. Based on this
information, you tentatively diagnose her as having some
variant of clinical depression and proceed with counseling.
But how do you proceed? Do you focus on her automatic
thoughts and her core beliefs about herself that might
be contributing to her depressive symptoms? Do you
help her get a tutor, thinking that improved grades might
lift her depressive symptoms? Do you recommend she
begin an exercise routine? Do you explore her childhood,
wondering if she has a trauma experience that needs to
be understood and worked through? Do you teach her
mindfulness skills and have her practice meditation? Do
you have her role play and rehearse solutions to her problems? Do you focus on listening, assuming that if you
provide her a positive therapy environment, she'll gain
insight into herself and move toward greater psychological health? Do you help her recast herself and her life into
a story with a positive ending with a more adaptive identity? Do you ask her to sit in different chairs—speaking
from different perspectives to explore her here and now
feelings of success and failure? Any or all of these strategies might help. Which ones seem best to you?

You have many choices for how to proceed, depending upon your theoretical orientation. Here's our advice.
Don't get stuck too soon with a single theoretical orientation. It's unlikely that all humans will respond to the
same approach. As suggested in Putting It in Practice 1.2,
experiment and reflect before choosing your preferred
theory. (Complete the ratings in Table 1.2 and then look
through Table 1.3 to see which major theoretical perspectives might fit best for you.)

Table 1.2   What's Your "Natural" Theoretical Orientation?

Instructions: Use the following scale to rate each statement under each theory heading:

0 - - - - 1 - - - - 2 - - - - 3 - - - - 4 - - - - 5 - - - - 6 - - - - 7 - - - - 8 - - - - 9 - - - - 10

0 = Completely Disagree   5 = On the Fence   10 = Completely Agree

Theory 1   1. Most client problems consist of repeating dysfunctional relationship patterns; these patterns are very difficult to change unless clients can become more aware of where their patterns come from. RATING _____

2. Because clients bring developmental baggage into therapy with them, they invariably project their old child–caretaker (parent) relationship dynamics onto the therapist and repeat or reenact their child–parent or child–caretaker relationship patterns. RATING _____

3. The main job of the therapist is to remain quiet and listen for the client's unconscious patterns of dealing with inner conflict or unhealthy relationship patterns and then to interpret or share these patterns with the client in an effort to increase client awareness. RATING _____

Theory 2   1. An unhealthy individual who needs counseling or psychotherapy typically feels discouraged in his/her efforts to face the major tasks of life (this also might involve a lack of courage to face the demands of life). RATING _____

2. People are built to strive forward in their lives toward future goals, seeking to improve themselves and seeking purpose and meaning. RATING _____

3. The relationship between therapist and client should be like that of a friendly teacher with one's student. RATING _____

Theory 3   1. The inevitable conditions humans face during life, such as death, responsibility, freedom, and meaning or purpose, can and should be a primary focus of counseling and psychotherapy. RATING _____

2. When clients are troubled by anxiety or guilt they're better served by embracing and seeking to understand the meaning of these emotions than they are by learning skills for avoiding their emotional reactions. RATING _____

3. Therapy works best when therapists are fully present and engaged in a relationship with the client and, at the same time, are, when appropriate, both empathic and confrontational. RATING _____

Theory 4   1. The client is the best expert on the direction therapy should go and consequently therapists should trust their clients to lead them to the most important topics to talk about. RATING _____

2. Clients (and all people) have within them a deep actualizing or formative tendency. If this force is activated it can pull or push clients toward positive growth and development. RATING _____

3. Successful therapy occurs because the therapist has established a relationship with clients based on authenticity, respect, and empathic understanding. This is the foundation for change and sometimes may be all that's needed for therapy to succeed. RATING _____

Theory 5   1. The most important focus for therapy is on client self-awareness in the present moment. This awareness should include physical and sensory awareness; intellectualizing or thinking should be de-emphasized. RATING _____

2. The main purpose of therapy techniques is to bring unfinished business from the past into the present so it can be dealt with more directly and effectively. RATING _____

3. In therapy clients should be pushed to stay in touch with their feelings and take responsibility for all of their behaviors. RATING _____

Theory 6   1. Therapy interventions should be based on solid scientific evidence (i.e., laboratory experimentation). RATING _____

2. Adaptive and maladaptive human behaviors are acquired and maintained in the same way: through learning. RATING _____

3. Successful therapy does not require clients to change their thinking. In fact, trying to change clients' thinking is often irrelevant. Instead, successful therapy only requires that clients change their behavior. RATING _____

Theory 7   1. It's not what happens to individuals that causes them misery; it's what they think about what happens to them. RATING _____

2. Therapy should be an educational process, with therapists teaching and clients learning. RATING _____

3. For therapy to result in a positive outcome, therapists need to challenge or question the irrational or maladaptive thinking that's linked to the client's problems. RATING _____

Theory 8   1. Humans act, not on the basis of external rewards and punishments, but based on internal values and things we want or wish for. RATING _____

2. The only person whose behavior you have complete control over is your own. Moreover, the only person's behavior that you should seek to control is your own. RATING _____

3. Therapy involves detailed planning for how clients can achieve what they want. A good plan is very specific and doable. RATING _____

(continued)

Table 1.2 What's Your "Natural" Theoretical Orientation? *(continued)*

Theory 9 1. Raising client consciousness of social oppression and gender-based limits is a crucial part of effective therapy. RATING _____
2. Psychopathology is primarily caused by gender and social-related norms that inhibit and oppress women and minorities. RATING _____
3. The therapy relationship should be mutually empathic and egalitarian. RATING _____

Theory 10 1. It is crucial for therapists to help clients apply whatever strengths they bring with them into the therapy office to their personal problem situations. RATING _____
2. Sometimes only a very small change is needed to address very big problems. RATING _____
3. Client resistance is natural and not the fault of the client. RATING _____

Theory 11 1. In most cases, the proper focus of therapy is the family system and not the individual. RATING _____
2. Individual problems are created and maintained by the family and serve a purpose within the family. RATING _____
3. Therapy that focuses on family systems, community systems, and other factors outside the individual constitute some of the most powerful approaches to human change. RATING _____

Theory 12 1. Ethnically diverse clients are better served by ethnically specific therapy, services oriented to the cultural needs of clients. RATING _____
2. To work effectively with minority clients, therapists need specific training in multicultural sensitivity and knowledge. RATING _____
3. Psychopathology is not a problem existing within individuals; instead, psychopathology is usually created by oppressive social forces outside individuals. RATING _____

Theory 13 1. There is no single best or right theory of counseling or psychotherapy. RATING _____
2. Therapy is most effective when there's a good match between the client's problem, the specific technique, and the therapist's style. RATING _____
3. Effective therapy involves an emotionally charged relationship and a process that includes a socially sanctioned myth (about the cause of the problem) and an appropriate ritual that enhances positive expectations. RATING _____

Scoring Instructions: Add up your scores for each theory. The lowest possible score is 0; the highest possible is 30. The theories linked to your highest scores are your natural theoretical inclination. Those linked to your lowest scores are inconsistent with how you think about therapy now. Check Table 1.3 for brief descriptions of each theory.

Table 1.3 An Overview of 13 Theoretical Perspectives

Theory 1: Psychoanalytic or psychodynamic theory (Chapter 2). Psychoanalytic theories hold the common belief that early childhood relationships shape personality and behavior. The main goal of psychoanalytic therapies is to bring maladaptive unconscious relationship dynamics into consciousness. This involves an exploration of past relationships, development of insights into current relationship dynamics, and an application of these insights to contemporary relationships.

Theory 2: Adlerian or individual psychology (Chapter 3). Individual (Adlerian) psychology views each client as a unique, whole individual who strives toward improvements and idiosyncratic personal goals. Psychopathology develops when people become discouraged due to belief systems that interfere with their ability to face and deal with the tasks of life. Therapists help clients have insight into the "basic mistakes" imbedded in their belief systems. Therapy is effective because of a friendly, collaborative relationship, insight into maladaptive aspects of the lifestyle, and education about how to remediate the maladaptive lifestyle.

Theory 3: Existential (Chapter 4). Existential approaches are derived from existential philosophy. Individuals must grapple with core life issues such as death, freedom, isolation, and meaninglessness. Anxiety is part of normal human experience. Psychopathology arises when individuals avoid, rather than confront and cope with, life's core issues. Existential therapists can be gentle or confrontational and strive to develop a deep and authentic relationship with clients. Preplanned techniques are generally not used. Therapy is effective when clients are able to face their ultimate concerns and constructively embrace anxiety in ways that enhance personal meaning.

Theory 4: Person-centered (Chapter 5). Person-centered therapy is an optimistic, humanistic, and phenomenological approach to therapy. Person-centered theory posits that individuals have within themselves a capacity for dramatic and positive growth. This growth is stymied and psychopathology arises when clients, usually in childhood relationships, begin to believe they are not worthwhile or lovable unless they meet specific behavioral conditions (i.e., conditions of worth). In person-centered therapy, clients can talk about whatever they believe is important, especially whatever is emotionally significant. Person-centered therapy is effective when therapists are genuine, accepting and respectful, and empathic.

Theory 5: Gestalt (Chapter 6). Gestalt theory views humans as having both natural growth potential and natural defensiveness from experiential contact. Gestalt therapy focuses on developing an I-Thou relationship between client and therapist and then works in the here and now to deal with unfinished emotional and behavioral experiences from the past. Intellectualization is discouraged and action within the session is encouraged. Gestalt therapists don't engage in authoritative interpretation, but instead confront clients to come to their senses and make their own interpretations via Gestalt experiments.

Theory 6: Behavioral (Chapter 7). Behaviorists believe in basing all therapy approaches on scientific research. Behaviorists view humans as a function of their environment. Psychopathology is directly caused by maladaptive learning, either from classical or operant conditioning models. Behavior therapy consists of relearning; the focus of therapy is primarily on the present. Therapy is effective when therapists teach clients to apply basic behavioral learning principles within and outside therapy.

Theory 7: Cognitive behavioral (Chapter 8). Cognitive theory and therapy are usually used in combination with behavioral approaches. Cognitive approaches emphasize vicarious learning and that it's not what happens to individuals that causes them distress but what they think or believe about what happens to them that causes distress. Maladaptive or irrational thinking styles and beliefs about the self and maladaptive inner speech produce psychopathology. Therapy is effective when clients are taught new and more adaptive or rational ways of thinking about themselves and their lives.

Theory 8: Reality therapy/choice (Chapter 9). Choice theory holds that individuals are responsible for choosing their thoughts and behaviors; thoughts and behaviors directly influence feelings and physiology. All humans are motivated to satisfy one or more of their five basic needs: survival, love and belonging, power, freedom, and fun. Psychopathology develops because clients choose to restrain anger, want to receive help from others, or are choosing to avoid important issues. Therapy focuses on the present and is effective because the therapist forms a positive therapy relationship with clients and then teaches choice theory from within the context of that relationship.

Theory 9: Feminist (Chapter 10). Feminist theory was developed to address the social and cultural oppression and unequal treatment of women. Feminists view psychopathology as arising from social, cultural, and masculine-based power inequities and oppression. Feminist therapy involves recognizing inequities and empowering women and minorities. Therapy is based on a strong, mutual, supportive, and empowering relationship between therapist and client. When therapy is effective, clients are empowered to use their strengths to further and deepen mutual relationships in their lives.

Theory 10: Constructive (Chapter 11). Constructive theory emphasizes the power of language, information processing, and cybernetics in influencing human behavior and change. Psychopathology is a function of each individual client's construction of reality. The focus is on the future, solutions, and reshaping the narrative or story the client is living. Therapy is effective when the therapist and the client have a conversation or dialogue and co-create a reality wherein clients engage in positive, solution-focused strategies for constructing and maintaining their world.

Theory 11: Family systems (Chapter 12). Family systems theorists view problems as emanating from dysfunctional family processes, rather than being owned by individuals. Psychopathology is viewed as a function of interpersonal transactions and interactions within the family context. Interventions focus on changing family dynamics or behaviors within the family, rather than on changing individuals. Therapy strategies range from being strategic and paradoxical to straightforward and behavioral.

Theory 12: Multicultural (Chapter 13). Multicultural theory focuses on the power of culture in influencing human behavior, emotions, and values. Psychopathology is a product of social and cultural oppression. Many multicultural approaches acknowledge and embrace religious and spiritual perspectives. Clients benefit from therapy when they are accepted and empowered to behave in ways consistent with their culture.

Theory 13. Integration/eclectic (Chapter 14). No single theory is viewed as more correct or inherently better than any other. Diverse theoretical perspectives are woven together with common factors, technical eclecticism, and theoretical integration. There are several evidence-based, new generation integrative approaches to counseling and psychotherapy. The nature of humans, psychopathology, and theoretical constructs shifts, depending upon the specific approaches employed. Effective therapy involves applying different approaches that best fit clients and their problems.

OUR BIASES

Good qualitative researchers try to acknowledge their personal biases when reporting their research results. We think the same should be true for textbook authors. We therefore provide you with a brief overview of some of our main biases.

Our Theoretical Roots

In a sense, we were born and raised eclectic. Our graduate program at the University of Montana in the 1980s included a psychoanalytic/hypnoanalytic professor, a cognitively oriented professor, a person-centered professor, and two behaviorists. John went to a strictly psychoanalytic predoctoral internship at a medical center in New York in 1985 and Rita went to a family systems child and family clinic in Oregon in 1988. After licensure,

John spent time teaching, working as a health psychologist in an industrial setting, in private practice, and as director of a parent education program. Rita has consulted with two different Veteran's Centers, established a part-time private practice, and taught 24 years as a professor of counselor education. During this time, we lived in Montana, New York, Washington, Oregon, Central America, and Northampton, England.

John's favorite theoretical figures are Carl Rogers, Alfred Adler, and Irvin Yalom. Rita's are Jean Baker Miller and the feminists, Alfred Adler, and Viktor Frankl. John loves to quote Freud and Rita loves to dethrone Freud, considering him overrated and antithetical to her feminist beliefs.

Our generalist background makes us slow to jump on contemporary bandwagons. We're especially cautious of new theories or techniques that claim remarkable recovery rates for distressed clients. Hopefully, this doesn't

---

PUTTING IT IN PRACTICE

1.2 Your Emerging Personal Theory
Reproduced with permission of Dr. Kurt Kraus

Dr. Kurt Kraus of the Department of Counseling and College Student Personnel at Shippensburg State University shares his thoughts on theories:

I am afraid that students are encouraged to identify their emerging theoretical identity way too early. Students write papers for professors of Introduction to Counseling and Survey of Theoretical Approaches espousing their growing theoretical identities. Nonsense! Take time to learn about mental health professionals who have practiced for many years, study their contributions, write about them and their experiences, their beliefs, their skills, the benefits and liabilities inherent in their practices. Only after you have explored the journeys of many others can you really begin to make a decision about your own. Heck, you are only beginning; how dare we imply that you should know where you want to be? (K. Kraus, personal communication, August 2002)

Another colleague who teaches theories of counseling and psychotherapy to graduate students, **Janice DeLucia-Waack** of the State University of New York, Buffalo, gives the following advice to her students (reproduced with permission of Janice DeLucia-Waack):

I tell my students that I don't expect or even want them to marry any particular theory while they're taking my course. However, I *do* tell them that I expect them to spend at least a week dating each theory before the semester ends. (J. DeLucia-Waack, personal communication, April 2002)

---

mean we're not open to new ideas. We're just reluctant to believe that having clients pop a pill or hum a few tunes will cure their longstanding problems.

Balance and Uncertainty

We have a strong bias against certainty. Several years ago we attended a workshop conducted by the great structural family therapist and theorist Salvador Minuchin. The subtitle of his presentation was "Don't be too sure." We agree. No theory holds the key to all problems. No theory entirely explains what it means to be human. When we get too sure about our theory, we close ourselves off to different perspectives; even worse, being too sure places us in danger of forcing the client to fit our theory, rather than the other way around.

We're skeptical about empirical research. The biggest problem with research is that it's tremendously difficult to conduct studies that reflect what happens in the therapy offices of practitioners around the world. As W. Silverman (1996) wrote, "Efficacy studies do not reflect models and they do not represent psychotherapy as practiced in the field" (p. 210).

However, we also deeply value counseling and psychotherapy research. Good research is essential to

guiding mental health professionals. When a particular form of treatment makes great claims of effectiveness in the absence of empirical research, we become very suspicious.

The Zeitgeist, Ortgeist, and Poltergeist

The **zeitgeist** is defined as "the spirit of the time." It explains why several individuals can, without consulting each other, make a significant discovery at around the same time. This spirit of the time explains why Pierre Janet and Sigmund Freud, in France and Austria, could both independently begin suspecting that working directly with client unconscious processes might help resolve longstanding and troublesome symptoms. In the late 1890s the time was right to begin working with the unconscious.

The **ortgeist** refers to the "spirit of the place." It explains why people in close proximity often move toward similar discoveries. Perhaps the ortgeist spirit was operating in Europe in the late 1890s. Bankart (1997) speaks of the zeitgeist and ortgeist in relation to Freud: "A genuine understanding of Freud's psychoanalysis, for example, requires (and at the same time provides) a reasonably deep understanding of middle-class life in turn-of-the-century Europe" (Bankart, p. 8).

Similarly, National Public Radio's show "The Writer's Almanac" featured a quotation on Freud from the plainspoken philosopher Eric Hoffer:

> Ah, don't talk to me about Freud. Freud lived in a tight little circle in Vienna, and inside that tight little circle was another tight little circle, and inside that tight little circle was still *another* tight little circle. What applies to that poor man, Freud, does not necessarily apply to me. (Keillor, 2002)

A **poltergeist** is a mischievous spirit or ghost. We reference poltergeists because, in our experience, conducting psychotherapy or counseling sometimes includes mysterious and mischievous surprises. An example of a poltergeist is given in the famous Harry Potter book series:

> Peeves the Poltergeist was worth two locked doors and a trick staircase if you met him when you were late for class. He would drop wastepaper baskets on your head, pull rugs from under your feet, pelt you with bits of chalk, or sneak up behind you, invisible, grab your nose, and screech, "GOT YOUR CONK!" (Rowling, 1997, p. 132)

We're not big believers in ghosts, but the idea of mischievous spirits is one way to bring your attention to the fact that you should prepare for the unexpected. Sometimes clients will say and do outrageous things. Other times, you'll suddenly feel the urge to say or do something inappropriate. For whatever reason, sitting privately with another individual for long periods of time can produce unusual and profound experiences. Just when you least suspect it, your videorecording equipment will malfunction or you'll feel like crying or you'll want to fidget or want to leave the room or the clock hanging on the wall in your office will stop or your client will tell you something shocking. Our point: be ready for surprises.

REFLECTIONS

Keeping the zeitgeist, ortgeist, and poltergeist in mind, what spirits of time, place, and mischief are operating in counseling and psychotherapy right now? What will be the next big discovery or controversy?

CONCLUDING COMMENTS

In this chapter we've taken you on a quick tour of major issues in counseling and psychotherapy. From historical context to contemporary research to ethical essentials, the field of counseling and psychotherapy is filled with amazing and interesting information. We wish you the best as you explore the main theories of therapy in greater depth.

CHAPTER SUMMARY AND REVIEW

Theories are central to the understanding and effectiveness of counseling and psychotherapy. Theories are important because they provide mental health practitioners with direction and guidance on how to practice. This book reviews many different traditional and contemporary theoretical perspectives, all of which have some research support and have made efforts to address unique issues salient to diverse populations.

Counseling and psychotherapy theories involve the gathering together and organizing of knowledge about how people develop emotional or behavioral problems, what can help them make positive changes, and how they're likely to respond to therapeutic interventions. All theories develop within a particular context. Most people consider modern theories of psychotherapy to have started with Sigmund Freud, but many other people and contextual factors were operating in combination.

At least four different cultural and historical perspectives have shaped the development of counseling and psychotherapy. These included: (1) biomedical, (2) religious/spiritual, (3) psychosocial, and (4) feminist/multicultural.

Many different definitions for counseling and psychotherapy have been offered over the years. Psychotherapy tends to be seen as a longer, deeper, and more expensive process as compared to counseling. The definition of counseling and psychotherapy is complex, including at least 12 different dimensions.

In 1952, Hans Eysenck conducted a review of psychotherapy outcomes and concluded psychotherapy was less effective than no treatment whatsoever. This finding was controversial and stimulated substantial research on psychotherapy outcomes. Currently, most researchers and practitioners agree that counseling and psychotherapy are very effective, but there are still heated arguments over which approaches are more effective with which problems.

There are two main positions constituting the *great psychotherapy debate*. One position claims that specific therapy procedures are superior to other procedures and therefore should constitute most of what therapists provide. The other position claims that there are common factors within all approaches that account for the fact that research generally shows all therapy approaches have equal efficacy or effectiveness.

Counseling and psychotherapy approaches are evaluated in either highly controlled research protocols or real-world settings. Tightly controlled research protocols are called treatment efficacy studies; research in real-world settings are called effectiveness studies.

Counselors and psychotherapists are required to abide by professional ethics. Essential ethical topics include: (a) competence and informed consent; (b) multicultural sensitivity, competence, and humility; (c) confidentiality; (d) multiple roles; and (e) beneficence. It's important for counseling and psychotherapy professionals to be aware that some treatment approaches are potentially harmful. To avoid harming clients, therapists should focus on establishing a strong therapy alliance, integrate empirically supported treatments, use evidence-based principles, individualize therapy, and use culturally sensitive assessments to monitor client progress.

Neuroscience is increasingly seen as having significant implications for how counselors and psychotherapists practice. New terms integrating neuroscience into therapy have been introduced. Over time, neuroscientific findings have supported the ideas that counseling and psychotherapy relationships and techniques cause changes in the brain that contribute to positive outcomes.

As you read this book you will have a chance to explore your own ideas about counseling, psychotherapy, and human change. This will help you integrate your own ideas, values, and ways of being into existing therapy approaches. As authors, we have our own biases. These include a preference for having broad theoretical roots, recognizing that even scientific research leaves room for uncertainty, and the importance of recognizing that the spirit of the time, place, and other mysterious forces will continue to influence counseling and psychotherapy theory and practice.

INTRODUCTORY KEY TERMS

Axon

Beneficence

Biomedical perspective

Common therapeutic factors

Competence

Confidentiality

Context

Corpus Callosum

Dendrite

Dodo bird effect

Effect size

Effectiveness research

Efficacy research

Empirically supported treatment (EST)

Empirically validated treatment

Evidence-based principles

Expectancy

External validity

Extratherapeutic factors

Feminist/multicultural perspective

Frontal lobe

Great psychotherapy debate

Hemisphere

Informed consent

Internal validity

Left hemisphere

Limbic system

Meta-analysis

Mirror neurons

Multicultural competencies

Multiple roles

Negative outcomes

Neurogenesis

Neurons

Neurotransmitters

Nonspecific factors

Occipital lobe

Ortgeist

Parietal lobe

Poltergeist

Potentially harmful therapies (PHTs)

Practice-based evidence

Primum non nocere (first, do no harm)

Progress Monitoring (PM)

Psychosocial perspective

Randomized controlled trials (RCTs)

Religious/spiritual perspective

Right hemisphere

Temporal lobe

The talking cure

Theory

Therapeutic relationship

Trephining

Working alliance

Working definition of counseling and psychotherapy

Zeitgeist

CHAPTER 2

Psychoanalytic Approaches

LEARNER OBJECTIVES

- Define psychoanalytic psychotherapy and its variants
- Identify historical dynamics in Freud's development of psychoanalysis
- Describe core psychoanalytic theoretical principles
- Outline the evolution and development of psychoanalytic theory
- Describe and apply psychoanalytic psychotherapy principles, strategies, and techniques
- Analyze cases that employ psychoanalytic approaches
- Evaluate the empirical, cultural, gender, and spiritual validity of psychoanalytic psychotherapy
- Summarize core content and define key terms associated with psychoanalytic theory and therapies

A famous psychotherapist once wrote, "There are many ways and means of conducting psychotherapy. All that lead to recovery are good."

Surprisingly, this broadly accepting statement came from Sigmund Freud. As you'll see in this chapter, Freud's reputation wasn't one of flexibility and openness. Psychoanalysis was a rigid and tightly controlled process. When you think of Freud and psychoanalysis you might have images come to mind of patients lying on couches with their analysts behind them. These analysts would speak only occasionally and mysteriously, guiding their patients toward important insights into the deep (usually sexual) meaning underlying their behaviors. However, as you'll learn, psychoanalytic and psychodynamic psychotherapies have morphed far from Freud's original theorizing.

Freud's approach established the headwaters from which all contemporary psychotherapies and counseling have flowed. This chapter is the story of psychoanalysis and its evolution.

INTRODUCTION

Contemporary psychoanalytic psychotherapy is based on the writing and theories of Sigmund Freud. However, beyond Freud, many other writers, practitioners, and clients have contributed to the vastly different ways in which psychoanalytic psychotherapies are practiced today.

What Is Psychoanalytic Psychotherapy?

This is a question with many answers.

Sigmund Freud developed psychoanalysis and psychoanalytic theory. Although he had stimulating discussions of his theory and approach with others while he was alive, Freud had the final word. **Psychoanalysis** is the term used to describe Freud's approach and classical Freudian psychoanalytic theory is his theoretical model. **Classical Freudian psychoanalytic theory** is a one-person intrapsychic model where the psychotherapist acts as a blank slate and listens for unconscious conflicts and motivations that underlie repetitive, maladaptive patterns of behavior.

Many other psychoanalytic and psychodynamic psychotherapies developed from Freud's original theorizing. These include, but are not limited to: (a) ego psychology, (b) object relations, (c) self psychology, and (d) relational (or two-person) psychoanalysis. These are broadly referred to as **modern psychoanalytic approaches**. Modern psychoanalytic practitioners generally treat therapy as a two-person field, where the psychotherapist's and client's unconscious, intrapsychic, and relationship interactions are used to shed light on interpersonal patterns that are troubling the client (Bass, 2015; Renik, 1993; Wachtel, 2010).

The most general term is psychodynamic psychotherapy. **Psychodynamic psychotherapy** refers to approaches that emphasize unconscious behavior patterns and use insight as a primary therapeutic tool for psychological change.

Counseling and Psychotherapy Theories in Context and Practice: Skills, Strategies, and Techniques, Third Edition. John Sommers-Flanagan and Rita Sommers-Flanagan. © 2018 John Wiley & Sons, Inc. Published 2018 by John Wiley & Sons, Inc.
Companion website: www.wiley.com/go/sommers-flanagan/theories3e

Sigmund Freud has maintained his place as the central figure in psychoanalytic theory since the early 1900s. Some contemporary theorists and practitioners view him as an inspiration. For others, he's almost reflexively seen in a negative light and his ideas are ignored or unfairly criticized. The fact that speaking his name in public still produces strong emotional and intellectual reactions is a testament to his widespread influence. We begin with a brief examination of his childhood and personal history, because, frankly, Freud himself wouldn't have it any other way.

Sigmund Freud

A man like me cannot live without a hobby-horse, a consuming passion—in Schiller's words a tyrant. I have found my tyrant, and in his service I know no limits. My tyrant is psychology.

—Sigmund Freud, 1895, in a letter to W. Fliess

Sigmund Freud

Sigmund Freud was born in Freiberg, Moravia, in 1856. He was the firstborn of the union between his father, Jakob, and his mother, Amalie (Jakob's second wife). Although Jakob had two children from a previous marriage, Sigmund held the favored position of eldest son in a family with three boys and five girls. Jakob, a wool merchant, was authoritarian, while Amalie was protective and nurturing. Due to financial constraints, the family lived together in a small apartment.

Freud's intellectual potential was obvious early on. For example, he and a friend taught themselves Spanish because they wanted to read *Don Quixote* in its original language. His parents supported his intellectual appetite as much as they could. Freud obtained a medical degree from the University of Vienna with the goal of becoming a research scientist. Given his later fascination with psychosexual development and the unconscious sexual meaning of many behaviors, it's especially interesting that his first major research project involved a search for the testes of the eel.

Freud was unable to continue his research career due to financial needs. Instead, he went into the private practice of neurology.

As a neurologist, Freud worked with patients diagnosed with hysteria. **Hysteria** included various unexplained symptoms, including, but not limited to, numbness, paralysis, and tremors. Many European women in the late nineteenth century were afflicted with hysteria.

During a visit to France, Freud became familiar with the work of Jean Charcot. Charcot was a French neurologist who was using hypnosis to *produce* hysterical symptoms. Charcot's work convinced Freud that he also might use hypnosis to treat hysteria. Freud began using hypnosis to get patients to talk about important incidents that they couldn't typically recall.

After experimenting with hypnosis and reporting that it made him feel like "a miracle worker," Freud began working alongside Viennese physician Josef Breuer. Breuer was successfully treating hysteria symptoms—without hypnosis—simply by having patients talk about emotionally laden childhood experiences. In the early 1880s Breuer worked extensively with a patient named *Anna O.* (a pseudonym for Bertha Pappenheim), discussing her hysteria symptoms and treatment in great detail with Freud. Together, they published *Studies in Hysteria* (Breuer & Freud, 1895). Eventually, Freud became impressed with this "talking cure" and stopped using hypnosis. The rest, as they say, is history.

HISTORICAL CONTEXT

As noted in Chapter 1, psychological theories are reflective of the culture and historic period in which they were developed. Freud was obsessed with the sexual origins of mental disorders (Bankart, 1997), but he also lived in Vienna in the late 1800s, a reputedly extremely sexually repressed society. No doubt, Freud's Viennese culture and personal history influenced his theory.

A good illustration of psychoanalytic historical context is Freud's development and subsequent recanting of his **seduction hypothesis** (the hypothesis that repression of early childhood sexual abuse caused hysteria). Interestingly, there's conflict over the truth of this story. As you read about the seduction hypothesis, keep in mind that certain points have been contested, but the unfolding of a spectacular drama around sexuality, sexual fantasy, and sexual abuse in a sexually repressed society appears accurate.

The Seduction Hypothesis

In 1885, Freud went to France to study with Jean Charcot. According to Jeffrey Masson, former projects director of the Freud Archives, it's likely that Freud visited the Paris

Morgue, observing autopsies of young children who had been brutally physically and sexually abused (Masson, 1984). Masson speculated that Freud's exposure to the grisly reality of child abuse combined with his patients' stories of abuse led him to believe that child sexual abuse caused hysteria.

Later, Freud presented a paper titled "The Aetiology of Hysteria" at the Society for Psychiatry and Neurology in Vienna (Freud, 1896). He presented 18 cases (12 women and 6 men), all of which included childhood sexual abuse. Freud's critics contended (then and now) that Freud never provided the facts of his case histories (Wilcocks, 1994). They have also noted that he may have constructed the sexual memories by pressuring patients and by distorting what he heard to fit with his preexisting ideas (Esterson, 2001).

Freud's (1896) seduction hypothesis included the following components:

1. Very early "premature" sexual experiences cause symptoms of hysteria.

2. At the time of the abuse, there are no hysterical symptoms; the sexual memories are repressed.

3. Unconscious memories are "aroused after puberty."

4. Hysterical symptoms (e.g., fainting, paralysis) are manifest.

5. Psychoanalysis can address symptoms of hysteria.

Freud apparently believed in this etiological foundation and treatment process, as well as the reality of his clients' sexual abuse stories, until the late 1800s or early 1900s (Ahbel-Rappe, 2009).

Recanting the Seduction Hypothesis

Imagine yourself alone with a profound and horrible insight. In Masson's version of the seduction hypothesis story, this was Freud's situation. Masson (1984) described the reception Freud received after presenting his hypothesis (there is no dispute over this part of the seduction hypothesis story):

> The paper … met with total silence. Afterwards, he was urged never to publish it, lest his reputation be damaged beyond repair…. But he defied his colleagues and published "The Aetiology of Hysteria." (pp. xviii–xix)

Five days after presenting his paper, Freud wrote about the experience to his friend and otolaryngologist (ear, nose, and throat physician) Wilhelm Fliess. Freud's anger was obvious:

> [My] lecture on the aetiology of hysteria at the Psychiatric Society met with an icy reception from the asses, and from Kraft-Ebing [the distinguished

professor and head of the Department of Psychiatry at the University of Vienna] the strange comment: "It sounds like a scientific fairy tale." And this after one has demonstrated to them a solution to a more than thousand-year-old problem, a "source of the Nile!" They can all go to hell. (Schur, 1972, p. 104)

Although it's clear that Freud's lecture received "an icy reception" it's less clear why the audience was unimpressed. According to Masson, the reception was icy because Freud was bringing up sex and sexual abuse and that most professionals and citizens at the time were uncomfortable with this topic. Others have suggested that Freud's arrogance along with an absence of scientific rigor, moved the audience to rebuke him. Wilcocks (1994) wrote:

> The inferential support offered—without detail, of course—is that in eighteen cases out of eighteen, Freud has "discovered" the same etiological factors. But since neither we nor his audience are/were privy to the circumstances of any of his cases, this claim—whatever it's other inferential mistakes—is simply useless. (p. 129)

Freud's life during the years following the "Aetiology of Hysteria" lecture were difficult. His private practice was in decline and his professional life in shambles. This is when Freud embarked on "his lonely and painful self-analysis" (Prochaska & Norcross, 2003, p. 29). His 2-year self-analysis included uncovering memories of yearning for his mother and equally powerful feelings of resentment toward his father (Bankart, 1997).

Eventually, Freud discarded his seduction hypothesis in favor of the Oedipus complex (wherein a boy holds unconscious wishes to have sexual relations with his mother). Some suggest this was because he began noticing seductive patterns in so many parent–child interactions that it was unrealistic to assume that child sexual abuse occurred at such a high rate. Others believe Freud was ahead of his time in discovering child sexual abuse, but buckled under the social and psychological pressure, abandoning the truths his patients shared with him. Still others contend that while Freud was constructing his theoretical principles, he was projecting and mixing his own fantasies into his clients' stories. This appears to be the case in the following passage:

> I found in myself a constant love for my mother, and jealousy of my father. I now consider this to be a universal event in childhood. (R. A. Paul, 1991)

In 1925, long after he recanted the seduction hypothesis, he reflected on how he was naïve to have believed his patients:

> I believed these stories, and consequently supposed that I had discovered the roots of the subsequent neurosis in

these experiences of sexual seduction in childhood.... If the reader feels inclined to shake his head at my credulity, I cannot altogether blame him.... I was at last obliged to recognize that these scenes of seduction had never taken place, and that they were only fantasies which my patients had made up. (Freud, 1925, cited in Masson, 1984, p. 11)

The creation and recanting of the seduction hypothesis offers a glimpse into Viennese culture, Freud's personal psychology, and the challenge of discerning fact from fantasy. Were Freud's patients recalling real memories or reporting fantasies? Did Freud finally discern the truth or did he unconsciously mix (or project) his own personal issues into the plot? This process, sorting out our own ideas from the facts of what clients tell us, remains a challenge to all professional helpers. In the end, it may be that we create Kraft-Ebing's "scientific fairy tale" or something with lasting and meaningful significance. More likely, we create a combination of the two.

REFLECTIONS

What's your impression of Freud's struggles with the seduction hypothesis? How might "hysteria" back then be related to post-traumatic stress disorder now?

THEORETICAL PRINCIPLES

Freud's theory is one of the "giant theories" of developmental psychology (P. Miller, 2010, p. 108). One of our psychoanalytic colleagues refers to classical Freudian theory as a "museum theory," not so much because it belongs in a museum (although a case can be made for that as well) but because, as noted previously, classical Freudian theory is a one-person intrapsychic model that treats clients as separate, individual artifacts to be objectively examined. Classical Freudian theory includes several models or "approaches."

The Dynamic Approach

Freud's dynamic approach forms the foundation of his overall theory. Other names for the **dynamic approach** include **drive theory** or **instinct theory**. Freud posited that mental or psychic energy fills and energizes humans. This energy comes from two sources: **eros**, defined as energy associated with life and sexual instincts, and **thanatos**, defined as externally and internally directed aggression (Freud, 1964).

Freud used physical models to describe drive theory. He believed that psychic energy could be built up, transformed, connected to certain images, distributed,

and discharged. Sometimes he wrote about searching for concrete, physical manifestations of his theoretical speculations. Nevertheless, psychic energy was and is a distinctly psychological force. Although parallel physical processes may exist, they have not been identified (Brenner, 1973).

Psychic determinism is foundational to the dynamic approach. Freud believed that nothing that occurs within the mental realm is random. Instead, preceding physical and psychological events link to and determine all subsequent psychological experiences (Brenner, 1973).

If psychic determinism exists, that means there's an underlying psychological motivation or explanation for every emotion, thought, impulse, and behavior. If you oversleep, you're probably avoiding something or someone. If you party too hard, maybe you're expressing antagonism toward your parents' demands for responsible behavior. If you forget your professor's name, perhaps you're experiencing an unconscious aggressive impulse toward that professor. Or perhaps that professor reminds you, in some unconscious way, of someone you felt sexual feelings for and not recalling the name is one way to defend against your sexual impulses.

Freud referred to eros-related energy as **libido**. Thanatos or destructive energy was unnamed. Based on Freudian drive (dynamic) theory, every impulse has an origin, aim, object, and intensity. An impulse originates from some place in the body. For example, in very young children, most pleasure (or libidinal) impulses arise from the oral region. This is why young children put everything into their mouths. Their aim (or goal) is oral gratification.

If we stay with a small child example, the dynamic approach might look like this:

- *Origin of impulse*: baby experiences physical hunger sensations.

- *Aim of impulse*: get food! (gratification).

- *Object of impulse*: breast or bottle (caregiver).

- *Intensity of impulse*: strength of hunger sensation varies.

One of the easiest ways to understand the contemporary relevance of the dynamic approach is to think about it with the help of a case example.

As a baby and toddler, Katie was consistently deprived of food and repeatedly experienced hunger and distress. Often, she had to wail and cry very loudly and forcefully to have her oral needs for sustenance fulfilled. This pattern involved her (a) physical need for food, (b) impulse (and strategy) to obtain impulse gratification, and (c) eventual gratification. This pattern was repeated so many times that it became internalized. For Katie, it became an internal working model for how relationships and gratification patterns work around hunger and food. An **internal working model** is a repetitive impulse–energy–relationship pattern that informs individuals about what to expect and how to react to the world.

When, at age 22, Katie arrives for psychotherapy, she's experiencing distress over the **repetition compulsion** of the pathological impulse–relationship cycle that's continuing to manifest itself in her life. Several of her hunger/food-related behaviors are causing problems in her new romantic relationship. Among other patterns, to avoid experiencing intense distress, Katie began hoarding food. Her food hoarding behavior is minor, but her emotional distress to having it interrupted is extreme. Given her current life situation, her response to lack of food availability constitutes an over-reaction; she recognizes this, but feels unable to break the pattern…and the pattern is causing conflict in her relationship. In psychoanalytic therapy, Katie comes to understand these patterns and their origins. She is then able to develop more positive coping responses.

The Topographic Approach

Freud described the topography of the mind:

> Let us…compare the system of the unconscious to a large entrance hall, in which the mental impulses jostle one another like separate individuals. Adjoining this entrance hall there is a second, narrower, room—a kind of drawing-room—in which consciousness, too, resides. But on the threshold between these two rooms a watchman performs his function: he examines the different mental impulses, acts as a censor, and will not admit them into the drawing-room if they displease him. (Freud, 1963, p. 295)

The psychoanalytic mind is divided into three interrelated regions: (a) the **unconscious** (the relatively large space where mental impulses outside of awareness are jostling one another); (b) the **preconscious** (where both consciousness and unconsciousness reside with the "watchman" sorting out unacceptable thoughts and tossing them back into the unconscious); and the (c) **conscious** (the narrow and relatively small drawing room where conscious thoughts reside). According to the theory, human consciousness constitutes only a small portion of this psychological topography; there's much more activity happening at the unconscious level than at the conscious level.

The main **purpose of psychoanalysis** is to make the unconscious conscious. Psychoanalysts help clients gain insight of unconscious impulses or maladaptive internal working models. By bringing these unconscious dynamics into awareness, clients are better able to manage them, because when existing outside awareness, primitive impulses can become indirect and destructive influences.

For example, if a young man has an unresolved Oedipus complex, he may become overly aggressive and competitive. His lack of awareness of the origin, aim, intensity, and object of these impulses allows for their escalation. As a consequence, one night while out with friends, he becomes belligerent toward a police officer (whom he unconsciously views as a substitute for his father) and ends up in jail. If the young man had received psychoanalytic therapy, he might recognize this pattern, manage his competitive and combative impulses, and avoid jail time. Note that, loosely associated with the Greek myth, the **Oedipus complex** involves a male child's sexual attraction and wish to possess or marry his mother. This conflict emerges at the phallic stage (see below) and is resolved when the boy identifies with his father (and the police officer). Freud thought that resolution of this conflict led to development of the superego. C. G. Jung postulated a similar dynamic involving female development, referring to it as the **Electra complex**.

The Developmental Stage Approach

Over the past decade, early brain development has been emphasized in the popular press and in the schools (Olson, 2014; Siegel & Bryson, 2015). For many, this emphasis seems like common sense, but in the early 1900s, the idea that adult functioning was shaped by early childhood experiences was groundbreaking. Freud was the first to outline an extensive developmental theory explaining how early childhood experiences influence later adult functioning.

Freud's **developmental stage approach** is a psychosexual developmental model; it involves an integration of psychological and sexual or sensual concepts. Each developmental stage focuses on a part of the body linked to gratification or pleasure.

- *Oral*: birth to 1 year old.
- *Anal*: 1 to 3 years old.
- *Phallic*: 3 to 5 or 6 years old.
- *Latency*: 5 or 6 to puberty.
- *Genital*: puberty to adulthood.

During the first five or six years of life, the drive for pleasure shifts from oral to anal to phallic regions of the body. How children get these needs met is both physical and interpersonal. Consequently, interpersonal patterns and emotions linked to need gratification in childhood eventually form the psychological foundation for later (adult) need gratification.

Progress through stages is driven by biological maturation—which forces individuals to confront demands inherent to each stage. At each stage, if parents are overly indulgent or withholding, children can end up with fixations or complexes. A **fixation** or **complex** is an unresolved unconscious conflict (aka dysfunctional internal working model).

Some contemporary psychoanalysts remain interested in Freud's developmental stages, but others are not. Nevertheless, most contemporary developmental theories grew, in one way or another, from Freud's original theorizing. Overall, Freud's general premise that individuals have developmentally based dysfunctions that can be treated via analysis remains alive and well within psychoanalytic circles. Beyond Freud, contemporary analysts consider a variety of developmental theories when working with clients (Erikson, 1963; Loevinger, 1976; Mahler, Pine, & Bergman, 1975; Stern, 1985).

The Structural Approach

Freud's **structural approach** to human personality involves interrelationships among the id, ego, and superego. As discussed previously, powerful, unconscious forces flow through the body and mind. If not for the system's structural components, sexual and aggressive forces or drives would directly dictate human behavior. However, because these primal forces flow through the id, ego, and superego, humans can constructively manage their urges; we learn to wait, watch, and control ourselves.

The *id* is the seat of biological desire. As a structural entity within the person, it functions on the pleasure principle. Freud (1964) described the id as "a chaos, a cauldron full of seething excitations" (p. 73). The **pleasure principle** is an instinctive drive toward pleasure; it represents hedonistic impulses and the desire for immediate gratification.

Id impulses are primarily unconscious. However, it's possible to glimpse these impulses—as in cases when individuals seek immediate sexual or aggressive gratification. Additionally, we can view id impulses within ourselves via dreams, fantasies, and powerful pleasure-seeking urges. **Primary process thought**, another facet of id functioning, is characterized by hallucination-like images of fulfilled sexual or aggressive desires.

The id is mother of the ego. Constant gratification is impossible, so you must learn to wait for what you want. This is how the ego develops. The **ego** represents the individual's conscious decision-making processes; these processes steer behavior in more safe and adaptive directions. To accomplish this "steering," the ego has resources of its own. Ego functions include memory, problem-solving abilities, and logical thought. These functions are labelled **secondary thought processes** and help us cope with sexual and aggressive drives. The ego operates on the **reality principle**—the realities associated with the external world.

The **superego** develops when children resolve their Oedipus (or Electra) issues and begin identifying with same-sex parents and parental demands or expectations. There are two parts of the superego: there is the **conscience**. The conscience develops from parental prohibitions. When mom, dad, or caregiver says, "No!" or "Stop that!" or administers punishment, these admonitions are internalized within the child's psyche and later used as a means of self-punishment or prohibition. The conscience becomes an inner source of punishment.

The superego also includes the ego-ideal. In contrast to the negative, punishing conscience, the **ego-ideal** is positive, and consists of a desire to emulate adult standards or operate on moralistic standards. When parents model healthy and rational behaviors, children strive to behave similarly. Using the language of behavioral psychology, the conscience is the "stick" or punishment motivator, while the ego-ideal is the "carrot" or reinforcement motivator.

Overall, the ego acts as mediator within the human personality. It mediates and settles conflicts between and among (a) the id's primitive impulses, (b) admonitions and expectations of the superego, and (c) realities of the external world. This is no easy task; therefore the ego often uses defense mechanisms to deal with anxiety linked to internal battles among these intrapsychic forces.

Defense mechanisms are designed to ward off unpleasant anxiety feelings associated with internal conflicts among the id, superego, and reality. Defense mechanisms have four primary characteristics:

1. They are automatic: individuals use them reflexively.

2. They are unconscious.

3. They ward off unacceptable impulses.

4. They distort reality (to a greater or lesser extent, depending upon the defense mechanism employed).

From an applied perspective, most therapies are ego supportive; they help the ego—a rational and logical entity—deal more effectively with primitive desires, internalized parental and societal standards, and the real world. Eight common ego defense mechanisms are described in Table 2.1.

Psychopathology and Human Change

Psychoanalytic theorists view psychopathology as arising from early childhood experiences. Freud believed in a **normal–abnormal continuum**, with healthy individuals showing occasional signs of pathology. Miller (1983) summarized:

Table 2.1   Ego Defense Mechanisms

Defense mechanism descriptions and examples
Repression involves forgetting an emotionally painful memory. When clients repress a memory, there may be behavioral evidence that it exists, but there's genuine absence of recall: "Nope. I don't remember anything unusual about my childhood."
Denial is expressed more forcefully than repression. Shakespeare's famous line about protest[ing] too much captures its essence. Clients using denial might say, "No way, that's not true" and repeat their denial forcefully.
Projection occurs when clients push unacceptable thoughts, feelings, or impulses outward, onto another person. Clients may accuse another person of being angry, instead of owning their anger: "Why are you so angry?"
Reaction formation occurs if it's dangerous to directly express aggression, and so the opposite behavior (obsequiousness) is expressed instead. Instead of expressing sexual attraction, individuals might act disrespectfully toward whomever they're feeling attracted.
Displacement occurs when the aim of sexual or aggressive impulses is shifted from a dangerous person to a less dangerous person. Aggressive displacement involves the proverbial "kicking the dog." Sexual displacement occurs when sexual feelings toward a forbidden person are displaced on to a more acceptable person.
Rationalization occurs when clients use excessive explanations to justify their behavior. Students who make a hostile comment in class might overexplain and justify their comment.
Regression involves reverting to less sophisticated methods of doing things. Traumatized children may regress to wetting the bed or pooping their pants rather than using more advanced toileting skills. Adults who are skillful communicators may regress to shouting rather than logical argument.
Sublimation occurs when sexual or aggressive energy is channeled into positive loving or vocational activities. Sexual energy is thought to be sublimated into creative tasks and aggression into hard work (e.g., house cleaning, yard work).

Note: Several more defense mechanisms have been identified and described, including regression, dissociation, acting out, introjection, identification, compensation, and compartmentalization. Also, depending on the extent to which they distort reality, defense mechanisms may be more adaptive or more maladaptive.

In an abnormal personality, psychological processes are exaggerated or distorted. A melancholic patient has an overly strong superego. A sadistic killer has a strong, uncontrolled aggressive drive. An amnesiac must repress all of a painful past. Yet every normal personality has traces of melancholia, sadism, and unaccountable forgetting. (p. 128)

Several key issues pertaining to psychopathology and human change have remained relatively constant in psychoanalytic theory and therapy. First, therapy focuses on psychopathology that arises from internalized, dysfunctional childhood experiences. Second, dysfunctional childhood experiences are not completely understood, recalled, or dealt with consciously. Consequently, repetitive maladaptive behavior and thinking patterns exist; changing these patterns can feel beyond the client's control. Third, a cornerstone of human change involves insight (a consciousness-raising experience). Fourth, human change isn't instantaneous; it requires a working-through process where practicing new ways of understanding and dealing with inner impulses and human relationships occurs.

EVOLUTION AND DEVELOPMENT IN PSYCHOANALYTIC THEORY AND PRACTICE

Despite Freud's charismatic appeal, two prominent members of his inner circle had deep conflicts with him. First, Alfred Adler stepped away (see Chapter 3) and later Carl Jung broke from Freud (see Putting It in Practice 2.1 and online at www.wiley.com/go/counselingtheories). Both Adler and Jung developed their own insight-oriented approaches to psychotherapy. This fragmentation of the psychoanalytic inner circle is part of what makes the evolution and development of psychoanalysis complex and multifaceted.

One way of understanding how psychoanalysis has evolved is to follow Pine's (1990) four stages of psychoanalytic theory development. Pine described the evolution of psychoanalytic thinking as a progression of focus from (a) drive to (b) ego to (c) object to (d) self.

Pine's first stage was drive theory. Drive theory is the foundation of Freudian psychoanalysis. Having covered that in the preceding sections, we now move on to an

---

PUTTING IT IN PRACTICE

2.1 The Former Heir Apparent: Carl Gustav Jung

Carl Gustav Jung was born in Kesswil, Switzerland, in 1875. He died in Zurich in 1961. At one point, Freud, Adler, and Jung were personally and intellectually close. Freud considered Jung to be his heir apparent, at least briefly, but this was before Jung began questioning Freud's ideas and formulating new concepts.

For instance, Jung redefined libido as creative life energy, rather than exclusively sexual energy. He also didn't view the unconscious as a bubbling cauldron of primitive impulses, but as a source of both peril and wisdom. Jung believed our psyches were self-regulating systems, seeking balance between opposing forces and impulses.

Jung divided the unconscious into the personal unconscious and the collective unconscious. The personal unconscious is unique to individuals and the collective unconscious is a shared pool of human inherited motives, urges, fears, and potentialities. Jung believed the collective unconscious was far larger than the personal unconscious and that it was universally shared by all members of the human race.

Although Jungian therapy and analysis are less common, some of Jung's concepts have become part of our modern lexicon. Many people speak of archetypes, complexes, shadows, and collective knowing.

Jung also believed that certain mental functions and attitudes organize our personalities and determine how we habitually or preferentially orient to the world. Along with the attitudes of introversion and extraversion, Jung identified four functions: the perceptional functions, sensation or intuition, and the rational functions, thinking or feeling. These concepts were used in developing the Myers–Briggs Type Indicator (Myers, 1995), a popular psychological questionnaire.

Many Jungian ideas are widely known, but perhaps not fully appreciated nor understood as Jung intended. This short box cannot do justice to Jung's ideas or their potential applications. We encourage you to read our online Jungian chapter to further expand your understanding of this important early figure (url: www.wiley.com/go/sommers-flanagan/theories3e).

---

early psychoanalytic innovator—who also happened to be named Freud. This is the story of Anna Freud (Sigmund's youngest daughter) and her influence on ego psychology.

Anna Freud
(photo reproduced under CC BY-SA 3.0 NL)

Anna and the Ego: Psychoanalytic Ego Psychology

Sigmund Freud controlled psychoanalytic theory and psychoanalysis. Part of his control included the insistence that his disciples submit to a course of psychoanalysis by the master. During this time, there were no state licensing boards or professional ethics codes. Thus, Freud was able to take what we would now consider a most unusual and unethical step of accepting his youngest daughter, Anna, into analysis. As Bankart (1997) wrote, Anna was barely out of her teens when she began analysis, and "From those days until the end of her life, Anna had room for only one man in her life, and that man was her father" (p. 183).

Anna was one of the few practicing psychoanalysts without an official professional degree. Essentially, she was "home schooled" with an experiential apprentice approach.

Anna Freud ushered in a new generation of psychoanalysis. As you may recall, Sigmund Freud based his theoretical propositions about child development on his intensive study of adults through psychoanalysis. In contrast, Anna Freud studied children directly. She listened as children shared their dreams and fantasies. Perhaps more importantly, she discovered how to observe children's unconscious mental processes through play. Although she never directly disputed her father's belief in the dominance of id impulses in human development and functioning, she helped shift the psychoanalytic focus from the study of instinctual drives to **ego psychology**—the study of ego development and function.

Beginning in about the 1930s, ego psychology began claiming a portion of the psychoanalytic landscape. These theorists didn't completely break with Freud; rather, following Anna Freud's lead, they extended his ideas, emphasizing that certain ego functions were inborn and autonomous of biological drives (Hartmann, 1958; Loevinger, 1976; Rapaport, 1951). These ego functions included memory, thinking, intelligence, and motor control. As Wolitzky and Eagle (1997) wrote, "Following … ego psychology, there was now room in psychoanalytic theory for behavior and functions relatively autonomous of the vicissitudes of drive" (p. 44). The greater emphasis on ego functioning as separate from id impulses brought the interpretation of ego defenses to the forefront.

The new focus on ego had ramifications for both psychoanalytic theory and practice. A profound development during this period came from one of Anna Freud's analysands and followers, Erik Erikson.

Like Anna Freud, Erikson had little formal academic training. Nonetheless, he outlined and described a highly regarded theory of human development. In his **eight-stage epigenetic psychosocial theory of development**, Erikson (1963) deviated from Freudian developmental theory in two key ways: he emphasized psychosocial development instead of psychosexual development and he emphasized the continuous nature of development into old age, rather than ending his theorizing in early adulthood. Erikson's eight stages of development are summarized in most introductory and developmental psychology textbooks. For a glimpse into the ever-evolving nature of developmental theories, we recommend Joan Erikson's (Erik's wife) video on the ninth stage of human development (F. Davidson, 1995).

Object Relations

In the 1950s, object relations theorists began conceptually reformulating Freudian psychoanalytic theory. Whereas traditional Freudian theory focused primarily on parent–child dynamics during the Oedipus crisis, **object relations theory** focuses on the dynamics and motivation captured within the context of earlier parent–child relationships. These dynamics are referred to as pre-oedipal. Keep in mind that *objects* are not things; they are internalized versions of people.

The most profound object relations shift in psychoanalytic thinking is captured by Fairbairn's (1952) famous statement:

Libido is object seeking, not pleasure seeking. (p. 82)

Fairbairn was emphasizing that human behavior is not fueled by instinctual (libidinal) drives for sexual and aggressive gratification; instead, behavior is influenced and motivated by desire for human connection. Wolitzky and Eagle (1997) wrote, "In contrast to Freud's psychic world which is populated by unconscious wishes and defenses against those wishes, Fairbairn's psychic world is populated by internalized objects and internalized object relations" (p. 56).

Object relations theorists believe that humans mentally internalize a representation of self and a representation of early caretaker figures (Scharff & Scharff, 2005). These self and other representations are carried within the individual into adulthood. If early childhood interpersonal relationships included trauma or repeating destructive patterns, remnants of these early self-other relationship patterns can dominate contemporary relationships. A major goal of object relations therapy is to "exorcise" the old maladaptive internalized representations and "replace the 'bad object' with a 'good object'" (Fairbairn, 1952; Wolitzky & Eagle, 1997, p. 59). This process is similar to Alexander and French's (1946) concept of the **corrective emotional experience**, which was defined as: "Re-exposing clients, under more favorable circumstances, to emotional situations which" they couldn't "handle in the past" (p. 66). Therapists act as good objects and through this experience clients can replace their original bad internalized objects.

The focus of interpretive work in object relations therapy is different from traditional Freudian analysis. In particular, whereas Freudian analysis focused on Oedipal conflicts and sexual and aggressive wishes and drives, object relations therapy focuses on relationship wishes and pre-Oedipal interpersonal dynamics as played out in the regressive analytic situation. As a "good object," the therapist makes efforts to respond empathically to client struggles (Horner, 1998).

Self-Psychology

Pine's (1990) fourth phase of psychoanalytic evolution centers on Heinz Kohut's (1971, 1977, 1984) writings. In contrast to the preceding theoretical perspectives, Kohut considered needs for self-cohesiveness and self-esteem to be the overarching motivations that fuel human behavior. His **self-psychology** focused not on instincts, ego, or even object relations, but instead on the development of healthy narcissism within individuals.

Kohut also focused on self-defects and the noncohesive self. He believed self-defects and noncohesion stemmed from early childhood experiences. In particular, he emphasized that the development of a "cohesive self requires the parental provision of empathic mirroring and the later availability of a parental figure permitting idealization" (Wolitzky & Eagle, 1997, p. 67). In contrast to his psychoanalytic predecessors, Kohut's approach emphasized psychoanalyst empathy and authenticity in therapy relationships.

In Kohutian psychotherapy, the following process is emphasized:

- Due to early childhood developmental defects, clients quickly establish a mirroring and idealizing transference in psychotherapy.

- This mirroring and idealizing transference is regressive and progressive; clients try to reengage a mirroring and ideal object to repair and build up their psychic structure.

- Clients fear retraumatization; this fear produces resistance.

- The therapist interprets the resistance.

- The therapist is imperfect and therefore fails to provide perfect empathy and is not a perfect figure for idealizing.

- The client then retreats from intimacy with the therapist.

- If the therapist's deficiencies and failures aren't traumatic, then this retreat can be interpreted along with the therapist's acknowledgment of failures to be perfectly empathic.

- These failures, if handled well, will be "optimal failures," and then a "new self structure will be acquired and existing ones will be firmed" (Kohut, 1984, p. 69).

Wolitzky and Eagle (1997) summarized Kohut's approach: "For Kohut, empathic understanding and the repeated working through of optimal failures in empathy constitute 'the basic therapeutic unit' of treatment" (p. 69).

Contemporary Movements

Up to this point in our discussion, the evolution of psychoanalytic thinking might be described, following Pine (1990), as a progression of focus from drive to ego to object to self. Unfortunately, although Pine's distinctions are helpful, the evolution of psychoanalytic thought hasn't been so simple and linear. Gedo (1979) described the progression as "piecemeal patching" rather than an organized effort at theoretical evolution (p. 9).

Around the time of ego psychology, Karen Horney's work, similar to Alfred Adler (see Chapter 3), focused on how social and cultural factors powerfully affect personality development (Horney, 1950). Horney provided many early feminist critiques of Freudian theory. (See Putting It in Practice 2.2 for a taste of her opposition to Freudian views of female sexuality.) Horney's work is labeled **neo-Freudian** (or new-Freudian) because, like Adler, she started with some of Freud's ideas, but emphasized social and cultural factors. Some contend it would be more accurate to refer to her as neo-Adlerian (Carlson, 2015).

Alternative theoretical developments were amalgamations, or attempts at integration. For example, Margaret Mahler's formulations include components of drive, ego, object relations, and self-psychology. Her observations of mother–child interactions, in combination with attachment research, as well as Donald Winnicott's object relations work, provided the foundation for contemporary attachment-based psychotherapy models (Ainsworth, 1969; Bowlby, 1978, 1988a; Hughes, 1998; Winnicott, 1965, 1975).

Time-Limited Psychodynamic Psychotherapy

The first psychoanalyst to push for active, directive, and briefer psychoanalysis was one of Freud's closest friends, Sandor Ferenczi (1920, 1950). Ferenczi claimed that because all therapy techniques were more or less suggestive, being more active was an acceptable option.

Many other analysts have recommended modifying psychoanalytic procedures. Notably, Alexander and French (1946) experimented with methods of time-limited psychoanalysis at the Chicago Institute of Psychoanalysis. They developed a procedure called the corrective emotional experience, designed to speed the curative therapeutic process. Alexander and French recommended that analysts adopt a compensatory role toward clients. If the client suffered from an overly critical parent and therefore, due to the transference phenomenon, expected criticism from the analyst, then the analyst would instead adopt a positive and supportive role. This manner of interacting was supposed to produce a corrective emotional experience, thereby reducing the time required for a complete analysis.

Other theorists advocated that analysts purposely act in ways to activate and deepen transference. This might involve an analyst's behaving in a cold and critical manner toward the patient who had cold and critical parents. Horowitz and colleagues (1984) wrote,

> The technique of "seeding," or manipulating, the transference has the apparent advantage of accelerating its development and the possible disadvantage of traumatizing the patient, causing him to feel manipulated or to disavow his own contribution. (p. 6)

Another strategy for speeding up analysis was advocated by French (1958) and Balint, Ornstein, and Balint (1972). These theorists recommended that analysts stop short of a complete analysis and instead focus their work on one significant conflict or problem. This modification is sometimes referred to as **focal psychotherapy**.

During the 1980s, Luborsky (1984) and other psychoanalytic thinkers (Strupp & Binder, 1984) developed a variety of different short-term psychoanalytic psychotherapy models. Luborsky identified the internalized and repeating dysfunctional interpersonal patterns as the client's **core conflictual relationship theme**. The purpose

---

PUTTING IT IN PRACTICE

2.2 Karen Horney versus Freudian Orthodoxy: The Battle of the Sexes

Karen Horney grew up in an era when both men and (some) women feared female emancipation. Otto Weininger wrote in *The Emancipated Woman*, "All women who really strive for emancipation are sexual intermediate forms" (from Quinn, 1987, p. 103).

Despite the odds, Karen Horney obtained her medical degree in 1911. This was the same year she gave birth to her first child, Brigitte.

Alfred Adler may have been the first Freudian disciple with feminist leanings (see Chapter 3), but as a woman herself, Horney took the battle of the sexes to new and exciting depths.

She did not believe in Freud's penis envy and she did not believe that women were inferior. Despite her traditional psychoanalytic training, she found her voice and made strong arguments against masculine formulations of female sexuality. She wrote:

How far has the evolution of women, as depicted to us today by analysis, been measured by masculine standards and how far therefore does this picture fail to present quite accurately the real nature of women?

and further:

[I]f we try to free our minds from masculine mode of thought, nearly all the problems of feminine psychology take on a different appearance.

She then turns the tables on penis envy:

When one begins, as I did, to analyze men only after a fairly long experience of analyzing women, one receives a most surprising impression of the intensity of this envy of pregnancy, childbirth, and motherhood, as well as of breasts and of the act of suckling.

Finally, she interprets male behavior from a new, feminist perspective:

Is not the tremendous strength in man of the impulse to creative work in every field precisely due to their feeling of playing a relatively small part in the creation of living beings, which constantly impels them to an overcompensation in achievement?

Later in her career, she focused even more on male inferiority:

One of the exigencies of the biological differences between the sexes is this: that the man is actually obliged to go on proving his manhood to the woman. There is no analogous necessity for her. Even if she is frigid, she can engage in sexual intercourse and conceive and bear a child. She performs her part by merely *being*, without any doing—a fact that has always filled men with admiration and resentment. (Horney, 1932, pp. 348–360)

Karen Horney was steady and forthright in her views. She accepted some of what psychoanalysis offered, but articulated and rejected erroneous assumptions about females. She's a role model, at least with regard to the need to look long and hard at the perspectives of all sexual identities before formulating a more complete psychology of humanity.

---

of Luborsky's (1984) and other psychoanalytic therapy approaches is to bring automatic, dysfunctional impulse-gratification cycles (and their interpersonal dynamics) into awareness so they can be replaced with more adaptive and intentional behavior patterns.

The Relational Psychoanalytic Movement

Originally psychoanalysis reflected Freud's image of a thoroughly analyzed, dispassionate, objective psychoanalyst expertly interpreting derivatives from the client's unconscious mind in order to eradicate maladaptive childhood fixations and neuroses. Renik (1993) described the classical Freudian position: "The image [is] of the analyst as detached psychic surgeon, dissecting the patient's mental operations in an antiseptic field" (p. 553).

For many psychoanalysts, the analyst as a detached psychic surgeon is gone. This paradigm shift began in the 1980s. The new paradigm is usually referred to as **relational psychoanalysis** (Mitchell, 1988), although **two-person psychology** and **intersubjectivity** are also used (E. Balint, 1950; Ghent, 1989; Marks-Tarlow, 2011). Two-person psychology emphasizes that the psychoanalyst is always subjective:

> Instead of saying that it is *difficult* for an analyst to maintain a position in which his or her analytic activity objectively focuses on a patient's inner reality, I would say that it is impossible for an analyst to be in that position even for an instant: since we are constantly acting in the analytic situation on the basis of personal motivations of which we cannot be aware until after the fact, our technique, listening included, is *inescapably* subjective. (Renik, 1993, p. 560)

Many psychoanalysts, including French psychoanalyst Jacques Lacan, view relational psychoanalysis as "the most fertile line of thought traced out since Freud's death" (Lacan, 1988, p. 11). In relational psychoanalysis the analyst is viewed as a fully engaged participant-observer. As a participant-observer, psychoanalysts cannot help but be part of what's influencing clients during therapy sessions (Renik, 1993).

This line of thinking parallels the paradigm shift from Newtonian to Einsteinian physics. Consequently, the inherent relativity and subjectivity of the psychoanalyst is now an important focus of study in and of itself.

This new perspective has dramatic implications for psychoanalysis and psychoanalytic psychotherapy. Therapist and client are considered a psychoanalytic couple. Analysts no longer have the authority to make independent and authoritative "interpretations" of their clients' unconscious derivatives. Instead, interpretations are cast as an alternative viewpoint for clients to consciously consider while making up their own minds. Moreover, not only are the clients' enactment of transference considered important therapeutic information, but so are the analysts' enactment of countertransference. Contemporary writers strongly recommend greater psychoanalyst spontaneity, countertransference enactment, and emotional involvement (Bass, 2015; Marks-Tarlow, 2011; Wachtel, 2008).

REFLECTIONS

Relational psychoanalysis changes much of traditional psychoanalytic thinking. What are your reactions to the idea of a psychoanalyst who's much more engaged—but still focused like a laser on your personal psychodynamics?

Attachment-Informed Psychotherapy

Attachment, both as a model for healthy child development and as a template for understanding human behavior is immensely popular within the United States (Berry & Danquah, 2016; Cassidy & Shaver, 2008). This is especially ironic because attachment theory's rise to glory parallels decreasing interest in psychoanalytic models. If you were to ask a sample of mental health professionals their thoughts on attachment theory, you'd elicit primarily positive responses. Oddly, these same professionals might dismiss psychoanalytic theory. **Attachment-informed psychotherapy** uses attachment theory and attachment styles as the theoretical foundation for psychodynamic psychotherapy.

John Bowlby, who was raised primarily by a nanny and sent to boarding school at the age of seven, began writing about the importance of parent–child interactions in the 1950s. He was a psychoanalyst. Similar to other neo-Freudians, Bowlby's thinking deviated from Freud's. Instead of focusing on infant or child parental fantasies, Bowlby emphasized real and observable interactions between parent and child. He believed actual caretaker–infant interactions were foundational to personality formation (aka the internal working model).

In 1970, Mary Ainsworth, a student of Bowlby's and scholar in her own right, published a study focusing on children's attachment styles using a research paradigm called the **strange situation** (Ainsworth & Bell, 1970). Ainsworth brought individual mother–child (6 to 18 months) pairs into her lab and observed them in a series of seven 3-minute episodes or interactions.

1. Parent and infant spending time alone.

2. A stranger joins parent and infant.

3. The parent leaves infant and stranger alone.

4. Parent returns and stranger leaves.

5. Parent leaves; infant left completely alone.

6. Stranger returns.

7. Parent returns and stranger leaves.

During this event sequence, Ainsworth observed the infant's:

- Exploration behavior.

- Behavioral reaction to being separated from parent.

- Behavioral reaction to the stranger.

- Behavior when reunited with parent.

Based on this experimental paradigm, Ainsworth identified three primary attachment styles:

1. **Secure attachment**: These children become distressed when their parent leaves, but are comforted upon their return. They seem to trust that their parent will return and use their parent as a source of emotional support or refueling.

2. **Anxious-resistant insecure attachment**: These children are highly distressed over exploring their surroundings when the parent is absent. Further, they continue to have significant anxiety even when the parent returns and may display anger toward the parent.

3. **Anxious-avoidant insecure attachment**: These children tend to show minimal emotion when parents depart or return. They also tend not to explore their environment very much.

In 1986, Ainsworth's student and colleague Mary Main (Main & Solomon, 1986), identified a fourth attachment style that could be reliably coded. They labeled it: **disorganized/disoriented attachment** (these children will display disorganized behaviors such as wandering, freezing, confused expressions, and unorganized interactions with the parent).

Many contemporary therapists view attachment theory in general, and Ainsworth and Main's attachment style formulations in particular, as having powerful implications for human relationships and therapy process (Berry & Danquah, 2016; Holmes, 2010; Wachtel, 2011). For example, one of the most popular approaches to couple counseling relies heavily on attachment theory principles (Johnson, 2010). In addition, attachment theory has profoundly influenced child development and parent training programs (J. Sommers-Flanagan & Sommers-Flanagan, 2011; Yaholkoski, Hurl, & Theule, 2016).

Attachment theorists hold a core belief that early child–caretaker interactions are internalized and subsequently serve as a model for interpersonal relationships. This is, again, the internal working model—with an emphasis on how real (and not fantasized) early relationships have become a guide or template for all later relationships. Byrd, Patterson, and Turchik (2010) described how attachment theory can help with selecting appropriate and effective interventions. They wrote that clients often vary regarding their comfort with interpersonal closeness. Consequently, therapists can use in-session relationship dynamics and insight-oriented approaches as therapeutic factors with clients who are comfortable with closeness. In contrast, when working with clients who have insecure attachment styles, therapists might maintain more relational distance and use more behavioral or skill-based approaches.

Despite its popularity, many criticisms of attachment theory exist. Perhaps the greatest criticism is that theorists and practitioners feel free to take Mary Ainsworth's 21 minutes of behavioral observations with one primary (female) caregiver and generalize it to the entire global population (Field, 1996). In this sense, the theory is not multiculturally sensitive. It seems obvious that not all cultures subscribe to the "American" preoccupation with an infant's relationship with a single caregiver (usually the mother).

Although scientific critiques have sought to reign in attachment theory as it has galloped its way into pop psychology and the media (Rutter, 1995), its popularity continues to escalate and the consequences seem to magnify the importance of an overly dramatized dance of love between a child and his or her mother. In the following excerpt from *A General Theory of Love* (2001), you can see the language is absolute and sexist—in that children are typically portrayed as male and parents as female.

> One of a parent's most important jobs is to remain in tune with her child, because she will focus the eyes he turns toward inner and outer worlds. He faithfully receives whatever deficiencies her own vision contains. A parent who is a poor resonator cannot impart clarity. Her inexactness smears his developing precision in reading the emotional world. If she does not or cannot teach him, in adult-hood he will be unable to sense the inner states of others or himself. Deprived of the limbic compass that orients a person to his internal landscape, he will slip through his life without understanding it. (Lewis, Amini, & Lannon, 2001, p. 156)

This is a good place to take a break to speculate on how Karen Horney or Mary Ainsworth might respond to this overgeneralization of attachment concepts and blaming of mothers for their adult children's emotional deficiencies.

THE PRACTICE OF PSYCHOANALYTIC PSYCHOTHERAPY

The following review of therapy techniques won't prepare you to conduct psychoanalytic psychotherapy. Instead, our goal is to help you see and feel how psychoanalytic principles are applied. If your interest is piqued, you can obtain further education and training in this area. The following section describes standard methods, techniques, and concepts that are still employed by contemporary psychoanalytically oriented therapists (see Putting It in Practice 2.3).

Overall, the methods and techniques of psychoanalytic psychotherapy have the following goals:

- Make the unconscious conscious (or increase client awareness).

- Help clients develop greater control over maladaptive impulses.

- Help clients rid themselves of maladaptive or unhealthy internalized objects and replace them with more adaptive internalized objects.

PUTTING IT IN PRACTICE

2.3 Informed Consent from the Psychodynamic Perspective
Contributed by Nicki Nance, PhD (reproduced with permission of Nicki Nance)

A note from your psychotherapist:

As you complete your intake forms, you may be wondering, "What have I gotten myself into?" Beginning therapy is similar to taking a trip to an unknown destination with someone you don't know well yet. Knowing what to expect can be helpful, so before we begin I want to tell you more about how we'll work together.

The Map: I will get to know you by learning what brought you to therapy at this time. I will guide you in an exploration of your history to determine how you developed your current patterns of thinking, feeling, and acting. Together, we'll set goals to decrease your current discomfort and help you develop resources for moving forward. We will venture into the past and future to find help for what brought you here today.

The Vehicle: The relationship between client and therapist is the foundation of successful therapy. Gaining insight about what you experience in our relationship may help you become more insightful about other relationships. In the context of our relationship, you may also develop skills for identifying and expressing feelings, and taking emotional risks. I encourage you to be open and honest in our communications and I will support you in doing so by providing a safe space and a nonjudgmental response. However, I will also sometimes explore with you how your reactions to me may be similar to your reactions to other people in your life.

The Journey: People often struggle because they're bound to troublesome past experiences. Therefore, I'll be using techniques that help you put the past in a better perspective and live more fully in the present. During therapy, I may ask you to recall early experiences. Remembering can be uncomfortable, but what you discover from the past will help you to make changes for the future. I'm honored to be a part of this process and I look forward to working with you.

- Repair self-defects through mirroring, presenting a potentially idealized object, and expressing empathy during optimal therapeutic failures.

Assessment Issues and Procedures

Psychoanalytically oriented clinicians use two primary assessment procedures: clinical interviewing and projective testing. **Projective testing** involves the presentation of an ambiguous stimulus that clients interpret. It is believed that clients project their intrapsychic or internalized interpersonal models onto the ambiguous stimulus. Projective tests include the Rorschach Inkblot Test, the Thematic Apperception Test, free association to specific words, and human figure drawings. Psychoanalytic therapists don't usually implement objective, standardized questionnaires or assessment procedures.

For example, during a 2-hour weekly assessment seminar on my (John's) psychoanalytic internship, the supervisors spent 10 minutes reviewing results from the

Wechsler Adult Intelligence Scales and the Minnesota Multiphasic Personality Inventory (MMPI) and 1 hour and 50 minutes talking about the Rorschach and human figure drawings. One supervisor enjoyed turning the MMPI profile upside down and sideways to make fun of objective testing procedures. Although this behavior was a bit over the top, we interns had long stopped caring about his MMPI jokes. He had already won our respect and admiration; in one of the first cases presented in the seminar, he accurately predicted that a woman he'd never met had been sexually abused solely on the basis of her first response to Card 1 on the Rorschach.

Despite their frequent use by psychoanalytically oriented clinicians, the empirical or scientific status of projective assessment is questionable (Wood, Nezworski, Lilienfeld, & Garb, 2008; Wood et al., 2010). It may be true that some Rorschach experts are exceptions to the empirical rule, but most reasonable scientists agree that projective assessments are not a valid means for establishing diagnoses, determining child custody, or predicting behavior. However, there are other reasons clinicians might find projective assessment procedures useful. These include: (a) rapport building through mutual exploration of deeper issues with clients; (b) determination of the presence or absence of more subtle thought disorders (e.g., psychotic symptoms); and (c) examination of ongoing therapy process and progress.

Critics of psychoanalytic approaches contend that projective assessment procedures are invalid and unethical (Lilienfeld et al., 2003), but in the big domain of psychotherapy practice, there's room for many perspectives. Psychoanalytic therapists use projective assessments, along with clinical interviewing, for many purposes.

REFLECTIONS

What are your thoughts on projective assessment procedures? How can practitioners use them appropriately... or perhaps you don't think there's any appropriate use for projective assessments?

The Basic Rule

Traditional psychoanalysts begin each session the same way. They encourage clients to "Say whatever comes to mind." This is **the basic rule** in psychoanalysis; it's also referred to as **free association**. A variation of free association is used in most psychoanalytically oriented therapies. Following the basic rule facilitates emergence of unconscious impulses and conflicts. The following guidelines are important:

- *Minimize distractions or external stimuli*: Minimizing distractions allows unconscious impulses and conflicts to rise to consciousness. This is why Freud used a couch. If the client lies on a couch and the analyst sits behind it, the analyst's distracting facial expressions are eliminated. Greater emphasis can be placed on what facial expressions (or thoughts and feelings) the client imagines the analyst is experiencing.

- *Minimize the client's internal stimuli*: When free associating, it's best that clients are not physically uncomfortable. For instance, if clients come to analysis hungry, thoughts about food will block their free association.

- *Reduce conscious planning*: Free association is designed to counter intentional or planned thought processes. If a client comes to therapy with a list of things to talk about, psychoanalytic practitioners might interpret this as resistance. You may wonder, "How can the client's planning for the session be considered resistance?" The answer is that conscious planning is a defense for keeping control over sexual, aggressive, and other

impulses. These impulses may be adversely affecting the client and need to be brought to consciousness.

To summarize, following the basic rule involves (a) minimizing external distractions, (b) minimizing internal distractions, and (c) encouraging spontaneous (and unplanned) talk.

Interpretation

Even free association won't give you direct access to clients' unconscious conflicts and psychodynamics. Instead, ego defenses protect clients from unconscious conflicts and distort information rising up from the unconscious, resulting in what's called unconscious derivatives. **Unconscious derivatives** can be fantasies, recollections, or symptoms that require translation—usually through interpretation—to be understood. The content of unconscious derivatives may reflect intrapsychic conflicts or relationship or attachment conflicts.

The analyst's job is to listen for and interpret unconscious derivatives. **Interpretation** involves the explaining or reframing the meaning of something, but when it comes to the unconscious, the process is anything but simple. The analyst cannot just sit back and make interpretation after interpretation of unconscious derivatives. As Fenichel (1945) wrote:

> The unprepared patient can in no way connect the words he hears from the analyst with his emotional experiences. Such an "interpretation" does not interpret at all. (p. 25)

Fenichel is saying that analysts must prepare clients before using interpretation. Proper client preparation involves the following steps.

Developing a Working Alliance

You may recall from Chapter 1 that the working alliance is viewed as a common factor contributing to positive therapy outcome. In 1911, Freud emphasized that a reality-based attachment (or bond) between analyst and client was crucial and needed to coexist with the simultaneously occurring positive or negative transference distortions. Later, Zetzel (1956) was the first to actually use the term therapeutic (or working) alliance. Consistent with Freud, she believed that if clients had early parent–child interactions characterized by trust and affection, their ability to develop a positive therapeutic alliance was enhanced. You may recognize the common sense fact that it's easier to defensively disregard input—even potentially helpful feedback—if you don't like the source.

Role Induction

Clients need clear information about how all therapies proceed, but explanations about therapy process are especially important in psychoanalytic therapy. For example, it's advisable to explain that you'll be using interpretations before you use one:

> As we do therapy, I may notice patterns related to your early childhood relationships, your relationship with me, or your descriptions of your relationships outside therapy. Is it okay if I occasionally mention these patterns so we can explore them together and hopefully come to a better understanding about how they might be affecting your life?

The term **role induction** refers to a process wherein therapists educate clients about their role in therapy (Swift & Greenberg, 2015).

Timing

Once a therapeutic relationship is established and role induction information provided, interpretation becomes a potential therapy tool. However, even then, psychoanalysts should proceed carefully. Fenichel (1945) noted:

> Since interpretation means helping something unconscious to become conscious by naming it at the moment it is striving to break through, effective interpretations can be given only at one specific point, namely, where the patient's immediate interest is momentarily centered. (p. 25)

As Fenichel emphasized, timing is essential. Here are several tips for **timing of interpretations**:

- Watch for when the client is just a step away from becoming aware of something new.

- Wait for the client to show positive regard for you.

- Wait until you can say the interpretation clearly and articulately; if the interpretation is muddled in your mind, it won't be helpful.

- Wait until you have data to support your interpretation; you should be able to link your interpretation to your client's concrete behaviors or specific statements.

To make matters even more complex, good timing isn't everything. When conducting psychoanalytic therapy, the therapist also needs to know what to interpret.

Transference

One of the unique and lasting contributions of Freud's work was his discussion of transference (Luborsky, 1985). In the past half century, more than 3,000 books and professional journal articles have been published on transference phenomena (Kivlighan, 2002). **Transference** is defined as:

> The client's experience of the therapist that is shaped by the client's own psychological structures and past and involves displacement, onto the therapist, of feelings, attitudes and behaviors belonging rightfully in *earlier significant relationships*. (Gelso & Hayes, 1998, p. 51, italics in original)

Transference is characterized by inappropriateness. Freud (1958) stated, transference "exceeds anything that could be justified on sensible or rational grounds" (p. 100). This is because transference involves using an old map to try to get around on new terrain; it doesn't work very efficiently (J. Sommers-Flanagan & Sommers-Flanagan, 2017). One way to detect transference is to closely monitor for when clients misperceive or mistreat you. Of course, to effectively monitor for inaccuracies in client perceptions, you must know yourself well enough to identify when your client is treating you like someone you aren't.

In one clinical case, I (John) had a client accuse me of being the most insensitive man she had ever had the displeasure of meeting. At one point, she shouted, "You're like a robot! I bet if I cut open your arms, I'd find wires, not veins."

As it turns out, this woman was having a transference reaction toward me. In her past, the consistent pattern was for men (including her father) to be unresponsive until finally erupting into a rage toward her. This was what she was expecting and finding so frustrating. My nonaggressive response to her may have provided a corrective emotional experience.

Countertransference

Freud (1957) originally defined **countertransference** as an interpersonal process wherein client transference triggers the psychoanalyst's unresolved childhood issues or conflicts. It's like transference, but it occurs when the transference is directed from the analyst toward the client. Freud viewed psychoanalyst countertransference reactions as negative: "Recognize this counter-transference... and overcome it," he counseled, because "no psychoanalyst goes further than his own complexes and internal resistances permit" (Freud, 1957, p. 145).

Contemporary psychoanalysts view countertransference differently than Freud. The **totalistic countertransference** perspective is that countertransference involves any and all reactions that therapists have toward clients (Gelso & Hayes, 2007). These reactions may be inappropriate. For example, during a session you may notice mild irritation or annoyance with a client. In some cases these feelings may not be important. However, when your annoyance is strong (intensity), comes up often (frequency), and sticks with you over time (duration), you may be suffering from countertransference.

As you may have guessed, in the case where I (John) was accused of acting like a robot, there was also evidence of countertransference. As my client's complaints about me increased in volume, I found myself in an emotional retreat. The fact is that I've never been comfortable with highly intense emotional demands; my typical response is to emotionally distance myself. Her transference had pushed my buttons. In a way, she was right: although I didn't have wires for veins, I was becoming less emotionally responsive to her. I was experiencing a countertransference reaction. Exploring my reactions through a relational or two-person psychoanalytic lens might have been therapeutic.

Using a broader (totalistic) conceptualization of countertransference, writers of different theoretical orientations have described two potential beneficial aspects of countertransference (Cartwright, 2011; Gordon et al., 2016).

- Countertransference awareness can help you have a deeper understanding of your own issues. This can help you sort out your own issues from your clients' issues and improve your diagnostic accuracy and ethical behaviors.

- If you have a strong and unusual reaction, your reaction probably has more to do with the client than you. For example, if you're feeling afraid, the client may be subtly saying or doing something threatening. Your reaction helps you glimpse how the client may affect other people and provide data for making a transference interpretation.

From the two-person psychology frame within psychoanalytic theory, a key question to keep in mind is "Who am I being asked to be in this situation?" Your reactions may be subtle, but still an important source of information.

You might think countertransference is only relevant to psychoanalytic approaches. However, even traditional behaviorists recommend that therapists recognize that their own "emotional reactions" to clients are an important source of clinical information (Goldfried & Davison, 1976, p. 58). There is also significant empirical research pointing to the fact that countertransference exists, is measurable, and that when therapists attend to and work through their countertransference, treatment outcomes improve (Betan, Heim, Conklin, & Westen, 2005; Fatter & Hayes, 2013; Hayes, Gelso, & Hummel, 2011).

Triangles of Insight

Psychoanalytic psychotherapists often use interpretation to focus on client resistance. Interpretive statements can begin as simple reflections that include potential client psychodynamics:

> It seems to me like you usually plan out in advance what you talk about in here. I'm wondering if you feel worried about what you might talk about if you just let yourself be spontaneous?

Beyond resistance, psychoanalytic therapists often focus their interpretations on triangles of insight. These triangles address conflict-based or transference-based dynamics.

A **conflict-based triangle of insight** includes (1) the client's wish, aim, or drive; (2) the threat or imagined threat that makes the direct gratification of the wish impossible; and (3) the defensive compromise (see Figure 2.1). Although in traditional Freudian analysis the client's wish has sexual or aggressive roots, in an object relations model the client's wish might have an interpersonal focus. For example, a young man might wish for greater emotional liberation from his father. However, because when he asserted himself while growing up, his father emotionally abandoned him, he feels too anxious to directly assert his independence needs. Then, although he feels confused when his father places demands on him, he denies and minimizes the issue by saying, "That's just my dad being my dad; I don't like it, but there's nothing I can do." Using the triangle of insight model, an interpretation might focus on one or more of these three issues:

1. *The wish*: You wish you could have more independence from or be more assertive with your dad.

2. *The threat*: You don't say or do anything because you're afraid you'll hurt him or he'll turn away from you in anger, like he's done before.

3. *The defensive compromise*: You've tried to shrink the problem by saying it's no big deal, but you still end up feeling anxious, guilty, and confused more than you'd like.

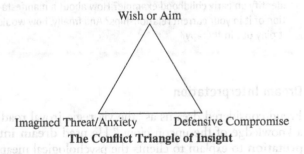

The Conflict Triangle of Insight

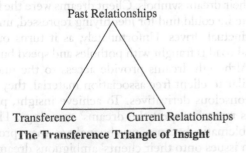

The Transference Triangle of Insight

FIGURE 2.1 Two Psychoanalytic Triangles of Insight

In contrast to a conflict-based approach, the **transference-based triangle of insight** includes:

- Observations based on an in-session transference relationship.
- The client's reports of childhood relationship dynamics.
- The client's reports of contemporary, outside-of-therapy relationships.

In the preceding case, to facilitate insight, the therapist (who happens to be a man and is 20 years older than the client) might say:

- Sometimes I feel you pulling away in a sort of charming way; you laugh and joke, but you seem to want to keep me away from knowing more personal or intimate things about you.
- You've told me before about how your dad would cling to you until finally you'd break free and then he'd punish you by being unavailable, and this seems connected to how we relate to each other in here.
- How hard it is now for you to really open up to your male friends is partly because you fear they'll clamp on and use you, or get angry and abandon you.

The transference triangle of insight may emerge and repeat itself in the client's dreams and waking narratives.

REFLECTIONS

Triangles of insight can be elusive phenomena. Try it out on yourself. Identify a repeating interpersonal pattern. Can you identify an early childhood example? How about a manifestation of it in your current relationships? And finally, how would it play out in therapy?

Dream Interpretation

Freud considered dreams as "the via regia [royal road] to a knowledge of the unconscious." He used **dream interpretation** to explain to clients the psychological meaning of their dream symbols. Client dreams were the best access route he could find for identifying repressed, unconscious, instinctual drives. Unfortunately, as it turns out, Freud's royal road is fraught with potholes and speed bumps.

Although dreams provide access to the unconscious, similar to client free association material, they consist of unconscious derivatives. To achieve insight, psychoanalysts must interpret the dreams' meanings. This can be problematic because psychoanalysts may project their own issues onto their clients' ambiguous dream symbols. Even Freud, because of his own interest (and perhaps

preoccupation) with sexual issues, might have overinterpreted or misinterpreted client dream images as representing sexual wishes. Additionally, based on his own theory, his own phallic (achievement) issues might have led him to insist to clients that his interpretations (rather than the clients') were correct.

This may be why psychoanalytically oriented therapists have a reputation for giving out authoritarian, symbol-based interpretations of dream content. For example, in an old, classical psychoanalytic dream analysis, if a male client dreams of struggling while climbing a tree, the tree trunk is interpreted as a penis and his struggle might represent his problems associated with feeling sexually adequate. Similarly, a woman client with the same dream might be told she's experiencing penis envy and her efforts to climb the tree are symbolic of her wish to become a man.

In reality, contemporary psychoanalytic dream work doesn't rely on authoritarian, symbol-based, analyst-centered interpretations. Instead, it's a personal and interactive process. Levy (1984) wrote:

> Using dreams to their fullest advantage requires that the patient be encouraged to free associate to dream elements. The patient must be an active collaborator in dream interpretation in order to avoid a sense of speculation.... Whenever possible, the patient's own ideas should be sought so that he becomes familiar with unconscious mechanisms that are sometimes most clearly seen in dream material. (p. 48)

This description is a reminder that psychoanalytic dream analysis is interactive. Although the analyst's perspective is important, the method involves asking clients to free associate to their dreams, thus facilitating a collaborative exploration.

Psychodynamic Psychotherapy in Action: Brief Vignettes

In traditional psychoanalysis, psychological defenses are interpreted before the underlying conflicts. If you interpret the underlying conflict first, clients will use preexisting defense mechanisms (e.g., denial) to resist the interpretation. For example, if you tell your client that the reason for her silence is fear of rejection, then she's likely to withdraw by using more silence. Instead, if you interpret the defense first, by opening up a discussion of how she uses silence to protect herself, then she may be able to begin being more open, giving you a clearer glimpse of underlying conflicts. She may then be more able to understand and accept deeper conflict interpretations.

Vignette I: A Poor Application of Interpretation

Defenses don't promptly disappear when interpreted. In fact, especially when used in an authoritarian or confrontational manner, interpretations can produce defensive reactions (W. R. Miller & Rollnick, 2013). Consider this example:

Client: There's nothing about my past that causes me any trouble. I hated my older brother, but he's dead now. There's no point in talking about that. The past is over. It doesn't help to talk about it.

Therapist: I've heard you say this before. You close down an entire subject for discussion when, very possibly, there could be something uncomfortable worth talking about. It's like you put up a wall and say, "There's nothing there, end of subject."

Client: There really *is* nothing in my past to talk about!

Therapist: There's that wall again.

This example of interpretation illustrates several problems. First, interpretations work best when nested in an empathic therapy alliance. In this case, the therapist doesn't start with empathy, but rushes right to a confrontational interpretation. Second, timing is critical for success. This therapist wants to share what she knows and isn't following Fenichel's rule of waiting until the interpretive material is very close to the surface. Third, the therapist doesn't back off and focus on what might be so hard about talking about the brother. Instead, the interpretation is repeated, without empathic understanding of what's happening in the room.

Vignette II: Analysis of Resistance Leading to Transference Material

This example emphasizes the importance of gently exploring resistance as something valuable—something to be collaboratively explored in pursuit of the meaning of the resistance. In this case, the client falls silent. During the past several sessions the therapist noticed his client was having difficulties speaking freely and usually followed these struggles with apologies and deprecating self-critique. The bracketed information that follows is in the original text.

Patient: I'm sorry. I feel like I don't have anything to say. [Silence, lasting a minute or two.]

Therapist: Let's try to understand the silence together and see what it tells us about you.

Patient: I just seem to run out of things to say. [Silence.]

Therapist: When you run out of things to say, how do you begin to feel?

Patient: I feel stupid. In fact, often, in the car on the way over here I worry about whether I'll have enough things to talk about to fill the time.

Therapist: You feel stupid.

Patient: After I've told you the news since my last appointment, I can't think of anything important to tell

you. My mind wanders to dumb things, what to cook for dinner, my hair, stupid things like that.

Therapist: You label your more personal thoughts dumb or stupid. What does that bring to mind?

Patient: My parents. They were always telling me I was stupid, that my opinions were stupid if they were different from theirs.

Therapist: So when you are silent, you keep more personal things to yourself. I think you may do this to ward off the possibility that I, too, may find your more personal thoughts stupid, even if that doesn't consciously occur to you.

Patient: You know, I do worry that you'll think I'm stupid, although I never put that together with being silent. Stupid was a word my mother used constantly. She still does, whenever I don't do things her way. (Levy, 1984, p. 82)

This case shows how exploring resistance (in this case, silence) can produce transference material and insight. The transference-related feelings of being stupid won't magically disappear, but their emergence provides new and useful information leading to further work on the client's internalized harsh and critical self. It's also important to notice how the therapist uses empathy and is gently and collaboratively exploring the resistance.

CASE PRESENTATION

In a published case example, Wachtel (2010) described his psychoanalytic work with Andrew, a male client who was struggling with feelings of disconnection in his marriage. As you read the following case, think about how Andrew's childhood experiences created an internalized interpersonal model for relationships. Also, notice how Wachtel uses attachment theory to guide his interactions and interventions with the client. This case is integrated with an abbreviated treatment plan based on a four-point outline:

- The Problem List (or Goal List).

- Problem Formulation (the theory-based explanation for what creates and/or sustains the client's problem).

- Interventions.

- Outcomes Assessment.

Wachtel (2010) initially described Andrew's problems and provided case formulation information.

Andrew … experienced his wife as "controlling" him, though a broader look at the pattern between them made it clear that her "control"—as is often the case—was in good measure a function of his own acquiescence. Put differently, part of what happened was that Andrew—both because of his concerns about his daughter and because of his own guilt over his wish to pull back from his wife—often went out of his way to be compliant with Jane's wishes, and then felt intruded on and "controlled." (pp. 562–563)

The Problem List

Andrew reports feeling controlled. Wachtel noted he acquiesces or backs down from speaking about his personal needs. Additionally, Andrew experiences depressive and anxious symptoms associated with his perception of being trapped in an unhappy marriage. The problem list for Andrew's treatment plan might look like this:

- Difficulty speaking up (aka subassertiveness).

- Anxiety (associated with speaking up and associated with feeling trapped).

- Depression (and related feelings of hopelessness linked to his perception of being trapped in an unhappy relationship).

Wachtel discussed his integration of attachment theory into the psychoanalytic case formulation:

[H]aving been stimulated by a recent immersion in the attachment literature and the related literature on mother–infant interaction, I articulated my understanding of Andrew's experience just a little differently.... Instead of saying that Jane's comment had felt intrusive (though it did, and though that would certainly have also been an empathically responsive comment), I said that it felt like Jane had been "overtracking" his experience. His [Andrew's] eyes lit up, and he said, excitedly: "Yes, that's exactly it. I love that word, overtracking, that's it!" (p. 563)

Wachtel used overtracking because it fit with attachment theory dynamics. He had been reading about how infants do best when mothers engage in moderate tracking to their emotional cues and physical needs. Too little tracking is obviously undesirable, but it appears too much tracking also can be a negative interpersonal experience. He goes on:

The babies of mothers who undertrack tend to be insecure in the fashion that is called ambivalent or resistant in the attachment literature. They keep flailing about trying to get their mothers to be more responsive. But the babies of mothers who overtrack, who are too in sync, seem to have difficulties too; they tend to be insecure in the fashion that is described as avoidant. They withdraw from contact in order to have any room for autonomy at all. (p. 564)

Problem Formulation

Psychoanalytic case formulations have interpersonal foundations (Binder, 2004). These foundations are built on repeated child–caretaker interactions, subsequently internalized, that later manifest themselves in clients' daily lives. Consequently, Andrew's depressive and anxiety symptoms are traced to early childhood interpersonal experiences (or perceptions), observed within the therapy relationship (transference), and triggered in his contemporary interpersonal relationships (i.e., using the transference-based triangle of insight).

From an attachment-informed psychoanalytic perspective, Andrew's difficulty speaking up and associated anxiety and depression are created and maintained by an unconscious internalized working model. Specific relational interactions with his wife trigger this dynamic. If Andrew becomes aware of his part in this interpersonal dynamic or dance, then he can proactively and intentionally deal with his underlying fears (of being emotionally suffocated) and develop new behaviors that allow him to initiate more desirable interpersonal patterns in his marriage. This will help him address his needs for autonomy in a way that doesn't trigger anxiety over rejection or abandonment (being alone).

Wachtel discusses the therapeutic process he uses with Andrew—a process based on the problem formulation. Take special note of how Wachtel gathers detailed observations of Andrew before offering specific interventions:

As Andrew and I continued to talk about the experience I had labeled as overtracking, Andrew conveyed both his great pleasure at the way I had labeled the experience and his experience of almost horror at what it felt like to be overtracked. In the midst of this, he suddenly did something I found very striking.... What happened was that Andrew continued to talk to me about the experience, but, while he was doing so, he turned his head so that he was not only facing away from me but was basically looking at right angles to me while he spoke. This continued for a few seconds, and then he turned back to look at me. He did not seem to notice at all that he had done this....

What Andrew did...seemed to me to be both a confirmation and a poignant playing out of the very concern about overtracking we had just been discussing. Andrew had clearly felt keenly understood by me in my labeling of his "overtracking" experience. In many respects this was a gratifying and positive experience for him. But the very fact that I had understood him so well, I believe, also raised the anxiety that I too would understand him too well, that I too would overtrack, not leave him room for his needed zone of privacy. From that vantage point, turning away from me was a way of seeing whether he could still control our interaction, whether he could be understood and in contact when he felt like it rather than as an inexorable consequence of my "looming empathy."

...In this instance, I think that the unconscious test that Andrew was posing was whether he could control the degree of contact between us and whether we could remain in contact on his terms—that is, with his regulation of the intensity and nature of the contact. (p. 565)

Intervention

As he worked with Andrew, Wachtel was formulating hypotheses based on his experience and observations of Andrew, Andrew as a child, attachment theory, and what he knew about Andrew's current relationships. At the same time, Wachtel was listening closely to Andrew and adjusting his therapist behaviors. An analysis of Wachtel's considerable multitasking illustrates why psychoanalytic or psychodynamic psychotherapies require rigorous training and supervision.

Working from a psychoanalytic model, Wachtel was developing a relationship with Andrew that respected Andrew's anxiety around closeness. As Wachtel provided emotional space, Andrew started having insights that allowed him to begin taking greater responsibility for his relationship behaviors. In fact, as Wachtel acknowledged, because of Andrew's sensitivity to too much closeness, he (Wachtel) needed to avoid too much early interpretation as it might be viewed as "overtracking." This experiential component of therapy is similar to what Alexander and French (1946) referred to as the corrective emotional experience. Wachtel noted that in this therapy situation, traditional interpretations should be employed secondarily—after indirectly communicating sensitivity to the therapeutic relationship dynamic. Toward the end of his case description, Wachtel described how he carefully offered an indirect suggestion for Andrew to consider. He did this in a way to avoid activating Andrew's interpersonal anxiety; if he were to activate Andrew's anxiety, he might have also activated Andrew's resistance.

> Later in the session I suggested that what he wished was…to be able to talk to [Jane] and not have to be gazing into her eyes at every moment, to be able to know that she is there and listening, but that he can glance over at the mail or do something else while talking to her.…Andrew was enthusiastically receptive to this comment, saying that yes, it captured very well what he longed for, and it seemed to create at least a small opening for him to imagine a way of approaching Jane rather than having to retreat from her in order to prevent himself from feeling invaded.

Wachtel's work with Andrew resulted in the possibility for new and more adaptive behaviors in Andrew's marriage relationship. This is an important example because although psychoanalytic therapists are traditionally criticized for only focusing on insight, in fact, effective psychoanalytic therapists also focus on behavior change. Binder (2004) described the typical change process in psychodynamic psychotherapy as including four parts:

1. Cognitive insight (usually of a repeating maladaptive interpersonal pattern).
2. Practice in detecting maladaptive mental and interpersonal patterns.

3. Creating new and more satisfying interpersonal experiences.
4. Internalization of new and more satisfying interpersonal experiences and the consequent modification of interpersonal schemas and corresponding internal working models of interpersonal relations (pp. 132–133).

Outcomes Measurement

Traditional psychoanalytic psychotherapists tend to underutilize outcomes assessment. Nevertheless, if psychoanalytic treatment practitioners want to provide services within medical systems, research support and valid outcomes assessment is necessary. It's not enough for psychoanalytic approaches to base their proof—as they have historically—on case studies and anecdotal reports.

Instead of using projective assessments, contemporary psychodynamic outcome researchers generally use a combination of symptom-oriented measures (e.g., the *Beck Depression Inventory-II*; BDI-II; Beck, Steer, & Brown, 1996) and interpersonal process measures that can be used to predict positive treatment outcomes or in-session therapy aliance (e.g., the 24-item *California Psychotherapy Alliance Scale*; CALPAS; Bachelor, 2013; Gaston, 1991).

In his work with Andrew, Wachtel could use the CALPAS and/or the BDI-II to track process and symptom change every session or less often, depending upon what they collaboratively agree on as a means of monitoring progress. Specific measures focusing on anxiety and relationship satisfaction would also be appropriate. Establishing a collaborative agreement on process and outcome measures is consistent with psychoanalytic ideas about building a working alliance.

EVALUATIONS AND APPLICATIONS

Psychoanalytic approaches have a long, storied, and controversial history. Many contemporary practitioners dislike Freud and psychoanalytic ideas. Others openly embrace psychoanalytic principles and practices. Still others, and perhaps the majority, apply psychoanalytic principles in their clinical work, but do so unknowingly. No matter where you end up in the future, it will be good for you to understand how psychoanalytic approaches address important issues in contemporary society.

Evidence-Based Status

Conducting rigorous research on longer-term treatments, such as psychoanalytic therapy, is challenging and cost prohibitive. Psychoanalytic approaches are often less symptom- or diagnosis-focused, seeking instead to facilitate

BRAIN BOX

2.1 The Contributions of Neuroscience to Psychoanalytic Theory

Chad Luke, Tennessee Technological University
Fred Redekop, Kutztown University

Modern neuroscience holds promise for the reconceptualization of counseling theories and for the reformulation of clinical practice. Neuroscience integration offers insights into the major theories and how practitioners might work with depression, anxiety, addictions, and other clinical concerns (Luke, 2016). It holds particular promise for the contemporary application of psychoanalysis. Indeed, this view is precisely the view of the journal, *Neuropsychoanalysis*, which has as its stated aim to publish empirical research and theoretical papers that integrate contemporary psychoanalysis and neuroscience. Fascinatingly, rather than suggesting that psychoanalysis is passé, modern neuroscience elaborates on some of Freud's ideas and is consistent with relational psychoanalysis.

Brief Background on the Brain

A brief discussion of brain function and development contextualizes the contributions of neuroscience to psychoanalysis. First, researchers focusing on brain lateralization generally support the idea that the two hemispheres of the brain perform distinct, but highly integrated, functions. The left hemisphere focuses on language, logic, literality, and linearity and is responsible for critical thinking and information processing (Siegel & Hartzell, 2003). The right hemisphere focuses on the big picture, creativity, sensory perception, and orientation to time and space (Badenoch, 2008). Interestingly (and despite our wishes to think of ourselves as primarily guided by logic and reason), the right hemisphere is dominant in many respects. Why? Because "emotional" processes are largely responsible, in evolutionary terms, for survival. Threat assessment requires "fast-track" processing; the quicker right-mode processing (RMP), as it's sometimes called, provides the best chance for responding soon enough to ensure survival. In contrast, while left-mode processing (LMP) may be more accurate, its slowness relative to RMP creates a hazard for the organism.

Attachment, the Unconscious, and Memory

Returning to specific interplay between neuroscience and psychoanalysis, we find that neuroscience researchers provide substantial input into three basic psychoanalytic concerns: (a) early relationships serving as a template for later relationships; (b) unconscious (or preconscious) influences, particularly in relationships and intuited threats in the environment; and (c) memory and the encoding and retrieval of cognitive, affective, and contextual cues.

Many theorists subsequent to Freud developed ideas about how early attachment relationships provide a template for subsequent functioning (Ainsworth, Blehar, Waters, & Wall, 1978; Bowlby, 1969; Marcia & Josselson, 2013). It is from the secure base of the primary caregiver that children learn to explore their world and express their needs and get those needs met in adaptive ways (Bowlby, 1988b). It is vital, in considering attachment, to understand that we are talking about largely unconscious mechanisms—both in the initial parenting relationship and in the counseling relationship—that are seen as a kind of re-parenting, an idea first suggested by Freud (1964).

In the words of one researcher, the "consolidation of information in the behaving brain rarely stops" (Dudai, 2012, p. 241). Instead of prior views of stable memory consolidation, we find that memories are highly malleable, and that researchers are now concerned with memory reconsolidation (Nader & Einarsson, 2010). In reconsolidation, long-term memory is reactivated, and in this process, long-term memory appears to become fragile and destabilized (Dudai, 2012); memory destabilization offers the potential for therapeutic reconsolidation through insight, interpretation, and working through.

The Right Brain Implicit Self

One useful model that illustrates neuroscientific principles in psychoanalytic practice is Schore's (2010, 2011a, 2011b) right brain implicit self model. Building on the idea of brain lateralization, he suggests that, in effect, humans have a conscious left brain and an unconscious right brain—and the unconscious right brain is dominant in the context of attachment relationships. This is consistent with psychoanalysts' insistence on the importance of unconscious processes. In caretaking attachment relationships, there is a dynamic, nonverbal, interaction between the caretaker's unconscious right brain processes and the developing child's right brain processes, interactions that form the working model for how the child understands attachment to function and that are stored for later retrieval—both later in the caretaking relationship and during later intimate relationships. In this intense less-than-conscious process, memory is a key mediator, since the attachment relationship is influenced not only by current overt behavior and covert clues but by reconstructions of past interactions.

Schore (2011b), using neuroscience language, suggests that:

> ...as a result of this interaction with caregivers, the infant forms internal working models of attachment that are stored in right-lateralized nonverbal implicit-procedural memory.... Security of attachment relates to a physiologic coding of an expectation that during times of stress, homeostatic disruptions will be set right.... The infant's ability to develop more complex self-regulatory coping capacities, to regulate stressful alterations of psychobiological state(s) ... emerges out of ... experiences with the social environment. (p. 236)

In simplified terms, the attachment relationship helps infants to self-regulate, teaching them strategies that are relatively less-than-conscious, encoded in the incredibly rich, implicit, nonverbal "conversations" that caregivers and children are regularly having. Furthermore, Schore suggests that there are two primary goals of this attachment process—to dampen negative affective states and to enhance and sustain positive ones.

However, what happens when children do not develop this "physiological encoding"? Attachment is adversely effected and need satiation is less adaptive; this may lead to global deficits in attachment, which may lead to the need for counseling. In counseling, counselors serve as surrogate attachment figures that use their own right-brain, implicit selves to resonate self-regulatory responses to dysregulated clients. This RMP attunement allows for healing attachment, often called re-parenting or corrective emotional experience in psychoanalytic approaches, and is made possible based on the plasticity principle of brain change. These suggestions can be seen as the neuroscientific elaboration of Freud's (1958) famous dictum that in confronting the freely associated unconscious material that patients produce in session, an analyst must "turn his own unconscious like a receptive organ towards the transmitting unconscious of the patient" (p. 115). These suggestions also support Frieda Fromm-Reichmann's (1948) adage that, "The patient needs an experience, not an explanation."

client insight and improve interpersonal relationships. Because empirically supported treatments focus on whether a specific psychological procedure reduces symptoms associated with a medical diagnosis, "proving" the efficacy of complex therapy approaches is difficult—especially when compared to the lesser challenges inherent in evaluating symptom-focused treatments. Partly because of these complexities, some reviewers have contended that psychoanalytic psychotherapies are less efficacious than cognitive and behavioral therapies (Busch, 2015; Tolin, 2010).

The good news for psychoanalytic therapy fans is that evidence is accumulating to support treatment efficacy.

The less good news is that some of the research support remains methodologically weak and the wide variety of psychoanalytic approaches makes it difficult to come to clear conclusions. Nevertheless, the most recent meta-analytic studies, literature reviews, and randomized controlled studies support the efficacy of psychoanalytically oriented therapies for the treatment of a variety of mental disorders. According to Leichsenring, Klein, and Salzer (2014), there is empirical support for the efficacy of psychoanalytic psychotherapies in treating:

- Depressive disorders.

- Anxiety disorders.

- Somatic symptom disorders.

- Eating disorders.

- Substance-related disorders.

- Borderline personality disorder.

The evidence for the efficacy of psychodynamic approaches for depressive disorders is strong. In a recent meta-analysis, Driessen and colleagues (2015) evaluated 54 studies, including 3,946 patients. They reported that short-term psychodynamic psychotherapy (STPP) was associated with improvements in general psychopathology and quality of life measures ($d = 0.49$–0.69) and all outcome measures ($d = 0.57$–1.18); they also noted that patients continued to improve at follow-up ($d = 0.20$–1.04). Further, no differences were found between STPP and other psychotherapies. On anxiety measures, STPP appeared significantly superior to other psychotherapies at post-treatment ($d = 0.35$) and follow-up ($d = 0.76$).

In a previous meta-analytic review, Shedler (2010) also concluded that psychodynamic therapies were equivalent to "…other treatments that have been actively promoted as 'empirically supported' and 'evidence based'" (p. 107). He also reported that psychodynamic therapies had more robust long-term effects.

Table 2.2 provides a sampling of meta-analytic evidence supporting psychodynamic therapies. For comparison purposes, the original meta-analyses conducted by Smith and colleagues are included (M. L. Smith & Glass, 1977; M. L. Smith et al., 1980). Notably, Smith, Glass, and Miller reported that psychodynamic approaches were significantly more efficacious than no treatment and approximately equivalent to other therapy approaches.

Table 2.2 also includes the average effect size (ES or d; see Chapter 1) for antidepressant medications (ES = 0.31 for serotonin-specific reuptake inhibitors or SSRIs). This comparison data shows that psychodynamic psychotherapy is more effective than SSRI treatment for depression. Additionally, the benefits of psychoanalytic therapy tend to increase over time (Driessen et al., 2015; Shedler, 2010). This implies that psychoanalytic psychotherapy clients develop insights and acquire skills that continue to improve their functioning into the future—which is clearly not the case for antidepressant medication treatment (Whitaker, 2010). One of the ways psychotherapists explain this difference in longer term efficacy is with the statement: "A pill is not a skill."

We recommend you take the preceding research findings (and Table 2.2) with a grain of salt. Conducting systematic research on something as subjective as human mental and emotional problems always includes error. One source of error is the allegiance effect (Luborsky et al., 1999). The

Table 2.2   A Sampling of Psychodynamic Psychotherapy Meta-analyses

Authors	Outcome focus	Number of studies	ES or d
Abbass et al. (2006)	General psychiatric symptoms	8	0.97
Anderson & Lambert (1995)	Various	9	0.85
de Maat et al. (2009)	Long-term treatment	10	0.78
Driessen et al. (2015)	Depression	54	0.57–1.18
Comparison research			
Turner et al. (2008)	Meds for Major depression	74	0.31
Smith et al. (1977)	Different therapies Many problems	375	0.68
Smith et al. (1980)	Different therapies Many problems	475	0.75

Note: This is a sampling of meta-analytic psychoanalytic psychotherapy reviews. We've omitted several reviews with very high effect sizes partly because of criticisms related to their statistical methodology (see Driessen et al., 2015, and Shedler, 2010, for more complete reviews). This table is not comprehensive; it's only a reasonable representation of psychoanalytic psychotherapy meta-analyses.

allegiance effect is the tendency for the researcher's therapy preference or allegiance to significantly predict outcome study results. Specifically, Luborsky and colleagues (1999) analyzed results from 29 different adult psychotherapy studies and reported that about two thirds of the variation in outcome was accounted for by the researcher's theoretical orientation (e.g., psychoanalytic researchers reported more positive outcomes for psychoanalytic therapy and behavior therapists discovered that behavior therapy was more effective).

The implications of the allegiance effect help explain why, shortly after Shedler's (2010) publication extolling the virtues of psychodynamic psychotherapy, several critiques and rebuttals were published (Anestis, Anestis, & Lilienfeld, 2011; McKay, 2011). The critics claimed that Shedler's review was biased and accused him of overlooking weaknesses within the meta-analyses he reviewed (e.g., poor outcome measures, pooling the effects of small samples with little power and poor designs, lack of treatment integrity effects). Although Shedler's critics raised important points, the critics themselves had their own biases. The problem is that all researchers (and writers) have an allegiance of one sort of another.

One of our favorite ways of understanding the allegiance effect is articulated in a story about the great New York Yankee baseball player, Yogi Berra. One day, when a player on Yogi's team was called out on a close play at second base, Yogi went charging onto the field to protest. The umpire explained that he, unlike Yogi, was an objective observer and that he, unlike Yogi, had been only about 5 feet from the play, while Yogi had been over 100 feet away, in the dugout. When Yogi heard the umpire's logic, he became even angrier and snapped back, "Listen ump, I wouldn't have seen it, if I hadn't believed it" (adapted from Leber, 1991).

The "I saw it because I believed it" phenomenon is also called confirmation bias (Masnick & Zimmerman, 2009; Nickerson, 1998). **Confirmation bias** involves seeking, interpreting, and valuing evidence that supports pre-existing beliefs, while ignoring and devaluing evidence contrary to preexisting beliefs. Consequently, psychoanalytically oriented individuals see support for their perspective and behavior therapists see support for theirs. However, despite these caveats, based on accumulating research, psychodynamic approaches have a reasonably good record of efficacy.

Cultural Sensitivity

Beginning with Freud, psychoanalytic theorists and therapists haven't been especially sensitive to cultural issues. More recently, C. E. Watkins reported on a 50-year (1960–2010) review of 104 psychodynamically oriented treatment studies. He summarized: "Approximately 75% of the studies provided no information about race or ethnicity whatsoever" and "Psychodynamic treatment data on non-white subjects are exceedingly rare" (2012, p. 292).

Consistent with Watkins's review, in the chapter case presentation, Wachtel (2010) never mentions Andrew's ethnic background. He also never mentions that social/cultural factors could be influencing Andrew's wish for more independence in his marriage relationship. This is disappointing because it's difficult to imagine that Andrew, being a married man in the twenty-first century, hasn't been bombarded by social media messages about what it means to be a man. Andrew likely has learned that "real men" are not "controlled" by their wives. Andrew's beliefs about marriage cannot help but be influenced by factors other than his early relationship with his mother. His marriage-beliefs are probably more directly and immediately linked to his ethnic or cultural orientation and gender-based expectations.

Although Wachtel's use of attachment theory to inform how he talks with Andrew is intellectually interesting and has intuitive appeal, attachment theory isn't a good fit for many individuals raised outside Middle Class American culture (Morelli, 2015). If Andrew were raised within an Israeli Kibbutz or African community, his "attachment" style might not neatly fit into an American model. In this chapter's featured case, Wachtel described a very personalized treatment plan for Andrew. This plan is based on Andrew's unique (a) concerns, (b) self-reported history, and (c) interactions within the therapy hour. Given this perspective, attachment-informed psychoanalytic therapists could claim they're exceptionally multiculturally sensitive. Although there are still questions about the cultural appropriateness of treating an individual who has collectivist cultural values with individually oriented psychoanalytic techniques, Andrew doesn't hail from a collectivist culture. The depth and exploration associated with psychoanalytic approaches lends support to its potential for individualized and multiculturally sensitive adaptation (Tummala-Narra, 2016).

Traditional psychoanalytic training has a strong focus on internal psychological processes. This "internal world" focus can cause psychoanalytic trainings to neglect the "external world" and may result in ethnically and sexually diverse students (trainees) feeling marginalized (Ciclitira & Foster, 2012, p. 370). Although it appears that there has been some progress toward including social and cultural factors in psychoanalytic training—especially within the intersubjectivity movement—overall progress in this area has been slow.

Gender and Sexuality

Without question, psychoanalytic theory and practice has a substantial history of being anti-women. Girls and women have been repeatedly pathologized, in part, simply for not having penises. As Karen Horney and others have articulated, psychoanalytic perspectives have been phallocentric and patriarchal (Flax, 2012). Females and the feminine were consistently framed as less than, more irrational than, weaker than, and less morally developed than males.

Psychoanalytic theory also hasn't been a friend to sexual diversity. Specifically, psychoanalytic explanations for "homosexuality" blamed parents (i.e., a smothering mother and distant father) for this so-called deviance. The ways in which psychoanalysis has treated women and sexual minorities in the past has been so abysmal that the only relevant question is whether contemporary psychoanalytic thinkers have improved in this area.

Looking back at Wachtel's featured case in this chapter, there's ample material to make a robust feminist critique. Specifically, when discussing attachment theory, Wachtel always uses "mother" instead of "father, parent, or caretaker." Consistent with the history of psychoanalytic discourse, this linguistic style places mothers in positions of great child-rearing responsibility and can lead to mother-bashing or blaming (Tummala-Narra, 2016). In keeping with this frame, all of Andrew's needs for freedom and his sensitivity to being controlled are traced to having a mother whom he experienced as overtracking his every move throughout childhood. Although his relationship with his mother is no doubt important and relevant to therapy, the fluidity of attachments and attachment dynamics suggests that Andrew's repeating relationship problems (aka Core Conflictual Relationship Theme) shouldn't be viewed as an internalized working model that Andrew rigidly carries around in his head (Luborsky, 1984). To his credit, Wachtel acknowledged this oversimplification and generalization.

> Attachment status is not a quality residing inside a single individual.... We describe people as securely or insecurely attached, as avoidantly or ambivalently attached, and so forth, as if they were that way with everyone and at all times—as if, that is, this was just "the way they are." This linguistic form, seeming to suggest that attachment status is a property the individual simply carries around with him in his head, reflects what Mitchell (1995, p. 65) called "a view of mind as monadic, a separable, individual entity," in contrast to "a view of mind as dyadic, emerging from and inevitably embedded within a relational field." (pp. 567–568)

As is the case with most theoretical perspectives, psychoanalytic theorists began moving toward a more inclusive paradigm in the early 1990s (Tummala-Narra, 2016). Although this more inclusive theoretical stance hasn't produced much empirical research on women and sexual minorities, it's now acceptable to think about sex and gender beyond the biological binary. Specifically, gay psychoanalytic practitioners have written about belonging

and lesbian psychoanalytic "foremothers" have been identified and the "Lavender couch" reconstructed (Beneditti, 2015; Zand, 2004). Affirmation of diverse sexual identities is common; gay, lesbian, and other sexual ways of being have been reformulated "as a positive developmental achievement."

In contrast to its narrow historical lens, Tummala-Narra (2016) has written that psychoanalytic perspectives are "uniquely suited" for understanding "gender, race, culture, sexual orientation and identity, social class, and dis/ability" (p. 29). Going forward, it's time for psychoanalytic proponents to let go of their regressive inhibitions, embrace a broader swath of humanity, and move closer to their potential.

Spirituality

Freud was no fan of religion. He often referred to himself as a "Godless Jew." Gay (1978) wrote that Freud "advertised his unbelief every time he could find, or make, an opportunity" (p. 3). Freud (1918) viewed religious beliefs as irrational, projective, and regressive. In return, most religious people are no fans of Freud. Casey (1938) captured some of the disdain early psychoanalysts held toward religion, "Even in the higher religions with their impressive theological facades there is always ... a myth, a rule of piety, a cult, which is rationalized but which neither begins nor ends with reason" (p. 445).

Despite this poor start, psychoanalytic theorists and practitioners have made strides in accepting religion and integrating spirituality into psychotherapy. A common psychoanalytic position is that religious and spiritual experiences are meaningful and therefore deserve the same level of analysis and respect as sexuality, family relationships, work, and other life domains (Rizzuto & Shafranske, 2013). This respectful stance toward religious experiences is exciting territory for practitioners who want to integrate religion and spirituality into psychoanalytic approaches.

As one example, Rizzuto and Shafranske (2013) wrote that, "God representations always involve a representation of the self in relationship with the sacred" (p. 135). They view client disclosures about religion as opportunities for a deeper understanding of clients. God representations are not only respected but also explored as multidimensional components of human experience that can exert both positive and negative influence on individual's lives. They believe, "Religion and spirituality can serve as a foundation for the healthy appreciation of the self and for the resolution of psychic pain and trauma" (p. 142). Clearly, this perspective plays better with religious clients than beginning with an assumption, like Freud, that all religious views and experiences are immature and irrational.

CONCLUDING COMMENTS

Anyone whose collected works fill 24 volumes is likely to have—as we psychoanalytically informed mental health professionals like to say—"achievement issues." Dr. Freud might even accept this interpretation. He said it himself, "A man who has been the indisputable favorite of his mother keeps for life the feeling of a conqueror, that confidence of success that often induces real success" (E. E. Jones, 1953, p. 5).

Judging him based on his own theoretical perspective, Freud clearly suffered from some Oedipus conflicts, and these were, in part, manifest in his intense striving for recognition. It may have been his penchant for stature that caused him to invent and then recant his seduction theory.

In 1937, 2 years before Janet's death, Edouard Pichon, Pierre Janet's son-in-law, wrote to Freud, asking him to visit Janet. Freud responded:

> No, I will not see Janet. I could not refrain from reproaching him with having behaved unfairly to psychoanalysis and also to me personally and never having corrected it. He was stupid enough to say that the idea of sexual aetiology for the neuroses could only arise in the atmosphere of a town like Vienna. Then when the libel was spread by French writers that I had listened to his lectures and stolen his ideas he could with a word have put an end to such talk, since actually I never saw him or heard his name in the Charcot time: he has never spoken this word. You can get an idea of his scientific level from his utterance that the unconscious is *une façon de parler*. No I will not see him. I thought at first of sparing him the impoliteness by the excuse that I am not well or that I can no longer talk French and he certainly can't understand a word of German. But I have decided against that. There is no reason for making any sacrifice for him. Honesty the only possible thing; rudeness quite in order. (Jones, 1957, pp. 633–634)

There was no special reconciliation for Freud. Toward the end of his life he suffered from many medical and psychological problems. His addiction to tobacco led to cancer and jaw surgery and considerable physical pain. In September 1939, he asked a fellow physician and friend, Max Schur, to assist in his suicide. Freud asked, "Schur, you remember our 'contract' not to leave me in the lurch when the time had come. Now it is nothing but torture and makes no sense" (Gay, 2006, p. 651). After Schur responded, Freud replied, "I thank you" and followed this with, "Talk it over with Anna, and if she thinks it's right, then make an end of it" (p. 651). Although Anna was initially against the plan, Schur argued otherwise and on two consecutive September days, he administered enough morphine to finally result in Freud's death on September 23, 1939.

Freud's legacy is often linked to negativity or pessimism. There are good reasons for this; Freud focused on issues like the death instinct and primitive instinctual impulses, impulses that we have little awareness of or control over. However, he was sometimes hopeful. One of his more optimistic statements is carved in a memorial to him in Vienna which reads,

> The voice of reason is small, but very persistent.

CHAPTER SUMMARY AND REVIEW

In the late 1800s and early 1900s, Sigmund Freud developed psychoanalysis. Along the way, Freud experimented with hypnosis, but finally settled on treating hysteria symptoms by having patients talk about their childhood experiences. Freud's original model is called classical Freudian theory or drive theory.

Early in the development of psychoanalysis, Freud hypothesized that childhood sexual abuse caused hysteria (i.e., the seduction hypothesis). His ideas were not well-received. Later, for unknown reasons, he recanted his seduction hypothesis in favor of the fantasized Oedipus complex. He lived in a time when and a place where sex and sexuality were not generally spoken of openly.

Freud developed one of the giant theories of human development. Four main parts (or approaches) to his theory include the: (1) dynamic approach, (2) topographic approach, (3) developmental stage approach, and (4) structural approach. Freud believed that everyone has the potential to develop psychopathology if exposed to the right type and amount of stress.

Following Freud, psychoanalytic thought continued to develop in different directions. Adler and Jung both left Freud's inner circle to develop their own theory and approach. Pine (1990) categorized the evolution of psychoanalytic thought as encompassing four stages: (1) drive, (2) ego psychology, (3) object relations, and (4) self-psychology. However, there are many other contemporary psychoanalytic or psychodynamic movements. These include time-limited psychodynamic psychotherapy, relational psychoanalysis, and attachment-informed psychotherapy.

Psychoanalytic practitioners sometimes use projective assessment to better understand underlying client psychodynamics. More often, they use free association (aka the basic rule) to help clients articulate underlying unconscious processes. Then, as clients experience transference and resistance, the psychotherapist carefully uses interpretation to clarify and bring unconscious patterns into awareness. Interpretation works best if therapists establish a strong working alliance, explain how psychoanalytic therapy works, and use good timing.

Psychoanalytic therapists observe for client transference and work to become aware of their countertransference reactions. Interpretations frequently focus on problematic repeating interpersonal themes or patterns in the client's life. These patterns can often be seen in two different types of triangles of insight. The transference triangle of insight focuses on (a) current client relationships, (b) the client–therapist relationship (transference), and (c) past client relationships. Psychoanalytically oriented therapists also use dream interpretation.

Generally, psychoanalytic approaches have been viewed as less scientific than behavioral or cognitive approaches. However, meta-analyses conducted over the past 10 years have shown that psychoanalytic therapies are efficacious for several different mental health problems.

Historically, psychoanalytic approaches have not focused much on cultural issues. Most research studies do not provide any information about race or ethnicity. Additionally, beginning with Freud, the psychoanalytic perspectives on women, sexual diversity, and spirituality have been negative and judgmental. Contemporary psychoanalytic approaches and publications have been more diversity-sensitive and open to spirituality.

PSYCHOANALYTIC KEY TERMS

Aetiology of hysteria

Allegiance effect

Anal

Anxious-avoidant insecure attachment

Anxious-resistant insecure attachment

Attachment-informed psychotherapy

Basic rule

Classical psychoanalytic theory

Confirmation bias

Conflict-based triangle of insight

Conscience

Conscious

Core conflictual relationship theme

Corrective emotional experience

Countertransference

Defense mechanisms

Denial

Developmental stage approach

Disorganized/disoriented attachment

Displacement

Dream interpretation

Dynamic approach

Ego

Ego-ideal

Ego psychology

Eight stage epigenetic psychosocial theory of development (Erikson)

Eros

Fixation

Focal psychotherapy

Free association

Genital

Hysteria

Id

Internal working model

Interpretation

Latency

Libido

Modern psychoanalytic approaches

Neo-Freudian

Normal–abnormal continuum

Object

Object relations theory

Oedipus complex

Oral

Phallic

Pleasure principle

Primary process thought

Preconscious

Projection

Projective testing

Psychic determinism

Psychoanalysis

Psychodynamic psychotherapy

Purpose of psychoanalysis

Rationalization

Reaction formation

Reality principle

Regression

Relational psychoanalysis (also two-person psychology or intersubjectivity)

Repetition compulsion

Repression

Role induction

Secondary thought process

Secure attachment

Seduction hypothesis

Self-psychology

Strange situation

Structural approach

Sublimation

Superego

Thanatos

Timing of interpretations

Topographic approach

Totalistic countertransference

Transference

Transference-based triangle of insight

Two-person psychology or intersubjectivity

Unconscious

Unconscious derivatives

CHAPTER 3

Individual Psychology and Adlerian Therapy

LEARNER OBJECTIVES

- Define individual psychology and Adlerian therapy
- Identify key figures and historical trends in the development, evolution, and application of individual psychology and Adlerian therapy
- Describe core principles of individual psychology
- Describe and apply Adlerian therapy principles, strategies, and techniques
- Analyze cases that employ Adlerian therapy techniques
- Evaluate the empirical, cultural, gender, and spiritual validity of Adlerian therapy
- Summarize core content and define key terms associated with individual psychology and Adlerian therapy

We often wonder about Alfred Adler. Who was this man whose theories and approach predate and contribute substantially to ego psychology (Chapter 2), the cognitive therapies (Chapter 8), reality therapy (Chapter 9), feminist therapy (Chapter 10), and constructive perspectives (Chapter 11)? How did he develop—over 100 years ago—influential and diverse ideas that are foundational to so many different approaches to therapy *and* so thoroughly infused into contemporary culture? His beliefs were so advanced that he seems an anomaly: he's like a man from the future who landed in the middle of Freud's inner circle in Vienna.

INTRODUCTION

Despite the ubiquity of Adler's ideas, many contemporary mental health professionals don't recognize, acknowledge, or appreciate his contributions to modern counseling and psychotherapy (Carlson & Englar-Carlson, 2017). Perhaps this is because Adler provided services for working class people, rather than the wealthy elite, or because he was an early feminist, or because his common sense ideas were less "sexy" than Freud's.

What Is Individual Psychology? (...and What Is Adlerian Therapy?)

Individual psychology was the term Adler used to describe the psychotherapy approach he founded.

Watts and Eckstein (2009) recounted Adler's rationale for choosing "individual psychology": "Adler chose the name individual psychology (from the Latin, *individuum*, meaning indivisible) for his theoretical approach because he eschewed reductionism" (p. 281).

Most people know individual psychology as Adlerian therapy, the contemporary applied term. **Adlerian therapy** is described as "a psychoeducational, present/future-oriented, and brief approach" (Watts & Pietrzak, 2000, p. 446). Similar to psychoanalytic psychotherapy, Adlerian therapy is also insight-oriented. However, therapists can use direct educational strategies to enhance client awareness.

Adler was a contemporary—not a disciple—of Freud. During their time, Adler's ideas were more popular than Freud's. Adler's first psychology book, *Understanding Human Nature*, sold over 100,000 copies in six months; in comparison, Freud's *Interpretation of Dreams* sold only 17,000 copies over 10 years (Carlson & Englar-Carlson, 2017). Jon Carlson (2015) referred to Adler as "the originator of positive psychology" (pp. 23–24).

Adler wove cognition into psychotherapy long before Albert Ellis and Aaron Beck officially launched cognitive therapy in the 1950s and 1960s. In the following quotation, Adler (1964; originally published in 1933) easily could be speaking about a cognitive rationale for a computerized virtual reality approach to treating fears and phobias (now growing in popularity in the twenty-first century):

Counseling and Psychotherapy Theories in Context and Practice: Skills, Strategies, and Techniques, Third Edition. John Sommers-Flanagan and Rita Sommers-Flanagan. © 2018 John Wiley & Sons, Inc. Published 2018 by John Wiley & Sons, Inc.
Companion website: www.wiley.com/go/sommers-flanagan/theories3e

I am convinced that a person's behavior springs from his [or her] idea....As a matter of fact, it has the same effect on one whether a poisonous snake is actually approaching my foot or whether I merely believe it is a poisonous snake. (pp. 19–20)

In his historical overview of the talking cure, Bankart (1997) claimed, "Adler's influence on the developing fields of psychology and social work was incalculable" (p. 146). This chapter is an exploration of Alfred Adler's individual psychology and his vast influence on modern counseling and psychotherapy.

Alfred Adler

Alfred Adler (1870–1937) was the second of six children born to a Jewish family outside Vienna. His older brother was brilliant, outgoing, handsome, and also happened to be named Sigmund. In contrast, Alfred was a sickly child. He suffered

Alfred Adler

from rickets, was twice run over in the street, and experienced a spasm of the glottis. When he was 3 years old, his younger brother died in bed next to him (Mosak, 1972). At age 4, he came down with pneumonia. Later Adler recalled the physician telling his father, "Your boy is lost" (Orgler, 1963, p. 16). Another of Adler's earliest memories has a sickly, dependent theme:

One of my earliest recollections is of sitting on a bench bandaged up on account of rickets, with my healthy, elder brother sitting opposite me. He could run, jump, and move about quite effortlessly, while for me movement of any sort was a strain and an effort. Everyone went to great pains to help me, and my mother and father did all that was in their power to do. At the time of this recollection, I must have been about two years old. (Bottome, 1939, p. 30)

In contrast to Freud's childhood experience of being his mother's favorite, Adler was more encouraged by his father. Despite his son's clumsy, uncoordinated, and sickly condition, Adler's father Leopold, a Hungarian Jew, firmly believed in his son's innate worth. When young Alfred was required to repeat a grade at the same middle school Freud had attended 14 years earlier, Leopold was his strongest supporter. Mosak and Maniacci (1999) described Adler's response to his father's encouragement:

His mathematics teacher recommended to his father that Adler leave school and apprentice himself as a shoe-maker. Adler's father objected, and Adler embarked upon bettering his academic skills. Within a relatively short time, he became the best math student in the class. (p. 2)

Adler's love and aptitude for learning continued to grow; he studied medicine at the University of Vienna. After obtaining his medical degree in ophthalmology in 1895, he met and fell in love with Raissa Timofeyewna Epstein, and married her in 1897. She had the unusual distinction of being an early socialist and feminist. She was good friends with Leon and Natalia Trotsky and she maintained her political interests and activities throughout their marriage (Hoffman, 1994).

HISTORICAL CONTEXT

Freud and Adler met in 1902. According to Mosak and Maniacci (1999), Adler published a strong defense of Freud's *Interpretation of Dreams*, and consequently Freud invited Adler over "on a Wednesday evening" for a discussion of psychological issues. "The Wednesday Night Meetings, as they became known, led to the development of the Psychoanalytic Society" (p. 3).

Adler was his own man with his own ideas before he met Freud. Prior to their meeting he'd published his first book, *Healthbook for the Tailor Trade* (Adler, 1898). In contrast to Freud, much of Adler's medical practice was with the working poor. Early in his career, he worked extensively with tailors and circus performers.

In February 1911, Adler did the unthinkable (Bankart, 1997). As president of Vienna's Psychoanalytic Society, he read a highly controversial paper, "The Masculine Protest," at the group's monthly meeting. It was at odds with Freudian theory. Instead of focusing on biological and psychological factors and their influence on excessively masculine behaviors in males and females, Adler emphasized culture and socialization (Carlson & Englar-Carlson, 2017). He claimed that women occupied a less privileged social and political position because of social coercion, not physical inferiority. Further, he noted that some women who reacted to this cultural situation by choosing to dress and act like men were suffering, not from penis envy, but from a social-psychological condition he referred to as the masculine protest. The *masculine protest* involved overvaluing masculinity to the point where it drove men and boys to give up and become passive or to engage in excessive aggressive behavior. In extreme cases, males who suffered from the masculine protest began dressing and acting like girls or women.

The Vienna Psychoanalytic Society members' response to Adler was dramatic. Bankart (1997) described the scene:

After Adler's address, the members of the society were in an uproar. There were pointed heckling and shouted abuse. Some were even threatening to come to blows. And then, almost majestically, Freud rose from his seat. He surveyed the room with his penetrating eyes. He told them there was no reason to brawl in the streets like uncivilized hooligans. The choice was simple. Either he or Dr. Adler would remain to guide the future of psychoanalysis. The choice was the members' to make. He trusted them to do the right thing. (p. 130)

Freud likely anticipated the outcome. The group voted for Freud to lead them. Adler left the building quietly, joined by the Society's vice president, William Stekel, and five other members. They moved their meeting to a local café and established the *Society for Free Psychoanalytic Research*. The Society soon changed its name to the *Society for Individual Psychology*. This group believed that social, familial, and cultural forces are dominant in shaping human behavior. Bankart (1997) summarized their perspective: "Their response to human problems was characteristically ethical and practical—an orientation that stood in dramatic contrast to the biological and theoretical focus of psychoanalysis" (p. 130).

Adler's break from Freud gives an initial glimpse into his theoretical approach. Adler identified with common people. He was a feminist. These leanings reflect the influences of his upbringing and marriage. They reveal his compassion for the sick, oppressed, and downtrodden. Before examining Adlerian theoretical principles, let's note what he had to say about gender politics well over 90 years ago:

All our institutions, our traditional attitudes, our laws, our morals, our customs, give evidence of the fact that they are determined and maintained by privileged males for the glory of male domination. (Adler, 1927, p. 123)

Raissa Epstein may have had a few discussions with her husband, exerting substantial influence on his thinking (Santiago-Valles, 2009).

> **REFLECTIONS**
>
> What are your reactions to Adler as a feminist? Do you suppose he became more of a feminist because he married one? Or did he marry a feminist because he already was one?

THEORETICAL PRINCIPLES

Adler and his followers have written extensively about IP's theoretical principles. Much of what follows is from Adler (1958), Ansbacher and Ansbacher (1956), Mosak and Maniacci (1999), Carlson, Watts, and Maniacci (2006), Sweeney (2015), and Carlson and Englar-Carlson (2017).

People Are Whole and Purposeful

Adler emphasized **holism** because he believed it was impossible "… to understand an individual in parts"

(Carlson & Johnson, 2016, p. 225). Instead of dichotomies, he emphasized unity of thinking, feeling, acting, attitudes, values, the conscious mind, the unconscious mind, and all aspects of human functioning. This holistic approach was in direct contrast to Freud's id, ego, and superego. The idea of an id entity or instinct separately pushing for gratification from inside a person was incompatible with Adler's holism.

A central proposition of individual psychology is that humans are purposeful or goal-oriented (Sweeney, 2015). We don't passively act on biological traits or react to the external environment; instead, we behave with purpose. Beyond nurture or nature, there's another force that influences and directs human behavior; Adler (1935) referred to this as "attitude toward life" (p. 5). Attitude toward life is composed of a delightful combination of human choice and purpose.

Everyday behavior is purposeful. When Adlerian therapists notice maladaptive behavior patterns, they focus on behavioral goals. They don't aggressively interrogate clients, asking "Why did you do that?"—but are curious about the behavior's purpose. Mosak and Maniacci (1999) articulated how Adler's holism combines with purposeful behavior:

For Adler, the question was neither "How does mind affect body?" nor "How does body affect mind?" but rather "How does the individual use body and mind in the pursuit of goals?" (pp. 73–74)

Rudolph Dreikurs (1948) applied the concept of purposeful striving to children when he identified "the **four goals of misbehavior**" (see Putting It in Practice 3.1).

Social Interest or Gemeinschaftsgefühl

Adler believed that establishing and maintaining healthy social relationships was an ultimate therapy goal. He developed this belief after working with shell-shocked soldiers from World War I (Carlson & Englar-Carlson, 2017). He became convinced that individualism and feelings of inferiority were destructive; in contrast, he viewed social interest and community feeling as constructive. Another way of thinking about this theoretical principle is to consider humans as naturally interdependent. Lydia Sicher (1991) emphasized this in the title of her classic paper "A Declaration of Interdependence." When we accept interdependence and develop empathy and concern for others, social relationships prosper.

Adler used the German word, **Gemeinschaftsgefühl**, to describe what has been translated to mean **social interest** or **community feeling**. Carlson and Englar-Carlson (2017) elaborated on the meaning of this uniquely Adlerian concept.

PUTTING IT IN PRACTICE

3.1 Why Children Misbehave

Adler's followers applied his principles to everyday situations. Rudolph Dreikurs posited that children are motivated to grow and develop. They're naturally oriented toward feeling useful and a sense of belonging. However, when children don't feel *useful* and don't feel they *belong*, less positive goals take over. In his book *The Challenge of Parenthood*, Dreikurs (1948) identified the four main psychological goals of children's misbehavior:

1. To get attention.
2. To get power or control.
3. To get revenge.
4. To display inadequacy.

Children's behavior isn't random. Children want what they want. When we discuss this concept in parenting classes, parents respond with nods of insight. Suddenly they understand that their children have goals toward which they're striving. When children misbehave in pursuit of psychological goals, parents and caregivers often have emotional reactions.

The boy who's "bouncing off the walls" is truly experiencing, from his perspective, an attention deficit. Perhaps by running around the house at full speed he'll get the attention he craves. At least, doing so has worked in the past. His caregiver feels annoyed, but gives him attention for misbehavior.

The girl who refuses to get out of bed for school in the morning may be striving for power. She feels bossed around or that she doesn't belong; her best alternative is to grab power whenever she can. In response, her parents might feel angry and activated—as if they're in a power struggle with someone who's not pulling punches.

The boy who slaps his little sister may be seeking revenge. Everybody talks about how cute his sister is and he's sick of being ignored, so he takes matters into his own hands. His parents feel scared and threatened; they don't know if their baby girl is safe.

There's also the child who has given up. Maybe she wanted attention before, or revenge, or power, but no longer. Now she's displaying her inadequacy. This isn't because she *is* inadequate, but because she doesn't feel able to face the Adlerian *tasks of life* (discussed later). This child is acting out learned helplessness (Seligman, 1975). Her parent or caregiver probably feels anxiety and despair as well, or, as is often the case, they may pamper her, reinforcing her behavior patterns and self-image of inadequacy and dependence.

Dreikurs's goals of misbehavior are psychological. Children who misbehave may also be acting on biological needs. Therefore, the first thing for parents to check is whether their child is hungry, tired, sick, or in physical discomfort. After checking these essentials, parents should move on to evaluating the psychological purpose of their child's behavior.

Gemein is "a community of equals," *shafts* means "to create or maintain," and *Gefühl* is "social feeling." Taken together, *Gemeinschaftsgefühl* means a community of equals creating and maintaining social feelings and interests; that is, people working together as equals to better themselves as individuals and as a community. (p. 43, italics in original)

Adlerians encourage clients to behave with social interest (Overholser, 2010). Watts (2003) emphasized that, "The ultimate goal for psychotherapy is the development or enhancement of the client's social interest" (p. 20). Research has shown that social interest is positively related to spirituality, positive psychology, and health (Leak, 2006; Leak & Leak, 2006; Nikelly, 2005), and inversely related to anger, irritability, depression, and anxiety (Newbauer & Stone, 2010). Some writers consider the positive aspects of religion to be a manifestation of social interest. This was Adler's position as well (Manaster & Corsini, 1982; Watts, 2003).

Various writers, and Adler himself, noted that Gemeinschaftsgefühl essentially boils down to the edict "love thy neighbor" (Watts, 2003). Carlson and Englar-Carlson described it as being the "same as the goal of all true religions" (p. 44). Although Adler wasn't especially religious, he had no difficulty embracing the concept of love thy neighbor as a social ideal. In contrast, Freud (1961) concluded, "My love is something valuable to me which I ought not to throw away without reflection" (p. 56). This is one of several distinctions between Adler and Freud; for Adler, love is valuable, powerful, and abundant and should be freely given; for Freud, love is also valuable, but should be conserved.

Striving for Superiority

Adler believed that the basic human motive is the striving for superiority. However, like Gemeinschaftsgefühl, this concept requires a detailed explanation.

The term superiority is an oversimplification. Heinz Ansbacher provided a more comprehensive description of Adler's **striving for superiority** in a published interview:

> The basic striving, according to Adler, is the striving for Vollkommenheit. The translation of Vollkommenheit is completeness, but it can also be translated as excellence. In English, only the second translation was considered; it was only the striving for excellence. The delimitation of the striving for excellence is the striving for superiority.
>
> Basically, it all comes from the striving for completeness, and there he said that it is all a part of life in general, and that is very true. Even a flower or anything that grows, any form of life, strives to reach its completeness. And perfection is not right, because the being does not strive—one cannot say to be perfect—what is a perfect being? It is striving for completeness and that is very basic and very true. (Dubelle, 1997, p. 6)

Striving for individual superiority can take on a Western, individualistic quality. This wasn't Adler's perspective. He viewed excessive striving for **self-interest** as unhealthy; Adler once claimed he could simplify his entire theory by noting that all neurosis was linked to vanity. Striving for self-interest translates into striving for superiority rather than for social interest (Watts & Eckstein, 2009).

When it comes to basic human nature and potential, Adlerian theory is like Switzerland: Adler was neutral. He didn't believe in the innate goodness or destructiveness of humans. He believed we are what we make ourselves; we have within us the potential for good and evil.

Striving for superiority is an Adlerian form of self-actualization. More concretely, it occurs when individuals strive for a perceived "plus" in themselves and their lives. Mosak and Maniacci (1999) applied this concept to a clinical situation:

> How can self-mutilation move someone toward a plus situation? Once again, that may be a "real" minus, especially in the short-term situation. Long-term, however, that person may receive attention, others may

"walk on eggshells" when near that person (so as to not "upset" him or her), and he or she may gain some sense of subjective relief from the act, including a sense of being able to tolerate pain. (p. 23)

Adler observed that people often compensate for their real or perceived inadequacies. Individual inadequacies can be in any domain (e.g., physical, psychological, social). Adler may have believed in compensation partly because he experienced it himself, while growing up. Being inadequate or deficient is motivating. "The fundamental law of life is to overcome one's deficiencies" (Ansbacher & Ansbacher, 1956, p. 48). **Compensation** is the effort to improve oneself in areas perceived as weak. The existential philosopher Friedrich Nietzsche expressed the same sentiment, "What does not kill me makes me stronger."

In an ideal situation, individuals strive to (a) overcome their deficiencies, (b) with an attitude of social interest, and (c) to complete or perfect themselves. Watts (2012) has argued that the Adlerian social interest and striving for superiority are foundational to positive psychology—despite the fact that Adler's work remains largely unacknowledged within the positive psychology discipline.

Phenomenology

After reading the quote from Ansbacher about flowers and completeness and humans and individuality, it's natural to think of existentialism (and Chapter 4). You may be wondering, was Adler an existentialist? Did he predate modern existentialism in psychotherapy?

Adlerians would answer with a resounding, enthusiastic "Yes!" and they would have a point. In fact, consistent with **phenomenology**, Adler believed that consciousness is subjective and unique to each individual (Carlson & Johnson, 2016). He emphasized subjective internal perceptions over external reality. The term Adlerians use for this is private logic.

Private logic refers to the idiosyncratic reasoning that individuals use to invent and justify their style of life or personality. Private logic is subjective. Although there may be broad similarities, the particulars of every client's private logic is unique. This is another way in which Adlerian theory is distinctively post-modern and constructive; individual clients construct their subjective reality.

Adler was writing about experiences of neuroses at around the same time and same place as Edmund Husserl, the founder of the school of phenomenology (Mosak & Maniacci, 1999). As we will see in Chapter 4, Adler influenced two key architects of modern existential theory, Viktor Frankl and Rollo May.

An Idiographic Approach

Adler valued the study of individuals over the study of groups—an **idiographic approach**. General statements about humans and human psychology can be helpful, but have limited utility. Ansbacher's description of a flower growing to completeness is an excellent example. Although it's an accurate statement about flowers in general, it tells us nothing about the particular completeness associated with a daisy, a rose, or a sunflower. Similarly, if you read about sunflowers in a book, the statements contained therein may tell you a lot about sunflowers in general, but not much about the particular sunflower plant that you're trying to grow in your shady garden in upstate New York. In Adler's words, "a human being cannot be typified or classified" (Adler, 1935, p. 6).

Individual psychology is all about the psychology of the single, unique, whole individual. Therefore, general (or nomothetic) information about schizophrenia is only minimally helpful in your work with an individual who happens to have the diagnosis of schizophrenia. In the practical, sensible manner common to Adlerian approaches, it's more important to meet and spend time with individual clients than it is to provide them with diagnostic labels. Research is best if it's idiographic, not nomothetic (Kelly & Main, 1978).

Soft Determinism

IP is not deterministic. Adler did not emphasize causal determinants of human behavior, but instead embraced soft determinism. **Soft determinism** is the idea that multiple interacting factors influence behavior.

Soft determinism is the midpoint between deterministic, cause-and-effect thinking and nondeterminism, which assumes no causal connections. Many factors influence everyday choices. Human behavior is a function of multiple interacting forces. There is no single cause for a given behavior. Instead, there are many influences or *contributing* factors.

Adler believed individuals freely choose from a menu (sometimes a limited menu) of behavioral options. Adlerians hold individuals responsible for their behaviors, although it's possible for people to not completely understand the consequences of their actions. Mosak and Maniacci described this: "People are not to be blamed, but to be educated" (1999, p. 19).

Adler was hopeful and optimistic. If you think about Adler and his life, his hope and optimism seem well founded. To begin as a young boy who was pronounced lost, who flunked a year of middle school, and who was hit by various vehicles in the street, and to then end up as one of the most influential psychological thinkers of all time—how could he not become an optimist?

Style of Life (aka Lifestyle): The Adlerian Personality

Based on his own theory, it appears that Adler had a positive, socially useful, style of life. **Style of life** or **lifestyle** is an individual's way of seeing and interacting with the world, the self, and the future. It shapes how people think about everything. Adler probably became an optimist before age 8 or 9, and more likely by age 5 or 6—which is when Adlerians believe the style of life is formed (Ansbacher & Ansbacher, 1956; Watts, 2013b).

Hans Vaihinger, a philosopher who wrote, *The Psychology of "As If"* was a big influence on Adler (Watts, Peluso, & Lewis, 2005). According to Vaihinger (1911), we each create our own world and then live by our self-created rules. This world is subjective and fictional—it's fictional because it's based on our implicit and explicit personal beliefs (our phenomenology) rather than objective fact. Early in his career, Adler described fictional goals or **fictional finalism**. Fictional finalism represents future-oriented goals that pull an individual's present behavior toward the future. Later, he stopped using the term *fictional*, instead using **guiding self-ideal** or subjective final goal (Watts & Holden, 1994).

Vaihinger's philosophy contributed to the cognitive flavor of Adler's individual psychology and his style of life concept, as illustrated in the following anecdote (Adler, 1931):

> Perhaps I can illustrate this [style of life concept] by an anecdote of three children taken to the zoo for the first time. As they stood before the lion's cage, one of them shrank behind the mother's skirts and said, "I want to go home." The second child stood where he was, very pale and trembling and said, "I'm not a bit frightened." The third glared at the lion and fiercely asked his mother, "Shall I spit at it?" The three children really felt inferior, but each expressed his feelings in his own way, consistent with his style of life. (p. 50)

An individual's style of life is subjective, created, conscious, and unconscious. In contemporary terms, lifestyle is a cognitive schema or map. As a child, if you learned that men are harsh, critical, and scary, you will likely carry that schema with you into the future. At times, you may be conscious of this belief, but you also may avoid being around men or respond to men in ways outside your awareness.

The style of life also has similarities to what attachment theorists call the internal working model (Peluso, Peluso, Buckner, Kern, & Curlette, 2009). It includes your beliefs or internalized model of your real and ideal self, of how the world works, your personal ethical convictions, and your understanding of interpersonal dynamics. Your style of life influences career decision-making, responses to stress, parenting behaviors, romantic relationship choices, conflict style, and everything else (Barclay & Wolff, 2011; Stoltz, Wolff, Monroe, Farris, & Mazahreh, 2013). Lydia Sicher (1935) claimed that you can understand the apparently nonsensical behavior of psychotic patients through their lifestyle:

> To the person not acquainted with the life history and life-style of this woman, her utterances would probably seem completely confused and incoherent, just as dreams seem when one tries to interpret them according to their content rather than in the light of their psychological purposes. To one fully acquainted with her life history and life-style, everything she said can be construed in connection with actual experience and real people. (Sicher, 1935, p. 55)

Lifestyle is more or less stable and leads people to behave consistently over time. The past, present, and future reflect continuity. Although Adler usually avoided typologies, he identified four different lifestyle types. Subsequently, other Adlerians have expanded on his list (Boldt & Mosak, 1997; adapted from Carlson & Englar-Carlson, 2017):

- *Ruling type*: This is an aggressive style; it includes efforts to dominate and control others; it may stem from compensation for underlying fears of helplessness.
- *Getting type*: This style involves passivity and going along with others; these individuals may fear personal responsibility and decision-making.
- *Avoiding type*: Individuals with this lifestyle type fear problems and disappointments in relationships, back away from social responsibilities, and experience isolation.
- *Driving type*: Driving types are all about achievement. They often view life as involving "winning" or "losing." To win or avoid losing, they focus excessively on self-interest.
- *Controlling type*: Order is highly valued. Social interest and relationships take a back seat to planning, predicting the future, and avoiding surprises.
- *Victimized type*: Victimized types tend to view life as unfair. They perceive themselves as being hurt, treated unfairly, and as not having much power to change their lives.
- *Being good type*: For these individuals superiority involves being the best and most competent person in the room. This type can also be very self-righteous.
- *Socially useful type*: These individuals feel they have control over their lives and strive to make positive contributions to society.

An individual's style of life may be adaptive, maladaptive, or somewhere in between. Some people hold on to beliefs about the self, world, and others that repeatedly cause emotional pain and distress to themselves or others. Adler referred to these beliefs as *basic mistakes*; these cognitive mistakes are an obvious target of therapy. As you might expect, given his optimistic lifestyle, Adler was hopeful about helping individuals change their lifestyle through therapy or through therapeutic life experiences. We review Adlerian approaches to style of life assessment and analysis later in this chapter.

Tasks of Life

Adlerian theory isn't just a psychological theory of the individual; it also includes assumptions about demands that come from life. Adler believed all individuals face three interrelated life tasks or challenges:

1. Work or occupation.
2. Social relationships.
3. Love and marriage.

Later, Dreikurs and Mosak (1966, 1967; Mosak & Dreikurs, 1967), both of whom worked directly with Adler, identified two additional life tasks:

4. Self.
5. Spirituality.

Other Adlerian practitioners, Dinkmeyer, Dinkmeyer, and Sperry (1987) identified a sixth task:

6. Parenting and family.

These six tasks constitute the challenges of life.

For the most part, clients come to therapy because of difficulties with one or more life tasks. The difficulties arise from inaccuracies, basic mistakes, and maladaptive perceptions associated with their style of life. Therefore, the overarching therapy goal is to help clients modify their style of life in ways that help them accomplish life tasks. This often involves using encouragement to enable clients to find the courage necessary to face the challenges inherent in the tasks of life.

Work or Occupation

Adler believed the best way to address work or occupation was by solving the second life task, social relationships, through "friendship, social feeling, and cooperation" (Adler, 1958, p. 239). When people are unable to work cooperatively, divide labor responsibilities, and maintain friendly relations, they struggle with work. Here's an example of how Adler described one particular occupational problem and its origin:

> There are some people who could choose any occupation and never be satisfied. What they wish is not an occupation

but an easy guarantee of superiority. They do not wish to meet the problems of life, since they feel that it is unfair of life to offer them problems at all. These, again, are the pampered children who wish to be supported by others. (Ansbacher & Ansbacher, 1956, p. 429)

Adler is linking the past to the present. He believed clients who were pampered as children will have occupational difficulties. However, if clients have corrective experiences, inside or outside therapy, then occupational problems may be solved.

Social Relationships

The need for positive social relationships is also referred to as the *need to belong* (Baumeister & Leary, 1995; Gere & MacDonald, 2010). Not meeting this life challenge can result in personal distress and/or misbehavior. For example, Dreikurs (1950) articulated that children who don't feel they belong are more likely to misbehave. Researchers also point to the negative consequences of "not belonging." These include: (a) decreased cognitive functioning (Chen, Williams, Fitness, & Newton, 2008), (b) increased cortisol and/or stress levels (Blackhart, Eckel, & Tice, 2007; Zwolinski, 2008), and (c) increased preoccupation with social stimuli (Gardner, Pickett, Jefferis, & Knowles, 2005; Pickett, Gardner, & Knowles, 2004). It appears that everyone needs to belong to some social group.

Social belonging is more likely among individuals who balance social and self interest. Additionally, as an Adlerian construct, social interest includes empathy, compassion, and valuing of others. As noted previously, social interest or Gemeinschaftsgefühl is Adler's primary indicator of psychological health. Developing and sustaining healthy, balanced, and empathic relationships is a cornerstone of Adlerian therapy.

Love and Marriage

Some theorists refer to this life task as love; others refer to it as sex (Mosak & Maniacci, 1999). For the purposes of our discussion, we use Adler's original terms, love and marriage (Ansbacher & Ansbacher, 1956).

Adler's writing and speaking about love and marriage were quite popular during his lifetime. His writing is very accessible, and sometimes romantic. A brief excerpt of his original work follows, with the male-oriented language of his time shifted to plural as we're certain that if Adler were alive today, he would be sensitive to gender identity issues:

[E]ach partner must be more interested in the other than in [the self]. This is the only basis on which love and marriage can be successful.

If each partner is to be more interested in the other partner than in [themselves], there must be equality. If

there is to be so intimate a devotion, neither partner can feel subdued nor overshadowed. Equality is only possible if both partners have this attitude. It should be the effort of each to ease and enrich the life of the other. In this way each will be safe; each will feel that [they] are worthwhile and that [they] are needed. The fundamental guarantee of marriage, the meaning of marital happiness, is the feeling that you are worthwhile, that you cannot be replaced, that your partner needs you, that you are acting well, and that you are a fellow [person] and a true friend. (Ansbacher & Ansbacher, 1956, p. 432)

Many clients come to therapy with intimacy problems, both sexual and nonsexual. The Adlerian road to recovery for these clients is predictable: modify the style of life, develop empathy (community feeling), take decisive action by thinking and acting differently, and view your partner as an equal.

Self

Dreikurs and Mosak (1967) and Shulman (1965) wrote about the life task of self. This task was implied, but not fully developed, in Adler's original work. The nature of your relationship with yourself develops during childhood.

Mosak and Maniacci (1999) described four dimensions of the self-life task:

1. *Survival of self*: Am I taking good care of my physical self? Am I taking good care of my psychological self? Am I taking good care of my social self?

2. *Body image*: Is my body image congruent with my actual body?

3. *Opinion*: What is my opinion of me? To evaluate this in an interview, Adlerians ask clients to complete the incomplete sentence, "I _____ me" (Mosak & Maniacci, 1999, p. 107).

4. *Evaluation*: Some clients have extreme perspectives of themselves. From the object relations perspective, the question might be "Am I good or am I bad?"

The optimal resolution of the self-task includes good self-care, an accurate perception and expectations of your body, a reasonably accurate and positive opinion of yourself, and a balanced view of yourself as not overly good or overly bad.

Spirituality

Adler valued community feeling, social interest, and cooperation and brought these values into his views of religion. He wrote: "The most important task imposed by religion has always been, 'Love thy neighbor'" (Adler, 1958, p. 253).

Mosak and Maniacci (1999) described five issues related to spirituality. Everyone must approach and deal with these issues:

- *Relationship to God*: Do individuals believe in God? If so, what kind of God? If not, then what are their core spiritual beliefs?

- *Religion*: Organized religion is different from God. Does the individual embrace religious beliefs or avoid them? How are guilt and repentance dealt with (Mosak, 1987)?

- *Relationship to the universe*: Mosak and Maniacci wrote, "Some individuals see humans as simply another animal. Others see humans as the pinnacle of God's creation" (p. 108). The question is: What is the relationship of humans to the rest of the world and the universe?

- *Metaphysical issues*: Most individuals have beliefs about heaven, hell, reincarnation, karma, salvation, and other metaphysical issues. How individuals view these issues is a function of lifestyle and can have implications for daily living.

- *Meaning of life:* A special emphasis is placed on the importance of meaning in life. Adlerians believe that healthy individuals lead meaningful lives in cooperative relationships with other members of the human community.

Parenting and Family

Giving birth to and raising children, and functioning as a family, are extensions of the love and marriage task. However, these activities also constitute a task in and of themselves. Some individuals function as single parents and raise children outside marriage. Individual parents also develop strong feelings and beliefs about how children *should* be raised. How individuals face the parenting and family task is a function of and a challenge to their style of life.

Adler viewed parents or caregivers as having tremendous influence on children's personality development and well-being (Adler, 1927). Rudolph Dreikurs, a follower-colleague of Adler's wrote extensively on parenting. Dreikurs's work has been exceptionally influential. In contrast to many popular parenting approaches at the time, the Adlerian–Dreikurian parenting approach has the following core characteristics (Gfroerer, Kern, & Curlette, 2004):

- The relationship between parent and child should be democratic–authoritative and not too autocratic/authoritarian or permissive.

- Parents should be responsive to their children's needs and yet firm in setting limits and boundaries.

- Discipline is designed to help teach children problem-solving and therefore should be respectful, emphasizing natural and logical consequences.

- Instead of overusing praise, parents should encourage their children.

- Parents should "get curious, not furious" and work to understand the purpose of their children's misbehavior.

- Punishment is avoided because it is not an effective means of teaching children.

Many contemporary parenting authorities attribute their ideas to Adler and Dreikurs (J. Sommers-Flanagan & Sommers-Flanagan, 2011).

Theory of Psychopathology and Change

Adler defined psychopathology and the primary mechanism of psychotherapeutic change in two words: discouragement and encouragement.

Discouragement

Discouraged individuals are unable or unwilling to deal with essential life tasks. **Discouragement** is defined as lacking courage to face challenges inherent in the basic life tasks (Watts, 2013b). With regard to mental disorders, one or more life tasks have become overwhelming. This is where discouragement fits in. When struggling to face life tasks, clients become discouraged. They feel inferior or unable to address the life tasks and symptoms arise.

Symptoms become an answer to the question "What shall I do if I cannot successfully manage this life task?" Symptoms have a purpose—they are a maladaptive effort to address life tasks. This is sometimes referred to as a psychology of use. Thoughts, emotions, behaviors, and symptoms have a purpose and are used to accomplish goals. Here are examples:

- If I steal, I won't have to communicate, cooperate, divide labor, or perform other social functions needed in the workplace.

- If I become depressed, I can communicate anger and dissatisfaction indirectly. I will be taken care of and in control of the household.

- If I become anxious, I won't have to approach one or more life tasks. Perhaps I can avoid marriage or work. If I collapse from anxiety, surely someone will rescue me from the demands of life.

Adler wrote about different mental disorders. He bluntly described the etiology of anxiety problems: "Anxiety neurosis is always symptomatic of a timid attitude towards the three problems of life, and those who suffer from it are invariably 'spoiled' children" (Adler, 1964).

Inferiority is a dominant theme in Adlerian psychopathology. Feelings of inferiority are natural because small children grow up in the presence of caretakers who are bigger, stronger, and smarter. However, inferiority can become pathological. Carlson and colleagues (2006) described three inferiority levels:

1. **Objective inferiority**: Inferiority is measurable and contextual. Some people are taller, stronger, faster, more musically talented, or more intelligent. Objectively, most of us can identify when others are superior and consequently feel objectively inferior in their presence.

2. **Inferiority feelings**: "Global, subjective and evaluative" generalizations can be believed despite contrary evidence. "For example, [a] 5-foot, 10-inch man...may feel short no matter who is in the room with him" (Carlson et al., 2006, p. 58). This would be true if there was objective evidence of his shortness (e.g., being in a room with a 6 foot 5 inch person) or no objective evidence (e.g., being in a room alone or only with shorter people). Individuals may have inferiority feelings, but these feelings are contained and not acted on.

3. **Inferiority complexes**: Whether an inferiority complex develops depends on whether inferiority feelings cause significant impairment. For example, a woman might feel test anxiety because she feels intellectually inferior. This anxiety may cause distress, but if she's able to cope with it and it doesn't interfere with her life goals (she attends college, graduates, and moves successfully into the employment world), then she has consistent inferiority feelings, but not an inferiority complex. In contrast, if her intellectual inferiority complex results in debilitating test anxiety and she fails tests, doesn't graduate from college, and is unable to pursue her intellectual interests, then she has an inferiority complex.

Encouragement

Encouragement is central to Adlerian therapy. When clients are discouraged and unable to face life tasks, encouragement is in the recipe for therapy success. Adler wrote, "In every step of treatment, we must not deviate from the path of encouragement" (Ansbacher & Ansbacher, 1956, p. 342). What does this mean? At the very least, it means that counselors and psychotherapists are positive and friendly sources of influence who are confident in their clients' capacity for positive change and who

collaboratively set goals and support clients toward goal attainment.

This bears repeating. If you're doing Adlerian therapy, you never deviate from the path of encouragement.

Writers and practitioners define encouragement in different ways. Wong (2015) offered a broad definition of **encouragement**, "...affirmation through language or other symbolic representations to instill courage, perseverance, confidence, inspiration, or hope in a person(s) within the context of addressing a challenging situation or realizing a potential" (p. 182).

There are at least two general approaches to encouragement in therapy and parenting education.

1. *The "You can do it" Approach*: This involves counselors or educators taking on a supportive role. "You can do it" can be expressed directly or indirectly, but the general message from the helper is that the client or parent or child is capable and competent.

2. *The Reflective Approach*: This approach is more subtle and is often expressed with the words, "I noticed..." For example, a therapist might say, "I noticed this week that your voice sounds stronger and you sound more confident in your ability to deal with your stresses at work."

Clients don't absorb or internalize encouragement via passive means. Although it's encouraging to feel belonging, belonging in and of itself isn't enough. As Dreikurs emphasized, children (and adults) also need to feel useful and feeling useful usually involves doing something. From an Adlerian perspective the "doing something" that best facilitates psychological health is the "doing" that involves positive social action or Gemeinschaftsgefühl.

To summarize, for Adler, the key to psychotherapy, psychological health, and well-being is encouragement (Dinkmeyer & Dreikurs, 1963; Watts & Pietrzak, 2000). In contrast, the road to psychological ill health is paved with discouragement. The following quotation captures Adler's ideas about psychopathology and treatment, as well as his optimistic attitude:

> When a doctor once said to Adler: "I do not believe you can make this backward child normal," Dr. Adler replied: "Why do you say that? One could make any normal child backward; one should only have to discourage it enough!" (Bottome, 1936, p. 37)

See Table 3.1 for a summary of Adlerian theoretical principles.

Table 3.1   Theoretical Principles of Individual Psychology

Theoretical Assumption	Description
Holism and purposeful striving	Humans are a single complete unit; a whole that cannot and should not be divided into separate parts. The whole human purposefully strives toward specific goals in life.
Gemeinschaftsgefühl or social interest	Humans strive to connect socially, both with individuals and with the community. This motivating factor is called social interest or community feeling (or Gemeinschaftsgefuhl). If humans strive for superiority without social interest, they're likely to become driven, selfish, and arrogant in pursuit of their goals.
Superiority striving	Humans strive; we are active, creative, and persistent in our drive toward completion and excellence. We can become discouraged and resigned due to unfortunate life circumstances, but our natural state is forward moving.
Phenomenology	Individual experience is subjective and based on each individual's perception. Individuals actively create their own personal reality.
An idiographic approach	Although general information about humans can be helpful, every individual is unique. To really understand an individual, a couple, or a family, you must work with that individual, couple, or family. Group or nomothetic research is of little value.
Soft determinism	Biology, the environment, and other factors don't directly cause specific behaviors to occur; instead, a myriad of influencing factors determine behavior.
Style of life	The individual cognitive map each of us uses to navigate through life is established in childhood. This map, referred to as lifestyle or style of life, is our personality. It gives us continuity and tells us about ourselves, others, and how the world works. The map can include basic mistakes, but can be modified through therapy and education.
Tasks of life	Adler (and his followers) identified 6 tasks of life. These included: (a) work/occupation; (b) social relationships; (c) love and marriage; (d) self; (e) spirituality; and (f) parenting and family. One therapy goal is to help clients develop the courage to face challenges inherent in the tasks of life.
Psychopathology and change	Discouragement leads to psychopathology. Encouragement leads to health and change. When clients are encouraged, they have the courage to face the basic tasks of life. Encouragement also gives clients the strength to look at themselves and accept feedback and facilitates potential for insight. Insight contributes to motivation.

THE PRACTICE OF ADLERIAN THERAPY

Adlerian therapy is a sensitive and complex process, requiring rigorous training to do well; it involves a friendly and collaborative process consisting of four stages (Carlson et al., 2006).

Stage 1: *Forming the therapeutic relationship*.

Stage 2: *Lifestyle assessment and analysis*.

Stage 3: *Interpretation and insight*.

Stage 4: *Reorientation*.

Forming the Therapeutic Relationship

Adlerian therapists and clients have an egalitarian relationship that includes empathic listening and caring. Therapists and clients sit on chairs of equal status and look more or less directly at one another. Of all therapist types, Adlerians may seem most like a friendly teacher or business consultant whose business it is to

help clients negotiate life more successfully (see Putting It in Practice 3.2: Informed Consent from the Adlerian Perspective).

Therapists intentionally foster collaboration and communicate interest in the client as a person. Here's a description of how Adlerian counselors might open a first session:

> We often start an interview with "What do you want me to know about you?" rather than, "What brought you in?" or "What did you want to talk about today?" Meeting and valuing the person is essential to positive change; the relationship may not be everything that matters, but [it] is *almost* everything that matters. (Bitter, Christensen, Hawes, & Nicoll, 1998, p. 98)

Clients are encouraged to be active participants in therapy. Therapists are experts who teach, but clients are active learners.

Goal Alignment

One way therapists communicate respect is by working hard to understand the client as a person and the client's

---

PUTTING IT IN PRACTICE

3.2 Informed Consent from the Adlerian Perspective

Hello. I'd like to welcome you to my office and provide you with information about how I typically work with clients.

Usually people come to counseling due to problems or concerns with relationships, work, or family issues. My first goal is to make a connection with you so we can work together collaboratively. At the same time, I'll be gathering information to better understand what's going on in your life now ... and I'll ask many questions about your past, your family of origin, and your future goals.

The counseling approach I use is called *Adlerian*. Let me explain what that means.

Our counseling together may be brief or longer. The length of counseling depends on your concerns and how efficiently we work together. The Adlerian approach emphasizes that we all develop ideas about ourselves, the world, and the future based on early childhood experiences. Sometimes ideas from the past don't work perfectly well in the present. As a consequence, we'll take a good hard look at your beliefs or automatic assumptions about yourself, the world, other people, and the future. Then we'll work together to change or tweak those assumptions so they fit with the challenges you're facing in your life. Sometimes I'll give you assignments to try out new behavior or new attitudes and then we'll talk about how well those new behaviors or attitudes work for you. At other times I'll offer you my opinion or recommendations about what I think you could try to do to improve yourself and your life. Usually these recommendations will have to do with making sure the purpose of your specific behaviors and attitudes are a good fit for what you want from life. We'll also probably focus on how you can improve your personal relationships—because, from an Adlerian perspective, having healthy and balanced social relationships is very important.

Overall, counseling is about developing greater awareness of old patterns so you can change old patterns into more effective and efficient new patterns. This usually just involves small changes in how you think about yourself, others, the world, and the future. Therapy is like a tune-up of your basic assumptions about life.

I look forward to working with you.

---

goals for therapy. In particular, for therapy to proceed successfully, therapist and client must align their goals. **Goal alignment** is associated with positive counseling and psychotherapy outcomes (Tryon & Winograd, 2011).

Although goal alignment is important, Adlerian therapists also have preset ideas about appropriate therapy goals. Mosak (1995) identified common Adlerian goals:

- Fostering client social interest or community feeling.

- Helping clients overcome feelings of inferiority and discouragement.

- Helping clients change their basic mistakes.

- Shifting client motivation from self-focused superiority to a community focus.

- Helping clients feel as equals in their relationships.

- Helping clients become contributing members to society.

In contrast to contemporary cognitive behavior therapy, therapists are unlikely to formulate "problem lists" with clients. The problem and the person are one entity and need not be separated, except for specific therapeutic purposes.

Focusing on Positives and Not Pathologizing

Adlerians focus on client strengths as well as problems. It's common to ask about positive personal qualities (e.g., "What were some of your best traits as a child?" and "Tell me a story about one of your childhood successes"). Focusing on client virtues, signature strengths, and other positive qualities is common (Hamm, Carlson, & Erguner-Tekinalp, 2016). Unlike solution-oriented approaches, therapists show interest in the whole person, both problems and strengths. The goal is to establish an encouraging environment.

Psychopathology involves basic mistakes imbedded in the clients' lifestyle. However, Adlerians also consider basic mistakes as a part of normal human experience. This might be best articulated by one of Adler's most famous quotations, "The only normal people are the ones you don't know very well."

Initial Lifestyle Interpretations

One of our old supervisors with an Adlerian-humanistic bent used to tell us, "Near the end of your first session, you should be able to share with your clients a few important things you've learned about them." Although we didn't know it at the time, our supervisor was talking about making an initial style of life interpretation. Early interpretations can further therapist and client connection and begin deeper problem analysis. Because it occurs early in counseling, early interpretations are more collaborative guesses and should be phrased tentatively.

Therapist: May I offer my thoughts from our session today?

Client: Yes, of course.

Therapist: I'm struck by how much energy you spend avoiding conflict. It must be exhausting in some ways. Maybe during our next meeting we could explore this pattern in more detail. How does that sound?

An initial lifestyle interpretation prepares clients for engaging in an Adlerian approach. Initial surface interpretations can lay the foundation for later exploration and other Adlerian techniques.

Lifestyle Assessment and Analysis

Several approaches to lifestyle assessment are available, including self-report questionnaires (e.g., the Basic Adlerian Scales for Interpersonal Success – Adult Form [BASIS-A Inventory]; Wheeler, Kern, & Curlette, 1991). Extensive pretherapy questionnaires are also used. In addition, Adlerian intake interviews integrate three key assessment strategies:

1. The family constellation interview.

2. The question.

3. Earliest recollections.

The Family Constellation Interview

The **family constellation interview** (FCI) is Adler's version of what's popularly known as a genogram in couple and family therapy (Shulman, 1962). The FCI is a distinct approach to obtaining pertinent information about childhood experiences. Topics covered include descriptions of each family member and how they interacted with one another, how the client viewed different family members, who fought, who didn't fight, and much more. Adler considered **psychological birth order** to be a strong contributor to style of life (see Putting It in Practice 3.3). He emphasized that every individual is born into a different family; with the addition of each new family member, family dynamics change, and a new family is born.

PUTTING IT IN PRACTICE

3.3 Psychological Birth Order and Lifestyle

Popular psychology oversimplifies Adler's ideas about birth order. At the worst, birth order is used like astrology to describe personality and predict human behavior. This occurs despite Adler cautioning against a simplistic birth order approach to understanding lifestyle. He wrote:

> There has been some misunderstanding of my custom of classification according to position in the family. It is not, of course, the child's number in the order of successive births which influences his character, but the situation into which he is born and the way in which he interprets it. (Adler, 1937, p. 211)

Birth order is psychological, not chronological. If a first-born daughter has illnesses or disabilities that reduce her abilities, a second-born daughter may adopt personality characteristics more commonly associated with first-born daughters. The chronological second born can become the psychological first born.

Psychological birth order contributes to the style of life. Keeping Adler's caution in mind, consider the following birth order tendencies (Eckstein et al., 2010).

Child's position	Lifestyle characteristics
Oldest	Oldest children may be initially spoiled and later dethroned. They may be bossy, strict, and authoritarian; it's as if they have a right to power. They also may take responsibility for others. Oldest children may identify with the father because they turn to him for support after the second child's birth.
Second	Second children have an older rival; this may make them competitive. The challenge is to develop a unique identity; this may make second born children natural rebels. There's often an unfulfilled wish to be bigger, stronger, smarter, and more capable.
Middle	Middle children are even-tempered, developing a "take it or leave it" attitude. They may be sensitive to the overlooked or underprivileged. They can feel cheated of their chance for privilege and harbor resentments, sometimes quietly manipulating others to achieve their ends. They may have trouble finding their niche in life.
Youngest	Youngest children are never dethroned; they may feel they should be treated like royalty. They're likely to have unrealistic aspirations, dreaming of being more powerful than everyone else, but follow-through is often lacking. Youngest children may be chronically frustrated. They might choose to stay the baby in the family, getting others to take care of them.
Only	Only children usually have attention from both parents; they feel special, especially liking adult attention. There may be problems with peer relationships, especially problems with give and take and tolerance. They may believe they should be "taken care of."
Only boy among girls	He may need to prove he's a man, but also be sensitive to feminine issues. He may be treated like a hero and hold high self-expectations. He also may expect that others will quickly recognize his specialness and feel disappointment when he's treated like everyone else.
Only girl among boys	She may become overly feminine or a tomboy, trying to compete with her brothers. She also may feel she has a special designation and, depending upon her relations with her brothers, may expect abuse or protection from males. She may feel disappointment when her specialness is unrecognized.

The Question

Adlerians consider all behavior as purposeful. **The question** can uncover the purpose of client symptoms. The question is, "How would your life be different if you were well?" It can be phrased differently (e.g., "What would you be doing in your life if you no longer had your symptoms?"), but always involves a search for underlying purpose. The question can help determine if clients are obtaining special treatment or secondary gain for having problems. Secondary gain includes advantages associated with having medical or psychological symptoms.

After asking the question, Adlerians listen for activities or relationships clients might resume should their problems be resolved. In this way, identification of the life tasks the symptoms help clients avoid is possible. Carlson et al. (2006) described how the question assists with case formulation:

> The answer…typically reveals what is being avoided by using the presenting problem. For example, one client may say, "If I didn't have this anxiety, I'd be able to work better." He may be using anxiety as a safeguarding mechanism…as well as using it to buy double insurance. Another client

may respond with "If I weren't so depressed, I'd be able to be nicer." She may be using depression to cover up some aggression and depreciation tendencies. (p. 110)

REFLECTIONS

How do you think "the question" might help in formulating a treatment approach for an individual client? What if the question were posed to you? What would your answer be?

Earliest Recollections

Adler considered early memories as one his most important discoveries. The **early recollection** is a projective technique for understanding client lifestyle and guiding self-ideal (Clark, 2013). Therapists ask,

> Think back to a long time ago when you were little, and try to recall one of your first memories, one of the first things that you can remember. (Clark, 2013, p. 41)

Sweeney (2015) described the Adlerian perspective on early recollections: "Early recollections are not a reflection of the past but a forecast of the future" (p. 105).

This perspective can be difficult to grasp. Early memories are not so much memories as they are projections…a message from the past, still active in the client's present life (Clark, 2002, 2013). As such, the accuracy of the memory is irrelevant. The memory or projection is an active expression of the client's living lifestyle and shaped to correspond with the client's current thoughts, feelings, and attitudes (see Putting It in Practice 3.4 for a summary of how to use early recollections).

In his Adlerian therapy text, Sweeney (2015) provided questions that can help you understand client memories at a deeper level:

- Is the individual active or passive, giving or taking?

- Is he or she alone or with others?

- What are the relationships to others? Inferior? Superior?

- What emotion is used?

- Are detail and color mentioned?

PUTTING IT IN PRACTICE

3.4 The ABCs of Gathering and Interpreting Early Recollections

Like many projective assessments, early recollections offer clients little structure and don't have a rigorous scoring system that allows for reliability and validity studies. Instead, early recollections are a collaborative and meaning-making process between therapist and client. The purpose of early recollections is not to predict behavior or produce a diagnosis. Instead, early recollections facilitate insight and reveal lifestyle patterns.

To conduct an early recollection assessment, use the following steps:

1. Introduce the assessment and ask permission: "One way I have of getting to know you is to ask about a few of your earliest memories. Is that okay with you?"

2. Explain the memories you want: "It's best if you can come up with memories from age 10 or earlier. The earlier the better. Some people can go back to three or earlier. It's important to use a real memory and not a memory of a video you've recently seen of yourself. And it's helpful if the memory is a single event that's clear, like a snapshot, but that includes what happened before and after the snapshot."

3. Ask the recollection question: "Try to go back in time and tell me a very early memory."

4. Listen, show empathy, and ask questions of clarification: "What happened next?" "What were you feeling?" "Who else was there?"

5. Gather additional early memories as needed. Depending on the clarity of the first memory, you may ask for several more early memories. Some Adlerians recommend three to eight memories (Clark, 2013).

6. Provide a collaborative interpretation. Adler was intuitive in his approach to early recollection interpretation. More recently, Clark (2013) developed a structured framework for analyzing early recollections. His framework includes:

   (a) Thematic Topics (e.g., what's the content or theme?).
   (b) Personality Dimensions (e.g., what "ways of being" jump out?).
   (c) Perceptual Modalities (e.g., what are the sensory qualities of the experience?) (see Clark, 2013, for additional information).

Case Example 1
Sarah relates an early childhood memory: "I remember sliding down a hill near my house. I was sitting on a red sled in front of my mother, and was all bundled up in a cozy snow suit. We were laughing together as we went down the hill. The snow was nice and fluffy, and I turned the sled a little by pulling on the rope. I can still feel how pleasant the tingling snow felt on my cheeks."

Thematic topics: Affectionate relationships and stimulating experiences are central. Sarah reports a close, supportive relationship with her mother.

Personality dimensions: Sarah's activity is high; she's fully engaged in the experience. There may be an elevated level of social interest because Sarah participates in a cooperative activity and contributes to its enjoyment. Sarah reports a positive affect, which might indicate an optimistic orientation. Sarah is involved in an activity that requires self-efficacy. Her attention to the sledding task and assumption of responsibility may reflect conscientiousness.

Perceptual modalities: Sarah's sensory modalities of vision and touch are prominent. Her reporting the red sled suggests aesthetic awareness or sensitivity. The outdoor location evokes a sense of place for Sarah within an interpersonal context.

Formulations from the three perspectives of her early recollection contribute to an assessment of Sarah's wellness and positive outlook on life.

Case Example 2

Keith is in counseling for an anxiety disorder. He recounts an early recollection: "I was about six years old, sitting in a car with my father in a parking lot. When the car wouldn't start, he began yelling and hitting the steering wheel. My father kept turning the key. The engine made a grinding noise. His eyes were bulging. He was yelling and swearing. It was scary and I felt sad."

Applying the multiple perspective early recollection interpretation model to Keith yields a less favorable outlook on life in comparison with Sarah. He endures a distressing and anxiety-laden experience from which he has no escape and passively observes a futile event. An awareness of Keith's ingrained convictions and perceptions enables the counselor to be more empathic and formulate a supportive treatment plan in counseling.

- Do stereotypes of authorities, subordinates, men, women, old, young, reveal themselves?

- Prepare a "headline" that captures the essence of the event.

- Look for corroboration in the family constellation information (adapted from Sweeney, 2015, pp. 104–105).

Consistent with modern therapies, Adlerians engage in case formulation. This includes identifying a client's "basic mistakes." Mosak (1995) described five examples of basic mistakes:

1. *Overgeneralization*: There's no fairness in the world. I'm always the one who has to take care of everything.

2. *False or impossible goals*: I have to be the boss to be acceptable. Alternatively, others should always take care of my needs.

3. *Misperceptions of life and life's demands*: The world is against me. Alternatively, the world is my oyster.

4. *Denial of one's basic worth*: I'm totally worthless. No one could ever love me.

5. *Faulty values*: A set of values at odds with social interest; I must win and be the best no matter how much it hurts others.

REFLECTIONS

What basic mistakes do you make over and over again? Don't worry about your answer because Adler believed we all repeatedly make *basic mistakes*—it's only a matter of whether the mistakes are large or small.

Interpretation and Insight

Adlerian therapy is insight-oriented. However, in contrast to a bubbling cauldron of primitive unconscious impulses in psychoanalytic theory, Adlerians view the unconscious as accessible. It's not repressed; it's out of awareness. Different tools can be used to help clients achieve insight, including education.

There's a strong link between insight, motivation, and action. Insight stimulates motivation, which stimulates action. Think about it. You discover a maladaptive lifestyle pattern or assumption in yourself (e.g., I think I must be perfect and in control at all times) and notice the cost to yourself of that maladaptive assumption (e.g., I'm always the one planning, organizing, and managing things; I never relax and have fun). This insight might motivate you to make changes in your life. Insight without action isn't true insight, but a sign that clients are playing at therapy, rather than taking it seriously.

Adlerian therapists use interpretation, confrontation, and education to facilitate insight. Interpretation can elucidate repetitive basic mistakes within the lifestyle; showing a causal connection between past and present isn't required. Confrontation also brings maladaptive patterns into focus (e.g., "On the one hand, you say you want more freedom, but you continue to get into trouble, and each time you do, you end up with more restrictions and less freedom"). Once repetitive basic mistakes or maladaptive patterns become clear to clients, the final phase of therapy, reorientation, begins.

Reorientation (Specific Therapy Techniques)

Adlerian therapists use specific techniques to deepen client insight and facilitate change during the reorientation phase. Action-oriented techniques that foster client learning are desirable. Mosak (1989) described the therapist's role and function: "There comes a time in psychotherapy when analysis must be abandoned and the patient must be encouraged to act in lieu of talking and listening. Insight has to give way to decisive action" (p. 91).

We now review several Adlerian techniques.

The Future Autobiography

The **future autobiography** involves assessment and intervention; it flows from the Adlerian idea that future goals guide and shape everyday behavior. It can help clients intentionally shape their future. This technique is especially useful for clients who like to write. However, it can be adapted for clients who prefer drawing or storytelling.

You can use the future autobiography in at least two ways. However, because Adlerians support counselor creativity, you may discover your own way to use this technique.

First, the future autobiography provides assessment information. You might say:

> You could write a great story about everything you've experienced in your past. That would be interesting, but I'd like you to do something even more interesting. Between now and next week, write a story about the rest of your life. Look at who you are now and project your life into the future. Finish your life story in whatever way you'd like it to go. We can read it together next week.

The future autobiography shines a light on clients' guiding self-ideal (or fictional life goals). It can clarify whether fictional life goals are helpful or harmful to everyday living. Discussing your clients' future autobiography can inspire them to take greater conscious responsibility for directing and shaping their lives.

Second, the future autobiography is also a therapy technique. If this is your preference, you should use it *after* gathering information about your client's past and lifestyle. Then, using your understanding of your client's basic beliefs about the world, self, and others, you can coach your

client to write a realistic and adaptive future autobiography. You might ask your client to address a basic mistake:

> We've been talking about how you think you need to be perfect all the time. This causes you constant anxiety. As an assignment for this week, write the rest of your life story, from here on out. As you're writing, be sure to write a story in which you're not perfect. Write a story in which you make mistakes but, overall, live in an acceptable and loving way in the world. Okay?

The future biography assignment focuses on the lifestyle and related future goals or ideals. Oral or pictorial future autobiographies are recommended for clients who prefer not to write.

Acting As If

Most people occasionally wish for traits they don't have. Some wish for self-confidence and others wish they were calm, instead of nervous and edgy. Still others wish they could focus, get organized, and follow through on a project.

Acting as if involves having clients pretend they already possess desirable traits they're striving toward. You can initiate the *as if* process by asking: "What if you were self-confident? How would that look?" Then, if your client shares an image of self-confidence, you might suggest, "For the rest of today and throughout this week, how about you act *as if* you were filled with self-confidence." This is followed with a detailing of exactly what "self-confident" would look and sound like. Of course, your client might refuse this suggestion and claim that acting self-confident would be phony. Your job at that point is to encourage your client to try it anyway. Mosak (1989) provided an example of encouragement: "[E]xplain that all acting is not phony pretense, that one can try on a role as one might try on a suit" (p. 91).

This technique gives clients permission to try on new ways of being. Acting as if can bypass resistance because it frames new behavioral experiments as "just acting." By engaging in these experiments and then talking about them in therapy, clients gain new perspectives and perhaps new motivation for behaving in different and more adaptive ways.

Reflecting As If

Watts (2003) created a modification of the classical Adlerian as if technique. This modification, **reflecting as if** (RAI), is based on an integration of Adlerian and social constructionist theoretical perspectives. Watts (2003) described this integration as it applies to couples counseling:

> The ... reflecting as if procedure asks clients to take a "reflective" step back prior to stepping forward to act as if. This process encourages clients to reflect on how they would be different in their relationship if they were acting as if they were the couple they desire to be. By using

reflective questions, counselors can help clients construct perceptual alternatives and consider alternative behaviors toward which they may begin moving. (p. 73)

There are three phases to RAI:

1. *Reflecting*: Counselors ask clients to reflect on how they wish they might act differently. For example: "If you were acting as if you were the person you would like to be, how would you be acting differently? If I were watching a videotape of your life, what would be different?" (Watts, 2013a, p. 49) and "What would be the first signs or signals that you're beginning to act in this way you'd like to act?"

2. *Planning*: This involves building a hierarchy of specific behaviors linked to the reflected upon self-ideal. Counselor and client collaboratively brainstorm a list of specific behaviors likely to emerge in the acting as if scenario. Then, the counselor guides the client in ranking the relative difficulty of the various as if behaviors.

3. *Implementing*: As a homework assignment, the client identifies one or two as if behaviors that would be easiest to implement. Watts (2013a) described the rationale for this:

> Beginning with the least difficult behaviors increases the potential for client success because success is typically encouraging for clients and often increases their perceived self-efficacy. Success typically increases the client's motivation to courageously engage the more difficult tasks on his or her list. (p. 51)

The RAI procedure is simple and straightforward. It's also a good example of not only the theoretical compatibility of Adlerian approaches but also of their empirical base. Specifically, RAI employs several evidence-based techniques, including (a) collaborative goal setting, (b) collaborative brainstorming as a step in problem solving, (c) a focus on concrete and measurable behaviors, and (d) concrete behavioral planning (Sommers-Flanagan, 2015). RAI can be used with individuals (Watts & Peluso, 2005), couples (Watts, 2003), and children (Watts & Garza, 2008).

The Push-Button Technique

Adler believed that cognitions underlie feelings. Based on this assumption, Mosak (1985) described the push-button technique. The **push-button technique** encourages clients to recognize how their cognitions elicit specific emotions. These preidentified cognitions are then used for clients to push their own emotional buttons. The goal is greater emotional control. Mosak described how to introduce this technique to clients:

> This is a three-part experiment. Please close your eyes and keep them closed until all three parts are over. First, I'd like you to dig into your memory and retrieve a very pleasant memory—a success, a beautiful sunset, a time when you

were loved—and project that in front of your eyes as if you were watching it on a TV screen. Watch it from beginning to end and attach to it the feelings you had when the incident occurred. Go! Remember how wonderful it was! When you are through, hold up a finger to signal that you are through, and we'll go on to the next part....
>
> Now I'd like you to fish back in memory and retrieve a horrible incident. You failed. You were hurt or ill. Life screwed you. Someone died. You were humiliated. Watch that one from beginning to end as if it were on TV and attach to it the feelings you had at the time the incident occurred. Go! Remember how terrible it was! When you are through, hold up a finger to signal that you are through and we'll go on to the last part....
>
> Now I'd like to go into your memory and retrieve another pleasant memory. If you can't come up with another pleasant memory, go back to the first pleasant memory you had. Watch it on the TV screen from beginning to end and attach to it the feelings you had when the incident occurred. Go! Remember how wonderful it was! When you are through, please open your eyes. (1985, pp. 211–212)

The push-button technique is an ABA reversal experimental design that teaches clients the power of thoughts and images over feelings. After clients experience affective changes with this procedure, you can make the point, "It's no wonder that depressed people feel depressed. It's because they're consistently thinking depressing thoughts." In the end, the therapist sends the client home with two make-believe push buttons (one happy and one sad) and the following persuasive statement:

> [I]f you come back next week and are *still* depressed, I'm going to ask you to explain why you *choose* to continue to feel depressed when you have the happy button at your disposal. We'll find out what your investment in being depressed is. (Mosak, 1985, p. 212)

In this example, Mosak described how to use the push-button technique in a session with a depressed adult. We modified the push-button technique for use with children and adolescents in therapy and as a general emotional education technique in schools. We call this the three-step emotional change trick (J. Sommers-Flanagan & Sommers-Flanagan, 2001, 2007b).

Spitting in the Soup

Clients frequently avoid demands and responsibilities associated with basic life tasks. **Spitting in the client's soup** is both a metaphor and technique for spoiling the client's use of avoidance. Spitting in the client's soup enhances client awareness/insight and spoils the future use of maladaptive thoughts or behaviors. After all, who can enjoy eating his soup after someone has spat in it?

Spitting in the soup is confrontational. Confrontation is an appropriate intervention when there is a good client–therapist bond and the therapist is aware of a discrepancy between what the client wants and what the client is doing (J. Sommers-Flanagan & Sommers-Flanagan, 2017). For example, spitting in the client's soup is appropriate for adolescent clients who repeatedly engage in destructive behaviors that threaten their freedom (e.g., theft and dishonesty) despite the fact that they profess to want greater personal freedom.

Carlson et al. (2006) provided a simple example of how spitting in the soup can spoil a client's underlying motive:

A male client who is too worried what other people must think of him whenever he goes in public is confronted with his vanity: Obviously, everybody must be noticing him. (p. 142)

This particular version of spitting in the soup has dimensions of paradox and reframing; it becomes difficult for the man to worry about others without simultaneously becoming aware of the fact that it's also a signal of his vanity.

Spitting in the client's soup works best if therapists follow these guidelines:

- Develop a friendly and supportive relationship with clients.

- Identify an unhelpful behavior or thinking pattern (basic mistake) that clients use repeatedly and likely will use in the future.

- Obtain your clients' permission to share an insight.

- Succinctly share the repeating and unhelpful pattern.

- Be open to discussing client reactions to having their soup spat in!

Another example of spitting in the soup is included in a counseling vignette later in this chapter.

Creating New Images

Clients naturally have images of themselves in the past, present, and future. These images are a product of the style of life and guiding self-ideal. **Creating new images** is a technique that helps clients stretch or shift a less-than-optimal style of life. This procedure has several variations. For example, Graham and Pehrsson (2011) included descriptions of several expressive art techniques that help children create new images or goals toward which they can strive. Additionally, Watts and Garza (2008) described using visualization or drawing combined with the traditional Adlerian acting as if technique. They recommended encouraging students to respond either verbally or with drawings to questions:

If you were acting as if you were the person you would like to be, how would you be acting differently? If I were watching a movie of your life, what would be different? (p. 115)

Creating new images encourages clients to develop new and adaptive self-images. After analyzing your client's early recollections and basic mistakes, you can work to come up with a "new visual" (as our artistic friends like to say). This new visual is a self-generated image that can replace old more negative or maladaptive self-images.

Catching Oneself

Self-awareness and self-control are foundational to Adlerian theory. **Catching oneself** involves teaching clients how to catch themselves when they slip into old, unhelpful behaviors. For example, a college basketball player came to therapy because of problems with his explosive temper during practice. His coach had issued an ultimatum: "Deal with your anger more constructively or leave the team." Step one in therapy involved having this young man catch himself when he began thinking or acting in ways that led to his angry outbursts. For this client, the primary dynamics related to his anger were perfectionism and blame. He was given these instructions:

We'll be focusing on what leads to anger outbursts at practice. This includes you thinking you need to be perfect, feeling terrible inside, and then attacking and blaming others. Your only job this week is to notice when you're thinking critically about yourself. Just notice it, catch yourself, and think—ah, there it is again, that tendency to criticize myself. Also, notice when you shift from self-criticism to blaming others for your performance. Just notice it; there's no need to do anything about it for now.

Catching oneself is an historical predecessor of behavioral and cognitive self-monitoring and thought stopping (see Chapters 7 and 8).

Task Setting and Indirect Suggestion

Adler employed an engaging and sometimes indirect therapy style. In the next section we talk about his most indirect strategy: paradoxical instruction. However, he sometimes combined a direct task-setting strategy and an indirect or suggestive method for implementing it. This style reminds us of the renowned hypnotherapist Milton Erickson, who become famous for this approach several decades after Adler's death (see Chapter 11).

Adler described using a two-stage social interest-oriented task-setting procedure for patients with depression:

Stage One: Adler would offer several suggestions to his patients. To start, he would say, "Only do what is agreeable to you." When the patient protested that nothing was agreeable, he shifted to, "Then at least…do not exert yourself to do what is disagreeable." In this first stage Adler is being empathic in that he had found that most depressed patients had been advised to engage in all sorts of activities that the patient experienced as unpleasant.

Stage Two: Later, Adler would provide his "Second rule of conduct." He framed this rule in advance, by saying, "It is much more difficult and I do not know if you can follow it."

Adler then described himself as becoming silent, and looking "doubtfully at the patient." His goal was to stimulate his patient's curiosity. Then, he would state, "If you could follow this second rule you would be cured in fourteen days. It is—to consider from time to time how you can give another person pleasure. It would very soon enable you to sleep and would chase away all your sad thoughts. You would feel yourself to be useful and worthwhile."

Adler's second rule of conduct is designed to move patients away from self-interest and toward social interest. However, he noted that his patients always found his prescription for social interest "too difficult to act upon." Adler described the sorts of discussions that would subsequently ensue:

> If the answer is, "How can I give pleasure to others when I have none myself?" I relieve the prospect by saying, "Then you will need four weeks." The more transparent response, "Who gives *me* pleasure?" I counter with what is probably the strongest move in the game, by saying, "Perhaps you had better train yourself a little thus: do not actually *do* anything to please anyone else, but just think about how you could do it!" (this and all preceding quotations in this section are from Adler, 1964, pp. 25–26)

There are several fascinating components to Adler's description of how he worked with his depressed patients. First, he is deeply engaged. He has thought through the typical responses and is anticipating the client's reactions. Second, his task setting for the client would be completely ineffectual without having a therapeutic alliance. Third, Adler is combining at least five approaches at once: (1) task setting; (2) spitting in the client's soup; (3) paradox; (4) indirect suggestion; and (5) use of a social interest activity.

Although you might make the case that Adler is being ingenuine or manipulative during this exchange, you can also make the opposite argument. Perhaps he's being so much himself that he's able to let out his playful, artistic, and Socratic self—all in an effort to move the patient away from depression and toward social interest or community feeling.

Paradoxical Strategies

Many different authors have written about paradoxical instruction, but Adler was one of the first. **Paradoxical instruction** involves prescribing the symptom. If your client is overly self-critical, you might suggest that she criticize herself at a higher rate and intensity during the coming week.

Paradoxical approaches have empirical support, but they're generally considered high-risk (Hill, 1987; Sexton, Montgomery, Goff, & Nugent, 1993). Consequently, we recommend using paradox in moderation. For example, with a 43-year-old woman who "worries constantly," we don't tell her to "worry more," but instead tell her to take 20 minutes twice daily to schedule time to worry intensively. Often, the positive outcome of a paradoxical prescription is that clients feel more in control than they did previously. Chapter 4 includes additional information on paradoxical strategies.

Advice, Suggestion, and Direction

Adlerian therapists offer advice freely. Of course, they do so within the context of a friendly, collaborative, positive relationship.

Corsini (1998) described a directive, advice-giving technique he referred to as "*I'll Betcha.*" He wrote:

> [This technique] is called "I'll Betcha." It goes as follows: Say that I suggest that a client do a particular thing to achieve a particular end and the client says it will not work. I will persist and finally will say, "I'll betcha it will." Then I outline the bet—always for exactly $2.00. If the client accepts my bet, the conditions are the following: He or she is to do exactly what I say. If it does not work, he or she wins the bet; if it does work, I win the bet. I have made about 50 such bets over the years and have not lost one. The interesting part is that my opponent decides whether it worked or not. (Corsini, 1998, p. 54)

Offering **advice**, **suggestions**, and **direction** occur within the reorientation stage of counseling. This is because insight and motivation are present and clients are ready for action. The motivation ignited through insight is motivation for excellence and a drive toward self-improvement.

Adlerian Play Therapy

Terry Kottman (Kottman, 1994; Kottman & Warlick, 1989) developed and evaluated an approach that she explicitly named Adlerian play therapy. Kottman and her colleagues described **Adlerian play therapy** as an approach that recognizes all children as (a) unique and creative, (b) striving toward connection and belonging, (c) creating fictional goals, and (d) valuing social interest (Meany-Walen & Teeling, 2016).

Similar to Adlerian therapy, Adlerian play therapy includes four treatment phases: (a) building the therapy relationship, (b) investigating the lifestyle, (c) gaining insight, and (d) reorientation/reeducation (Meany-Walen & Teeling, 2016). Parent and teacher consultation is also part of the Adlerian play therapy process. Specifically, Adlerian play therapists integrate the "Crucial C's" into their play therapy with children and consultation with adults. The Crucial C's include: "the child's need to connect, feel that they are competent and capable of caring for themselves, feel that they count, and have courage" (p. 288).

REFLECTIONS

Adlerians use lots of different techniques to facilitate client insight and change. Which of the preceding techniques stand out in your mind? Which ones can you imagine using in therapy? Which ones would you avoid?

Adlerian Therapy in Action: Brief Vignettes

The following vignettes illustrate two common Adlerian interventions. As you read these vignettes, imagine yourself as either the client or the therapist. How might it feel to have someone work with you in this way... and how might it feel to work this way with clients?

Vignette I: Using an Early Interpretation

This first vignette is an excerpt from a session John did with a 17-year-old male. It illustrates how a basic mistake can be surfaced quickly and then an early interpretation used to engage the client's interest and motivation.

The young man in this interview is a Job Corps student. He was referred due to repeated anger episodes. The young man described himself as "half black and half white" (J. Sommers-Flanagan & R. Sommers-Flanagan, 2004).

John: I don't know you, you don't know me.... I have different ways of trying to get to know people. One is just to ask you some things about what you like and what you don't like.

Sean: Alright.

John: So, I'll just do that if that's okay. [Asking permission; an invitation to collaborate.]

Sean: That'll work.

John: Okay... tell me, what's your favorite thing to do, your favorite recreational activity?

Sean: Um, there's a couple things. I like playing football. I like playing basketball. Um, I like to draw and write music.

John: Yeah? You write music or lyrics?

Sean: Um, lyrics.

John: Write lyrics, okay.

Sean: And that's about it.

John: Yeah. So those are the things you really like. Enjoy a lot.

Sean: Mmm hmm.

John: How about some things you hate? Sometimes you can tell a lot about somebody by finding out some things that they just hate.

Sean: The same things.

John: You hate football, you hate basketball, you hate drawing?

Sean: Those are my favorite things to do but they make me mad.

John: Yeah?

Sean: Cause I get frustrated when I like, when I play basketball if I don't play so well, it'll make me mad. Well, you know, I like to be QB when I play football. If I don't get a good pass or if somebody drops it I get

mad. Um, when I draw if I can't think of nothin' to draw or mess up, I get mad. Or um, when I'm writing music if I can't think of anything I get writer's block, I get really mad. So, yeah, they're like my worst things to do, like what somebody wouldn't want me to do, but they're my favorite things to do, so I do them anyways.

John: That's interesting. So, I can tell you what the issue is already. [This offer to interpret the problem is premature. It would be more in keeping with an Adlerian approach if John asked permission to share his perspective. However, when working with adolescents this quick problem formulation can provide a concrete issue to work on collaboratively.]

Sean: Alright.

John: You ready?

Sean: Yeah.

John: So, you know what the problem is about anger for you? You're a perfectionist.

Sean: I don't try to be. I don't really mean to be, though. [Sean accepts the perfectionist frame and begins talking about how his perfectionism feels out of control.]

John: Yeah.

Sean: I don't like to be because if I don't play as good as I want to play in basketball, for example. If I miss a shot and I know I can make it, I know I should make it, it makes me mad. I mean really mad. I don't just be like "oh darn" you know, I'm a little mad now. I'll flip out. [The client continues to share his style of life dynamic and the distress it causes him.]

John: You think you should do things right all the time. [This is a cognitive reflection.]

Sean: Yeah.

John: Yeah, that's tough. Man, you've got a huge burden. [This is an emotionally empathic statement.]

Sean: Yeah, well I don't mean to.

John: That's a lot of pressure.

Sean: Kind of. It's, it's a lot of stress because you know, it's just kind of the way that I was brought up. You know, I never wanted to lose at anything. I never wanted to be less than anybody. I've always wanted to be the best, but I've never gotten there yet. [Sean naturally links his lifestyle problem or basic mistake to childhood experiences.]

The purpose of insight is to enhance motivation for change. Immediately following the early interpretation, Sean begins sharing information that may be useful for making personal changes.

Later in therapy Sean discloses ways in which his biracial ethnic identity feeds into his needs to be perfect. This discussion is especially interesting because it's consistent with the literature on biracial identity development theory and validates the Adlerian emphasis on social and cultural factors shaping human behavior (Csizmadia & Ispa, 2014; Poston, 1990).

Vignette II: Spitting in the Client's Soup

A 15-year-old boy named Mark, who identified as white, was referred for therapy because he had taken explosives to school. He had seen John previously and they had a positive working alliance. Partway through the session John noticed Mark was using criminal thinking errors to remain blame-free and began working to spoil those thinking errors.

Mark: Yeah. This whole thing is stupid. Everybody's just overreacting. It was just a big firecracker.

John: It seems to you like a big overreaction about a not-so-big deal.

Mark: Right.

John: You know what, I bet I can guess exactly what you were thinking just before you decided to take those explosives to school.

Mark: No you can't.

John: I bet I can.

Mark: I bet you can't.

John: I bet you were thinking, "I won't get caught."

Mark: How did you know I thought that?

John: [Smiling.] It must be my psychic powers.

For this boy, the belief "I won't get caught" is an idea related to his basic mistake of thinking he is invincible. His style of life included something like this: "I can do what I please and never be responsible."

As Sweeney (2015) noted, after the spitting in the soup intervention, the client "may continue the behavior, but it won't taste as sweet any longer!" (p. 141). In this case, the boy illustrates how sometimes clients will cling to maladaptive beliefs associated with their style of life.

John: I guess it turned out you were wrong.

Mark: No I wasn't.

John: You're kidding right?

Mark: No. I wasn't wrong.

John: Wait. You just admitted that you were thinking to yourself, "I won't get caught" and then you took the explosives to school and then you got caught, so you were wrong.

Mark: No I wasn't. I didn't get caught. Somebody narked on me.

Mark is denying that John spit in his soup. He's saying, "Yeah I was thinking I won't get caught but because someone narked on me I can still say I didn't get caught

so that in the future it will be just as sweet because you spit in the wrong soup." This is one of several creative maneuvers clients can use to justify continuing with their basic mistakes. Consequently, John switches his approach to creating a new image.

John: I wonder if thinking "I won't get caught" could be a signal for you. Maybe it means trouble is coming. What if every time you thought "I won't get caught" you also saw a bunch of red stop lights flashing in your mind. You could see the warning and choose not to do whatever you're about to do and avoid getting in trouble.

Mark: That's dumb.

John: Let's try it anyway. I'll say the words and you think of flashing lights. Okay. "I won't get caught." Did you see the lights?

Mark: I guess.

John: Cool. Good. Now let's try it again and try to see the red lights as brightly in your mind's eye as possible. "I won't get caught."

Mark: Okay.

John: Let's try one more thing. What if, right after you see those flashing lights, you thought, "I'm the kind of guy who makes good decisions!" Try that out. Go ahead and say it.

Mark: I'm the kind of guy who makes good decisions.

John: All right. I want to make a deal with you for next week. I know you're into collecting baseball cards and so when you step into my office next week, I'll ask: "What kind of guy are you?" and if you say, "I'm the kind of guy who makes good decisions," I'll give you this pack of baseball cards. Deal?

Mark: Definitely. That's a deal.

In this case John tried spitting in Mark's soup, but Mark resisted the intervention and so John switched to creating a new image combined with a behavioral strategy for reinforcing Mark for adopting a new self-statement to replace the basic mistake of "I won't get caught." The Adlerian approach is flexible and mixes well with other approaches. In the end, John has linked Mark's basic mistake to (a) flashing red lights, (b) the phrase "I'm the kind of guy who makes good decisions," and (c) positive reinforcement (or a positive logical consequence) for making good decisions. Hopefully, the "I won't get caught" cognition has been spoiled and replaced.

CASE PRESENTATION

In this section we include an example of a family constellation interview. There are many such examples in the literature, including one H. Mosak conducted with a

17-year-old girl. We highly recommend that you read his interview (Mosak, 1972, pp. 232–247). In the following case, Dr. Murray is interviewing an 18-year-old named Kisha.

Dr. Murray's family constellation interview picks ups with Dr. Murray asking Kisha about her perceptions of her younger brother, Shane. As Dr. Murray gathers information, she occasionally connects with Kisha through gentle interpretations:

Dr. M.: I'm curious about your memories growing up. You've mentioned your brother a couple of times. What was he like?

Kisha: He's always been the family clown, but his jokes were on me most of the time. But he was nice enough.

Dr. M.: You don't sound all that convinced.

Kisha: Well, other people thought he was funny, and he included me sometimes.

Dr. M.: Did he hurt people's feelings when he was funny?

Kisha: Yeah, but not really on purpose. He tries to be a good kid.

Dr. M.: So, he was funny, sometimes at other people's expense, but not on purpose. When he wasn't being funny, what was he like?

Kisha: He was kind of athletic. He liked basketball, especially in middle school. My parents went to all the games, but he wasn't all that good. My dad didn't think Shane tried hard enough.

Dr. M.: So, that must have been kind of hard for him. If you were going to describe Shane, in middle school, what word comes to mind?

Kisha: Um. I don't want to be mean, but the word screwup came to mind.

Dr. M.: Hmmm. Okay.

Kisha: But that's not the only way I see him.

Dr. M.: Yes, I can tell. And I have a word I might offer. A long hyphenated one. Could I?

Kisha: Sure.

Dr. M.: I'd say Shane was an under-achiever.

Kisha: Yeah. He was. It's a family trait.

As Dr. Murray collected information, she consistently validated Kisha's perspective, staying friendly, supportive, and perceptive, but also offering words to help Kisha share deeper information.

The Problem List

Dr. Murray asked Kisha about her brother as a means to evaluate Kisha's style of life. Asking about the brother works as an assessment tool because Kisha defines herself both as similar and in contrast to her brother. Her brother plays a role in how Kisha sees herself.

Children often compete to find successful niches within the family system. Each child needs to belong and feel useful. Even very young children can sense whether they have a chance at being the "successful" one in the family on a particular dimension. This is why birth order and gender can play significant roles. In Kisha's case, the birth of a younger brother displaced her role as the only child, and her brother's irreverence and humor made him a favorite, even though he didn't live up to his father's sports expectations. Without parental support, the younger child might develop inferiority issues stimulated when he tries hard in the area in which the older child excels, and discouragement can ensue. In contrast, the older child may feel displaced by a successful younger child, valued for his gender or his humor.

A tentative initial problem list for Kisha includes:

Protective feelings for her brother, combined with resentment, with an inability to see how his actions hurt her.

A range of different maladaptive behaviors and cognitions. These include Kisha's conception of herself as needing to step aside for younger, attention-seeking males. She is at risk for getting into relationships where she is subordinate (and resentful) to a "screw-up who gets away with it." She isn't able to focus on her own identity, her own strengths, or grow her own potential.

Next, Dr. Murray continues to identify Kisha's unique status in the family and how it relates to her conception of herself.

Dr. M.: Who's the most active in your family, and who's the least?

Kisha: Depends. Shane tries more crazy things. I stay home and study.

Dr. M.: Who would you say behaves better and who is more likely to try things that might get them in trouble?

Kisha: Shane is the go-getter, dare-devil, for sure. And I try to be, um, good, I guess.

Dr. M.: Try?

Kisha: Yeah. Because I'm not sure if I want to be that good.

Dr. M.: Okay. So, in your family, who does more of what they want?

Kisha: Shane and Dad.

Dr. M.: Who gets their own way the most?

Kisha: Well, on the surface, Shane and Dad, but when it matters, my mom can make sure she gets her way.

Dr. M.: And you?

Kisha: I don't get my way. I don't even know what my way would be sometimes.

Problem Formulation

Dr. Murray is starting to get a picture of Kisha's role in this family. Kisha's sense of herself is ill-defined and subordinate. Kisha seems to have decided that not asserting herself is the best way to get along in the family (a basic mistake). Her underlying perception is that she must value her brother's attempts at humor and athletics, even when it hurts her feelings or she feels ignored. Kisha wants her parents' acceptance and approval, but obtaining approval for being subordinate is interfering with her development. She is at risk of developing an identity of being unimportant; she also is at risk of becoming resentful of her brother.

The preceding is only a small segment of a much longer interview. Dr. Murray has started a process of connecting Kisha's descriptions of her brother to Kisha's functioning in the family. During the interview Dr. Murray also explores the parental dynamics. Kisha's mother is generally unassertive except when something really matters to her. Kisha's father aligns with Shane, and they both get their way more often. In a typical family constellation interview, the therapist closes with an initial lifestyle interpretation. Dr. Murray's initial lifestyle interpretation also works as a problem formulation (Mosak, 1972).

Dr. M.: Well, Kisha, I want to offer a sort of summary so far. Is that okay with you.

Kisha: Sure. Whatever you think.

Dr. M.: But what do you think? What do you remember from us talking together?

Kisha: We talked about my brother a lot…and my parents.

Dr. M.: Maybe we should have just talked about you?

Kisha: But I'm boring.

Dr. M.: Actually, I think we should have talked about you the whole time. Just Kisha. Only Kisha. How about we meet again and that's ALL WE DO.

Kisha: That would be weird.

Dr. M.: Just weird?

Kisha: Weird and nice too. I get tired of talking about my brother all the time.

Dr. M.: What I noticed today is that growing up in your family hasn't helped you figure out who you are, or who you want to be. The questions: Who is Kisha…and what does Kisha want?…are important. Maybe you feel unnoticed and not valued as much as Shane. It's not your fault or Shane's fault. This happens in lots of families where personalities are different. Now, you need to find time to figure out who you are and how you want to be in the world. Does this ring true to you at all?

Kisha: Yeah, I guess. Sometimes I feel like I'm on the sideline or the edge and not really involved in anything.

Dr. M.: And so next time, we're just talking about Kisha, 100%. Okay?

Kisha: That will be weird.

Dr. M.: And nice and good and about time.

Interventions

Throughout the process leading to the interpretation, Dr. Murray is empathic, supportive, encouraging, hopeful, and direct. She is so much of these qualities that Kisha can easily digest the less positive interpretive feedback—that she doesn't believe in or even know herself very well—without becoming defensive. Kisha can entertain the idea that it might be "nice" to spend a session talking about herself.

Dr. Murray's interpretation explicitly articulates what many psychodynamic interpretations imply: she asks Kisha if she wants to change her old, outdated, way of thinking about herself and the world. If the timing is right, Kisha's motivation to strive toward excellence and completion will cause her to answer this important therapy question with, "Yes! I want to change!" This affirmation leads directly to the reorientation phase.

If we had access to additional therapy interactions with Kisha and her Adlerian therapist, we know they would focus primarily on action, encouragement, and support. The following techniques could be applied to Kisha and her situation, based on her family constellation interview.

Acting as if: "During this next week, Kisha, I'd like you to act 'as if' you know exactly what you want. As you practice this new way of thinking, notice the ways you feel, think, and act differently. Also, notice what activities spark your interest."

Spitting in the client's soup: When the therapist notices Kisha talking about her brother's need, this comment might be helpful, "When you put the spotlight on Shane, you can't see your own direction. Let's put it back on you."

Creating new images: "Until now, you've seen Shane as someone who gets away with things, and who can do what he wants. How would it feel to see yourself as someone who can do what she wants?"

Adlerian therapy involves using a variety of active techniques to help clients develop more adaptive lifestyles. Adler sums up the modest nature of therapy goals for Kisha or other Adlerian therapy recipients: "Our method enables us to replace the great mistakes by small ones…. Big mistakes can produce neuroses but little mistakes a nearly normal person" (Adler, 1964, p. 62).

Outcomes Measurement

Assessment occurs at the beginning of therapy and continues throughout. As noted in Dr. Murray's work with Kisha, it's possible to obtain information regarding Kisha's lifestyle while discussing her brother's childhood behaviors during a family constellation interview. However, gathering lifestyle information based on family constellation interviews, early memories, and psychological birth order doesn't focus enough on diagnostic symptoms to meet contemporary scientific standards for outcomes research.

A primary goal is for clients to develop social interest. Additionally, Adlerians focus on helping clients to face and accomplish the tasks of life. These goals are measurable and relevant to treatment outcomes. Higher scores on the Sulliman Scale of Social Interest are associated with fewer psychiatric symptoms and lower diagnostic rates (Mozdzierz, Greenblatt, & Murphy, 2007). Common Adlerian measures include:

- Basic Adlerian Scales for Interpersonal Success–Adult Form (Wheeler, Kern, & Curlette, 1991).

- Sulliman Social Interest Scale (Mozdzierz, Greenblatt, & Murphy, 1988; Sulliman, 1973).

- Social Interest Index (Greever, Tseng, & Friedland, 1973).

- Social Interest Scale (Crandall, 1975).

Although some life tasks are integrated into the existing social interest scales, the ability to face and accomplish the tasks of life also can be measured using scales focusing on functional impairments or specific symptoms. For example, it would be useful and interesting to have clients who receive Adlerian therapy complete standard outcomes measures, such as the Outcome Questionnaire-45 (OQ-45; Lambert et al., 1996). The OQ-45 has three subscales: (a) symptom distress, (b) interpersonal relationships, and (c) social role (difficulties). Additionally, there are a wide variety of self-efficacy scales that could be used to evaluate Adlerian therapy treatment outcomes (DiIorio et al., 2001; Forcehimes & Tonigan, 2008). Bandura's self-efficacy concept (the belief in one's ability to accomplish a specific task) holds promise for Adlerian therapists interested in monitoring treatment outcomes (see Chapter 8 for more information on self-efficacy).

EVALUATIONS AND APPLICATIONS

Many contemporary therapists aren't especially familiar with Adlerian therapy approaches. Nonetheless, Adler's influence on counseling and psychotherapy has been immense. In this section we review how well Adlerian approaches have stood the test of time.

Evidence-Based Status

Adler's hopes of creating a useful psychology have been affirmed: professionals, teachers, and parents around the globe apply IP principles within educational settings, for parent education and for group, family, couple, and individual therapy (Carlson & Englar-Carlson, 2017; Sperry & Carlson, 2012). Even further, numerous contemporary approaches to therapy borrow extensively from IP, including cognitive behavioral, solution-focused, existential therapy, and reality therapy (Carlson, 2015; see Putting It in Practice 3.5 for a practitioner commentary on the broad utility of Adlerian theory).

Despite the prominent use of Adler's concepts, empirical research attesting to the efficacy of individual, marriage, family, and group forms of Adlerian therapy is sparse. This may be because Adler found nomothetic research focusing on group outcomes to be relatively useless. Adlerians are more inclined to report idiographic case studies.

Some research exists that focuses on Adlerian therapy outcomes, birth order, social interest, and the style of life. Highlights of this research includes:

- Smith, Glass, and Miller (1980) reported that Adlerian individual psychotherapy (four studies) was slightly more effective than placebo treatment and had efficacy similar to psychoanalytic and person-centered therapy.

- Several studies, including one small RCT ($n = 58$) indicate that Adlerian group play therapy reduces disruptive classroom behavior among elementary school students (Meany-Walen, Bratton, & Kottman, 2014; Meany-Walen, Bullis, Kottman, & Taylor, 2015; Meany-Walen, Kottman, Bullis, & Taylor, 2015; Meany-Walen & Teeling, 2016).

- Social interest and encouragement form the foundation of several different school-based curricula. *Ready to Learn*, a prekindergarten through first grade program, has empirical support (Villares, Brigman, & Peluso, 2008). A research-based school counselor intervention program titled *Student Success Skills* had a positive effect on math and reading (Brigman, Villares, & Webb, 2011; Webb, Lemberger, & Brigman, 2008). A small Turkish study also showed positive outcomes for Adlerian encouragement-oriented group counseling with Turkish college students (Ergüner-Tekinalp, 2017)

- The relationship of birth order to specific personality traits is complex (Eckstein et al., 2010; Pollet, Dijkstra, Barelds, & Buunk, 2010; Sulloway & Zweigenhaft, 2010). This is probably related to challenges in discerning between psychological and chronological birth order. However, in a review of 200 studies, Eckstein and colleagues (2010) concluded: "Research overwhelmingly supports general differences in birth-order characteristics" (p. 418).

- Social interest is associated with better health. Several researchers report that individuals with higher social

PUTTING IT IN PRACTICE

3.5 Adlerian Theory Development

This essay was contributed and reproduced with permission by Dr. Veronica I. Johnson of the University of Montana.

In graduate school, I felt immediately drawn to Adlerian theory. This attraction only solidified as I developed as a professional counselor and has continued now as a counselor educator. Adlerian theory fits with my belief system as to what causes human suffering and what promotes change. I feel these two factors are the most important components in choosing a theoretical orientation. From Carl Rogers we learn how important the counselor–client relationship is in promoting change and growth. Although Rogerian relationship principles are key, Adler goes further when he describes the concept of encouragement and how pathology develops as a result of discouragement.

My professional counseling identity is further articulated with Adler's view that all humans strive for superiority or purpose in life and what we need to thrive is encouragement. This isn't an illness-oriented theory, but a wellness perspective—consistent with our counseling roots. Adler went beyond the relationship, emphasizing technique and purpose in his theory.

As I've learned more about Adler over the years, I'm affirmed in my belief that, as Adler would suggest, we choose counseling for a reason, often based on our own personal experiences, and those experiences shape how we see the world ... and the theory that we choose to practice from and live our lives by. Our families are our first communities and we strive to belong to something. From our families we learn about ourselves and the world and we transfer that knowledge to our adult relationships and to our communities.

My passion is in working with couples and fostering healthy relationship skills and attitudes in young adults. I use Adlerian theory to describe how we develop our worldview and how this contributes to our behavior in romantic relationships. I love to see that "Aha!" look in client's faces when they develop insight as to how they came to think a certain way about their significant other, or why they behave the way they do in their relationships. Adler provides us with an explanation of human nature—thoughts, feelings, and actions—that just makes good sense.

Adler also helps me to be optimistic in my view of humanity. I'm optimistic to begin with, but working in the mental health field, it's easy to become less hopeful about clients' prognoses. I've worked with sexual abuse survivors, adolescents diagnosed with severe emotional disturbance, and adults with severe and persistent mental illness. Adlerian theory has given me a strong foundation from which to understand the human experience, communicate and connect with clients, and work effectively towards change. As long as I believe in the creativity of the human spirit, the ability to overcome obstacles with encouragement, and the power of striving with purpose, I remain hopeful that any client can change and grow. I acknowledge the uniqueness of all clients and identify what strengths they already possess that can aid in their current functioning. Adler also introduced humor to the counselor–client relationship, which I believe is very important. Adler was human with his clients, not simply a mirror or an objective bystander.

I love Adler's forward thinking. I wish that current and future theories gave more credit to how much Adler contributed to the human services field. There are glimpses of Adler in Cognitive Behavioral theory, Choice theory, Existentialism, Constructive theories, and Feminist theory, just to name a few. As psychotherapy continues to move towards an integrative model of helping, Adlerian theory represents the epitome of integration. It's one of the most comprehensive, holistic, wellness-oriented theories I've encountered. This theory works with various populations. I've yet to find its flaws in working with couples, families, individuals, and diverse cultural groups. Because of its emphasis on uniqueness, it

> is flexible and malleable to most client situations. I use Adlerian theory to make sense out of situations that I confront in my own life; I use it to relate to and understand students; I use it in supervision; I use it with clients. I continue to be fascinated by and in admiration of Alfred Adler—his strength, courage, and foresight. I will continue to credit him in the courses I teach as one of the great contributors to what we know about human nature.

interest have fewer psychiatric symptoms, fewer negative emotions, and increased well-being (Mozdzierz et al., 2007; Newbauer & Stone, 2010). Social interest also tends to predict positive psychology and spirituality (Leak, 2006; Leak & Leak, 2006).

• Many research studies (mostly before 1988) show that Adlerian-based parenting programs are effective, although these evaluations were not RCTs (Burnett, 1988; Gfroerer et al., 2004; Spence, 2009). Two prominent parenting education programs are distinctly Adlerian: Systematic Training for Effective Parenting (STEP; Dinkmeyer, McKay, & Dinkmeyer, 1997) and Active Parenting (AP; Popkin, 2014).

Although many therapy practitioners use Adlerian approaches, a relatively small body of research supports Adlerian therapy efficacy. Despite the Adlerian theoretical aversion to group efficacy studies, additional empirical research support is needed (Curlette & Kern, 2016).

Cultural Sensitivity

Adler's focus on individuals may lead you to think that his approach is insensitive to cultural groups with collectivist values. Such is not the case. Adler was the first modern theorist and practitioner to emphasize social and family dynamics in shaping individuals (Carlson, Watts, & Maniacci, 2006). Also, Adler's clinical practice focused primarily on lower socioeconomic clients (circus performers and tailors); this made him sensitive to social justice issues and struggles among the working class.

Social equality is deeply woven into Adlerian theory. This is true regarding broad social policy, contemporary publications, and therapist–client interactions. In the historical 1954 case of *Brown v. Board of Education*, Adlerian theory was part of the argument to the Supreme Court to advocate for equality in schools (Carlson & Englar-Carlson, 2017). In keeping with Adler's social justice values, the *Journal of Individual Psychology* has featured articles focusing on parenting across cultures (Oryan, 2014), racism (Hanna, 1998), sexism (Bitter, 2008), and other diversity issues. Also, Adlerian approaches emphasize social justice: there should be a "fundamental valuing of each person as a social equal" (Sweeney, 2015, p. 28).

It's unlikely that Adlerian approaches, like birth order and the family constellation interview, can be directly applied to specific minority groups. As with many theory-based approaches, cultural adaptation is necessary. Several examples of modifying Adlerian approaches for minority populations or integrating Adlerian principles into multicultural work are in the literature (Aleksandrov, Bowen, & Colker, 2016; McLean, La Guardia, Nelson, & Watts, 2016). For example, Roberts, Harper, Caldwell, and Decora (2003) administered a modified version of the Adlerian Lifestyle Scale to a group of Lakota women and subsequently engaged in a focus group discussion of the questionnaire items. More research like this is needed to better understand how lifestyle assessment and other Adlerian procedures apply to nontraditional or culturally diverse family systems.

Gender and Sexuality

Adler was a radical feminist in the early 1900s. Some of what he wrote remains radically feminist now. He spoke directly about ways in which a prejudiced society drives women's psychopathology:

> It is a frequently overlooked fact that a girl comes into the world with a prejudice sounding in her ears which is designed only to rob her of her belief in her own value, to shatter her self-confidence and destroy her hope of ever doing anything worthwhile. If this prejudice is constantly strengthened, if a girl sees again and again how women are given servile roles to play, it is not hard to understand how she loses courage, fails to face her obligations, and sinks back from the solution of her life's problems. (Quoted in J. B. Miller, 1973, p. 41)

He also believed strongly in the equal capabilities of women (Adler, 1958): "If we investigate … closely we learn that the story of the lesser capability of women is a palpable fable" (p. 109). Adler is unarguably one of the first modern feminists in psychology.

Like many older theories, the literature on the sensitivity of Adlerian approaches for sexually diverse clients is mixed. Three tendencies are prominent:

1. Early formulations of same sex attraction—even Adler's description of the masculine protest—tend toward pathologizing sexual diversity (Mansager, 2008).

2. Many Adlerian approaches have yet to fully acknowledge, address, and integrate sexual minorities as important and unique populations. This has led

to individuals with sexual minority identities feeling excluded (Aleksandrov, Bowen, & Colker, 2016; Fox, 2008).

3. Recent efforts have begun to integrate sexual minority issues—in nonpathologizing ways—into Adlerian therapeutic approaches (LaFountain, 2013; Shelley, 2009).

Overall, Adlerian approaches appear to be on the road toward becoming more diversity inclusive.

Spirituality

Over the years, Adlerian theory has been open to client spirituality and has attracted practitioners and writers with strong religious convictions (Cashwell & Watts, 2010; Johnson, 2013; Sweeney, 2015). This is probably because of Adler's emphasis on social equality and justice, but also because, as Carlson and colleagues (2006) wrote:

> The cardinal tenet of Adlerian theory is social interest, something Adler equated with the mandate to "Love one's neighbor as oneself" and the Golden Rule. (pp. 33–34)

The Golden Rule is an ancient theological/philosophical concept that Adlerians openly embrace; they also embrace multiple other religious and spiritual perspectives. In particular, Johansen (2010) provided guidelines for integrating IP concepts into Christianity, Judaism, Buddhism, Hinduism, and Islam. Overall, as described in the theoretical principles section of this chapter, Adlerians view spirituality as a life task that can contribute encouragement and meaning into clients' lives (Bluvshtein, Belangee, & Haugen, 2015).

Consistent with what is known about Adler, the specifics of client spirituality and religious belief is of minimal importance. What's important is how religion is used. Does the client use religion to promote separation and violence? Or is religion used to bring people together as a working and compassionate community? The latter of these alternatives is clearly the Adlerian way.

CONCLUDING COMMENTS

In the end, there's little debate about the significance of Adler's contribution as a person, theorist, and practitioner to the fields of counseling and psychotherapy. Albert Ellis, not typically one to lavish praise on anyone, wrote a tribute to Alfred Adler, in which he referred to him as the "true father of modern psychotherapy" (Ellis, 1970, p. 11). Similarly, Ellenberger (1970) wrote, "It would not be easy to find another author from which so much has been borrowed from all sides without acknowledgement, than Adler" (p. 645).

If you know what you're looking for, you'll find Adlerian psychology everywhere. Sometimes he's cited; other times he isn't. One explanation for Adler's omnipresence in modern counseling and psychotherapy is that he employed a psychology of common sense. It has been only a matter of time until the rest of the field began catching up with him.

Adler's writings are a treasure of quotations. We leave you with two of our favorites:

> "An incalculable amount of tension and useless effort would be spared in this world if we realized that cooperation and love can never be won by force." (Adler, 1931, p. 132)
>
> "Everything is a matter of opinion." (Adler, 1983, p. 1)

CHAPTER SUMMARY AND REVIEW

Alfred Adler developed individual psychology (IP) in the early 1900s. Many of his theoretical and political ideas were ahead of his time. Although he was part of Freud's inner circle, he was a contemporary, not a follower, of Freud, having established himself and published a book before meeting Freud. Adler's influence on contemporary therapy approaches has been substantial.

Adler had a difficult childhood. He experienced physical illness and educational challenges. IP includes many different theoretical concepts, some of which seem directly connected to Adler's childhood experiences. IP includes the central idea that individuals are whole persons who strive for purpose and superiority. Social interest (or Gemeinschaftsgefühl) is valued over self-interest. Individuals are viewed as unique, behavior is determined by multiple factors, and people develop an internal cognitive map or "style of life" for how to accomplish tasks of life. These tasks include: (a) work or occupation, (b) social relationships, (c) love and marriage, (d) self, (e) spirituality, and (f) parenting and family.

Adlerian theory and therapy deemphasizes psychopathology. Individuals who seek (or need) counseling are viewed as discouraged or as lacking the courage to directly face the challenges of the tasks of life. The therapeutic process involves encouragement.

Adlerian therapy is practiced in four overlapping stages. These include: (1) forming a friendly and egalitarian therapy relationship, (2) obtaining information leading to a comprehensive lifestyle (or style of life) assessment and analysis, (3) using collaborative interpretation to help clients achieve insight into their style of life, and (4) reorientation or a changing of one's style of life to better meet the tasks of life. Distinct Adlerian assessment principles and techniques include goal alignment, psychological birth order, the family constellation, the question, and earliest recollections. Adlerian therapy principles and techniques include the future autobiography, acting as if, reflecting as if, the push-button technique, spitting in the soup, creating new images, catching oneself, task setting and indirect suggestion, paradoxical strategies, and advice.

IP principles are used in schools, parenting, and individual, couple, group, and family counseling. However, there's little systematic empirical research supporting its efficacy. This may be because Adler and Adlerians tend to value idiographic analysis of individuals over group or nomothetic sources of knowledge. Recent research supports the effectiveness of Adlerian play therapy and parenting programs. Additionally, research supports Adler's concepts of social interest, encouragement, and, to some extent, psychological birth order. Additional research is needed to demonstrate the efficacy of Adlerian therapies.

Although focusing on individuals, Adler's approaches are also sensitive to family dynamics and social/cultural settings. Adler was especially far ahead of his time in terms of his views on social justice, women, and on egalitarian relationships. Like many older theories, Adler's ideas about sexual diversity were antiquated and pathologizing. Contemporary Adlerians are working to be more sensitive and affirming of sexual diversity. Adler's views on spirituality were centered around the principle "Love thy neighbor." From an Adlerian perspective, religion and spirituality should be used to bring people together as a working and compassionate community.

INDIVIDUAL PSYCHOLOGY KEY TERMS

Acting as if

Adlerian therapy

Basic mistakes

Catching oneself

Community feeling

Compensation

Creating new images

Discouragement

Early recollection

Encouragement

Family constellation interview

Fictional finalism

Forming the therapeutic relationship

Four goals of misbehavior

Four stages [of Adlerian therapy]

Future autobiography

Gemeinschaftsgefühl

Goal alignment

Guiding self-ideal

Holism

I'll betcha

Idiographic approach

Individual psychology

Individuum

Inferiority complexes

Inferiority feelings

Interpretation and insight

Lifestyle assessment

Masculine protest

Need to belong

Objective inferiority

Offering advice, suggestions, and direction

Paradoxical strategies

Phenomenology

Private logic

Psychological birth order

Push-button technique

Reflecting as if

Reorientation

Secondary gain

Self-interest

Social interest

Soft determinism

Spitting in the client's soup

Striving for superiority

Style of life/lifestyle

Task setting and indirect suggestion

Tasks of life

The masculine protest

The question

Existential Theory and Therapy

This chapter is about life's big quandaries. Together, we explore meaning, death, responsibility, and the ambiguity and suspense inherent in human existence. Although many contemporary therapy approaches are oriented toward the great American quick fix, existentialists believe that reducing psychotherapy into a technical procedure that focuses on symptom reduction is unhealthy and wrong (van Deurzen & Adams, 2016).

INTRODUCTION

Psychoanalysis (Chapter 2), evolved primarily from medical practice with disturbed patients. Behavior therapy (Chapter 7) arose from experimental psychological research. Person-centered therapy (Chapter 5) and individual psychology (Chapter 3) have roots in clinical practice, humanistic-existential philosophy, and, to some degree, psychotherapy research. In contrast, existential therapy is derived from existential philosophy. **Existential philosophy** focuses on the inevitable conditions humans face during life, such as death, responsibility, freedom, and the pursuit of meaning (van Deurzen, 2014a; Yalom, 2008).

What Is Existential Therapy?

Existential psychotherapy (or **counseling**) is grounded in existential philosophy; it focuses on self-awareness,

facing the unavoidable conditions of human existence, and authentic living. Existential therapists believe humans are more than their chemical composition, more than their DNA, and more than their childhood and educational experiences (van Deurzen & Adams, 2016). Humans are meaning-makers. Viktor Frankl, an early existential psychotherapist, expressed it this way:

> I have been told in Australia, a boomerang only comes back to the hunter when it has missed its target, the prey. Well, man also only returns to himself, to being concerned with his self, after he has missed his mission, has failed to find meaning in life. (1969, p. 9)

Existential approaches prioritize the deeper meanings of life. When symptoms occur, they're viewed as meaningful. Symptoms aren't cured or minimized. Instead, clients are encouraged to lean into their symptoms, learning everything they can from the whole of their existential experience.

Existentialists often eschew scientific research because of its inauthentic artificiality. Instead, philosophy and a particular therapeutic attitude guide therapy. As Irvin Yalom, a renowned existential therapist, has written, "I have always felt that the term 'existential therapy' reflects not a discrete, comprehensive body of techniques, but, instead, a posture, a sensibility in the therapist" (Serlin, 1999, p. 143).

Counseling and Psychotherapy Theories in Context and Practice: Skills, Strategies, and Techniques, Third Edition. John Sommers-Flanagan and Rita Sommers-Flanagan. © 2018 John Wiley & Sons, Inc. Published 2018 by John Wiley & Sons, Inc.
Companion website: www.wiley.com/go/sommers-flanagan/theories3e

KEY FIGURES AND HISTORICAL CONTEXT

No single philosopher represents all existential thought. Most texts point to the nineteenth century philosophers Søren Kierkegaard and Friedrich Nietzsche as major players in the formulation of existentialism. In fact, Kierkegaard and Nietzsche capture the diversity of thinking inherent in existentialism.

Søren Kierkegaard

The Danish philosopher Søren Kierkegaard (1813–1855) lived nearly his entire life in Copenhagen. Kierkegaard was devoutly religious. He was shaken when he discovered, at age 22, that his father had not only cursed God, but also seduced his mother prior to marriage. Subsequently, Kierkegaard's writings focused primarily on religious faith and the meaning of Christianity. Eventually he concluded that religious faith was irrational and attainable only via a subjective experiential "leap of faith." For Kierkegaard, virtuous traits such as responsibility, honesty, and commitment are subjective choices—often in response to a subjective religious conversion. Kierkegaard did not describe himself as an existentialist, but his work is a precursor to the existential philosophical movement, which formally began some 70 years following his death.

Friedrich Nietzsche

In contrast to Kierkegaard who began from a position of religious faith, the German philosopher Friedrich Nietzsche (1844–1900) had negative feelings about Christianity. It was he who, in his book *Thus Spake Zarathustra*, wrote, "God is dead." Although he may have been referring to societal emptiness, he also claimed that religion used fear and resentment to pressure individuals into moral behavior. Instead of following a religion, he believed, individuals should channel their passions into creative, joyful activities. Irvin Yalom offers a fascinating view of Nietzsche's psychological suffering in a historical fiction piece titled *When Nietzsche Wept*. In this novel, Yalom (1992) weaves existential principles into a fictional therapeutic encounter between Breuer, Freud, and Nietzsche.

Kierkegaard and Nietzsche represent an interesting paradox or dialectic in existential thinking. A **dialectic** is a process where learning is stimulated from the integration of opposites. On the one hand, some existentialists embrace deep religious faith, whereas others are staunchly atheistic. Still others claim an agnostic middle ground. These differences in fundamental beliefs represent a wide sweep of human intellectual diversity and provide for fascinating philosophical exploration. You will glimpse existential dialectics intermittently in this chapter.

Jean–Paul Sartre: The Existentialist Prototype

French philosopher Jean-Paul Sartre (1905–1980) may have introduced the most succinct description of existentialism when he wrote: "Freedom is existence, and in its existence precedes essence" and "Man's essence is his existence" (Sartre, 1953, p. 5).

If Sartre's description of pure existentialism isn't clear to you, you're not alone. Existential philosophy is sometimes so abstract that distilling the practical implications is difficult. Grasping meaning from existential philosophy is especially challenging for practicing therapists and students of counseling and psychotherapy who are looking for concrete advice about exactly how to behave during a therapy session. We have only this minor reassurance for you: in many ways, the entire purpose of existential philosophy is to struggle with personal meaning (Adams, 2016). Therefore, as you grope and flail for meaning within the philosophy that embodies this chapter, you will also be experiencing existential psychology.

Rollo May (1962) explained Sartre's statement *Freedom is existence, and in its existence precedes essence*: "That is to say, there would be no *essences*—no truth, no structure in reality, no logical forms, no *logos*, no God nor any morality—except as man in affirming his freedom makes these truths" (pp. 5–6).

Sartre is claiming there are no absolute or essential truths (essences). Instead, individuals create their own truth and reality. This is pure existentialism. You may recognize that many Adlerian (Chapter 3) ideas (e.g., style of life, acting as if, and fictional finalism) are consistent with existentialism; Adler also believed that individuals construct their realities.

Paul Tillich, a renowned German American existential philosopher and theologian, discussed Sartre's second statement, "Man's essence is his existence."

> There are, however, only rare moments…in which an almost pure existentialism has been reached. An example is Sartre's doctrine of man. I refer to a sentence in which the whole problem of essentialism and existentialism comes into the open, his famous statement that man's essence is his existence. The meaning of this sentence is that man is a being of whom no essence can be affirmed, for such an essence would introduce a permanent element, contradictory to man's power of transforming himself indefinitely. According to Sartre, man is what he acts to be. (Tillich, 1961, p. 9)

This description speaks to a key existential proposition: *humans contain no permanent elements*. It's like the popular phrase in the contemporary media, "to reinvent oneself." If you reinvent yourself, you're using existentially based concepts of impermanence and emergence. For existentialists, transformation is within reach.

Much of existentialism boils down to self-awareness, personal choice, and personal responsibility. If humans construct their own reality and are capable of self-reinvention, then individuals must take responsibility for their behaviors. For Sartre, humans create and humans are responsible for their creations. He expressed this in four words: "I am my choices" (Sartre, 1953, p. 5).

Existentialism is antideterministic. If you suggest to existentialists that particular factors, events, or mental processes determine their behavior, they're likely to roll their eyes. This is because existentialists reject unconscious or instinctual drivers of human behavior; they also reject environmental stimulus–response determinants. Instead, existentialists embrace human freedom and choice. The past does not determine the future. Our choices in this moment determine the now, and our choices in the next moment determine the future now.

However, what determines our daily, moment-to-moment choices? For Sartre, the answer is this: human reality "identifies and defines itself by the ends which it pursues" (Sartre, 1953, p. 19). This theme should sound familiar because, once again, it resonates with Adler's ideas about purposeful, goal-oriented behavior and the style of life. The following quotation from Yalom clarifies this important theme:

> The difference is between drive and strive. In our most essential being, in those characteristics that make us human rather than animal, we are not driven but instead actively strive for some goal.... "Striving" conveys a future orientation: we are pulled by what is to be, rather than pushed by relentless forces of past and present. (Yalom, 1980, p. 445)

Although existentialists believe in the unconscious, their particular unconscious is not Freudian. Reflecting on Yalom's words of being *pulled by what is to be*, we turn our attention to how existential philosophy was transformed into existential therapy.

Viktor Frankl and the Statue of Responsibility

Viktor Frankl
(*photo by Professor Dr. Franz Vesely, CC BY-SA 3.0*)

Viktor Frankl was the leading existentialist in Europe during his time. He was born to a Jewish family in Vienna and studied medicine at the University of Vienna before marrying Tilly Grosser in 1941. He, Tilly, and his parents were deported to a concentration camp less than a year later. Initially, Frankl worked as a physician and then as a psychiatrist in the concentration camp, with a focus on suicide prevention. He reported that sometimes his terrible circumstances led him to dissociate and deliver lectures to imaginary audiences. On October 19, 1944, his plight became even worse; he was transported to Auschwitz and then to a Nazi concentration camp affiliated with Dachau. While in these camps, his father died and his wife and mother were murdered. In April 1945, Frankl was liberated from Dachau. He later married Eleonore Katharina Schwindt, a practicing Catholic; they honored each other's religious beliefs, attending both the Catholic Church and the Jewish synagogue, and celebrating both Hanukah and Christmas (Redsand, 2007).

Frankl is author of the most widely read existential work of all time, *Man's Search for Meaning* (Frankl, 1963). This book, originally published as *Trotzdem Ja zum Leben Sagen: Ein Psychologe Erlebt das Konzentrationslager* (*Saying Yes to Life in Spite of Everything: A Psychologist Experiences the Concentration Camp*; 1946), includes vivid descriptions of Frankl's concentration camp experiences and outlines his particular therapeutic approach, logotherapy.

Logotherapy focuses on helping clients find meaning. Frankl frequently quoted Nietzsche, stating, "He who has a why to live can bear with almost any how" (Frankl, 1963, p. 121). Frankl distinguished his perspective from Freud and Adler:

> The striving to find a meaning in one's life is the primary motivational force in man. That is why I speak of a will to meaning in contrast to the pleasure principle (or, as we could also term it, the will to pleasure) on which Freudian psychoanalysis is centered, as well as in contrast to the will to power stressed by Adlerian psychology. (1963, p. 121)

Although he was a strong proponent of freedom, Frankl believed freedom would degenerate without responsibility. He recommended building a statue of responsibility on the West Coast of the United States to balance the Statue of Liberty on the East Coast (Frankl, 1963; see http://stephendpalmer.com/statue-responsibility/ for a video promoting Frankl's idea of a statue of responsibility).

Rollo May: From Existential Theory to Existential Practice

Most historians credit Rollo May with bringing existential thought into American counseling and psychotherapy (May, Angel, & Ellenberger, 1958). May obtained his bachelor's degree in English from Oberlin College in Ohio. Then he became a missionary teacher in Greece for 3 years in the early 1930s. During that time, he traveled to Vienna in the summer, where he enrolled in seminars with Alfred Adler. In a 1987 interview, May contrasted his experiences with American psychology and Adler:

> Well, in college, I took one course in psychology and [although] I didn't learn much about human beings... I did learn a lot about pigeons and dogs. So I dropped the whole thing and majored in English literature.
>
> So the next summer, I went up to Alfred Adler's seminar in Vienna and there I learned what psychotherapy can really be. It changed me very deeply. It opened up a great deal of new possibilities in my life. (Schneider, Galvin, & Serlin, 2009, p. 425)

Next, May returned to the United States, where he obtained a bachelor's degree in divinity, working with and befriending the existential theologian Paul Tillich at Union Theological Seminary in New York.

May gave up the life of a pastor at a New Jersey church to study clinical psychology at Columbia University. Shortly thereafter, he fell ill with tuberculosis and was on the brink of death; he spent 18 months being treated in a sanitarium. Eventually May returned to Columbia, where he was granted a doctoral degree in clinical psychology in 1949 (DeCarvalho, 1996). In his dissertation, *The Meaning of Anxiety* (1977; published much later), he argued that anxiety was an essential component of the human condition.

May integrated self-awareness with an action orientation. He wrote: "The crucial question always is that I happen to exist at this given moment in time and space, and my problem is how am I going to be aware of that fact and what am I going to do about it?" (May, 1958, p. 12). One thing May consistently did "about it" was to continue to write. His major works include his edited volume, *Existence: A New Dimension in Psychiatry and Psychology* (May, Angel, & Ellenberger, 1958), *Love and Will* (1969), and *Freedom and Destiny* (1981).

Learning from Dialectics

As promised, we've now covered existential philosophers and practitioners who are deeply religious and others who are staunchly atheist. We've discussed essence and existence, freedom and responsibility, drive and strive, and death (which implies life). From the existential perspective, these contrary or polarized positions (aka dialectics) are natural and predestined (Schneider, 2013). As Fritz Perls emphasized in his existentially based Gestalt therapy approach (Chapter 6), humans are drawn toward polarizing positions. He wrote: "Every psychological phenomenon... [is] experienced as a polarity" (F. Perls, 1969a, p. 3).

Georg Wilhelm Friedrich Hegel (1770–1831) believed human reasoning and ideas evolve through a *dialectical process* that involves: (a) a concept or idea is developed, which then (b) fuels the generation of the opposite idea, which (c) produces conflict between the ideas. It is through this conflict between polarized ideas that (d) a new, synthesized, and higher level of truth is understood.

Hegel's dialectic is relevant to counseling and psychotherapy. One popular evidence-based approach, dialectical behavior therapy (DBT; Chapter 14), involves a direct application of Hegel's dialectic (Linehan, 1993). DBT practitioners adopt a dialectical position of radical acceptance when working with clients: "I accept you as you are, and I am committed to helping you to change for the better" (J. Sommers-Flanagan & Sommers-Flanagan, 2017, p. 491).

The ongoing polarized struggles within individuals can be seen as a primary pathway toward deeper understanding of the true nature of the self. This seems an appropriate outcome of the existential struggle because, for most existential practitioners, regardless of religious orientation, the overarching goal of therapy is to help the client discover and explore the authentic self.

Then again, as we consider the big questions, even the existence of the self is in doubt. Some multicultural and post-modern worldviews not only question the usefulness of thinking about an authentic self but they question its very existence. Hoffman and colleagues (2009) described the "crisis of the self":

> The influence of Eastern thought, particularly Buddhist philosophy, introduced recognition of no-self as an ideal.... Cultural analyses provided examples of cultures which did not have a traditional conception of self, but rather understood what is referred to as the self in Western thought in terms of roles which are much more fluid over time.... In the end, the necessity of a self conception, so basic to Western psychology, is now in question. (Hoffman, Stewart, Warren, & Meek, 2009, p. 136)

Therefore, we should keep in mind the following:

- Humans naturally create polarities.

- These polarities generate conflict.

- Through this conflict, there is potential for synthesis and intellectual development.

- Some traditional theorists emphasize the centrality of the self, while post-modern and culturally diverse perspectives deemphasize the self.

- We learn from both perspectives—self as central and no-self as ideal—and develop a more wise and balanced view of self.

- This process links directly to existential practice.

One final historical footnote: some writers speculate that the Zeitgeist or context of the 1940s was ripe for existentialism, especially European existentialism. This is because the devastation of World War I, followed by further global conflict in World War II, including the murder of millions of Jewish people, gay and lesbian people, and others in and around Germany, stimulated an introspective process focusing on death, personal responsibility, freedom, love, and other related existential topics.

Past, Present, and Future

Existential philosophy didn't abruptly start (and doesn't stop) with Kierkegaard, Nietzsche, Sartre, and Hegel. Existential therapy practice doesn't end with Adler, Frankl, and May. Many other historical and contemporary existential philosophers and practitioners have continued and are continuing to popularize and develop existential perspectives (Bakewell, 2016; Schneider, 2013; Shapiro, 2016). Major figures in existential psychotherapy and some of their key publications include:

- James Bugental (1915–2008): *The Art of the Psychotherapist* (1987); *Psychotherapy Isn't What You Think* (1999).

- Irvin Yalom (1931–): *Existential Psychotherapy* (1980); *Love's Executioner* (1989); *Staring at the Sun* (2008).

- Emmy van Deurzen (1951–): *Existential Counselling in Practice* (1988, as van Deurzen-Smith); *Everyday Mysteries: Existential Dimensions of Psychotherapy* (2nd ed.) (2010).

- Kirk Schneider (1953–): *Rediscovery of Awe: Splendor, Mystery, and the Fluid Center of Life* (2004); *Existential–Humanistic Therapy* (Schneider & Krug, 2010); *The Polarized Mind: Why It's Killing Us and What We Can Do About It* (2013).

THEORETICAL PRINCIPLES

An amalgamation of existential theorists and therapists have created the rich and creative approach to human change that we call existential counseling and psychotherapy. In the previous section, we started discussing existential concepts. In this section, we continue an examination of big theoretical principles that define the existential approach.

The I-Am Experience

The **I-am experience** is the experience of being, of existing (R. May et al., 1958). This experience of being is often referred to as **ontological experience** (*ontos* means "to be" and *logical* means "the science of"). Literally, then, a major focus of existential therapy consists of exploring immediate human experience. You might think of it as suddenly waking up and completely tuning into what it's like to exist and be here and now in this particular moment in time.

Existentialists like to use hyphens to capture the interconnectedness of phenomenological experience. For example, in contrast to May's I-am experience, Boss (1963) and Binswanger (1933) used *Dasein* (which is translated to being-in-the-world) to describe the sense-of-existence. Also, the phrase, "*Dasein choosing*," which is translated to the-person-who-is-responsible-for-his-existence choosing is used. We should note that this practice is in no way related to our own hyphenated last names, although it has inspired John to consider adding a hyphenated middle name so he can refer to himself in the third person as, "John-who-is-responsible-for-his-existence-Sommers-Flanagan," which he thinks sort of rolls right off the tongue.

It follows, as-if-anything-really-follows-from-the-preceding, that existential therapy is nearly always in the service of self-awareness or self-discovery. However, unlike psychoanalysts, existentialists expand and illuminate client self-awareness rather than interpreting client unconscious processes. This is because existentialists believe the entirety of an individual's human experience is accessible to consciousness.

Four Existential Ways of Being

There are four primary existential ways of being-in-the-world. They include:

1. *Umwelt*: Being-with-nature or the physical world.

2. *Mitwelt*: Being-with-others or the social world.

3. *Eigenwelt*: Being-with-oneself or the world of the self.

4. *Uberwelt*: Being-with-the-spiritual or over world.

Boss (1963), Binswanger (1963), and May et al. (1958) described the first three of these existential ways of being, and van Deurzen (van Deurzen-Smith, 1988) added the fourth.

These dimensions of existence are ubiquitous and simultaneous. Some people focus more on one dimension than others or shift from one to another depending on particular intentions or situations. For example, while on a hike up the Stillwater gorge in Montana, it's easy to experience being-with-nature as water powerfully cascades around you. However, depending on other factors, this experience can take people inward toward eigenwelt, toward an uberwelt spiritual experience, or stimulate a deep mitwelt (albeit a nonverbal one). In most cases, the direction your being-ness moves in a given situation is likely a combination of several factors, such as: awareness, anxiety, previous experiences, intention, and/or your spiritual predisposition.

The Daimonic

According to Rollo May, "The daimonic is any natural function which has the power to take over the whole person" (1969, p. 123). Historically, *Daimon possession* was used to explain psychotic episodes and is popularly referred to as *demonic possession*. However, May repeatedly emphasized that daimonic and demonic are not the same concept: "I never use the word demonic, except to say that this is not what I mean" (May, 1982, p. 11).

The **daimonic** is an elemental force, energy, or urge residing within all persons that functions as the source of constructive and destructive impulses. May wrote, "The daimonic is the urge in every being to affirm itself, assert itself, perpetuate and increase itself.... [The reverse side] of the same affirmation is what empowers our creativity" (May, 1969, p. 123).

Similar to C. G. Jung, May considered harnessing and integrating the daimonic as a central psychotherapy task. He viewed psychotherapy as an activity that plumbs the depths of an individual's most basic impulses ... the purpose of which is to acknowledge, embrace, and integrate every bit of being and energy into the whole person. May commented specifically about the danger of leaving the daimonic unintegrated:

> If the daimonic urge is integrated into the personality (which is, to my mind, the purpose of psychotherapy) it results in creativity, that is, it is constructive. If the daimonic is not integrated, it can take over the total personality, as it does in violent rage or collective paranoia in time of war or compulsive sex or oppressive behavior. Destructive activity is then the result. (May, 1982, p. 11)

The goal is to integrate natural daimonic urges and energies in ways that maximize constructive and creative behavior.

The Nature of Anxiety

Within existential philosophy, anxiety leads to authenticity and freedom (Wulfing, 2008). Following this tradition, R. May (1953) conceptualized anxiety as a good thing. He emphasized that anxiety was a normal and essential by-product of human existence. May's formulation of anxiety encourages ownership of anxiety as a part of human experience. Anxiety should be explored, experienced, engaged, and redirected into constructive activities. We should not seek to avoid it.

There are two types of anxiety: normal anxiety and neurotic anxiety. **Normal anxiety** is directly proportional to the situation. It is meaningful as it enters awareness and stimulates constructive action. It doesn't require repression or other defensive processes. In contrast, **neurotic anxiety** is disproportionate to the situation; it is usually repressed, denied, or avoided; it's not used for creative or constructive purposes. It is destructive.

For example, as you read this chapter, you may simultaneously be aware of mounting anxiety over time pressures in your life. Perhaps you need to finish reading this chapter and study for an exam in your theories class. You also need to finish writing a proposal for a research class. At the same time, you're thinking about how you should get the oil changed in your car before your weekend road trip. You also haven't found anyone to dog-sit for you while you're away. The pressure is rising.

If, in response to your pressure-packed situation, you respond with creativity and efficiency, you're experiencing normal anxiety. Perhaps you decide to write your research proposal on an existential topic and hire your nephew to stay at your apartment and take care of your dog. You study as efficiently as you can, and then get your oil changed on the way out of town. In the end, you sigh with relief. You faced your anxiety and dealt with the situation effectively.

In contrast, if you avoid your rising anxiety by going out and partying with your friends, blowing off your theories exam, writing up a minimal research proposal, and taking your misbehaving dog with you on the road in your car without rechecking the oil—then you're experiencing neurotic anxiety. The three key differences are:

1. You deny the importance of your life demands.

2. You respond or react to the situation out of desperation, rather than responding proactively and with creativity.

3. You end up increasing your chances of having difficulties down the road (literally) because you haven't responsibly maintained yourself (or your vehicle).

Existential therapy isn't about eliminating normal anxiety; the goal is to reduce neurotic anxiety. Therapists help clients live with and cope effectively and creatively with the normal anxiety that accompanies existence.

May emphasized that a "neurosis" isn't a failure to adapt, but instead an adaptation that hasn't addressed the core life problem(s). When anxiety is suppressed or avoided, it's impossible to deal with it creatively or effectively. This leads to a neurotic adaptation. The effort is still self-protective (e.g., anxiety is avoided), but the real life problem isn't addressed (R. Milner, personal communication, September 16, 2016).

Normal and Neurotic Guilt

Guilt, like anxiety, has positive and negative qualities. Normal guilt is good. Guilt inspires people to act in thoughtful and conscientious ways. **Normal guilt** is like a sensor: it alerts us to what is ethically correct and guides us toward morally acceptable behavior.

Psychopathology arises from neurotic guilt. **Neurotic guilt** usually consists of a twisted, exaggerated, or minimized version of normal guilt. For example, when a victim of intimate partner violence feels guilty for provoking a partner to violence, it may not serve a productive purpose. Similarly, the person who feels transient or minimal guilt after physically battering a romantic partner often denies or minimizes personal responsibility. The person who behaves violently may experience relief from guilt after delivering a quick apology and a dozen roses. Even worse, blaming the partner and demanding an apology may relieve guilt.

In contrast, some individuals feel massive guilt and responsibility for even minor, normal, human ethical transgressions. Excess guilt may make such people think they should be punished or make restitution for their unacceptable behaviors. For example, after making a mistake that cost an employer several hundred dollars, a guilt-ridden employee may commit unending hours of compensatory service in an effort to be relieved of guilty feelings—and even then, the guilt feelings may continue. As with anxiety, guilt—when experienced—is best dealt with directly and constructively.

Existential Psychodynamics

Similar to psychoanalytic theorists, existentialists believe humans are in conflict with powerful internal forces. However, instead of helping clients cope with instinctual drives or rework internalized object relations, existential therapists help clients face and embrace **existential psychodynamics** or "ultimate concerns" of existence (Yalom, 1980, 1995). **Ultimate concerns** produce anxiety; these concerns must be dealt with directly or indirectly via defense mechanisms (although for existentialists, defense mechanisms are not an elusive, automatic unconscious process, but a style or pattern of avoiding anxiety that can and should be brought to awareness).

Yalom (1980) described four ultimate concerns relevant to psychotherapy. These concerns are:

1. Death.
2. Freedom.
3. Isolation.
4. Meaninglessness.

Everyone must confront these four demands and conditions inherent in human existence.

1. Death

Yalom (1980) described two propositions about death. First, he emphasized that death and life exist simultaneously:

> [D]eath whirs continuously beneath the membrane of life and exerts a vast influence upon experience and conduct. (p. 29)

The possibility of death cannot be ignored. Death can happen in the next moment, next day, or next week—

or we may live decades longer. Death is knowable and unknowable. We will die; it's only a question of when, where, and how. Death is a reality of life.

Second, Yalom claimed death is a "primordial source of anxiety" and a main source of psychopathology (1980, p. 29). If you've faced death, then you probably know about death anxiety. "There is a huge difference between knowing about something and knowing it through your own experience" (Yalom, 2008, p. 42).

Facing death is one method for experiencing life more deeply and fully. Yalom (2008) refers to this as the potential that facing death has for self-awakening. To face death is to motivate oneself to drink with greater enthusiasm from the cup of life. This is *not* a call for morbid preoccupation about your eventual demise, but instead a call to shed external trappings and roles and to live in the now as an individual self with freedom of choice. Researchers have affirmed that when individuals embrace the present, they can approach death without increased psychopathology or emotional distress (Lichtenthal et al., 2009; Strang, Henoch, Danielson, Browall, & Melin-Johansson, 2014).

REFLECTIONS

A hospice chaplain told us that often people with terminal diseases make peace with their impending death and their lives become more rich and full. In contrast, a famous Dylan Thomas poem urges, "Do not go gently into that good night. Rage, rage against the dying of the light." Peace or resistance? Rage or acceptance? Where do you find yourself?

2. Freedom

Freedom is generally considered a positive part of human experience, but this isn't the existentialist's view. Sartre wrote that humans are *condemned to freedom*. Existential therapists have followed suit by articulating the many ways in which freedom is an anxiety-laden burden (Sartre, 1971). More recently, feminist author Vivian Gornic has written regarding the mystifying tendencies of people to resist change, even when the change would result in greater freedom. She reflected on how, for millions of women, potential freedoms associated with the equal rights amendment could feel threatening:

> An old-time revivalist movement seemed to sweep through the land, the kind that arises when a society, like an individual, being forced to face its own deepest conflicts, cries out against the potential loss of familiar dysfunction, so great is its fear of coming to consciousness. After all, what feminism both promised and threatened was a level of self-knowledge that would make it almost impossible to go on living with the old social agreements (July 16, 2017; http://bostonreview.net/politics-gender-sexuality/vivian-gornick-feeling-paranoid).

Personal responsibility is the primary burden of freedom. If you are free, you are also responsible for your actions. There is no one to blame for your mistakes. Perhaps you were misled and made a poor choice, but the fact is that *you* were a participant in the misleading. You cannot even defend yourself with the pesky Freudian unconscious. As Yalom (1980) wrote, "To a patient, who insists that her behavior is controlled by her unconscious, a therapist says, 'Whose unconscious is it?'" (p. 216).

Complete and total responsibility is inescapable. In the end, the more freedom you experience, the more choices you have; and the more choices you have, the more responsibility you have; and having a large load of responsibility potentially translates into a large load of anxiety.

To make matters more daunting, you're responsible not only for your choices but also for your *nonchoices*. This is because every choice you make represents the death of hundreds of other possibilities. You have chosen to study counseling and psychology and are choosing to read this text in this moment. You may be aware that you could be volunteering at a homeless shelter, helping a family member in need, or selling Internet scams. In some ways, you're also choosing how aware you want to be about these various choices. As Sartre and Yalom have emphasized, even ignorance can be framed as a human choice.

Personal responsibility is a heavy burden. Many individuals can't bear the weight and defend themselves with denial, displacement, and blaming. For example, when employees underperform, they often blame the situation ("I didn't have time to do a good job") or a coworker ("Bob is impossible to work with") or the employer ("I'm not paid enough to work harder").

Sartre's "I am my choices" is roughly the equivalent of former U.S. President Harry Truman's "The buck stops here." If you meditate on this, you can feel empowered, which is why existentialists doggedly focus on personal freedom. For existentialists, the best and most direct route to personal empowerment is awareness of personal responsibility, including fully experiencing the angst that comes along with it.

The main point of freedom and responsibility is this: you and you alone are the author of your experiences. Don't bother pointing the finger of blame toward anyone other than yourself.

REFLECTIONS

Governments vary dramatically in the amount of individual freedoms available to citizens. States vary, cities vary, even families and couples vary in this domain. What makes freedom safe or dangerous within human groups? Should human freedom sometimes be limited?

3. Isolation

Every individual is fundamentally alone. Being alone can be a terrifying truth; we enter life alone and we exit the same way. This is existential isolation. Existential therapists help clients connect as deeply as possible with others, while at the same time acknowledging their incontrovertible separateness.

Martin Buber, a Jewish philosopher and theologian, wrote extensively on the I-Thou relationship (Buber, 1970). An **I-Thou relationship** involves the deepest of all possible connections between two individuals. It's a mutual and celebratory relationship, in which both self and other are fully experienced. Unfortunately, according to Buber, legitimate I-Thou moments are rare and brief. I-Thou relationships are ideal, even though it's impossible to stay constantly in an I-Thou connection.

The practical interpersonal problem that most of us face is the problem of isolation versus fusion. Like a newborn, sometimes we luxuriate in the illusion that someone will anticipate and meet our every need. Alternately, in the blush of powerful infatuation, we're intoxicated by the possibility of complete fusion with another individual. Sometimes, even a glimpse of the reality of existential aloneness can cause clinging to whatever potential love object may be in our vicinity, often with less than desirable outcomes.

Denial is a common way that humans deal with frightening existential isolation. One way to deny isolation is through love or fusion with another person. In *Love's Executioner*, Yalom (1989) complained of working with clients who are in love:

> I do not like to work with patients who are in love. Perhaps it is because of envy—I, too, crave enchantment. Perhaps it is because love and psychotherapy are fundamentally incompatible. The good therapist fights darkness and seeks illumination, while romantic love is sustained by mystery and crumbles upon inspection. I hate to be love's executioner. (p. 15)

No doubt you've been around friends, relatives, acquaintances, or clients who desperately seek social or intimate contact. These individuals loathe being alone, and if their intimate relationship ends, they act quickly to replace their former partner. Existentialists contend that these individuals haven't developed the inner strength, identity, and sense of completeness necessary to face the piercing anxiety associated with isolation. Instead, frantically seeking interpersonal connection gives them brief and intermittent experiences of completeness.

Earlier in this chapter, we noted that the goal of existential therapy is to help clients discover and explore their authentic self. We should extend that definition to include the discovery and exploration of the authentic and complete, individual self—separate from others.

Heightening clients' awareness of existential isolation should improve their ability to form healthy interpersonal relationships. Similar to death anxiety and angst over personal freedom, getting in touch with and embracing existential isolation can have positive consequences. To admit to and face aloneness gives us the strength to face the world and motivates us to connect with others in deep and meaningful ways.

Many individuals find the existential musings about love and eternal aloneness depressing. Viktor Frankl (1963), while being prodded by the butts of Nazi rifles, offered a more uplifting existential perspective on love:

> A thought transfixed me: for the first time in my life
> I saw the truth as it is set into song by so many poets,
> proclaimed as the final wisdom by so many thinkers.
> The truth—that love is the ultimate and the highest
> goal to which man can aspire. Then I grasped the
> meaning of the greatest secret that human poetry and
> human thought and belief have to impart: The salvation
> of man is through love and in love. I understood how a
> man who has nothing left in this world still may know
> bliss, be it only for a brief moment, in the contemplation
> of his beloved. (p. 37)

REFLECTIONS

Eastern philosophies often stress that our separations are illusions. We are all part of the great web of life. Does this argue against accepting and embracing our isolation? Is one view or the other true, or do they somehow both speak to ultimate reality?

4. Meaninglessness

The classic existential crisis or neurosis occurs when an individual faces the question "What is the meaning of my life?" Seeking life's meaning can be agonizing. The agonizing nature of this search may be why it's so easy to stay busy on Facebook or Snapchat instead of grappling with meaning. Leo Tolstoy captured the pain and torment associated with thinking too much about the meaning of one's life:

> The question, which in my fiftieth year had brought
> me to the notion of suicide, was the simplest of all
> questions, lying in the soul of every man from the
> undeveloped child to wisest sage: "What will come
> from what I am doing now, and may do tomorrow?
> What will come from my whole life?" otherwise
> expressed—"Why should I live? Why should I wish for
> anything? Why should I do anything?" Again, in other
> words: "Is there any meaning in my life which will not
> be destroyed by the inevitable death awaiting me?"
> (Tolstoy, 1929, p. 20)

Existentialists would respond to Tolstoy's musings with something like, "Life has no inherent meaning. It's up to you to invent, create, or discover meaning in your life. Your challenge is to find meaning in an apparently meaningless world." One existential mantra is: humans are meaning makers.

Meaninglessness should be confronted, embraced, and dealt with directly. Frankl wrote of his own personal struggle with meaninglessness:

> As a young man I had to go through the hell of despair
> over the apparent meaninglessness of life, through total
> and ultimate nihilism. But I wrestled with it like Jacob
> with the angel did until I could say "yes to life in spite
> of everything," until I could develop *immunity* against
> nihilism. (Gould, 1993, p. 9)

Frankl believed the "will to meaning" is a primary motive, more important than Freud's pleasure principle and Adler's superiority striving. He also emphasized that meaning isn't a drive or push; instead, meaning involves striving or willing.

Many clients are suffering from an absence of meaning in their lives. C. G. Jung also wrote about the preponderance of meaninglessness among clients with whom he worked:

> Absence of meaning in life plays a crucial role in the
> etiology of neurosis. A neurosis must be understood,
> ultimately, as a suffering of a soul which has not
> discovered its meaning.... About a third of my cases are
> not suffering from any clinical definable neurosis but
> from the senselessness and aimlessness of their lives.
> (Jung, 1953, p. 83)

A sense of meaningfulness, religiosity, and spirituality are predictive of positive mental health—especially in cases of personal loss (Fry, 2001; Vos, Craig, & Cooper, 2015).

Is Life Meaningful?

Frankl claimed that humans are pulled toward meaning. However, the question remains, is there inherent meaning in life toward which all humans can or should strive? The ever-optimistic (just kidding here) Sartre said no:

> All existing things are born for no reason, continue
> for no reason, continue through weakness and die by
> accident.... It is meaningless that we are born; it is
> meaningless that we die. (Cited in Hepburn, 1965)

Frankl was more optimistic: "We do not just attach and attribute meaning to things, but rather find them; we do not invent them, we detect them" (1967, p. 16).

Frankl was claiming two things. First, humans have a will to meaning. Second, meaning *does* exist in the world—it's up to us to find it. Further, Frankl emphasized that individuals don't find meaning through preoccupation with the self. Instead, we must look outside ourselves to find meaning.

Frankl's approach to helping clients find meaning was **logotherapy** (*logos* = meaning; *therapeia* = healing). As noted previously, he developed this approach after being imprisoned in Nazi concentration camps in Germany. During this time, he affirmed his beliefs in meaning as essential to human survival.

In logotherapy, clients are pushed to deal directly with the need for meaning, but specific meaningful activities are not prescribed. Logotherapy celebrates individual responsibility: clients are responsible for their choices regarding the pursuit of meaning. Although Frankl wrote about religion and spirituality, he emphasized that logotherapy is a secular theory and practice.

Humans can resolve existential neuroses through a number of paths toward meaning. The following possibilities are from Yalom (1980) and Frankl (1967):

- *Altruism*: Clients can serve others through kindness and unselfishness.

- *Dedication to a cause*: Clients can dedicate themselves to political, religious, medical, familial, scientific, or other causes. The key is for the cause to take the person beyond selfishness.

- *Creativity*: Clients can create something beautiful, powerful, and meaningful.

- *Self-transcendence*: Guilt, depression, personal salvation, and other self-oriented goals are put aside to pursue selflessness.

- *Suffering*: Clients can face suffering with optimism, dignity, and integrity.

- *God/religion*: Clients can serve God or their religion instead of serving self or pursuing material goals.

- *Hedonism*: Clients can live life to the fullest each moment and drink up the excitement, joys, and sorrows of daily life.

- *Self-actualization*: Clients can dedicate themselves to self-improvement and meeting their potential.

Yalom discussed these last two potentially meaningful pursuits (hedonism and self-actualization). However, Frankl might dismiss them as unsuitable because they focus on the self, rather than on something outside the self.

In summary:

1. Humans have an internal striving for meaning.

2. Meaningful pursuits exist in the world.

3. Counselors can help clients pursue and embrace meaning.

Self-Awareness

Self-awareness is central to existential therapy. Earlier, we said the goal of therapy was to help clients get in touch with their authentic selves. Consistent with existentialist thought, we're revising the goal of existential therapy again (recall that because existence precedes essence, we are continually reinventing, revising, and updating ourselves). Bugental (2000) wrote:

> There is no final or definitive statement to be made. About psychotherapy, about human psychology, about life. We are always in the process of sketching possibilities, of discovering, of becoming. (p. 251)

Therefore, for now, the goal of existential therapy is to facilitate self-awareness—including the awareness of death, freedom, isolation, and life's meaning. However, stay alert (and aware) because before this chapter ends we'll shift the focus of self-awareness once again—next time we'll be talking about existential integration (Schneider, 2008, 2010).

Theory of Psychopathology

Existentialists view psychopathology from several different perspectives. The first, and perhaps most ubiquitous, involves psychopathology as diminished self-awareness. Bugental (2000) described this:

> Most of us spend the greater portion of our lives on tape. Without awareness we carry out preprogrammed actions, feel preset emotions, and act on predetermined judgments. This taped living comes not because we are helplessly the creatures of our habit systems, our environments, our glands, or our ancestry, but because we have lost our centers.

For many existentialists successful therapy is about expanding self-awareness and helping clients live fully in the moment (Schneider, 2010; van Deurzen & Adams, 2016).

Diminished self-awareness might include some or all of the following characteristics:

- Emotional numbness or automaton living.

- Failure to acknowledge and reconcile life's ultimate concerns.

- Avoidance of anxiety, guilt, or other meaningful emotions.

Avoidance is often at the root of neurotic or maladaptive behavior. As clients disavow natural urges and avoid ultimate concerns, they become decentered and develop psychological, emotional, or behavioral symptoms. The cure involves facing oneself, facing life, and embracing the realities of death, freedom, isolation, and meaninglessness. This doesn't make life easy. However, clients who face ultimate concerns with an integrated sense of self experience normal anxiety and guilt, rather than neurotic anxiety and guilt.

Existential therapists also focus on how well individuals are able to lead meaningful lives with authentic purpose. Keshen (2006) described the following psychopathology sequence:

1. There is a will to meaning (or purpose) in life.

2. The individual is unable to "find or fulfill" authentic meaning or purpose.

3. The individual therefore experiences an "existential vacuum."

4. Symptoms associated with this vacuum may include: anhedonia, worthlessness, boredom, anxiety, apathy, emptiness, low self-esteem, or low mood.

5. The individual engages in a "purpose substitute" instead of directly addressing the need for purpose or meaning in life. This purpose substitute might involve addictions, excessive television viewing, or overzealous emphasis on acquisition. (See Keshen, 2006, p. 288.)

Van Deurzen and Adams (2016) described yet another psychopathology prototype: "The prototypical dysfunction in the personal world is to take responsibility for things one does not have responsibility for and deny responsibility for things one does have responsibility for" (p. 133). Overall, existentialists describe psychopathology in many different ways, but none of these descriptions translate well to mental disorder diagnosis and the medical model.

THE PRACTICE OF EXISTENTIAL THERAPY

Providing informed consent to clients is especially important for practitioners who use existential approaches. Informed consent is essential when therapy includes confrontational components. (See Putting It in Practice 4.1.)

PUTTING IT IN PRACTICE

4.1 Informed Consent from an Existential Perspective

Welcome to therapy! As you may already know, therapy is an intense, engaging, exciting collaborative process. When you arrive for therapy, be prepared for a full-on interpersonal encounter. We will talk about anything and everything. I will give you feedback about every aspect of yourself that I can.

The purpose of therapy is for you to discover who you are, what you want, and how to get it. The philosophy underlying my work is that life should be lived to the fullest. This means that during our sessions we won't focus on how you can control your emotions more completely; instead, we will focus on how you can feel all of your emotions and experiences with more depth and authenticity than ever.

During therapy, I will do my best to honor you and your personal experience and perspective. However, I will also consistently provide you with feedback about your thinking patterns, feelings, gestures, and other behaviors that may be outside your awareness. In some ways, you should think of me as a mirror, designed to help you get to know yourself better. This means that I won't be playing any social games or dancing around the truth of what I see. Often, I will simply describe what I see, what I think, and the emotional reactions I have to you and your behavior.

When you come to therapy, be prepared to have emotions stirred up. Therapy is not a calm place where you come to relax and detach from the world and your personal experiences. Our purpose together is to help you face and embrace all of life, rather than running from it. Therefore, much of what we do together will be a real, authentic, mini-life experience wherein you confront the challenges of life and existence within the relatively safe confines of the therapy office. We will use therapy for practicing life, rather than for avoiding life.

In addition to providing presession informed consent, initial here and now interactions with clients should proceed gently and educationally. This is true whether the interaction is feedback about personal responsibility or involvement in an existentially oriented Gestalt experiment (see Chapter 6). Later in this chapter, we illustrate educational therapist–client interactions within the context of specific skills and case examples.

Existential Therapy Relationships

Existential practitioners view technical interventions as artificial or phony. Frankl (2000) was blunt about this: "We can see the therapist as a technician only if we have first viewed the patient as some sort of machine" (p. 26).

Techniques detract from the authentic I-Thou interpersonal existential encounter. Brief and superficial quick-fix therapy is anathema to existential therapists. It's good and healthy to feel negative emotions and, in doing so, clients become more open to positive emotions.

Instead of techniques, the primary therapeutic force that existentialists use is the interpersonal therapeutic encounter. Buber's (1970) I-Thou relationship is the best descriptor of the existential therapy encounter. By being present with the client in the immediate moment, existential therapists collaborate with clients toward self-discovery and growth. As the therapeutic encounter develops, therapists may apply specific skills designed to facilitate awareness, creativity, and self-development (Adams, 2016).

Forming an I-Thou Relationship and Using It for Positive Change

Existential practitioners prioritize development of an I-Thou relationship with clients (van Deurzen, 2010). This relationship includes depth, mutuality, connection, and immediacy.

Existentialists also emphasize therapist transparency and authenticity. The therapeutic endeavor flows from an interpersonal encounter where therapists are spontaneous and open to their sensations, emotions, and intuition.

Therapist authenticity and spontaneity can bring certain liabilities. Given that self-deception is a common characteristic among clients and therapists alike, it's possible for therapists to have intuitive impulses that are more attuned to and designed to address their own issues and agendas than that of their clients (Schneider, 2010). Of course, therapist self-deception is a concern for all therapy approaches, but it's a particular ethical concern for existential therapists because of their endorsement of therapist intuition and spontaneity.

Personal Responsibility

Personal responsibility has direct implications for existential therapists (Adams, 2016; Sapienza & Bugental,

2000). As a therapist, you're completely responsible for your behavior within the therapy session. In Sartre's frame, you are your therapeutic choices. Also, although you aren't responsible for your client's welfare, you are responsible for the therapy process to which your client is exposed. It's your job to create conditions that facilitate an interpersonal therapeutic encounter and to avoid behaviors (e.g., too much self-disclosure) that might inhibit therapy progress (Geller, 2003).

Presence

Presence describes therapists who are alert, interested, and as fully in-the-room as possible during every minute of every session. If you feel bored or distracted (signs of what psychoanalysts refer to as countertransference), it is your responsibility for getting reconnected and reengaged. Sapienza and Bugental (2000) noted that therapists who feel boredom or disconnection should look within and then engage in activities designed to recapture their aliveness.

Schneider (2010) described presence as a critical component in the experiential liberation portion of his existential integrative approach:

> Presence serves three basic therapeutic functions: it holds or contains the therapeutic interaction; it illuminates or apprehends the salient features of that interaction; and it inspires presence in those who receive or are touched by it. (p. 7)

For some clients, focused existential presence and an I-Thou relationship might be too intense. This could serve as one indicator of whether or not an existential approach is a good fit for a given client. Additionally, existential therapists should shift their intensity level depending on the particular client and, in most cases, begin with less intensity and move toward deeper interpersonal connection as the relationship warms up.

Empathic Mirroring and Focusing

Existentialist therapists tune in as much as possible to what's happening within clients. Although this tuning in always falls short of complete accuracy, mirroring back to clients what's happening in the room is a powerful part of existential therapy. **Existential integrative therapy** (EIT) is an approach that Schneider (2008, 2010) developed. In EIT, empathic mirroring and focusing are components of (a) presence and (b) invoking the actual. **Invoking the actual** involves a "calling of attention [to] help clients to experience the expansive rage, for example, beneath their oppressive sadness, or the contractive melancholy beneath their expansive bravado" (p. 8). This description helps to articulate how invoking the actual overlaps with therapist presence and is designed to take clients deeper into their emotions.

Schneider (2010) identified three specific verbal invitations (i.e., techniques) to aid in invoking the actual. These include:

- *Topical focus*: "Take a moment to see what's present for you," "What really matters right now?" and "Can you give me an example?" (p. 9).

- *Topical expansion*: "Tell me more," "Stay with that (feeling) a few moments," or "You look like you have more to say" (p. 9).

- *Content-process discrepancies*: "You say you are fine, but your face is downcast" or "Your body hunches over as you talk about your girlfriend, I wonder what that's about" or "When you talk about that job, your eyes seem to moisten" (p. 9).

Schneider's verbal invitations are skills, not prescriptive techniques; existential therapists don't plan ahead to use these particular scripts in a therapy session. Instead, topical focus, topical expansion, and content-process discrepancies are ways therapists can be responsive or facilitative in the moment within therapy sessions.

Feedback and Confrontation

Feedback in psychotherapy involves therapists providing clients information about what they see and hear in the session. **Confrontation** is feedback that focuses on client inconsistencies or discrepancies (J. Sommers-Flanagan & Sommers-Flanagan, 2017). Both feedback and confrontation flow directly from presence and empathic mirroring. When therapists are present and mirroring back what they're seeing, hearing, and experiencing, feedback and confrontation are implicit.

Depending on your personality style and approach, the feedback you give clients may be more or less confrontational. Fritz Perls tended toward in-your-face confrontation (see Chapter 6), whereas Rollo May was more reflective. Our advice is to begin gently and progressively become more direct. This is because without a strong working alliance, feedback and confrontation can be too painful to integrate. For example, when discussing client resistance, Yalom and Leszcz (2005) and Schneider (2010) emphasized the longstanding protective function of defense mechanisms and the need to treat defensiveness with respect and care. Further, Schneider noted that although there are no perfect guidelines for when to confront, confrontation is generally more reasonable when a strong therapy alliance exists, along with a chronic pattern of unhealthy client behaviors. Confrontation examples include:

- You say you can't [discuss this with] your wife, but [I think] you mean you won't!

- How many times are you going to keep debasing yourself [in ways you hate]?

- You'd rather argue with me than get on with your life! (These examples are from Schneider, 2010, p. 12.)

Mindfulness

Mindfulness is a traditional Buddhist approach to daily living (Nanda, 2009). **Mindfulness** emphasizes awareness and acceptance of thoughts and life situations. Although not specifically "existential," we include mindfulness here because of its compatibility with the existential approach. The case example detailed later features an integration of mindfulness and existential therapy (Nanda, 2010).

Mindfulness meditation is a component of dialectical behavior therapy (DBT; Linehan, 1993), acceptance and commitment therapy (ACT; Hayes, Stroshahl, & Wilson, 1999), and the foundation of mindfulness-based cognitive therapy (MBCT; Segal, Williams, & Teasdale, 2002). Mindfulness approaches emphasize the acceptance, instead of rational disputation, of internal cognitive thought processes. Nanda (2010) described commonalities of mindfulness and existential therapy principles:

> Some common attitudes that are valued in Mindfulness … and Existential therapy … are the stance of a beginner's mind, openness to discover, allowing experience to be disclosed, suspending judgment, nonstriving, letting go of any agenda of curing, fixing. All these approaches encourage "being with" experience, and an acceptance of what is present. (p. 332)

Mindfulness fits with the existential approach as long as it's integrated into therapy in a way that honors authenticity and the I-Thou relationship.

Existential Therapy Skills

Adams (2016) made an important distinction between techniques and skills: "Techniques are tools, skills are owned ways of being; they are how we do being. A hammer is only useful if you have the skill to use it. Otherwise it is dangerous" (p. 60).

Both Frankl and Fritz Perls wrote extensively about technical interventions in therapy. Perls referred to "experiments," a term that captures the immediate experiential nature necessary in an existential encounter (see Chapter 6). Frankl wrote about paradoxical intention and reframing.

Paradoxical Intention

Alfred Adler originally used **paradoxical intention** or antisuggestion. In a case example, Frankl discussed using paradox with a bookkeeper who was suffering from chronic writer's cramp. The man had seen many physicians without improvement; he was in danger of losing his job. Frankl's approach was to instruct the man to:

> Do just the opposite from what he usually had done; namely, instead of trying to write as neatly and legibly as possible, to write with the worst possible scrawl. He was advised to say to himself, "now I will show people what a good scribbler I am!" And at that moment in which he deliberately tried to scribble, he was unable to do so. "I tried to scrawl but simply could not do it," he said the next day. Within forty-eight hours the patient was in this way freed from his writer's cramp.... (Frankl, 1967, p. 4)

Frankl attributed the success of paradox, in part, to humor. He claimed that paradox allows individuals to place distance between themselves and their situation. New (humorous) perspectives allow clients to let go of symptoms. Frankl considered paradoxically facilitated attitude changes to represent deep and not superficial change.

Given that Frankl emphasized humor as the therapeutic mechanism underlying paradoxical intention, it fits that he would use a joke to explain how paradoxical intention works:

> The basic mechanism underlying [paradoxical intention]...can best be illustrated by a joke....A boy who came to school late excused himself to the teacher on the grounds that the icy streets were so slippery that whenever he moved one step forward he slipped two steps back again. Thereupon the teacher retorted, "Now I have caught you in a lie—if this were true, how did you ever get to school?" Whereupon the boy calmly replied, "I finally turned around and went home!" (Frankl, 1967, pp. 4–5)

Frankl believed paradoxical intention was especially effective for anxiety, compulsions, and physical symptoms. He reported on numerous cases, similar to the man with writer's cramp, in which a nearly instantaneous cure resulted from the intervention. In addition to ascribing the cure to humor and distancing from the symptom, Frankl emphasized that paradox teaches clients to intentionally exaggerate, rather than avoid, their existential realities.

REFLECTIONS

Think of a time when you had an annoying physical symptom that seemed beyond your control (e.g., an eye twitch, excessive sweating). Do you think intentionally "trying" to produce the symptoms could give you more control over them?

Cognitive (Meaning) Reframing

Cognitive reframing has its origins in Adler's individual psychology. However, Frankl also employed this technique, as well as cognitive therapists Albert Ellis and Aaron Beck.

Frankl (1967) described reframing (although he didn't refer to it as reframing) in the following case example:

> An old doctor consulted me in Vienna because he could not get rid of a severe depression caused by the death of his wife. I asked him, "What would have happened, Doctor, if you had died first, and your wife would have had to survive you?" Whereupon he said: "For her this would have been terrible; how she would have suffered!" I then added, "You see, Doctor, such a suffering has been spared her, and it is you who have spared her this suffering; but now you have to pay for it by surviving and mourning her." The old man suddenly saw his plight in a new light, and reevaluated his suffering in the meaningful terms of a sacrifice for the sake of his wife. (pp. 15–16)

Frankl's emphasis was on helping his clients find meaning. His meaning reframes flowed from the classic Nietzsche quote offered earlier—"He who has a why to live." In the preceding case, suffering without meaning produced clinical depression. However, when Frankl gave the man contextual meaning for his suffering, the depression lifted.

As we discuss existential skills (or interventions), we're reminded that Adams (2016) recently offered a warning of how skills can degrade into techniques:

> In our work the danger of slipping from skills into technique is ever present and existential therapists are certainly not immune to this danger; it is a human failing that we can fall into looking for short cuts— but if we adhere to existential and phenomenological principles of reflexivity we will both reduce the danger and increase the awareness of its occurrence. (p. 60)

Awareness and Existential Integration

As an existential therapist, how do you know what directions to go with clients? The general answer to that question is toward self-awareness. During counseling, there are moment-to-moment dimensions to self-awareness that can and should be developed and harnessed to move clients toward existential integration (Schneider, 2008). These include:

- Constriction.

- Expansion.

- Centering.

It is helpful for existential therapists to understand these here and now phenomenological therapeutic moments.

Constriction, Expansion, and Centering

Mahoney (1991) wrote that all individuals experience natural human rhythms of expansion and constriction. This involves intermittent drawing inward (constriction) and venturing outward (expansion). Expansive periods involve growth, risk, and moving forth assertively into the world. Constrictive periods involve inhibition and a retreat from contact with others and the outside world.

As individuals deal with threatening life circumstances or opportunities, shifting from expansion to constriction to expansion is healthy. There are obvious times when we should shrink and other times to enlarge ourselves. Different situations produce a natural rhythm between expansion and constriction.

In existential integrative psychotherapy, Schneider (2008, 2010) focuses clients not only on awareness of their personal constriction and expansion experiences, but also on understanding the meaning of these natural patterns. As clients work on developing awareness and understanding their personal meanings, existential integrative therapy moves clients toward a centering experience or "the capacity to be aware of and direct one's constrictive and expansive potentialities" (Schneider, 2010, p. 2). The goal is to be in the center while observing and intentionally embracing constriction and expansion behaviors.

Existential Therapy in Action: Brief Vignettes

In existential therapy, therapists are intermittently nondirective and directive, sometimes tracking their clients' emotions, anxiety, and avoidance and other times directing or leading them into deeper emotional waters. Existential therapy emphasizes the therapist as an instrument of change—therapists develop an I-Thou relationship and then respectfully push clients to face and address difficult issues. Being an instrument of change places a burden on therapists. Doing existential therapy requires substantial training. Existentialists also recommend personal psychotherapy for therapists.

Vignette I: Using Paradox

Reginald was a 29-year-old biracial history professor. He came to therapy for a variety of reasons and worked extensively on these issues over about nine months.

BRAIN BOX

4.1 Existential Problems with Neuroscience

Existentialists have a problem with neuroscience. Actually, because existentialists often don't agree much with each other, it would be more accurate to say that some existentialists have a problem with neuroscience. Better yet, some existentialists have problems (plural) with neuroscience.

Existentialists worry that neuroscience cannot adequately address concepts like *love* and *free will*. I should note that this worry is a normal worry, not a neurotic worry. Speaking for existentialists, which is always a risky business, I'd venture to say that they don't feel the least bit neurotic about neuroscience.

Also, existentialists doubt that electrical, chemical, cellular, and structural analysis of an individual can do justice to that individual's nuanced decisions, emotions, relationships, and impulses. To be honest, what I just wrote is a vast understatement. Existentialists believe there's no chance in hell that human understanding of neural networks can ever match the awe and mystery of humans and humanity.

It should be noted, however, that despite their worry and doubt, existentialists see potential value in neuroscience. However, there can't be any value in neuroscience if neuroscientists and neuroscience fans band together to boil down human experience into neatly wrapped packages of neurochemicals. Instead, as van Deurzen has recommended, going forward, neuroscientists should collaborate with psychotherapists and philosophers to ensure that neuroscience conclusions don't oversimplify and mislead the public or helping professionals about the intricacies of human experience. Existentialists always eschew oversimplification.

About halfway through his therapy, Reginald brought up a relatively minor issue that caused him significant distress. The issue was excessive sweating. He reported feeling out of control. These feelings typically began when he felt anxiety and began sweating profusely. He had tried various strategies to control his sweating, but had been unsuccessful. He told a story of when he was challenged on a lecture issue by a student in class. During the exchange, he started sweating so badly that his glasses fogged over and he had to remove them.

The therapist guided Reginald to explore his feelings of being out of control. Reginald shrank away from that part of his experience. He was intelligent, athletic, and in control of his life. He told his therapist:

> I like feeling in control. It's who I am. It's what I'm comfortable with.

The therapeutic discussion ranged back and forth from Reginald's intellectual talk of being comfortable to his gut-level distress over sweating. There weren't many therapeutic openings, so the therapist gave Reginald the following assignment:

> Reginald, trying harder to control your sweating hasn't worked. I have a new idea, but it's just an experiment. The next time you're in a situation and you begin sweating, just notice it and say to yourself—in your head, not aloud—"Go ahead and sweat away. Sweat as much as you want. Sweat as much as you need." Try to make yourself sweat more.

Reginald reluctantly agreed to the homework assignment. The next week he came to therapy with good news:

> I tried to make myself sweat more and I think the reverse happened. I stopped sweating sooner!

In their discussion that day, Reginald's therapist guided him toward a number of resolutions. These were cognitive and behavioral resolutions rooted in existential philosophy. Reginald resolved to:

- Embrace his sweating.

- Tell people he sweats a lot sometimes, rather than trying to hide it.

- Tell people—including himself—"I'm glad I sweat easily because it's a great way for the body to cool and cleanse itself."

- Tell himself that he loves himself—even when feeling out of control and even when sweating profusely.

At the end of therapy Reginald's decreased need for control had a positive effect on several different areas of his life.

Vignette II: Using Confrontation and Visualization to Increase Personal Responsibility and Explore Deeper Feelings

Francie, a Native American counselor-in-training, was working with Sophia, an 18-year-old Latina woman. Sofia agreed to attend counseling to work on her sarcastic and disruptive behaviors within a residential vocational training setting. Her behaviors were costing her freedom at the residential setting and contributing to the possibility of being sent home. Sofia wanted to stay in the program and complete her training, but her behaviors seemed to communicate otherwise.

Sofia: I got in trouble again yesterday. I was walking on the grass and some "ho" told me to get on the sidewalk so I flipped her off. Mr. Baker saw me. So I got a ticket. That's just bullshit.

Francie: You sound unhappy about getting in trouble, but you also think the ticket was stupid.

Sofia: It WAS stupid. I was just being who I am. All the women in my family are like this. We don't take shit.

Francie: We've talked about this before. You just don't take shit.

Sofia: Right.

Francie: Can I be straight with you right now? Can I give you a little shit?

Sofia: Yeah. In here it's different.

Francie: On the one hand you tell me and everybody that you want to stay here and graduate. On the other hand, you're not even willing to follow the rules and walk on the sidewalk instead of the grass. What do you make of that?

Sofia: Like I've been saying, I do my own thing and don't follow anyone's orders.

Francie: But you want to finish your vocational training. Why not walk on the sidewalk? That's not taking any shit. That's the same rule that everybody has. All you're doing is giving yourself trouble.

Sofia: I know I get myself trouble. That's why I need help. I do want to stay here.

Francie: What would it be like for you then...to just walk on the sidewalk and follow the rules?

Sofia: That's weak brown-nosing bullshit.

Francie: Will you explore that with me? Are you strong enough to look very hard right now with me at what this being weak shit is all about?

Sofia: Yeah. I can take whatever. What do you want me to do?

Francie: Let's get serious. Relax in your chair and imagine yourself walking on the grass and someone asks you to get on the sidewalk and then you just see yourself smiling and saying, "Oh yeah, sure." And then you see yourself apologize. You say, "Sorry about that. My bad. You're right. Thanks." What does that bring up for you?

Sofia: Goddamn it! It just makes me feel like shit. Like I'm f-ing weak. I hate that.

In this counseling scenario Sofia is using reactive, angry behaviors to compensate for inner feelings of weakness and vulnerability. Francie used Sofia's own language to confront the discrepancy between what Sofia wants and her provocative behaviors. As you can see from this dialogue, the confrontation (and Francie's use of an interpersonal challenge) gets Sofia to look at what her discrepant behavior is all about. This cooperation wouldn't be possible without an earlier development of a therapy alliance … an alliance that seemed deepened by the fact that Sofia saw Francie as, in her words, "another Brown woman." After the confrontation and cooperation, Francie shifted into a visualization designed to focus and vivify Sofia's feelings. This process enabled Sofia to begin exploring why cooperating with rules triggered intense feelings of weakness. Later in counseling, Sofia articulated what it meant for her to feel weak and how that meaning permeated and affected her life.

CASE PRESENTATION

Existential therapy focuses on moment-to-moment experiences inside and outside therapy. As such, this approach is not well-suited to the diagnostic and treatment planning components of the medical model. Generally, existential therapists aren't keen on treatment planning. If therapy is a spontaneous and authentic interpersonal encounter designed to open individuals to their deepest sensations and emotions, how can we design a concrete treatment plan with objective and measurable goals?

When discussing existential treatment planning, it's best to begin with apologies and caveats. Our efforts to capture existential depth psychotherapy will fall short. Our treatment plan will be either too narrow or too broad. Nevertheless, in this section we try squeezing an existential therapy perspective into a medical model treatment plan.

Jyoti Nanda (2010) originally reported the following case. Nanda described using the popular mindfulness-based cognitive therapy (MBCT; Segel, Williams, & Teasdale, 2002) approach within existential psychotherapy to facilitate awareness of existential-phenomenological client themes. Nanda referred to integration of mindfulness and existential psychotherapy as **mindfulness-based existential therapy** (MBET).

Nanda was working with John, a man who came to therapy with depressive symptoms. John was on antidepressant medications. The event that triggered his depressive symptoms was the stillborn death of his second child. He came to see Nanda about five months after the stillborn delivery. Nanda reflected on their first session:

> John spoke of his immense sorrow and loss at the death of their child. As I listened attentively sharing the space, the silences, and offering my understanding of his pain, what felt palpable for me was the human to human connection we had. While I have never experienced loss of this nature, I am no stranger to the human condition of pain and suffering. Perhaps John sensed that I felt his pain with him. (pp. 338–339)

During the second session John asked Nanda for direct advice.

John: You must have had other people come to you with similar issues. In your experience, what do you think we should do, should we try for another baby?

Jyoti: You are asking me to choose for you whether you and your wife should try for another baby?

John: What do you think?

Jyoti: I can see it is a difficult situation, and choosing one way or another is really hard. It is a real dilemma. I really don't know what the right choice is for you John. What do you and your wife want? [John looked crestfallen.]

John: That's not very helpful. If I knew I wouldn't ask you.

Jyoti: You're looking for an answer from me, and I am not telling you what to do! [Pause.] I can understand you are perhaps disappointed and perhaps annoyed with me. But you are assuming that I should know what the right choice is for you. [John looked perplexed and thoughtful.]

Jyoti: [Silence.] Perhaps the answer will emerge as we find greater clarity about what is really important for you. (p. 339)

This exchange illustrates several features of existential therapy. First, the therapist doesn't offer advice. Existentialists don't believe one individual (even therapists) should usurp another person's choice. Recall the theoretical concept of dasein choosing. This doesn't mean Nanda never provides information to clients; it just means that when it comes to big life decisions, existential therapists don't presume to know what's best for another person (Sapienza & Bugental, 2000).

Second, Nanda is transparent and open about discomfort she has in response to her client's direct question. There's no muted, emotionally neutral response followed by unguided exploration. Nanda states bluntly: "I really don't know what the right choice is for you John."

Third, Nanda is modeling an existential way of being. In reflecting on this interaction, she noted:

> Over the course of therapy, my feeling comfortable with the not knowing, and moving away from being the expert who knows the "right" answers from the "wrong" ones and someone who provides explanations of what is "wrong" and knows how to fix it, perhaps facilitated for John a greater comfort in staying with his own not knowing, and uncertainty. (p. 339)

Accepting one's inability to control or know everything is a tenet of existential therapy. To some extent, Nanda is *teaching* or demonstrating this value to her client by refusing to take on the role of an all-knowing expert and modeling an ability to acknowledge not knowing.

The Problem List

Although existentialists don't like shrinking their clients' existential being-in-the-world into a problem list, an initial and tentative list for John might look like this:

1. The client has grief and sadness related to profound disappointment and loss associated with the stillborn death of his second child.

2. The client is partially alienated from or avoiding his own experiences (taking antidepressants and wishing for a quick fix or answer to a question that is so deep it deserves greater reflection).

3. Contemporary world values are acting on the client in ways that suggest he should somehow know the right thing to do and/or control uncontrollable life events.

As they continued working together, John reported that he was having strong negative feelings about not having a second child—and these feelings were often triggered by seeing other couples with two children. His feelings also were linked to a sense of personal failure. Nanda empathized with John's feelings, while, at the same time, gently confronting his failure feelings. After John disclosed what seeing "two-child" families brought up for him, Nanda stated:

Jyoti: It feels like a reminder yet again, and of course it is painful. But I am not sure I understand why you see this as personal failure.

John: I didn't do enough to save our baby.

Jyoti: [After a silence, then saying softly.] Didn't do enough to save your baby?

John: I should have saved our baby, somehow.

Jyoti: Of course, you wish you could save your baby. So do I. But I am still not sure I understand why you see this as personal failure.

John: It is pathetic, I feel helpless that as a father I couldn't somehow save our baby.

Jyoti: [After a silence, saying softly.] Of course, it feels helpless. Both of us wish it had been different. But can either of us control outcomes in matters like birth and death, which are beyond our control? Can either you or I know when and how we or our loved ones are going to die?

At this point Nanda is helping John face an ultimate concern of death. She explains her reasoning:

> The existential theme that we have choice only within the givens of our human limitations…informed my intervention. I acknowledged our shared desire for life, and our shared helplessness of what is beyond our control—birth and death. This intervention was possible within the strength and quality of our relationship. Without the relationship itself, it could sound quite clinical. Our being together with the pain and suffering of the human condition, sharing the space and the silences allowed John to reflect and re-consider what was beyond our control, that possibilities arise within limitations. (Nanda, 2010, p. 340)

In addition to the confrontation, Nanda is existentially sharing space with John. This involves helping him "be" rather than moving into an urgent sense of "doing" (as if there is really anything to be done in this situation).

Problem Formulation

From the existential perspective, client problems are usually related to diminished awareness, avoidance of death anxiety, and avoidance of acknowledging the limits of his personal control. As we look back at John's problem list and construct a problem formulation, it's important to note that John's three identified problems are overlapping and interrelated. Existentialists see human existence as indivisible.

Chronic grief and sadness are directly related to John's other two problems. As he contemplates trying to conceive another child so soon after his loss, he's avoiding a full experience of his grief. In this way if he and his wife can deny their anxiety and sadness by focusing on hope for another child, they can postpone facing their human limitations. Additionally, he is allowing his personal illusions of control over the uncontrollable to protect him from fully facing death and other parts of life over which he has no control.

The problem formulation involves John's impulses to do something to eradicate his and his wife's suffering. His efforts to do things and not feel things or be with the situation indicate an avoidance pattern. Actively avoiding his experience isn't working for John. He needs an intervention that helps him to be more fully with his grief and loss.

Interventions

The therapy process that helps John overcome his problems isn't brief or surface-focused. The interventions, if we can call them that, include the therapy skills discussed previously in this chapter. These include: (a) establishing a therapeutic presence (i.e., I-Thou relationship), (b) empathic mirroring, (c) feedback and confrontation, (d) cognitive reframing, and (e) monitoring of John's constrictions and expansions with the goal of him becoming a more centered, self-aware, and intentional being.

Earlier in the therapy Nanda challenged John's beliefs about himself being a failure. She described this confrontation:

> Acceptance of his personhood did not prevent me from challenging his "sedimented" beliefs. Our relationship could be seen close to Buber's I-Thou relationship. It offered inclusion of John's way of being by me, while also confronting him with my own being. (p. 340)

As individuals work in existential therapy, they have intermittent insights into why they are the way they are. Although behavioral and cognitive therapists dismiss the importance of insight, insight can provide fuel for change in the form of enhanced motivation.

Nanda and John worked together for just over two years. During therapy John was able to face the domineering nature of his father, his suppressed interest in art (he was in the finance industry, a choice his father made for him), and the connection between his moods and fluctuations in the stock market. He also faced many other issues.

When John experienced a regression to deep sadness and grief during the one-year anniversary of his child's death, he asked Nanda for specific techniques to deal with his emotions. As a mindfulness-based practitioner, Nanda felt the tug to teach John mindfulness strategies. She also experienced the prohibition against techniques commonly associated with existential therapy. She articulated her dilemma:

> I was aware that the Existential approach is technique averse. I needn't have offered mindfulness. I could have stayed with John's distress in the manner that I had, and clearly that was helpful to John. Yet there was this whole body of research that I was aware of. Should I deny John a practice that I believed would be helpful? (p. 341)

After an internal debate about whether to integrate mindfulness into existential therapy, Nanda decided to go ahead, primarily because of the compatibility between mindfulness and existential acceptance of self. This decision included an open discussion with John that she had never previously provided mindfulness training to a client. Consequently, for several sessions, Nanda provided 30 minutes of mindfulness training for John, without charge, prior to beginning their usual therapy sessions.

As John became more skilled with mindfulness and continued with existential therapy, he decided to discontinue his antidepressant medication. Another open discussion occurred and then John worked with his medical provider to titrate down and discontinue the antidepressants. Nanda described John's experience:

> As the effect of the medication started waning, John reported experiencing his feelings with greater intensity, with greater nuances to them. The irritations and frustrations had greater intensity, but so did the pleasures and the joys. Colours seemed more vivid, and sharper. What he was noticing had a wider range to them. (p. 345)

When therapy ended, John was able to function well without medication. He reported being more confident, less self-critical, not depressed, more calm, more able to be assertive with his father, and better able to talk about his needs with his wife. He also wrote Nanda a long description of the benefits he attributed to learning mindfulness techniques.

Outcomes Measurement

Determining how to measure treatment outcomes from an existential perspective is a perplexing conundrum. Therefore, before describing how to measure existential treatment outcomes, we focus first on existentialist arguments for why treatment outcomes are not measured.

Traditional existential therapists don't believe in using assessment instruments. You can probably guess why that's the case, but here's a short story describing their rationale.

I (John) recall talking with colleagues over lunch at the University of Portland about their possible Myers-Briggs Type Indicator scores. The resident existentialist was clearly offended. She countered with, "You wouldn't use a questionnaire like that with a client, would you?" When I said I might, because I thought questionnaires and personality assessment could sometimes be therapeutic, she explained how using such an instrument was unethical and inauthentic. She had an important point: all assessment measures fall short of measuring a real, complete person—and labels can be constrictive. Existential therapy should expand, and not narrow, an individual's self-conception. The danger is that psychometric assessment procedures can be antitherapeutic and/or unethical because they label and limit people, and can detract from the human encounter.

Despite philosophical opposition, all practitioners are called to monitor outcomes and demonstrate accountability. Perhaps the best solution to this predicament is to use a few standardized outcome measures focusing on depression, personal misery, meaninglessness, or positive dimensions of life (e.g., happiness), while acknowledging that these are wholly insufficient for measuring existential therapy outcomes.

Another approach is to narrow the focus for existential therapy and then seek to measure specific behaviors or behavior patterns linked to this narrower focus. In this regard, Keshen (2006) recommended "a more succinct, well-defined, and research-friendly model of existential psychotherapy" (p. 285). In his model, the focus is on purposelessness (or meaninglessness). He explained his rationale:

> I have decided to focus on purposelessness because, in my opinion, this concept is more tangible and amenable to quantitative evaluation than other existential foci (e.g. scales are available to evaluate purpose in life).

If you're operating from an existential perspective (or if Nanda wanted to employ specific outcome measures in her work with John), tools for monitoring client outcomes might include some of the following:

- Life Regard Index (Battista & Almond, 1973).

- Purpose in Life Test (Crumbaugh, 1968; Crumbaugh & Henrion, 1988).

- Seeking of Noetic Goals Test (Crumbaugh, 1977).

- Spiritual Meaning Scale (Mascaro, Rosen, & Morey, 2004).

- Toronto Mindfulness Scale (Lau et al., 2006).

For a discussion on psychometric evaluations of meaning measures, see Mascaro and Rosen (2008).

EVALUATIONS AND APPLICATIONS

Existential philosophers, therapists, and clients are meaning makers. They embrace and value awareness. In theory, these are good things. However, what's the empirical, cultural, gender, and spiritual status of contemporary existential therapy practice?

Evidence-Based Status

Schneider (2010) described several concrete changes clients can experience if and when they achieve existential integration:

> The result for ... clients is that they experience more centeredness, less panic, and a greater capacity to respond to rather than react against their fears. For some clients, moreover, and for many at varying degrees of intensity, there is a whole new orientation toward life following [existential integrative] therapy; I call this orientation awe-inspiring: a renewed sense of the humility and wonder, indeed, amazement before, the whole of life. (p. 12)

Schneider's description of existential therapy outcomes poses significant challenges for efficacy and effectiveness researchers. How can "a renewed sense of the humility and wonder, indeed, amazement before, the whole of life" be measured? Schneider isn't using modernist scientific language.

For many students imbedded in a society where individuals who are experiencing emotional distress or behavioral disorders go to see a medically oriented provider, receive a treatment, and then experience symptom relief, it can be difficult to think like an existentialist. Philosopher-empiricists are looking at the whole research enterprise differently. To them, existentialism makes psychotherapy more empirical, more experiential, and more real (May, 1983). Existentialism also questions the philosophical presumptions of various scientific methods. What scientists see depends on the lenses they're wearing.

Rather than pursuing so-called empirical support, existentialists want to expose how the ubiquity of subjectivity makes modernist science no more valid than other ways of knowing (van Deurzen, 2014b). The modernist scientific paradigm is only one lens for examining therapy outcomes; many other are available. May (1983) wrote:

> [As] Helen Sargent has sagely and pithily remarked, "Science offers more leeway than graduate students are permitted to realize." (pp. 45–46)

Existentialists contend that scientific outcome studies only represent a single perspective on the nature and effectiveness of therapy. Of course, you (and psychotherapy efficacy researchers) may see this position as a cop-out—especially because based on contemporary scientific standards, no RCTs attest to the efficacy of existential therapy. There are case studies and anecdotal reports, but even those usually don't meet scientific standards for single-case controlled research with psychometrically acceptable measures.

Very little modernist empirical research on existential therapy efficacy or effectiveness exists. In the most recent meta-analysis study, 15 studies were reviewed, including 1,792 participants. The researcher (Wong) concluded that meaning therapies had positive effects on meaning-related measures; other approaches were less consistent in their outcomes, but the potential for existential approaches to produce positive outcomes was affirmed. In particular, the researchers noted there was "Particular support for structured interventions incorporating psychoeducation, exercises, and discussing meaning in life directly and positively with physically ill patients" (Vos, Craig, & Cooper, 2015, p. 115).

Specific outcomes research also has shown the following: one research team found significant changes in endocrine and immune functioning in breast cancer patients who participated in existential group therapy (van der

Pompe, Duivenvoorden, Antoni, & Visser, 1997). This and other studies suggest that existential group therapy is both meaningful and helpful to individuals facing life threatening illnesses (Kissane et al., 2003; Page, Weiss, & Lietaer, 2002).

Related to, but not exactly addressing, broad existential approaches, published research on the effectiveness of paradoxical intention is positive. For example, in a meta-analysis, paradoxical intention was shown to have a 0.99 effect size (K. A. Hill, 1987). This suggests that the average client treated with paradoxical approaches is better off than about 84% of clients not receiving treatment. This is a large effect and slightly better than the .80 effect size typically attributed to psychotherapy in general (M. L. Smith, Glass, and Miller, 1980). A separate meta-analysis of paradoxical techniques was similarly positive (Shoham-Salomon & Rosenthal, 1987).

In support of existential common sense, there's also research attesting to the importance of meaning in psychological well-being (Wong, 2015, 2017). Fry (2001) reported that personal meaning, religiosity, and spirituality predicted psychological well-being more significantly than other factors, such as physical health and social support. There is also substantial evidence attesting to the contribution of meaningfulness as an aid in acculturation (Pan, Wong, Chan, & Joubert, 2008; Pan, Wong, Joubert, & Chan, 2008), buffering of stress (Mascaro & Rosen, 2006), and in reducing depressive symptoms (Mascaro & Rosen, 2005). More recently, an intensive analysis of four existential therapist–client dyads showed promising and positive results (Alegria et al., 2016).

We should be clear that based on contemporary scientific standards, none of the preceding research establishes existential therapy efficacy. However, in a review of Schneider's *Existential Integrative Psychotherapy* book, renowned psychotherapy researcher Bruce Wampold (2008) wrote: "I have no doubt that [existential integrative] approaches would satisfy any criteria used to label other psychological treatments as scientific. Our current consensus on what is scientific is excruciatingly narrow." Wampold's statement is based on the primacy of common relationship factors and integrative principles in the implementation of existential therapy (Alegria et al., 2016; Wong, 2015).

At this point, quantitative counseling and psychotherapy research emphasize symptom reduction, and although symptom reduction can be a very good thing, it's not everything. Existentialists might ask: "Would you rather experience symptom reduction as your therapy outcome or a renewed sense of amazement before the whole of life?" Now that's a therapy outcome worth striving for (see Putting It in Practice 4.2 for musings from an existentially oriented practitioner).

Cultural Sensitivity

White, male, European philosophers originally articulated existential theory. Although many of these philosophers were part of an oppressed Jewish minority, multiculturalists and feminists still critique the existential perspective and approach as too narrow. Prochaska and Norcross wrote, "Only in existentialism and the movies do people possess unlimited freedom, construct their own meanings, and execute boundless choices. Save it for the wealthy, worried well" (Prochaska & Norcross, 2003, p. 133).

Despite the Prochaska and Norcross critique, existential approaches *can be* diversity sensitive. As is often the case, it seems diversity insensitivity lies less with specific theories and more with individual practitioners and how theories are applied.

- Vontress and Epp (2015; Vontress, Johnson, & Epp, 1999) have written about cross-cultural counseling cases and issues from an existential perspective.

- The research of Paul Wong (2008a, 2008b, 2017) has shown the importance of meaningfulness as a broad common therapy factor and as a specific contributor to acculturation.

- Schneider (2010) noted in his existential integrative approach that when therapists confront client resistances, they should be careful not to do so out of cultural misunderstanding.

Writing from an existential perspective, counselor educator Kurt Kraus articulated the need for cultural sensitivity:

I remember a time in my career when with great anticipation I moved far away to be able to work with more clients of color, specifically Native American and African American peoples. When I found myself, White, for the first time in the minority, still experiencing life as a majority person, it dawned on me: Being well-trained and embracing a multicultural experience did not make me ready; privilege is a skin that is hard to shed.

When a supervisee errantly says, "I know how you feel" in response to a client's disclosure, I twitch and contort. I believe that one of the great gifts of multicultural

---

PUTTING IT IN PRACTICE

4.2 Existential Musings

Reproduced with permission of Dr. Kurt Kraus

Kurt Kraus of Shippensburg State University wrote the following commentary:

As an existentially oriented phenomenologist I am often caught, conflicted by my theoretical belief and my clients' desire for someone in my chair whose beliefs are not mine. For me, the honoring of suffering, the anxiety of limited time, and the continuous presence of opportunities for personal meaning are often the very things that clients initially wish to be rescued from. It is a conflict that I very much appreciate, one that makes for the most interesting therapeutic alliances.

I often ask myself, "How can theory help me better understand some aspect of the client with whom I am working?" Then, when I have located one or two meaningful theoretical explanations, I store them in some recess of my mind—sort of as a backdrop or a map. I then proceed with my client to construct a personal meaning for his or her experience. One thing I try to remember is that no map gets you where you want to be: movement does. It is, at least in therapy, the actual journey that gets the client where he or she chooses to go. Learning theories is a valuable means to an end, but the path is not paved in theory; it is paved with experience.

Sometimes theory texts afford great fantasy. If I adhere to one theory I will be clear in my professional identity, "I am a reality therapist, or I am Rogerian, or I do rational emotive behavior therapy." At times through these fantasies I can be Melanie Klein, or Alexander Wolfe, or Judith Jordan. I've never held on long enough to emerge as anyone other than myself—full of doubts about the veracity of any one theory over all others. Instead I study those that fit me, content in the notion that the theories of counseling and psychotherapy are quite occasionally transmogrified through my interpretation and through my unique relationship with each and every client with whom I sit.

---

awareness...for me [is] accepting the limitations to the felt-experience of empathy. I can only imagine how another feels, and sometimes the reach of my experience is so short as to only approximate what another feels. This is a good thing to learn. I'll upright myself in my chair and say, "I used to think that I knew how others felt too. May I teach you a lesson that has served me well?" (K. Kraus, personal communication, August, 2002)

Kraus's multicultural lesson reminds us of Yalom's (1980, 1989, 1999, 2003) discussions of existential isolation. As individual entities traveling through human existence, we're destined to be separate from everyone else. To say "I know how you feel" is a violation of existential reality. It's an easily detectable interpersonal deception. Perhaps the best we can do is to communicate to clients, regardless of their cultural background, "I'm trying my best to understand how you feel," keeping in mind that we'll never fully succeed.

Gender and Sexuality

After decades of discrimination and disrespect, affirmative psychotherapy for gay, lesbian, and other sexual minority clients has become the standard of care. Beginning with

an affirmation of sexual identity is viewed as making counseling or psychotherapy more accessible for vulnerable sexual minorities who seek therapy. However, for an approach like existential therapy, where meaning and identity are a central focus of therapeutic questioning, the fit between affirmation and therapy process is less than ideal (du Plock, 2014).

If sexuality and existential thought is of interest to you, *Sexuality: Existential Perspectives* (Milton, 2014) is recommended. This text takes you through a rather classic intellectual and existential look at sexuality, where everything is questioned. The pros and cons of affirmative therapy are presented. Naturally, the existentialists who wrote *Sexuality* embrace the idea that nearly everything is about sex, except sex, which can hold meaning about virtually everything else.

Whether we're talking about feminism or sexual diversity, existential approaches can be enlightening and threatening—which from an existential perspective is likely to be the whole point: hardly anything should be comfortable. For practitioners who use this approach, what's most essential is the use of a clear informed consent form, so clients can know, up-front, exactly what they're getting themselves into.

Spirituality

A deeply spiritual client was engaging in guided imagery with an existential therapist. The client "discovered" a locked door in the basement of his "self."

"What's behind the door?" the therapist asked.

"It's darkness," he said. With shivers of fear, he added, "There's dread. It's dread of being unacceptable. Unacceptable to God. Even worse, it's my dread of being unforgiveable."

"Shall we go in?" asked the therapist.

Silence.

"Let's wait a moment and breathe. I'm wondering if you can even get in the door. I'm wondering if you want to get in. There's no rush. We know where the door is. We can wait. Or we can create a key and try to get in. But first let's wait here and breathe before deciding anything."

For two minutes, client and therapist sat breathing together. The paralyzing fear diminished and the client said, "I have a key. Let's look inside."

"Yes. Let's look inside."

The key opened the lock. The door creaked open. In the dreaded darkness, there was light. In a dialogue with the dread and unforgiveable, the client found a broad sense of love and acceptance. There were tears of relief. His spiritual load was lightened. His basement demons were exorcised.

In this chapter we've discussed the deep and profound quality of existential psychotherapy. Schneider (2010) called it "Rediscovery of Awe." Frankl and Wong referred to it as the pursuit of meaning. In existential therapy, meaning and awe are individualized, as is spirituality. There's great potential in combining the existential and the spiritual in psychotherapy, but clients should be forewarned and informed: combining the spiritual and existential isn't about formulaic or surface explanations; it requires a commitment to go deep and explore doubts, uncertainties, and core vulnerabilities.

CONCLUDING COMMENTS

Existential therapy is about finding meaning. It's about facing that we die and that often we are very much alone. Existential therapy is also about taking personal responsibility for the glorious choices we have before us each day…each hour…each minute…each second. To quote Mary Oliver (1992), "What is it you plan to do with your one wild and precious life?"

CHAPTER SUMMARY AND REVIEW

Existential approaches to counseling and psychotherapy are based on existential philosophy. Existential philosophy focuses on self-awareness of the inevitable conditions of human existence, including personal responsibility, isolation, death, and meaning. Existential counseling, psychotherapy, and philosophy are at odds with the quick-fix mentality of the medical model.

Many different existential philosophers (and therapists) have contributed to the development of existential therapy. These include, but are not limited to, Søren Kierkegaard, Friedrich Nietzsche, Jean-Paul Sartre, Georg Hegel, Viktor Frankl, Rollo May, James Bugental, Irvin Yalom, Emmy van Deurzen, and Kirk Schneider. Existentialists tend to view life in dialectical extremes; knowledge and meaning are derived from integrating extremes. For example, Viktor Frankl suggested a Statue of Responsibility on the West Coast to balance the Statue of Liberty on the East Coast. Experiencing and embracing personal freedom, combined with complete responsibility for one's actions, stimulates individuals to learn and grow.

Key principles of existential theory cover a vast range of human experiencing. These key principles are: (a) the I-Am experience; (b) the four existential ways of being (i.e., umwelt, mitwelt, eigenwelt, uberwelt); (c) the daimonic; (d) the nature of anxiety and guilt; (e) existential psychodynamics or ultimate concerns (i.e., freedom, death, isolation, meaninglessness); and (f) self-awareness. Based on these principles, existential therapists don't believe in contemporary models of psychopathology. Instead, they work with individuals and groups to achieve greater awareness, meaning, and to embrace all of what life has to offer—including death. Embracing all of existence allows life to be lived to the fullest.

Existential therapists don't use prescribed techniques or procedures. Instead, they seek to form an "I-Thou" relationship with clients and use it for therapeutic change. Existential therapy process typically involves an intense interpersonal encounter that includes deep emotional sharing, feedback, confrontation, and encouragement. The therapist is fully present, and may use empathic mirroring, focusing, paradoxical intention, reframing, and other skills, as needed. The goal is to achieve greater awareness and existential integration.

Existential approaches aren't a good fit with modern empirical science. Existentialists even define the word empirically differently than contemporary scientists. Nevertheless, among other positive outcomes, recent research indicates that existential approaches have a positive effect on clients' sense of meaning in life. Also, from a common factors perspective, existential approaches meet criteria for being considered scientifically supported.

Depending on individual practitioners, existential approaches may or may not be sensitive to culture, gender, sexuality, and spirituality. As a general approach, there are signs of exquisite sensitivity to these client variables, but the number of publications that systematically examine culture, gender, sexuality, and spirituality are limited. Overall, existential therapists are open to helping clients boldly explore whatever issues they bring into therapy.

EXISTENTIAL KEY TERMS

Cognitive reframing

Confrontation

Daimonic

Dasein

Dasein choosing

Dialectic

Dialectical process

Eigenwelt

Existential integrative therapy

Existential philosophy

Existential psychodynamics

Feedback

I-Am experience

Invoking the actual

I-Thou relationship

Logotherapy

Mindfulness

Mindfulness-based existential therapy

Mitwelt

Neurotic anxiety

Neurotic guilt

Normal anxiety

Normal guilt

Ontological experience

Paradoxical intention

Presence

Uberwelt

Ultimate concerns

Umwelt

CHAPTER 5

Person–Centered Theory and Therapy

LEARNER OBJECTIVES

- Define person-centered theory and therapy
- Identify key figures and historical trends in the development, evolution, and application of person-centered theory and therapy
- Describe core person-centered theoretical principles
- Describe and apply person-centered therapy principles, strategies, and techniques
- Analyze cases that employ person-centered approaches
- Evaluate the empirical, cultural, gender, and spiritual validity of person-centered therapy
- Summarize core content and define key terms associated with person-centered theory and therapy

If Freud was a pessimist and Adler and Jung were optimists, then Carl Rogers—the primary force behind person-centered counseling—was a super-optimist. He was a staunch believer in the capacity for persons, when unfettered by social and familial obstacles, to develop into positive, creative, flexible, and altruistic beings.

Beginning in the 1940s and through the 1960s, Rogers developed his distinct approach to psychotherapy. His foundational, groundbreaking idea was to trust the client's own sense of what was wrong and what to work on. He wrote:

[I]t is the client who knows what hurts, what directions to go in, what problems are crucial. (Rogers, 1961, pp. 11–12)

Initially, Rogers named his approach "nondirective counseling." Later, he renamed it "client-centered therapy." In the 1960s, he renamed it "person-centered therapy."

INTRODUCTION

Rogers developed a radical new approach to therapy; he advocated respectful listening and an authentic counselor–client connection. Additionally, in all aspects of his life, he strove to be a genuine and open person; he strove to be himself. As he engaged with clients, he put himself so deeply into their worlds that he could sometimes feel their feelings right along with them.

What Is Person–Centered Therapy?

Person-centered therapy is a humanistic or existential-humanistic approach. **Person-centered therapy** includes the following characteristics:

(a) The therapist trusts the client.

(b) Therapists hold attitudes toward clients of congruence, unconditional regard, and empathic understanding.

(c) The therapeutic relationship is the mechanism of change.

(d) Therapists don't educate clients, interpret their conflicts, or identify faulty thoughts or behaviors; instead, they establish relational conditions that allow clients to engage in natural self-discovery and personal growth.

Person-centered therapy isn't a good fit with the medical model. This is partly because person-centered therapists view clients (and not therapists) as the ultimate experts. Other professional helpers, even existential theorists, sometimes viewed Rogers's optimistic perspective as frustratingly naïve. For example, Rollo May, who regarded Rogers quite highly, once wrote to Rogers:

You paint a seductive and enticing picture, and anyone would like to believe it. But I recall the words of Warren Bemis in the film of you and him, when he characterized your viewpoint as "devilishly innocent." (Kirschenbaum & Henderson, 1989, p. 242)

We hope, despite his innocence, that you will embrace Carl Rogers and his person-centered theory and therapy with every part of your being. As one of the best listeners to walk the planet, Rogers deserves to have us stop whatever else we might be doing and, for the moment, listen to him.

Carl Rogers

Carl Rogers
(*photo courtesy of the Department of Special Collections, Davidson Library, University of California, Santa Barbara*)

Carl Ransom Rogers was born in 1902. He was the fourth of six children raised on a farm in Illinois. His parents were rigid fundamentalist Christians, whom Rogers later described as "absolute masters of repressive control" (quoted in Bankart, 1997, p. 292). His parents taught him to keep his distance when socializing with outsiders:

Other persons behave in dubious ways which we do not approve in our family. Many of them play cards, go to the movies, smoke, dance, drink, and engage in other activities, some unmentionable. So the best thing to do is to be tolerant of them, since they may not know better, and to keep away from any close communication with them and live your life within the family. (Rogers, 1980, p. 28)

As an adult, Rogers embraced a philosophy starkly different than what he experienced growing up with his parents. In contrast to the flavor of the preceding quotation, as a therapist Rogers worked to create an accepting, nonjudgmental therapeutic environment where clients were free to be themselves.

Rogers went to college, initially following the family policy of majoring in agriculture. He became involved in the campus Young Men's Christian Association and was one of 12 students chosen to attend the World Student Christian Federation Conference in Peking, China (Rogers, 1961).

It was on this trip that, according to Bankart, "Rogers appears to have become Rogers" (Bankart, 1997, p. 292). He was away 6 months. This experience produced at least the following changes in Rogers: (1) he rejected his parents' conservative religious ideology, (2) he decided to marry his childhood sweetheart, and (3) he decided to pursue graduate studies at the liberal Union Theological Seminary in New York City.

HISTORICAL CONTEXT

After two years at Union Theological Seminary, Rogers transferred (across the street) to Columbia University

Teachers College to study clinical psychology. His training was squarely within the domain of American academic psychology. At the time, Columbia University was a bastion of John Watson's behaviorism (see Chapter 7). Consequently, Rogers was more oriented toward psychological science than other theorists we've discussed to this point. He had a strong interest in research and was the first person to tape-record actual therapy sessions. This drive to understand the mechanics and effectiveness of therapy led some to refer to him as "the founder of psychotherapy research" (Bohart, 1995, p. 87; Rogers, 1942b).

Professional and Personal Influences

Rogers's first clinical position was at the Adlerian-oriented Rochester Child Guidance Center. During this time, academic psychologists were staunchly behavioral, while clinicians were trained in either psychoanalytic or Adlerian (neoanalytic) theory. Rather than work in a laboratory, Rogers wanted to help people, so he was trained in a diagnostic-prescriptive analytic approach:

Rogers originally went to … Rochester … believing in this diagnostic, prescriptive, professionally impersonal approach, and it was only after actual experience that he concluded that it was not effective. As an alternative, he tried listening and following the client's lead rather than assuming the role of the expert. This worked better, and he discovered some theoretical and applied support for this alternative approach in the work of Otto Rank and his followers. (Raskin & Rogers, 1989, pp. 160–161)

Rogers attended a 3-day seminar with Otto Rank (Kramer, 1995). He later reported to his biographer, "I became infected with Rankian ideas" (Kirschenbaum, 1979, p. 95). He also learned a great deal from a Rank-trained social worker, Elizabeth Davis, whom he hired to work for him in Rochester. Ms. Davis was able to tune into and articulate clients' feelings in a way that fascinated Rogers; he credits her as an inspiration. "What later came to be called the reflection of feeling sprang from my contact with her," he noted (Rogers & Haigh, 1983, p. 7).

During his 12 years in Rochester, Rogers wove many elements of Rankian practice into his approach, including the following ideas:

- Clients have creative powers.

- Therapy should help clients accept their personal uniqueness and self-reliance.

- The client is the central figure in the therapy process; the therapist only helps clients access their powers of self-creation.

- Therapists shouldn't seek to educate clients.

- Therapists shouldn't foster dependency with clients by becoming love objects.

- Therapy works when clients are able to experience the present within the therapy setting (adapted from Raskin & Rogers, 1989).

President Franklin D. Roosevelt and his social policies influenced Rogers. Roosevelt was optimistic, empowered individuals by involving them in social and political activities, and supported the creativity of his subordinates (Bohart, 1995). Rogers also was influenced by the philosophy of John Dewey, whose statements about human development goals are similar to Rogers's goals for and attitudes toward psychotherapy: "Not perfection as a final goal, but the ever-enduring process of perfecting, maturing, refining, is the aim in living" (Dewey, 1920, pp. 176–177).

Rogers's relationship with his wife powerfully affected him. She was the first person with whom he ever had a caring and sharing relationship. In 1980, at the age of 75, he wrote,

> During the first two years of marriage we learned … through some chance help, that the elements in the relationship that seemed impossible to share—the secretly disturbing, dissatisfying elements—are the most rewarding to share. This was a hard, risky, frightening thing to learn, and we have relearned it many, many times since. (Rogers, 1980, p. 32)

Honoring Clients and a Way of Being

Consistent with his theory, Rogers gave the most credit for the development of his theory to his clients; he learned from them about what helped and what didn't help. In a published interview, his daughter, Natalie, articulated this, "… like Carl, I stayed open to learning from my clients. They are always our best teachers." (J. Sommers-Flanagan, 2007, p. 122).

Rogers's first book, *The Clinical Treatment of the Problem Child* (1939), helped him obtain a professorship in psychology at Ohio State University. He then published *Counseling and Psychotherapy* (1942a), which pioneered the use of audiotape recordings to study therapy. This was another example of his emphasis on learning from his clients.

As Rogers articulated and expanded his approach, it became clearer that traditional terminology used to describe how psychotherapists behaved didn't fit. Instead of technical strategies, Rogers was developing and emphasizing a way of being with clients. His *way of being* incorporated his deep trust for clients and his trust in the power of healing relationships.

Struggles with Psychiatry and Psychology

Rogers developed client-centered therapy in a climate openly hostile to his ideas. He was a radical, who rapidly built a devoted following both within academia and out in the real world. He fought the behaviorism of academic psychology as well as the psychoanalysis that ruled the clinical world. One of his biggest battles was with psychiatry, a battle that he described as "an all-out war" (Rogers, 1980, p. 55).

During the 1930s and 1940s, psychiatry opposed letting non-physicians practice psychotherapy. They also fought desperately to keep psychologists from assuming leadership roles within mental health agencies. At Rochester, Rogers battled with psychiatry to maintain his leadership position at the guidance clinic. Later, at the University of Chicago counseling center, he was accused of practicing medicine without a license and launched a "blistering counterattack" to earn psychologists the right to practice psychotherapy (Rogers, 1980, p. 54).

Rogers also had his battles with mainstream academic psychology. His ongoing debates with the noted behaviorist B. F. Skinner are legendary (see Chapter 7).

Professional counselors, social workers, and educators often have been more receptive to Rogers and his work than psychologists. He summarized his feelings about his impact on psychology:

> I believe an accurate statement would be that we have had very little influence on academic psychology, in the lecture hall, the textbook, or the laboratory … by and large, I think I have been a painfully embarrassing phenomenon to the academic psychologist. I *do not fit*. Increasingly I have come to agree with that assessment. (Rogers, 1980, p. 51)

Rogers was indeed an unusual academic psychologist. He fraternized with social workers, counselors, and teachers, even publishing in their journals. He rebelled against assigning course grades, allowing students to be their own teachers and evaluators. He participated in encounter groups and expressed disdain for the class lecture. Nevertheless, Rogers still earned significant respect from academic psychology. He was elected president of the American Psychological Association in 1946 and received a prestigious award for scientific contribution in psychology in 1956. These honors led Rogers to refer to himself as a "respected gadfly" within psychology (1980, p. 53).

Evolution of Person-Centered Therapy

Rogers's practice of person-centered theory and principles fit into four developmental periods.

- *Nondirective counseling*: This period began in the 1940s. It included Rogers's growing aversion to directive, traditional therapy methods. He published *Counseling and Psychotherapy* (Rogers, 1942).

- *Client-centered therapy*: In the 1950s Rogers changed the name of his approach from nondirective counseling to client-centered therapy. Rogers published *Client-Centered Therapy* (1951); he changed from a nondirective process to an honoring of the client's ability to lead in therapy.

- *Person-centered therapy*: During the 1960s, Rogers focused on self-development. His work was associated with the human potential movement. He published *On Becoming a Person* (1961) and moved from academia at the University of Wisconsin to California in 1964. In 1968, Rogers founded the Center for the Study of the Person in La Jolla, California. He applied person-centered theory to new situations, publishing *Freedom to Learn: A View of What Education Might Become* (1969). He changed the name of his approach to person-centered therapy (PCT).

- *Worldwide issues*: In the 1970s and 1980s, Rogers began dedicating much of his work to improving interracial relations and world peace. He met with Irish Catholics and Protestants, visited South Africa

and the Soviet Union, and conducted cross-cultural workshops in Brazil, Dublin, and Hungary. He published *Carl Rogers on Personal Power* (1977) and *A Way of Being* (1980).

As happens with most enduring theories, person-centered principles have moved beyond Rogers (Cain, 2010). Contemporary variations on PCT, including motivational interviewing, are discussed later in this chapter.

REFLECTIONS

Can you let clients lead during therapy? Try on the idea of letting go of your direction and goals, and letting clients talk about whatever they view as important.

THEORETICAL PRINCIPLES

The person-centered approach includes a theory of personality and a theory of psychotherapy. The theory of personality has 19 propositions (Rogers, 1959). Rogers noted that his personality theory "is the most thoroughly ignored of anything I have written" (Rogers, 1980, p. 60). The reason it gets ignored might be due to its complexity and idiosyncratic language (see Table 5.1 for our "translation" of Rogers's 19 propositions).

Table 5.1   Rogers's 19 Theoretical Propositions—Translated

Rogers's original statements	First person translations
1. All individuals (organisms) exist in a continually changing world of experience (phenomenal field) of which they are the center.	I am at the center of understanding myself, other people, and the world—although my perspective is constantly changing.
2. The organism reacts to the field as it is experienced and perceived. This perceptual field is "reality" for the individual.	I have a unique sense of reality. I base this on my direct experiences and my perceptions of my experiences.
3. The organism reacts as an organized whole to this phenomenal field.	When I react, I am an indivisible whole.
4. A portion of the total perceptual field gradually becomes differentiated as the self.	Over time, I learn who I am from personal experiences.
5. As a result of interaction with the environment, and particularly as a result of evaluational interaction with others, the structure of the self is formed—an organized, fluid but consistent conceptual pattern of perceptions of characteristics and relationships of the "I" or the "me", together with values attached to these concepts.	Evaluations from others have an especially significant influence on my sense of self. My own direct experiences also influence my sense of self. I organize a "self" and develop values from these experiences.
6. The organism has one basic tendency and striving—to actualize, maintain and enhance the experiencing organism.	More than anything else, I move in directions toward self-maintenance and self-actualization.
7. The best vantage point for understanding behavior is from the internal frame of reference of the individual.	If you want to understand me, you should tune into how I see myself, others, and the world.

8. Behavior is basically the goal-directed attempt of the organism to satisfy its needs as experienced, in the field as perceived.

9. Emotion accompanies, and in general facilitates, such goal-directed behavior, the kind of emotion being related to the perceived significance of the behavior for the maintenance and enhancement of the organism.

10. The values attached to experiences, and the values that are a part of the self-structure, in some instances, are values experienced directly by the organism, and in some instances are values introjected or taken over from others, but perceived in distorted fashion, as if they had been experienced directly.

11. As experiences occur in the life of the individual, they are either, (a) symbolized, perceived, and organized into some relation to the self, (b) ignored because there is no perceived relationship to the self structure, (c) denied symbolization or given distorted symbolization because the experience is inconsistent with the structure of the self.

12. Most of the ways of behaving that are adopted by the organism are those that are consistent with the concept of self.

13. In some instances, behavior may be brought about by organic experiences and needs which have not been symbolized. Such behavior may be inconsistent with the structure of the self but in such instances the behavior is not "owned" by the individual.

14. Psychological adjustment exists when the concept of the self is such that all the sensory and visceral experiences of the organism are, or may be, assimilated on a symbolic level into a consistent relationship with the concept of self.

15. Psychological maladjustment exists when the organism denies awareness of significant sensory and visceral experiences, which consequently are not symbolized and organized into the gestalt of the self structure. When this situation exists, there is a basic or potential psychological tension.

16. Any experience which is inconsistent with the organization of the structure of the self may be perceived as a threat, and the more of these perceptions there are, the more rigidly the self structure is organized to maintain itself.

17. Under certain conditions, involving primarily complete absence of threat to the self structure, experiences which are inconsistent with it may be perceived and examined, and the structure of self revised to assimilate and include such experiences.

18. When the individual perceives and accepts into one consistent and integrated system all her sensory and visceral experiences, then she is necessarily more understanding of others and is more accepting of others as separate individuals.

19. As the individual perceives and accepts into his self structure more of his organic experiences, he finds that he is replacing his present value system—based extensively on introjections which have been distortedly symbolized—with a continuing organismic valuing process.

I act in ways designed to meet my needs, as I perceive them.

My emotions are motivating forces and influence me in determining what is important.

My values come from my experiences, but sometimes I take them in from others, as if they were my own.

When I have experiences, I either:

- Take them into my sense of self.
- Ignore them because they seem irrelevant.
- Deny or distort them to fit my sense of who I am.

Most of the time I behave in ways that are consistent with my sense of self.

Sometimes underlying factors that I don't completely understand leak through and influence my behavior. When this happens, I may not take responsibility for my behavior.

When I am tuned into and accept my whole experience, I feel integrated, adjusted, and congruent.

When I disconnect from or deny my organismic experience, I experience tension and disturbance.

When my experiences are inconsistent with how I see myself and the world, I feel threatened. The more threatened I feel, the more rigid I am in clinging to my perspective.

When I feel safe, I can consider new experiences and I can change the ways I view myself and the world.

When I am accepting of myself, I am more accepting and understanding of others.

The more I'm able to be aware of and accept my direct life experiences, the more I am able to become a person of my own making, rather than adopting the ideas and perspectives of others.

Note: First person translations were inspired by the Palace Gate Counselling Service Blog: https://palacegatecounsellingservice.wordpress.com/

Theory of Personality

Rogers's 19 theoretical propositions can be overwhelming. Therefore, we've collapsed them into four core features. His original 19 propositions are summarized in Table 5.1.

Self-Theory

In the tradition of William James, Mary Calkins, and Gordon Allport, the person-centered theory of personality is a self-theory (Bankart, 1997). Rogers postulated that every person exists within an ever-changing world in which that person is the center. In addition, he believed the self is not a fixed structure, but a structure in process that includes both stability and change.

Rogers used the term **organism** to refer to the locus of all psychological experience. The organism is a holistic entity that responds to the ever-changing world. The organism is the entire realm of an individual's experience, while **the self** is the portion of the organism that becomes the "me" part of personal identity. Rogers's self has both conscious and unconscious components.

The distinction between organism and self makes it possible for an individual's self to be inconsistent with its overall psychological experience. This discrepancy is **incongruence**. When the self's experiences and perceptions are consistent with the organism's total experience, there is congruence. Congruence between self and organism is desirable; it leads to adjustment, maturity, and optimal functioning. The developmental goal is for the "me" or self to grow so that it takes up the entire organism (and in the process, the self becomes more fully aware—meaning that self-awareness is a key part of human or self-development).

Phenomenology and the Valuing of Experience

Rogers summarized his personality theory, "This theory is basically phenomenological in character and relies heavily upon the concept of self as an explanatory concept" (Rogers, 1951, p. 532). Person-centered theory places a premium on direct personal experience. Although both intellectual/rational thinking and feelings/emotions are valued and crucial informational sources, experiencing is considered a more direct way of accurately knowing oneself and the world. Bohart wrote, "experiencing is the direct, nonverbal sensing of patterns and relationships in the world, between self and world, and within the self. It includes what is often called 'intuitive knowing'" (Bohart, 1995, p. 91).

In part, person-centered therapy (PCT) helps clients be more open to all personal or organismic experiences. True learning, inside and outside therapy, occurs through lived experience wherein the "self" evaluates whether a particular action or feeling is enhancing or not.

Learning and Growth Potential

Rogers believed people have a single source of energy within them that moves them forward "toward actualization, involving not only the maintenance but also the enhancement of the organism" (Rogers, 1980, p. 123). The energy includes moment-to-moment learning. He called this an **actualizing or formative tendency**, a tendency to "move toward greater order, complexity and interrelatedness" (Bohart, 1995, p. 89).

Some of this viewpoint came from his childhood farming and outdoor experiences; he saw the potential for many things in nature to grow and evolve toward completeness. He also attributed this viewpoint to writers and philosophers, including Kurt Goldstein, Harry Stack Sullivan, Abraham Maslow, and Karen Horney.

The Rogerian actualizing tendency is similar to Adler's striving for superiority and Freud's small, but persistent, voice of reason. The idea of an actualizing tendency or developmental force underlying human behavior is an oft-repeated theoretical concept (J. Sommers-Flanagan & Sommers-Flanagan, 2011).

Conditions of Worth

Along with the organism's need to maintain and enhance itself, there are additional, learned needs. The main two are the need for positive regard and the need for self-regard. The **need for positive regard** is defined as the need to be prized and loved; the **need for self-regard** involves individuals' need to view themselves in a positive light.

As babies and toddlers grow in relationship with caretakers, two things happen. First, the baby begins developing greater self-consciousness. Second, the growing child develops a need for positive regard or approval; this need becomes so powerful that children automatically look to caretakers and significant others for approval.

Rogers describes an ideal situation:

> If an individual should *experience* only *unconditional positive regard*, then no *conditions of worth* would develop, *self-regard* would be unconditional, the needs for *positive regard* and *self-regard* would never be at variance with *organismic evaluation*, and the individual would continue to be *psychologically adjusted*, and would be fully functioning. (Rogers, 1959, p. 224, italics in original)

Unfortunately, no child's home life is ideal, so although children consistently watch and listen for approval, it's not always forthcoming. Consequently, children begin distinguishing between approved and disapproved feelings and actions. They sense and understand the conditions of worth present in their lives (Kohn, 2005). **Conditions of worth** are the standards that children and adults believe they must meet to be acceptable and worthy of love. Over time, these conditions lead individuals toward an external locus of evaluation.

Eventually, children internalize caretakers' appraisals, despite the fact that these appraisals are inconsistent with their overall organismic experiences; the alternative is to suffer painful **negative self-regard** (i.e., self-deprecatory thoughts and feelings). For example, if a young girl who loves to play roughly and aggressively consistently experiences disapproval from her parents, she is forced to one of three conclusions:

1. When I play rough, I am bad (negative self-regard).

2. My parents don't like me because I play rough (negative regard from others).

3. I don't like to play rough (denial of a desirable organismic experience).

None of these conclusions honor the child's organismic love of rough-and-tumble play. Consequently, one way or another, she experiences incongruence.

Over time, if children continually experience conditions of worth incongruous with their organismic values, a conflict or discrepancy may develop between their conscious, introjected values and their unconscious genuine values. Hall and Lindzey (1970) described this seed of psychopathology:

> If more and more true values of a person are replaced by values taken over or borrowed from others, yet which are perceived as being his [sic] own, the self will become a house divided against itself. Such a person will feel tense, uncomfortable, and out of sorts. He will feel as if he does not really know what he is and what he wants. (p. 532)

When individuals lose touch with their true selves and desires, they experience anxiety or distress. This involves a discrepancy or incongruence between the real self and ideal self. The **real self** is the total organismic self—the self linked to actualization. In contrast, the **ideal self** has unattainable shoulds derived from dysfunctional societal and familial conditions of worth. Incongruence can be associated with a growing but vague awareness of discomfort, of something being wrong. This discomfort likely arises when clients experience organismically desirable feelings, actions, or opportunities, but have internalized values from others that prohibit these feelings.

For example, when the little girl with aggressive impulses grows up and has an opportunity for aggressive expression, difficult internal events may take place. She may project her desires for aggressiveness onto others, she may become aggressive and then condemn herself, or she may let loose with her aggression but then deny that she experienced any anger or gratification. Unless her self becomes congruent with reality, she will continually reinterpret reality to fit whatever self-picture she needs to maintain, no matter how much this violates her true experience and external reality.

Rogers believed individuals are capable of perception without awareness. He referred to this process as subception (McCleary & Lazarus, 1949). **Subception** occurs when a person unconsciously perceives a threatening object or situation (see *The Gift of Fear*, de Becker, 1997, for a related example). The object or situation is threatening because it represents an inner conflict between real desires and introjected desires. Subception is likely to result in visceral reactions (e.g., increased heart rate, high blood pressure, rapid respiration, and other anxiety sensations).

To summarize, Rogers emphasized several concepts in his personality theory: it's a theory of self, of experience, of striving for maintenance and enhancement of the self, and of learned needs for positive regard. It's also a theory of discrepancy, because it's the discrepancy between self and organismic experience, between what the caretakers value and what the organism values, that contributes to psychopathology.

Theory of Psychopathology

Elucidating psychopathology from a person-centered perspective, Bohart (1995) wrote:

> Psychological problems are neither faulty beliefs or perceptions nor inadequate or inappropriate behavior per se. As humans confront challenges in life they will periodically misperceive, operate on mistaken beliefs, and behave inadequately. Dysfunctionality occurs if we *fail to learn* from feedback and therefore remain stuck in our misperceptions or inadequate behavior. Dysfunctionality is really a failure to learn and change. (p. 94)

The failure to learn from experience best characterizes person-centered psychopathology. This is why person-centered therapists work so hard to help clients become open to and evaluate their experiences. Rogers posited that threats to the "self-structure" could cause rigidity. Rigidity is consistent with a state of being threatened. Safe environments can help clients return to a state of openness to experiencing and learning.

Psychopathology occurs when clients accept introjected parental conditions of worth instead of modifying their self-concept based on moment-by-moment, day-by-day personal experiences. Since every moment is an opportunity for new learning, closing down and avoiding or ignoring these moments is pathological. Similarly, in their person-centered approach, **emotion-focused therapy**, Greenberg and colleagues focus especially on the importance of openness to emotional processing in normal human functioning (Greenberg, 2015). When clients are unaware of or unable to access important emotional information, dysfunctional behavior or interpersonal interactions result.

Theory of Psychotherapy

Rogers's theory of psychotherapy flows from his theory of personality. If psychopathology stems from judgment or invalidation of the self, then a nonjudgmental atmosphere will facilitate psychological health. This is the foundation of Rogers's theory of psychotherapy.

If therapists trust clients and provide a therapeutic relationship, then clients will begin trusting themselves to process their (emotional) experiences and move toward greater psychological health. Rogers described his theory of psychotherapy in one sentence:

> If I can provide a certain type of relationship, the other person will discover within himself the capacity to use

that relationship for growth, and change and personal development will occur. (Rogers, 1961, p. 33)

Rogers (1957) outlined six conditions of effective psychotherapy in a landmark article, "The Necessary and Sufficient Conditions of Therapeutic Personality Change."

For constructive personality change to occur, it is necessary that these conditions exist and continue over a period of time:

1. Two persons are in psychological contact.
2. The first, whom we shall term the client, is in a state of incongruence, being vulnerable or anxious.
3. The second person, whom we shall term the therapist, is congruent or integrated in the relationship.
4. The therapist experiences unconditional positive regard for the client.
5. The therapist experiences an empathic understanding of the client's internal frame of reference and endeavors to communicate this experience to the client.
6. The communication to the client of the therapist's empathic understanding and unconditional positive regard is to a minimal degree achieved. (Rogers, 1957, p. 95)

Although six conditions are listed, when professionals talk about Rogerian or person-centered core conditions, they're typically referring to the big three relational conditions: (a) congruence, (b) unconditional positive regard, and (c) empathic understanding.

Congruence

Congruence is authenticity or genuineness. Rogers claimed, "The more that I can be genuine in the relationship, the motre helpful it will be" (Rogers, 1961, p. 33). Rogers was specific about why therapist congruence is essential. He stated, "It is only by providing the genuine reality which is in me, that the other person can successfully seek ... the reality in him" (1961, p. 33).

Congruence implies that therapists should acknowledge and express both positive and negative feelings in therapy. Rogers emphasized the importance of expressing less positive feelings when he wrote, "I have found this to be true even when the attitudes I feel are not attitudes with which I am pleased, or attitudes which seem conducive to a good relationship. It seems extremely important to be real" (1961, p. 33).

REFLECTIONS

What do you think helps congruence be therapeutic? If you were a client, what sorts of congruence would you find helpful? Along with your classmates, make a list of genuine therapist disclosures that could be destructive.

Unconditional Positive Regard

Unconditional positive regard includes acceptance and respect. Clients are valued as separate individuals whose thoughts, feelings, beliefs, and entire being are openly accepted, without conditions. If therapists accept clients, then clients can explore who they are and what they want. Through acceptance, therapists lead clients toward self-acceptance.

Rogers described unconditional positive regard:

> The more acceptance and liking I feel toward this individual, the more I will be creating a relationship which he (sic) can use. By acceptance I mean a warm regard for him as a person of unconditional self-worth— of value no matter what his condition, his behavior, or his feelings. It means a respect and liking for him as a separate person, a willingness for him to possess his own feelings in his own way. (Rogers, 1961, p. 34)

Rogers went on to say that therapists should accept moment-to-moment changes and inconsistencies that clients manifest during sessions. He took a stand against more directive interventions, such as confrontation and interpretation. At one moment a client may identify feelings of love and kindness toward someone, and at the next there may be rage. To person-centered therapists, both love and rage are important, valid, and equally worthy of attention. By listening and reflecting back the depth of both feelings, therapists allow clients to accept or modify self-expression. Rogers believed complete acceptance combined with accurate empathy could lead clients to awareness of previously unknown parts of the self.

Empathic Understanding

Empathic understanding is the therapeutic condition professionals most directly link to Carl Rogers and PCT. Rogers became increasingly skilled at noticing and reflecting his clients' feelings. When listening to audiotapes of his work, you can hear him slip into the client's world, seeing and experiencing what the client sees and experiences. He sometimes shifted from using second-person pronouns ("When he left, you felt betrayed and alone") to using first-person pronouns ("If I'm getting this right, it's almost like, here I was, wanting to be close, and then he just up and left, and I felt betrayed and alone"). This pronoun shift is called **walking within**.

A tremendous amount of research has focused on empathy in psychotherapy (Elliott, Bohart, Watson, & Greenberg, 2011; Watson, Steckley, & McMullen, 2014). Nearly everyone acknowledges that empathy is central to psychotherapy. It has been referred to as a prerequisite for therapy (Freud, 1923), a necessary condition (Bohart & Greenberg, 1997), and an enabling factor (Hamilton, 1995). Empathy has many effects and functions. It's the basis for forming a patient–therapist bond (Kohut, 1959); it dissolves client fear and denial (Barrett-Lennard, 1981); and it enhances client safety (Jenkins, 1997).

Empathy is multidimensional (Clark, 2007, 2010; Elliott, Bohart, Watson, & Greenberg, 2011). In 1964, Rogers implied three ways of empathic knowing.

- *Subjective empathy*: Identifying with clients in the here and now through intuition, and imagining your clients' experiences.

- *Interpersonal empathy*: Communication back and forth about clients' phenomenological experiences (including feedback from clients).

- *Objective empathy*: Using theoretical knowledge and resources to better understand clients (Clark, 2010).

More recently, neuroscience researchers have identified brain structures, networks, and neurochemicals underlying empathic responsiveness (Gonzalez-Liencres, Shamay-Tsoory, & Brüne, 2013; see Brain Box 5.1).

Empathic understanding is used in conjunction with the other two therapeutic conditions, congruence and unconditional positive regard. In the following excerpt, Rogers (1961) discussed the importance of experiencing and conveying *both* empathy *and* unconditional positive regard:

> Acceptance does not mean much until it involves understanding. It is only as I understand the feelings and thoughts which seem so horrible to you, or so weak, or so sentimental, or so bizarre—it is only as I see them as you see them, and accept them and you, that you feel really free to explore all the hidden nooks and frightening crannies of your inner and often buried experience. (p. 34)

Despite all the research confirming that empathy is crucial to therapy, Natalie Rogers has described it as the most underestimated condition leading to positive change in therapy (J. Sommers-Flanagan, 2007). Many professionals don't seem to comprehend the power of empathic responding.

The Magic of Person-Centered Listening

Person-centered listening requires a commitment to taking the time and creating the space. The whole approach goes against the "quick fix" attitude that many people have toward mental health problems.

Years ago, when I (John) was deep into the "Carl Rogers" stage of my development, I recruited a volunteer from an introductory psychology course to create a person-centered video demonstration. I obtained informed consent and started listening.

The session didn't start smoothly. I was trying to demonstrate paraphrasing, feeling reflections, summarizing, and walking within, but mostly I felt inarticulate and dull. About halfway through the 50 minute session, I offered a poorly worded summary. I was doing what I could to be present in the room and connect, but not with much skill. After the summary, there was silence. I stayed with the silence, worried about not having been very clear, but trying to trust that the woman knew where to go next. She did. She seemed to gather courage, and then disclosed a sexual abuse experience. She told her story, cried, and spoke about her journey toward inner strength. I listened supportively, in awe of the magic of person-centered listening.

As Rogers (1961) said, "The client knows what hurts." It's up to us to provide an environment where clients can find and express their pain, and reactivate their actualizing tendency (see Putting It in Practice 5.1: An Interview with Natalie Rogers).

PUTTING IT IN PRACTICE

5.1 Why Is the Person-Centered Approach Undervalued in the United States?

An Interview with Natalie Rogers

In the following excerpt from two telephone interviews, Natalie Rogers discusses why person-centered approaches tend to be undervalued or overlooked in the United States.

John Sommers-Flanagan (JSF): Other than the managed-care focus and an emphasis on quick fixes, can you think of any reasons why more American therapists aren't practicing PCT?

Natalie Rogers (NR): That's a good question. Most psychology students I know only get a chapter or two in the academic world, and they don't really understand in any depth what the person-centered approach is about. And, most importantly, I think they haven't experienced it. They've read [about] it and they've talked about it and they've analyzed it, but my own belief is that it really takes in-depth experiencing of the client-centered approach to know the healing power of empathy and congruence and unconditional positive regard.

JSF: Students get more of an intellectual understanding, but you're just not seeing them get the experiential part.

NR: Even the intellectual understanding is very superficial, because they read maybe a chapter and watch the old Gloria film (Rogers, 1965). The fact that there have been 16 books written on client-centered therapy and a lot of other books now that Carl's passed away and the research that he did is so profound ... the in-depth research on what actually helps clients go deeper into their feelings and thoughts.

JSF: Right.

NR: You know, [how therapists can help clients go deeper into their feelings and thoughts] is hardly ever mentioned in academia as far as I know.

JSF: And what I remember from our last conversation was that you said you thought it didn't happen in the U.S. at all and maybe a little bit in Europe?

NR: I think it does happen a lot more in Europe, and most particularly in the United Kingdom, Scotland, and England. They have really excellent training programs in the client-centered approach ... in Germany they have a several-year, very extensive training program that's also linked in, I believe, to becoming accredited or licensed as a therapist ... none of that is here in the States.

JSF: That seems to reflect our own emphasis on the surface or the quick fix as well in that people just really haven't gone deeper and experienced the power of PCT.

NR: Right. And then again I think the other point is that the ego needs of the therapists [appear] to be strong here. Therapists in this country seem to need to have the attitude that "I have the answers" or at least that "I know more," and it's ... the old medical model that we still hold on to in this country a lot. The doctor knows what he needs to diagnose and treat, knows what's wrong and that there are ten steps to fix it.

JSF: Right, which seems to be the opposite of the person-centered therapy of "trust the individual, trust the person."

NR: Not just seems to be, it is the opposite. So, to actually believe, to have faith in the individual, to have faith that each person has the answers within himself or herself if given the proper conditions, and that's a big if. That philosophy takes a great deal of humility on the part of the therapist.

JSF: For us to realize that we don't have all the answers for another person.

NR: Right. I kind of like the gardener metaphor. That I'm the gardener and I help till the soil and I help water the plants and fertilize the plants, and care for them. And I need to understand what the plant needs, what conditions that plant needs for it to actually grow and become its full potential. That's very different. That's what I see as one metaphor for being a therapist. I don't know all the answers, but I'm a person who creates the conditions for the person to grow.

JSF: What would you tell beginning therapists that would help them see the tremendous value of following person-centered principles?

NR: Well, I always ask my students to examine their own beliefs about psychotherapy and about what it is that creates psychological feelings and growth. I think it's a philosophical, spiritual belief system that we're looking at. People are using the words "methods" and "techniques," which always puts me off, because although there certainly are methods that we use, it's much bigger than that. It's a belief system about the connection between mind, body, and emotional spirit. And so I ask them what do they believe creates personal growth, and what have they experienced themselves that creates growth, and we get them to think and talk about their religious experiences, their psychotherapy experiences, their experiences in nature, and their experiences in relationships. I think they're all profound. And then when we focus in on relationships, which is what psychotherapy is about, then I want them to experience ... from me or my colleagues in hour-long demonstrations what it means to be client-centered. So then they experience it as witnesses and they can experience it as a client.

JSF: So more students need to directly experience, or at least witness, client-centered therapy.

NR: Let me give an example. I was talking to a colleague once who had some of my training and who said that he was now using brief therapy, brief psychotherapy, and I admitted I didn't really know what that was. We decided that he'd have to give me some ideas on what that's like. So I listened to him describe the theory and practice for quite a while and questioned him about it. And as he was describing it, I was wondering, how would I feel if I were in the client's chair and this was what was being done to me. And so then I felt pretty uncomfortable, and thought, "I guess I wouldn't like it." So I asked him, "Have you ever been a client in this kind of brief therapy yourself?" And he said "No," and I thought that was inexcusable. To practice something on somebody else that you haven't experienced in-depth yourself. I think it is inexcusable. So that illustrates in a kind of negative way the point that I wanted to make. You really need to have in-depth experience of that which you are going to have other people do.

REFLECTIONS

What might be some problems with having too much empathy? If you have issues that overlap with a client who you're seeing, what challenges could arise? Would having issues similar to your client make it harder or easier to sit back and let the client talk freely, without your commentary?

THE PRACTICE OF PCT: A WAY OF BEING WITH CLIENTS

Generally speaking, there are two types of person-centered therapists: classical and contemporary. **Classical person-centered therapists** hold at least the following beliefs:

1. The six core conditions (Rogers, 1957) are necessary and sufficient.

2. The 19 Rogerian (1959) theoretical propositions remain definitive.

3. Nondirective therapist attitudes and behaviors are "essential to practice" (from Cain, 2010, p. 44).

In contrast, **contemporary person-centered therapists** believe in person-centered principles, but are sometimes active and directive. They also blend PCT with other approaches. For example, focusing therapy (Gendlin, 1981, 1996), emotion-focused therapy (Greenberg, 2015), and motivational interviewing (Miller & Rollnick, 2013) are all foundationally person-centered, but use alternative methods to facilitate client self-exploration and self-development.

Natalie Rogers
(*photo reproduced with permission of Fiona Chang*)

Decades of psychotherapy research confirm that the relationship between therapist and client is a fundamental, active therapeutic factor (Bachelor, 2013; Lambert, 1992; Norcross, 2011). Because Rogerian principles, like Adlerian principles, are integrated into virtually every other contemporary therapeutic approach, learning PCT is an excellent foundation for becoming any sort of therapist you want to become (J. Sommers-Flanagan & Sommers-Flanagan, 2017).

Assessment Issues and Procedures

Classical person-centered therapists don't employ standardized assessment or diagnostic procedures. Rogers believed that diagnosis was unnecessary and possibly "detrimental to the therapeutic process" (Rogers, 1951, p. 220).

Diagnostic labels can increase psychopathology because they function like conditions of worth. External assessment is intrinsically judgmental and anathema to internal judgments that classical person-centered therapists support. Also, using diagnoses makes it harder to view clients as unique individuals. The person-centered perspective is that designing treatments for specific disorders (e.g., generalized anxiety disorder or post-traumatic stress disorder) misses the point—which is to treat the individual, not the disorder.

Despite problems with diagnosis, person-centered therapists may have to use diagnostic procedures for insurance billing. Also, when communicating with other professionals, therapists may employ diagnostic terminology, but they take care to treat the client as a unique individual who's much more than a label.

Contemporary person-centered approaches sometimes employ assessment procedures. For example, in emotion-focused therapy (EFT) the therapist assesses specific areas of client functioning (Greenberg, 2015). Goldman and Greenberg (1997) explained that assessment procedures are used for idiographic case formulation, that assessments are never performed a priori, and that assessment data emerge best within the safety of a PCT environment. EFT is covered in Chapter 14.

The Therapist's Opening Statement

The opening message given to clients is "You talk and I'll listen and try my best to understand what you're experiencing in your life and in yourself." Rogers provided an excellent model for starting a person-centered therapy session:

> Anything you'd like to tell me about yourself that will help me to know you better, I'd be very glad to hear. (Rogers, 1963)

This opening is similar to the psychoanalytic basic rule or free association. Both approaches use a process where clients talk while therapists listen intently. Despite this commonality, psychoanalytic therapists are listening for material to judge and interpret, while person-centered therapists are listening in order to go as deeply as possible into the client's inner world—without judging. (See Putting It in Practice 5.2: Informed Consent from the Person-Centered Perspective.)

PUTTING IT IN PRACTICE

5.2 Informed Consent from the Person-Centered Perspective

I'm looking forward to working with you in counseling. The purpose of this form is to share information with you about your rights as a client and to tell you what to expect during typical counseling sessions.

The first thing is there's no such thing as a typical counseling session. You are unique and the problems and challenges in your life are unique. As a counselor, it's my job to help you express what you're thinking, feeling, and experiencing. You should think of me as a companion. I will accompany you as you explore yourself, your problems, your life situation, and your personal experiences. I won't tell you what to do in your life. Instead, because the form of counseling I provide is "person-centered" I'll help you focus on your own thoughts and feelings. There are two reasons why I don't "advise" clients. First, you're a different person than I am and therefore I can't and shouldn't tell you how to live your life. Your personal decisions are up to you and I respect and trust your ability to make decisions about your life. Second, I also don't give out expert advice because I've discovered that clients rarely benefit from such advice. You'll benefit more from reflecting on your experiences and then deciding what's right for you.

Even though I won't offer advice, that doesn't mean I won't sometimes express my opinions or feelings during counseling. At times, when I have a strong feeling or reaction, I'll tell you what I'm thinking or feeling as honestly as I can.

Being in counseling isn't easy and it's never an emotionally neutral experience. Sometimes you may feel good because you're getting to express everything you're feeling and thinking while I'm trying my best to listen and understand. At other times you may feel upset because you're talking about emotions that are hard and painful. Counseling isn't a neutral experience because it requires you to face yourself more completely than you do in your ordinary life. It's like scrutinizing yourself in a mirror. Even though the mirror doesn't judge you, you may feel judgmental about things you see. As you explore yourself on the inside and outside, you may feel both pain and joy.

If you have questions or concerns about counseling, ask them any time. I'll do my best to respond to your questions. Overall, my view is that counseling is an excellent opportunity for you to explore, in greater depth, who you are, what you want, and how you want to live. I'm delighted to accompany you on your journey of self-discovery.

Experiencing and Expressing Congruence

Therapists sometimes struggle to understand how to best communicate congruence (Cain, 2010). The most basic question is: "Does being congruent mean I need to tell the client about my every thought and feeling?"

The answer to this question is "No." Although therapists shouldn't be overly cautious about self-disclosing, offering random self-disclosures, no matter how spontaneous, aren't especially therapeutic. Rogers (1957) discussed this issue:

> Certainly the aim is not for the therapist to express or talk about his own feelings, but primarily that he should not be deceiving the client as to himself. At times he may need to talk about some of his own feelings (either to the client, or to a colleague or superior) if they are standing in the way. (pp. 97–98)

Therapist verbal self-censoring is required (Cain, 2010). An excellent way to see how much self-disclosure is appropriate from a person-centered perspective is to listen to Rogers doing therapy. In his therapy recordings, Rogers only occasionally self-disclosed, and did so in the service of furthering the client's therapy work, not for his own ego needs. If you're honest with yourself, most of the time you won't need to disclose because your disclosure won't be relevant or helpful to the client.

Rogers viewed therapist techniques in a manner similar to self-disclosure. When asked if it's ever appropriate for therapists to use techniques, Rogers said "Yes," but only when techniques come up spontaneously, from a genuine or congruent place, and not when they're preplanned.

Experiencing and Expressing Unconditional Positive Regard

Is it possible for therapists to always feel unconditional positive regard toward clients? You're probably shaking your head "no," and if so, you're in good company. Even Rogers didn't think so, referring to his use of the phrase as "an unfortunate one" (1957, p. 98). However, this is the wrong question. The more realistic question is whether it's possible for therapists *to try to feel* unconditional positive regard toward their clients? The answer to this revised question is a cautious "yes." (See Putting It in Practice 5.3.)

The problem of how to best express positive regard remains. Should you do it directly? Would it be appropriate to say, "I accept you completely and totally as the person you are" or "I prize and value your total being?" After all, these are the attitudes that you're trying to experience and convey.

However, the answer to that question is "Absolutely not!" Most therapists eventually get themselves in trouble when they directly express unconditional positive regard

---

PUTTING IT IN PRACTICE

5.3 Stretching Your Ability to Experience Unconditional Positive Regard

Trying to experience and express unconditional positive regard for clients is hard. In the following situations, see if you can imagine yourself feeling that elusive Rogerian attitude.

- You're working with a sex offender who's talking about the gratification he gets from sexual encounters with young children.
- You're working with a battered victim of domestic violence who insists her husband loves her and that she must go back and live with him again—for the fifth time.
- You're working with a pyromaniac. He tells you about how he masturbated after setting a local historical building ablaze.
- You're working with a teen girl. She tells you about using strangulation or the drug ecstasy to increase her sexual gratification.

Do you think you could experience unconditional positive regard in the preceding situations? What might get in the way? Which situations would be easier for you? Which ones would be harder?

One way to experience partial positive regard in these situations is to find compassion within yourself for the suffering human being in the room with you—not positive regard for the behaviors, but for the yearnings, longings, losses, and fears the behaviors represent. Rogers believed every person was born with the potential to develop in positive, loving ways, given the right environment, but some folks don't get much of a chance. When doing person-centered therapy, you become their next chance, maybe their last chance, to be welcomed, understood, and accepted. Your acceptance may create the conditions needed for change.

to clients. First, clients may react by wanting to break down therapy boundaries. Upon hearing positive, loving statements they naturally seek more closeness, perhaps a friendship or romantic relationship. Alternatively, some clients may react with fear. These clients may move away from the intimacy the therapist is offering.

Second, saying "I care about you" or "I won't judge you" can be viewed as phony or unrealistic, especially if you haven't had much time with the client. These statements often backfire because eventually your client will notice ways in which you're judgmental or don't seem to care enough.

If it's inappropriate to directly express unconditional positive regard to clients, then how can you communicate this important message? In our *Clinical Interviewing* text, we've detailed several ways that therapists can indirectly communicate unconditional positive regard (from J. Sommers-Flanagan & Sommers-Flanagan, 2017, pp. 224–225):

1. You arrive on time, ask your clients how they like to be addressed (and then remember to address them that way), listen sensitively, show compassion, and carefully guard the time boundaries around appointments.

   • How would you like me to address you? Do you prefer Mrs., Ms., or something else?

2. You allow clients freedom to talk about themselves in their natural manner.

   • I have information about you from your physician. She said you're experiencing anxiety, but I'd like to hear from you what that anxiety has been like.

3. By remembering your clients' stories, you communicate interest and a valuing of what they're telling you.

   • Earlier today you mentioned wishing your roommate respected you. And now I hear you saying again that you find her behavior disrespectful.

4. When you respond with compassion or empathy to clients' emotional pain without judging the content of that pain, clients can feel accepted.

   • The loss of your job really has you shaken up right now. You're feeling lost about what to do next.

5. Because clients are sensitive to your judgments and opinions, by simply making a sincere effort to accept and respect your clients, you're communicating a message that may be more powerful than any other therapy technique.

   • I know you're saying I can't understand what you've been through, and you're right about that. But I'd like to try to understand, and hear as much about your trauma as you're willing to share.

6. Although direct expression of unconditional positive regard is ill-advised, researchers suggest that direct expressions of encouragement and affirmation for specific behaviors can have a positive effect.

   • "I didn't see you as submissive or weak. In fact, since showing emotion is so difficult for you, I saw it as quite the opposite" (Farber & Doolin, 2011, p. 173).

   • I have confidence in your ability to do this.

   • Thank you for sharing so much about yourself with me.

Most person-centered writers acknowledge a difference between completely accepting all client thoughts, feelings, and behaviors and practical applications of unconditional positive regard. In most cases, a line is drawn between accepting clients' thoughts and feelings versus accepting or endorsing all client behaviors (Cain, 2010). Natalie Rogers described this:

> In terms of Carl's theories about education, I remember hearing him talk and audiences asking about permissiveness and freedom, but I think the permissiveness often has been misunderstood. He said that any thoughts and feelings are OK, but not all behavior is acceptable. Unless that is really made clear, both in the theory and in the practice, it can be disastrous. (J. Sommers-Flanagan, 2007, p. 122)

Experiencing and Expressing Empathic Understanding

Consistent with the existential-humanistic tradition, person-centered therapists don't believe it's possible for one individual to directly know another individual's feelings (Rogers, 1959). As with unconditional positive regard, what appears important regarding empathy is not that therapists perfectly experience and express empathy, but they *try their best* to do so. Rogers described the empathic way of being:

> The way of being with another person which is termed empathic has several facets. It means entering the private perceptual world of the other and becoming thoroughly at home in it. It involves being sensitive, moment to moment, to the changing felt meanings which flow in this other person, to the fear of rage or tenderness or confusion or whatever, that he/she is experiencing. It means temporarily living in his/her life, moving about in it delicately without making judgments, sensing meanings of which he/she is scarcely aware, but not trying to uncover feelings of which the person is totally unaware, since this would be too threatening. (Rogers, 1975, p. 4)

The following sections are organized around Rogers's (1975) description of what it means to be empathic (see also Brain Box 5.1).

BRAIN BOX

5.1 The Neuroscience of Empathic Listening as Meditation

In recent years, neuroscientists have begun studying brain activity associated with empathy. The fact that there are many different definitions of empathy makes this research challenging. Nevertheless, it appears that empathic responses are linked to several different brain structures, networks, and neurochemicals. Researchers have also hypothesized that empathy consists of three core subprocesses:

1. *Emotional stimulation*: You can probably recall a time when you felt emotions in response to someone else's emotions. It could have involved tearing up or experiencing anger in resonance to another person's anger. Emotional stimulation involves mirror neurons, the limbic system, neurochemicals (e.g., oxytocin), the bilateral dorsomedial thalamus, and the insula.

2. *Perspective-taking*: Perspective-taking is the cognitive part of empathy. It involves using intellectual processes to see or think about the world from someone else's perspective. This intellectual inference process probably involves the prefrontal and temporal cortices.

3. *Emotional regulation*: When emotionally activated in therapy, therapists need to appraise, soothe, and possibly express their own emotions. This might involve noticing an emotional response and then offering a reflection of feeling or self-disclosure. Researchers think that this involves the orbitofrontal cortex and prefrontal and right inferior parietal cortices. What makes empathy even more fascinating and complex is that it involves all three of these cortical subprocesses happening simultaneously. Empathic listening activates many different structures and networks in the brain.

In 1949, Donald Hebb hypothesized that when neurons repeatedly fire in a particular sequence, the stronger those neural connections will become. This idea has been summarized as "Neurons that fire together, wire together" (Jones-Smith, 2016, p. 638). Consequently, whatever you practice will change your brain to make it better at producing that practiced behavior. This is likely true with regard to empathy.

As a former full-time therapist, I (John) recall becoming aware of "something happening" as I regularly engaged in empathic listening. Often, before meeting with my first client, my thoughts were bouncing around in my head like ping-pong balls. I was thinking about family, business, finances, interpersonal conflicts, or community issues. Perhaps, in an ideal world, I would have been settled and centered before inviting my first client into the room. Instead, I would just sit down with clients and attend to them.

On most days, as soon as I started listening, my personal thoughts drifted away. My clients' disclosures landed me in their emotional world. Most likely, I slipped in via mirror neurons and my anterior insular cortex. The emotional and psychological shift from my world to my clients' worlds felt like meditation. Now I know that researchers have found that repeated compassion (lovingkindness) meditation is linked to insula growth. Repeated empathic listening is like repeated compassion meditation. Most likely, it changes your brain, increasing your capacity for empathic responding.

Entering and Becoming at Home in the Client's Private Perceptual World

Entering the client's private world requires preparation and intentionality. You need to be open to feeling what the client feels and willing to ask the subjective empathy question "How would I feel if I were _____ and saying these things?" (Carkuff, 1987, p. 100). To enter the client's world you might use reflection of feelings, empathic exploration, walking within, and clarification.

We have a colleague who likes to say that the door to children's emotions locks from the inside (J. Sommers-Flanagan & Sommers-Flanagan, 2011). The same applies to adults. We can't barge in, without doing damage. As Rogers demonstrated, we must establish safety and trust, so clients will unlock their emotional doors and let us into their private and personal worlds.

Being Sensitive from Moment to Moment with the Client's Changing Meanings and Emotions

Moment-to-moment sensitivity requires focused attention to clients' constantly changing ways of being. For example, in emotion-focused therapy, Goldman and Greenberg (1997) recommended that therapists listen to client narratives with attention focused on internal questions such as "What is the core meaning or message [being communicated]?" or "What is most alive?" or "What is being felt?" (p. 408). These questions help therapists maintain a focus on new information or new emotions occurring in the now.

Being all too human, clients can be unintentionally inconsistent. They'll say one thing one moment ("I miss my mom") and another thing the next ("I'm glad I live 1,000 miles from my mother"). As a careful and rational listener, you may want to jump in and confront client inconsistencies ("Wait a minute, you just said you miss your mother and now you're saying you're glad you live far away from her. Which is really true?"). Instead, as Rogers taught, it's your job to keep listening to these moment-to-moment changes. Confrontation is undesirable because it can reduce trust and increase resistance (Miller & Rollnick, 2013).

Temporarily Living, and Moving About Delicately, in the Client's Life

Rogers suggested we live in the client's life only *temporarily—not permanently*. It can be dangerous to dive too deeply into another's world. In 1967, Rogers wrote of becoming too involved with a client:

> I stubbornly felt that I should be able to help her and permitted the contacts to continue long after they had ceased to be therapeutic, and involved only suffering for me. I recognized that many of her insights were sounder than mine, and this destroyed my confidence in myself, and I somehow gave up my self in the relationship. (Rogers, 1967, p. 367)

Ideally, your goal is to have one foot in the client's world and one foot firmly planted in your own world, letting yourself flow into the client's being for periods of time without losing a more objective perspective on what's happening in therapy. As noted in Chapter 4, Martin Buber referred to this sort of experience as an

I-Thou relationship and emphasized that it's impossible to constantly maintain such a relationship. For a transcript of a 1957 dialogue between Rogers and Buber, see Kirschenbaum and Henderson (1989).

Sensing Deep Meanings, But Not Uncovering Feelings That Are Too Far Out of Awareness

Rogers sometimes talked about working on the edge of his clients' consciousness. This idea is consistent with psychoanalytic practice. You may recall from Chapter 2 that psychoanalytic therapists try to interpret unconscious material *just as* insights are about to break through. Similarly, Rogers respected the client's pace and comfort. As a person-centered therapist moving about gently within your client's world, your main job is to follow the client's lead, not to forge your own path.

Motivational Interviewing: A Contemporary Application of PCT

PCT principles are the heart and soul of most therapies (Duncan, Miller, Wampold, & Hubble, 2010). Of course, there's debate about what's classical PCT, what's second generation PCT, and what shouldn't be considered PCT. Carl Rogers addressed this himself:

> After one demonstration counseling session, a workshop participant confronted Rogers: "I noticed that you asked questions of the client. But just last night a lecturer told us that we must never do that." Rogers responded, "Well, I'm in the fortunate position of not having to be a Rogerian" (Farber, Brink, & Raskin, 1996, p. 11; as quoted in Hazler, 2016).

With this anecdote in mind, we feel safe that Rogers would accept our list of second generation person-centered therapies. These include:

1. *Focusing* (Gendlin, 1996).

2. *Motivational interviewing* (Miller & Rollnick, 2013).

3. *Emotion-focused therapy* (Greenberg, 2015).

4. *Child-centered (nondirective) play therapy* (VanFleet, Sywulak, & Sniscak, 2010).

5. *Expressive art therapy* (Rogers, 1996).

In the interest of space, we limit our discussion to motivational interviewing. Due to its integrative qualities, emotion-focused therapy is covered in Chapter 14. Many resources on focusing, nondirective play therapy, and expressive art therapy can be found online.

What Is Motivational Interviewing?

In the latest edition of *Motivational Interviewing* (2013), Miller and Rollnick offer "Layperson's," "Practitioner's," and "Technical" definitions of MI. For practitioners, **motivational interviewing** is:

> ... a person-centered counseling style for addressing the common problem of ambivalence about change. (p. 29)

As a person-centered approach to therapy, MI relies substantially on four central listening skills, referred to as OARS (open questions, affirming, reflecting, and summarizing). MI helps clients change from less healthy to more healthy behavior patterns. However, consistent with PCT, MI practitioners don't interpret, confront, or pressure clients in any way. Instead, they use listening skills to encourage clients to talk about their reasons and motivations for positive change.

Moving Away from Confrontation and Education

In his research with problem drinkers, William R. Miller was studying the efficacy of behavioral self-control techniques. To his surprise, he found that structured behavioral treatments were no more effective than an encouragement-based control group. When he explored the data for an explanation, he found that regardless of treatment protocol, therapist empathy ratings were the strongest predictors of positive outcomes at 6 months ($r = 0.82$), 12 months ($r = 0.71$), and 2 years ($r = 0.51$) (W. R. Miller, 1978; W. R. Miller & Taylor, 1980). Consequently, he concluded that positive treatment outcomes with problem drinkers were less related to behavioral treatment and more related to reflective listening and empathy. He also found that active confrontation and education generally triggered client resistance. These discoveries led him to develop motivational interviewing (MI).

Miller met Stephen Rollnick while on sabbatical in Australia in 1989. Rollnick was enthused about MI and its popularity in the UK. Miller and Rollnick began collaborating and subsequently published the first edition of *Motivational Interviewing* in 1991. Rollnick is credited with identifying client ambivalence as a central focus for change (Jones-Smith, 2016, p. 320).

Client Ambivalence

Client ambivalence is a primary target of MI. Miller and Rollnick (2013) have consistently noted that ambivalence is a natural part of individual decision-making. They wrote: "Ambivalence is simultaneously wanting and not wanting something, or wanting both of two incompatible things. It has been human nature since the dawn of time" (2013, p. 6).

Although MI has been used as an intervention for a variety of problems and integrated into many different treatment protocols, it was originally a treatment approach for addictions and later became popular for influencing other health-related behaviors. This focus is important because ambivalence is especially prevalent among individuals who are contemplating their personal health. Smokers, problem drinkers, and sedentary individuals often recognize they could choose more healthy behaviors, but they also want to keep smoking, drinking, or not exercising. This is the essence of ambivalence, as it relates to health behaviors. When faced with a client who is ambivalent about whether to make changes, it's not unusual for professional helpers to be tempted to push clients toward health. Miller and Rollnick (2013) call this the "righting reflex" (p. 10). They described what happens when well-meaning helping professionals try to nudge clients toward healthy behaviors:

> [The therapist] then proceeds to advise, teach, persuade, counsel or argue for this particular resolution to [the client's] ambivalence. One does not need a doctorate in psychology to anticipate [how clients are likely to respond] in this situation. By virtue of ambivalence, [clients are] apt to argue the opposite, or at least point out problems and shortcomings of the proposed solution. It is natural for [clients] to do so, because [a client] feels at least two ways about this or almost any prescribed solution. It is the very nature of ambivalence. (2013, pp. 20–21)

The ubiquity of ambivalence leads to Miller and Rollnick's (2013) foundational person-centered principle of treatment:

> Ideally, the client should be voicing the reasons for change (p. 9).

MI is both a set of techniques and a person-centered philosophy. The philosophical MI perspective emphasizes that motivation for change is not something therapists should impose on clients. Change must be drawn out from clients, gently, and with careful timing. Motivational interviewers do not use direct persuasion.

The Spirit of MI

The "underlying spirit" of MI "lies squarely within the longstanding tradition of person-centered care" (Miller & Rollnick, 2013, p. 22). They identified four overlapping components that the spirit of MI "emerges" from. These include:

- Collaboration.
- Acceptance.
- Compassion.
- Evocation.

MI involves partnership or collaboration. It's described as dancing, not wrestling. Your goal is not to "pin" the client; in fact, you should even avoid stepping on their toes. This is consistent with the first principle of person-centered therapy. The counselor and client make contact, and in that contact there's an inherent or implied partnership to work together on behalf of the client.

Person-centered (and MI) counselors deemphasize their expertness. Miller and Rollnick refer to this as avoiding the expert trap where you communicate "that, based on your professional expertise, you have the answer to the person's dilemma" (p. 16). In writing about collaboration, Miller and Rollnick (2013) sound very much like Carl Rogers, "Your purpose is to understand the life before you, to see the world through this person's eyes rather than superimposing your own vision" (p. 16).

Consistent with Rogerian philosophy, MI counselors hold an "attitude of profound acceptance of what the client brings" (p. 16). This **profound acceptance** includes four parts:

1. *Absolute worth*: This is Rogerian unconditional positive regard.

2. *Accurate empathy*: This is pure Rogerian.

3. *Autonomy support*: This part of acceptance involves honoring each person's "irrevocable right and capacity of self-direction" (p. 17).

4. *Affirmation*: This involves an active search or focus on what's right with people instead of what's wrong or pathological about people.

In the third edition of *Motivational Interviewing*, Miller and Rollnick added compassion to their previous list of the three elements of MI spirit. Why? Their reasoning was that it was possible for practitioners to adopt the other three elements, but still be operating from a place of self-interest. In other words, practitioners could use collaboration, acceptance, and evocation to further their self-interest to get clients to change. By adding **compassion** and defining it as "a deliberate commitment to pursue the welfare and best interests of the other," Miller and Rollnick are protecting against practitioners confusing self-interest with the client's best interests.

Evocation is somewhat unique, but also consistent with person-centered theory. Miller and Rollnick contend that clients have already explored both sides of their natural ambivalence. As a consequence, they know the arguments in both directions and know their own positive motivations for change. Additionally, they note, "From an MI perspective, the assumption is that there is a deep well of wisdom and experience within the person from which the counselor can draw" (p. 21). It's the counselor's job to use evocation to draw out (or evoke) client strengths so these strengths can be used to initiate and maintain change.

A Sampling of MI Techniques

One distinction between MI and classical PCT is that Miller and Rollnick (2013) identify techniques that

practitioners can and should use. These techniques are generally designed to operate within the spirit of MI and to help clients engage in change talk instead of sustain talk. **Change talk** is defined as client talk that focuses on their desire, ability, reason, and need to change their behavior, as well as their commitment to change. **Sustain talk** is the opposite; clients may be talking about lack of desire, ability, reason, and need to change. Overall, researchers have shown that clients who engage in more MI change talk are more likely to make efforts to enact positive change.

MI appears simple, but it's a complicated approach and challenging to learn (Atkinson & Woods, 2017). Miller and Rollnick (2013) have noted that having a solid foundation of person-centered listening skills makes learning MI much easier. The following content is only a sampling of MI techniques.

MI practitioners use techniques from the OARS listening skills. In particular, there's a strong emphasis on the skillful and intentional use of reflections instead of questions or directives. Here are some examples.

Simple reflections stick very closely to what the client said.

Client: I've just been pretty anxious lately.

Simple Reflection: Seems like you've been feeling anxious.

Client: Being sober sucks.

Simple Reflection: You don't like being sober.

Simple reflections have two primary functions. First, they convey to clients that you've heard what they said. This usually enhances rapport and interpersonal connection. Second, as you provide a simple reflection, it lets clients hear what they've said. Hearing their words back—from the outside in—is sometimes illuminating for clients.

Complex reflections add meaning, focus, or a particular emphasis to what the client said.

Client: I haven't had an HIV test for quite a while.

Complex reflection: Getting an HIV test has been on your mind.

Client: I only had a couple drinks. Even when I got pulled over, I didn't think I was over the limit.

Complex reflection: That was a surprise to you. You might have assumed "I can tell when I'm over the limit" but in this case you couldn't really tell.

Complex reflections go beyond the surface and make educated guesses about what clients are thinking, feeling, or doing. Clients tend to talk more and get deeper into their issues when MI therapists use complex reflections effectively. Also, if your complex reflection is correct, it's likely to deepen rapport and might evoke change talk.

An **amplified reflection** involves an intentional overstatement of the client's main message. Generally, when therapists overstate, clients make an effort to correct the reflection.

Client: I'm pissed at my roommate. She won't pick up her clothes or do the dishes or anything.

Interviewer: You'd like to fire her as a roommate.

Client: No. Not that. There are lots of things I like about her, but her messiness really annoys me (from J. Sommers-Flanagan & Sommers-Flanagan, 2017, p. 440).

Client: My child has a serious disability and so I have to be home for him.

Interviewer: You really need to be home 24/7 and have to turn off any needs you have to get out and take a break.

Client: Actually, that's not totally true. Sometimes, I think I need to take some breaks so I can do a better job when I am home (from J. Sommers-Flanagan & Sommers-Flanagan, 2017, p. 441).

Sometimes MI practitioners accidentally amplify a reflection. When intentionally amplifying reflections, it's important to be careful, as it can feel manipulative.

The opposite of amplified reflection is undershooting. Undershooting involves intentionally understating what your client is saying.

Client: I can't stand it when my mom criticizes my friends right in front of me.

Therapist: You find that a little annoying.

Client: It's way more than annoying. It pisses me off.

Therapist: What is it that pisses you off when your mom criticizes your friends?

Client: It's because she doesn't trust me and my judgment (from J. Sommers-Flanagan & Sommers-Flanagan, 2017, p. 441).

In this example, the therapist undershoots the client's emotion and then follows with an open question. Clients often elaborate when therapists undershoot.

As noted, the preceding content is a small taste of MI technical strategies; if you want to become a competent MI practitioner, advanced training is needed (Atkinson & Woods, 2017).

REFLECTIONS

Take a few moments to reflect on what you see as the similarities and differences between MI and PCT. What thoughts, feelings, and reactions come up for you when you imagine intentionally using amplified reflection?

PCT in Action: Brief Vignettes

In classical PCT, therapists are nondirective and follow their clients' lead. Meier and Davis (2011) refer to this as *pacing* and write eloquently about the difference between pacing and leading. For beginning therapists, it's crucial to recognize when you're pacing and when you're leading. Another way to think of this is to know the difference between following your client's agenda versus following your own agenda. In the first vignette, we provide an example of a cognitive behavior therapist conducting an intake interview.

Vignette I: Person–Centered Therapy (Not!)

In contrast to PCT, cognitive behavior therapy (CBT) involves setting an explicit agenda and then working from that agenda (see Chapter 8). The following excerpt from Ledley, Marx, and Heimberg (2010) illustrates how, in CBT, therapists lead and push their agenda. In this excerpt, all bracketed comments are added by us and are not in the original:

Clinician: So, you consider the panic attacks your biggest problem right now?

Client: Yeah. For sure.

Clinician: Hmmmm. That surprises me a bit. During our assessment, you told me that you have panic attacks pretty infrequently. [In this situation the therapist is using the word "surprise" to move toward a confrontation—where the discrepancy between what the client rates as most troubling is contrasted with what the therapist views as most troubling.]

Client: Yeah, I do. But they're pretty awful when they come on.

Clinician: So, when they do happen, they get you pretty stressed out and kind of foul up your day? [This is a motivational interviewing technique, called *amplified reflection* (Rosengren, 2009). The therapist slightly overstates the client's position, hoping the client will respond with a more moderate statement.]

Client: Yeah. They definitely stress me out. I don't know about fouling up a whole day, though. They don't last that long, you know. [As predicted from the motivational interviewing perspective, the client pulls back from the more extreme statement.]

Clinician: How about the problems with your eating? Can they foul up a whole day? [Now the cognitive behavior therapist is confronting, albeit somewhat indirectly, the client's choice to work on her panic attacks instead of her eating behaviors.]

Client: They foul up every day. I already told you—I'm bingeing like three times a day. And then I throw up. And I feel so gross that I have to have a shower to get cleaned up and calm down. It's awful. I've missed five classes in the past week. [The client concedes that the eating problem is more disruptive to her daily life.]

Clinician: So, it sounds like the bulimia might be interfering more than the panic attacks. [This is a person-centered reflection of content or paraphrase that highlights what the therapist wants the client to admit.]

Client: I guess. [The client concedes, but seems less than enthused.]

Clinician: It sounds like you might be feeling like working on the eating is a bit more stressful right now than working on the panic. [Non-leading paraphrase.]

Client: Well, obviously.

Clinician: It can be very hard, I agree. Is it worth giving it a try for a few weeks and seeing how it goes? [The therapist acknowledges the client's perception that working on the eating "can be very hard," but follows that with, "How about we do this my way first and then evaluate?" Person-centered therapists would not put their goals and strategies as a higher priority than the client's.]

Client: I guess. [Again, the client concedes, but perhaps without much motivation.] (pp. 78–79).

Vignette II: Person-Centered Goal-Setting

Let's revisit this scene, reworked to be consistent with PCT. Note how the person-centered therapist respects both sides of the client's ambivalence and works to help the client decide for herself how to move forward.

Clinician: So, you consider the panic attacks your biggest problem right now. [From the PCT perspective, this is framed (and phrased) as a statement, not as a question.]

Client: Yeah. For sure.

Clinician: When you were talking earlier you said you're really struggling with your eating. And now I hear you saying your feelings of panic are also a priority. [In the PCT approach, the therapist, having listened closely, simply brings the two conflicting statements together in space and time and lets the client clarify the discrepancy. There's no judgment or "surprise," just a gentle noticing.]

Client: They're both priorities. They both make me feel miserable.

Clinician: It's like you're saying, "They both make me feel so miserable that I'm not even sure which one to talk about first." [This is an example of the PCT method of "walking within." The therapist is metaphorically stepping into the client's psychological world and speaking from that perspective using first-person pronouns. When done well, clients typically don't notice this wording shift. When done poorly, it can sound

phony—which is why Rogers would likely recommend using this method only when it bubbles up naturally.]

Client: I wish I could deal with the eating, but it's overwhelming. It takes over my whole life. I'm afraid if we try to work on this first, we'll fail and then I'll know I'll never be able to change. [This process allows the client to begin articulating deeper fears.]

Clinician: It feels like, "If I were to try to change my eating behaviors and fail, then things will be hopeless." Do I have that right? [Another walking within, centered on fear of failure and hopelessness.]

Client: Exactly. It just feels too risky. What do you think I should do? [It's not unusual, when prompted to self-reflect, for clients to ask the therapist for direct guidance.]

Clinician: I hear you wishing you could deal with your eating struggles, but you're scared. You also would like my advice on what to do. I wish I knew the perfect answer, but you're the one experiencing this and so you're the only one who knows the risk and feels the fear you feel inside. Do you mind if I just tell you what I think? [The therapist summarizes the internal dynamic the client is struggling with and then asks the client's permission to be open.]

Client: That's exactly what I'd like you to do. [Of course, the client affirms this, because she's already asked for it.]

Clinician: I may eventually come to the point where I feel clear enough to give you advice on whether to start with the eating or with the panic. But I'm not there yet. For now, I hear you saying you're afraid to work directly on your eating behavior. Before we decide what you should work on first, it seems important for us to respect your fears and keep talking. It also seems important for us to focus on how you can be your own best guide in this process, with me along for clarification and support. [This is PCT. The rule is to respond to every client question, but not to answer every question. This is also an example of role induction where the therapist leads the client back toward self-exploration, rather than to a reliance on external guidance. From the PCT perspective, many client problems exist or are exacerbated because of nonreliance on the self. For example, an eating disorder can be conceptualized as a repeated pattern where the client is feeling out of control and not in charge of her own behavior. Additionally, she may have body image issues related to self-rejection instead of self-acceptance. Consequently, self-rejection and denial of her personal power could contribute to her eating disorder. Even in cases of modified PCT, where therapists integrate more directive approaches (e.g., CBT), initially a deeper exploration of the self and self-acceptance are emphasized.]

Client: It's so hard being me right now. I just want to have someone else take over and rescue me from myself. [The client acknowledges her feelings of self-alienation and wish to have someone else take over her decision-making.]

Looking at this case through the PCT and CBT lenses allows for consideration of the pros and cons of working from each perspective. It's quite possible that the client needs to be actively guided toward working on her bulimia. Alternatively, providing more time to explore her fear and waiting until she's "ready" could be preferable.

REFLECTIONS

What do you think about quickly directing the client to work on bulimia versus more gently exploring her fears? Discuss with your classmates the pros and cons of being directive and nondirective in this situation.

CASE PRESENTATION

In this case example, Carl Rogers is conducting a single-session demonstration with a hospitalized woman, identified as Ms. PS (Rogers, 1963). This is an abridged version of the session, with ellipsis following responses where portions were deleted. This case is integrated with an abbreviated treatment plan and our comments are in brackets.

Carl Rogers (CR): What'd I like is for you to tell me anything you're willing to tell me about yourself and your situation and how you feel about yourself and your situation. Or I guess another way of putting it is, anything you're willing to tell me that would help me to know you better, I'd be very glad to hear. [This is a vintage Rogers opening.]

PS: Where do you want me to start?

CR: Where ever you would like to. [This is a PCT response to the client's hesitation over where to begin. Rogers gives the client freedom to begin where she likes.]

PS: Well, I'll start with my childhood. When I was, uh, when I was a little girl, I had this cross eye since I was about 7 years old. And, I mean kids poked fun of me and as the years got longer and I start going into the higher grades. I mean I never had no boyfriends or anything. I mean I had girlfriends but after the girls started going around with the boys I mean and the boys would tell them, don't go around with me or something like that. And actually I ended up without any girlfriends at all. And around my neighborhood

there was no girls my age so I was counting on the school and they sort of let me down. And I felt just like I, I wasn't wanted.

CR: So you sort of wound up with no friends at all and am I getting it right, that you feel that was due, basically, due to your eye condition, or.... [As Wickman and Campbell (2003) described, Rogers commonly provided "invitations for repair" (p. 179). These invitations allow clients to correct Rogers, in case his perceptions are inaccurate.]

PS: [There's a 2-minute gap and then the interview continues.] That's what I always say [5 seconds of silence]. And then my home situation now, is um, well that's part of it, my husband won't let me go anyplace. But then there's my mother too. My husband's brother's staying downstairs with my mother and I just don't, I don't like the idea of it. I mean, my mother isn't married to him, and yet he acts like he's a father to my two brothers and we're living upstairs in my mother's place and even though I'm married, he tries to boss me around.

CR: So that's another thing you don't like, you don't quite like the situation your mother is in and you don't like him, because he acts like he's married to her.... [Rogers initiates a pattern where, when the client goes silent, he waits expectantly for her to continue. The client is focusing on what she *doesn't* like; Rogers is staying with her.]

PS: No, she's only living on 20 dollars a month for food already and with having to have him stay there and eat and, my God, they practically eat beans all the time, it wouldn't be that bad if he wasn't there. Gotta be buying cigarettes and all that stuff. They could be saving that money for food. Actually with the little money she gets he's actually living off her.

CR: Sounds like you feel pretty resentful of that. [This is Rogers's first response that can be categorized as a "reflection of feeling."]

PS: Yes, well, I mean I don't care for it. I mean everybody's up against it, like my mother's mother. [The feeling reflection with the word *resentful* may have disorganized the client; she appears to struggle expressing herself.]

CR: I'm sorry. I didn't get that. [A clarification.]

PS: My mother's mother don't like it either.

CR: I see, um hmm.

PS: She don't like to have her daughter talked about by my mother's brothers and sisters.

CR: Uh huh. Uh huh. So I guess you're saying, "I'm not the only one that feels that way about her and her situation." [Rogers uses a first-person quotation—for the first time in this session—to deepen the empathic connection. This is an example of "walking within." He also steers clear of his client's muddled verbal output.]

PS: Yes. I mean, I'm not the only one, but if anybody tells her anything, she's so bull-headed and knot-headed that she, she just, if somebody tells her to do something or get away from him or something, she just stay with him. I mean she just wants to do things her own self. But, even though I'm married, she wants to try to run my life. I mean. I hate the idea of everybody telling me what to do. Even my husband, he'll tell me what to do. Even though I'm young and I'm married, I mean I'm a human being and I like to run my life myself. I mean I don't want to feel like I'm still in a baby buggy or something like that.

CR: You feel that your mother and your husband and everybody tries to run your life. [Another paraphrase.]

PS: Yes. That's why I feel, I was old enough to bear a baby and that's surely a lot of pain. But yet they won't let me make up my mind for myself.

CR: Here I was old enough to have a child and yet nobody thinks I can make my decisions or run my own life. Is that what you're saying? [Here he's walking within and using an invitation for repair.]

The Problem List

Person-centered therapists usually don't think about problem lists. However, even though Rogers hasn't yet asked a problem-oriented question, a tentative problem list can already be generated. The initial problem list for Ms. PS might look like this:

1. Unspecified social problems (feeling disconnected or alienated).

2. Problems with assertiveness and self-esteem (Ms. PS reports difficulties speaking up for herself and feels controlled by others; this could be related to self-esteem issues).

3. Unresolved anger/resentment (Ms. PS is angry toward several people; she may need help exploring this and dealing with it effectively).

4. Thinking difficulties that may be exacerbated by either anger or anxiety (Ms. PS seems to have difficulties expressing herself clearly, which could be related to mental disorganization).

The interview continues....

PS: Yes. I mean like, this is when my husband and I went to California, with our little boy.... But, being back in the whole situation it's just not good. His mother is the kind of person who would talk behind her own brother's back. Uh, I mean her own son's. My husband has six brothers and one sister. And I mean she'll talk to one of her sons about one of her other sons. I mean, she's that kind of person. And although she don't come right out and tell me to my face that she don't like me, I know by the way she's talking about the other people behind their backs, that she's talking about me, too.

CR: You feel she's just a gossip and you feel she doesn't like you. [Another paraphrase.]

PS: Oh, I know she don't like me. [Laughs.]

CR: No doubt about that. [Rogers resonates with the client's correction of his paraphrase.]

PS: Oh, no doubt. [11 seconds of silence.] Uh, mostly that's, uh, that's the point. And my little girl she passed away a couple of months ago. And my mother did another thing. See, when my little girl was born, I asked my mother, I said, um, "How come her leg, her one leg, is turned a little bit?" and she said, "All babies are like that when they're small." She said, "You can't expect them to get up and walk right away," and I said, "I know that." And she said, "Don't worry about it" and so I didn't worry about it and then after my little girl passed away, my mother told me that my daughter was cripple. She kept it from me again. She keeps things from me like that. And, and in a way I felt responsible for my little girl's death. You know, she would be sitting down and um, well, I'd sit her up in the davenport, in the corner and I'd put her little legs in, but if I would have known she was cripple, I surely wouldn't do that. [Following Rogers's validation of her correction of his paraphrase, the client becomes silent. Rogers stays with the silence. Then, Ms. PS moves to an emotionally significant issue. His responses have allowed her to go deeper.]

CR: That really concerns you that that was kept from you and it concerns you that maybe you didn't deal with her right, not, not knowing that she was crippled.... [Paraphrase.]

PS: She let me down. I mean, my mother she, I always took the blame home. My mother always, always liked my oldest brother. I always took the blame home, whether I did something wrong or not. I got along a lot better with my father. Then my father passed away and then, and well actually, I mean I took most, I took all the blame I wanna say, than my brother and now my youngest brother that's home, he's going through the same darn thing I am. He's taking all the blame home.

CR: You feel when you were home, whatever went wrong, you took the blame for it, within yourself. [Even though he uses the word "feel" this is just a paraphrase.]

PS: No, uh, my brother would say that I did this and that.

CR: I see. That's what I wasn't quite clear about, you were blamed for everything. [This is an example of a correction or repair.]

PS: Yeah.

CR: Whether you had done it or not. Is that …?

PS: Yes I was.

CR: It isn't so much you felt you were to blame, but, but, others blamed you. [Repair continues.]

PS: I mean my brother actually got away with everything.

CR: I guess you feel that was sort of true with everybody except your father. Is that…. That things went somewhat better between you and your father. [Rogers leads the client toward talking about her father.]

PS: Yes. Yes they did. I mean, I could go and he'd take me, well, my mother and my father we used to go out a lot of times, but they went sort of late you know and by that time I'd be asleep and I used to fool 'em all the times because I knew they were gonna stop at the hamburger shop. And I'd make believe I was asleep and when they'd stop and I'd say, "Oh, I'm awake, I'm awake, you gotta get me one too." And I mean, I used to have a lotta fun when I used to go out with my mother and father and mostly when I went away with my father I used to help him pile wood and I mean we had a lotta fun, the neighborhood kids would come over, boys and girls and they'd help my father pile up the wood and help him cut it with a saw and after that, we'd all pile in the car and went down got an ice cream cone.

CR: Those are really kind of pleasant memories. [A simple reflection of feeling.]

PS: Uh hmm.

CR: [10 seconds of silence.] I don't know, but it looks as though, thinking about those things, make you feel a little bit weepy, or am I wrong? [Rogers lets the silence do its work and then comments on the client's affect.]

PS: A little bit.

CR: A little bit.

Problem Formulation

Ms. PS has experienced conditions of worth. She has not relied on her own judgments, perhaps because of not trusting herself. She has allowed others to control her or tell her how to lead her life. This pattern of submitting may have led to her feeling anger and resentment and yet there's also the question of whether she's developed herself enough to make mature and healthy decisions on her own. This problem formulation implies that part of the therapy work will involve this client exploring her experiences and values. This will help her to begin relying on herself and her own judgment, while at the same time considering input from others.

It's also likely that her low self-worth adversely affects her ability to express anger directly. Although a behavioral approach might emphasize skill development through practice and role playing, PCT works on improving her self-worth and her situational appraisal skills so she can become confident enough to speak up appropriately.

Finally, it may be that she has unresolved feelings of loss and guilt around the death of her daughter. The guilt seems associated with her self-evaluation that she should have relied on her own feelings or beliefs when her mother was misleading her about her daughter's health condition.

The session continues….

PS: I can remember, I don't exactly know how it went, but I know I was pretty young, but um, we went over by, my father, yes his brother, we went over by, it was I and David, my oldest brother. Anyway, the two guys, they decided to go out and then my mother and my aunt and my brother were there and two children, gee, I don't know if I'm getting this quite clearly. [The client is able to go deeper into an early childhood memory.]

CR: It's hard to remember. [A process-focused paraphrase.]

Toward the end of the session the client commented on her counseling experience with Rogers:

PS: Gee, that's funny, I never said these things before to the other doctors (16 seconds of silence). [The patient's comment reflects that Rogers is, indeed, different than the other doctors. As Natalie Rogers has put it, her father's approach uses a different language and is revolutionary (N. Rogers, personal communication, May, 2003). Thus far, he has shown interest in the client as a person, while showing no interest in her symptoms.]

Toward the session's end the client admits to having previously wanted pity from others, but says she wants to start making her own decisions and no longer wants pity. In one of her final apt references to her self-development, she stated: "It's just like everyone's got a part of me … like one's got one leg the one's got one arm (laughs), just like they all got part of me and I ain't got none of myself."

Interventions

The PCT intervention is always the same, but always unique. Ms. PS needs Rogers's "certain kind of environment" characterized by congruence, unconditional positive regard, and empathic understanding. As this environment (intervention) is provided, she will develop greater insight into what she wants. She also will begin trusting her own judgment. Her actualization tendency will be activated.

For the most part, Rogers will track what Ms. PS says in therapy. He will reflect his understanding back to her. Through this treatment process, he will help her become more aware and sensitive to her own emotions and judgments. At times, as he did in this interview when he guided Ms. PS toward talking about her father, Rogers will lead her to explore new psychological and emotional territory. He will help her to freely "explore all the hidden nooks and frightening crannies of" her "inner and often buried experience" (p. 34).

For those of us oriented toward psychotherapy and medicine, this approach raises questions. What good does this exploration do? How can we understand what Rogers is offering via PCT?

It may be helpful to think about PCT using behavioral terminology (see Chapter 7). PCT's freedom to explore the self can be reformulated as exposure treatment, using a classical conditioning model. As Ms. PS talks about her fears and emotional pain within an accepting environment, she is exposed to her fears and is systematically extinguishing them. In the end, she can leave therapy without fear of herself or her judgments. She may be able to identify her feelings and opinions, while considering others' input. In this way PCT can facilitate her development or maturation into a more fully functioning person.

Outcomes Measurement

Person-centered therapists don't typically use objective, pencil-paper outcomes measures. Therapy focuses on self-development and not on symptom reduction; behaviorally oriented measures may not be optimal for measuring outcomes. However, researchers with humanistic perspectives have begun using symptom-based measures in combination with measures sensitive to changes that humanistic therapies are likely to produce. For example, in an "allegiance-balanced randomized clinical trial" comparing the efficacy of cognitive-behavioral therapy (CBT) and process-experiential therapy (PE; aka emotion-focused therapy) for treating clinical depression, two self-report measures sensitive to person-centered outcomes were used (Watson, Gordon, Stermac, Kalogerakos, & Steckley, 2003):

1. A 10-item version of the Rosenberg Self-Esteem Inventory (Bachman & O'Malley, 1977).

2. The 127 item Inventory of Interpersonal Problems (Horowitz, Rosenberg, Baer, Ureño, & Villaseñor, 1988).

These measures were used in addition to symptom-based inventories like the Beck Depression Inventory (BDI; Beck, Ward, Mendelson, Mock, & Erbaugh, 1961). With Ms. PS or other person-centered cases, brief instruments evaluating her self-esteem, assertiveness, and depression/anxiety might be appropriate and not interfere

with the person-centered treatment process. Additionally, Hubble, Duncan, and Miller (1999) developed a four-item Outcomes Rating Scale, a humanistic-oriented process-outcome measure used every session as a means for both tracking progress and empowering clients to provide therapists with feedback about how the therapy process is going (Duncan, Miller, Wampold, & Hubble, 2010).

EVALUATIONS AND APPLICATIONS

Rogers strove to be genuine, accepting, and empathic with all clients, regardless of culture, gender, sexuality, and spirituality. This is a good start toward being inclusive. In this section we review how well person-centered therapy stands up to scientific scrutiny and addresses diversity issues.

Evidence-Based Status

Rogers was the first modern scientist-practitioner. He took the unusual step of recording and empirically evaluating his therapeutic approach. He also applied PCT to challenging clinical populations and openly reported his less-than-stellar findings.

One of Rogers's most ambitious studies was with hospitalized schizophrenics in Wisconsin. This study examined client-centered relationship variables in the treatment of 16 hospitalized schizophrenics. Rogers reported:

> It is a sobering finding that our therapists—competent and conscientious as they were—had over-optimistic and, in some cases, seriously invalid perceptions of the relationships in which they were involved. The patient, for all his psychosis … turned out to have more useful (and probably more accurate) perceptions of the relationship. (Rogers, Gendlin, Kiesler, & Truax, 1967, p. 92)

The patients made little progress in this treatment study. However, consistent with later research pointing to the crucial nature of empathy in positive treatment outcomes, patients who rated themselves as experiencing a higher degree of empathy, warmth, and genuineness had shorter hospital stays than patients with therapists whom they rated as less empathic, warm, and genuine.

Research on PCT effectiveness tends to yield small, but positive results. For example, in their large meta-analysis, Smith and Glass reported an effect size of 0.63 for client-centered therapy, a moderate-size effect (Smith & Glass, 1977; Smith et al., 1980). In contrast, behavioral and cognitive therapies obtained effect sizes ranging from 0.73 to 1.13 (Smith & Glass, 1977; Smith, Glass, & Miller, 1980).

The following research summaries support PCT's effectiveness.

• In a review of 18 client-centered treatment versus no treatment studies, emotional-focused therapy researchers Greenberg, Elliot, and Lietaer (1994) reported a large effect size ($d = 0.95$) for client-centered therapy.

- Two research teams reported no significant differences between cognitive behavior therapy, psychodynamic therapy, and PCT (Stiles, Barkham, Mellor-Clark, & Connell, 2008) or between cognitive therapy and PCT (Marriott & Kellett, 2009).

- In a five-year U.K. study of PCT in routine clinical practice, PCT had an effect size of $d = 1.2$ as compared to $d = 0.24$ for wait-list controls (Gibbard & Hanley, 2008).

- Another U.K. study showed that time-limited PCT and low-intensity CBT were equivalent in treating mild depression and preventing depressive episodes (Freire et al., 2015).

Most professionals, academics, and students believe cognitive and behavioral treatments are more effective than PCT. Although this may be the case, there's another perspective. It may be that PCT appears less effective on the typical measures used in outcome studies. In fact, it would be surprising to discover that a phenomenological treatment outperforms structured educational treatments on symptom-focused measures. As existentialists would inevitably argue, it's impossible for empirical research to quantify and measure people's capacity to love, accept, and prize themselves—outcomes toward which PCT strives. Also, PCT is much more difficult to manualize and deliver in structured ways necessary for empirical research.

Despite limitations of PCT research, Michael Lambert, an esteemed outcomes researcher noted, "The efficacy of client-centered psychotherapy for the client rests on 50 years of outcome and process research" and "Few therapies have such a long, storied, and successful research base" (Lambert & Erekson, 2008, p. 225).

Research on motivational interviewing is extensive and robust. MI is viewed as an empirically supported and preferred treatment for substance-related problems. In a large-scale study of an early four-session form of MI, MI was equivalent to 12 session 12-step and cognitive-behavioral therapy at immediate outcome and more effective than CBT with less motivated clients. A meta-analysis of 72 studies showed MI was equivalent to other more long-term and directive treatments (Hettema, Steele, & Miller, 2005). Additionally, several different studies show that MI may also be effective for different populations, problems, and settings. Specifically, meta-analytic reviews on MI are positive for reducing gambling behaviors (Yakovenko, Quigley, Hemmelgarn, Hodgins, & Ronksley, 2015), improving adolescent health behaviors (Cushing, Jensen, Miller, & Leffingwell, 2014), and reducing alcohol consumption in young people treated in emergency care settings (Kohler & Hofmann, 2015).

Before leaving this section, we should comment on the empirical status of Rogers's bold claim, made in 1957, that a special relationship between therapist and client is *necessary* and *sufficient* for positive therapy outcome. Most researchers have "disproven" this claim, at least to their satisfaction. Parloff, Waskow, and Wolfe (1978) wrote:

> ... the evidence for the therapeutic conditions hypothesis [as necessary and sufficient] is not persuasive. The associations found are modest and suggest that a more complex association exists between outcome and therapist skills than originally hypothesized.

These writers show a typical lack of understanding of PCT. They make the common mistake of evaluating Rogers's therapeutic conditions as "therapist skills" rather than therapist attitudes. This oversimplified articulation of PCT could produce poorer outcomes and may be linked to the allegiance effect. Natalie Rogers would contend that most U.S. researchers "don't get" PCT and therefore are unlikely to represent it adequately (J. Sommers-Flanagan, 2007). Rogers himself came to despair "parrot-like" translations of PCT.

Cultural Sensitivity

Core principles of PCT include trust in and respect for individuals. Rogers developed PCT because, like Rank, he thought therapy was too therapist-centered (Cain, 2010). His approach focuses on and addresses the needs and interests of unique clients, while activating their inner potential for positive change and growth.

Despite this profoundly respectful foundation, there are several ways in which PCT isn't culturally sensitive or appropriate. First, PCT focuses on individuals—which may not fit for culturally diverse clients with collectivist worldviews. PCT's emphasis on the self and self-actualization may not work for clients who have familial-community-collectivist goals.

Second, person-centered therapists focus on emotions and emotional expression, but some cultures don't value emotional expression. Within the Latino or Asian cultures, male emotionality can be viewed as weakness. Many First Nations or Native American people, as well as Asians, don't talk about personal issues outside the family (Sue & Sue, 2016).

Third, researchers report that culturally diverse clients often expect and value expert advice, and prefer directive therapies (Atkinson, Lowe, & Mathews, 1995). This makes classical PCT a poor treatment choice for some culturally diverse clients.

Fourth, person-centered approaches may be too indirect for some cultures, but in other cases they may be too direct. For example, if counselors are too congruent they may express thoughts and feelings in ways that are unacceptable within some cultures. If so, instead of facilitating therapy, counselor congruence might increase client anxiety and impair the therapy process.

On the other hand, a case can be made for PCT as a diversity-sensitive approach. Many Rogerian ideas have an Eastern flavor. He discussed the Taoist principle of wu-wei, sometimes referred to as the principle of nonaction. PCT remains a force in international approaches to therapy and is popular in Japan and the United Kingdom (Cain, 2010).

Although PCT may not be a perfect fit for clients from diverse or collectivist backgrounds, competent PCT practitioners are unlikely to use it in ways that are insensitive. Bottom line: it's hard to imagine Rogers ever advocating that PCT be applied to anyone who isn't comfortable with PCT.

Gender and Sexuality

Rogers held an empowering stance toward women. This makes his approach acceptable to feminist therapists, but mostly as a foundation, not as a finished product (Brown, 2010). In the case presentation on Ms. PS, he followed her lead, listened to her, and empowered her (albeit indirectly) to articulate her wants and needs.

The main feminist critique of PCT is that it's not directly activist—PCT doesn't advocate for clients, but waits for clients to become ready to advocate for themselves. Additionally, person-centered therapists and the PCT literature haven't focused extensively on oppressive, patriarchal social forces. Nevertheless, the bridge between person-centered principles and feminist perspectives is strong (Jordan, 2010).

PCT offers a solid foundation for working with sexually diverse, transgender, or gender nonconforming clients. Person-centered therapists view clients as the ultimate authority on their emotional pain and counseling goals. This is consistent with affirmative approaches where transgender and gender nonconforming clients "are in charge of their own mental health [and where] goals and aspirations ... are client driven" (Singh & Dickey, 2017, p. 1). However, in addition to operating from foundational Rogerian principles, it would be crucial for therapists to educate themselves on sexually diverse culture, language use, and specific affirmative approaches to psychotherapy (Kort, 2008; Singh & Dickey, 2017).

Spirituality

On his journey to developing person-centered theory and therapy, Carl Rogers renounced traditional Christianity. Given that all religions, including Christianity, can be viewed as directly imposing judgmental conditions of worth, Rogers's renouncing Christianity as antithetical

to his beliefs is not surprising. In particular, Rogers may have been especially reactive to religious dogma because of his childhood experiences in an extremely conservative Christian family. Thorne (1990) proposed that Rogers broke from Christianity, at least in part, over the doctrine of original sin.

Although he died an agnostic, toward the end of his life, Rogers began speaking about transcendental or mystical experiences (Thorne, 1992). These spiritual statements were mostly made in the context of interpersonal mutuality and human connection, derived from person-centered or I-Thou experiences. Within the person-centered world, his statements about spirituality have been viewed as controversial (Fruehwirth, 2013). In an interview with Elizabeth Sheerer, one of Rogers's early colleagues at the University of Chicago Counseling Center, Sheerer was asked about why Rogers never formally addressed spirituality. Her response included:

> That's Carl. This was an area of difficulty for Carl. We learned early in the game not to talk about religion with Carl ... it was uncomfortable for him.... But, of course, his work is so profoundly influenced by his background in Christianity. I don't think he could have developed it without that background. (Barrineau, 1990, pp. 423–424)

There have been contemporary efforts to build a bridge between spirituality and PCT. One example is Fruehwirth's (2013) work connecting PCT and Christian contemplation. He proposed that if wordless contemplation can be regarded as "the heart of the Christian spiritual tradition" (p. 370), then parallels can be drawn to wordless contemplation and the PCT experience. Similarly, a case can be made connecting the acceptance doctrine of Christian, Buddhist, and other religious viewpoints with the PCT process.

Overall, it seems reasonable that, for some therapists and clients, the deep interpersonal acceptance inherent in the PCT experience might have religious, spiritual, or mystical components. Spiritual-based acceptance is probably the main place where an integration of PCT and religion/spirituality can occur. In contrast, wherever and whenever judgment flows from religious doctrine, religion and PCT are incompatible.

CONCLUDING COMMENTS

Rogers understood the central role of relationship in therapy. The person of the therapist and attitudes the therapist holds are more important than problems or techniques. We can't generate a more apt or succinct concluding comment than that of Rogers himself:

> [T]he relationship which I have found helpful is characterized by a sort of transparency on my part, in

which my real feelings are evident; by an acceptance of this other person as a separate person with value in his own right; and by a deep empathic understanding which enables me to see his private world through his eyes. (Rogers, 1961, p. 34)

CHAPTER SUMMARY AND REVIEW

Carl Rogers was a super-optimist and the creator of person-centered therapy. His central idea was to trust clients because they knew what was hurting and could lead therapists in the best therapeutic directions. Originally, his approach was called nondirective therapy. Later, he changed it to client-centered therapy, and finally, to person-centered therapy (PCT).

PCT is an existential-humanistic approach. Rogers held a very positive view of human nature. Although he was born and raised in a fundamentalist Christian family, his approach to psychotherapy was remarkably nonjudgmental. In the 1930s, Rogers was influenced by the work of Otto Rank; he also learned about the healing power of relationships from his clients and through his marriage. The development of Rogers's therapy approach included four phases: (1) nondirective counseling, (2) client-centered therapy, (3) person-centered therapy, and (4) worldwide issues.

Rogers developed a complex 19-point theory of human personality, focusing on self-development. He emphasized the full development of a self that is consistent with an individual's total organismic experience. Unfortunately, most children are exposed to conditions of worth that cause them to have conflicts between their real (what they want) and ideal (what they should want) selves. This contributes to a negative self-regard and to individuals not trusting themselves. Psychopathology is defined as a failure (of the self) to learn from personal experiences.

All people are viewed as having an actualizing or formative tendency. PCT is designed to activate the actualizing tendency through a therapeutic relationship that includes: (1) congruence, (2) unconditional positive regard, and (3) empathic understanding. Natalie Rogers, Carl's daughter, contended that most U.S. practitioners don't understand person-centered therapy.

In practice, PCT is a way of being with clients. This way of being is not skill-based, but instead based on therapist attitudes (the core conditions). It's the therapist's role to experience and express congruence, unconditional positive regard, and empathic understanding. Assessment is viewed as either unimportant or potentially damaging. The three core conditions are expressed indirectly. Recent neuroscience research has affirmed that empathic responding can affect the brains of therapists and clients.

Although PCT conditions are at the heart of most therapies, there are a number of therapy approaches that are second generation forms of PCT. These include (a) focusing, (b) motivational interviewing, (c) emotion-focused therapy, (d) child-centered play therapy, and (e) expressive art therapy. Of these, motivational interviewing (MI) is the most prominent. MI, initially developed for working with alcohol-abusing clients, uses reflective, empathic techniques to focus on client ambivalence and help clients develop their own motivation for change. The underlying spirit of MI and MI techniques are consistent with person-centered theory and practice.

There is strong evidence to support some of PCT's key concepts. In particular, empathy is generally considered a robust therapist variable influencing positive treatment outcome. Most empirical research indicates that classical PCT is better than no treatment, but less efficacious than more structured and explicitly educational therapies. However, this may be related to researcher bias. In contrast, motivational interviewing has strong empirical support for treating a number of different mental disorders and health problems.

To some degree, PCT is very culturally sensitive. However, because it focuses on the treatment of individuals, clients from collectivist backgrounds may prefer more directive approaches. Due to its empowering foundation, feminist therapists tend to view PCT in a positive light. However, for both feminists and sexually diverse clients, traditional PCT may not be as affirmative or advocating as desired. Additionally, if clients hold nonjudgmental spiritual or religious values, then PCT may be a good fit.

PERSON-CENTERED KEY TERMS

Absolute worth

Accurate empathy

Actualizing or formative tendency

Affirmation

Amplified reflection

Autonomy support

Change talk

Classical PCT

Client ambivalence

Client-centered therapy

Compassion

Complex reflections

Conditions of worth

Congruence

Contemporary PCT

Emotion-focused therapy (aka process-experiential psychotherapy)

Emotional regulation

Emotional stimulation

Empathic understanding

Ideal self

Incongruence

Interpersonal empathy

Moment-to-moment sensitivity

Motivational interviewing

Necessary and sufficient conditions

Need for positive regard

Need for self-regard

Negative self-regard

Nondirective counseling

Objective empathy

Organism

Pacing

Person-centered therapy

Perspective-taking

Profound acceptance

Real self

Simple reflections

Subception

Subjective empathy

Sustain talk

The self

Unconditional positive regard

Walking within

Worldwide issues

CHAPTER 6

Gestalt Theory and Therapy

- Define Gestalt therapy
- Identify key figures and historical trends in the development, evolution, and application of Gestalt theory and therapy
- Describe core principles of Gestalt theory
- Describe and apply Gestalt therapy principles, strategies, and techniques
- Analyze Gestalt therapy cases
- Evaluate the empirical, cultural, gender, and spiritual validity of Gestalt therapy
- Summarize core content and define key terms associated with Gestalt theory and therapy

Fritz and Laura Perls developed Gestalt theory and therapy. Fritz was charismatic and controversial. One of his most famous descriptions of Gestalt therapy was: "Lose your mind and come to your senses" (1969a, p. 69). This statement captures the physical and experiential nature of Gestalt therapy; it also implies that you should try to move beyond an intellectual understanding of this chapter and directly experience Gestalt therapy.

INTRODUCTION

Gestalt therapy is primarily a process-oriented therapy. Perls typically downplayed or dismissed the content of client talk. He also tended to lament all things intellectual. Perls was much more likely to demonstrate Gestalt therapy than talk about it.

What Is Gestalt Therapy?

During an interview with a professional journalist (Bry, 1973), Fritz was asked, "What is Gestalt therapy?"

He responded: "Discussing, talking, explaining is unreal to me. I hate intellectualizing, don't you?"

He then refused the interview, instead convincing the journalist to experience Gestalt therapy in the *here and now*. He urged her to *be the patient* so he could teach her Gestalt therapy (and not teach her *about* Gestalt therapy).

This anecdote illustrates what Gestalt therapy is *not*: Gestalt therapy is not a time to sit around and talk *about* your experiences; instead, Gestalt therapy is experiential.

A formal definition: **Gestalt therapy** is an existential-humanistic-phenomenological therapy. It focuses on using here and now sensory experiences to enhance self-awareness and facilitate personal growth. Gestalt therapy occurs within a relational context.

Similar to how he handled professional interviews, when asked to lecture, Perls complained that learning was unlikely to occur. He viewed lectures as too intellectual and sterile for real learning to occur. Likely, he'd view this textbook the same way, which leads to a conundrum for us: How can we use a textbook (a format steeped in the intellectual tradition) to teach Gestalt therapy? Although the challenge is significant, we'll do our best to engage you in a Gestalt experience.

This chapter is sprinkled with experiential activities. Feel free to skip them if you like. You might even choose to snooze, but you'll just be avoiding an opportunity to "Wake up, lose your mind, and come to your senses."

Fritz Perls and Laura Posner Perls

Take a moment to get in touch with your current sensory experience. Look at the words on this page as if you were seeing letters and words for the very first time. Notice your face. How does *your face* feel? Do you notice any facial tension? Now pay attention to your whole body. Where's the tension? Where's the calmness? Intentionally breathe in. Intentionally let your breath out. Now, notice your posture. Are you in the posture you aspire toward? Deliberately assume a learning posture. Assume *your* learning posture.

A defining feature of Gestalt therapy involves cultivating self-awareness by paying attention to your body. As we travel through this chapter together, pay attention to your body. Do that now.

Think about that word.

Now.

Later, we'll come back to talking about now.

Shift your attention again, this time to your imagination. As you read historical anecdotes about Fritz and Laura, go into your imagination. Visualize and feel what you're reading. To help bring this historical information to life, we'll follow singer-songwriter Joni Mitchell's advice from the song, *Chelsea Morning*.

> Oh, won't you stay
> We'll put on the day
> And we'll talk in present tenses (Mitchell, 1969)

Frederick Salomon Perls is born and lives in Berlin. He and his family are Jewish. He is a middle child, with an older sister and a younger sister.

Fritz is a difficult boy—a boy who challenges his lower middle-class parents. He flunks 7th grade. He flunks it again. He is enrolled in the conservative Mommsen Gymnasium that has a reputation for rigidity and anti-Semitism. They ask him to leave the school.

For a short time Frederick works for a merchant, but he's dismissed for being a prankster. He returns to school at the more liberal Askanishe Gymnasium at age 14. Somehow, he turns his life around and perseveres. He decides to study medicine. At age 23, he volunteers and serves as a medical corpsman in World War I. He works in the trenches and is gassed and wounded. Later he earns his medical degree with a specialization in psychiatry from Friedrich-Wilhelm University.

In the early to mid-1920s Fritz moves to Vienna for psychoanalytic training. He spends 7 years in psychoanalysis with three leading analysts, Otto Fenichel, Wilhelm Reich, and Karen Horney. He describes his experience:

> In 1925, I started seven years of useless couch life. I felt stupid. Finally, Wilhelm Reich, then still sane, began to make some sense. Also, there was Karen Horney, whom I loved. ... From Fenichel I got confidence; from Reich, brazenness; from Horney, human involvement. (1969a, p. 38)

During this time, Perls works for Kurt Goldstein at the *Goldstein Institute for Brain-Damaged Soldiers* in Frankfurt. Goldstein, best known for first coining the term self-actualization, uses a Gestalt psychology approach to help soldiers focus on their perceptions. His emphasis on placing "the total organism of the individual in the

foreground" (Goldstein, 1939, p. 17) is an intellectual and practical predecessor of Gestalt therapy.

Lore Posner is born in Pforzheim, Germany, to a wealthy family as Fritz was flunking 7th grade. She is fabulously bright and ambitious. She is in modern dance, is a concert-caliber pianist, attends law school, obtains a doctorate in Gestalt psychology, and studies existential psychology with Paul Tillich and Martin Buber. Prior to collaborating with Fritz, Lore is a dynamic force of her own.

While working on her PhD in Gestalt psychology, Lore studies with Kurt Goldstein. She meets Fritz Perls in 1926. She is 21; he is 33. Frederick and Lore are married in 1929. Together they are Fritz and Laura, a union that produces one of the most provocative personal change strategies ever.

Not long after their marriage they flee Germany and the Nazis with the clothes on their backs and about $25, moving briefly to Amsterdam and then to South Africa.

HISTORICAL CONTEXT

In Germany in the 1930s, several different ideas about psychotherapy were vying for attention and dominance. Psychoanalysis was central among these. Perls was a fan of Freud. One of his training analysts was Wilhelm Reich.

A Muscular Digression

As we follow our moment-to-moment awareness, we should briefly digress and note that Wilhelm Reich is both famous and infamous (Reich, 1975; Reich, Higgins, Raphael, Schmitz, & Tompkins, 1988). He developed a psychotherapy that focused on observing clients' facial expressions and body positions. He believed libido was a positive life force or energy characterized by excitement. This excitement could be viewed in the human body, but it was suppressed by society. He came up with the term **character armor** to describe muscular resistance through which clients defended against their libido.

Reich moved to the United States and turned away from his psychoanalytic work, developing a telephone booth–size device he called the orgone accumulator. This device (purportedly used by J. D. Salinger and written about by Jack Kerouac and Orson Bean) supposedly charged the body with so-called "orgone" collected from the atmosphere. The U.S. Food and Drug Administration obtained a federal injunction banning interstate distribution of orgone boxes or written materials. Reich violated the injunction, was arrested, and sent to prison where he died of heart failure (Mann, 1973; Sharaf, 1994).

Now we return to our main story.

Fritz and Laura in South Africa

In 1934, Fritz and Laura settle in South Africa for about 12 years. They quickly establish the *South African Institute for Psychoanalysis*. Then, in 1936, Fritz has a profound experience that further shapes his life…he meets Sigmund Freud at a conference in Europe. Fritz describes this meeting in his autobiography, *In and Out the Garbage Pail*:

> I made an appointment, was received by an elderly woman (I believe his sister) and waited. Then a door opened about 2½ feet wide and there he was, before my eyes. It seemed strange that he would not leave the door frame, but at that time I knew nothing about his phobias.
>
> "I came from South Africa to give a paper and to see you."
>
> "Well, and when are you going back?" he said. I don't remember the rest of the (perhaps four-minute long) conversation. I was shocked and disappointed. (F. Perls, 1969b, p. 56)

For Perls, this meeting is ultimately invigorating and motivating. It frees him from the dogma of psychoanalytic thinking and propels him to embrace existentialism and his own psychotherapeutic approach.

In South Africa, Fritz and Laura collaborate on their first major written work, *Ego, Hunger and Aggression* (F. S. Perls, 1945). Although Laura writes several chapters she receives only an acknowledgment and even that is deleted from future editions.

Laura reports that their initial discoveries begin when she is mothering their two children in South Africa (Rosenfeld, 1978). She observes their children's eating and chewing behaviors. This leads to linking the real chewing of food to the metaphorical process of assimilating ideas.

Chewing, eating, and digesting become consistent themes in Gestalt theory and therapy. When people eat, they bite off what they can chew. When they experience ideas, they take in what they can and mentally chew it to digest the ideas. They use the term **mental metabolism** to describe this process.

REFLECTIONS

Let's explore mental metabolism. What foods "go down easy"? What ideas do you find yourself easily digesting? What foods give you a stomach ache? What ideas give you a headache? Now, one step further: What foods make you want to vomit? What ideas do you find repulsive?

The Gestalt Therapy Bible

Laura described how Gestalt therapy is named:

> Actually when we first started we wanted to call it "Existential therapy", but then existentialism was so much identified with Sartre, with the nihilistic approach, that we looked for another name. I thought that with Gestalt therapy, with the word "Gestalt", we could get into difficulties. But that criticism was rejected by Fritz and Paul [Goodman]. (Rosenfeld, 1978, p. 11)

The second major work of Fritz and Laura's, *Gestalt Therapy: Excitement and Growth of the Human Personality*, is published in 1951 (F. Perls, Hefferline, & Goodman, 1951). Once again, Laura receives no credit. The book is primarily written by Goodman. The first half of the book includes Gestalt activities Hefferline uses with his students at Columbia University. The second half of *Gestalt Therapy* is a dense immersion into Gestalt theoretical principles. Although not initially well received or accessible (Goodman is apparently a rather plodding writer), this book remains a cornerstone of contemporary Gestalt therapy. Margherita Spagnuolo Lobb, founder and director of the *Istituto di Gestalt* in Italy, wrote:

> Our founding book, Gestalt Therapy, is strange and difficult to understand because it does not lend itself to rational categorizations, but it is provocative and intellectually challenging. It stimulates readers to reflect and generate new ideas. This effect is not dependent on culture or time or place; it happens any time one reads it—50 years ago or today. For this reason, it is often referred to as the "bible" of Gestalt therapists. (Lobb & Lichtenberg, 2005, pp. 22–23)

Although Lobb is referring to the theoretical section of the book, this is a good time for you to drop everything and fully participate in the Gestalt therapy activity, **Feeling the Actual** (see Putting It in Practice 6.1).

Fascism and World War II

Gestalt therapy is developed in the wake of World War II. Bowman and Nevis (2005) describe the conditions:

> The rise of fascism, the Holocaust, and World War II were arguably the most influential factors in the development of Gestalt therapy since Freud and Breuer's development of the "talking cure." The list of indispensable contributors to Gestalt therapy who were forced to flee their homelands in search of safety and freedom from fascism is extensive—The Perlses, Buber, Lewin, Goldstein, Wertheimer, Koffka, Kohler, and Reich, to name but a few. Many lost entire families, and all lost loved ones and their worldly belongings. (p. 12)

Given this context, it's not surprising that Gestalt therapy has anarchistic roots. The resulting skepticism toward bureaucracy leads to friction between Gestalt practitioners and bureaucratic systems in psychology and medicine (Bowman & Nevis, 2005). Consistent with sensitivity to authoritarian control and oppression, after 12 years in South Africa, in 1946, Fritz and Laura move away from the growing Apartheid regime and toward the freedom of New York City.

From 1948 to 1951, Fritz, Laura, and Paul Goodman conduct Gestalt therapy workshops. In New York,

---

PUTTING IT IN PRACTICE

6.1 The Gestalt "Feeling the Actual" Experiment

This is experiment 1 from *Gestalt Therapy* (1951). It illustrates a concrete therapy technique *and* captures the basic philosophy of Gestalt therapy. After you've experienced it, you may want to try it with someone else, possibly a fellow student, or a willing practicum client.

This experiment tunes you into what is actual and now. Too often, our attention is divided and we're numb to life or we experience anxiety or apprehension that focuses our attention. However, true contact with the environment and with your self is different from an anxiety state.

To participate in this experiment, follow these instructions: "Try for a few minutes to make up sentences stating what you are at this moment aware of. Begin each sentence with the words 'now' or 'at this moment' or 'here and now'" (F. Perls et al., 1951, p. 37).

For example, "Now, as I type, I'm aware of soreness in my lower back. Now I'm thinking about what I've done to myself and why I've chosen to sit for so long. Now I think I should move. Now I'm aware of thinking I should stop thinking. At this moment I wonder what my body wants. Here and now it wants to lie down and rest, but at this moment I remain sitting, resisting what I know is good for me. Now I'm fighting with myself about whether to type another word or to stretch my back and stare at the ceiling."

Okay. Now it's your turn. Start "feeling the actual" now.

Debriefing section [Don't read any further until you've spent five minutes feeling the actual.]

How did it feel to participate in this experiment? For some, it feels silly or awkward. For others, it seems phony and contrived. Still others feel resistance or opposition. In Gestalt experiments, your individual here and now reaction to the experiment is just as important as any "content" you generate. You're a total being, capable of simultaneously experiencing an experience and reacting to the experience.

If you felt this experiment to be phony, don't be surprised. Sometimes, after living in disconnected ways, it's possible to feel like you're acting when you're beginning to really experience life.

If you felt opposed and resistant to this experiment, perhaps you're using deflection. You're avoiding contact with the environment by pulling back and being uninvolved.

Gestalt therapy can be repetitive, but the purpose of repetition isn't in the service of numbness. Instead, it's to awaken you. To "wake up" is to value your physical-sensory experience. Repeatedly experiencing the mundane (even this book!) as well as the extraordinary as fully and completely as possible means your awareness is elevated and consciousness expanded.

Cleveland, and then California, Fritz's already big personality grows even bigger. He relocates to Big Sur, California, as a member of the Esalen staff and prominent figure in the human potential movement. Fritz stops doing individual psychotherapy work in favor of large group demonstrations, sometimes called "circuses" (Bowman & Nevis, 2005).

For Gestalt therapy specifically, the most unfortunate effect of … Perls's circuses was a perception of Gestalt therapy as, ironically, significantly less than the sum of

its parts. Gestalt therapy became known as a therapy of techniques, quick cures, or even gimmicks. (p. 15)

Toward the end of his life, Fritz flees from what he perceives as increasing fascist trends in the United States under the Nixon administration. He settles in Cowichan, B.C., establishing a communal utopian anarchy. Fritz dies in 1970.

Although the contributions of Laura Posner Perls to Gestalt therapy practice were immense, she never receives much credit, partly due to the flamboyant extraversion of

Fritz and partly due to the fact that her name, somewhat mysteriously (at least to us) is not on many publications. She does, however, comment freely on Fritz's productivity at the twenty-fifth anniversary of the New York Institute for Gestalt Therapy (an organization that she co-founded with Fritz).

> Without the constant support from his friends, and from me, without the constant encouragement and collaboration, Fritz would never have written a line, nor founded anything. (L. Perls, 1990, p. 18)

Gestalt Therapy's Roots and Branches

Gestalt therapy is an integration of several different intellectual and historical forces. These include:

- Psychoanalysis.
- Developmental psychology.
- Gestalt psychology.
- Field theory.
- Existential philosophy.
- World War II, fascism, and anarchist rebellion.
- Reich's focus on body awareness.
- Experiential learning during workshops and demonstrations.

Gestalt theory and therapy is an amalgam, an integration, a flourish of immediacy, a powerfully human encounter, and more. It's an open system where everything is interrelated and where, consistent with anarchistic roots, the concepts of friction, rebellion, and reconfiguration prevail.

Like all systems and cultures, Gestalt theory and practice continues to evolve. Two big developments, woven into this chapter, are relational Gestalt therapy (Yontef, 2010) and emotion-focused therapy (Greenberg, 2015).

THEORETICAL PRINCIPLES

Gestalt theoretical principles are praised and castigated. On the one hand, Fritz and Laura were onto something profound. On the other hand, as Laura Perls noted, Fritz was not very adept at writing in English (Rosenfeld, 1978). This may have been partly why he preferred demonstrations over traditional academic publications.

To provide a caveat to our theoretical discussion, we quote Wagner-Moore's (2004) helpful summary of the status of Gestalt theory:

The "Perlsian" form of Gestalt therapy primarily embodies the history and personality of Perls himself, rather than a scientific, structured, empirically derived or theoretically consistent model of psychotherapy. Gestalt theory is an intellectually fascinating, philosophically complex set of diverse but poorly articulated and poorly substantiated beliefs.

Examining Gestalt theoretical principles is challenging. There is classical Gestalt theory derived from the previously mentioned *Gestalt Bible* (F. Perls, Hefferline, & Goodman, 1951). There is the less formal and more accessible *Gestalt Therapy Verbatim* (F. S. Perls, 1969a), a compilation of verbatim transcripts of Perls's weekend dream retreats and 4-week intensive workshops. Many contemporary Gestalt figures consider these transcripts to be the best representation of his work (Prochaska & Norcross, 2014). There are also several theoretical modifications and extensions of his work (E. Polster & Polster, 1973; Yontef, 1988).

Our look at Gestalt theory is an effort to honor Fritz's and Laura's original thinking while incorporating ideas, revisions, and new emphases provided by recent and contemporary Gestalt theorists and practitioners.

Existential and Gestalt Psychology Foundations

Gestalt theory and therapy has existential-humanistic and Gestalt psychology roots. Similar to other existential-humanistic therapies (e.g., person-centered theory), there's an underlying belief that individuals have self-actualizing potential. Gestalt experiments can activate the actualizing potential and move clients toward their potentials.

Self-Actualization and Self-Regulation

Instead of self-actualization per se, Gestalt theory focuses on individuals' **self-regulation**. If you notice that the term self-regulation has a physical feel, you're sensing an important component of Gestalt theory. Gestalt has a greater emphasis on physical awareness and the body or musculature than other therapy approaches.

Self-regulation relies on awareness. We can't self-regulate until self-awareness brings the need for self-regulation into focus. The process includes:

- An initial state of equilibrium. All is well in the organism.
- Disruption of equilibrium through emergence of a need, sensation, or desire. Disequilibrium begins to occur, but may still not have completely emerged from the background.
- Development of awareness of the need, sensation, or desire. Individuals may need a therapist to facilitate this awareness (i.e., moving the need from the background to the figure).

- Taking actions or making contacts to deal with disequilibrium. The aware individual takes intentional action to address the situation and finish whatever "business" needs finishing.

- Return to equilibrium. All is well again, until the next moment when another disequilibrating experience occurs.

Based on this natural self-regulation model, the therapist's primary role is to help clients become aware of their needs, sensations, and desires. Therapists then help clients deal with these experiences more directly and authentically.

The Gestalt (Holism)

Gestalt is a German word referring to the unified whole or complete form. A primary idea associated with Gestalt is that "the whole is different or greater than the sum of its parts." This idea can be traced to at least Aristotle's *Metaphysica* in 350 b.c. (Warrington, 1956). During Perls's time, the term **holism** was coined by South African Prime Minister Jan Smuts, author of *Holism and Evolution* (Smuts, 1927).

The following comment about holism helps articulate how individual components can combine to form new, unique, and unpredictable qualities.

> Carbon atoms have particular, knowable physical and chemical properties. But the atoms can be combined in different ways to make, say, graphite or diamond. The properties of those substances—properties such as darkness and softness and clearness and hardness— are not properties of the carbon atoms, but rather properties of the collection of carbon atoms. Moreover, which particular properties the collection of atoms has depends entirely on how they are assembled—into sheets or pyramids. The properties arise because of the connections between the parts. I think grasping this insight is crucial for a proper scientific perspective on the world. You could know everything about isolated neurons and not be able to say how memory works, or where desire originates. (Christakis, 2011; retrieved July 2, 2011, from http://www.edge.org/q2011/q11_6.html)

Mind–body is an inseparable whole; Gestalt is a physical–mental–emotional theory. Gestalt therapists actively comment on their client's physical positions, postures, and gestures because these motor movements represent emotional and cognitive events within the person. Much of this comes from Reich's influence on Perls. "Gestalt therapists consider repression as essentially a muscular phenomenon" (Wallen, 1970, p. 7). We'll return to the body when we discuss Gestalt therapy techniques.

Phenomenology

Like Adlerian and Rogerian theories, Gestalt theory is phenomenological, meaning it has to do with consciousness and direct experiencing. In Gestalt theory, the phenomenological field involves the study of experience through subjective observations. Therapists are interested in their own and their clients' reports of direct experiencing. Direct experiencing and authenticity in therapy and life facilitates growth.

Field Theory

Kurt Lewin (1951) originally discussed field theory. **Field theory** includes propositions that individuals and the environment are together within a field of constant interaction. Field theory is holistic. Everything is relational within field theory (Yontef, 2002).

Field theory can fundamentally guide therapist behavior and practice (adapted from Parlett & Lee, 2005, pp. 47–51).

1. The therapist is not detached or separated from the field. This concept is consistent with subatomic physics. People are both in the field and of the field.

2. Therapist and client explore the field together. All fields have patterns and interrelationships that repeat and are interdependent. Gestalt therapists are saying (metaphorically), "Let's wade right into the field and try to see it as a functioning whole and, at the same time, become more intimately familiar with how its parts work."

3. Gestalt therapists work in the immediate, here-and-now field. Time is relative and captured in memories; everything of import is in the here and now field.

Gestalt therapists attend to what's happening within the whole field; the contact or boundary between the person and environment is of special interest. As these boundary contacts are explored, awareness is stimulated in clients and therapists. Awareness, in turn, stimulates self-regulation.

The Figure-Formation Process

Humans constantly shift their cognitive or perceptual focus. This is especially true in our contemporary, media-based society where distractibility is normative (Freedman & Honkasilta, 2017).

An amazing human quality is the ability to intentionally shift the focus of consciousness. If you're reading these words, your focus (figure) is the words on this page (or screen) and their meaning. This process puts you in your head—literally. You're all eyes and intellectual processing.

This visual and intellectual experience is a function of your focus, but you could focus on something else. If, as you read these words, you intentionally shift focus to your ears, what happens? Alternatively, if you are listening to this book instead of reading, you could shift to the smells in the room. Can you simultaneously focus completely on every sound wave or every odor bouncing around you without losing your intellectual focus? You may still be seeing or hearing the words, but now they've drifted into the background. If you consciously focus on auditory perception, sound will take over the foreground or figure. If we take this further, you could alternate between different sounds and smells in your environment (maybe there's music or a dull hum of lights, or your breathing, or someone's perfume/cologne, or your gym clothes in the corner, or...). In each case, the **figure-formation process** is happening; it involves your attention shifting, more or less, placing different perceptions at the forefront.

Perhaps an everyday example will help. Let's say you're driving the Interstate in Montana, going 80 mph. There aren't many cars on the road, because you're in Montana. A signal from your cell phone pops into your awareness, triggering a social need, which produces disequilibrium; you decide to take action and check your new text message. You steer with one hand, hold your phone with the other, and shift your eyes from the road to the phone. Three seconds on the road, 3 seconds reading text on the phone. At first, the road is figure and the phone in your hand is background. Then, the phone becomes figure and the road is background.

Suddenly, you have a background thought about what you're doing. Having passed your driver's test, you possess internal knowledge about how far you travel in three seconds at 80 mph. You're covering 352 feet—well over the length of a soccer or football field—every 3 seconds. This internal memory emerges from background to figure along with a realization that you could have run over approximately 117.3 deer on the highway standing side-by-side while checking three seconds of your text message. Another linked thought crystalizes into figure; you can almost hear your parents telling you they love you so much that they'd like you not to text and drive.

The figure-formation voice in your head brings a surge of anxiety. You tap your brake and slow down to an unheard of 55 mph so that you're only covering 243 feet every 3 seconds. Somehow you rationalize and justify that you're safe enough to read your text; equilibrium is restored.

The point is not that you're endangering your life and the lives of hundreds of innocent deer, but that when figure recedes into background, you always miss something, but you gain something when figure-formation occurs. This losing or gaining is, to some extent, under voluntary control. You may choose to miss out on the text message or you may choose to miss out on the 352 feet of road—but you can't have it both ways; something has to be figure and something has to be ground.

From the Gestalt perspective, you're always just a little bit aware of the ground (or background). Part of therapy involves turning up background noise by refocusing your awareness. This lets you evaluate whether whatever's bubbling around in the background might be important. Not everything you focus on in therapy will be important. However, many parts of your human experience (including unfinished business from the past that's affecting you in the present) might prove important and helpful.

This is the essence of Gestalt therapy: shift your focus and then shift it again to embrace here and now awareness and the personal development it might stimulate. At the same time, you recognize that not every 352-foot stretch of Montana highway will be immediately and profoundly important, but you stay with that focus because to do otherwise threatens your existence.

Primary or dominant needs of an individual can emerge from background (ground) into focus (figure) at any given moment. This is why Gestalt therapists believe a here and now focus will inevitably bring unfinished business from the past into the present.

REFLECTIONS

Think of some ways in which the figure-formation process happens in your life. What triggers old memories for you? How do they "emerge" from background to foreground?

I and Thou, Here and Now, What and How

Yontef (2010, p. 31) used nine words to describe Gestalt therapy. These words speak to three core theoretical processes in Gestalt therapy:

1. **I and Thou**: An authentic therapist–client relationship.

2. **Here and Now**: Immediacy or being present in the here and now.

3. **What and How**: An emphasis on process over content; moment-to-moment examination of what's happening.

1. I and Thou

Perls was dynamic and confrontational. Much of his work occurred in group contexts. He often intentionally frustrated clients to produce reactions and worked in ways considered adversarial. His approach is often not directly generalizable to individual or group psychotherapy. However, many historical and contemporary Gestalt therapists have moved away from trying to *be like Fritz* and have instead expanded on the original Gestalt theoretical model, deemphasizing the therapist as authoritative and confrontational (Hycner & Jacobs, 2009; Yontef, 2005).

The Gestalt therapy relationship is viewed as an authentic contact between two collaborative experts working to develop and refine client self-awareness. Therapists are experts on the Gestalt change process; clients are experts on their own experiences. These two parties are interdependent and mutually responsible for therapy process and success (Yontef, 2002). Although in keeping with an existential framework, therapists hold clients responsible for their experiences; they don't blame them for their problems or for impasses in therapy. E. Polster (1966) described this kinder and gentler Gestalt therapy relationship:

> They may engage simply, saying and doing those things which are pertinent to their needs, the therapist offering a new range of possibility to the patient through his willingness to know the truth and to be an authentic person. Ideally this would be enough. It is curative for both to speak freshly, arouse warmth, and encounter wisdom. (pp. 5–6)

In keeping with Buber's (1970) I-Thou relationship, Gestalt therapists strive to connect deeply with their clients. They work toward compassion. They acknowledge moving in and out of an I-Thou connection; they do so to guide clients toward greater self-awareness and personal discovery.

2. Here and Now

> I maintain that all therapy that has to be done can only be done in the now. (F. S. Perls, 1970, p. 16)

We have a friend with an old-fashioned hour-hand, minute-hand, and second-hand wristwatch. However, in place of numbers around the watch dial the same word sits in each number's usual position. The word is NOW.

The opposite of Here and Now is Then and There. The operation of Then and There is to distance ourselves from ourselves. We can tell stories about our experiences rather than accessing our experiences directly. Although this may feel safer, it's more dead and less alive. For Gestalt therapists, the lively Now is all that's worthy of focus.

Gestalt therapists emphasize that the past can only be accessed in the Now. This is because the past is unchangeable. It's over. The only way the past is accessible is to bring it into Now. Perls made his position clear in Atlanta in 1966:

> This is why I am absolutely dogmatic in regard to the fact that nothing exists except in the now, and that in the now you are behaving in a certain way that will or will not facilitate your development, your acquisition of a better ability to cope with life, to make available what was unavailable before, to begin to fill in the voids in your existence. (F. S. Perls, 1970, p. 18)

Perls believed that a psychoanalytic focus on the past causes clients to remain infantile or childish. He claimed that when clients *talk about* themselves they (a) give over authority to therapists who then profess to understand or interpret client behavior and (b) remain in a dependent, child-like position. In Gestalt therapy, the past comes into the Now. This allows clients to choose

personal responsibility. He stated, "We are infantile because we are afraid to take responsibility in the now" (Perls, 1970, p. 17).

Perls talked about the fear of taking responsibility for oneself in the Now as a form of "stage fright" (F. S. Perls, 1970, p. 15). He based his reasoning on a quotation from Freud: "Denken ist probearbeit" ("Thinking is trial work"). Perls noted that thinking about ourselves and the future is all simply rehearsal for the main event of living. For better or worse, living in the moment requires stepping up and out onto the stage.

Consider a client who's focusing on the future and wondering, "How will I talk with my parents about wanting to study dance instead of computer science?" A Gestalt therapist might bring the future into the present with an empty chair technique. The empty chair conversation would bring the stage fright into the client's control; then, moment-to-moment sensory awareness could be explored—giving the client practice at talking about his desire to dance professionally and increased awareness of unfinished business from the past and anxieties imported from the future.

3. What and How

We should re-emphasize that Gestalt therapy focuses on process over content. To support this process orientation, Gestalt therapists generally avoid using the question "Why?" because why questions promote intellectualization. Instead, therapists use "What" questions ("What would your feet tell you right now if they could speak?") or "How" questions ("How would you describe the sound of your voice as you say that?").

Contact and Resistance to Contact

> The Gestalt concept of *contact* can be defined as the exchange of information between I-ness and otherness. (Tønnesvang, Sommer, Hammink, & Sonne, 2010, p. 588; italics added)

Individuals are organisms in and of the world (field) that come in contact with other objects and organisms. Contact is perceptual. We recognize contact through our senses.

Imagine yourself on a nature walk. You're smelling flowers, seeing green leaves and grass, hearing the river, touching rough bark on a tree, feeling yourself move. You're making contact with various objects in nature. Now imagine that you meet a person on the trail. You smell the person's scent in the breeze. Is it perfume, cologne, or body odor?

Contact implies boundaries. When another person's scent reaches your nose and into your brain, two human boundaries are in contact. Depending on the odor and your mental representations of that odor in your past, you may approach or withdraw; you may try to prolong or shorten your boundary contact. Boundaries function to connect and to separate.

Erving and Miriam Polster (1973) consider contact the "lifeblood of growth" (p. 101). All learning possibilities involve contact. As you read these words you're making contact with Gestalt theory and therapy. As you make contact with Gestalt theory and therapy, you experience one of five different boundary disturbances, which we discuss next.

BRAIN BOX

6.1 Neuroscience and Gestalt Feedback Loops

If we boil Gestalt theory and therapy down to dust, we might be left with awareness. The next logical question is: "Awareness of what?" As a holistic theory, the answer would seem to be: "Everything." More specifically, Gestalt theory includes self, field (including others), and contact. So we're talking about awareness of the whole of the self, all of the field, and contact experiences.

In some ways, Gestalt therapy is the original body-work. Some have argued that Gestalt theory paved the way for integration of neuroscience findings into counseling and psychotherapy (Lobb, 2016). Gestalt theory and therapy is about the whole of the self, including neurons, neurochemicals, and neural networks. Gestalt theory and therapy are also precursors to contemporary somatic experiencing therapy (Levine, 2010).

It's possible to think of neurofeedback as having Gestalt roots. **Neurofeedback** is a form of biofeedback where individuals are provided with EEG (electroencephalogram) feedback and coached (sometimes using video game imagery) to change their EEG patterns in specific ways. As a therapeutic modality, neurofeedback is partly popular and partly dismissed (Chow, Javan, Ros, & Frewen, 2017). There's little (but growing) scientific evidence to support its efficacy, but the neurofeedback process is mostly about monitoring the body/brain to enhance self-awareness. At least, neurofeedback represents a contemporary effort to establish a feedback loop between what's happening in the brain and what's happening (a) in the body; (b) in behavioral, cognitive, emotional, and interpersonal domains; and (c) in the environment (aka field).

Daniel Siegel (2010), among others, has articulated ways in which interpersonal relationships influence neurobiology. He refers to this as interpersonal neurobiology. Gestalt theorists view interpersonal neurobiology as evidence for how what resides in the brain makes it possible for individuals to make creative adjustments to whatever is sensed and experienced at the contact boundary (Lobb, 2016). Interpersonal neurobiology is also consistent with the relational movement in Gestalt therapy and greater emphasis on the I-Thou relationship. Siegel (2010) wrote:

> The physiological result of presence and attunement is the alignment of two autonomous beings into an interdependent and functional whole as each person influences the internal state of the other. With resonance we come to "feel felt" by the other. This joining has profound transformative effect on both people. Resonance is what our human nervous system is built to require for a sense of connection to others early in life.... The need for such intimate and vulnerable connection persists throughout our lives. (p. xx)

Let's return to the idea that neurons that fire together, wire together (see Chapter 1, Hebb's Law). If so, then Gestalt interpersonal resonance and Gestalt experiments become methods that can be viewed as stimulating and developing new and more adaptive neural networks. Proponents of Gestalt theory and therapy see Gestalt theory as having established the groundwork for neuropsychotherapy or neurocounseling; they also see great potential for neuroscience to validate Gestalt therapeutic process and practice (Day, 2016; Lobb, 2016).

Theory of Psychopathology

Healthy functioning in the Gestalt world is characterized by contact, full awareness, full sensory functioning, choice, and spontaneity. In this state, the individual experiences excitement and a sort of graceful flow. There's little need for overthinking or planning as being oneself in the spontaneous moment is possible.

Psychopathology as Contact Disturbance

Psychopathology occurs when natural processes of contact, excitement, self-regulation, and new learning are disturbed. Gestalt therapists view psychopathology through the lens of contact and **resistance to contact** (i.e., defenses against the intrusion that contact can represent).

Every contact evokes excitement and presents the possibility of new learning. However, some contacts are especially challenging and can potentially damage individuals. These challenging contacts must be faced and assimilated or integrated into one's being. The individual or organism needs to face the contact, bring it into figure (awareness), bite into it (the experience of contact), and then using maximal self-awareness, digest what is organically vital and intentionally discard the rest.

Given this model, psychopathology is defined as an individual's or organism's (client's) "creative adjustment" in a difficult situation:

> If a young girl spontaneously feels the desire to hug her father and she encounters his coldness, she stops her spontaneous movement toward him, but she doesn't stop her intentionality to contact him. The excitation of "I want to hug him" is blocked in an inhaling movement (where she holds her breath), and she becomes anxious. To avoid this anxiety, she learns to do other things and eventually may even forget the anxiety. What she does is establish contact via styles of interrupting or resisting spontaneity. (Lobb & Lichtenberg, 2005, p. 33)

Individuals may have characteristic styles of interrupting or resisting contact. Because learning is an essential by-product of contact, repeatedly interrupting or resisting contact constitutes psychopathology. Five different **boundary disturbances** (aka ways of having resistance to contact) and examples are described in Table 6.1.

Table 6.1   The Five Boundary Disturbances

1. **Introjection:** This boundary disturbance involves uncritical acceptance of other's beliefs and standards. Contact occurs; whatever values and standards are associated with the contact are swallowed whole. Not much thinking or chewing is involved.	Miguel meets Marlon on the nature walk. Miguel tells Marlon he has found a special plant off the trail that produces a "natural high" when ingested. Marlon joins Miguel in eating some of the plant. [Reflect for a moment on what consequences you think might be associated with Marlon's uncritical acceptance and swallowing of Miguel's ideas and values (as well as the plant!).]
2. **Projection:** This boundary disturbance occurs when people place (or project) their emotions or traits onto others. Often the emotions or traits are those we would like to disown or those that make us uncomfortable, but that we can identify with.	Susan meets Latisha on the nature walk. Susan was just in a fight with her romantic partner and has some residual anger. After stopping and having a short conversation with Latisha, Susan walks on, thinking to herself: "Wow, that was one angry woman. I'm glad I'm not like that." [Susan projected her uncomfortable angry feelings onto Latisha.]
3. **Retroflection:** This disturbance has two variations. First, it occurs when people turn back on themselves something they would like to do to another person. For example, when working with suicidal clients, one of our former supervisors used to always ask: "Who is the client wanting to commit suicide at?" Second, it involves the doing to ourselves what we would like someone in the environment to do to or for us.	Marco meets Polo on the nature walk. Marco falls immediately in love with Polo, but Polo doesn't return his affection. After they separate, Marco comes upon a lake. He looks into the clear water, sees his reflection, and falls in love with himself. [Marco does to/for himself what he wished Polo had done for him.]
4. **Deflection:** This boundary disturbance involves a distraction that diffuses or reduces contact. This can include avoiding physical contact, using humor excessively, and talking about others instead of the self. This is similar to what Perls calls "Aboutism," which involves talking about things or about the self instead of directly experiencing contact.	LeBron meets Veronica on the nature walk. They walk together for over two hours. During this time LeBron tells Veronica all about his athletic accomplishments from 20 years ago. As a consequence, LeBron and Veronica never feel an intimate connection.
5. **Confluence:** This occurs when boundaries merge. There can be a feeling of not really knowing where one person stops and the other begins. This style can be associated with overaccommodating behavior among people who desperately want to be liked and approved by others.	Romeo meets Juliet on the trail. In a few minutes they begin holding hands. They feel they're experiencing something mystical, like they've known each other forever. It doesn't take long and they're completing each other's sentences. They discover they agree on everything.

THE PRACTICE OF GESTALT THERAPY

Doing Gestalt therapy is tricky business. As modeled by Fritz, it's provocative and powerful. However, because Fritz was a showman and used frustration and confrontation to facilitate dramatic change, it's all the more important for beginning and advanced practitioners alike to understand the process, be sensitive to client responses, and use caution when implementing Gestalt techniques. In a research review, Lilienfeld (2007) noted that Gestalt and experiential treatments can increase risk for negative therapy outcomes.

Polster (1966) identified three specific therapeutic devices or phases within the Gestalt approach. These included:

1. Encounter.

2. Awareness.

3. Experiment.

Our discussion on Gestalt therapy practice is organized around Polster's three general therapeutic categories, but first we provide guidelines for assessment and training.

Assessment Procedures and Training Guidelines

Gestalt therapy approaches have underused formal assessment and diagnostic processes. There are several reasons for this. First, as we've seen in previous chapters, existential-humanistic therapists typically avoid assessment and diagnosis. Second, Gestalt therapy was modeled by Fritz during workshops and retreats; there was little focus on screening participants or formal problem assessment. Third, Gestalt techniques were formulated as growth stimulators, meaning there was more focus on pushing people toward growth than on a systematic problem assessment. Finally, in some ways, the entire Gestalt therapy approach involves self-assessment. It is through self-awareness that humans change. Without self-awareness, there can be no self-regulation. Assessment occurs continuously as Gestalt therapists help clients focus on moment-to-moment self-awareness (Clarkson, 2003; Melnick & Nevis, 1998). Of course, this assessment approach translates poorly to the modernist scientific paradigm.

In recent years Greenberg and colleagues have conducted extensive research on emotion-focused therapy (formerly called process-experiential therapy; Elliott & Greenberg, 2007):

> Drawing together person-centered, Gestalt and existential therapy traditions [emotion-focused therapy] provides a distinctive perspective on emotion as a source of meaning, direction and growth. (p. 241)

Because Gestalt therapists typically don't use formal assessment procedures, minimizing client risk includes two main factors: (1) emphasizing collaboration and (2) clinical training guidelines related to goodness of fit.

Emphasizing Collaboration

Early Gestalt therapy applications were about therapy tasks and experiments designed to facilitate self-awareness. Less time and attention was spent on cultivating the therapy bond or relationship (Greenberg & Watson, 1998). More recently, developing positive, collaborative client–therapist relationships has been emphasized.

Working toward a positive therapy relationship is consistent with classical Gestalt therapy, but needed this renewed emphasis. A number of contemporary Gestalt theorists and therapists have been advocating for this rededication to a therapy relationship as a manifestation of Buber's I-Thou relationship and characterized by presence, inclusion, nonexploitiveness, and authenticity (Day, 2016; Hycner & Jacobs, 2009).

Adopting a phenomenological stance implies that therapists should work collaboratively with clients to determine whether a Gestalt approach is appropriate. This collaborative work begins with informed consent—where clients read about what a Gestalt approach entails and begin appraising whether the approach sounds appealing (see Putting It in Practice 6.2). However, naïve clients can't be considered responsible for understanding Gestalt therapy after reading a short description. It's also the therapist's job to explain and discuss the Gestalt approach. Therapists can also introduce small and relatively nonthreatening Gestalt experiments to help assess goodness of fit for specific clients.

In contrast to many of Fritz's demonstrations, ethical Gestalt therapists don't jump right into here-and-now Gestalt experiments. Instead, there's a warming up period, collaborative exploration of client problems, and communication of empathy, compassion, and respect. Without this collaborative foundation, Gestalt experiments carry a heightened client risk.

Clinical Training Guidelines Based on Goodness of Fit

Goodness of fit between the client and therapy approach is a predictor of treatment outcomes (Beutler, 2009). Researchers have identified three specific client types for whom Gestalt and experiential therapies are likely a poor fit. These include:

1. Clients with depressive symptoms who are also highly reactive or sensitive to feedback.

2. Clients with depressive symptoms who also have tendencies to externalize their problems (e.g., these clients more naturally blame others or their environment for their depressive symptoms).

3. Clients who exhibit observable deterioration when engaging in an expressive-experiential, emotionally activating treatment.

6.2 Informed Consent from the Gestalt Perspective

Reproduced by permission of Nicky Nance, PhD, LMHC

A note from your counselor:

Often a new client will say, "If I knew what therapy was, I'd have been here a lot sooner." In fact, it's common to put off a first appointment for fear of the unknown. Now that you've taken that important first step, I want to tell you more about how we will work together.

Ownership: You are the owner of yourself, your struggles, and your solutions, and, as such, your experiences are the map for our sessions. What we address in any session will be determined by your ongoing experiences in the session. I will actively guide that process to help you become more deeply aware of how you think, act, and feel, but I'll try my best to avoid telling you what to believe, how you should feel, or what you should do.

Genuineness: You may have heard that I'm a "straight shooter." I do, in fact, constantly search for the most excellent truth and the clearest way to state it. Sometimes the sudden revelation of a truth is like a bright light being turned on in a dark room—uncomfortable at first, but ultimately helpful for finding your way. I encourage you to be genuine as well. It may be uncomfortable to confront reality, disclose personal experiences, or speak your mind, so our sessions are intended to provide a safe place where you can be your most authentic self.

Presence: Although a review of the past may provide a context for understanding your current experience, the past doesn't get any better. Our primary focus will be less about *why* you are the way you are and more about *how* to connect with yourself and engage in your current life. For that reason, I'll be vigilant in keeping our work in the "here-and-now."

Enactment: At times, I will challenge you to try alternative statements or behaviors during our sessions. Talking about your issues is valuable, but allowing yourself to participate in actual experiences is often more effective in deepening your knowledge of yourself. The action-based techniques will also help me to know you better, and therefore provide you with more precise feedback.

Connection: Our ability to work together is based on mutual respect, commitment to a common goal, and the knowledge that our work is time-limited. The relationship itself can be richly rewarding and serve as a foundation for your future interpersonal successes. I hold the opportunity to be a part of your process in high regard, and I look forward to working with you.

Gestalt and experiential therapists should develop methods for identifying clients who exhibit these patterns. When these patterns are identified, approaches that are less intense and less emotionally activating should be employed (Castonguay, Boswell, Constantino, Goldfried, & Hill, 2010).

There are additional guidelines in the literature for when and how to use experiential techniques. These include:

• When clients have a borderline personality disorder diagnosis or show similar emotional instability, therapists should take more time to establish a therapeutic alliance before implementing therapeutic tasks; this means using Gestalt experiments such as the empty chair technique less often early in therapy and more sparingly throughout.

• Therapists should avoid using interpretations when implementing Gestalt experiments. Using interpretations can leave clients feeling disempowered and pushed around by an expert therapist. Although Fritz was often highly confrontational, Gestalt theory and therapy (as articulated by Fritz himself) strongly emphasized that therapists don't engage in interpretation; interpretation is left to the client. For example, with regard to dreamwork, Fritz stated: "In working with a dream, I avoid any interpretation. I leave this to the patient since I believe he knows more about himself than I can possibly know" (F. S. Perls, 1970, p. 32).

These cautions regarding Gestalt therapy are an example of why counseling and psychotherapy is taught, tutored, and supervised within rigorous professional training programs. Experiential approaches are emotionally activating. Other therapies are more ego-supportive and/or intellectually educational. Professional training and supervision will help you develop skills for determining when and how to apply these powerful techniques collaboratively, ethically, and respectfully (Wheeler, 2006).

Encounter: The Dialogic Relationship in Gestalt Therapy

Polster identified the **therapeutic encounter** as the initial phase of the Gestalt therapy process:

> First is encounter, the interaction between patient and therapist, each of whom is in the present moment a culmination of a life's experiences. They may engage simply, saying and doing those things ... pertinent to their needs, the therapist offering a new range of possibility to the patient through his willingness to know the truth and to be an authentic person. (Polster, 1966, pp. 5–6)

Dialogic Relationship

Gestalt therapists strive for a dialogic relationship with clients. A **dialogic relationship** involves full presence, authenticity, acceptance, and willingness for open communication. This stance is aspirational, meaning that therapists shouldn't expect to continuously achieve it. Of greatest importance is for therapists to hold the intention to be in a dialogic relationship (Joyce & Stills, 2014).

In the 1990s, Gestalt writers began integrating concepts from relational psychoanalytic psychotherapy (Jacobs, 1992). Relational psychoanalysis and **relational Gestalt therapy** hold a common belief; both the therapist and client bring subjectivity into therapy. Both subjective viewpoints are considered phenomenological, rather than an inherent truth (Hycner & Jacobs, 2009; Yontef, 2005).

Gestalt therapists encourage clients to attend to moment-to-moment experiences. The therapist tries to create a safe therapeutic environment where clients can explore experiences, enhance awareness, and engage in Gestalt experiments. To help make the therapy environment safe, Gestalt therapists try to act as a nonjudgmental partner in the client's self-awareness journey. Yontef (2002) emphasized that this dialogic relationship requires therapist humility, respect for client–therapist differences, personal therapy, and the ability to bracket or suspend one's own thoughts, emotions, and judgments.

Brownell (2016) noted that it is essential, but difficult, for therapists to mindfully bracket their first impressions; it's natural to instantly make up a diagnostic narrative. Similarly, countertransference is inevitable. **Bracketing** is the cognitive tool therapists use to keep their own judgments and countertransference from spoiling the dialogic relationship.

Therapist Self-Disclosure

Therapist self-disclosure is relatively common among existential therapies. In Gestalt therapy, therapist disclosures flow from the experience of being with a particular client. Of primary importance is for therapist disclosures to be descriptions of how the therapist is affected by the client. Self-disclosures are both relational and technical. Brownell (2016) provided an example: "I notice that your mouth turns down when you talk about people misunderstanding you at work and criticizing you, ... and that makes me sad" (p. 419).

There are two key parts to Brownell's disclosure. First, he bases it on a description of what he sees. He doesn't interpret the "mouth turning down" as sadness, but just says what he sees. Second, as he shares his experience; he is feeling sadness himself.

Awareness

Polster's (1966) second phase of Gestalt therapy is awareness. **Awareness** runs the gamut from body sensations to emotions and values.

> An inward look is required, one which goes beyond taking life for granted. This look encompasses the breathing process, tightness of sphincters, awareness of movement and an infinite number of similar details ranging from small and physical aspects to larger awarenesses like expectancy, dread, excitement, relief, etc. (p. 6)

Gestalt therapists emphasize body awareness (see Brain Box 6.1). They attend to movements, gestures, flushing, and other physical manifestations of emotional and psychological responses to contact.

Grounding: Developing a Mindful Orientation

Gestalt therapists consistently engage clients in mindful focusing. **Grounding** is one label therapists use to guide clients to a mindful orientation. Often, the best initial grounding is to have clients pay attention to their breathing in the present moment (Joyce & Sills, 2014). It can be expanded to include feeling your (a) feet on the floor, (b) body in the chair, (c) muscular tension wherever it appears, (d) body in space, and much more.

Grounding might occur regularly at the opening of therapy. Grounding is also used intermittently, as needed, to center clients in their bodies and in the present moment. Joyce and Sills (2014) noted that therapists also need to regularly come back to their own body awareness. They wrote, "A grounded, embodied counsellor, breathing steadily, will model and encourage self-support" (p. 93). Gestalt ideas about holding a mindful orientation to the body (or soma) is consistent with, and a theoretical predecessor to, somatic experiencing therapy (Levine, 2010).

Body Feedback

As therapy proceeds, Gestalt therapists consistently notice and sometimes point out client nonverbal behavior. This process, referred to as **body feedback**, can be intense. You may recall from personal experience that having someone comment on your posture or facial expression can feel too intimate or intrusive.

REFLECTIONS

Think of a time when someone commented on your emotional or physical self. Maybe they said you looked sad or angry. Perhaps they noticed your leg bouncing or some flushing on your neck. What was it like to have someone noticing your physical behaviors?

In a series of studies focusing on emotional expression, Pennebaker and colleagues (Pennebaker, Zech, & Rimé, 2001) tested the idea that physical–emotional inhibition adversely affects health. In one study, two groups of college students engaged in a personal journaling assignment. One group was randomly assigned to keep a journal of trivial daily events. The other group was instructed to keep journals that focused on their deeper thoughts and feelings.

The researchers reported that students who had been instructed to express deeper thoughts and feelings were healthier as measured by number of visits to the university health service and blood tests of immune functioning. Although this study was unrelated to Gestalt therapy, it can be viewed as supportive of the notion that resistance to contact (or in this case, authentic disclosure) may have a bodily dimension.

Gestalt therapists also contend that emotional inhibition exacts an emotional price, and can be observed physically. They might be inclined to comment, relatively freely, on any of the following physical observations.

- Tightness in a client's jaw.
- Repeated opening and closing his fists.
- The movement of one hand to the neck several times when talking about father.

- Grimacing or puckering of the lips.
- Redness or flushing of the neck begins to emerge.

In the following example, Naranjo (1970) illustrates the Gestalt therapist's focus on the physical (in the dialogue T is the therapist and P is the patient):

P: I don't know what to say now....

T: I notice that you are looking away from me.

P: (Giggle.)

T: And now you cover up your face.

P: You make me feel so awful!

T: And now you cover up your face with both hands.

P: Stop! This is unbearable!

T: What do you feel now?

P: I feel so embarrassed! Don't look at me!

T: Please stay with that embarrassment.

P: I have been living with it all my life! I am ashamed of everything I do! It is as if I don't even feel that I have the right to exist! (p. 78)

In this next example, Engle and Holiman (2002) use physical observations and feedback as a foundation for initiating a Gestalt empty-chair experiment:

Therapist: I'm struck by how much your face changes as you move from talking about your son to talking about work. It's an important conflict for you, and you seem to rush past your tenderness about your son and move quickly back to your struggles with work. Let me offer you a way to address this struggle and to acknowledge both parts of yourself. Let me set up two chairs facing one another, and, if you are willing, you can dialogue between those two parts of yourself... the part that loves the role of mother and the part that can't resist the high-profile career. (p. 156)

Engle and Holiman's (2002) Gestalt approach includes the therapist as an interpretive authority. The therapist says, "It's an important conflict for you." This is an interpretation, because the client didn't say "this is important." Additionally, when the therapist says, "Let me offer you a way..." the therapist is acting as an authority. Although there is variability in how much interpretation and authority is included in Gestalt therapy, generally speaking, less interpretation and less authority is more consistent with Gestalt theory and practice.

Language and Voice Quality

Gestalt therapists attend closely to client language and voice quality. Common examples of using language and voice to enhance awareness include:

- *Moving clients from using "it" or "you" to "I"*: "When you talk about yourself it can be helpful to use the word 'I.' Are you willing to try that on?"

- *Moving clients from talking in past tense to talking in present tense*: "I noticed that you're talking about your relationship with your daughter and telling me a story about what happened yesterday. Instead of telling me a story about what happened, describe it as if it's happening right here and right now."

- *Having clients transform their questions into statements*: Perls (1970) wrote:

  You may have wondered about the fact that I almost never answer questions during therapy. Instead I usually ask the patient to change the question in to a statement.... You will find that nothing develops your intelligence better than to take any [client] question and turn it into a genuine statement. (pp. 30–31)

- *Noticing when clients use passive language*: Clients will frequently use language that represents passivity or disempowerment. They speak with qualifiers like "maybe," "sort of," "kind of," and "I don't know." Gestalt therapists have clients use more direct language and drop the qualifiers. As clients speak more directly therapists check in on how the change feels.

- *Notice client voice tone and quality*: Client voice tone and quality may change significantly when they speak about different issues or people. These changes may reflect unfinished business or emotions like guilt (resentment) or fear. Gestalt therapists encourage clients to speak with a different voice tone or volume and then examine how it feels. For example, clients who speak softly might be asked to raise their voice and then talk about what sensations, thoughts, and emotions this change stimulates.

Because clients are whole beings, they can't help but express part of who they are and what they've experienced in the past through language and voice tone. Gestalt therapists take advantage of this to turn the client's inner world inside out—what the client is experiencing internally is open to examination.

Unfinished Business

In many ways Gestalt therapy is a here and now therapy that's all about there and then. The purpose is to get clients to bring their baggage or **unfinished business** out of their crusty old closet and into the present moment. When that happens, change is possible.

Bankart (1997) described this Gestalt process:

  How does Gestalt psychotherapy help the individual become self-regulating again? Here, I think, Perls showed us the true genius of the talking cure. Perls believed that the conflicts manifest in the unconscious

must be brought out of the past—out of the demilitarized zone of fantasy, dream, and memory—and into the here and now. The therapeutic session must become a living theater of the mind where dreams and impulses are lived out, usually symbolically but always immediately and fully. As awareness bursts into consciousness, the person must become the reality of what she or he is experiencing. The empty chair next to the client becomes the mother who withheld love; the foam bat placed in the client's hands becomes the sword with which she or he can "stab" the betraying father in the heart.... (p. 321)

The Gestalt approach pulls the long-dead but still influential past into the living present. Because everything is happening *now*, we can watch personal issues unfold in the therapy session.

Another example from Naranjo (1970) illustrates how the past is pulled into the present.

P: I would like to face this fear and bring out whatever it is that I am avoiding.

T: Okay. That is what you want now. Please go on with your experiences in the moment.

P: I would like to make a parenthesis to tell you that I have felt much better this week.

T: Could you tell me anything of your experience while making this parenthesis?

P: I feel grateful to you and I want you to know it.

T: I get the message. Now please compare these two statements: "I feel grateful" and the account of your well-being this week. Can you tell me what it is you felt that makes you prefer the story to the direct statement of your feeling?

P: If I were to say, "I feel grateful to you," I would feel that I still have to explain.... Oh! Now I know. Speaking of my gratefulness strikes me as too direct. I feel more comfortable in letting you guess or just making you feel good without letting you know my feeling.

T: Now see what it feels like to tell me of your gratefulness as directly as possible.

P: I want to thank you very much for what you have done for me. I feel that I would like to recompense you for your attention in some way.... Wow! I feel so uncomfortable saying this. I feel that you may think that I am being a hypocrite and a boot-licker. I guess that I feel that this was a hypocritical statement. I don't feel that grateful. I want you to believe that I feel grateful.

T: Stay with that. How do you feel when you want me to believe that?

P: I feel small, unprotected. I am afraid that you may attack me, so I want to have you on my side.

In this example the client is in the moment and has two incidents where he spontaneously has an insight (self-awareness shifts) and changes course. Additionally, although the final statement may be associated with unfinished business, the therapist makes no interpretation or connection. If the client makes a connection to the past, the therapist will track and reflect.

Gestalt Experiments

Polster's (1966) third phase of Gestalt therapy process involves implementation of **Gestalt therapy experiments**:

> The third therapeutic force is the experiment, a device which creates new opportunities for acting in a safely structured situation. Included are suggestions for trying one's self out in a manner not readily feasible in everyday life. (p. 6)

The Gestalt experiment is a powerful treatment method. Unfortunately, powerful psychological methods can be abused. This abuse can take place unintentionally. Well-intended therapists may feel frustrated with a plodding therapy pace and implement Gestalt experiments based on their own needs and not on a schedule in sync with client readiness.

Perls tended to model an excessive use of Gestalt experiments. They were certainly more dramatic than Rogerian reflections. In defense of Perls, he was aware of the dangers of abusing techniques:

> A technique is a gimmick. A gimmick should be used only in the extreme case. We've got enough people running around collecting gimmicks, more gimmicks and abusing them. These techniques, these tools, are quite useful in some seminar on sensory awareness or joy, just to give you some idea that you are still alive.... But the sad fact is that this jazzing-up more often becomes a dangerous substitute activity, another phony therapy that *prevents* growth. (F. Perls, 1969a, p. 1)

Perls is saying that Gestalt therapy is not technique-driven. He's also emphasizing that therapy is about facilitating self-awareness and personal growth in the long run (not the short term). He's open to the possibility that Gestalt techniques, inappropriately used, can be phony and antitherapeutic.

Although the following techniques are designed for use with adult clients, Gestalt therapy also has been used with child and adolescent populations (Blom, 2006; Oaklander, 1978, 2006, 2015).

Staying with the Feeling

Gestalt therapy places an emphasis on immediate feelings. Feelings are to be faced and confronted, not avoided. **Staying with the feeling** is less a specific technique than a general therapy strategy or philosophy.

Gestalt therapists use several techniques to encourage clients to stay with (rather than avoid) feelings:

- Therapists persistently ask questions like: "What are you aware of now?" or "What are you noticing inside yourself right now?"

- Clients are instructed to "voice" their feelings and sensations (e.g., "Let your anxiety have a voice; what would it say right now?").

- Clients are encouraged to act out their feelings in the here and now. Perls had clients pull on and "stretch" him when they felt inner tension and conflict. He believed that acting on feelings could help clients identify and reintegrate disowned feelings.

- As in the preceding Naranjo (1970) case example, sometimes therapists simply say, "Stay with that."

Therapists encourage clients to stay with feelings because doing so enhances full contact, improves awareness (sometimes including an "Ah ha!" or "Wow!" exclamation of insight), and stimulates self-regulation and personal development.

I Take Responsibility For...

This experiment fulfills a basic underlying Gestalt therapy principle. As Baumgardner wrote, "Gestalt therapy is an existential therapy, concerned with the problems evoked by our dread of accepting responsibility for what we are and what we do" (Baumgardner & Perls, 1975, p. 9).

To use this experiment, clients use **I take responsibility for** as a prefix to what they say in therapy. If clients are feeling bored, they might be instructed to say, "I'm bored and I take responsibility for my boredom." The technique is especially useful when clients are externalizing symptoms.

REFLECTIONS

Think about how you might use "I take responsibility for" with clients who are having anxiety and depression symptoms. How does it feel to imagine having clients say, "I'm depressed and I take full responsibility for my depression?" How about "I take responsibility for my anxiety?"

Playing the Projection

Much of Gestalt therapy as practiced by Perls was conducted in group settings. He routinely put group participants in the hot seat, engaged them in Gestalt experiments, and then gave feedback. An old supervisor of ours was in a Perls-facilitated group. He reported—with enthusiasm—that being in the hot seat was one of the most frightening and exhilarating experiences in his life.

Playing the projection is especially applicable to group therapy. Perls believed that much of what happens in interpersonal relationships is projective. In therapy groups, when Perls observed a member making a statement about someone else, Perls would ask the participant to play the projection. For example, if the participant commented that Robert (another group member) was too critical, Perls might say, "Try that on. Stand up and be critical of everyone here. Go around the room and criticize everyone."

Another way to apply this technique is to direct clients, "Tell me something especially annoying you've noticed about someone else." When a client states, "I hate it when Juan is so selfish and insensitive," the client is asked to act selfish and insensitive. You can also have clients amplify these selfish and insensitive feelings using an empty-chair dialogue, with one part being selfish and insensitive and the other part being unselfish and sensitive. As the dialogue ensues, clients are encouraged to focus on what thoughts and feelings come up while playing the two roles. We discuss the empty-chair technique in more detail in an upcoming section.

The Exaggeration Experiment

In **the exaggeration experiment** clients are instructed to exaggerate subtle nonverbal behaviors. Exaggerating subtle nonverbal behaviors helps clients reclaim their entire self—including their bodies—and can amplify the meaning of behaviors outside of awareness.

This experiment is used with specific instructions. For example, a client who brushes her hand past her neck when speaking might be asked to exaggerate the motion and then to focus on what she feels. The therapist might say, "Speak again and make that motion again, only make it bigger. What are you aware of now?"

The Empty-Chair or Dialogue Experiment

This technique is the best known and best researched of all the Gestalt experiments (Greenberg & Foerster, 1996). There are two ways to use the **empty-chair dialogue**.

1. *Working out an internal conflict*: In the first version of the empty-chair, clients switch seats while playing two different parts of the self. Typically, this approach to the empty-chair results in the client taking on the "topdog" and "underdog" polarities. For example, if a client is having trouble getting her college assignments and projects completed on time, the following interaction might ensue:

Therapist: I'd like you to try an experiment. It involves putting your two most extreme attitudes about doing class assignments into these chairs. In this chair [pointing] you put all your feelings and beliefs about getting assignments done on time; in this other chair, put all your procrastination feelings and beliefs. Then you move back and forth between the chairs and have a dialogue. Okay?

Client: Okay. I'll try it.

Therapist: Which chair would you like to start in?

Client: I'll be in this one [moves into chair]. It's the procrastination side. It doesn't want to do any homework at all.

Therapist: Okay. Good. Now that you're sitting in that seat, use the word "I" instead of "it" and keep everything in the present tense and try it again.

Client: I don't want to do any homework at all!

Therapist: Nice. Now stay with that and keep looking at the empty chair and saying how you feel.

Client: Homework sucks. What's the big deal? I don't know why I have to do it. Mostly professors give out busy work. I really don't care at all about homework. [Pause.]

Therapist: Sit in the other chair and see what comes up.

Client: What should I do?

Therapist: Look at the chair you were just in and respond to what you heard.

Client: You're so irresponsible. If you don't do your projects, you'll get bad grades. Then you might flunk. Then you'll lose your scholarship. Then you might as well plan on flipping burgers at a fast food restaurant all your life. Is that what you want?

Therapist: How do you feel as you say that?

Client: This is totally my mom. I think she took over my body and spoke for me. That's weird.

Therapist: What else?

Client: It's like I want to do homework, but when I hear that voice I want to punch myself.

Therapist: What's that about?

Client: I don't want to do the homework because of being afraid to get bad grades. I don't want to do anything out of fear. I want to do homework because I want to do something with my life, not because someone's scaring me or forcing me.

Therapist: Okay. Stay in that chair that wants to do homework and say what you're feeling.

Client: I want to do homework because I want to be smart. [Client takes a deep breath.]

Therapist: What's that like?

Client: That feels right. It feels nice.

Therapist: Okay. See what's left in the other chair.

Client: [Switches.] I'm not afraid of flipping burgers. You won't scare me into doing anything. But I can totally honor what you're saying about wanting to be smart.

Therapist: What do you want when you sit in that chair?

Client: I don't want to flip burgers, but I'm not afraid to. I do want to have some fun. I won't let you study all the time and forget about having fun. If you try to do that I'll screw everything up.

Therapist: What sort of fun do you want?

Client: Just to be with friends. To hang out. To talk and laugh. I just want two things. I want to have fun with my friends and I want you to stop with all the crazy threats about flipping burgers. That doesn't help. It just makes me want to sabotage everything.

Therapist: What does the other side think of that?

Client: [Switches.] I think we can make a deal. I will own my desire to be smart and do well in school. I think I can stop with the threats. And I'm totally okay with having some fun.

This is a simplified illustration of the Gestalt **topdog/ underdog** phenomenon. Perls wrote about this split:

> [O]ne of the most frequent splits in the human personality...is the topdog–underdog split. The topdog is known in psychoanalysis as the superego or the conscience. Unfortunately, Freud left out the underdog, and he did not realize that usually the underdog wins in the conflict between topdog and underdog. I give you the frequent characteristics of both. The topdog is righteous, some of the time right, but always righteous....The topdog always says you should and the topdog threatens.... However, the topdog is pretty straightforward. Now the underdog looks for the different method. The underdog says, yeh, or I promise, or I agree...or...if only I could. So the underdog is a very good frustrator. And then the topdog, of course, doesn't let him get away with it and praises the use of the rod and the self-torture game or self-improvement game, whatever you want to call it, goes on year in and year out, year in and year out and nothing ever happens. Right? (F. Perls, 1973, p. 125)

One goal of the empty-chair technique is to help clients break out of a self-torture game. In the preceding example, as the dialogue proceeds, polarization begins, but the client suddenly becomes aware of her own desire to do well in school. It appears she may have introjected (swallowed whole) threatening ideas about what might happen if she has any fun (instead of studying). When she spits out the threatening piece of her self-torture game, she's able to make contact with her own motivation and begins depolarizing. She's able to negotiate a "deal" between her competing internal demands.

In this case, the topdog entity that wants class assignments completed was connected with an early parent figure; the underdog was the child. The conflict represented unfinished business. By bringing the unfinished business into the here and now, the empty-chair experiment provided an opportunity to finish the unfinished business. When this exchange occurs, it's desirable for emotions to run high, which seems to facilitate resolution (Malcolm & Greenberg, 2000).

2. *Working out interpersonal conflicts*: In the second empty chair alternative, clients act out old or contemporary life conflicts in the now. For example, if a female client is in the midst of a conflict with her husband, she would play both parts of a dialogue with her husband while simultaneously examining the feelings that emerge. Although this procedure begins differently from the first version of the empty-chair dialogue, it often progresses into the topdog versus underdog dialogue. In the first case, the dialogue emerges from an inner conflict. In the second case, the dialogue emerges from an external conflict. However, considering the dynamic of defensive projection, intense conflicts can involve projected parts of the self onto others and the empty chair helps the disowned parts of the self to become reintegrated. When working out an old or contemporary interpersonal conflict using an empty-chair technique, sometimes the focus is entirely on monitoring, reflecting, and coming to terms with the client's emotional experiences. This approach, during which the client remains in one chair, is illustrated in the extended case example in this chapter.

The Gestalt Approach to Dream Work

Dream work was central to traditional Gestalt psychotherapy. Fritz worked with dreams in workshop settings and viewed them as especially important.

> The dream is an existential message. It is more than an unfinished situation; it is more than an unfulfilled wish; it is more than a prophecy. It is a message of yourself to yourself, to whatever part of you is listening. The dream is possibly the most spontaneous expression of the human being, a piece of art that we chisel out of our lives. And every part, every situation in the dream is a creation of the dreamer. (Perls, 1970, pp. 31–32)

Dreams are the royal road to integration. They should be experienced, not interpreted. In keeping with existential philosophy, the dreamer is 100% responsible for all dream images. If your client dreams of a monster murdering an innocent victim, it's important to remember that both monster and victim were "created by" the dreamer. There are four main steps to Gestalt dream work.

1. The dreamer tells the dream story.

2. The dreamer "revives" the dream by changing the language. Instead of telling the dream in past tense, it's reported in present tense.

3. The dreamer becomes a director and organizes the dream as a play, moving around, setting the stage, and describing where everyone is and where every object is.

4. The dreamer then acts out the dream, always using the personal pronoun "I" to enhance identification with each object and character in the dream.

Overall, the goal of dream work is for the dreamer to

[b]egin on his own to re-identify with the scattered bits and pieces of his personality, which had only been held together superficially by the expression "I." Then when the click comes, the dynamic, the Elan vital, the life force that has been disowned and projected into others will begin to follow into his own center and he will begin to be himself again. (Baumgardner & Perls, 1975, p. 119)

Gestalt Therapy in Action: Brief Vignettes

The following vignettes focus on how repetitive phrasing with dream work and how conversing with body parts can help clients increase personal awareness and achieve insights leading toward positive change.

Vignette I: And This Is My Existence

Perls had an uncanny ability to use repetitive phrases to produce client insight. He used the **and this is my existence** technique with dreams, fantasies, and other repeating images. The technique is formulaic. You ask clients to describe a dream image with a brief phrase and then follow the phrase with the statement "and this is my existence." The technique often feels silly or phony, but clients are instructed to just focus on their inner experience. The following example illustrates the technique with a 26-year-old male who came for treatment because of anxiety about academic achievement.

Client: I dreamt I was racing my brother home. We were kids again. He got ahead of me and cut me off. I tackled him from behind. The next thing I knew we were all muddy and my mom was scolding us.

Therapist: Just go through the dream one thought at a time. Say it slowly and clearly. Then, after each thought, add the statement "and this is my existence." I know this sounds silly and phony, but just try it and see what it feels like.

Client: I'm racing my brother ... and this is my existence. We're heading home ... and this is my existence.

Therapist: That's it. Keep your focus on your body and your feelings and see what happens.

Client: He's ahead ... and this is my existence. I can't catch up because he's blocking me ... and this is my existence. I'm tackling him from behind ... and this is my existence. I'm muddy and a big mess ... and this is my existence. My mom is standing over me ... and this is my existence. She's telling me I'm stupid ... and this is my existence. And that I should leave my brother alone ... and this is my existence.

Therapist: What's happening?

Client: This dream is my life. I don't believe it!

Therapist: What is there you don't want to believe?

Client: I don't want to believe that I'm still competing with my brother. I'm still losing. I'm still worried about what my mother will think.

Therapist: How do you want to change the dream?

Client: What do you mean?

Therapist: You can go ahead and change the dream. It's your dream. Tell it to me again. This time change it into how you want it to be right now.

This example illustrates several Gestalt therapy principles.

• The dreamer owns the dream, whether he wants to or not. The simple "existence" technique only amplifies reality as it is.

• The therapist facilitates, but doesn't interpret. Interpretation is the job of the client, not the therapist.

• As the client sinks into the process, he begins sensing connections. These connections fit into his reality like pieces of a puzzle. It feels like an "aha" experience. The client's insight represents the unfinished business that's dominating his life. As awareness increases, the client can take control and guide his life in the present, rather than spending energy battling the unfinished business from the past.

• When the therapist asks the client to recreate his dream, the client is empowered to actively live his life, rather than being an automaton trudging forward without an independent spirit.

Vignette II: Hand-to-Hand Conversation

This vignette is from a therapy session John had with an 11-year-old African American boy named DeWayne. The client was having trouble with impulsive and aggressive behavior. During the following exchange, John was working with DeWayne on a repeating aggressive behavior pattern. DeWayne would sometimes hit his younger sister and other times hit inanimate objects (e.g., trees, walls).

John: Hey I noticed you've got a scab on your hand. What happened?

DeWayne: I got mad and punched a tree in my yard.

John: And you ended up with that scab.

DeWayne: Yeah. It doesn't hurt.

John: Yeah. You're tough and strong and so I'm not surprised it doesn't hurt.

DeWayne: Yeah.

John: Do you mind if we try something weird? I mean you're tough and strong and all that and so I think you can do this, but it's pretty weird.

DeWayne: I can do it. What is it?

John: It's like acting. I want you to have a conversation with your hand.

DeWayne: That is weird.

John: Let me show you what I mean. [John looks at his hand and begins talking.]

John: Hey, how's it going?

John's hand: Uh, pretty good.

John: Yeah, well, what'cha been doing?

John's hand: I'm just hanging here on the end of your arm.

John: Yeah. I know that. But what have you been doing lately?

John's hand: Not much. Staying out of trouble I guess. Sometimes I've been grabbing food and stuffing it into your mouth.

John: And you do a really good job of that … thanks for keeping me well fed!

John: Okay. Do you see what I mean?

DeWayne: Yeah. I get it.

John: Now which hand do you usually hit things with … is it the one with the scab?

DeWayne: Yeah. I always hit things with my right hand.

John: All right. Go for it. Just be yourself and then have a conversation with your hand like I did. When you're talking I might ask you a question or I might ask your hand a question, and you just keep right on going. Okay?

DeWayne: Okay.

DeWayne: How you doing down there?

DeWayne's hand: I'm all right. I just hit a tree this week and got this scab.

DeWayne: [Looks at John.] This is weird.

John: True. But you're doing great. Just go with it like you're acting in a play. Forget about everything else and let yourself have an interesting conversation with your hand.

DeWayne: Yeah. I can see your scab. It looks kind of cool.

DeWayne's hand: Yeah. I think it makes me look tough. But it hurt a little when it was bleeding.

DeWayne: Yeah. I remember.

DeWayne's hand: Yeah. I don't always like scabs. And I don't like it when you pick at scabs.

DeWayne: But it's hard not to.

John: Can I ask your hand a question?

DeWayne: Sure.

John: [Looking at DeWayne's hand.] Do you always like hitting things?

DeWayne: Not always.

John: So sometimes you'd like not to hit things?

DeWayne: Yeah, but it's hard when somebody makes me mad I just swing.

John: [Still looking at DeWayne's hand.] What do you think you could do instead of swinging at things?

DeWayne: I could get put in a pocket.

John: Cool. I suppose you'd be safe in there.

DeWayne: Yep.

John: What else could you do?

DeWayne: I could hold my dad's hand. Then I wouldn't hit my sister.

John: So sometimes it would be nicer to get close to your dad and hold his hand. Sometimes you'd rather do that instead of hitting your sister?

DeWayne: Yeah.

John: [Looking up at DeWayne.] What do you think it would be like to tell your dad this?

DeWayne: I could do that.

John: Let's practice that. Let's pretend your dad is in that empty chair. Tell him what your hand would rather do than hit your sister. Start off with, "Hey Dad…"

DeWayne: Hey Dad. Sometimes if I feel like hitting Josie would you mind if I held your hand instead?

John: What did that feel like?

DeWayne: It felt good. I think my dad would like that because he doesn't like me to hit Josie. I think it would be good.

It becomes clear that DeWayne would prefer contact with his father over expressing his anger aggressively. Although we can't know for sure, it's possible that some of DeWayne's anger was related to jealousy. This possibility made DeWayne's solution a reasonable behavioral alternative. He can get the closeness he wants with his father and not experience the negative consequences associated with his aggressive behavior.

At the end of the session DeWayne's father was invited in and DeWayne offered his suggestion. The father was receptive and later reported that DeWayne was being less aggressive.

CASE PRESENTATION

This is a case from Watson, Goldman, and Greenberg (2007), *Case Studies in Emotion-Focused Treatment of Depression: A Comparison of Good and Poor Outcome*. The book is an important contribution to the literature for several reasons: (a) the authors' report detailed descriptions of six prototypical therapy cases, (b) three cases have positive outcomes and three cases have neutral or negative outcomes, (c) the sequence of therapeutic tasks is explained well, and (d) the authors employ a variety of standardized psychological measurements to track treatment process and outcomes.

The following is a summary of a 20-session case with Gayle, a 37-year-old woman who was married and mother of two children. She was diagnosed with major depression, as well as other mental disorders. This was one of the positive outcome cases reported by Watson et al. (2007).

Before beginning, we should note that emotion-focused authors and researchers consider EFT as primarily a person-centered approach that employs the Gestalt empty-chair technique as a means of focusing on emotion. We include it here as an illustration of the empty-chair technique and discuss the EFT model in more detail in Chapter 14.

The Problem List

Watson et al. (2007) describe Gayle's problems in a narrative:

> [Gayle] was concerned about being viewed as a "bad mother," was dissatisfied with her parenting, and felt like giving up. She was afraid of perpetuating her family history with her children. She was also concerned with having been unfairly considered "the screwed up one" by her parents and her parents-in-law. She felt unsupported and judged by everybody. She also perceived her life as a "mess" and was afraid of being disdained for being depressed. The stressors that were identified when she entered therapy were her inability to parent her children, conflict with her family of origin, and lack of support. (p. 53)

Gayle also reported feeling "screwed up," "not good enough," "stupid," and ashamed of her binge eating (p. 53). She very much wanted to fix her problems with her parents and gain their approval.

A pretherapy *DSM* multiaxial diagnosis was provided (Watson et al., 2007, p. 54):

Axis I: Major depressive disorder.

Axis II: Borderline, dependent, and fearful/anxious personality features.

Axis III: Back and weight problems.

Axis IV: Problems with primary support system, discord with parents and brother, and discord between son and daughters.

Axis V: GAS = 49.

Gayle's pretherapy Beck Depression Inventory (BDI) score was 33 (in the severely depressed range).

Problem Formulation

Watson et al. (2007) described the case formulation:

> Gayle's core maladaptive emotion scheme was of sadness and a sense of abandonment. These feelings became the central focus of therapy early in the treatment within the context of working on her unresolved feelings toward her mother. The goals of therapy were to resolve her unfinished business with her mother and to have Gayle become less self-critical and more self-validating.... One of the primary tasks was to help her change her behavior so that she could become more expressive of her feelings and needs and differentiate herself from significant others. (p. 55)

There are several specific stages within this therapy model. These include: (a) bonding and awareness, (b) evoking and exploring feelings, and (c) transformation. From the beginning Gayle was extremely emotional in her therapy sessions. The authors reported "510 coded emotion episodes" during Gayle's 20-session treatment. This is about double the average with this therapy model. They also reported that by the third session, a bond and collaborative focus had been established so they could begin working on "[Gayle's] unfinished business with her mother and her need for support" (p. 56).

Interventions

In Session 3 the therapist introduced the empty-chair technique.

Therapist: I'd like us to try something. I think it might be helpful.

Gayle: [Blowing nose.] OK.

Therapist: What I'd like to try is for you to imagine your mom here.

Gayle: OK.

Therapist: In this chair. Can you imagine her here and have a dialogue with her? How does that sound?

Gayle: [Laughs.] I don't know. I do it in my head all the time [laughs].

Therapist: Yeah. OK. Why don't we see where it goes, and I'll be right there next to you. We'll just see what happens, OK? Can you imagine your mom there?

Gayle: Sort of.

Therapist: What do you see?

Gayle: Well, she wants to be accepted, and she doesn't think she's doing anything wrong.

After intermittent discussion of the technique, the empty-chair dialogue begins in earnest. This is the intervention. The therapist functions as a facilitator and supporter while expressing empathy as the empty-chair dialogue proceeds.

Gayle: Yeah. You hurt me so bad as a kid, Mom.

Therapist: That's so deep, yeah. What do you want from her?

Gayle: I want some space right now.

Therapist: Can you tell her that? "Mom, I just…"

Gayle: [Sighs, blows nose.] I'm sorry.

Therapist: That's OK.

Gayle: I'm a cry baby. It happens [laughs]….

Therapist: Good. That's why you're here [laughs]. This is the place to cry.

Gayle: Well, Mom, I'd really like some space. I know you don't understand, and it's not that I don't care, but I feel like you control me, and I can't be myself when you're around.

The therapy process is fairly repetitive. As Gayle exhibits escalating emotions (as viewed through her body, voice tone, and speech content) the therapist initiates repeated empty-chair dialogues. These dialogues enable Gayle to focus on her emotions and become clearer about where these feelings originate and how she can deal with them behaviorally. In this next excerpt, the focus is on a sexual abuse incident.

Gayle: I was really angry [crying] that nobody was there to help me. Why wasn't my mother there when I needed her?

Therapist: Yeah. Do you want to put your mother in the chair, Gayle, and tell her now?

Gayle: [Crying.] Why weren't you there when I needed you, Mom?

Therapist: Yeah.

Gayle: Why did you let me go to a stranger's house, and you didn't really know them?

Therapist: Yeah. Tell her what it was like for you.

Gayle: I felt very mad and wrong, and I felt very ashamed and scared, and I wanted to be protected. It's like I couldn't trust you again because you didn't protect me.

Therapist: Yeah. "So I didn't trust you after that."

Gayle: And I always felt that I had to meet your needs because you never met mine, I needed to be protected.

Therapist: "I was a little girl; I was only 5."

Gayle: I was so little.

Therapist: Yeah…

Gayle: And I bottled it so much to the point where it was just exploding, and you didn't see any of it; you didn't recognize it.

Therapist: Yeah. "So you didn't protect me from the abuse, and then you didn't see pain."

Gayle: And you didn't help me.

Therapist: "As a result you didn't help me."

Gayle: It was very painful.

Therapist: What did you need from her then?

Gayle: I needed it not to happen.

Therapist: Yeah. "I needed you to be an adult."

Gayle: And then when it did happen [cries], I needed you to hug me and tell me it was OK and that she would get disciplined and that you would still love me, that it wasn't my fault. (pp. 76–77)

Outcomes Measurement

This case was a part of a research protocol and so several outcomes measures were employed. In a real-world setting fewer measures would be used to track progress. Most likely, the BDI would be used to track depressive symptoms.

Gayle's outcomes were very positive. After 20 sessions she "was able to function normally" and "was no longer afraid of becoming depressed" (p. 81). Her BDI score went from 33 at pretherapy to zero. Her scores on other distress-related measures also dropped to zero. These positive outcomes were "maintained at 18-month follow-up" (p. 81).

EVALUATIONS AND APPLICATIONS

Like psychoanalysis, Adlerian therapy, and person-centered therapy, Gestalt theory and therapy was originally the product of an individual and his inner circle. Also, like these other theories and approaches, Gestalt theory and therapy has evolved. In this section we examine whether Gestalt therapy has matured in a way that addresses important contemporary issues.

Evidence-Based Status

Based on anecdotal reports and observations of Gestalt therapists in action, it appears that Gestalt therapy is powerful and meaningful. However, research on Gestalt therapy outcomes is sparse. Even further, from the tough-minded, empirically oriented scientist perspective, most Gestalt therapy ideas are untestable and unverifiable. To talk of confluence and of physiological manifestations of resistance is one thing, but to scientifically demonstrate that such things exist and influence lives in a measurable way is another. Although Gestalt theorists talk about leaps of insight, they haven't taken even the smallest steps toward empirically validating their interesting ideas.

This is strong criticism, but Fritz always encouraged directness. No doubt, he would reciprocate with criticism of academia and science. Here's one example of how Fritz regarded scientific verification.

> The first approach is science, or as I call it, "aboutism," which lets us talk about things, gossip about ourselves or others, broadcast about what's going on in ourselves, talk about our cases. Talking about things, or ourselves and others as though we were things, keeps out any emotional responses or other genuine involvement. In therapy, aboutism is found in rationalization and intellectualization, and in the "interpretation game" where the therapist says, "This is what your difficulties are about." This approach is based on noninvolvement. (1970, p. 12)

Perls didn't engage in or appreciate therapy outcome studies and nomothetic approaches to understanding individuals. He believed that discovering what works should not and cannot be determined through research. Instead, to determine the effectiveness of an approach, the focus should be on individuals: "[W]e present nothing that you cannot verify for yourself in terms of your own behavior" (F. Perls, Hefferline, & Goodman, 1951, p. 7).

Perls's perspective notwithstanding, the sparse empirical research on Gestalt therapy is modestly positive. The results were initially articulated by M. L. Smith et al. (1980) in their meta-analysis of 475 outcome studies (which also included several Gestalt therapy studies). Further research has consistently shown that Gestalt therapy is slightly better than placebo treatment and perhaps somewhat less effective than cognitive and behavioral treatments (Greenberg, Elliott, & Lietaer, 1994). It also appears most effective with reserved, internalizing clients who are open to participating in Gestalt experiments (Daldrup, Beutler, Engle, & Greenberg, 1988). Some researchers have suggested that the slightly lower effectiveness of Gestalt therapy during clinical studies can be more than accounted for by the researcher allegiance effect. The bias of cognitive and behavioral researchers may contribute to the overall slight advantage of CBT over Gestalt therapy (Elliot, Greenberg, & Lietaer, 2002).

More recent research and reviews are promising.

- In a large-scale practice-based U.K. study, Gestalt therapy outcomes were equivalent to cognitive-behavioral, person-centered, and psychodynamic approaches (Stevens, Stringfellow, Wakelin, & Waring, 2011). Effect sizes were large, ranging from 1.12 to 1.42.

- A study in Iran showed Gestalt therapy to be equivalent to logotherapy in treating aggression and anxiety symptoms in college students (Yousefi et al., 2009).

- In Hong Kong, researchers reported that Gestalt therapy improved emotional well-being and hope (Man Leung, Ki Leung, & Tuen Ng, 2013).

- Several well-respected psychotherapy outcome researchers have reaffirmed the view that established process-oriented existential-humanistic approaches should be considered evidence-based (Lambert, 2013a; Wampold, 2008).

- Perhaps most promising is the growing empirical base for using an empty-chair to facilitate process, resolve personal conflicts, and contribute to positive therapy outcomes (Carpenter, Angus, Paivio, & Bryntwick, 2016; Paivio & Greenberg, 1995; Watson, McMullen, Prosser, & Bedard, 2011).

Cultural Sensitivity

A case can be made that Gestalt approaches are compatible with multicultural work (Wheeler, 2005, 2006). Gestalt experiments in general, and the empty-chair technique in particular, can help bicultural and culturally diverse clients living in the dominant white culture deepen their self-awareness and live more authentically within challenging cultural situations. However, this cultural compatibility is more theoretical than real. In fact, many clients from diverse cultural backgrounds are reluctant to engage in emotionally focused, experiential therapies (D. W. Sue & D. Sue, 2016). The emotional focus can be inconsistent with collectivist cultural values and with cultural rules about emotional expression (Joyce & Sills, 2014).

To date, an explicit valuing of multicultural contact and awareness has not been a major focus in Gestalt professional journals. Specifically, in a database search of all Gestalt professional journals, less than 10 articles included the words diversity, multicultural, or cultural in the title. Of course, a title search doesn't speak to the implicit valuing of all forms of contact and learning inherent to Gestalt approaches. The usual position is that Gestalt therapy can be sensitive to all clients because Gestalt practitioners focus on the subjective phenomenological experience of each client. Also, there are Gestalt training texts that discuss diversity issues directly (Joyce & Sills, 2014; Wheeler & Axelsson, 2015). However, it appears that a greater emphasis on reaching out to and addressing diversity issues is both possible and needed.

Gender and Sexuality

Similar to Gestalt therapy and culture, the situation regarding Gestalt therapy's sensitivity to women and feminist issues is also mixed. Although women have been involved in the development and evolution of Gestalt therapy, this hasn't resulted in many publications focusing on how Gestalt approaches address women's issues. Most of the articles published in professional journals (five) were commentaries focusing on a single featured piece (Amendt-Lyon, 2008). Perhaps of greater significance was the fact that there were no professional Gestalt journal articles with titles that included the word "feminist" or the word "women."

On the other hand, because it's an approach that emphasizes emotional focusing, Gestalt therapy may be easier for women than men. Due to gender-based expectations, female clients may be more interested in and comfortable with an intensive and active focus on emotions. Additionally, Laura Posner Perls and Miriam Polster were central to the training of Gestalt therapists worldwide (Polster, 1991).

Gestalt therapy could also do a better job of explicitly focusing on LGBTQ issues. There have been writings that focus on applications of Gestalt approaches to (a) the coming out process (Iaculo & Frew, 2004), (b) gay survivors of domestic abuse (Kondas, 2008), and (c) lesbian couple counseling (Brockmon, 2004), but these publications represent a small minority of articles in Gestalt journals. There isn't yet a systematic or rigorous effort within the Gestalt professional community to articulate and address LGBTQ therapy needs and concerns.

Spirituality

Although not always visible or palpable, Gestalt theory and therapy have deep spiritual roots. Laura Perls studied with Martin Buber and had interests in Taoism. Fritz Perls studied Zen Buddhism. Paul Goodman had interests in Taoism and Gestalt writer Dave Mann (2010) contended that Goodman's book, *Nature Heals*, is consistent with his Taoist beliefs about living with nature in accordance with nature. It may be that Gestalt experiments are consistent in style with the Zen Buddhist koan, a puzzle or riddle designed to open Zen novices to deeper levels of consciousness. At the very least, Zen Buddhism and Gestalt therapy share an attitude of acceptance of the now and an exploration of experience.

There are, of course, differences between Gestaltists regarding the role and nature of spirituality in Gestalt theory and practice. For some, the I-Thou connection is where the transcending and spiritual contact happens. Boundaries dissolve and deeper connections and insights blossom. This may have been what led Jesse Thomas (1978) to publish an early Gestalt-spiritual work titled, *The Youniverse: Gestalt Therapy, Nonwestern Religions, and the Present Age.* Spirituality, from the Gestalt perspective, is both personal and universal (or youniversal ☺).

At the other end of the continuum are individuals who don't see spirituality as warranting a place in Gestalt theory and practice (Mann, 2010). Mann (2010) recommended that Gestalt therapists, like clients, need to decide where they stand on religion and spirituality, recognizing, at the same time, that where they stand may well change. This brings us to perhaps the most famous words Fritz Perls ever wrote, the Gestalt prayer:

> I do my thing and you do your thing.
> I am not in this world to live up to your expectations,
> And you are not in this world to live up to mine.
> You are you, and I am I,
> and if by chance we find each other, it's beautiful.
> If not, it can't be helped.
> (F. Perls, *Gestalt Therapy Verbatim*, 1969a, p. 24)

CONCLUDING COMMENTS

In the final scene from *The Gestalt Approach and Eyewitness to Therapy*, Fritz Perls has switched seats with his client. She is playing Fritz, while Perls is playing a resistant client. After battling his resistance, she moves Perls toward a breakthrough. The following dialogue took place as a live demonstration.

Barbara: I notice that no matter what happens, the burden returns to me. No matter what I suggest, you say no, you do it for me, I don't know how.

Fritz: Of course. If I weren't so incapable, I wouldn't be here. This is my illness, don't you see?

Barbara: Talk to your illness.

Fritz: But my illness isn't here. How can I talk to my illness? And if I could talk to the illness, the illness wouldn't listen, because this is the illness.

Barbara: I'll listen. Did someone give you the illness?

Fritz: [Slowly.] Yes.

Barbara: Who?

Fritz: Sigmund Freud. [There is much laughing among the group at this point.]

Barbara: I realize that Sigmund isn't here, that he's...

Fritz: But for seven years I got infected.

Barbara: [Giggling.] Oh, I'm three years above you because I spent 10 years with an analyst. Don't tell me how bad it is! Could you talk to Sigmund?

Fritz: Oh no, I can't. He's dead.

Barbara: You've changed. That's the first time you've slipped. What are you aware of now?

Fritz: [Soberly.] A great sorrow that Freud is dead before I really could talk as man to man with him.

Barbara: [Gently.] I think you could still talk to him. Would you like to?

Fritz: Uh huh.

Barbara: Fine. [Pause.] I'd like to listen.

Fritz: Now I'm stuck. I would like to do it. I would like to be your patient in this situation, and uh … [speaking very slowly] Professor Freud … a great man … but very sick … you can't let anyone touch you. You've got to say what is and your word is holy gospel. I wish you would listen to me. In a certain way I know more than you do. You could have solved the neurosis question. And here I am … a simple citizen … by the grace of God having discovered the simple secret that what is, is. I haven't even discovered this. Gertrude Stein has discovered this. I just copy her. No, copy is not right. I got in the same way of living—thinking—with her. Not as an intellectual, but just as a human plant, animal—and this is where you were blind. You moralized and defended sex; taking this out of the total context of life. So you missed life. [There is quiet in the room for several moments. Then Fritz turns to Barbara.] So, your copy of Fritz wasn't so bad. [Gives Barbara a kiss.] You did something for me.

Barbara: Thank you, Fritz. (F. Perls, 1973, pp. 207–208)

Gestalt therapy is about much more than isolated sexual and aggressive impulses, or altering reward schedules or errant cognitions. Gestalt therapy is a about living life to the fullest in the present moment.

CHAPTER SUMMARY AND REVIEW

Fritz Perls and Laura Posner Perls were the primary developers of Gestalt theory and therapy, an existential and experiential approach to counseling and psychotherapy. Fritz and Laura met at Kurt Goldstein's lab in Germany, but soon afterwards moved to South Africa to flee the Nazis. In South Africa and later in New York, they collaborated with others to produce several publications leading to the theory and practice of Gestalt therapy. The experiential nature of Gestalt theory and therapy includes an emphasis on self-awareness and being in the here and now.

Gestalt theory is an existential-humanistic approach, but also is a composite or integration of many different theoretical perspectives. There is a foundation of psychoanalysis combined with Gestalt psychology, muscular or physical defenses, field theory, existentialism, phenomenology, holism, and the personalities of Fritz and Laura. Gestalt therapists form an I-Thou relationship with clients, work in the here and now during sessions, and ask clients what and how questions about their moment-to-moment experiences. Therapy focuses on process, experiential activities, and physical sensations/experiences.

Although personal growth is a major focus, Gestalt theory focuses more on self-regulation than self-actualization. Contact with other people and experiences are the lifeblood of Gestalt therapy. Contact can create boundary disturbances and disequilibrium, but through self-awareness and self-regulation, people are able to integrate their experiences, channel them toward learning and growth, and regain equilibrium. For various reasons, people develop stylistic resistances to contact and therefore lead lives characterized by numbness. The ways in which people resist contact and experience boundary disturbances include: (a) introjection, (b) projection, (c) retroflection, (d) deflection, or (e) confluence.

Polster identified three stages of Gestalt therapy. First, there is a relational encounter or dialogic relationship. Second, awareness of physical and emotional experience is cultivated. Third, clients are engaged in here and now experiments that deepen awareness and facilitate change. Gestalt experiments are emotionally activating for clients; therefore therapists should work collaboratively and follow counseling and psychotherapy training guidelines. Gestalt therapy is not a good fit for all clients. Typically, clients enter therapy with unfinished business from the past that can be brought into the present and worked on actively. Gestalt therapists use a variety of techniques and experiments to facilitate client awareness, including, but not limited to: (a) staying with the feeling, (b) I take responsibility for …, (c) playing the projection, (d) the exaggeration experiment, (e) the empty-chair technique, and (f) dream work.

Anecdotal reports and observations of Gestalt therapy in action suggest it is a powerful and meaningful approach, but empirical evidence supporting Gestalt therapy is sparse. This may be because Fritz Perls had an existential orientation and was not interested in modernist scientific research. A smattering of research studies have shown Gestalt therapy to be equivalent to other contemporary therapies. In particular, emotion-focused therapy, an approach that integrates person-centered therapy with empty chair dialogues, has shown empirical promise.

Gestalt experiments can be uncomfortable for individuals or groups from diverse cultures who don't value direct individualist emotional focusing and expression. Diversity issues have just begun to be addressed in the Gestalt literature. There also hasn't been much exploration of the compatibility of Gestalt therapy and feminism or diverse sexualities. Eastern spirituality has long been associated with Gestalt approaches, but whether or not religion and spirituality is addressed in therapy is largely a function of individual therapist and client preference.

GESTALT THERAPY KEY TERMS

And this is my existence

Awareness

Body feedback

Boundary disturbances

Bracketing

Character armor

Confluence

Contact

Deflection

Dialogic relationship

Dream work

Emotion-focused therapy

Empty-chair dialogue

Feeling the actual

Field theory

Figure-formation process

Gestalt

Gestalt experiments

Gestalt therapy

Grounding

Here and now

Holism

I and Thou

I take responsibility for

Introjection

Mental metabolism

Playing the projection

Projection

Relational Gestalt therapy

Resistance to contact

Retroflection

Self-regulation

Staying with the feeling

The exaggeration experiment

Theraputic encounter

Topdog

Underdog

Unfinished business

What and how

CHAPTER 7

Behavioral Theory and Therapy

LEARNER OBJECTIVES

- Define scientific behaviorism and behavior therapy
- Identify key figures and historical trends in the development, evolution, and applications of behavior therapy
- Describe theoretical models and core theoretical principles from the behavioral perspective
- Describe and apply behavior therapy principles, strategies, and techniques
- Analyze cases that employ behavior therapy techniques
- Evaluate the empirical, cultural, gender, and spiritual validity of behavior therapy
- Summarize core content and define key terms associated with behavioral theory and therapy

In the late 1800s and early 1900s, psychology was, arguably, more philosophy and less science. Although Wilhelm Wundt's first psychology laboratory was established in 1879, counseling and psychotherapy practice was mostly psychoanalytic/neoanalytic and then existential-humanistic. However, other perspectives were also brewing. The pendulum of psychology was swinging in the direction of modernist science.

INTRODUCTION

Conflict and disagreement are ubiquitous in psychiatry, psychology, counseling, and other clinically oriented fields. Some writers claim that psychoanalysis was the first theory to dominate, referring to it as the first force. Others identify behaviorism as the first force and put psychoanalysis second. By all accounts, existential-humanism came third, as an alternative to psychoanalytic and behavioral theories.

What Is Scientific Behaviorism and Behavior Therapy?

Scientific behaviorism is the focus of this chapter and the foundation of much of academic psychology. Originating in the late 1800s and early 1900s, **scientific behaviorism** holds the premise that psychology is an objective, natural science, and therefore is the study of observable

and measurable human (and animal) behavior; behaviorists view the study of the mind, or internal mental states, as unscientific.

Scientific behaviorism and behavior therapy were, in part, reactions to less scientific experimental (e.g., introspection) and therapeutic (e.g., psychoanalytic) approaches within academic and applied psychology (Fishman & Franks, 1997). Scientific behaviorism was primarily laboratory-based for many decades. It wasn't until the 1950s that the term behavior therapy was coined; this explains why this behavior therapy chapter (as a first or second force) comes after coverage of the existential-humanistic therapies (third force). **Behavior therapy** is the therapeutic application of scientific behaviorism.

In some ways, behaviorism is philosophically opposed to psychoanalysis. In other ways, the two approaches are similar. The biggest difference between behaviorism and psychoanalysis is that psychoanalysts focus on inner mental dynamics, whereas behaviorists strictly focus on observable phenomena or materialistic concepts (Lazarus, 1971). In addition, behaviorists use therapy techniques derived from scientific research, whereas psychoanalytic techniques are rooted in clinical practice. However, both perspectives are highly mechanistic, positivistic, and deterministic approaches to understanding humans. These similarities led the late Michael Mahoney, an influential behavior therapist, to refer to psychoanalysis and behaviorism as the "yin and yang" of determinism (Mahoney, 1984).

For behaviorists, human learning is the crucible through which complex human behaviors develop. New learning (or behavior modification) is the behaviorist's tool for creating therapeutic change. This chapter explores the history and application of scientific behaviorism and behavior therapy.

KEY FIGURES AND HISTORICAL CONTEXT

Behavioral approaches to human change came in three major stages:

1. Behaviorism as a scientific endeavor.

2. Behavior therapy approaches.

3. Cognitive behavior therapy.

Behaviorism

John B. Watson
(*photo courtesy of Furman University*)

In the early 1900s, North American scientific psychology was on the move. Led by the ambitious John B. Watson, a new and different view of humans was becoming popular. This view, dubbed behaviorism, was in stark contrast to prevailing perspectives. Most early twentieth century academic psychologists were using **introspection** (the subjective observation of one's own mental state) to study human consciousness. In contrast, behaviorists rejected subjective introspection, focusing instead on objective observations. They also believed in determinism, rather than free will (Watson, 1913).

Prior to Watson, William James, the innovative thinker credited with launching psychology as an academic discipline, was more comfortable as a philosopher than as a scientist. When, in 1889, the president of Harvard University told James that he would soon be appointed their first *Alford Professor of Psychology*, James allegedly responded with great drama: "Do it, and I shall blow my brains out in front of everyone at the first mention of my name" (Bankart, 1997, p. 218). James had little regard for the scientific foundation of psychology; in 1892, he claimed it was:

> ... a string of raw facts; a little gossip and wrangle about opinions; a little classification and generalization on the mere descriptive level; a strong prejudice that we *have* states of mind, and that our brain conditions

> them: but not a single law in the sense in which physics shows us laws, not a single proposition from which any consequence can causally be deducted.... This is no science, it is only the hope of a science. (James, 1992, p. 433)

John Watson (1913, 1924) held a contrasting perspective. For Watson, behaviorism was a legitimate science. In publishing his behaviorist manifesto in 1913, he redefined psychology as pure science: "Psychology as a behaviorist views it is a purely objective branch of natural science" (Watson, 1913, p. 158). The young field of psychology was ready for Watson's ideas. He became president of the American Psychological Association in 1915, at the age of 35.

In opposition to James's emphasis on free will and human autonomy, Watson's scientific behaviorism focused on the prediction and control of human behavior. Similar to Pavlov and Thorndike, much of his work focused on animal behavior. Watson viewed humans and other animals as indistinguishable. His claims about the potential of behaviorism in predicting and controlling human behavior were bold and startling.

> Give me a dozen healthy infants, well-formed, and my own specified world to bring them up in and I'll guarantee to take any one at random and train him to become any type of specialist I might select—doctor, lawyer, artist, merchant-chief and yes, even beggar-man and thief, regardless of his talents, penchants, tendencies, abilities, vocations, and race of his ancestors. (Watson, 1924, p. 104)

From the beginning, Watson was interested in applying scientific behaviorism to human suffering. This may have been because he experienced a "nervous breakdown" as a young man and had not found psychoanalysis helpful (Bankart, 1997).

Little Hans and Little Albert

Watson began testing his beliefs about human psychopathology partly as a reaction to what he viewed as unscientific psychoanalytic treatments. In 1909, Freud reported an analysis of a 5-year-old boy who experienced a profound and debilitating fear of horses. Freud explained that his patient, Little Hans, was afraid of being bitten by a horse because of unresolved Oedipal issues and castration anxiety (Freud, 1909).

Watson wanted to demonstrate that direct classical or respondent conditioning caused severe fears and phobias (and that Freud's obscure psychoanalytic constructs were irrelevant). In his now famous experiments with 11-month-old Little Albert, Watson quickly made his point. After only five trials in which Watson and his research assistant Rosalie Rayner paired the presentation of a white rat to Albert with the striking of a metal bar, Albert developed a strong fear of and aversion to white rats (Watson & Rayner, 1920). Classical conditioning was quick and efficient, despite the fact that Albert had previously been a calm and happy baby. Even worse (for Little Albert), his conditioned fear response generalized to other furry or fuzzy white objects, including a rabbit, a dog, cotton wool, and a Santa Claus mask. Although Watson had further conditioning and deconditioning plans for Little Albert, after the initial five trials the boy's mother removed Little Albert from Watson's experiments (Beck, Levinson, & Irons, 2009).

Mary Cover Jones and Little Peter

In 1924, Watson's former student, Mary Cover Jones, conducted an investigation of the effectiveness of counterconditioning or deconditioning to eliminate anxiety with a 3-year-old boy named Little Peter. **Counterconditioning** is the pairing of a positive (and often incompatible) stimulus with a stimulus that elicits a negative or undesirable response (e.g., fear). It was Jones's study and not Watson's that dramatically illustrated how classical conditioning techniques could remediate fears and phobias.

Mary Cover Jones
(*photo courtesy of*
G. Paul Bishop)

Jones reported that Little Peter exhibited fear in response to several furry objects, including rabbits, fur coats, and cotton balls (Jones, 1924b). Then Jones systematically deconditioned Little Peter's fear reaction by pairing the gradual approach of a caged rabbit with Peter's involvement in an enjoyable activity—eating his favorite foods. In the end, Peter could touch the rabbit without fear; Jones extinguished his fear response.

Jones's work on counterconditioning was extensive and profound. Over time, she worked with 70 different children, all of whom had marked and specific fear responses. The children upon whom she conducted her experiments were from an institution; her efforts were to eliminate their fears, not create them. Overall, her conclusions were clear, and remain the basic framework for contemporary (and scientifically verifiable) behavioral approaches to treating human fears and phobias (Jones, 1924a). She wrote:

> In our study of methods for removing fear responses, we found unqualified success with only two. By the method of direct conditioning we associated the fear-object with a craving-object, and replaced the fear by a positive response. By the method of social imitation we allowed the subjects to share, under controlled conditions, the social activity of a group of children especially chosen with a view to prestige effect. [Other] methods proved sometimes effective but were not to be relied upon unless used in combination with other methods. (Jones, 1924a, p. 390)

The behavioral emphasis on observable behavior and rejection of mental concepts is well suited to laboratory research with animals and humans. Watson, Jones, and other early behaviorists made many important contributions to psychological science. Highlights include:

- The discovery by Pavlov, Watson, and their colleagues that classical or respondent conditioning procedures can produce involuntary physical and emotional responses.

- The discovery by Mary Cover Jones that deconditioning fear responses were possible through either (a) replacing (counterconditioning) the fear response with a positive response or (b) social imitation.

- The discovery by Thorndike (of the law of effect) and its later elaboration by Skinner that antecedents and consequences powerfully shape animal and human behaviors.

REFLECTIONS

If you're comfortable, take a minute to think about your fears. How well does classical conditioning explain their origin? Can you imagine using Mary Cover Jones's two components (deconditioning and social imitation) to successfully conquer your fears?

Behavior Therapy

In a testament to the behavioral zeitgeist of the 1950s, three different research groups in three different countries independently introduced the term behavior therapy to modern psychology.

B. F. Skinner in the United States

Skinner's early work involved an immense experimental project on operant conditioning with rats and pigeons in the 1930s (Skinner, 1938). At that time, he was trying to expand Thorndike's *law of effect*. He demonstrated the power of positive reinforcement, negative reinforcement, punishment, and stimulus control in modifying animal behavior. Within the confines of his well-known Skinner box, he taught pigeons to play ping-pong via operant conditioning procedures.

In the 1940s, Skinner began extending operant conditioning concepts to human social and clinical problems. His book *Walden Two* was a story of how operant conditioning procedures could be used to create a utopian society (Skinner, 1948). His next book, *Science and Human Behavior*, was a critique of psychoanalytic concepts and a reformulation of psychotherapy in behavioral terms (Skinner, 1953). Finally, in 1953, Skinner and his colleagues began using behavior therapy as a clinical term to describe the application of operant conditioning procedures to modify the behavior of psychotic patients (Skinner, Solomon, & Lindsley, 1953).

Joseph Wolpe, Arnold Lazarus, and Stanley Rachman in South Africa

Joseph Wolpe's interest in conditioning procedures as a means for resolving neurotic fear began with his doctoral thesis (Wolpe, 1948). Later, he conducted "experiments in neurosis production" with 12 domestic cats (Wolpe & Plaud, 1997, p. 968). Although Mary Cover Jones's counterconditioning work predated Wolpe, because she was a laboratory behaviorist and Wolpe was a clinician, Wolpe is considered to have established the first nonpsychoanalytic, empirically supported behavior therapy technique (Wolpe, 1954, 1958). His book *Psychotherapy by Reciprocal Inhibition* outlined the therapeutic procedure now called systematic desensitization (Wolpe, 1958). In the late 1990s, Wolpe reflected on his treatment technique:

> As the therapy procedure has evolved, the anxious patient is first trained in progressive muscle relaxation exercises and then gradually exposed imaginally or *in vivo* to feared stimuli while simultaneously relaxing. (Wolpe & Plaud, 1997, p. 969)

Wolpe's approach is similar to Jones's first counterconditioning principle wherein a conditioned negative emotional response *is replaced with* a conditioned positive emotional response (Jones, 1924b). Wolpe's revolutionary work attracted the attention of two South African psychologists, Arnold Lazarus and Stanley Rachman. Both contributed significantly to the behavior therapy movement.

Lazarus also was the first behavior therapist to embrace eclecticism. Early on, and throughout his career, he integrated laboratory-based scientific procedures into counseling practice (Lazarus, 1958, 1991). He adamantly opposed narrow therapy definitions or conceptualizations. His eclectic clinical approach, multimodal behavior therapy, is described in Chapter 14.

Stanley Rachman also influenced behavior therapy. For decades, he was editor of the journal *Behaviour Research and Therapy*. His unique contribution involved the application of aversive stimuli to treating what he described as neurotic behavior, including addictions (Rachman, 1965).

Hans Eysenck and the Maudsley Group in the United Kingdom

Although most famous for his personality theory, British psychiatrist Hans Eysenck used behavior therapy to describe the application of modern learning theory to the understanding and treatment of behavioral and psychiatric problems (Eysenck, 1959). Eysenck's publication, a behaviorally based textbook of abnormal psychology and a collection of case studies in behavior therapy, led to the widespread dissemination of behavior therapy for treating symptoms of neurotic conditions, instead of their underlying psychodynamics (Eysenck, 1960, 1964).

Cognitive Behavior Modification

Behavior therapy continues to evolve. As Cyril Franks wrote, behavior therapy is designed to evolve: "Above all, in behavior therapy a theory is a servant that is useful *only until better theory and better therapy* come along" (Franks & Barbrack, 1983, pp. 509–510; italics added).

Most behavior therapists now acknowledge and work with cognition. In the compilation *The Best of Behaviour Research and Therapy*, many articles (selected over a 35-year period) specifically focused on thoughts, expectations, and emotions (Rachman, 1997). Additionally, in 2005, the Association for the Advancement of Behavior Therapy (AABT) renamed itself the Association for Behavioral and Cognitive Therapies (ABCT). More recently, the Association for Contextual Behavioral Science (ACBS) was established. ACBS focuses primarily on theory and science underlying acceptance and commitment therapy (ACT). As an integrative behavior therapy, ACT is covered in Chapter 14.

THEORETICAL PRINCIPLES

There have been many formulations and reformulations of behavioral theory and therapy (Farmer & Nelson-Gray, 2005). Two primary convictions characterize behaviorists and behavioral theory—both then and now:

1. Behavior therapists employ techniques based on modern learning theory.

2. Behavior therapists employ techniques derived from scientific research.

Some behaviorists have criticized even these most basic behavioral tenets. For example, Lazarus wrote:

> Eysenck's ... insistence that behavior therapy denotes "methods of treatment which are derived from modern learning theory" amounts to little more than a beguiling slogan....
>
> The danger lies in a premature elevation of learning principles into unwarranted scientific truths and the ascription of the general term of "modern learning theory" to what in reality are best described as "modern learning theories." (Lazarus, 1971, pp. 4, 5)

Lazarus's point is that there is no single "learning theory," but instead, many learning theories (in the plural). He asserted that even psychoanalytic formulations constitute learning hypotheses, many of which remain unsubstantiated.

Theoretical Models

We turn now to a brief description of the two main models of learning that form the theoretical foundation of behavior therapy (Farmer & Nelson-Gray, 2005; Fishman & Franks, 1997). In Chapter 8, we look at two additional learning models that focus on cognitive learning.

Operant Conditioning: Applied Behavior Analysis

Applied behavior analysis is a clinical term referring to a behavioral approach based on operant conditioning principles. **Operant conditioning** (also called instrumental conditioning) is a form of behavior modification that involves manipulation of behavioral antecedents and consequences. The operant conditioning philosophy is: *Behavior is a function of its consequences.*

B. F. Skinner expanded on Thorndike's (1932) original learning theory and developed operant conditioning. Thorndike hypothesized that behavior followed by a "satisfier" would strengthen responses and behavior followed by an "annoyer" would weaken responses. Skinner (1938) changed the terminology and conducted extensive research. The term operant refers to how behaviors operate on the environment, thereby producing specific consequences. **Positive reinforcement** occurs when a specific behavior is followed by Thorndike's satisfier, and therefore the likelihood of the specific behavior is strengthened.

Operant conditioning is a **stimulus–response (SR) theory**, meaning that no cognitive or covert intervening variables mediate the relationship between the stimulus and response. Applied behavior analysis focuses solely on observable behaviors. Therapy proceeds primarily through manipulating environmental variables to produce behavior change.

Applied behavior analysts primarily employ reinforcement, punishment, extinction, and stimulus control. These procedures are used to manipulate environmental contingencies (e.g., environmental rewards and punishments). The goals are to increase adaptive behavior through reinforcement and stimulus control and to reduce maladaptive behavior through punishment and extinction.

In theory, and sometimes in practice, positive reinforcement and punishment concepts are simple. For example, when your cat meows at the front door and gets a bowl of tasty cat food, the likelihood of your cat returning to your front door and meowing again increases. In contrast, if you spray cold water on your cat when it meows (or administer an aversive electric shock), the meowing behavior is likely to diminish (or, as sometimes occurs with punishment, erratic or aggressive behaviors may develop).

Unfortunately, operant conditioning procedures are not always straightforward in real life. Take, for example, hypothetical parents of 5- and 15-year-old girls. The parents are trying to teach their 5-year-old to tie her shoes. Therefore, whenever she engages in shoe-tying behavior they coo and clap, and when she finally gets it right they give big bear hugs and high fives. In this situation, the parents' cooing and clapping are serving as positive reinforcements and the 5-year-old's shoe-tying behavior increases.

At the same time, the parents are trying to teach their 15-year-old daughter to speak to them respectfully. Because positive reinforcement worked so well with their 5-year-old, they decide to try cooing, clapping, and hugging in response to their daughter's respectful communication. Unfortunately, when they hug her, she recoils (especially in front of her teenage friends) and responds by saying, "Get away from me!" After discovering that positive reinforcement doesn't work with their older daughter, the parents decide to try punishment. They resolve to shout and scold her whenever she speaks disrespectfully. This time their efforts completely backfire— she responds by shouting right back at them.

In desperation, the parents visit a counselor. When the counselor suggests using a behavioral plan, the parents roll their eyes and exclaim, "We've already tried that, it doesn't work!" In reality, the only thing the parents discovered is that operant conditioning is more complex than most people understand.

Whether we're talking about parenting or teaching your cat fun new tricks, you have four operant conditioning tools: two types of reinforcement and two types of punishment (see Table 7.1).

Classical Conditioning: The Neobehavioristic, Mediational Stimulus–Response Model

The **neobehavioristic mediational SR model** involves classical conditioning principles. Pavlov, Watson, Mowrer, Wolpe, and others developed classical conditioning principles.

Classical conditioning (also referred to as respondent conditioning) involves an association or linking of one environmental stimulus with another. In Pavlovian terms, an **unconditioned stimulus** is one that naturally produces a specific physical-emotional response. Unconditioned stimuli elicit smooth muscle reflex responses; higher-order cognitive processes are not required for conditioning to occur. The following clinical example described by Wolpe illustrates how fear responses are classically conditioned.

A 34-year-old man's four-year fear of being in automobiles started when his car was struck from behind while he was waiting for a red light to change. At that moment he felt an overwhelming fear of impending death; subsequently he was afraid to sit inside even a stationary car. That the fear was purely a matter of classical autonomic conditioning (automatic response to the ambience of a car's interior) was evidenced by the fact that he had no expectation of danger when he sat in a car. (Wolpe, 1987, pp. 135–136)

Table 7.1 Reinforcement and Punishment

	Apply (adding something)	Withdraw (removing something)
Something Positive (+)	*Positive reinforcement*	*Negative punishment* (aka response cost)
Often referred to as a "reward"	Parents give their 5-year-old hugs and high-fives after shoe-tying behavior. Another example is the giving of allowance or company bonuses following positive behavioral performance.	Caregivers take away something positive, like allowance or cell phone privileges, in response to undesirable behavior. This is the taking away of something positive (e.g., a privilege).
	Positive reinforcement occurs when a stimulus is applied that *increases* the likelihood of the behavior it follows.	**Negative punishment occurs when the removal of a stimulus *decreases* the likelihood of the behavior it follows.**
Something negative (–)	**Positive punishment* (aka punishment or aversive conditioning)	*Negative reinforcement*
Often referred to as something aversive.	When caregivers use spanking, verbal insults, or physical pain to modify behavior.	When the seatbelt alarm beeps when you're not belted in and stops when you are is an example of negative reinforcement. Also, when physical and emotional pain decreases immediately after using a drug or alcohol.
	Positive punishment occurs when a stimulus is applied (usually called an aversive stimulus) that *reduces* the likelihood of the behavior it follows.	**Negative reinforcement occurs when the removal of an aversive stimulus *increases* the likelihood of the behavior it follows.**

*Note: Although it's common language, we don't support the use of the term "positive punishment." This is because it implies that punishment is "positive" despite the fact that it involves a universally negative or aversive consequence or stimulus and the adverse effects of "positive punishment" are well-documented. Instead of positive and negative punishment, we prefer "punishment" and "response cost."

Being struck from behind while waiting for a red light is the unconditioned stimulus (Wolpe, 1987). An unconditioned stimulus is a stimulus that automatically (or autonomically) produces an unconditioned response. An **unconditioned response** is a reflexive fear response. As a consequence of the accident, the 34-year-old man developed a **conditioned response** (which in this case is fear—and is always the same as the unconditioned response) in response to the conditioned stimulus. The **conditioned stimulus** (which involves a learned association with the unconditioned stimulus) was the interior of automobiles. As Wolpe emphasized, this scenario represents classical autonomic conditioning or learning because the man has no cognitive expectations or cognitive triggers that lead to his experience of fear when sitting inside an automobile.

Classical conditioning principles also include stimulus generalization, stimulus discrimination, extinction, counterconditioning, and spontaneous recovery.

Stimulus generalization is the extension or generalization of a conditioned fear response to new settings, situations, or objects. In the preceding example, if the man begins experiencing intense fear when sitting in an airplane, stimulus generalization has occurred. Similarly, for Little Albert, stimulus generalization occurred when Albert experienced fear in response to objects (stimuli) similar in appearance to white rats (e.g., Santa Claus masks or cotton balls).

Stimulus discrimination occurs when a new or different stimulus doesn't elicit a conditioned fear response. For example, if the 34-year-old man can sit in a movie theater without experiencing fear, stimulus discrimination has occurred. The movie theater (stimulus) is different enough from the car (stimulus) that it doesn't elicit the conditioned response.

Extinction involves the gradual elimination of a conditioned response. It occurs when a conditioned stimulus is repeatedly presented without a previously associated unconditioned stimulus. For example, if Watson had kept working with Little Albert and repeatedly exposed him to a white rat without a frightening sound of metal clanging, eventually Little Albert might lose his conditioned fear response to rats. Extinction is not the same as forgetting; it involves relearning that the conditioned stimulus is no longer a signal that precedes the unconditioned stimulus.

Jones's work with Little Peter is an example of successful counterconditioning or deconditioning. **Counterconditioning** involves new associative learning. The subject learns that the conditioned stimulus brings with it a positive emotional experience. For example, when Jones repeatedly presented the white rat to Little Peter while he was eating some of his favorite foods, eventually the conditioned response (fear) was counterconditioned. Counterconditioning is part of Wolpe's systematic desensitization process.

Pavlov (1927) initially discussed spontaneous recovery. **Spontaneous recovery** occurs when an old response suddenly returns after having been successfully extinguished or counterconditioned. For example, if after successful counterconditioning, Wolpe's client suddenly begins having fear symptoms associated with the interior of automobiles, he is exhibiting spontaneous recovery.

Theory of Psychopathology

Learning causes maladaptive behavior. There are two usual remedies: extinction of maladaptive behavior or replacing maladaptive behavior with new learning. The idea that human learning is at the core of human behavior guides behavior therapy assessment and treatment.

Psychopathology can also involve a skill deficit. An underlying premise of assertiveness or social skills training is that individuals who exhibit too much passive or too much aggressive behavior haven't learned how to appropriately use assertive behavior in social situations. Consequently, the purpose of assertiveness skills training (a behavioral treatment) is to teach clients assertiveness skills through modeling, coaching, behavior rehearsal, and reinforcement.

Either classical or operant conditioning can explain successful outcomes associated with assertiveness training. For example, Wolpe would have considered assertive behavior as incompatible with anxiety; when anxiety is counterconditioned, assertive behavior may emerge (Wolpe, 1973). In contrast, contemporary assertiveness trainers usually focus more on operant conditioning contingencies—reinforcements and punishments—that establish and maintain passive, aggressive, and assertive social behavior (Alberti & Emmons, 2017).

As a means of better understanding client psychopathology, behaviorists apply scientific methods to clinical or counseling settings. Behaviorists systematically:

- Observe and assess client maladaptive or unskilled behaviors.

- Develop hypotheses about the cause, maintenance, and treatment for maladaptive or unskilled behaviors.

- Test behavioral hypotheses with empirically supported interventions.

- Observe and evaluate the results of their intervention.

- Revise and continue testing new hypotheses about how to modify maladaptive or unskilled behavior(s) as needed.

Behaviorists are on the cutting edge when it comes to applying specific treatment procedures to specific clinical problems. More than any other practitioner group, behavior (and cognitive behavior) therapists insist on empirical support for their treatment methods. Consequently, most empirically supported treatments (ESTs) are behavioral or cognitive behavioral (Chambless et al., 1998, 2006).

THE PRACTICE OF BEHAVIOR THERAPY

When preparing to do behavior therapy, be sure to get out your clipboard, because behavior therapists take notes, think like scientists, and act like educators. You may even need graph paper or a white board for illustrating concepts to clients. Your job is to help clients unlearn old, maladaptive behaviors and learn new, adaptive behaviors.

A sample excerpt from a behavioral informed consent is in Putting It in Practice 7.1.

What Is Contemporary Behavior Therapy?

In this chapter we include a description of therapeutic interventions that are primarily behavioral, but that occasionally include cognition. Not all therapies in this chapter are purely behavioral. Similarly, although the next chapter includes cognitive therapy interventions and are predominantly cognitive in nature, we recognize that nearly all cognitive therapies are used in conjunction with the behavioral techniques described in this chapter.

This leaves us in a conundrum regarding the definition of cognitive behavior therapy (CBT). As you may know, CBT is currently the most popular and scientifically evaluated approach to psychotherapy. This approach explicitly combines cognitive and behavioral techniques, with both technical strategies viewed as compatible and mutually enhancing.

To make matters more complex, there are now several third wave cognitive behavior therapies. These include:

- Dialectical behavior therapy (DBT).

- Acceptance and commitment therapy (ACT).

- Eye movement desensitization reprocessing (EMDR).

Some theorists place these third wave behavior therapies in the behavior therapy domain. However, partly because we'd rather not risk the wrath of the late, great Joseph Wolpe, we view them as horses of a different therapeutic color. Consequently, we review DBT, ACT, and EMDR in Chapter 14.

Assessment Issues and Procedures

The main goal of behavioral assessment is to determine the external (environmental or situational) stimuli and internal (physiological and sometimes cognitive) stimuli

---

PUTTING IT IN PRACTICE

7.1 A Behavioral Informed Consent Form

The following is a sample excerpt from a behavior therapy informed consent. As you read it, pretend you're sitting in a therapist's waiting room, about to go in for your first behavior therapy session.

I specialize in behavior therapy, a research-based and highly effective form of therapy based on modern learning theories.

Humans are constantly learning. As you know from experience, humans learn everything from how to read or ride a bicycle to complex emotional responses, like love, jealousy, and nervousness. Everyone has a tremendous capacity for learning.

Whether you've come to therapy because of a difficult situation, a problem relationship, or a troubling emotion, I'll help you unlearn old troubling habits and learn new, more positive habits. Research has proven that behavior therapy is very helpful for many problems.

In therapy, we'll work as a team, and we'll talk in detail about some of the hardest things you're facing in life. Then, we'll develop a plan for helping you overcome the problems and symptoms that cause you distress.

In most cases, our plan will include several different approaches to learning. Some learning will happen right in our sessions, and some will happen outside our sessions. That means I'll give you assignments to complete between our meetings. If you complete your assignments, the positive changes will happen even faster.

Behavior therapy is a brief therapy. You won't come to therapy forever; depending on your problem and your situation, it may take only a few therapy sessions or it may take several months. We'll regularly evaluate our work together and talk openly and directly about your progress.

My job is to work in partnership with you to improve your life and relieve your uncomfortable symptoms. I'll regularly explain exactly what we're doing and why we're doing it. Whenever you have questions, feel free to ask; I'll do my best to provide you with the answers you deserve.

---

that directly precede and follow adaptive and maladaptive client behaviors. In a perfect behavioral world, behavior therapists would directly observe clients in their natural environments to obtain specific information about exactly what happens before, during, and after adaptive and maladaptive behaviors. Direct observation is the behavioral assessment gold standard.

Functional Behavior Assessment

Behaviorists refer to a formal assessment of behavior contingencies as a **functional behavior assessment** (FBA) (Drossel, Rummel, & Fisher, 2009). An FBA involves assessment of the **behavioral ABCs** (Spiegler & Guevremont, 2016):

- A = The behavior's **antecedents** (everything that happens just before maladaptive behavior is observed).

- B = The **behavior** (the problem as defined in concrete behavioral terms; e.g., rather than being called an "anger problem" it's "yelling or swearing six times a day and punching others twice daily").

- C = The behavior's **consequences** (everything that happens immediately following the problem behavior occurs).

FBAs help determine the function of specific behaviors. The basic question we're trying to answer is: What reinforcements are operating that maintain a problem behavior? FBAs assist practitioners (especially in schools) in developing a functional causal model (or hypothesis) to explain behavior (O'Brien & Carhart, 2011). For example, if a child is disrupting class, therapists can gather data and watch for patterns via direct behavior observation. A particular stimulus may precede the child's disruptive behaviors. Perhaps a stimulus (e.g., in-class reading assignments) produces an aversive, uncomfortable state (i.e., anxiety). Consequently, the child's avoidant (i.e., disruptive) behavior is negatively reinforced (see Table 7.1). In addition, or alternatively, perhaps the child is obtaining positive reinforcement (e.g., attention from the teacher and classmates) when engaging in disruptive behavior.

There are a number of obstacles to direct behavioral observation. First, most therapists can't afford the time required to observe clients or students. Second, many clients object to having their therapist come into their home or workplace to conduct a formal observation. Third, even if the client or student agrees to have the therapist come perform an observation, the therapist's presence can influence the client's behavior. The therapist as observer is more than an observer, also becoming a participant within the client's environment—this means that a truly objective and natural observation is often impossible (J. Sommers-Flanagan & Sommers-Flanagan, 2017). When direct behavioral observations are used, they should be as unobtrusive as possible. Also, computerized assessment applications have created many unobtrusive measurement alternatives (Medin, Astrup, Kåsin, & Andersen, 2015).

Because behavior therapists cannot always use direct behavioral observation, they usually employ a variety of less direct methods to gather data and construct a functional causal hypothesis.

The Behavioral Interview

During behavioral clinical interviews, behavior therapists directly observe client behavior, inquire about antecedents, problem behaviors, and consequences, and operationalize the primary therapy targets (Cormier, Nurius, & Osborn, 2017). For behaviorists, the **operational definition** or specific, measurable characteristics of client symptoms and goals are crucial behavioral assessment components.

Defining the client's problem(s) in precise behavioral terms is the first step in a behavioral assessment interview. Behavior therapists aren't satisfied when clients describe themselves as "depressed" or "anxious" or "hyper." Typical queries during a behavior therapy intake interview might include:

- Tell me everything that happens during a day when you're depressed. Let's start with when you wake up in the morning and cover everything that happens

until you go to bed at night. Then we'll talk about how you're sleeping.

- Describe the physical sensations you experience in your body when you're feeling anxious.

- You said you were acting "hyper." Tell me what that looks like. Describe it to me as if I were watching it happen.

Behaviorists value information about both the internal (cognitions, mood, physiology) and the external (behavior), as long as the information is clear, specific, and measurable.

Despite many practical advantages of behavioral or clinical interviews, this assessment procedure also has several disadvantages:

- Low interrater reliability.

- Lack of interviewer objectivity.

- Inconsistency between behavior during an interview and behavior outside therapy.

- False, inaccurate, and subjective reports from clients.

Behavior therapists compensate for the inconsistent and subjective nature of interviews through two strategies. First, they employ structured or diagnostic interviews such as the *SCID* (*Structured Clinical Interview for DSM-5*; First, Williams, Karg, & Spitzer, 2016). Second, they use additional assessment methods—such as self-monitoring and standardized questionnaires (J. Sommers-Flanagan & Sommers-Flanagan, 2017).

Self-Monitoring

Behavior therapists often train clients in self-monitoring. **Self-monitoring** occurs when clients observe and record their own behaviors. For example, clients can monitor food intake or keep track of the number of cigarettes they smoke. In cognitive behavior therapy, clients frequently keep thought or emotion logs that include at least three components: (1) disturbing emotional states, (2) the exact behavior engaged in at the time of the emotional state, and (3) thoughts that linked to the emotions. Teaching clients to self-monitor is an easy and essential therapist skill (see Table 7.2 for a sample A-B-C log; S. Kuhlenschmidt, personal communication, March 27, 2016).

Table 7.2   Sample A-B-C Log

Date/Time	Place	Antecedents	Behavior	Consequences	Notes
11/2/17 1:00pm	At work	Lunch	Smoked 1 cigarette	Enjoyed talking; got nicotine fix; felt good	Walked outside; smoked with friends
11/2/17 8:00pm	At home	Finished eating ice cream	Smoked 1 cigarette	Peace and quiet outside noisy house; got nicotine fix; felt better	Wanted to get away and smoke

Client self-monitoring has advantages and disadvantages. On the positive side, self-monitoring is inexpensive and practical, and cell phone and computer apps can make self-monitoring easy and convenient (Carter, Burley, & Cade, 2017; Tregarthen, Lock, & Darcy, 2015). The other big benefit is that self-monitoring is not simply an assessment procedure, it also typically shows therapeutic benefits; clients can begin improving solely as a function of self-monitoring (Davies, Jones, & Rafoth, 2010; Mairs & Mullan, 2015). The downside is that clients may collect inadequate or inaccurate information, or resist collecting any information at all.

REFLECTIONS

Have you ever tried self-monitoring as a method for changing behavior? Either way, consider starting a self-monitoring project now. Identify an undesirable behavior. Then, find a way to diligently track it. You might want to find a cool smartphone app to help make it easier.

Standardized Objective Questionnaires

Behaviorists famously prefer "objective" assessment measures over "subjective" projective assessment procedures (Groth-Marnat & Wright, 2016). Objective psychological measures include standardized administration and scoring. Additionally, behaviorists prefer instruments with established reliability (i.e., internal consistency and consistency over time) and validity (i.e., the instrument measures what it purports to measure). Applied behavior analysts emphasize that objective measurement must focus solely on overt, observable behaviors rather than internal mental processes. Case examples in this chapter illustrate behavior therapist's use of standardized questionnaires.

Operant Conditioning and Variants

In the tradition of Skinner and applied behavior analysis, perhaps the most straightforward application of behaviorism to therapy is operant conditioning. Skinner emphasized environmental manipulation. In one of his more dramatic statements, he noted:

> I see no evidence of an inner world of mental life. … The appeal to cognitive states and processes is a diversion which could well be responsible for much of our failure to solve our problems. We need to change our behavior and we can do so only by changing our physical and social environments. (Skinner, 1977, p. 10)

Contingency Management and Token Economies

Using operant conditioning for human problems requires an analysis of naturally occurring behavioral consequences

in the client's physical and social environments. This process is also called contingency management. **Contingency management** (CM) is:

> The systematic delivery of reinforcing or punishing consequences contingent on the occurrence of a target response, and the withholding of those consequences in the absence of the target response. (Schumacher et al., 2007, p. 823)

Institutional, educational, family, and drug treatment settings often employ CM strategies.

To illustrate CM in action, here's a brief summary of how an applied behavioral analyst (ABA) conducted therapy with the parents who wanted their 15-year-old to stop speaking disrespectfully. If you recall, the parents' efforts to modify their teen's behavior using positive reinforcement and punishment backfired because they didn't use the procedure appropriately. Operant conditioning involves several systematic steps.

First, the ABA therapist collaborated with the parents to operationalize the target behaviors and identify behavioral objectives. This requires precisely defining behaviors of interest. It also requires determining whether they want to increase or decrease the frequency of each target behavior. They agreed on the following behavioral goals:

- Decrease profanity in the home or toward the parents.

- Decrease disrespectful gestures or nonverbal behaviors (e.g., giving "the finger," rolling her eyes, long heaving sighs).

- Decrease derogatory comments about the parents or their ideas, such as "You're stupid," "That sucks," or "This family sucks."

- Increase their 15-year-old's smiling behavior, compliments toward the parents and younger sibling, and compliance with parental suggestions and advice.

Second, their therapist helped the parents develop a system for measuring target behaviors. They used an electronic notebook to track their 15-year-old's behaviors and a digital audio recorder to keep an ongoing record of verbal interactions preceding and following their daughter's behaviors.

After analyzing the parents' notebooks and audio data, the therapist helped the parents identify contingencies that were maintaining disrespectful speech. During a 2-week baseline monitoring period, 16 incidents of undesirable behavior and 3 incidents of desirable behavior were recorded.

It was determined that the parents' reaction to the disrespectful speech—giving into demands, getting emotionally upset, or engaging in a protracted argument—were positively reinforcing the problem behaviors, whereas their relative lack of response to pleasant behaviors was extinguishing the behaviors they wanted to increase. Put another way, they were engaging in **backward behavior modification** (i.e., reinforcing undesirable behaviors and extinguishing desirable behaviors; J. Sommers-Flanagan & Sommers-Flanagan, 2011).

A variety of potential positive reinforcements were identified, including (a) taking their daughter to dinner, (b) allowing her to stream movies online, and (c) taking her for driving lessons. This analysis led to the third stage of treatment: modification of existing environmental and social contingencies.

The therapist instructed the parents in a reinforcement and extinction procedure.

- The parents initiated a $20 weekly allowance program. This program provided their teen with money to spend as she wished. However, whenever the 15-year-old engaged in an undesirable behavior, a response cost (negative punishment) was implemented. For profanity, she lost $2 of the allowance; for disrespectful gestures or derogatory comments, she lost $1 of the allowance.

- The parents provided a reinforcement after their teen displayed one of the target behaviors. They used a variable-ratio reinforcement schedule (see Putting It in Practice 7.2).

- The therapist taught the parents to continuously monitor and evaluate the effects of their new contingency schedule. This is a key factor in operant conditioning. The therapist explained this principle to the parents:

> As behaviorists, we believe the only way to tell if something is a positive reinforcement is to test it. What you discovered last time around was that hugging and high fives were positive reinforcements for your 5-year-old, but not for your 15-year-old. Perhaps the most important part of our intervention with your 15-year-old is for us to evaluate her response to the consequences you provide. This will help us understand how to increase and decrease the target behaviors.

After using this operant conditioning program for eight weeks, the parents ended therapy and said, "Thank you for your help. It's like we have a brand-new daughter."

PUTTING IT IN PRACTICE

7.2 Understanding and Applying Schedules of Reinforcement

B. F. Skinner's work with rats and pigeons led him to introduce the concept of reinforcement. Skinner hypothesized, tested, and proved that behaviors that are reinforced tend to increase, while behaviors that are not reinforced tend to die out or become extinguished. Descriptions of positive and negative reinforcement are given in Table 7.1.

Skinner also developed graphs to visually represent his laboratory findings. In repeated experiments, he tested animal responses to different schedules of reinforcement. He described (and visually displayed; see Figure 7.1) five reinforcement schedules.

1. **Continuous reinforcement**: Reinforcement is provided every time the desired (target) behavioral response occurs. *Example*: A child gets a star or for every completed homework assignment. *To think about*: You get a kiss from your romantic partner every time you do the dishes.

2. **Fixed ratio reinforcement**: Reinforcement is provided after a predetermined number of desired behaviors. *Example*: A child gets a star after every fourth completed homework assignment. *To think about*: You get a kiss from your romantic partner after every fourth time you do the dishes.

3. **Fixed interval reinforcement**: Reinforcement is provided after a predetermined time period, as long as the target behavior has occurred at least once. A child gets a star each week, as long as one homework assignment was completed. You get a kiss from your romantic partner every 24 hours, as long as you've done the dishes at least once.

4. **Variable ratio reinforcement**: Reinforcement is provided after an unpredictable number of target behaviors occur. A child gets a star after having completed an unpredictable number of homework assignments (we call this surprise rewards; J. Sommers-Flanagan & Sommers-Flanagan, 2011). *To think about*: You get a kiss from your romantic partner

after washing the dishes, but sometimes it occurs after 3 washings, sometimes after 7, sometimes after 1. *Real life examples*: Fishing, golfing, gambling.

5. **Variable interval reinforcement**: Reinforcement is provided after an unpredictable time period, as long as the target behavior has occurred at least once. A child gets a star after unpredictable time periods pass (sometimes after 1 day; other times 3 days; other times 1 week, etc.). *To think about*: You get a kiss from your romantic partner after a variable time period has passed.

Note: Think about how these schedules of reinforcement might affect you. See Figure 7.1 for graphed results from four common reinforcement schedules (not including continuous reinforcement).

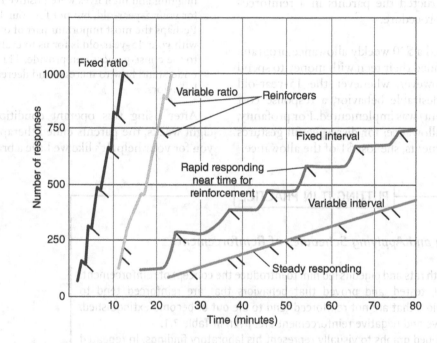

FIGURE 7.1 Graphs of Four Schedules of Reinforcement

Following Skinner's original work aimed at modifying the behavior of psychotic patients, operant conditioning or CM within institutions came to be known as token economies (Ghezzi, Wilson, Tarbox, & MacAleese, 2009; Skinner, 1954). Within **token economy** systems, patients or students earn points or poker chips (aka symbolic rewards) for positive or desirable behaviors. These tokens function like money, to obtain goods (e.g., food or toys) or privileges (e.g., computer or recreational time).

Token economies have been lauded as highly effective, but they've also been criticized as coercive and as not generalizing to the real world (Coelho et al., 2015; Glynn, 1990; Wakefield, 2008). In an ideal behavioral setting, reinforcements and punishments would be tightly controlled and then, after desirable behavior patterns are well established, behavioral contingencies would be slowly decreased. The term for this is **fading**. Fading helps to generalize learning from over time and across settings (Gross, Duhon, & Doerksen-Klopp, 2014). The

desired outcome occurs when a child, teen, or institutionalized adult internalizes the contingency system and continues positive behaviors independent of a token system.

Critics of behaviorism contend that people have a natural or intrinsic desire to behave in positive ways and that CM can interfere with that desire. Specifically, Kohn (2005) contended that applying tangible rewards to people who are already motivated undermines intrinsic motivation. Many studies have shown that positive reinforcement adversely affects intrinsic motivation (Deci, 1971; Ma, Jin, Meng, & Shen, 2014; Ryan, Lynch, Vansteenkiste, & Deci, 2011). Of course, there's also a body of literature rebutting this hypothesis and claiming that positive reinforcement, when properly conceptualized and administered, can increase intrinsic motivation (Maag, 2001; Pope & Harvey, 2015). Advanced training and supervision is necessary in order to employ operant techniques in a consistently helpful fashion.

Although positive reinforcement has had its share of criticism, punishment or aversive conditioning as a therapeutic technique generates far more controversy. Historically, Thorndike (1932), Skinner (1953), and Estes (1944) all concluded that punishment led to behavior suppression but wasn't effective for controlling behavior. Punishment was viewed as insufficient to eliminate learned responses. Somewhat later, Solomon (1964) reopened the book on punishment by reporting that punishment alone could generate new, learned behavior. Currently, although punishment is considered a powerful behavior modifier, it's also viewed as having major drawbacks.

Despite problems with punishment as a learning tool, **aversive conditioning** (the term used to describe the use of punishment for behavior modification purposes) can reduce undesirable or maladaptive behavior. It has been applied with some success to smoking cessation and alcohol abuse or dependency (Arzi et al., 2014).

Former American Psychological Association President and renowned behaviorist Alan Kazdin (2008) provided an excellent description of what the research says about using punishment (including spanking children):

> Study after study has proven that punishment all by itself, as it is usually practiced in the home, is relatively ineffective in changing behavior....
>
> Each time, punishing your child stops the behavior for a moment. Maybe your child cries, too, and shows remorse. In our studies, parents often mistakenly interpret such crying and wails of I'm sorry! as signs that punishment has worked. It hasn't. Your child's resistance to punishment escalates as fast as the severity of the punishment does, or even faster. So you penalize more and more to get the same result: a brief stop, then the unwanted behavior returns, often worse than before....
>
> Bear in mind that about 35 % of parents who start out with relatively mild punishments end up crossing the line drawn by the state to define child abuse: hitting with an object, harsh and cruel hitting, and so on. The surprisingly high percentage of line-crossers, and their general failure to improve their children's behavior, points to a larger truth: punishment changes parents' behavior for the worse more effectively than it changes children's behavior for the better. And, as anyone knows who has physically punished a child more harshly than they meant to—and that would include most of us—it feels just terrible. (pp. 15, 16, 17)

Kazdin's point about how using punishment changes the parent's behavior for the worse is another example of operant conditioning. Specifically, when parents spank children, immediate compliance often occurs, which relieves parents of tension and discomfort. This cycle gives parents a powerful dose of negative reinforcement for using physical punishment.

In a meta-analysis of the effects of corporal punishment on children's behavior (Gershoff, 2002), punishment was associated with 1 desirable outcome (i.e., immediate behavioral compliance) and 10 undesirable outcomes, including less internalization of moral principles, potential abuse, delinquent behavior, and later abuse within adult relationships. Harsh physical punishment has also been associated with adverse effects on brain development, increased rates of adult mental disorders, and poorer adult physical health (Afifi, Mota, Dasiewicz, MacMillan, & Sareen, 2012; Afifi, Mota, MacMillan, & Sareen, 2013; Gershoff, 2016). These and other findings led a group of Canadian and U.S. researchers to recommend classifying spanking as an "adverse childhood event" (Afifi et al., 2017). Despite scientific indictment of corporal punishment, many adults remain in favor of its use as a disciplinary technique.

REFLECTIONS

It's not unusual for people to have strong reactions to the preceding scientific critique of punishment. What's your reaction? Is your reaction based more on alternative scientific research or on your own personal experiences?

Behavioral Activation

Over half a century ago, Skinner suggested that in individuals who have normal moods, behavioral activity produces ongoing positive reinforcement. However, when these activities are interrupted, positive reinforcement is reduced and depression ensues. Later, Ferster (1973) and Lewinsohn (Lewinsohn, 1974; Lewinsohn & Libet, 1972) elaborated on this idea, leading to the hypothesis that:

> Depressed individuals find fewer activities pleasant, engage in pleasant activities less frequently, and obtain therefore less positive reinforcement than other individuals. (Cuijpers, van Straten, & Warmerdam, 2007a, p. 319)

From the behavioral perspective, the thinking goes like this:

• *Observation*: Individuals experiencing depression engage in fewer pleasant activities and obtain less daily positive reinforcement.

• *Hypothesis*: Individuals with depressive symptoms might improve or recover if they change their behavior (while not paying attention to thoughts or feelings associated with depression).

Like good scientists, behavior therapists have tested this hypothesis and found that behavior change—all by itself—produces positive treatment outcomes for clients with depression. This treatment is now called behavioral activation. **Behavioral activation** was initially referred to as **activity scheduling**; it involves working with clients to schedule activities that increase the rate of naturally occurring positive reinforcement. Originally, activity scheduling was one component of cognitive therapy (CT) for depression (Beck, Rush, Shaw, & Emery, 1979; Lewinsohn, Steinmetz, Antonuccio, & Teri, 1984).

However, in 1996, Jacobson and colleagues conducted a dismantling study on CT for depression. They compared the whole CT package with activity scheduling included (which they referred to as behavioral activation), with behavioral activation (BA) only and with CT for automatic thoughts only. Somewhat surprisingly, BA by itself was equivalent to the other treatment components—even at two-year follow-up (Gortner, Gollan, Dobson, & Jacobson, 1998; Jacobson et al., 1996).

This research finding stimulated further research on behavioral activation. Two separate research teams developed behavioral activation treatment manuals. Jacobson and colleagues (Jacobson, Martell, & Dimidjian, 2001) developed an expanded BA protocol and Lejuez, Hopko, LePage, Hopko, and McNeil (2001) developed a brief (12-session) behavioral activation treatment for depression (BATD) manual and a more recent 10-session revised manual (Lejuez, Hopko, Acierno, Daughters, & Pagoto, 2011). Implementation of the BATD protocol is in a short vignette later in this chapter.

Relaxation Training

Edmund Jacobson was the first modern scientist to write about relaxation training as a treatment procedure (Jacobson, 1924). In the book, *Progressive Relaxation*, he outlined principles and techniques of relaxation training that therapists still employ in the twenty-first century (Jacobson, 1938). **Progressive muscle relaxation** (PMR) was initially based on the assumption that muscular tension is an underlying cause of a variety of mental and emotional problems. Jacobson claimed: "Nervous disturbance is at the same time mental disturbance. Neurosis and psychoneurosis are at the same time physiological disturbance; for they are forms of tension disorder" (Jacobson, 1978, p. viii). Jacobson believed that individuals can cure neurosis through relaxation. Currently, PMR is conceptualized as either a counterconditioning or extinction procedure. By pairing a muscle-tension conditioned stimulus with pleasurable relaxation, relaxation can extinguish or reduce muscle tension as a stimulus or trigger for anxiety.

Progressive muscle relaxation remains a common relaxation training approach, although others—such as breathing retraining, meditation, autogenic training, imagery, and hypnosis—are also popular (Benson, 1976; Bowden, Lorenc, & Robinson, 2012; Reiss et al., 2016). Clinical training guidelines suggest that beginning

therapists understand how, when, and for how long relaxation procedures should be implemented (Castonguay, Boswell, Constantino, Goldfried, & Hill, 2010; Lilienfeld, 2007). This is partly because of the well-documented research finding that, ironically, relaxation can trigger anxiety (Braith, McCullough, & Bush, 1988; Heide & Borkovec, 1984).

Information on implementing relaxation procedures with clients is outlined in Putting It in Practice 7.3.

Systematic Desensitization and Exposure-Based Treatment

Joseph Wolpe (1958) formally introduced systematic desensitization as a treatment technique. In his original work, Wolpe reported a controversial treatment success rate of 80 %. Other therapists (especially psychoanalysts) criticized and challenged his procedures and results (Glover, 1959). Wolpe staunchly defended his success rates (Wolpe & Plaud, 1997).

Systematic desensitization is a combination of Jones's (1924a) deconditioning approach and Jacobson's PMR procedure. Jacobson wrote, "to be relaxed is the direct physiological opposite of being excited or disturbed" (Jacobson, 1978, p. viii).

After clients receive PMR training, they build a fear hierarchy in collaboration with the therapist. Systematic desensitization usually proceeds in the following manner:

- The client identifies a range of fear-inducing situations or objects.

- Using a measuring system referred to as **subjective units of distress** (SUDs), with the support of the therapist, the client rates each fear-inducing situation or object on a 0 to 100 scale (0 = no distress; 100 = total distress).

- Early in the session the client engages in PMR.

- While deeply relaxed, the client is exposed, in vivo or through imagery, to the least feared item in the fear hierarchy.

- Gradually, the client is exposed to each feared item, gradually progressing to the most feared item in the hierarchy.

- If the client experiences significant anxiety during the imaginal or *in vivo* exposure process, the client reengages in PMR until relaxation overcomes anxiety.

- Treatment continues until the client achieves relaxation competence while simultaneously being exposed to the entire range of his or her fear hierarchy.

PUTTING IT IN PRACTICE

7.3 Prepping Clients (and Yourself) for Progressive Muscle Relaxation

Before using relaxation training with clients, you should experience the procedure yourself. You can accomplish this by going to a behavior therapist, using a PMR CD or podcast, or asking your professor to demonstrate the procedure in class.

After learning the basics, we recommend you make your own PMR recording and use it for practicing. Getting comfortable with the right pace and voice tone for inducing a relaxed state is important. It's also helpful to try out your relaxation skills with your classmates and ask for feedback.

When working with clients, keep the following issues in mind:

- Have a quiet room and a comfortable chair available. Noise and discomfort are antithetical to relaxation. Reclining chairs are useful. Lighting should be dim, but not dark.

- Give clients clear information as to why you're teaching PMR. If the rationale isn't clear, they may not participate fully.

- Explain the procedure. Say something like "I'll be instructing you to create tension and then let go of tension in specific muscle groups. Research shows that tensing your muscles first and then relaxing them helps you achieve a deeper relaxation than if you just tried to relax them without tensing first." You might demonstrate this by flexing and then relaxing your arm or shoulder muscles.

- Seat yourself in a position that's not distracting. A face-to-face arrangement can make clients uncomfortable. Instead, place seats at a 90° to 120° angle.

- Emphasize that relaxation is a learnable skill and, like most skills, repeated practice is the best way to learn.

- Tell your clients that to become relaxed, all they have to do is listen to you and follow along, but whether they listen and follow along is totally their choice.

- Warn clients that they may feel unusual body sensations: "Some people feel tingling, others feel light and maybe a little dizzy, and still others feel heavy, like they're sinking into the chair. I don't know how you'll feel, but we'll talk afterward about how it felt to you."

- Let clients know they can keep their eyes open or shut. Some clients are uncomfortable closing their eyes. Respect that preference. Relaxation is possible either way and more likely if the client is doing whatever is comfortable.

- Let clients know they can move around if it helps them be comfortable. If they wear glasses, they might want to remove them. Facilitate physical comfort.

- Check for physical conditions (e.g., knee or back problems) that might be aggravated. Omit painful body parts from the procedure.

- Let clients know their minds may wander while you're talking and they're relaxing. "If your mind wanders, just bring your attention back to whatever I'm saying."

- Help clients have realistic, but optimistic, expectations: "Most people who do progressive relaxation find that it helps them relax, but don't find it amazing or dramatic. Some people find it extremely relaxing and wonderful."

- Acknowledge that practicing relaxation can cause some people to feel anxiety. This can be due to unusual sensations, trauma history, feeling a loss of control, or fears that something bad may happen during the process (Castonguay et al., 2010; Lilienfeld, 2007).

Additional detailed information about using PMR is available from several sources (Bernstein & Borkovec, 1973; Field, 2009; Goldfried & Davison, 1994).

In the traditional systematic desensitization protocol, clients were taught PMR and exposed to feared stimuli using visual imagery. More recently, it appears that PMR may not be necessary and that *in vivo* exposure is superior to imaginal exposure (D. Dobson & K. S. Dobson, 2009).

Imaginal or In Vivo *Exposure and Desensitization*

Systematic desensitization is an example of an exposure treatment. **Exposure treatment** is based on the principle that clients are best treated by exposure to the very thing they want to avoid (i.e., the stimulus that evokes intense fear, anxiety, or other painful emotions). Mowrer (1947) used a two-factor theory of learning, based on animal studies, to explain how avoidance conditioning works. First, he explained that animals originally learn to fear a particular stimulus through classical conditioning. For example, a dog may learn to fear its owner's voice when the owner yells due to the discovery of an unwelcome pile on the living room carpet. Then, if the dog remains in the room with its angry owner, fear continues to escalate.

Second, Mowrer explained that operant conditioning processes reinforce avoidance behavior. Specifically, if the dog hides under the bed or dashes out the front door, it's likely to experience decreased fear and anxiety. Consequently, the avoidance behavior—running away and hiding—is negatively reinforced because it relieves fear, anxiety, and discomfort. **Negative reinforcement** is defined as the strengthening of a behavioral response by reducing or eliminating an aversive stimulus (like fear and anxiety).

Exposure via systematic desensitization and the other procedures detailed here are distinctively behavioral. However, the concept that psychological health improves when clients face and embrace their fears is consistent with existential and Jungian theory (van Deurzen, 2010; see the online Jungian chapter: www.wiley.com/go/sommers-flanagan/theories3e).

There are three ways to expose clients to their fears during systematic desensitization. First, you can use mental imagery or **imaginal exposure**. This approach is convenient and allows clients to complete treatment without leaving their therapist's office. Second, you can use *in vivo* **exposure** (direct exposure to the feared stimulus). This option can be more complex (e.g., going to a dental office to provide exposure for a client with a dental phobia), but may sometimes produce outcomes superior to imaginal exposure (Agren, Björkstrand, & Fredrikson, 2017; Armfield, 2008). Third, you can use computer simulation (virtual reality exposure) to expose clients to feared stimuli (Cardoş, David, & David, 2017; Emmelkamp, Bruynzeel, Drost, & van der Mast, 2001).

Psychoeducation is critical for effective exposure treatment. D. Dobson and K. S. Dobson (2009) wrote:

A crucial element of effective exposure is the provision of a solid rationale to encourage your client to take the risks involved in this strategy. A good therapeutic alliance is absolutely essential for exposure to occur. (p. 104)

D. Dobson and K. S. Dobson (2009) provided a sample client handout that helps inform clients of the exposure rationale and procedure.

Exposure treatment means gradually and systematically exposing yourself to situations that create some anxiety. You can then prove to yourself that you can handle these feared situations, as your body learns to become more comfortable. Exposure treatment is extremely important in your recovery and involves taking controlled risks. For exposure treatment to work, you should experience some anxiety—too little won't be enough to put you in your discomfort zone so you can prove your fears wrong. Too much anxiety means that you may not pay attention to what is going on in the situation. If you are too uncomfortable, it may be hard to try the same thing again. Generally, effective exposure involves experiencing anxiety that is around 70 out of 100 on your Subjective Units of Distress Scale. Expect to feel some anxiety. As you become more comfortable with the situation, you can then move on to the next step. Exposure should be structured, planned, and predictable. It must be within your control, not anyone else's. (p. 104)

Massed (Intensive) or Spaced (Graduated) *Exposure Sessions*

Behavior therapists continue to optimize methods for extinguishing fear responses. One question being examined empirically is this: Is desensitization more effective when clients are directly exposed to feared stimuli during a single prolonged session (e.g., one 3-hour session; aka **massed exposure**) or when they're slowly and incrementally exposed to feared stimuli during a series of shorter sessions (such as five 1-hour sessions; aka **spaced exposure**)? Initially, massed exposure was thought to result in higher dropout rates, greater likelihood of fear relapse, and a higher client stress. However, researchers have reported that both massed and spaced exposure desensitization strategies are similarly effective (Lang & Hoyer, 2007; Ost, Alm, Brandberg, & Breitholz, 2001).

Virtual Reality Exposure

Technological advancements have led to potential modifications in systematic desensitization procedures. Specifically, **virtual reality exposure**, a procedure wherein clients are immersed in a real-time computer-generated virtual environment, has been empirically evaluated as an alternative to imaginal or in vivo exposure in cases of acrophobia (fear of heights), flight phobia, spider phobia, and other anxiety disorders (Cardoş et al., 2017; Ruwaard, Broeksteeg, Schrieken, Emmelkamp, & Lange,

2010). Some researchers have concluded that virtual reality exposure is more effective than in vivo exposure (Cardoş et al., 2017; Powers & Emmelkamp, 2008).

Interoceptive Exposure

Panic-prone individuals may be highly sensitive to internal physical cues (e.g., increased heart rate, increased respiration, and dizziness). They become especially reactive when they interpret those cues as linked to people or situations causing anxiety (Boettcher, Brake, & Barlow, 2017; Story & Craske, 2008). For example, if clients interpret specific physical sensations as signs of physical illness, impending death, or imminent loss of consciousness (and associated humiliation), then anxiety escalates. Although specific cognitive techniques are available to treat catastrophically overinterpreted bodily sensations, a more behavioral technique, interoceptive exposure, has been developed to help clients learn, through exposure and practice, to deal more effectively with physical aspects of intense anxiety or panic (Boettcher et al., 2017; Stewart & Watt, 2008).

Interoceptive exposure is identical to other exposure techniques except that the target exposure stimuli are internal physical cues or somatic sensations (Boettcher et al., 2017). At least six interoceptive exposure tasks reliably trigger anxiety (Lee et al., 2006). They include:

- Hyperventilation.
- Breath holding.
- Breathing through a straw.
- Spinning in circles.
- Shaking head.
- Chest breathing.

Before interoceptive exposure is initiated, clients receive education about body sensations, learn relaxation skills (e.g., breathing training), and learn cognitive restructuring skills. Through repeated successful exposure, clients become desensitized to previously feared physical sensations (Forsyth, Fusé, & Acheson, 2008).

Response and Ritual Prevention

Recall Mowrer's (1947) two-factor theory. He posited that, when clients avoid or escape a distressing situation, the maladaptive avoidance behavior is negatively reinforced. As clients feel relief from aversive anxiety, fear, or distress, avoidance or escape behaviors are reinforced or strengthened (Spiegler & Guevremont, 2016). Many examples of this negative reinforcement cycle are present across mental disorders. For example, clients with bulimia nervosa who purge after eating "forbidden" foods are relieving themselves from anxiety and discomfort they experienced after eating the foods (Agras, Schneider, Arnow, Raeburn, & Telch, 1989). Therefore, purging behavior is negatively reinforced. Similarly, when phobic clients escape from a feared object or situation, or when clients with obsessive-compulsive symptoms engage in a repeated washing or checking behavior, negative reinforcement of maladaptive behavior occurs (Franklin, Ledley, & Foa, 2009).

It follows that, to be effective, exposure-based desensitization treatment must include response prevention. **Response prevention** involves therapists guiding and supporting clients to not engage in an avoidance response. For example, clients with bulimia are prevented from vomiting after ingesting a forbidden cookie, agoraphobic clients are prevented from fleeing a public place when anxiety begins to mount, and clients with obsessive-compulsive disorder are prevented from washing their hands following exposure to a "contaminated" object. Without response or ritual prevention, treatments may exacerbate anxiety conditions. Researchers have reported that exposure plus response prevention can produce significant brain changes, sometimes in as few as three psychotherapy sessions (Freyer et al., 2011; Schwartz, Gulliford, Stier, & Thienemann, 2005).

Participant Modeling

In addition to operant principles, researchers have also evaluated social learning as a treatment for anxiety (Bandura, Blanchard, & Ritter, 1969). Recall that, in her work with Little Peter and other fearful children, Jones reported that social imitation (now known as **participant modeling**) was one of two effective deconditioning strategies (Jones, 1924a).

Like most behavioral techniques, participant modeling should be applied using clinical skills and sensitivity. For example, individuals with airplane or flight phobias don't find it helpful when they watch other passengers calmly getting on a plane; such observations can increase feelings of humiliation and hopelessness. Seeing others easily confront fears can be discouraging to clients who have phobias. The problem is that the gap in emotional state and skills between the model and the observer is too large, so vicarious learning doesn't occur. Instead of providing clients with completely competent and fear-free participant models, effective behavior therapists provide models of successful coping that are closer to what clients are capable of accomplishing. This is partly why various forms of group therapy are effective for anxiety disorders (Craske, 1999; Kocovski, Fleming, Hawley, Ho, & Antony, 2015).

Skills Training

Skills training is an approach primarily based on skill deficit psychopathology models; it involves using behavioral techniques to teach clients new skills. Behavior therapists evaluate their clients' functional skills during the assessment phase of therapy and then use skills training to remediate client skill deficits. Traditional targets include assertiveness and other social behavior, as well as problem solving.

Assertiveness and Other Social Behavior

In the behavioral tradition, Wolpe, Lazarus, and others consider assertiveness a learned behavior (Alberti & Emmons, 1970; Lazarus, 1973). **Assertiveness** is defined as a social competence that involves being able to stand up for your rights, while not infringing on the rights of others. Individuals may have one of three social behavior styles: passive, aggressive, or assertive. **Passive** individuals behave submissively; they say yes when they want to say no, avoid speaking up and asking for instructions or directions, and let others take advantage of them. **Aggressive** individuals dominate others, trying to get their way through coercive means. In contrast, **assertive** individuals speak up, express feelings, and actively seek to meet their own needs without dominating others.

Assertiveness training became popular in the 1970s as an individual, group, or self-help treatment for social difficulties. A number of self-help books on assertiveness were published, including *Your Perfect Right: Assertiveness and Equality in Your Life and Relationships*, now in its tenth edition (Alberti & Emmons, 2017). Common social behaviors targeted in assertiveness training are (a) introducing oneself to strangers, (b) giving and receiving compliments, (c) saying no to requests from others, (d) making requests of others, (e) speaking up or voicing an opinion, and (f) maintaining social conversations. Behavioral approaches to teaching assertiveness include:

- *Instruction*: Teaching clients to use assertive eye contact, body posture, voice tone, and verbal delivery.

- *Feedback*: Therapists or group members give clients feedback regarding other's efforts at assertive behavior.

- *Behavior rehearsal or role playing*: Clients practice assertive behaviors, such as asking for help or expressing disagreement.

- *Coaching*: Therapists whisper instructions in the client's ear as role-play progresses.

- *Modeling*: Therapists or group members demonstrate appropriate assertive behaviors.

- *Social reinforcement*: Therapists or group members offer positive feedback and support for improved assertive behaviors.

- *Relaxation training*: Relaxation training can reduce anxiety in social situations and increase skill acquisition.

Developed in the 1970s, assertiveness training remains a viable treatment option for many clients. However, most practitioners will use the terms skills training or social skills training instead of assertiveness. Components of assertiveness training for individuals with social anxiety and social skills deficits are still of great interest. For example, social phobia—a condition where individuals fear interpersonal scrutiny and evaluation—is frequently treated with a combination of relaxation and social skills training (e.g., instruction, feedback, behavior rehearsal, social reinforcement). Additionally, dialectical behavior therapy has a substantial social skills or assertiveness training component (see Chapter 14).

Problem-Solving Therapy

D'Zurilla and Goldfried (1971) originally described a therapeutic approach that eventually became problem-solving therapy. **Problem-solving therapy** (PST) is a behavioral treatment that focuses on how to approach and solve personal problems. The rationale for PST is that effective problem solving is a mediator or buffer that helps clients manage stressful life events and achieve improved personal well-being (D'Zurilla & Nezu, 2010; Nezu, Nezu, & D'Zurilla, 2013).

There are two main components to problem-solving therapy:

1. Problem orientation.

2. Problem-solving style.

Problem orientation involves teaching clients to have positive attitudes toward problem solving. These attitudes include: (a) seeing problems as a challenge or opportunity, (b) seeing problems as solvable, (c) believing in one's own ability to solve problems, and (d) recognizing that effective problem solving requires time and effort (Bell & D'Zurilla, 2009).

Problem-solving style refers to how individuals approach social problems. In PST, clients are taught a rational problem-solving style that includes four steps (Nezu & Nezu, 2016):

1. *Problem definition*: Clarifying a problem, identifying goals, and identifying obstacles.

2. *Generating alternatives*: Brainstorming potential solutions for overcoming obstacles and solving the problem.

3. *Decision-making*: Predicting likely outcomes, conducting a cost–benefit analysis, and developing a solution plan (means-ends thinking or consequential thinking are alternative names for this part of the process).

4. *Solution implementation and verification*: Trying out the solution, monitoring outcomes, and determining success.

PST has been employed as an intervention for coping with and resolving a wide range of problems, including depression, suicide ideation, and many other stressful life circumstances (Kirkham, Choi, & Seitz, 2016; Malouff, Thorsteinsson, & Schutte, 2007; Nezu & Nezu, 2010). PST is also used for working with youth diagnosed with conduct disorder (Kazdin, 2010). Components of PST (though not necessarily the whole package) are often emphasized as a practical part of working with young clients (Shure, 1992; J. Sommers-Flanagan & R. Sommers-Flanagan, 2007b; Spivack, Platt, & Shure, 1976). One of the chapter vignettes features Step 2 of the problem-solving approach (generating alternatives).

Behavior Therapy in Action: Brief Vignettes

Traditional approaches to counseling and psychotherapy emphasized clients achieving insight through talking (i.e., the talking cure). In contrast, many contemporary therapies focus on therapists providing clients with education. Behavior therapy is a good example of an approach that actively teaches new life skills. Although behavior therapy also involves experiential client-learning activities, therapists place a strong emphasis on psychoeducation. The following case vignettes capture this style.

Vignette I: Behavioral Activation Treatment for Depression (BATD)

This vignette briefly illustrates the revised behavioral activation treatment for depression (BATD-R). The full BATD-R manual was published in *Behavior Modification*. Forms for this therapy are free online (Lejuez et al., 2011). Although BATD-R is a 10-session manualized protocol, researchers support its flexible application.

The authors (Ruggiero, Morris, Hopko, & Lejuez, 2007) describe the case:

Adrienne was a 17-year-old European American high school student referred for treatment to address symptoms of depression as well as difficulties in her relationship with her foster mother. She was socially pleasant and was of average intelligence. She lived with her foster mother and several younger children, all of whom were unrelated to Adrienne (two were foster children, two were the foster mother's biological children). (p. 233)

During the initial assessment session, Adrienne was accompanied by her caseworker (the foster mother could not attend). The behavior therapist conducted a semi-structured clinical interview to determine presenting symptoms and possible comorbid complaints. Behavioral antecedents and consequences were explored and analyzed. Ruggiero and colleagues reported that Adrienne had:

[S]everal symptoms of depression and expressed concern about verbal conflicts with her foster mother that had been escalating in frequency. When asked for details about her daily routine, Adrienne described that she typically had minimal time to herself, rarely spent time with friends after school, and had numerous household and babysitting responsibilities. (p. 68)

The fundamental premise of BA is that clients with depressive symptoms are experiencing too few positive reinforcements and too many aversive stimuli. Consequently, Adrienne was engaged in a thorough behavioral assessment process. She completed two assessment instruments: (1) the *Beck Depression Inventory-II* (BDI-II; Beck, Steer, & Brown, 1996), and (2) the *Daily Activity Log* (DAL; Hopko, Armento, Cantu, Chambers, & Lejuez, 2003).

Adrienne obtained a BDI score of 13 (mildly depressed). Her DAL responses capture the rigor of behavioral assessment:

The completed DAL covered 152 hours (6.3 days) during which her activities were allocated roughly as follows: 50 hours of sleep (about 8 hours per day), 35 hours in school, 24 hours of chores and responsibilities unrelated to school (e.g., cleaning the house, chores for her foster mother), 22 hours of school-related and miscellaneous activities (e.g., homework, preparation for school and church, meals), and 21 hours of discretionary time. Perhaps most striking, of her 21 hours of discretionary time, none were used to communicate and/or visit with similar-age peers and nearly all were spent watching television and using the Internet. One hour was used to interact with adult neighbors, and 2 to 3 hours were used to entertain young children. (p. 69)

Based on this assessment information, combined with information from the initial clinical interview, two goals were established:

1. Reduce frequency of verbal conflict between Adrienne and her foster mother.

2. Reduce depressive symptoms.

The therapist gathered additional information pertaining to antecedents and consequences associated with Adrienne–Foster Mom verbal conflicts. Although delineating specific patterns was challenging, the therapist found:

• Parent–child conflict was "temporally connected" to the foster mother's increased after-school volunteer activities.

• Adrienne had to babysit the four younger children for several hours after school.

- Because the foster mother was fatigued, she was asking Adrienne to complete additional household tasks.

- Conflicts were also "linked to unpredictable, uncontrollable, and/or short-notice requests to babysit or perform household tasks" (p. 70).

- Partly due to her increased workload at home and partly due to poor choices regarding healthy social and physical behavior, Adrienne had discontinued enjoyable activities (e.g., going to the mall with friends, photographing birds).

Key BATD components included (a) the foster mother's acknowledgment that Adrienne needed additional discretionary time and (b) the following behavioral interventions.

> Three feasible and pleasurable activities were prescribed for the following week and monitored with the Weekly Behavior Checkout (form 8). The three activities were (a) to make at least one phone call to at least one friend on each of 5 days, (b) to exercise for at least 30 minutes on each of 3 different days, and (c) to take one or more pictures of animals or natural settings on at least 1 day. These activities were selected because they were identified by Adrienne as pleasurable, were related to multiple life-goal domains, and were all clearly within household rules. Also, they had all been activities in which she had engaged at least once during the prior month, suggesting that likelihood for success was satisfactory. (p. 71)

The authors reported a positive outcome in this case. At her final BATD session, Adrienne obtained a score of 2 (no depression) on the BDI. She also recognized the relationship between her daily routine and depressive symptoms and reported a wider range of healthy social and recreational activities, and expanded social contacts.

BA treatment as reported in this case and as described in treatment manuals doesn't address client cognitive processes. This is an advantage for some clients—especially clients who are less cognitively oriented or perhaps inclined to overthink life situations. Hopko and colleagues (2015) provide a nice description of the distinction between behavioral activation and cognitive approaches to treating depression, along with a fitting conclusion to this case vignette:

> Activation partially involves teaching patients to formulate and accomplish behavioral goals irrespective of certain aversive thoughts and mood states they may experience. This clear focus on action makes it unnecessary to attempt to control and change such thoughts and mood states directly. (Hopko, Ryba, McIndoo, & File, 2015, p. 703)

BA is a promising approach for clients and therapists who prefer to focus on behaviors rather than cognitions.

Vignette II: Generating Behavioral Alternatives with an Aggressive Adolescent

Problem-solving therapy (PST) focuses on teaching clients steps for rational problem solving. In this case vignette, the therapist (John) is trying to engage a 15-year-old white male heterosexual client in stage 2 (generating alternatives) of the problem-solving model. At the beginning of the session, the client had reported that, over the weekend, a male peer had tried to rape his girlfriend. The client was angry and planning to "beat the shit out" of his fellow student. During the session, John worked on helping the boy identify behavioral alternatives to retributive violence.

The abridged transcript below begins 10 minutes into the session.

Boy: He's gotta learn sometime.

JSF: I mean. I don't know for sure what the absolute best thing to do to this guy is, but before you act, it's important to think of all the different options you have.

Boy: I've been thinking a lot.

JSF: Well, tell me the other ones you've thought of and let's write them down so we can look at the options together.

Boy: Kick the shit out of him.

JSF: Okay, I know 2 things, actually maybe 3, that you said. One is kick the shit out of him, the other one is to do nothing.

Boy: The other is to shove something up his ass.

JSF: And, okay, that's kinda like kicking the shit out of him. I mean to be violent toward him. [Notice John is using the client's language.]

Boy: Yeah, Yeah.

JSF: So, what else?

Boy: I could nark on him.

JSF: Oh.

Boy: Tell the cops or something.

JSF: And I'm not saying that's the right thing to do either. [Although John thinks this is a better option, he's trying to remain neutral, which is important to the brainstorming process; if the client thinks John is trying to "reinforce" him for nonviolent or prosocial behaviors, he may resist brainstorming.]

Boy: That's just stupid. [This response shows why it's important to stay neutral.]

JSF: I'm not saying that's the right thing to do. I might even have the same kind of impulse in your situation. Either, I wanna beat him up or kinda do the high and righteous thing, which is to ignore him. And I'm not sure. Maybe one of those is the right thing, but I don't know. Now, we got three things—so you could nark on him. [John tries to show empathy and then encourages continuation of brainstorming.]

Boy: It's not gonna happen though.

JSF: Yeah, but I don't care if that's gonna happen. So there's nark, there's ignore, there's beat the shit. What else?

Boy: Um. Just talk to him, would be okay. Just go up to him and yeah ... I think we need to have a little chit-chat. [The client is able to generate another potentially prosocial idea.]

JSF: Okay. Talk to him.

Boy: But that's not gonna happen either. I don't think I could talk to him without, like, him pissing me off and me kicking the shit ... [Again, the client is making it clear that he's not interested in nonviolent options.]

JSF: So, it might be so tempting when you talk to him that you just end up beating the shit out of him. [John goes back to reflective listening.]

Boy: Yeah. Yeah.

JSF: But all we're doing is making a list. Okay. And you're doing great. [This is positive reinforcement for the brainstorming process—not for the content of his brainstorming.]

Boy: I could get someone to beat the shit out of him.

JSF: Get somebody to beat him up. So, kind of indirect violence—you get him back physically—through physical pain. That's kind of the approach.

Boy: [This section is censored. You can imagine what an angry 15-year-old might say that would require censoring for a textbook.]

JSF: So you could [do another thing]. Okay.

Boy: Someone like ...

JSF: Okay. We're up to six options. [John is showing neutrality or using an **extinction** process by not showing any affective response to the client's provocative maladaptive alternative that was censored for this book.]

Boy: That's about it....

JSF: So. So we got nark, we got ignore, we got beat the shit out of him, we got talk to him, we got get somebody else to beat the shit out of him, and ... [Reading back the alternatives allows the client to hear what he has said.]

Boy: Um ... couple of those are pretty unrealistic, but. [The client acknowledges he's being unrealistic, but we don't know which items he views as unrealistic and why. Exploring his evaluation of the options might be useful, but John is still working on brainstorming and now decides to join with the client.]

JSF: We don't have to be realistic. I've got another unrealistic one. I got another one.... Kinda to start some

shameful rumor about him, you know. [This is a verbally aggressive option which can be risky, but illustrates a new domain of behavioral alternatives.]

Boy: That's a good idea.

JSF: I mean, it's a nonviolent way to get some revenge.

Boy: Like he has a little dick or something.

JSF: Yeah, good, exactly. [John inadvertently provides positive reinforcement for an insulting idea rather than remaining neutral.]

Boy: Maybe I'll do all these things.

JSF: Combination.

Boy: Yeah.

JSF: So we've got the shameful rumor option to add to our list.

Boy: That's a good one. (Excerpted and adapted from J. Sommers-Flanagan & Sommers-Flanagan, 2007b)

This case illustrates what can occur when therapists conduct PST and generate behavioral alternatives with angry adolescents. Initially, the client is blowing off steam and generating aggressive alternatives. This process, although not producing constructive alternatives, is important because the boy may be testing John to see if he will react with judgment. During this brainstorming process, therapists should remain positive and welcoming of all options, no matter how violent or absurd; being judgmental can be perceived and experienced as a punishment and adversely affect the therapy relationship. As the boy produced various aggressive ideas, he appeared calmer.

During PST, behavioral alternatives are repeatedly read back to the client. This allows the boy to hear his ideas from a different perspective. Finally, toward the end, John joins the boy in brainstorming, adding a risky, verbally aggressive response. John is modeling a less violent approach to revenge and hoping to get the boy to consider nonphysical alternatives. This is a harm reduction approach. **Harm reduction** approaches help clients consider less violent or less risky behaviors (Marlatt & Witkiewitz, 2010). Next steps in this problem-solving process include:

• Decision-making.

• Solution implementation and verification.

As the counseling session proceeded, John employed a range of different techniques, including "reverse advocacy role playing" where John plays the client and the client plays the counselor and provides reasons that particular attitudes are maladaptive or dysfunctional (Nezu, Nezu, & D'Zurilla, 2013).

CASE PRESENTATION

Most behavior therapists use cognitive treatments and most cognitive therapists use behavioral treatments. This is why the most popular current terminology for these approaches is cognitive behavior therapy (CBT).

Although the following case illustrates a cognitive-behavioral approach, in this chapter we focus on the behavior therapy techniques for panic disorder. The next chapter (Chapter 8) includes a continuation of this case, with cognitive components from a comprehensive cognitive behavioral approach for panic disorder and agoraphobia added (Craske, 1999).

Richard, a 56-year-old white male, referred himself for therapy due to anxiety, phobic, and depressive symptoms. Richard was afraid to leave his home because of fears of having a panic attack. He had experienced 10+ attacks in the past month. These attacks were increasing in intensity. During his intake, he indicated that panic attacks trigger fears that he's having a heart attack. Richard's father died of a massive heart attack at 59.

Richard's health was excellent. He was taken to the emergency room during two recent panic episodes. In both cases, Richard's cardiac functioning was within normal limits. Nonetheless, his fear of panic and heart attacks was escalating, and his increasing seclusion was adversely affecting his employment as a professor at a local vocational college. His wife, Linda, accompanied him to his intake session. At the time of the referral, Richard had stopped driving; his wife was transporting him.

Richard was administered the *Anxiety Disorders Interview Schedule for DSM-IV* (Grisham, Brown, & Campbell, 2004). This semi-structured interview indicated that Richard met the diagnostic criteria for panic disorder with agoraphobia.

During the intake interview, Richard learned self-monitoring procedures and was given a packet of panic and agoraphobic rating scales. He also learned how to use the self-monitoring scales to rate the duration, intensity, situational context, and symptom profile of each panic attack that occurred during the 10 days between his intake interview and his first treatment session. Richard kept a food and beverage log during this 10-day period to determine if there were any links between food and beverage consumption and his anxiety symptoms.

Richard's therapist referred him for an adjunct medical consultation. There were two reasons for the consultation. First, panic and agoraphobic symptoms can be linked to various medical conditions. These conditions include heart disease, diabetes, hypoglycemia, hyperthyroidism, mitral valve prolapse, stroke, and others. Second, clients who obtain behavioral treatment for panic and agoraphobia often receive pharmacological treatment. Adding medications appears to help some clients while adversely affecting others due to physical side-effect sensitivity and motivation reduction. Empirically oriented behavior therapists often consult with medical professionals to determine whether pharmacological treatment is appropriate.

Because he didn't have any medical conditions that were causing or maintaining his anxiety symptoms, Richard was diagnosed with primary rather than secondary panic symptom. Additionally, after a conference with Richard and his physician, it was determined that behavioral treatment should initially proceed without adjunctive pharmacological treatment.

The Problem List

Behavior therapy includes the generation of a clear and concrete problem list. Problems are defined in measurable behavioral terms.

Richard's problem list included:

1. *Specific fears of having a panic attack*: Fear of heart attack, fear of death, and fear of public humiliation (these were measured in terms of frequency, intensity, and duration).

2. *Repeated un-cued panic attacks*: Physical symptoms included heart palpitations, sweating, dizziness, shortness of breath. Richard's symptoms triggered catastrophic thoughts of death and dying (a cognitive symptom also associated with Problems 1, 3, and 4).

3. *Social isolation/withdrawal*: Richard reported diminished social contact (i.e., less than one social contact outside the home each week).

4. *Loss of independence*: Richard had begun relying on his wife and others to transport him to various destinations (driving himself = 0).

5. *Depressive symptoms*: Richard also had depressive symptoms including low mood most days, anhedonia, and self-deprecatory thoughts; these symptoms were secondary to his anxiety and therefore not a primary target of treatment.

Each behavior therapy session included four parts: (1) check-in and homework review, (2) educational information about panic and behavior therapy, (3) in-session behavioral or cognitive tasks, and (4) new homework assignments.

Sessions 1 and 2. Richard and his therapist reviewed his homework. During the 10 days since his intake interview, he left home eight times and had four panic attacks. Although he was unable to identify specific environmental cues for every panic attack, his panic symptoms were associated with caffeine consumption: three of four panic episodes occurred after he consumed caffeinated sodas, coffee, or both.

The first two sessions primarily focused on psychoeducation.

Therapist: Richard, excellent job on your homework. Looking this over gives us a much better idea of how to get you back on track.

Richard: Thanks.

Therapist: One of our main goals for today is to talk about what your panic symptoms mean. Let's start there.

Richard: That sounds good.

Therapist: First, even though the intense panic feelings you've been getting seem strange, they're completely natural. Humans are designed to experience panic just like you've been experiencing it. Why do you suppose that is? [Psychoeducation.]

Richard: Um. I've always figured that when my heart starts pounding and I get dizzy and all that, it must mean that something is terribly wrong.

Therapist: Exactly! The human internal panic response is an alarm system. Some people call it the fight-or-flight response. When it's working properly, the panic alarm is a great survival device. It increases blood pressure, tenses up muscles, and gets you ready to deal with danger. It's supposed to go off during moments of extreme danger—like when you're crossing a street and a car is barreling straight at you, or if you're attacked by someone. Your main problem is that your alarm is misfiring. It goes off when you don't need it. You've been having false alarms. Think about that. When you've had your panic attacks, have there been any extreme dangers you're facing? [Psychoeducation.]

Richard: Not exactly. But when I feel panicked, I'm sure I must be having a heart attack, just like my dad did when he was about my age.

Therapist: What have the doctors said about that?

Richard: They've told me my heart is fine. That it's in good shape.

Therapist: So the false alarm you're feeling has two parts. There are physical symptoms of heart pounding, dizziness, and shortness of breath—that's one part. Then there's the thought of "I'm going to die from a heart attack just like my dad" that grabs you. Both these signals, the physical sensations and the thought of dying, are false. There is no immediate big danger, and your heart is fine. Right?

Richard: That's what they say.

Therapist: I know it feels incredibly scary and it's a horrible feeling. I don't expect you to instantly believe what I'm saying or what your doctor is saying, because the feelings are real and you've been having them repeatedly. But let's take it a step further. What would happen if you were in a movie theater and a false alarm went off? What would happen if you just sat there, because you *knew* it was only a false alarm?

Richard: I—um, I think, uh, I'd get pretty freaked out sitting there if everybody else was rushing out.

Therapist: Perfect. So you'd feel fear, but let's say you just sat there anyway and felt your fear, but you *realize* it's a false alarm and so you *know* that jumping up and running out isn't necessary. What would eventually happen?

Richard: I guess the fear would eventually go away.

Therapist: That's right. Just like we talked about during your intake interview, eventually your heart stops pounding and returns to normal, your breathing slows down, your body's alarm shuts off, and it returns to normal.

Problem Formulation

During the preceding exchange the therapist is using psychoeducation to inform Richard about the natural role of panic and anxiety in humans. This education is both an initial component of a behavioral intervention as well as an example of collaborative problem formulation.

During these sessions, the following points are highlighted:

- Anxiety is composed of three parts: thoughts, feelings, or sensations, and actions.

- With practice, Richard can become better at objectively observing his anxiety-related thoughts, feelings, and actions.

- His panic symptoms, although very disturbing and uncomfortable, are harmless.

- There's no "chemical imbalance" linked to his panic symptoms. Anxiety and panic are natural human responses to danger.

- When Richard feels physical sensations associated with panic, but there is no clear external danger, his mind searches for an explanation for his panic.

- Even though his father died from a heart attack when he was Richard's age, there's no medical evidence that the same thing will happen to Richard. (We explore this cognitive dimension to his panic in Chapter 8.)

- Because Richard leaves or avoids situations where he expects he might have a panic attack and then his symptoms decrease or abate, he's experiencing negative reinforcement (reduction of aversive feelings when leaving or avoiding stressful situations). This contributes to Richard's panic. He's not giving himself a chance to learn that his symptoms will subside even when he stays in the situation.

Based on this formulation, solutions to Richard's panic include the following: (a) learn new skills for coping with the symptoms, (b) use these skills to face the panic symptoms, (c) relearn through deconditioning that there's nothing to fear from physical panic symptoms.

Interventions

Richard's therapist used a five-component panic disorder protocol (Barlow & Craske, 2000; Craske, 1999). These included:

1. Education about the nature of anxiety (which has already begun).

2. Breathing retraining.

3. Cognitive restructuring.

4. Interoceptive exposure.

5. Imaginal or *in vivo* exposure.

In the preceding excerpt, Richard didn't completely buy the new explanation for his panic. Nevertheless, the next steps are distinctly behavioral: Richard needs to (a) cut down on his caffeine intake, (b) develop behavioral coping skills, and (c) directly experience panic, face it, and deal with it effectively.

Therapist: Okay, Richard, we're about done for today, but I've got some homework for you again. This week I'd like you to slowly cut back on the caffeine intake. How do you think you might accomplish that?

Richard: I can get some of that caffeine-free soda. Actually my wife already picked some up.

Therapist: Excellent. So you've got an option waiting at home, and your wife is very supportive. Make that same switch to decaf coffee.

Richard: Okay.

Therapist: And keep up your self-monitoring panic log. The more we know about the patterns and symptoms, the better our work together will go.

Session 3. After a discussion of Richard's homework (he managed to make it one week without caffeine, had only one panic attack, and completed his panic log very thoroughly) the therapist moves into a learning activity.

Therapist: Richard do you remember us talking about your panic symptoms being a natural, but false, alarm?

Richard: Yeah, I remember.

Therapist: I got the impression that you weren't convinced of that idea, so if you want, we can discuss it further, do a brief demonstration, and then focus on a new breathing technique that will help you calm yourself.

Richard: I'm a skeptic about everything. But I'm feeling a little better, and I think the no caffeine rule is helping.

Therapist: Yes, like we've talked about, caffeine produces physical sensations that can trigger a panic attack. When the caffeine hits your system and your heart rate and breathing increase, your body notices it, and the false alarm can start that much easier.

Richard: Yeah. That seems right to me.

Therapist: What we want is for you to turn off the false alarm. One of the best ways to do that is to practice a little controlled breathing. Watch me. [Therapist demonstrates diaphragmatic breathing, inhaling for about 7 seconds and exhaling for about 11 seconds.] Okay, now you try it. The point is to breathe in slowly and then breathe out slowly. It works best if your out-breath is a little longer than the in-breath. Some people call it 7-11 breathing because you do 7 seconds in and then 11 seconds out. But really, what's best is for the pace to work for you. Let's try it. [Richard places one hand on his abdomen and begins the breathing process.]

Therapist: Okay, that's great. Now let's have you try it for 1 minute.

Richard: Okay. [Richard breathes slowly for 1 minute.]

Therapist: Nice job, Richard. You had a slow and steady pace. How did it feel?

Richard: It was fine. I felt uptight to start, but it got easier, smoother as I went along.

Therapist: Excellent. Now I'm going to show you something that's called overbreathing or hyperventilation. Watch. [Therapist stands up and breathes deeply and rapidly, as if trying to quickly blow up a balloon. After about 1 minute, he sits down and slows down his breathing again.] So, Richard, what did you see happening to me as I did the overbreathing?

Richard: I don't know what you felt like on the inside, but your face got red and when you sat down you looked a little unsteady.

Therapist: Right. I got dizzy, light-headed, and my hands felt tingly. When I sat down and did the diaphragmatic breathing I could feel my heartbeat slowing back down.

Richard: That's intense.

Therapist: You can probably guess what's next. I want you to try the same thing. Then, as soon as you feel any dizziness or heart pounding or physical distress, you should sit down and do your diaphragmatic breathing until the feelings subside. Got it?

Richard: How do you know I won't have a full-blown attack?

Therapist: Actually, that's a big part of this activity. If you have a full-blown attack, I'll be here and guide you through the breathing and the symptoms will pass. Our goal is for you to just feel a tiny bit of the symptoms, and then sit down and relax and breathe. But even if it gets extreme, we have plenty of time, so I'll be here and you'll get control back over your body. Ready?

Richard: Okay. [Richard rises from his chair, overbreathes for about 30 seconds, then sits down and, guided by his therapist, breathes steadily and slowly for about 90 seconds.]

Therapist: Now, Richard, tell me what you felt when overbreathing and what you're feeling now.

Richard: I'm okay now, but I did get dizzy. My hands got tingly. It was just like my attacks. But I'm okay, maybe a little shaky, but okay.

Therapist: So you feel okay now. Actually, you look good too. And you gave your body an excellent lesson. Your body will learn that the panic alarm can get turned on intentionally and that you can turn it back off yourself.

Richard and his therapist continue debriefing his overbreathing experience. The therapist explains the physiological mechanisms associated with hyperventilation. At the end, the therapist asked Richard to practice diaphragmatic breathing for 10 minutes, twice daily, until his next session. He was also to continue abstaining from caffeine and keep his panic logs.

At the beginning of Session 4, Richard and his therapist begin working on cognitive restructuring. The next phases of Richard's cognitive behavior therapy for panic disorder are in Chapter 8.

Outcomes Measurement

Richard completed several standardized objective assessment instruments to provide treatment planning, monitoring, and outcomes information. These included:

- *Body Sensations Questionnaire* (Chambless, Caputo, Bright, & Gallagher, 1984).

- *Mobility Inventory Questionnaire* (Chambless, Caputo, Gracely, Jasin, & Williams, 1985).

- *Agoraphobia Cognitions Questionnaire* (Chambless et al., 1984).

Depending on client problems and symptoms, behaviorists use many other behaviorally oriented questionnaires to monitor progress and outcomes.

EVALUATIONS AND APPLICATIONS

From the beginning, behavioral researchers and practitioners embraced scientific principles. This scientific orientation aligns well with the medical model. Many of the strengths and criticisms of contemporary behavior therapy are also strengths and criticisms of the medical model.

Evidence-Based Status

Behavioral and cognitive therapies are the largest producers and consumers of therapy outcomes research. A thorough review of this research is beyond the scope of this text. Instead, we offer an overview of research related to intervention approaches discussed in this chapter.

The most recent APA Division 12 list of ESTs includes 60 different treatment protocols, most of which are behavioral or cognitive behavioral. The approaches featured in this chapter have a substantial empirical base. The following is a brief sampling of this support:

- Token economies and contingency management (CM) systems are used in institutional programs. A meta-analysis of CM outcomes with individuals who were both homeless and abusing cocaine showed that day treatment and CM and CM alone were more effective in producing drug abstinence than day treatment alone (Schumacher et al., 2007). CM also has shown short-term effectiveness in alcohol and drug treatment (Benishek et al., 2014; Sayegh, Huey, Zara, & Jhaveri, 2017).

- Extensive research indicates that individual and group administered behavioral activation is effective in treating depression in a wide range of different clinical populations (e.g., college students, hospitalized patients, clients with suicide ideation; Chan, Sun, Tam, Tsoi, & Wong, 2017; Cuijpers, van Straten, & Warmerdam, 2007a; Sturmey, 2009).

- Progressive muscle relaxation and other forms of relaxation are often used as a treatment component in behavioral and cognitive behavior therapies. However, for treating insomnia and panic disorder, relaxation training alone shows efficacy (Morin et al., 2006; Ost et al., 1995; Spiegler & Guevremont, 2016).

- Exposure plus response or ritual prevention is one of the most well-researched procedures, consistently producing robust outcomes. It has demonstrated its efficacy as a treatment for many different anxiety disorders as well as bulimia nervosa (DiMauro, 2014; McIntosh, Carter, Bulik, Frampton, & Joyce, 2011).

- In a meta-analysis of 18 outcome studies, Powers and Emmelkamp (2008) reported that virtual reality exposure had a large effect size (d = 1.11) as compared to no treatment and a small effect size (d = 0.35) when compared to *in vivo* control conditions. In particular, recent research using virtual reality exposure for flight anxiety is especially robust (Cardoş et al., 2017). Virtual reality exposure may be as efficacious or more efficacious than *in vivo* exposure.

- Problem-solving therapy has substantial research support for treating depression and for contributing to effective treatment with children and adolescents with behavioral disorders (Cuijpers et al. 2007; Kazdin, 2010; Kirkham et al., 2016; Nezu & Nezu, 2010).

BRAIN BOX

7.1 Brain Science May Be Shiny, but Exposure Therapy Is Pure Gold

In honor of Joseph Wolpe, let's start with mental imagery.

****

Imagine you've travelled back in time to your first week of high school. You look around and see that one of your classmates is named Mary Jones.

Mary is an ordinary girl with an ordinary name. Over the years, you don't notice her much. She seems like a nice person, a fairly good student, and someone who doesn't get in trouble or draw attention to herself.

Four years pass. A new student joined your class during senior year. His name is Daniel Fancy Pants. Toward the end of the year, Daniel does a fantastic Prezi presentation about a remarkable new method for measuring reading outcomes. He includes cool video clips and boomerang Snapchat. When he bows at the end, he gets a standing ovation. Daniel is a good student and a hard worker; he partnered up with a college professor and made a big splash. Daniel deserves recognition.

However, as it turns out, over the *whole* four years of high school, Mary Jones was quietly working at a homeless shelter; week after week, month after month, year after year, she was teaching homeless children how to read. In fact, based on Daniel's measure of reading outcomes, Mary had taught over 70 children to read.

Funny thing. Mary doesn't get much attention. All everybody wants to talk about is Daniel. At graduation, he wins the outstanding graduate award. Everyone cheers.

Let's stop the visualization and reflect on what we imagined.

****

Like birds and raccoons, humans tend to like shiny things. Mary did incredible work, but hardly anyone noticed. Daniel did good work, and got a standing ovation and the top graduate award.

The "shiny-thing theory" is my best explanation for why we tend to get overly excited about brain science. It's important, no doubt, but brain imaging isn't therapy; it's just a cool way to measure or validate therapy's effects.

Beginning from at least 1924, when Mary Cover Jones was deconditioning fear out of little children, behavior therapy has shown not only great promise, but great outcomes. However, when researchers showed that exposure therapy "changes the brain," most of the excitement and accolades were about the brain images; exposure therapy was like background noise. Obviously, the fact that exposure therapy (and other therapies) change the brain is great news. It's great news for people who have anxiety and fear, and it's great news for practitioners who use exposure therapy.

This is all traceable to neuroscience and human evolution. We get distracted by shiny objects and miss the point because our neural networks and perceptual processes are oriented to alert us to novel (new) environmental stimuli. This is probably because change in the form of shiny objects might signal a threat or something new and valuable. We therefore need to exercise self-discipline to focus in and not overlook that behavior therapy in general, and exposure therapy in particular, has been, is, and probably will continue to be, the most effective approach on the planet for helping people overcome anxiety and fear. In addition, you know what, it doesn't really matter that it changes the brain (although that's damn cool and affirming news). What matters is that it changes clients' lives.

Exposure therapy, no matter how you package it, is highly effective for treating anxiety. This statement is true whether we're talking about Mary Cover Jones and her evidence-based counterconditioning cookies or Francine Shapiro and eye movement desensitization reprocessing (EMDR). It's also true whether we're talking about virtual reality exposure, imaginal exposure, massed exposure, spaced exposure, in vivo exposure, interoceptive exposure, response prevention (in obsessive-compulsive disorder), or the type of exposure that acceptance and commitment therapists use (note that they like to say it's "different" from traditional classical conditioning exposure, but it works, and that's what counts).

In the end, let's embrace and love and cheer brain imaging and neuroscience, but not forget the bottom line. The bottom line is that exposure therapy works! Exposure therapy is the genuine article. Exposure therapy is pure gold.

Mary Cover Jones is the graduate of the century; she was amazing. Because of her, exposure therapy has been pure gold for 93+ years, and now we've got cool pictures of the brain to prove it.

Mary Cover Jones passed away in 1987. Just minutes before her death, she said to her sister: "I am still learning about what is important in life" (as cited in Reiss, 1990).

We should all be more like Mary.

Cultural Sensitivity

Behavior therapy focuses directly on client problems and symptoms. Client cultural background is less important than symptom presentation. When a client like Richard (in the Case Presentation) comes to counseling with anxiety symptoms, behavioral practitioners are inclined to offer an evidence-based intervention—regardless of the client's culture or ethnicity.

When introducing themselves and their services, behavior (and cognitive behavior) therapists are likely to inform prospective clients that they use "techniques that have been shown to be effective in carefully performed research studies" (Ledley, Marx, & Heimberg, 2010, p. 86). Using a statement like "proven effective" is generally true. However, with culturally diverse clients, the question of whether or not behavior therapy techniques are research-based is still open.

Michelle Craske (2010), a prominent cognitive behavior therapist, commented on this issue:

The empirical support for CBT [cognitive behavior therapy] derives almost entirely from studies with white middle class Europeans or Westerners. In general, CBT is aligned with European and North American values of change, self-disclosure, independence and autonomy, and rational thinking, all of which are at odds with values of harmony, family and collectivism, and spirituality that define many other cultures. (p. 123)

There are several reports that behavioral treatments are effective with minority clients (Penedo et al., 2007; Pina, Silverman, Fuentes, Kurtines, & Weems, 2003; Weber, Colon, & Nelson, 2008). However, behavior therapies are not yet proven efficacious in the multicultural domain (Craske, 2010;

Ortiz & Del Vecchio, 2013). That's not to say behavioral researchers and practitioners are culturally insensitive. Over the past decade, training programs and clinical research studies have included significant efforts to address diversity issues (Fong, Ficklin, & Lee, 2017; Forehand & Kotchick, 2016; Hofmann, 2014). There has also been greater attention paid toward cultural validity in behavioral assessment (Shulman & Hope, 2016). Although these efforts are laudable, behavior therapists still need to make multicultural adjustments. Therapy with culturally diverse clients should proceed cautiously, with openness to the client's reaction to specific treatments. For example, if Richard happened to be a Native American client, the therapist might say:

> You have symptoms that fit with a panic disorder diagnosis. Fortunately we have a scientifically supported treatment for panic disorder available. However, I should also tell you that most of the research has been with white clients, although there have been a few Native Americans and clients from other cultures involved in the research studies. It's likely this approach will be helpful to you, but as we proceed, let's talk about how it's working for you. If there's anything about this treatment that doesn't feel right, please let me know and we'll make adjustments. Is that okay with you?

When working with Native Americans (or other culturally diverse clients), Richard's therapist might integrate indigenous ways of healing into the therapy approach (e.g., participation in Native American sweat lodge ceremonies; D. W. Sue & Sue, 2016).

As another example, a behavioral activation protocol like the one implemented with Adrienne might not work if Adrienne and her family had strong collectivist values. It could be offensive to conceptualize solutions to Adrienne's problem as requiring time away from the family. Also, Adrienne might resist behavioral activation homework if she doesn't view her personal and independent pleasure as important.

This discussion may lead you to worry that offering diverse clients treatments that have been validated with white clients is culturally insensitive. However, it turns out that regardless of empirical support for treatment outcomes, many ethnic minority clients prefer an active, directive, problem-focused form of therapy over less-directive insight oriented therapies (Atkinson, Lowe, & Mathews, 1995). D. W. Sue and Sue (2016) discussed why diverse clients might prefer directive therapies:

> We contend that the use of more directive, active, and influencing skills is more likely to provide personal information about where the therapist is coming from (self-disclosure). Giving advice or suggestions, interpreting, and telling the client how you, the

counselor or therapist, feel are really acts of counselor self-disclosure … [and] … a culturally diverse client may not open up (self-disclose) until you, the helping professional self-disclose first. (p. 277)

Overall, like most contemporary counseling and psychotherapy approaches, behavior therapists have more work to do to determine the cultural acceptability and efficacy of specific behavioral interventions (Craske, 2010; Hofmann, 2014).

REFLECTIONS

With more diverse students enrolling in counseling and psychology programs, minority therapists will be working with white clients. How do you think trust issues might affect white clients working with African American, Latino, Asian, or Native American therapists?

Gender and Sexuality

There's not much scientific literature available on feminist behavior therapy (Hunter & Kelso, 1985). That's probably because behavior therapy doesn't specifically address or ignore women's issues. Instead, behavior therapy practitioners integrate feminist perspectives into their practice on an individual basis. However, as in the vignette with Adrienne, behavior therapy can be very empowering for women, even though it doesn't explicitly endorse a political agenda.

Consistent with the medical model, behavior therapists tend to conceptualize mental disorders or personal problems as centered within individuals. This perspective could be seen as ignoring systemic social, political, and familial factors that create and exacerbate women's problems. Overall, as long as behavior therapy is implemented in a way that supports women and helps them feel empowered to address their symptoms, it can be seen as supporting a feminist perspective.

Historically, behavior therapy researchers and practitioners haven't had much emphasis on therapy approaches with sexual minority clients. However, over the past five years, this has changed. In particular, researchers have conducted randomized controlled trials (RCTs) on the efficacy of LGB-affirmative psychotherapy (Millar, Wang, & Pachankis, 2016; Pachankis, Hatzenbuehler, Rendina, Safren, & Parsons, 2015), adapted specific behavioral approaches for specific sexual minority populations (Craig, Austin, & Alessi, 2013), and identified clinical principles and techniques for working with gay and bisexual men (Pachankis, 2014). If you're interested in using behavioral and cognitive behavioral approaches with sexual minority clients, you'll be able to find many intellectual and practical resources.

Spirituality

Strict behaviorists don't believe in cognition. Problems are behaviors. Treatments involve new learning to facilitate behavior change. If you stick with the perspective that cognition is irrelevant—which is the perspective we're sticking with in this chapter—then client religious or spiritual beliefs are also not relevant.

Considering religious and spiritual beliefs as irrelevant doesn't imply disrespect for religious and spiritual beliefs. Behaviorists would be respectful of beliefs, but the focus of therapy would be on behaviors—which could include religious or spiritual behaviors. If you're following the logic here, then behavior therapy is 100 % compatible with religion and spirituality.

The focus of behavior therapy with religious and spiritual clients could be on behaviors that are related to religion and spirituality. From a behavioral model, the question would be, "Are your religious/spiritual behaviors causing you distress or contributing to your well-being?" The good news about this is that behavior therapy is an evidence-based approach for modifying behavior, including the development of positive and healthy habits (and behaviors commonly thought of as representing self-control and self-discipline). The focus on enhancing self-control and self-discipline is a good fit for clients with religious or spiritual orientations (Shapiro, 1978).

Researchers have explored the relationship between behavioral activation and client values. In one study, it was found that when individuals with high intrinsic religious values engaged in a greater frequency of religious behaviors, then they reported reduced depressive symptoms (Agishtein et al., 2013). Conversely, for individuals with low intrinsic religious values, increasing religious behaviors were associated with more depressive symptoms. In conclusion, despite disregard for religious/spiritual beliefs, a strict behavioral approach can be used to increase or decrease specific religious and spiritual behaviors.

CONCLUDING COMMENTS

During their careers, B. F. Skinner, a strong proponent of behavioral determinism, and Carl Rogers, long an advocate of free will and human dignity, had numerous professional interactions. In the following excerpt, Rogers (1960) was commenting on an exchange they had while presenting their work together on a conference panel.

> A paper given by Dr. Skinner led me to direct these remarks to him. "From what I understood Dr. Skinner to say, it is his understanding that though he might have thought he chose to come to this meeting,

might have thought he had a purpose in giving his speech, such thoughts are really illusory. He actually made certain marks on paper and emitted certain sounds here simply because his genetic make-up and his past environment had operantly conditioned his behavior in such a way that it was rewarding to make these sounds, and that he as a person doesn't enter into this. In fact if I get his thinking correctly, from his strictly scientific point of view, he, as a person, doesn't exist." In his reply Dr. Skinner said that he would not go into the question of whether he had any choice in the matter (presumably because the whole issue is illusory) but stated, "I do accept your characterization of my own presence here." I do not need to labor the point that for Dr. Skinner the concept of "learning to be free" would be quite meaningless. (pp. 15–16)

Although Rogers offers an amusing critique of Skinner, contemporary behavior therapy has moved beyond rigid determinism. In fact, behavior therapy represents not only a flexible approach to therapy but is also open to incorporating new techniques. The only rigidity inherent in the behavioral approach is its strict adherence to scientific validation of therapeutic techniques. Most of the behavior therapy perspective can be summed up in one sentence: if it can't be empirically validated, then it's not behavior therapy.

Overall, behavior therapists deserve credit for demonstrating that their particular approaches are effective—based on a quantitative scientific-medical model. Even more impressive is the fact that behavior therapy research has begun identifying which specific approaches are more likely to be effective with which specific problems. However, the question remains open regarding whether behavior therapy techniques are generally more effective than other techniques or whether behavior therapy researchers are simply better at demonstrating efficacy. Either way, we close with Skinner's remarks as an apt summary of the behavioral scientist's credo:

> Regard no practice as immutable. Change and be ready to change again. Accept no eternal verity. Experiment. (Skinner, 1970, p. viii)

CHAPTER SUMMARY AND REVIEW

Scientific behaviorism, the perspective that psychology is the study of objective, observable behavior, strongly shaped American psychology beginning in the early 1900s. John Watson, Mary Cover Jones, and other researchers studied the behavioral acquisition and treatment of fear. In particular, Jones's work produced the principles that continue to guide contemporary treatment of fears and anxiety. Later, in the 1950s, B. F. Skinner, Joseph Wolpe, Arnold Lazarus, and other leading researchers and practitioners officially began researching and practicing behavior therapy.

Behavior therapists are scientists. They use assessment and therapy procedures that are observable and supported by established learning theories and scientific research.

There are two primary behavioral theoretical models: (1) operant conditioning (aka applied behavior analysis) and (2) classical conditioning (aka the neobehavioristic, mediational stimulus–response model). These models emphasize that human behavior is a function of environmental stimuli that precede and follow it. Extensive scientific research on schedules of reinforcement, stimulus generalization, stimulus discrimination, extinction, and other behavioral principles underlie behavior therapy. For all behavior therapists, psychopathology is caused by maladaptive learning and is treated by providing clients with new learning experiences.

Contemporary behavior therapy consists of a variety of empirically based assessment and intervention procedures; it also usually includes cognitive approaches. In this chapter the focus is on assessment and therapy approaches that are more strictly behavioral and less cognitive. Behavioral assessment approaches include (a) functional behavioral assessment, (b) the behavioral interview, (c) self-monitoring, and (d) standardized objective questionnaires. Although there are many evidence-based behavior therapy procedures, this chapter includes descriptions of (a) contingency management and token economies, (b) behavioral activation, (c) relaxation training, (d) systematic desensitization and exposure treatment, and (e) skills training.

Behavior therapy is proven efficacious and effective for a wide range of problems for members of the dominant culture. This is partly because behaviorists are inclined to conduct research, embrace the modern scientific paradigm, and are comfortable with the medical model. Most of the therapies listed as highly efficacious or likely to be efficacious by Division 12 of the American Psychological Association are either behavior therapies or cognitive-behavioral therapies.

Behavior therapy tends to focus exclusively on symptoms, sometimes ignoring social, political, and gender-related factors that contribute to client problems. Although this focus is helpful for symptom reduction, feminists and multiculturalists complain that behavior therapy can blame clients for their problems. More recently, behavior therapy researchers have begun addressing cultural variables and efforts toward making cultural adaptations are under way. Research with sexual minority clients is also accumulating, providing practitioners with new guidance. Although behavior therapists don't focus on religious or spiritual beliefs, behavior therapies can help religious/spiritual clients increase or decrease specific religious or spiritual behaviors.

BEHAVIOR THERAPY KEY TERMS

Activity scheduling

Aggressive

Antecedents

Applied behavior analysis

Assertiveness

Assertiveness training

Aversive conditioning

Backward behavior modification

Behavior

Behavior therapy

Behavioral ABCs

Behavioral activation

Classical conditioning

Contingency management (CM)

Conditioned response

Conditioned stimulus

Continuous reinforcement

Counterconditioning

Exposure treatment

Extinction

Fading

Fixed interval reinforcement

Fixed ratio reinforcement

Functional behavioral analysis

Imaginal exposure

In vivo exposure

Interoceptive exposure

Introspection

Massed exposure

Negative punishment

Negative reinforcement

Neobehavioristic mediational SR model

Operant conditioning

Operational definition

Participant modeling

Passive

Positive punishment (note: authors strongly prefer "punishment")

Positive reinforcement

Problem-solving therapy (PST)

Progressive muscle relaxation (PMR)

Response prevention

Scientific behaviorism

Self-monitoring

Skills training

Spaced exposure

Spontaneous recovery

Stimulus discrimination

Stimulus generalization

Stimulus–response (SR) theory

Subjective units of distress (SUDs)

Systematic desensitization

Token economy

Unconditioned response

Unconditioned stimulus

Variable interval reinforcement

Variable ratio reinforcement

Virtual reality exposure

CHAPTER 8

Cognitive Behavioral Theory and Therapy

LEARNER OBJECTIVES

- Define cognitive behavior therapy (CBT)
- Identify key figures and historical trends in the development, evolution, and application of cognitive theory and CBT
- Describe core principles of social learning theory and cognitive appraisal theories and their integration into cognitive behavioral theory and therapy
- Describe and apply CBT principles, strategies, and techniques
- Analyze CBT cases
- Evaluate the empirical, cultural, gender, and spiritual validity of CBT
- Summarize core content and define key terms associated with cognitive behavioral theory and therapy

We have many ideas about how to open a chapter about cognition. John wanted to say something pithy like, "You are what you think," but Ralph Waldo Emerson got there first. Rita was considering, "As a woman thinketh" (a feminist version of James Allen's 1903 book titled, *As a Man Thinketh*), but John countered with "As a person thinketh" and by then we'd grown weary of the word thinketh. Then Rita waxed Shakespeare-esk, saying, "There is nothing either good or bad but thinking makes it so," which seemed a little better than the Buddha's, "What you think you become" until we found the writings of Hafiz (a fourteenth-century Persian poet):

> Zero
> Is where the Real Fun starts
> There's too much counting
> Everywhere else!
>
> *(Ladinsky, 1996, p. 47)*

Although Albert Ellis might respond to this poem by asking, "What the Holy Hell are you thinking?" we thought it was about clearing a cognitive space for meditation. Let's start with zero.

INTRODUCTION

In the beginning, most behaviorists didn't want to think about cognition, but cognition found its way into their work anyway. Joseph Wolpe opened Skinner's

black box just wide enough to let in mental imagery—for the purposes of doing systematic desensitization (Wolpe, 1958).

Wolpe wouldn't appreciate being implicated in the cognitive revolution. At the 1983 annual meeting of the Association for the Advancement of Behavior Therapy (AABT then, Association for Behavioral and Cognitive Therapy now, ABCT), we listened as Wolpe condemned Michael Mahoney's use of "streaming" with a client. Streaming involved having the client free-associate while looking at himself in a mirror (Williams, Diehl, & Mahoney, 2002). Wolpe was adamant: *There were events happening at the conference far outside the behavior therapy realm*. Mahoney and other "cognitive types" had stepped over the line.

However, this wasn't the first behavioral-cognitive spat. As Meichenbaum (2003) noted years later, a 1970s zeitgeist caused a split between behaviorists who embraced cognition and behaviorists who eschewed cognition. In an interview, he recalled:

- [A] letter by a very senior and prominent behavior therapist was circulated in AABT to have individuals who advocated for cognitive factors in therapy to be kicked out of the behavior therapy association.

- The number of presentations on cognitive factors at AABT conferences were limited, if not excluded.

Counseling and Psychotherapy Theories in Context and Practice: Skills, Strategies, and Techniques, Third Edition. John Sommers-Flanagan and Rita Sommers-Flanagan. © 2018 John Wiley & Sons, Inc. Published 2018 by John Wiley & Sons, Inc.
Companion website: www.wiley.com/go/sommers-flanagan/theories3e

- Certain behavioral journals would not permit the use of the word "cognition" in any articles.
- Researchers in … CBT were professionally threatened if they continued to challenge the behavioral approach.
- CBT researchers were challenged as being "oxymoronic" and were labeled as "malcontents." (Meichenbaum, 2003, p. 127)

The pressure from behaviorists didn't dampen the "cognitivists'" resolve. They pushed back, and in 1977, a new journal, *Cognitive Therapy and Research*, was founded, with Michael Mahoney as editor.

Although there were initial conflicts and a split between staunch behaviorists and cognitivists, the past three decades have brought rapprochement and integration. Now, it's nearly impossible to distinguish between cognitive therapy and cognitive behavior therapy. In keeping with this trend, Judith Beck (Kaplan, 2011) announced:

[W]e are changing our name from the Beck Institute for Cognitive Therapy to the Beck Institute for Cognitive Behavior Therapy because people now seem more familiar with the term CBT. (p. 36)

What Is CBT?

Judith Beck
(photo courtesy of Beck Institute for Cognitive Behavior Therapy)

CBT is the popular term for cognitive behavior therapy. The following statements define **cognitive behavior therapy**:

- CBT is brief or time-sensitive.
- CBT is structured.
- CBT is present oriented.
- CBT involves teaching and learning.
- CBT seeks to change BOTH dysfunctional thinking and maladaptive behavior (see https://www.beckinstitute .org/get-informed/what-is-cognitive-therapy/).

CBT is an integration of cognitive and behavior therapies. In Chapter 7, we focused on behavior therapy. In this chapter, we focus on the cognitive dimension of CBT. We explore the origins and practice of integrating cognition into the behavior therapy process (see Putting It in Practice 8.1 for Judith Beck's explanation of why she's a cognitive behavior therapist).

PUTTING IT IN PRACTICE

8.1 Why Do I Practice Cognitive Behavior Therapy?

The following commentary was written and reproduced with permission by **Judith S. Beck**, PhD, president of the Beck Institute for Cognitive Behavior Therapy at the University of Pennsylvania.

Why do I practice cognitive therapy? Aside from the familial connection (my father, Aaron T. Beck, MD, is the "father" of cognitive therapy), it is the most widely researched form of psychotherapy; it has been shown in several hundred research studies to be effective. If I had an ear infection, I would first seek the treatment that has been demonstrated most efficacious. Why should it be different for psychiatric disorders or psychological problems?

Other than research efficacy, it is the one form of psychotherapy that makes sense to me. Take a typical depressed patient. Nancy, a 32-year-old married sales clerk with a young child, has been clinically depressed for almost a year. She has quit her job, spends much of the day in bed, has given over most of her child-rearing responsibilities to her mother and husband, goes out only infrequently, and has withdrawn from family and friends. She is very sad, hopeless, weighted down, self-critical; she gets little if any pleasure from activities or interactions with others and little sense of achievement from anything she does.

It just makes sense to me to work directly on the problems Nancy has today, teaching her cognitive and behavioral skills to get her life in order and decrease her depression. Behaviorally, I help Nancy plan a schedule: getting out of bed at a reasonable time each morning, getting bathed and dressed immediately, and preparing breakfast for herself and her daughter. We include calling friends, doing small household tasks, taking walks, and doing one errand. Cognitively I help her identify and respond to her negative thinking. Some of her dysfunctional thoughts are related to the behavioral tasks I have suggested: "I'll be too tired to get out of bed. I won't know what to make for breakfast. [My friend]

Jean won't want to hear from me. It won't help to take a walk." Other dysfunctional thoughts are about herself ("I'm worthless"), her world ("Life is too hard"), and the future ("I'll never get better").

We tackle Nancy's problems one by one. In the context of discussing and solving problems, I teach her the skills she needs. Cognitive skills include identifying her depressed thoughts, evaluating her thinking, and developing more realistic, adaptive views. I also help her respond to her deeper-level ideas, her beliefs or basic understandings that shape her perception of her experience, ideas that, left unmodified, might contribute to a relapse sometime in the future.

While doing cognitive therapy, I need to use all my basic counseling skills to establish and maintain a strong therapeutic alliance. I am highly collaborative with the patient, working with her as a "team" to help her get better; I provide rationales for the strategies I use; I use active listening and empathy, and I provide support. I also ask for feedback at every session to make sure that I have understood the patient correctly and that the process of therapy is amenable to her. But perhaps most importantly, I am quite active in the session—providing direction, offering suggestions, teaching her skills. Doing all of these things helps the patient recover most quickly.

Why do I specialize in cognitive therapy? Because it is humane, it is effective, and it is the quickest way to alleviate suffering.

KEY FIGURES AND HISTORICAL CONTEXT

Wilhelm Wundt used introspection as a scientific technique when he established the first psychology laboratory in 1879. Then, introspection was viewed as a method for studying cognition (Wozniak, 1993). Although 1879 seems like long ago, introspection didn't begin with Wundt. It dates at least back to Socrates, who used an approach now referred to as **Socratic questioning** to uncover an individual's method of reasoning.

In the first half of the twentieth century, John Watson and B. F. Skinner had mostly banished introspection from academic psychology. They could have held a memorial service celebrating its death, but as far as we know, that particular cognition never crossed their minds.

It's just as well. Cognition is a slippery and persistent phenomenon that keeps popping up. Have you ever tried to banish particular cognitions (thoughts) from your own mind? Typically, when humans try to stop thinking about something, the banished thoughts return ... sooner or later. Despite Watson's and Skinner's best efforts, cognition (now sometimes disguised as "information processing") returned to academic psychology and is central to contemporary counseling and psychotherapy.

Three primary historical figures and trends capture the history and evolution of cognitive therapy.

- Albert Ellis and Rational Emotive (Behavior) Therapy.

- Aaron Beck and Cognitive Therapy.

- Donald Meichenbaum and Self-Instructional Therapy.

Albert Ellis and Rational Emotive Behavior Therapy

Albert Ellis
(*photo courtesy of the Albert Ellis Institute*)

Albert Ellis is credited with the discovery and promotion of modern rational (cognitive) approaches to psychotherapy. Ellis was born in Pittsburgh, Pennsylvania, in 1913 to Jewish parents. Similar to Adler (see Chapter 3) he had a challenging childhood. Eldest of three children, he described his father as a minimally successful businessman who was often away from home. He described his mother as self-absorbed and as having bipolar tendencies. Ellis became very sick with a kidney ailment at age 5 and was hospitalized eight times from age 5 to 7 years. He believed his health struggles taught him to confront feelings of inferiority. His parents divorced when he was 12 years old.

Initially, Ellis wanted to be a writer, but his first eight novels were rejected. Eventually he entered the Columbia University clinical psychology program in 1942. After graduating, he pursued training in psychoanalysis and, like Fritz Perls (see Chapter 6), was analyzed by Karen Horney.

Ellis formulated his approach after discovering he was ineffectual in his traditional psychoanalytic practice, but he used his awareness of being ineffectual as a source of learning and discovery:

I realized ... that although people have remarkable differences and uniquenesses in their tastes, characteristics, goals, and enjoyments, they also have remarkable sameness in the ways in which they disturb themselves "emotionally." People have, of course, thousands of specific irrational ideas and philosophies (not to mention superstitions and religiosities) which they creatively invent, dogmatically carry on, and stupidly upset themselves about. But we can easily put almost all these thousands of ideas into a few general categories. Once we do so, and then actively *look for* these categories, we can fairly quickly find them, show them to disturbed individuals, and also teach them how to give them up. (Ellis & Grieger, 1977, pp. 4–5)

Ellis began using directive therapy approaches in the late 1940s and early 1950s. Many of his contemporaries were already heading in the same direction—away from traditional psychoanalysis and toward more active-directive, cognitive-oriented therapy. He wrote:

Actually, they attributed to me more originality than I merited. By the late 1940s quite a few other therapists, most of them trained as I was in the field of psychoanalysis, had begun to see the severe limitations and myths of the analytic approach and had, whether they consciously acknowledged it or not, moved much closer to Adler than to Freud. (Ellis & Grieger, 1977, p. 4)

Despite Ellis's humility (which some may view as uncharacteristic), Beck views Ellis as "the first to attempt to develop a comprehensive cognitive model of psychopathology. He theorized that psychopathology was the result of processing events through an irrational belief system" (Beck & Haigh, 2014, p. 7).

Ellis also credited Epictetus, a Roman philosopher and stoic, for his "rational psychotherapy" approach. J. W. Bush (2002) described Epictetus's history.

The first cognitive behavior therapist, so to speak, in the Western world was the philosopher Epictetus (c. 50–138 a.d.). He was born a slave in the Greek-speaking Roman province of Phrygia, in what is now central Turkey.

One day when Epictetus was working in the fields chained to an iron stake, his master approached him with the idea of tightening his leg shackle. Epictetus suggested that making the shackle tighter was not needed to keep him from running away, but would merely break his leg. The master was not persuaded, and sure enough Epictetus's leg was broken. But he did not protest or give any sign of distress. His master asked him why, and was told that since the leg was already irreversibly broken, there was really no point in getting upset about it. His master was so impressed by this demonstration of unflappability that he eventually set Epictetus free, and sent him away with money so he could become an itinerant philosopher. Epictetus considered this preferable to being a philosopher chained to a stake, and eventually came to Rome, then the capital of the Western world. Among the prominent Romans he influenced was the emperor Marcus Aurelius.

Initially, Ellis referred to his therapy approach as rational psychotherapy, later changing the name to rational-emotive therapy. In 1993, he added the word *behavior*, thus creating **rational emotive behavior therapy** (REBT). He considered REBT to be a philosophical, behavioral, and cognitive approach (Ellis, 1999c).

Ellis was one of the big characters in the history and practice of psychotherapy. His influence was profound, from the publication and dissemination of many rational humor songs (including the infamous Albert Ellis Christmas Carols) to the direct training of thousands of REBT practitioners. When we heard him speak, there were two consistent occurrences. First, he found a reason to break into song (despite his extremely poor singing ability). Second, he always managed to slip the "F" word into his presentations.

Given Ellis's eccentric, direct, and sometimes abrasive characteristics, it's tempting to minimize his accomplishments, but he produced more than 700 scholarly journal articles and 60 professional books. Additionally, he probably provided therapy to more individuals than any other practitioner in the history of psychotherapy. In 1987 alone, he reported he was working with 300 individual clients and five groups, while demonstrating his procedures at weekly "Five-Dollar Friday Night Workshops" in New York City (Ellis, 1987). Moreover, he continued this incredible pace into the twenty-first century—amassing more than 50 years of applied clinical experience. For detailed information on Ellis's personal history, see Dryden (1989).

Not long after Ellis began formulating his rational approach to psychotherapy another formal cognitive approach entered the scene.

Aaron Beck and Cognitive Therapy

Aaron Beck
(*photo courtesy of the Beck Institute for Cognitive Behavior Therapy*)

Aaron Beck was born in 1921 in Providence, Rhode Island. His parents were Russian Jewish immigrants. He was the youngest of five children. By the time he was born an older brother and older sister had died of influenza, causing his mother to become very depressed. Beck saw himself as a replacement for his deceased older siblings (Weishaar, 1993).

Similar to Adler and Ellis, Beck also had a physical problem during childhood. He broke his arm and missed a substantial amount of school due to a long recovery period in the hospital. During this time he was held back a year in school and began believing he was not very smart. He overcame this difficult situation and his negative beliefs about himself, eventually obtaining a medical degree from Yale in 1953.

Like Adler, Rogers, Perls, and Ellis, Beck was psychoanalytically trained. Early on, he became interested in validating Freud's anger-turned-inward-upon-the-self theory of depression. Instead he ended up rejecting Freud's theory and articulating his own (Beck, 1961, 1963, 1970).

Psychoanalytic colleagues ostracized Beck for questioning Freud (Weishaar, 1993). However, over time, Beck's work on depression was recognized as empirically valid. His theory of depression and specific approaches to its treatment are two of the best-known and most scientifically supported discoveries in counseling and psychotherapy.

Beck discovered the centrality of cognition to human functioning while conducting psychoanalysis:

> [T]he patient volunteered the information that while he had been expressing anger-laden criticisms of me, he had also had continual thoughts of a self-critical nature. He described two streams of thought occurring at about the same time; one stream having to do with his hostility and criticisms, which he had expressed in free association, and another that he had not expressed. He then reported the other stream of thoughts: "I said the wrong thing ... I shouldn't have said that ... I'm wrong to criticize him ... I'm bad ... He won't like me ... I'm bad ... I have no excuse for being so mean." (Beck, 1976, pp. 30–31)

This led Beck to conclude that focusing on this "other stream of consciousness" was more valuable than psychoanalytic free association.

Beck's approach to therapy is known as cognitive therapy. He reasoned:

> [P]sychological problems can be mastered by sharpening discriminations, correcting misconceptions and learning more adaptive attitudes. Since introspection, insight, reality testing, and learning are basically cognitive processes, this approach to the neuroses has been labeled cognitive therapy. (Beck, 1976, p. 20)

Similar to Ellis's REBT, cognitive therapy has taken on Beck's personal qualities. Beck was recognized as collaborative and practical. He was gentle and inquiring. Beck wasn't interested in rational argument with clients. Instead, cognitive therapists using Beck's approach use collaborative empiricism. **Collaborative empiricism** involves therapists working together with clients to elucidate the maladaptive nature of clients' automatic thoughts and core or primal beliefs. A key distinction between these two therapists is that whereas Ellis emphasizes the forceful eradication of irrational thoughts, Beck emphasizes the collaborative modification of maladaptive thoughts (Beck, Rush, Shaw, & Emery, 1979; Clark, Beck, & Alford, 1999).

Donald Meichenbaum and Self-Instructional Strategies

Unlike Adler, Ellis, and Beck, Donald Meichenbaum started practicing behavior therapy, then shifted to cognitive therapy, and then became a constructivist (Neimeyer, Meichenbaum, & Stanley, 2015). Looking back on his life, he recalled learning to be a people-watcher as he grew up in New York City. Specifically, he noticed people on the streets sometimes talking to themselves.

Meichenbaum's early research focused on impulsive school children and hospitalized adults diagnosed with schizophrenia. He discovered that both schizophrenics and children, similar to people on the New York streets, could improve their functioning after being taught to talk to themselves (aka think aloud; Meichenbaum, 1969; Meichenbaum & Goodman, 1971).

A consummate observer and researcher, Meichenbaum's perspective has evolved over time. Initially, he integrated the work of Soviet psychologists Vygotsky (1962) and Luria (1961) with Bandura's (1965) vicarious learning model and the operant conditioning principle of fading. Using these disparate perspectives, he developed a systematic method for teaching children to use self-instructions to slow down and guide themselves through challenging problem-solving situations. His work with self-instruction led him to conclude that

> [E]vidence has convincingly indicated that the therapist can and does significantly influence what the client says to [the therapist]. Now it is time for the therapist to directly influence what the client says to himself. (Meichenbaum & Cameron, 1974, p. 117)

Meichenbaum's early focus was on self-instructional training (SIT). Consistent with his behavioral roots, he referred to SIT as cognitive behavior modification (Meichenbaum, 1977). He emphasized that "[b]ehavior change occurs through a sequence of mediating processes involving the interaction of inner speech, cognitive structures, and behaviors and their resultant outcomes" (Meichenbaum, 1977, p. 218).

He later developed **stress inoculation training** (also SIT), a specific approach for helping clients manage difficult stressors (Meichenbaum, 1985). Throughout this early and middle phase of his career, Meichenbaum focused on empirical research and validation of highly practical approaches to helping clients. His style was similar to Beck; he collaboratively worked with clients to change their inner speech. His style was (and is) more openly empathic and emotionally oriented than most cognitive therapists.

Along with other behavioral and cognitive therapists, Meichenbaum has now shifted toward an empirically oriented constructive model (Hoyt, 2000; Meichenbaum, 1992). At the Second Evolution of Psychotherapy Conference (1992), he made statements that redefined his view of CBT:

[Cognitive behavior therapy,] which is phenomenologically oriented, attempts to explore by means of nondirective reflective procedures the client's world view. There is an intent to see the world through the client's eyes, rather than to challenge, confront, or interpret the client's thoughts. A major mode of achieving this objective is for the [cognitive behavior] therapist to "pluck" (pick out) key words and phrases that clients offer, and then to reflect them in an interrogative tone, but with the same affect (mirroring) in which they were expressed. The [cognitive behavior] therapist also may use the client's developmental accounts, as well as in-session client behavior, to help the client get in touch with his or her feelings. (Meichenbaum, 1992, pp. 117–118)

Meichenbaum's progression—from behavior therapy, to cognitive behavior modification, to cognitive behavior therapy, to constructive cognitive behavior therapy—reflects a trend toward integration that we explore later (see Chapter 14).

THEORETICAL PRINCIPLES

Like behavior therapy, CBT is based on learning theory. This means that when we examine cognitive behavioral theory, we're also considering the two learning theories discussed in the previous chapter:

1. Classical conditioning.
2. Operant conditioning.

Cognitive behavior therapy also incorporates at least two additional learning theories: (1) social learning theory and (2) cognitive appraisal theory. These theories emphasize cognition's role in initiating and sustaining specific behaviors.

Social Learning Theory

Albert Bandura developed social learning theory (Bandura & Walters, 1963). It is viewed as a theoretical extension of operant and classical conditioning. Social learning theory includes stimulus-influence components (classical conditioning) and consequence-influence components (operant conditioning), but also adds a cognitive mediational component.

Social learning theory includes two main cognitive processes: observational learning and person-stimulus reciprocity.

Much of human learning is observational (Bandura, 1971). **Observational learning** is also called **vicarious learning**; it occurs when individuals learn indirectly, from watching or listening to the experiences of others. It can involve the increase or decrease of behaviors and/or new skill development. For example, in Bandura's famous Bobo doll experiment, he showed that observational learning strongly influenced children's behavior (Bandura, Ross, & Ross, 1963). Observational learning includes covert or private mental processes that cannot be directly observed by experimenters (or therapists). Observational learning is commonly known as **modeling**.

Social learning theory also focuses on **reciprocal interactions** that occur between an individual's behavior and the environment (i.e., person-stimulus reciprocity; Bandura, 1978). Bandura postulated that individuals can have thoughts about the future, behavioral consequences, and goals. These thoughts form a feedback loop and influence current behavior. In combination with observational learning, it becomes possible for clients to learn how to approach or avoid specific situations, never having directly experienced positive or negative reinforcement—based completely on observing what happened to someone else. These reciprocal interactions make individuals capable of self-directed behavior change. In contrast to Skinner and Watson, Bandura sees free will and self-determination as possible.

One of Bandura's most important concepts is self-efficacy (Bandura & Adams, 1977; Bandura, 1977). **Self-efficacy** is defined as:

The conviction that one can successfully execute the behavior required to produce an outcome. (Bandura, 1977, p. 193)

Self-efficacy is different from self-esteem or self-confidence. Its specificity has made it more helpful to researchers and clinicians. There are many different self-efficacy measures in the scientific literature (Kurtz, Olfson, & Rose, 2013; Lee & Bobko, 1994).

Self-efficacy can have an interactive or reciprocal influence on client behavior. As a positive expectation or belief about the future, higher self-efficacy is associated with more persistence, greater effort, and willingness to face obstacles. If you really believe in your skills to study and successfully pass an upcoming midterm in this class, you have high self-efficacy and will behave in ways that make your success more likely. In contrast, lower self-efficacy is associated with negative self-talk or preoccupation, giving up easily, and reduced concentration. Low self-efficacy won't help with your exam-taking success.

Several factors can increase or improve client self-efficacy:

- Incentives.
- Knowledge and skills.

- Positive feedback.

- Successful performance accomplishment.

Based on Bandura's reciprocal interactions model, a primary therapy goal is to help clients develop and strengthen their self-efficacy. For example, a client who comes to therapy to quit smoking cigarettes may have little confidence in her ability to quit. If therapy is to be successful, it will be necessary to enhance the client's smoking cessation self-efficacy. This may come about when the therapist teaches self-monitoring procedures, progressive muscle relaxation, and strategies for coping with uncomfortable nicotine withdrawal feelings. As the client's skills develop, so might her belief in her ability to successfully quit smoking. Therapists also may model a positive belief in their client's success. In this way cognitive techniques produce change indirectly; they provide clients with tools that positively modify their beliefs toward greater self-efficacy.

Cognitive Appraisal Theories

Cognitive appraisal theory can be summarized in one sentence that Ellis attributes to Epictetus (Ellis & Dryden, 1997):

> People are disturbed not by things, but by the view which they take of them.

Consider Watson's (Chapter 7) position that "Introspection forms no essential part of [behavior therapy] methods" (Watson, 1924, p. 158). Watson's objection was scientific; introspection was subjective and not measureable and so it was outside the purview of behaviorism. In contrast, for cognitive theorists, discovering the client's subjective interpretation of reality is the whole point. For example, many clients have classically conditioned fear responses, but these responses are cognitively mediated. Research supports cognitive mediation of client symptoms. Individuals with anxiety disorders tend to:

- Pay too much attention to negative incidents or cues.

- Overestimate the likelihood of a negative event occurring.

- Exaggerate the significance or meaning of potential or real negative events. (Davey, 2006)

Similarly, if we look at Skinner's theoretical position, "Behavior is a function of its consequences," then cognitive theory transforms "consequences" away from an exclusively objective phenomenon. Now, behavior is a function of *what the organism thinks about its consequences*.

The cognitive revision of behavioral stimulus–response (S–R) theory is **stimulus–organism–response (S–O–R)**

theory, with the organism (person) appraising stimulus and response. Beck (1976) stated it this way:

> [T]here is a conscious thought between an external event and a particular emotional response. (p. 27)

Cognitive theory emphasizes the individual organism's processing of environmental stimuli as the force determining specific responses

Three Basic REBT Philosophies

Ellis has identified three REBT philosophies underlying REBT process and guiding therapy interventions. These philosophies are:

1. *Unconditional self-acceptance (USA)*: REBT self-acceptance is similar to the self-acceptance person-centered therapists advocate. Although Ellis wrote several USA definitions, one version goes like this: "I do not have intrinsic worth or worthlessness, but merely aliveness. I'd better rate my traits and acts, but not my totality or 'self.' I require no other kind of self-rating" (Ellis, 1999a, p. 6). USA doesn't mean you're complacent about self-improvement; the purpose is for you to stop self-flagellation when failures or rejection or other adverse experiences occur (Dryden, 2013, p. 108).

2. *Unconditional other-acceptance (UOA)*: Accepting others as they are, without preconditions. Dryden (2013) wrote: "Seeing others as human, unique, complex, in flux and fallible and that this is true about them no matter what conditions exist in the world." (p. 110)

3. *Unconditional life-acceptance (ULA)*: Fully accepting your life and ongoing existence regardless of whether you get what you want. This involves recognizing that rejection, failure, and other adverse life experiences are part of life. Although you would prefer avoiding them, accepting them as an overall part of your life experience is essential.

These philosophies are health-promoting. They are aspirational and require effort. In contrast, irrational beliefs are easy and natural, often leading to "absolutistic musts," and then to more profound problems including: (a) low frustration tolerance, (b) self-denigration, and (c) awfulizing or spoiling personal experiences (see Ellis & MacLaren, 2005).

The REBT ABCDEF Cognitive Model

In Ellis's REBT model humans have the potential to think rationally, but have a strong tendency to think in exaggerated, tangled, contradictory, mistaken, and irrational ways. Irrational thinking is the primary source of human misery.

Ellis used an ABCDEF model to describe and discuss S–O–R theory. In REBT, "A" represents the **activating event** or stimulus that has occurred in an individual's life; "B" refers to the **belief** about the activating event; and "C" refers to **consequent emotion** and behavior linked to the belief.

The **REBT ABCs** are best illustrated through an example.

Jem comes to therapy feeling angry, depressed, hurt, and resentful. Last night his romantic partner, Pat, wasn't home at 6 p.m. for dinner as they had arranged. This event troubled him greatly. Jem began thinking, "Pat doesn't care enough about me to be home for dinner on time." He also started imagining Pat was romantically involved with someone else. Jem found himself thinking over and over: "Pat doesn't really love me and prefers to spend time with someone else."

Pat finally arrived home at 7:45 p.m. The explanation, "I was stuck in a meeting at work and couldn't call because my phone battery was dead" didn't convince Jem; his feelings continued escalating. He yelled at Pat for being so insensitive and then said, "I know what's going on. You can't fool me. I've seen the way you look at that new tech person in your office."

When Jem shows up for his appointment with Dr. Ellis, the doctor says: "What the hell. You can blame Pat for your problems if you want, but you're making yourself miserable." He spells out the ABCs:

A. Jem's Activating Event: Pat is late for dinner.

B. Jem's Belief: Pat doesn't love or respect him anymore. Pat's probably having an affair.

C. Jem's Consequent Anger: sadness, hurt, resentment, and jealousy.

D. Feelings and Behavior: yelling and accusing Pat of having an affair.

The main thrust of REBT is to show Jem that his current belief about Pat's lateness is irrational. Ellis referred to this as an **irrational belief** (iB). Through REBT procedures a **rational belief** (rB) is substituted for an irrational belief (iB). This should result in a more positive and comfortable **new feeling** (F).

Ellis was well known for his direct and confrontational therapy style. Although it's easy to directly associate Ellis's style with REBT, not all Rational Emotive Behavior therapists are direct and confrontational.

Ellis's main intervention is to *dispute* (D) the irrational belief. He might directly dispute Jem's belief by asking,

- Is it true that Pat must always be home right on time to prove you're loved?

- Isn't it true that sometimes Pat can be late and that it's really not all that awful—it doesn't mean you're not

lovable, but instead it's an inconvenient behavior that sometimes happens to all couples?

Disputation (D) of Jem's irrational belief (and Jem's own subsequent and ongoing disputations of his irrational belief) will have an **emotional effect** (E) on Jem. Hopefully, this effect will teach Jem to question his irrational conclusions and to develop alternative, rational beliefs. If therapy is successful, Jem will experience a **new feeling** (F).

Rational-emotive therapists would work with Jem (and others) using the five bedrock components of Ellis's approach:

1. People dogmatically adhere to irrational ideas and personal philosophies.

2. These irrational ideas cause people great distress and misery.

3. These ideas can be boiled down to a few basic categories.

4. Therapists can find these irrational categories rather easily in their clients' reasoning.

5. Therapists can teach clients to give up their misery-causing irrational beliefs.

REFLECTIONS

Jem concluded that because Pat was late, Pat is having an affair. What other interpretations or beliefs could Jem use to explain Pat's lateness? Have you had similar experiences? What thoughts (rational and irrational) pop into your head?

Beck's Cognitive Theory: Distinctions from Ellis

The theoretical principles of Beck's cognitive therapy are similar to Ellis's REBT. Similarities include:

- Cognition is at the core of human suffering.

- The therapist's job is to help clients modify distress-producing thoughts.

Cognitive therapy and REBT have a few distinctive differences. Beck criticizes Ellis's use of "*irrational*" to describe the rules by which people regulate their lives. Beck (1976) wrote:

Ellis (1962) refers to such rules as "irrational ideas." His term, while powerful, is not accurate. The ideas are generally not irrational but are too absolute, broad, and extreme; too highly personalized; and are used too arbitrarily to help the patient to handle the exigencies of his life. To be of greater use, the rules need to be remolded so that they are more precise and accurate, less egocentric, and more elastic. (p. 33)

Beck's cognitive theory includes the following components:

1. No one is cognitively perfect. Psychopathology is an exaggeration of normal cognitive biases.

2. All individuals develop deep beliefs about the self—also referred to as **self-schema** (note that this is similar to Adler's style of life).

3. Due to biogenetic predisposition, modeling by early caregivers, and/or adverse life events, individuals' schemas include negative and/or inaccurate beliefs about the self.

4. These beliefs aren't necessarily problematic until activated by stressful life events or negative mood states, especially events and mood states that match or are consistent with the underlying belief or schema.

5. When these beliefs are activated, faulty information processing increases and negative or positive biases spread to several cognitive domains like (a) selective attention, (b) memory, and (c) interpretation of events/experiences. These biases often emerge in the form of automatic thoughts (which are consistent underlying beliefs), and that, in turn, contribute to increasing emotional dysfunction and maladaptive behaviors.

6. Information processing has two interacting subsystems: automatic and reflective. The automatic subsystem processes information rapidly, but categorizes incoming data into broad categories and produces errors. The reflective subsystem is slower, requires more cognitive resources, and is more nuanced and accurate.

7. Repeated information processing—especially the rapid, automatic processing—tends to be repetitive and confirmatory; there is repeated activation and confirmation of underlying negative beliefs, some of which have cognitive content consistent with specific mental disorders.

8. When therapists engage the reflective subsystem, automatic thoughts, intermediate beliefs, core (or primal) beliefs, and their associated emotional and behavioral disturbances, can be modified. (Adapted from Beck & Haigh, 2014.)

The contrasting point is that Ellis views clients as having irrational thoughts; Beck views the thoughts as too broad or inaccurate based on rapid, automatic, and maladaptive information processing. The difference is subtle. One way to summarize the distinction: Ellis used the label irrational; in contrast, Beck uses maladaptive.

Collaborative, Not Confrontational
Beck's cognitive theory uses a different procedure (than REBT) for modifying client thinking. Although both theorists advocate teaching and learning, cognitive therapists use collaborative empiricism, to help clients discover inaccurate or maladaptive thoughts. Collaborative empiricism includes three main components:

1. Client and therapist work together in partnership.

2. The therapist employs Socratic questioning to uncover the client's idiosyncratic and maladaptive thinking patterns.

3. The therapist uses Socratic questioning and other techniques to help clients test the validity or usefulness of their automatic thoughts and core beliefs.

This approach requires therapists to try to see the world through the client's eyes (Shaw & Beck, 1977). It emphasizes that clients aren't irrational or defective but may need to adjust the lens through which they're viewing the world (J. S. Beck, 2011).

Ellis considered Beck's collaborative empiricism to be an inelegant solution. Instead, he would present clients with worst case scenarios and then directly dispute the terribleness of the scenario. Ellis believed his approach was an elegant solution because it provided clients with a way to cope with worst case scenarios in case they ever occur. Beck's approach is inelegant because clients aren't given a healthy emotional response for situations where reality matches their distorted cognitions.

For example, let's say a college student fears failing a test. Then, she actually fails the test. Ellis wants the student to be ready so if she fails the test, she feels healthy sadness and disappointment, but still believes she's a valuable person (unconditional self-regard; USA). He doesn't want her to embrace ideas like, "I must pass the test" or "I must be loved" to be a valuable or worthy person (D. Shea, personal communication, August 15, 2016). For Ellis, pushing the conclusion, "You are a valuable person, no matter what happens" is more elegant than working with clients on their inaccurate information processing.

Meichenbaum's Self-Instructional Theory
Meichenbaum's cognitive self-instructional model emphasizes internal speech or verbal mediation. He wrote,

> [B]ehavior change occurs through a sequence of mediating processes involving the interaction of inner speech, cognitive structures, and behaviors and their resultant outcomes. (Meichenbaum, 1977, p. 218)

His model is a reciprocal one; it emphasizes an interactive relationship between the individual and the environment.

Meichenbaum's self-instructional model is one small step from behavior therapy. He takes inner speech or self-talk out of the client's head, bringing it into the therapy office. Then he works with clients to develop more adaptive speech. Finally, he works with clients to internalize these adaptive ways of talking to themselves.

Similar to REBT and cognitive therapy, **self-instructional training** (SIT) focuses on patterns of responding to stressful life events (e.g., activating events or emotional triggers). How clients handle stressful events is addressed in a three-stage sequence.

- **Preparation**: Inner speech that occurs before the stressful situation.

- **Coping**: Inner speech that occurs during the stressful situation.

- **Aftermath**: Inner speech that occurs after the stressful situation.

When clients learn to give themselves helpful instructions before, during, and after stressful events, the events are handled more smoothly and competently.

REFLECTIONS

Meichenbaum's model emphasizes inner speech. Is his model compatible with Ellis's and/or Beck's? Where would you place Meichenbaum's ongoing, coping-oriented inner speech in Ellis's ABC model and Beck's model?

Theories of Psychopathology

Cognitive theories of psychopathology were described in the preceding section. Here, we provide brief, contrasting summaries.

Ellis and REBT Psychopathology

Psychopathology is a function of irrational beliefs. Ellis summarized his views with his usual flair:

> [E]very single time my clients talk about their depression, obsession, or compulsion, I can quickly, when using RET, within a few minutes, zero in on one, or two, or three of their major musts: "I *must* do well; you *must* treat me beautifully; the world *must* be easy." I then show these clients that they have these *musts* and teach them to surrender them. Now, they have many subheadings and variations on their musts but they all seem to be variations on a major theme, which I call "musterbation, absolutistic thinking or dogma," which, I hypothesize, is at the core of human disturbance. (Ellis, 1987, p. 127)

To further capture his perspective, another quotation is pertinent: "I said many years ago, that masturbation is good and delicious, but musterbation is evil and pernicious" (Ellis, 1987, p. 127).

For Ellis, psychopathology is aligned with his basic REBT philosophies (USA, UOA, and ULA):

- USA: I *must* do well and be approved by *significant* others. This irrational belief leads to depression, anxiety, despair, and self-doubting. I have to do well or *I'm* no good.

- UOA: Other humans must, ought, and should treat me considerately and fairly. If they don't they should roast in hell. This belief results in anger, rage, and homicide.

- ULA: Conditions under which I live must give me what I want. If not, I can only be miserable or kill myself! This belief results in low frustration tolerance or poor coping (adapted from Ellis, 1987, p. 126).

Beck and Cognitive Psychopathology

Beck emphasized **cognitive distortions** or faulty assumptions and misconceptions. These distortions, triggered by external or internal events (e.g., a romantic break-up or drug/endocrine reaction), produce **automatic thoughts**, which are linked to **core beliefs or schemas**. Beck defined seven different types of cognitive distortions, some of which overlap with one another and are similar to Ellis's irrational beliefs (Beck, 1976). Other authors have identified up to 17 different distorted thinking styles (Burns, 1989; Leahy, 2003).

Beck also theorized that specific automatic thoughts and core beliefs were indicative of particular mental disorders (Beck, 1976). Early on, he identified a cognitive triad associated with depressive conditions. Beck's **negative cognitive triad** consists of:

- Negative evaluation of self: "I am unworthy."

- Negative evaluation of the world or specific events: "Everything is just more evidence that the world is falling apart."

- Negative evaluation of the future: "Nothing will ever get better."

To help make Beck's cognitive triad clearer, we like to present it as the adolescents with whom we work express it:

- I suck.

- The world sucks.

- Everything will always suck.

Beck's theoretical work on depression has had an immense impact on the formulation and treatment of depressive disorders.

Meichenbaum and Self-Instructional Psychopathology
Psychopathology is dysfunctional inner speech. Individuals with anxiety engage in disturbing inner speech long before facing stressful situations. To prepare for difficult situations they're saying unhelpful things to themselves (e.g., "Lions, tigers, and bears, oh my!"). Instead of engaging in coping self-talk during an incident, they may be engaging in a self-critique that takes away from their ability to deal with the situation. After the incident ends, people with mental health problems are probably talking to themselves about how they're failures who will never handle difficult tasks.

THE PRACTICE OF COGNITIVE BEHAVIOR THERAPY

Sometimes CBT seems ever so simple. It's as easy as 1, 2, 3:

1. Access clients' irrational or maladaptive thoughts or dysfunctional inner speech.

2. Instruct clients in more adaptive or more rational thinking and/or teach internal verbal instructional coping strategies.

3. Support clients as they apply these new and developing skills in their lives.

Unfortunately, cognitive therapy isn't as easy as it appears. Whatever model you follow, you'll need extensive training and supervision to achieve competence. In the now classic text *Cognitive Therapy of Depression*, Beck and his colleagues included an 85-point checklist to measure therapist competency (Beck et al., 1979).

CBT begins with the initial contact between therapist and client. During this initial contact cognitive behavior therapists focus on developing a positive therapy relationship and on educating clients about CBT (a sample excerpt from a cognitive behavior informed consent is included in Putting It in Practice 8.2).

PUTTING IT IN PRACTICE

8.2 Cognitive Behavior Informed Consent

I specialize in cognitive behavior therapy. Cognitive behavior therapy (or CBT for short) has more scientific research supporting its effectiveness than any other therapy approach.

CBT is an active, problem-focused approach to helping you improve your life. There are several important and unique parts of CBT.

CBT is collaborative: When many people think of therapy they sometimes think they'll be coming to see an all-knowing therapist who will make pronouncements about their problems. That's not the way CBT works. Instead, because you're the best expert on what's going on in your life, we'll work together to develop ideas and plans for how to reduce whatever symptoms or troubles you're having.

CBT is educational: As we work together, I'll share with you essential information about how thinking and behavior patterns effect emotions. This doesn't mean I'll be lecturing; I'll offer demonstrations about the ways in which situations, thoughts, behaviors, and emotions affect each other.

CBT is time-limited and active: Research shows that CBT is most effective when we work together actively to address your problems. This means there will be outside-session projects or homework. I'll be coach and cheerleader to help you face problems and complete your homework.

CBT focuses on current thoughts and behaviors: Most people develop problems due to events that happened during childhood or due to traumatic experiences. Even though your past is important, we'll spend most of our time talking about what's happening right now in your life.

CBT is not for everyone: Although CBT has more scientific evidence behind it than any other treatment approach, it's not perfect for everyone. You may have uncomfortable reactions to some parts of CBT. When this happens I want you to tell me; hopefully we can work it through. Therapy isn't always comfortable and I'll be encouraging you to face and deal with problems that are blocking you from what you want in life. However, if you have strong cultural or personal values that don't fit well with CBT, we should talk, and I can connect you with a professional who can provide the treatment you want.

I look forward to working with you to solve your problems. Please feel free to ask me questions at any time. My goal is for us to work together to achieve your treatment goals.

Assessment Issues and Procedures

According to Ledley, Marx, and Heimberg (2010), two primary goals are associated with CBT assessment.

1. Arriving at a diagnosis that best describes client symptoms.

2. Developing a tentative cognitive behavioral treatment formulation that can be used for treatment planning (p. 40).

To accomplish these goals, cognitive behavior therapists employ various assessment strategies. These strategies include collaborative interviewing, setting an agenda, developing an initial problem list, self-rating scales, cognitive behavioral self-monitoring, and case formulation.

Collaborative Interviewing

CBT practitioners are collaborative. They also value the therapy relationship and take care to establish rapport and an alliance in the initial interview (Dobson & Dobson, 2017; Friedberg & McClure, 2015). That said, some (probably a minority of) CBT practitioners consider the therapy relationship to be secondary. This is because CBT has remediation of client problems as its primary focus (Kazdin, 2007). As we'll discuss later, Ellis is the main voice that advocated for less emphasis on the therapy relationship. His main reasoning was that he didn't want clients to become dependent upon him for their irrational love and acceptance needs (Shea, 2016).

Cognitive behavior therapists emphasize collaboration. The client and therapist join together to identify and move toward treatment goals. Practitioners using the Beck or Meichenbaum models generally use collaborative empiricism; in contrast, REBT practitioners may use more authority-based interventions to work toward what Ellis considered an elegant solution.

Setting the Agenda

CBT is agenda-driven. Therapist and client collaboratively engage in **setting the agenda** for the session during the first few minutes. During an initial session the therapist might begin with an organizing statement:

> Welcome to therapy. We have a number of items to take care of today, but there's also flexibility. The first two items on my list are the consent form and confidentiality. After that I'd like to ask you questions about the problems and symptoms that bring you to therapy. Toward the end we can talk about an initial plan for how we can best address the problems we discuss today. How does that sound to you?

Depending on the therapist's style and preference a more formal structured clinical interview might be used (e.g., the *Structured Clinical Interview for DSM-5*; aka

SCID-5-CV; First, Williams, Karg, & Spitzer, 2016) or a less formal interview loosely focused on generating a problem list could be initiated (Dobson & Dobson, 2017; J. Sommers-Flanagan & Sommers-Flanagan, 2017).

The Problem List

A central assessment task is to establish a clear and comprehensive problem list. A **problem list** includes client concerns described in simple, descriptive, concrete terms. Persons and Tompkins (1997) recommended including about five to eight items on a problem list. Susanna, a 25-year-old heterosexual female, generated the following problem list during an initial interview:

1. *Depressive thoughts*: Susanna reports depressive thoughts. She believes she is worthless (negative evaluation of self), that the world is a rotten place (negative evaluation of the world), and that her life will stay miserable (negative evaluation of the future).

2. *Social isolation*: She is greatly dissatisfied with her social life. She has social contact outside of work only once weekly or less.

3. *Procrastination and lack of self-discipline*: She struggles with timely payment of bills, keeping her house clean, personal hygiene, and organization.

4. *Internet preoccupation*: She spends many hours a day on the Internet. She enjoys this, but her Internet activity increases markedly when she needs to pay bills, has a social opportunity, or is facing deadlines.

5. *Lack of academic progress*: She would like to finish her bachelor's degree, but after enrolling quits attending class.

6. *Disrupted sleep patterns*: She has difficulty sleeping.

Generating a problem list is helpful in several ways. First, it gives therapists a chance to show interest in and compassion for clients. Second, as clients describe their problems, cognitive and behavioral antecedents and consequences are identified and initial hypotheses about client core beliefs can be generated. Third, as therapists use Socratic questioning to explore problems, clients become oriented to the CBT process.

Greenberger and Padesky (2016) provided specific examples of questions for exploring client automatic thoughts. These questions can be used in an interview or as part of the automatic thought section of a client's thought record; they help elucidate the client's cognitive world:

- What was going through your mind just before you started to feel this way?

- What images or memories do you have in this situation?

- What does this mean about you ... your life ... your future?

- What are you afraid might happen?

- What is the worst thing that could happen?

- What does this mean about the other person(s) or people in general?

- Did you break any rules, hurt others, or not do something you should have done? (adapted from Greenberger & Padesky, 2016, p. 54).

In Susanna's case, she reported feeling like "a loser" who had "no willpower" and who had always "been a miserable failure at initiating social relationships." She also thought others were critiquing her inadequacies. These core beliefs became the main target for change in therapy.

Self-Rating Scales

At the beginning and throughout therapy, cognitive behavior therapists use self-rating scales. For example, Beck developed the widely used *Beck Depression Inventory* (*BDI*; now *BDI-II*) to evaluate and monitor depression during treatment (Beck, Ward, Mendelson, Mock, & Erbaugh, 1961). Empirically minded therapists often have clients complete the BDI at the beginning of each session. Similar rating scales include the *Beck Anxiety Inventory* (Beck, Epstein, Brown, & Steer, 1988), the *Penn State Worry Questionnaire* (Meyer, Miller, Metzger, & Borkovec, 1990), and the *Children's Depression Inventory* (Kovacs, 1992).

Cognitive Behavioral Self-Monitoring

Cognitive behavioral self-monitoring is a method for helping clients to develop awareness of automatic thoughts, automatic behaviors, and associated emotions.

Cognitive behavioral self-monitoring begins within therapy sessions, but self-monitoring homework is also important (Kazantzis et al., 2016).

Many different cognitive behavioral self-monitoring procedures are available. Persons (1989) recommended using a generic "thought record." A **thought record** is a system for clients to record the following information immediately after experiencing a strong emotional response:

- Date and time of the emotional response.

- Situation that elicited the emotional response.

- Behaviors the client engaged in.

- Emotions that were elicited.

- Associated thoughts that occurred during the situation.

- Other related responses.

The thought record provides a foundation for cognitive interventions. Therapists can transform generic thought records into specific theory-based tools by having clients use the language of automatic thoughts, cognitive distortions, and rational responses. Table 8.1 is a sample of a generic thought record. Therapists operating from an REBT perspective would use the ABCDEF model (Ellis, 1999a).

Many self-monitoring mobile phone "apps" are now available. In a recent review, Huguet et al. (2016) identified 117 different mobile telephone apps available for self-monitoring/self-help for depression. Of these, only 12 were consistent with evidence-based practice, but no effectiveness or efficacy studies using the different apps were available. Consequently, they didn't recommend general clinical use of phone apps to monitor or implement CBT.

Table 8.1 Thought Record Sample

Situation	Emotion	Automatic thoughts	Cognitive distortion	Rational response	Outcome/new feeling
Briefly describe the situation linked to the unpleasant emotion	Specify and rate the emotion (Sad, Anxious, Angry) on a 0–100 scale	State the automatic thought that accompanied the emotion (Note: You could add automatic behaviors here too)	Classify the cognitive distortion present within the automatic thought	Replace the automatic thought (or behavior) with a more rational (or adaptive) response	Rate the feelings again to see if the rational response modified them
Home alone on Saturday night	Sad: 85	"I'm always alone. No one will ever love me. No one will ever want to be with me."	Dichotomous thinking and catastrophizing	Being home alone is better than being with someone I don't like. Not being in a relationship now doesn't mean I'll never be in one.	Sad: 45

REFLECTIONS

Can you imagine using a cognitive self-monitoring log or thought record on a regular basis? What might stop you from using this assessment procedure on yourself? What would motivate you to use a thought record?

Case Formulation

Cognitive behavior therapists emphasize case formulation (aka case conceptualization) as an essential bridge from assessment to treatment. A **CBT case formulation** identifies an underlying psychological (cognitive and behavioral) mechanism and describes how they are maintaining client problems. Case formulations help practitioners develop treatment plans that address client issues.

Persons (2008) described four key elements for CBT case formulations:

1. Creating a problem list.
2. Identifying mechanisms underlying or causing disorders and problems.
3. Identifying precipitants activating current client problems.
4. Consideration of the origins of the client's current problems.

You may be surprised to see a CBT problem formulation that includes "consideration of the origins of the client's current problems." Consistent with Beck's original work, cognitive therapists are open to talking about the past—even though the past is not a primary focus. Cognitive behavior therapists focus on the past when (a) clients want to, (b) clients are stuck in dysfunctional thinking, or (c) cases are especially complex (J. S. Beck, 2011). Talking about the past can facilitate rapport and give therapists greater insight into the thoughts and behaviors that are maintaining the problem in the present.

Psychoeducation

Psychoeducation is an educational process that focuses on information about client diagnosis, treatment process, prognosis, and intervention strategies (J. Sommers-Flanagan & Sommers-Flanagan, 2017). Cognitive behavior therapists consider psychoeducation an essential treatment component (J. S. Beck, 2005, 2011; Dobson & Dobson, 2017). Just as physicians educate patients about medical rationale, problems, and procedures, cognitive behavior therapists educate their clients about their treatment (CBT) rationale, problems, and procedures.

Psychoeducation for CBT Rationale

Lecturing clients is not desirable (Ledley et al., 2010). Instead, many therapists use stories, demonstrations, and life examples to illustrate CBT rationale (Friedberg & McClure, 2015). We sometimes use a "bump in the night" scenario to discuss how cognition can influence emotion.

Therapist: I know it's hard to believe that what you think has such a big influence on your emotions. Let me give you an example.

Client: Okay.

Therapist: Let's say you're lying in bed at night, trying to go to sleep, and suddenly, from nowhere, you hear a thud in your house. What would you feel?

Client: I'd be terrified.

Therapist: Okay, so the first thing that comes to mind is that you'd feel scared. What if you were taking care of a pesky dog for a friend of yours, how would you feel then?

Client: Well, if I knew it was the dog, then I'd feel annoyed. I'd feel irritated that the dog was making noise while I'm trying to sleep.

Therapist: Perfect. So, it's not the thud that produces your emotion, but the thoughts you have about the thud. Tell me, when you said you'd "be terrified" in reaction to the thud, what thoughts were you imagining?

Client: I thought the thud meant a burglar had broken into my house. Then I'd be scared.

Therapist: Exactly. Without knowing what caused the thud, you inserted a burglar, and that would, of course, produce fear. But if you think it's a pesky dog, then you feel annoyed. What if your grandmother was staying with you and you heard a thud, what might come to mind then?

Client: I'd be worried that she might have hurt herself. I'd get up and go check on her.

Therapist: So, what you think not only directly affects your emotions, but also your behavior, because if you thought it was a burglar you might do something different, right?

Client: I'd hide under the covers in my bed and call 911!

Therapist: Right. That's one option. But my point is that it's not the thud that produces your emotions and behavior, it's what you're thinking about a situation. It's your assumption or beliefs about the situation that cause you to feel and act in particular ways.

Client: I see what you mean.

In this example the therapist used Socratic questioning and dialogue to educate the client about the cognitive theory of emotional disturbance.

Psychoeducation about Client Problems

J. Beck (2005) provided an example of using psychoeducation to discuss depression.

Therapist: You know, these are all important questions you have, essential questions. And I think therapy can help you figure out some of the answers, though many of us struggle with them to some degree throughout our lives. (Pause.) What we've found, though, is that people find these questions almost impossible to answer when they're depressed. (Pause.) Once they get [therapy] for the depression and the depression lifts, then they have more success.

Arthur: Hmmm.

Therapist: What do you think about that? (p. 148)

This is a good template for how psychoeducation can occur during CBT. In the midst of assessment or therapy, the therapist senses a need to provide information and does so slowly and clearly. Then the therapist checks to determine the client's reaction. This process is crucial because it's important to know how clients are reacting to psychoeducation.

Psychoeducation for CBT Rationale, Client Problems, and CBT Procedures
The following excerpt illustrates how a skilled cognitive-behavior therapist can simultaneously provide psychoeducation about CBT rationale, client problems (i.e., anxiety and avoidance), and CBT procedure (i.e., exposure):

Clinician: You've mentioned your problems with anxiety. One big research finding about anxiety is that it tends to lead to something called avoidance behaviors. Have you noticed yourself avoiding things?

Mitchell: Yeah. I feel anxious in groups, so I avoid groups. I also feel anxious around women, so I avoid them too.

Clinician: I know you're here to work on anxiety, so this question might seem silly, but what's the pay off for avoiding the things that trigger your anxiety? [The therapist wants the client to dig into a potential rationale for avoidance.]

Mitchell: I feel better. If I can avoid the anxious things, I don't feel as much anxiety.

Clinician: So avoidance feels good, probably mostly in the short run. What about avoidance in the long run. [This is Socratic questioning.]

Mitchell: Not so good. Avoidance makes my life so small. I want to get stronger and braver. [Like with motivational interviewing, it's best if the client makes the case for change.]

Clinician: That seems to be the case for lots of people. Avoidance feels good in the moment, but it can start to control you and feel restrictive, that you're not all that keen on avoidance as a longer term strategy. [The therapist is mostly paraphrasing the limited usefulness of avoidance behavior.]

Mitchell: Right. But my anxiety is so terrible.

Clinician: What would do you think you need to do to make your anxiety less terrible?

Mitchell: Face it. That's why I'm here.

Clinician: You're totally right. It's pretty much impossible to get over anxiety through avoidance. That's why part of our therapy will involve exposure. We'll do some pretend or imaginary exposures to the things that trigger anxiety and then we'll do some direct exposures too. We'll have you do the scary things to prove you can handle them. [Now the therapist makes a pitch for exposure treatment.]

Mitchell: Right. I don't want to face my anxiety, but I really want to face it too.

Clinician: How about this? We'll start making a plan for you to confront your anxiety, but as we talk, I'm sure you'll start having some negative thoughts about how this won't work, or how you're too weak, or other thoughts that could—if you listen to them too closely—might sabotage our work. Will you share those thoughts with me as they come up?

Mitchell: They're already coming up.

Clinician: Great. Let's start there.

Following this exchange, intermittent psychoeducation continues throughout therapy.

Methods for Exploring and Identifying Automatic Thoughts and Core Beliefs

Early CBT work often focuses on helping clients develop awareness of their automatic thoughts and core beliefs. Sometimes clients develop this awareness quickly. For other clients, developing cognitive awareness is more challenging. Fortunately, many techniques exist for helping clients become more tuned into their cognitions (Leahy, 2003).

Guessing the Thought
Clients can have difficulty identifying the thoughts that underlie their emotions and behaviors. When this occurs, J. Beck (2011) recommended the strategy of guessing the thought. When **guessing the thought**, therapists use their knowledge and experience to make an educated guess at the content of the client's underlying thought. We've found this strategy useful in our work with adolescents who have anger and aggression issues.

John: You said you end up in fights even when you didn't even plan to get in a fight. What thoughts are usually going through your head when that happens?

Pedro: I don't know. I just black out.

John: What might the other person say that gets you so mad you black out? [John hits a dead end regarding exploration of thoughts; he shifts to exploring a concrete anger trigger; information about specific anger triggers can help with later efforts to guess underlying thoughts.]

Pedro: If somebody disses my family. Then I'm all over them.

John: So if someone disses your family. But, what does that make you think? Like, someone says something nasty about your mom. What goes through your mind? [John goes for underlying thoughts again.]

Pedro: I don't know. I just go crazy on them.

John: Let me take a guess. Is that okay with you? [John asks permission to take a guess.]

Pedro: Fine with me.

John: Maybe you start thinking, "That F—ing son of a B— has got no business saying that sh—. I'm gonna teach that A— a lesson for saying that." [John uses profanity to show empathy for the thoughts or inner speech the client is likely experiencing.]

Pedro: Yeah (smiles). That's exactly what I'm thinking.

In this case it was easy for John to take an educated guess about what the young man was thinking. When doing this technique with youth who get extremely angry it helps to throw in profanity because that's the type of self-talk that gets activated in provocative situations (J. Sommers-Flanagan, Richardson, & Sommers-Flanagan, 2011).

Vertical Descent (aka the Downward Arrow)

The purpose of **vertical descent** or **downward arrow** is to uncover underlying core beliefs (Burns, 1989; McLachlan, Eastwood, & Friedberg, 2016).

Therapist: You said you fear you might have cancer, even though the doctor has reassured you that you're okay. What would it mean to you if you did have cancer?

Patient: I'd be afraid I might die.

Therapist: Almost everyone fears dying, at least a little. But let me ask you about your particular fears of dying. Complete this sentence: "I'd be afraid of dying because …"

Patient: I'd be afraid I wasn't really dead—that I was only in a coma—and that I would wake from the coma in my grave, buried alive (Burns, 1989, p. 20).

This is a great illustration of how sometimes client underlying fears or beliefs can be different from what we expect.

Chasing Cognitive Distortions

In the early 1960s, Beck began identifying *cognitive distortions* associated with mental and emotional problems (Beck, 1976). Following Beck, other authors have also written about these distortions (see Burns, 1989; Leahy, 2003). Five common cognitive distortions are given in Table 8.2.

Table 8.2   Five Common Cognitive Distortions in CBT

The following cognitive distortions are adapted from Leahy (2003) and Beck (1976). Leahy's book, *Cognitive Therapy Techniques: A Practitioner's Guide*, includes more than 100 techniques and many useful forms for assigning CBT homework. Leahy (2003) lists 17 possible cognitive distortions, but only five are listed here.

Dichotomous or polarized thinking: People and situations are evaluated as black or white, good or bad. Clients with polarized (aka black–white) thinking come often to either love or hate their therapist, with automatic thoughts like "This is the best therapist ever. She's incredible." Similarly, situations are described as "wonderful" or "terrible."

Labeling and mislabeling: Labels are used inaccurately, with emotional cost. For example, when a client consistently labels himself a "loser" or a "wimp," the labels can have a negative effect on client behavior and may be linked to depression. Overly positive labels can have maladaptive features (e.g., a woman with narcissistic qualities labels herself "The Queen").

Magnification and minimization: Also known as *overestimation and underestimation*. It occurs when clients make a mountain out of a molehill (and vice versa). When clients exaggerate the likelihood that they will flunk a test, magnification has occurred. When clients minimize the extent of their hard work, minimization has occurred. Magnification is common among anxiety disorders and this style is also known as **catastrophizing**.

Mind reading: This involves clients thinking they know what other people think. For example, clients might conclude: "He thinks I'm a loser" or "I can tell she doesn't like me." Although these thoughts may or may not be accurate, clients who use this distortion are fairly certain their mind reading assumptions are correct.

Personalization: Clients using this distortion tend to take everything personally. If someone doesn't say hello, they conclude it's their fault. If the cashier gives them back incorrect change, they think the person is purposely taking advantage of them for some specific reason. Automatic thoughts might include, "I know she's out to get me; she's been out to get me ever since I came in this store."

Cognitive distortions are typically related to core beliefs or self-schema. All of the techniques discussed in this chapter can help reveal cognitive distortions. Once distortions are clarified and clients become aware of them, therapists can use many different techniques to question the validity or utility of these distortions. Leahy (2003) recommended:

1. *Conducting a cost–benefit analysis (to mind reading)*: Do you think mind reading (or another distorted thinking style) gives you valuable information? How would your thoughts, feelings, and behavior change if you did less mind reading?

2. *Applying the double standard technique (to dichotomous thinking)*: Would everyone see it this way? Why not? How might someone else describe this situation?

There are many other techniques for exploring the validity and usefulness of particular cognitive distortions (see J. S. Beck, 2011; Dobson & Dobson, 2017; Leahy, 2003).

Specific Therapy Techniques

There are numerous, highly accessible, and highly practical cognitive therapy techniques practitioners can employ. The following techniques come from Ellis, Beck, and Meichenbaum, but many other excellent resources for specific CBT techniques are available.

Vigorous and Forceful Disputing

Albert Ellis described vigorous and forceful disputing in a book titled *Favorite Counseling and Therapy Techniques* (Rosenthal, 1999). **Vigorous and forceful disputing** involves clients offering a forceful and rational counterattack against their irrational beliefs.

Ellis suggested explaining to clients that "vigorous, forceful, and persistent" disputing of irrational beliefs is often needed to "actually replace them with rational beliefs" (Ellis, 1999b, p. 76). Clients are provided with written instructions, encouraging them to partake in this homework assignment:

> One way to do highly powerful, vigorous disputing is to use a tape recorder and to record one of your strong Irrational Beliefs into it, such as, "If I fail this job interview I am about to have, that will prove that I'll never get a good job and that I might as well apply only for low-level positions!" Figure out several Disputes to the Irrational Belief and strongly present them on this same tape. For example: "Even if I do poorly on this interview, that only will show that I failed this time, but never will show that I'll always fail and can never do well in other interviews. Maybe they'll still hire me for the job. But if they don't, I can learn by my mistakes, can do better in other interviews, and likely can get the kind of job I want."

> Listen to your Disputing. Let other people, including your therapist or members of your therapy group, listen to it. Do it over in a more forceful and vigorous manner and let them listen to it again, to see if you do it better and more forcefully, until they agree that you are getting more powerful at doing it. Keep listening to it until you see that you are able to convince yourself and others that your Disputing is becoming more and more powerful and more convincing. (Ellis, 1999b, pp. 76–77)

Ellis's homework involves repeated practice at forceful cognitive disputations. This assignment flows from his therapy style: if clients can mount a forceful and rational counterattack against their irrational beliefs, they can minimize and eliminate irrational thinking.

Shame Attacking

In 1968, Ellis created his "now famous shame-attacking exercise" (Ellis & MacLaren, 2005, p. 95). Therapists may assign shame attacking exercises or clients may create them independently as a self-help activity. **Shame attacking exercises** are defined as situations where clients intentionally act in ways that are socially inappropriate in public settings. The purpose is for clients to learn to accept themselves while tolerating discomfort. Common shame attacking exercises include singing in public, wearing bizarre clothing, and shouting out the time in a classroom or crowded public setting. Robertson (2010) noted that shame attacking dates back to the ancient Cynic philosophers who intentionally practiced extreme shamelessness.

Practitioners trained at the Ellis Institute are often assigned shame attacking exercises. After training with Ellis himself, a colleague of ours reported that Ellis had given him in vivo and imaginal shame attacking exercises. This colleague found the experience invigorating and was impressed with how quickly and efficiently Ellis was able to inspire him to get to work on his irrational shame. Looking back to behavior therapy (Chapter 7), it seems obvious that Ellis was a master at practicing a "no holds barred" form of direct, imaginal exposure.

Thinking in Shades of Gray or Graduated Thinking

Beck and colleagues (1979) identified dichotomous thinking as a cognitive distortion associated with depression. Dichotomous thinking is the tendency to perceive everything in absolutistic black–white terms. The recommended intervention for dichotomous thinking is to demonstrate to clients, via Socratic questioning and collaborative empiricism, that "events may be evaluated on a continuum" (Beck et al., 1979, p. 261).

One technique—with several names—is commonly used with clients who present with dichotomous thinking. Burns (1989) referred to the technique as **thinking in shades of gray**; Judith Beck called it a **cognitive continuum** to modify beliefs; Dobson and Dobson (2017) used the term **graduated thinking**. This technique involves taking automatic thoughts, assumptions, or conclusions about a specific event or performance and placing them on a concrete, measurable scale. The technique often begins with a verbal inquiry and client response:

Therapist: You said you've been suicidal before, what helped then?

Client: Nothing. Nothing ever helps.

This is a common response from an extremely depressed client. The next steps involve expressing empathy and building a continuum.

Therapist: I hear you saying nothing ever helps. That feels very discouraging.

Client: It's true.

Therapist: I see. I believe it feels totally true to you. But I'd still like to go over some of the different things you've tried. You mentioned exercising and talking with friends and medication and therapy. If we line those up, which would you say was the absolute worst and least helpful? (Adapted from J. Sommers-Flanagan & Sommers-Flanagan, 2017.)

You may notice that the therapist focused first on what was "worst." With an extremely depressed client, this is important because the worst option will resonate with their negatively biased information processing.

There are many other ways to build a continuum or help clients think in shades of gray. One of the upcoming chapter vignettes provides another example.

Stress Inoculation Training

Stress inoculation training (SIT) is a three-phase method to help clients with stress management (Meichenbaum, 1985, 1996; Novaco, 1979).

1. *Conceptualization*: This phase includes (a) developing a collaborative relationship, and (b) using Socratic questioning to educate clients about stress and how to view stressful situations as "problems-to-be-solved" (Meichenbaum, 1996, p. 4). When stress is viewed as a challenge, the therapist begins assisting clients in formulating methods for preparing for, confronting, and reflecting on stressful experiences.

2. *Skills acquisition and rehearsal*: Specific coping skills are taught and practiced in the office and eventually in vivo. Skills taught are related to the individual's problems. Examples include relaxation training, self-instruction, emotional self-regulation, and communication skills.

3. *Application and follow-through*: Clients apply their new coping skills to increasingly challenging stressors. Personal experiments are used to help inoculate

clients from later stressful situations. Relapse prevention strategies, attribution procedures (in which clients take credit for their accomplishments), and booster sessions are built into the final phase of SIT.

The unique component of Meichenbaum's theory is his emphasis on three types of self-statements. For example, counselors teach clients preparation self-statements. **Preparation self-statements** are internal self-instructions that prepare clients for a challenging situation. Here's an anger example:

- This could be a rough situation, but I know how to deal with it.
- I can work out a plan to handle this. Easy does it.
- Remember, stick to the issues and don't take it personally (Novaco, 1979, p. 269).

Counselors also teach **coping self-statements**; these are internal instructions that focus on how to deal effectively in the moment:

- My muscles are getting tight. Relax and slow things down.
- Time to take a deep breath. Let's take the issue point by point.
- I'm [dealing] with [this] constructively (Novaco, 1979, p. 269).

Finally, counselors teach clients to use **reinforcing self-statements**; these are internal statements that focus on positive outcomes and look to a positive future:

- I did all right. I stayed calm.
- I can do even better next time if I focus more on my breathing.

Stress inoculation training has empirical support for treating stress and preventing post-traumatic stress disorder (Hourani et al., 2016; Saunders, Driskell, Hall, & Salas, 1996). The application of self-instructional procedures in the treatment of children with impulsive behavioral problems continues to influence current treatment and research, but outcomes in that area have been mixed (Kendall, 2000).

Other Cognitive Techniques

There are many more cognitive techniques available to cognitive therapists. Most of these techniques focus on using mental strategies—usually verbal, linguistic, or based on visual imagery—to manage or eliminate problematic symptoms.

Cognitive Behavior Therapy in Action: Brief Vignettes

One fascinating thing about doing counseling or psychotherapy from different theoretical perspectives is that you can get really good at focusing on different dimensions of human functioning. In the following vignettes three techniques for focusing on cognitions are illustrated. Although these techniques focus on cognitions, cognitions are always linked with situations, behaviors, and emotions. Cognitive behavior therapists can use cognitions narrowly or to initiate a focus on multiple dimensions of human functioning.

Vignette I: Generating Alternative Interpretations

In Chapter 7 we gave an example of the technique of generating behavioral alternatives. **Generating alternative interpretations** is based on the same model, with the specific focus being on thoughts or interpretations rather than behaviors.

Generating alternative interpretations is a useful technique with clients who hold maladaptive or irrational automatic thoughts despite the fact that other, more reasonable, explanations exist. As McMillin (1986) noted, the first interpretation of a scene is often the worst, most negative, or most catastrophic. Unfortunately, first interpretations can be difficult to counter. This technique teaches clients to immediately counter first interpretations with at least four reasonable alternatives, using the following guidelines:

1. Clients keep a written log of the worst emotions experienced during a 1-week period. This log includes a brief description of the activating event or situation and a brief description of the first interpretation (what Ellis would call an iB).

2. At the next session homework is reviewed and clients are given an additional assignment: "After logging your initial interpretation, add four different but equally plausible interpretations." The following example is adapted from McMillin (1986):

   Situation: Sophia, a single 25-year-old female just broke up with her boyfriend.

   First interpretation: There's something wrong with me. I'm inadequate. I'll never find a life partner.

   Alternative interpretations:

   - I haven't met the right guy.

   - I'm not interested in giving up my freedom right now.

   - My boyfriend and I didn't have the right chemistry.

   - My boyfriend was afraid of commitment (McMillin, 1986, p. 12).

3. At the next session, the therapist (Karla) helps determine which interpretation has the most supporting evidence. She guides Sophia through an objective review of data rather than subjective impressions or hunches by asking questions like:

   - What's the evidence supporting the possibility that there's something wrong with you and you'll never have a long-term relationship?

   - How about the idea that you haven't met the right guy? What evidence do you have to support that?

4. Sophia is instructed to continue using this four alternative interpretation procedure when an emotionally distressing event occurs. Additionally, she's coached to write down alternative interpretations, but to wait and decide which interpretation is best only after time has passed to distance her from the event. Karla asks Sophia to practice this procedure with every upsetting event for the next month until it becomes an automatic response (McMillin, 1986).

Like generating behavioral alternatives (see Chapter 7), this technique is especially useful with adolescents. In a series of studies, it was demonstrated that youths with aggressive behavior problems often are engaging in the **misattribution of hostility**; they quickly and incorrectly interpret the behavior of other youths as hostile (Dodge, 1980; Dodge & Frame, 1982; Dodge & Somberg, 1987). For example, if a youth who often behaves aggressively is walking through the hall at school and another student bumps him, the youth is likely to attribute the bump to an intentional hostile act. This attribution increases the likelihood of retaliation.

In our work with aggressive youths, we've used this technique with two minor modifications. First, in-session we use a stopwatch to add real-world pressure to the process: "Okay, you've got 60 seconds to come up with as many alternative explanations as possible. Starting now!" Second, we sometimes add incentives (stickers, money, sports/entertainment cards) to enhance motivation: "I'll give you one baseball card for every 'good' alternative you come up with" (J. Sommers-Flanagan & Sommers-Flanagan, 2007b).

Vignette II: Thinking in Shades of Gray and Exploring the Consequences of Giving Up the "Should" Rule

Jackson, a 35-year-old engineer, was referred to therapy because his perfectionistic standards were causing extremely slow work performance. He was also experiencing various depressive symptoms, most of which seemed related to work. He produced the following written description of himself and his core beliefs or self-schema:

I'm defective. To prove I'm not defective, I have to do a better, higher quality job on my work than everyone

Table 8.3   Jackson's "Dichotomous" Rating Scale

96–100	Complete success
75–95	Complete failure
50–74	Complete failure
25–49	Complete failure
0–24	Complete failure

else. Every task I do must be flawless, or it's more proof that I'm defective. Accomplishing one or two tasks perfectly isn't sufficient. I've got to keep being perfect ... or I've failed. To fail at one task is to fail altogether."

Jackson was suffering from a terrible case of the "tyranny of the shoulds" (Horney, 1950). Although several cognitive and behavioral procedures are employed in his overall treatment, we started with thinking in shades of gray.

Jackson's therapist worked with him to develop a 100-point performance rating scale. Initially, Jackson confided that a normal scale might include ratings from zero to 100, but for him the meaning of each rating from zero to 95 would be "failure." To illustrate, he drew the scale shown in Table 8.3.

In Jackson's cognitive world, the only way to achieve complete success was to have a performance in the 96 to 100 range.

Collaborating with his therapist, Jackson developed a new rating scale that he could experiment with when evaluating his work-related performance. His new scale is shown in Table 8.4.

Jackson's new scale represented a compromise between him and his therapist. To continue thinking in shades of gray, Jackson took his new scale for a "test drive," using it for a week at work. His assignment was to rate himself using this new scale and to occasionally double-check his ratings with his supervisor's feedback. To Jackson's surprise, his supervisor always rated the quality of his performance in the top two categories. Jackson also discovered that all of his self-ratings were also in the top two categories. Even more important, Jackson's supervisor was pleased that Jackson was completing his projects more quickly.

This technique is a variation of response prevention discussed by Beck and colleagues (Beck et al., 1979; Shaw

Table 8.4   Jackson's "Shades of Gray" Rating Scale

96–100	Complete success
85–95	Partial success
75–84	Marginally acceptable
0–74	Complete failure

& Beck, 1977). It was employed in Jackson's case because much more work was needed to help him change his self-schema. Specifically, Jackson was instructed to clearly verbalize his "should" rule, to predict what would happen if the should was not followed, to carry out an experiment to test the prediction, and to revise his should rule according to the outcome of the experiment (Beck et al., 1979, p. 255).

Jackson was given a series of activities to test his should statement: "Every task I do must be flawless, or it's more proof that I'm defective." He predicted that he might receive a reprimand from his boss if he ignored this should and turned in poor-quality work. His homework was to perform several work tasks as quickly as he could, while keeping his overall work quality within the 75 to 84 "marginally acceptable" range. Jackson successfully completed this test of his should rule and discovered that instead of receiving a reprimand from his boss, he received a pat on the back for a job well done.

CASE PRESENTATION

In Chapter 7, we described the first three sessions of the case of Richard, a 56-year-old professor at a vocational college who referred himself for CBT due to recurring panic attacks. This case continues, with a focus on cognitive components of Richard's treatment.

The Problem List

Five items were included on Richard's initial problem list. The main cognitive item was Problem 1:

1. *Specific fears of having a panic attack*: Fear of a heart attack, fear of death, and fear of public humiliation.

Richard believed his physical symptoms signal an imminent heart attack. This can be viewed as either an irrational or maladaptive belief. The following sessions address many issues, including Richard's belief that he will have a heart attack and die.

Session 4. Richard's homework was reviewed. Between sessions he had one full-blown panic attack and two minor incidents that he coped with using diaphragmatic breathing. He reported no caffeine or other stimulants. He also reported practicing diaphragmatic breathing 12 times over the 7 days. During his major panic episode, Richard was out with his wife shopping, became separated from her, and then began worrying about her because she never leaves him alone when they're out together. The entries in his panic log included several references to catastrophic thoughts and overestimations (see the Problem Formulation section for more on these distorted thinking processes).

The first item on the Session 4 agenda was a review of Richard's homework. This review stimulated a psycho-educational discussion about maladaptive thoughts.

Therapist: I see here on your panic logs that when you got separated from your wife, Linda, your mind started running a hundred miles an hour. Tell me about what you were thinking and feeling when you couldn't find her.

Richard: She said she was just going to the restroom. I was browsing around the restrooms and never saw her come out. I kept waiting and waiting; it felt like forever. I got all worked up. Ever since this panic stuff started, she's been my constant companion. When she didn't come out I kept thinking that she must be hurt or sick or, my God, that maybe she was passed out or dead. I finally got a woman to go in and check on her, and she wasn't in there, and then my mind really started racing. I thought she'd left me. I was sure that she'd gotten sick and tired of dealing with me and had snuck away. [Richard does a nice job articulating his anxiety-producing thoughts.]

Therapist: Where was she?

Richard: Oh, I guess there was an elderly woman in the bathroom who had gotten confused, and Linda took her to the help desk and they asked a bunch of questions. She felt terrible about being gone so long, but she had to help this woman, and then the woman got frightened and didn't want her to leave. I must have wandered away a little ways when Linda came out with the woman, since I never saw them at all.

Therapist: How did you and Linda get back together and then what happened?

Richard: Linda found me in a cold sweat by the restrooms. I was trying to figure out why she would leave me and was imagining life without her. She dashed up and started explaining, but I was in such a panic, I just had to go home. I couldn't focus and breathe and calm down. I had to go home to settle down. I'm sorry.

Therapist: It sounds like that was terribly frightening. There's no need to apologize. Like we've talked about before, those false panic alarms aren't going away all at once. You've been making great progress. What's important is that we take a good look at what happened and learn from it so you can keep getting the upper hand on the panic.

Richard: But I can't help feeling I disappointed myself and you, too.

Therapist: Well, overall, it looks like you had an excellent week. You practiced the diaphragmatic breathing and used it to calm yourself. And we can use the incident that happened with Linda to understand even more about what's causing the panic. [The therapist provides an in-session counter to Richard's overestimation of the importance of his panic attack.]

Richard: You think so?

Therapist: Absolutely. The next item on today's agenda is for us to talk about this thing we call "automatic thoughts." As most people go through the day, things happen and then their minds quickly produce automatic thoughts about whatever just happened. When you were waiting for Linda and she didn't come out, you immediately concluded that something terrible was wrong. You thought she was hurt or sick or dead in the bathroom. Those are extremely stressful thoughts. And when the woman went in there and told you the bathroom was empty, your first thought was that Linda was so sick of you that she had up and left you. Is that right?

Richard: Yeah. That's right.

Therapist: Okay, now that you're calm, I want to ask some questions about what you were thinking in the store. Ready?

Richard: Yeah.

Therapist: Has Linda ever gotten hurt or injured in a public restroom before? [Socratic questioning begins.]

Richard: No. I know. That's a crazy thing for me to think.

Therapist: Actually, it's not totally crazy, it's just an over-estimation. Based on the fact that she's in good health and the fact that this has never happened before makes the odds that she would get hurt in the bathroom very unlikely. Possible, but very unlikely.

Richard: Okay.

Therapist: Another question: Do you think you can tell the difference between a thought and a fact?

Richard: I'm not sure what you mean.

Therapist: This happens to lots of people. We have a thought—yours was that Linda got hurt and maybe even died in the bathroom. But that's not a fact. One thing that helps people sometimes is to get clear in your mind about the difference between a thought and a fact.

Richard: I think I follow.

Therapist: Let's test it: Sometimes when your heart starts beating faster you say to yourself "I'm having a heart attack." Is that a thought or a fact?

Richard: That's a thought. But it could happen.

Therapist: Yes. Good point. Many of our thoughts could happen … but when we think they'll happen it's called fortune-telling. But now let me ask you, the fact that your heart is beating faster than usual, is that a thought or a fact?

Richard: That's a fact.

Therapist: Right. And so the trouble starts not with the facts, but with your thoughts about what the facts might mean. If it's okay with you, I'm going to put a little "Thoughts or facts" assignment in your homework package.

Richard: That's fine.

Therapist: And here are some more questions. Does Linda love you?

Richard: Yes. I'm sure of that.

Therapist: And has she ever said that she's tired of being with you?

Richard: Nope.

Therapist: And were the two of you in a fight or having a bad time at the store?

Richard: Oh no. We like to shop together. We have fun shopping. We don't buy much, but we have a good time looking.

Therapist: Okay, so the thought that she'd up and left you is not really overestimating. It's what we call a catastrophic thought. You automatically thought of the worst possible relationship catastrophe—even though there was no evidence to support it. You and Linda have been together for thirty years. She says she loves you and is happy to be with you and you were having a good time, but somehow you assumed that she must be tired of you and therefore she had left you permanently.

Richard: Man. That does sound pretty crazy. You're right. When we talk about this it's like that thought came out of left field. Maybe I'm a little tired of myself, but Linda hasn't ever complained. But you know, at the time, for about five horrible minutes, I had myself convinced it was true.

Therapist: So you had a catastrophic thought that came out of the blue. It might be related to your own weariness with yourself. Your brain grabbed onto a convenient explanation. You've been tired of yourself, and so the best, ready-made explanation for Linda's absence was the same, that she was tired of you, too.

Problem Formulation

In Session 4 the therapist is working through the problem formulation at a deeper level than can be done in an initial session. Although Richard received previous psychoeducation about how thoughts affect emotions and behavior, now his thoughts are being categorized. This will help make it easier for him to engage in cognitive self-monitoring.

Richard's problem formulation includes the following components:

- He has automatic thoughts that include overestimations (of bad outcomes), catastrophizing, and fortune-telling.

- He has a core belief that he's physically defective.

- He has a secondary core belief that gets activated when he's feeling defective. His secondary core belief is that because he's defective he's also undesirable and will end up alone in the world.

- When something happens that activates (i.e., activating event) Richard's core beliefs, he has automatic thoughts that distort reality and produce debilitating anxiety.

Interventions

Cognitive interventions target Richard's core belief that he's defective, his associated core belief that he's undesirable, and his distorted and unhelpful automatic thoughts. Five main interventions were used, some of which have already been applied and others that will be soon:

1. *Psychoeducation*: It's natural, but not helpful, to have inaccurate or distorted automatic thoughts.

2. *Cognitive self-monitoring*: Richard focused on tracking his distorted thinking.

3. *Socratic questioning*: Used to help Richard recognize his overestimation and catastrophizing and respond with curiosity and reflection.

4. *Distinguishing thoughts from facts technique* (Leahy, 2003): The therapist used Socratic questioning to help Richard discern between thoughts and facts.

5. *Generating alternative interpretations technique* (McMillin, 1986): This was used to teach Richard to gently dispute his automatic thoughts and replace them with more accurate interpretations.

Sessions 5–8: The therapist continues implementing the preceding five interventions.

Psychoeducation: Richard and his therapist discussed and explored differences between maladaptive overestimation, catastrophizing, and fortune-telling. An overestimation is the inflation of the likelihood of a negative outcome. Since it was possible that Linda was sick or hurt in the bathroom, Richard's automatic thought was an overestimation. However, his assumption that Linda had left him was a catastrophic thought. The thought that he will die of a heart attack was fortune-telling.

Richard's homework included a thought record. This record included a column for the situation (e.g., standing in line at a movie theater), behaviors engaged in (e.g., fidgeting and shallow breathing), emotions or feelings (e.g., anxiety and worry), and automatic thoughts (e.g., oh no, we won't get into the movie and it's my fault, and if we don't get in Linda will be disappointed, and she'll get so sick of me that she'll want a divorce). Richard categorized his automatic thoughts on the thought record.

Richard had one panic attack between Sessions 5 and 6. Upon arrival he expressed discouragement and disappointment. The therapist was empathic and then used Socratic questioning to help Richard examine his distorted thinking. Together, Richard and his therapist reviewed that he's in the process of teaching his body how to turn off a false alarm system that's been functioning for years. After using empathy, reassurance, and psychoeducation, the therapist began interoceptive exposure.

Therapist: Richard, today we have a 90-minute appointment so we can get started on some anti-panic practice. Is that still okay with you?

Richard: Uh, okay. If you think I'm ready.

Therapist: I'm sure you're ready. Our first activity is the chair spin. It will get you feeling dizzy, which is one of the symptoms you have when your panic alarm goes off. You spin yourself till you're slightly dizzy, and then you can use your coping skills. Once you're dizzy, do the breathing and the rational thinking activity.

Richard: What should I say to myself for the rational thinking?

Therapist: Remember, last week you had some great rebuttals for your overestimations, catastrophizing, and fortune-telling. For today, the main thing is to identify whatever automatic thought comes into your mind and replace it with one of those four rebuttals.

Richard: I can't remember them very well.

Therapist: Okay. I'm glad you mentioned that. It's good to get prepared. I've got them here in my notes. [Therapist pages through file.] Here they are. When you feel your body's alarm going off, you can say, "This is my false alarm. I can get my body back to normal with deep breathing" or "I have proof from my doctor that my heart is in great shape." You also wrote: "I can ignore minor physical sensations" and "These sensations will go away on their own ... they always do." Remember?

Richard: Yeah. I've got it.

Therapist: Let's write those thoughts out on a piece of paper and, if you like, for today you can say them out loud while doing your breathing, okay?

Richard: Yeah. Good idea. That way I don't have to suffer from brain lock like I do sometimes.

The therapist led Richard through three interoceptive exposure activities. These included chair spinning, breathing through a straw until panic feelings emerged, and hyperventilation. Richard calmed himself down each time. During the third activity, he chose to think his automatic thought-counters internally instead of saying them out loud. Richard left the session more optimistic than when he arrived.

Richard didn't have any panic episodes during these sessions 5–8. His optimism continued to rise, and he and his therapist began talking about termination in session 8. During these sessions he continued interoceptive exposure practice and diaphragmatic breathing.

REFLECTIONS

What problems or worries do you imagine facing as you lead clients through interoceptive exposure activities? How could you prepare yourself to use these empirically supported strategies?

Session 9. Richard had two panic attacks between Sessions 8 and 9 and came into therapy very discouraged. Much of this session focused on Richard's "explanation" for his relapse.

Richard: I went backwards this week. I'm a basket case. This stuff works for most people, but I'm weaker than most people.

Therapist: Richard, you had a relapse. That's the reality. You also had several weeks of amazing success. But I hear you coming up with a fictional explanation for your relapse. I know we've been working hard on the breathing and dealing with your automatic overestimations, catastrophizing, and fortune-telling and so I'm pretty sure you can figure this out. What type of thought is this explanation that you're too weak to be successful?

Richard: Geez. You mean this is just another one of those crazy thoughts?

Therapist: It's not a crazy thought. It's that old unhelpful overestimation thought combined with fortune-telling. You had a relapse and then came up with an explanation. What would you say about the work we've done together ... is that the work a weak person does?

Richard: You're right. I'm working hard and it's going well, but not perfectly.

Therapist: I agree. You've been dealing with this stuff like a hero. You've kept going to work; you've shown great self-discipline. Let's toss your weakness theory and come up with a better explanation.

Richard: I'm stumped on that one.

Therapist: What did we talk about for about 15 minutes last week?

Richard: [20 seconds of silence.] Um. We talked about me stopping therapy in a few weeks.

Therapist: Right. That's a better explanation. So what you're telling me with these two panic attacks is that we need to deal with the end of counseling slowly and carefully because your *thoughts* of ending counseling are a new *trigger* for your false alarm system. The other thing it reminds me of is your tendency to quickly think that Linda will abandon you forever for one reason or another. Let's look at another trigger for your panics that we haven't really focused on much yet. Those automatic thoughts you have about Linda and about being weak seem to be what we call "defect thoughts." Somewhere inside, you think you're weak and defective, and so when something goes wrong, you've got an instant explanation. Unfortunately, your explanation makes things worse.

Richard: Do you really think it's possible for me to overcome this?

Therapist: I'll answer that, but first, how about you look at the evidence and tell me what you think? What do you think your chances of recovery are?

Richard's response to this question revealed significant optimism; his therapist let him take the lead in a discussion of what he needed for counseling to end smoothly. Richard suggested they continue counseling for a total of 15 sessions. He said he wanted two more weekly sessions and then to cut back to every other week for two sessions and then possibly do monthly sessions. The therapist added that even after therapy was over, Richard could still do telephone check-ins or schedule a booster session. These possibilities seemed to greatly relieve Richard, which led to a deeper discussion about his abandonment anxiety. When discussing abandonment, the therapist stuck with the cognitive behavioral model and recommended that Richard begin some imaginal exposure to losing Linda in their next session. After that, they progressed to in vivo exposure where Richard spent time away from Linda.

Sessions 10–15. During these sessions Richard began spending short periods of time away from Linda to practice dealing with abandonment anxiety. He continued practicing his breathing, and worked to insert new and better explanations for situations that previously caused him panic. In the end, Richard was seen for a total of 15 sessions and one additional follow-up at 6 months after treatment.

Outcomes Measurement

CBT is a problem (or symptom) focused treatment. Consequently, the best way to measure treatment success is to measure Richard's symptoms before, during, after, and at 6-month follow-up.

As noted in Chapter 7, Richard was administered the following questionnaires at intake and then intermittently.

- *Body Sensations Questionnaire* (Chambless et al., 1984)

- *Mobility Inventory Questionnaire* (Chambless et al., 1985)

- *Agoraphobia Cognitions Questionnaire* (Chambless et al., 1984)

Although he also was given the Anxiety Disorders Interview Schedule for *DSM-IV* at intake, this was not readministered. Richard's scores on these three measures were consistent with him not experiencing panic or agoraphobia symptoms at termination and at 6-month follow-up.

EVALUATIONS AND APPLICATIONS

When it comes to psychotherapies in the contemporary world, CBT is the bomb—meaning it's the most widely accepted and respected approach available today. However, CBT isn't for everyone. We have many friends and colleagues (in the mental health business) who proudly say things like, "I'd never get CBT." This could be because many mental health professionals could just do CBT on themselves; there are a plethora of CBT self-help guides available (e.g., Greenberger & Padesky, 2016). It also could be because counselors and psychotherapists are interested in digging deeper into their problems and achieving insight and having an interpersonal connection with another professional. However, we digress. Let's see what the recent research and literature has to say.

Evidence–Based Status

The efficacy of CBT is so well established that there isn't space available to provide a detailed review of the scientific studies evaluating the efficacy and effectiveness of CBT packages and components. CBT is effective across a wide range of mental disorders and client.

Two caveats are given before presenting a summary of CBT outcomes research in Table 8.5. First, much of the CBT efficacy evidence focuses on immediate effects. As Dobson and Dobson (2017) noted in their review, it's difficult to conduct longer-term studies and to measure longer-term effects via meta-analysis. Second, CBT outcomes research is usually conducted by researchers with a CBT orientation (and allegiance); clearly there's the possibility of conscious or unconscious allegiance bias (Luborsky et al., 1999). With those caveats in mind, Table 8.5, adapted from Dobson and Dobson (2017) summarizes the research.

In addition to the preceding review, various entities publish empirical supported treatment (EST) lists (e.g., American Psychological Association, Division 12; SAMHSA, etc.). These lists usually categorize psychological treatments as either (a) well-established, (b) probably efficacious, or (c) possibly efficacious. Overall, about 80% of adult and child treatments classified as ESTs are CBT. These numbers are impressive. The scientific treatment of choice is nearly always CBT.

Table 8.5 Evidence for CBT by Diagnosis

Disorder or problem	Treatment	Evaluation
Specific phobia	Exposure and cognitive restructuring	Treatment of choice; better than medication
Social anxiety disorder	Exposure and cognitive restructuring	Treatment of choice; equivalent to medication
Panic disorder	Exposure and cognitive restructuring	Treatment of choice; equivalent to medication
Generalized anxiety disorder	Exposure and cognitive restructuring	Positive evidence; equivalent to medication
Posttraumatic Stress Disorder	Exposure and cognitive restructuring	Treatment of choice; equivalent to medication
Obsessive-compulsive disorder	Exposure and response prevention	Treatment of choice; better than medication
Hoarding disorder	Exposure and cognitive restructuring and declutter training	Positive evidence
Major depression	Activity scheduling, cognitive restructuring, and schema change	Positive evidence; equivalent to medication
Bipolar	Affect regulation and cognitive restructuring	Positive evidence; better than medication alone
Substance-related and addictions	Affect regulation, behavioral control, and cognitive restructuring	Positive evidence; equivalent to medication
Eating disorders	Eating regulation and cognitive restructuring	Positive evidence; better than medication
Sleep disorders	Behavioral control and cognitive restructuring	Treatment of choice; better than medication
Chronic fatigue syndrome	Activity scheduling and cognitive restructuring	Treatment of choice; better than medication
Anger and aggression	Cognitive restructuring and emotional control	Positive evidence; equivalent to medication
Psychosis	Affect regulation and cognitive restructuring	Positive evidence; better than medication alone
Somatic symptom disorders	Distress tolerance and cognitive restructuring	Positive evidence
Irritable bowel syndrome	Distress tolerance and cognitive restructuring	Positive evidence
Borderline personality disorder	Dialectical behavior therapy	Positive evidence

Notes: Treatment of choice indicates CBT is viewed as having stronger empirical support than other psychotherapies (in other cases, non-CBT approaches may be equivalent); for these disorders, CBT is equivalent to or better than medication treatments; if no statement is made, then there isn't enough data available to make an efficacy statement relative to medication treatment; keep in mind that even in cases where medication treatment is equivalent (e.g., panic disorder), side effects or addiction potential may make CBT the preferred treatment option.

However, there are other competing conclusions. Non-CBT practitioners claim that federal grants are biased toward CBT and that CBT researchers and organizations promote CBTs. Additionally, perhaps the clearest statement about CBT is that it's a treatment approach consistent with the medical model and therefore it fits with the dominant modernist scientific paradigm. CBT is also much more amenable to manualization than other treatments and, if nothing else, it's clear that CBT researchers have pursued their research agendas with great vigor and determination.

In an effort to depoliticize EST lists, Rosen and Davison (2003) advocated a shift away from treatment lists and toward treatment principles. They noted that many treatment packages have an entrepreneurial side and consequently there becomes more potential for bias in research process, outcomes, and reporting. This bias is clearer in medicine and with pharmaceuticals, but Rosen and Davison imply that the same sort of bias that affects psychotropic drug research might also influence psychotherapy outcomes research (and likely already has on a smaller scale).

Most contemporary cognitive behavioral practitioners are warm, empathic, and collaborative with clients. Consistent with common factors research, they incorporate a positive working alliance into CBT. In contrast, Ellis (1973) held a different viewpoint, commenting on warmth in psychotherapy with his usual charm:

> I am deliberately not very warm or personal with my clients, even those who crave and ask for such warmth, since I quickly explain to them, their main problem is usually that they think they need to be loved, when they actually do not; and I am here to teach them that they can get along very well in this world *without* necessarily being approved or loved by others. I therefore refuse to cater to their sick love demands. (p. 155)

We include Ellis's perspective partly because of its entertainment value, but he also makes an important point. Sometimes therapists over-focus on therapy relationships, wanting to be liked or admired, and catering too much to client perspectives. This pattern might make it easier to avoid serious therapeutic work or, as Ellis contended, clients may become too dependent on their therapists for approval and support.

REFLECTIONS

What's your reaction to Ellis's comment about clients' "sick love demands"? What might be an ideal degree of closeness to facilitate optimal outcomes? Might that closeness vary with different clients and different forms of therapy?

Cultural and Diversity Considerations

CBT focuses on symptoms as manifest within individuals. This position can be (and is) sometimes viewed as disregarding important culture, gender, and sexual diversity issues. For most cognitive behavior therapists, culture, gender, and sexuality aren't primary factors that drive successful outcomes.

This position is a two-edged sword. In the featured case, Richard is a white male living a life squarely in the middle of the dominant culture. The therapist was committed to Richard's well-being. If the client had been an Asian Indian or a bisexual or a woman experiencing domestic abuse the cognitive behavior therapist would have been equally committed to the client's well-being. This is the positive side of CBT being diversity insensitive.

The negative side is that CBT can be viewed and experienced as blaming clients for their symptoms, when the symptoms may be a function of diversity bias. Dobson and Dobson (2009) articulated the potential for clients to experience blame,

> By virtue of looking for distorted thoughts, cognitive-behavioral therapists are more likely than other therapists to find them. Furthermore, some clients do react to the terms distorted, irrational, or dysfunctional thinking. We have heard clients say something to the effect—"Not only do I feel bad, but now I've learned that my thoughts are all wrong." (p. 252)

Awareness of the possibility of client blaming is crucial. For example, what if Richard were a black American male? And what if his therapist noticed that Richard's thought record included numerous personalization examples? If so, instead of concluding that Richard is displaying oversensitivity and paranoid cognitions, his therapist should explore the possibility of microaggressions in Richard's daily life.

The term microaggression was initially coined by Chester Pierce (1978). **Microaggressions** were originally defined as "the everyday subtle and often automatic 'put-downs' and insults directed toward black Americans" but now this is expanded so they "can be expressed toward any marginalized group in our society" (Sue, 2010b, p. 5).

Microaggressions are typically unconscious. For example, we had a female client come to us in great distress because her vocational instructor had told her "You're pretty strong for a girl." Although the vocational instructor defended his "compliment," the young woman clearly didn't experience the statement as a compliment. In this circumstance if a therapist is insensitive to culture and gender issues, the young woman might feel blamed for having irrational thoughts and overreactive behaviors. Sue (2010) recommends that mental health professionals exercise vigilance to address microaggression issues inside and outside of counseling. One way in which cognitive behavioral practitioners have addressed the potential for committing microaggressions against sexually diverse clients is by using LGBTQ affirmative CBT (Pachankis, Hatzenbuehler, Rendina, Safren, & Parsons, 2015).

Returning to racial/cultural microaggressions, let's briefly pretend that Richard is a 6'7" black American male. In his thought record he notes:

Situation: Walking into the local grocery store. Young female makes eye contact with me and then quickly turns around and goes back and locks her car.

Thoughts: She thinks I'm going to steal her car.

Emotions: Anger.

Behavior: I act rude toward her and toward other white people I see in the store.

If the black American version of Richard has a therapist who looks at this thought record and then talks with Richard about the distorted thinking style of mind-reading ("Richard, you didn't really know what she was thinking, did you?") this therapist is showing cultural insensitivity and will likely be fired by Richard. This is an example of one of the many growing edges CBT should address with respect to women and minority clients.

Spirituality

Like all therapists, cognitive behavior therapists work with religious or spiritual clients. Given that cognitively oriented therapists routinely identify and challenge (either through disputation or collaborative empiricism) client beliefs, there's a risk that clients' deeply held religious or spiritual beliefs might also be challenged. Additionally, practiced as a radical modernist scientific paradigm, CBT has been critiqued for overlooking transcendence, grace, and evil (Stewart-Sicking, 2015).

Looking at the situation logically (which cognitive theorists would appreciate), CBT practitioners have three options:

1. Ignore client religion and spirituality.

2. Freely challenge religious beliefs, whenever they cause emotional distress.

3. Integrate religious/spiritual knowledge into practice in a way that supports nuanced discussions of religion and spirituality. Unhelpful or irrational thoughts might be questioned, as needed, but not central religious values (Johnson, 2013).

Historically, cognitive therapists have followed these first two options, mostly ignoring religion, or questioning its rational foundations (Andersson & Asmundson, 2006; Nielsen & Ellis, 1994). However, in the past decade or two, interest in integrating religion/spirituality into counseling and psychotherapy has increased (Stewart-Sicking, 2015).

It can help to think about client religion/spirituality as a multicultural/diversity issue. If so, the general guide is for therapists to (a) seek awareness of their own spiritual and religious attitudes and how they might affect counseling process and specific clients, (b) obtain relevant knowledge about religion/spirituality, (c) learn religion/spirituality specific skills, and (d) advocate for individuals who are oppressed on the basis of religion/spirituality as needed and as appropriate. Each of these cultural competence components can be stimulating for individual practitioners.

For practitioners interested in religion/spirituality integration with cognitive approaches, the following two areas can provide focus for further training and development.

Gain and Apply Scriptural Knowledge with Clients

Gaining knowledge regarding how to use specific religious scriptures to dispute irrational or maladaptive cognitions may seem daunting. However, from an REBT perspective, Nielsen (2001) wrote:

> Since clients usually upset themselves through their awfulizing, demanding, frustration intolerance, and human rating, REBTers need only search Scriptures that decatastrophize life, suggest forbearance in the face of uncontrollable people and situations, tolerance of life's frustrations, and that affirm basic human equality. The prominent religious writings of most major world religions emphasize such rational values. (p. 38)

Using scriptural knowledge would be most appropriate when working with clients who have similar religious beliefs. Nielsen (2001) is advocating general knowledge, but general knowledge could prove problematic. For example, if a Jewish therapist quoted the Koran to a Muslim client, the discussion might quickly shift away from being therapeutic. On the other hand, having general knowledge, if used sensitively, could represent appreciation of religious diversity and enhance the working alliance.

Use Spiritual Principles of Acceptance for Managing Disturbing Cognitions.

Contemporary CBT approaches (covered in Chapter 14) offer an alternative way of viewing and handling so-called irrational or maladaptive cognitions. These approaches include acceptance and commitment therapy (ACT), dialectical behavior therapy (DBT), and mindfulness-based cognitive therapy (MBCT). ACT, DBT, and MBCT integrate religious/spiritual philosophy (e.g., Buddhism, contemplative Christian, etc.) and generally view cognitions as disturbing, but not necessarily pathological. Acceptance of all cognitions is advocated; encouraging clients to dispute or restructure their thoughts, memories, and experiences can increase suffering (Hayes, 2016).

CONCLUDING COMMENTS

There's little doubt about the efficacy of CBT. In a relatively short time period, cognitive therapies have garnered considerable scientific support. So have we arrived? Do cognitive behavioral techniques provide the ultimate answer to human suffering? Is cognitive therapy the way forward for human growth and actualization? Wherever there is certainty, there is always room for doubt, and Mahoney provides us with some. He stated:

> I do not believe that the simple cueing, recitation, or reinforcement of positive self-statements or the rationalistic "reconstruction" of explicit beliefs are optimal or sufficient approaches for facilitating significant and enduring personal development. (Mahoney, 1985, p. 14)

Even further, in his magnum opus, *Human Change Processes* (Mahoney, 1991), he quoted Hayek (1979), suggesting there may even be a superstitious quality to scientific validation:

> An age of superstitions is a time when people imagine that they know more than they do. In this sense the twentieth century was certainly an outstanding age of superstition, and the cause of this is an overestimation of what science has achieved. (Hayek, 1979, p. 176)

Hayek's comments suggest that it might be possible to ask larger, more complex questions than "does this technique make this symptom go away?" Cognitive and cognitive behavioral approaches are very effective. Failing to at least think about using cognitive and behavioral techniques in certain situations and with certain diagnoses might be unprofessional. Nevertheless, CBT is not effective for everyone; it's essential for researchers and practitioners to continue searching for even more optimal approaches for facilitating enduring personal development.

CHAPTER SUMMARY AND REVIEW

Cognitive behavior therapy (CBT) represents a combination of behavioral and cognitive approaches to human change. Initially, including cognitive variables in behavior therapy was resisted, but now most practitioners and researchers consider the two approaches as an integrated form of counseling and psychotherapy.

Key figures in CBT's development include Albert Ellis, Aaron Beck, and Donald Meichenbaum. In the 1940s and 1950s Ellis was a leader in promoting more directive cognitive therapy procedure, naming his approach rational-emotive therapy (which he later changed to rational emotive behavior therapy). Not long after Ellis, Beck developed cognitive therapy. While Ellis's approach was confrontational and focused on irrational thoughts, Beck's approach was more collaborative, focusing on maladaptive thoughts. Later, Meichenbaum developed a third slightly distinctive cognitive behavioral approach named self-instructional training.

Cognitive behavior therapies have several underlying theoretical principles. These include the classical and operant conditioning theories discussed in Chapter 7, as well as social learning theory and cognitive appraisal theories. *Social learning theory*, developed by Albert Bandura, focuses on observational or vicarious learning as well as reciprocal person-environment interactions. His concept of self-efficacy has been especially important to CBT. Cognitive appraisal theories focus on how individuals subjectively interpret their environments. Psychopathology is defined as the presence of persistently irrational, maladaptive, or dysfunctional patterns in thinking and internal speech.

In CBT, therapists develop a collaborative and educational relationship with clients. Assessment includes a collaborative interview during which therapists collaboratively set an agenda, identify a problem list, use self-rating scales and procedures, develop a case formulation, and provide psychoeducation. Early in therapy, cognitive therapists explore and identify their clients' automatic thoughts and core beliefs. Therapists may sometimes guess the underlying thoughts, use the vertical descent technique, and use monitoring procedures to chase down and identify distorted or irrational thinking patterns. Among the many CBT interventions available, using vigorous and forceful disputing, stress inoculation training, generating alternative interpretations, and cognitive restructuring were illustrated.

CBT primarily focuses on providing treatment for individuals. Attention to cultural, gender, sexuality, and spiritual issues has sometimes been minimized. More recently, CBT practitioners have begun integrating culturally sensitive concepts like microaggressions and LGBTQ affirmative therapy into CBT protocols. When working with religious or spiritual clients, CBT practitioners need to be careful about challenging central religious and spiritual beliefs. Gaining awareness, knowledge, and expertise for working with religious and spiritual clients is recommended.

COGNITIVE BEHAVIOR THERAPY KEY TERMS

Activating event (A)

Aftermath

Association for Behavioral and Cognitive Therapy (ABCT)

Automatic thoughts

Belief (B)

CBT case formulation

Cognitive appraisal theory

Cognitive behavioral self-monitoring

Cognitive continuum

Cognitive distortions

Collaborative empiricism

Consequent emotion (C)

Coping

Coping self-statements

Core beliefs or schemas

Dichotomous or polarized thinking

Disputation (D)

Emotional effect (E)

Generating alternative interpretations

Graduated thinking

Guessing the thought

Irrational belief (iB)

Labeling and mislabeling

Magnification and minimization

Microaggressions

Mind reading

Misattribution of hostility

Modeling

Negative cognitive triad

New feeling (F)

Observational or vicarious learning

Personalization

Preparation

Preparation self-statements

Problem list

Psychoeducation

Rational belief (rB)

Rational emotive behavior therapy (REBT)

REBT ABCs

Reciprocal interactions

Self-efficacy

Self-instructional training (SIT)

Self Schema

Setting an agenda

Shame attacking exercises

Social learning theory

Socratic questioning

Stimulus–organism–response (S–O–R) theory

Stress inoculation training (SIT)

Thinking in shades of gray

Thought record

Unconditional life-acceptance (ULA)

Unconditional other-acceptance (UOA)

Unconditional self-acceptance (USA)

Vertical descent (aka downward arrow)

Vigorous and forceful disputing

CHAPTER 9

Choice Theory and Reality Therapy

LEARNER OBJECTIVES

- Define choice theory and reality therapy
- Identify key figures and historical trends in the development, evolution, and application of choice theory and reality therapy
- Describe core principles of choice theory
- Describe and apply reality therapy principles, strategies, and techniques
- Analyze cases that employ reality therapy techniques
- Evaluate the empirical, cultural, gender, and spiritual validity of reality therapy
- Summarize core content and define key terms associated with choice theory and reality therapy

Reality therapy was officially birthed when *Reality Therapy: A New Approach to Psychiatry* (Glasser, 1965) was published. As is true of many therapies, reality therapy was initially the product of one person, William Glasser. Glasser wrote and spoke of the inspiration he got from mentors and colleagues, and the guidance his students and patients offered. Prior to Glasser's death in 2013, other certified reality therapists had taken over much of the national and international training programs in reality therapy (Burdenski et al., 2009; Robey, 2011; Wubbolding, 2000, 2011).

INTRODUCTION

Reality therapy is often oversimplified and confused with confrontational therapeutic approaches. In this chapter we describe and explain the nuances and clarify the confusion.

What Is Choice Theory and Reality Therapy?

Glasser developed reality therapy in the 1960s. Later, recognizing that he needed a theoretical foundation for his therapeutic approach, he began exploring cybernetics and control system theory (Powers, 1973; Wiener, 1948). Initially, following Powers, Glasser used control theory to explain reality therapy. Later, he adapted the theoretical model and shifted to using choice theory (Glasser, 1998).

Choice theory is based on the idea that conscious behaviors are chosen in an effort to satisfy one of five internal basic human needs (Wubbolding & Brickel, 2017). The human mind or brain acts as a "negative input control system," providing feedback to individuals so that they can correct out behaviors and continue getting what they need and want (Wubbolding, 2011, p. 13).

Reality therapy is a present-focused, directive therapeutic approach designed to help individuals identify and satisfy their needs and wants more consistently and adaptively. As Wubbolding (2011) has written, "If choice theory is the track, reality therapy is the train that delivers the product" (p. 5).

William Glasser

William Glasser was born May 11, 1925, in Cleveland, Ohio. In keeping with a reality therapy focus on the present (and not the past), we provide only minimal biographical information here. For additional information, you can read his biography: *William Glasser: Champion of Choice* (Roy, 2014).

William Glasser
(photo courtesy of the William Glasser Institute)

Counseling and Psychotherapy Theories in Context and Practice: Skills, Strategies, and Techniques, Third Edition. John Sommers-Flanagan and Rita Sommers-Flanagan. © 2018 John Wiley & Sons, Inc. Published 2018 by John Wiley & Sons, Inc.
Companion website: www.wiley.com/go/sommers-flanagan/theories3e

As a young adult, Glasser initially became a chemical engineer, but changed his focus and began a PhD program in clinical psychology. He obtained his master's degree in clinical psychology in 1948, but his advisors apparently rejected his dissertation. Subsequently, he was admitted to medical school at Western Reserve University and obtained his MD, accomplishing all this by age of 28. In 1957, Glasser completed his psychiatric residency at the Veterans Administration and UCLA. He became board certified in psychiatry in 1961.

During his psychiatric residency, Glasser began questioning "the basic tenets of conventional psychiatry" (Glasser, 1965, p. xxv). In *Reality Therapy* (1965), he shared a story of how he told his mentor, psychiatrist G. L. Harrington, MD, of his doubts about traditional psychiatry: "When I hesitatingly expressed my own concern, he reached across the desk, shook my hand and said 'join the club'" (p. xxv). Glasser had deep gratitude to Harrington, whom he referred to as "my mentor ... [and] the most skillful psychiatrist I've ever known" (1998, p. 5).

HISTORICAL CONTEXT

Sometimes it's difficult to determine the inspiration and roots of a particular individual's thinking. There are clear historical and theoretical predecessors to Glasser, but exactly how these earlier thinkers influenced him is unclear.

At first glance, because reality therapy involves teaching clients how to think, plan, and behave more effectively, some textbooks classify it as a cognitive behavioral approach. However, basing our conclusions on Glasser's work and conversations with Glasser and other reality therapists, we believe that classifying reality therapy as a cognitive or behavior therapy is inaccurate (Glasser, 1998). In fact, Glasser was adamantly opposed to behaviorism (Onedera & Greenwalt, 2007).

Much of Glasser's approach is consistent with humanistic-existential theory (Prochaska & Norcross, 2014). Glasser's emphasis on personal choice—each individual's inherent freedom—has an existential feel. His orientation toward personal responsibility is in the tradition of great existentialists such as Viktor Frankl and Irvin Yalom (see Chapter 4). Additionally, Glasser focused almost exclusively on the present and placed immense value on the authentic encounter between therapist and client. He viewed the therapy relationship as a key factor in treatment success (Onedera & Greenwalt, 2007). For Glasser, the relationship between therapist and client emphasized kindness, connection, and a genuine desire to help (along with teaching choice theory principles). The following statement illustrates his emphasis on authenticity and connection:

> [T]herapy is not perfect. Psychiatrists make mistakes like everyone else. I handled that mistake by admitting

it and learning something from it. When I admit a mistake, it makes me more human and increases the connection. If I don't admit it, I risk harming our connection or looking stupid. (Glasser, 2000, p. 91)

Other writers have speculated on the roots of Glasser's thinking. Croll (1992) described how reality therapy's emphasis on personal responsibility can be traced to Ralph Waldo Emerson's concept of self-reliance. Rozsnafsky (1974), Whitehouse (1984), Petersen (2005), and Carlson (Carlson & Glasser, 2004), linked Glasser's theory to Alfred Adler's individual psychology. Although Glasser claimed minimal awareness of the fine points of Adler's theory, substantial overlap exists (Robey, Wubbolding, & Malters, 2017).

QUESTION FOR REFLECTION

What are your first impressions of where choice theory fits as a theoretical perspective? As you read this chapter contemplate the historical factors and bodies of knowledge that may have influenced Glasser and his development of choice theory.

THEORETICAL PRINCIPLES

Choice theory holds that humans are internally motivated. If you compare this central assumption of choice theory to the primary theoretical assumption of behaviorism, you can appreciate the fundamental contradiction between choice theory and behaviorism. You may recall, B. F. Skinner believed *behavior is a function of its consequences* (see Chapter 7). Skinner's position implies that humans have little internal choice over their behavior, because environmental factors control behavior. In contrast, the choice theory perspective is that environmental factors only provide humans with information; after obtaining and processing external information, we then choose our behaviors.

Glasser (1998) claimed that behaviorism—which he unaffectionately refered to as **external control psychology**—currently dominates human thinking and reasoning. He stated:

> The simple operational premise of the external control psychology the world uses is: Punish the people who are doing wrong, so they will do what we say is right; then reward them, so they keep doing what we want them to do. This premise dominates the thinking of most people on Earth. (pp. 5–6)

Glasser blamed many contemporary social and psychological problems on external control psychology. In his words,

> [T]his psychology is a terrible plague that invades every part of our lives. It destroys our happiness, our health, our

marriages, our families, our ability to get an education, and our willingness to do high-quality work. It is the cause of most of the violence, crime, drug abuse, and unloving sex that are pervasive in our society. (1998, p. 7)

Glasser advocated discarding external control psychology and replacing it with choice theory. He viewed choice theory as the road to human happiness. In contrast, Wubbolding noted that it is not choice theory, per se, that leads to human happiness, but learning and utilization of an internal control psychology system (R. E. Wubbolding, personal communication, September 17, 2011). Internal control psychology can make us happy because it helps people to (a) stop trying to control others and (b) recognize we can only control our own behaviors. This shift in thinking allows people to meet their basic human needs in more direct, healthy, and adaptive ways.

From a behavioral paradigm, you're reading this book to evade punishment, to obtain reinforcement, or both. You might be reading to avoid failing an upcoming test or to gain rewards associated with knowledge acquisition—perhaps your professor will compliment you if you make an intelligent comment in class. In contrast, from the choice theory perspective, you're reading this book because you're choosing to read this book. You might, at any time, for internal reasons, decide to put this book down and stop reading. Decisions are always based on internal factors.

If choice theory posits that humans make decisions based on internal factors, the next reasonable question is one that philosophers and psychologists have struggled with for centuries. What internal forces or factors guide human decision-making? Or, as Glasser (1998) put it, what is the "underlying motivation for all our behavior"? (p. 25).

The Five Basic Human Needs

All humans are motivated to satisfy one or more of **five basic human needs**. These needs are genetically encoded and include:

1. Survival.

2. Love and belonging.

3. Power (or inner control).

4. Freedom.

5. Fun.

Choice theory may be simple, but it's not simplistic. As we explore the needs in greater detail, you'll discover that humans are often motivated simultaneously by two or more basic needs. Sometimes survival needs are linked with needs for love or power; needs can also be in conflict, as when love and belonging needs interfere with freedom needs (or vice versa).

Glasser (1998) viewed personality as stemming from the relative strengths of these needs within each individual. He wrote, "The strength of each need is fixed at birth and does not change" (p. 91). Some individuals have high needs for power and freedom, while others have high needs for love and belonging and fun. Typically friends and romantic partners have better relationships when their need strength profiles are similar (Glasser, 1998).

Each individual experiences a unique blend of human need states. It's as if the human needs derived from choice theory are five separate primary colors on an artist's palette. Consider the unlimited number of colors you could generate by mixing these colors. If you can imagine a skilled artist noticing the unique hue or texture in an original painting, then you can probably imagine the skilled reality therapist noticing the unique blend of human needs being articulated by the behavior, thoughts, feelings, and physical condition of individuals in therapy. Consistent with an Adlerian viewpoint, in the end all behavior is purposeful; individuals engage in behaviors that move them toward their internalized values or needs (Robey et al., 2017).

In contrast to the other needs, the first human need, survival, is a physical need. Glasser (1998) has written extensively about the five basic human needs in *Choice Theory*. In the following sections, we summarize each.

Survival

The **need for survival** is defined as the instinct to stay alive. When faced with potential death or nonexistence, humans will fight back mightily. However, struggling for survival isn't a salient issue for most people most of the time. Directly confronting life-threatening conditions on a regular basis is rare. Glasser (1998) provided an example of conceptual survival, the kind of survival we can talk about from an intellectual distance:

All living creatures are genetically programmed to struggle to survive. The Spanish word *ganas* describes the strong desire to engage in this struggle better than any word I know. It means the desire to work hard, carry on, do whatever it takes to ensure survival, and go beyond survival to security.... If you are looking for a mate you can count on to help build a family and a life with you, find one with *ganas* and treat him or her well. Try not to criticize this motivated mate; you don't want the *ganas* turned against you. (p. 31)

Often, abstract theoretical discussions about survival take people to the related topic of species survival and evolutionary biology. Glasser addressed this issue in choice theory, noting that sexual pleasure, a genetically wired-in human response, is an effective means of insuring species survival. Individual survival needs are expressed through total behavior (including our thoughts, behaviors, feelings, and physiology).

Love and Belonging

Glasser posited that while some individuals may be genetically predisposed toward needs for power or freedom, in most cases, love and belonging is dominant. This is consistent with Adler's social interest concept. It is also true that we need to be involved with others in order to meet the rest of our needs (Robey et al., 2017).

The influence and primacy of love and belonging are everywhere; just check Facebook or Instagram, or turn on the television. There are more songs, jokes, books, podcasts, and other materials about love, sex, and friendship than any other topic, including survival. Shakespeare's play, *Romeo and Juliet*, articulates the dominance of love. Romeo and Juliet choose love over survival.

From the perspective of choice theory, suicide is usually a choice that arises out of a conflict between survival and another basic need. Recall Patrick Henry, who spoke eloquently of his choice between survival and freedom when he said, "Give me liberty, or give me death." Similarly, young children, in their uniquely direct manner, articulate their preference for power and fun over survival when they threaten to hold their breath until they get what they want.

One bit of advice Glasser provided for anyone looking for romantic love is this: "Especially ask yourself, 'If I were not hormonally attracted to this person, would he or she be someone I would enjoy as a friend?' If the answer is no, there is little chance for that love to succeed" (1998, p. 36).

The **need for love and belonging** includes acquaintanceship, sexual love, friendship love, and romantic love. Unfortunately, needs for love and belonging can be confounded with the need for power. Glasser (1998) wrote:

> To keep any love, sexual or not, going, we need to go back to … friendship…. Unlike lovers or even many family members, good friends can keep their friendship going for a lifetime because they do not indulge in the fantasies of ownership. (pp. 35–36)

Love relationships are often derailed by power needs.

REFLECTIONS

Think about love relationships you've seen in friends, family, or clients. How might power needs interfere with love relationships? Can you think of examples where power needs damaged or destroyed a loving relationship?

Power

The **need for power or inner control** is defined as a desire for influence and control. However, Wubbolding (2000) has noted that power needs are often viewed negatively. He prefers more positive descriptors of this basic human need, such as inner control or achievement.

Most humans enjoy having at least a little power. Complete powerlessness is usually aversive, and in most cases, having power and influence is gratifying. Imagine you're very hungry. You walk into a restaurant, but no one greets you or offers to serve you. You call out for help, but there's no response. In desperation, you pull cash out and wave it around, but still no one offers to help you. The frustration of having no power to meet even your own basic needs can be debilitating. Minority groups through history have repeatedly faced damaging situations of powerlessness.

In contrast to the preceding example, some individuals in the world, due to wealth or status, wield immense power. For example, the queen of England or the crown prince of Saudi Arabia will probably never experience powerlessness and helplessness frequently associated with poverty, gender, or racial/ethnic/sexual discrimination.

From the perspective of choice theory, excessive striving for power *or* experiencing oneself as powerless may result in unhappiness and a need for counseling. Glasser (1998) considered an excess need for power to be a deeply destructive force within our Western culture:

> Driven by power, we have created a pecking order in almost everything we do; social position, neighborhoods, dwellings, clothing, grades, winning, wealth, beauty, race, strength, physique, the size of our breasts or biceps, cars, food, furniture, television ratings, and almost anything else you can think of has been turned into a power struggle. (p. 38)

Glasser discussed early childhood as a time when our human needs for power, and the gratification associated with meeting those needs, become recognized. He stated:

> As infants, once we get a taste of power through seeing our parents or others jump to attention to give us what we want, our need for more power starts to take over. By the time we are teenagers, power pushes us far beyond what we would do if our only motivation was to survive and get loving attention. (p. 38)

Often, when we teach or counsel parents of young children, the parents bitterly complain about having a "manipulative" child. Based on choice theory, it's natural for children to try to manipulate or gain power in their family situation. As noted previously, all behavior is purposeful and children are pursuing the pictures in their world of wants. It's the parents' job to guide children toward more responsible and safe ways for them to get what they want (Buck, 2013).

However, as Glasser (2002) pointed out in his book, *Unhappy Teenagers*, children become too focused on power and freedom primarily when their needs for love and belonging are unmet (this is also a basic concept in individual psychology; see Chapter 3). Many parents focus in on control and "why" their children misbehave instead of looking specifically at which needs their children are trying to fulfill. If, instead, they could ask themselves what their child is trying to get, they could perhaps help their child achieve more balance (Buck, 2013).

Unfortunately, instead of tuning into what children want and letting them pursue their wants in safe and responsible ways, parents try setting limits, have difficulty, and then begin applying external control, basing their relationship on the exchange of goods and services. Consequently, the children's primary means of having needs fulfilled gets transferred into power and freedom. Glasser (2002) described this process in the case of Jackie, a teenager featured in *Unhappy Teenagers*:

> If she is unable to satisfy her need for love and belonging, she turns to the two needs, power and freedom, that may seem easier to satisfy but which will further disconnect her if she succeeds in satisfying them. She uses all that violent language for gaining both power and freedom. If she can't find a way to get connected again, she'll stay the same or get worse. (p. 85)

It's tempting to cast a negative light on the human need for power. However, from the choice theory perspective, power is just another human need: "By itself, power is neither good nor bad. It is how it is defined, acquired, and used that makes the difference" (Glasser, 1998, p. 38). As with other human needs, individuals can become preoccupied with power and they can go about obtaining their power needs in cruel, insensitive, or overly selfish ways. From the Adlerian perspective, this would be framed as excessive superiority striving.

People get preoccupied with power, freedom, or fun for two main reasons. First, their preoccupation is caused by their inability to be involved in a satisfying relationship. The need for love and belonging is primary, so when it's not fulfilled, efforts to meet other needs may get out of control. Second, some people incorrectly turn to external control theory as a means for getting their love and belonging needs met. This causes them to pursue power or fun needs because, somewhere inside, they think having more property, more power, more toys, and more fun will get them what they really want: a loving and fulfilling relationship.

People who use power as a substitute for intimacy often seem addicted to power. They want to get ahead, to dominate the competition, to greedily acquire money and property, to win at all costs, or to control the lives and livelihoods of others. Without the concept of potential power-addiction, it's hard to explain why very wealthy people continue to accumulate massive material possessions, often at the cost of meeting other basic needs.

In contrast, and consistent with the writings of Carl Rogers and Alfred Adler, Glasser claimed power can be used for positive purposes. He even admits to his own power needs: "[M]any people gain power working for the common good.... I have written this book to try to help people, and if I succeed, I will feel very good and very powerful" (1998, p. 38). In addition, Wubbolding (2000) emphasized

that having an internal sense of achievement or accomplishment is a strong, positive, and constructive basic need.

Freedom

Many teens long for their driver's license and their very own car. When they get behind the wheel and drive away from their family home for the first time, they sometimes want to shout in joy at their new-found freedom. The **need for freedom** includes the desire for independence and creative impulses.

It's not unusual for toddlers and teenagers to view their parents as denying their freedom (J. Sommers-Flanagan & Sommers-Flanagan, 2011). In fact, many parents throughout the world use the psychology of external control with children (Glasser, 2002; Kohn, 2005). Consequently, toddlers and teenagers often strive hard to establish freedom or autonomy. Glasser (1998) wrote, "I believe that the need for freedom is evolution's attempt to provide the correct balance between your need to try to force me to live my life the way you want and my need to be free of that force" (p. 40).

Creativity is connected to freedom. If you can't express yourself, or if no one listens when you do express yourself, you may channel your creative impulses into destructive behaviors or a so-called illness. Glasser (2000) described the case of a college-age woman who was experiencing auditory hallucinations:

> Rebecca is fearful that the life she is choosing to lead ... will alienate her from her mother and family. This fear, coupled with all the pressure she is putting on herself to give up that satisfying life, is triggering her creativity to produce the voices [auditory hallucinations]. My task is to create a good-enough relationship with her so that I can encourage her to live the life she wants. (p. 123)

This case illustrates how a problem related to limited freedom—or the perception of limited freedom—can cause clients to produce creative symptoms. From the choice theory perspective, many women of Freud's era who were experiencing hysteria symptoms were probably creatively expressing their pain and frustration at the limits and abuses that society was imposing on them.

Glasser also noted that creativity, when unburdened from external controls, is often much less focused on the self and used naturally to benefit others.

REFLECTIONS

Glasser (1998) wrote, "Freedom concerns us mainly when we perceive that it is threatened" (p. 39). What are current situations where individuals perceive their freedom as threatened? Try to think of national and international political situations, as well as freedom-limiting behaviors that occur in families or romantic relationships? What factors contribute to the perceptions that one's freedoms are being limited?

Fun

When we teach graduate courses in psychology and counseling, many students are pleased to find fun on Glasser's short list of human needs. Glasser (1998) believed "the need for fun became built into our genes" (p. 41). He directly links the **need for fun** to play, and, even further, he links playing to learning, asserting that "[t]he day we stop playing is the day we stop learning." He went on to assert that the need for fun is the easiest one to satisfy and "is best defined by laughter" (p. 41). Having your need for fun met is commonly linked to or blended with having other needs met. For many people, fun is deeply intertwined with the need for love and belonging.

Your Quality World

According to choice theory, **your quality world** or your world of wants "may be best thought of as a mental 'picture album' that holds images of all that we value and/or possess, or wish to eventually value and/or possess" (Smith, Kenney, Sessoms, & Labrie, 2011, p. 54). These mental pictures or memories are typically associated with obtaining one or more basic needs. If someone helped you survive, experience love, or have fun, you're likely to put that person into your quality world. Glasser believed that your quality world includes three categories:

1. People.

2. Things or experiences or activities.

3. Ideas or systems of belief.

He stated that:

> ... the overwhelming reason we chose to put these particular pictures into our quality worlds is that when we were with these people; when we owned, used, or experienced these things; and when we put these beliefs into action, they felt much better than did other people, things, or beliefs. (1998, p. 45)

Everyone's quality world is different. For example, one person might have Hillary Clinton (person), baseball (activity), and Buddhism (belief system) in her quality world and be married to someone with Donald Trump (person), butterfly collection (activity), and Christianity (belief system) in his. At the same time, somehow the two of them got into each other's quality worlds!

The quality world of most people is a relatively stable place. With the possible exception of romantic love interests, the pictures in our quality worlds tend to come and go rather slowly. In fact, it can be difficult for people to let someone get out of their quality world—which, as you can imagine, may result in some serious problems, including stalking or murder.

Therapists need to do two things with respect to a client's quality world. First, you need to do your best to understand what's in your client's quality world. Second, it also helps if the therapist gets into the client's quality world as a need-satisfying person.

Glasser and other reality therapists use different strategies to get into a client's quality world. These strategies are founded on this underlying principle: act with clients in a way that gives them both hope for, and an experience of, having their basic human needs met. In a 2007 interview, Glasser described the initial process of a reality therapy session as including the following steps:

1. The client tells the story.

2. You reflect back that the client does not seem to be a very happy person.

3. The client agrees.

4. You propose working together to understand the unhappiness and make changes that increase happiness and improve relationships.

5. The client agrees.

6. You guide the client toward examining his/her/their important relationships.

7. You both discover that the client's important relationships are far less than ideal. (Onedera & Greenwalt, 2007, p. 82)

In this excerpt, Glasser offers the client an invitation to collaborate on working toward happiness. By doing so, he discovers unhappy relationships and simultaneously begins entering the client's quality world as a need-satisfying person.

Total Behavior

Choice theory includes a concept referred to as total behavior. **Total behavior** includes four distinct, but inseparable, components that are always occurring simultaneously:

1. *Acting*: What you do.

2. *Thinking*: What you think.

3. *Feeling*: How you feel.

4. *Physiology*: What your body does.

Total behavior is often described using an automobile analogy (see Figure 9.1). Imagine you're sitting in the driver's seat of a front-wheel-drive vehicle. You place the key in the ignition and turn on the engine. The engine represents your basic needs; your desire to have those needs fulfilled powers your overall system. As you step on the

THEORETICAL PRINCIPLES   235

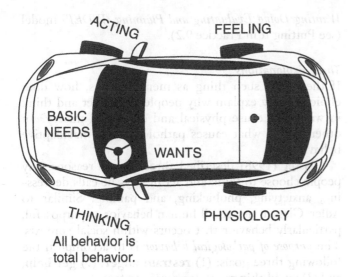

ACTING   FEELING

BASIC
NEEDS

WANTS

THINKING   PHYSIOLOGY

All behavior is
total behavior.

FIGURE 9.1   The Reality Therapy Car

accelerator, you keep a firm grip on the steering wheel. When you get up in the morning and hop in your choice theory car, you almost always steer toward the same exciting destination—you steer toward your quality world or your inner world of wants. That's because you learned early in your life that doing so gives you the best possible chance of meeting your five basic human needs.

If you're interested in love and belonging, you may steer your car toward making breakfast for your romantic partner. If you want power, you may down a triple latte from the drive-through espresso stand on your way to work. If your first thoughts focus on survival, you may immediately head somewhere that provides you with food, water, shelter, and clothing. If you have a strong need for freedom or fun, you can imagine where those needs might take you.

In the car analogy, the two front wheels represent acting and thinking. These parts of total behavior are under direct control. We act and think in ways to get what we want. Although sometimes it feels like we have little control over our thoughts, Glasser believed that thoughts, like behaviors, are chosen. The back wheels of the car represent feelings and physiology. According to the total behavior concept, feelings and physiology are indirectly chosen. The ways in which we choose to act and think pull our feelings and physiology in the same direction.

Choice Theory and Psychopathology

Glasser's view of psychopathology isn't shared by all practitioners of reality therapy.... Keep this in mind as you read about Glasser's three primary principles of psychopathology. As is true with any theory, one can make use of much of the theory, and the resulting techniques, without ascribing unilaterally to all the tenets of the theory.

Glasser's perspective on psychopathology includes three primary principles.

There Is No Such Thing as Mental Illness

Glasser often wrote that he did not believe in mental illness. He expressed this position in 1965, while working as a psychiatrist at a school for delinquent girls, and did not waver. He wrote: "The philosophy which underlies all treatment at the Ventura School is that mental illness does not exist" (Glasser, 1965, p. 85). Glasser was not alone in his views. Other prominent writers and psychiatrists have held similar beliefs (e.g., Thomas Szasz, 1970; Peter Breggin, 1991).

Glassser believed the term mental illness should only be used when brain pathology is clearly present (e.g., as in Alzheimer's disease, brain injury). Despite his medical background, he didn't prescribe or recommend psychotropic medications. He believed such medications were harmful. In 2003, he published a book titled, *Warning: Psychiatry Can Be Hazardous to Your Health*. On many occasions he has made statements similar to the following:

> Other mental health professionals don't talk about mental health, don't think about mental health. They focus on what psychiatrists and other people now believe are mental illnesses and focus on telling you that there is something wrong with your brain, that you need some kind of psychiatric drug to correct what's wrong with your brain, which they claim is some sort of a chemical imbalance. And [they] tell you that you can do nothing to help yourself. You should never tell anyone that he or she can do nothing to help himself or herself. That's a terrible thing to say. And certainly if you diagnose people as mentally ill who are not, and treat them with drugs that could harm them, this is a disaster in the country where we are not only spending billions of dollars doing that, which is bad enough, but the billions of dollars … harm the mental health of the people we are spending it on. (Onedera & Greenwalt, 2007, p. 80)

Glasser's position was that we choose our behavior and are completely responsible for all our emotional, behavioral, and some physical problems. Sometimes this perspective evokes a negative reaction, but Glasser was adamant that people are more likely to change if they view themselves as fully responsible for their symptoms. He went so far as to use verbs like headaching, depressing, and angering to describe human problems. These verbs were used to help clients feel more in control and to help them have more hope for change.

Glasser viewed himself as holding individuals responsible for their symptoms. When he worked with clients, he was respectful, never blaming or scolding. Though some claim Glasser's stance blames the so-called "mentally ill" for their problems, Glasser was very much against blaming. He encouraged people to think and act in ways that would give them more power over their symptoms and life situation, and remember, even if you find you cannot go as far as Glasser's view on psychopathology, choice theory and reality therapy practitioners aren't required to adopt every viewpoint of William Glasser. Many reality therapists are quite comfortable working within the traditional medical model and are open to referring clients for medication evaluations.

Clients who come for counseling may not be the least bit interested—at least initially—in using a choice theory model to explain and resolve their problems. It's often more appealing to use an external control theory model and abdicate personal responsibility. However, from the choice theory perspective, hanging on to external explanations for problems may feel better, but, in the end, believing you have no control over your symptoms will increase your suffering and decrease your chances of recovery.

Unhappy Relationships

Glasser contended that most clients come to therapy because of unhappiness in an important relationship. He believed unhappiness is usually caused by one person trying to control another person. The two antidotes to this particular problem are:

1. Learning the first axiom of choice theory: "The only person whose behavior we can control is our own."

2. Activating the positive therapeutic relationship inherent in reality therapy.

For Glasser, symptoms—even symptoms of psychosis—are generally efforts to control others, or to feel in control, or obtain basic needs in life. He explained how his approach to counseling psychotic clients is consistent with how he counsels all other clients:

> Contrary to much current thinking, there is no problem doing psychotherapy with a person who hears voices or suffers from delusions. Although I accept that the symptoms are there, I rarely refer to them in therapy. Most psychotic people can be reached if you concentrate on what they do that is sane.... I focus on these sane behaviors and work hard to try to create what I know every client I have ever seen, psychotic or not, wants: *good relationships that start with me.* (2000, p. 122)

Your ability to relieve clients of problems and suffering hinges on two main factors: how well you can establish a positive therapy relationship (and thereby enter into your client's quality world) and how effectively you can teach your client to use choice theory in his or her life. Teaching clients to use choice theory can involve the distinct process of teaching clients to use Wubbolding's

Wanting Doing Evaluating and Planning (WDEP) model (see Putting It in Practice 9.2).

Three Explanations

If there's no such thing as mental illness, how does choice theory explain why people would act and think in ways that cause physical and emotional misery? In other words, what causes pathological or maladaptive behavior?

Glasser (1998) described three logical reasons why people choose to think and act in ways he calls depressing, anxietying, phobicking, and paining. Similar to Adler, Glasser viewed all human behavior as purposeful, particularly behavior that occurs within social contexts. The *purpose of pathological behavior* is to accomplish the following three goals: (1) **restrain anger**, (2) **get help**, and (3) **avoid things** we don't want to face.

Restrain Anger

Depressing is the most common solution to the problem of anger. Similar to—but not the same as—the psychoanalytic conceptualization of depression as anger turned inward, depressing is viewed by reality therapists as a means by which anger is restrained or managed. Using the language of choice theory, here's how the process works.

Something in your life doesn't go just the way you want. For example, you wanted your boyfriend to meet you at the movies, but he doesn't show up. When this happens, you probably feel upset, frustrated, and out of control. Then, like most people, on the heels of your frustration, you're likely to have an immediate impulse to anger.

Anger is a normal survival-related response built into our genes. As Glasser said, "Angering is the first total behavior most of us think of when someone in our quality worlds does something that is very much out of sync with what we want the person to do" (1998, p. 80). Although Wubbolding also views anger as a natural reaction, he emphasizes that "Hurt and fear are the primary feelings—then comes anger" (personal communication, September 17, 2011).

To return to Glasser's perspective, you probably learned that angering is not a very effective or acceptable choice for getting your love and acceptance needs met, so you may choose instead to depress. Depressing is, for the most part, safer than angering, but it also has many drawbacks, not the least of which is that it feels miserable. While discussing the case of "Todd," Glasser described the immediate benefits of depressing over angering:

> Depressing prevented Todd from going after his wife, harming her, and even killing her, a common behavior in this country where weapons are so available. It also might have prevented him from killing himself.

Suicide is another total behavior that people choose when they have given up on the idea that they will ever be able to get their lives back into effective control. (1998, p. 81)

If, like Todd, you're restraining anger by depressing, reality therapy can help you find a better way (a better choice) to regain control over your need for love and acceptance. Part of this better way will undoubtedly include understanding the first axiom: You can only control yourself! Of course, everyone knows it's possible to control others—but what we believe Glasser meant is that ultimately, we're healthier when we focus on ourselves rather than on controlling others.

Getting Help

Depressing and other forms of misery are often ways for us to get the love, power, or freedom we crave. Unfortunately for everyone involved, depressing can be an effective method of controlling important people in life. It can also be an effective method for gaining sympathy, support, and medications. This is one reason why Glasser firmly believes mental health professionals should be compassionate, and yet not pay too much attention to clients' symptoms. He stated, "If it is coupled with compassion, not allowing anyone to control us with depressing helps them to see that there are much better choices than to depress" (1998, p. 82).

Reality therapists must sometimes pay attention to their clients' symptoms, because to ignore them is incompatible with being compassionate. The challenge is to gently and empathically help clients critically evaluate whether their symptoms are helping them fulfill their basic needs (Wubbolding, Brickell, Loi, & Al-Rashidi, 2001).

Avoiding Things

Everyone engages in avoidance. It may have to do with fear, aversion to doing something, or lack of motivation. For example, you may need to talk to your advisor about a thesis or dissertation topic, but you're nervous about your advisor's reaction. In that case, it would be easy to find other things to do and avoid scheduling an advising session. Alternatively, maybe you've had conflicts with your parents (probably because they're trying to control or advise you in one way or another), and so you're reluctant to call or visit them on your semester break. As it turns out, depressing, panicking, and obsessing are excellent ways to avoid dealing with life situations that need to be addressed. Glasser would say you have two choices: "Change what you want or change your behavior" (1998, p. 83). In other words, if you want more happiness in your life, take more responsibility for attaining it—there's almost always

more we can do to fulfill our needs than what we're currently doing.

Choice Theory in a Nutshell

As a review of the theoretical material covered so far and a preview of upcoming sections focusing on reality therapy, Glasser's (1998) *Ten Axioms of Choice Theory* are listed below.

1. The only person whose behavior we can control is our own.

2. All we can give another person is information.

3. All long-lasting psychological problems are relationship problems.

4. The problem relationship is always part of our present life.

5. What happened in the past has everything to do with what we are today, but we can only satisfy our basic needs right now and plan to continue satisfying them in the future.

6. We can only satisfy our needs by satisfying the pictures or specific wants in our quality world.

7. All we do is behave.

8. All behavior is total behavior and is made up of four components: acting, thinking, feeling, and physiology.

9. All total behavior is chosen, but we only have direct control over the acting and thinking components. We can only control our feeling and physiology indirectly through how we choose to act and think.

10. All total behavior is designated by verbs and named by the part that is the most recognizable.

THE PRACTICE OF REALITY THERAPY

To do reality therapy you must learn and apply choice theory. Even better, you can obtain a reality therapy certification through the Willam Glasser Institute-US (http://www.wglasser.com/), William Glasser International (http://www.wglasserinternational.org/), or the Center for Reality Therapy (http://www.realitytherapywub.com/). See also Putting It in Practice 9.2 by Robert Wubbolding to better understand the interface between choice theory and reality therapy (and see Putting It in Practice 9.1 for a sample reality therapy informed consent).

PUTTING IT IN PRACTICE

9.1 Informed Consent from the Choice Theory/Reality Therapy Perspective

Welcome to therapy! I'm glad you've chosen to meet with me to work on improving yourself and your life situation.

My approach to working with clients is called reality therapy. Reality therapy is refreshingly straightforward. We will spend almost all our time focusing on the present—what's going on in your life right now—and your future. This approach to therapy doesn't involve digging around in your past. The only reason I might ask you about your past would be to find out about some of your past successes or if something about your past is "alive" for you in the present. Overall, as I work with you in reality therapy, I like to focus on three primary goals.

First, we'll need to spend time getting to know each other and getting comfortable. I'm interested in helping you accomplish your goals and so I'll be asking you questions to understand what you value and what you want in life.

Second, reality therapists use choice theory. Choice theory emphasizes that we only have control over ourselves and although it's tempting to try to control others, things usually don't work out very well when we focus on changing other people. We'll focus on what you want, what you're doing, and whether what you're doing is getting you what you want. Choice theory is about helping you make the choices that get you what you want.

Third, an important part of choice theory involves active and detailed planning to help you achieve what you want in life. We'll focus a lot on your personal planning, making sure you have the best plan in place for accomplishing your goals.

Overall, I'm delighted to be working with you. What I want is to help you identify what's meaningful in your life and then to help you successfully accomplish your personal goals.

PUTTING IT IN PRACTICE

9.2 The Interface Between Choice Theory and Reality Therapy
Reproduced with permission of Robert E. Wubbolding

Robert E. Wubbolding (right)
(*photo courtesy of John Sommers-Flanagan*)

Robert E. Wubbolding, EdD, director of the Center for Reality Therapy, provided the following commentary:

Reality therapy, based on choice theory, has long been criticized as a short-term, symptom-oriented problem-solving method. Now that brief, outcome-based counseling has become fashionable, reality therapy is gaining prominence and acceptance. To gain its rightful place in academia, however, will require more extensive research-based studies. Nevertheless, contrary to common belief, there are studies validating its effectiveness.

I have found that when students learn the theory accurately they see it as a comprehensive explanation of human behavior. To enhance its practicality, I have summarized the delivery system WDEP. W means exploring clients' wants and perceptions (i.e., what they want from the world around them and how hard they are willing to work to satisfy their wants). They also examine how they perceive themselves in the world as well as what they can control and not control. In the D component, the counselor helps clients describe their choices, their self-talk (e.g., "even though my choices are ineffective, I'll continue to do the same thing"), and their feelings—such as hurt, fear, anger, depression, and many others. The cornerstone in the practice of reality therapy is E, self-evaluation. No one changes a behavior without first determining that current choices are ineffective. In *Reality Therapy for the 21st Century*, I describe 22 types of reality therapy self-evaluation based on choice theory. A few of the self-evaluation questions follow:

- "Is what you're doing helping or hurting?"
- "Is what you want realistically attainable?"
- "Does your self-talk help or impede need satisfying choices?"

I have found this component to be increasingly necessary with clients, many of whom come from substance abusing, attention-deficit/hyperactivity disordered, or simply tumultuous families in which expectations are, to say the least, inconsistent. In such an environment children grow up lacking the ability to self-evaluate; hence the need for a mentor to teach this skill.

In counseling any client my goal is to become part of his or her inner discourse. I cannot do this by communicating a lack of interest in the presenting issue—depression, blaming others, external perceived locus of control. I *always* deal directly with these issues and *then* proceed to discuss his or her relationships and choices by listening carefully for wants. For me, anything less demeans clients, worsens their frustration, and communicates that my agenda is more important than their pain.

The WDEP system is clearly based on an environment that avoids the **toxic ABCs**: arguing, blaming, criticizing, demanding, and getting lost in excuses. The helpful components of the environment include being determined, courteous, and enthusiastic; using paradoxical techniques; using informed consent; respecting boundaries; creating a sense of anticipation; discussing problems not as problems but as client solutions that have not helped; suspending judgment; using reflective listening; and many others.

One of my missions as a counselor, psychologist, and university professor is to make reality therapy academically both respected and respectable. A second goal is to promote it as a usable system, not as a cult. So I urge you, as students hoping to be respected therapists and helpers, to realize that reality therapy is a system practical *for you*. You need not imitate the style of anyone else. Adapt it to your own personality: assertive, laid-back, action-centered, or more cognitive. Select one, two, or three ideas from this excellent chapter that you will use!

Assessment Issues and Procedures

Glasser didn't use standardized assessment procedures. He relied exclusively on choice theory to guide his treatment approach. Other reality therapy practitioners may or may not use traditional assessment procedures. This distinction is another good example of why it's important to separate the theorist from the therapeutic practice. Glasser is generally against testing, medications, and diagnostic procedures, but many reality therapists find choice theory and reality therapy compatible with these standard mental health practices.

Choice theory assessment initially focuses on an assumption regarding the primary reason why humans become unhappy and seek therapy. Glasser articulated the root problem as always involving an unsatisfying relationship:

> From … forty years of psychiatric practice, it has become apparent to me that all unhappy people have the same problem: They are unable to get along well with the people they want to get along well with. (Glasser, 1998, p. 5)

This stance makes the therapist's assessment task straightforward.

During clinical interviews, reality therapists reflect on the following assessment questions related to choice theory. These aren't necessarily questions that reality therapists ask clients directly; these are questions reality therapists are thinking about (and sometimes asking) when providing counseling (for many additional questions, see Wubbolding, 2000).

- What is the nature of the client's unsatisfying relationship or relationship-related conflict?
- Will the client be able to understand and use choice theory to better meet the basic needs? If so, the therapist can move quickly into explaining choice theory. If not, the therapist will need to use various strategies, such as in-session demonstration, rational persuasion, and reframing, to help the client understand how choice theory works.
- Who and what is within the client's quality world?

- How is the client meeting needs for survival, love and belonging, power, freedom, and fun?

- Is the client overemphasizing any basic human needs?

- What's going wrong as the client tries to meet the basic needs?

- Have there been past successes that can show the client how choice theory can help meeting their needs now and in the future?

- What are the perceptions of other people and how do they act in relation to you? What is the impact of their behaviors on you?

Reality therapy practitioners have developed at least three different assessment instruments designed to measure the basic human needs. These include: (1) the *Basic Needs Self-Assessment* (Mickel & Sanders, 2003), (2) the *Contextual Needs Assessment* (T. Brown & Swenson, 2005), and (3) the *Student Need Survey* (Burns, Vance, Szadoki-erski, & Stockwell, 2006).

Building the Relationship

Glasser wrote about relationship-building and relationship-destroying behaviors or habits that he considered as consistently positive or negative for all relationships, both within and outside therapy. His seven caring habits and seven deadly habits provide guidelines for how reality therapists should and shouldn't behave toward clients. Glasser's **seven caring habits** are listed here along with brief descriptions and examples.

1. *Supporting*: Reality therapists show support by helping clients focus on what they want and how to obtain it in a direct and constructive way. Reality therapists also communicate support through collaboration on specific tasks. For example, to a client who wanted to write a letter to an important person, Glasser suggests, "Write the letter and bring it in to me. We'll look it over together before you send it. Is that okay?" (1998, p. 68).

2. *Encouraging*: Reality therapists are positive and encouraging. This emerges in several forms. When focusing on the person or, in rare cases, on the person's past, the reality therapist emphasizes successes and positive identity. With a client who was struggling with a reluctance to talk, Glasser used an encouraging statement: "Well, say it anyway. This is the place to say hard-to-say things" (1998, p. 65).

3. *Listening*: Many nonreality therapists view reality therapy as directive and confrontational. In truth, reality therapists emphasize the caring habit of listening (Wubbolding, Brickell, Burdenski, & Robey, 2012).

Reality therapists actively listen and respond when clients talk about their successes, plans, and efforts to connect with others, and listen less actively when clients' talk about symptoms or negative past experiences. Consistent with the WDEP model, reality therapists listen for what clients want (W); what clients are doing (D); self-evaluations (E); and plans (P).

4. *Accepting*: Reality therapists accept that all clients want to fulfill their five basic human needs. This provides an excellent foundation for empathy and connecting within therapy sessions. However, reality therapists don't accept client statements that externalize responsibility. This is probably why many students and professionals inaccurately view reality therapy as being confrontational. Reality therapists use teaching techniques—not harsh confrontation—when clients externalize responsibility.

5. *Trusting*: Reality therapists communicate trust. For example, in the Case Analysis later in this chapter, when Glasser tells Teresa to call him and that he'll call her back, he's building a trust relationship.

6. *Respecting*: Reality therapists respect what people want. The following excerpt from a case in which Glasser is working with a married man who wants to become a woman illustrates his emphasis on both connecting with clients and respecting them:

> I could turn him over to someone else, but we've made a good connection. He may think I am afraid to deal with his problem, and we'll lose the connection. It's that connection that's all important. Even his wife will look for that connection—that I really want to help him; that I respect him even though he wants to be a woman. (2000, pp. 90–91)

7. *Negotiating differences*: A basic assumption of choice theory is that although all individuals have the same five basic needs, there are unique ways in which they want those needs fulfilled. Reality therapists help clients negotiate differences between what they want from life and what they're getting. In couple therapy, reality therapists use "the solving circle" to help clients negotiate their differences (Robey, Wubbolding, & Carlson, 2012). The solving circle is a "place" in therapy where both parties are willing to step in and negotiate, rather than argue.

Reality Therapy and Confrontation

Because reality therapy has been misconstrued as harshly confrontational, once again we want to emphasize that reality therapy is gently confrontational. The confrontational component almost always involves therapists encouraging clients to engage in self-evaluation (Wubbolding, 2017). Reality therapists strive to avoid the **seven deadly habits** of choice theory:

1. Criticizing.

2. Blaming.

3. Complaining.

4. Nagging.

5. Threatening.

6. Punishing.

7. Bribing or rewarding to control.

Glasser was direct and clear about the negative consequences of using the seven deadly habits. He stated: "There is nothing intangible about any of them; they are clear and explicit. Exhibiting them in any relationship will damage that relationship. If you keep doing so, the relationship will be destroyed" (2002, p. 13). Therapists should choose the seven caring habits as a guide for them and their clients, while remaining aware of and moving away from using the seven deadly habits.

Helping Clients Develop Effective Plans

Wubbolding (1988, 1991, 2000, 2011) has written extensively about how reality therapists help clients develop plans for making positive life changes. Therapists help clients make positive and constructive plans. Wubbolding (1988) uses the acronym $SAMI^2C^3$ to outline the essential ingredients of an effective plan:

S = *Simple*: Effective plans are simple. If a plan generated in reality therapy is too complex, the client may become confused and therefore not follow through.

A = *Attainable*: Effective plans are attainable or realistic. If the plan is unattainable, the client can become discouraged.

M = *Measurable*: Effective plans are measurable. Clients need to know if the plan is working and if they're making progress.

I = *Immediate*: Effective plans can be enacted immediately, or at least very soon. If clients have to wait too long to implement a plan, motivation may be compromised.

I = *Involved*: Helping professionals can be involved with their client's or student's planning. This should be done ethically and in ways that promote client independence.

C = *Controlled*: The planner has exclusive control over effective plans. Avoid having clients develop plans that are contingent on someone else's behavior.

C = *Committed*: Clients need to commit to their plans. If a client is only half-heartedly invested in the plan, the plan is less likely to succeed.

C = *Continuous*: Effective plans are continuously implemented. When the process is going well, reality therapy clients have continuous awareness of what they want and of their plan for getting what they want. This high level of awareness reminds us of mindfulness or conscious-raising therapeutic techniques.

Wubbolding (1988) also recommended that individuals learning to conduct reality therapy develop a plan for themselves. He noted that to be effective reality therapists, practitioners should obtain consultation and/or supervision from certified reality therapists (in addition, we recommend that you practice living your life using choice theory rules; see Putting It in Practice 9.3).

PUTTING IT IN PRACTICE

9.3 Living Choice Theory: The Four Big Questions

Four questions have been developed to help students and clients live the choice theory lifestyle (Wubbolding, 1988). These questions are derived from Wubbolding's *WDEP* formula. During one full week, do your best to keep these four reality therapy questions on your mind:

1. What do you want? (Wants)

2. What are you doing? (Doing)

3. Is it working? (Evaluation)

4. Should you make a new plan? (Planning)

Every day you're operating with a personal plan. The plan may or may not be any good and it may or may not be clear. The point is this: You're thinking and doing things aimed toward getting your basic needs met. Therefore, consistently ask yourself the four preceding questions. This will help make your plan and choices more explicit.

Wubbolding's four questions are powerful and practical. Think about how you might apply them when doing therapy with a teenager. Now think about how you might apply them as a consultant for a local business. Whether you're consulting with a teenager or a business leader, there are hardly any other four questions that are more relevant and practical.

In the space that follows each question, answer the four questions for yourself today.

1. What do you want?

   _____

2. What are you doing?

   _____

3. Is it working?

   _____

4. Should you make a new plan?

   _____

After you've answered the questions, go back and think about what you've written as your answer for Question 1.

Reality Therapy in Action: Brief Vignettes

Similar to Adlerian therapy, reality therapy involves encouragement and intentional planning. The counselor establishes a positive working relationship and then persistently keeps the therapeutic focus on what's within the client's solving circle or circle of control. Maintaining a clear focus on positive actions and thoughts is what makes reality therapy an efficient and brief counseling approach.

Vignette I: Using Encouragement—Not Critical Confrontation

The following is an example of the type of confrontation often *inaccurately* associated with reality therapy. The counselor is confronting a teenage client on his efforts to find a job.

Counselor: Where else did you go?

Client: I tried a couple other [gas] stations, too. Nobody wants to look at me. They don't pay too good anyway. [Screw] them!

Counselor: So you haven't really done too much looking. Sounds like you want it served on a silver plate, Joe. Do you think looking at a couple of gas stations is really going to get you a job? (Ivey et al., 2002, p. 219).

Based on this brief exchange it appears the counselor is trying to help the client be successful in obtaining employment. Consequently, we can assume that having gainful employment (or at least making money) is a "want" (the W in WDEP) and in the client's quality world. Although this counselor is supposedly doing reality therapy, his critical statements ("you haven't done too much looking" and "you want it served on a silver platter") are inconsistent with reality therapy principles. A reality therapist would use a more supportive and encouraging approach. For example:

Counselor: Where else did you go?

Client: I tried a couple other [gas] stations, too. Nobody wants to look at me. They don't pay too good anyway. [Screw] them!

Counselor (Reality therapy response): It sounds like you really want a job and you feel very frustrated. What else could you do to help get what you want?

Notice that the reality therapist keeps the focus on what the client wants, empathizes with the frustration, and ignores the client's desire to quit trying. This approach is encouraging because the counselor is expressing confidence in the client's ability to act and think in ways that will move him toward his quality world.

Generally, when counselors use confrontation, the goal is to help clients engage in self-examination. The process for nearly all therapy approaches is similar—counselors help clients increase their awareness or have insights, which then leads to motivation and eventual change. Consistent with this process, Wubbolding referred to client self-evaluation as a "prelude to change" (1999, p. 196).

In working with this young man on employment issues, the following exchange uses concepts and questions adapted from Wubbolding (1999):

Counselor: Hey Joe, do you think the overall direction of your life is more of a plus or more of a minus?

Client: I don't know. I suppose it's kind of a neutral. I don't have a job and I'm not really going any direction.

Counselor: That's interesting. No direction. I guess my question about that is whether going no direction is really the direction you want … or whether maybe you want something else?

Client: Yeah. I'd love to have some money. Right now the economy sucks, so I don't really see the point of looking for work.

Counselor: The odds of getting a job right now aren't great, that's for sure. Do you suppose the odds are better if you stay home or better if you get out and drop off a few applications?

Client: I see what you're saying. My odds are a little better if I get out there. But I think my odds of making money are probably better if I just got out there and sold drugs, like some other guys I know are doing.

Counselor: I'm just trying to follow along and track what you want. It does sound like you want money. And you might be right about the drug-selling scene, I don't know much about that. But let's be serious, do you think selling drugs would genuinely be good for you? I guess another way of asking that is, "Will selling drugs help or hurt you in getting what you want in the long run?" [This confrontation does what a reality therapy confrontation is supposed to do: it directly questions the usefulness of excuses.]

Client: I'm not saying I think selling drugs is a good thing to do. I'm just frustrated and sick of being broke and poor.

Counselor: Yeah. It's very hard. But I'm your counselor and it's my job to keep pushing you in positive directions. I'm asking you this because I think you can do better than how you're doing. Is the way you're thinking about this—that it's too hard, the economy sucks, and you're likely to fail—is that line of thinking helping you get a job or hurting your prospects?

Client: Yeah. I guess having a pity-party isn't helping much.

Counselor: I'm sure having a pity-party can feel good sometimes. But I'm with you on the fact that it's not helping much. So we've got to try out something different.

Because the preceding questions ask the client to look at himself and self-evaluate, they're inherently confrontational, but also supportive and encouraging. Many additional reality therapy questions that help clients self-reflect and plan are in Wubbolding's (2000, 2017) publications.

Vignette II: Collaborative Planning

This vignette extends the previous case into the reality therapy collaborative planning process.

Client: Well. What sort of different approach do you suggest?

Counselor: If it were up to me, I'd suggest we make a very clear plan for you to try out this week. The plan would focus on how you can get what you want: a job so you can start earning money. And we'd develop this plan together and we'd be honest with each other about whether our ideas would give you the best chances to get a job.

Client: How about I go down to the Job Service and sign up there?

Counselor: That's one good idea. It doesn't guarantee you a job, but nothing will because you don't have control over whether someone hires you, you only have control over your strategy or plan. Do you know what I mean?

Client: Not really.

Counselor: Thanks for being honest about that. When you make a plan or set a goal, it's important for it to be completely within your control and not dependent on anyone else. That's because the only behavior you can control is your own. For example, if your plan is to "get hired," you can be doomed to frustration and anger because you don't make the hiring decision. Instead, a good plan involves developing a detailed, step-by-step process. Your plan could be to revise your resume and then submit it along with a well-crafted cover letter to 10 places where you think your skills are a good fit. You have complete control over all that.

Client: Okay. I get it. I could do that, but I'm not very good with writing and resumes and all that.

Counselor: How can you make sure those things are in good shape then?

Client: I could get my sister to look it over.

Counselor: When could you do that?

Client: Next week, I suppose.

Counselor: What would make it possible to do that sooner, like this week?

Client: You know, you're really kind of pushy.

Counselor: Do you think you'd do better with someone who lets you put things off until next week? Would that be more helpful in getting you a job sooner?

Client: Right. Right. Okay. I call my sister tonight and ask if she can help me as soon as she's available.

Counselor: That's sounds like a great start. What time will you call her tonight?

Client: Seven o'clock. I know. Why not six? Well I figure she'll be done with dinner by seven, that's why.

Counselor: Good planning. Maybe I don't have to be so pushy after all.

The preceding dialogue illustrates how counselors can use gentle and persistent questioning to lead clients toward planning that's consistent with Wubbolding's principles (i.e., $SAMI^2C^3$). It also illustrates how reality therapists function as collaborators to help clients or students plan for success. Burdenski (2010) noted that this collaborative or "coaching" model distinguishes reality therapy from solution-focused postmodern approaches:

> ... the [choice theory/reality therapy] practitioner is encouraged to use his or her knowledge and experience to help clients widen their perception of choices and new possibilities. I don't think of [choice theory/reality therapy] as an "expert" model, but rather as a "coaching model." (p. 14)

When it comes to planning for success, reality therapists are engaged with students and clients in the here-and-now. In contrast to some postmodern approaches, reality therapists offer ideas and push an agenda. As with the case example in this section, reality therapists work to make the planning process simple, straightforward, and concrete. This emphasis on concreteness is in contrast to postmodern approaches (e.g., the miracle question; see Chapter 11) that can be more challenging for children who haven't yet developed abstract thinking skills. Burdenski (2010) offers an example of how a school counselor might apply the practical and concrete aspects of this model with elementary students:

> When working with an elementary-aged child struggling with paying attention in class, the counselor using reality therapy might ask: "How did your morning go in Ms. Smith's class?" "How did you spend your time?" "What did you try doing to help you pay attention better?" "What can you try later today?" "Are you willing to make a plan and tell me how it goes?" "Can you show me your commitment to the plan by giving me a nice firm handshake?" (p. 14)

Finally, we should note that Burdenski's inclusion of the "nice firm handshake" is a signature piece from reality therapy. Not only does the handshake symbolize the collaborative partnership, it emphasizes the human connection between counselor and client. The human connection—love and belonging—is so central to choice theory and reality therapy that some Glasser Quality

School consultants recommend that teachers begin their day standing at the classroom door and shaking hands or fist-bumping or somehow making a connection as each student enters the classroom.

CASE PRESENTATION

The following case example is from *Counseling with Choice Theory* (2000). The client, Teresa, is a woman with depressive symptoms that appear primarily associated with her husband "leaving her."

Before meeting with Teresa, Glasser had access to her mental health history. He was aware of her marital break-up and depressive symptoms. Based on this information, he formulated his approach.

Prior to presenting the case, Glasser (2000) articulated the thinking that guides his initial behavior with Teresa:

> I was determined not to ask Teresa to tell me her story and, especially, not to ask her how she felt. I had to try to convince her that she was making ineffective choices in her life, knowing full well that my claim that she was making choices, especially choosing to depress, would be the furthest thing from her mind. If I couldn't begin to convince her on the first visit, there was little chance of any measurable progress. (p. 129)

In this excerpt, Glasser is illustrating several reality therapy concepts. First, he prepares himself to focus on the positive. He plans to avoid asking Teresa about her symptoms. Second, his goal is to "try to convince her" that she's making poor choices. As you can see from his language, he understands that she won't be expecting to be held responsible for her depressive symptoms. Third, Glasser is set on working quickly. He wants to convince her of the merits of choice theory before she leaves his office.

Although reality therapy is predominantly an educational approach, it also includes experiential components. Note Glasser's next move:

> I started by rising briskly, greeting her warmly, and offering my hand. Teresa was surprised by my energy and enthusiasm to see her. I was not the first therapist she had seen, and she was used to using her depressing to take over the interview. (p. 129)

Glasser anticipates that Teresa will use her depressing style to disempower the therapy and depress the therapist. This illustrates an early assessment and educational rule for reality therapists: do your best to determine how clients use people to confirm their external control view of the world, and then behave in a way that doesn't validate their style. This can also be seen through a behavioral lens: instead of reinforcing his client's depressing style, Glasser ignores depressive behaviors and models choice theory and remains upbeat and positive, despite the client's interpersonal cues for depressing and hopelessness.

The Problem List

In the case of Teresa, Glasser doesn't use any formal assessment procedures. Instead, even before Teresa enters the office, he assumes she is *depressing*. This assumption is based on diagnostic referral information and generalization from his previous experiences as a therapist and with choice theory. As Fulkerson (2015) wrote, "With a reality therapy perspective, diagnoses are viewed as a symptom of a much larger problem: an inability to form healthy, need-satisfying relationships" (p. 3).

Glasser could be completely incorrect in his initial assumptions. If so, he would likely modify his behavior to fit with the client's unique needs ... while maintaining his initial counseling objectives of teaching choice theory and connecting with the client.

At this point, the problem list is brief.

1. Unhappiness, probably related to problems with important relationships (Teresa is presumed to be engaging in a pattern of *depressing total behaviors*).

Most reality therapists would engage in a more systematic assessment or problem/goal identification process. As discussed previously, Wubbolding (2000) recommends a series of very specific questions aimed at stimulating self-evaluation. From Wubbolding's more systematic orientation, the initial focus would be on identifying Teresa's wants (W), what she's doing (D), evaluating/determining whether her total behavior is getting her what she wants (E), and components of a new plan (P). Then, the problem list might include the following four items:

1. Depressed mood (Teresa wants to be happier).

2. Social disconnection (Teresa complains of social isolation or inactivity).

3. Lack of energy (Teresa wants to feel more energetic).

4. Unhappiness with herself. (This might also be formulated as the depressive symptom of low self-esteem. From a choice theory perspective, Teresa's self-critical thoughts are not helpful and therefore a problem that needs to be changed.)

Goal: Develop a (SAMI^{2}C^3) plan for increasing social connection.

As the case proceeds, Glasser uses psychoeducation to inform Teresa about what to expect from him and from therapy. His explanation is also functioning as an intervention:

Teresa, therapy is not easy. I have to ask you some hard questions that may even confuse you a little, but I'm doing it because I want very much to help you. But please, if I say anything that you don't think is right, ask me why, and I'll explain as well as I can. This isn't really a hard question, but I'd like you to try to do your best to answer it. What do you think a psychiatrist can do for you? (pp. 130–131)

When he says, "I want very much to help you" and "I'd like you to try to do your best" Glasser is directly expressing what he wants and then leaving the rest to Teresa, a strategy in line with choice theory Axiom 2: All we can give another person is information.

Teresa's response to Glasser's question about what a psychiatrist can do for her is: "Help me to feel better." He then uses a positive cognitive frame to direct Teresa toward the positive and toward experiencing hope. He responds, "Fine, that's the answer I was hoping for: You think you can use some help; you haven't given up" (p. 131). This is an example of Glasser beginning to impose choice theory onto Teresa's situation and symptoms.

Teresa has preconceived notions about therapy and mental illness stemming from previous therapy experiences. She has learned external control concepts that are compatible with the medical model, but incompatible with choice theory (Fulkerson, 2015). In particular, Teresa expects to talk about her past and believes she's suffering from clinical depression, an illness that may require medication. The question is: How can Glasser introduce his beliefs about the nonexistence of mental illness without offending Teresa?

Glasser: Now I'm going to ask you a question that may not make much sense. Are you willing to try to answer it?

Teresa: You're the doctor, ask me, and I'll try to answer.

Glasser: Is it okay if we don't talk at all about how you feel or about your life? You said it was a disaster; I'd just as [soon] not talk about it. (p. 131)

Not only does Glasser ask Teresa a question, he also states that his preference is to not talk about Teresa's feelings. He's continuing to apply his choice theory model.

It's likely that Teresa is taken aback by Glasser's question and perspective. She probably can't help but wonder what's up with this therapist who doesn't want to talk about her troubles. From her point of view, if he doesn't want to talk about her troubles and misery, then what on earth could he want to talk about?

Problem Formulation

It may even seem strange that Glasser doesn't want to listen to Teresa talk about her problems, but this position flows from his problem formulation: Teresa is not suffering from a condition called clinical depression, *she is depressing*; that is, *the total behaviors that she's choosing are depressing her.*

Like solution-oriented therapists (see Chapter 11), Glasser has reasons for avoiding depressing talk (Dermer, Robey, & Dunham, 2012). The main reason is that Teresa has been habitually meeting her love and belonging or power needs through depressing behaviors. It may be that people take care of her, listen to her, and think about her when she acts depressed, or it may be that somewhere inside she feels better, because if she's depressed, then she

has a good, legitimate reason for being lonely (and for not having her needs for love and belonging met).

A practical issue that reality therapists must address is the issue of timing and client readiness. Unlike Glasser in this case, it's often best for reality therapists to talk with clients about their symptoms and their misery. Otherwise, it's likely they won't return therapy. Glasser is obviously very direct—which may be more palatable to clients when the therapist is an elderly, caring man who happens to be the creator of his own therapy approach (see Putting It in Practice 9.4).

PUTTING IT IN PRACTICE

9.4 The Risks of Insensitivity

To begin with, consider this: Glasser's approach to psychiatry, psychology, and counseling is radical. His beliefs that mental illness doesn't exist and that anxiety, depression, and schizophrenia are the responsibility of the client run counter to most contemporary approaches. Consequently, if you choose to fully imitate Glasser rather than integrating reality therapy principles into your practice, you may end up offending clients or even other mental health professionals because of your unorthodox views and approach.

In addition, reality therapy is sometimes viewed as a directive and insensitive form of therapy that permits therapists to simply confront clients with the reality of the consequences of their choices. For example, in the case of Teresa, at one point Glasser tells her, "You don't have to tell me how you feel. I know how you feel" (p. 132). This statement can be considered blatantly insensitive and in direct violation of existential-humanistic principles of an empathic I-Thou relationship.

From our perspective, Glasser's work with Teresa is neither unsympathetic nor unethical. However, taken out of context, Glasser's words are insensitive and blunt. This is where the main ethical danger lies.

Sometimes reality therapy may appeal to students and professionals who are bossy and directive in their personality styles. Reality therapy becomes most offensive and potentially unethical when employed in a confrontational manner by naturally directive therapists who don't understand choice theory or how to use reality therapy appropriately.

We have especially seen this tendency in poorly trained professionals who work with juvenile delinquents. The end result is that the professional becomes demanding, bossy, confrontational, and insensitive—all in the name of "reality therapy." Of course, in our opinion, demanding, bossy, confrontational, and insensitive therapist behavior isn't reality therapy; it's just bad behavior and possibly unethical. When practiced in this manner, reality therapy is transformed into just another effort to apply external control tactics to difficult youths (who are already reacting to adult efforts at external control).

In conclusion, this is our advice. It's quite possible for you to read this chapter or Glasser's or Wubbolding's work and be able to try out reality therapy ideas, strategies, and techniques immediately. There's nothing wrong with integrating reality therapy approaches into your counseling or psychotherapy practice. However, if you develop an interest in reality therapy, we recommend that you take advantage of advanced reality therapy training and perhaps become a certified reality therapist yourself. On the other hand, if you choose to inappropriately twist reality therapy approaches into another form of external control psychology because you haven't obtained adequate training on how to really conduct reality therapy, then you shouldn't refer to yourself as a reality therapist.

Although he's been operating on choice theory from the beginning, in this next exchange, Glasser formally introduces choice theory. However, Teresa pushes back and expresses her interest in talking about her feelings.

Glasser: Please, Teresa, tell me. Has it done any good to talk about your misery to anyone? Like, do you choose to feel better after telling someone how miserable you are? [I'm tangentially introducing the idea that she can choose to feel better. I wonder if she'll pick up on it? She didn't.]

Teresa: Wait a second, you're getting me confused. I've got to tell you how I feel. How can you help me if you don't know how I feel?

A little later, Glasser is even more direct about choice theory. Again, Teresa resists his perspective.

Glasser: Everyone who comes in here is choosing to feel bad. No one who chooses to feel good ever comes in. At least they've never come to see me. I don't think it's [feeling bad] a very good choice. That's why I don't want to talk about it.

Teresa: I don't know what you're talking about. I don't choose to feel bad. (p. 132)

Teresa makes it clear that she's not giving up her external control theory without a fight. When practicing reality therapy, you must be prepared to use skills and strategies to teach clients choice theory. You often must be doggedly persistent, repetitive, and ready to provide evidence and demonstrations.

Unlike Glasser, many reality therapists are much less blunt, more empathic, and more patient as they help clients understand the power of their choices. Glasser's version of reality therapy is similar to Ellis's version of cognitive therapy. There are kinder, gentler ways to use both approaches.

Rarely do clients grasp choice theory immediately. This is partly because most individuals are steeped in external control psychology. They come to therapy believing they have a chemical imbalance, or believing they have a thing called schizophrenia or anxiety, and they've often been taught to think of themselves as having little personal control over their symptoms.

Interventions

Reality therapy interventions will naturally focus on helping Teresa change her actions and thoughts. Common reality therapy techniques include questioning (both for the purpose of confrontation and rational analysis or persuasion), reframing, staying focused on the positive, in-session demonstrations, and out-of-session experiments or homework.

In his session with Teresa, Glasser frequently uses questioning designed to persuade Teresa to adopt a choice theory mind-set.

Glasser: Well, if you don't choose to feel bad, then how come you feel bad?

Teresa: I feel bad because my life is a disaster. What else could I feel?

Glasser: But does choosing to feel bad help you in any way to feel better? I realize I'm confusing you, but I'm trying to help you. How you feel is a part of the way you choose to live your life. You chose what you did all day yesterday. Did you feel good or bad yesterday? (p. 132).

He then moves quickly to an in-session demonstration:

Glasser: Think about how you feel now and how you felt a few minutes ago when you walked in the door. Let's say hello again. Here, give my hand a good shake. [I reach out my hand, and she gives it a much more vigorous shake than she did when she came in.]

Teresa: Okay, you're right. I feel a little better. I do.

Glasser: Aren't you choosing to feel better? You could have chosen to continue to feel the way you did when you came in.

And then he moves back to questioning for the purposes of rational persuasion:

Glasser: If you were suffering from clinical depression, how could you feel better all of a sudden?

Glasser is persistent in teaching Teresa that her "depression" is a function of her choice to depress, not of a chemical imbalance or a diagnostic label. Further, he eventually emphasizes to every client that their problems are a result of their unsuccessful efforts to deal with an unsatisfying relationship or the lack of any relationships at all (Fulkerson, 2015). With Teresa, he used the following question to get her to focus on her relationship loss and loneliness.

Glasser: When you give up on your life, what is it that you really give up on? Think a minute. If you can answer that question, I think you can really get some help (p. 134).

For Teresa, giving up on life coincided with her husband's walking out on her. Like many people who respond well to choice theory, she had previously felt better and functioned better because she was previously making more positive choices. Consequently, at least one avenue for helping Teresa make good choices was to have her reflect, even if briefly, on the fact that she made positive choices in the past. This is one exception to the general rule that reality therapy does not focus on the past; there is a focus on the past if the focus includes something positive or successful. Then, Glasser used more questioning:

Glasser: When you felt good, what did you choose to do that you've totally stopped doing now (p. 134)?

When Teresa answers, Glasser uses reframing to mold her response into something that better fits with choice theory.

Teresa: I did things, I saw people, I took care of my children, I wasn't broke all the time. I had a life.

Glasser: That's a perfect answer except for one little detail. You chose all those good things; you chose to have a life.

Teresa: Okay, okay, but that's all gone. In your words, tell me how I can choose to have a life now (p. 134).

Teresa is signaling to Glasser that she's willing to give his theory a try. Once a client has accepted parts of choice theory, it's time to move toward application. Subsequently, Glasser assigns homework that captures two themes. First, the assignments help Teresa experience the fact that front-wheel actions and/or thinking directly affects rear-wheel feelings and physiology. In our work using reality therapy with teens, we often sketch out the reality therapy car to illustrate total behavior concepts (see Figure 9.1). Second, reality therapy homework includes active and effective planning. In the following excerpt, both forms of homework are illustrated.

Glasser: That's right, you can't separate choosing how you feel from choosing what you do. They go together. But you can go home and spend the rest of the day saying to yourself: *Teresa, face it. Good or bad, happy or sad, you're choosing everything you do all day long* (p. 135; italics in original).

A bit later, Glasser uses a homework assignment to help Teresa establish a short-term plan.

Glasser: All right, let's start…. What could you choose to do tomorrow that would be better than today?

Teresa: I could choose not to sit around all day.

Although Teresa generated a plan, she generated a negative and vague plan. As a result, Glasser uses confrontation and rational persuasion to help her establish a more positive plan.

Glasser: No, that won't work. It'd be like trying to choose not to eat so much. I'm not looking for you to choose not to do anything. I'm looking for you to start to choose to do something better than you're doing now. Something active, so that you have to get up

and get going. [Then she said something that made us both smile. She was getting it.]

Teresa: I could choose to clean the house. It's a mess (p. 135).

Rather quickly in this exchange Teresa is ready to go home and choose different, more positive, constructive behaviors. But the next thing Glasser does is somewhat surprising. After a brief period of praising Teresa for "getting it," he makes a special, spontaneous-sounding contractual agreement with her. He asks her to call and leave him a message every time she chooses to do something all week. He also asks her to leave her number on his answering machine and tells her he'll find time to call her back.

At the end of Teresa's therapy, Glasser takes another step that's somewhat unusual. He asks Teresa if she's read *The Divine Secrets of the Ya-Ya Sisterhood.* Then he offers to help her start her very own "Ya Ya group" (p. 138). He concludes with this charge:

Glasser: For thousands of years, women have supported women. It may even be why the human species has survived. I say, take advantage of your genetic good fortune. Care for each other (p. 138).

Outcomes Measurement

Choice theory and reality therapy practitioners help people take responsibility for their thinking, actions, feelings, and physiology. It follows that the general goal of reality therapy is for clients to gain a sense of personal control over their choices. This intrinsic control should help clients become more capable of meeting their basic human needs in ways that are responsible and satisfying (Fulkerson, 2015).

Given these general goals, reality therapy treatment outcomes can focus on virtually any issue related to personal control and need-fulfillment. Not surprisingly, locus of control measures have often been used as outcome measures in reality therapy research (Rose-Inza & Mi Gu, 2001). However, nearly any measure linked to client total behavior (thoughts, actions, feelings, physiology) would be acceptable. For example, if a client comes in with an anger/aggression problem (angering) then an anger or aggressive behavior measure would be appropriate for monitoring progress. Reality therapists also use measures of personal satisfaction, emotional control, or relationship satisfaction as a way of determining treatment efficacy. For Teresa, a specific depressive symptom scale would be appropriate (e.g., the *Beck Depression Inventory*). Additionally, when working with student populations, Burdenski and Faulkner (2010) have developed several basic need measures that can be used by teachers or school counselors to measure baseline student need satisfaction and any gains made over time in the classroom or counseling setting.

EVALUATIONS AND APPLICATIONS

Wubbolding (2016a) and others have emphasized that reality therapy is a practical system that can be applied to most issues that educators and therapists face. Indeed, choice theory and reality therapy has been applied widely and internationally. Whether it lives up to contemporary evidence-based and diversity standards is a complex issue.

Evidence-Based Status

Overall, given the relatively high frequency with which choice theory and reality therapy is and has been practiced in schools and in counseling settings, very few well-controlled efficacy or effectiveness studies have been conducted. This may be due to four reasons:

1. Existential therapists have historically discounted the validity of the scientific research paradigm and outcomes research.

2. Reality therapy has been extensively and pragmatically applied within school settings. This particular setting is often burdened and underfunded, which may have contributed to a minimalist research agenda.

3. Certification in reality therapy does not include research training.

4. Large-scale grant funding typically goes toward cognitive behavioral research and not reality therapy research.

The paucity of empirical research also may be related to Glasser's attitude toward outcomes. For example, when asked about evidence-based treatment, he stated:

> Well, I have a lot of evidence about what I do, it's in my books, it's in other books.... There's a group of references that will support what I am saying. And therefore when you use choice theory, you have tremendous evidence. But the biggest evidence of all is that it works. The people will say to you, "My goodness gracious, I'm much happier than I was, and I owe it to you because I've changed the way I'm living my life." (Onedera & Greenwalt, 2007, p. 83)

Consistent with the existential tradition, Glasser's response focuses on anecdotal and experiential evidence. Unfortunately, the evidence he's talking about is not viewed as significant within the dominant scientific efficacy or effectiveness paradigms.

Other reality therapy proponents acknowledge the need for more scientific evidence to support reality therapy's efficacy. Wubbolding (2011) emphasized that although substantial anecdotal and less-controlled research evidence exists, future research should include studies that are (a) more tightly controlled, (b) longitudinal, and (c) conducted by objective evaluators. Similarly, Burdenski (2010) noted that reality therapy's less prominent position within academic counseling and psychology may be related to a lack of empirical research.

Highlights of the existing scientific research include:

- Researchers in Taiwan have published three recent studies on the effectiveness of reality therapy in the treatment of women with drug offenses (Law & Guo, 2014, 2015, 2017). In each study, Law and Guo reported positive results for short-term therapy (12 sessions) with modest sample sizes ($n = 40$–48). Positive results attributed to reality therapy included (a) improved hope, goal-setting, and persistence (2017); (b) higher self-efficacy in decision-making, planning, coping, and social skills (2015); and (c) improved self-determination and sense of self-control (2014).

- In a comparison study of a 12-week choice theory-based (CT) group intervention ($n = 93$) versus a 12-week motivational interviewing (MI) group intervention ($n = 98$) for college students with an alcohol-related violation, no differences were found between the CT and MI approaches on the *Daily Drinking Questionnaire* and self-reported negative alcohol-related incidents (B. Smith, Kenney, Sessoms, & Labrie, 2011). This is a positive outcome for the choice theory intervention because CT was shown to be as effective as MI, an empirically supported treatment (EST).

- A meta-analysis of 43 studies conducted in Korea showed that students within educational institutions receiving reality therapy interventions scored higher on self-esteem and locus of control outcome measures than students in control or comparison groups (Kim & Hwang, 2001).

- Reality therapy, cognitive coping training and their combination were more effective in helping empty nester Nigerian retirees with their adjustment than participants in a control group (Chima & Nnodum, 2008).

- A 15-week reality therapy-based group guidance program for underachieving Taiwanese elementary students learning Mandarin produced improved learning attitudes, motivation, learning strategies, and grades (Liu et al., 2010).

- Using a small pre-test, post-test, control group design, Azekhueme and Adegoke (2010) reported that reality therapy significantly reduced HIV risk among 20 Nigerian high school students.

- In a study of a reality therapy-based group therapy for chronic pain management, 22 veterans reported increased coping skills, greater need satisfaction, and overall satisfaction with the treatment (Sherman, 2000).

Looking back, the research evidence supporting reality therapy is primarily international and of relatively small scale. Going forward, the good news about reality therapy and research is that reality therapy is a short-term, directive form of therapy that should be relatively easy to evaluate. The potential for future research on the educational and therapeutic benefits of reality therapy is promising.

Cultural Sensitivity

Choice theory and reality therapy has been practiced with an impressively wide range of ethnic groups. As seen in the preceding section, reality therapy research is substantially international, including research studies in Korea, Nigeria, and Taiwan. Additionally, there are William Glasser Institutes in at least 30 different countries (http://www.wglasser.com/). The lead journal, the *International Journal of Choice Theory and Reality Therapy* (formerly the *International Journal of Reality Therapy*, 1997–2009, and formerly the *Journal of Reality Therapy*, 1980–1996) has a distinctly international flavor with many articles from international practitioners (Jusoh, Mahmud, & Ishak, 2008; Liu, Ting, & Cheng, 2010). In 1998, Wubbolding and associates published an article promoting reality therapy as an approach that can be modified and adapted to many cultures (Wubbolding et al., 1998). Emphasizing an international flavor, this article was prepared by 11 signatories from 10 different countries.

Glasser, in an interview with Wubbolding, emphasized his perspective on the multicultural applicability of choice theory:

[C]hoice theory is strongly based on the idea that built into our genetic structure are five basic human needs, and that all people on earth today, regardless of their size, shape, color, or anything else, have exactly the same genetic structure. We are all one race. (Wubbolding, 2000, p. 61)

From a multicultural perspective, Glasser's comment captures only one of two important realities. Although he emphasizes the culturally universal, he completely neglects the culturally specific (D. W. Sue & D. Sue, 2016). In his writings he doesn't address the potential genetic differences and nonshared environmental experiences common to ethnically diverse populations.

In contrast, others (Wubbolding et al., 2004) have written with more balance and sophistication about the application of choice theory and reality therapy to non-Western individuals and groups. As an example of Wubbolding's pioneering efforts to apply reality therapy to Japanese individuals, he notes: "There is no exact Japanese translation for the word 'plan,' just as there is no exact word for 'accountability'" (2000, p. 181).

Wubbolding's (2016a) message is that reality therapists must respect specific language and cultural differences and modify their approach when applying choice theory to individuals from different cultures. He emphasizes that asking questions like "What do you want?" or "Would that help?" may be too direct and possibly difficult for Asian clients to interpret. Instead, he suggests modifications such as "What are you looking for?" and "Would that be a minus or a plus?" Asian students with whom we have worked concur with Wubbolding's ideas for modifying choice theory for Asian clients.

REFLECTIONS

Consider Wubbolding's ideas about shifting CT/RT language for minority clients. What ideas do you have for how you might change the language for clients who are sexual minorities or clients who have strong spiritual beliefs?

Gender and Sexuality

From a feminist perspective, choice theory and reality therapy have potential for empowerment, but also do not address important social power dynamics. Specifically, Ballou (1984) criticized the fact that reality therapists hold individual women completely responsible for their behaviors when there are external forces, both historical and contemporary, that limit women's rights and power. More than 20 years later, Linnenberg (2006) reviewed Ballou's concerns and found they had, for the most part, not been addressed. Perhaps in the next 20 years reality therapists will begin to more systematically and effectively incorporate social issues and feminist perspectives into their practice.

There are some signs that women clients find reality therapy useful and helpful. As noted, the research agenda on reality therapy in Taiwan focuses on women with drug problems (Law & Guo, 2017). Also, various professional journals have included articles that apply choice theory to specific female populations. These have ranged from an analysis, critique, and application of choice theory to the "Strong Black Woman" archetype (Holmes, White, Mills, & Mickel, 2011), to an exploratory study of reality therapy-based group work for Korean expatriate women in the United States (Suh & Lee, 2006). Also, as you may recall, one of Glasser's recommendations to Teresa (in the case example) was for her to start her own women's support group.

Other than dated critiques of CT/RT as being less than optimally sensitive to sexual diversity (LaFontaine, 1994, 1995), very little professional literature focuses on reality therapy with sexual minority populations. This is disappointing because the straightforward and naturally empowering nature of choice theory and reality therapy might be useful for sexual minorities. However, it may be that the overall emphasis on personal responsibility and minimal focus on social/cultural factors make CT/RT a poor fit for some diverse populations.

It should be emphasized that Glasser held a strong cultural universalist perspective. What is interesting about his version of a universal cultural orientation is that although he didn't specifically write about feminist values or the social/cultural oppression of women and sexual minorities, if you read his work, you'll see that Glasser was extremely liberal and supported people of all ethnicities and sexualities. In his reality therapy casebook (written when he was in his 70s), he featured a case involving support and acceptance for a man transitioning to a woman and a young girl exploring her appetite for sexual gratification (Glasser, 2002). Although Glasser may have problems with the color blindness of cultural universalism (D. W. Sue & Sue, 2016), he was always ready and willing to work with all clients and students, without prejudice.

Spirituality

In the 1989 Spring issue of the *Journal of Reality Therapy*, Brent Dennis, a certified reality therapist, wrote an article titled, "Faith: The fifth psychological need." Glasser (1989) responded later that year. He noted that he found the discussion interesting, but that there is "no possible way to resolve an argument about belief" (p. 29). He concluded with a statement embracing inclusiveness toward whatever anyone might place in their quality world. Consistent with this perspective, contemporary reality therapists have published book chapters on how to help interfaith and multicultural couples succeed in their partnerships and marriages (Minatrea & Duba, 2012; Olver, 2012).

In an article on integrating reality therapy into Malaysian Islamic culture, Jusoh and Ahmad discussed many ways in which choice theory is consistent with Islam and can be practiced in Asian cultures. Specifically, they orient toward the WDEP and $SAMI^2C^3$ systems and emphasize their compatibility with Islamic concepts. They conclude that "choice theory and reality therapy have universal attributes, and these can be interpreted in any religion or culture" (2009, p. 7). This statement seems consistent with Glasser's (1989) inclusive statement on spirituality as a potential human need.

Overall, aside from the content summarized here, very little information exists on the integration of spirituality into reality therapy. However, given the growing international flavor of CT/RT, progress in this area seems inevitable.

CONCLUDING COMMENTS

The mission of the William Glasser Institute is to teach all people Choice Theory® and to use it as the basis for training in reality therapy, lead management, and Glasser Quality School education (http://www.wglasser.com/). The institute has existed for more than 44 years and there are now approximately 8,000 certified reality therapists worldwide and over 86,000 who have obtained substantial advanced reality therapy training.

William Glasser passed away in 2013. Although his advocacy for conscious, noncoercive human choice is missed, there are many other contributors to the national and international dissemination of choice theory and reality therapy. As examples, Robert Wubbolding is the director of the Center for Reality Therapy. Thomas Parish is the editor of the *International Journal of Choice Theory and Reality Therapy*. Patricia Robey, Nancy Buck, Jim Roy, and John Brickell are prolific contributors to the CT/RT literature (Buck, 2013; Parrish, 2017; Robey, 2017; Roy, 2014, 2017; Wubbolding & Brickell, 2017).

In Dr. Glasser's eulogy, Wubbolding shared the following anecdote:

> Quite recently, a woman approached him at his home and begged him for advice for how to deal with her 3-year-old son. He paused for a long time and then reached deep down inside his soul and gave her 2 suggestions: "Always treat him as if he is good." And "Set up circumstances where he can only succeed." These wise words could serve as his suggestions for all counselors. They represent for us a worldview, an attitude toward clients and his perception of all human beings. These two sentiments transcend a particular counseling system in that they summarize his legacy (September 10, 2013; http://www.realitytherapywub.com/index.php/easyblog/entry/dr-william-glasser).

In support of Glasser's legacy, we end this chapter with a quotation that reflects his idealism and ambition:

> *It is my vision to teach choice theory to the world.*
> *I invite you to join me in this effort.*

—William Glasser, *Unhappy Teenagers* (2002, p. 190)

CHAPTER SUMMARY AND REVIEW

Choice theory and reality therapy is the brainchild of William Glasser (1965). Initially conceived in the 1960s, reality therapy is a present-focused and directive therapy approach. Reality therapy has strong existential and

Adlerian components, but due to its focus on actions (behavior) and thoughts (cognition), it's frequently miscategorized as a cognitive behavioral approach.

Choice theory posits that humans are internally motivated to fulfill five basic needs. These needs include (1) survival, (2) love and belonging, (3) power or recognition, (4) freedom, and (5) fun. All humans seek to have these needs met and if one or more are not met, then there may be efforts to meet them by overemphasizing one need over the others. All humans also have an internal quality world or inner world of wants. The quality world, developed and established during childhood, consists of deeply valued people, things or activities, and ideas or systems of belief. Total behaviors (acting, thinking, feeling, and physiology) are used to help individuals meet their human needs and pursue the pictures that exist in their quality worlds.

Glasser's position is that mental illness does not exist. This is a controversial position and not held by all reality therapy practitioners. He also believed that much of human psychopathology stems from unhappy relationships and most unhappy relationships develop because one or more people in the relationships are engaging in controlling behaviors. Glasser posited that individuals display "psychopathology" in order to restrain their anger, get help, or avoid things. The ten axioms of choice theory provide a foundation for reality therapy practice.

Reality therapy does not rely on formal assessment procedures, but individual practitioners may integrate such procedures into their practice as they see fit. Individuals are evaluated through an interview process focusing on how well they're functioning in the world using choice theory. Often, the focus is on unsatisfying relationships. The therapy process is based on choice theory principles and is characterized by building the relationship, asking direct questions focusing on the four reality therapy questions: (1) What do you want? (2) What are you doing? (3) Is it working? (4) Should you make a new plan? Once there is clarity around these four questions (wants, doing, evaluation, plan: WDEP), then much of therapy involves planning for how clients can successfully obtain their wants.

Although reality therapy is frequently employed in counseling and schools, there's relatively little systematic research on its efficacy. Recent research includes positive outcomes for women with drug offenses in Taiwan, college students with alcohol-related violations, and other specific populations. Future research needs to include larger and more tightly controlled studies.

Choice theory and reality therapy have a wide range of international practitioners and researchers. Consequently, there have been efforts to adapt reality therapy for use with different cultures. However, Glasser is a cultural universalist and was less sensitive to culturally specific issues. Although reality therapy could be applied to women's issues and sexual diversity in ways that are empowering, there hasn't been much focus on these issues in the literature. However, several of Glasser's case examples have focused on sexual diversity and gender issues in ways that were affirming. Very little information exists on the integration of spirituality into reality therapy.

CHOICE THEORY AND REALITY THERAPY KEY TERMS

Accepting

Acting

Avoid things

Choice theory

Depressing

Encouraging

External control psychology

Feeling

Five basic human needs

Get help

Ideas or systems of beliefs

Listening

Need for freedom

Need for fun

Need for love and belonging

Need for power (or inner control)

Need for survival

Negotiating differences

People

Physiology

Power as a substitute

Purpose of pathological behavior

Reality therapy

Respecting

Restrain anger

SAMI^{2}C^3

Seven caring habits

Seven deadly habits

Supporting

Ten axioms of choice theory

Things or experiences or activities

Thinking

Total behavior

Toxic ABCs

Trusting

Wanting Doing Evaluating Planning (WDEP)

Your quality world

CHAPTER 10

Feminist Theory and Therapy

With Maryl J. Baldridge

LEARNER OBJECTIVES

- Define feminist theory and therapy
- Identify key figures and historical trends in the development, evolution, and application of feminist theory and therapy
- Describe core principles of feminist theory
- Describe and apply feminist therapy principles, strategies, and techniques
- Analyze cases that employ feminist therapy techniques
- Evaluate the empirical, cultural, gender, and spiritual validity of feminist therapy
- Summarize core content and define key terms associated with feminist theory and therapy

Some years ago, at the national conference of the American School Counselor Association, 90-year-old Georgie Bright Kunkel delivered the keynote address. She bounded onto the stage—not looking a day over 80. She introduced herself as the oldest stand-up comic in Washington state. (Was there an older stand-up comic somewhere else on the planet?) She proceeded to crack jokes about everything from sex to ... well ... sex, and then sex again. In the middle of her routine, she slipped in a serious story that went something like this:

> I was working as a school counselor at an elementary school. To kick off our career day, I contacted a woman friend of mine who was an airplane pilot. She agreed to land her one-person plane in the middle of our schoolyard. We were all very excited. We gathered the students outside and watched as she guided the plane down, smoothly landing on the playground. The students crowded around as she emerged from the tiny plane, helmet in hand. When it became apparent she was a woman, a male student turned to me and asked, "Where's the pilot?" It was clearly a one-person plane, but in this boy's mind, *men were pilots and women were stewardesses*. This was a sad truth for many of our students. But what interested me more was the impact of this event on our students' career ambitions. We had decided to take a student

survey before and after career day. Before my friend landed on our playground, exactly 0% of our female elementary students listed "airplane pilot" as one of their potential career choices. After career day, about 40% of the girls listed airline pilot as a career to consider in the future.

Ms. Kunkel's story is a feminist story. She was raising awareness about equal opportunity and facilitating development, change, and liberation.

INTRODUCTION

Feminist theory doesn't have neat boundaries; it can't be easily described and there are many ways to put it into practice. Feminist therapy, like feminist theory, reflects the work of many women, men, and sexually diverse minorities in grass-roots, multidisciplinary movements; concerns and new ideas were and are formulated from the ground up. If you're interested in working with people who struggle with real problems and you believe gender-based social norms, politics, power-driven hierarchies, economics, and other patriarchal cultural factors oppress individuals and groups, thus contributing to their problems, then feminist theory and therapy may be an excellent fit for you.

What Is Feminism?

Feminism simultaneously exists and evolves in grassroots settings and within different academic disciplines. There is feminist philosophy, sociology, psychology, social work, anthropology, and more. Feminism also exists within the sociopolitical sphere and consequently is regularly defined, redefined, represented, and misrepresented in the media. In this chapter we do our best to sort through and describe the many dimensions of feminist theory and therapy. We will inevitably fall short. However, in the spirit of an inclusive and interactive feminist community, we invite feedback and commentary (go to: johnsommersflanagan.com).

Funderburk and Fukuyama (2001) defined **feminism** as:

The belief that human beings are of equal worth and that the pervading patriarchal social structures which perpetuate a hierarchy of dominance, based upon

gender, must be resisted and transformed toward a more equitable system. (p. 4)

Of course, feminism has never been easy to define. We should consider the famous quote by Rebecca West who lived from 1892 to 1983.

I myself have never been able to find out precisely what feminism is: I only know that people call me a feminist whenever I express sentiments that differentiate me from a doormat.

Feminism boils down to the central belief that females are equal to males and consequently deserve equal rights, opportunities, and freedoms. This idea is sometimes labeled as radical because it pushes against boundaries and realities of what most people are taught via the dominant social and cultural media. However, we believe that the central feminist idea of equality is *not the least bit* radical: believing in equity and equality among all people is rather ordinary.

PUTTING IT IN PRACTICE

10.1 An Opening Feminist Reflection

Feminist ideas may be ordinary, but they also fly in the face of common social discourse. This is why consciousness-raising around all dimensions of femaleness and maleness is an important part of feminist work. With this in mind, read the quotation below and see what rises up within your consciousness:

For years, psychiatric journals have touted the salutary effects of antidepressants by printing "before" and "after" pictures showing a woman leaning on a mop looking despondently at her kitchen floor, and then happily mopping it after taking her medication. (Kaschak, 1992, p. 22)

As you process your reactions to the image of a woman needing medication to help her feel happy about mopping the floor, we invite you to consider whether the feminist idea that no one should have to take medications so they can complete their socially constructed roles and expectations is common sense or radical.

What Is Feminist Therapy?

Feminist therapy was born in the 1960s. At that time, women were gathering together, building awareness, and beginning to recognize that they were being oppressed from systemic inequality and inequity. Brown (2017) described **feminist therapy** as an approach that is grounded in multicultural feminist scholarship that "leads both therapist and client toward strategies and solutions advancing feminist resistance, transformation and social change in daily personal life, and in relationships with the social, emotional and political environments." Feminist therapy is also diversity-oriented.

Feminist knowledge comes from voices that have been traditionally silenced or ignored. These voices include "people of color, lesbian, gay, and bisexual people, gender variant people, poor people, people with disabilities, immigrants, and refugees" (retrieved, July 26, 2017, from: http://www.drlaurabrown.com/feminist-therapy/).

What Is Subversive?

In *Subversive Dialogues* (1994b), Brown framed feminist therapy as a subversive partnership. She described **subversive** as:

... a concept that broadly represents the psychotherapeutic strategies by which therapist and client, working together collaboratively, use the tools of psychotherapy to undermine the internalized and external patriarchal realities that serve as a source of distress and as a brake on growth and personal power for all humans. (Brown, 2010, p. 4)

Brown isn't suggesting that psychotherapy *could* be subversive, she's contending it *should* be subversive. As you'll read later, subversive feminist psychotherapy is a transformative leap from the oppressive psychotherapy Chesler wrote about in 1972.

What Is Patriarchy?

In the preceding (and following) pages we use the word patriarchy. It can be easy to look at that word and assume it represents anger towards men or criticism of so-called male leadership. To clarify, patriarchy isn't necessarily male-blaming. Many women participate heartily in the dominant hierarchical patriarchy, and oppress, discriminate, and hold others back. Criticizing patriarchy isn't about blaming men. It's about holding **egalitarian** (i.e., equality across all domains) values and working together across gender, racial, cultural, spiritual, and other individual and group identities to develop awareness and solutions.

Patriarchy consists of social hierarchies where male attributes are privileged and female attributes are undervalued. Brown (2010) referred to them as "toxic social hierarchies" (p. 5). Feminists are critical of damaging social hierarchies and the pathological use of power to oppress (Enns, 2004).

REFLECTIONS

One of our reviewers bluntly recommended: "You need to answer the questions: Where did patriarchy come from? Why was it maintained? Why is it so hard to fight against?"

Wow. These are huge questions. We fear we cannot do them justice. Therefore, we want to do the honorable thing ... pass them onto you.

Seriously. Your ideas about this are valuable. There are many theories about this. They include: (a) evolution-sociobiology, (b) religion, and (c) power.

There are no perfect answers to huge questions. We hope you'll grapple with your ideas, discuss the origins and maintainers of patriarchy with each other, and do some of your own reading and research.

What Is Intersectionality?

Kimberlé Crenshaw (1989, 1991) introduced the term intersectionality, but the roots of intersectionality theory date back to black female abolitionists. In the 1860s, Sojourner Truth articulated black women's uniquely oppressive experiences. She focused on simultaneous classism, racism, and sexism. Later, Claudia Jones (1915–1964) referred to this as "triple oppression" (Boyce Davies, 2008).

Intersectionality is the idea that overlapping or intersecting social identities within an individual create a whole that's different from the sum of its parts. Social identities that intersect include, but are not limited to, gender, sexual orientation, sexual identity, race, ethnicity, religion, nationality, mental disorder, physical disability/illness, citizenship, and social class.

Intersectionality includes "tremendous heterogeneity" within itself (Collins & Bilge, 2016). Intersectionality is a big concept, but can be quickly and easily understood. For example, we often open class discussions with the question: "Which individuals or groups do you think are the most oppressed in our society?" The answers roll out and usually include: transgender people, Muslims, poor people, the physically and mentally disabled, Native Americans, etc. At some point, someone inevitably brings up the idea of cumulative oppression. Then, the class acknowledges that, "Yes, multiple social identities exist, and they add to, subtract from, or multiply the social oppression or privilege that particular individuals experience." A common conclusion is that a transgender, African American who is poor, identifies as female, has a mental disorder, physical disability, and who is labelled obese would experience multiple and complex discrimination and substantial social and political oppression.

The uniting perspective of everyone interested in feminist therapy (including males) is an acknowledgment that without greater awareness, therapists will directly or indirectly contribute to their clients' experiences of oppression and psychological wounds, and be complicit in pathologizing natural reactions to abuse, denial of freedom, and denial of human rights. Remembering this unifying thread will be useful.

REFLECTIONS

At this early point in the chapter, try calling yourself a feminist. Say aloud, "I'm a feminist therapist." Notice how that feels. What are your gut reactions? What are your intellectual musings? Can you embrace that label? Can you let it embrace you? What might get in the way?

HISTORICAL CONTEXT

Social activists outside the counseling and psychotherapy disciplines continue to influence feminist theory and therapy. Consequently, we begin our journey by examining recent evolutionary movements in feminist thought within the United States.

Four Feminist Waves

Themes of feminist thought have emerged, receded, reemerged and developed further throughout history. For example, although he wrote of women as inferior to men, Plato (c. 440 b.c.) included consideration of women for leadership positions within the ruling elite. John Stuart Mill, influenced in part by his friendship and marriage to feminist Harriett Taylor, wrote essays decrying the oppression of women, pointing out great costs to society that resulted from this oppression. Historically, women's rights and freedoms have ebbed and flowed in ways that make it difficult for women and gender diverse individuals to be secure in their progress.

To understand how feminism applies to modern counseling and psychotherapy, it's useful to have an awareness of feminist history in the United States. This is a topic worth volumes; we hope this limited synopsis will help you understand how feminism evolved over time and glimpse how it has influenced counseling and psychotherapy today.

Recent feminist history is typically organized into four movements. These movements are referred to as different "waves" of feminism, a descriptor that highlights the influence each time period had on the next and the continuous nature of feminism's evolution.

First Wave Feminism

First wave feminism refers to the feminist and liberation-oriented activities occurring around and before the women's suffrage movement. Some of the roots extended into the anti-slavery movement, before the focus shifted to equal rights for women. During this time, feminists lobbied for all women's rights to vote, own property, and be fully acknowledged as citizens. Sometimes students ask us about the relevance and contribution of feminism in their lives. The first wave answer is, "If you're female and can vote and own property or you're a male who thinks females should be able to vote and own property, then you owe a debt to first wave feminism."

Contemporary feminists honor the first wave feminism period and its leaders, while also acknowledging its limits. For instance, stories of racial minorities who were working hard for change are rarely linked to the suffrage movement. As feminist consciousness expands, more inclusive historical representations of early feminism are deepening our understanding of first wave feminism (see Boyce Davies, 2008; Collins, 2009).

Second Wave Feminism

Betty Freidan is often recognized as starting second wave feminism with the publication of her book, *The Feminine*

Mystique (1963). Freidan's book became the bestselling nonfiction book in 1964. In her book, Freidan took on Freud, surveyed women and discovered their discontent with marriage and mothering, and debunked myths that women shouldn't be educated lest they lose their femininity or capacity for sexual gratification.

Second wave feminism included the Women's Liberation movement, the formation of NOW (National Organization of Women), and a focus on women's political and personal experiences. In particular, there was an emphasis on workplace, family, sexuality, and reproductive rights. Many people think of second wave activists when they hear the word, "feminism," as this was when feminist activists were highlighted (and often demonized) in the media (Collins, 2009). This wave also initiated feminist explorations of masculinity and the oppression of men under patriarchy.

Although minority women's voices were included in second wave feminism, the movement is retrospectively seen as predominantly white and middle class. For example, when "Women's Lib" advocated for a woman's right to work, the fact that many poor women and women of color had no choice and had to work low-wage jobs was largely ignored. At that time the women who were fighting for the right to work were generally wealthy enough to have the option of working or not working (although it was difficult for women to work in positions of power equal to men). Second wave feminism was sometimes associated with a "women versus men" mentality.

Third Wave Feminism

Beginning in the 1990s, third wave feminism was an expansive and inclusive feminism (Espín, 1993). In contrast to second wave feminism, **third wave feminism** broadly focused on how sexism and patriarchy impact all members of society (Barrett et al., 2005; Espín, 1997; Kawahara & Espín, 2007; Yakushko & Espín, 2010). The concept of women versus men—the battle of the sexes—popular back in the 1970s and early 1980s, was viewed as too simplistic. Third wave feminism brought women and men together to work against social injustice and raise consciousness related to patriarchal injuries. Third wave feminism challenged underlying systems of oppression and introduced a clearer focus on power analysis. Third wave feminists fought against all systems that oppress and limit societal members regardless of where they fall along the gender continuum (Enns, 2004).

Although second and third wave feminists address many of the same issues, they do so somewhat differently. Second wave feminism challenged the meaning of and limits associated with being a woman in addition to challenging the restrictive social construct and patriarchal norms (Collins, 2009). For example, women were encouraged to move beyond their traditional employment options and into traditionally male-dominated vocations (e.g., firefighting, police work, medicine, welding).

This chapter's opening story of the woman airplane pilot is second wave feminism.

Similar to the second wave, third wave feminism honored all occupations and roles as legitimate and valuable, and took these concepts further. The mothers' movement was one of many examples of this shift (Bridson, 2010). Another distinction was that, in the past, great emphasis was placed on minimizing differences between men and women (Collins, 2009). With the third wave, feminism focused on respecting and celebrating potential differences between men and women, while also highlighting the fluidity of gender and the individual experiences of each person's gender definition. In this respect, wearing make-up or spike heels were considered women's (and men's) choices—as long as those choices were made with awareness and empowerment of alternative ways of being.

Fourth Wave Feminism

Fourth wave feminism includes a plethora of different issues. Most descriptions of **fourth wave feminism** emphasize technology and the Internet, reproductive justice, spirituality, and support for transgender persons, plus-size fashion, and sex work, all in the service of gender equity and social justice.

Without a retrospective perspective, fourth wave feminism is difficult to define. There are many simultaneous and competing feminist voices. However, at its core, fourth wave feminism is an inclusive feminism that fights for the marginalized and oppressed. Intersectionality and its emphasis on multiple social identities is a core fourth wave construct. Fourth wave feminism uses technology and other means to include disparate voices arising from collectives, groups, and individuals.

Feminism Continues to Evolve

Whether considered first, second, third, or even fourth wave, at the core feminism is about liberation. Feminist and English professor, bell hooks (2000), has emphasized that feminism is for everyone:

> … females can be just as sexist as men. And while that does not excuse or justify male domination, it does mean that it would be naïve and wrongminded for feminist thinkers to see the movement as simplistically being for women against men. (pp. viii)

In many ways, feminism continues to evolve because it's about partnership, partnership of everyone to work for liberty, equality, and justice for all.

Key Figures and Factors in the History of Feminist Theory and Therapy

Despite many obstacles women faced in the early 1900s, there were many original feminist thinkers within psychotherapy and counseling. Two of the most promi-

nent were Raissa Epstein Adler (see Chapter 3) and Karen Horney (see Chapter 2), although a case could be made for including many others (e.g., Laura Perls and Joan Erikson, both of whom contributed substantially to their husbands' theories, but received little formal credit).

Raissa Epstein Adler was a radical socialist and intellectual from a wealthy Jewish family in Russia. She moved from Russia to study zoology, biology, and microscopy in Zurich because, at the time, women weren't allowed to attend Russian universities. While in Vienna she met and married Alfred Adler in 1887. Although she took the lead in raising the couple's four children (two of whom, Alexandra and Kurt, became psychiatrists), Raissa was deeply involved in the development of Individual Psychology. Raissa took minutes at meetings of the Society for Free Psychoanalytic Research and undoubtedly influenced Alfred Adler's views on women (R. Adler, 1982). Alfred Adler's public comments on sexual equality remain progressive today.

As we've seen from previous chapters, Karen Horney was a powerfully influential woman within psychology

Karen Horney
(photo courtesy of Mrs. Patterson, reproduced under CC BY-SA 3.0)

and psychoanalysis. She analyzed at least two very influential historical figures within psychotherapy (i.e., Fritz Perls, Chapter 6, and Albert Ellis, Chapter 8). Her work on "tyranny of the shoulds" is viewed as an intellectual predecessor of REBT and cognitive therapy. She was persistent and sometimes provocative. She provided a strong "push back" to traditional Freudian psychoanalytic theory. Her views on womb envy and other feminist psychological phenomena are featured in Chapter 2.

From the early twentieth century forward, in psychiatry, as in many fields, women slowly, against great odds, began joining the ranks of educated male professionals. The inclusion of women in doctoral programs was vehemently resisted. Prior to second wave feminism, many educational institutions, including Harvard, didn't allow women into the labs. One of the most effective rationales for excluding women had to do with their limited brainpower … aka, the smaller and less capable female brain (Fine, 2010, 2017; see Brain Box 10.1).

Three Groundbreaking Feminist Publications

Many different publications contributed to how second wave feminism affected psychology and counseling. In this section we describe three groundbreaking publications (Brown, 2010).

Kinder, Kuche, Kirche as Scientific Law: Misogyny in the Science of Psychology was written by Naomi Weisstein and published in 1968. Weisstein was studying comparative and physiological psychology at Harvard University in the 1960s. As a woman, she had substantial obstacles: she wasn't allowed access to laboratory facilities or the library. The article was subsequently included in a feminist anthology, *Sisterhood Is Powerful* (Morgan, 1970). Weisstein's article was especially provocative because she used the German words Kinder (children), Kuche (kitchen), and Kirche (church), words that had been endorsed by the Nazi Third Reich.

Weisstein described ways in which experimental psychologists made broad and inaccurate generalizations about women—even when women weren't included in the research studies. Brown's (2010) description of Weisstein's argument (and reflection back to Karen Horney) captures the content:

> Weisstein—perhaps echoing Karen Horney's (1967) earlier observation that the concept of penis envy might simply reflect the egocentric musings of a now-grown male child who was himself so attached to his penis that he could not imagine how those not possessing one would not envy him—critiqued then-pervasive psychoanalytic formulations of women as being less morally capable, more dependent, and less fully adult than men. She pointed out the complete absence of empirical, research-based support for these assertions upon which most of psychotherapy with women was founded. While today such assertions about women might seem outrageous, rereading Weisstein reminds us that in 1968 and for many years afterward, they were the conventional wisdom about women ascribed to by almost all practicing psychotherapists. (pp. 15–16)

This quotation deserves a brief commentary. When she refers to "almost all practicing psychotherapists" Brown isn't referring to Carl Rogers whose approach to psychotherapy focused on valuing all persons (yes, even women). Also, although "such assertions about women" might be seen as "outrageous" today, if you conduct a brief Internet search you can easily uncover many examples of individuals and groups that demean women and strongly express their views that women are inferior beings.

Sex-role Stereotypes and Clinical Judgments of Mental Health by Broverman, Broverman, Clarkson, Rosencrantz, and Vogel (1970) included results from a study on how 79 psychiatrists, psychologists, and social workers judged healthy males, healthy females, and healthy adults. Not surprisingly, it turned out that healthy males and healthy adults were essentially identical. The authors described their findings as:

> … a powerful, negative assessment of women. For instance, among these items, clinicians are more likely to suggest that healthy women differ from healthy

men by being more submissive, less independent, less adventurous, more easily influenced, less aggressive, less competitive, more excitable in minor crises, having their feelings more easily hurt, being more emotional, more conceited about their appearance, less objective, and disliking math and science.

In conclusion, Broverman et al. (1970) didn't blame the mental health professionals. They emphasized that the professionals had merely accepted sex role stereotypes prevalent in society.

Women and Madness: Exposing Patriarchy in the Consulting Room was written by Phyllis Chesler (1972), a psychological researcher. Following the 1969 meeting of the American Psychological Association (APA) where she attended a feminist protest, she decided to use her skills to support the movement. *Women and Madness* was a scathing critique of mental health treatment. Her main points:

- Psychotherapy for women was sexist and oppressive toward women.

- Women who didn't want to engage in full-time parenting, or wanted to venture into the working world, were labeled as disturbed.

- Many women were sexually violated during psychotherapy.

In 1969, Chesler and other women psychologists founded the independent and inclusive Association for Women in Psychology (AWP). Chesler and her colleagues presented many demands to the American Psychological Association. Eventually, in 1973, APA established a division focusing on the Psychology of Women (Division 35). AWP and APA's Division 35 still work together to promote women and gender issues.

Overall, the mental health system and psychotherapists that Weisstein (1968), Broverman et al. (1970), and Chesler (1972) were critiquing were simply reflecting the social climate (Collins, 2009). Women were devalued. Women were considered inferior—even childlike in their ability to reason. However, as Broverman et al. (1970) emphasized, the psychotherapists should have known better; they were scientists; they were supposed to be objective. As it turned out, they were scientists—but they weren't objective. To steal (and paraphrase) a line from the film *Network* (1976), the women of psychology were mad as hell and weren't going to take it any more.

Consciousness-Raising Groups and Relational–Cultural Therapy

In the late 1960s and early 1970s, there was a bubbling grassroots feminist phenomenon in the United States. This phenomenon was referred to as feminist consciousness-raising groups. **Feminist consciousness-raising groups** were loosely structured and nonhierarchical meetings sweeping through the United States and catalyzing the women's movement within and outside psychology. Worell and Remer (2003) described how these groups promoted psychological awareness:

> In response to their growing awareness of personal dissatisfaction and unexplained malaise, groups of women began to congregate to discuss their life situations. In sharing experiences of restricted and stereotyped expectations for how they should conduct their lives, they discovered that their problems were voiced and mirrored by others. (p. 6)

Feminist consciousness-raising groups illustrated a two-sided principle associated with women's positive psychological development.

- Isolating women enables oppression, but ...

- Connecting women with each other facilitates awareness, motivation, and change.

More recent contributors to feminist thinking have pursued this and other core principles. For example, Jean Baker Miller (1976), Judith Jordan (1997, 2010), and other therapists/scholars were instrumental in developing **relational-cultural therapy (RCT)**. RCT is a contemporary feminist-informed therapy approach currently gaining popularity (Frey, 2013; Jordan, 2017; Oakley et al., 2013). Jordan (2010) described RCT's feminist principles:

> RCT is based on a new model of human development that places connection at the center of growth. The fundamental principles of RCT, as it emerged over the years, posit that we grow in relationship throughout our lives. RCT sees the ideal of psychological separation as illusory and defeating because the human condition is one of inevitable interdependence throughout the lifespan. (p. 3)

RCT holds that psychological connection for women (and men) has growth producing effects (Gilligan, 2003; Jordan, 2010). This principle of connection is consistent with how the women's consciousness-raising groups worked, years earlier. Additionally, RCT is an example of the migration in thinking from second wave to third wave feminism. No longer are women competing to fit men's theories of healthy development. Instead, women's ways of being are valued in their own right and used to describe human health and well-being.

THEORETICAL PRINCIPLES

Feminist theory is complex and simple, innocent and insidious, common sense and deeply profound. What can

be more obvious (at least to the Western European mind) than the notion that every baby born deserves to pursue her, his, or their calling to the fullest, with no arbitrary sex, gender, race, or cultural obstacles?

Fairness and equal opportunity are deeply disturbing to some individuals and groups. The problem is apparent on many levels. Universal fairness and equal opportunity immediately call into question the status quo. It disrupts the natural (or unnatural) order of things. If your sex should not in any way determine your role in culture or excuse you from culturally identified adult obligations, what are the implications?

- Equal responsibility for serving in the military.

- Equal responsibility for providing income to your family.

- Equal responsibility for nurturing your children.

- Equal opportunity for all employment options.

- Equal opportunity to attend the college of your choice.

- No limits based on skin color, body shape, native language, or ethnic origin.

About 30 years ago, in a psychology of women class at a small, private university, Rita asked the 14 female students, "Do you believe you should have the options of either being a stay-at-home mom with your children or joining the workforce and hiring nannies or using a day care to take care of your children?"

The response was unanimous. These young women were adamant: Yes! The choice to either stay home or enter the workplace should be theirs. Rita then posed a second question: "If you're in a heterosexual partnership or marriage, should your children's father have the same option? Is it totally okay for him to choose to be a stay-at-home dad?"

This time the response was muted and mixed. A few women dared to share that they wouldn't want to marry someone who chose to stay at home with the children and expected her to work. A thoughtful discussion followed. When we ask this question now, depending on the group, the age of the respondents, etc., the responses are different, but what's clear is that men's and women's rights and choices are inextricably bound together. Allowing men equal freedom to choose to stay home and take care of a baby affects his partner. One respondent recently pointed out, "The bottom line is this: We're in this together and so we'd better start talking and negotiating to develop more functional, mutual, and fair partnerships."

Sex and Gender Powerfully Affect Identity

The first principle of feminist psychological theory is that *both* biologically determined sexual characteristics *and* socially constructed gender-role expectations play a central role in understanding client experiences. As we explore this principle, keep in mind distinctions between the scientific meaning of the words sex and gender.

- **Sex** refers specifically and exclusively to the biological, physiological, and anatomical characteristics associated with being female or male. (Keeping in mind that intersex conditions within the general populations require the consideration of more than two dichotomous "sexes.")

- **Gender** refers to the socialized or socially constructed roles, behaviors, activities, and attributes associated with identifying as female or male.

Put another way, female and male refer to sex differences and feminine and masculine refer to gender differences (see Putting It in Practice 10.1 for an activity focusing on sex and gender distinctions). Maleness and femaleness doesn't vary a great deal across cultures, but what is considered feminine or masculine can vary drastically.

PUTTING IT IN PRACTICE

10.2 Distinguishing Between Sex and Gender

To help make sex and gender distinctions even clearer try out the following activity.

After reviewing our examples, make a list of different sexual characteristics associated with females and males:

- Females have uteruses, fallopian tubes, and vaginas—males do not.

- Males have penises, prostates, and testicles—females do not.

Now try generating some sex differences on your own:

- Females _____—males do not.

- Males a _____—females do not.

In terms of gender, there are no hard and fast rules and so caveats are included to note the differences are not universal:

- In the United States, females wear skirts and dresses—what about males?

- In the United States, males can go topless in public—what happens if females go topless?

- In the United Kingdom, both females and males play "football."

- In some Arabic countries, men drive cars—women do not.

- In some African countries, women tend gardens—men do not.

As you read through the preceding list, did you agree, disagree, or think about exceptions? Have you noticed any gendered behaviors evolving during your lifetime? Now generate your own gender differences list:

- In _____, males _____ is context—females do not.

- In _____, females _____—males do not.

Did you focus on any particular cultures or countries as you made your distinctions? What did notice about your own male/female biases?

Biological Sex

There are a few biological distinctions that classify humans as male or female. These include the sex chromosomes and sex-determining genes, the H-Y antigen, gonads, certain hormones, and internal reproductive organs. The majority of those classified as female are born with clitorises, labia, vaginas, and uteruses and at puberty will develop breasts capable of milk production and begin a menstrual cycle that will last until midlife. The majority of those classified as male will have testicles and penises and at puberty will experience a hormonally driven change in their vocal cords that lowers their voices.

Although well over 90% of human biology is identical across all humans, there are important physical and hormonal differences that contribute to binary (male versus female) sex identification. These physical and hormonal differences vary greatly within any group of males or females. If you randomly select two females or two males, on average, the males will be more similar to the males and females more similar to the females, but the two males and two females will also be different from one another. Typically, physical variations within one biological sex are underestimated, while variations between the binary sexes are overestimated.

A significant number of babies (about 1.0% to 1.5%) are born with less pronounced physical sexual characteristics (Reis, 2009). These babies are commonly labelled as having **intersex conditions**. In the DSM-5 (APA, 2013), intersex conditions were renamed as **disorders of sexual development** (*DSD*) and listed as a possible specifier for gender dysphoria disorder. Some writers have advocated for less pathologizing labels, recommending that intersex conditions be referred to as variations instead of disorders (see Kraus, 2015; Meyer-Bahlburg, 2017; Reis, 2007, 2009). We agree. Cultural insistence that male and female are dichotomous entities causes distress that might lead to psychopathology.

Transgender people represent another, often marginalized, sexual diversity. **Transgender** is the term used for people who have a gender identity or gender expression that is different from their biological sex. **Cisgender** is the term for people who have a gender identity that matches their biological sex. Transgender people continue to struggle for equal rights and protection; sometimes they even struggle for the right to exist in society. The feminist perspective on hot button issues like "transgender bathroom legislation" is based on the following principles:

1. Movements to protect the majority from oppressed sexual minorities stem from the uncomfortable (or phobic) reactions that many Americans have to natural sexual diversity.

2. The presence of sexual diversity in the population disturbs the neat and tidy social norms around binary sexual divisions between male and female.

3. Psychiatry, mental health, and the general public have a long tradition of pathologizing and ostracizing sexual minorities.

4. Pressure to conform to a dichotomous sexual classification system is a primary causal factor in gender dysphoria.

5. If the culture accepted intersex conditions and sexual diversity as part of normal human variation, the pathology assigned to these conditions would disappear.

Gender

Beyond biology, humans add many layers to the male/female binary. Much of the behavior we classify as male or female is culturally constructed, not biologically determined. Based on the latest science, women are not from Venus and men are not from Mars—we are all from planet Earth in complex and diverse culturally and biologically diverse bodies, working things out as best we can, and we may not be as different as we think. In a comprehensive review of 46 meta-analyses, Hyde (2005) reported that females and males are strikingly similar across a wide range of psychological variables; more recent research on intelligence and cognitive abilities are consistent with Hyde's findings (Iliescu, Ilie, Ispas, Dobrean, & Clinciu, 2016; Makel, Wai, Peairs, & Putallaz, 2016; Pezzuti & Orsini, 2016).

Gender is a social construction. As such, it's surprisingly fluid across cultures and surprisingly rigid within them. In some cultures, it's feminine to be emotional. In others, it's feminine to be stoic, centered, and a source of family stability. Some cultures prefer physically aggressive males. Others value intellectual skills in males. Sometimes gender-related behaviors will shift in a matter of minutes as when an executive transitions from the office, to the car, and to home or the nightclub. Determining what's biological and what's socially constructed has been the goal of many research projects, the source of much controversy, and fuel for heated arguments at the dinner table. Regardless of where divisions lie, feminist theory rejects the notion that biology is destiny and holds suspect most claims of innate male–female behavioral differences, noting that such differences are often used to exclude, exploit, or devalue individuals on the basis of sex or gender (see Brain Box 10.1).

Human Development

Human development theorists believe our first self-defining insight is the realization, occurring during infancy, that primary caregivers are distinct from the self (Mahler, Pine, & Bergman, 1975). The second, identity-delineating insight is an awareness of biological sex. Researchers believe that, as early as 18 months, many toddlers know their sexual identity and are selectively processing information accordingly. This is highly significant for identity formation. Think about it. The first two human developmental insights are:

1. I am a separate individual.

2. I am a girl; I am a boy; or I am unsure if I'm a girl or a boy.

This awareness—and associated drive to fit with one's sexually identified group—opens the door for culture to step in and offer developing boys and girls (and those with intersex characteristics) all sorts of potentially useful and harmful guidance. From religious instruction to Saturday morning cartoons, from popular music lyrics to parental role modeling, young people generally follow cultural rules for expressing gender identity (Flynn, Craig, Anderson, & Holody, 2016).

No matter what you believe about the relative contributions of biology and environment on human behavior, sexual identity is a powerful and defining feature. Think about how often male and female differences get magnified and broadcast into your homes on television or through the Internet. For the most part, social forces in the United States seem to want the differences between females and males to be large and unequivocal, and sometimes, when comparing individuals to individuals, the differences do seem substantial and obvious. However, there are many exceptions to these marked differences between the dichotomous sexes. This is in keeping with what Gilbert and Scher (1999) dubbed the **iron rule**, which states that "for any psychological or cognitive variable studied by psychologists, the differences within each sex are always greater than the differences between the two sexes" (p. 37). Hyde's (2005) meta-analytic review and other contemporary research has supported the iron rule.

Deviance Comes from Dysfunctional Culture

Much of human suffering and distress comes from inequities suffered by women and others who were not born into the white, male, privileged class in North America and Western Europe. In these dominant cultural settings, male is normative.

Male as Normative

Although male and female babies are born at roughly the same rate throughout the world, most cultures place greater value on male babies and regard maleness as normative (Enns, 2004; Nutt, 2005). However, what does "male as normative" mean?

Male as normative means that maleness sets the standard for whatever is considered normal, average, or representative (Kaschak, 1992). Conversely, it means that anything deviating from male can be considered abnormal and inferior (Beauvoir, 1952).

Male as normative also includes an inherent assumption that male is valuable. If you're not male and you regularly experience maleness as more normal and valuable than your other-than-maleness, then you will likely also regularly experience distress. This distress may or may not be completely conscious … just as distress of

undervalued minority populations may not always be consciously accessible. If you're male, take a moment to pretend you live in a world that devalues your existence and considers you less than normal, and as not inherently valued. This is a world where you can be labeled abnormal or inferior simply because of what you're not.

New Research: Similarities and Differences

The first thing you should notice about this section is that it's labelled "New Research" but it contains old research. It would be understandable for you to conclude: "John and Rita are just getting old and, therefore, old research still seems new to them." However, our reason for presenting this as new research is that most people—even in highly reputable professional positions—aren't aware of these research-based reformulations that expand the concept of male as normative.

Remnants (and more) remain of male as normative in psychology, although some progress has been made. For example, while working with the renowned moral development theorist, Lawrence Kohlberg, Carol Gilligan began wondering if Kohlberg's stages of moral development were complete, since he had done most of his research using male subjects. Gilligan's (Gilligan, 1982; Gilligan & Attanucci, 1988) research led her to hypothesize that an **ethic of caring** for others might constitute a different moral reasoning, one that some females might more readily embrace within the dominant culture. For example, someone who makes decisions based on relieving someone else's emotional pain might be using moral reasoning that's just as highly developed as people who base decisions on a rational analysis of fairness.

Gilligan's revised perspective on moral development has generated controversy for moral philosophers and feminists alike. What's important about Gilligan's contributions is that she provided an example of what's left out when we don't include multiple perspectives. Having a diverse moral model that includes women's voices creates a more complete model.

Stress researcher and social psychologist Shelly Taylor made a similar contribution when researching the well-known **fight or flight phenomenon** (Taylor et al., 2000). She and her colleagues wrote:

A little-known fact about the fight-or-flight response is that the preponderance of research exploring its parameters has been conducted on males, especially on male rats. Until recently, the gender distribution in the human literature was inequitable as well. Prior to 1995, women constituted about 17% of participants in laboratory studies of physiological and neuroendocrine responses to stress. (2000, p. 412)

Reanalysis of existing data and new research revealed significant differences in the ways in which females and males respond to stressful situations. Consequently, Taylor and colleagues (2000) proposed an alternative female stress response pattern, referring to it as "**tend-and-befriend**." To summarize, there was evidence that female responses to stress frequently (but not always) involved caring for others, "joining social groups to reduce vulnerability," and communal management of responsibilities and resources (p. 422).

To summarize, white male ways of being aren't always normative for all females, or even for all males. There are physical and psychological similarities between females and males, but also differences. It's inappropriate to claim that the fight-or-flight response is superior to a tend-and-befriend response. There may be benefits to both stress-related behavior patterns (Master et al., 2009; Taylor & Gonzaga, 2007; Taylor & Master, 2011). Anecdotally, Rita is more likely to directly confront (and chase) a male mugger than tend to the friend the mugger just knocked down. Remember the iron rule: There will be more within-group variation than between-group variation. Neither behavior pattern represents psychopathology and neither will always be the superior response to threat.

Despite research and theoretical modifications linked to Gilligan, Taylor, and others, behavior and beliefs remain strongly oriented toward male as normative. Old ways of thinking are hard to change. Gender bias also remains a significant factor in medical research (Karp et al., 2017).

Old Patterns: Can Men Understand Women?

Men sometimes playfully, yet hurtfully, perpetuate male as normative and female as deviant. At a public lecture, John was presenting with a panel on the "Amazing Brain." Off and on during the panel discussion there were observations and comments about differences between male and female brains. Toward the end of the evening, a man in the back raised his hand and asked: "I don't suppose anyone can ever really answer this, uh, this age-old question, but how can you understand women?" His question was carefully intoned and worded in such a way that it was clear that he wasn't (a) complimenting women because of their sophisticated complexity or (b) speaking about his own shortcomings or inabilities to comprehend women. This comment was an articulation of the age-old belief—perpetuated primarily by men—that women are irrational and therefore impossible for rational-logical-superior men to understand.

John responded to this man's question by stating:

I'm not really going there, but I guess I'd say that to understand women you'd actually have to spend time with them, listen to them, and be interested in what they have to say.

We encourage you to watch and listen for additional subtle or direct examples of male as normative in your everyday experiences. Additional examples we've seen or that we've read about in the literature include:

- White males are overrepresented in politics, entertainment, and literature: spend an evening counting the number of male versus female characters on television shows or in movies. The *Sesame Street* puppets continue to provide a prime example.

- When vocations are all or mostly male, the average salary is higher. Welders and custodians are generally paid more than teachers. Garbage collectors make more than child-care workers.

- When males have problems, efforts will be made to deny those problems, explain them as failures of the system, or reframe them as hidden strengths. We once had a man at a workshop explain that male suicide rates were 3 to 4 times higher than female suicide rates because "men know how to get the job done."

- When women or minorities have problems it will be interpreted as due to their inherent weakness or defectiveness. Think of how high rates of depression and anxiety in women are explained.

- When a women or person from a minority group gains power or recognition, groups of primarily white males will make extreme, inaccurate, and inflammatory statements about that individual's character, mental health, or legitimacy. This seems to be tolerated more fully in recent times.

- If an entity has no stereotypically male or female features, it will be referred to as male until proven otherwise. How else could Big Bird or Bugs Bunny have been construed as male?

- Traditional masculine adjectives can be used as compliments for males and females (i.e., she or he is so active, dominant, strong!); in contrast, traditional feminine adjectives can't be effectively used for complimenting both sexes and even have less positive valence for females. Try calling one of your male friends soft or demure. Also, using these same terms on women isn't necessarily complimentary. As Kaschak (1992) noted, "Women are subject to censure not only for behaving too much like men, but for behaving too much like women" (p. 40).

- Women's activities are referred to as *women's* activities. Male activities are simply activities. Women's work, versus work. Women's ways of knowing, versus ways of knowing.

Cumulatively, these examples illustrate the point that maleness has been and still is the primary normative definition of being human. This is *the* core tenet of feminist (and multicultural) therapy. When a culture treats certain members as exemplary, or normal, and other members as different from normal and therefore inferior, it creates psychological burdens (Enns, 2004). The blame for the problems these burdens cause people rests with the culture, not the individual.

Consciousness–Raising Is Part of Healing and Change

Another key feminist principle is that consciousness-raising facilitates healing and growth. To change, clients must recognize cultural oppression. They must stop blaming themselves for not being heterosexual, white, male, or for being the wrong kind of male. They must free themselves from the burden of self-blame.

Without consciousness-raising, clients might continually try to change themselves to survive in patriarchal, sexist environments. Empirical research supports that this "taking of responsibility" will add stress and distress. Denial of sexism, whether in the form of macro- or microaggressions, is linked to higher distress (Moradi & DeBlaere, 2010; Sue, 2010a).

The Personal Is Political

The **personal is political** was a second wave rallying cry; it refers to the fact that personal experiences are intertwined with, and cannot be separated from, the social-political cultural setting (Brown, 2010; Enns, 2004). Personal transformation facilitates social transformation and vice versa. One measure of success in feminist therapy might be increased social interest and awareness—an optimistic desire to change the world for the better. As Worell and Remer (2003) wrote:

> Overall, our feminist psychological practice approach seeks a dual outcome: assisting women toward empowerment in their own lives and seeking change in whatever social power structures form the basis of many of their problems. (p. 18)

The personal is political is directly related to consciousness-raising or feminist-inspired insights; it involves recognizing the connection between one's personal misery and related political practices. This is why consciousness-raising groups were so powerful. As women met together and spoke of their experiences and feelings, they began to recognize the political significance of their personal situations and the negative force of isolation. From the personal is political perspective, the goal is change—change in the women, but more importantly, change in the structure and function of the politics (or power arrangements) within their environments.

THE PRACTICE OF FEMINIST THERAPY

Feminist therapy is primarily feminist theory-driven. The therapy process is distinctively focused on awareness (consciousness-raising) and empowerment. Feminist therapy isn't linked to specific techniques and, similar to existential-humanistic approaches, in some cases techniques might be contraindicated.

Enns (2004) described feminism as an "umbrella framework" for psychotherapy practice (p. 8). One way of thinking about what Enns is saying is that technical strategies don't define what feminist therapists do; instead, feminist theory drives what feminist therapists do. Feminist therapists are therefore free to be technically eclectic. They're comfortable using techniques from a broad range of therapy orientations (e.g., Adlerian, person-centered, existential, cognitive behavioral). However, the work they do must be compatible with their underlying feminist philosophy.

The overarching **goals of feminist therapy** are not eclectic. They include:

- Helping clients see the patterns and social forces that have diminished their sense of power and control.

- Encouraging clients to reclaim power, authority, and direction in their lives.

- Allowing clients to experience this shared power in the therapy relationship.

- Honoring and facilitating female ways of being or feminist consciousness, including growth stemming from deep, connected, intimate relationships.

Worell and colleagues (Worell & Chandler, 1996; Worell, Chandler, & Robinson, 1996; Worell & Johnson, 2003) articulated and described a feminist approach to therapy. Their essential ingredients include: (a) empowerment, (b) an analysis of power, and (c) evocation of feminist consciousness. We weave Worell's essential feminist therapy ingredients into the following sections.

Informed Consent

Traditionally, **informed consent** involves a written document that describes the process and purpose of therapy, along with likely benefits and potential risks (see Putting It in Practice 10.2). Informed consent is also an ongoing process in most counseling relationships. For feminist therapists, informed consent is a particular process that includes empowerment and partnership.

Feminist therapists are open about themselves and their therapeutic purpose. They tell clients why they engage in certain activities, assign homework, or focus on specific topics. They also regularly check in on the counseling relationship to make sure they're respecting their client's wishes. Consider the following exchange:

C: It says in your paperwork that you're a feminist. I didn't know that when I made the appointment.

T: Yes. Thanks for noticing. It's important for us to talk about that part of my professional identity. Probably some other parts, too.

C: I don't know if I would have come in if I'd known you're a feminist.

T: Sounds like you're unsure about working with someone like me.

C: Yes, I am. And I only have six visits total with my managed care.

T: I can see why this would feel bad. How about this? Let's explore what I mean in my paperwork, and let's explore what brought you in, and if you feel it would be better to work with someone else, I won't turn this session in to your company.

C: Wow, really? Yes. That works for me. Thanks.

T: What happened inside you when you read that informed consent?

C: Well, I'm not comfortable with gays and I think women need to raise their children at home, and I know it isn't good for animal testing and all, but I like wearing make-up and I respect my husband, at least when he's sober. [Client gets a little emotional.]

T: You know, I can tell you've got a lot on your mind, both from what you filled out and the way you just said that. I want to assure you about a couple things and then hear more about what's troubling you. Would that be okay?

C: Yeah. Sorry. I'm pretty strung out.

T: That's okay. You've made a good choice to get help. I just want you to know that my counseling work is about you, not me. I don't need to change you at all. I just want to help you change in the ways you think are best for you. We don't need to talk about people who are gay. I don't have any hard and fast rules about the ways women should dress or raise kids or anything. I just believe women deserve a fair shake, and I think it can be useful for us to look at the ways women sometimes get the short end of the stick. But I don't push it. I mostly listen and reflect things back to you.

C: But I like men. I think they deserve our support, working and all. My dad worked himself to death, basically. [Client gets teary again.]

T: [Smiles.] I like men too. And I believe we need to support both men and women. So far, I don't think we really disagree in ways that will matter in our work together, but I'm open to talking about it along the way. And I can see that your dad meant a lot to you. [Therapist makes two statements, giving her client the choice to respond to further concerns about the feminist orientation or to move into some of what is troubling her.]

C: He was my savior. That's why I got together with my husband. They seemed so much alike. Boy, was I wrong. That's why I need help. I need perspective or something. I want to just get on with talking about it. It's okay what you believe as long as you're not going to push it or judge me. I've got to talk about it, or I'm going to just up and leave him.

T: Okay. Seems really important for you to start talking right now. But if you feel worried about what I'm thinking, or if you feel like I'm pushing an agenda, will you please tell me?

C: Yeah. I will. Thanks.

From this interaction, it's possible to see how a feminist therapist might work effectively with clients who may not envision becoming feminists themselves. For most people, feeling empowered and respected is a welcome experience. However, having an honest, careful exchange is both necessary and in keeping with ethical practice.

PUTTING IT IN PRACTICE

10.3 Aspects of a Feminist Informed Consent

Mental health professionals work from different theoretical perspectives. They have different beliefs about what hurts, limits, or damages people and what it takes to heal or change. My own perspectives will influence the ways I will work with you.

As a feminist, I believe women and men deserve equal chances for jobs, recreation, and other things that make life meaningful. I believe gender matters a great deal and can sometimes get in the way of our development. I also believe our culture can make things tough on men or women because of how narrowly being male and female has been defined. Often, people find that exploring gender issues makes a big difference in the ways they feel about themselves. Because being a feminist means being sensitive to minority groups and people who are systematically disadvantaged, I'm also a big supporter of people who are diverse or different from the mainstream culture.

What does this mean in my work with you?

First, it's important for you to know I won't try to change your beliefs. I will respect our differences.

Second, we'll be partners in our work together. You're the expert on you, and I hope I can offer my education and experiences as you work on the issues bringing you to counseling.

Third, as we explore the distress you're feeling in your life, we may talk about social and cultural forces outside of yourself that are increasing your distress. We may also talk about how you've come to believe unhelpful messages given to you by our culture.

Fourth, because therapy is about you and your life, we'll focus on what you can do, what you can think or believe, and how you can act to help you feel better about yourself and your life situation. Sometimes this will involve changing the way you think or other things inside yourself. Other times it will involve changing your life situation or learning to deal with your life situation more assertively.

Fifth, the overarching goal of therapy is to empower you as a person. I want you to be able to look at yourself and your life and make the decisions that will help you learn and grow in ways that are meaningful to you.

Assessment Issues and Procedures

Feminists approach assessment in a therapeutic and constructive manner. Assessment doesn't involve one person judging another person's well-being. Instead, assessment is a mutual exploration of what's happening in the client's inner world and real life, all within a cultural context. Because mutual assessment and exploration of clients and the world they live in is inherently therapeutic, feminist therapists generally use nontraditional assessments. Symptoms are viewed as communications about what's wrong in the client's world and are explored in a safe environment (Enns, 2004).

Standardized Assessment

Feminist therapists are familiar with standard assessment procedures, but avoid using them unnecessarily. This is because assessment and diagnosis place problems within the psyche of individuals—even when there's ample evidence to suggest the problem is initiated and maintained by destructive social, political, and patriarchal forces.

Feminists eschew labeling nonconforming thoughts and behaviors as pathological. Ballou and Brown (2002) describe the rationale:

> The decision to call nonconforming thoughts, values, and actions psychopathology does two things. First,

it discounts [the person] described as such. Second, it blocks our ability to look outside the individual to see forces, dynamics, and structure that influence the development of such thinking, values and actions. (p. xviii)

The goals of feminist therapy include *not* discounting clients and *not* being seduced into thinking that the whole of the problem resides within the person who entered the office. If standardized assessments are used, they're used collaboratively and sensitively. Results are shared carefully, within the crucible of context; women and persons from other cultures have often experienced assessment processes that marginalize and label them.

Diagnosis

The *Diagnostic and Statistical Manual of Mental Disorders* (*DSM*) has an abysmal history when it comes to sex, gender, and racial sensitivity (Caplan, 1995; Caplan & Cosgrove, 2004; Cosgrove & Wheeler, 2013). Although the fourth (2000) and fifth (2013) editions included sections discussing culture and gender issues, most of the emphasis of the *DSM* system as well as the *International Classification of Diseases*, 9th edition (*ICD-9*) is on the medicalization of emotional and psychological distress.

From a feminist perspective, diagnoses, like all labels, can be oppressive and marginalizing. Diagnosis can hold people back from their potential. This is one among many reasons feminists are reluctant to make use of the *DSM-5* and *ICD-9*. In addition, feminist critiques have revealed that every edition of the *DSM* has included an unfair and biased distribution of mental disorders toward females (Ali, Caplan, & Fagnant, 2010; Kupers, Ross, Frances, & Widiger, 2005). More recently, conflicts of interest between the *DSM* task force and work group members and the pharmaceutical industry have been documented (Cosgrove et al., 2014; Cosgrove & Wheeler, 2013). For example, 61% of *DSM* task force members were identified as having a financial conflict of interest involving testing medications for new *DSM* disorders (Cosgrove et al., 2014). Although feminist therapists don't refuse to diagnose clients, when they diagnose, they do so in an educational and collaborative manner that involves the client in diagnostic decision-making.

Power Analysis and Empowerment

Power analysis is a feminist assessment approach that examines how clients give away, acquire, and maintain power in different life domains. **Empowerment** is defined as the process of increasing interpersonal strength and confidence, especially as it pertains to personal control and assertiveness. As clients acquire insight into ways they might acquire personal power, feminist therapists work with them to feel an accompanying sense of empowerment. Brown (2010) described four *power types* that can become targets for feminist therapy interventions.

1. *Somatic power.* This is related to body image and comfort. When individuals are disempowered, it's often manifest through negative body image or physical dissociation. Healthy personal power with regard to the body involves feeling safety and security and acceptance of one's body as it is, rather than preoccupation with unattainable media-based body ideals.

2. *Intrapersonal/intrapsychic power.* When there are power shortages in this dimension, individuals can be overly focused on other people's thoughts and feelings or they can be consumed with a focus on past interactions that cannot change. Many oppressed individuals are so focused on taking care of others that they're out of touch with what they feel and what they want. Healthy intrapersonal/intrapsychic power is linked to self-understanding, clarity of purpose, and emotional awareness.

3. *Interpersonal/social-contextual power.* Lack of power in the interpersonal domain is common among oppressed persons. Often this situation is associated with feeling helpless, hopeless, or isolated. Individuals might feel invisible or irrelevant. Healthy interpersonal power includes the ability to be assertive. Healthy interpersonal power involves confidence in one's ability to help oneself and to make a difference in the world.

4. *Spiritual/existential power.* When power is low in this domain, individuals feel meaninglessness and disconnection. Healthy spiritual/existential power involves feeling free to embrace culturally preferred spiritual or religious rituals and practices, or to develop one's own, or to find meaning in ways consistent within the definition of intrapsychic power.

Self-Esteem and Self-Efficacy

Many women continue to evaluate themselves based on the success of their mating and nurturing accomplishments. Although these are important life dimensions, completely basing self-esteem on mating and nurturing can be patriarchy driven, distracting from a focus on personal development. To check for imbalance in these areas consider the impact of answering the following questions:

- How desirable or attractive am I to potential sexual partners?

- How much status does my current romantic partner have?

- What do others think of how I look?

- Is my house clean enough?

- Are my offspring getting all the opportunities they expect?

- How many people am I able to nurture or take care of?

In contrast to first and second wave feminism (where balancing mating and nurturing activities with activities outside the family was viewed as optimal), third and fourth wave feminists accept mothering as a primary focus—with one caveat: the choice to embrace mothering should be a conscious choice that's not solely a function of the dominant patriarchy. Third and fourth wave feminists celebrate motherhood in all its forms, including lesbian motherhood, feminist mamas, and matricentric feminism (O'Reilly, 2011, 2016).

For girls and women, success outside of family life can be a double-edged sword. It can increase self-esteem, but there may be costs associated with venturing beyond stereotypical female behaviors.

The same dilemma (but in reverse) is true for many boys and men. The expectations to make money, be emotionally rugged, and achieve success outside the home are strong. Men who want to be stay-at-home dads may face raised eyebrows, accusations of laziness, or even be suspected of nefarious activities. For feminist therapists, the focus on men's self-esteem and self-efficacy remains embedded in consciousness-raising and conscious choosing. The question of "What do men want?" is more relevant than ever. Perhaps even more importantly, feminist therapists assess the support that males have, especially gay and minority males, from parents, family, partners, coworkers, and friends (Kocet, 2014).

In feminist therapy, self-esteem and self-efficacy are assessed through reflective conversation, not standardized questionnaires. Questions that can stimulate conversations about self-esteem, self-efficacy, and life decisions might include:

- What brings you joy?
- In what directions do you long to grow and develop yourself?
- If you strip away all of society's expectations, where do you think your true skills and talents lie?
- Where could you go to take an hour or a day or a week to reflect on what you want in your life?

Gender-Role Comfort, Development, and Satisfaction

Gender role is defined as culturally based behavioral expectations for males and females. Women and men are often expected to conform to limited definitions of what it means to be male or female. In one dimension of the traditional scenario, females are cast as helpmates (wives) who support their husband's needs, career, and ambitions. An offensive old Groucho Marx joke captures the status of a traditional wife:

> Behind every successful man is a woman, behind her is his wife.

Examining how clients' feel about their gender role in social, intimate, and work relationships is an important part of feminist assessment. Many women and men seek counseling when their storybook marriage or partnership takes a bad turn and it's clear that "happily ever after" isn't happening. Profound disappointments around gender roles in social and employment settings also contribute to clients' distress. Although the dynamics are unique to different relationship configurations (e.g., LGBTQ), explicitly negotiating couple, family, social, and employment-related gender roles and expectations is critical.

Within heterosexual relationships women continue to bear a disproportionate burden of household and parenting responsibilities (Askari, Liss, Erchull, Staebell, & Axelson, 2010). This may be a conscious and intentional choice for some couples, but a feminist analysis of gender role comfort can help bring gender-based expectations into awareness.

Important questions within domestic or romantic relationships include:

- How do you feel about sharing of household workloads within your relationship?
- Are you satisfied with your parenting role?
- Have you and your partner had intentional discussions about your individual and family budgets and your respective contributions?
- How do you and your partner decide the relative worth of what each of you contribute to your relationship and household?

Over the last two decades, several writers have identified a crisis in male identity and achievement (Hymowitz, 2011; Kimmel, 2010). This crisis is partly manifest in an apparent lack of career ambition among young men, including males who are ethnic or racial minorities (Matthews, 2014; Pérez, 2017). Recent estimates are that about 55% to 60% of enrolled college/university students are female (Swanson, Vaughan, & Wilkinson, 2017). Based on our own observations of university students seen in a campus-based career counseling clinic, a significant number of distressed females are balancing employment, school, and romantic relationships. These young women are doing the lion's share of household work, attending college, and bringing more income into the relationship. In contrast, at least some of the males are more interested in recreational pursuits than academic or vocational success.

Feminist approaches to evaluating and empowering males to set and achieve academic goals may be especially salient. Specifically, researchers with White, Latino, and African American males all point, in one way or another, toward college experiences that focus on increasing interpersonal connection (Matthews, 2014; Pérez, 2017; Swanson et al., 2017). Similarly, as early as middle school, researchers have identified emotional stoicism as a predictor of school avoidance and disengagement (Rogers, Gendlin, Kiesler, & Truax, 1967). Feminist assessment with male college students should focus on physical versus emotional risk-taking and identifying male role models who are academically successful.

Females, Males, and Bodies

Negative body image among girls and women has been prominent in the psychological literature for many decades (Levin & Kilbourne, 2009). More recently, boys and men have been experiencing greater body dissatisfaction than ever before (Cheng, McDermott, Wong, & La, 2016). Clearly, the U.S. marketing media has pushed images of unattainable bodies onto the general public with such force that there have been dramatically negative consequences.

Honoring the body is an important element of feminist therapy and clients' attitudes toward their bodies is a core assessment domain. Eating disorders, obesity, sexual dysfunctions, self-mutilation, psychosomatic disorders, and other body-related distresses are more common among females than males (Touchette et al., 2011). Noncombat post-traumatic stress disorder is also more common in females; this disorder has important physical/somatic dimensions. Many females who come to counseling have a history of physical or sexual abuse or rape. They may or may not focus on this trauma, but such experiences are likely to affect their relationship with their bodies. Feminist therapists will often inquire about how clients feel about their bodies.

Feminist therapists are concerned with the physical experiences of all clients and have been centrally involved in the shift in psychology toward acknowledging the negative effects of psychological and physical trauma.

About 25 years ago, influential psychiatrist Judith Herman (1992) highlighted the resistance of mainstream society to grapple with these negative outcomes. When providing assessment and treatment, feminist therapists recognize the adverse physical and emotional effects of trauma and conduct assessments in a manner that is simultaneously therapeutic.

Transgender clients typically have strong feelings toward and sometimes preoccupation with specific body parts (McGuire, Doty, Catalpa, & Ola, 2016). When working with transgender clients, or other clients experiencing body dissatisfaction and intense self-criticism, the purpose of assessment isn't to judge or evaluate; instead, the purpose is to understand. Sitting with transgender clients and listening nonjudgmentally as they share their body-related critiques, hopes, and fears is an example of feminist assessment and therapy.

BRAIN BOX

10.1 Feminist Theory and Interpersonal Neurobiology: Natural Parallels

Feminist therapy is about connection.

So is neuroscience.

Neuroscience involves the study of synaptic interconnections, neural networks, brain structures and their electrochemical communications.

Feminist therapy involves egalitarian interconnection, empathy, mutual empathy, and empowerment of the oppressed, neglected, and marginalized.

As a highly sophisticated, interconnected entity, the human brain is metaphorical support for feminist theory and therapy. In the brain, cells don't operate in isolation. In feminist therapy in general, and relational-cultural therapy (RCT) in particular, isolation is unhealthy. Connection is healthy.

Healthy brains are connection-heavy. Whether humans are awake or asleep, brain cells are in constant communication; they problem-solve; they operate sensory and motor systems; they feed back information to and from the body, inhibiting, exciting, and forming a connected, communicating, community.

Using modern brain research as a foundation, Jordan (the developer of RCT) described how empathic relationships can change clients:

Empathy is not just a means to better understand the client; in mutually empathic exchanges, the isolation of the client is altered. The client feels less alone, more joined with the therapist. It is likely that in these moments of empathy and resonance, there is active brain resonance between therapist and client (Schore, 1994), which can alter the landscape and functioning of the brain. Thus, those areas of the brain that register isolation and exclusion fire less and those areas that indicate empathic responsiveness begin to activate (Jordan, 2010, p. 32).

Jordan is talking about how therapist–client interactions change the brain. Many others have made the same point: "It is the power of being with others that shapes our brain" (Cozolino, 2006, p. 9). In her review of RCT theory and outcomes, Frey (2013) emphasized that "research on mirror neurons, the facial recognition system, lifelong neuroplasticity and neurogenesis, and the social functions of brain structures" (p. 181) supports feminist theory and feminist therapy process.

Neuroscience research is supportive of feminist therapy in ways that are both real and metaphorical. There is unarguably great potential here. However, before we wax too positive, it's important to heed a warning. Beginning with Plato (at least) and throughout the history of time, the main way in which physical (or brain) differences between the sexes have been used is to marginalize females and undercut their viability as equal partners in the human race.

With that caveat in mind, let's respect feminism with some multitasking. Let's celebrate the positive parallels between human neurology and feminist theory, while simultaneously keeping a watchful eye on how neuroscience is being used to limit or oppress girls and women.

Here are two quick examples of neurosexism in the popular press (there are many more).

The Essential Difference: Male and Female Brains and the Truth about Autism (Baron-Cohen, 2003). Baron-Cohen is an autism researcher. His book allegedly, "... proves that female-type brains are better at empathizing and communicating, while male brains are stronger at understanding and building systems—not just computers and machinery, but abstract systems such as politics and music."

The Female Brain (Brizendine, 2006). Brizendine is a neuropsychiatrist. Her book is touted as bringing "... together the latest findings to show how the unique structure of the female brain determines how women think, what they value, how they communicate, and who they love."

Genderizing the brain marginalizes and limits females, but also does the same for males. For a thorough and cogent argument for brain equality, see *Delusions of Gender* by Cordelia Fine (2010). Fine examines the scientific evidence and refutes Baron-Cohen's and Brizendine's arguments. She even describes how empathy research discriminates against males. One of her main recommendations for neuroscience writers is "don't make stuff up."

Therapy Relationships

Mutual partnership is the foundation of love. A feminist practice is the only movement for social justice in our society which creates the conditions where mutuality can be nurtured. (hooks, 2000, p. 104)

Feminists place great emphasis on therapy relationships. Feminist therapy relationships are egalitarian, and involve mutuality and empowerment (J. Sommers-Flanagan & Sommers-Flanagan, 2017). Rader and Gilbert (2005) wrote that egalitarian feminist therapy relationships occur when therapists:

1. View clients as their own experts

2. Inform clients of the therapy process and their role and rights in that process (e.g., a client's right to "shop around" for a therapist or to understand the potential risks of therapy)

3. Use strategies that promote client autonomy and power

4. Encourage anger expression

5. Model appropriate behaviors for clients (adapted from Rader & Gilbert, 2005, p. 427)

Gilbert's (1980) fourth item, "encourage anger expression," warrants explanation. Anger expression is encouraged because: (a) direct expression of anger has been traditionally discouraged for females; (b) anger stimulates insight or consciousness-raising; (c) anger helps clients clarify how they've been mistreated and identify counseling goals; (d) feminist counselors recognize and welcome anger directed toward them, and are prepared to explore its potential underlying insights; (e) anger is an appropriate emotional response to oppression and abuse that should not be suppressed. Overall, nurturing client anger can facilitate feminist consciousness. **Feminist consciousness** involves becoming aware of balance and equality in roles and relationships.

The feminist therapy relationship is similar to the person-centered therapy (PCT) relationship. There is congruence, unconditional positive regard, and empathy. Also, similar to Rogers (1957), the relationship itself is seen as a healing force. Feminist therapists also emphasize mutuality, mutual empathy, and self-disclosure.

Mutuality

Mutuality means that power, decision-making, goal selection, and learning are shared. Although other psychotherapies consider treatment a mutual process wherein clients and therapists are open and human with one another, nowhere are egalitarian values and the concept of mutuality emphasized more than in feminist therapy (Evans, Kincade, & Seem, 2011; J. Sommers-Flanagan & Sommers-Flanagan, 2017).

Mutual Empathy

Mutual empathy is defined as clients seeing–experiencing–knowing their emotional effect on their therapists within a safe environment. When achieved, mutual empathy allows clients to see their therapists experiencing empathic resonance. This connection—as opposed to the withdrawing–isolation–punishment that caregivers often have in response to their children's deep emotions—is viewed as healing in and of itself and as stimulating self-acceptance of painful emotions (J. Sommers-Flanagan & Sommers-Flanagan, 2017).

Self–Disclosure

Self-disclosure occurs when therapists share their thoughts or feelings with their clients. Self-disclosure can facilitate therapy in several ways (Jordan, 2010; R. Sommers-Flanagan, 2012). First, therapists self-disclose to model openness and transparency. Second, self-disclosure is used to enhance relationship connection. As therapists and clients come to know one another, trust builds. Third, self-disclosure is used to share experiences and wisdom in a non-hierarchical manner. It's not that the therapist is the only one who has knowledge and life experiences; it's just that to hold back helpful knowledge and experience is anti-therapeutic. The client's knowledge and experience is equally valued. Fourth, self-disclosure can facilitate an egalitarian relationship. Again, the more this type of relationship is established, the more trust develops, and the more open clients can be about their challenging

situations and traumatic experiences. Examples of self-disclosure are included in the case vignettes and case presentation.

There are limits on self-disclosure. The therapy office shouldn't become a place where therapists focus too much on their own pain or try to develop future friendships. As with all therapies the self-disclosure must be therapeutic and focused for the good of the client. Supervision is a good place to learn how to balance your self-disclosure in ways that maximize its usefulness for clients.

Focusing on Sex and Sexuality

Sexuality is a topic where many men and women feel rigid about gender roles and ashamed or confused if they don't fit into the male–female cultural norms. Female sexuality is still less well-understood than male sexuality. In an article titled "Female Sexual Disorders: Psychiatric Aspects," the author stated bluntly, "Knowledge of female sexuality has consistently lagged behind our knowledge of male sexuality" (Segraves, 2002, p. 420). This lagging may be changing, as a quick search for woman and sexuality on your favorite online bookseller's site will provide you with plenty of information ranging from how women can have great sex all the time, to how they can guard their bodies and remain pure.

Despite online educational resources, many people don't understand their own bodies well and might be unable to express their sexual needs in their intimate relationships or might fear their needs are abnormal or shameful. The female orgasm has been the subject of many books and much lively debate for centuries. Many male authority figures have asserted their knowledge of this uniquely female experience. Part of the women's movement in the 1960s focused on women reclaiming their orgasms and their bodies. Healthy female sexuality and rights to reproductive health and choices continue to be a focus in feminism today, as is analyzing the rigidity of attitudes about sexual orientation and the effect of homophobic attitudes on all people.

Feminist therapists provide an open and safe space for discussing relationships, sexuality, and intimacy. These discussions should be sensitive to the client's preferred pace. Information may be explored or offered, without a rigid idea of what's normal or acceptable. Clients are encouraged to determine their own sexual identity and boundaries.

What about Men?

Feminist theory and science directly examines how society damages individuals who don't fit into gender stereotypes (e.g., from sissies and tomboys to transgender people) but that's not all. Contemporary feminism also focuses on the price individuals pay when they fit too well! Many problems men face, such as homophobia, aggression, workaholism, and the inability to relate to women, children, or even their own emotions, are by-products of male socialization (Levant & Pollack, 1995). The painful costs of devaluing all things feminine and strict rules for being male were evidenced in William Pollack's (2000) book, *Real Boys' Voices*. Scotty, a 13-year-old boy from a small town in the Northeast, said,

Boys are supposed to shut up and take it, to keep it all in. It's harder for them to release or vent without feeling girly. And that can drive them to shoot themselves. (p. ix)

The challenge for feminists and men's movement advocates is to engage males who are trapped in male stereotypes that confer privilege, but limit full human development. Reading about Pollack's boy code is one way to increase awareness of the ways that contemporary gender-based stereotypes adversely affect males (see Putting It in Practice 10.4).

PUTTING IT IN PRACTICE

10.4 The Boy Code

In the 1990s, Harvard professor William Pollack conducted qualitative interviews with boys. The goal was to determine what they viewed as implicit social-emotional rules that influence boy behavior. He called these rules the *boy code*. The boy code includes:

- Stand on your own two feet.
- Separate from your mother and all things female ASAP.
- Never show any feelings—except anger.
- Stay on top, in control, and in the limelight.
- Remember, sex is a conquest.
- Bullying and teasing is normal boy behavior.
- Never give in, never apologize, and never really listen to anyone else (these are signs of weakness).
- Don't show any fear of violence.
- Never "rat" or "nark" on another boy. (Pollack, 2000)

Overall, Pollack's boy code is viewed as contributing to unhappy intimate relationships, poor emotional health, and increased violence (for a short video promoting emotional expression in boys and men, see India's #startwiththeboys campaign: https://www.youtube.com/watch?v=0Nj99epLFqg).

For gender balance, we searched for a *girl code*, but didn't find anything comparable. Consequently, we conducted an informal survey with our students and obtained the following gender-based rules for girls. Check them out and see if you've got rules to add to either list.

- Always look pretty.
- Always be clean and smell good.
- Be as thin as you can be.
- Strive to be a mom.
- Take care of other people and the family home.
- Be sexy, but not too sexy.
- Defer to your man—especially in public.

- Always be nice—if not, you're a bitch.

- You need a man to be complete.

- Be emotionally expressive. But don't be angry. Because, if you're angry, either you're a bitch ... or you're on your period.

- Don't compete with men or boys, or, if you do, don't win.

Feminist Therapy in Action: Brief Vignettes

As you read these vignettes look for therapy interactions that you believe are distinctly feminist. Watch for assessment conversations, mutuality, mutual empathy, self-disclosure, empowerment, and valuing of feminine consciousness.

Vignette I: Laura Brown

Laura Brown
(*photo courtesy of Lynn Brown*)

This vignette is excerpted from a demonstration videotape featuring Laura S. Brown, PhD, working in her third session with a client named Ellen (L. Brown, 1994a). The client–therapist interactions are paraphrased rather than verbatim. Ellen is a 34-year-old client mandated to counseling because of a drug problem.

Early in the session, Ellen explains that she went to a Narcotics Anonymous (NA) meeting in Baltimore. Dr. Brown lifts her eyebrows, saying "Baltimore?" in a surprised tone. Ellen acknowledges that it is quite a distance from her home, but she doesn't want to be seen by anyone who might know her locally. This leads to an assessment question: "Ellen, what will people see if they see the real Ellen?"

Ellen defends herself against this question, talking about clothes, jewelry, and the desire she believes everyone shares to stay hidden. Dr. Brown stays on the theme, asking about what dark secrets Ellen fears that people might see. Ellen talks about her drug use and her feelings that this is her own business, not something people need to know about or judge her on. She claims that her drug use hasn't interfered with her life, but catches herself, just as Dr. Brown says, with warmth, "Wait a minute. What's wrong with this picture?"

Ellen admits that her drug use caused a slight problem, in that she lost her job and has to go to counseling, but she denies most of the problem. Rather than going after the denial, Dr. Brown comments:

Dr. Brown: How things look is very important to you, and it is very hard for you to keep it up. It's very tiring.

Ellen: Yes, I work hard at how I look. And I'm not saying it isn't tiring.

Dr. Brown: Let yourself notice the tiredness. Don't talk about it. Just notice your body and how tired it is in there. Feel how hard it is to keep that pretty picture in place.

Ellen relaxes her body and is quiet. Dr. Brown encourages her to keep relaxing. Ellen tears up and talks about how hard she tries and how much she wishes her father would be proud of her. She spontaneously explores her father's gender messages—either be a lawyer like him or a wife and mother. Ellen explains that she can't do either. She faces how alone that makes her feel. Dr. Brown asks a strategic question: "Ellen, when did you get yourself to be at peace that your father will never, ever say he's proud of you, no matter what you do?" Ellen admits that though her father will never say that, she isn't at peace about it and at 34 is still letting that wish drive her life. Together, for a short time, Dr. Brown and Ellen explore how alone she is and how no one has taken care of her. At this point, Dr. Brown tells Ellen she would like to revisit something Ellen mentioned last session—the fact that when Ellen was in college, someone she knew broke into her apartment and raped her.

Ellen: Yeah, I don't think there's that much to talk about. It was college. I was trying things out, you know. Freedom. Being an adult. Lots of sex and stuff. I was giving it away for free anyway, so I didn't think there was much to do. I told my brother later. He said I should tell the police and see a psychologist, but I didn't. I mean I sort of chose that life. I thought, hey, if guys can sow their wild oats, so can I. So I was pretty out there. I tried it all. No inhibitions. I guess the drugs aided that. I can say that back then, I really was a drug addict.

Dr. Brown: So, you felt like, I can do this. It's my choice, and if it hurts or feels bad, it's my own fault?

Ellen: Yeah, I chose it. That's how I feel about the rape, I guess. I don't know.

Dr. Brown: Ellen, what's your body saying as you say, "I don't know"?

Ellen: It's tired ... I didn't stand up for my own body. It's a little sad. But I can't go back now and change it.

Dr. Brown: No, but we can explore how that experience might be affecting things now—how being an adult, sexual woman is for you now. What do you wish would have happened?

Ellen tearfully admits her wish that someone might have helped her. She condemns herself as well, claiming that she should have handled it, wishing she had fought her assailant but noting that her drug-induced state made that unlikely. She ends with a wistful statement: "I wish someone would have been there, but there wasn't anyone. So I dealt with it."

As the session ends, Dr. Brown asks Ellen to consider doing two things during the week: going to one more NA meeting and using her art, either in writing or painting, to explore the question: "What does Ellen want?" Ellen agrees, saying that she has neglected her painting. Smiling, Ellen also says that the painting will have to be a Monet, because she only has impressions, but no clarity. Dr. Brown counters with support and the observation that even a Monet, from the right position, is clear. Ellen is surprised and pleased.

At the conclusion of the recording, Dr. Brown reflects on the session. Her goals for Ellen were to help the relationship develop and encourage Ellen to listen to her emotional self, which Dr. Brown explains is especially important with women who have used substances to numb emotions after traumatic experiences. She also notes her intention to begin exploring gender issues. In Ellen's case, as in many, it's important for the client to know that she will not be abandoned, judged, or overpowered as she begins to explore her pain and seek ways to make changes (adapted from Brown, 1994a).

Vignette II: Relational-Cultural Therapy

Relational-cultural therapy (RCT) is a feminist-oriented therapy developed by Jean Baker Miller, Judith Jordan, and other collaborators at the Stone Center (Frey, 2013; Jordan, 2010). RCT founders were trained in psychoanalysis. RCT is a depth psychotherapy that closely examines relationship connections, disruptions, and growth potential from mutually empathic intimate relationships. Core concepts of RCT include (from Jordan, 2010):

1. People grow through and toward relationship throughout the life span.

2. Movement toward mutuality rather than separation characterizes mature functioning.

3. Relationship differentiation and elaboration characterize growth.

4. Mutual empathy and mutual empowerment are at the core of growth-fostering relationships.

5. Authenticity is necessary for real engagement and full participation in growth-fostering relationship.

6. In growth-fostering relationships, all people contribute and grow or benefit. Development is not a one-way street.

7. One of the goals of development from a relational perspective is the development of increased relational competence and capacities over the life span. (p. 24)

Jordan (2010) describes a case in which she worked with a woman named Barbara, a "well-educated White woman who had seen six therapists before she began" working with Jordan (p. 53). Barbara's previous therapy experiences were negative. She had been labeled with various mental disorders and was in the hospital due to a suicide attempt when Jordan began RCT with her.

The therapy included open exchanges in both directions. Barbara made her evaluation of Jordan clear: "She [Jordan] was not much better than the other clinicians she had seen" (p. 53). Jordan worked intermittently through long silences to resonate with Barbara's fears and express what she could provide:

> I did not press her to give up her fears, acknowledged it had been a hard road, and told her that while I could not guarantee that I would understand her any better than the others, I was committed to trying. But I also suggested she had no real reason to trust me.

A turning point in therapy occurred when Barbara came to a session following a fresh self-mutilation incident (she had scratched her arm until it bled). Barbara became provocative. She asked if she might be "fired" as a client. She asked if perhaps Jordan would be embarrassed or worried that she was seeing a client who had blood dripping from her arm. Jordan (2010) described her response:

> I hesitated and agreed that the thought had crossed my mind (what her colleagues might think), but that I also could see she was in real pain and needed to be able to communicate that to me. She looked at first triumphant (at my admission of personal concern about my "reputation") but then genuinely relieved (perhaps that I had spoken a piece of truth about myself that she knew anyway). We then had a truly collaborative conversation about how she might be able to really let me know her conversation about her pain and whether she could trust my response. (p. 54)

You can see from these descriptions that RCT involves authentic interpersonal exchanges. There are rough patches (challenges, ruptures, and disconnections), but as therapists stay with empathy, honest self-disclosure, and focus on therapy process, positive changes can happen. Jordan reported that after over 2 years of challenging therapy, the process settled down. In the end, Barbara made remarkable process (immensely improving her job status, beginning to date a gentle and kind woman, and moving beyond her self-destructive behaviors). In ending, Jordan quotes Barbara's reflections on mutual empathy:

> Isn't it ironic that when you showed yourself as most fallible and vulnerable, I had the most trust in you? You didn't always get it right … and often it took a while for you to get it at all, but you almost always came back, trying and clearly imperfect. That made you feel safe to me. (p. 55)

REFLECTIONS

RCT has a strong emphasis on authenticity. Think about how that might work for you. What would help you become therapeutically authentic? Experience? Supervision? Both? What else?

CASE PRESENTATION

In an interesting twist, we're featuring a case with a male therapist and male client in the feminist chapter to illustrate how working within a feminist model can work for boys and men. This case focuses on a 16-year-old male's struggle with emotional expression. John is the therapist.

Josh was a white, 16-year-old heterosexual sophomore in high school. He had never met his biological father and lived in a middle-class neighborhood with his mother and three younger sisters. His mother was diagnosed with bipolar disorder. Josh's main loves were consistent with his gender identity. They included basketball, cars, girls, and sarcasm. He very much disliked school.

Josh and I met for therapy for several years. At the beginning of one of our sessions Josh handed me a packet of photos.

"Hey, what's this about?" I asked.

He responded with a half-mumble about a recent awards ceremony. I thought I discerned pride in that mumble. I looked through the pictures while he told me about each one. There was one in particular that he gently lifted from my hands. It was a picture of him in a line-up with five other people. He carefully pointed out that he was standing next to the Lieutenant Governor of Oregon. I teased him because there were no pictures of him and the *actual* governor.

"What's the deal?" I asked. "Wouldn't the Guv pose with you?" Josh rolled his eyes and signaled for me to move on to the next photo.

The Problem List and Problem Formulation

Unlike CBT, feminist therapy doesn't involve collaboratively generating a concrete problem list and formulating

problems as if the problems resided in the client. Instead, because problems and problem-formulation are inseparable, we can't talk about the problems without also talking about cultural factors creating and contributing to the problems.

If client issues are discussed as problems, they're likely discussed as situational challenges. In Josh's case, his mother initially had brought him to therapy for anger management. Anger was consistently a regular focus in Josh's therapy. Like many 16-year-old boys immersed in the dominant U.S. culture, Josh's emotional life was highly constricted. He was living by Pollack's boy code (2000) and unable or unwilling to risk feeling anything other than anger and irritation. From the feminist worldview, this wasn't Josh's problem; his issues around anger stemmed from him living in a culture that kept him in an emotional straitjacket.

Josh's issues (and case formulation from a feminist perspective) looked like this:

1. Learning to deal more effectively with sadness, grief, and anger within the context of a repressive emotional environment.

2. Coming to an understanding that his beliefs and views of emotional expression were not in his best interest, but instead, foisted upon him by toxic cultural attitudes about how boys and men should experience and express emotion.

3. Developing trust and confidence in himself—despite not having a father figure or a mother who could provide him and his sisters with a consistently safe and stable home environment.

4. Learning to talk about what he really feels inside and pursue his life passions whatever they might be instead of reflexively pursuing culturally "manly" activities.

5. Expanding Josh's limited emotional vocabulary through consciousness-raising.

Interventions

Feminist therapists are technically eclectic and use a wide range of interventions imbedded in an egalitarian and mutually empathic relationship:

1. Encouraging Josh to speak freely and openly about his life experiences.

2. Empathic listening with intermittent focusing on more tender emotions, depending on how much of this Josh was willing or able to tolerate.

3. Therapist self-disclosure and modeling.

As Josh and I looked at photos together, I responded with interest and enthusiasm. Because interpersonal connection is a core part of therapy, I didn't rush him to move on to our therapy agenda. Instead, I shifted back and forth between saying, "Cool" or "What's going on there?" to making sarcastic wisecracks like "Why exactly did the government let you into the capital building?" Sarcasm was used to express interest and affection indirectly, mirroring Josh's humor and style. After seeing most of the photos I asked, "Who's the person standing next to you?" I could tell from his response that I had asked a good question.

"Oh, yeah, her. Her name is Sharice; her mentor was getting the same award as my mentor. I danced with her. She's a good dancer."

We talked about dancing and what it was like for him to feel attracted to her. We were ten minutes into therapy and both of us had completely ignored the fact that we hadn't been able to see each other for five weeks. Finally, I decided to break the avoidance pattern. I asked "So … how are you doing with all that's been going on?"

He looked toward me, glancing downward.

"I'm doing okay, I guess."

Because this was a young man who had been socialized to keep his emotions tightly wrapped, I probed, but gently.

"I understand it's been pretty wild times?"

He looked up, eyes fixed on some invisible spot on the ceiling. I recognized this strategy—a surefire way to avoid crying in public. An upward gaze constricts the tear ducts; tears cannot flow.

He looked back down and said, "I've been busy. My mom's been in the hospital for about a month."

"I heard she had a pretty hard time."

He grunted and then, in a quiet growly voice, the words, "Let-me-tell-you-about-it" seeped out from behind his teeth. Silence followed. I cautiously probed a bit more by sharing more of what I knew.

"I talked with your mom yesterday. She told me that she got pretty caught up in some housing project." This statement lit a fire in Josh and he plunged into the story.

"You won't believe what she did. It was so f*ing stupid. Some punk developer is gonna build three houses. Three houses at the end of our street. This is *no big deal*. She just f*ing freaked out. She chained herself up to a tractor to stop them from building a house. Then she called the f*ing senator and road department and I don't know who in hell else she called. She was totally nuts. So I told her she had a choice. I told her that she could go back home or I'd call the police and have her committed. She wasn't taking care of my sisters. She was being a shit for a mom. So I just gave her a choice."

I nodded and said, "You must be practicing to be a parent. That's the kind of choice parents give their kids."

His voice grew louder as he continued: "I gave her the choice five times. Five f*ing times! She tried to buy a Mercedes and a Volvo over the phone. So I called the cops. And the woman asked *me* what to do. I'm f***ing 16 years old and they f*ing ask me what to do. I didn't know what to say. I told 'em to come get her. They finally sent some really big cops over to take her away."

"Then what happened?"

"My mom was still acting nuts and my sisters were crying. So I just picked them up and held them and they took her away. We sat and they cried and we snuggled a while. And then I drove us home. I don't have my license, but I can drive. My mom is still pissed at me about that, but I don't give a shit!"

While listening to Josh, I formed an image of him in my mind. I saw an awkward and 16-year-old boy "snuggling" his sobbing sisters, as the cops take their mother away. The girls were 9 and 6 and 4 years old—the same sisters he had complained about in previous therapy sessions.

Talking with teenage boys about emotional issues is tricky. Too much empathy and they retreat. No empathy and you're teaching the wrong lesson. Throughout Josh's storytelling, I used sarcasm, empathy, and emotional exploration, like, "What was that like for you to gather up your sisters and take care of them?" I suspected that if I asked too much about feelings or forced him to go too deep too fast, I would lose my "coolness rating" and there would be a relationship rupture.

Much of the session focused on empathy for Josh's anger. Josh ranted and I listened. He was immensely angry and disappointed and hurt about his mother's behavior. But I wanted to find a way to let Josh know that it's okay, even a positive thing, for boys and men to feel and express more tender feelings.

About halfway through our session, I asked:

"So Josh," I said. "When was the last time you cried?"

After a short pause he spoke with extreme deliberation, "I … don't … cry … I … just … get … pissed."

Josh expressed this masculine emotional principle very efficiently and then offered more about his socially coerced, but internalized emotional philosophy.

"Crying doesn't do any good. It doesn't change anything. It's just stupid."

"I know, I know," I said. "The whole idea of crying sounds pretty stupid to you. It's not like crying will change your mom and make her better."

"Nothing will ever change her."

I renewed my pursuit of when he last cried. He insisted that was so long ago that he couldn't really recall, but we both knew that several years ago, after an especially hard week with his mother, he had sat on my couch and sobbed himself to sleep. Instead of bringing that up, I asked him what might make him cry now. Would he cry if his girlfriend broke up with him … if he lost his cell phone … if one of his sisters got cancer … if he didn't graduate from high school? Josh fended off my questions about tears by repeating his resolve to get "pissed" about everything that might make him feel sad, but the question about one of his sister's getting cancer stumped him. He admitted, "Yeah, I might cry about that …" while quickly adding "… but I'd do it alone!"

I responded, "Right. Absolutely. Some things might be worth crying about … even though it wouldn't change things … but you'd want to do the crying alone."

We talked indirectly and intellectually about sadness and tears, trying to model that we can talk about it—once removed—and if he cried some day, it would be perfectly okay, there would be no need to feel ashamed.

Toward the end of the session, I decided to lighten things up by teasing Josh about his social insensitivity. I said, "I can't believe that we've talked this whole hour and you never asked me a single thing about myself."

Josh grinned. He knew therapy was all about him and not about me. He probably thought I was playing some sort of therapy game with him. He was a good sport and played along.

"Okay. So what am I supposed to ask?"

I acted offended, saying, "After all those questions I asked you, at least you should ask me when I last cried."

"God you don't know when to drop things. Okay. So when did you cry?"

I said, "I think it was yesterday."

Our eyes met. He looked surprised. I continued, "Yeah. I feel sad sometimes. It can be about really hard stories I hear in here or it can be about my own life. Even though it doesn't change anything, it feels better to let my sadness out."

It was time for the session to end. We both stood and I said, "We have to stop for today, but we can talk more about this or whatever you want to talk about next time."

Outcomes Measurement

Feminists generally don't use outcomes assessments (Santos de Barona & Dutton, 1997). Assessment involves labelling and can add to pressure and expectations to behave in particular ways. Josh's progress was mainly monitored through verbal updates. However, it might have been reasonable to have him respond to a few measures that focus on the degree to which the therapist is collaborative and shares power.

- *The Working Alliance Inventory* (Horvath & Greenberg, 1989).
- *Client Therapy with Women Scale* (Worell et al., 1996).

Additionally, RCT researchers developed a measure called the Relational Health Indices (Liang et al., 2002; Liang, Tracy, Kenny, Brogan, & Gatha, 2010). This is a 37-item questionnaire that measures three dimensions of growth-fostering relationships: engagement,

authenticity, and empowerment/zest. Having Josh complete this questionnaire might help us evaluate his relationships and be a structured way to focus on relationship issues.

Feminist therapists can also complete questionnaires about their own therapy behaviors. Therapist questionnaires shed light on how closely therapists are following a feminist therapy model. For example, as I worked with Josh I could have repeatedly completed the *Feminist Self-Disclosure Inventory* (FSDI; Simi & Mahalik, 1997). The FSDI could help me monitor whether and how I was using self-disclosure as a therapy technique.

EVALUATIONS AND APPLICATIONS

Feminists have distinct ways at looking at the world. There's no question that feminist thought and feminist therapy has inspired many individuals to be more fully free to be themselves. In this section we look at more formal evaluations and applications of feminist therapy.

Evidence-Based Status

Before accepting scientific evidence supporting or refuting particular therapy approaches, feminist therapists are inclined to critique the traditional research paradigm and question the validity of specific therapy outcome measures. In an early feminist critique, Klein (1976) noted that focusing on client distress and self-esteem for outcomes is unacceptable; measures of distress are inadequate because distress is an adaptive and appropriate response to feeling trapped in negative sex-role situations. Additionally, stress or distress is likely to rise when clients are breaking out of old patterns and starting to pursue what they really want. Klein (1976) also noted that self-esteem measures are infused with traditional sexist stereotypes, leaving them of questionable validity. Instead, she recommended using measures that evaluate the freedom to be emotionally expressive within interpersonal relationships.

Broadly speaking, similar to Adlerian, existential, and multicultural practitioners, feminist therapists tend to discount the validity of large group research on therapy outcomes. Additionally, from a philosophical perspective, feminists aren't interested in measuring up to medical model standards that they view as a means through which oppressed minorities can be further controlled and marginalized.

Despite this general negative attitude toward therapy outcomes research, there's a modest body of anecdotal and empirical evidence supporting feminist therapy as a distinct and effective approach to positive change. Several examples are summarized.

Simi and Mahalik (1997) found evidence that feminist therapy is a distinctly open and egalitarian approach. Compared to non-feminists, feminist therapists were more likely to: (a) create an egalitarian relationship in therapy, (b) encourage their clients to select a positive role model during therapy, and (c) inform clients of their sexual orientation. Several other studies support Simi and Mahalik's (1997) findings (Chandler, Worell, Johnson, Blount, & Lusk, 1999; Worell & Chandler, 1996; Worell et al., 1996). Overall, it appears that feminist therapists provide a distinctive product characterized by power sharing, an egalitarian relationship, self-disclosure, client empowerment, and support for feminist goals. Worell and Remer (2003) also concluded that existing research shows that feminist therapy reduces client distress.

Frey (2013) summarized research on RCTs theoretical assumptions, practice applications, and treatment outcomes. Overall, she reported that RCT is theoretically distinct and that it has been applied in a variety of settings and to a range of problems. She also reported two favorable effectiveness studies, one in which a 16-session manualized form of RCT was equivalent to 16 sessions of CBT in the treatment of bulimia nervosa or binge-eating disorder (Tantillo & Sanftner, 2003).

In a well-controlled effectiveness study, a brief form of RCT was evaluated (Oakley et al., 2013). The research team reported that in their 91 all-female sample, significantly positive outcomes were obtained on all eight outcome measures, including traditional measures (e.g., the *Beck Depression Inventory*, 2nd edition; BDI-II). The study was the first of its kind to show that a feminist approach focusing on connection is effective.

Cultural Sensitivity

Professional cynics might argue that feminist therapy has been limited to special populations or to just one special population—discontented white women with feminist leanings. Historically, there was some truth to this complaint. In 1992 Brown and Brodsky published an article titled "The Future of Feminist Therapy" (1992). They stated,

> Currently, feminist therapy theory is neither diverse nor complex in the reality it reflects. It has been deficient from the start in its inclusiveness of the lives and realities of women of color, poor or working class women, non-North American women, women over sixty-five, or women with disabilities. (p. 52)

However, as discussed throughout this chapter, third and fourth wave feminism has transformed feminist therapy to include and address oppression as experienced by all marginalized and minority populations. Feminists are vocal advocates for diverse and multicultural perspectives in the practice of counseling and psychotherapy. Therefore, depending on how it's applied, feminist theory can be applicable to other populations suffering from externally imposed limits, stereotypes, abuse, and exploitation, which, as one of our reviewers noted, might include everyone.

Sexuality

Feminists openly embrace all sexual identities. For feminists, sexual self-agency, consent, and mutuality are defining features of healthy sexual relationships (Williams & Jovanovic, 2015). Individuals should be free to self-identify their sexual orientations; coerced sexual behaviors or foreclosing on sexual identity without consciousness are unacceptable.

Feminist theory and feminist therapists don't define gender and sexuality in binary terms. Gender and sexuality are pluralistic, with individual choice emphasized and labels or judgments of deviance de-emphasized. However, this doesn't mean that everyone under the large umbrella of feminism agrees on sexual language and values. For example, conflict exists among individuals identifying as queer, transgender, bisexual, gay, and lesbian (Josephson, Einarsdóttir, & Sigurðardóttir, 2017; Marx & Donaldson, 2015). Perhaps the most important point is that everyone under the feminist umbrella values diversity and resists sexual limitations that the dominant patriarchal culture forces onto individuals.

Feminists have leveled strong critiques at traditional, medical model, sex therapy (Tiefer, 2012). These critiques are extensions of the personal is political view into the sexual realm. For feminists, sex therapy cannot move forward unless accompanied by a nuanced and open analysis of power, privilege, desire, and the real emotional, psychological, and situational challenges that individuals are facing in their lives (Trice-Black & Foster, 2011).

Spirituality

Most dominant world religions have rules or practices that restrict women's freedoms. In some cases, feminists view religion as abusive, coercive, and dangerous toward women. In most cases, feminists view dominant religions as laden with conservative, patriarchal values (Hagen, Arczynski, Morrow, & Hawxhurst, 2011; Jiménez, Almansa, & Alcón, 2017).

The naturally activist orientation of feminism can create tension between feminist therapists and specific religious practices. For example, female genital mutilation is considered a male-perpetuated human rights violation that sanctions systemic violence toward girls and women. Despite the feminist general philosophy of openness to diverse ways of being, feminists view systematic oppression of females in the name of religion to be intolerable (Jiménez et al., 2017).

Feminists see potential for affirmation and liberation in spiritual alternatives. Specifically, feminist writers have discussed ways in which sexually diverse women can use spirituality to enhance their resilience within oppressive sociocultural contexts (Hagen et al., 2011). Integrating affirming spirituality into feminist therapy is an acceptable and, for many clients and therapists, preferred practice (Funderburk & Fukuyama, 2001; Hagen et al., 2011).

Adherents to male-oriented religious or cultural norms are unlikely to welcome feminist critique on their values. This is where the potential for conflict is highest and where feminists could be viewed as imposing their values on other cultural or religious groups. Feminists view the systematic oppression of women as unacceptable, regardless of political, religious, or cultural justifications that might be used to support oppression.

CONCLUDING COMMENTS

Feminist theory and therapy tend to get students and readers riled up. Sometimes there's opposition to feminist ideas; at other times students decide they want to self-identify as feminists. Either response is fine. More important than agreement or disagreement, we hope you consider and learn from the feminist perspectives discussed in this chapter; it could make you a better therapist.

REFLECTIONS

It's time to try on the feminist label again. Now, what's it like to say, "I'm a feminist therapist"? What are your gut reactions? What goes through your mind? Are you closer or further from embracing a feminist therapist label?

CHAPTER SUMMARY AND REVIEW

Feminist theory and therapy is part of a grassroots historical effort to bring inequities based on sex or gender into awareness, and resolve them through egalitarian and nonpatriarchal solutions. Feminism is the belief in equality and equity for all human beings and that egalitarian principles can be achieved through resistance and transformation of existing patriarchal systems. Feminist therapy is grounded in multicultural feminist scholarship, consciousness-raising, subversion, intersectionality, and is socially transformative.

The feminist movement in the United States is generally divided into four stages: (1) first wave feminism:

striving for universal suffrage and property rights were central; (2) second wave feminism: an emphasis on obtaining equal rights for women; (3) third wave feminism: inclusive worldwide and multicultural efforts to address oppression; and (4) fourth wave feminism: orienting toward technology, sexual diversity, reproductive justice, and spirituality.

Many factors contributed to the development and implementation of feminist therapy. Early figures like Riassa Adler and Karen Horney provided inspiration and then, as women became established within academic and scientific communities, they produced numerous groundbreaking publications. Simultaneously, women's consciousness-raising groups helped move women to take action together to improve their situations. Recently, relational-cultural therapy (RCT) has emerged as an approach to therapy founded on interpersonal connection instead of independence-striving.

Three primary feminist theoretical principles guide feminist therapy in practice. These included: (1) sex and gender powerfully affect identity; (2) deviance comes from a dysfunctional culture, including the idea that maleness is normative and preferred; and (3) consciousness-raising is a part of healing and change, including the important concept of the personal is political.

Other than operating on a feminist theory foundation, feminist therapy isn't theory or technique driven. Overarching goals include consciousness-raising, empowerment, and nonhierarchical interpersonal connection. Feminist philosophical principles pervade the therapy process through informed consent, nonstandardized assessment of feminist-related issues, development of a therapeutic relationship, self-disclosure, empowerment, and development of feminist consciousness. Additionally, feminist therapists focus on sex, sexuality, body image issues, self-esteem, gender role comfort, and men's issues. Technically, feminist therapists are open to a variety of techniques, but emphasize mutuality and mutual empathy.

Feminists tend to be critical of outcome measures and outcome research, emphasizing that these systems for determining therapy efficacy need to be modified to fit feminist values. Researchers have affirmed that feminist therapy is a distinct approach. Recent evidence is limited, but accumulating, and indicates that relational-cultural therapy may be effective for specific issues.

Although first and second wave feminism didn't adequately incorporate issues of cultural diversity, third and fourth wave feminism have been much more explicitly inclusive. Cultural and sexual minorities are generally and specifically affirmed and supported. Due to rules and practices restricting women's freedoms, it has been less easy for feminists to openly embrace religion and spirituality. However, some feminists are working to integrate nontraditional spirituality into feminist therapy.

FEMINIST KEY TERMS

Boy code

Cisgender

Disorders of sexual development (DSD)

Egalitarian

Empowerment

Ethic of caring

Feminism

Feminist consciousness-raising groups

Feminist therapy

Fight or flight phenomenon

First wave feminism

Fourth wave feminism

Gender

Gender role

Girl code

Goals of feminist therapy

Informed consent

Interpersonal/social-contextual power

Intersectionality

Intersex conditions

Intrapersonal/intrapsychic power

Iron rule

Kinder, Kuche, Kirche as Scientific Law

Male as normative

Mutuality

Mutually empathic

Patriarchy

Personal is political

Power analysis

Relational-cultural therapy (RCT)

Second wave feminism

Self-disclosure

Sex

Somatic power

Spiritual/existential power

Subversive

Tend and befriend

Third wave feminism

Transgender

Women and madness

Constructive Theory and Therapy

LEARNER OBJECTIVES

- Define constructivism, social constructionism, solution-focused therapy, and narrative therapy
- Identify key figures and historical trends in the development, evolution, and application of constructive psychotherapies
- Describe core principles of post-modern and constructive theories
- Describe and apply solution-focused and narrative therapy principles, strategies, and techniques
- Analyze cases that employ solution-focused and narrative therapy techniques
- Evaluate the empirical, cultural, gender, and spiritual validity of solution-focused and narrative therapy
- Summarize core content and define key terms associated with constructive theory and solution-focused and narrative therapy

Constructive theories and therapies help clients reconstruct or re-story their lives in more adaptive and satisfying ways. This emphasis requires that therapy interactions focus primarily on the present and future. To explore constructive theories is to dive more deeply into the abyss of "as if," a concept Hans Vaihinger (1911) introduced to philosophers (and Alfred Adler) in the early twentieth century.

INTRODUCTION

The best way to begin a chapter on constructive theory and therapy is with a story.

> Once upon a time a man and a woman met in the forest. Both being academic philosophers well-steeped in epistemology, they approached each another warily. The woman spoke first, asking, "Can you see me?"
>
> The man responded quickly: "I don't know," he said. "I have a plethora of neurons firing in my occipital lobe and, yes, I perceive an image of a woman and I can see your mouth was moving precisely as I was experiencing auditory input. Therefore, although I'm not completely certain you exist out there in reality—and I'm not completely certain there even is a reality—I can say without a doubt that you exist ... at least within the physiology of my mind."

> Silence followed.
>
> Then, the man spoke again.
>
> "Can you hear me?" he asked.
>
> This time the woman responded immediately. "I'm not completely certain about the nature of hearing and the auditory process, but I can say that in this lived moment of my experience I'm in a conversation with you and because my knowledge and my reality is based on interactive discourse, whether you really exist or not is less important than the fact that I find myself, in this moment, discovering more about myself, the nature of the world, and my knowledge of all things."

There are two main branches of constructive theory. These branches are similar in that both perspectives hold firmly to the post-modern idea that knowledge and reality are subjective.

What Is Constructivism and What Is Social Constructionism?

Constructivism, as represented by the man in the forest, includes people who believe knowledge and reality are constructed within individuals. In contrast, **social constructionism**, as represented by the woman in the forest, includes people who believe knowledge and reality are constructed through discourse or conversation.

Constructivists focus on what's happening within the minds or brains of individuals; social constructionists focus on what's happening between people as they join together to create realities. Guterman (2006) described these two perspectives:

> Although both constructivism and social constructionism endorse a subjectivist view of knowledge, the former emphasizes individuals' biological and cognitive processes, whereas the latter places knowledge in the domain of social interchange. (p. 13)

In this chapter, we deemphasize distinctions between constructivist and social constructionist perspectives. Mostly, we lump them together as constructive theories and therapies and emphasize the intriguing intervention strategies developed within these paradigms. This may upset staunch constructivists or radical social constructionists, but we take this risk with full confidence in our personal safety—because most constructive types are nonviolent, strongly preferring to think, write, and engage in intellectual discussion. Therefore, within our own socially or individually constructed realities, we've concluded that we're in no danger of bodily harm from angry constructive theorists or therapists.

What Is Post-modern Philosophy

Post-modern philosophy emphasizes the fact that objectivity and reality are individually or socially constructed. These constructive ideas are philosophically and psychologically compelling, especially within our contemporary multidimensional and multicultural society. According to this philosophical position, humans cannot stake a claim to objectivity. Everything is perspective and perspective is everything. Hierarchical structures of expert and nonexpert are challenged. Each of us views reality through our own particular lenses or created social discourse. The prominent social psychologist and social constructionist Kenneth Gergen (2009a) explained:

> At the outset, constructionist ideas alert us to the absence of foundations (rational, empirical, ethical, or otherwise) for any position that one advocates. All articulated positions emerge from social process, and even the attempt to elaborate foundations must ultimately beg the question of how its elaborations are to be warranted. This scarcely suggests that we should abandon the positions we occupy. Rather, it is to become aware that we live within traditions that may or may not be adequate to the contingencies of today. Reflection, curiosity, and doubt must all be encouraged. (p. 99)

With reflection, curiosity, and doubt as our guides, we now look at the roots of constructive psychotherapy.

KEY FIGURES AND HISTORICAL CONTEXT

Constructive approaches to counseling and psychotherapy also have roots in traditional talk therapy. As an example, Steven de Shazer, a co-originator of solution-focused therapy, used a phrase from Sigmund Freud (*words were originally magic*) as a title for one of his solution-focused books (de Shazer, 1994). In the 1915 writings from which de Shazer was quoting, Freud wrote,

> Nothing takes place in a psycho-analytic treatment but an exchange of words.... The patient talks.... The doctor listens.... Words were originally magic and to this day words have retained much of their ancient magical power. By words one person can make another blissfully happy or drive him to despair.... Words provoke affects and are in general the means of mutual influence among men. (Freud, 1963, p. 17)

As Freud noted, the magical power of words began long before psychoanalysis. Ancient healers, storytellers, and religious evangelists knew the power of words. Regardless of your particular religious or spiritual beliefs, it's difficult to argue over the word and story power included in the I Ching, the Bible, the Koran, the Talmud, the sayings of Confucius, the Book of Mormon, and other religious documents.

Early philosophers who contributed to constructive theory and therapy include Immanuel Kant and Hans Vaihinger. Kant's view was that knowledge of reality can only be approximated. Vaihinger believed that there were many individual fictional realities. Both of these claims are at the root of contemporary constructive theory. Constructive thought is in opposition to modernism or objectivism. Both constructivism and social constructionism hold that individuals actively construct reality based on either their own perceptual experiences or jointly held social agreements. Both these perspectives make reality quite flexible. In contrast, objectivism holds that individuals know reality by passively receiving sensory information directly from the environment (aka the real world).

George Kelly, Personal Construct Theory, and Preposterous Interpretations

With the publication of *The Psychology of Personal Constructs*, George Kelly (1955) developed the first unarguably constructive approach to psychotherapy. He wrote,

> Life provides man with no scientific footholds on reality, suggests to him no narrative plots, offers no rhythmic metaphor to confirm the moving resonance of a human theme. If he chooses to write tragedy, then tragedy it will be; if comedy, then that is what will come of it; and if burlesque, he, the sole reader, must learn to laugh

at his misanthropic caricatures of the only person he knows—himself. (Kelly, 1969, p. 24)

Kelly described many foundational constructive psychological concepts. Although Vaihinger and other philosophers influenced him, his theoretical work was primarily a product of his clinical observations. For example, early in his transformation from Freudian analysis to personal constructs, Kelly began "deliberately" offering clients preposterous interpretations. His only criteria were that the interpretative statements (a) integrate his clients' current perspective and (b) have ramifications for how clients might approach their personal futures differently. Somewhat to his surprise, Kelly discovered that his preposterous interpretations often worked very well in moving clients toward positive behavior and emotions.

Milton Erickson, Strategic Hypnotherapy, and Solution-Based Approaches

Milton Erickson
(photo courtesy of The Milton H. Erickson Foundation, Inc. www.erickson-foundation.org)

Stephen de Shazer and others trace the origin of solution-focused constructive thinking to the late, great hypnotherapist Milton Erickson (de Shazer, 1985; Haley, 1973; O'Hanlon, 1988). Erickson is also considered the innovative inspiration for the strategic therapy approach with individuals and families (Goldenberg, Stanton, & Goldenberg, 2017). In his therapeutic work, Erickson made no effort to correct "causative underlying maladjustments" lurking in his clients' unconscious, self, past, or environment (Haley, 1967, p. 393). Instead, he focused on how to deconstruct and reconstruct the skills and strengths his clients brought with them to therapy. The following case, summarized in O'Hanlon and Bertolino (1998), illustrates Erickson's strength-based approach.

A 70-year-old woman named Ma met with Erickson. She was unable to read despite many years of sincere effort. She had resolved to learn how to read at age 16 but had subsequently become frightened and blanked out whenever someone tried to teach her. Erickson promised her that she would be reading and writing within three weeks.

Erickson's approach to teaching Ma to read was innovative. He told her that she wouldn't have to learn anything that she didn't already know. The core of his message was that she already had within her all of the skills and strengths needed to learn to read and write.

He asked her to pick up a pencil in any old way she wanted. Then, he had her make some marks with the pencil on paper, just scribbling, like any baby might do. Progressively, he had her make straight lines at various angles, donut holes, donut halves, and two sides of a gabled roof. As a way to decrease her anxiety about writing, Erickson did not have the woman learn to copy letters but instead had her draw objects that she had been familiar with during her lifetime. He had her practice making these familiar marks on paper between sessions.

During their next meeting, Erickson explained to Ma that the only difference between a pile of lumber and a house was that the house was put together in a particular way. Ma agreed but didn't see the relevance between building a house from lumber and turning pencil marks on a page into letters. Then, Erickson helped Ma make a series of 26 new marks, based on the marks she had previously produced. Of course, these marks were the 26 letters of the English alphabet.

Erickson's work with Ma continued along the same lines. He coaxed her into naming the different letters and words she produced. After all, just as farm animals needed names, so did the marks she produced on a piece of paper. Eventually, he had her write a sentence: "Get going Ma and put some grub on the table." This was a statement she had frequently heard from her late husband, which helped Ma realize that reading was just like talking. In the end, without causing Ma any anxiety whatsoever, Erickson taught her to read and write in less than three weeks.

Erickson was a powerful and creative individual whose work is still highly regarded (Haley, 2015; Rogers & White, 2017). He made many contributions to what we know about psychotherapy today. He's best known for brief hypnotherapeutic techniques and innovative approaches to working with individual cases. One of his most significant contributions to therapy is the intervention referred to as utilization (Erickson, 1954).

Utilization is both an intervention and a theoretical concept; it involves guiding clients to utilize whatever strengths they brought with them to therapy. Client strengths might include humor, work experiences, language style, personal resources, and nonverbal behaviors. As with Ma, Erickson incorporated or utilized the personal qualities his clients possessed into their therapeutic work.

Erickson's legacy is characterized by three of his personal attributes. We believe these qualities continue to shine through and shape the contemporary practice of many constructive therapies and therapists. Erickson was many things, but in particular he was:

- Optimistic (and confident).
- Clever (and intelligent).
- Indirect (and collaborative).

Erickson was so positive and creative with clients that, before long, often without even realizing what had happened, clients would experience a doubling or trebling of their previously unnoticed and underutilized personal strengths and resources. As we see later, he was a masterful listener and had a knack for constructing solutions that his clients could instantly understand.

REFLECTIONS

Consider the following: How much of Erickson's personality is reflected in the evolving nature of constructive theory and therapy? Have you noticed how the personalities of other major theorists (e.g., Freud, Adler, Rogers, Beck) shaped how their therapies are practiced? How might feminist and multicultural life experiences shape theory?

The Palo Alto Projects and Brief Therapy in Italy

In 1952 Gregory Bateson began the Double-Bind Communications Project (DBCP) with Jay Haley, John Weakland, and Donald Jackson (as consultant) in Palo Alto, California. This project focused on communication patterns in so-called schizophrenic families. Shortly after this project started, Haley and Weakland became interested in communication patterns that occur between hypnotherapist and client. With Bateson's encouragement, Haley and Weakland began attending Milton Erickson's hypnosis workshops and visited him regularly in Phoenix.

In 1958 Jackson established the Mental Research Institute (MRI) along with Virginia Satir and Paul Watzlawick, also in Palo Alto. This project and the DBCP both focused on the power of verbal and nonverbal communication in influencing human behavior. The project boundaries were somewhat blurred because Jackson was heavily involved in both. Together, they produced more than 200 professional publications, including numerous books (Bateson, Jackson, Haley, & Weakland, 1963; Watzlawick, Beavin, & Jackson, 1967; Weakland, 1962).

In 1968, the Brief Therapy Center was established at MRI. By then the DBCP had ended and Haley and Weakland had joined MRI. Around the same time, four Italian psychiatrists led by Mara Selvini-Palazzoli broke away from their psychoanalytically trained colleagues and formed the Milan Center for the Study of the Family. Their goal was to work with family systems using briefer therapy models. The Milan group was strongly influenced by the Palo Alto group and, in particular, by the publication *Pragmatics of Human Communication* (Watzlawick et al., 1967). Watzlawick became the main consultant for the Milan group.

Haley and Cloe Madanes (who was trained at MRI) later married and developed the strategic approach to family and individual therapy (Madanes & Haley, 1977; see Chapter 12). The essence of strategic therapy is to devise a unique strategy for each particular client or family problem. There are numerous strategic therapy techniques, but the most relevant to our discussion is **positive relabeling or reframing**, both of which refer to helping clients perceive things from a different (more positive) perspective.

In one famous case, Haley informed a woman whose husband had recently chased her around the house with an ax that her husband "was simply trying to get close to her" (Goldenberg & Goldenberg, 2008, p. 280). Obviously Haley's positive relabeling in that case was a bit over the top, but strategic therapy approaches were boldly positive. Similarly, in her work at the Milan Center, Selvini-Palazzoli and her group (Selvini-Palazzoli, Boscolo, Cecchin, & Prata, 1974) developed an active-directive family therapy technique called *positive connotation*, in which negative symptoms or behaviors are recast in a positive light (e.g., "Your child is setting fires in order to get your attention and some emotional warmth in his life").

REFLECTIONS

Some writers have strongly criticized the extremely positive reframing approaches that Haley and Selvini-Palazzoli popularized. What are your thoughts on this issue? How do you think provocatively positive reframes might affect clients?

Efran and Fauber (1995) offer the following criticism of overly positive therapy interventions based on "verbal magic":

> In our view, some workers have stretched the meaning of such terms as reframing and positive connotation ... to the breaking point. They underestimate the solidity of a constructed reality and assume that because something is language dependent, it is insubstantial and can be easily modified by relabeling problems willy-nilly. They feel free to portray faults as virtues, failures as successes, and selfishness as altruism. Some therapists will say almost anything for strategic effect. Critics have attacked such ad hoc conceptualizations as superficial and manipulative—an uncomfortable melding of the roles of therapist and con artist.... We tend to agree. (p. 291)

A significant danger associated with constructive approaches is the minimization or denial of what Efran & Fauber (1995) refer to as the solidity of constructed reality.

Discovering Solutions and Narratives

The work of Kelly, Erickson, Bateson, MRI, the Milan Group, and Haley and Madanes are directly related to contemporary constructive theory and therapy. Within the constructive paradigm, this chapter focuses primarily on two distinct therapeutic movements and approaches: solution-focused and narrative therapies.

Solution-Focused Brief Therapy

Steve de Shazer and Insoo Kim Berg cofounded the Brief Family Therapy Center (BFTC) in Milwaukee in 1978 and developed solution-focused brief therapy (SFBT). **Solution-focused brief therapy (SFBT)** is a goal-oriented and collaborative brief therapy approach that narrowly focuses on client solutions and minimizes any talk about problems. In particular, de Shazer and Berg emphasized that clients don't need to know anything about why or how their problem originated. Even further, therapists also don't need to know anything about how clients' problems developed—and they need to know very little about the problem itself. Instead, solution-focused brief therapy primarily (and often exclusively) focuses on helping clients generate solutions (de Shazer et al., 2007). De Shazer refers to standard therapy interventions as **formula tasks** and **skeleton keys** (de Shazer, 1985, p. 119). In the following, he describes the similarity of his approach to that of the Milan group:

> [The Milan group's] prescription (which follows a formula) and our "formula tasks" (each of which are standardized) suggest something about the nature of therapeutic intervention and change which has not been clearly described before: interventions can initiate change without the therapist's first understanding, in any detail, what has been going on. (de Shazer, 1985, p. 119)

Also, de Shazer was inspired by Ludwig Wittgenstein's (1968) concepts of language games as interpersonal determinants of reality. Berg and de Shazer (1993) articulated this linguistic development:

> As the client and therapist talk more and more about the solution they want to construct together, they come to believe in the truth or reality of what they are talking about. This is the way language works, naturally. (p. 6)

Not long after solution-focused brief therapy emerged on the scene, William O'Hanlon and Michele Weiner-Davis developed **solution-oriented therapy** (later known as possibility therapy; O'Hanlon, 1988). The solution-oriented approach is derived from three main theoretical-practical precursors: (1) Milton Erickson's work, (2) strategic intervention and problem-solving techniques developed at MRI, and (3) de Shazer and Berg's solution-focused brief therapy. O'Hanlon (1998) described the evolution of his approach:

> In the early 1980's I began a correspondence with Steve de Shazer.... [H]e and some colleagues had begun what came to be called the Brief Family Therapy Center.... De Shazer and I shared a common view that mainstream

therapies that saw clients as pathological and resistant were all wrong. People were naturally cooperative if approached in the right way and treated as resourceful and competent. De Shazer's work began to take shape and has turned into "solution-focused therapy." ... My work took shape and I began to call it "solution-oriented therapy." ... Because the two were often confused and I have some major differences with the Milwaukee approach, I began to speak of my approach as "possibility therapy." (p. 139)

The differences between SFBT and possibility therapy are small but important. As compared to SFBT, O'Hanlon's possibility therapy is described as,

- Having more focus on validating clients' emotions and experience.

- Somewhat less directive and less formulaic.

- More collaborative.

- More open to considering political, gender, and historical factors as important in problem development.

O'Hanlon also believes that therapists must take responsibility for pursuing issues that clients don't bring up—especially if the issues lead to violent, dangerous, or painful life outcomes. In contrast, de Shazer (Hoyt, 1994) has gone on record to say that therapists should avoid reading "between the lines" and instead simply stick with what the client is saying is the problem and whatever is working (e.g., "[if] he says he doesn't drink too much and it's not a problem. Leave it alone. Take it seriously"; pp. 29–30).

Narrative Therapy

Michael White of Australia and David Epston of New Zealand met in 1981 at an Australian–New Zealander family therapy conference and subsequently developed a therapeutic approach based on **narrative metaphor** (Goldenberg et al., 2017). The personal narrative metaphor is the story that defines and organizes each individual's life and relationship with the world. As we live and accumulate experiences, we each develop a personal narrative that gives our lives meaning and continuity. Much like a well-written story, our personal narrative includes an organized plot, characters, points of tension and climax, and a beginning, middle, and end.

White was strongly influenced by Michel Foucault (1965), a French intellectual and social critic. Foucault accused dominant culture of oppressively maintaining power and control over minority groups by eliminating alternative historical perspectives. Eventually, the dominant culture turns its historical stories into objective truth, and alternative ways of being are pathologized. White's application of Foucault's thinking to the therapy process allows individuals who have oppressed themselves through personal narratives to deconstruct and reconstruct their life stories into more complete, adaptive, and personally meaningful storylines (White & Epston, 1990). **Narrative therapy** is a respectful approach that empowers clients to be experts in their own lives; it separates the person from the problems and helps individuals break free from internalized social, cultural, and political oppression and rewrite their life stories with adaptive themes.

David Epston introduced narrative metaphor concepts to White (Goldenberg, Stanton, & Goldenberg, 2017). He also has pioneered the use of letters to clients as an extension of therapy (Epston, 1994). In collaboration with Stephan Madigan of Canada, Epston cofounded the **Anti-anorexia/Anti-bulimia League**, an organization that turns so-called eating disordered patients into empowered community and political activists. According to Madigan, narrative approaches spring from diverse sources, including Foucault, Bateson, feminism, anthropology, geography, and post-modernism (Carlson & Kjos, 2000; Madigan, 2011). These approaches also carry the distinct flavor of George Kelly's (1955) psychology of personal constructs.

THEORETICAL PRINCIPLES

Constructive therapies are approaches that begin with the recognition that humans are meaning makers who construct, not simply uncover, their psychological realities. They are based on "the construction that we are constructive."
— Michael F. Hoyt, *The Handbook of Constructive Therapies* (1998, p. 3)

A powerful conceptualization of constructive therapy comes from Michael White (1993), who described therapists as not just "taking history" but "making history." Certainly, in their own particular and sometimes peculiar way, constructive theorists and therapists are currently making history in counseling and psychotherapy.

Post-modernism

The most basic position that post-modernists hold is antirealism (aka subjectivism). Post-modernists firmly believe there is no such thing as objective fact. This position is, of course, at once illogical, subjective, nonlinear, and essentially unprovable, but from the post-modernist's perspective, such is the inherent nature of all things. De Shazer articulates the subjective and socially constructed nature of client symptoms when he writes, "There are no wet beds, no voices without people, no depressions. There is only *talk* about wet beds, *talk* about voices without people, and *talk* about depression" (de Shazer, 1993, p. 93).

Let's take a moment to deconstruct post-modernism. As a term, **post-modernism** derives from art and literature. It originally referred to a movement or perspective that was in opposition to or in reaction against modern art or literature. To define post-modernism adequately, we must first define modernism. Technically, modernism is associated with the scientific, objective, and deterministic paradigm of an external reality. In some ways, however, defining modernism is like trying to catch a snowflake because all things modern melt away very quickly with the passage of time. It's possible to define the modern art and modern science period and style, but when doing so, we're struck with the fact that using the word *modern* in that context is a misnomer. Modern art is no longer "modern" art in the sense that it is no longer contemporary but instead representative of a static period in time. It is most likely that post-modernism, too, will come to represent a period of time and a way of thinking that emphasizes the profound subjectivity of reality.

If you're feeling confused, that's exactly the point. Milton Erickson sometimes based his therapeutic interventions on what he referred to as the **confusion technique** (Erickson, 1964). In an effort to produce positive change, he would speak to clients in ways that were circular, nonlinear, and confusing.

Once confusion set in, client responsiveness to hearing and accepting alternative ways of thinking were increased. As discussed in Chapter 8, Albert Ellis helped clients deconstruct irrational beliefs through vigorous disputation—a forceful approach, based on modernist, rational thinking. In contrast, like Erickson, constructive therapists help clients deconstruct and reconstruct specific beliefs as well as personal narratives through a careful and subtle use of words and language. This theoretical perspective encourages cognitive activity that involves what Gergen (2009a, 2009b, 2011) described earlier—reflection, curiosity, and doubt.

REFLECTIONS

Think about what it's like to experience confusion. What might be the purpose of Erickson's confusion tactics? When you're confused about something do you reach out and grab onto the first thing that makes sense? Could that work as a therapy strategy?

Language and Languaging

Constructive therapists focus on how language builds, maintains, and changes each individual's worldview (H. Anderson, 2007; H. Anderson & Burney, 2004). As Hoyt (1998, p. 4) wrote, "Language and languaging are the ways we make meaning and exchange information."

Language determines reality. Efran and Fauber (1995) described,

> Language is where people live.... It allows people to have names, to "know" who they are, and to carve separable things out of the interconnected flux that they take to be the universe. One can manage to play baseball without a shortstop, but not without the words and symbols that differentiate first base from home plate. Without language, it would not be possible for a person to engage in self-conscious thought, to keep an appointment book, or to have problems. (p. 279)

Given their focus on language, constructive therapists are open to an entire domain of therapy interventions including relabeling, reframing, solution-focused questioning, re-storying, and problem externalization (Guterman, 2013; Murphy, 2015; Sklare, 2014). We review these approaches in the Practice of Constructive Psychotherapies section.

Change Is Constant and Inevitable

Solution-focused and narrative therapists believe change is constant and inevitable. Change happens every day,

both in the domain of internal human perception (what you see, hear, etc.) and the domain of social discourse. From the constructive perspective, because change is inevitable, therapists should actively guide the change in positive directions. Perhaps more importantly, constructive theorists believe that only a small change is required to change so-called big problems (de Shazer et al., 2007).

Problems Are Co-created

Constructive theory holds that you can change the past from the present. This is because problems are either creations (constructivist) or co-creations (social constructionist). The client—as creator/author/architect—can deconstruct the problem and then reassemble it differently.

Therapy conversations are opportunities to reconstruct, re-story, or accommodate experiences from the past. You may recall the concept of introjection or "swallowing whole" from Chapter 6 (Gestalt therapy). In constructive therapy, particularly its narrative therapy format, therapists help clients cough up their old life stories and chew them up in new and different ways before trying to swallow and digest them again.

BRAIN BOX

11.1 Memory Consolidation, Memory Reconsolidation, and Memory Re-reconsolidation

In the old modernist world, we thought of memory as a relatively stable entity. It went something like this: (a) you experience an event; (b) your experience is stored in short-term memory; (c) after about 20–30 seconds, memory consolidation starts happening and the memory is converted from short- to long-term memory; (d) for various reasons, you recall (or retrieve) the memory; and then (e) the memory goes back into storage, to be retrieved again later.

For better or worse, when it comes to humans and the human brain, nothing is particularly simple or linear. The brain has millions of connections and memories are distributed into various parts of the brain, where they're electrochemically stored. The hippocampus is especially important for memory storage and recall, but it doesn't work alone.

What's new about this process is the discovery of memory reconsolidation. As it turns out, when memories are retrieved, they're pulled out of storage and into active memory. It's during this moment that the process becomes post-modern. Once they're out and in active memory, old memories may be reexperienced and reconstructed. Then, the memories—along with new information—are reconsolidated.

The key point for counseling and psychotherapy is that when memories are pulled out of storage, they're open to and vulnerable to modification.

Reconsolidation opens up the possibility of **re-remembering** (Quirk & Mueller, 2008; Rüegg, 2009). This means every remembering is an opportunity to re-remember things differently. Of course, as humans we often re-remember things differently (depending on mood, who we're with, time of day, etc.).

Narrative therapists call this process the deconstruction and reconstruction of the problem. As clients tell their stories, narrative therapists act as script writers. They help clients recast their original experiences in a new light. They reframe. They emphasize sparkling moments. They reinterpret trauma as strength and resilience.

Many of the trauma-focused therapies operate directly on memory reconsolidation. These include EMDR, emotion-focused therapy, trauma focused CBT, narrative exposure therapy, and many more. In each of these therapies, disturbing memories are taken out of storage and clients are engaged in conversations or activities that might facilitate positive reconsolidation.

There's a new story in town. It's a better story. Our job, as therapists, is to help our clients remember it.

Therapy Is a Collaborative, Cooperative, Co-constructive Conversation

Constructive therapists establish collaborative relationships with clients. Guterman (2013) noted: "Borrowing from the field of anthropology, some social constructionists have described their role as a participant–observer" (p. 15). This idea implies an interconnection between client and therapist and leads to a process wherein therapists "act with" their clients collaboratively rather than "acting on" their clients as an outside modernist influencer.

Constructive therapists denounce the concept of resistance. If you recall, much of the old modernist psychoanalytic model was based on the therapist as an authority who interpreted reality to clients and then helped clients work through their resistance to psychoanalytic reality. In contrast, constructive therapists view resistance as natural and as the responsibility of the therapist—and not the fault of the client. For example, O'Hanlon and Weiner-Davis (1989) wrote:

> [C]lients do not always follow therapists' suggestions
> … this is not viewed as resistance. When this happens,
> clients are simply educating therapists as to the most
> productive and fitting method of helping them change.
> (pp. 21–22)

Moving responsibility for cooperation and resistance from clients to therapists is a major contribution of constructive theory. It's not surprising that many involuntary clients are relieved when an appointed therapist focuses on strengths and possibilities, rather than trying to break down denial and get them to admit to owning the problem. The gentle, collaborative, and positive approach that constructive therapists advocate may be why many therapists and agencies that work with involuntary or mandated clients find constructive approaches so useful (J. Sommers-Flanagan, Richardson, & Sommers-Flanagan, 2011; Tohn & Oshlag, 1996).

Therapy Focuses on Strengths and Solutions

With the preceding emphasis on collaboration, cooperation and co-construction of new stories, you might think constructive therapists strive for an absolutely equal sharing of power in their relationship with clients. After all, egalitarianism is a basic constructive theoretical position. Even further, the client is respected and viewed as her own best expert. Not long ago, a student in one of our theories classes queried us about this egalitarian theoretical position. As we lectured on solution-focused methods for leading clients toward solutions, she exclaimed, "But just a few minutes ago you said constructive theory embraces equality between therapist and client and views the client as the best expert on her own reality. I thought that meant constructive therapists don't lead their clients."

The truth is, although constructive therapists respect and accept their client's perspectives, they also direct and lead clients in a preplanned direction—toward personal strengths and positive problem-solving abilities. As Weakland (1993) stated, "Just as one cannot not communicate, one cannot not influence" (p. 143). Weiner-Davis (1993) asked, "Since we cannot avoid leading, the question becomes, 'Where shall we lead our clients?'" (p. 156).

The answer to this question is simple. Constructive therapists lead clients toward (a) solutions, (b) exceptions to their problem-centered viewpoint, (c) optimism and self-efficacy, and (d) new versions of personal stories that promote greater psychological health (Monk, 1997; Winslade & Monk, 2007). In this way, constructive theory and therapy are laden with Erickson's utilization concept.

Theory of Psychopathology

Constructive theory doesn't support or use traditional psychopathology models. Diagnosing clients is unhelpful. Client symptoms such as anxiety and depression are not objective entities but part of an individual's personal emotional experience cast within a personal life narrative and social context. Instead of using diagnostic categories, constructive therapists meet clients where they are, emphasizing unique strengths that clients bring to therapy.

On the other hand, constructive therapists are practical and in touch with contemporary needs for diagnostic assessment and categorization (Guterman, 2013). As most of us recognize, diagnosis and labeling constitute a means of professional communication, and this form of communication is used, but also simultaneously questioned. Solution-focused, possibility, and narrative approaches are routinely applied to the treatment of many different problems. These applications include alcoholic narratives, grief therapy, eating disorders, domestic violence, dissociative disorders, and more (Connie & Metcalf, 2009; Hoyt, 1998; Metcalf, 2008).

Broadly speaking, there are two main determinants of client problems, regardless of whether the client is an individual, couple, or family:

The client has gotten stuck using ineffective solutions. This view, derived from Erickson's work and the Mental Research

Institute approach, emphasizes that individuals become stuck repeating maladaptive behavior patterns even though they possess personal strengths and resources. Clients become stuck because they construct their experiences, using language and other meaning-making procedures, in a manner leading to stuckness. Constructive therapists examine client symptoms, problems, and psychopathology for the purpose of deconstruction. Many solution-focused therapists almost completely ignore client statements about problems and reorient therapy conversations toward solutions.

The client believes in an unhealthy, pathology-based self-, couple-, or family-narrative. Narrative therapists believe that human problems develop when clients write themselves into their self-narratives as inadequate, problem-plagued victims. Clients often show up in therapy because they have constructed a narrative in which the dominant theme of an "internalized personal problem" is obscuring a nondominant theme of "personal strength and resourcefulness" (and external social-cultural problem maintainers). Deconstructing and reconstructing of the client's personal narrative is the road to improvement.

THE PRACTICE OF CONSTRUCTIVE PSYCHOTHERAPIES

Being collaborative, constructive therapists, don't emphasize psychoeducation or role induction procedures. Instead of formally introducing clients to therapy, constructive therapists continuously collaborate with clients to identify goals, strategies, and the therapy direction. (See Putting It in Practice 11.1: Informed Consent from a Constructive Perspective.)

PUTTING IT IN PRACTICE

11.1 Informed Consent from a Constructive Perspective

I'm looking forward to working with you in counseling. This next section describes a little bit about my theoretical orientation and my ways of working with people. Questions are always welcome!

There are many words used to describe the kind of work I do, but some people call it constructivist. This means that I believe people construct many aspects of their lives, and when things aren't going well, it's possible to change the way things are constructed. Each of us has our own reality, and our own beliefs about things. Sometimes, problems can be changed or pushed back by working on the way we see things and experience them.

As we work together, I will be excited to hear your life story and help you notice the way you tell your story. I will help you turn your attention to your successes and your strengths. We will explore how to build on these successes and strengths. We will also work to get a grip on those pesky problems that creep into our lives, and experiment with ways to see them differently.

I believe words can be magic. Just talking together, paying attention to the words we use, can bring about change. We don't need to go over every detail of your past, and

> we won't necessarily need to meet for very long. Sometimes my clients only need a few sessions to make the changes they want to make.
>
> In my work with people who are fighting back problems in their lives, I am curious and optimistic. Each individual has a unique reality that I am always excited to learn about. Believe it or not, we can tinker with your reality in ways that can make your life seem new, better, and more under your own control.

Assessment Issues and Procedures

Constructive therapy approaches use minimal formal assessment procedures. In keeping with de Shazer's (1985) emphasis on keys to solution and White and Epston's (1990) emphasis on client narratives, the primary therapy focus is either on identifying and implementing solutions or on deconstructing problem narratives and constructing more satisfying narratives (White, 2007; White & Denborough, 2011). Narrative therapists spend more time assessing and exploring client problems than solution-focused brief therapists, but, overall, too much time spent discussing problems might only strengthen, build, and further deepen the client's problem-focused worldview. The main therapy goal is to help clients move past their problem focus and develop solution- and strength-focused worldviews and adaptive personal narratives.

Even though solution-focused brief therapists want clients to shift from problem talk to solution talk, it's still important to begin therapy by allowing clients to tell their stories. If therapists ignore the client's problem, rapport can be damaged. The general rule for solution-focused brief therapists at the beginning of therapy is to follow the client's lead. This rule flows from Erickson's indirect hypnotic approach with clients, in which therapists begin by pacing clients and later take the lead and make indirect and direct suggestions (Haley, 1967). Insoo Kim Berg articulated this philosophy when she wrote about *leading from behind* (Berg & Miller, 1992).

The primary therapist tool in solution-focused and narrative therapy is questioning. However, excessive questioning can be problematic. To help address potential negative outcomes associated with using too many questions, Monk (1997) described a role induction statement in narrative therapy with a young client:

> A therapy of questions can easily make the client feel like the subject of an interrogation. To avoid the power imbalance that might follow from this kind of conversation, I sought permission from Peter to ask him some more questions, saying that if I asked too many questions, he could either not answer them or tell me he was "questioned out." (p. 9)

As we explore constructive assessment strategies, keep in mind the possibility that clients could get tired of answering questions or being **questioned out**.

Opening the Session

Discovering the client's goals is a main initial focus for constructive therapists. Therapists usually begin therapy with questions that stimulate clients to begin moving up a positive path. The following opening questions fit with a solution-focused/narrative model:

- What could happen during our time today that will make your visit with me worthwhile?

- If this session goes very well, what will we accomplish together?

- How did you decide to come to counseling?

Usually, these questions prompt clients to identify specific goals they want from treatment. Identifying or constructing reasonable goals is an important assessment component of solution-based therapies.

Narrative therapists generally want to know more about the original construction of the problem; this involves gathering information about how the problem first started and how it initially affected the client's view of herself (Monk, 1997). Early narrative-based assessment questions include:

- How will your life go forward if [the problem] continues into the future?

- How will your life go forward if [the problem] gets smaller or goes away completely?

A key concept to keep in mind when constructing assessment questions from the narrative perspective is to work on externalizing the problem from the person or the family. This involves referring to problems as separate from the self. We discuss externalizing questions later in this chapter.

Scaling Questions

Solution-focused therapists use scaling questions as a means of assessment and treatment (Murphy, 2015).

Scaling questions are used to ask clients to rate problems, progress, or any therapy-related issue on a 0 to 10 scale. Typically, 0 is considered the lowest or worst possible rating and 10 the highest or best possible rating. Scaling questions are used in a variety of creative ways.

Following a qualitative examination of scaling questions in therapy, Strong, Pyle, and Sutherland (2009) described how scaling questions operate in terms of constructive theory:

> Asking how a client will move from a 6 on a scale to a 7 requires a linguistic ladder of sorts to be constructed and serve both client and counselor in constructing still-to-be articulated solutions. (p. 182)

The following therapy excerpt illustrates how a solution-focused therapist might use scaling questions to (1) obtain an initial client rating of the problem's size, (2) monitor progress, (3) identify intermediate therapy goals, and (4) make plans for improvement.

(1) Therapist: Tell me, on a scale from 0 to 10, with 0 representing feeling completely and totally depressed and 10 representing feeling the best a person can possibly feel, how would you rate your feelings today?

Client: I'm about the same as last week.

(2) Therapist: Last week you gave yourself a rating of 2. What rating would you give yourself today?

Client: Hmm. I guess I think I'm still at about a 2.

(3) Therapist: So if you're still at a 2 right now, exactly what would need to be different to bump your rating up to a 3?

Client: I don't know. Maybe if I could get up in the morning without feeling so damn tired. Or if I could make it through the workday without thinking about how stupid and meaningless my job is.

(3) Therapist: So if you weren't tired in the morning that would make it a 3? Or would you need to have both those changes happen, both waking up refreshed and thinking that your job is meaningful?

Client: Either waking up feeling good or feeling better about my job would make it a 3. Both of those would make it a 4 or maybe even a 5.

(4) Therapist: Let's look at your job first. What exactly do you need to do to make it feel just a little more meaningful? What would make your job meaningful enough to bump your daily rating up to a 3 for tomorrow?

Percentage Questions
Percentage questions are similar to scaling questions; they give therapists a simple method for measuring exactly what change would look like. Typical percentage questions include: "How would your life be different if you were 1% less depressed?" "How about if you were 10% less depressed?" and "How about if you were 100% less depressed?"

Assessing Client Motivation
Solution-focused therapists categorize clients in terms of three motivational levels (Murphy, 2015):

1. *Customers for change*: These clients are eager to work in therapy and ready to make changes.

2. *Complainants*: These clients are interested in therapy because of the insistence or interest of a significant other.

3. *Visitors to treatment*: These are typically mandated clients who aren't interested in change and show up only because they have to.

Ideally, therapists can indirectly convince clients who are complainants or visitors to become customers for change (de Shazer, 1988).

To assess motivation and obtain commitment for change, at the end of the first session, a narrative therapist might ask:

> Are you more interested in finding a way to move beyond that depression that's got a hold on you and your life, or are you more interested in accepting that your depressed state is permanent and therefore you just need ways of coping with depression?

Of course, the motivated and committed client will voice an interest in the former option as opposed to the latter.

The Credulous Approach to Assessment
In his usual common sense manner, Kelly pioneered the **credulous approach to assessment**. He summarizes this approach by stating, "If you don't know what is wrong with a person, ask him [sic]; he may tell you" (1955, p. 322). Kelly's approach—and every approach associated with constructive therapy—emphasizes that clients are the best experts on their own lives.

Is Formal Assessment Really Required for a Constructive Therapist?
The radical solution-focused view of assessment holds that traditional assessment is unnecessary. De Shazer (1985) articulated this:

> For an intervention to successfully fit, it is not necessary to have detailed knowledge of the complaint. It is not necessary even to be able to construct with any rigor how the trouble is maintained in order to prompt solution.... All that is necessary is that the person involved in a troublesome situation does something different, even if that behavior is

seemingly irrational, certainly irrelevant, obviously bizarre, or humorous. (p. 7)

Despite his irreverent position regarding assessment of client problems, de Shazer has a straightforward but complex method for evaluating client complaints and providing solutions. His approach doesn't involve traditional or formal assessment, but it does offer therapists a menu of potential formula solutions linked to client complaints. The de Shazer system is summarized in Putting It in Practice 11.2.

PUTTING IT IN PRACTICE

11.2 De Shazer's Complaint–Solution Assessment System

In his complaint–solution assessment system, de Shazer (1985) identified 12 typical complaints that he viewed as leading to specific solutions. This complaint–solution system is summarized below:

Client complaint	Formula solution prescription
The client complains about a *sequence of behavior*: "When I'm depressed, I can't get myself out of bed in the morning."	Assign a specific task: "On the days when you do get out of bed in the morning, what's the first thing you do? Go ahead and do that each morning."
The client complains about the *meanings ascribed to a situation*: "My wife won't stop nagging me about getting a better job. She thinks I'm a lazy good-for-nothing husband."	Use reframing: "It's clear your wife loves you very much and is concerned about your happiness."
The client complains about the *frequency of a problem behavior or experience*: "I'm always worrying about everything—my husband's health, my daughter's marriage, our financial situation."	Assign a specific task: "You're worrying is important. I'd like you to schedule a half hour every day to just focus on worrying. What time would work best for you?"
The client complains about the *physical location where the problem occurs*: "I only drink when I'm out with my buddies on Friday after work."	Suggest a new location: "Where could you and your buddies go after work and not drink?"
The client complains that *the problem is involuntary*: "I can't stop myself from pulling out hair from my eyebrows."	Prescribe the symptom, ask for exceptions to the rule, or suggest a new location: "I notice you still have plenty of eyebrow hairs left; would you get to work on that this week?" or "What's happening during those times when you don't pull out your eyebrow hairs?" or "Where are you when you don't pull out your eyebrow hairs?"
The client complains about *significant others involved in the problem*: "And then my wife totally sabotages my diet by baking all these cakes and cookies."	Ask when guilt will be resolved or what difference it will make to them: "When will your wife be free from guilt over contributing to your weight problem?" or "What difference will it make to your wife if you choose not to eat her cakes and cookies?"
The client complains about *who or what is to blame* for the problem: "This whole situation is my brother's fault. He is totally insensitive and selfish."	Ask when guilt will be resolved: "When is it likely for your brother's guilt in this matter to be resolved?"
The client complains about *an environmental factor or situation* such as job, economic status, living space, etc.: "My job sucks. My boss rides me constantly and I don't like any of my coworkers."	Suggest a new location: "You could either quit your job or spend time with your boss and coworkers at some place where you might actually enjoy them."

Client complaint	Formula solution prescription
The client complains about *a physiological state or feeling*: "I weigh about 190 pounds and have tried everything to lose weight. I'd like to weigh 125 to 130 pounds."	Use symptom prescription: "The first thing you need to do is go home and start eating. When you get up to 220 pounds, come back and I can help you" (adapted from Haley, 1973, pp. 115–119).
The client complains about *the past*: "My parents were abusive and critical of me when I was young. They favored my sister."	Talk about a past success: "You were able to graduate from high school with high honors."
The client complains about *likely future situations that are catastrophic or dire*: "I know I'm gonna flunk my history test."	Talk about a past success or focus on new expectations: "How did you pass your last one?" or "What would you have to do to get a D on your exam?"
The client has *excessively idealistic or utopian expectations*: "I know I'll be able to get a job this summer, no problem."	Focus on new expectations or focus on a minimal change: "What if it is hard to get a job this summer? How would you cope with that?" or "Tell me what it would look like if you just put 10% more effort into getting a job."

Source: Adapted from de Shazer (1985).

Specific Therapy Techniques

In this section we review therapy techniques derived from solution-focused brief therapy, solution-oriented therapy (or possibility therapy), and narrative therapy. We make theoretical distinctions regarding techniques when possible, but constructive therapists use many overlapping technical procedures.

The Pretreatment Change Question

Solution-focused therapists cite research that indicates clients often begin improving between the time they call for an appointment and the first session (Beyebach, Morejon, Palenzuela, & Rodriguez-Arias, 1996). To help clients focus on how they're already using their strengths and resources effectively, therapists ask a **pretreatment change question** to prompt clients to reflect on the positive changes that have already started happening:

> What changes have you noticed that have happened or started to happen since you called to make the appointment for this session. (de Shazer et al., 2007, p. 5)

Solution-focused brief therapists report that a large percentage of clients have begun making changes prior to their first session and that using positive language during initial interviews can reduce client symptoms (Richmond, Jordan, Bischof, & Sauer, 2014).

Unique Account and Redescription Questions

White (1988) developed unique account and redescription questions. We refer to **unique account** and **redescription**

questions as "How did you manage that?" questions. These questions are central to narrative and solution-based approaches. They're phrased in many different ways and accompanied by genuine interest, and used whenever clients say anything that can be framed as progress. Narrative therapists typically refer to these glimmers of hope as **unique outcomes** or **sparkling moments** (Monk et al., 1997; White & Epston, 1990). Examples include:

- How did you beat the fear and go out shopping?

- How did you manage to get yourself out of bed and come to this appointment despite the depression?

- You stopped drinking for two whole days last week! How did you accomplish that?

- What were you telling yourself when you were feeling a little better last month?

The client's personal narrative can never match the depth and richness of the client's lived experiences. Unfortunately, what usually gets dismissed or pruned away from the client's story are the moments of strength, the courage in the face of adversity, and experiences of positive decision-making. Consequently, it's crucial for therapists not only to highlight sparkling moments, but also to help clients articulate and repeat them, using words, images, and even movements. The key is to acknowledge, not ignore, positive, lived moments. Monk (1997) compares the therapist's nurturance for sparkling moments to building a fire:

> These sparkling moments, or new developments in relation to the problem-saturated story, need to

be historicized so that they do not hang lifeless and disconnected. I like to describe this stage of the narrative interview as similar to … building a fire. To keep the first flickering flame alive, you place tiny twigs very carefully and strategically over the flame. If the twig is too large, the flame could be suffocated. If there is only one twig, it will quickly be spent and the flame will be extinguished. The fire needs to be gently nurtured by the placing of twigs in such a way that oxygen can feed the flames. Larger sticks are then placed on the fire, and soon the fire has a life of its own. (pp. 16–17)

Monk's analogy is a warning for therapists who might jump in too enthusiastically when sparkling moments first emerge. If therapists are too excited about client progress, clients may retreat to their safe, but maladaptive life stories.

In a qualitative study of unique outcomes imbedded in abuse experiences, Draucker (2003) summarized her findings:

Six types of unique outcomes stories were identified in the women's narratives (rebellion, breaking free, resurgence, refuge, determination, confidant) and three types in the men's narratives (reawakening, buddy and normal guy, champion). Findings suggest that unique outcomes stories are common in narratives otherwise focused on abuse. (p. 7)

Helping clients uncover the sparkling moments or unique and positive twists on their challenging life experiences is at the heart of narrative therapy. Although Draucker (2003) observed substantial male–female differences in her study, it's important for therapists practicing narrative therapy to be open to whatever general or specific positive and unique outcomes their clients generate.

Externalizing Conversations

Virtually everyone recognizes the tendency for clients (and other humans) to blame themselves or others when things go awry. Blaming is a natural, but often unhelpful, human phenomenon.

Many clients come to therapy in distress because the narratives or stories they tell themselves about themselves are saturated with problems for which they are responsible. **Externalizing conversations** are designed to help clients, couples, and families push their problems outside the intrapsychic realm. Ramey, Tarulli, Frijters, and Fisher (2009) defined externalizing:

Externalizing involves using language to position problems and other aspects of people's lives outside of themselves in an effort to separate people from dominant, problem saturated stories. (p. 263)

Through problem externalization, clients can dissociate from problems, look at them from greater distances,

and develop strategies for eliminating them. Potential externalizing questions include:

- How long have you been working against this opiate problem?

- What exactly are you doing when you're free from the grip of that anger?

- Who are you with when you feel lighter and happier and like you've thrown off the weight of that depression?

- How might you tell your anxiety thank you and good bye? (Adapted from J. Sommers-Flanagan & Sommers-Flanagan, 2017.)

In our work with youth, we've found it helpful to use drawings to help young clients visualize their problems as outside of themselves. Similarly, Conner (2017) reported using art in group settings with substance using clients. The experiential nature of drawings and artwork may be a creative method that some clients can use to enhance their externalizing process.

When individual clients, couples, or families engage in therapeutic externalizing conversations, they usually experience relief (Hill, 2011). This may be because often clients come to counseling worrying that the counselor's all-seeing and all-knowing eye will pierce their defenses and hold them 100% responsible for their problems. Externalizing conversations reduce defensiveness, allowing client and therapist to work collaboratively against the problems.

REFLECTIONS

Think of a challenging problem in your own life. Then talk to yourself about it using externalizing language.

What comes up when you imagine using externalizing questions with clients? Consider how you might initiate an externalizing conversation with: (1) A client who complains of "biological" depression or (2) a parent and teenager who want to work on the teen's delinquent behaviors.

Carl Rogers with a Twist

O'Hanlon (1998) credits Carl Rogers with teaching him the importance of showing empathy and compassion for clients. He also describes a unique technique for showing empathy and compassion while simultaneously helping clients move beyond their negative or traumatic feelings from the past. **Carl Rogers with a Twist** involves reflecting back the content of what clients said, but shifting the tense (from present to past), the perception (from global to partial) or the certainty (from factual to perceptual):

Client: I feel like cutting myself.

Therapist: You've felt like cutting yourself (O'Hanlon & Bertolino, 1998, p. 47).

[The therapist validates the client, but shifts to past tense.]

Client: I have flashbacks all the time.

Therapist: You have flashbacks a lot of the time.

[The therapist transforms the client's description from global to partial.]

Client: I'm a bad person because I was sexually abused.

Therapist: So you've really gotten the idea that you're bad because you were sexually abused.

[The therapist shifts the client's words from factual to perceptual.]

O'Hanlon's Carl Rogers with a twist technique is an excellent example of a subtle, indirect, linguistically based strategy for shifting client perspectives. It's also a good example of solution-oriented therapists intentionally directing clients toward the positive.

Positive Relabeling and Reframing

Positive relabeling and reframing are core therapy tools. For example, clients are customers for change (not clients) and therapy is a conversation (not counseling or an interview). In fact, some therapists aren't therapists at all; they're coaches and consultants. Constructive therapists relabel and reframe any part of therapy necessary to gain access to clients and engage them in social discourse.

We've seen therapy-reluctant teens start cooperating when we relabel therapy. For example, teens who boldly claim, "I think therapy is stupid" and "You can't make me talk in here" suddenly calm down and talk openly when we relabel therapy,

Okay, let's not do therapy today. How about if we have a consultation meeting instead? I won't be your therapist; I'll just be your consultant. (See J. Sommers-Flanagan & Sommers-Flanagan, 2007b)

In his solution-focused book on working with adolescents, Selekman (1993) recommended using a forced-teaming reframe with an adolescent who was referred by a probation officer. **Forced-teaming** involves aligning yourself with clients and against something else. Selekman suggested that he and the client team up to surprise the probation officer, and prove that the boy can avoid trouble and be successful. This approach captured the boy's attention, intriguing him and motivating him to work harder with the counselor.

Similarly, many parents resist using positive reinforcement approaches with their children because they view reinforcement as bribery. In our work with difficult adolescents, it has been helpful when we define bribery and reframe positive reinforcement.

Do you know the definition of bribery? It's when you pay someone, in advance, to do something illegal. What we're talking about is positive reinforcement. Positive reinforcement is what you get AFTER you do something LEGAL. It's like you getting paid for your job. How about we set up a positive reinforcement system with your daughter, focusing on homework completion. Then we can evaluate, together, whether or not the positive reinforcement is helping.

Using relabeling and reframing can motivate parents to try out positive reinforcement and other therapy strategies (J. Sommers-Flanagan & Sommers-Flanagan, 2007b).

Presuppositional Questions

Goal setting is a powerful force for change. Surprisingly, it wasn't until 1970 that goal setting was conceptualized as a direct way to modify individual and group behavior (Ryan, 1970). Locke and Latham (2002) and others have demonstrated that individuals perform better when they have specific, difficult goals.

Constructive therapists use presuppositional questions to co-create therapeutic and life goals with clients (de Shazer et al., 2007). **Presuppositional questions** involve pretending that a positive change has already been made and then asking for specific descriptions of these changes. O'Hanlon and Bertolino (1998) illustrate a presuppositional question using an approach they refer to as **videotalk**:

Let's say that a few weeks, months, or more time has elapsed and your problem has been resolved. If you and I were to watch a videotape of your life in the future, what would you be doing on that tape that would show that things were better? (p. 90)

There are many creative presupposition questions, using language ranging from crystal balls to letters (or postcards) from the future (White & Epston, 1990). The main point is to construct a question that helps clients hear, feel, and picture themselves functioning in the future without problems; this could involve asking clients what they might post on Snapchat or Instagram after successfully getting over a problem. Some therapists believe that the longer clients can linger with positive, problem-free, goal-attained futures within a session, the greater likelihood they have of making the solution-focused future happen.

The Miracle Question

The miracle question is one of the most well-known of all solution-focused therapy techniques (Murphy, 2015).

De Shazer's (1988) original version of the miracle question is:

> Suppose you were to go home tonight, and while you were asleep, a miracle happened and this problem was solved. How will you know the miracle happened? What will be different? (p. 5)

The miracle question is a presuppositional question that helps clients focus on a positive future. When clients respond, counselors follow up with an additional question to obtain clear, concrete, and behaviorally specific descriptions of what would be different. This question can help clients develop and maintain a positive future vision. The question also builds rapport with clients; when therapists validate and nurture each answer the client provides, the alliance is deepened.

The miracle question can be modified for use with various populations. Bertolino (1999) suggested an alternative wording with young clients:

> Suppose that when you went home tonight and went to sleep, something strange happened to you and your life changed for the better. You may or may not know what actually happened, but you knew that your problem had gone away. What will be different? (p. 75)

Bertolino used word *strange* instead of *miracle*. He also suggested using the word *weird* or an alternative word the client has previously used in therapy. He advised therapists to modify their language style when working with young clients.

Tohn and Oshlag (1996) described a different version for use with mandated clients:

> **Suppose** that tonight, after our session, you go home and fall asleep, and while you are sleeping a miracle happens. The miracle is that **the problems that brought you here today** are solved, but you don't know that the miracle has happened because you are asleep. When you wake up in the morning, what will be some of the first things you will **notice** that will be different that will tell you this miracle has happened? (pp. 170–171, bold in original)

Tohn and Oslag explained that beginning with the word suppose is crucial because it leads clients toward pretending that the miracle has already happened, rather than speculating on whether it will or won't happen. They also noted that saying "the problems that brought you here" focuses the question on the reality of the situation. In contrast, they claimed that when therapists use "your problem is solved," clients are likely to respond with a more grandiose disappearance of the problem. Finally, they used the word *notice* toward the end of the intervention to focus clients on different sensory experiences.

Formula Tasks

In addition to the pretreatment change question discussed previously, there are other solution-based formula tasks (de Shazer & Molnar, 1984). De Shazer originally developed the formula task concept, but following his lead others have created additional formula tasks. Positive expectancy is a significant component in successful formula tasks:

> By expecting that change/difference will occur for the client, based on the way that it makes most sense for the client, the therapist is sending a message to the client(s) that a new more useful mode of operation is not only possible, but will occur sometime in the near future. (Reiter, 2007, p. 28)

The **first-session formula task** shifts clients from a focus on the past and negative expectations to a present–future focus and positive expectations. This task is based on the assumption that, in general, many positive qualities already exist within most people who come for treatment.

> Between now and next time we meet, we [I] would like you to observe, so that you can describe to us [me] next time, what happens in your [pick one: family, life, marriage, relationship] that you want to continue to have happen. (de Shazer, 1984, p. 15)

Reiter (2007) described how the first-session formula task works:

> This formula task is designed to shift clients' lenses from that of a problem-focused orientation to a solution-focused orientation. Instead of doing the typical thing that the client has been doing (i.e., focusing on when things are not going well), the client now is doing something different and focusing on times of strength and resources. (p. 31)

Selekman (1993) reported that when he uses the first-session formula task, clients usually return to their second session with two or three specific descriptions of positive interactions they would like to have continue.

Reiter (2007) also described another popular de Shazer formula task, the **write–read–burn task**:

> This intervention involved spending at least one hour, but no more than one-and-a-half hours per day, on odd-numbered days, writing down good and bad memories (of a boyfriend). On even-numbered days, the client was to read the previous day's notes and then burn them. After this first case, this task was generically used for clients who had complaints dealing with obsessive thoughts or depressive thoughts. (p. 33)

Write–read–burn has a Milton Erickson feel to it. It includes paradox and the likelihood is that clients will insightfully decide they've had quite enough of writing, reading, and burning in a relatively short time period.

Exception Questions

Exception questions are a commonly employed solution-based intervention (de Shazer et al., 2007; Murphy, 2015). In keeping with the theoretical position that only small changes are needed to instigate larger changes, **exception questions** solicit minor evidence that the client's problem is not always present. Bertolino (1999) provided several examples of exception questions with teenage clients:

- It seems that when this problem is happening, things are pretty difficult. When does the problem seem less noticeable to you? What is everyone doing when it's less noticeable?

- When does the problem appear to happen less?

- What is your son/daughter doing when he/she is not in trouble?

- Tell me what it's like when the problem is a little less dominating.

Exception questions build hope and identify small behavioral patterns or sequences when the problem is occurring less, or not occurring at all. Constructive therapists use exception sequences to build a case for pre-existing client strengths and resources. These sequences can build up or feed the client's adaptive storyline, instead of the problem-saturated storyline.

The Do Something Different Task

The **do something different task** is a direct but nonspecific intervention that's especially well-suited for disrupting repeating and dissatisfying behavior sequences. For example, if a parent comes to therapy complaining about her son's recurrent tantrums, the therapist might tell the parent to do something totally different the next time a tantrum occurs (J. Sommers-Flanagan & Sommers-Flanagan, 2011).

As is the case with direct, but nonspecific interventions, the therapist doesn't know in advance what different behavior the client may select. This unknown and unknowable component of the intervention fuels creativity and danger. It releases clients from entrenched behavior patterns, but may implicitly give them permission to act out inappropriately. In one case reported by de Shazer (1985), the father of a young boy with a pattern of lying came up with the idea of rubbing his son's face in actual bullshit whenever a lie was suspected. Fortunately, the boy's mother wouldn't allow such an intervention, so the father chose a less violent option of buying a can of "bullshit repellent" from a local novelty shop and spraying his son with it on the next occasion of a lie. Although de Shazer reported success, it illustrates how clients may come up with bad or abusive ideas for "doing something different."

Letter Writing

To deepen the therapy process and stimulate alternative storylines, Epston (Epston, 1994; White & Epston, 1990) pioneered the use of **letter writing** as a narrative therapy technique. Epston used and recommended several letter formats, some of which we'll cover next. For detailed examples, see White and Epston's (1990) *Narrative Means to Therapeutic Ends* and other letter writing publications (S. Alexander, Shilts, Liscio, & Rambo, 2008).

In the **summary letter**, narrative therapists write to clients immediately following a therapeutic conversation. Summary letters are written from the therapist's perspective, but highlight sparkling moments and use the client's words to produce a strength- and hope-based storyline.

Letters of invitation are written to family members who are reluctant to attend therapy. These letters highlight the person's status in the family, focusing on positive reasons for attending a session, rather than negative consequences of nonattendance. Such letters are a therapeutic art, requiring supervision and feedback. Some examples in the literature include far too much counselor self-disclosure, or other contraindicated content.

At the end of therapy, **letters of prediction** are written to help clients continue strength-based storylines into the future. Epston asks clients permission to make predictions for the future and then mails the letters—usually with a "private and confidential" label and an instruction "not to be viewed until [6 months after the final session]" (White & Epston, 1990, p. 94). He cites two reasons for using prediction letters. First, he notes that the letters serve as a 6-month follow-up or review that is both interesting and potentially helpful (White & Epston, 1990, p. 94). Second, he suspects that most clients will not wait 6 months to open the letter and that it therefore serves as a possible positive prophesy.

Both Epston and White discuss writing many other types of letters, letters that spring from the issues and concerns expressed to them during sessions. Some of these additional letter variations include letters of reference, counter-referral letters, and letters for special occasions. White, in particular, includes several examples of what he refers to as brief letters designed to strengthen the positive therapeutic narrative. An example follows in which White maps a client's personal influence in her own life:

> Dear Molly,
>   Anorexia nervosa had claimed 99% of your life. You only held 1% of your own territory. You have said that you now hold 25% of your own territory. This means that you have reclaimed 24% of yourself from anorexia nervosa, and you achieved this over the last eight months. And yet, you despair for all those lost years, for the two-thirds of your life under its influence.
>   Tell me, if you were to pick up another 24% over the next eight months, and then 24% over the next eight

months and so on, how long would it take you to reach 200% and be experiencing double value in your life? And should you keep on in this way, how old would you be at the point when you have regained all the time that was lost? And what will it mean that your life is accelerating right at the time that others are slowing down in their lives?

Just curious,

M.W. (White & Epston, 1990, p. 116)

White's letter illustrates problem externalization using scaling information for feedback, a linguistic flexibility intervention, and personal influence mapping.

Writing letters has great potential for influencing clients. In our work with young clients, we've experimented with in-session note-passing. We've noticed that clients are often surprised and touched at receiving a written communiqué from a concerned and interested therapist (J. Sommers-Flanagan & Sommers-Flanagan, 2007b). White (1995) estimated that a single letter may have a potency equivalent to four to five therapy sessions.

Reflecting Teams or Therapeutic Breaks

Reflecting teams originated with Norwegian psychiatrist Tom Andersen's approach to family therapy (1987, 1991, 1995). Following his lead, many therapists have integrated **reflecting teams** or **therapeutic breaks** into individual, couple, and family therapy (Cox, Bañez, Hawley, & Mostade, 2003; de Barbaro et al., 2008; de Oliveira, 2003; Fishel, Buchs, McSheffrey, & Murphy, 2001). This approach, which emphasizes multiple perspectives or realities, is highly consistent with constructive thinking.

Andersen's (1987) reflective team provides a feedback procedure that's much different from the traditional one-way mirror in family therapy training. In the one-way mirror paradigm, a supervisor and fellow students sit behind a one-way mirror and observe family therapy sessions. Sometimes the supervisor communicates with the therapist about appropriate therapeutic interventions via a bug-in-the-ear device. Overall, the standard procedure emphasizes supervisory input and a rich discussion of "the case" either midway during the session or immediately afterward.

Consistent with post-modern constructive thinking, Andersen's reflecting team breaks down hierarchical boundaries of traditional one-way mirror supervision by introducing a two-way mirror reflecting team. Originally, his reflecting team procedures consisted of the following:

1. During an impasse when the therapist is unsure how to proceed, or at a preplanned time, a reflecting team meeting is initiated.

2. The therapy session stops as the therapist and family turn to the mirror and the lights and sound system are reversed.

3. The therapist and family watch and listen as the reflecting team spontaneously provides hypotheses about the family's problem issues.

4. During the reflecting team meeting, care is taken to talk about the family in a respectful, non-pathologizing manner.

5. When the reflecting team meeting ends, the lights and sound system are again reversed and family members and therapist have a conversation about the reflecting team's conversation.

Reflecting teams honor the family, while providing fresh perspectives. Usually, families feel important, listened to, and accepted. After using the reflecting team approach for a number of years, Andersen (1995) described some of his discoveries:

When we finally began to use this mode we were surprised at how easy it was to talk without using nasty or hurtful words. Later it became evident that how we talk depends on the context in which we talk. If we choose to speak about the family without them present, we easily speak "professionally," in a detached manner. If we choose to speak about them in their presence, we naturally use everyday language and speak in a friendly manner. (p. 16)

The reflecting team approach is a gentle and collaborative experience. Andersen emphasized that reflecting teams should speak with uncertainty, with inclusive both–and language ("*both* this could be true *and* this other thing could be true, too"), and without negative connotations (1991, p. 61).

Andersen's (2007) approach is in contrast to the more provocative and sometimes confusing or double-binding approaches derived from Erickson's work, the MRI group, and the preceding White and Epston narrative letters. For example, de Shazer (1985) reported using the following feedback intervention with a couple whose drug use was, in the eyes of the woman, adversely affecting their marriage.

You've got a problem.

It seems to us, Ralph, that your marital problems are being exacerbated by the drugs, or fogged over by the drugs, or perhaps even created by the drugs. Perhaps you need to stop the drugs, just to see what is going on. But, on the other hand, we agree with you Jane, that if you two were to stop the drugs, then there might be nothing there. And, you might not have time to create anything before the marriage broke up. In short, we don't know what the fuck you are going to do.

I suggest you think about what I just said, and decide what actions you are going to take ... first. (p. 52)

De Shazer reported that the clients cut down on their drug use immediately after the intervention.

Within weeks, both clients stopped using drugs and managed to stay married and to develop healthier common interests.

REFLECTIONS

As you contrast Andersen's and de Shazer's styles, what differences do you notice? How would it feel to you, to use the more provocative style? Which approach are you more comfortable with and why?

Narrative Exposure Therapy

Narrative exposure therapy (NET) is an evidence-based treatment approach that integrates traditional exposure therapy principles with narrative storytelling to help individuals who have experienced repeated traumatic events (Schauer, Neuner, & Elbert, 2011). NET is a manualized treatment, developed by *Vivo*, an international organization focusing on trauma, international health, humanitarian aid, and human rights (see www.vivo.org). Originally, NET was created to be implemented in refugee camps and sometimes implemented by nonmental health providers (Robjant & Fazel, 2010).

In NET, following psychoeducation about the nature of trauma, clients create a timeline narrative of their lives. The constructed timeline includes both positive and negative events in chronological order. Timelines are reported verbally, but include symbols. For example, a rope can be used to symbolize the timeline, with flowers and stones to represent the positive and negative events. The timeline can also be drawn, along with the flowers and stones (Colville, 2017). There's a version of NET for children (i.e., KIDNET) that follows the same general procedure, but uses developmentally appropriate techniques.

As positive and trauma memories are recalled, therapists employ person-centered listening strategies. Contextual details of the events are drawn out and discussed. NET practitioners focus on both cold and hot memories. **Cold memories** are declarative, descriptive, and specific. They contain information, but affective components may be detached. **Hot memories** are more affective; they include extensive sensory information, as well as physical and motor responses.

Clients are coached to narrate their traumatic experiences in great detail. Emotional involvement is combined with using words to describe the experiences. The therapist records or takes notes on the narrative. Between sessions, therapists write up the narrative to clarify details and understanding, but also to be prepared to reexpose the clients to the memory in the next session. After the re-reading of the narrative, clients move on to what hap-pened next in their lives. This may involve additional traumatic events. When using a rope to symbolize the timeline, a portion of the rope at the end remains coiled to represent the future, yet-to-be-lived life.

NET and KIDNET are evidence-based (Robjant & Fazel, 2010; Schauer, Neuner, & Elbert, 2011). More information about research support for this approach is discussed later in this chapter.

Constructive Therapy in Action: Brief Vignettes

Solution-focused therapy emphasizes a collaborative relationship, but also includes active use of a variety of techniques. Most of these techniques involve questioning. In contrast, narrative therapy is less technically focused and more oriented toward a deeper relationship, although when narrative therapists use interventions, they also tend to use questions similar in content to those used by solution-focused therapists.

Vignette I: A Resistant (Reluctant) Teenager

This is a brief case excerpt from Dr. Brent Richardson illustrating several solution-focused therapy techniques. Richardson is the author of *Working with Challenging Youth: Seven Guiding Principles* (Richardson, 2016). The case is from a journal article (J. Sommers-Flanagan, Richardson, & Sommers-Flanagan, 2011).

As a father and his teenage son, Brian, begin therapy, they're in conflict, struggling to communicate. Richardson uses solution-focused techniques to increase positive feelings and to get the father and son working together more productively.

Dad: I can't get a word in edgewise. There's no respect. He's always interrupting me.

Brian: Me?! He never lets me finish a sentence. My opinion doesn't matter.

BR: I can see both of you are really frustrated with times in the past that you haven't felt heard. [Carl Rogers with a twist.] How long have the two of you been fighting against this interruption habit? [Externalizing question.]

Dad: I would say about 2 years now.

BR: Interesting, so does that sound about right to you Brian—that this interrupting habit has been winning much of the time over the past 2 years? [Continuing to externalize the problem.]

Brian: Yeah, that's about right.

BR: So, it sounds like that for most of your life Brian, you and your dad have gotten along better. Tell me about a time when you felt like you and your dad were on the same page. [Exception-oriented question.]

Brian: I remember when he coached me in Little League baseball. We got along then.

BR: Brian, I notice that your body language seemed to relax as you remembered those times. Mr. Jones, tell me about a recent time in which you and Brian were relating in a way that felt better to you. [Exception-oriented question.]

Dad: Well, there aren't many.

BR: That's okay. Take your time and pick one.

Dad: [Pause.] After the baseball game the other night, we were driving home and Brian asked me about hitting the ball to the opposite field. I felt like he really listened.

BR: I can tell that felt good. BR continues: This question is for both of you. Tonight, when the two of you are really listening to one another, what will that look like? How are you going to make that happen? [Presuppositional question.] (J. Sommers-Flanagan et al., 2011, p. 74)

One principle of solution-focused therapy is: Whatever you spend time doing or thinking tends to stay the center of your focus, and grows in strength and salience. In this case, Richardson persists and skillfully gets father and son to focus on positive interactions they've had and continue to have.

Vignette II: Leila and the Tiger

This vignette is a case story presented by a psychiatrist, Glen Simblett, in *Narrative Therapy in Practice: The Archaeology of Hope* (1997). We selected this case because it focuses on making therapeutic connection across a multicultural divide.

Leila was Maori [a New Zealand native]. Twenty-four years old. A woman. A patient. She stood in my office and handed me a drawing. Neither of us sat down. I was puzzled. This was meant to be a routine outpatient follow-up to Leila's recent discharge from a psychiatric unit. Pictures are not normally a part of that.

Simblett has described the routine contact with a patient that has quickly become not routine.

Previously, Simblett met this patient twice. The most recent was difficult. She was actively hallucinating. The hallucinations were commanding her to hurt herself … and her family. Consequently, as psychiatrists can do, he coerced her into agreeing to hospitalization. While she was in the hospital she stopped eating, drinking, and talking.

Against the advice of her doctors, she had stopped treatment and persuaded her family to discharge her from the hospital to see a tohunga [a Maori healer]. Some incredulity had been expressed about that by the white mental health workers. They asked if potatoes in her shoes were going to stop a depressive psychosis or schizophrenia.

Simblett looked at the drawing. It was a partial profile of the head of a tiger.

"It's a tiger," I said lamely.

She waited silently. There had been some words written beside the tiger. I could still see the erasure marks.

"Was something written there?"

Leila nodded—the slightest tilt of her head. "There was a story to go with it. I changed my mind about writing it."

I knew that I was holding something significant in my hands but did not have the faintest idea how to respond. I was outside my psychiatric training. Outside the country I was born in. Outside my culture. I knew enough to register that, but not enough to know how to proceed.

Finally, Simblett admitted to Leila that he didn't understand the meaning of the picture. She asked,

"Do you want to hear the story?"

We still hovered uncertainly. I noticed that she was nearer the door than I was, and the door was still open. She avoided my gaze.

"Yes, I would like to."

Leila took a deep breath. "This is a tiger. A tiger has nine lives. This tiger only has five lives left. Do you want to know what happened to the other lives?"

I did, but I didn't. Part of me knew what was coming next, and I didn't want to hear it.

"Yes I do," I lied.

"It lost its first life in the family it was born in because of their abuse and punishment. It lost its second life to drugs and alcohol. She lost her third life in a marriage where there was no room for her hopes and ideas." She paused, for the first time catching my gaze with culturally surprising boldness. "She lost her last life when she was admitted to a psychiatric unit."

Another pause.

"She hasn't got many lives left now," Leila added.

She waited silently. Patiently. It was not an accusation. Just a statement. The way it was for her.

Where do you go from here? You begin again, maybe. I invited her to sit down. We closed the door and we talked. We tried to understand each other's point of view. We tried not to blame.

I still find it hard to understand why she gave me another chance like that, why she did not just give up on yet another Pakeha [white] doctor who did not understand. I often wonder if I would have been so generous if the roles had been reversed. The tiger drawing still hangs on the wall of my office. It acts as a gentle caution and constant reminder to me of the dangers of dominant discourse. (Simblett, 1997, pp. 121–122)

Simblett's experience with Leila, and his exposure to White and Epston's narrative approach transformed the way he practices psychiatry. He now reads referral letters from other physicians aloud to his patients and asks for their comments. He also formulates client problems differently. For example, rather than viewing clients with anorexia symptoms as having family relationship problems and internal psychological problems, he provides them information about the Auckland Anti-Anorexia/Anti-Bulimia Leagues to help empower them to fight against anorexia. The story of Leila and the tiger is about Simblett's personal experience, but it may have relevance to you as you listen to client stories.

CASE PRESENTATION

The following case example is excerpted from Tammie Ronen's book, *Cognitive-Constructivist Psychotherapy with Children and Adolescents* (Ronen, 2003). We selected this case because it illustrates how constructive approaches can be integrated with more traditional cognitive approaches. This is the case of a 12-year-old girl named Sharon. Sharon was a bedwetter. She had a diagnosis of primary nocturnal enuresis (p. 162).

Ronen employed a diverse approach to assessment. In addition to a standard interview wherein she evaluated the specific enuresis antecedents, behaviors, and consequences, she had Sharon lead the family in a family sculpture activity and then had Sharon draw her family as a group of animals. The results helped in the development of a problem and strengths list.

Problem–Strengths–Goals List

Constructive approaches focus on strengths and goals. Although Sharon had a specific problem, it can be transformed into a positive goal. For example, her problem of wetting her bed once a night about 5 to 6 nights a week, can be transformed into:

Sharon is working toward having a dry bed every night.

Similarly, the problem of reduced social contact can be reworded to reflect what she wants to accomplish, instead of focusing on the problem using problem language:

Sharon is increasing her confidence and will soon be able to go on overnight social outings.

In keeping with a constructive model, Sharon's strengths included:

- Sharon has good relationships with her parents and a close family.
- Sharon is a good student and reports having many friends.
- Sharon is motivated and was cooperative during the initial session.

Problem and Strengths Formulation

The initial interview revealed that Sharon and her parents had tried many different strategies to address the bedwetting. She had play therapy for 2 years, beginning when she was 6 years old. She used the bell-and-pad device at age 10. After trying the bell-and-pad, she tried medications. None of these interventions was successful.

Ronen formulated the bedwetting problem as having two main contributing factors. These included (a) Sharon appeared to have poor self-control and (b) the parents seemed overprotective of Sharon. Ronen reflected on the problem formulation:

I could not give a full explanation as to the cause of enuresis, but I could see how the parents were ineffective in handling it. I noted that Sharon was a nice, intelligent girl, yet she had been overly dependent on her parents when it came to her previous attempts to cease her bedwetting. For example, it was the parents who had ensured she took her medication every night, because "she tended to forget." While using the bell-and-pad technique, the parents set up the equipment every night and came to awaken her when the alarm rang, because "she couldn't hear anything while sleeping." In addition, Sharon construed herself as a bedwetting girl who couldn't control her behavior. This particular narrative of her not having control over bedwetting incidents that just seemed to happen was also a target of treatment.

The treatment goals included: (a) have Sharon take more responsibility for the bedwetting; (b) have Sharon learn self-control strategies.

Interventions

Ronen employed at least five different interventions:

1. She asked the parents to require Sharon take care of the wet laundry, wash it, and make the bed when there was a bedwetting incident.
2. Explore and understand Sharon's "meaning making" of the bedwetting experience.
3. Shift Sharon's ideas about the bedwetting to within her control through Socratic questioning and paradoxical examples.
4. Homework monitoring of bedwetting and internal sensations.
5. Psychoeducation and demonstrations of how the brain controls bladder functioning.

Therapist: What do you think, why do you wet your bed at night?

Sharon: I don't feel anything when I'm asleep. It's not my fault. It's not up to me.

T: Let's check this out. How many times do you fall out of your bed at night?

S: Never.

T: How come?

S: Because I don't move when I sleep.

T: Really? Let's check it out: Please find a nice position in which you'll feel comfortable. Now, I want you to stay in the same position and not move at all.

[We continued talking and after 2 minutes Sharon started fidgeting from side to side.]

T: You see, Sharon, after 2 minutes you already moved. Why?

S: It hurts. I can't stay in the same position all day long.

T: You know, the same thing happens at night. You feel uncomfortable, and for that reason you move from one side to the other.

S: Well, then, I guess that when I get close to the edge of the bed I just turn to the other side. (p. 168)

Ronen also provided psychoeducation. She taught her about how drinking fills up the bladder and how the bladder's pressure of filling up sends the message to the brain to eventually open up the valve and let the bladder drain out. She wrote:

> It was important for me to help Sharon realize that it was she who conceptualized herself as of being enuretic, and she was responsible for the meaning she put into her own behavior. We looked at books with illustrations of the human body and of the bladder, and we discussed the brain and its role.

Therapist: Could you stand up please?

Sharon: Sure [standing up].

T: How did you do that?

S: What do you mean?

T: What made you stand up? From what you already learned about the brain.

S: Oh, yes, the brain commanded me to stand up. (p. 169)

After six weeks of therapy, Sharon's bedwetting had reduced to only one to two times weekly. Although she had considerable success, she still tended to minimize her control over the bedwetting. An additional intervention was applied. Ronen had her keep a nightly chart predicting whether she would have a bedwetting incident. As Sharon's confidence in her ability to control her enuresis increased, so did her success at staying dry.

After Sharon had three consecutive dry weeks her therapy frequency was reduced to one session every three weeks. These sessions focused on relapse prevention, especially helping Sharon from slipping back into an "I have no control over this" narrative when she had regressions.

Ronen described Sharon's status at the end of treatment:

> After three months of being dry, the follow-up stage was terminated. Sharon stayed dry even when she went to sleep late, drank before going to sleep, or forgot to empty herself before going to bed. The charts emphasized the change in her wetting behavior and showed that Sharon was dry and did not regress. Follow-up by telephone revealed that Sharon stayed dry. (p. 173)

Outcomes Assessment

In Sharon's case outcomes assessment included ongoing parent reports as well as charts that Sharon completed, tracking her enuresis. Typically, both narrative and solution-focused professionals are open to using a variety of traditional and creative self-report outcome assessment instruments.

EVALUATIONS AND APPLICATIONS

Solution-focused and narrative therapy approaches share in their post-modern foundation, but differ in therapeutic approach. Although both therapies liberally employ questions to guide clients toward positive perceptions and outcomes, they are stylistically distinct. In this section, we review how both of these post-modern therapeutic approaches fare with respect to empirical research and cultural, gender, sexual, and spiritual applications.

Evidence-Based Status

Solution-focused and narrative therapies have separate and distinct research foundations.

Solution-Focused Therapy Research

Solution-focused therapists and researchers are enthusiastic supporters of solution-focused therapy (SFT). Over the years they've consistently made claims pertaining to SFT effectiveness (DeJong & Hopwood, 1996; Sklare, 2014). Their positive claims are consistent with their theoretical perspective of persistently focusing on the positive. However, sorting through all the positive assertions of SFT effectiveness makes it difficult to objectively evaluate SFT effectiveness.

In a 1996 review published in the *Handbook of Solution-Focused Brief Therapy* it was concluded that no definitive empirical research existed:

> Not only does no single collection of studies exist, but for the most part there simply are no research

studies to report! In fact, in spite of having been around for ten years, no well-controlled, scientifically sound outcome studies on solution-focused therapy have ever been conducted or published in any peer-reviewed professional journal. (Miller, Hubble, & Duncan, 1996, p. 2)

Gingerich and Eisengart (2000) conducted a literature review of outcomes studies on SFT (aka SFBT). They identified 15 studies, only five of which they considered relatively well-controlled. They summarized their findings by stating:

Since none of the five studies met all of the stringent criteria for efficacy studies, and all five studied different populations (that is, there were no replications by independent investigators), we cannot conclude that SFBT has been shown to be efficacious. We do, however, believe that these five studies provide initial support for the efficacy of SFBT. (Gingerich & Eisengart, 2000, p. 493)

Gingerich and Eisengart's conclusions were reasonable, but there were significant shortcomings in the five "well-controlled" studies. For example, Gingerich and Eisengart (2000) included a one-session SFT intervention for depressed college students compared to a one-session interpersonal psychotherapy intervention for depression ($n = 40$). Although the authors' claimed this study was well-controlled and compared SFT with another well-established treatment, the other treatment also was delivered in a one-session format—which is not how IPT was designed to be delivered (and there's no evidence of IPT's efficacy as a single session treatment). What the study showed was evidence that providing "depressed" college students with one session of counseling may be helpful, although the positive outcomes could have been a function of placebo effects.

The next review of SFT efficacy/effectiveness was reported by a Dutch research group (Stams, Deković, Buist, & de Vries, 2006). They conducted a meta-analysis of 21 studies with 1,421 clients and reported a small to medium positive SFBT effect ($d = 0.37$). They concluded:

Although SFBT does not have a larger effect, it does have a positive effect in less time and satisfies the client's need for autonomy. Therefore, it is reasonable to consider this form of therapy when it is tuned to the client and his problem. (p. 81)

Kim (2008) conducted a meta-analysis of 22 SFT studies. He reported that 10 of the 22 studies had no statistical significance, but positive results were linked to 12 studies focusing on internalizing disorders (e.g., depression, anxiety, low self-esteem). Kim reported an effect size of $d = 0.26$ for these 12 studies. This indicates a small but positive effect of SFT over control groups within these studies. Kim also noted that these studies are more representative of effectiveness research rather than efficacy research.

Reviewing the research, Corcoran and Pillai (2009) concluded:

The most striking finding is that very little research has still been conducted on solution-focused therapy. That only ten studies met the basic criteria of having two groups with which to compare treatment response is remarkably low.... Overall, this study indicates that the effects of solution-focused therapy are equivocal and more rigorously designed research needs to establish its effectiveness. Therefore, practitioners should understand there is not a strong evidence basis for solution-focused therapy at this point in time. (pp. 240–241)

More recent SFT research continues on the same theme. Schmit, Schmit, & Lenz (2016) reported results from a meta-analysis of 26 studies representing 2,968 clients. The studies included youth and adults, as well as individual and group therapy. Overall, the researchers concluded there were "modest effect sizes for SFBT when treating internalizing disorders (Schmit et al., 2016, p. 21).

Several SFT research studies have been conducted outside the United States. In Finland, a series of comparisons of short- and long-term psychodynamic psychotherapy and solution-focused therapy showed that the shorter term treatments were more effective at one year (Knekt et al., 2008; Lindfors, Knekt, Virtala, & Laaksonen, 2012). However, at three-year follow-up longer term psychotherapy was shown to have more lasting effects.

The strongest empirical support for SFT to date was found in a meta-analysis of nine SFT studies in China (Kim et al., 2015). Specifically, Kim et al. (2015) reported an effect size ranging from 0.49 to 3.22. They concluded that the "... results highlight the positive impact SFBT has on Chinese clients with mental health-related problems" (p. 187).

On a smaller scale, positive outcomes have been reported that support having clients focus on the positive at the beginning of therapy. Specifically, in two small randomized studies designed to evaluate pretreatment or initial interview change, the results were significant and positive (Richmond et al., 2014). First, clients who completed a solution-focused intake form were more able to describe prospective solutions (and fewer problems) than clients who completed a problem-focused intake questionnaire. Second, clients who experienced a solution-focused intake interview reported significant symptom improvement compared to clients who experienced a traditional diagnostic intake interview. These results support using solution- or goal-oriented language during initial intake screenings and interviews.

Establishing SFT as an empirically supported treatment has been a long-term effort with inconsistent success. Although it is listed as an evidence-based group treatment for substance abuse on SAMHSA's National Registry of Evidence-Based Programs and Practices, the standards for achieving that status are low. Time will tell whether solution-focused outcomes research will live up to the enthusiasm that solution-focused practitioners have for their craft.

Narrative Therapy Research

Empirical research on narrative therapy generally falls into one of three categories: (a) generic narrative approaches, (b) narrative exposure therapy (NET); and (c) personal construct therapy. Summary reviews for these areas follow.

Generic approaches to narrative therapy have only a small research literature. Most publications focus on qualitative themes that emerge in the treatment of specific populations. In one study of individuals who had experienced dating violence, the researchers reported: "Six categories of unique outcome stories were identified: facing-facts stories, standing-up-for-myself stories, cutting-it-off stories, cutting-'em-loose stories, getting-back-on track stories, and changing-it-up stories" (Draucker et al., 2016, p. 112). These unique outcome themes were viewed as potentially therapeutic storylines that could be elaborated on in narrative therapy.

Gonçalves (Gonçalves, Batista, & Freitas, 2017) has conducted several studies on innovative moments (IMs) in psychotherapy. IMs are defined as "exceptions to the inflexible meaning systems present in psychopathological suffering" (Gonçalves et al., 2017, p. 146). Targeting these narrative meaning systems is viewed as a promising therapeutic strategy.

Over the past 15–20 years, research on narrative exposure therapy (NET and KIDNET) has been accumulating. A meta-analytic review of NET for traumatized adults indicated that a brief manualized treatment (4 to 10 sessions) produced positive outcomes in six small studies ($n = 9$ to $n = 111$). These studies included traumatized Romanian adults, Sudanese refugees, Rwandan and Somali refugees, and Rwandan orphans (Vromans & Schweitzer, 2011). Effect sizes ranged from $d = 0.71$ to 3.15. (We should note here that we're not sure how an effect size of 3.15 was attained.) A slightly more recent meta-analysis of seven quantitative studies showed more modest results, with a total average effect size of $d = 0.63$ (Gwozdziewycz & Mehl-Madrona, 2013).

More recent research also includes positive outcomes. NET has shown effectiveness with (a) traumatized Saudi Arabian firefighters (Alghamdi, Hunt, & Thomas, 2015), (b) traumatized South Africans living in unstable conditions (Hinsberger et al., 2017), (c) adult earthquake survivors in China (Zang, Hunt, & Cox, 2013), and (d) traumatized clients diagnosed with borderline personality disorder (Steuwe et al., 2016).

Limited support exists for KIDNET. Positive results were reported for three studies using NET for children. These studies were very small ($n = 6$ to 16) and not amenable to meta-analysis. Overall, KIDNET is viewed as a promising treatment for children exposed to repeated trauma (Vromans & Schweitzer, 2011).

There are at least two major reviews of the efficacy of personal construct therapy. Personal construct therapy is a form of narrative therapy developed by Robert Neimeyer and based on Kelly's (1955) work.

Holland and colleagues (Holland, Neimeyer, Currier, & Berman, 2007) conducted a meta-analysis on 22 personal construct therapy research studies. They reported a small, but positive effect size of $d = 0.38$. In contrast, Metcalfe and colleagues (Metcalfe, Winter, & Viney, 2007) reported a meta-analysis of 20 studies showing that personal construct theory had an effect size of $d = 0.55$ when compared to no treatment, but no differential effectiveness when compared with alternative treatments. Overall, outcomes data suggest that personal construct therapy may have modest positive treatment effects.

Cultural Sensitivity

Constructive approaches are naturally aligned with culture. There is an emphasis on respect for the individual, respect for personal language, the process of languaging, and narrative. Each individual's construction of reality is valued. The strong focus on problem externalization fits well with multicultural and feminist perspectives emphasizing the destructive effect of outside social factors. However, in practice, constructive therapies may not always live up to their theoretical ideals.

Overall, multicultural sensitivity among constructive therapies seems to fall along a continuum. On one end of the continuum lies narrative therapy, the most multiculturally oriented of all constructive approaches. This approach has been used successfully with traumatized children and adults from low-income countries (Schauer et al., 2011; Vromans & Schweitzer, 2011). The approach is inherently sensitive to human diversity, perhaps because White and Epston were influenced by their work with aboriginal tribal populations in Australia and New Zealand as well as theoretical origins associated with Foucault's philosophy. There also have been research and practice initiatives supporting narrative therapy with Latino youth (Malgady, 2010; Malgady & Costantino, 2003).

O'Hanlon's possibility therapy (previously solution-oriented therapy) also values and honors human diversity. However, his approaches are somewhat more formulaic and therefore could be practiced in ways reflecting a less-than-ideal multicultural orientation and gender sensitivity.

At the other end of the continuum lies solution-focused brief therapy. With its emphasis on brevity, formulaic interventions, and disinterest in each individual's unique problem, solution-focused brief therapy has the greatest potential among constructive approaches of being multiculturally insensitive. However, this approach is not inherently insensitive and has attracted a strong international following. As you may recall, much of the empirical research on solution-focused therapy has been conducted outside the United States. Recently Kim (2014) published *Solution-Focused Brief Therapy: A Multicultural Approach*. This is an edited volume with chapters on working with Asian American, African American, Latino, American Indian, Asian immigrant, LGBTQ clients, clients with disabilities, economically poor clients, and spiritual or religious clients. Unfortunately, to date, no research exists evaluating the efficacy of solution-focused or narrative approaches with specific cultural or minority groups. Constructive approaches may be unarguably more culturally sensitive than many others, but much work remains to be done.

Gender and Sexuality

Although constructive therapists emphasize respecting clients, traditional constructivist use of confusion, provocation, and cleverness may cause these approaches to be perceived as disrespectful. For example, de Shazer described giving a client feedback of: "we don't know what the fuck you are going to do." Obviously, this feedback could be viewed as disrespectful.

If solution-focused and narrative therapists focus too much on using confusion or on being provocative or clever, they risk offending all clients, but especially clients from oppressed people or minority groups (including females and the sexually diverse). This risk is all the more present because of the virtual absence of gender or sexual diversity as a formal focus in solution-focused and narrative publications. Although many LGBTQ publications mention narratives, not many focus on the application of a narrative approach for transforming unhealthy narratives into healthy narratives. Additionally, solution-focused therapy has been critiqued for ignoring gender and power dynamics and differences (Dermer, Hemesath, & Russell, 1998).

With this critique in mind, over the years there has been a variety of journal articles and book chapters that address feminism and sexual diversity. Of special interest are articles integrating feminism into narrative approaches on women's bodies (Brown, Weber, & Ali, 2008). Instead of relying on individualistic, self-management approaches to women's body-related issues, Brown and colleagues (2008) recommended resistance to dominant genderized scripts of women's appearance. In a similar vein and consistent with the Simblett case example, feminists have advocated for openness with respect to medical/psychological records. Fors and McWilliams (2016) proposed collaborative reading of medical records in psychotherapy as a means of feminist empowerment for otherwise oppressed clients.

The literature also includes some limited content on sexual diversity. These include articles and book chapters on narrative sex therapy with lesbian partners (Hall, 2012), working with gay males from a narrative perspective (McLean & Marini, 2008), and narrative views of gay and lesbian sexual identity over the lifespan (Frost, 2010).

Spirituality

For constructive theorists and therapists, spirituality and religion are either individual or social constructions. That doesn't mean faith is unimportant or irrelevant. In fact, narrative and solution-focused approaches can attract highly religious and spiritual individuals. However, within the scientific literature, there aren't many publications focusing on the integration of spirituality and constructive therapies.

A PsycInfo title search identified only a handful of publications combining solution-focused or narrative and religious or spiritual. These included an article on solution-focused counseling with clients who have spiritual or religious concerns (Guterman & Leite, 2006) and a meta-analysis of spiritual/narrative interventions on quality of life among cancer patients (Kruizinga et al., 2016).

Guterman and Leite (2006) proposed implementing a standard solution-focused approach with clients who have religious or spiritual problems. They reasoned that because problems are socially constructed and can be addressed via solution-focused strategies, then religious or spiritual problems could be addressed in the same manner. In particular, they advised that the change process involves helping clients to identify and amplify exceptions until the problem is resolved (p. 45). Further, they recommended that a thorough understanding of client worldview was needed to facilitate generation of appropriate and effective solutions.

In the meta-analysis of spiritual/narrative approaches, 12 trials with 1,878 clients were included. Results indicated a moderate immediate effect on overall quality of life ($d = 0.50$). However, at 3–6 months, the quality of life was no longer significantly improved. The researchers recommend additional studies to understand better how spiritual/narrative interventions might come to have a longer-term effect.

CONCLUDING COMMENTS

There's probably no single existing theoretical orientation containing the breadth of diversity associated with constructive theory. On the one hand, solution-based approaches emphasize formulaic, brief, and surface-oriented techniques designed to produce relatively small changes. These small changes are then viewed as having a potential ripple effect in producing bigger and more profound changes over time. It's not surprising that solution-based approaches are sometimes criticized for ignoring client problems and denying the significance of human emotional pain and suffering.

On the other hand, narrative approaches use language to produce profound, transformative client changes. Although there's some overlap in technique, in contrast to solution-based therapists, narrative therapists aren't in a hurry to fix clients and send them out the door in a minimum amount of time and with a minimum of human intimacy. Instead, narrative therapists spend more time listening to the depths of clients' personal stories, searching for tiny sparkling moments in the rubble of difficult lives. Narrative therapists join with clients in attacking maladaptive personal narratives in a manner that often involves deep connections with clients.

Overall, based on our review of constructive therapy approaches, we think it's appropriate to caution mental health professionals about becoming too cavalier or clever. Although most constructive therapists are focused and respectful, we occasionally read examples of therapy interventions that appear insensitive and unprofessional. Of course, this is a warning to be heeded by therapists associated with all theoretical orientations. Doing no harm to the client is always the highest ethical mandate.

CHAPTER SUMMARY AND REVIEW

Post-modern philosophy is the foundation for constructive theory and therapies. In contrast to modern-objectivist philosophy, post-modern philosophy emphasizes that everything is subjective and reality is a construction. There are two main constructive perspectives: (1) constructivism and (2) social constructionist.

The roots of constructive theory and therapy are also linked with the work of George Kelly, Milton Erickson, and Gregory Bateson and the Palo Alto projects. Kelly discovered that his clients would improve when he used preposterous interpretations. Erickson was a strategic hypnotherapist who could construct new realities and options for clients. Bateson led a team that focused

extensively on language in human interaction. From these beginnings narrative therapy and solution-focused therapy were developed.

The primary theoretical principles underlying constructive approaches include: (a) post-modernism; (b) language and languaging; (c) change is constant and inevitable; (d) problems are co-created; (e) therapy is a collaborative, cooperative, co-constructive conversation; and (f) therapy focuses on strengths and solutions. There are two main ways that constructive therapists think of psychopathology. These include the development and maintenance of negative and maladaptive personal narratives and getting stuck using unhelpful solutions.

Constructive therapists generally don't employ formal assessment procedures. Instead, narrative therapists encourage clients to tell their personal and problem-saturated stories and solution-focused therapists ask questions to simultaneously initiate an assessment and treatment process.

Solution-focused and narrative therapists use overlapping techniques to help clients change. Some of the main techniques include: (a) scaling questions, (b) the pretreatment change question, (c) unique account and redescription questions, (d) focusing on unique outcomes or sparkling moments, (e) externalizing conversations, (f) Carl Rogers with a twist, (g) positive relabeling and reframing, (h) presuppositional questions, (i) the miracle question, (j) formula tasks, (k) exception questions, and more.

Evidence supporting solution-focused and narrative approaches is accumulating. Initially, the enthusiasm for solution-focused therapy outpaced the empirical evidence. However, more recently solution-focused research shows it may be mildly effective. For narrative therapies, there is a modest number of studies indicating that narrative exposure therapy is efficacious with traumatized populations. Otherwise, research on narrative therapy is limited.

Narrative therapies tend to be culturally sensitive. In contrast, because solution-focused therapists have little interest in client problems, they may come across as less sensitive. Given the positive orientation of solution-focused and narrative therapies, both approaches have potential for working with gender issues, sexuality, and spirituality.

CONSTRUCTIVE THERAPY KEY TERMS

Anti-anorexia/Anti-bulimia League

Carl Rogers with a twist

Cold memories

Complainants

Confusion technique

Constructivism

Credulous approach to assessment

Customers for change

Do something different task

Exception questions

Externalizing conversations

First session formula task

Forced teaming

Formula tasks

Hot memories

Letter of invitation

Letter writing

Letters of prediction

Narrative exposure therapy (NET)

Narrative therapy

Percentage questions

Positive relabeling or reframing or positive connotation

Post-modern philosophy

Post-modernism

Presuppositional questions

Pretreatment change question

Questioned out

Reflecting teams

Relabeling and reframing

Re-remembering

Scaling questions

Skeleton keys

Social constructionism

Solution-focused brief therapy (SFBT)

Solution-oriented therapy (aka possibility therapy)

Summary letter

The miracle question

Unique account and redescription questions

Unique outcomes or sparkling moments

Utilization

Visitors to treatment

Write–read–burn task

CHAPTER 12

Family Systems Theory and Therapy

With Kirsten W. Murray

LEARNER OUTCOMES

- Define family systems theory and family therapy
- Identify key figures and historical trends in the development, evolution, and application of family systems theory and family therapy
- Describe core principles of family systems theory
- Describe and apply family therapy principles, strategies, and techniques
- Analyze cases that employ family therapy techniques
- Evaluate the empirical, cultural, gender, and spiritual validity of family systems therapy
- Identify key terms and resources associated with family systems theory and therapy

In the film *Annie Hall* (1977), there's a joke about a patient who goes to a psychiatrist. He complains to the psychiatrist, "My brother thinks he's a chicken." Then, when the psychiatrist recommends to the patient that perhaps he should send his brother for treatment, the patient tells the psychiatrist, "… but I need the eggs!"

As concerning as it is to have a brother laying eggs and clucking like a chicken, his behavior serves a purpose for the family. Eventually, a sibling who thinks he's a chicken becomes predictable and normal within the family. This egg-laying brother not only provides food for the family, but ultimately contributes to the family dynamics in other ways too. There's no time to worry about Dad's drinking because his son thinks he's a chicken; Mom is too busy taking care of her chicken/son to address strife in her marriage; because his brother is so busy clucking around the house, no one puts energy into addressing Tommy's failing grades.

Welcome to the world of systems theory … a theoretical perspective where we intentionally step away from thinking about individuals in isolation.

INTRODUCTION

There are many family therapy approaches. Although not all family therapies are pure applications of systems theory, if the family is the target of treatment, then

knowledge of family systems theory is needed (Smith-Acuña, 2011).

Systems theory encompasses more than just family therapy. Systems theory is applied to businesses, organizations, and, somewhat recently, internal family systems theory for individuals has become popular (Schwartz, 1995; Sweezy & Ziskind, 2013). In this chapter we focus on family systems theory and therapy and describe several different distinct family therapy approaches.

What Is Systems Theory?

Systems theory is an approach that focuses not on individual components but on unifying principles regarding how entities within organizations (i.e., systems) operate or function. A **system** is an organized whole that has interacting parts and the interacting parts maintain the system.

Systems theory is naturally relational. Just as the moon's orbit around the Earth affects ocean tides, the behavior of your siblings, parents, and other caretakers (e.g., grandparents, foster or adoptive parents) affect your mood, thoughts, and behaviors. All systems approaches share the common principle: when clients have disturbing symptoms, the symptoms are a function of and maintained by relationships. Therefore, if counseling is to be effective, the client's primary system, usually the family, is the best treatment focus.

Counseling and Psychotherapy Theories in Context and Practice: Skills, Strategies, and Techniques, Third Edition. John Sommers-Flanagan and Rita Sommers-Flanagan. © 2018 John Wiley & Sons, Inc. Published 2018 by John Wiley & Sons, Inc.
Companion website: www.wiley.com/go/sommers-flanagan/theories3e

Although systems theory is critical for understanding and working with families, it's also relevant in many other contexts, including individual therapy. Smith-Acuña (2011) described her dismay regarding the underappreciation of systems theory.

> It is very common for a student to tell me, "I find systems theory very interesting, but I probably won't use it, since I don't want to work with families." Depending on the day, the poor student making this comment may get a long diatribe about the relevance of systems theory to all of psychology, not simply to families. (p. 5)

Depathologizing Individuals

When working with families, problems are no longer solely in the purview of individuals; instead, problems are created and maintained by and for the family. As demonstrated in the opening scenario from *Annie Hall*, our symptoms (believing to be a chicken) are often maintained to meet the needs of our families (providing eggs).

Family systems theorists consider all symptoms as purposeful. Although other theoretical models consider the family when formulating treatments, the idea that problems are central to the family and therefore the family must be treated remains a radical and new way to think about psychopathology. A core principle in family systems thinking is that the problem resides in and is shared by the whole family system, not in the individual—even though the individual (e.g., the brother who thinks he's a chicken) appears to own the problem.

REFLECTIONS

If you go to a family systems therapist, the therapist will view every family member's behavior as serving a function. When you look back, what problem behaviors occurred in your own family? What functions did those so-called problems serve in your family? This isn't to blame anyone. When family systems therapy works well—everyone changes.

HISTORICAL CONTEXT AND HIGHLIGHTS

Family dynamics have been a powerful force to deal with since the beginning of time. There is no doubt that prehistoric couples had conflicts. Then, when children came along, conflicts became more complex and voilà, relationships within the family emerged as something to talk about (or avoid talking about). At some point it's likely that the community around the family noticed and other people stepped in and tried to help. These other people probably included resident community experts such as elders, clergy, doctors, lawyers, and neighbors or friends.

Likely, most of these well-intended outside entities probably had no idea what they were getting themselves into. We pick up on the long story of family dynamics beginning in the early 1900s.

Adler's Contributions: Child Guidance Clinics

Alfred Adler (1927) was probably the first modern theorist to focus on family dynamics. *Individual psychology* was an early systems theory; Adler emphasized family constellations as a means of understanding individuals. However, no matter how important family dynamics were to Adler, Adlerian therapy primarily focused on treating individuals. Referring to this tendency to think like a family therapist, while working with individuals, Blume (2006) wrote:

> Family therapy with one person has a long and proud history. (p. 5)

Adler established more than 30 **child guidance clinics** in and around Vienna following World War I. He offered family therapy demonstrations at these clinics, observed by parents, teachers, and community members. Adlerian-oriented child guidance clinics spread to the United States, but the Nazi regime eliminated them from Vienna.

Following Adler, child guidance clinics and then marriage and family clinics became popular in the United States (Goldenberg, Stanton, & Goldenberg, 2017). These clinics focused on helping families handle child-rearing responsibilities, infidelity, divorce, financial conflicts, and sexual problems. Most of this initial work involved therapy with children and/or parents separately.

Nathan Ackerman in New York

American psychiatrist, Nathan Ackerman, is considered the first modern family therapist. His intellectual openness, combined with direct experiences working with children and parents in an Adlerian-style clinic, inspired him to experiment with new ways of working with families. In the following quotation from a 1948 article, he discussed the importance of including fathers in child guidance interventions:

> If the therapy … is to be child-oriented, the primary need is an intimate knowledge of the relationship between the parents, and the relationship of each parent to the child. The father's personality, as well as the mother's must be understood, and the emotional interaction between these two persons must be dealt with. Often, the father must receive treatment as well as the mother, if adequate results are to be achieved. (Ackerman & Neubauer, 1948, p. 86)

Similarly, mothers' support groups were routinely used at his New York clinic. In a 1959 publication, he discussed an example of the strong, emotionally charged material generated from these group experiences (note that this excerpt precedes the women's consciousness-raising groups that contributed to feminist therapy movements discussed in Chapter 10; this note from Ackerman captures the convergence of group therapy, feminist psychology, and family dynamics that was happening during the late 1950s):

> The mother had an outburst of anger at the therapist when she discovered in group therapy sessions for mothers that women could enjoy sex and even experience orgasm. She felt bitter that her husband had withheld this information from her all these years. Until now she believed that men had a corner on sex and that women submitted purely out of a sense of duty. She was hurt and angry at her husband, but blew up at her female therapist. (Ackerman & Lakos, 1959, p. 62)

Ackerman's work provides an apt illustration of how different streams of thought, clinical experiences, and social movements were simmering together in the crucible that would eventually produce family therapy.

A Timeline of Family Therapy History

The following timeline includes highlights of the many threads contributing to the tapestry of modern family therapy.

1910s

- Richmond (1917) published *Social Diagnosis*. An early social worker, she advocated including fathers in welfare interviews and the family in treatment; she paid particular attention to emotional bonding and cohesion.

1920s

- Adler established child guidance clinics in Vienna; later, Adlerian clinics were established in the United States.
- The Marriage Consultation Center in New York opened its doors in 1929, thanks to the work of Abraham and Hannah Stone.

1930s

- Ackerman (1938) published "The Unity of the Family" in the *Archives of Pediatrics*.
- Rogers (1939) published *The Clinical Treatment of the Problem Child*; he acknowledged that it was impossible to have lasting effects on children's problems without involving parents.

1940s

- The American Association of Marriage Counselors was formed in 1941 (later to become the American Association for Marriage and Family Therapy in 1978).
- Bowen began treating schizophrenic children at the Menninger Clinic in 1946. His work led to rich theory development emphasizing family member differentiation and triangles.
- Levy (1943) and Fromm-Reichmann (1948) began attending to the mother's role and parenting style when treating schizophrenic children.
- Whitaker began conducting biannual conferences in 1946 where colleagues met to observe and discuss family therapy.
- Bowlby (1949) began using family interviews to complement his individual approach.

1950s

- In his *Field Theory* manuscript (1951), Lewin established that groups are more than the sum of their parts.
- Don Jackson (1954) documented patterns of shifting disturbance among family members: when treatment was successful with one family member, symptoms would arise in another.
- Bateson, Jackson, Haley, and Weakland focused on communication among family members in schizophrenia, publishing *Toward a Theory of Schizophrenia* (1956).
- Lidz, Cornelison, Fleck, and Terry (1957) focused on the role fathers and marital relationships play in what was referred to at that time as "schizophrenic families."
- Whitaker (1958) developed an experiential approach for working with families at the Atlanta Psychiatric Clinic.
- Jackson and Weakland (1959) published the thesis that symptoms preserve homeostasis among family members, emphasizing that problems occur in contexts.

1960s

- Satir (1964), a contributing member of the Palo Alto Group, published *Conjoint Family Therapy*.
- Minuchin began focusing on family patterns and structures with urban poor families. He was named the director of the Philadelphia Child Guidance Clinic in 1965.
- In 1967 Selvini-Palazzoli and colleagues formed the Institute for Family Studies in Milan.

The 1970s and 1980s are referred to as *the golden age of family therapy*, when treatments, centers, theoretical concepts, and core publications flourished (Nichols & Schwarts, 2007, p. 27). There was excitement and optimism. Although inspiration was generated from these innovative and creative therapists, the originality of their concepts began dissipating over the years, and the energy they generated in the 1970s and 1980s leveled off. In more recent years, new energy began forming around evidence-based, feminist, multicultural, and post-modern perspectives. Despite a diversity of approaches, family therapy's roots lie in fundamental systemic concepts.

THEORETICAL PRINCIPLES

The stimulus to attend to family systems rather than individuals in isolation came from outside the counseling and psychotherapy world.

Cybernetics

At the Josiah Macy Foundation conferences held from 1946 to 1953, a multidisciplinary group of science, mathematics, and engineering professionals gathered to discuss systems issues. Conference participants examined machine-like systems, evaluated their efficiency and stability, and deciphered how systems communicated and used feedback loops to achieve regulation. This shift in thinking towards systems was the birth of cybernetics. Wiener (1948) defined **cybernetics** as "the entire field of control and communication theory, whether in the machine or in the animal" (p. 11).

Gregory Bateson (1972) used his anthropological roots to shift cybernetics from engineering and mathematics to the social sciences. He focused on human communication, viewing families as cybernetic systems. Because families can achieve self-regulation and stability through their norms, Bateson began examining family communication patterns associated with psychopathology. In particular, with his Mental Research Institute (MRI) colleagues, Bateson (Bateson, Jackson, Haley, & Weakland, 1956) looked at families that had a child diagnosed with schizophrenia. Bateson observed patterns between mothers and their children characteristic of a double-bind scenario. **Double-bind communication** is defined as an emotionally distressing communication that includes contradictory messages, with one message negating the other; double binds often feel like no-win situations. For example:

Mother: [Appears agitated and disappointed about something.]

Child: "Mom, are you okay?"

Mother: "I'm fine," she answers in a short and irritated tone.

Child: [Turns away from his mother to continue playing his game.]

Mother: "Well, won't you talk to me? Can't you see that I've had a hard day?"

Child: [Pursuing further and standing, reaches to give her a hug.]

Mother: "Never mind, I'm fine, please just go play."

No matter how he responds, the boy in this scenario is in a lose-lose, double-bind situation. If the boy carries on without his mother, he fails her. When he pursues her, he disappoints her. After observing many families, the MRI group reported that many families with a schizophrenic child displayed double-bind communications. As a result, a **double-bind theory** was developed to explain schizophrenic symptoms (Bateson et al., 1956). Bateson (1972) gave an example describing the nature of the double-bind in their original article:

> In the Eastern religion, Zen Buddhism, the goal is to achieve Enlightenment. The Zen Master attempts to bring about enlightenment in his pupil in various ways. One of the things he does is to hold a stick over the pupil's head and say fiercely, "If you say this stick is real, I will strike you with it. If you say this stick is not real, I will strike you with it. If you don't say anything, I will strike you with it." We feel that the schizophrenic finds himself continually in the same situation as the pupil, but he achieves something like disorientation rather than enlightenment. (pp. 175–176)

The double-bind theory was soundly refuted as an etiological factor in schizophrenia. However, attending to double-bind communication highlighted the importance of studying and modifying family interactional patterns (Cullin, 2006; Stark & von der Haar, 1977). After the Bateson project was discontinued, Jackson carried on with many of the ideas, especially focusing on how families can maintain homeostasis via mental health symptoms.

Many studies related to schizophrenia and family systems emerged before and after Bateson's work. Levy (1943) theorized about overprotective mothers and Fromm-Reichmann (1948) discussed dominating, rejecting, and insecure **schizophrenogenic mothers** (i.e., mothers who "cause" schizophrenia). Jay Haley (a member of the MRI research team) was quoted as sarcastically saying, "We discovered that schizophrenics had mothers!" (Napier & Whitaker, 1978, p. 48).

Given the sociopolitical status of women at the time, it's no surprise that mothers were first in line to get blamed for family problems and children's mental disturbances (although Bateson et al., 1956, made it clear that the double-bind communicator was not necessarily the mother—it could be a father or a sibling). Somewhat later, however, researchers apparently *discovered the existence of fathers* and began examining fathers' roles in family interactions (Lidz et al., 1957). As family interaction patterns and contexts were recognized as major contributors to mental health, attending to systems and treating families gained prevalence. Systems formulations were evolving.

General Systems Theory

Unlike cybernetics—a model derived from strict, rule-bound, closed systems with mechanical structures—**general systems theory** considers nuances among human actors within systems. Developed by biologist Ludwig von Bertalanffy (1950), general systems theory included the idea that human systems function more like organisms and less like machines.

Human systems aren't closed; they're open and have fluid boundaries that accept and give influence. This is in stark contrast to cybernetic mechanical and rule-bound systems. Living systems don't function in closed loops where "A" always leads to "B" and eventually "C." General systems theory recognizes that all parts of a system can impact the others, leaving room for many possible outcomes.

Consider a couple with a new baby. Adding this tiny player to a two-person system changes family dynamics. The couple's family responsibilities shift toward providing and caring for their child. From changing diapers, to night-time feedings, to navigating a new sleeping schedule, the couple is powerfully influenced. Further, there are many possible responses to this new family addition. The couple may maintain an egalitarian relationship and divide tasks, they may take on specific provider or caretaker roles, or their culture may include godparents and extended family in caretaking responsibilities. Potential outcomes in response to a systemic change are theoretically infinite; living systems can discover various means to multiple ends.

General systems theory not only accounts for many possibilities, but also explains the many systems and subsystems layered around and within the family. **Subsystems** are smaller, self-sustaining parts of a larger system. Individuals are made of many subsystems: from cells, to tissues, to organs such as the heart, to the circulatory system, to the individual as a whole; we are all layers of subsystems that contribute to larger systemic functioning. Families contain subsystems (e.g., the parent subsystem and sibling subsystem) and simultaneously function as a part of a larger system themselves. From the family, to neighborhoods, to schools, to communities, to counties or states, to nations, and to the world, there are points of influence from various subsystems that impact families and vice versa.

Urie Bronfenbrenner (1979) developed **ecological systems theory** to organize, explain, and differentiate systemic forces that influence children's development. He postulated six levels of influence. These included:

1. *The child (or individual)*: The child is an entity that's affected and influenced by the other five forces or factors.

2. *The microsystem*: The setting where the child lives. The microsystem includes parents, siblings, classmates at school, and others with whom the child has regular contact.

3. *The mesosystem*: The interaction between micro- and exosystems. An example would be the interaction between the child's family and the school administration.

4. *The exosystem*: This includes entities or systems outside the microsystem with which the individual or microsystem interacts. Examples include parents' employers, extended family, the school board, and mass media.

5. *The macrosystem*: This refers to culture, laws, politics, and socioeconomics of a region or country.

6. *The chronosystem*: This refers to changes occurring in the other five domains over time. For example, children develop increasing cognitive skills; families experience divorce, instability, and restabilize; schools change administrations; and laws, cultural values, and socioeconomics change with time.

Subsystems influence families in constant and significant ways. Let's go back to the couple with a new baby. Imagine now that their child has been diagnosed with Down's syndrome. This diagnosis impacts the child's internal functioning and ripples out to the family (microsystem) as they seek support from the medical community, their neighborhood, church, extended family, and community (exosystem). Now imagine the parents are a lesbian couple. How they interact with and are affected by the macrosystemic factors of political climate, religious groups and attitudes, as well as the exosystem (their neighborhood, friends, and families of origin), will affect their interactions and support for their child.

General systems theory revealed that systems are more than the sum of their parts. This shift in systemic epistemology laid the groundwork for second-order cybernetics.

Second-Order Cybernetics

In the original cybernetics movement (now termed **first-order cybernetics**), observers of a system were immune to its influence. With the development of quantum physics, post-modern philosophies, and constructive epistemologies (see Chapter 11), questions arose regarding experts as outside observers with no influence on the family system. A shift occurred. **Second-order cybernetics** emerged as the application of cybernetics to itself. No longer was the family counselor an expert-observer; now family counselors were participant-observers.

At first contact, family therapists enter or join the family system. They go from being external to internal. This happens very quickly and can catch therapists by surprise. For example, Dr. X is sitting in her office doing paperwork. Her telephone rings. She answers:

Dr. X: Hello. This is Dr. X's family counseling clinic.

Father: Uh. Yeah. Hello. My name is Robert and my wife told me to call for a family therapy appointment.

Dr. X: Okay. I have appointments available next Tuesday and next Thursday after 3 p.m.

Father: Hmm. Now I'm not so sure. I didn't realize you would be a woman. Are there any men who work in your office?

Dr. X: Actually no, there's just me. I'm a licensed family counselor.

Father: Damn. I guess I'd better take that 3 p.m. time. My wife will be pissed if I don't get this done.

One way or another family dynamics often emerge during initial telephone or face-to-face contacts. From the moment the father hears Dr. X's voice, Dr. X is in the family system. She's no longer a dispassionate expert-observer. This is a second-order cybernetics rule: When therapists work with families, they immediately become an influence, if only by their presence. Counselors are nonexperts whose role is to co-construct meanings and solutions with the family. New interactions evolve in partnership (Goldenberg, Stanton, & Goldenberg, 2017).

The critical underpinnings of any systemic counseling theory are grounded in the cybernetic and general system theories. These concepts include, but are not limited to: circular causality, the identified patient, first- and second-order change, the ability to attend to process, and homeostasis. We now explore these crucial elements that guide a family counselor's conceptualization and intervention strategies when working with families.

Where's the Problem and Where's the Solution?

Similar to feminist, constructive, and multicultural perspectives, family systems theory places "the problem" outside the individual. If we look at this through ecological systems theory, feminist and multicultural theorists point to macrosystems (e.g., culture) as the source of the problem and intervention target. Constructive theorists will look at both micro- and macrosystems. In contrast, family systems theorists and therapists primarily focus on the microsystem of family as (a) the source of the problem and (b) the location where the intervention should occur.

If you're coming from a Western cultural perspective, viewing individual symptoms as family problems might contradict your individualistic values of independence and personal responsibility. Family counselors, however, are known for seeing everything through their family lens. To work within a systemic approach, we must let go of the idea that symptoms are contained and maintained within individuals and view problems and symptoms as belonging to the whole family system.

Circular Causality

To embrace an entire family as one client, it helps to understand **circular causality**. Everyone, in one way or another, contributes to the process that maintains problems and successes. Most of us are accustomed to engaging in a more linear thinking style. Linear thought is clear, logical, and seeks answers in a direct-causation manner. For an example, let's consider the Stevens family. The father in the family is struggling with alcohol addiction. Linear thinking would be:

A (Dad) + B (Alcohol Abuse) = C (Unhappy Family)

Given this conceptualization, if Dad stops drinking, the Stevens family will be happy. The solution is straightforward. It examines Dad in isolation. Circular thinking, however, asks us to take contexts and other players into consideration.

When expanding our scope beyond Dad's specific drinking behavior, we discover he has a family … and his family has dynamics. We notice the following:

- Mom regularly berates Dad.

- This berating escalates when the 17-year-old son misbehaves.

- When the son misbehaves, Dad doesn't intervene, instead he laughs.

- Dad's laughing bothers Mom.

As you can see, Dad's alcohol-related behavior is now nestled comfortably within a multidimensional family system—which makes things complex and circular. The family becomes lost in a pattern where behaviors are influenced by and support alcohol use. An equation for circular thinking might resemble something like this, where there's no clear beginning or end point, only a process that is maintained between two (or more) variables (see Figure 12.1).

FIGURE 12.1 Simple Circular Causality

Transitioning into circular thinking requires focus and discipline. When a family comes to see you, they'll likely have what family counselors refer to as an **identified patient (IP)**. An IP is the person to whom other family members ascribe the problem. In the case of the family described above, Dad would be the IP. Often, IPs are described with phrases like, "If he would just change, things would be better for our family." You often learn who the IP is immediately when the family calls for an appointment; it's whoever the complaints are about. Having an IP provides safety and comfort for the family, as it keeps the problem localized to one person. When the IP holds the problem in its entirety, the rest of the family can avoid examining their own problem behaviors as well as any responsibility for the IP's problem.

Reconceptualizing Problems and Clients

Initially, almost everyone attending the family counseling session wants to talk about the IP. Getting family members to shift to a family systems lens is a significant challenge.

Helping a family see the circular causality present in their family system begins when the counselor shifts the conversation away from the IP and has family members look at themselves and their relationships with each other. Asking all family members to examine their own contributions to the family problem is threatening. Family members will feel vulnerable and defensive. Anderson and Stewart (1983) described this process:

> While all therapists encounter resistance, the resistance experienced by family therapists is particularly challenging. Since most families present with one symptomatic member, other family members may fail to see the relevance of involving the whole family, or fear that requests for such family involvement amount to the therapist's blaming them for their problem member's difficulties. (p. 2)

If you practice family therapy, there will be many tempting moments to collude with family members and view the IP as the "true client." If this happens, you might as well do individual counseling. To engage the family, you must help all family members recognize and grapple with their roles, reactions, and contributions to the problem. Your focus will be on relational interactions.

Shifting a family's perspective from linear to circular requires patience and finesse. The Stevens family has invested substantial energy in maintaining dad as "the keeper of the family problems." In the following family therapy dialogue, the goal is for the family to begin seeing dad's symptoms in relational contexts:

Counselor: After talking with you on the phone, Mom, I gathered that one concern bringing you to family counseling is your husband's drinking.

Mom: That's correct. I want to support him in getting better. Our family can't keep going like this.

Dad: [Crosses arms, sits back in his chair, and glares at his wife.] I told you, I'd come here with you, but I'm done being yelled at and blamed for everything. I don't want this to turn into another lecture.

Counselor: [Addressing Dad.] So, it seems like this is an old topic between the two of you. I wonder, Dad, if you had to describe the difficulties present in your family, what would they be?

Dad: Well for one, she's in my business all the time. Poking around, asking questions about where I am? Did I do this? Did I forget that? She's always looking over my shoulder and yelling at me if I did something wrong. I can't stand it. She's the same way with Scotty. For God's sake, our son is nearly an adult, and she can't let him do a damn thing on his own. And she always wants me to discipline him.

Son: [Fidgets, looking uncomfortable in his seat.]

Counselor: [Addressing the son.] How would you sum up what's happening in your family?

Son: They just fight all the time. Well, not all the time. But they're either fighting or not paying attention to each other. I wish they would just divorce and get it over with already. I'm sick of it.

Counselor: When your parents fight, what do you do?

Mom: Oh, he's a good kid, usually. He's graduating with honors. Really, he's not who we need to worry about. I hate that he sees his dad drunk all the time. His dad is a horrible example, and never corrects Scotty when he acts up. Thank God Scotty is doing the best he can even without a good father.

Counselor: Scotty, what do you do when your parents fight?

Scotty: Just zone out, basically. I hang in my room, text with friends, leave the house, do my thing. Just ignore them.

Counselor: It sounds like you escape what's happening in your family by closing yourself in your room. Your Dad might be escaping what's happening in your family by drinking. And your mom is alone.

Counselor: [Looking toward Mom.] I'm wondering if you feel alone in your family? Like you're not sure how to connect with your husband and son anymore. It seems like you're working hard to stay connected, but I'm not sure if it's working.

Mom: When are we going to talk about his drinking? That's why we're here.

Counselor: I'm sure we'll get to that. But this is family counseling and so what I'm doing now is getting a better idea of what's happening with the *whole* family. I think this is the best way to get a picture of the three problems you've all mentioned so far: Dad's drinking, Scotty's isolation and occasional acting out, and the strain on you and your husband's relationship. So, while you see the problem as Dad's drinking, the more we understand the whole family, the better.

Mom: Yes, but if he stopped drinking, he'd spend more time with Scotty, I would stop nagging, and things would be better.

Counselor: That's quite possible. But it's also possible that the drinking will decrease if he spends more time with you and Scotty doing things that are enjoyable. Or maybe if you spend more time with Scotty, Dad will feel jealous and try harder to connect with Scotty. My hope is that we can come up with shared ideas for what all three of you can do to make family life better. The word that keeps coming to mind for me is loneliness. Everyone sounds lonely. Mom tries to connect by being bossy. It doesn't work. Dad, feeling angry and disconnected, drinks. Angry and hurt about the drinking, Mom becomes more directive and more bossy. Scotty, hearing his parents fight, escapes from home. Even though you're all under the same roof, everyone sounds lonely. And the lonelier you feel, the more you try to escape the problem by drinking, arguing, or isolating.

With the Stevens family, the counselor had a challenge trying to shift how the family talks about the problem. The counselor shifted the focus away from Dad (the IP), and began co-constructing a new language for the problem(s), gaining input from all of the family members. Making this shift is difficult for Mom; she's invested in addressing Dad's drinking. In cases like this, the counselor must be assertive and empathic, managing the ebb and flow of building a relationship with Mom while also challenging her to embrace a new way of thinking. The counselor expands the problem to highlight family members' roles and contributions to the problem. When shifting away from alcohol abuse and looking at deeper isolation patterns, the counselor sets the groundwork for second-order change.

First- and Second-Order Change

Systemic perspectives focus on two types of change: **first-order change** (addressing symptoms) and **second-order change** (addressing underlying patterns). Making changes to symptoms themselves is first-order change. This involves making surface behavioral changes, while ignoring underlying family system dynamics. For the Stevens family, first-order change involves Dad attending AA and getting sober, while the family maintains their same old interactional patterns. The symptom itself can be addressed but system patterns often hold strong. First-order changes are

sometimes referred to as shallow, as the behavior itself can be changed, but it's often difficult to maintain a new behavior (not drinking) in the light of unchanging systemic patterns (disconnection and nagging). Becoming sober without addressing family patterns places Mr. Stevens at greater risk for relapse.

Second-order change involves deeper interaction patterns. For the Stevens family, the patterns would be the same no matter what symptoms brought them to counseling (isolation and loneliness are central themes whether or not the family discloses Dad's drinking, Mom's nagging, or Scotty's disengagement). Because symptoms indicate underlying family patterns, second-order change is the ultimate goal. When conceptualizing the Stevens family, a counselor may wonder:

- What's happening in the family that maintains Dad's drinking?

- What relational purpose does Dad's drinking serve for the family?

From a family systems perspective, there's no clear beginning or "root cause," but rather a circular pattern where the behavior of one family member influences and sustains the behavior of another. Nichols and Schwarts (2007) wrote:

> The essence of family therapy is to see patterns of connection where others see only isolated events. (p. 7)

By looking at family process and not getting lost in problem content, counselors can identify family patterns more efficiently and can predict family behaviors, regardless of content that surfaces within a session.

Homeostasis

Family interaction patterns are grounded in homeostasis. **Homeostasis** is the tendency for a system to maintain a relatively stable state. Body temperature is an excellent example. The body's homeostatic mechanisms maintain a normal temperature.

Families have their own unique homeostatic mechanisms. Maintaining homeostatic balance creates safety and familiarity. An important note on homeostasis: the patterns that are familiar to a family, even if uncomfortable, seem safer than new or unknown patterns. Recall the saying, "Better the devil you know than the devil you don't." This applies to families in homeostasis: there's security in embracing well-known family patterns.

When beginning counseling, families are asked to surrender their old, homeostatic ways. This will create great anxiety, as change stimulates disequilibrium. Once in flux, systems usually need time to accommodate. Times of change are often followed by times of rest, allowing families to adapt to the new normal.

Attending to Interaction Patterns

Attending to a family's interaction patterns is vital, whether referencing circular causality, establishing the family as the client, creating second-order change, or remaining mindful of homeostasis. Given the natural multidimensional interactive complexity of families, what exactly should be the focus for family therapists? Here's a short list of interaction patterns from family systems theories: subsystems, boundaries, coalitions, alliances, triangles, hierarchies, roles, and rules.

Subsystems

As noted earlier, sibling and parental units are the most common family subsystem. The goal of attending to subsystems isn't to find causal factors, but to look into the relationships central to maintaining family symptoms. In the case of the Stevens family, this may lead to the parental subsystem. When counseling this family, one may begin to tease out the nuances of the marital relationship that maintain the couple's isolation.

Boundaries

Imagine a family as a Venn diagram, with circles around every person, every subsystem, and the whole family. Although these lines are invisible, these boundaries are in the counselor's mind's eye when deciphering where one individual or subsystem ends and another begins.

Boundaries in family systems can be healthy or dysfunctional. In their healthiest form, boundaries protect and enhance systemic functioning. Within functional family systems, boundaries are opened and closed with intentionality; the family's boundaries are considered clear when they intentionally open their boundaries to accept new influence and then close their boundaries to allow the system to adjust to the recent influence. Boundaries that are too rigid or diffuse often have troublesome consequences.

Rigid boundaries are thick, inflexible, and difficult to penetrate. A family with rigid boundaries won't accept influence and attempts to keep the same impenetrable boundaries across time and contexts. Imagine a family with a 14-year-old daughter who is beginning to form friendships outside the home. She's engaging in new behaviors: going to movies with friends and attending school dances. The parental subsystem sets a summer curfew of 9:30 p.m., enforcing a mutually agreeable boundary between their daughter and subsystems outside the family.

Five years later, when their 19-year-old daughter returns home after her first year of college, her parents stick to the 9:30 p.m. curfew. The parents' refusal to change boundaries given new contexts is an overly rigid boundary.

Diffuse boundaries are loose, open, or absent. Diffuse boundaries can be common between a dysfunctional parental subsystem and the child subsystem. Consider a husband and wife with marital difficulties. They have a 9-year-old daughter. As the couple's troubles persist, they cope by leading parallel lives, rarely communicating to each other directly; instead, they find family connection with their child. Over time, Dad becomes more absent and Mom turns to her daughter to "vent" about her disappointing marriage. The daughter is elevated to a "companion" and becomes Mom's personal counselor. In this case, the boundary between Mom and daughter has become diffuse. Mom talks to her daughter about sex, physical abuse, and drug use in ways that are unhealthy for a parent–child subsystem. These diffuse boundaries can set the stage for other concerning patterns: triangulation, alliances, and coalitions.

Alliance, Coalition, and Triangulation

Imagine that you're in a conflict with someone, but you're alone: no one sees the world as you, there's no one to encourage and empathize with you, and most of all, there's no one to affirm your perspective. This state is so uncomfortable that you may actively seek **alliances** to ease your distress.

Forming alliances is a natural means for gaining connection and support. Alliances occur when family members position themselves in support of one another. One type of alliance seen in families is the coalition; a **coalition** occurs when two family members side together against a third.

In the family mentioned above, as Dad drifts away and the boundary between mother and daughter becomes increasingly diffuse, the stage is set for a coalition. Mom could begin confiding in her child about the disappointment she feels over Dad's absence and her anger about him not only ignoring her, but the daughter as well. To comfort her mom, the daughter speaks of her disappointment in her father. The relationship between mother and daughter is strengthened as a result of their alliance and mutual perceptions of Dad.

Another fascinating shift in family structures during conflict is triangulation. Although sometimes confused with coalitions because it also involves three people and is used as a means to provide comfort, the aim of a triangulation is different. **Triangulation** happens when a dyad in conflict *pulls in* a third party. The third party holds the focus to relieve relationship distress. This enables the dyad to ignore their own struggle and come together as they place energy into the third party. Consider a couple that have been married 13 years and are parents to Maria, a 12-year-old girl. After discovering an intimate e-mail exchange between his wife and a co-worker, the father approaches his wife with concern about his daughter's choice of friends. Instead of focusing on their relationship troubles, the couple colludes to regain a sense of connection by coming together "for their daughter's sake." Typically, the dyad pulls in a more vulnerable or less powerful family member. For example, a child having academic problems or a recently divorced sibling; it's easier to hold the focus on someone lower in the family's hierarchy. If a family therapist suspects that presenting issues involve triangulation, they might ask "If Maria weren't the problem, what would the problem be?"

Roles and Rules

Family roles involve the consistent emotional and behavioral patterns that family members take on within the family. Some systems theories go into great depth describing these roles. For example, when exploring family roles, renowned family therapist Salvador Minuchin would often ask families:

- Who's the sheriff in this family?
- Who's the lawyer?
- Who's the social worker?

As family members develop expectations for one another (i.e., for homeostasis—remember, systems are predictable), roles become more prevalent. Family roles are limitless. Examples can include: breadwinner, caretaker, disciplinarian, cook, jester, problem solver, protector, logical one, reactive one, needy one, and more. To make it more interesting, family members can hold more than one role. Family counselors examine roles to help identify family norms. Roles are one piece of the family system puzzle.

Family rules set expectations for behavior and can be spoken or unspoken. Like roles, family rules support predictability or homeostasis. **Overt rules** are spoken and direct. Examples of overt rules might include curfews, bed times, and household chores. **Covert rules**, on the other hand, are unspoken, but usually well-established; covert rules often are powerful partly because they're not openly discussed or questioned, but, rather, quietly followed. Covert rules might include:

- Don't talk about Mom's drinking.
- When you really want something, ask Grandma first.
- When you're sad, keep it to yourself.
- Don't talk about bills until payday.
- Hug every family member when you say goodbye.
- Never directly express approval or affection.

When working with families, counselors enter the family system's patterns and rules. To form a clear picture of a family, counselors must view rules, roles, alignments, coalitions, triangulations, boundaries, and subsystems from various perspectives. Even when a fairly clear family picture is established, it's hard to know what to do next. This is where theory translates into practice.

FAMILY SYSTEMS THERAPY IN PRACTICE

Family therapists practice in many ways. Some family therapists employ traditional theoretical models. There are psychodynamic family therapists, Adlerian family therapists, behavioral family therapists, feminist family therapists, and many more.

In this chapter, we explore four approaches. Although these approaches have traditional theoretical roots (e.g., psychoanalytic or humanistic-existential), they developed directly out of family therapy research and practice. They include:

1. Murray Bowen's Intergenerational Family Therapy.

2. Salvador Minuchin's Structural Family Therapy.

3. Jay Haley's Strategic Family Therapy.

4. Virginia Satir and Carl Whitaker's Humanistic and Experiential Family Therapy.

These approaches share a systems perspective, but employ distinct ways of joining and working with families (see Putting It in Practice 12.1 for a sample informed consent for family therapy).

Intergenerational Family Therapy

Developed by Murray Bowen (1978), **intergenerational family therapy** (aka Bowenian therapy) is a family therapy approach with psychodynamic foundations; it focuses primarily on family history and patterns established across generations. Bowen was the first to define triangulation, emotional cutoff, enmeshment, and differentiation of self. He was also the first to use genograms.

From an intergenerational perspective, differentiation (aka differentiation of self) is an ideal therapy outcome. **Differentiation** has two parts, including the ability to (a) self-regulate and (b) manage or balance the relational challenge of togetherness and independence (Jankowski & Hooper, 2012). Practically speaking, this translates into the ability to establish a calm, observant, and logical self (even in the face of pulls toward dependence or pushes toward independence). Once family members attain differentiation, they're emotionally and intellectually self-sufficient and able to resist the unconscious grasp of their family's rules and roles (Bowen, 1978).

PUTTING IT IN PRACTICE

12.1 Informed Consent from the Family Systems Perspective

As you read this sample written, informed consent, pretend you're sitting in the counselor's waiting room, about to go in for your first session along with your family.

I'm glad to see the entire family here, ready to begin counseling together. Family counseling takes commitment from the whole family. Your presence here is a sign of the love and support you have for one another.

In the beginning, it can be difficult to understand why *everyone* has to come to counseling when it seems that only one, or maybe a few of you, are having difficulties. One thing you'll notice in family counseling is that I'm working with the whole family and not just one person in the family. We'll work together to understand where your family is stuck in old patterns of relating. This is important because the patterns your family has created together is what causes people to have problems. When the family starts to grow and change, everyone will get better because you can intentionally create healthier patterns in your family. This doesn't mean that anyone is to blame for problems in your family. It does mean that everyone will get to consider making changes that could contribute to healthier family patterns.

So, what will we do in counseling to help your family grow?

- Everyone will share their ideas of what the problem is and how they see the family. Together we'll make a drawing called a genogram that maps out your relationships and family events. This will help all of us understand your family in new ways.

- We'll focus on how you communicate and react to one another "in the moment." We'll also create and practice new ways of communicating to help you speak directly to one another with genuineness and empathy. I will help you express your feelings to one another more directly; this is so you can have stronger connections.

- Sometimes, I may coach you to try new things in a session. I might ask you to move from one seat to another or try new behaviors.

Learning to relate to one another differently can be scary and risky. There are times I'll ask you to express yourself and take risks with your family that seem unusual. My hope for counseling is that you'll experiment with new ways of relating to each other and then later try them out at home.

Last of all, I want to welcome your whole family to counseling. I'm glad you care enough about each other to come together to create some new and healthier family patterns.

REFLECTIONS

After reading the Informed Consent description of family therapy in Putting It in Practice 12.1, what do you think family counseling might be like? What are your impressions of the counselor? How would your family respond to this approach?

Role of the Therapist

The counselor or therapist serves as an investigator and later as a coach, looking into the past to identify a family's interactional patterns and then directing them toward differentiation. The therapist's role is consistent with psychodynamic theory: objective, detached, and explicitly unaffected by the family. A primary objective is to maintain a safe distance and avoid enmeshment when working with families. In this way, the therapist maintains and models successful differentiation.

Key Concepts

Therapists investigate the family's intergenerational family style. As therapists assess levels of differentiation present in the family, they look for indicators of triangulation, emotional cutoff, and enmeshment. Emotional

| Emotionally Cutoff | Differentiation | Enmeshment |

FIGURE 12.2   The Differential Continuum

cutoffs and enmeshments are viewed as polar positions on the differential continuum (see Figure 12.2).

Successful differentiation is marked by gaining intellectual and emotional independence from one's family. **Emotional cutoff** involves either physical or emotional distance, and may involve relational disconnection and include rigid, thick boundaries (Nichols & Schwarts, 2008). **Enmeshment,** on the other hand, involves incredibly diffuse boundaries and fusing together of individuals. In enmeshed families, there may be so much overidentification that it's difficult to tell where one family member ends and another begins. When exploring family relationships on the differentiation continuum, the task is to help family members understand their current functioning and move toward optimal differentiation.

Intergenerational family systems therapy has a strong individualist value system. As a consequence, families within cultural groups with collectivist orientations (e.g. Latino, Asian, African American, Native American) may appear highly enmeshed. If the therapist is operating from a collectivist orientation, families from the dominant U.S. culture may appear emotionally cut off. This illustrates how a therapist's cultural perspective can determine whether a family (or individual) appears functional or dysfunctional (pathological).

Facilitating Change
The main goal is to help family members achieve differentiation while remaining connected. In the evaluation interview, therapists gather historical information about presenting problem(s) and family members' perceptions of what creates and sustains the problem(s). This process often involves using a genogram.

The **genogram**, invented by Bowen, is a tool for teaching family members about relationship dynamics in their system. Similar to a family tree (or Adlerian family constellation), genograms include all family members, with symbols to note gender, age, alliances, coalitions, triangles, enmeshments, cutoffs, addictions, and mental health concerns. Events such as births, deaths, marriages, separations, and divorces are included.

In intergenerational family therapy, genograms extend back at least three generations. By seeing family patterns across generations, patterns of triangulation, enmeshment, and cutoff become clearer. Patterns from previous generations are clues to current family functioning. When constructing and looking at a genogram, family members can reflect on their family from a new (more differentiated) perspective. Families can stand back and take on objective roles, seeing ingrained family patterns across

generations. Throughout the process, the family can be shown new ways to think about family relationships, while supporting emergence of an emotionally regulated and differentiated family structure. Bowenian therapists use genograms creatively, sometimes using art to help clients express emotions and attain insight (Gatfield, 2017).

Constructing a Genogram
Genogram work can involve vulnerability and risk. Genogram construction can include disclosures about family events and relationships, revealing family structure and illuminating unique family meanings.

Taking a curious, respectful stance allows therapists to guide and join in the conversation with the family, while supporting a deeper and richer understanding. Common symbols are used when constructing genograms (see Figure 12.3). When family structure and interaction patterns are represented using these symbols, family themes become clearer. (See Putting It in Practice 12.2 for the Griswold family description, and Figure 12.4 for the beginning of their genogram.)

Structural Family Therapy

Salvador Minuchin
(photo courtesy of Salvador Minuchin)

Although Bowen's intergenerational approach examines family structure, it primarily attends to differentiation across and within generations. In contrast, the **structural family therapy** approach emphasizes homeostasis, subsystems, boundaries, and coalitions as they relate to family organization and functioning.

Salvador Minuchin (1974) developed structural family therapy. Minuchin worked with poor and ethnically diverse families. His theory's trademark is its focus on changing the organizational structure of families. The goal of structural family therapy remains the same today: create a path for new behavior through organizational changes to a family's dysfunctional power hierarchies and boundary structure (McAdams et al., 2016; Minuchin, 1974).

Role of the Therapist
To change family structure, structural family therapists take a directive role in leading families toward change. Structural family therapists engage families and develop a relationship characterized by increased kinship and trust.

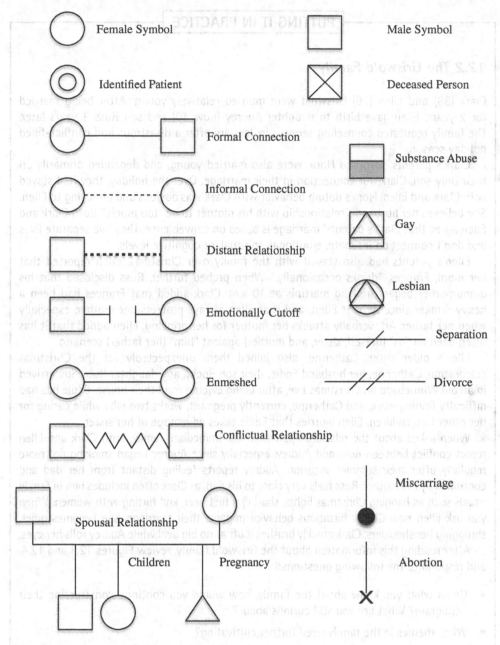

FIGURE 12.3 Common Genogram Symbols
(adapted from McGoldrick, Gerson, & Shellenberger, 2005)

The relationship between therapist and family is essential to this approach; the therapist makes personal adjustments to foster a meaningful connection and adapt to a unique family's style of relating. Therapists make efforts to accommodate cultural diversity (Minuchin, Reiter, & Borda, 2014).

Key Concepts
Structural family therapy is built around the principle that family member behavior is a function of family structure. The primary focus and objective is to change family structure to better nurture the growth of its members.

Structural family therapists focus on family membership hierarchy and boundaries to understand and change family structure. This allows therapists to understand rigid and diffuse relational styles within the family. In structural family work, you attend to boundaries around individual family members, but also examine how boundaries are defined between subsystems, urging the development of clear and intentional boundary making.

| PUTTING IT IN PRACTICE |

12.2 The Griswold Family

Clark (38) and Ellen (36) Griswold were married relatively young. After being married for 2 years, Ellen gave birth to daughter Audrey (now 16) and son Russ 3 years later. The family requested counseling services in January after a disastrous and conflict-filled holiday season.

Clark's parents, Sam and Nora, were also married young, and depended primarily on their only son, Clark, for connection in their marriage. Over the holiday, they had stayed with Clark and Ellen. Nora's doting behavior with Clark was obvious and annoying to Ellen. She believes her husband's relationship with his mother to be "too much." Both Clark and Ellen agree that Clark's parents' marriage is based on convenience. They live separate lives and don't connect on intimate, emotional, spiritual, or cognitive levels.

Ellen's parents had also stayed with the family over Christmas. Ellen reported that her mom, Frances, "drinks occasionally." When probed further, Russ disclosed that his grandmother began drinking martinis at 10 a.m. Clark added that Frances had been a heavy drinker since he met Ellen, and that Ellen always protects her mother, especially when her father, Art, verbally attacks her mother for her drinking. Ellen added that it has often been an "us" (herself, sister, and mother) against "him" (her father) scenario.

Ellen's older sister, Catherine, also joined them unexpectedly for the Christmas celebration. Catherine, her husband Eddie, their son Rocky, and daughter Ruby Sue arrived in an old Winnebago on Christmas Eve, after being evicted from their house. Eddie has had difficulty finding work, and Catherine, currently pregnant, works two jobs while caring for her other two children. Ellen worries that Eddie takes advantage of her sister.

When asked about the relationships within the immediate family, both Clark and Ellen report conflict between Russ and Audrey, especially since Audrey began smoking pot more regularly after their summer vacation. Audrey reports feeling distant from her dad and controlled by her mother. Russ feels very close to his dad, as Clark often includes him in family rituals such as hanging Christmas lights, sharing a first beer, and flirting with women. When you ask Ellen how Clark's flirtatious behavior impacts their marriage, she becomes quiet, shrugging her shoulders. Clark quickly brushes it off as no big deal while Audrey rolls her eyes.

After reading this information about the Griswold family, review Figures 12.3 and 12.4, and respond to the following questions:

- Given what you know about the family, how would you continue constructing their genogram? What are you still curious about?

- What themes in the family need further cultivating?

- How would you approach the family to gather further information?

- What events or relationships would you want to have represented on the genogram?

- Considering the information you've gathered so far, what will be some of your treatment goals?

An ideal structure consists of a parental unit in leadership with clear boundaries over the child subsystem. When a family maintains boundaries that are too rigid or diffuse, the result is a structure that supports coalitions, overinvolvement, scapegoating, abuse, and conflict.

Facilitating Change

The big (and challenging) question is: How can you help a family develop healthy boundaries and maintain a fair hierarchical structure, while also eliminating coalitions and attending to homeostasis? A structural approach breaks the actions for accomplishing these tasks into several steps.

1. The therapist joins the family. Structural therapists refer to joining as mimesis. **Mimesis** is defined as joining with the family in ways that set the foundation for trustworthy and open relationships. Specifically, mimesis involves making an effort to "fit in" with the

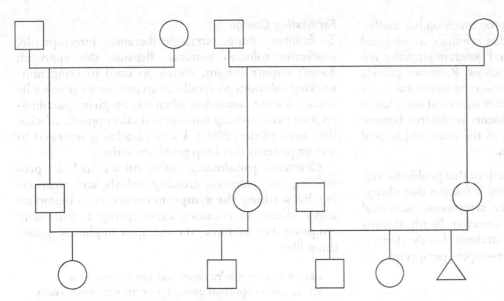

FIGURE 12.4 Griswold Family Genogram Shell

family. Similarities between the family and therapist in affective styles and mannerisms are highlighted.

2. While joining with the family, therapists simultaneously begin conceptualizing family structure, attending to (a) who is in the scapegoated role of identified patient (note that **scapegoating** refers to the more or less universal blaming of one person for general problems within a system), (b) who holds power in the family, (c) what coalitions are in place, and (d) where conflict resides. To track relational structures, therapists rely on a shorthand referred to as family mapping. **Family mapping** involves using symbols to summarize power, boundaries, conflict, coalitions, and scapegoating.

3. Therapists gain further insight through family enactments. **Family enactments** occur when therapists bring family conflict into the here and now to witness the conflict process and outcomes. This allows the dysfunctional structure of the family to be seen, rather than merely described. During family enactments, therapists focus on what's happening with every family member; this helps expand the problem beyond the identified patient and into other family members.

4. Once the family organization is understood and dysfunction processes observed, the therapist intervenes through **restructuring**. Interventions include an awareness of when to push family to open boundaries and accept influence and when to encourage families to strengthen or close boundaries.

5. Three techniques facilitate structural change: (a) unbalancing, (b) intensifying, and (c) reframing.

   (a) Unbalancing occurs when therapists intentionally align with a family member who is disempowered

in the family hierarchy. For example, if a family structure includes a father and child in a coalition against the mother, the therapist might align with the mother to unbalance the coalition. In this example, unbalancing is an effort to destabilize the father/child coalition and supports emergence of a new structure.

   (b) Intensifying also stimulates new structuring. **Intensifying** involves encouraging family members to engage in strong, here and now, emotional expression to enhance motivation for change. As emotions heighten, internal pressure for system change builds, and therapists can introduce change more easily. Intensifying increases family discomfort; distress linked to change becomes less than the pain involved with remaining the same.

   (c) Reframing is used throughout counseling. **Reframing** is a restatement of the family's problem from a novel perspective. The problem can be softened so that its purpose is more easily understood and a greater sense of empathy among family members is fostered. Imagine a family whose daughter is getting married; over the course of the planning, the mother of the bride becomes hurt as she's left out of decision-making. The mother responds with increasing efforts to take over planning. A reframe of the mother's behavior could sound like: "Mom seems worried about being pushed out of her daughter's life. Asserting herself into the wedding plans is one way to remind everyone that she loves her daughter and wants to stay close to her." Another possible reframe would be that the parents have done a great job raising a daughter who is able to function independently, and thus able to plan her wedding without leaning too much on her mother for help. Keep in mind that reframes are designed to expand perspectives and generate empathy, not to excuse or endorse behavior. Reframes provide ideas about how to address core structural issues more effectively. A common structural issue has to do with boundary adjustments as children become adults. Reframing is one of the most widely used family therapy techniques.

Structural family therapists believe that problems with family structure create symptoms. It follows that changing family structure can reduce symptoms. Structural family therapy is a moderately directive family therapy approach. The next approach, strategic family therapy, has an even stronger counselor-as-expert perspective.

Strategic Family Therapy

Strategic family therapy is a product of the Mental Research Institute in Palo Alto, California. Jay Haley and Chloe Madanes, prominent names in both constructive therapy and strategic family therapy, believed insight wasn't needed for change (Haley, 1976; Madanes & Haley, 1977). Instead, they believed families can change by simply following the therapist's guidance.

Role of the Therapist

The therapist is the primary change mechanism in strategic family therapy. Strategic therapists use their expert role and power to direct families toward change. These directives are determined through observation of family relationships and communication processes, with an especially close focus on how family members are trying to solve their problems and on the power dynamics within the family. Consultation with a reflecting team is sometimes part of this process.

Key Concepts

Strategic family therapists assume that families engage in ineffective problem-solving strategies. Often family members use strategies that produce outcomes that are the opposite of what they say they want. Consequently, strategic therapists focus on the methods families have used to try and solve problems. Strategic therapists have identified three common but inadequate solutions:

1. Needing to act, but failing to do so.

2. Needing to stop acting, but failing to stop acting.

3. Solving a problem at a level that is ineffective (Nichols & Schwarts, 2007).

Strategic interventions target one of these three problems. Once the problem is identified, therapists facilitate change by interrupting these failing solution patterns.

Facilitating Change

To facilitate change, strategic therapists interrupt old, ineffective solution patterns. Because this approach doesn't require insight, there's no need to bring non-working solutions to family awareness or to process its impact. Rather, counselors often rely on giving paradoxical directives, advising families to do the opposite of what they need (Bitter, 2009). Using paradox is intended to disrupt patterns that keep problems active.

Common paradoxical interventions include prescribing the symptom, creating ordeals, and positioning. **Prescribing the symptom** occurs when therapists advise clients to continue experiencing a distressing symptom. For example, the therapist might say something like:

> I know you say you're depressed, but I'm not sure you're quite depressed enough. For the next week, really commit to your depression; make it obvious and allow it to really get in your way.

An **ordeal** involves prescribing an activity that is a greater "ordeal" than just continuing on with the usual problem behavior. The therapist creates an ordeal that overshadows the current problem with a different problem or task. Haley often recommended that families engage in ordeals that were distressing, but also healthy. For example, he might prescribe exercise, diet, or other self-improvement regimens (Haley, 1984).

Positioning is a technique wherein therapists align with a family member's position, but then exaggerates it in ways that make it less palatable. For example, if a parent has lost hope in a child's academic achievement, the therapist might take an even more extreme position, advocating dropping out, trade school, or other options that the parent would find even more distasteful.

As discussed in previous chapters, paradoxical strategies remain controversial and have drawn ethical questions since their inception. Consistent with Miller and Rollnick (2013), we don't recommend using paradox with families in ways that come across as manipulative. Further, if used at all, we believe these strategies require supervision and advanced training.

Humanistic and Experiential Models

Virginia Satir and Carl Whitaker were central figures in the humanistic and experiential movement in family therapy. Although each developed a distinct approach, they share common factors.

The relationship between the therapist and the family is central to experiential and humanistic approaches. Therapists remain in the here and now with the family during therapy sessions. Slowing the process down and attending to communication styles and metaphors sets an attentive and emotionally attuned tone. Above all else, when working from this framework, families are encouraged to explore, discover, and make changes in the moment (Satir, 1983; Whitaker & Malone, 1981). Change isn't intellectually discussed or assigned as homework; it's spontaneously created and experienced in the here-and-now.

Role of the Counselor

Counselors remain attuned to their own internal experiences and emotions throughout the counseling process. They actively engage families and use themselves and experiential activities to facilitate change (Thompson, Bender, Cardoso, & Flynn, 2011). Counselors also self-disclose, model personal congruence, and authentically engage the family. Intuition often serves as the spark to ignite family change. As counselors allow their congruent and spontaneous selves to emerge, the stage is set for families to let go of stagnant patterns and become open to new experiences. To use themselves effectively, experiential and humanistic counselors remain committed to their own personal growth. The counselor's continued engagement in personal growth and discovery is central to their capacity to facilitate growth in others. In this spirit, experiential and humanistic counselors grow and benefit from therapeutic encounters alongside the families they help.

The use of a co-therapy team is recommended. Working in tandem with another therapist not only allows for two sets of eyes and ears, but also places the relationship between the co-therapists front and center for families. The co-therapy relationship can be used to model authenticity, connectedness, freedom of expression, communication, and conflict management. Napier and Whitaker's book, *The Family Crucible* (1978) provides an illuminating example of a co-therapy relationship and the process of counseling one family over time using symbolic experiential family therapy.

Key Concepts

Humanistic and experiential counselors de-emphasize diagnosis and psychopathology. Instead, they use reframing and other methods to shift the meaning of symptoms and view families as stuck in their unique growth process. Growth is embraced as an inherent drive within all families and individuals. To become "unstuck," counselors help families value one another equally, openly articulate feelings, accept differences, and take risks to remain flexible, and move into the unknown. Counselors seek to break down rigid structures and processes (Thomas & Krum, 2015).

Virginia Satir developed the human validation process model (Loeschen & Suarez, 2008; Satir, Banmen, Gerber, & Gomori, 1991). The **human validation process model** is a humanistic family therapy approach focusing on modifying communication patterns to help families move beyond unhealthy and inflexible roles and rules. Satir identified five common communication styles (or stances):

1. Placating.
2. Blaming.
3. Super-reasonable.
4. Irrelevant.
5. Congruent.

The **placating** position is self-deprecating; it places others above the self. When taking a **blaming** position, responsibility is deflected, little thought or concern is given to others, and an air of self-importance flows from the communicator. **Super-reasonable** communicators are cool and logical. They sometimes become super-reasonable to excuse themselves and others from needing to work on uncontrollable factors. Irrelevant communicators behave in ways that are distracting; they're sometimes seen as the family clown. Irrelevant communicators put their energy into shifting the focus away from the self, others, or other relevant factors.

When families use congruent communication, they have more flexibility to express and reach their potential; they're also able to achieve a greater sense of connection. **Congruent communication style** involves authenticity, sensitivity, and clarity. Congruent communicators share their inner experience while valuing themselves and others (see Putting It in Practice 12.3 for an activity to help you understand Satir's communication styles).

Facilitating Change

Within humanistic/experiential frames, direct experiencing is the mechanism through which change happens (Keith & Whitaker, 1982; Thomas & Krum, 2015). The primary goal is to create an in-session experience with families that allow for freedom of expression and new interaction patterns. To foster risk-taking, counselors must establish rapport with families. Congruent interactions with family members foster trust. Demonstrating "realness," being genuinely expressive, and sending level messages are building blocks for rapport.

Drawing on the ability to remain attuned in the moment, counselors recognize unspoken, rigid processes and structures that limit family growth. Once aware of these covert themes, counselors promote experiences that break down barriers with open, expressive, here and now communication. Potential techniques are limited to the counselor's imagination. Techniques can be fun, spontaneous, and responsive to family needs in the moment, but they must also be aligned with an open, accepting, and connected process.

PUTTING IT IN PRACTICE

12.3 Getting in Touch with Satir's Communication Styles

The following scenario illustrates the communication styles identified by Satir. Imagine yourself as a single mother waiting up late to greet your adolescent daughter. She arrives home 1 hour after curfew. When she walks through the door, your response is:

Placating: "I'm so glad you're home. I've been waiting up to see if you need anything. Did you have a good time?"

Blaming: "You've ruined my night. I was supposed to enjoy my night off from work, but instead I had to sit here worrying about you. This is ridiculous. You have no concern or respect for me and I'm sick of it."

Super-reasonable: "We really need to check your cell phone. It must not be working."

Irrelevant: "Hey. Wanna watch a movie?"

Congruent: _____. What would be a congruent response for you here? It should be a response that's respectful, but that also is an open and genuine expression of feelings.

Now, try practicing these styles of communicating when responding to the following family predicaments, giving voice to the placating, blaming, super-reasonable, and irrelevant styles:

You're the oldest son, age 15, in a family of five. You just learned your parents are divorcing. Your response is _____.

You and your partner have been together 29 years. Your partner recently informed you that he/she has been diagnosed with lung cancer. Your response is _____.

You're a grandfather living with your daughter, her husband, and their three children. You find pot and condoms in your 13-year-old grandson's school bag. Your response is _____.

After constructing Satir's communication styles to the given scenarios, consider the inner processes of the family member you have taken on in your role. What underlying dynamics might lead to each response you thought of? What would a congruent response sound like? Accessing unspoken responses and becoming attuned to emotions is the heart of an experiential counselor's conceptualization process. Once attuned to these inner workings, counselors then rely on intuition to construct here and now experiences that foster change.

Family sculpting is a classic experiential technique (Hearn & Lawrence, 1981) that involves the family agreeing to become moldable. Either the counselor or a family member guides everyone into physical positions that represent their relationships. Family sculpting is a nonverbal technique designed to bring the unspoken into the room. To depict a placating and blaming relationship, for example, a counselor might position the family member in a blaming role on top of a chair or table towering over placating family members who are on their knees. Experiences like these sculptures can evoke emotion and foster new communication patterns. Throughout the process, the counselor encourages family members to own their feelings and share them openly. The counselor creates an environment where experimentation and change are possible.

CONTEMPORARY FAMILY THERAPY DEVELOPMENTS

Intergenerational, structural, strategic, and experiential family therapy are foundational perspectives in the family systems movement. Elements of these approaches are often at the core of more recent family therapy developments. Now, we turn to more contemporary family therapy approaches, most of which are broadly evidence-based.

Functional Family Therapy

James Alexander and Bruce Parsons (J. Alexander & Parsons, 1982; Onedera, 2006) developed **functional family therapy** (FFT), which is an integration of behavioral and systemic approaches, with particular focus on the purpose (or function) of family member behavior. Functional family therapists believe that family member behaviors create and define interpersonal relationships, generate and maintain intimacy, and contribute to other meaningful life experiences.

Consistent with its behavioral roots, FFT has an evidence base. Researchers have focused on adolescents across cultures and ethnicities, treating youth with disruptive behavior problems (Robbins, Alexander, Turner, & Hollimon, 2016). Specifically, youth struggling with violence, drug abuse, and other criminal behaviors have been a main treatment target.

Role of the Counselor

FFT therapists focus on making the specific functional qualities of family member behaviors explicit. They operate on the underlying premise that family member behavior is purposeful (i.e., the behavior has a functional purpose). The goal is to help family members change risky and damaging behavior, while working to address or fulfill the behavior's original intent (i.e., function) through alternative, healthier means.

FFT is a strength-based approach. Sexton (2011) wrote:

> FFT's core belief about youth and their families is that they have an inherent strength and a natural ability to be resilient, and that despite the most difficult of situations, they do their best in the context. (p. 10)

The strength-based perspective makes FFT respectful to youth and their families.

Functional family therapists use a style that's been compared to a curious researcher. Therapists ask questions and explore client symptoms, as well as family member reactions to behavioral improvements and escalation. The therapist seeks to answer the question: What is the interpersonal payoff of the identified behavior of concern?

Consider a family that has a teenage son who has engaged in violent behaviors. They arrive at a court-ordered appointment with an FFT clinician. The clinician is likely to ask questions about the violent behavior, but also gather information about behavioral antecedents and consequences. These questions help the clinician formulate the family-based function of the teenager's behavior. Internally, the clinician might be musing about:

- Is this the son's way of maintaining a connection with Dad, albeit a tumultuous one?

- Do Mom and Dad use the son's behavior to maintain their roles as disciplinarian and consoler? Or to ignore their marital troubles?

- Is there an element of attention-seeking that contributes to the son's behavioral motivations?

While remaining curious about behavioral functions, the counselor simultaneously works to create a nonblaming environment and fosters relationships attentive to interpersonal needs.

Key Concepts and Change Strategies

All behavior is purposeful and serves to create either distance or intimacy in family relationships (Sexton, 2011). A goal of FFT is to help families understand their behaviors in these terms, rather than labeling behavior as good or bad. The systemic concept of circular causality is central, as the family is encouraged to see the problem beyond the identified patient and consider the IP's behavior to be serving a family purpose.

The family is encouraged to recognize everyone's contribution to problem maintenance. After understanding the behavior's purpose for the family, the next goal is behavior change. Therapists help families fulfill the behavioral purpose in less risky and more relationally responsive ways.

Following analysis and discussion of family member behaviors, therapists implement change techniques. Relabeling, similar to the reframing technique discussed earlier, is used to explain family member's behavior in a compassionate way, revealing positive underlying behavioral motives.

Consider a family that brings their daughter, Jill, for counseling. With all family members present, it becomes clear that Jill's recent drug use has brought Jill's mom and dad closer together. Relabeling Jill's behavior and defining it in circular terms could sound something like this:

> You've all said the two of you (mom and dad) used to really get into intense arguments, but you're really on the same page. Maybe part of what Jill's drug use is doing is bringing mom and dad closer together. Jill, you're making quite the sacrifice to help your parent's marriage.

Relabeling helps family members restructure cognitions around the problem and can lead to softer affective responses that are more sensitive to each family member's interpersonal needs. After greater understanding is reached, and more empathy is fostered among family members to eliminate blaming, therapists help the family change their behaviors using behavioral interventions. The ultimate aim of these interventions is to help the family remain true to the initial intent of their behaviors, but find other means to achieve the same function. For Jill's family, this could mean that instead of deescalating parental conflict and bringing her parents together through drug use, the three of them could find a common recreational pursuit (e.g., a community art class, music lessons, fishing, four-wheeling, etc.). It also might be a relief to Jill if her parents agreed to go to couple counseling.

Multidimensional Family Therapy

Multidimensional family therapy (MDFT) focuses on individual, family, and environmental factors in an effort to remediate adolescent behavior problems. Many of the cases described in the MDFT literature include youth and/or parents with substantial alcohol and drug problems (Liddle, 2016). The MDFT approach focuses on youth and family strengths and natural motivations, but also directly addresses problems that are occurring on multiple levels. These problem areas often include:

- Poor family communication.
- Family relationship distress.
- School truancy, suspension, or dropout.
- School achievement challenges.
- Legal issues that youth and their parents are facing.
- Community disengagement.
- Youth skill deficits.
- Parenting skill deficits.

Although many different researchers and practitioners have been involved, Howard Liddle is the primary architect of MDFT (Dakof, Tejeda, & Liddle, 2001; Diamond & Liddle, 1996; Liddle, 1985). MDFT is an integration of diverse intellectual perspectives and empirical research; it includes dimensions from Bronfenbrenner's developmental model, systems theory, adolescent identity development, parenting effectiveness, and, from the beginning, had a systems and empirical orientation (Coyne & Liddle, 1992). This empirical orientation has resulted in MDFT having an exceptionally strong research base (Liddle, 2016).

Role of the Counselor

Multidimensional family therapists approach therapy from a practical perspective, focusing on initial distress, subtle signs of motivation, and client strengths. Initial engagement with clients is crucial to successful outcomes. Engagement focuses on four major areas: (a) the adolescent, (b) the parent, (c) the interactions between parent and adolescent, and (d) the "extrafamilial" (e.g., school, probation services; Liddle, 1995, p. 39).

Therapists hone in on parent and youth fears to understand their distress and enhance motivation. Therapists also make themselves available to provide services in whatever setting makes practical sense. This flexibility serves to reduce treatment obstacles. If the youth needs a school mentor or tutor, meetings might take place at school or in an educational facility. If probation services are involved, meeting in a probation office might be warranted. No matter what the setting, the aim is to help youth and parents develop the skills they need to strengthen family relationships and succeed in school and community contexts.

Key Concepts and Change Strategies

MDFT is a skills-based, goal-oriented treatment. Youth and parents are coached and counseled to directly take on the problems in their lives. The problems and events that precipitate treatment usually involve family relationship distress, school truancy or suspension, substance abuse, and negative peer relationships.

Typical MDFT treatment objectives include: (a) reduce or eliminate delinquency, criminal behavior, and substance abuse; (b) improve parent and child mental health; (c) improve school functioning; and (d) improve family functioning. Several different counseling strategies are used to achieve these objectives. For example, focusing on adolescent identity development and personal goals can be used to enhance motivation and help adolescents develop prosocial interests. Treatment also often involves facilitating constructive communication between youth and parents. Additional treatment strategies include parenting skills training, communication skills training, and developing personal skills for coping with mental health challenges and stressful life situations.

Multisystemic Therapy

Multisystemic therapy (MST) is a "comprehensive family and community-based treatment" (Henggeler & Schaeffer, 2016, p. 514). MST has three theoretical foundations: (a) Bronfenbrenner's (1979) theory of social ecology, (b) social validity or the orientation toward providing assessment and interventions in the client's real-world settings, and (c) the reciprocal nature of human interaction. MST practitioners assess multiple social factors that contribute to behavioral problems and then intervene at one or more systemic levels (Henggeler

---

12.4 Exploring Other Family Therapy Approaches

There are many other family therapy approaches. Based on content from several recently published family therapy texts (Capuzzi & Stauffer, 2015; Gehart, 2018; Goldenberg et al., 2017), the following primary approaches were identified.

1. Psychoanalytic and Intergenerational Family Therapies

2. Systemic and Strategic Therapies

3. Structural Family Therapy

4. Experiential Humanistic Family Therapies

5. Behavioral and Cognitive Behavioral Family Therapies

6. Solution-Focused Family Therapies

7. Collaborative and Narrative Family Therapies

8. Research-Based Approaches (e.g., Multisystemic Family Therapy and Functional Family Therapy)

In this chapter we summarized several, but not all, of the most common family therapies. If you're interested in pursuing family therapy training, there is a plethora of information, and there are many training programs available.

& Borduin, 1990; Henggeler, Schoenwald, Borduin, Rowland, & Cunningham, 2009).

Role of the Counselor

MST is delivered via treatment teams. Teams include from two to four master's level therapists, a supervisor, and administrative support (Henggeler & Schaeffer, 2016). Treatment is brief (3 to 6 months), but intensive (60–100 hours of contact). Meetings and interventions focus on problems and settings consistent with the youth and family's social ecology. MST is comprehensively strength-based. Therapists are optimistic in their communication with clients and stakeholders throughout assessment and treatment. Child, parent, family, peer, school, and community strengths are identified. Strengths are then used to address issues that contribute to problem behaviors. For example, a family friend with a positive affective bond with the youth might be recruited to provide after-school supervision (or mentoring or tutoring). Specific intervention strategies are constructed to address what MST therapists define as the drivers of the problems.

Key Concepts and Change Strategies

MST is founded on the proposition that "caregivers are the key to achieving and sustaining positive long-term outcomes" with youth (Henggeler & Schaeffer, 2016, p. 515). There is a practical focus on caregiver competencies, since caregivers need support and skill-building to improve their caregiving competencies. Therapists advocate for caregivers to make sure they're provided with social support from friends, family, and the community. As caregiver skills progress, therapists guide treatment toward reducing factors contributing to the youth's problems and increasing, among other issues, positive peer support.

REFLECTIONS

When engaging the informed consent process with a family, how will you handle confidentiality? How will this be different than handling confidentiality in an individual session? Discuss these questions with classmates and instructor.

CASE PRESENTATION

The following is an excerpt from an experiential and humanistic family therapy session. The Jackson family has been court-ordered to counseling after Jake, their 17-year-old son, was arrested on drug charges. The family consists of Jake's mom, dad, 14-year-old sister, Anna, 10-year-old brother, Luke, and 8-year-old sister, Sarah. This is the family's third session. It was previously established that Mom and Dad both have a long history of methamphetamine use and production. Two years prior, the children were placed in state custody while Mom served a three-year prison sentence.

Counselor: I'm glad you all made it back this week. I know you all said it was important to do this for Jake, but I'm wondering if you also might be getting something out of this time together?

Mom: I just want to be out of the damn system, get them off our backs.

Counselor: Yeah, the system has been a big part of your family for a while now. You're ready to move on. Wash your hands of them.

Mom: Yup.

Counselor: And, they're still hanging on.

Dad: They're going to be sticking their nose in our business forever.

Counselor: So, there are things, like child protection services and the legal system that won't let go of this family. No matter how hard you try to move on, they don't let go.

Sarah: Yeah, we work really hard.

Counselor: I bet you do. I've seen you work very hard in here. You work so hard to comfort your mom. Whenever someone begins to feel angry with your mom, you cuddle right up next to her.

Mom: She's my baby girl.

Counselor: That's a big job, a lot of protecting to do, and you're so little, the baby even? I think you should carry this big shield. (Counselor hands Sarah a toy shield resembling a knight's armor.) While we're together I want you to use this shield to protect who needs protecting.

Anna: [Rolls her eyes.]

Counselor: What's up Anna?

Anna: Nothing.

Counselor: [Using a playful tone.] I saw your eyes go back in your head. Jake, what do you think Anna might be thinking?

Jake: That this is a bunch of bullshit.

Counselor: [To Anna.] Is that about right?

Anna: Yeah.

Luke: [Giggles.]

Counselor: It seems like you guys have put up with a lot of bullshit lately. Piles and piles of bullshit. Let's make a pile in here, of the unfair, stupid shit you've had to deal with. I'll start. [The counselor writes on a piece of paper *alone*, shows the family the word, crumples the piece of paper, and throws it in the middle of the room.]

Counselor: I think it's crap that you kids feel alone in the world, like everyone is against you.

Dad: What are you trying to say? That I'm not doing my job? You f***ing people have no idea.

Sarah: [Hides behind shield.]

Counselor: Sarah, do you need some protecting right now?

Dad: [Exhales loudly.]

Sarah: [Cuddles into her mom. Mom puts her arm around Sarah, kissing her on the head.]

Counselor: [To Dad.] What's it like to see Sarah like this?

Dad: I hate it. I hate how she (Mom) babies her.

Counselor: It seems like Mom does the comforting in the family and you draw the hard line. It must be tough sometimes, playing the bad guy.

Dad: Somebody's got to do it.

Counselor: Would you say that it's bullshit that it always has to be you?

Dad: [Reluctantly.] Sure.

Counselor: [Hands Dad a piece of paper to add to the pile.]

Counselor: [To Sarah.] It looks like you might be feeling afraid.

Sarah: [Shakes her head.]

Counselor: Dad, what do you think Sarah might need right now, while she's cuddled into Mom, holding up her shield?

Dad: She wants her mom.

Counselor: I'm thinking you might be able to do something for her too. Why don't you move over to this couch and sit next to Sarah. Sarah, would that be okay?

Sarah: [Nods her head.]

Dad: [Moves next to Sarah, puts his arm around her.]

Counselor: So Jake, what would you add to the pile?

Jake: No one here used to give a shit about me. I was never taken care of like Sarah is now.

Counselor: [Hands Jake paper and pen to add to the pile.] Talk to your mom about this. Tell her about your anger and your hurt.

Jake: Mom, you weren't there for me. I took care of these kids most of the time. I'm sick of cleaning up your messes.

Mom: [Tears up, looks down.]

Counselor: Mom, let's let Dad sit with Sarah, so you can focus on Jake. Move over here so you can face him.

Mom: [Moves over, avoids looking at Jake.]

Counselor: It's even hard to look at him. You're feeling a lot of guilt. Tell Jake about your tears.

Mom: I'm just really sorry.

Jake: You being sorry don't take it away. It doesn't fix everything.

Sarah: [Moves toward Mom, climbs into her lap.]

Counselor: Sarah, you're doing your job for the family so well. Working hard to keep your mom happy. [To Mom.] Is this a job you want Sarah to have?

Mom: Well, I like her hugs, but it's not her job to keep me happy.

Counselor: Sarah, I wonder if you could be brave and try something new for me. Let's let Mom feel what she needs to feel and talk to Jake. This is going to be a scary, being so new. Who would you like to sit with while Mom and Jake tell each other about their hurt and sorrow?

Anna: [Opens her arms for Sarah. Sarah walks over and is held next to her. An authentic conversation between Mom and Jake continues while the counselor supports congruent communication in the moment.]

The Problem List

Experiential family counselors attend to problems emerging in the moment while working to facilitate an awareness of deeper family issues. In this case, the first problem to emerge was the family's struggle with the legal system. The counselor acknowledged this as a problem, while also bringing the family into the moment and addressing the communication patterns and structural issues that were impeding the family's growth. Based on what was observed and addressed in the moment, the problem list includes (notice this doesn't include Jake's legal issues because that's a problem linked to his IP role):

- Sarah's rigid role to protect her mother.

- Mom and Dad's inflexible caretaker and disciplinarian roles.

- The parentification and later role dismissal of Jake.

- Dad and Anna's resistance/fear of the counseling process.

- The family's covert rule not to talk about past hurts, current fears, and anger regarding their drug use history and the children's removal from the home.

- Mom and Dad's marriage (with the focus on their children, more information is needed to assess the parents' marriage).

Problem Formulation

To gain a deeper understanding of the family's problems, the counselor looks into the processes and structures that keeps the family stuck. The Jackson family has been engaging in dysfunctional relationship patterns. These include: (a) not speaking directly to each other, (b) not disclosing authentic reactions to one another (especially where past hurts are concerned), and (c) triangulating outside systems like child protective services and legal authorities to foster family connectedness.

The Jackson family structure, although able to shift in times of crisis (e.g., Jake taking on a parenting role when his parents were unavailable), is also quite rigid. Sarah is entrenched in her mother-placating role, Luke is intermittently irrelevant, Dad blames, and Mom placates. The family isn't a pleasant or supportive place for the members. As the problem formulation becomes clearer, the counselor creates experiences where the family can experiment with new, more authentic ways of being, including ways in which they might experience positive feelings and support from one another.

Interventions

In an experiential model, the counselor's interventions are activity-based. Change doesn't occur primarily through talk or insight. Change happens through action in the now. When facilitating change with the Jackson family, the counselor spontaneously creates experiences responsive to the family's moment-to-moment needs. When the counselor witnesses Sarah placating Mom, the counselor intervenes by emphasizing the role and giving Sarah a toy shield to shift it into a playful (and overt) experience. As Sarah relies on Mom for comfort, the counselor intervenes by asking Dad to move near Sarah to provide comfort, creating flexibility in his disciplinarian role. Further, the counselor empathizes with the family's frustration about being in counseling and in the system.

Instead of allowing the family to collude in opposing counseling, the counselor connects and joins with their frustration and then prompts the family to uncover other sources of "unfairness" using a spontaneous experience to create a metaphorical pile of bullshit in the counseling session. This experience freed the family to express frustrations about what was happening to the family as well as within the family. Eventually the counselor coached Sarah into temporarily letting go of her placating role and guided Jake toward congruent communication with his mom.

> **REFLECTIONS**
>
> Pretend you're a member of the Jackson family. How would it feel to be involved in this therapy process? Can you think of anything that you'd find uncomfortable or unacceptable from a cultural or personal perspective?

Outcomes Measurement

Many formal tests and rating scales for measuring family therapy efficacy or effectiveness exist. Additionally, less formal assessments, such as reconstructing a genogram to look for evidence of change or repeated family sculpting can also be used.

Family counselors tend to rely on self-report and direct observations to determine counseling effectiveness.

When using self-report, counselors seek family member perspectives about family roles, rules, relationships, and satisfaction with family functioning. When relying on observation, counselors use their knowledge and perceptions, evaluating families from an "outsider" perspective.

The *Family Adaptability and Cohesion Evaluation Scale* (FACES) is a commonly used self-report instrument for assessing family members' satisfaction. This 20-item scale has family members rate their current and ideal family situation in terms of flexibility and connectedness (Olson, 2000). The closer the two scores are, the greater the satisfaction. This assessment could be utilized as a pre- and post-intervention measure with the families like the Jackson family.

The *McMaster Clinical Rating Scale* (Epstein, Baldwin, & Bishop, 1983) is another common family functioning assessment tool that evaluates six areas: (1) roles, (2) communication, (3) problem solving, (4) affective responsiveness, (5) affective involvement, and (6) behavioral control. Additional formal assessments that could be considered include:

- The *Beavers Interactional Competence and Style* (BICS).

- The *Circumplex Clinical Rating Scale* (CCRS).

A final note: When selecting assessment procedures for measuring outcomes, you should be aware that there are well over 1,000 couple and family assessments available (Goldenberg, Stanton, & Goldenberg, 2017). No doubt many were constructed in alignment with specific theoretical concepts. When selecting an outcomes assessment, be sure to find one or more that share a similar lens to your theoretical orientation and are representative of what you intend to measure.

EVALUATIONS AND APPLICATIONS

Families come in many different shapes and sizes, and so do family therapies. No doubt there's likely a family therapy out there that will fit, more or less, for nearly every family type. In this section we look at how well the family therapies do in terms of empirical research and sensitivity to cultural, gender, sexual, and spiritual issues.

Evidence-Based Status

Evaluating the empirical status of family therapies is a daunting task. As noted, there are many different family therapy models. Some models or theoretical approaches are more specific than others. In some ways, it's difficult to know whether positive outcomes are based on simply getting the whole family together in the same room for therapy or whether a specific systems-based intervention is the helpful factor.

Research on family therapy is generally positive. In an early review, Shadish and Baldwin (2002) reported on 20 meta-analyses of couple and family research. They reported a combined (couple and family outcomes) overall effect size of $d = 0.65$ compared to no treatment controls. This is a moderately positive effect size; the efficacy of couple therapy was slightly better than family therapy.

The Traditional Family Therapies

Compared to contemporary evidence-based family therapies, the traditional models (i.e., intergenerational, structural, strategic, and humanistic-experiential) have much less empirical research.

There's very little controlled empirical research focusing on Bowen family systems therapy outcomes (Shadish, Ragsdale, Glaser, & Montgomery, 1995; Shadish & Baldwin, 2002; Stanton & Shadish, 1997). A recent Iranian study showed that eight 90-minute Bowen family therapy sessions were more effective than no treatment in reducing marital conflict (Yektatalab, Oskouee, & Sodani, 2017). There's also research supporting the validity of Bowenian constructs (e.g., differentiation of self, fusion, triangulation; Charles, 2001; Jankowski & Hooper, 2012). Overall, it appears that Bowenian approaches are valued for their depth of analysis.

Research on structural therapy has generated a few positive outcomes over the years. Specifically, it may be effective for substance abuse, psychosomatic disorders, and conduct disorders (Shadish et al., 1995; Shadish & Baldwin, 2002; Stanton & Shadish, 1997). In a more recent review, four outcome studies were summarized (McAdams et al., 2016). The reviewers reported that structural family therapy improved well-being in HIV seropositive women, and generally supported the utility of the structural approach.

Research evaluating the efficacy of humanistic and strategic family therapy is even sparser and more equivocal. There is no evidence of these approaches producing positive outcomes (Stanton & Shadish, 1997; Shadish et al., 1995; Shadish & Baldwin, 2002). However, integrating experiential activities into family therapy was reported to improve adherence and family engagement (Thompson, Bender, Cardoso, & Flynn, 2011; Thompson, Bender, Windsor, & Flynn, 2009).

Multidimensional Family Therapy

MDFT has substantial research support. This support includes several meta-analyses, many RCTs, and numerous individual studies across a variety of problems and treatment populations. Overall, Liddle (2016) reported MDFT efficacy for reducing substance abuse and related problems, improving school performance, reducing symptoms of co-occurring mental disorders, decreasing delinquent behaviors and delinquent peer socializing, reducing out-of-home placements, and reducing high-risk sexual behaviors.

Multisystemic Therapy

Multisystemic therapy (MST) also has significant research support. In a 2016 review, Henggeler and Schaeffer reported over 100 journal articles and 55 published outcome and implementation studies. They summarized, "Outcome research has yielded almost uniformly favorable results for youths and families" (p. 514). Treatment fidelity was noted to be important to treatment efficacy/effectiveness.

Functional Family Therapy

FFT had been empirically evaluated across more than 300 clinical settings (Robbins, Alexander, Turner, & Hollimon, 2016; Sexton & Turner, 2010). Although the results sometimes have been mixed, a meta-analysis of 14 studies showed FFT as clearly superior to untreated control groups and slightly superior to other established treatments (e.g., cognitive behavior therapy). Most of the research has focused on various delinquent behaviors among adolescents. Interestingly, in the 14 study meta-analysis, FFT's effects were not significantly different than treatment as usually conducted in mental health settings (Hartnett, Carr, Hamilton, & O'Reilly, 2017).

Other Family Therapy Findings

APA's Division 12 includes family therapy as efficacious or probably efficacious for four different treatment populations. These include:

- Family-based treatment for anorexia nervosa.

- Family-based treatment for bulimia nervosa.

- Family-focused therapy for bipolar disorder.

- Family psychoeducation for schizophrenia.

Family therapy also appears promising for assisting families who have children with health problems such as childhood obesity and asthma (Ng et al., 2008; Young, Northern, Lister, Drummond, & O'Brien, 2007) and adolescent suicide ideation (Diamond et al., 2010).

Cultural Sensitivity

The cultural sensitivity of family therapy varies considerably across the different theoretical models reviewed in this chapter. Bowen's intergenerational approach, with its focus on individuation and pathologizing of emotional cutoff and enmeshment, has the potential to be insensitive to diversity issues. Further, it's difficult to think of which cultural group, including members of the dominant culture, that Haley's strategic approach wouldn't potentially offend.

In contrast, Minuchin's structural family therapy was used respectfully with minority populations in and around Philadelphia. In a recent review, the cultural sensitivity of structural family therapy was affirmed (McAdams et al., 2016).

In her work with families, Satir strove for authenticity and empathy with all clients. However, the interpersonal, here and now focus that she and Carl Whitaker employed in humanistic-experiential family therapies might be uncomfortable for some cultural groups.

The evidence-based multisystems models have great potential for cultural sensitivity. Broadly, a multisystems approach is formulated as addressing up to nine different levels in clients' lives (Boyd-Franklin, Cleek, Wofsy, & Mundy, 2013). These levels are integrated into the clients in their real worlds in ways that are inclusive, strength-based, and respectful. The levels include:

- Level I: Individual.

- Level II: Subsystems.

- Level III: Family household.

- Level IV: Extended family.

- Level V: Nonblood kin and friends.

- Level VI: Churches, schools, and community resources.

- Level VII: Social service agencies and outside systems.

- Level VIII: Work.

- Level IX: External societal forces (e.g., poverty, racism, discrimination, sexism) (from Boyd-Franklin, Cleek, Wolfsy, & Mundy, 2013, p. 205).

Gender and Sexuality

Historically, family therapy was no friend of mothers. Fortunately, with increasing consciousness partly inspired by feminist psychology and counseling, most family therapy approaches no longer explicitly blame mothers for their children's psychopathology.

There may be some concerns that family therapies may orient too specifically to traditional family structures and roles. In particular, functional family therapy has been critiqued for promoting traditional family roles, although Alexander provided a rebuttal for that critique (Alexander, Warburton, Waldron, & Mas, 1985; Avis, 1985).

In a recent survey, only 45.6% of couple and family therapy faculty members reported having received training in LGBTQ affirmative therapies (Corturillo, McGeorge, & Carlson, 2016). However, over the past decade LGBTQ sensitivity in family therapy training and practice has increased. Many publications, including the Handbook of LGBT-affirmative couple and family therapy (Bigner & Wetchler, 2012) are now available to help practitioners gain awareness, knowledge, and skills for working with non-traditional families.

Spirituality

Until the 1990s, religion and spirituality in family systems theory and family therapy was mostly absent (Harris, 1998). However, since then, researchers and practitioners have surveyed student satisfaction with the spirituality dimensions of family therapy training. In most cases, these surveys have revealed that students would prefer more training in how to integrate religious/spiritual issues into family work (Carlson, Kirkpatrick, Hecker, & Killmer, 2002; McNeil, Pavkov, Hecker, & Killmer, 2012). Finding that students want more training in this area makes rational sense because most families have spiritual or religious values.

A variety of books, book chapters, and articles that focus on spirituality and religion in family therapy have been published over the past decade (Daneshpour, 2017; Marterella & Brock, 2008; Walsh, 2009). The orientation of these publications tends to be broad and inclusive of various faith practices, although Daneshpour's book is specifically geared toward working with Muslim families. From a more generalist perspective, Walsh (2009) described her approach:

> The authors in this volume bring varied spiritual vantage points to inform clinical assessment and intervention. All are grounded in a strengths-based family systems orientation and a collaborative approach to practice. (p. 3)

At this point in time, using strength-based and collaborative models is the trend in family therapy. If you wish to integrate faith systems into your family therapy work, operating from a strength-based collaborative model is still strongly recommended, and likely compatible with potential strengths located within the family's faith systems.

CONCLUDING COMMENTS

This chapter underlines the notion that no one exists in isolation. Instead, we exist in living, breathing systems with all of their intricate structures, deep-rooted patterns, and powerful relationships. Treatment at the systemic level must address these complexities and also engage families in ways that facilitate change. Regardless of the systemic model embraced, the driving conceptual forces in family counseling (homeostasis, rules and roles, the notion of the identified patient, boundaries, alliances, coalitions, and triangles) remain consistent over time and approach. Further, common factors in family therapy are

what appear to garner the most research support. This involves facilitation of counseling relationships where an alliance with the family sets a foundation for accessing familial resources and generating hope, which, in turn, stimulates risk taking, new learning, and positive change in families.

CHAPTER SUMMARY AND REVIEW

Systems theory is an approach that focuses not on individual components but on unifying principles regarding how entities within organizations operate or function. Family systems theory considers the whole system, rather than individuals, as the source of individual problems and the target for therapy interventions.

Alfred Adler was one of the first modern therapists to consider the family as relevant to treatment of individuals. Following Adler, Nathan Ackerman began working directly with families and family dynamics in the 1930s. Progress was slow, but family systems approaches greatly gained in popularity during the golden age of family therapy (the 1970s and 1980s).

As a derivative of cybernetics, general systems theory, and second-order cybernetics, family systems theory incorporated concepts from outside counseling and psychology to better understand how families operated and how individuals affect other individuals within family systems. Family systems models emphasize that family member problems serve a purpose within the family system. Family systems theory doesn't employ a linear model for understanding families. Instead, concepts such as circular causality, homeostasis, first- and second-order change, alliances, subsystems, triangulation, and coalitions became the language of family therapy. Family systems therapists shift the focus away from pathologizing identified patients, and instead focus on the family microsystem for treatment.

There are four traditional family systems approaches that have shaped contemporary family therapy. These include: (a) intergenerational family therapy, (b) structural family therapy, (c) strategic family therapy, and (d) humanistic-experiential family therapy. Although overlapping, each of these traditional approaches have distinct therapist roles, key concepts, and change principles.

There are also several contemporary family therapy approaches that are multisystemic and empirically oriented. These include: (a) functional family therapy, (b) multidimensional family therapy, and (c) multisystemic therapy. Other theory-based family therapies (e.g., behavioral, narrative, feminist) are also used for treating families.

The evidence base for functional family therapy, multidimensional family therapy, and multisystemic therapy is strong. Each of these approaches appear effective, especially with youth who engage in delinquent, substance abusing, or other challenging behaviors. The traditional family systems models have much less empirical support.

Although most family therapies are culturally sensitive, intergenerational family therapy and strategic family therapy tend to be less sensitive to individual client and family dynamics. In contrast, structural family therapy and the contemporary multisystemic therapies have been used extensively with minority populations. These approaches also appear to be strength-based and sensitive to nontraditional family systems. However, most family therapy students would like more training in how to work effectively with minority clients, especially clients who are sexually different and who hold distinct religious or spiritual beliefs.

FAMILY SYSTEMS KEY TERMS

Alliances

Blaming

Boundaries

Child guidance clinics

Chronosystem

Circular causality

Coalition

Congruent communication style

Covert rules

Cybernetics

Differentiation

Diffuse boundaries

Double-bind theory

Ecological systems theory

Emotional cutoff

Enmeshment

Exosystem

Family enactments

Family mapping

Family roles

Family rules

Family sculpting

First-order change

First-order cybernetics

Functional family therapy

General systems theory

Genogram

Homeostasis

Human validation process model

Identified patient (IP)

Intensifying

Intergenerational family therapy

Irrelevant

Macrosystem

Mesosystem

Microsystem

Mimesis

Multidimensional family therapy

Multisystemic family therapy

Ordeal

Overt rules

Placating

Positioning

Prescribing the symptom

Reframing

Restructuring

Rigid boundaries

Schizophrenogenic mothers

Second-order change

Second-order cybernetics

Strategic family therapy

Structural family therapy

Subsystems

Super-reasonable

System

Systems theory

The golden age of family therapy

Triangulation

Unbalancing

CHAPTER 13

Developing Your Multicultural Orientation and Skills

LEARNER OBJECTIVES

- Define multicultural theory and therapy
- Identify key figures and historical trends in the development, evolution, and applications of multicultural therapy
- Describe theoretical principles associated with the multicultural perspective
- Describe and apply multicultural therapy principles, strategies, and techniques
- Analyze cases that employ multicultural approaches
- Evaluate the empirical, gender, and spiritual validity of multicultural therapy
- Identify key terms and resources associated with multicultural therapy

Although culture is a force that shapes every human being, many of us are unaware of the extent of our own culture's influences. It could be argued that those in majority cultures have less awareness of their cultural underpinnings because these values and ways of being frequently go unexplored and unquestioned. Recognizing the benefits and engaging in the challenges of multiculturalism are important to maturing as a human being and mental health professional.

Perhaps, in a more evolved world, this chapter's content would be seamlessly integrated into the other 13 chapters. Certainly, most theoretical approaches now embrace diversity in varying degrees, but there's not enough research and practice literature within each theoretical model to justify eliminating this chapter and integrating diversity material into other chapters.

The historical position of multiculturalism, as the fourth force in counseling and psychotherapy suggests, influenced the placement of this content in this chapter. However, the content is flexible enough for instructors to use as an initial orientation chapter or a closing chapter. Either way, our goal in this chapter is to help you integrate diversity awareness, knowledge, and skills into all counseling and psychotherapy approaches.

INTRODUCTION

Because cultures have both overlapping and contrasting dimensions that distinguish individuals from each other,

we believe all counseling and psychotherapy is inherently multicultural. That makes this chapter different. This chapter is an orientation to multicultural counseling fundamentals. Some principles discussed here have been covered briefly in previous chapters, but we hope all of the principles here will inform and influence you if you choose to practice counseling or psychotherapy.

In Chapter 11 we discussed how language shapes thought. The reverse is also true; thought shapes language. In addition, culture shapes language and language shapes culture. If there's one overarching summary of multicultural psychology, it's that we live in a multidimensional universe, with a wide variety of ways of seeing and experiencing the world. This can be exciting, daunting, and, at times, disturbing.

What Is Culture?

Defining **culture** is a task with political overtones. Christopher (1996) stated:

> Culture permeates our lives much more thoroughly
> or pervasively than we tend to consider. Because of
> Western culture's individualistic orientation, we tend
> to think of the individual first and of culture second....
> What this tendency to give primacy to the self overlooks
> is the manner in which culture precedes us. (p. 17)

Using the influential anthropologist Geertz's (1973) definition of culture as webs of significance that give coherence and meaning to our lives, Christopher wrote, "Our social practices, institutions, family structures, and daily life make sense and 'hang together' because of these webs of significance" (p. 17). Further, he pointed out that culture shapes us and tells us both what should be considered a good life and what should be considered deviant (Christopher, 2001; Christopher & Bickhard, 2007).

Alternatively, Wade Nobles (2006), an African American scholar, defined culture as:

> [T]he vast structure of behaviors, ideas, attitudes, values, habits, beliefs, customs, language, rituals, ceremonies, and practices peculiar to a particular group of people which provides them with a general design for living and patterns for interpreting reality. (p. 71)

Culture permeates our lives, it precedes us (we are born into it), and culture constitutes a general design for living and pattern for interpreting reality (see Putting It in Practice 13.1).

In our work with young people, we've claimed that children belong to a different culture than adults (J. Sommers-Flanagan & Sommers-Flanagan, 2007b). This concept illustrates the constantly changing nature of culture; even though you were a member of a group once, you don't necessarily know what it means to be a member now. Parents and young people can easily attest to enormous group and cultural pressures on young people—pressures that adults may or may not fully understand. Failing to look, speak, act, and dress within defined

youth–cultural bounds can be a source of painful harassment. Counselors working with young people can find the application of multicultural counseling principles helpful.

What Is Multiculturalism?

Multiculturalism is a relatively new term that carries political baggage. It's broadly defined as the appreciation and validating of diverse perspectives. Multiculturalists believe all cultures have positive and enriching dimensions. A multiculturalist agenda involves the valuing and promotion of cultural diversity. For better or worse, attempting to accommodate more than one culture is a political act and therefore generates controversy, opposition, and sometimes violence.

Multiculturalism isn't a specific theory of psychotherapy. As Derald Wing Sue and others (J. Sommers-Flanagan et al., 2009) have emphasized, we shouldn't have 12 "other theories" of psychotherapy and then add a 13th multicultural theory. Instead, all counseling and psychotherapy theories and approaches must become multiculturally oriented—or cease to exist. Culturally diverse clients should not be expected to change to fit a dominant culture. Theoretical approaches must have the capacity to serve all clients.

D. W. Sue and Sue (2016) defined multiculturalism as:

> The integration, acceptance, and embracing of cultural differences that include race, gender, sexual orientation, and other sociodemographic identities. (p. 747)

PUTTING IT IN PRACTICE

13.1 Dimensions That Vary across Cultures

Culture permeates our lives and affects our beliefs and practices on many dimensions. The following list includes several of these dimensions. We challenge you to articulate the practices or beliefs of your own culture on each of these. Then, either through direct observation or through readings, explore how other cultures vary on these dimensions. Add and share with your classmates additional dimensions you discover.

- Eye contact
- Conception of time and timeliness
- Signs of respect
- Language
- Spirituality and religion
- Kinship systems
- Directness in communication style
- Collectivist versus individual orientation
- Aging
- Clothing (especially hats)
- Gender roles
- Definitions of the good life
- Educational practices
- Family definitions and duties

A glance at this definition reminds us of intersectional theory (defined and discussed in Chapter 10). Every individual simultaneously has multiple identities; these identities range along a continuum of strong to weak, and their existence can trigger responses of privilege or oppression from the individual's environmental or cultural context. Intersectional theory was derived from the experiences of black women who were not white, and black people who were not male. In the midst of this negative identity were real people who were experiencing double jeopardy or triple oppression (Crenshaw, 1989, 1991).

The cultures represented in the term multicultural are often dependent on the speaker. Many argue that the worst discrimination and abuse has occurred across racial divides. Others argue that history provides horrifying examples of religious discrimination. Gender, disability, sexual orientation, and class also represent cultures within the meaning of multicultural. Citizens of the United States tend to resist the idea of class as a source of cultural discrimination, but as columnist Ellen Goodman (2003) wrote,

> Through thick and thin, boom and bust, we tenaciously hold on to the belief that we are, fundamentally, a classless society. This self-image survives even though we have the most unequal distribution of wealth in the Western world. It survives even though 1 percent of us owns 40 percent of the wealth. And even though there's less income mobility between generations in our country than in any other but South Africa and Great Britain. (p. 4)

Goodman was writing in 2003. Since then, wealth inequality has increased. Global wealth distribution is highly correlated with nations. For example, to rank in the top 1% in the world, you would need to have about $770,000 in net worth. In contrast, to rank in the top 1% in the United States, you would need about $7 million in personal net worth.

This brief and insufficient analysis leads us to believe the term multicultural should include class, nation, as well as other overlapping categories with distinct values and patterns of living. Although there are problems with defining multiculturalism, the idea of multiculturalism is profound and will be pivotal in coming decades.

What Is Multicultural Therapy?

Nhu, a 44-year-old Vietnamese woman, comes to you for counseling. She identifies herself as Lesbian and female. She speaks English, but not especially well. She brings her 19-year-old daughter to serve as translator. Her presenting concern is distress over the pain "her sexuality" has caused her ex-husband and family.

How should you approach this case? Should you offer psychoanalytic psychotherapy? Feminist therapy?

Jumping into either of these distinct therapy approaches might cause termination after a single session.

D. W. Sue and Sue (2016) defined **multicultural counseling/therapy**:

> A helping role and a process that uses modalities and defines goals consistent with the life experiences and cultural values of diverse clients. (p. 749)

With this definition in mind, imagine how you might proceed with Nhu as your client and her daughter as your translator.

Multicultural therapy requires that you conduct counseling in a way that's consistent with Nhu's life experiences and cultural values. Her perspective comes first; your theoretical orientation comes second. The challenge is how you can integrate her perspective with your theoretical approach.

Practicing multicultural therapy also involves modifying the diagnostic process. Clearly, what constitutes a mental disorder in one cultural context may or may not constitute one in a different context. To address cultural context in diagnosis, the *DSM* (now *DSM-5*; American Psychiatric Association, 2012), includes specific sections that focus on culture and gender (and has since 1994). There should be no consideration of psychiatric diagnosis without an examination of culture (duPlessis, 2015; Paniagua, 2014).

As is true with the definition of multiculturalism, there's controversy within multicultural counseling about which groups to include under the umbrella of diversity (D. W. Sue & Sue, 2016). As we noted earlier, in one sense, all counseling is multicultural in that the counselor and the client are always from different families, have different life experiences, possibly different sexes, and different socioeconomic status. Most multicultural thinkers acknowledge these differences but believe that to call all counseling multicultural misses the point of the power of culture in our lives. Many multiculturalists adhere to an inclusive model of diversity that includes race, religion, sex, disability, and socioeconomic class. In contrast, some authors argue that broadening the definition of diversity weakens the power of certain cultural domains, most notably race, and can lead to color blindness (Helms, 1994).

HISTORICAL AND CONTEMPORARY CONTEXT

Multicultural theory and therapy didn't spring to life as a result of abstract speculation about the nature of humans and human need. Instead, it came into being—or was driven into being—by the painful recognition that the privileged white male worldview was often damaging to individuals other than healthy white economically secure males. Unfortunately, there are endless examples of how racial, ethnic, sexual, and other minorities have suffered from cultural oppression.

Historical Examples of Cultural Oppression

Acts of oppression predate Western civilization, but for our purposes, the most relevant historical examples come from the recent past in the United States.

Not infrequently, persons of color and females have been viewed as possessing limited moral and intellectual potential. When viewed from a multicultural perspective, these judgments are remarkably bigoted. However, at the time, these statements were framed as multiculturally sensitive. Take, for example, the following statement from the highly regarded *Southern Literary Messenger* in 1843.

We are not friendly to slavery. We lament and deplore it as the greatest evil that could be inflicted on our country. We lament it not for the sake of the black race but of the white. The former, who are slaves, are not only far happier in a state of slavery than of freedom, but we believe the happiest class on this continent. (Quoted in Kutchins & Kirk, 1997, p. 204)

Considering slavery as a benefit to blacks might be more stunning if it were simply an isolated example of multicultural insensitivity and racism. Unfortunately, there are many other examples where dominant white American–European physicians, psychologists, counselors, and social workers displayed profound insensitivity toward diverse cultures. A few examples are in Putting It in Practice 13.2.

PUTTING IT IN PRACTICE

13.2 Historical Examples of Multicultural Insensitivity

In 1851 physician S. A. Cartwright claimed discovery of two mental diseases peculiar to Africans. The first, *drapetomania*, caused slaves to have uncontrollable urges to run away from their masters. The cure? Whipping the devil out of them. The second disease, *dysaethesia*, affected mind and body, causing disobedience and disrespect. The cure? Extra hard labor, causing blood to finally reach the brain and give liberty to the mind (Szasz, 1970).

Among his many conclusions about women's inferiority, Freud claimed women had underdeveloped superegos:

They show less sense of justice than men, that they are less ready to submit to the great necessities of life, that they are more often influenced in their judgments by feelings of affection or hostility—all these would be amply accounted for by the modification in the formation of their superego. (Freud, 1948, pp. 196–197)

Unfortunately, from Freud's perspective, there's no cure for being born a woman. Baca and Cervantes (1984) quote Lewis Terman (1916), author of the Stanford-Binet Intelligence Scale, as having written:

A low level of intelligence is very, very common among Spanish-Indians and Mexican families of the Southwest and also among Negroes. Their dullness seems to be racial.... Children of this group should be segregated into special classes and be given instruction which is concrete and practical. They cannot master abstractions but they often can be made efficient workers, able to look out for themselves. There is no possibility at the present in convincing society that they should not be allowed to reproduce, although from a eugenic point of view they constitute a grave problem because of their unusually prolific breeding. (p. 147)

These examples amply illustrate how tolerance for differences is often limited and those in power or in the majority have defined cultural differences as representing genetic inferiorities or mental disorders. Inaccurate labeling is especially likely if these differences irritate or frighten those in power because, as Thomas Szasz (1970) noted, categorization of so-called mental illness is a subjective process:

Which kinds of social deviance are regarded as mental illnesses? The answer is, those that entail personal conduct not conforming to psychiatrically defined and enforced rules of mental health. (p. xxvi)

It is not unusual for individuals in power to justify their behavior with the explanation that they're acting to benefit the minority. In *For Your Own Good*, Alice Miller (1984) articulated this same dynamic from the perspective of children who are hit, kicked, slapped, and physically abused, all for the sake of helping them develop properly. Similar arguments have been made by various religious groups seeking to save individuals from their "homosexual" behaviors (L. White, 1994).

The dominant culture is both intentionally and inadvertently oppressive. Gushue and Constantine (2007) commented on the **color-blind phenomenon** that exists within professional mental health settings:

> Unlike more overt forms of racism, the color-blind perspective does not necessarily make explicit claims about White superiority. Rather, color-blind attitudes reflect the seemingly benign position that race should not and does not matter. Included in this stance, however, is a denial that racism continues to benefit White individuals. (Gushue & Constantine, 2007, p. 323)

Unconscious or unintentional racism or sexism is another reason why studying counseling and psychotherapy in context is so important. Context and culture affect everything.

REFLECTIONS

Does the dominant U.S. culture:

- Seek to understand the perspective of nondominant groups by asking them for their opinion—and then listening to their answers?
- Step into the alternative culture to deepen mutual understanding and respect?
- Consider that minority group members might fear reprisal for speaking openly?

The Recent History of Multicultural Competency and Practice Guidelines

The multicultural movement in psychology and counseling was made possible in part by shifting awareness with the U.S. populace and political changes within the U.S. government. For example, passage of the Civil Rights Act of 1964 led to positive changes in educational, housing, and employment access for many minority groups. The Act bolstered the confidence of persons of color and empowered them to organize (Arredondo & Perez, 2006). Within psychology, the Association of Black Psychologists was formed in 1968, followed by the Asian American Psychological Association, the National Hispanic Psychological Association (now known as the

National Latina/o Psychological Association), and the Society of Indian Psychologists. Together, these groups combined to form the Council of National Psychological Associations for the Advancement of Ethnic Minority Interests (CNPAAEMI; see Arredondo & Perez, 2006).

The development of guidelines for training counselors and psychologists was stimulated by a number of events and people. In particular, there was a group of "multicultural advocates and allies" who, being members of both the American Counseling Association and the American Psychological Association, pushed for progress in addressing multicultural competencies (Arredondo & Perez, 2006, p. 1).

Patricia Arredondo, who has been active as a multicultural leader and reformer in both ACA and APA, described several critical historical events leading to formal adoption of multicultural guidelines (Arredondo & Perez, 2006).

- In 1981, Allen Ivey, president of APA Division 17, Counseling Psychology, commissioned a report from the Professional Standards Committee, headed by Derald Wing Sue, to address cross-cultural issues. The first multicultural competencies document, listing 10 competencies, was published as "Position Paper: Cross-Cultural Counseling Competencies" (D. W. Sue et al., 1982).

- In 1991, Thomas Parham, president of the Association of Multicultural Counseling and Development (AMCD), a division of ACA, commissioned the Professional Standards Committee to review and revise the 1982 cross-cultural competencies document. The AMCD committee produced 31 multicultural counseling competencies in the document "Multicultural Counseling Competencies and Standards: A Call to the Profession" (D. W. Sue, Arredondo, & McDavis, 1992). Two years earlier, APA published *Guidelines for Providers of Psychological Services to Ethnic, Linguistic, and Culturally Diverse Populations* (APA, 1990).

- To amplify the 1992 and 1993 multicultural counseling competencies, another AMCD Professional Standards Committee produced a document with 119 explanatory statements for the 31 competencies, which was published as "Operationalization of the Multicultural Counseling Competencies" (Arredondo et al., 1996). The Arredondo et al. publication also introduced the dimensions of the personal identity model ... highlighting the concept of multiple or intersectional identities and multiple contexts.

- Three competencies related to organizational change were added, bringing the AMCD competency list to 34. The result was the book *Multicultural Counseling Competencies: Individual and Organizational Development* (D. W. Sue et al., 1998).

- A task force composed of members of APA Divisions 17 and 45, co-chaired by Nadya Fouad and Patricia Arredondo, developed "Guidelines on Multicultural Education, Training, Research, Practice, and Organizational Change for Psychologists," the task force document, and was unanimously approved by the APA Council of Representatives in August 2002 and published in *The American Psychologist* (APA, 2003). In a collateral action, in 2002, the ACA endorsed the 31 AMCD multicultural guidelines in 1992 (Arredondo & Perez, 2006, p. 2).

Following the preceding changes supporting persons of color and ethnic minorities, national, state, and local professional organizations focusing on the interests and rights of other minority groups flourished. For example, in 1985, APA's Division 44 (The Society for the Psychological Study of Lesbian and Gay Issues) was founded. The APA also has many other divisions that focus on issues pertinent to minority groups, including aging (Division 20), disabilities (Division 22), intellectual and developmental disabilities (Division 33), women (Division 35), religion (Division 36), and ethnic minorities (Division 45).

Organizational action to help educate mental health professionals regarding how to work effectively with cultural groups outside the ethnic–racial domain continue. For example, the ACA's Association for Lesbian, Gay, Bisexual, and Transgender Issues in Counseling's (ALGBTIC) published Competencies for Counseling LGBQIQA Individuals (2012) and the APA published "Guidelines for Psychological Practice with Transgender and Gender Nonconforming People" (APA, 2015). The ACA and APA have specific competency or practice guidelines for working with many different minority groups. Specific information and resources are at the organizations' websites (ACA: http://www.counseling.org/; APA: http://www.apa.org/).

Multicultural Leaders: Many Cultures, Many Paths

As noted in the previous section, there have been and continue to be many contributors to the multicultural movement in counseling and psychology. These leaders come from diverse cultural backgrounds, including American Indian (or Native American or First Nations People); African American (or Black American); Arab American (or Middle Eastern), Asian American; Latino/a (or Hispanic), and more. Additionally, other minority groups including lesbian, gay, bisexual, transgender, and queer (LGBTQ) people and individuals with disabilities are often part of the communal voice of multiculturalism.

Rather than providing a long list of names of prominent individuals here, we feature two to give you a taste of the multidimensional flavor of multicultural psychology and counseling.

Lillian Comas-Diaz

I inherited a healing lineage. My ancestors drank in the fountains of shamanism, Christian healing, spiritualism, gitano (Gypsy) wisdom, and Oricha beliefs. As a result, my dharma was to become a psychotherapist. Like many underprivileged Puerto Ricans of their generation, my parents migrated to the continental United States in search of work. Poor in their pockets, but rich in their hearts, they received their first born with acceptance and hope: I was born with a cleft palate. Longing to hear my voice, my father named me after his favorite singer—Lily Pons. My parents armed themselves with perseverance and prayed for a miracle. Physicians at the University of Illinois answered their prayers when they repaired my cleft palate in an experimental operation. A medical expert examined me 50 years later and declared my cleft palate repair "one of the best surgeries" she had seen. "Medicine did not have the correct technique at the time of your surgery" (Comas-Díaz, 2008). Almost in disbelief, the doctor dried her tears and declared my cleft palate operation a "divine intervention." (Comas-Diaz, 2010, p. 162)

Lillian Comas-Diaz recounted her dharmic path using words that mainstream psychology might view as mystical. Her words help us glimpse multiculturalism. There are so many unique pathways in individual, family, and communal life, that adhering to one rigid psychology for everyone is unacceptable.

Comas-Diaz is executive director of the *Transcultural Mental Health Institute* in Washington, DC. She's also a clinical professor of psychiatry at George Washington University School of Medicine. She has edited or co-edited several books and videos, including:

- *Clinical Guidelines in Cross Cultural Mental Health* (Comas-Diaz & Griffith, 1988)

- *Women Psychotherapists: Journeys in Healing* (Comas-Diaz & Weiner, 2011)

- *Womanist and Mujerista Psychologies* (Bryant-Davis & Comas-Diaz, 2016)

- *Latina Psychologists: Thriving in the Cultural Borderlands* (Comas-Diaz & Vazquez, 2018)

Derald Wing Sue

Many Whites, for example, fail to realize that people of color from the moment of birth are subjected to multiple racial microaggression from the media, peers, neighbors, friends, teachers, and even in the educational process and/or curriculum itself. (Derald Wing Sue, 2010b, p. 7)

Derald Wing Sue
(photo courtesy of Derald Wing Sue)

Derald Wing Sue was born to a Chinese American family in Portland, Oregon. Raised in a primarily white neighborhood, he reported being taunted and bullied due to his racial background.

Currently, he is professor of psychology and education at Teacher's College, Columbia University. His work crosses the boundaries between the counseling and psychology disciplines and he is one of the most cited multicultural authors of all time. He and his brothers, Stanley Sue and David Sue (all of whom are trained in psychology) have been strong voices in multicultural theory and practice for 30-plus years. Derald Wing Sue and David Sue are coauthors of the renowned multicultural text, *Counseling the Culturally Different* (D. W. Sue & D. Sue, 2016). Derald Wing Sue also has published many other books, including:

Microaggressions in Everyday Life: Race, Gender and Sexual Orientation (2010).

Microaggressions and Marginality (2010).

Race Talk and the Conspiracy of Silence: Understanding and Facilitating Difficult Dialogues on Race (2015).

THEORETICAL PRINCIPLES

Multicultural theory as applied to counseling and psychotherapy provides a distinct focus. Although somewhat fragmented and constantly evolving, multicultural theory for therapists includes three main principles.

Multicultural Principles

These are the foundational principles for multicultural theory and practice.

Principle I: Cultural Membership Is Linked to Disadvantage and Privilege

In a now-classic paper titled, "White Privilege: Unpacking the Invisible Knapsack," Peggy McIntosh (1998) articulated the invisible nature of privileges accorded to the dominant culture. She pointed out that in the United States, middle- and upper-class white people carry (in their invisible knapsack) unearned assets. Sue and Sue (2016) defined **white privilege** as: "The unearned advantages and privileges that accrue to people of light-colored skin (usually white European descent)" (p. 753). Unfortunately, one advantage white privilege doesn't offer is awareness; many white people don't immediately understand, discern, or agree that they're holders of privilege (see Putting It in Practice 13.3).

One obvious problem facing multicultural theorists and practitioners is that "we are all of us as individuals already mixed ethnically and culturally; our roots are historically constructed out of subtly mediated cultural strands" (Fernandez, 2001, p. ix). We share attributes and beliefs with many groups and the salience of our membership varies for each of us and across the lifespan. Being from Montana seemed unremarkable to us until we lived in upstate New York, Belize City, and the United Kingdom. In those contexts, our Montana identities took

---

PUTTING IT IN PRACTICE

13.3 Exploring Examples of White Privilege

Prochaska and Norcross (2010) described three perhaps-dated examples of white privilege.

1. White privilege is when you can get pregnant at age 17 and everyone is quick to insist that your life and that of your family is a personal matter, and that no one has a right to judge you or your parents, even as black and Latino families with similar challenges are regularly typified as irresponsible and pathological.

2. White privilege is when you are a gun enthusiast and do not make people immediately scared of you.

3. White privilege is when you can develop a painkiller addiction, having obtained your drug of choice illegally, go on to beat that addiction, and everyone praises you for being so strong, while being an ethnic minority who did the same thing is routinely labeled a drug addict who probably winds up in jail (p. 408).

Consider whether you agree with these examples. What examples of white privilege can you identify in your life now or in the lives of others? Have your examples changed much compared to the 2008 examples provided here? If so, what do you see as having changed and what do you see as having stayed the same?

on more defined attributes. Consistent with constructive theory, multiculturalism suggests that we construct worldviews based on our cultural experiences and memberships. Consciously or not, we are privileged or disadvantaged by these memberships as well, and, as intersectionality theory predicts, our multiple identities can cause simultaneous privilege and disadvantage.

In the late 1980s, Rita organized a panel with four women of color to discuss multiple, intersecting identities. When asked, each participant claimed that her experience of racial prejudice was far greater and more damaging than her experience of sexism. For them, race outweighed sex in terms of cultural definition, power, and oppression. In more recent panels and classroom discussions we've noticed students making stronger arguments for class distinctions (and the concomitant economic limits) in the United States carrying even more negative judgments than sex or race.

REFLECTIONS

What are your reactions to the idea of intersecting multiple identities? Can you feel them within yourself? If you can, which ones dominate, and when? All things being equal (which they rarely are), what group(s) do you feel you fit best with?

Principle II: We Make Distinctions between Groups of People Based on Race, Religion, Sex, Sexual Orientation, Ethnicity, Physical and Mental Disabilities, and Socioeconomic Status

Implicit in multicultural theory is the notion of group differences. If you met a young woman who grew up in an Amish community in Pennsylvania, you'd probably assume you're different from her in many ways. If you met five of her friends and relatives, you might assume they have many commonly held beliefs, experiences, and ways of being. As you know, humans make meaning by noticing similarities and differences around them. Our brains are always sorting out salient attributes of a given set of stimuli. If a piece of furniture has four legs and a flat surface, we call it a table. When we use this same strategy with "types" of people, difficulties arise. Which are the best attributes to use when grouping people into cultures or subcultures? No human has exactly the same life experiences so members of a given group often seem more different than alike. We can learn all about a given group and then meet many members who violate the group norms. One great problem in applying cultural/racial knowledge is the tendency for practitioners to assume everyone from a particular group (e.g., Asian, Native American, LGBTQ) holds the same cultural values (S. Sue & Zane, 2009).

The human tendency to make distinctions between individuals and groups based on differences can lead to stereotyping. A **stereotype** is a standardized and oversimplified mental picture or idea about members of a group.

BRAIN BOX

13.1 Neuroscience and Social Justice: The Neural Costs of Poverty

Social justice advocates are very enthusiastic about brain-scans, developmental neurobiology, and cutting edge neuroscience research. We wondered why. Let's think it through.

Two babies are born on the same day. One is born to socioeconomic advantages. The city water and air are clean; the schools are high achieving; the neighborhood is safe; and the family is financially and socially supported. The other baby is born in a city (maybe Flint, Michigan, or St. Joseph, Louisiana) where, sadly, the water is contaminated with toxic substances; the air is polluted; the educational system is broken; the neighborhood is unsafe; and the family is stressed and chaotic.

It doesn't take a rocket scientist to see that the social-emotional–physical–mental health of the first child will naturally have a more positive and health-enhancing trajectory than the second one. It also doesn't take a social justice advocate to recognize that being born into worse socioeconomic and environmental circumstances is not the fault or responsibility of the baby.

Social justice involves the fight for fairness, equity, self-determination, and physical and psychological safety. Social justice advocates search for knowledge and information to support their goals. Neuroscience research offers a new plank in the social justice platform.

Neuroscientific findings help make the effects of poverty and social injustice clearer. There's a large and growing body of evidence showing that poverty, chronic stress, and other environmental factors have an adverse effect on children's brain development—from day one, or before. Lipina and Evers (2017) wrote:

> Evidence from neuroscience goes to show not only how poverty may breach human rights, but also how it may prevent a child's possibility of ever enjoying them. In other words, it importantly reveals how poverty may cause problems in the very prerequisites for attaining personal development and a good life. (p. 8)

Poverty is doubtless a barrier for healthy brain development. Lipina and Evers (2017) identified two complementary arguments for how neuroscience can be used to promote social justice. First, it can be asserted that all people have an inherent human right to environments free from factors that have detrimental effects on brain development. This argument is an appeal to social conscience and goodwill. Second, it can be argued that reducing poverty within society will serve the interests of the wealthy. Of course, neither of these arguments have helped much in the push for social justice, but neuroscience might help amplify the case for justice.

Neuroscientific findings can help us identify the unequivocally adverse effects of specific environmental conditions. Neuroscientific findings can also help us to improve our efforts to remediate poverty-related early and later childhood deficits. This is great news and provides leverage for social justice advocates. However, as Lipina and Evers (2017) noted, there are also risks to pushing forward with the neuroscience rationale. Two primary risks include:

1. Potential stigmatizing of people living in poverty (e.g., brain deficits; blaming individuals/families for not escaping poverty).

2. Overstating the implications of neuroscientific findings (e.g., making causal statements from correlational findings; exaggerating the adverse effects; exaggerating neuroscience-based treatments).

The take home, at least for us, is that neuroscientific findings can help support the social justice cause. However, we need to make sure we use it like a scalpel, not like a battering ram.

Principle III: A Multiculturalist Stance Can Foster Greater Understanding between Cultural Groups and Facilitate Equitable Treatment of All Humans

A multicultural stance isn't restricted to understanding and valuing diverse perspectives. Multiculturalism is also about social justice (D. W. Sue, Bingham, Porche-Burke, & Vasquez, 1999). **Social justice** "involves addressing issues of equity, power relations, and institutionalized oppression" (Goodman, 2011, p. 4). Social justice also includes goals for all people to be able to live "with dignity, self-determination, and physical and psychological safety" (p. 4).

Multicultural advocates have worked and are working vigorously to decrease stereotyping and discrimination, and to increase social justice (Ratts, Singh, Nassar-McMillan, Butler, & McCullough, 2016). However, social justice work is difficult and fraught with strong

emotional responses. Even class discussions can be overwhelming:

> Some students described physiological reactions of anxiety like a pounding heart, dry mouth, tense muscles and perspiration. One student stated: "I tried hard to say something thoughtful and it's hard for me to say, and my heart was pounding when I said it." Others described feeling intimidated in the discussions, stammering when trying to say something, being overly concerned about offending others, ... being overwhelmed by the mix of emotions they felt." (D. W. Sue & Sue, 2016, pp. 24–25)

In a qualitative study focusing on what white trainees fear about racial dialogues, the following five themes were identified (D. W. Sue, Rivera, Capodilupo, Lin, & Torino, 2010):

1. Denial of whiteness or white privilege.

2. Endorsement of color blindness.

3. Fear of appearing racist.

4. Feelings of having no right to dialogue on race.

5. Reactions of anxiety, helplessness, and feeling misunderstood. (pp. 209–210)

These and other research results, as well as multicultural education experiences, illustrate the challenges of living in culturally inclusive ways. Our values and beliefs aren't easily contained in ways that allow us to openly examine and acknowledge the validity of diverse values and beliefs. Although great progress has been made on this third multicultural principle, there's much more work to be done (T. B. Smith, Constantine, Dunn, Dinehart, & Montoya, 2006; D. W. Sue & Sue, 2016).

D. W. Sue et al. (2010) offered the following recommendations for continued progress in facilitating valuable multicultural and intercultural discussions:

- Instructor/facilitator validation of participant feelings and emotional reactions.

- Facilitation of open discussions.

- Instructor/facilitator role modeling of openness and honesty, as well as reflections on their own biases and weaknesses. (pp. 210–211)

In addition, instructor passivity was a negative or unhelpful strategy when facilitating multicultural discussions.

Theory of Psychopathology

Like feminist theory, multicultural theory considers social forces as the primary contributor to psychopathology.

Thus, professionals with a multicultural perspective are extremely cautious when using standardized assessment instruments and diagnoses that presume the problem resides within the individual (duPlessis, 2015; Paniagua, 2014). Also, multicultural therapists don't quickly impose pathological labels on troubling behaviors, but instead seek to understand the meaning of behaviors within cultural contexts.

The names of disorders, beliefs about causation, and symptoms vary greatly across cultures. Many cultures view human distress through religious or philosophical lenses (and not medical or psychological lenses), leading some writers to argue for indigenous psychologies. David Ho (1998) wrote:

> Much of Western psychology may be irrelevant or inapplicable in Asia. Western ideological presuppositions, such as individualism, are alien to the Asian ethos. Thus, a reliance on Western psychology can only lead to an incomplete, even distorted, understanding of Asia or of Asians. Moreover, the wholesale importation of Western psychology into Asia represents a form of cultural imperialism that perpetuates the colonialization of the mind. To an alarming degree, Asians are now confronted by stereotypes about themselves generated not only by Western researchers but also by Asian researchers relying on imported, mainly American, psychology. (p. 89)

A clinical example from cognitive behavior therapy (CBT) illustrates how imported Western ideas of psychopathology may not fit Asian clients. One common target for CBT interventions involves modifying negative self-statements. While this treatment target makes sense from the Western perspective, members of Asian cultures often view these internal self-statements as valuable and motivating (Craske, 2010; Hwang & Wood, 2007). Consequently, modifying or eliminating negative self-statements would make little sense to many Chinese, Japanese, or other Asian clients.

THE PRACTICE OF MULTICULTURALLY SENSITIVE THERAPY

Practicing multicultural therapy is linked to multicultural competence. However, as we begin exploring multicultural competency in greater depth, keep in mind that no one achieves multicultural competence. Complete multicultural competence would be akin to learning to speak every language in the world. Multicultural competency is a process, not an outcome. As professionals, we continually work on our competencies. Put another way, we like to think of therapists practicing with multicultural sensitivity or humility, which opens us up to lifelong learning about cultural diversity (J. Sommers-Flanagan & R. Sommers-Flanagan, 2011; see Putting It in Practice 13.4).

The Multicultural Competencies

In 2015, the Association for Multicultural Counseling and Development (AMCD) updated the multicultural counseling competencies (D. W. Sue, Arredondo, & McDavis, 1992). D. W. Sue et al. (1992) had defined **multicultural competencies** as broadly consisting of (a) **cultural self-awareness** (i.e., awareness of cultural background and biases), (b) **cultural knowledge** (i.e. possession of

---

PUTTING IT IN PRACTICE

13.4 Informed Consent and the Multicultural Perspective

I'm looking forward to working with you in counseling.... This next section describes a little bit about an important part of my orientation and my ways of working with people. Questions are always welcome!

I believe people are who they are as a result of many life experiences, choices, and circumstances. Each person is a unique blend of culture, genetics, and choice. Your cultural group, your race, your sex and sexual orientation, your spiritual or religious beliefs, your skills and abilities, and your struggles or limits are all important to who you are. I might not know very much about some of these aspects of you, but I will do my best to learn and understand. I will do my best to respect you and our differences. When possible, I will do some research and reading to better understand your culture or life experiences if they're new to me.

I believe all humans grow up with some fears and prejudices and I'm no exception. If you notice me being insensitive or if I say something that reveals ignorance, I sincerely hope you'll tell me. I'm a lifelong learner, and will appreciate your help in understanding your unique experiences, beliefs, and aspirations.

information about specific cultures), and (c) **culture-specific expertise** (i.e., using techniques that fit clients' culture). The new competencies were renamed the Multicultural and Social Justice Counseling Competencies (MSJCC; Ratts, Singh, Nassar-McMillan, Butler, & McCullough, 2016). The MSJC Competencies were reorganized from three to four broad categories (Ratts et al., 2016):

1. *Counselor Self-Awareness* (CSA): Being aware of your cultural values, beliefs, and biases. CSA requires self-reflection.

2. *Counselor Knowledge of Client Worldview* (CKCW): Understanding (or seeking to understand) client worldview. CKCW requires knowledge acquisition.

3. *The Counseling Relationship* (CR): Being sensitive to how culture, power, privilege, and oppression might influence the counseling relationship. Developing a CR or therapeutic alliance requires the integration of cultural and social justice knowledge with collaborative counseling or interviewing skills.

4. *Culturally Appropriate Counseling and Advocacy Interventions* (CACAI). Working collaboratively to apply strategies and interventions that are multiculturally sensitive and promoting social justice, when needed, through advocacy. CACAI requires continued collaboration and discernment regarding when it's appropriate to move out of the counseling office and into community advocacy. (These four competencies are summarized from Ratts et al., 2016.)

The MSJCC sequence, from counselor self-awareness to culturally appropriate counseling and advocacy interventions reflects the idea that social justice and multicultural competence begins from within the counselor. Despite the implication that practitioners might be able to achieve competence, the MSJCCs are "intended to be aspirational" (Ratts et al., 2016, p. 30). The AMCD MSJCCs are at: https://www.counseling.org/docs/default-source/competencies/multicultural-and-social-justice-counseling-competencies.pdf.

The American Psychological Association published their "Guidelines on Multicultural Education, Training, Research, Practice, and Organizational Change for Psychologists" in 2003. This document identifies six guidelines focusing on:

1. Self-awareness of biased attitudes and beliefs.

2. Multicultural sensitivity/responsiveness.

3. Multiculturalism in psychological education.

4. Culturally sensitive research.

5. Culturally appropriate clinical skills.

6. Culturally informed organizational change processes.

The complete APA guidelines are available at: http://www.apa.org/pi/oema/resources/policy/multicultural-guidelines.aspx.

Assessment Issues and Procedures

Multicultural assessment begins with sorting out your existing and potential biases. Developing self-awareness and adding cultural knowledge can prepare you to implement culturally specific assessment strategies. Let's start that process with an in-text reflection activity.

Consider the following scenarios:

• Imagine you have an opportunity to work with a gay client ... or a lesbian client ... or a transgender client ... or a bisexual, polyamorous client. As you imagine these scenarios, what are your first reactions, both emotional and cognitive? What are your biases? What stereotypes come to mind? Did your reactions come from family, the media, friends, religion, or other sources?

• Now imagine your next client has a disability. Perhaps it's a brain injury acquired later in life ... or a lifelong disability such as hearing impairment or cerebral palsy. Again, track your reactions, biases, stereotypes, and how you acquired your attitudes.

• Repeat this process, as needed, for whatever minority groups come to mind. Challenge yourself to venture outside your comfort zone. Then find a trusted friend, classmate, colleague, relative, or therapist to debrief your responses.

This reflective activity might feel overwhelming. On the other hand, you might believe you've worked through all your personal biases. Either way, time can help. We once had a Muslim student who shared that it made her feel nauseated when class lecture content and discussions focused on gay and lesbian people. Several years later, she shared her progress. It required difficult personal reflection and exploration, but she opened up her worldview, and became open and affirming of sexual diversity.

Diagnosis

The first problem with multicultural assessment is diagnosis. As noted earlier, there are horrifying historical examples of diagnostic abuse or insensitivity to diverse individuals, families, and communities.

In 1994, the *DSM-IV* introduced a section on "Specific Culture, Age, and Gender Features." Additionally, DSM's focus on cultural sensitivity has continued to expand. The DSM-5 includes statements emphasizing that "conflicts that are primarily between the individual and society are not mental disorders" (APA, 2013, p. 20). The DSM also includes the "Cultural Formulation Interview" (CFI). The CFI includes 16 culturally sensitive questions divided into four sections. These questions are designed to help clinicians collaboratively explore cultural dynamics that might be contributing to client problems (J. Sommers-Flanagan & Sommers-Flanagan, 2017).

It's important to emphasize that the whole premise upon which mental disorder diagnosis is based is inconsistent with multicultural theory. Specifically, if multiculturalism holds that social injustice and oppression cause and contribute to distress and deviance among individuals, families, and communities, then how can we use a system that locates the so-called disorder in the individual person? This dilemma is why many multiculturally oriented clinicians avoid diagnosis whenever possible.

Testing

Psychological and intellectual assessment has been used in biased and prejudicial ways with ethnic minorities and women. Appropriate training in psychological assessment is essential to ethical practice. Lack of such training when using testing instruments with minority populations is especially ethically egregious. There is a knowledge base and ethical codes to guide your use of assessment materials (see APA and ACA ethical codes).

To provide culturally competent assessment, therapists should use a culture-specific service delivery, possibly including test administration in the client's native language or use of an interpreter; evaluate the client as a cultural being prior to testing; observe for culture-specific syndromes; select culture-specific tests; and critically examine the standardization procedures and norms used in testing procedures (Dana, 1993, 1996; Hays, 2016; D. W. Sue & Sue, 2016). Additionally, all testing procedures should be used in conjunction with a collaborative interview.

Clinical Interviewing as a Collaborative Assessment Process

Counselors and psychotherapists should engage in collaborative assessment processes when working with diverse clients (D. W. Sue & Sue, 2016). Collaborative assessment involves, at a minimum, honoring the client's perspective, soliciting client input throughout the process, and jointly formulating hypotheses about the problem and strategies for treatment (Finn, Fischer, & Handler, 2012; J. Sommers-Flanagan & Sommers-Flanagan, 2017).

In her book, *Addressing Cultural Complexities in Practice: Assessment, Diagnosis, and Therapy*, Hays (2016) described a detailed and multicultural assessment process. She emphasized that family members or interpreters may be needed as a part of the assessment. She also recommended obtaining a client timeline and information linked to her ADDRESSING acronym (see Table 13.1). Among other functions, this acronym helps therapists attend to intersectionality during the assessment process. ADDRESSING includes a range of information related to multiple dimensions (intersections) of client identity.

Table 13.1 ADDRESSING Client Multiple Identities

Hays uses the following model to obtain comprehensive information about the many dimensions of her client's identities (see Hays, 2016). This approach helps therapists recognize the wide range of cultural and personal dimensions affecting client identity.

A	Age and generational influences
D	Developmental disabilities
D	Disabilities acquired later in life
R	Religion and spiritual orientation
E	Ethnic and racial identity
S	Socioeconomic status
S	Sexual orientation
I	Indigenous heritage
N	National origin
G	Gender

There are many culture-related issues, including (a) language, (b) norms and mores against speaking negatively about one's family, and (c) privacy issues related to religion, which can make it difficult for therapists to obtain reliable and valid information from clients. As you work with minority and diverse clients, we highly recommend seeking specific culturally informed consultation and supervision.

Attend to the Therapeutic Relationship with Humility

Trappist monk Thomas Merton (1974) wrote about his deep regrets for the ways religious missionaries contributed to cultural genocide. He asked the thought-provoking question, "What would the world be like if different cultures had encountered each other with questions instead of answers?" What if the questions went something like these?

- What can you tell me about yourselves?

- What would you like to know about us?

- What can you teach me about the Creator?

Merton's ideas about how to approach other cultures are a good reminder to value, rather than judge, the perspectives of diverse clients. Respecting client perspectives doesn't mean therapists should turn to diverse and minority clients for their personal education; it does mean we should have an attitude of valuing what we can learn from diverse perspectives. Without that attitude, multicultural clients will likely leave therapy prematurely. In fact, early research indicated that about 50% of ethnic diverse clients dropped out of treatment after only one therapy session (S. Sue, 1977).

Talking about Differences

When conducting therapy with diverse and minority clients you should be open to talking about your obvious differences. However, initiating a conversation about those differences early in every session may not be necessary. Therapists who make a practice of always bringing up cultural differences in a perfunctory or pre-planned manner (e.g., "I noticed you're an African American person and I want to let you know that I'll do my best to respect your cultural perspective") run the risk of forcing clients into conversations about race and diversity, even when the topic feels forced, irrelevant, and uncomfortable. The place for standardized multiculturally sensitive statements is in your informed consent (see Putting It in Practice 13.4). In session, it's best for direct conversations about diversity to come up in authentic ways, as the session content dictates. Additionally, having office décor that communicates multicultural sensitivity is recommended and might involve:

- Intentional efforts to be fully accessible to people with disabilities.

- Gay, lesbian, bisexual, and transgender sensitive materials in the office and waiting room.

- Art or knick-knacks that show interest and respect for a variety of cultures.

Rather than talking about specific cultural differences between you and your clients at the beginning of therapy, a more general statement about how you handle diverse perspectives can be helpful. For example, multiculturally sensitive counselors might say something like,

> In my work, I've come to believe that culture is very important. By culture, I mean things like race, religion, sexual orientation, and other things central to our identities. You and I are probably different in some ways and alike in some ways. When we bump into the ways we are different, I hope we can talk about them if they matter to you. I'll try to be open to your perspective. If you think I'm missing the boat, I hope you'll let me know.

Burdening clients with your educational needs is suboptimal. For example, a couple of decades ago, we had a gay student in our mental health counseling program who eventually became weary of answering student and faculty queries about gay and lesbian culture. He cleverly gave us the hint by purchasing three books he believed to be useful and donating them to the clinic library. Then, when asked a question, he refused to answer unless the person asking had shown interest by at least skimming through these books.

When the Therapist Has Minority Status

If you're a member of a minority culture and are training to be a mental health professional in the dominant culture, you face unique challenges. One counselor we know who was born and raised in Malawi worked out a gracious introduction that touched on her accent and cultural differences in a way that helped clients immediately feel more comfortable. She would open with something like:

> I imagine you might be a little surprised to find a counselor like me here in Montana. I grew up in Malawi, Africa, and my education is both from there and from here in the United States. Sometimes, people find my accent a little hard at first, so I want you to feel comfortable asking me to repeat myself. I mean, really. Can you imagine doing counseling if we can't understand each other?

Using her obvious accent, this counselor wisely opened the door to important questions clients may have when encountering therapists from different cultures: "Can this person really understand me enough to help? And can I understand her?"

Similar issues may arise for gay and lesbian therapists or therapists with visible or invisible disabilities. In each case it's important to consult—especially with professional mentors who have been through similar situations—about how to deal with the issues in ways that facilitate positive interactions with clients.

One challenging issue, especially for diverse therapists, is the potential for racism, sexism, or other discrimination expressed from clients toward the therapist. Ratts et al. (2016) provided examples of "privileged clients and counselors from marginalized groups" where discrimination toward therapists might happen:

> This relationship may involve a White client who seeks counseling from a counselor of color, a temporarily able-bodied client interacting with a counselor who has a disability, or a male client who receives counseling from a female counselor. (pp. 36–37)

Experiences of discrimination and oppression are unsettling. Obviously, there are no perfect solutions to how minority-status counselors should handle discriminating statements. One guide is to stay centered, absorb the comment, and respond with acceptance. For example,

> I hear you expressing concerns about whether or not I will be able to be helpful to you … and if I'm getting this right, your concerns seem to be related to the fact that [I'm Latina … or … my sexual identity … or … my disability, etc.]. I'm open to talking about your concerns, if you would like.

Beyond this general suggestion, we encourage you to discuss with your supervisors, your classmates, and others how to best manage and cope with discrimination directed toward you as a counselor.

Avoiding Generalizations and Stereotyping

One counselor we knew was seeing a Chinese American woman for an intake interview. After she complained that everyone seemed to treat her like a child, he (the counselor) asked about her family and her Asian heritage. She responded energetically with,

> I know you think Chinese women act quiet, like black-eyed Barbie dolls, but not me. It's not about being Chinese at all. It's about my coworkers and my stupid husband. I have something to say once in a while, and I say it. But they get all bent out of shape.

Multicultural counseling is like qualitative research; *you may not generalize*. Skin color, ethnicity, sexual orientation, disabilities, and other client characteristics all exist within unique individuals, groups, and communities. Just as you would never generalize your findings from eight clients in a phenomenological-qualitative study, you shouldn't use your knowledge of the preceding categories and generalize to the person or people in your office.

S. Sue and Zane (2009) commented on how a little bit of multicultural knowledge *does not* go a long way (and often a large amount of knowledge won't take you very far either):

> Perhaps the most difficult issue confronting the mental health field is the role of culture and cultural techniques in psychotherapy. We believe that cultural knowledge and techniques generated by this knowledge are frequently applied in inappropriate ways. The problem is especially apparent when therapists and others act on insufficient knowledge or overgeneralize what they have learned about culturally dissimilar groups. (p. 5)

One concept that can help us understand why cultural knowledge and techniques that are supposed to work with specific cultural groups often don't work is acculturation.

Understand Acculturation

Acculturation (aka **ethnocultural orientation**) is defined as "giving up ethnicity-based cultural values, beliefs, and traditions, while adopting values, beliefs, and traditions of the dominant social structure" (Atkinson, Lowe, & Mathews, 1995; D. W. Sue & Sue, 2016). Garrett and Pichette (2000) identified five cultural orientations within American Indian populations (Herring, 1996; LaFromboise, Trimble, & Mohatt, 1990):

1. *Traditional*: The individual thinks in the native tongue and practices traditional tribal customs and tribal worship methods.

2. *Marginal*: The individual is not fully connected with traditional Indian culture or mainstream society. Both languages may be spoken.

3. *Bicultural*: The individual is relatively comfortable and conversant in both sets of cultural values.

4. *Assimilated*: The individual is oriented toward the mainstream social culture and has little interest in traditional tribal practices.

5. *Pan-traditional*: The individual has been exposed to and perhaps adopted mainstream values but has made an intentional effort to return to traditional values.

Individual and communal acculturation can influence client openness to counseling or psychotherapy. For example, researchers evaluating Asian American students' attitudes towards professional counseling reported:

> The results indicate that acculturation status, loss-of-face concerns, and conceptions of mental illness appear to be significant moderators of Asian American college students' attitudes toward mental health, mental health professionals, and help-seeking. (Leong, Kim, & Gupta, 2011)

This study illustrates why two Asian American college students who appear nearly identical might hold widely differing attitudes toward mental health counseling.

Acculturation is directly related to the melting pot. **The melting pot** implies that, over time, cultures should melt down, adding their own flavor and color to the "American soup," while losing their distinguishing features. Many believe this was a thinly disguised way of asserting that minority groups should shed their inferior ways of being and in a generation or two become "White" (Axelson, 1999).

There are ways for culturally different people to live side by side, mix and marry, without losing their cultural integrity. New terminology to describe cultural mixing include the salad or stew metaphor. Cultures remain identifiable, each uniquely contributing to the whole. Of course, no metaphor is perfect, at the societal level nor at the individual level. Cultural identity and even racial identity, at the individual level, can entail unique mixtures and expressions. Take, for example, the famous golfer Tiger Woods, who is African-Indonesian-white American, or Thomas Jefferson's descendants from his wife's half-sister and slave, Sally Hemings, who was half-African, half-white. One branch of Sally's lineage developed a black identity and the other developed a white identity.

Multicultural counselors realize that cultural identity isn't static and that racial identity and affiliation cannot be assumed by glancing at skin color or eye shapes. However, culturally sensitive counselors also realize that client behavior can be greatly influenced by being a minority within a dominant culture. Family functioning and identity also can be challenged and severely stressed when second-generation members assume values and practices of the dominant culture (Ferrer-Wreder, Palchuk, Poyrazli, Small, & Domitrovich, 2008).

Practicing multicultural counseling involves following your clients' multicultural lead; this requires sensitivity and flexibility. For instance, consider the case of Jake, a young man from the Crow Indian Reservation in Montana. Jake was a busy physician who was having trouble relating to his son. His counselor asked about tribal affiliation, and Jake stated he was 75% Crow but that he "wasn't traditional." Jake claimed that being Crow was unrelated to his difficulties. A careful inquiry into what Jake meant by these statements revealed deeply conflicted feelings Jake had about the many cultures (Crow, medical professional, and father) to which he belonged and the pressures he was experiencing.

Even when clients insist their cultural background is irrelevant, it's wise to keep an open mind. Insisting on working directly with cultural material or conflicts is inadvisable, but awareness of potential cultural issues is informative.

Be Aware of Individualist versus Collectivist Orientations

A common dialectic in the multicultural literature is the individualist versus collectivist worldview (Rubin, Milanov, & Paolini, 2016). **Individualist** cultures, like the dominant U.S. culture, place enormous value on individual personal liberty and self-interest. Autonomy is regarded as a virtue and personality is viewed as separate from family and culture.

In **collectivist** cultures, values and norms are shared. The self and the personality are defined in terms of group memberships, and group needs and values are more central than the individual. Collectivists tend to evaluate themselves based on attaining group goals, whereas individualists orient toward individual responsibility and personal goals (Fouad & Arredondo, 2007; D. W. Sue & Sue, 2016).

Although individualism still dominates, theorists within Western culture point to problems with this orientation. Robert Hogan wrote,

A central theme in Western European history for about 800 years has been the decline of the medieval synthesis or, alternatively, the emergence of individualism. Two hundred years ago individualism was a moral and religious ideal capable of legitimizing revolutions and inspiriting sober and thoughtful minds. Sometimes in the last century, however, social thinkers began to regard individualism in more ambivalent terms, even in some cases as a possible indicator of social decay. (1975, p. 533)

If you have an individualist perspective, you may not perceive any difficulties with such a perspective. However, to push the nondominant point further, we offer another comment critical of individualism.

The defining mark of contemporary American culture is the celebrated idea of liberty without limits. Freedom is cast in purely individualistic terms, there being no notion of, nor respect for, the common good. The individual is entitled to do exactly as he pleases, short of the most blatant and egregious violation of another person's rights. There is endless talk of the rights of the individual, but nary a word spoken of any concomitant responsibilities. Right and wrong are relative, having no discernible objective reference or content. That which burdens the individual is seen as unfair, and anything that restricts choices is condemned. This is the heart and soul of the new freedom. It is also the heart and soul of our psychological and social disorders. (Donohue, 1990, p. 221)

Just as therapists with individualist values may have trouble understanding clients with collectivist values, clients with collectivist values may not see the need to focus on themselves; they may not value setting personal goals. They could see a critique of family members as a critique of themselves.

Bicultural clients and clients who are second-generation U.S. citizens may struggle with how to juggle newly discovered individualist desires while honoring their family's wishes and/or original cultural practices. For example, Native American college students may be attending college because of their own personal ambitions or they may be attending to bring honor to their family or tribe. Perhaps on some days they're in touch with their personal academic goals, but other days they're more in touch with their familial or tribal academic goals. Trying to balance and sort out conflicting values can cause clients personal and familial distress.

Make Cultural Adaptations

Multicultural counselors know their limits and seek consultation, supervision, and additional training when needed and proactively. **Cultural adaptation** occurs when therapists "incorporate culture specific variables and factors into specific treatment strategies, thereby making them more culturally relevant" (D. W. Sue & Sue, 2016, p. 757). For example, Hays (2016) recommended using experts for consultation. In the following excerpt, she described how a white therapist named Kate used a consultant in her work with a Muslim couple (Mouna and Majid):

The consultant told Kate that although it was likely (considering the couple's more recent immigration, Majid's strong Muslim identity, and the current political climate) that the couple disagreed with U.S. policies, it was also possible that they did not. The consultant explained that although more recently immigrated Arabs and Muslims tend to be less satisfied with U.S. foreign policy, up until the 1980s the majority of Arab Americans were Republican and tended toward assimilation into the dominant culture.... The consultant reminded Kate that there can be just as much diversity in the way Arab and Muslim people see the world and themselves as there is between ethnic and religious cultures. She encouraged Kate to continue her reading and look for community events at which she might meet a wide variety of Arab and Muslim people. (p. 164)

Consultation can be crucial. You can't be expected to know how to work effectively with every minority group on the planet. For most U.S. counselors and psychotherapists, working directly with a Muslim couple from Tunisia would require special preparation.

In addition to consultation, other cultural adaptations are associated with positive treatment outcomes (Griner & Smith, 2006; Smith, Rodriguez, & Bernal, 2011). In a meta-analysis of 65 studies, Smith and colleagues (2011) reported that when therapists make more cultural adaptations, outcomes are more positive. They recommended:

1. Align treatment with client culture, especially when clients are less acculturated.

2. Conduct therapy in the client's native or preferred language.

3. Make efforts to align therapy with client culture (the general effort may be more important than the specific procedures).

4. Adapt therapy approaches to client's specific cultural background/values. This might involve using metaphors or symbols that match the client's worldview (this summary was adapted from J. Sommers-Flanagan & Sommers-Flanagan, 2017, p. 422).

Practice Cultural Humility

Previously we described cultural competence. Over the past decade, cultural humility has been operationalized as an additional factor contributing to positive outcomes (Davis et al., 2016; Hook & Watkins, 2015). Cultural humility is related to the idea that individuals from dominant cultures may have a natural tendency to view their cultural perspective as right, good, and sometimes as superior. If therapists inherently view their culture as superior, this sense of superiority might override multicultural competence and contribute to poorer outcomes. To practice cultural humility, clinicians need to let go of their own cultural superiority and value the different perspective of their clients (Hook, Davis, Owen, Worthington, & Utsey, 2013).

Cultural humility is defined as:

1. Having an other-orientation instead of a self-orientation.

2. Holding respect for others and their values and ways of being.

3. Exhibiting an attitude that includes a lack of superiority.

Cultural humility is viewed as a supplement to multicultural competence. Cultural humility appears to independently contribute to clinician effectiveness. In a recent research study, cultural humility was identified as mediating or softening the effects of rupture in the counseling relationship (Davis et al., 2016). Previous researchers reported that when clients viewed therapists as more culturally humble, they endorsed higher working alliance ratings and perceived themselves as having better outcomes (Hook et al., 2013).

Learn Multicultural Therapy Skills

S. Sue (1998) identified three specific skills indicative of cross-cultural therapeutic competency:

1. *Scientific mindedness*: Therapists who use scientific mindedness form hypotheses about clients rather than jumping to premature conclusions. These therapists also test their initial hypotheses about minority clients and then act on the basis of the data they obtain, not their prejudices or prejudgments.

2. *Dynamic sizing*: Therapists who practice dynamic sizing know when to generalize and be inclusive and when to individualize and be exclusive. They also know when to apply general knowledge about a culture to an individual and when to focus more on the individual than the culture.

3. *Culture-specific expertise*: Culture-specific expertise involves acquiring knowledge about one's own culture and about the client's culture; it also involves the application of that knowledge in a culturally sensitive, nonstereotyping, and effective manner.

Invite Spirituality Back In

In cultures other than Western European, the title of this section would be ludicrous. Spirituality wouldn't be invited back in, because it would never have left. For most indigenous persons and those of Asian, African, or Latin American origin:

> Spirituality is a life force that undergirds our existence in the universe. (D. W. Sue, Bingham, Porche-Burke, & Vasquez, 1999, p. 1064)

In contrast, those reared and educated in the logical positivist psychology domain may find it challenging to be open to client spirituality. For multicultural therapists, being open to and inviting in spirituality isn't optional. Sue and colleagues (D. W. Sue, Bingham, Porche-Burke, & Vasquez, 1999) noted:

> [A] psychology based solely on the separation of science and spirituality and that uses primarily the segmented

and reductionistic tenets of the natural sciences is one that may not be shared by three quarters of the world nor by the emerging culturally diverse groups in the United States. (p. 1065)

If spirituality and psychology are reunited, serious implications for therapists and therapy follow. A psychotherapy that focuses on caring for the client's psychological symptoms fully within the context of the client's spiritual values and beliefs might be a very different psychotherapy. Of course, this chapter isn't the place to learn how to integrate spirituality into counseling; it's just a good place to start thinking about how to be open to a wide range of religious viewpoints. For many clients and therapists there is more to life than behavior change and more to their symptoms than can be addressed with cognitive restructuring. Even existential and humanistic approaches can be seen as missing something essential that many people seek (see Putting It in Practice 13.5).

Multicultural Therapy in Action: Brief Vignettes

The following two case vignettes illustrate applications of multicultural counseling and psychotherapy principles. However, keep in mind that applying these principles isn't a standardized process and these examples are examples, not norms.

Vignette I: Anger Management

Taylor Wind Runner, a 20-year-old Job Corps student studying the electrical trade, was referred for therapy due to problems with anger management. He was a member of the Salish tribe. His scores on the educational achievement test were high and he was doing well in all areas at the Job Corps center. He was required to see a mental health counselor because of three incidents where he used abusive language toward other students.

Taylor was open and honest about his problem.

Taylor: People here are stupid and they piss me off. It's not all my fault though. You wouldn't believe the stupid things people say here.

Counselor: Actually, I've heard lots of stories about lots of people saying stupid things here. It's amazing. I'd like to hear your stories if you're willing to tell me.

Taylor: It's mostly stupid racist stuff.

Counselor: I'm sorry to hear that. I imagine that would feel very bad, but I can't exactly know what it feels like. You can give me an example if you'd like, but you don't have to.

Taylor: I don't mind.

Counselor: What sorts of things are they saying?

Taylor: One guy came up to me yesterday and asked: "Why do Indians eat dogs." He thought he was funny. I started yelling and I threatened him and then I got in trouble.

Counselor: So this guy comes up to you and he thinks he's being funny, but he's being rude and racist.

Taylor: Yeah. I don't think I should have to put up with that here.

Counselor: You're absolutely right. We've got rules here about no racist talk. That's unacceptable.

Taylor: Well nothing ever happens to these guys ... so I take care of it myself.

PUTTING IT IN PRACTICE

13.5 A Dangerous Assignment

This homework assignment is from the book *Favorite Counseling and Therapy Homework Assignments* (Breggin, 2001, pp. 58–59).

Based on the therapy principle, "Do unto others as you would have others do unto you," I rarely assign homework to my clients....

There is, however, one exception: a homework assignment that I guarantee will improve my clients' lives and the lives of almost everyone they touch. If only as an experiment for a week or two, I suggest that they try being nice to everyone they meet. I explain, "Before we get together again, try being courteous and kind to everyone you deal with, even people you find unworthy or aggravating."

Some religions speak of greeting the God within each person we meet; the Quakers talk about addressing "that of God" which is in other people with respect and even reverence. Naturally, like most of us, my clients are tempted to dismiss "being nice" as utopian, unmanly, embarrassing, and even dangerous. Rarely does anyone gratefully declare, "That's a great idea, Peter. An application of universal truths to my personal life. I can't wait to put it into action."

Counselor: I've heard you say some pretty nasty things back sometimes. I guess it's like basketball … one guy does something dirty, a cheap shot, then they always catch the guy who's trying to get even and call a foul on him.

Taylor: That's exactly how it is. The other guy starts it and I get caught. It's totally not fair.

Counselor: You're right about that too. Now it's just a matter of us figuring out how to deal with it.

Taylor: Yeah I know. I've been told we can do some dormitory education or mediation or I can file a complaint, but no way am I doing any of that shit. That just makes things worse.

Counselor: Okay. I hear you. It sounds like you know some of the options, but you don't want any part of that.

Taylor: Yeah.

Counselor: So, if you're okay with this, you and I can work together and talk about what else you can do … in the moment … to handle this without getting in trouble. But I want you to know that I agree with you. It's not your fault. You shouldn't have to deal with it. I wish we could stop these guys from saying racist crap.

Taylor: Yeah, but I always have to deal with it. You can't just make somebody shut up. You know, I've tried and it just doesn't work. You can slam their head into the ground, but people just keep on yapping.

Taylor and his counselor formed an alliance and worked together to help Taylor develop skills for dealing with racism. During their discussion, Taylor came to the conclusion: "People who make stupid racist jokes are ignorant." Then he and his counselor talked about how ignorant people might get educated. Taylor had been physical in the past and had tried using verbal abuse and threats. Both Taylor and the counselor agreed verbal abuse and threats weren't working. Then Taylor came up with the idea of using each racial slur as an opportunity to educate people. Because Taylor was very intelligent, they reframed the problem as an intellectual challenge. The question was: How can Taylor educate students who are uneducated about Indian people? The discussion continued off and on in further sessions. Taylor was empowered to use his brain to work with the counselor to develop programs at the Job Corps on valuing all cultures and all races. In the end, Taylor felt heard, empowered, contributed to cultural education at Job Corps, and graduated.

In this case the counselor listened and empathized with Taylor's situation, but also went further than typical nondirective listening to openly validate Taylor's anger. Validating Taylor's perspective is important because it communicated to Taylor that the counselor was on his side on the racism issue and Taylor's anger wasn't identified as strictly "his" problem. Then, although Taylor decided to make changes in how he approached the situation, they worked together on a social problem Taylor was facing and not a "Taylor problem" that others were facing. Finally, the counselor followed Taylor's lead, using advocacy to empower him to "educate" other students in ways that Taylor found personally and culturally meaningful. The counselor avoided taking over the issue. Instead he was respectful of Taylor's agenda.

Vignette II: What's Good about You?

In collaboration with our colleague Dudley Dana, PhD, we developed an informal self-esteem assessment and intervention activity called "*What's good about you?*" To initiate the activity, the therapist obtains client consent or assent and then says, "I'm going to ask you the same question 10 times. The only rule is that you can't use the same answer twice. So, I'll ask you the same question 10 times, but you have to give me 10 different answers."

The question asked is, "What's good about you?" Most young clients immersed in the dominant culture enjoy the activity and it provides material for discussion. This activity is described in greater detail elsewhere (J. Sommers-Flanagan & R. Sommers-Flanagan, 2007b).

One day when John was working with an Asian American teen, he decided to initiate *What's good about you?*

JSF: Okay. Are you ready for the question?

Client: Yes. I'm ready.

JSF: What's good about you?

Client: (Silence, about 5 seconds.) "I don't want to do this."

JSF: Sure. Absolutely. That's totally fine. We don't have to do this activity or anything in particular in here.

Client: I'm not comfortable with that. I don't talk like that about myself and I don't want to.

JSF: Right. I'm very sorry. I guess this was a dumb idea. I didn't intend to make you uncomfortable.

Client: This is the kind of thing my parents want me to do all the time. They want me to focus on the positive and think happy things and all that crap.

JSF: But it's not really something you want to do.

Client: It's not what Asian people do. My grandmother is totally humble. I don't want to brag about myself. I'd rather be like her.

JSF: Even though your parents want this sort of thing, it doesn't fit with your culture, and you like your grandmother's way of being better anyway.

Client: My parents want me to be more like my friends. They want me to live the happy American life. That doesn't fit for me. I'm more serious and intense.

JSF: There are lots of different thoughts and feelings you're having. You don't want to be the way your parents want you to be ... it doesn't fit for you. You feel attracted to being more humble like your grandma and your Asian culture. But then there's a little feeling of wanting to be a bit more like your friends, too.

Client: Yeah. It's all a big mess, huh?

This case illustrates several points in working with diverse clients.

- John tries using an individualist technique with a client who has collectivist values (a poor idea to start with).

- Rather than pressing forward with an activity that causes a brief rupture (and client discomfort), the process is stopped (Safran & Kraus, 2014).

- John apologizes and expresses interest in the client's perspective.

- As many multicultural writers suggest, the client has multiple identities. He's Asian and he's American. He's a teenager pushing away from his parents' influence and is identifying with his Chinese grandmother's way of being.

The key is to stay open to exploring the client's multiple identities of self and of being part of a collective. He has a variety of mixed feelings and likely needs support as he engages in a bicultural-adolescent identity development process.

CASE PRESENTATION

Shonda was a 19-year-old athlete whose father was half-Latino and whose mother was an enrolled member of the Blackfeet tribe. She came to college on a full-ride basketball scholarship. In high school, Shonda was a local legend, leading her team to three state titles. She was the pride of her tribe and her small town.

College was a different story. Almost on arrival, she got involved with a young man from another tribe and began partying. Her grades slipped; she missed practices or arrived late. Although still occasionally spectacular on the court, she was progressively more inconsistent. Her coach finally contacted Dr. N., a counselor in town known to work successfully with athletes and American Indian families. Shonda's coach insisted that she try counseling; he made the call himself, even offering to accompany Shonda to the first session. Over the telephone he told Dr. N. that Shonda seemed down, unresponsive to guidance, and irritable. When she engaged and asserted herself on the court, it wasn't unusual for her to blow up and get into a shoving match with a teammate. Shonda's coach was worried about her alcohol use.

Comment: Shonda embodied multiple cultural identities. She identified herself as American Indian, but her father's heritage was half-Latino and half European American, and Shonda spoke a little Spanish as well as a little Blackfeet. Besides these racial-ethnic identities, Shonda had a strong identity as an athlete. Athletes, as a cultural group, don't easily admit weakness and don't typically seek counseling (Maniar, Curry, Sommers-Flanagan, & Walsh, 2001). Dr. N., having worked with reluctant athletes before, was aware of this attribute.

Shonda arrived for her first session alone. She immediately told Dr. N. that she didn't want to come, but that she'd rather come herself than have her coach drag her in. After the usual informed consent discussions and after Dr. N. told Shonda what the coach had said, she asked, "But I'm interested in what might bring *you* in to see me, Shonda. From your perspective."

Shonda responded with humor: "My feet brought me, I guess."

Dr. N. laughed, smiled, and said, "Good answer. Sometimes I ask questions in a weird way. My feet brought me here today, too. I'm guessing from what you said before, that your feet just *barely* brought you here today."

Shonda smiled, apparently pleased that Dr. N. liked her joke.

Comment: Dr. N. knew that American Indians often enjoy laughter and joking. Rather than interpreting Shonda's joke as sarcastic hostility, she felt included and trusted with the humor.

Encouraged, Dr. N. decided to get a few cultural cards on the table. She asked, with genuine interest, "I know you played ball for Benton. Are you a member of the Blackfeet tribe?"

Shonda nodded, averting her gaze, but smiling. "Yeah. My mom's from there, and all my folks. But I have cousins who are white and cousins who are very dark. Strange, huh? And my boyfriend's only half, so if we had kids, they wouldn't even meet the quota."

Comment: Dr. N's entry into the cultural arena produced a variety of cultural and personal information and illustrates how a short client disclosure can present a large range of counseling options, such as:

- Shonda's mentioning of the blood quota may be a test for Dr. N. because blood quota is not a well-known issue outside Indian country. How should Dr. N. respond? Should she ignore the blood quota issue? Should she act informed or uninformed? Shonda shares her multiracial identity. Should Dr. N. pursue this area in order to gather more specific information about Shonda's thoughts and feelings about her racial identity?

- When Shonda mentions having "kids" with her boyfriend it might indicate a pregnancy, hope of a pregnancy, and all that becoming pregnant means symbolically and literally. Should Dr. N. directly ask about whether Shonda is pregnant or thinking about getting pregnant?

- Overall, Shonda's openness gave Dr. N. hope for connection. Shonda's averted gaze also may indicate respect (or shyness, or both). Should Dr. N. comment on Shonda's openness?

Dr. N. nodded sympathetically. Her mind was filled with the preceding options. Dr. N. knew that she and Shonda didn't have enough of a relationship to ask directly about underlying issues yet, so she continued listening carefully and stayed with the central content of what Shonda was saying, instead of trying to interpret deeper possibilities.

"Wow. That blood quota controversy is something. I don't know much, but I've been following the news on it a little bit. What do you think?"

"It sucks. In my Native American studies class, the professor compared it to genocide. A planned way to make sure that, pretty soon, there won't be Indians at all."

"Yeah, it's pretty awful. Lots of those policies seem to be more destructive than helpful. And some of the policies are so complicated that you have to come to college to learn more about them. Who's your Native American studies professor?"

"It's Dr. Cleland. He's got Blackfeet in him too. Mostly I like it. But English sucks and I can't even make myself go to my math class."

"Yeah," Dr. N. smiled. "It must be a big adjustment, coming away to college, taking classes you don't like, and keeping up with basketball, all at the same time."

"Nah. My cousin Sidney is here. He introduced me to Derrick. It's been fun. But the coach. He's the one having a problem. I can play ball, if he'll just get off my case."

The Problem (and Strengths) List

Remember that from the multicultural perspective the problems Shonda is facing are not indicators of individual pathology. The problems exist in a sociocultural context and create challenges for Shonda. They include:

- Understanding and managing her multiple identities and how they influence her in positive and less positive ways.

- Dealing with the adjustment to college; this adjustment is historically a big challenge for Native students who feel pressure to represent themselves, their tribes, and their families.

- Shonda is engaging in behaviors (e.g., alcohol use) that may or may not be self-destructive.

Shonda also has several strengths that might help her deal with her challenging situation. These include, but are certainly not limited to:

- Excellent athletic abilities.

- Warm sense of humor and skilled use of humor.

- A strong family connection.

- A strong tribal connection.

Problem Formulation

To this point Dr. N. has been working at establishing a working alliance and on helping Shonda become comfortable in the room. Shonda is responsive, but as soon as Dr. N. mentions "adjustment" and "basketball," Shonda disagrees, asserting that the adjustment is no problem and that her coach is her problem. At this point Dr. N. could directly ask about what the coach does that's a problem, but instead she used a person-centered reflection, rather than aggressively probe for a viewpoint that Shonda doesn't agree with.

"So you've been having fun and the adjustment hasn't been too hard and it sounds like you still want to play ball. It's just the coaching and practice that aren't going well?"

Shonda looked around the office, not immediately responding to Dr. N. She yawned. Then she smiled and asked, "How many times do I need to come in here?"

Comment: It's hard to say whether Dr. N.'s paraphrase fell flat or whether it made Shonda consider a longer-term relationship. Either way, what was important was for Dr. N. to acknowledge that Shonda had choices about therapy.

"I don't know. At this point I haven't even heard anything that makes me think you need therapy. It might be good for you to talk with me about what's happening in your life. But I'm interested in what you think. How about we talk about counseling and whether it might be helpful for you before we make any decisions either way about how many times you should come, or even if you need to come at all. Is that okay with you?"

Comment: Dr. N. stayed open to the possibility that Shonda may not engage in counseling. She also invited collaboration on deciding if counseling could be helpful.

Shonda paused, looking down. Dr. N. sat quietly. Finally, Shonda said, "I don't know. I don't even know if I can stick around here very long. College isn't what I thought it would be."

Comment: Shonda indirectly answered the question by opening up a new area of discussion. It's not unusual for Indian clients (or other clients) to be subtle and indirect in their verbal responses.

Dr. N. glanced at Shonda and looked downward herself for a few seconds before cautiously asking, "What's making it hard for you to want to stick around?"

Shonda fidgeted in the silence that followed. Dr. N. reminded herself to breathe and wait. Shonda was deciding what to say and what not to say, and it was important for that process to be respected. Finally, she said, "It's really stupid. College is okay. It just feels weird. I've been on the res 18 years. I know everybody and everybody knows me. It's home. This isn't home. It's that simple. I like my cousin and I like Derrick, but I miss my mom and my family back home."

Comment: Therapy has now started. Dr. N. shouldn't return to her original question. Shonda answered it indirectly. Now is a time to accept Shonda's offering and gently explore her feelings. Dr. N. should avoid stock questions like, "How do you feel about that?"

"When you put it that way," Dr. N. began, "I get an image of you with some bad feelings on the inside. What about being on the reservation would help make the weird feelings get better?"

"I'd be around my family. I'd know everybody and everybody would know me. There's no strangers on the res. Around here, aside from my cousin and Derrick, everybody's a stranger. Especially my God-damn coach. He's strange."

Comment: In diagnostic terms, Dr. N. might categorize Shonda's description of her experience as separation anxiety. If Dr. N. was behaviorally oriented, she might systematically evaluate Shonda's anxiety symptoms, and then teach her skills for anxiety reduction. In psychodynamic terms, Shonda might be seen as recapitulating her dilemma in the counseling session. The issue is, "Shall I stay here where I feel uncomfortable and anxious, or shall I go away to some place where I'm comfortable and not anxious?"

The problem formulation that makes the most sense at this point is necessarily general. Getting specific or diagnostic would be premature and unhelpful. Shonda is anxious and homesick, both related to adjusting to college. She's is also adjusting to her basketball coach and the change in setting. It would be easy for Dr. N. to try and generalize Shonda's problems: "Hey, did you know that most Indian people who leave the reservation feel incredibly homesick?" or normalize and align with the coach, "Yeah, you know your coach is weird, but really he cares a lot about your well-being." Most likely, neither would be helpful. Continuing to listen in an informed, nonjudgmental manner will be Dr. N's wisest course of action.

Interventions

As the session progressed, Dr. N. engaged Shonda in a brainstorming activity focusing on what might make being at college "feel better" if she decided to stay. During the activity, Dr. N. used humor on occasion (at one point asking Shonda about the possibility of having her family come live in her dorm room). Overall, the session proceeded smoothly. Toward the end Dr. N. asked Shonda if she would come for three more sessions just to sort out whether to stay in college or go home. Shonda agreed and they scheduled an appointment.

Dr. N. didn't assign Shonda homework to complete between sessions. Instead, because the therapy connection was fragile, Dr. N. did some homework herself. She went online to gather information about the reservation where Shonda grew up.

Shonda showed up 15 minutes late for her second session. Neither she nor Dr. N. commented on the lateness. Among some Native Americans there's a concept called Indian time. Indian time means that things happen when they happen. Although Shonda's lateness might reflect Indian time, it also might reflect her ambivalence about therapy. However, interpreting lateness is a bad idea early in therapy with an Indian client. This is also an example of scientific mindedness; Dr. N. has hypotheses about Shonda's lateness, but doesn't come to any conclusions. Dr. N. also chose to open the session with two gifts, one metaphorical and the other edible.

After greeting and as soon as they sat down, Dr. N. opened with, "Hey, Shonda. I picked up a chocolate chip cookie from the bakery down the street. They're pretty good. Would you like one?" Dr. N. handed a small bakery bag to Shonda and pulled an identical bag for herself out of her purse. "I figured with all that basketball practice, you probably get pretty hungry."

"Thanks," Shonda replied. "I love chocolate chip cookies."

"You know, after our talk last time I thought I should find out a little more about what life is like up on your reservation, so I got on the Internet and found a couple of websites that had some information."

"Really? I didn't know my res had a website. What'd you find out?"

"Well, of course there was some info about the Indian Health Services. And I found a little café or bar or something that had a website."

"Yeah. That musta been the Brown Horse Bar and Grill. That's where the drunks hang out."

"Right. Okay, let me check to see if we know some people in common. The Indian Health Services website had a staff directory. Turns out I know a couple of the people."

Comment: Socializing and gift giving are very important in most Indian cultures. Dr. N. wants her therapy office to be a comfortable place for Shonda, so she's making efforts to connect with her and understand her cultural experiences. Typically, if Shonda was on the reservation and feeling distress, she might go talk with an aunt or grandmother and some sort of food would be included in the interaction. Further, knowing people in common is often reassuring for people who feel isolated and in the minority in a new setting.

"So, Shonda, last time we talked about how it feels pretty weird for you to be here, away from the res. Have you had any thoughts or reactions to our conversation from last time?"

"Well yeah," Shonda began, "I kept thinking about the one thing you said about having my family come live in my dorm room. The idea made me feel good. I thought about what it would be like having my mom in my dorm room making me fry bread and waking me up in the morning."

"That sounds like a nice scene. Do you think she'd come down and do the same for me?"

Shonda giggled. "I bet she would. You'd love her fry bread. Everybody loves her fry bread. You know, that's probably why I know everybody on the res, 'cause everybody's had my mom's fry bread."

"How often have you been talking to your mom?" Dr. N. asked.

"About twice a week. Just enough to make me miss her crazy like."

"Well, I guess that totally sucks," Dr. N. offered.

The multiculturally sensitive interventions in this session included:

- Collaborative brainstorming of what will help Shonda be more comfortable at college.

- Humor designed to connect.

- Providing food and eating together.

- Socializing to connect with Shonda's culture and her strengths and familiarity with the reservation.

- Empathy for her missing home.

Overall, Dr. N. is hoping to help Shonda adjust to being with her and in counseling, and this adjustment may eventually generalize to her being at college.

As therapy proceeded, Dr. N. continued working with Shonda using a culture-sensitive frame. She helped Shonda focus on, notice, and change the ways in which she was coping with her homesickness or separation anxiety. Sometimes through humor, and sometimes through more serious but indirect communication, Dr. N. guided Shonda to create a home away from home. This involved joining the campus Native American Club, learning calming and soothing techniques to use instead of alcohol, and developing a support system on and off campus. Shonda's relationship with Derrick continued, and Dr. N. and Shonda talked directly about using birth control, rather than risking a pregnancy that would almost certainly land her back on the reservation. Shonda was able to see that returning to the reservation was an option for her, but that if she decided to return, she wanted to do so intentionally and on her own terms.

Outcomes Measurement

Determining appropriate outcome measures for Shonda is a challenge. There are standardized measures of adjustment. There are also symptom checklists that might be appropriate. As long as Dr. N. uses a culturally sensitive

approach, doesn't take the results too seriously, and employs process and outcomes measurement collaboratively, it would be possible to use virtually any brief outcome measure.

REFLECTIONS

What are your thoughts and reactions to Dr. N.'s therapy approach? How do you suppose Dr. N. introduced herself? Do you think Dr. N. insisted that Shonda call her Dr. N. or that she used her first name?

EVALUATIONS AND APPLICATIONS

Multicultural approaches can be difficult to define and even more difficult to quantitatively evaluate. To date, there is much more qualitative research and anecdotal information than empirical research. The leaning toward anecdotal material in the professional literature may be a function of the utility of stories in understanding and communicating multicultural experiences. In this section we tell the story of how multicultural therapy is viewed from the perspectives of empirical research, gender and sexuality, and spirituality.

Evidence-Based Status

The rational foundation for establishing multicultural or culturally sensitive therapy approaches is unarguable. Taking each client's individual cultural background into consideration is the rational and logical thing to do.

In contrast, the empirical foundation for multicultural therapy is more controversial (G. C. N. Hall, 2001). Problems associated with empirical validation of culturally sensitive treatments are legion. It's hard to imagine how researchers could collect data to support multicultural treatment efficacy. Think about cases involving American Indians, Somali refugees, Asian Americans, or Latino immigrants. How could researchers accurately measure the concerns of all these clients as they enter treatment? In many cases, the client's conception of the problem may be dramatically different from a traditional Western diagnostic label. Further, can you imagine using a manualized treatment approach with a young Latino immigrant suffering from susto? (*Susto* can occur when a frightening incident causes a person's soul to leave his or her body. The result is depression and physical malady. The customary treatment in Mexico and Central America includes ritual healings in which the person's soul is called back to the body.) Even if a manualized treatment was acceptable, could researchers find the right standardized questionnaires to determine treatment efficacy? As with Shonda, although questionnaires might be employed, they should be used collaboratively, for exploratory purposes, and not taken too seriously.

Treatment Outcomes Research

Perhaps due to the preceding challenges, there hasn't been much therapy outcomes research with ethnic-minority clients. In a review of the status of ethnic minorities in treatment outcomes studies, S. Sue and Zane (2009) reported:

> Since 1986, about 10,000 participants have been included in RCTs evaluating the efficacy of treatments for certain disorders. For nearly half of these participants (N = 4,991), no information on race or ethnicity was given. For another 7% of participants (N = 656), studies only reported the general designation "non-white." For the remaining 47% of participants (N = 4,335), very few minorities were included; not a single study analyzed the efficacy of the treatment by ethnicity or race. (p. 331)

Given the lack of research in this area, a more practical and answerable question is this: What therapy situations and counseling skills produce positive outcomes among culturally diverse populations?

Ethnic Matching

Research on **ethnic matching** is equivocal. In some cases ethnic matching seems to have salutatory effects on outcomes, but in other cases it seems unimportant (S. Sue, Fujino, Takeuchi, & Zane, 1991). In their meta-analysis of 76 studies on culturally adapted therapies, Griner and Smith (2006) found an inverse relationship between ethnic matching and positive outcomes.

S. Sue and colleagues also evaluated the relationship of ethnic-specific services on treatment outcomes (Takeuchi, Sue, & Yeh, 1995). **Ethnic-specific services** are defined as treatments that try to respond to the cultural needs of clients (e.g., culturally sensitive greetings are used, Chinese clients are offered tea as well as coffee). Overall, research showed that ethnic clients stay in treatment longer when offered ethnic-specific services. Additional research indicated that clients benefit from a cognitive match, in which the therapist and client use similar ways of identifying goals and resolving problems and have similar degrees of acculturation (S. Sue, 1998).

Cultural Adaptation and Multicultural Training

Research on cultural adaptation as a strategy for improving treatment outcomes is positive. Based on a meta-analysis of 76 studies, Griner and Smith (2006) reported:

- Overall, the effect size from 76 studies was *d* = 0.45 (a positive effect of moderate magnitude).

- Diverse clients who were less acculturated benefited more from cultural adaptations.

- In particular, older Latino/a clients who were less acculturated had very positive outcomes.

- Although general multicultural adaptation was good, specific multicultural adaptation had more positive outcomes.

- Although ethnic matching showed no positive effects (and were generally associated with more negative outcomes) **language matching** (i.e., matching the language of client and provider) produced outcomes twice that of nonlanguage matching.

- Interventions provided in same race groups were approximately four times more effective than interventions provided in mixed race groups.

The effects of multicultural training on therapy outcome are similarly positive. Therapists with greater multicultural competence report higher self-efficacy and treatment outcomes are generally better (T. B. Smith, Rodriguez, & Bernal, 2011). T. B. Smith and colleagues (2006) also reported that multicultural education is linked to more positive educational outcomes.

Overall, the research consistently points to the conclusion that culture, multicultural education and training, and multicultural competence do matter.

Cultural Sensitivity

Multicultural counseling is designed to be culturally and gender sensitive. For instance, in Shonda's case, Dr. N. is an interesting combination of directive and nondirective. She's directive in that she actively explores Shonda's culture, changes her own behavior to connect with Shonda, and asks Shonda challenging questions. However, she's also very nondirective in that she never tells Shonda what she should do or how she should live her life. This combination of directiveness and nondirective respect for Shonda's perspective is multiculturally sensitive. Directiveness, like other counseling techniques and styles, should be calibrated to fit individual and cultural preferences and practices.

Gender and Sexuality

In the world of sexuality, Shonda currently would identify herself as a heterosexual, as would Jake, our angry electrician-in-the-making. Nevertheless, many of the issues these young people will face in life have to do with unfair discrimination that marginalizes them as people and as tribal members. Shared experiences of oppression can sometimes lead to similar struggles and needs.

There's a relatively new approach to working with LGBTQ clients called **affirmative therapy**; this approach includes ideas that can be helpful for working with non-LGBTQ clients (see Putting It in Practice 13.6 for a story about a young therapist who discovers affirmative psychotherapy).

PUTTING IT IN PRACTICE

13.6 Becoming an Affirmative Therapist for LGBTQ Clients

Reproduced with permission of Nick Heck, PhD.

Note: Dr. Heck is an assistant professor of psychology at Marquette University. He wrote this essay when he was a doctoral student at the University of Montana.

To complete a final assignment for my first graduate-level interviewing course, I reviewed a book (Fox, 2006) that described affirmative psychotherapy with bisexual clients. I kept careful notes as I read each chapter and it soon became clear that I had no idea what any of the book's contributors meant when they used the term affirmative psychotherapy. I thought to myself, "How can I become a psychologist who practices affirmative psychotherapy with lesbian, gay, bisexual, and transgender (LGBT) clients when I have no idea what affirmative psychotherapy is?" I needed a definition so I continued to read and search PsychINFO for answers.

Before I share more of my experiences, ask yourself, "What is affirmative psychotherapy?" and "What does it mean to be an affirmative therapist or counselor for LGBTQ clients?" You might be thinking, "Is affirmative psychotherapy a brand of psychotherapy similar to cognitive behavior therapy (CBT) or functional analytic psychotherapy?" That was my assumption, and I knew there had to be interventions specific to this new brand of psychotherapy. Where was the affirmative psychotherapy equivalent to CBT's seven-column thought record for identifying and correcting maladaptive thinking patterns? Where was the affirmative psychotherapy intervention manual? When I read the *Handbook of Counseling and Psychotherapy with Lesbian, Gay, Bisexual and Transgender Clients* (Bieschke, Perez, & DeBord, 2007) I was sure one of the chapters would outline interventions specific to affirmative psychotherapy. That chapter was nowhere to be found.

When I began practicum, everything I thought I knew about psychotherapy went out the window. For example, I had a preconceived notion that after I finished my first intake interview (during which I would administer a semi-structured interview), my supervisor would say, "Your client has [insert disorder X here]. You should read [insert treatment manual for disorder X here]." You may laugh at my naïveté, but that's the impression I had of psychotherapy when I finished my undergraduate studies. I quickly realized that psychotherapy involved more than routinized administration of specific therapeutic interventions. Before I could even think about successfully implementing specific interventions, I would have to learn how to develop a therapeutic relationship with my clients.

To develop relationships with LGBTQ clients, I had to unlearn some "bad habits" that develop as a result of living in a heterosexist society that embraces a dichotomous view of gender. I could no longer make implicit or explicit assumptions about sexual orientation or gender identity. It took time to become comfortable asking a client who has a child, "Is there a second parent in your child's life?" The first time I asked this question, the client simply responded by saying "Yes." I didn't know what to say next; I mean I could have said, "Is this second parent a man or a woman?" but that would have been awkward and invalidating of transgender people.

Later in my second year I co-facilitated a therapy group for transgender clients. In planning to co-facilitate this group, I met regularly with my supervisor to discuss readings related to group therapy and therapy with transgender individuals. Initially, I approached supervision with the same simplistic views that I had when I started seeing clients individually. I envisioned meetings with my supervisor where we would discuss specific readings, but I also thought we would be reviewing treatment manuals to identify specific interventions that might be helpful for working with transgender clients within a group therapy framework.

When speaking about my development (as a therapist in training) at our clinic "graduation," my supervisor shared how she had initially been "apprehensive" in allowing me to co-facilitate a therapy group for transgender clients, because I wouldn't stop talking about empirically supported treatments. Clearly, she recognized that no such treatment existed, and so she helped us become validating, supportive, and affirmative group therapists. As my co-facilitator and I became more confident in our abilities and group cohesion increased, we were eventually able to integrate a greater number of interventions consistent with experiential-process group therapy, as described by Yalom and Leszcz (2005). Supervision, in addition to ongoing reading and self-reflection, challenged and changed my views of gender and helped further my development as an affirmative therapist.

In addition to my group work and supervision experiences, I frequently read (and reread) books and journal articles related to affirmative psychotherapy with LGBT clients. In addition, professional associations have published reports on counseling and psychotherapy with LGBT clients. Some of these include the American Psychological Association's "Guidelines for Psychotherapy with Lesbian, Gay, and Bisexual Clients" (APA, 2000) and the Association of Lesbian, Gay, Bisexual, and Transgender Issues in Counseling's *Competencies for Counseling with Transgender Clients* (ALGBTIC, 2009). I also joined APA's Division 44 (Society for the Psychological Study of Lesbian, Gay, Bisexual, and Transgender Issues), which offers a Listserv with LGBT practice, research, and policy information.

Not long ago, a request came across the Listserv asking when the term "gay affirming" emerged and for the original definition and description of LGBT affirmative psychotherapy. Senior LGBT scholars replied and directed the member toward a special edition of the *Journal of Homosexuality* that contained the seminal article on affirmative psychotherapy. For those of you interested, you should read Alan Malyon's 1982 article titled, "Psychotherapeutic Implications of Internalized Homophobia in Gay Men." I truly wish someone had directed me to this article earlier in my career and I hope it will help you begin (or continue) your journey toward becoming an LGBT affirmative therapist.

Spirituality

As noted previously, **spirituality**, the belief in a higher interconnecting power, is a natural part of multicultural therapy. The main challenge for traditional clinicians is to discern how to integrate spirituality in ways that contribute to, rather than detract from, therapy process and outcome. Research on spirituality and psychotherapy can provide foundational guidance.

In a meta-analysis of 46 studies and 3,290 clients, Worthington, Hook, Davis, and McDaniel (2011) reported that clients who received religious or spiritually oriented therapy experienced greater improvements than clients who received secular-only therapy. The differences were small, but they were obtained on psychological, as well as spiritual, outcome measures.

Worthington et al. (2011) summarized their results and recommendations:

- Religious or spiritually oriented therapy is effective, at least in the short run, and there are possibly long-term positive effects.

- When religious or spiritual concepts are integrated in therapy with clients who desire religious or spiritual accommodation, spiritual well-being outcomes are enhanced.

- Whether to integrate spiritual or religious content into therapy should be done based on the "desires and needs of the client" (Worthington et al., 2001, p. 212; adapted from J. Sommers-Flanagan & Sommers-Flanagan, 2017).

Overall, similar to recommendations for using assessment with diverse clients, whether and how to integrate religious or spiritual content should flow from collaborative discussions. There may be religious perspectives that practitioners find more or less challenging to integrate, but the effectiveness of integrating spirituality with diverse clients will likely be a function of collaborative agreement. When agreement occurs, it's likely that integrating spirituality will deepen the process and improve outcomes.

REFLECTIONS

Outcomes research with multicultural populations is lacking. As a budding researcher and practitioner, how would you address this issue? Try to think of a thesis or dissertation that focuses on outcomes research with a minority group.

CONCLUDING COMMENTS

Conceptually, multicultural theory is simple. What could be simpler than a theoretical stance pointing out that culture is central in human development and human perception? However, as D.W. Sue et al. (1999) stated unequivocally, multicultural theory isn't value neutral. In fact, the theory itself entails a belief in social justice. Harvard philosopher John Rawls (1971) proposed that social justice could be achieved only if we chose our social policies from behind a veil of ignorance so that we could not know where or who we might be in the society for which we were making the rules. We might be white, black, poor, rich, prematurely disabled, male, female, old, young, and so on. If we had absolutely no way of knowing where we would step into life, what would we consider the best social policy?

Many argue that even Rawls gets it wrong because his system insinuates that humans achieving a consensus will then fail to take into account minority views (Tjeltveit, 1999), and, of course, such a veil is impossible. We can only approximate understanding the experiences of other people, and we can never rid ourselves of our own cultural identities. The best we can hope for is a rich understanding of ourselves as members of our cultural communities and a constantly evolving appreciation and understanding of other cultures, other values, and other people.

CHAPTER SUMMARY AND REVIEW

Culture is ubiquitous; therefore, all approaches to counseling and psychotherapy must address cultural issues. Culture, multiculturalism, and multicultural therapy are all relatively new to the counseling and psychotherapy scene. Understanding these terms and pursuing cultural knowledge is crucial to successful therapy. These terms also contain political baggage.

Throughout the world and in the United States there's a long history of cultural oppression. In many cases when people are different they're labeled deviant and treated with disrespect and discrimination.

The passing of the Civil Rights Act in 1964 opened up greater opportunities for cultural minorities. Subsequently, groups with racial and cultural interests were formed (e.g., the Association for Black Psychologists). More recently, additional growth and development in

multicultural thinking has resulted in many organizations supporting gender issues, including publication of the "Guidelines for Psychotherapy with Lesbian, Gay, and Bisexual Clients" (APA, 2000) and the ALGBTIC *Competencies for Counseling with Transgender Clients* (ALGBTIC, 2009). There are now many multicultural and diversity leaders within counseling and psychology.

Multicultural theory has three underlying principles. These include: (1) cultural membership is linked to disadvantage and privilege; (2) we make distinctions between groups of people based on race, religion, sex, sexual orientation, ethnicity, physical and mental disabilities, and socioeconomic status; and (3) a multiculturalist stance can foster greater understanding between cultural groups and facilitate egalitarian treatment of all humans. Flowing from these principles, like feminist theory, a multicultural perspective doesn't locate psychopathology within the individual. Instead, psychopathology is a function of oppressive social forces.

The multicultural competencies are foundational to multiculturally sensitive practice. The recently revised competencies include: (a) *counselor self-awareness*, (b) counselor knowledge of client worldview, (c) the counseling relationship, and (d) culturally appropriate counseling advocacy interventions.

In the past, assessment and diagnosis have been used with minority clients in ways that were insensitive or abusive. As a consequence, assessment and diagnosis with minority clients should proceed collaboratively and with caution, sometimes talking with clients about cultural differences and always avoiding overgeneralizations and stereotyping. Multiculturally sensitive therapists should also: (a) understand acculturation, (b) be aware of individualist versus collectivist orientations, (c) make cultural adaptations (especially language-matching when indicated), (d) practice cultural humility, (e) learn multicultural therapy skills, and (f) be open to spirituality.

Evaluating the efficacy and effectiveness of multicultural approaches is challenging. Historically, counseling and psychotherapy researchers have not conducted many efficacy or effectiveness studies focusing on cultural, gender, or disability variables. Gathering more research data on these important variables is a challenge for the future. A multicultural counseling orientation is inherently sensitive to client gender, sexuality, and spirituality.

MULTICULTURAL KEY TERMS

Acculturation (aka ethnocultural orientation)

ADDRESSING

Affirmative therapy

Assimilated

Bicultural

Collectivist

Color-blind phenomenon

Cultural adaptation

Cultural knowledge

Cultural self-awareness

Culture

Culture-specific expertise

Drapetomania

Dynamic sizing

Dysaethesia

Ethnic matching

Ethnic-specific services

Individualist

Language matching

Marginal

Multicultural competencies

Multicultural counseling

Multiculturalism

Pan-traditional

Scientific mindedness

Social justice

Spirituality

Stereotype

Susto

The melting pot

Traditional

What's good about you?

White privilege

CHAPTER 14

Psychotherapy and Counseling Integration

LEARNER OBJECTIVES

- Define the four types of psychotherapy integration
- Identify key figures and historical trends in the development, evolution, and application of technical eclecticism, common factors, theoretical integration, and assimilative integration approaches
- Describe core principles of eclectic, common factors, theoretical integration, and assimilative integration approaches
- Describe strategies and techniques associated with eclectic and integrative approaches to counseling and psychotherapy
- Evaluate the empirical status of third wave therapies
- Summarize core content and define key terms associated with psychotherapy integration and third wave therapies

The future is always connected to the past, through a road we call the present. In this chapter, we use the past to springboard into the contemporary emphasis on psychotherapy or counseling integration. We examine seven psychotherapy systems. Each of these systems is multi-theoretical, practical, and evidence-based. As such, each contributes to the future of counseling and psychotherapy, both as art and science.

INTRODUCTION

At this point in studying theories of counseling and psychotherapy, it's easy to feel like throwing up your hands and shouting, "Enough!"

That would be an understandable response, but there's still work to be done. The exciting, but sometimes daunting, truth is, there always will be. This chapter will help you put things together (for now) and glimpse the possibilities of counseling and psychotherapy integration.

One Theory or Many?

Early researchers and practitioners engaged in heated disputes over which approach counseling or psychotherapy was best. Whether it was Freud rising to push out Adler, or Wolpe and the behaviorists opposing the cognitive movement, or de Shazer burying resistance in his backyard, or feminist therapists rejecting patriarchal dominance—friction and conflict have been the norm. Looking back on early conflicts among theorists, Parloff referred to it as a "dogma eat dogma" world. Everyone wanted everyone else to see things their way.

Disagreements over how to best do psychotherapy continue. Some authors have reported over a thousand different counseling and psychotherapy theories (Consoli, Beutler, & Bongar, 2017; Lebow, 2008). Why so many? We have two main explanations: individuality/cultural specificity and human conflict.

Individuality/Cultural Specificity

Every individual is unique. One size does not fit all. There's truth to both cultural universality and cultural specificity. These are all parts of the psychology of individual differences. We're like snowflakes; even identical twins experience the world differently. How could we expect uniformity in counseling and psychotherapy theory and practice?

Imagine how you would explain your particular counseling approach to a Wyoming cattle rancher. Imagine doing the same for a Wall Street stockbroker or Syrian refugee or transgender teen. Considering these diverse perspectives gives us a glimpse of why having a single system to explain everything might eventually break down. Values imbedded within different cultural and subcultural perspectives will always influence whether contemporary therapy is viewed as a valuable service, witchcraft, hocus-pocus, a waste of time, a growth opportunity, or a final act of desperation. Integrating many theoretical perspectives gives us a better chance of addressing the real needs of real people in the real world.

Human Conflict

So far, you've learned about 12 relatively distinct theoretical approaches to therapy. Do you have a favorite? Do your classmates have the same favorite? We'd wager that we could call 12 different friends together (some of whom we've cited in the preceding chapters) and start a heated debate over which theory is best.

Although many people like to avoid conflict, conflict can lead to positive transformations. If people approach differences with mutual respect and a willingness to learn, a good debate can stimulate creative thought and synthesis. Consider the following:

- In 1896 Freud was ostracized for suggesting that sexual abuse was at the roots of hysteria. Freud later recanted the seduction hypothesis, but along the way he developed a fascinating (but flawed) theory of human personality and psychotherapy.

- In 1911 Adler had the audacity to suggest that women wanted equal power (and not penises). For that insight, Freud and his psychoanalytic cronies sent Adler packing; he quickly established his own professional society.

- In the late 1920s Adler dismissed Frankl from his study group. One would have hoped that Adler, so empathic toward the oppressed and working-class citizens, wouldn't have squelched alternative viewpoints, but history and humans often disappoint. Frankl rose like a phoenix after World War II, championing *meaning* as central to psychotherapy and human development.

- In the 1920s and 1930s Karen Horney wrote forcefully about the neglected feminine voice in psychoanalysis. Instead of submitting to proper authority, she entered into conflict with her colleagues. Her influence was substantial.

- When rebuffed by Freud in 1936, Fritz Perls didn't slip away into obscurity. Instead, he emerged with the attitude, "I'll show you—you can't do this to me" and, along with Laura, became remarkably influential (F. Perls, 1969b, p. 57).

- In the 1950s and 1960s Carl Rogers didn't bow down to B. F. Skinner, and Skinner didn't bow down to Rogers. Their debates still stimulate productive conversations.

- In the 1960s and continuing into the present, second, third, and fourth wave feminist therapists have reshaped counseling and psychotherapy in ways that honor and empower females and oppressed minorities.

- In the 1970s behaviorists, including Joseph Wolpe, threatened to exile cognitivists, such as Beck, Goldfried, Meichenbaum, and Mahoney, from behavior therapy. This brush with exile proved fruitful, as a new journal, *Cognitive Therapy and Research*, was born.

- In the 1980s multicultural perspectives became prominent, sometimes clashing with the established hegemony. These perspectives helped integrate cultural awareness, knowledge, skills, and advocacy into therapy process (D. W. Sue & Sue, 2016).

- As you'll see later in this chapter, in the 1990s Francine Shapiro's Eye Movement Desensitization Reprocessing (EMDR) received sharp criticism. Fortunately, instead of wilting, Shapiro worked to validate her treatment approach.

Conflicts about how to best conduct counseling and psychotherapy have contributed to the depth and breadth of the approaches available today. Adler, Jung, Frankl, Horney, Perls, Mahoney, Meichenbaum, feminists, multicultural advocates, Shapiro, and many others didn't go quietly into the night. Instead, the history of psychotherapy theory is replete with examples of how conflict and rejection are great motivators. We hope your future debates with your classmates, professors, and eventual colleagues are equally illuminating and productive.

REFLECTIONS

Is conflict inevitable? Would we have attained the theoretical diversity and sophistication we now have in counseling and psychotherapy without intense arguments, debates, division, and conflict?

What Is Psychotherapy (or Counseling) Integration?

Psychotherapy or counseling integration is the effort to move beyond individual theoretical systems; it involves bringing together diverse theories, models, strategies, and techniques. There are four main psychotherapy integration subtypes (Norcross, Goldfried, & Zimmerman, 2017): technical eclecticism, theoretical integration, common factors, and theoretical assimilation. These subtypes are defined in the next section.

PSYCHOTHERAPY INTEGRATION: HISTORICAL AND THEORETICAL TRENDS

Five options are available for practicing ethical, theory-based counseling and psychotherapy:

1. Ideological purity.

2. Theoretical integration.

3. Common factors.

4. Technical eclecticism.

5. Assimilative integration.

Having 1,000+ options available to you might lead you to seek the security of a single theoretical model. If so, you won't be alone. Many practitioners embrace one model and have excellent outcomes.

Ideological Purity

Ideological purity involves studying and learning one therapy model and striving to apply it ethically and competently. Ideological purity emphasizes depth over breadth. It's appealing in a practical sense; it allows you to become a master of one approach, rather than a jack-of-all-trades. It can ease ambiguities inherent in practicing therapy.

Taken to an extreme, ideological purity can turn into dogmatism. As can be seen throughout history, one can close off alternative ways of thinking and practicing. The underlying message of the ideological dogmatist is this: I've found my theoretical orientation, I live by its tenets, and I treat it as sacred and unalterably true.

Even in today's diverse world, many professionals are ideological purists—they practice one form of therapy and practice it well. Judith Beck's description of why she's a cognitive therapist (see Chapter 8) is an excellent example of ideological purity (but not dogmatism). Practicing as an ideological purist, or specialist, is still a reasonable alternative; it requires focus, knowing your limitations, and sometimes practicing within a specialized area (e.g., eating disorders, trauma, substance dependence).

Theoretical Integration

Theoretical integration involves combining two or more theoretical approaches to maximize therapeutic effectiveness. London (1986) elegantly called theoretical integration, "theory smushing." It also involves combining theoretically diverse technical interventions. Initial theoretical integrations usually involved weaving together psychoanalytic and behavior therapies.

Norcross and colleagues (2017) referred to early efforts at integration as representing a latent process that didn't become more active until the 1980s. Thomas French (1933) may have been the first to try to integrate psychoanalysis and classical conditioning. His effort was not especially well received (Norcross et al., 2017). In 1950, Dollard and Miller published *Personality and Psychotherapy: An Analysis in Terms of Learning, Thinking, and Culture*. This book was an impressive effort at integrating psychoanalytic and behavioral principles. French was ahead of his time, and so were Dollard and Miller.

During the ensuing 20 to 25 years, only a few select theorists discussed theoretical integration (Alexander, 1963; London, 1964). The next major effort at integration was Wachtel's (1977) publication of *Psychoanalysis and Behavior Therapy: Toward an Integration*.

Common Factors

Adherents to the **common factors** perspective value the overlapping or key ingredients that different theoretical orientations share (Norcross et al., 2017). If you recall from Chapter 1, common factors that contribute to positive therapy outcomes include, but are not limited to: (a) the therapy relationship or alliance, (b) positive expectations or hope, and (c) extratherapeutic client resources.

Early writings on common factors began to appear in the literature in the 1930s. Rosenzweig (1936), claimed that three factors contributed to psychotherapy effectiveness across all models: (a) hope, (b) interpretations that made client problems more understandable, and (c) the synergistic nature of change (Norcross et al., 2017). Somewhat later, Alexander and French (1946) articulated their overarching concept of **corrective emotional experience**:

> In all forms of ... psychotherapy, the basic therapeutic principle is the same: To re-expose the patient, under more favorable circumstances, to emotional situations which he could not handle in the past. The patient, in order to be helped, must undergo a corrective emotional experience suitable to repair the traumatic influence of previous experiences. (p. 66)

REFLECTIONS

Consider Alexander and French's corrective emotional experience concept. How does it fit for exposure therapies? How well does it explain skills training for assertive behavior? What about feminist and multicultural models?

Jerome Frank (1961, 1973; J. D. Frank & J. B. Frank, 1991) developed a comprehensive common factors model of psychotherapy. He wrote:

> All psychotherapeutic methods are elaborations and variations of age-old procedures of psychological

healing. These include confession, atonement and absolutions, encouragement, positive and negative reinforcements, modeling, and promulgation of a particular set of values. These methods become embedded in theories as to the causes and cures of various conditions which often become highly elaborated. (Frank, 1985, pp. 10–11)

Frank's (1961) study of historical and intercultural healing processes shaped his model, which still has relevance for therapists.

The Demoralization Hypothesis

Not only are there common factors of effective therapy, but people who come for therapy are also experiencing a common form of distress. He referred to this distress as the **demoralization hypothesis**:

Demoralization occurs when, because of lack of certain skills or confusion of goals, an individual becomes persistently unable to master situations which both the individual and others expect him or her to handle or when the individual experiences continued distress which he or she cannot adequately explain or alleviate. Demoralization may be summed up as a feeling of subjective incompetence, coupled with distress. (Frank, 1985, p. 17)

Frank (J. D. Frank & J. B. Frank, 1996) identified several demoralization symptoms, including low self-esteem, anxiety, sadness, and hopelessness. These symptoms are often the initial targets of therapy.

Shared Therapeutic Components

Frank (1961) defined the following shared therapeutic components.

- **An emotionally charged, confiding relationship**: Contemporary practitioners usually refer to this component as the therapeutic relationship or working alliance (Bordin, 1979; Norcross & Lambert, 2011).

- **A healing setting**: The setting elevates the therapist's prestige and provides a sense of safety.

- **A rationale, conceptual scheme, or myth**: Clients need a plausible explanation for their symptoms and for the treatment approach to be used. Explaining the therapy rationale to clients is crucial.

- **A ritual**: Clients (and therapists) need a process or ritual they both believe will bring about a cure or improved functioning.

Frank used the terms myth and ritual to convey universal dimensions of therapeutic approaches across cultures:

All therapeutic myths and rituals, irrespective of differences in specific content, have in common

functions that combat demoralization by strengthening the therapeutic relationship, inspiring expectations of help, providing new learning experiences, arousing the patient emotionally, enhancing the sense of mastery or self-efficacy, and affording opportunities for rehearsal and practice. (Frank, 1985, p. 22)

REFLECTIONS

Recall Lambert's common therapy factors from Chapter 1. How do you think they match up with Frank's formulations?

Technical Eclecticism

Technical eclecticism involves using logic and empirical data to choose the best treatment for a specific person with a specific problem. Practitioners who use technical eclecticism may or may not subscribe to the underlying theories. The multimodal approach of Lazarus (1989, 1997) discussed below is a good technical eclectic prototype.

Some professionals avoid singular theoretical commitments. Instead, these therapists choose one technique for one client, but use a different technique with the next. They might consider using two theoretically diverse techniques for a single client without concern for theoretical compatibility. Their selection of a particular therapy technique is usually based on one of three factors: (1) empirical research, (2) what's practical for the situation, or (3) clinical intuition. This approach is referred to as "eclectic." More disparagingly, one of our supervisors used to call it "flying by the seat of your pants."

Eclecticism has been lauded and criticized over the years. Despite occasional criticism, researchers typically find that an eclectic or integrative orientation is most common for every category of mental health therapist (clinical and counseling psychologists, counselors, social workers, and psychiatrists; Norcross, Karg, & Prochaska, 1997). More recently, practitioners appear to prefer integrative over eclectic (Norcross, Karpiak, & Lister, 2005).

In 1970 Esyenck referred to eclecticism as a "mishmash of theories, a hugger-mugger of procedures, a gallimaufry of therapies" (p. 145). Of course, it's ironic that Eysenck said this because in his famous 1952 psychotherapy efficacy review he identified 7,293 cases treated by eclectic means with a 64% "cure" or recovery rate. Perhaps what's most interesting in Eysenck's original review is that eclectic psychotherapy treatment was evaluated nearly 10 times as often as were other approaches, suggesting this "hugger-mugger of procedures" was remarkably common long before it was overtly fashionable.

Good and Bad Eclecticism

More recently, there has been a distinction made between "bad" (seat-of-the-pants) eclecticism and

---

| PUTTING IT IN PRACTICE |

14.1 Eclecticism Requires Expertise in Multiple Domains

A colleague of ours who worked as a rehabilitation counselor told us that in her first job interview, she was asked if she had a single theoretical orientation or if she was eclectic. The expected answer was eclectic. She later discovered her new boss believed adherence to a single theory was a sign of intellectual weakness and applied laziness. He insisted that his counselors display person-centered attributes, be comfortable with cognitive behavioral strategies, be aware of and sensitive to feminist and multicultural theory, and be well versed in many career and human development theories and assessment strategies. He also insisted on a well-articulated treatment rationale and encouraged counselors to pay attention to what worked and why. This wasn't an office for the theoretically faint of heart. In this setting, eclectic meant "you'd better know quite a bit about quite a lot and pay attention to what works."

"good" (empirical and/or planful) eclecticism. Lazarus, Beutler, and Norcross (1992) commented on therapy approaches blended together in "an arbitrary, subjective, if not capricious manner" (p. 11). When one chooses therapy techniques in a whimsical, unreasoned, or impulsive manner, it's called **syncretism** (Lazarus et al., 1992, p. 12). As one of our colleagues who thinks he's funny says, "Sometimes counselors mix up the words eclectic and electric—they think they can just do whatever turns them on" (Richardson, personal communication, November 2002).

Behavioral theory and therapy may be the most flexible of all theoretical orientations. Behaviorists practice therapy based on scientific research and observable processes. Their interest isn't in a static theory, but in what has been tested in the laboratory and demonstrated as effective in the real world. This makes behaviorists naturally eclectic. Consequently, it's not surprising that initial movements toward technical eclecticism came from the behavioral camp.

The Who–How–Whom Question
In 1969 Gordon Paul posed the following question to his behavioral colleagues: "What treatment, by whom, is most effective for this individual with that specific problem, under which set of circumstances, and how does it come about?" (p. 44). This question, sometimes referred to as **the who–how–whom question**, provides a solid rationale for technical eclecticism. It is consistent with matching specific therapy approaches with specific clients (and specific problems)—a goal that's openly endorsed by eclectic therapists. This approach is also consistent in principle with the medical model and the proliferation of psychiatric diagnosis and empirically supported treatment procedures. A main purpose of the *Diagnostic and Statistical Manual of Mental Disorders* (DSM) is to identify specific mental disorder entities that are best ameliorated

through the application of specific (often pharmacological) treatments.

What Is Assimilative Integration?
Assimilative integration involves a committed allegiance to one primary theoretical orientation, along with an openness to selectively incorporating or assimilating techniques or procedures from other systems (Norcross, Goldfried, & Zimmerman, 2017). An example is the person-centered therapist willing to incorporate self-monitoring homework and, as appropriate, solution-focused questions.

Practitioners who embrace psychotherapy integration share the belief that there's more than one mechanism of therapeutic change. For example, let's say Roberta, a pure (and novice) existential therapist, considers self-awareness as the prerequisite for client change. As Roberta gains experience and knowledge, she opens herself up to different change mechanisms. She wants to do more work with traumatized clients, so she obtains training in narrative exposure therapy (NET). Although NET includes exploration of the past and experiential components, insight isn't required. The mechanism(s) of healing aren't clearly known. The NET training and subsequent experiences with clients open Roberta to the principle of narrative, exposure, and the resulting desensitization as a change mechanism. Consequently, she assimilates NET into her practice and later becomes open to other procedures that may or may not facilitate client awareness. She has taken the first step and adopted assimilative integration. Later, she may progress into a full-fledged theoretical integrationist.

THE PRACTICE OF INTEGRATIVE THERAPIES: EARLY MODELS

Multimodal therapy and interpersonal psychotherapy are two early examples of integrative therapy.

Multimodal Therapy: The Technical Eclecticism of Arnold Lazarus

Multimodal therapy (MMT) was developed by Arnold Lazarus and is a technically eclectic approach that uses a pan-theoretical model for assessment and intervention. Lazarus has been a prolific and controversial clinician and writer for more than 50 years. He coined the term "technical eclecticism" in 1967, noting that,

> To attempt a theoretical rapprochement is as futile as trying to picture the edge of the universe. But to read through the vast amount of literature on psychotherapy, *in search of techniques*, can be clinically enriching and therapeutically rewarding. (Lazarus, 1967, p. 416)

Lazarus has not been interested in blending theories; as a self-identified behaviorist, he's only interested in practical application of approaches that are helpful to his clients.

Lazarus also has an opinion about why technical eclecticism is preferable to theoretical purity. In 1971, he claimed,

> [T]he most essential ingredients for an effective psychotherapist are *flexibility* and *versatility*. This implies

an ability to play many roles and to use many techniques in order to fit the therapy to the needs and idiosyncrasies of each patient. By contrast, therapists with pet theories or specially favored techniques usually manage, in their own minds at least, to fit their patients' problems within the confines of their particular brand of treatment. (p. 33)

Multimodal therapists apply specific techniques and adopt different interpersonal styles to help clients reach goals. Multimodal therapists focus on: assessment, technical applications, and therapist interpersonal style.

Assessment

Underlying Lazarus's assessment system is the assumption that psychological difficulties are multifaceted, and require assessment across at least seven different parameters. The seven modalities are described in Table 14.1. At the end of each description there's a question suggested by Lazarus to guide the clinician's thinking about the category (Lazarus, 2008). Lazarus used the acronym **BASIC I.D.** to represent the seven parameters of human functioning.

Assessment and diagnosis involve a thorough evaluation of the BASIC I.D. Treatment focuses on alleviating problems occurring within these seven domains.

Table 14.1   The BASIC I.D.

Area of functioning	Description
Behavior	*Behavior* includes observable and measurable behaviors. Therapists gather information about (a) frequent actions, (b) habits, and (c) frequent behavioral reactions. Examples: smoking, regular aerobic exercise (or lack thereof), hair pulling, nail biting, yelling. Question: What behaviors does the client want to increase or decrease?
Affective responses	*Affective responses* include emotions and moods. Therapists gather information about problematic or helpful emotions. Examples: anger, sadness, anxiety, guilt. Question: What affective reactions are proving disturbing?
Sensations	*Sensations* include taste, touch, smell, vision, and hearing. Therapists are interested in the client's pleasant or unpleasant sensations. Examples: pain, dizziness, palpitations, depersonalization. Question: What are the client's precise sensory pains and pleasures?
Imagery	*Imagery* includes mental pictures or visualization. Therapists ask clients about the images they see and experience during stress or distress and during functional or dysfunctional moments. Examples: helpful or success images that occur before and during a stressful event and unhelpful, disturbing, or failure images. Question: What intrusive images need to be replaced by positive visualizations?
Cognition	*Cognition* includes nonvisual thoughts. Therapists gather information about what clients think or say to themselves when functioning well and when functioning poorly. Examples: personal values, rational and irrational thoughts, cognitive distortions, maladaptive automatic thoughts. Question: What dysfunctional beliefs and faulty cognitions are in need of restructuring?
Interpersonal relationships	*Interpersonal relationships* includes all human interactions. Therapists gather information about the nature, quality, and quantity of satisfying and dissatisfying interpersonal relationships. Examples: friendships, romantic relationships, primary family relationships, family of origin relationships, and work relationships. Question: Who are the significant others and what essential processes are at play vis-à-vis his or her interpersonal network?
Drugs and biology	*Drugs and biology* includes all physical or biological areas, including substance use. Therapists gather information about the client's eating, sleeping, and activity levels as well as medications and drug use. Examples: physical exam information, amount of alcohol and drug use. Question: What are the important facts about the client's drug use (recreational or prescribed) and his or her general medical-biological well-being?

Source: Questions are from Lazarus (2000, pp. 93–94).

Technical Applications

Multimodal therapists use any therapy technique that seems appropriate based on empirical research, or on a logical or practical rationale. Sometimes multimodal therapists also use intuition when determining what therapy approach to use (Lazarus, 1997).

Multimodal therapy requires skill in numerous therapy interventions. In the glossary of his 1989 book, Lazarus listed 39 main techniques. Learning how to effectively use these techniques is one of the challenges inherent in being a multimodal therapist.

Therapist Style

Therapists should change their style based on each new client. Lazarus (1971) wrote: "a flexible therapist has no fixed pattern of approaching new patients. He usually perceives what his patient needs and then tries to fit the role" (p. 50). For example, Lazarus criticizes person-centered therapists for not shifting their interpersonal styles based on different client traits: "These person-centered counselors do not ask if individual differences may warrant a confrontational style for some, or point to an austere business-like atmosphere for others … or when a sphinx-like guru might be made to order" (Lazarus, 1993, pp. 404–405).

Lazarus (1993) refers to shifting a therapeutic style as becoming an **authentic chameleon**. Some interpersonal variables therapists should consider varying their style depending on clients' needs, preferences, or expectations, including:

- Level of formality or informality.
- Amount of personal disclosure.
- How much or how often a new topic of conversation is initiated.
- Level of directiveness.
- Level of supportiveness.
- Level of reflectiveness.

One method for determining what interpersonal style to adopt with new clients is to obtain specific assessment data prior to the initial meeting. Lazarus recommended using the *Multimodal Life History Inventory*, which includes questions pertaining to therapy expectations (A. A. Lazarus & C. N. Lazarus, 1991). For instance, if a client writes, "I hope therapy is like a mirror so I can start understanding myself better," a more person-centered approach may be desirable.

REFLECTIONS

What interpersonal style variables might you vary depending on the client you're seeing? How will you decide how to approach a given client? What factors will you consider when deciding your interpersonal approach?

Determining the best therapeutic style is often a judgment call you have to make on the spot. Lazarus (1993) shared a story in which he sensed that a particular client (a 39-year-old woman) would respond well to humor and sarcasm:

> When she first entered my office, she looked me up and down and asked, "Why do you have graves outside your office?" In perfect Rogerian style I said, "I have graves outside my office?" "Look out the window dummy!" she replied. I went to my office window and looked out. Two new flower beds had been installed alongside the front walk on the grass. It was early spring and the shoots had yet to emerge from the soil. "Well, since you ask," I said, "I have just buried one of my clinical failures in the one grave and the other is earmarked for you … if you turn out to be an uncooperative client." The twinkle in her eye told me that my response was an appropriate one. (p. 406)

Although Lazarus's humor apparently worked, if used with the wrong client at the wrong time (you can imagine the situation), his joke might have had a less favorable impact. Using humor and sarcasm and acting like an authentic chameleon in therapy carries significant risk, especially for those newer in the field. However, learning to modify your style with clients is a skill that may be worth cultivating—with reasonable caution and supervision.

The Evidence Base for MMT

The research base for MMT is small. All of the published research identified through PsycINFO was conducted prior to 2000. There were multiple case reports, but none that would meet the standards for a well-controlled single case research design (Edwards, 1978; Keat, 1985). Additionally, three publications utilized group designs with minimal controls. These group designs focused on different treatment populations (i.e., psychiatric inpatients: Kwee, Duivenvoorden, Trijsburg, & Thiel, 1987; individuals with anxiety disorders: Gross, 1989; developmentally disabled adults with sex abuse histories: Allen & Borgen, 1994). All of the case studies and small group research indicated that MMT was effective.

MMT is a practical model that some clinicians find useful. MMT clinicians would likely contend that because they're using research to inform the techniques they implement, the MMT model is broadly evidence-based. Although this may be true, the research evidence supporting MMT as a specific protocol is sparse.

Interpersonal Psychotherapy for Depression

Interpersonal psychotherapy for depression (IPT-D) is a short-term, focal approach to treating depression. IPT-D integrates attachment theory, interpersonal theory, CBT, and psychodynamic psychotherapy. Relatively speaking, it quickly established itself as an efficacious therapy for depression. IPT was developed in the 1970s by the late Gerald Klerman of Harvard University and a group of associates from Yale University. It was empirically validated in the 1980s.

IPT Development

Interpersonal psychotherapy has its roots in the interpersonal psychiatry of Harry Stack Sullivan and the attachment theories of John Bowlby and Mary Ainsworth (Ainsworth, 1969; Bowlby, 1977; Sullivan, 1953), which, in turn, have roots in psychodynamic principles. It also employs cognitive and behavioral interventions. It's unique in that it was designed, not as a general psychotherapeutic approach, but as a specific treatment for depression. Klerman and colleagues compared and contrasted their interpersonal approach with psychodynamic approaches:

> Both interpersonal and psychodynamic approaches are concerned with the whole life span, and both consider early experience and persistent personality patterns important. In understanding human transactions, however, the psychodynamic therapist is concerned with object relations while the interpersonal therapist focuses on interpersonal relations. The psychodynamic therapist listens for the patient's intrapsychic wishes and conflicts; the interpersonal therapist listens for the patient's role expectations and disputes. (Klerman, Weissman, Rounsaville, & Chevron, 1984, p. 18)

Interpersonal psychotherapy was established as an effective treatment for depression in adults principally due to positive outcomes achieved in one large-scale RCT (Elkin et al., 1989). It focuses on diagnosing and treating interpersonal problems associated with depression. These include grief, role disputes, role transitions, and interpersonal deficits. Because it focuses on real interpersonal relationships instead of internalized object relations, it's a step removed from a psychoanalytic treatment, but rooted in and guided by psychodynamic principles (Klerman, Weissman, Rounsaville, & Chevron, 1995; Weissman, Markowitz, & Klerman, 2000).

Characteristics and Protocol

IPT has the following characteristics:

- Time-limited.

- A focus on one or two interpersonal problem areas.

- A focus on current, rather than past, interpersonal relationships.

- Cognitive behavioral issues are addressed, but only as they affect social relationships.

- Personality variables are recognized, but not focused on.

- The medical model is emphasized. Clients are viewed as having a mental disorder for which a specific treatment is needed.

IPT focuses on helping clients (a) recognize the relationship between depressive symptoms and interpersonal problems and (b) find ways to deal more effectively with interpersonal problems, thereby alleviating depressive symptoms.

IPT includes three treatment phases.

Phase One: In the first three sessions, a diagnostic evaluation and psychiatric history are conducted and a framework for treatment is established. An interpersonal inventory is also obtained. This inventory reviews the client's current social functioning and interpersonal relationships. It also examines any relationship changes that may have occurred near the time when the depressive symptoms increased.

Consistent with the medical model, during this first phase of treatment the client is assigned the sick role. This strategy may seem foreign to those of us trained in providing psychosocial treatments. Assignment of the sick role includes the giving of a diagnosis (clinical depression), and carries with it two implications: (1) clients may be relieved of overwhelming social obligations and (2) clients are expected to work in treatment to recover their full functioning. Also during the first phase of treatment, clients are evaluated for possible antidepressant medication treatment, educated about the nature of depression, and offered an interpersonal formulation.

The **interpersonal formulation** involves linking the client's depressive symptoms to one of four possible specific interpersonal situations:

1. *Grief*: Complicated bereavement following a loved one's death.

2. *Interpersonal role dispute*: Conflicts in an important social relationship (spouse, family member, coworker, or close friend).

3. *Role transition*: A change in life status, including, but not limited to, the beginning or end of a relationship, retirement, graduation, and medical diagnosis.

4. *Interpersonal deficit*: When a client's social skill deficits contribute to relationship problems.

Phase Two: Therapists apply strategies to address interpersonal problems, as articulated in the interpersonal formulation. IPT strategies are reviewed and described in the treatment manual (see Klerman et al., 1984; Weissman et al., 2000). IPT sessions typically begin with the query, "How have things been since we last met?"

(Weissman et al., 2000, p. 21). The purpose of this question is to help clients focus on recent interpersonal events and recent mood. The therapist's job is to link these two issues and help clients make plans to address the interpersonal problems fueling their depressive symptoms.

Phase Three: The final treatment phase focuses on recognition and consolidation of treatment gains. Strategies for facing and coping with future depressive episodes are reviewed.

The Evidence Base for IPT

IPT for depression in adults was initially evaluated in the National Institute of Mental Health (NIMH) Treatment of Depression Collaborative Research Program (Elkin et al., 1989). This study randomly assigned 239 patients with depressive symptoms to an antidepressant medication (imipramine), cognitive therapy, or IPT. This study was tightly controlled and coordinated across three sites. All three treatments outperformed the placebo condition (which included a placebo pill and supportive meetings). Based on Beck Depression Inventory scores, 70% of the IPT patients recovered, as compared to 69% for imipramine, 65% for cognitive therapy, and 51% for placebo.

Research on IPT has continued at a substantial pace. In a recent meta-analysis, 62 RCTs were identified from 1979 to 2014 (Cuijpers, Donker, Weissman, Ravitz, & Cristea, 2016). Overall, IPT was reported as significantly more effective than control conditions in treating acute-phase depression; IPT was also equivalent to antidepressant medications and other psychotherapies. The researchers reported that IPT was more effective when implemented for 10 sessions or more. It was also concluded that IPT was efficacious for preventing depression. Several studies showed somewhat less conclusively that IPT was effective in treating eating disorders and anxiety (Markowitz, Lipsitz, & Milrod, 2014). Several additional studies published after 2014 continue to provide evidence supporting IPT's efficacy. Interestingly, this efficacy extends across diagnostic domains that the treatment was not initially designed for, thus supporting the idea that mental health problems are multideter-mined and can respond to different treatments.

IPT has also been shown to effectively treat depressive symptoms in adolescents (Mufson, Dorta, Moreau, & Weissman, 2004). In one school-based mental health study, IPT for adolescents (IPT-A) significantly reduced depressive symptoms and improved overall functioning as compared with treatment as usual (Mufson et al., 2004). It has also been successfully implemented as a prevention intervention with youth at risk for depression (Young, Mufson, & Gallop, 2010). In recent years a family-based version of IPT (i.e., FB-IPT) has been developed and shows promise as yet another IPT alternative for depressed youth (Dietz, Weinberg, Brent, & Mufson, 2015).

Although most research doesn't clearly demonstrate that antidepressant medications combined with psychotherapy improves outcomes, adding antidepressants to IPT has consistently increased positive outcomes (Cuijpers et al., 2016). This may be because IPT explicitly embraces the medical model and yet addresses interpersonal symptoms that don't respond well to medication treatments.

THE PRACTICE OF INTEGRATIVE THERAPIES: THIRD WAVE MODELS

This section provides a description of six contemporary therapy models with integrative qualities. Some of these models have been called "third wave behavior therapy." Each of these approaches combines two or more theories, has empirical support, and is garnering a significant following among mental health practitioners.

Acceptance as a Central Principle

Traditional behavioral and cognitive therapies were (and are) all about change. The process is something like this:

1. A person is in distress.

2. That person seeks professional help.

3. The helper, using CBT strategies, teaches the distressed person behavioral and cognitive coping and personal growth strategies.

4. Over time, the distressed person learns the skills and makes behavioral and/or cognitive changes that reduce distressing symptoms.

5. The formerly distressed person applies the skills and experiences improved adjustment.

Although vastly different in their specific technical strategies, new generation (or third wave behavioral) approaches have a common central principle: acceptance.

Instead of focusing on how distressed clients can and should make behavioral and cognitive changes, these newer therapy approaches generally focus on helping clients accept and/or process their disturbing cognitive and emotional symptoms. Here's a quick, simplified summary:

Dialectical Behavior Therapy (DBT): Radical acceptance is a core principle of DBT (Linehan, 1993). DBT practitioners help clients develop an accepting attitude, along with emotional regulation and interpersonal skills for dealing with difficult environments.

Eye Movement Desensitization Reprocessing (EMDR): EMDR practitioners tell clients, "There are no right or wrong responses." Clients are coached to "go with" whatever comes up. Whatever thoughts, memories, or emotions arise are greeted with acceptance, without analysis, interpretation, or judgment.

Emotion-Focused Therapy (EFT): EFT practitioners use person-centered principles to focus on and accept clients' emotional distress (Greenberg, 2017). A variety of empty chair techniques are used to process difficult emotions, thereby helping clients accept past experiences and move more fully into present functioning.

Acceptance and Commitment Therapy (ACT): Operating partly on the Buddhist principle of acceptance, ACT practitioners guide clients to stop trying to make their disturbing thoughts and emotions go away; instead, ACT practitioners engage clients in mindful acceptance and help them act on committed core values (Harris, 2009).

Mindfulness-Based Cognitive Therapy (MBCT): MBCT primarily involves helping clients learn and establish a mindfulness meditation practice (Segal, Williams, & Teasdale, 2013). MBCT practitioners make a distinction between situations where problem-solving can be applied and situations where mindful acceptance is necessary.

Eye Movement Desensitization and Reprocessing

Eye movement desensitization and reprocessing (EMDR) is an evidence-based treatment for trauma in adults and children. Francine Shapiro (1989) developed EMDR; it has an interesting history and unique treatment protocol.

EMDR Development

Francine Shapiro
(photo courtesy of Francine Shapiro)

Shapiro discovered EMDR while exploring her own personal trauma experience and disturbing memories. In 1979, while working on her doctorate in English literature at New York University, she was diagnosed with cancer. Rather than continuing with her doctoral work in English literature, she left New York to study clinical psychology. Years later, in 1987, as Shapiro was walking through a park, she felt distress stemming from past memories. After focusing on these memories for a few minutes she noticed her disturbing thoughts were gone. When she brought them back into her mind, she found these thoughts had lost much of their disturbing quality. She then tried to recreate what she had just experienced and discovered that her eyes were moving back and forth (horizontally) very rapidly. Later, she found that when she intentionally focused on a trauma-related memory and simultaneously moved her eyes back and forth, the memory became less distressing in what appeared to be a desensitization process. As she continued exploring eye movements and desensitization, she recognized that the eye movements alone weren't adequate for therapeutic benefits and so she added additional dimensions to her treatment protocol.

Shapiro initially called her treatment approach eye movement desensitization (EMD) (Shapiro, 1989). There was an emphasis on bilateral eye movements as a means for trauma desensitization. However, she later renamed her approach EMDR, primarily to capture the more complex information processing that she believed was related to its efficacy (Shapiro, 1995). Although other writers have classified EMDR as a behavior therapy and an exposure therapy, Shapiro considers EMDR an integrative treatment. It includes principles from the following theoretical perspectives:

- *Psychodynamic*: Therapists and clients focus on past traumatic events.

- *Behavioral*: Consistent with exposure therapy, there's a focus on present fear/anxiety and specific triggering stimuli.

- *Cognitive*: Clients are asked to identify negative and positive beliefs about the self; there is also activation of an information-processing model.

- *Person-centered*: EMDR therapists accept what clients say and often follow the client's lead rather than dictating the course or direction of therapy.

- *Physiological or body-centered*: Therapists and clients focus on physical-affective links associated with trauma experiences.

In the early years of its development and application, EMDR was viewed as controversial; some academics and professionals were highly critical. This may have been because of Shapiro's early claims that EMDR could have a positive effect in a single session. Interestingly, Prochaska and Norcross (2003) speculated that gender bias from the male-dominated professions of psychology and psychiatry also may have contributed to negative critiques of Shapiro's work. Whatever the reasons, even the mention of EMDR within some circles would stimulate unprofessional derisive reactions. Some authors even went so far as to classify it as a "power therapy" (which, by the way, is an insult in the psychotherapy world; Figley, 1997).

In response to her critics, Shapiro has consistently provided clarifying information and pointed to empirical research supporting EMDR as a valid treatment approach. Below is a sample of Shapiro's effort to clarify misconceptions associated with EMDR:

> Contrary to a common misconception, EMDR, as it is currently practiced, is not a simple, by-the-book

procedure dominated by the use of repeated eye movements (despite its name), but rather an integrated form of therapy incorporating aspects of many traditional psychological orientations ... and one that makes use of a variety of bilateral stimuli besides eye movements. The inaugural study ... did indeed stress directed eye movements as the primary component of the therapy. (Shapiro, 1999, p. 37)

Although some writers continue to discount or minimize EMDR as a clinical procedure (Lohr, 2011), research evidence supporting EMDR efficacy is impressive. It's a structured approach that has a strong cognitive component. Research supports EMDR as a means for addressing and reducing trauma symptoms in adults and adolescents.

EMDR Protocol

The standard EMDR protocol includes eight phases:

1. *History*: Assessment of client readiness and initial treatment planning.

2. *Preparation*: Making sure clients have skills for coping with stress that might be generated from the treatment process.

3. *Assessment*: A target memory is identified. A current negative belief about the self-linked to the target memory is identified and rated, along with a hoped-for positive belief. Associated emotional and physical characteristics are articulated.

4. *Desensitization*: Bilateral stimulation (eye movements, tapping, or audio stimulation) ensues. Therapist explains and initiates this process, but then follows the client's experiencing.

5. *Installation*: Bilateral stimulation is repeated linking the positive belief to the memory.

6. *Body scan*: There is a review of the client's physical/body sensations. Negative sensations are processed through bilateral stimulation.

7. *Closure*: The client is asked to keep a journal of experiences during the upcoming week and is reminded of the self-calming strategies used in Stage 2.

8. *Reevaluation*: When clients return for the next session a reevaluation of status and progress is conducted.

Detailed information regarding EMDR practice can be obtained from Shapiro's many works in the area (Shapiro 1989, 1995, 2001, 2002). EMDR training is available worldwide (see www.emdr.com) and has been used across cultures following traumatic human-caused and natural disasters.

The Evidence Base for EMDR

APA's Division 12 lists EMDR as a well-established treatment for noncombat PTSD. EMDR is also listed as an empirically supported treatment by the American Psychiatric Association, the Department of Veterans Affairs and Department of Defense, the California Evidence-Based Clearinghouse for Child Welfare, and several other organizations.

Research highlights include the following:

- Davidson and Parker (2001) reported a meta-analysis of 34 studies. The results indicated that EMDR has a significantly positive effect compared with no treatment and an equivalent effect compared with alternative treatments. The eye-movements showed no additive effects over the desensitization process without eye-movements.

- In a meta-analysis of EMDR versus exposure therapy versus relaxation training, EMDR and relaxation training produced equivalent results. Although EMDR and exposure treatment were equal in terms of attrition, worsening of symptoms, and reduction of numbing and hyperarousal symptoms, exposure therapy was faster at reducing avoidance symptoms, produced larger reductions in avoidance and trauma re-experiencing, and resulted in resolution of PTSD diagnosis at a higher rate (Taylor et al., 2003).

- A French review of EMDR versus CBT for a range of problems found that EMDR and CBT were equal with regard to PTSD outcomes, but CBT was superior for treating phobias and panic disorder (Bériault & Larivée, 2005).

- In seven direct comparisons between EMDR and trauma-focused CBT (TF-CBT) the two treatment procedures were determined equally efficacious (Seidler & Wagner, 2006).

- In a single study comparing 88 adults with trauma who were randomly assigned to EMDR versus fluoxetine (Prozac) versus pill placebo conditions, EMDR was more efficacious than medication. EMDR produced: "Substantial and sustained reduction of PTSD and depression in most victims of adult-onset trauma" (van der Kolk et al., 2007, p. 37).

- In a meta-analysis of seven studies that focused on EMDR for children who had experienced trauma, an effect size (versus no treatment) of $d = 0.56$ (moderate effects) was reported. EMDR was slightly superior to CBT, $d = 0.25$ (small effect size; Rodenburg, Benjamin, de Roos, Meijer, & Stams, 2009).

- In a review of eight studies on reducing distress among survivors of natural disasters, EMDR showed clinical significance, in some cases after just one session (Natha & Daiches, 2014).

• In a meta-analysis of 11 studies with 424 participants, EMDR was slightly superior to CBT (Chen, Zhang, Hu, & Liang, 2015). Specifically, although avoidance ratings were equivalent, EMDR was better than CBT at reducing intrusion and arousal severity. The authors noted that several of the studies were of poor quality and consequently cautioned drawing strong conclusions.

EMDR is not always efficacious and is not a panacea. However, the preceding research support is substantial; there is also accumulating evidence suggesting it may be effective in the treatment of other mental health problems.

As with many treatments, it has been difficult to definitively pinpoint why EMDR works. Some contend it's simply an alternative imaginal desensitization protocol. The eye-movements and other bilateral stimulation procedures may or may not add anything to treatment. EMDR includes a cognitive component focusing on client trauma-related beliefs. Positive expectations and a positive focus are also present. The process may (or may not) be related to memory consolidation and reconsolidation.

Shapiro has developed a theoretical explanation focusing on information processing (Adaptive Information Processing). She believes that trauma produces disturbing information that must be cognitively or neurologically processed. The overwhelming quantity and/or quality of the trauma experiences causes information processing to be disconnected from more adaptive ideas or information that ordinarily might be integrated into the negative event or events. The application of EMDR may help clients reconnect trauma memories with more adaptive memories and beliefs. This is similar to the underlying hypothesis for narrative exposure therapy of connecting hot and cold memories (NET; Schauer, Neuner, & Elbert, 2011). Shapiro's explanation is speculative, as is the NET explanation. Additional research is needed to further address underlying mechanisms associated with EMDR efficacy.

EMDR treatment has expanded into problem areas other than PTSD. In particular, EMDR is being used to treat acute stress related to natural disaster, war, and other large-scale traumatizing events. On a practice level, EMDR practitioners offer pro bono services to trauma victims through the EMDR Humanitarian Assistance Programs (see emdrhap.org). EMDR has been offered to many victims of natural and human-caused trauma in the Balkans, Bosnia, Haiti, Indonesia, Japan, Northern Ireland, Oklahoma City, New York City, San Salvador, and many other locales (see Putting It in Practice 14.2 for a story of two therapists who combined EMDR and DBT to address the needs of a traumatized population).

PUTTING IT IN PRACTICE

14.2 Two Counselors Integrate Two Integrational Theories—Together

This commentary was co-written and is reproduced with permission by Laura M. Schmuldt, PhD, University of the Cumberlands, and Troyann I. Gentile, PhD, University of Colorado-Denver..

Selecting a theory of counseling is an endeavor that makes most graduate students cringe. It has been compared to enrolling in medical school only to learn that you're expected to develop your own theory of surgery: overwhelming and, frankly, frightening. Many students find themselves surprised by the self-exploration required in the process.

We are two counselor educators who believe that development of theory demands self-reflection and exploration of research—but these experiences cannot exist in a vacuum. Our theoretical development (and it's always a work in progress!) was enhanced and finessed through our conversations—often informal and meandering—and our shared commitment to a very unique project. Our story will be described exclusively in the words of "us" and "we" and "our"; for although we each bring individual values, ideas, and knowledge to the equation, we've found our professional collaboration is inseparable from our work within a very specific set of circumstances.

Through amazing chance and circumstance, we became involved in a project working with the adult survivors of the Romanian orphanages. The collective histories of these individuals, now a cohort of more than 170,000, ranging in age from 18 to 34, are notoriously well-documented.

In 1989, shortly after the "fall" of communism in Romania, tragic images of undernourished children, tied to steel cribs, rhythmically banging their heads against the walls, locked in dimly lit rooms and supervised by custodial staff, attracted international attention. Though conditions have improved overall, a generation of "lost children"—adult survivors of the orphanages—remains. Having been taught nothing about money, work ethic, how to find a job or a place to live, paying bills, manners or even simple hygiene, many cannot fend for themselves and become jobless and homeless on the streets with other adult survivors. These individuals often turn to begging for and stealing food, drug addiction, and, worst of all, are vulnerable and subject to underground prostitution and human trafficking.

At this point in the story, you may be wondering: What could possibly be offered to individuals from such dreadful circumstances? This question helped our theoretical foundation evolve. We reasoned that such individuals grew up in the ultimate "invalidating environment," a term coined by Marsha Linehan, creator of dialectical behavior therapy (DBT). An invalidating environment is one that consistently communicates to a person that his or her interpretation of reality is somehow flawed, incorrect, and inaccurate. As such, it's a challenge for such individuals to trust their own sense of the world and their ability to meet and negotiate challenges (self-invalidation). A sentence from Linehan's work resonated with us: "Given what you've been through, this behavior makes sense." We've grown to believe that validation is perhaps the most important mediator of human relationships. At a minimum, we reasoned, these survivors needed to learn a set of skills—skills for accurately interpreting events and responding to them in a way that won't ultimately create more suffering. In other words, when deeply painful emotions are present, the mind seeks relief. Relief can come about in ways that work in the short term, but fail in the long term (e.g., drugs, reckless sexual behavior, overeating, overspending). We continually noticed that mindfulness—quieting the mind and focusing simply on what we were experiencing in the moment—was critical in our interpretation of the adults' behavior and our judgments about the complexities of this unfamiliar culture. As such, DBT became our tool for not simply approaching this population, but for also addressing our personal feelings of burnout (counselors need validation, just like clients).

However, what about the very real symptoms of post-traumatic stress disorder (PTSD) experienced by literally every adult survivor we encountered? To grow up in the Romanian orphanages meant experiencing negligence and abuse of an unspeakable, even ghastly, degree. Again, we turned to theory and were intrigued by the clinical efficacy of eye movement desensitization and reprocessing (EMDR). We discovered a means of reducing the power of traumatic memories while simultaneously prompting clients to rapidly connect the painful memory to memories that are holistic, resilient, and hopeful. Additionally, EMDR allowed processing of trauma without necessarily describing and discussing the trauma in intricate detail. This aspect of treatment is critically important in that these clients often lack language for describing their experiences.

Our project is in many ways "under construction"—and we believe that this is analogous to the development of one's personal theory of counseling or psychotherapy. We advise you, as we've strived to do, to establish a network of colleagues who thrive on learning about the process of human change and challenge you to grow as a clinician. Through this collaboration we've had opportunities to come together with each other's theoretical paradigms and create inspiration. Further, we encourage you to develop skills as generalists and specialists. Most importantly, perhaps, we challenge you, on a daily basis, to find hope in whatever dire circumstances and clinical difficulties you encounter.

Emotion–Focused Therapy

Emotion-focused therapy (formerly process-experiential therapy) was discussed briefly in Chapter 5 and illustrated in a case in Chapter 6. **Emotion-focused therapy (EFT)** is an integrative approach with roots in person-centered theory and that employs the Gestalt empty chair as a means of focusing on and deepening emotional experiencing, expression, and processing (Greenberg, 2015; Greenberg, Rice, & Elliott, 1993). EFT is broadly classified as an evidence-based neo-humanistic therapy approach.

EFT Development

Leslie Greenberg
(photo courtesy of Leslie Greenberg)

Leslie Greenberg developed EFT. Greenberg originally trained as a mechanical and industrial engineer, but was dissatisfied and decided to leave Johannesburg, South Africa, and came to York University to obtain his doctorate in counseling psychology. There, he studied with Laura Rice who had trained with Carl Rogers at the Chicago Counseling Center. Subsequently, Greenberg obtained training in Gestalt therapy and also in family therapy at MRI. EFT is a blend of person-centered therapy and Gestalt technique, but Greenberg and his colleagues emphasize that EFT has a person-centered foundation and is more person-centered than Gestalt (R. Elliott, personal communication, July 15, 2011). Greenberg also was involved in the development of emotion-focused couple therapy (Greenberg & Johnson, 1988; Johnson & Greenberg, 1985).

Over the past 25-plus years Greenberg and his colleagues have focused on ways in which anxiety, depression, and other disorders include a range of processing blocks or difficulties within the cognitive-affective domain (Greenberg, 2006; Paivio & Greenberg, 1995). EFT incorporates two main treatment principles. First, therapists provide an empathic therapy relationship; this relationship is viewed as a curative factor, in and of itself (Greenberg, 2015). Second, from the foundational empathic relationship, therapists facilitate emotional processing.

Pavio and Greenberg (1995) described the EFT rationale and process:

> Markers of unfinished business or lingering negative feelings toward a significant other commonly occur in therapy, and there is agreement across orientations that unresolved anger and sadness are among the generating conditions of anxiety, depression, and a variety of interpersonal problems.... Drawing on Gestalt therapy techniques,... an intervention for resolving such unfinished emotional issues has been devised....

Empty-chair dialogue intervention (ECH), in which the client engages in an imaginary dialogue with the significant other, is designed to access restricted feelings allowing them to run their course and be restructured in the safety of the therapy environment. The process of resolving unfinished business using ECH has been rigorously modeled,... and the model has been empirically verified.... Resolution consists of changed perceptions of self and other so that clients shift from viewing themselves as weak and victimized to a stance of greater self-empowerment and either view the significant other with greater understanding or hold them accountable for harm. (Paivio & Greenberg, 1995, p. 419)

As the name implies, emotions and emotional processing is central to EFT. Emotions are viewed as central to identity and growth (e.g., "I feel, therefore I am"; Greenberg, 2015). Acceptance of emotions is also central. Emotional change can't happen unless and until emotions are accepted and experienced. However, as Greenberg (2017) has noted, evoking too much or too little emotion is suboptimal.

Narrative components of EFT also have been discussed. When clients experience a facilitated empty chair dialogue from a person-centered perspective, they can shift existing personal narratives. Narrative therapists refer to these shifts as unique outcomes or sparkling moments and these experiences—reflected back to clients via person-centered listening—can open up the possibility and elaboration of new meaning. Essentially, clients begin to see themselves and others differently. This process was described in an article examining narrative change within an EFT case:

> Thus, unique outcomes—or, as we prefer, innovative moments (or i-moments)—can be defined as all occurrences (thought, acted, and imagined) that are different from the problematic self-narrative and are, in this sense, a representation of client self-change. They are openings to the elaboration of new meanings, challenging the hegemonic role of problematic self-narratives in clients' lives. (Gonçalves, Mendes, Ribeiro, Anus, & Greenberg, 2010, p. 269)

In a successful EFT case, Gonçalves et al. measured these i-moments (aka unique outcomes or sparkling moments) using the Innovative Moments Coding System (IMCS; Goncalves, Matos, & Santos, 2009; Gonçalves et al., 2010). They concluded that a reconceptualization of self and other was essential in producing change in counseling or psychotherapy.

Characteristics and Protocol

EFT process involves the formation of a relationship based on Rogers's core conditions for the first 2 or 3 sessions. Subsequently, from the trusting relationship foundation, unfinished emotional business is explored and resolved. Sometimes therapists need to provide clients with a rationale for intensely focusing on emotions (Greenberg, 2017). Although traditional person-centered therapists explicitly follow the client's lead, EFT is more of a balancing act that involves following and leading. Goldman and Greenberg (2015) explained:

> At times we follow our clients while they unfold their emotions and meanings, but at other times we lead clients and suggest that they engage in in-session tasks and exercises designed to deepen emotion and emotional processing and ultimately work toward transformation of painful emotion. For the EFT therapist, leading and following is a constant balancing act. (p. x)

Part of the "leading" in EFT involves therapists using case formulation. EFT case formulation focuses on explanations and understanding the client's core painful emotion. Consistent with the here and now philosophy of PCT, EFT practitioners are open to modifying their case formulation on a moment-by-moment basis; this involves tracking and responding to whatever is most painful in the moment.

The assessment and case formulation processes in EFT involve simultaneously experiencing and observing global and specific indicators of empathic markers. When these markers are identified, they lead toward a particular form or style of intervention, such as, reflective listening, emotional validation, or empty chair dialogue. Two sample empathy markers, therapist tasks, process, and desired resolution states for EFT are summarized in Table 14.2.

As emotion-focused therapists track empathy markers and guide clients in specific emotional processing tasks, movement toward emotional resolution can follow in several different ways. Examples include (a) emotional expression of previously blocked emotion, (b) meaningful shifts in client narratives or core beliefs, and (c) transforming one emotion with the presence of a different, more adaptive emotion (Greenberg, Warwar, & Malcolm, 2008).

Working directly with emotions is complex and not always intuitive for therapists. Therefore, therapists who practice EFT need training and supervised experience to increase their understanding of human emotion. For example, as Greenberg has noted, dramatic emotional expression can, at times, interfere with emotional experiencing. It's as if the dramatic expression makes it harder to step back and look at the emotional experience. Questions to clients like, "How does it feel to weep?" can help clients move from expression to reflection (Greenberg, 2015, p. 242).

EFT: The Evidence Base

As a neo-humanistic therapy, EFT isn't a naturally good fit for modernist empirical research. Nevertheless, research on EFT efficacy and effectiveness continues to accumulate. In particular, EFT researchers have done an admirable job of publishing intensive individual case studies that discuss differences between successful and unsuccessful outcomes. Highlights of the evidence base for EFT include:

- EFT has empirical support for treating depression (Greenberg, 2017; Ellison, Greenberg, Goldman, & Angus, 2009; Goldman, Greenberg, & Angus, 2006; Watson, Gordon, Stermac, Kalogerakos, & Steckley, 2003). It's listed on the Division 12 website as having modest empirical support.

- EFT also is listed as empirically supported for couple counseling and there's research suggesting its utility as a group therapy modality for reducing recidivism among individuals incarcerated for intimate partner violence (Pascual-Leone, Bierman, Arnold, & Stasiak, 2011).

- Two well-controlled outcome studies have focused on EFT for social anxiety disorder; one was a multiple baseline study of 12 clients (Shahar, Bar-Kalifa, & Alon, 2017) and the other a group design comparing EFT versus PCT (Elliott & Shahar, 2017). Both studies showed positive outcomes for EFT, leading to the

Table 14.2 Sample Empathy Markers, Tasks, Process, and End States in EFT

Empathy-marker	Therapist task	Process	Resolution state
Client vulnerability: painful emotions like shame or weakness emerge.	Empathic affirmation. Validate client experience. Allow feelings to unfold and deepen. Inner exploration or explanation is not encouraged.	Clients often hit rock bottom and bounce back up.	Affirmation of self. Client feels heard, understood, stronger, and perhaps ready for more activating work.
Enactment task marker. The client experiences a self-evaluative split characterized by self-criticism or "tornness."	The therapist gently prompts the client toward using a two-chair dialogue.	Clients assert themselves and the critical voice softens.	The client experiences increased self-acceptance and integration.

Note: These two empathic markers are a sampling of and adapted from Goldman and Greenberg (2015, p. 122–124).

conclusion that EFT has promise for this population (Elliott & Shahar, 2017).

• EFT has been found superior to psychoeducation in resolving old conflicts (unfinished business) and facilitating forgiveness (Greenberg, Warwar, & Malcolm, 2008; Malcolm & Greenberg, 2000).

Overall, EFT is a promising approach, especially for clients who have depressive symptoms linked to unresolved interpersonal relationships. Because EFT can also produce negative outcomes, therapists who are comfortable working with intense emotions and are interested in this therapy modality should seek additional training and supervision.

Dialectical Behavior Therapy

Dialectical behavior therapy (DBT) is a multitheoretical approach that blends cognitive behavioral and Eastern meditation practices with elements of psychodynamic, person-centered, Gestalt, strategic, and paradoxical approaches (Heard & Linehan, 1994). DBT is one of the most popular third wave behavior therapies—it even has a smartphone app (see DBT Diary Card). Although DBT has historically and primarily been applied in the treatment of borderline personality disorder (BPD), more recently it has been applied to other problem areas and clinical populations.

DBT Development

Marsha Linehan and her colleagues at the University of Washington Suicidal Behaviors Research Clinic developed DBT as a treatment for women who were exhibiting parasuicidal behavior and suffering from borderline personality disorder (BPD) (Linehan, 1993). Parasuicidal behavior includes all intentional self-injurious

Marsha Linehan
(photo courtesy of Marsha Lineham)

behavior, sometimes involving suicidal intent and sometimes not. Although often classified as a cognitive behavioral approach, DBT is an excellent example of psychotherapy integration.

DBT is a comprehensive approach directed toward a difficult clinical population. Therapists who work with clients who engage in repeated suicidal and self-destructive behaviors and who regularly experience emotional dysregulation can quickly become discouraged, cynical, and burned out. In the past, this often led therapists to criticize their clients, sometimes disparagingly referring to them as "borderlines." DBT helps therapists maintain a positive perspective; the

model weaves in support for therapists to cope with this difficult client population.

Characteristics and Protocol

DBT is based on a biosocial theoretical model of BPD. Therapists view **emotional dysregulation** as the primary deficit associated with BPD. BPD clients are viewed as being biologically predisposed to emotional dysregulation. Linehan believes "individuals with BPD have emotional responses to environmental stimuli that occur more quickly, are more intense, and have a slower return to baseline than the responses of non-BPD individuals" (Linehan & Schmidt, 1995, p. 562).

On the social side, BPD clients often come from or are currently living in environments that are a poor fit for their emotional sensitivity. Over time, this social environment can become "chronically and pervasively" emotionally invalidating—BPD clients consistently receive communications indicating that their emotional and behavioral responses are "incorrect, faulty, or inappropriate." A modern term that describes the BPD person's perspective is gaslighting. **Gaslighting** is a power-based strategy where the person in power questions the validity or accuracy of a victims perceptions.

DBT is founded on dialectical philosophy and integrates Buddhist concepts of acceptance. **Dialectical philosophy** emphasizes that reality includes opposing forces that constantly shift and change. The three-stage process through which change occurs is referred to as the dialectic. As applied to a suicidal client, the dialectic transformation occurs in the following stages:

• *First*: An initial proposition, "Life has meaning and positive possibilities," is experienced.

• *Second*: The initial proposition is negated through a contradictory experience: "Life has no relevance, meaning, or positive possibilities."

• *Third*: The contradiction is resolved through the negation of the negation: "Life can be both inherently meaningful and completely irrelevant."

Through DBT, clients are encouraged to grapple with both sides of this contradiction. The result is greater acceptance of transitory meaning and irrelevance in life and improved emotional regulation skills.

DBT also embraces another dialectic. Clients and their emotional condition are embraced and accepted (as in Eastern philosophy and person-centered theory). At the same time, the client is engaged in a purposeful change process to help with emotional dysregulation and environmental invalidation (Linehan, 1993). Essentially, the therapist is communicating the attitude: "I accept you as you are, and I am helping you to change." This statement is a therapy stance of **radical acceptance**.

DBT practice is comprehensive and includes five functions delivered in various modalities. The functions include:

1. Enhancing skills and capabilities.

2. Improving client motivation.

3. Generalizing skills and capabilities from therapy to outside therapy.

4. Improving the therapist's capabilities and motivation to treat patients with BPD.

5. Structuring the client's environment to support and validate the client's and therapist's capabilities. (Linehan, 1993)

To address these functions, therapists and clients engage in the following: (a) clients commit to 12 months of psychoeducational skills training in a group format; (b) clients work individually with a therapist to increase motivation, address skill acquisition and application barriers, and generalize specific skills to the real world; (c) therapists also commit to participating in a weekly professional consultation group for technical assistance and emotional support; (d) family sessions or consultations with the client's personal environment are conducted to facilitate client emotional validation and skill development.

DBT is not a therapy for the meek. It requires that both therapist and client make considerable commitments to training and ongoing skill development (see Putting It in Practice 14.3 for a DBT therapist's story of developing an interest in and acquiring DBT training).

DBT: The Evidence Base

DBT for BPD is evidence based. Division 12 lists it as having strong empirical support. Programmatic research shows positive outcomes after two years (Linehan et al., 2006; van den Bosch, Verheul, Schippers, & van den Brink, 2002). In particular, in a meta-analysis of five RCTs, DBT was significantly more efficacious than treatment as usual in reducing suicide attempts and parasuicidal behaviors (Panos, Jackson, Hasan, & Panos, 2014). In a recent study DBT was reported as approximately equivalent to the collaborative assessment and management of suicide in preventing suicidal behaviors and suicide attempts (CAMS; Andreasson et al., 2016).

DBT has also been used to treat nonsuicidal self-injury and depression in adolescent clients. In a preliminary meta-analysis of 12 studies, there was a large effect size for reducing self-injury (0.81) and a small effect size for reducing depressive symptoms (0.36). Further research is needed to confirm these results.

The popularity of DBT may be because it provides a means through which therapists can work effectively with a very challenging treatment population. It's also been formulated as a preventative strategy for challenging, but subthreshold, adolescents at risk for developing BPD (A. L. Miller, Rathus, & Linehan, 2007). DBT gives therapists hope for success with a treatment population that displays a range of disturbing behaviors.

Researchers have also adapted DBT for treating American Indian/Alaska Native adolescents with substance use disorders (Beckstead, Lambert, DuBose, & Linehan, 2015). In a pilot study of 229 adolescents, "96% of adolescents were either recovered or improved" (p. 84). Specific traditional and spiritual Native practices were integrated into the DBT treatment.

Overall, DBT is a well-established treatment for BPD. DBT also has potential for effectiveness in treating substance abuse (among whites and Native American populations), violent offenders, and elderly clients with depression and personality disorders. It also may contribute to prevention of the development of BPD. Interestingly, although the skills training component of DBT is often used as a standalone treatment, evidence for that particular use is equivocal (Valentine, Bankoff, Poulin, Reidler, & Pantalone, 2015).

PUTTING IT IN PRACTICE

14.3 On Becoming a "DBT Therapist"

Reproduced with permission of K. Michelle Hunnicutt Hollenbaugh, PhD, Texas A&M University, Corpus Christi

When I originally began attending local dialectical behavior therapy (DBT) trainings while working in a community mental health center, I never expected it to become an area of specialization. My supervisor was running DBT skills training groups and believed it was important for all her supervisees to attend the trainings. Basically, I had to go to the trainings.

At first I was dubious. However, as I attended weekly trainings for the next year, two things happened:

1. I found myself using DBT skills in my own life on a daily basis. This included mindfulness meditation and working to accept frustrating situations as reality—to reduce personal suffering.
2. I realized I was no longer afraid to work with clients others labeled *difficult*. In treatment team meetings, while other clinicians were reluctant to accept new clients with the dreaded borderline personality disorder (BPD), I was not. This was very empowering. It fueled my interest and further pursuit of DBT training. Then, I began running a DBT skills training group and started implementing as many aspects of DBT therapy as possible into my work with clients.

DBT is a complex therapy. Many facets are involved, training is a big commitment, and so I ran into barriers. Behavioral Tech (the organization founded by Marsha Linehan for DBT training) only offers the intensive 10-day DBT training to whole treatment teams; without financial support from the mental health center to form and fund a full team, I was unable to attend this training, and so, instead, I continued to attend and offer local trainings and worked with other local therapists in a consultation team to continue our DBT growth and development. When honing my behavioral reinforcement skills, I practiced in consultation team meetings, with my clients, but also with family members and friends.

There was never a specific time when I said, "Now, I'm a DBT therapist." For me, it has been a process happening over time and having a DBT therapist title didn't occur to me until others began referring to me as such.

The journey to becoming a DBT therapist is difficult. I floundered at times; there were skills group sessions that fell apart before my eyes and clients that dropped out and never returned. But I continue to work to develop my skills and improve. I'm certain I'll face barriers and failures in the future.

You don't need to specialize in BPD to learn and use DBT. Although the majority of published research is on its use with BPD, DBT skills training is helpful for a variety of diagnoses and settings.

There are several helpful basic assumptions in DBT:

- Clients are doing the best they can.
- Clients want to improve.
- Clients need to do better, try harder, and be more motivated to change.
- Clients may not have caused all of their problems, but they have to solve them anyway.
- The lives of suicidal, borderline individuals are unbearable as they are currently being lived.
- Clients must learn new behaviors in all relevant contexts.
- Clients cannot fail therapy.
- Therapists treating BPD need support (from Linehan, 1993, pp. 106–108).

Notice that these are assumptions. What we believe shapes what we do and DBT is a state of mind. To be a DBT therapist, you must believe your client is doing the best she can. You must also believe she can do better. You must believe that your client's life is unbearable as it's currently being lived and that your client cannot fail therapy. Above all, DBT therapists must incorporate a dialectical worldview—a view that's flexible and free from absolutes. This returns to the concept of accepting reality and a mantra often used in DBT—"everything is as it is; and everything is as it should be."

Acceptance and Commitment Therapy

Acceptance and commitment therapy (ACT) is a third wave behavior therapy that combines committed action with the Buddhist (or person-centered) idea of acceptance. Acceptance and commitment therapy is abbreviated as ACT, which is pronounced as a word and not as a set of initials. On the APA Division 12 website, ACT is listed as having strong research support for treating pain and modest research support for treating depression, mixed anxiety, obsessive-compulsive disorder, and psychosis.

The ACT developers identified their approach as integrational:

> Is ACT a behavior therapy, a cognitive-behavioral therapy, a type of clinical behavior analysis, a contextual therapy, or a humanistic/existential/Gestalt therapy? It is all of these. … We do not view the distinctions between these streams of thought to be important to the ACT work, and relish the fact that it spans several seemingly distinct traditions. (Hayes, Strosahl, & Wilson, 1999, p. 79)

ACT Development

ACT takes the novel position of rejecting existing diagnostic and medical models. ACT developers believe the assumptions of healthy normality (and abnormality as a disease) are flawed. The disease, disorder, or psychopathology model is viewed as incorrect and unhelpful (Hayes, Strosahl, & Wilson, 1999). They wrote:

> Considering how much attention has been afforded the medical model within psychology and psychiatry, it is a bit shocking to note how little progress has been made in establishing syndromes as disease entities. … The "comorbidity" rates in the current diagnostic system are so high as to challenge the basic credibility of the nosology.… Even if clients can be given a label such as panic disorder with agoraphobia, or obsessive-compulsive disorder, many of the issues within therapy will still have to do with other problems: jobs, children, relationships, sexual identity, careers, anger, sadness, drinking problems, or the meaning of life. (Hayes, Strosahl, & Wilson, 1999, p. 5)

Hayes and his colleagues believe that clinical researchers have been seeking support for an invalid model. They offer an alternative or supplemental view that they refer to as "destructive normality" (Hayes et al., 1999, p. 6). **Destructive normality** is the idea that a normal person can use normal psychological processes and end up feeling quite disturbed. For example, if you think about the common process of lying down to go to sleep at night, it not unusual for ordinary people to easily and naturally think themselves into distress.

Characteristics and Protocol

Acceptance and commitment therapists make a point that human thoughts do not represent reality; they're only thoughts. Further, ACT avoids judging negative cognitions as unhealthy or deviant. If therapists judge and label clients as having pathological thinking, it can worsen clients' symptoms. Instead, therapists accept clients' thoughts, and help clients accept their thoughts (using mindful acceptance). Then, helping clients clarify values and take committed action toward these values becomes the focus. In some ways, the ACT perspective that focusing too much on cognitions is unnecessary or problematic is similar to therapists who advocate behavioral activation therapy for depression instead of CBT. Here's how the reasoning goes:

- In CBT, clients are viewed as having negative (aka bad) cognitions that contribute to a depressive or anxious state.

- CBT expects clients to dispute or restructure their (bad) cognitions to eliminate them and doing so is thought to improve well-being and mental health.

- CBT contends that if these (bad) cognitions can't be managed it's dysfunctional.

- ACT contends that all thoughts are normal and natural and not deviant.

- ACT practitioners coach clients to use mindfulness approaches to accept their thoughts—instead of trying to fight their thoughts off—because the thoughts aren't bad things anyway.

- ACT also emphasizes values-based committed action, which is viewed as healthy in and of itself.

- ACT practitioners and researchers contend that pathologizing normal negative thoughts can worsen depression, anxiety, and other mental health conditions.

Relational frames theory is the theory underlying ACT (Hayes, Barnes-Holmes, & Roche, 2001). **Relational frames theory (RFA)** posits that the function of human language and other higher cognitive processes is to appraise associations or relationships between things. For example, language enables humans to quickly process similarities and differences, and the strength of those similarities and differences, along many different dimensions. Hayes developed RFA, and has noted that it is complex and difficult to digest easily. He attributes the fact that it took nearly 20 years for the first ACT book to be published as evidence of its complexity (Fletcher & Hayes, 2005). Following Hayes's lead, we attribute our limited discussion of RFA to its complexity.

ACT often focuses on two types of destructive normality: cognitive fusion and experiential avoidance (Hayes, 2016). Put simply, **cognitive fusion** occurs when individuals operate as if "I am my thoughts." As noted previously, thoughts are not reality and thoughts are not the only dimension of the self. Pulling thoughts too closely into the self is cognitive fusion and contributes to psychological suffering.

Experiential avoidance is defined as the tendency for individuals to engage in a struggle to escape and/or avoid unpleasant or unwanted private experiences. As is true with behavioral and existential models, avoidance is negatively reinforcing and is an effort to deny valid dimensions of human experience.

To address cognitive fusion and experiential avoidance, ACT incorporates six therapeutic components:

1. *Be here now*: Making contact with the present moment.

2. *Defusion*: Separating/detaching from private thoughts; holding on to thoughts lightly, not tightly.

3. *Acceptance*: Opening up and making room for all experiences, including so-called unpleasant ones.

4. *Self-as-context*: The observing self is the perspective from which context is established and through which awareness happens.

5. *Values*: The goals you desire and the activities/beliefs that matter to you.

6. *Committed action*: Doing what you need to do to move toward and live by your values.

ACT includes experiential components. For example, it's common for therapists to guide clients to engage in mindful breathing, participate in exposure activities, and do the hexaflexercise (an activity that incorporates all of the previously listed six therapeutic components; Harris, 2009).

In summary, ACT integrates mindfulness into clinical practice. That's why ACT begins with the word *acceptance*. It also emphasizes values-based committed action—which is where the word commitment comes from. Finally, it emphasizes action in the direction of values-based commitments, which is why the authors want us to say ACT all as one word, to emphasize action.

ACT: The Evidence Base

Given that ACT is comparatively new, its research based is extensive. To start, as noted previously, ACT is already included on the APA Division 12 list for five separate conditions. Below, we summarize two fairly recent meta-analyses.

Lee, An, Levin, and Twohig (2015) conducted a meta-analysis on ACT for the treatment of substance use, with 10 different RCTs where ACT was compared with other active treatments (i.e., 12-step programs, CBT, pharmacotherapy, and treatment as usual). The researchers reported a "small to medium effect size" favoring ACT and concluded that ACT appears promising as an intervention for smoking and other drug use (Lee, An, Levin, & Twohig, 2015, p. 1).

In a general meta-analysis of ACT in the treatment of "… mental and physical health problems," 39 RCTs were identified and included in the analysis (A-Tjak et al., 2015). The researchers reported that ACT had better outcomes than waitlist controls (0.82), psychological placebo (0.51), and treatment as usual (0.64). They also reported that when CBT was included as a comparator, ACT and CBT were essentially equivalent. It appears that ACT may be a treatment approach that is effective across different diagnostic conditions (i.e., having transdiagnostic value), but more research was recommended (A-Tjak et al., 2015).

Mindfulness–Based Cognitive Therapy

Mindfulness-based cognitive therapy (MBCT) is another third wave therapy that combines mindful acceptance and psychoeducation as a means of treating various mental health problems and life challenges. The most notable application of MBCT is in the treatment of clinical depression, particularly the prevention of depressive relapse. However, MBCT and mindfulness-based stress reduction have been adapted for addressing a wide range of life problems, including, but not limited to: (a) insomnia, (b) parental depression, (c) substance abuse relapse prevention, and (d) eating problems (Follette & Hazlett-Stevens, 2016).

MBCT Development

MBCT was developed as a variant of mindfulness-based stress reduction (MBSR). Jon Kabat-Zinn (1979) had been engaging in his own meditation practice. In the late 1970s, he decided to integrate meditation practice into a stress reduction clinic at the University of Massachusetts. He developed an 8-week curriculum, introducing Buddhist meditation to American medical patients. His MBSR protocol was used primarily with patients coping with chronic illness and chronic pain. MBSR is described in Kabat-Zinn's (1990) book, *Full Catastrophe Living*.

In 1993, cognitive therapy researchers Zindel Segal, Mark Williams, and John Teasdale (2002, 2013) observed Kabat-Zinn's MBSR program. Subsequently, they modified the MBSR protocol for medical patients who had recently recovered from a major depressive episode. The goal of the program was depression relapse prevention. The MBCT protocol was/is very similar to Kabat-Zinn's original protocol.

Characteristics and Protocol

The MBCT protocol for preventing depression relapse is an eight-session group format that combines meditation practice with psychoeducation for depression. Mindfulness meditation is used, in part, to address the negative cyclical ruminative nature of chronic, recurrent depression.

MBCT practitioners make a point of distinguishing between mental states or modalities associated with doing and being. Doing, although not viewed as inherently pathological, can become so because the doing modality motivates patients to act to solve their problems. The downside of this is that problem-solving isn't always possible. Consequently, negative rumination combined with frustrated actions usually results in increased negative rumination about how the problem "should" have been taken care of. Alternatively, MBCT teaches patients to, when appropriate, step back from problem-solving (the doing modality) and instead engage the brain's being modality. Engaging the being modality when problems are unsolvable generally provides relief from stress, rumination, and frustration.

Each of the eight sessions in MBCT has a title that articulates the session theme. These include:

1. Awareness and automatic pilot.

2. Living in our heads.

3. Gathering the scattered mind.

4. Recognizing aversion.

5. Allowing/letting be.

6. Thoughts are not facts.

7. How can I best take care of myself?

8. Maintaining and extending new learning.

MBCT is administered in a group format, although some practitioners and researchers have been experimenting with using it in individual therapy.

MBCT group leaders are expected to maintain their own mindfulness meditation practice. Segal, Williams, and Teasdale (2013) are clear in passing on this important prerequisite. The MBCT view is that if practitioners aren't engaging in their own mindfulness practice, they won't be able to adequately teach it or understand the challenges their patients might face.

MBCT: The Evidence Base

MBCT has a strong and growing evidence base. Based on several meta-analyses, it appears that MBCT is effective in preventing depression relapse among patients who have a history of recurrent depressive episodes. Specifically, in a meta-analysis of 1,258 patients, results were that patients receiving MBCT were at significant reduced risk of relapse after 60 weeks (Kuyken et al., 2016). Previous meta-analyses have been consistent with this finding,

with typical effect sizes in the 0.60 to 0.69 range (Galante, Iribarren, & Pearce, 2013; Piet & Hougaard, 2011).

As noted previously, not only is MBCT used for depression treatment and relapse prevention, it has also been adapted for other mental health problems and life challenges. Although most of the controlled outcomes research has focused on depression, MBCT has also shown promise in the treatment of insomnia, stress reduction among medical patients, various forms of anxiety, and substance abuse relapse prevention (Abbott et al., 2014; Larouche, Lorrain, Côté, & Bélisle, 2015).

STEPPING BACK AND LOOKING FORWARD

Earlier in this chapter we wrote about some authors making the claim that there are now over 1,000 therapies. We may have forgotten to say that we think that's a ridiculous and meaningless statement. Even if there were 1,000 therapies, they couldn't be that much different. This is probably why, when we read about a new and exciting therapy approach, our first reaction is to suspect that it is simply somebody rebottling, repackaging, relanguaging, or recombining one or more of the original approaches to counseling and psychotherapy.

Fortunately, there are alternative ways of viewing the supposed 1,000 different therapies. In particular, we find it helpful to focus higher order principles in an effort to better understand how to provide therapy to real people with real problems.

Higher Order Integration: The Transtheoretical Change Model

In the late 1970s James Prochaska began looking at theories of psychotherapy in a new way. While reviewing traditional psychotherapy systems, he discovered most theories emphasize personality and psychopathology, both of which orient therapists toward why people don't change rather than why people do change (Prochaska, 1995). Consequently, he and his colleagues began their groundbreaking work on developing a new theory of therapy—a transtheoretical model focusing on how people change (Prochaska, 1995; Prochaska & DiClemente, 1982; Prochaska, DiClemente, & Norcross, 1993).

The **transtheoretical model** is a higher-order theory of psychotherapy integration; it emphasizes both common factors and theoretical integration. The model seeks to:

• Respect the fundamental diversity and essential unity of therapy systems.

• Emphasize empiricism.

- Account for how people change inside and outside of therapy.

- Address physical and mental health problems.

- Encourage therapists to be innovators and not simply borrowers from various systems.

When the transtheoretical model was developed, counseling and psychotherapy were ripe for creative, integrative ideas. In the 1970s, eclecticism was very popular, but it was also associated with soft thinking, fragmentation, and superficiality, as described earlier in this chapter (Eysenck, 1970).

Prochaska (1995) considers his development of the transtheoretical model to be a product of increasing divergence in the field. Based on Guilford's (1956) model of intelligence he notes that periods of divergence need to be followed by higher levels of convergent thinking. Consequently, because therapy approaches had become so fragmented in the 1970s, the time was right for greater rapprochement or convergence in counseling.

The transtheoretical model focuses on three different dimensions of change:

1. Change processes.

2. Stages of change.

3. Levels of change.

Change Processes

Beginning with research focused on addictive behaviors, Prochaska and colleagues identified common **change processes** occurring across different theoretical orientations. They identified 10 primary change processes (Prochaska, 1995; Prochaska & Norcross, 2003). These processes, along with their likely theoretical roots, are listed in Table 14.3.

Stages of Change

Some clients come to therapy ready to change for the better. Other clients end up in therapy with little or no motivation for change. Recognizing these basic differences, as well as more subtle change levels, Prochaska identified six **stages of change**:

1. *Precontemplation*: During this stage, the individual has little or no interest in changing his behavior.

2. *Contemplation*: During this stage, the individual is aware that a problem exists, but she has not yet made a clear commitment to making a personal change.

3. *Preparation*: During preparation, there may be some intention and effort made toward change. For example, a sedentary individual may go out and buy running shoes or join a fitness club. There may be occasional forays into action, but mostly these individuals are so deep into contemplation that they're only beginning some minimal action toward change but are not yet into the action stage.

4. *Action*: During action, people are plunging into the change process. These are the clients whom most therapists love to see because their motivation is so high that they quickly engage in the therapy process and often make considerable and immediate progress. Prochaska (1995) defines this stage as the "successful alteration of a problem behavior for a period from 1 day to 6 months."

5. *Maintenance*: During maintenance, people continue with their action and deepen their commitment toward permanent change. There is continual work or action toward relapse prevention. This stage continues from 6 months to infinity, but relapse often occurs at some point during maintenance. For example, many alcohol- or drug-addicted individuals reach the maintenance stage only to experience relapse. Then,

Table 14.3 Common Change Processes and Theoretical Origins

Consciousness-raising	Processes of personal insight and awareness that stem from feedback and education	Psychodynamic theory and feminist theory
Dramatic relief	Catharsis and expressive procedures	Gestalt theory
Self-re-evaluation	An examination of self, self-schema, and other variables	Cognitive therapy, constructivist, and Adlerian
Environmental re-evaluation	Information processing with an environmental focus	Cognitive and constructivist theory
Self-liberation	A focus on personal freedom	Existential and choice theory
Social-liberation	A focus on freedom from social oppression	Feminist, existential, and constructivist
Counterconditioning	New learning that overcomes old learning	Behavioral
Stimulus control	Management of environmental stimuli	Behavioral
Reinforcement management	Management of environmental contingencies	Behavioral
Helping relationship	The healing potential of a helping relationship	Person-centered and feminist

they generally cycle back through the stages of change in an effort to obtain mastery over their problem. This recycling tendency is apparent in many nonclients as many individuals repeatedly make the same New Year's resolutions (for 5 or more years) until finally maintaining their goal for over 6 months (Norcross & Vangarelli, 1989).

6. *Termination*: During termination, people have 100% confidence that they will not engage in the problem behavior again. They also report having no urges to engage in the problem behavior again. Prochaska uses a 5-year criterion of symptom liberation, plus 100% confidence, for classification into this stage. In a study of recovering alcoholics and smokers, 17% and 16% of former drinkers and smokers were classified as being in the termination stage of change (Snow, Prochaska, & Rossi, 1992).

Levels of Change
Prochaska identified five different **levels of change**:

1. Symptom/situational problems.
2. Maladaptive cognitions.
3. Current interpersonal conflicts.
4. Family systems conflicts.
5. Intrapersonal conflicts.

Based on the transtheoretical model, efforts are initially directed toward the symptom-situation level because most clients come to therapy seeking relief from a particular distressing symptom or situation. However, as Prochaska points out, rarely does therapy proceed in a simple and straightforward manner that focuses solely on symptom elimination (Prochaska, 1995). Instead, as clients participate in therapy for longer periods, they delve deeper into cognitive, interpersonal, familial, and intrapsychic issues.

One advantage of the transtheoretical model is its emphasis on the interactive and integrative nature of therapeutic processes, stages, and levels. For example, when clients are in the precontemplative stage, it's likely they will resist action-oriented therapy interventions. Alternatively, when clients are in the contemplative or preparation stages, they may be ready to experience sudden, dramatic relief, followed by regression or relapse. It's best to focus on symptom and situational issues with clients in these early stages of change, as they're unlikely to be motivated to explore deeper, more personal issues (i.e., interpersonal, familial, or intrapsychic conflicts).

PUTTING IT IN PRACTICE

14.4 A Concluding Image: Group Therapy with Some Exceptionally Difficult Clients

There are indeed many ways to practice counseling and psychotherapy. There are also many ways to end a book. Because this is a textbook, we're tempted to end it with a logical and rational analysis of future trends in counseling and psychotherapy. However, because humans have difficulty predicting tomorrow's weather, we chose a different, more irreverent ending. We leave you with a fantasy.

After reading and writing about so many great therapy minds, one of us (you can guess which one) had a daydream.

Imagine many of the historical and contemporary therapy masters gathered together in one location. They form a circle and begin a discussion. Old friends and rivals are reunited. Freud appears and shakes hands with Jean Baker Miller, who has brought quite a number of impressive-looking women with her. Fritz Perls tries to kiss some of their hands. Alfred Adler brings Raissa, who quickly bonds with Jean Baker Miller. Carl Rogers signs a book for Prochaska. New friends are made, old rivalries rejuvenated. Insoo Kim Berg smiles quietly off to one side, hoping to engage Virginia Satir. Jung notes to himself that she (Berg) must be an introvert. What might happen in this circumstance? What might happen in *"An Encounter Group for the Major Theorists"*?

After some initial mingling, the group begins:

Rogers: I wonder where we might want to start.

Raissa Adler: Here's where I'm starting. I'm not taking minutes for this meeting. I did that back in 1912 for the Free Psychoanalytic Society, so I've put in my time. It's someone else's turn. I nominate a male, any male. Women have been taking notes in meetings for so long it's ridiculous. The problem with women's psyches has more to do with oppression than repression.

Feminists: [Including Jean Baker Miller, Judith Jordan, bell hooks, Lillian Comas-Diaz, and Laura Brown—all of whom, fully embracing the subversion concept, snuck into the group.] You go woman! We're with you.

Freud: [Turning his back, since there is no couch to hide behind.] That's it. Say whatever comes to mind.

Ellis: If you want to think that taking notes is oppression, that's up to you, but as far as I can tell, you're oppressing yourself with a bunch of damn crazy, irrational thinking.

Beck: You know Al, we've been through this before, but what I think you mean is that Raissa's thinking that taking notes is oppression could be maladaptive, but not irrational.

Glasser: Raissa can choose to take notes or choose not to take notes. She can also choose to think she's oppressed or choose not to think she's oppressed. Personally, Raissa, I recommend that you read my book, *Choice Theory*. I want you to read it, and I think it will help you, but of course, whether you read it or not, that's completely your choice.

F. Perls: Be here now, Raissa. Act out those feelings. Be the pen. Talk to the paper.

L. Perls: Fritz, she can be the pen without your assistance. If by chance she finds herself, that's beautiful.

Ellis: She won't find a goddamn thing in this group of love-slobs without a flashlight.

Skinner: Uh. Albert. I've been wanting to mention to you that if you could just keep quiet when people say inappropriate things, we might have a chance at extinguishing that particular behavior.

Ellis: Well, Burris, did you have an irrational thought that someone might actually care about your opinion before you engaged in that speaking behavior, or was it just a function of its consequences?

V. Satir: Albert, if you could just get up on that chair and talk down to Burris, I think you could get in touch with your placating style.

Skinner [whispering to Ellis]: Seriously man. Just ignore her. I'm talking about a complete extinction schedule. Just like I'm ignoring you—except for when you sit quietly and listen to me.

Rollo May: Freedom and dignity are the essence of being. There's far too much freedom, with very little dignity in this room.

I. K. Berg: If a miracle happened and we all got out of this group without anyone getting hurt, what would that look like?

A. Adler: My God! No wonder I felt so inferior. I just remembered an early memory.

Freud: Inferiority. I hate that word. It makes me feel so very small. I just want to be recognized for my contributions. It would make my mother proud.

Rogers: It's like, if only I can make my mother happy. Getting recognized, being remembered, that's one big way you can have that experience.

Ellis: Siggy, my man. Let me offer you an elegant solution. That crap about being recognized and making your mother proud is the most f—ing ridiculous thing I've ever heard. What's the big deal if everybody forgets you? What's the terrible, awful, very bad thing that will happen? You'll be dead and it won't make a white rat's ass difference if people remember you or not.

Feminists: That's right. We can't believe we're agreeing with Albert Ellis. White males can afford to play with such big ideas. Immortality. Do you have a clue about the legacy you've left? There have been decades of girls and women with destroyed self-esteems. Do you recognize that they litter your road to "greatness"?

Mahoney: I can see Freud as great and I can see feminism as great. Even this lived moment in our genetic epistemology exudes the potential for greatness. We're not a passive repository of sensory experience. Instead, we're co-constructing this reality right now.

Prochaska: This entire group seems to be in precontemplation.

D. W. Sue: Yeah, well, I might consider change if we could include a minority voice or two? Most of what I've heard so far is the construction of a very narrow, white reality. Culture is primary, and we need to include diversity if we're to meet the needs of everyone, including Raissa, who happens to have a strong Russian ethnocultural identity.

Raissa Adler: [Slowly stands and walks over and embraces D. W. Sue.]

Rogers: What I'm seeing and what I'm hearing, if I'm getting this right, is affection and appreciation. Two people who have, now and again, felt marginalized are able to connect more deeply with each other right now than with anyone else.

M. White: Actually, Carl, I think I'd just call this a sparkling moment.

Choosing Your Theory

As we come to the end of this text, we're tempted to tell you that you should choose a specific theory. We're tempted to encourage you to choose one that fits with your personality and values. We're also tempted to tell you not to choose a theory. As dialectic behavior therapists might suggest, such is the nature of the world. Sometimes the best path forward is to embrace both sides of the dialectic. So, our final advice: choose a theory, but don't grip it too tightly, and then get ready to integrate. At first you might feel like a syncretic eclectic, but later you might sense your growing ability to discern when to assimilate another theoretical approach or technical strategy. In the end, we think you'll discover that the practice of counseling and psychotherapy makes for a fabulous life-long learning process. Even though this book is ending, your learning will continue.

CONCLUDING COMMENTS

In every human domain, we have more information than we can possibly sort out and use effectively. Wisdom consists of knowing both *what* to know and *how* to use what you know. A careful analysis and synthesis of the material in this book will go a long ways toward helping you begin your journey as a mental health professional.

In the end, we challenge you to look beyond the face value of these theories. We encourage you to treat them as more than narrow historical artifacts. If you can view these theories as a product of time, place, deep contemplation, and a sincere desire to understand and alleviate human suffering, you'll be better served.

CHAPTER SUMMARY AND REVIEW

Over the years many theorists and therapists have argued over which of the many different therapy approaches is most effective. So far, no one has won that argument. Some writers have estimated that there are now over 1,000 different approaches to counseling and psychotherapy.

There are two good explanations for why there are so many different approaches to counseling and psychotherapy. First, therapy approaches need to deal with individuality and cultural specificity. Second, over time, human conflict has stimulated the proliferation of different theories.

There are five main ways of practicing counseling and psychotherapy. These include: (1) ideological purity, (2) theoretical integration, (3) common factors, (4) technical eclecticism, and (5) assimilative integration. There are advantages and disadvantages associated with each of these approaches.

In recent years there has been much more focus on integrating theoretical concepts and developing hybrid therapy approaches. Lazarus's technical eclecticism model was an early example of selecting strategies associated with different approaches to address unique client needs. More recently, five different "new wave behavior therapies" have come to the forefront as integrational and evidence-based approaches. These include: (1) EMDR, (2) IPT, (3) EFT, (4) DBT, (5) ACT, and (6) MBCT. Each of these approaches has a fascinating origin, a specific treatment protocol, and a strong evidence base.

The transtheoretical change model is a higher order integrative model designed to inform practitioners about common change processes, stages of change, and levels of change. Although it's tempting to want to choose a specific theoretical orientation, we recommend that you don't grip any orientation too tightly, staying open to integration possibilities.

INTEGRATIVE KEY TERMS

Acceptance and commitment therapy (ACT)

Action

Assimilative integration

Authentic chameleon

BASIC I.D.

Change processes

Cognitive fusion

Common factors

Contemplation

Corrective emotional experience

Demoralization hypothesis

Destructive normality

Dialectical behavior therapy (DBT)

Dialectical philosophy

Emotional dysregulation

Emotion-focused therapy (EFT)

Emotionally charged, confiding relationship

Experiential avoidance

Eye movement desensitization reprocessing (EMDR)

Gaslighting

Grief

Healing setting

Ideological purity

Interpersonal deficit

Interpersonal formulation

Interpersonal role dispute

Interpersonal psychotherapy for depression (IPT-D)

Levels of change

Maintenance

Multimodal therapy (MMT)

Precontemplation

Preparation

Psychotherapy or counseling integration

Radical acceptance

Rationale, conceptual scheme, or myth

Relational frames theory (RFA)

Ritual

Role transition

Stages of change

Syncretism

Technical eclecticism

Termination

The who–how–whom question

Theoretical integration

Transtheoretical model

References

Abbass, A. A., Hancock, J. T., Henderson, J., & Kisely, S. (2006). Short-term psychodynamic psychotherapies for common mental disorders. Cochrane Database of Systematic Reviews, Issue 4, Article No. CD004687.

Abbott, R. A., Whear, R., Rodgers, L. R., Bethel, A., Coon, J. T., Kuyken, W., et al. (2014). Effectiveness of mindfulness-based stress reduction and mindfulness based cognitive therapy in vascular disease: A systematic review and meta-analysis of randomised controlled trials. *Journal of Psychosomatic Research, 76*(5), 341–351.

Ackerman, N. (1938). The unity of the family. *Archives of Pediatrics, 55*, 51–62.

Ackerman, N. W., & Lakos, M. H. (1959). *The treatment of a child and family*. Oxford, England: Prentice-Hall.

Ackerman, N. W., & Neubauer, P. B. (1948). *Failures in the psychotherapy of children*. New York, NY: Grune & Stratton.

Adams, M. (2016). Existential therapy as a skills-learning process. *Existential Analysis, 27*(1), 58–69.

Adler, A. (1898). *Gesundheitsbuch fur die schneidergewerbe [Healthbook for the tailor trade]*. Berlin: C. Heymanns.

Adler, A. (1927). *Understanding human nature*. Garden City, NY: Garden City.

Adler, A. (1931). *What life should mean to you*. Oxford, England: Little, Brown.

Adler, A. (1935). Introduction. *International Journal of Individual Psychology, 1*(1), 5–8.

Adler, A. (1937). Position in the family constellation influence life-style. *International Journal of Individual Psychology, 3*(3), 211–227.

Adler, A. (1958). *What life should mean to you*. New York, NY: Capricorn.

Adler, A. (1964). *Problems of neurosis: A book of case histories*. New York, NY: Harper Torchbooks.

Adler, A. (1983). *The practice and theory of individual psychology* (P. Radin, Trans.). Totowa, NJ: Littlefield, Adams.

Adler, R. (1982). Minutes of the society for free psychoanalytic research: September 1912 to January 1913. *Individual Psychology: Journal of Adlerian Theory, Research & Practice, 38*(1), 22–27.

Afifi, T. O., Ford, D., Gershoff, E. T., Merrick, M., Grogan-Kaylor, A., Ports, K. A., et al. (2017). Spanking and adult mental health impairment: The case for the designation of spanking as an adverse childhood experience. *Child Abuse & Neglect, 71*, 24–31.

Afifi, T. O., Mota, N. P., Dasiewicz, P., MacMillan, H. L., & Sareen, J. (2012). Physical punishment and mental disorders: Results from a nationally representative US sample. *Pediatrics, 130*(2), 184–192.

Afifi, T. O., Mota, N., MacMillan, H. L., & Sareen, J. (2013). Harsh physical punishment in childhood and adult physical health. *Pediatrics, 132*(2), e333–e340.

Agishtein, P., Pirutinsky, S., Kor, A., Baruch, D., Kanter, J., & Rosmarin, D. H. (2013). Integrating spirituality into a behavioral model of depression. *Journal of Cognitive and Behavioral Psychotherapies, 13*(2), 275–289.

Agras, W. S., Schneider, J. A., Arnow, B., Raeburn, S. D., & Telch, C. F. (1989). Cognitive-behavioral and response-prevention treatments for bulimia nervosa. *Journal of Consulting & Clinical Psychology, 57*, 215–221.

Agren, T., Björkstrand, J., & Fredrikson, M. (2017). Disruption of human fear reconsolidation using imaginal and *in vivo* extinction. *Behavioural Brain Research, 319*, 9–15.

Ahbel-Rappe, K. (2009). "After a long pause": How to read Dora as history. *Journal of the American Psychoanalytic Association, 57*(3), 595–629.

Ainsworth, M. D. (1969). Object relations, dependency, and attachment: A theoretical review of the infant–mother relationship. *Child Development, 40*(4), 969–1025.

Ainsworth, M. D., & Bell, S. M. (1970). Attachment, exploration, and separation: Illustrated by the behavior of one-year-olds in a strange situation. *Child Development, 41*, 49–67.

Ainsworth, M. D. S., Blehar, M. C., Waters, E., & Wall, S. (1978). *Patterns of attachment: A psychological study of the strange situation*. Hillsdale, NJ: Erlbaum.

Alberti, R. E., & Emmons, M. L. (1970). *Your perfect right: A guide to assertive behavior*. San Luis Obispo, CA: Impact.

Alberti, R., & Emmons, M. (2017). *Your perfect right* (10th ed.). San Luis Obispo, CA: Impact.

Alegria, S., Carvalho, I., Sousa, D., Correia, E. A., Fonseca, J., Pires, B. S., & Fernandes, S. (2016). Process and outcome research in existential psychotherapy. *Existential Analysis, 27*(1), 78–92.

Aleksandrov, D. S., Bowen, A. R., & Colker, J. (2016). Parent training and cultural considerations. *The Journal of Individual Psychology, 72*(2), 77–89.

Alexander, F. (1963). The dynamics of psychotherapy in light of learning theory. *American Journal of Psychiatry, 120*, 440–448.

Alexander, F., & French, T. M. (1946). *Psychoanalytic psychotherapy*. New York, NY: Ronald.

Alexander, J., & Parsons, B. V. (1982). *Functional family therapy*. Monterey, CA: Brooks/Cole.

Alexander, J. F., & Parsons, B. V. (1973). Short-term behavioral intervention with delinquent families: Impact on family process and recidivism. *Journal of Abnormal Psychology, 81,* 219–225.

Alexander, J. F., Warburton, J., Waldron, H., & Mas, C. H. (1985). The misuse of functional family therapy: A non-sexist rejoinder. *Journal of Marital and Family Therapy, 11*(2), 139–144.

Alexander, S., Shilts, L., Liscio, M., & Rambo, A. (2008). Return to sender: Letter writing to bring hope to both client and team. *Journal of Systemic Therapies, 27*(1), 59–66.

Alghamdi, M., Hunt, N., & Thomas, S. (2015). The effectiveness of narrative exposure therapy with traumatised firefighters in Saudi Arabia: A randomized controlled study. *Behaviour Research and Therapy, 66,* 64–71.

Ali, A., Caplan, P. J., & Fagnant, R. (2010). *Gender stereotypes in diagnostic criteria.* New York, NY: Springer Science + Business Media.

Allen, B., & Borgen, K. (1994). Multimodal therapy for survivors of sexual abuse with developmental disabilities: An evaluation of treatment effectiveness. *Sexuality and Disability, 12*(3), 201–206.

Amendt-Lyon, N. (2008). Gender differences in Gestalt therapy. *Gestalt Review, 12*(2), 106–121.

American Counseling Association. (2014). *The American Counseling Association Code of Ethics.* Alexandria, VA: Author.

American Psychiatric Association. (2013). *Diagnostic and statistical manual of mental disorders* (5th ed.). Washington, DC: Author.

American Psychiatric Association. (2000). *Diagnostic and statistical manual of mental disorders* (IV-TR ed.). Washington, DC: Author.

American Psychological Association. (1990). *Guidelines for providers of psychological services to ethnic, linguistic, and culturally diverse populations.* Washington, DC: Author.

American Psychological Association. (2000). Guidelines for psychotherapy with lesbian, gay, and bisexual clients. *American Psychologist, 55,* 1440–1451.

American Psychological Association. (2003). Guidelines on multicultural education, training, research, practice, and organizational change for psychologists. *American Psychologist, 58,* 377–402.

American Psychological Association. (2010). *Ethical principles of psychologists and code of conduct.* Washington, DC: Author.

American Psychological Association. (2015). Guidelines for psychological practice with transgender and gender nonconforming people. *American Psychologist, 70,* 832–864.

Andersen, T. (1987). The reflecting team: Dialogue and meta-dialogue in clinical work. *Family Process, 26,* 415–426.

Andersen, T. (1991). *The reflecting team: Dialogues and dialogues about dialogues.* New York, NY: Norton.

Andersen, T. (1995). Reflecting processes: Acts of informing and forming: You can borrow my eyes, but you must not take them away from me! In S. Friedman (Ed.), *The reflecting team in action: Collaborative practices in psychotherapy* (pp. 11–37). New York, NY: Guilford Press.

Andersen, T. (2007). Reflecting talks may have many versions: Here is mine. *International Journal of Psychotherapy, 11*(2), 27–44.

Anderson, C. M., & Stewart, S. (1983). *Mastering resistance: A practical guide to family therapy.* New York: Guilford Press.

Anderson, E. M., & Lambert, M. J. (1995). Short-term dynamically oriented psychotherapy: A review and meta-analysis. *Clinical Psychology Review, 15,* 503–514.

Anderson, H. (2007). A postmodern umbrella: Language and knowledge as relational and generative, and inherently transforming. In H. Anderson & D. Gehart (Eds.), *Collaborative therapy: Relationships and conversations that make a difference* (pp. 7–19). New York, NY: Routledge/Taylor & Francis.

Anderson, H., & Burney, J. P. (2004). A postmodern collaborative approach: A family's reflections on "in-the-room" and "on-the-challenge course" therapy. It's all language. In T. Strong & D. Paré (Eds.), *Furthering talk: Advances in the discursive therapies* (pp. 87–108). New York, NY: Kluwer Academic/Plenum.

Andersson, G., & Asmundson, G. J. G. (2006). Editorial: CBT and religion. *Cognitive Behaviour Therapy, 35*(1), 1–2.

Andreasson, K., Krogh, J., Wenneberg, C., Jessen, H. K. L., Krakauer, K., Gluud, C., et al. (2016). Effectiveness of dialectical behavior therapy versus collaborative assessment and management of suicidality treatment for reduction of self-harm in adults with borderline personality traits and disorder—A randomized observer-blinded clinical trial. *Depression and Anxiety, 33*(6), 520–530.

Anestis, M. D., Anestis, J. C., & Lilienfeld, S. O. (2011). When it comes to evaluating psychodynamic therapy, the devil is in the details. *American Psychologist, 66*(2), 149–151.

Ansbacher, H. L., & Ansbacher, R. R. (Eds.). (1956). *The individual psychology of Alfred Adler.* New York, NY: Harper.

Armfield, J. M. (2008). An experimental study of the role of vulnerability related perceptions in spider fear: Comparing an imaginal and *in vivo* encounter. *Journal of Anxiety Disorders, 22*(2), 222–232.

Arredondo, P., & Perez, P. (2006). Historical perspectives on the multicultural guidelines and contemporary applications. *Professional Psychology: Research and Practice, 37*(1), 1–5.

Arredondo, P., Toporek, R., Brown, S., Jones, J., Locke, D. C., Sanchez, J., & Stadler, H. (1996). *Operationalization of the multicultural counseling competencies.* Alexandria, VA: Association for Multicultural Counseling and Development.

Arzi, A., Holtzman, Y., Samnon, P., Eshel, N., Harel, E., & Sobel, N. (2014). Olfactory aversive conditioning during sleep reduces cigarette-smoking behavior. *The Journal of Neuroscience, 34*(46), 15382–15393.

Asay, T. P., & Lambert, M. J. (1999). The empirical case for the common factors in therapy: Quantitative findings. In M. A. Hubble, B. L. Duncan, & S. D. Miller (Eds.), *The heart and soul of change* (pp. 33–56). Washington, DC: American Psychological Assocation.

Askari, S. F., Liss, M., Erchull, M. J., Staebell, S. E., & Axelson, S. J. (2010). Men want equality, but women don't expect it: Young adults' expectations for participation in household and child care chores. *Psychology of Women Quarterly, 34*(2), 243–252.

Association of Lesbian, Gay, Bisexual, and Transgender Issues in Counseling. (2009). *Competencies for counseling with transgender clients.* Alexandria, VA: Author.

A-Tjak, J., Davis, M. L., Morina, N., Powers, M. B., Smits, J. A. J., & Emmelkamp, P. M. G. (2015). A meta-analysis of the efficacy of acceptance and commitment therapy for clinically relevant mental and physical health problems. *Psychotherapy and Psychosomatics, 84*(1), 30–36.

Atkinson, C., & Woods, K. (2017). Establishing theoretical stability and treatment integrity for motivational interviewing. *Behavioural and Cognitive Psychotherapy, 45,* 337–350.

Atkinson, D. R., & Lowe, S. M. (1995). The role of ethnicity, cultural knowledge, and conventional techniques in counseling and psychotherapy. In J. G. Ponterotto, J. M. Casas, L. A. Suzuki, & C. M. Alexander (Eds.), *Handbook of multicultural counseling* (pp. 387–414). Thousand Oaks, CA: Sage.

Atkinson, D. R., Lowe, S. M., & Mathews, L. (1995). Asian-American acculturation, gender and willingness to seek counseling. *Journal of Multicultural Counseling and Development, 23,* 130–138.

Avis, J. M. (1985). The politics of functional family therapy: A feminist critique. *Journal of Marital and Family Therapy, 11*(2), 127–138.

Axelson, J. A. (1999). *Counseling and development in a multicultural society* (3rd ed.). Belmont, CA: Wadsworth.

Azekhueme, K. U., & Adegoke, A. A. (2010). The efficacy of reality therapy in the reduction of HIV/AIDS—Risk behaviour among adolescents in Nigeria. *The Nigerian Journal of Guidance & Counselling, 15*(1), 1–23.

Baca, L., & Cervantes, H. T. (1984). *The bilingual special education interface.* St. Louis, MO: Times Mirror/Mosby College.

Bachelor, A. (2013). Clients' and therapists' views of the therapeutic alliance: Similarities, differences and relationship to therapy outcome. *Clinical Psychology & Psychotherapy, 20*(2), 118–135.

Bachman, J. G., & O'Malley, P. M. (1977). Self-esteem in young men: A longitudinal analysis of the impact of educational and occupational attainment. *Journal of Personality and Social Psychology, 35*(6), 365–380.

Badenoch, B. (2008). *Being a brain-wise therapist: A practical guide to interpersonal neurobiology.* New York, NY: Norton.

Baker, T. B., & McFall, R. M. (2014). The promise of science-based training and application in psychological clinical science. *Psychotherapy, 51*(4), 482–486.

Baker, T. B., McFall, R. M., & Shoham, V. (2008). Current status and future prospects of clinical psychology: Toward a scientifically principled approach to mental and behavioral health care. *Psychological Science in the Public Interest, 9*(2), 67–103.

Bakewell, S. (2016). *At the existentialist café: Freedom, being, and apricot cocktails with Jean-Paul Sartre, Simone de Beauvoir, Albert Camus, Martin Heidegger, Maurice Merleau-Ponty, and others.* New York, NY: Other Press.

Balint, E. (1950). Changing therapeutic aims and techniques in psychoanalysis. *International Journal of Psychoanalytic Psychology, 31,* 117–124.

Balint, M., Ornstein, P. H., & Balint, E. (1972). *Focal psychotherapy.* Philadelphia, PA: Lippincott.

Ballou, M. B. (1984). Thoughts on reality therapy from a feminist. *Journal of Reality Therapy, 4*(1), 28–32.

Ballou, M., & Brown, L. S. (Eds.). (2002). *Rethinking mental health and disorder: Feminist perspectives.* New York, NY: Guilford.

Bandura, A. (1965). Vicarious processes; A case of no-trial learning. In L. Berkowitz (Ed.), *Advances in experimental social psychology,* Vol. 2 (pp. 49–91). New York, NY: Academic Press.

Bandura, A. (1971). Psychotherapy based on modeling procedures. In A. E. Bergin & S. L. Garfield (Eds.), *Handbook of psychotherapy and behavior change: An empirical analysis* (pp. 653–708). New York, NY: Wiley.

Bandura, A. (1977). Self-efficacy: Toward a unifying theory of behavioral change. *Psychological Review, 84,* 191–215.

Bandura, A. (1978). The self system in reciprocal determinism. *American Psychologist, 33,* 344–358.

Bandura, A., & Adams, N. E. (1977). Analysis of self-efficacy theory of behavioral change. *Cognitive Therapy and Research, 1,* 287–310.

Bandura, A., Blanchard, E. B., & Ritter, B. (1969). Relative efficacy of desensitization and modeling approaches for inducing behavioral affective, and attitudinal changes. *Journal of Personality and Social Psychology, 13,* 173–199.

Bandura, A., Ross, D., & Ross, S. A. (1963). Imitation of film-mediated aggressive models. *Journal of Abnormal & Social Psychology, 66,* 3–11.

Bandura, A., & Walters, R. H. (1963). *Social learning and personality development.* New York, NY: Holt, Rinehart, and Winston.

Bankart, C. P. (1997). *Talking cures: A history of Western and Eastern psychotherapies.* Pacific Grove, CA: Brooks/Cole.

Barclay, S. R., & Wolff, L. A. (2011). When lifestyles collide: An Adlerian-based approach to workplace conflict. *The Journal of Individual Psychology, 67*(2), 122–135.

Barlow, H., & Craske, M. G. (2000). *Mastery of your anxiety and panic.* New York, NY: Graywind.

Barnett, J. E., Lazarus, A. A., Vasquez, M. J. T., Johnson, W. B., & Moorehead-Slaughter, O. (2007). Boundary issues and multiple relationships: Fantasy and reality. *Professional Psychology: Research and Practice, 38*(4), 401–410.

Baron-Cohen, S. (2003). *The essential difference: Male and female brains and the truth about autism.* New York, NY: Basic Books.

Barrett, S. E., Chin, J. L., Comas-Diaz, L., Espin, O., Greene, B., & McGoldrick, M. (2005). Multicultural feminist therapy: Theory in context. *Women & Therapy, 28*(3–4), 27–61.

Barrett-Lennard, G. T. (1981). The empathy cycle: Refinement of a nuclear concept. *Journal of Counseling Psychology, 28,* 91–100.

Barrineau, P. (1990). Chicago revisited: An interview with Elizabeth Sheerer. *Person-Centered Review, 5,* 416–424.

Bass, A. (2015). The dialogue of unconsciouses, mutual analysis and the uses of the self in contemporary relational psychoanalysis. *Psychoanalytic Dialogues, 25*(1), 2–17.

Bateson, G. (1972). *Steps to an ecology of mind.* New York, NY: Dutton.

Bateson, G., Jackson, D. D., Haley, J., & Weakland, J. (1956). Toward a theory of schizophrenia. *Behavioral Science, 1,* 251–264.

Bateson, G., Jackson, D. D., Haley, J., & Weakland, J. H. (1963). A note on the double bind: 1962. *Family Process, 2*(1), 154–161.

Battista, J., & Almond, R. (1973). The development of meaning in life. *Psychiatry: Journal for the Study of Interpersonal Processes, 36*(4), 409–427.

Baumeister, R. F., & Leary, M. R. (1995). The need to belong: Desire for interpersonal attachments as a fundamental human motivation. *Psychological Bulletin, 117*(3), 497–529.

Baumgardner, P., & Perls, F. (1975). *Legacy from Fritz.* Oxford, England: Science & Behavior.

Beauchamp, T. L., & Childress, J. F. (2013). *Principles of biomedical ethics* (7th ed.). New York, NY: Oxford.

Beauvoir, S. D. (1952). *The second sex.* New York, NY: Knopf.

Beck, A. T. (1961). A systematic investigation of depression. *Comprehensive Psychiatry, 2,* 163–170.

Beck, A. T. (1963). Thinking and depression. *Archives of General Psychiatry, 9,* 324–333.

Beck, A. T. (1970). The core problem in depression: The cognitive triad. In J. Masserman (Ed.), *Depression: Theories and therapies* (pp. 47–55). New York, NY: Grune & Stratton.

Beck, A. T. (1976). *Cognitive therapy and the emotional disorders.* Oxford, England: International Universities Press.

Beck, A. T., Epstein, N., Brown, G., & Steer, R. (1988). An inventory for measuring clinical anxiety: Psychometric properties. *Journal of Consulting & Clinical Psychology, 56,* 893–897.

Beck, A. T., & Haigh, E. A. P. (2014). Advances in cognitive theory and therapy: The generic cognitive model. *Annual Review of Clinical Psychology, 10,* 1–24.

Beck, A. T., Rush, A., Shaw, B., & Emery, G. (1979). *Cognitive therapy of depression.* New York, NY: Guilford Press.

Beck, A. T., Steer, R. A., & Brown, G. (1996). *Beck depression inventory–II.* San Antonio, TX: Psychological Corporation.

Beck, A. T., Ward, C. H., Mendelson, M., Mock, J., & Erbaugh, J. (1961). An inventory for measuring depression. *Archives of General Psychiatry, 4,* 561–571.

Beck, H. P., Levinson, S., & Irons, G. (2009). Finding little Albert: A journey to John B. Watson's infant laboratory. *American Psychologist, 64*(7), 605–614.

Beck, J. S. (2005). *Cognitive therapy for challenging problems: What to do when the basics don't work.* New York, NY: Guilford Press.

Beck, J. S. (2011). *Cognitive therapy: Basics and beyond* (2nd ed). New York, NY: Guilford Press.

Beckstead, D. J., Lambert, M. J., DuBose, A. P., & Linehan, M. (2015). Dialectical behavior therapy with American Indian/Alaska Native adolescents diagnosed with substance use disorders: Combining an evidence based treatment with cultural, traditional, and spiritual beliefs. *Addictive Behaviors, 51,* 84–87.

Bell, A. C., & D'Zurilla, T. J. (2009). Problem-solving therapy for depression: A meta-analysis. *Clinical Psychology Review, 29*(4), 348–353.

Benedetti, R. (2015). Belonging: Ontogeny of a gay psychoanalytic candidate. *International Journal of Psychoanalytic Self Psychology, 10*(4), 398–407.

Benishek, L. A., Dugosh, K. L., Kirby, K. C., Matejkowski, J., Clements, N. T., Seymour, B. L., & Festinger, D. S. (2014). Prize-based contingency management for the treatment of substance abusers: A meta-analysis. *Addiction, 109*(9), 1426–1436.

Benson, H. (1976). *The relaxation response.* New York, NY: Avon Books.

Berg, I. K., & de Shazer, S. (1993). Making numbers talk: Language in therapy. In S. Friedman (Ed.), *The new language of change: Constructive collaboration in psychotherapy* (pp. 5–24). New York, NY: Guilford Press.

Berg, I. K., & Miller, S. D. (1992). *Working with the problem drinker: A solution-focused approach.* New York, NY: Norton.

Bériault, M., & Larivée, S. (2005). Guérir avec l'EMDR: Preuves et controverses. French review of EMDR efficacy: Evidences and controversies. *Revue De Psychoeducation, 34*(2), 355–396.

Bernstein, D. A., & Borkovec, T. D. (1973). *Progressive relaxation training: A manual for the helping professions.* Champaign, IL: Research Press.

Berry, K., & Danquah, A. (2016). Attachment-informed therapy for adults: Towards a unifying perspective on practice. *Psychology and Psychotherapy: Theory, Research and Practice, 89*(1), 15–32.

Bertolino, B. (1999). *Therapy with troubled teenagers: Rewriting young lives in progress.* New York, NY: Wiley.

Betan, E., Heim, A. K., Conklin, C. Z., & Westen, D. (2005). Countertransference phenomena and personality pathology in clinical practice: An empirical investigation. *American Journal of Psychiatry, 162*(5), 890–898. doi:10.1176/appi.ajp.162.5.890.

Beutler, L. E. (2009). Making science matter in clinical practice: Redefining psychotherapy. *Clinical Psychology: Science and Practice, 16*(3), 301–317.

Beutler, L. E. (2011). Prescriptive matching and systematic treatment selection. In J. C. Norcross, G. R. VandenBos, & D. K. Freedheim (Eds.), *History of psychotherapy: Continuity and change* (2nd ed.) (pp. 402–407). Washington, DC: American Psychological Association.

Beutler, L. E., Harwood, T. M., Bertoni, M., & Thomann, J. (2006). Systematic treatment selection and prescriptive therapy. In G. Stricker & J. Gold (Eds.), *A casebook of psychotherapy integration* (pp. 29–41). Washington, DC: American Psychological Association.

Beyebach, M., Morejon, A. R., Palenzuela, D. L., & Rodriguez-Arias, J. L. (1996). Research on the process of solution-focused therapy. In S. D. Miller, M. Hubble, & B. L. Duncan (Eds.), *Handbook of solution-focused therapy* (pp. 299–334). San Francisco, CA: Jossey-Bass.

Bieschke, K. J., Perez, R. M., & DeBord, K. A. (2007). *Handbook of counseling and psychotherapy with lesbian, gay, bisexual, and transgender clients* (2nd ed.). Washington, DC: American Psychological Association.

Bigner, J. B., & Wetchler, J. L. (2012). *Handbook of LGBT-affirmative couple and family therapy.* New York, NY: Routledge.

Binder, J. L. (2004). *Key competencies in brief dynamic psychotherapy: Clinical practice beyond the manual.* New York: Guilford.

Binswanger, L. (1933). *Ueber ideenflucht. Flight of ideas.* Oxford, England: Orell Fuessli.

Binswanger, L. (1963). *Being-in-the-world: Selected papers of Ludwig Binswanger.* New York, NY: Basic Books.

Bitter, J. R. (2008). Reconsidering narcissism: An Adlerian-feminist response to the articles in the special section of the journal of individual psychology. *The Journal of Individual Psychology, 64*(3), 270–279.

Bitter, J. R. (2009). *Theory and practice of family therapy and counseling.* Belmont, CA: Brooks/Cole.

Bitter, J. R., Christensen, O. C., Hawes, C., & Nicoll, W. G. (1998). Adlerian brief therapy with individuals, couples, and families. *Directions in clinical and counseling psychology* (pp. 95–111). New York, NY: Hatherleigh.

Blackhart, G. C., Eckel, L. A., & Tice, D. M. (2007). Salivary cortisol in response to acute social rejection and acceptance by peers. *Biological Psychology, 75*(3), 267–276.

Blom, R. (2006). *The handbook of Gestalt play therapy: Practical guidelines for child therapists.* London, England: Kingsley.

Blumberger, D. M., Maller, J. J., Thomson, L., Mulsant, B. H., Rajji, T. K., Maher, M., et al. (2016). Unilateral and bilateral MRI-targeted repetitive transcranial magnetic stimulation for treatment-resistant depression: A randomized controlled study. *Journal of Psychiatry & Neuroscience, 41*(4), E58–E66.

Blume, T. W. (2006). *Becoming a family counselor: A bridge to family therapy theory and practice.* Hoboken, NJ: Wiley.

Bluvshtein, M., Belangee, S., & Haugen, D. (2015). Adler's unlimited universe. *The Journal of Individual Psychology, 71*(2), 89–101.

Boettcher, H., Brake, C. A., & Barlow, D. H. (2016). Origins and outlook of interoceptive exposure. *Journal of Behavior Therapy and Experimental Psychiatry, 53*, 41–51.

Bohart, A. C. (1995). The person-centered psychotherapies. In A. S. Gurman & S. B. Messer (Eds.), *Essential psychotherapies* (pp. 85–127). New York, NY: Guilford Press.

Bohart, A. C., & Greenberg, L. S. (1997). *Empathy reconsidered.* Washington, DC: American Psychological Association.

Boldt, R. M., & Mosak, H. H. (1997). Characterological resistance in psychotherapy: The getter. *Individual Psychology, 53*, 67–80.

Booth, A., Shelley, G., Mazur, A., Tharp, G., & Kittok, R. (1989). Testosterone, and winning and losing in human competition. *Hormones and Behavior, 23*(4), 556–571.

Bordin, E. S. (1979). The generalizability of the psychoanalytic concept of the working alliance. *Psychotherapy: Theory, Research & Practice, 16*(3), 252–260.

Boss, M. (1963). *Psychoanalysis and daseins analysis.* Oxford, England: Basic Books.

Bott, N. T., Radke, A. E., & Kiely, T. (2016). Ethical issues surrounding psychologists' use of neuroscience in the promotion and practice of psychotherapy. *Professional Psychology: Research and Practice, 47*(5), 321–329.

Bottome, P. (1936). Limits to a human being—if any. *International Journal of Individual Psychology, 2*(4), 37–48.

Bottome, P. (1939). *Alfred Adler: Apostle of freedom.* New York, NY: G. P. Putnam's Sons.

Bowden, A., Lorenc, A., & Robinson, N. (2012). Autogenic training as a behavioural approach to insomnia: A prospective cohort study. *Primary Health Care Research and Development, 13*(2), 175–185.

Bowen, M. (1978). *Family therapy in clinical practice.* New York, NY: Aronson.

Bowers, K. S., & Meichenbaum, D. (1984). *The unconscious reconsidered.* New York, NY: Wiley.

Bowlby, J. (1969). *Attachment.* New York: Basic Books.

Bowlby, J. (1977). The making and breaking of affectional bonds: II. Some principles of psychotherapy. *British Journal of Psychiatry, 130*, 421–431.

Bowlby, J. (1978). Attachment theory and its therapeutic implications. *Adolescent Psychiatry, 6*, 5–33.

Bowlby, J. (1988a). Developmental psychiatry comes of age. *American Journal of Psychiatry, 145*(1), 1–10.

Bowlby, J. (1988b). *A secure base: Parent–child attachment and healthy human development.* New York, NY: Basic Books.

Bowlby, J. P. (1949). The study and reduction of group tensions in the family. *Human Relations, 2*, 123–138.

Bowman, C. E., & Nevis, E. C. (2005). *The history and development of Gestalt therapy.* Thousand Oaks, CA: Sage.

Boyce Davies, C. (2008). *Left of Karl Marx: The political life of black communist Claudia Jones.* Durham, NC: Duke University Press.

Boyd-Franklin, N., Cleek, E. N., Wofsy, M., & Mundy, B. (2013). *Therapy in the real world: Effective treatments for challenging problems.* Guilford Press, New York, NY.

Braith, J. A., McCullough, J. P., & Bush, J. P. (1988). Relaxation-induced anxiety in a subclinical sample of chronically anxious subjects. *Journal of Behavior Therapy and Experimental Psychiatry, 19*(3), 193–198.

Breggin, P. R. (1991). *Toxic psychiatry: Why therapy, empathy and love must replace the drugs, electroshock and biochemical theories of the "new psychiatry."* New York: St. Martins.

Breggin, P. R. (2001). A dangerous assignment. In H. G. Rosenthal (Ed.), *Favorite counseling and therapy homework assignments* (pp. 58–59). Washington, DC: Accelerated Development.

Breggin, P. R. (2016). Rational principles of psychopharmacology for therapists, healthcare providers and clients. *Journal of Contemporary Psychotherapy, 46*(1), 1–13.

Brenner, C. (1973). *An elementary textbook of psychoanalysis* (Rev. ed.). Madison, CT: International Universities Press.

Breuer, J., & Freud, S. (1895). *Studies on hysteria* (Standard Edition ed.). London: Hogarth Press.

Bridson, K. (2010). *Stunned: The new generation of women having babies, getting angry, and creating a mothers' movement.* Deerfield Beach, FL: HCI.

Brigman, G., Villares, E., & Webb, L. (2011). The efficacy of individual psychology approaches for improving student achievement and behavior. *The Journal of Individual Psychology, 67*(4), 408–419.

Brizendine, L. (2006). *The female brain.* New York, NY: Broadway Books.

Brockmon, C. (2004). The fish is in the water and the water is in the fish: A perspective on the context of gay and lesbian relationships for gestalt therapists. *Gestalt Review, 8*(2), 161–177.

Bronfenbrenner, U. (1979). *The ecology of human development.* Cambridge, MA: Harvard University Press.

Broverman, I. K., Broverman, D. M., Clarkson, F. E., Rosenkrantz, P. S., & Vogel, S. R. (1970). Sex-role stereotypes and clinical judgment of mental health. *Journal of Consulting and Clinical Psychology, 34*, 1–7.

Brown, C. G., Weber, S., & Ali, S. (2008). Women's body talk: A feminist narrative approach. *Journal of Systemic Therapies, 27*(2), 92–104.

Brown, L. (Director). (1994a). *Feminist therapy.* [Video/DVD] Washington, DC: American Psychological Association.

Brown, L. S. (1994b). *Subversive dialogues: Theory in feminist therapy.* New York, NY: Basic Books.

Brown, L. S. (2010). *Feminist therapy.* Washington, DC: American Psychological Association.

Brown, L. S., & Brodsky, A. M. (1992). The future of feminist therapy. *Psychotherapy, 29*, 51–57.

Brown, T., & Swenson, S. (2005). Identifying basic needs: The contextual needs assessment. *International Journal of Reality Therapy, 24*(2), 7–10.

Browne, E. G. (1921). *Arabian medicine.* New York, NY: Macmillan.

Brownell, P. (2016). Contemporary gestalt therapy: An early case of theoretical integration come of age. In H. E. A. Tinsley, S. H. Lease, & N. S. G. Wiersma (Eds.), *Contemporary therapy and practice in counseling and psychotherapy* (pp. 407–433). Thousand Oaks, CA: Sage.

Brunoni, A. R., Tortella, G., Benseñor, I. M., Lotufo, P. A., Carvalho, A. F., & Fregni, F. (2016). Cognitive effects of transcranial direct current stimulation in depression: Results from the SELECT-TDCS trial and insights for further clinical trials. *Journal of Affective Disorders, 202*, 46–52.

Bry, A. (1973). *Inside psychotherapy.* New York, NY: Signet.

Bryant-Davis, T., & Comas-Diaz, L. (2016). *Womanist and Mujerista psychologies: Voices of fire, acts of courage.* Washington, DC: American Psychological Association.

Buber, M. (1970). *I and thou.* New York, NY: Scribner.

Buck, N. S. (2013). *How to be a great parent: Understanding your child's wants and needs.* New York, NY: Beaufort Books.

Bugental, J. F. T. (1987). *The art of the psychotherapist.* New York, NY: Norton.

Bugental, J. F. T. (1999). *Psychotherapy isn't what you think: Bringing the psychotherapeutic engagement into the living moment.* Phoenix, AZ: Zeig, Tucker.

Bugental, J. F. T. (2000). Outcomes of an existential-humanistic psychotherapy: A tribute to Rollo May. *The Humanistic Psychologist, 28*(1–3), 251–259.

Burdenski, T. K., Jr. (2010). What does the future hold for choice theory and reality therapy from a newcomer's perspective? *International Journal of Choice Theory and Reality Therapy, 29*(2), 13–16.

Burdenski, T. K., Jr., & Faulkner, B. (2010). Empowering college students to satisfy their basic needs: Implications for primary, secondary, and post-secondary educators. *International Journal of Choice Theory and Reality Therapy, 30*(1), 73–97.

Burdenski, T. K., Jr., Faulkner, B., Britzman, M. J., Casstevens, W. J., Cisse, G. S., Crowell, J. L., et al. (2009). The impact of the Glasser scholars project on participants' teaching and research initiatives: Part 1. *International Journal of Reality Therapy, 29*, 43–49.

Burke, J. F. (1989). *Contemporary approaches to psychotherapy and counseling: The self-regulation model.* Pacific Grove, CA: Brooks/Cole.

Burnett, P. C. (1988). Evaluation of Adlerian parenting programs. *Individual Psychology: Journal of Adlerian Theory, Research & Practice, 44*(1), 63–76.

Burns, D. (1989). *The feeling good handbook.* New York, NY: Morrow.

Burns, M. K., Vance, D., Szadokierski, I., & Stockwell, C. (2006). Student needs survey: A psychometrically sound measure of the five basic needs. *International Journal of Reality Therapy, 25*, 4–8.

Busch, F. N. (2015). Discussion: Psychoanalytic research: Progress and questions. *Psychoanalytic Inquiry, 35*, 196–203.

Bush, J. W. (2002). Epictetus, the fundamentals. Retrieved October 12, 2011: http://www.anxietyinsights.info/read/page/jwb_epictetus_fundamentals.htm.

Byrd, K. R., Patterson, C. L., & Turchik, J. A. (2010). Working alliance as a mediator of client attachment dimensions and psychotherapy outcome. *Psychotherapy: Theory, Research, Practice, Training, 47*(4), 631–636.

Cain, D. J. (2010). *Person-centered psychotherapies.* Washington, DC: American Psychological Association.

Campbell, D. T., Stanley, J. C., & Gage, N. L. (1963). *Experimental and quasi-experimental designs for research.* Boston, MA: Houghton Mifflin.

Caplan, P. J. (1995). *They say you're crazy: How the world's most powerful psychiatrists decide who's normal.* Reading, MA: Addison-Wesley/Addison Wesley Longman.

Caplan, P. J., & Cosgrove, L. (Eds.). (2004). *Bias in psychiatric diagnosis.* Lanham, MD: Aronson.

Capuzzi, D., & Stauffer, M. (2015). *Foundations of couples, marriage, and family counseling.* Hoboken, NJ: Wiley.

Cardoş, R. A. I., David, O. A., & David, D. O. (2017). Virtual reality exposure therapy in flight anxiety: A quantitative meta-analysis. *Computers in Human Behavior, 72*, 371–380.

Carkuff, R. R. (1987). *The art of helping* (6th ed.). Amherst, MA: Human Resource Development Press.

Carlson, J. (2015, November/December). Overlooking Adler. *New Therapist, 100*, 22–25.

Carlson, J., & Englar-Carlson, M. (2017). *Adlerian psychotherapy.* Washington, DC: American Psychological Association.

Carlson, J., & Glasser, W. (2004). Adler and Glasser: A demonstration and dialogue. *The Journal of Individual Psychology, 60*, 308–324.

Carlson, J., & Johnson, J. (2016). In I. Marini & M. A. Stebnicki (Eds.), *Adlerian therapy* (2nd ed.) (pp. 225–228). New York, NY: Springer.

Carlson, J., & Kjos, D. (Directors). (2000). *Narrative therapy with Stephen Madigan.* [Video/DVD] Boston, MA: Allyn & Bacon.

Carlson, J., Watts, R. E., & Maniacci, M. (2006). *Adlerian therapy: Theory and practice.* Washington, DC: American Psychological Association.

Carlson, T. D., Kirkpatrick, D., Hecker, L., & Killmer, M. (2002). Religion, spirituality, and marriage and family therapy: A study of family therapists' beliefs about the appropriateness of addressing religious and spiritual issues in therapy. *American Journal of Family Therapy, 30*(2), 157–171.

Carpenter, N., Angus, L., Paivio, S., & Bryntwick, E. (2016). Narrative and emotion integration processes in emotion-focused therapy for complex trauma: An exploratory process-outcome analysis. *Person-Centered and Experiential Psychotherapies, 15*(2), 67–94.

Carter, M. C., Burley, V. J., & Cade, J. E. (2017). Weight loss associated with different patterns of self-monitoring using the mobile phone app my meal mate. *Journal of Medical Internet Research, 19*(2), e8.

Cartwright, C. (2011). Transference, countertransference, and reflective practice in cognitive therapy. *Clinical Psychologist, 15*(3), 112–120.

Casey, R. P. (1938). The psychoanalytic study of religion. *The Journal of Abnormal and Social Psychology, 33*(4), 437–452.

Cashwell, C. S., & Watts, R. E. (2010). The new ASERVIC competencies for addressing spiritual and religious issues in counseling. *Counseling and Values, 55*(1), 2–5.

Cassidy, J., & Shaver, P. R. (2008). *Handbook of attachment: Theory, research, and clinical applications* (2nd ed.). New York, NY: Guilford Press.

Castonguay, L. G., Boswell, J. F., Constantino, M. J., Goldfried, M. R., & Hill, C. E. (2010). Training implications of harmful effects of psychological treatments. *American Psychologist, 65*(1), 34–49.

Chambless, D. L., Baker, M. J., Baucom, D. H., Beutler, L. E., Calhoun, K. S., Crits-Christoph, P., et al. (1998). Update on empirically validated therapies, II. *The Clinical Psychologist, 51*, 3–16.

Chambless, D. L., Caputo, G., Bright, P., & Gallagher, R. (1984). Assessment of fear in agoraphobia: The Body Sensations Questionnaire and the Agoraphobia Cognitions

Questionnaire. *Journal of Consulting & Clinical Psychology, 52,* 1090–1097.

Chambless, D. L., Caputo, G., Gracely, S., Jasin, E., & Williams, C. (1985). Assessment of fear in agoraphobics: The Mobility Inventory for Agoraphobia. *Behaviour Research and Therapy, 23,* 35–44.

Chambless, D. L., Crits-Christoph, P., Wampold, B. E., Norcross, J. C., Lambert, M. J., Bohart, A. C., et al. (2006). What should be validated? In J. C. Norcross, L. E. Beutler, & R. F. Levant (Eds.), *Evidence-based practices in mental health: Debate and dialogue on the fundamental questions* (pp. 191–256). Washington, DC: American Psychological Association.

Chan, A. T. Y., Sun, G. Y. Y., Tam, W. W. S., Tsoi, K. K. F., & Wong, S. Y. S. (2017). The effectiveness of group-based behavioral activation in the treatment of depression: An updated meta-analysis of randomized controlled trial. *Journal of Affective Disorders, 208,* 345–354.

Chandler, R., Worell, J., Johnson, D., Blount, A., & Lusk, M. (1999). Measuring long-term outcomes of feminist counseling and psychotherapy. Annual Convention of the American Psychological Association, Boston, MA.

Chaouloff, F. (1997). Effects of acute physical exercise on central serotonergic systems. *Medicine & Science in Sports & Exercise, 29*(1), 58–62.

Charles, R. (2001). Is there any empirical support for Bowens' concepts of differentiation of self, triangulation, and fusion? *American Journal of Family Therapy, 29*(4), 279–292.

Chen, L., Zhang, G., Hu, M., & Liang, X. (2015). Eye movement desensitization and reprocessing versus cognitive-behavioral therapy for adult posttraumatic stress disorder: Systematic review and meta-analysis. *Journal of Nervous and Mental Disease, 203*(6), 443–451.

Chen, Z., Williams, K. D., Fitness, J., & Newton, N. C. (2008). When hurt will not heal: Exploring the capacity to relive social and physical pain. *Psychological Science, 19*(8), 789–795.

Cheng, H., McDermott, R. C., Wong, Y. J., & La, S. (2016). Drive for muscularity in Asian American men: Sociocultural and racial/ethnic factors as correlates. *Psychology of Men & Masculinity, 17*(3), 215–227.

Chesler, P. (1972). *Women and madness.* New York, NY: Doubleday.

Chima, I. M., & Nnodum, B. (2008). Efficacy of reality therapy and cognitive coping behaviour training in handling adjustment problems of empty-nester retirees. *The Nigerian Journal of Guidance & Counselling, 13*(1), 190–200.

Chow, T., Javan, T., Ros, T., & Frewen, P. (2017). EEG dynamics of mindfulness meditation versus alpha neurofeedback: A sham-controlled study. *Mindfulness, 8*(3), 572–584.

Christakis, N. A. (2011). Holism. In Edge: World Question Center, p. 6. Retrieved July 2, 2011 from http://www.edge.org/q2011/q11_6.html

Christopher, J. C. (1996). Counseling's inescapable moral visions. *Journal of Counseling & Development, 75,* 17–25.

Christopher, J. C. (2001). Culture and psychotherapy: Toward a hermeneutic approach. *Psychotherapy: Theory, Research, Practice, Training, 38*(2), 115–128.

Christopher, J. C., & Bickhard, M. H. (2007). Culture, self and identity: Interactivist contributions to a metatheory for cultural psychology. *Culture & Psychology, 13*(3), 259–295.

Ciclitira, K., & Foster, N. (2012). Attention to culture and diversity in psychoanalytic trainings. *British Journal of Psychotherapy, 28*(3), 353–373.

Clark, A. J. (2002). *Early recollections: Theory and practice in counseling and psychotherapy.* New York, NY: Brunner-Routledge.

Clark, A. J. (2007). *Empathy in counseling and psychotherapy: Perspectives and practices.* Mahwah, NJ: Erlbaum.

Clark, A. J. (2010). Empathy: An integral model in the counseling process. *Journal of Counseling & Development, 88,* 348–356.

Clark, A. J. (2013). *Dawn of memories: The meaning of early recollections in life.* Lanham, MD: Rowman & Littlefield.

Clark, D. A., Beck, A. T., & Alford, B. A. (1999). *Scientific foundation of cognitive theory and therapy of depression.* New York, NY: Wiley.

Clarkin, J. F., Levy, K. N., Lenzenweger, M. F., & Kernberg, O. F. (2004). The Personality Disorders Institute/Borderline Personality Disorder Research Foundation randomized control trial for borderline personality disorder: Rationale, methods, and patient characteristics. *Journal of Personality Disorders, 18*(1), 52–72.

Clarkson, P. (2003). *The therapeutic relationship* (2nd ed.). Philadelphia, PA: Whurr.

Coelho, L. F., Barbosa, D. L. F., Rizzutti, S., Muszkat, M., Bueno, O. F. A., & Miranda, M. C. (2015). Use of cognitive behavioral therapy and token economy to alleviate dysfunctional behavior in children with attention-deficit hyperactivity disorder. *Frontiers in Psychiatry, 6,* 9.

Cohen, J. (1977). *Statistical power analysis for the behavioral sciences* (Rev. ed.). Hillsdale, NJ: Erlbaum.

Collins, P. H. (2009). *Black feminist thought: Knowledge, consciousness, and the politics of empowerment.* New York, NY: Routledge.

Collins, P. H., & Bilge, S. (2016). *Intersectionality: Key concepts.* Cambridge, UK: Polity Press.

Colville, G. A. (2017). Narrative exposure therapy with parents who have been traumatized in pediatric settings: A case series. *Clinical Practice in Pediatric Psychology, 5*(2), 161–169.

Comas-Díaz, L. (2008). Latino psychospirituality. In K. J. Schneider (Ed.), *Existential-integrative psychotherapy: Guideposts to the core of practice* (pp. 100–109). New York, NY: Routledge/Taylor & Francis.

Comas-Díaz, L. (2010). On being a Latina healer: Voice, consciousness, and identity. *Psychotherapy: Theory, Research, Practice, Training, 47*(2), 162–168.

Comas-Díaz, L., & Griffith, E. E. H. (Eds.). (1988). *Clinical guidelines in cross-cultural mental health.* Oxford, England: Wiley.

Comas-Diaz, L., & Weiner M. B. (2011). *Women psychotherapists: Journeys in healing.* Lanham, MD: Jason Aronson.

Conner, S. (2017). Externalizing problems using art in a group setting for substance use treatment. *Journal of Family Psychotherapy, 28*(2), 187–192.

Connie, E., & Metcalf, L. (Eds.). (2009). *The art of solution focused therapy.* New York, NY: Springer.

Consoli, A. J., Beutler, L. E., & Bongar, B. (Eds.) (2017). *Comprehensive textbook of psychotherapy: Theory and practice* (2nd ed.). New York, NY: Oxford University Press.

Constantino, M. J., & Bernecker, S. L. (2014). Bridging the common factors and empirically supported treatment camps: Comment on Laska, Gurman, and Wampold. *Psychotherapy, 51*(4), 505–509.

Constantino, M. J., Morrison, N. R., MacEwan, G., & Boswell, J. F. (2013). Therapeutic alliance researchers' perspectives on alliance-centered training practices. *Journal of Psychotherapy Integration, 23*(3), 284–289. doi:10.1037/a0032357.

Corcoran, J., & Pillai, V. (2009). A review of the research on solution-focused therapy. *British Journal of Social Work, 39*(2), 234–242.

Corey, G. (2017). *Theory and practice of counseling and psychotherapy* (10th ed.). Boston, MA: Cengage.

Cormier, S., Nurius, P. S., & Osborn, C. J. (2017). *Interviewing and change strategies for helpers: Fundamental skills and cognitive-behavioral interventions* (8th ed.). Boston, MA: Cengage.

Corsini, R. (1998). Turning the tables on the client: Making the client the counselor. In H. G. Rosenthal (Ed.), *Favorite counseling techniques: 51 therapists share their most creative strategies* (pp. 54–57). Washington, DC: Accelerated Development.

Corsini, R., & Wedding, D. (Eds.). (2000). *Current psychotherapies* (6th ed.). Itasca, IL: Peacock.

Corturillo, E. M., McGeorge, C. R., & Carlson, T. S. (2016). How prepared are they? Exploring couple and family therapy faculty members' training experiences in lesbian, gay, and bisexual affirmative therapy. *Journal of Feminist Family Therapy: An International Forum, 28*(2–3), 55–75.

Cosgrove, L., Krimsky, S., Wheeler, E. E., Kaitz, J., Greenspan, S. B., & DiPentima, N. L. (2014). Tripartite conflicts of interest and high stakes patent extensions in the DSM-5. *Psychotherapy and Psychosomatics, 83*(2), 106–113.

Cosgrove, L., & Wheeler, E. (2013). Industry's colonization of psychiatry: Ethical and practical implications of financial conflicts of interest in the DSM-5. *Feminism & Psychology, 23*, 93–106.

Cox, J. A., Bañez, L., Hawley, L. D., & Mostade, J. (2003). Use of the reflecting team process in the training of group workers. *Journal for Specialists in Group Work, 28*(2), 89–105.

Coyne, J. C., & Liddle, H. A. (1992). The future of systems therapy: Shedding myths and facing opportunities. *Psychotherapy: Theory, Research, Practice, Training, 29*(1), 44–50.

Cozolino, L. J. (2006). *The neuroscience of human relationships: Attachment and the developing social brain*. New York, NY: Norton.

Craig, S. L., Austin, A., & Alessi, E. (2013). Gay affirmative cognitive behavioral therapy for sexual minority youth: A clinical adaptation. *Clinical Social Work Journal, 41*(3), 258–266.

Crandall, J. E. (1975). A scale for social interest. *Journal of Individual Psychology, 31*(2), 187–195.

Craske, M. G. (1999). *Anxiety disorders: Psychological approaches to theory and treatment*. Boulder, CO: Westview Press.

Craske, M. G. (2010). *Cognitive–behavioral therapy*. Washington, DC: American Psychological Association.

Crenshaw, K. (1989). Demarginalizing the intersection of race and sex: A black feminist critique of antidiscrimination doctrine, feminist theory and anti-racist policies. *University of Chicago Legal Forum, 140*, 139–167.

Crenshaw, K. (1991). Mapping the margins: Intersectionality, identity politics, and violence against women of color. *Stanford Law Review, 43*(6), 1241–1299.

Croll, M. (1992). The individualist roots of reality therapy: A textual analysis of Emerson's "self-reliance" and Glasser's reality therapy. *Journal of Reality Therapy, 11*, 22–26.

Crumbaugh, J. C. (1968). Cross-validation of purpose-in-life test based on Frankl's concepts. *Journal of Individual Psychology, 24*(1), 74–81.

Crumbaugh, J. C. (1977). The seeking of noetic goals test (SONG): A complementary scale to the purpose in life test (PIL). *Journal of Clinical Psychology, 33*(3), 900–907.

Crumbaugh, J. C., & Henrion, R. (1988). The PIL test: Administration, interpretations theory and critique. *International Forum for Logotherapy, 11*(2), 76–88.

Csizmadia, A., & Ispa, J. M. (2014). Black-white biracial children's social development from kindergarten to fifth grade: Links with racial identification, gender, and socioeconomic status. *Social Development, 23*(1), 157–177.

Cuijpers, P., Donker, T., Weissman, M. M., Ravitz, P., & Cristea, I. A. (2016). Interpersonal psychotherapy for mental health problems: A comprehensive meta-analysis. *The American Journal of Psychiatry, 173*(7), 680–687.

Cuijpers, P., Driessen, E., Hollon, S. D., van Oppen, P., Barth, J., & Andersson, G. (2012). The efficacy of non-directive supportive therapy for adult depression: A meta-analysis. *Clinical Psychology Review, 32*(4), 280–291.

Cuijpers, P., van Straten, A., & Warmerdam, L. (2007a). Behavioral activation treatments of depression: A meta-analysis. *Clinical Psychology Review, 27*(3), 318–326.

Cuijpers, P., van Straten, A., & Warmerdam, L. (2007b). Problem solving therapies for depression: A meta-analysis. *European Psychiatry, 22*(1), 9–15.

Cullin, J. (2006). Double bind: Much more than just a step "toward a theory of schizophrenia." *ANZJFT Australian and New Zealand Journal of Family Therapy, 27*(3), 135–142.

Curlette, W. L., & Kern, R. M. (2016). In support of empirical research in individual psychology. *The Journal of Individual Psychology, 72*(1), 1–3.

Cushing, C. C., Jensen, C. D., Miller, M. B., & Leffingwell, T. R. (2014). Meta-analysis of motivational interviewing for adolescent health behavior: Efficacy beyond substance use. *Journal of Consulting and Clinical Psychology, 82*(6), 1212–1218.

Dakof, G. A., Tejeda, M., & Liddle, H. A. (2001). Predictors of engagement in adolescent drug abuse treatment. *Journal of the American Academy of Child & Adolescent Psychiatry, 40*(3), 274–281.

Daldrup, R. J., Beutler, L. E., Engle, D., & Greenberg, L. S. (1988). *Focused expressive psychotherapy: Freeing the overcontrolled patient*. New York, NY: Guilford Press.

Dana, R. H. (1993). *Multicultural assessment perspectives for professional psychology*. Boston, MA: Allyn & Bacon.

Dana, R. H. (1996). Culturally competent assessment practice in the United States. *Journal of Personality Assessment, 66*, 472–487.

Daneshpour, M. (2017). *Family therapy with Muslims*. New York, NY: Routledge.

Davey, G. C. L. (2006). Cognitive mechanisms in fear acquisition and maintenance. In M. G. Craske, D. Hermans, & D. Vansteenwegen (Eds.), *Fear and learning: From basic processes to clinical implications* (pp. 99–116). Washington, DC: American Psychological Association.

Davidson, F. (Producer & Director). (1995). *On old age: A conversation with Joan Erikson at 90*. [Motion Picture] USA: Davidson Films, 668 Marsh Street, San Luis Obispo CA 93401.

Davidson, K., Perry, A., & Bell, L. (2015). Would continuous feedback of patient's clinical outcomes to practitioners improve NHS psychological therapy services? Critical analysis and assessment of quality of existing studies. *Psychology and Psychotherapy: Theory, Research and Practice, 88*(1), 21–37.

Davidson, P. R., & Parker, K. C. H. (2001). Eye movement desensitization and reprocessing (EMDR): A meta-analysis. *Journal of Consulting and Clinical Psychology, 69*(2), 305–316.

Davies, S. C., Jones, K. M., & Rafoth, M. A. (2010). Effects of a self-monitoring intervention on children with traumatic brain injury. *Journal of Applied School Psychology, 26*(4), 308–326.

Davis, D. E., DeBlaere, C., Brubaker, K., Owen, J., Jordan, T. A., II, Hook, J. N., & Van Tongeren, D. R. (2016). Microaggressions and perceptions of cultural humility in counseling. *Journal of Counseling & Development, 94*(4), 483–493.

Dawes, R. M. (1994). *House of cards: Psychology and psychotherapy built on myth.* New York, NY: Free Press.

Day, E. (2016). Field attunement for a strong therapeutic alliance: A perspective from relational gestalt psychotherapy. *Journal of Humanistic Psychology, 56*(1), 77–94.

de Barbaro, B., Drozdzowicz, L., Janusz, B., Gdowska, K., Dembinska, E., Kolbik, I., et al. (2008). Multi-couple reflecting team: Preliminary report. *Journal of Marital and Family Therapy, 34*(3), 287–297.

de Becker, G. (1997). *The gift of fear.* New York, NY: Dell.

DeCarvalho, R. J. (1996). Rollo R. May (1909–1994): A biographical sketch. *Journal of Humanistic Psychology, 36*(2), 8–16.

Deci, E. L. (1971). Effects of externally mediated rewards on intrinsic motivation. *Journal of Personality and Social Psychology, 18*, 105–115.

DeJong, P., & Hopwood, L. E. (1996). Outcome research on treatment conducted at the brief family therapy center, 1992–1993. In S. D. Miller, M. A. Hubble, & B. L. Duncan (Eds.), *Handbook of solution-focused brief therapy* (pp. 272–298). San Francisco, CA: Jossey-Bass.

de Maat, S., de Jonghe, F., Schoevers, R., & Dekker, J. (2009). The effectiveness of long-term psychoanalytic therapy: A systematic review of empirical studies. *Harvard Review of Psychiatry, 17*, 1–23.

Dennis, B. (1989). Faith: The fifth psychological need. *Journal of Reality Therapy, 8*, 39–56.

de Oliveira, A. S. B. (2003). An "appropriated unusual" reflecting team: Inviting parents to be on the team. *Journal of Family Psychotherapy, 14*(2), 85–88.

Dermer, S. B., Hemesath, C. W., & Russell, C. S. (1998). A feminist critique of solution-focused therapy. *American Journal of Family Therapy, 26*(3), 239–250.

Dermer, S., Robey, P., & Dunham, S. (2012). A comparison of reality therapy and choice theory with solution-focused therapy. *International Journal of Choice Theory and Reality Therapy, 31*(2), 14–21.

de Shazer, S. (1984). The death of resistance. *Family Process, 23*(1), 11–17.

de Shazer, S. (1985). *Keys to solution in brief therapy.* New York, NY: Norton.

de Shazer, S. (1988). *Clues: Investigating solutions in brief therapy.* New York, NY: Norton.

de Shazer, S. (1991). *Putting differences to work.* New York, NY: Norton.

de Shazer, S. (1993). Creative misunderstanding: There is no escape from language. In S. G. Gilligan & R. Price (Eds.), *Therapeutic conversations* (pp. 81–90). New York, NY: Norton.

de Shazer, S. (1994). *Words were originally magic.* New York, NY: Norton.

de Shazer, S., Dolan, Y., Korman, H., McCollum, E., Trepper, T., & Berg, I. K. (2007). *More than miracles: The state of the art of solution-focused brief therapy.* New York, NY: Haworth Press.

de Shazer, S., & Molnar, A. (1984). Four useful interventions in brief family therapy. *Journal of Marital & Family Therapy, 10*(3), 297–304.

Dewey, J. (1920). *Reconstruction in philosophy.* New York: Henry Holt.

Diamond, G., & Liddle, H. A. (1996). Resolving a therapeutic impasse between parents and adolescents in multidimensional family therapy. *Journal of Consulting and Clinical Psychology, 64*(3), 481–488.

Diamond, G. S., Wintersteen, M. B., Brown, G. K., Diamond, G. M., Gallop, R., Shelef, K., et al. (2010). Attachment-based family therapy for adolescents with suicidal ideation: A randomized controlled trial. *Journal of the American Academy of Child & Adolescent Psychiatry, 49*(2), 122–131.

Dietz, L. J., Weinberg, R. J., Brent, D. A., & Mufson, L. (2015). Family-based interpersonal psychotherapy for depressed preadolescents: Examining efficacy and potential treatment mechanisms. *Journal of the American Academy of Child & Adolescent Psychiatry, 54*(3), 191–199.

DiIorio, C., Dudley, W. N., Wang, D. T., Wasserman, J., Eichler, M., Belcher, L., et al. (2001). Measurement of parenting self-efficacy and outcome expectancy related to discussions about sex. *Journal of Nursing Measurement, 9*(2), 135–149.

DiMauro, J. (2014). Exposure therapy for posttraumatic stress disorder: A meta-analysis. *Military Psychology, 26*(2), 120–130.

Dimidjian, S., & Hollon, S. D. (2011). What can be learned when empirically supported treatments fail? *Cognitive and Behavioral Practice, 18*(3), 303–305.

Dinkmeyer, D. C., Dinkmeyer, D. C., Jr., & Sperry, L. (1987). *Adlerian counseling and psychotherapy* (2nd ed.). Columbus, OH: Merrill.

Dinkmeyer, D., & Dreikurs, R. (1963). *Encouraging children to learn: The encouragement process.* Oxford, England: Prentice Hall.

Dinkmeyer, D. C., McKay, G. D., & Dinkmeyer, D. C. (1997). *STEP—Systematic training for effective parenting.* Circle Pines, MN: AGS.

Dobson, D., & Dobson, K. S. (2009). *Evidence-based practice of cognitive-behavioral therapy.* New York, NY: Guilford Press.

Dobson, D., & Dobson, K. S. (2017). *Evidence-based practice of cognitive-behavioral therapy* (2nd ed.). New York, NY: Guilford Press.

Dodge, K. A. (1980). Social cognition and children's aggressive behavior. *Child Development, 51*, 162–170.

Dodge, K. A., & Frame, C. L. (1982). Social cognitive biases and deficits in aggressive boys. *Child Development, 53*, 620–635.

Dodge, K. A., & Somberg, D. R. (1987). Hostile attributional biases among aggressive boys are exacerbated under conditions of threat to the self. *Child Development, 58*, 213–224.

Dollard, J., & Miller, N. E. (1950). *Personality and psychotherapy: An analysis in terms of learning, thinking, and culture.* New York, NY: McGraw-Hill.

Donohue, W. A. (1990). *The new freedom: Individualism and collectivism in the social lives of Americans.* New Brunswick, NJ: Transaction.

Draucker, C. B. (2003). Unique outcomes of women and men who were abused. *Perspectives in Psychiatric Care, 39*(1), 7–16.

Dreikurs, R. (1948). *The challenge of parenthood.* Oxford, England: Duell, Sloan & Pearce.

Dreikurs, R. (1950). *Fundamentals of Adlerian psychology.* New York, NY: Greenberg.

Dreikurs, R., & Mosak, H. H. (1966). The tasks of life I: Adler's three tasks. *Individual Psychology, 4,* 18–22.

Dreikurs, R., & Mosak, H. H. (1967). The tasks of life: II: The fourth life task. *Individual Psychology, 4,* 51–55.

Driessen, E., Hegelmaier, L. M., Abbass, A. A., Barber, J. P., Dekker, J. J. M., Van, H. L., et al. (2015). The efficacy of short-term psychodynamic psychotherapy for depression: A meta-analysis update. *Clinical Psychology Review, 42,* 1–15.

Drossel, C., Rummel, C., & Fisher, J. E. (2009). Assessment and cognitive behavior therapy: Functional analysis as key process. In W. T. O'Donohue & J. E. Fisher (Eds.), *General principles and empirically supported techniques of cognitive behavior therapy* (pp. 15–41). Hoboken, NJ: Wiley.

Dryden, W. (1989). Albert Ellis: An efficient and passionate life. *Journal of Counseling and Development, 67,* 539–546.

Dryden, W. (2013). Unconditional self-acceptance and self-compassion. In M. E. Bernard (Ed.),. *The strength of self-acceptance* (pp. 107–120). New York, NY: Springer.

Dubelle, S. (1997, September). Part two: Excerpts from an interview with Heinz Ansbacher, Ph. D. *The Quarterly: Publication of the Adlerian Psychology Association of British Columbia,* pp. 5–7.

Dudai, Y. (2012). The restless engram: Consolidations never end. *Annual Review of Neuroscience, 35,* 227–247.

Duncan, B. L., Miller, S. D., & Sparks, J. A. (2004). *The heroic client: A revolutionary way to improve effectiveness through client-directed, outcome-informed therapy* (Rev. ed.). San Francisco, CA: Jossey-Bass.

Duncan, B. L., Miller, S. D., Wampold, B. E., & Hubble, M. A. (Eds.). (2010). *The heart and soul of change: Delivering what works in therapy* (2nd ed.). Washington, DC: American Psychological Association.

duPlessis Nelson, J. (2015). How do you solve a problem like Agbon? The trials and tribulations of applying diagnoses to children of a foreign culture. *Journal of Infant, Child & Adolescent Psychotherapy, 14*(4), 423–433.

du Plock, S. (2014). Gay affirmative therapy: A critique and some reflections on the value of an existential-phenomenological theory of sexual identity. In M. Milton (Ed.), *Sexuality: Existential perspectives* (pp. 141–159). Ross-on-Wye: PCCS Books.

D'Zurilla, T. J., & Goldfried, M. R. (1971). Problem solving and behavior modification. *Journal of Abnormal Psychology, 78*(1), 107–126.

D'Zurilla, T. J., & Nezu, A. M. (2010). *Problem-solving therapy.* New York, NY: Guilford Press.

Eckstein, D., Aycock, K. J., Sperber, M. A., McDonald, J., Van Wiesner, V., III, Watts, R. E., & Ginsburg, P. (2010). A review of 200 birth-order studies: Lifestyle characteristics. *The Journal of Individual Psychology, 66*(4), 408–434.

Edwards, A. C., Bacanu, S., Bigdeli, T. B., Moscati, A., & Kendler, K. S. (2016). Evaluating the dopamine hypothesis of schizophrenia in a large-scale genome-wide association study. *Schizophrenia Research, 176*(2–3), 136–140.

Edwards, S. S. (1978). Multimodal therapy with children: A case analysis of insect phobia. *Elementary School Guidance & Counseling, 13*(1), 23–29.

Efran, J. S., & Fauber, R. L. (1995). Radical constructivism: Questions and answers. In R. A. Neimeyer & M. Mahoney (Eds.), *Constructivism in psychotherapy* (pp. 275–304). Washington, DC: American Psychological Association.

Elkin, I. E., Shea, T., Watkins, J. T., Imber, S. D., Stotsky, S. M., Collins, J. F., et al. (1989). National Institute of Mental Health treatment of depression collaborative research program: General effectiveness of treatment. *Archives of General Psychiatry, 46,* 974–982.

Ellenberger, H. F. (1970). *The discovery of the unconscious: The history and evolution of dynamic psychiatry.* New York, NY: Basic Books.

Elliott, R., Bohart, A. C., Watson, J. C., & Greenberg, L. S. (2011). Empathy. *Psychotherapy, 48*(1), 43–49.

Elliott, R., & Greenberg, L. S. (2007). The essence of process-experiential/emotion-focused therapy. *American Journal of Psychotherapy, 61*(3), 241–254.

Elliott, R., Greenberg, L. S., & Lietaer, G. (2002). Research on experiential psychotherapies. In M. Lambert (Ed.), *Handbook of psychotherapy and behavior change* (5th ed.). New York, NY: Wiley.

Elliott, R., & Shahar, B. (2017). Emotion-focused therapy for social anxiety (EFT-SA). *Person-Centered and Experiential Psychotherapies, 16*(2), 140–158.

Elliott-Boyle, D. (1985). A conceptual analysis of codes of ethics. *Journal of Mass Media Ethics, 1,* 22–26.

Ellis, A. (1962). *Reason and emotion in psychotherapy.* New York, NY: Lyle Stuart.

Ellis, A. (1970). Tribute to Alfred Adler. *Journal of Individual Psychology, 26,* 11–12.

Ellis, A. (1987). The evolution of rational-emotive therapy (RET) and cognitive behavior therapy (CBT). In J. K. Zeig (Ed.), *The evolution of psychotherapy* (pp. 107–132). New York, NY: Brunner/Mazel.

Ellis, A. (1999a). *How to make yourself happy and remarkably less disturbable.* San Luis Obispo, CA: Impact.

Ellis, A. (1999b). Vigorous disputing of irrational beliefs in rational-emotive behavior therapy (REBT). In H. G. Rosenthal (Ed.), *Favorite counseling and therapy techniques* (pp. 76–77). Washington, DC: Accelerated Development.

Ellis, A. (1999c). Why rational-emotive therapy to rational emotive behavior therapy? *Psychotherapy: Theory, Research, Practice, Training, 36*(2), 154–159.

Ellis, A., & Dryden, W. (1997). *The practice of rational-emotive therapy* (Rev. ed.). New York, NY: Springer.

Ellis, A., & Grieger, R. (1977). *Handbook of rational-emotive therapy.* New York, NY: Springer.

Ellis, A., & MacLaren, C. (2005). *Rational emotive behavior therapy: A therapist's guide* (2nd ed.). Manassas, VA: Impact.

Ellison, J. A., Greenberg, L. S., Goldman, R. N., & Angus, L. (2009). Maintenance of gains following experiential therapies for depression. *Journal of Consulting and Clinical Psychology*, 77(1), 103–112.

Emmelkamp, P. M. G., Bruynzeel, M., Drost, L., & van der Mast, C. A. P. (2001). Virtual reality treatment in acrophobia: A comparison with exposure *in vivo*. *Cyber Psychology and Behavior, 4*, 335–339.

Engle, D., & Holiman, M. (2002). A case illustration of resistance from a Gestalt-experimental perspective. *Journal of Clinical Psychology, 58*(2), 151–156.

Enns, C. Z. (2004). *Feminist theories and feminist psychotherapies: Origins, themes, and diversity* (2nd ed.). New York, NY: Haworth Press.

Epstein, N. B., Baldwin, L. M., & Bishop, D. S. (1983). The McMaster family assessment device. *Journal of Marital and Family Therapy, 9*, 171–186.

Epston, D. (1994). Extending the conversation. *The Family Networker, 18*(6), 30–37, 62–63.

Ergüner-Tekinalp, B. (2017). The effectiveness of Adlerian-based encouragement group counseling with college students in Turkey. *The Journal of Individual Psychology, 73*(1), 54–69.

Erickson, M. H. (1954). Special techniques of brief hypnotherapy. *Journal of Clinical and Experimental Hypnosis, 2*, 109–129.

Erickson, M. H. (1964). The confusion technique in hypnosis. *American Journal of Clinical Hypnosis, 6*, 183–207.

Erikson, E. H. (1963). *Childhood & society* (2nd ed.). New York, NY: Norton.

Espín, O. M. (1993). Feminist therapy: Not for white women only. *The Counseling Psychologist, 21*(1), 103–108.

Espín, O. M. (1997). *Latina realities: Essays on healing, migration, and sexuality*. Boulder, CO: Westview Press.

Esterson, A. (2001). The mythologizing of psychoanalytic history: Deception and self-deception in Freud's accounts of the seduction theory episode. *History of Psychiatry, 12*, 329–352.

Estes, W. (1944). An experimental study of punishment. *Psychological Monographs, 57* (Whole No. 263).

Evans, K., Kincade, E. A., & Seem, S. R. (2011). *Introduction to feminist therapy: Strategies for social and individual change*. Thousand Oaks, CA: Sage.

Eysenck, H. J. (1952). The effects of psychotherapy: An evaluation. *Journal of Consulting Psychology, 16*, 319–324.

Eysenck, H. J. (1959). Learning theory and behaviour therapy. *Journal of Mental Science, 105*, 61–75.

Eysenck, H. J. (Ed.). (1960). *Behaviour therapy and the neuroses*. New York, NY: Pergamon.

Eysenck, H. J. (Ed.). (1964). *Experiments in behavior therapy*. New York, NY: Pergamon.

Eysenck, H. J. (1970). A mish-mash of theories. *International Journal of Psychiatry, 9*, 140–146.

Fairbairn, W. R. (1952). *Psychoanalytic studies of the personality*. Oxford, England: Routledge & Kegan Paul.

Farber, B. A., Brink, D. C., & Raskin, P. M. (Eds.). (1996). *The psychotherapy of Carl Rogers: Cases and commentary*. New York, NY: Guilford.

Farber, B. A., & Doolin, E. M. (2011). Positive regard and affirmation. In J. C. Norcross (Ed.), *Psychotherapy relationships that work: Evidence-based responsiveness* (2nd ed.) (pp. 168–186). New York, NY: Oxford University Press.

Farmer, R. F., & Nelson-Gray, R. O. (2005). *The history of behavior therapy*. Washington, DC: American Psychological Association.

Fatter, D. M., & Hayes, J. A. (2013). What facilitates countertransference management? The roles of therapist meditation, mindfulness, and self-differentiation. *Psychotherapy Research, 23*(5), 502–513. doi: 10503307.2013.797124.

Fenichel, O. (1945). *The psychoanalytic theory of neurosis*. New York, NY: Norton.

Ferenczi, S. (1920). The further development of an active therapy in psychoanalysis. In J. Rickman (Ed.), *Further contributions to the theory and techniques of psychoanalysis* (pp. 47–81). London, England: Hogarth Press.

Ferenczi, S. (1950). *The selected papers of Sandor Ferenczi*. New York, NY: Basic Books.

Fernandez, R. (2001). *Imagining literacy*. Austin: University of Texas Press.

Ferrer-Wreder, L., Palchuk, A., Poyrazli, S., Small, M. L., & Domitrovich, C. E. (2008). Identity and adolescent adjustment. *Identity: An International Journal of Theory and Research, 8*(2), 95–105.

Ferster, C. B. (1973). A functional analysis of depression. *American Psychologist, 28*(10), 857–870.

Field, T. (1996). Attachment and separation in young children. *Annual Review of Psychology, 47*, 541–561.

Field, T. (2009). *Progressive muscle relaxation*. Washington, DC: American Psychological Association.

Figley, C. (1997). The active ingredients of the power therapies. The Power Therapies: A Conference for the Integrative and Innovative use of EMDR, TFT, EFT, Advanced NLP, and TIR. Lakewood, CO.

Fine, C. (2010). *Delusions of gender: How our minds, society, and neurosexism create difference*. New York, NY: Norton.

Fine, C. (2017). *Testosterone rex: Myths of sex, science, and society*. New York, NY: Norton.

Finn, S. E., Fischer, C. T., & Handler, L. (2012). Collaborative/therapeutic assessment: Basic concepts, history, and research. In *Collaborative/therapeutic assessment: A casebook and guide* (pp. 1–24). Hoboken, NJ: Wiley.

First, M. B., Williams, J. B. W., Karg, R. S., & Spitzer, R. L. (2016). *Structured Clinical Interview for DSM-5® Disorders—Clinician Version* (SCID-5-CV) [Structured interview form]. Arlington, VA: American Psychiatric Association.

Fishel, A. K., Buchs, T., McSheffrey, C., & Murphy, C. (2001). Adding written reflections to the reflecting team. *Journal of Family Psychotherapy, 12*(3), 81–88.

Fishman, D. B., & Franks, C. M. (1997). The conceptual evolution of behavior therapy. In P. L. Wachtel & S. B. Messer (Eds.), *Theories of psychotherapy: Origins and evolution* (pp. 131–180). Washington, DC: American Psychological Association.

Flax, J. (2012). Can it come undone? Treating gender troubles in psychoanalytic discourses. *Sex Roles, 66*(7–8), 558–561.

Fletcher, L., & Hayes, S. C. (2005). Relational frame theory, acceptance and commitment therapy, and a functional analytic definition of mindfulness. *Journal of Rational-Emotive & Cognitive Behavior Therapy, 23*(4), 315–336.

Flynn, M. A., Craig, C. M., Anderson, C. N., & Holody, K. J. (2016). Objectification in popular music lyrics: An examination of gender and genre differences. *Sex Roles*, 75(3–4), 164–176.

Follette, V. M., & Hazlett-Stevens, H. (2016). Mindfulness and acceptance theories. In J. C. Norcross, G. R. VandenBos, D. K. Freedheim, & B. O. Olatunji (Eds.), *APA handbook of clinical psychology: Theory and research*, Vol. 2 (pp. 273–302). Washington, DC: American Psychological Association.

Fong, E. H., Ficklin, S., & Lee, H. Y. (2017). Increasing cultural understanding and diversity in applied behavior analysis. *Behavior Analysis: Research and Practice*, 17(2), 103–113.

Forcehimes, A. A., & Tonigan, J. S. (2008). Self-efficacy as a factor in abstinence from alcohol/other drug abuse: A meta-analysis. *Alcoholism Treatment Quarterly*, 26, 480–489.

Forehand, R., & Kotchick, B. A. (2016). Cultural diversity: A wake-up call for parent training. *Behavior Therapy*, 47(6), 981–992.

Fors, M., & McWilliams, N. (2016). Collaborative reading of medical records in psychotherapy: A feminist psychoanalytic proposal about narrative and empowerment. *Psychoanalytic Psychology*, 33(1), 35–57.

Forsyth, J. P., Fusé, T., & Acheson, D. T. (2008). Interoceptive exposure for panic disorder. In W. T. O'Donohue & J. E. Fisher (Eds.), *Cognitive behavior therapy: Applying empirically supported techniques in your practice* (2nd ed.) (pp. 296–308). Hoboken, NJ: Wiley.

Fouad, N. A., & Arredondo, P. (2007). *Becoming culturally oriented: Practical advice for psychologists and educators*. Washington, DC: American Psychological Association.

Foucault, M. (1965). *Madness and civilization: A history of insanity in the age of reason*. New York, NY: Random House.

Fox, R. C. (2006). *Affirmative psychotherapy with bisexual women and bisexual men*. Binghamton, NY: Haworth Press.

Francis, W., & Bance, L. O. (2016). Protective role of spirituality from the perspective of Indian college students with suicidal ideation: "I am here because God exists." *Journal of Religion and Health*, 56, 962–970. doi: /10.1007/s10943-016-0296-6.

Frank, J. D. (1961). *Persuasion and healing: A comparative study of psychotherapy*. Oxford, England: Johns Hopkins University Press.

Frank, J. D. (1973). *Persuasion and healing: A comparative study of psychotherapy* (Rev. ed.). Baltimore, MD: Johns Hopkins University Press.

Frank, J. D. (1985). Further thoughts on the anti-demoralization hypothesis of psychotherapeutic effectiveness. *Integrative Psychiatry*, 3(1), 17–20.

Frank, J. D., & Frank, J. B. (1996). Demoralization and unexplained illness in two cohorts of American soldiers overseas. *Journal of Nervous and Mental Disease*, 184(7), 445–446.

Frankl, V. (1959). The spiritual dimension in existential analysis and logotherapy. *Journal of Individual Psychology*, 15, 157–165.

Frankl, V. (1963). *Man's search for meaning*. Boston, MA: Beacon.

Frankl, V. (1967). *Psychotherapy and existentialism: Selected papers on logotherapy*. New York, NY: Clarion.

Frankl, V. (2000). *Man's search for ultimate meaning*. New York, NY: Basic Books.

Franklin, M. E., Ledley, D. A., & Foa, E. B. (2009). Response prevention. In W. T. O'Donohue & J. E. Fisher (Eds.), *General principles and empirically supported techniques of cognitive behavior therapy* (pp. 543–549). Hoboken, NJ: Wiley.

Franks, C. M., & Barbrack, C. R. (1983). Behavior therapy with adults: An integrative perspective. In M. Hersen, A. E. Kazdin, & A. S. Bellack (Eds.), *The clinical psychology handbook* (pp. 507–523). New York, NY: Pergamon.

Freedman, J. E., & Honkasilta, J. M. (2017). Dictating the boundaries of ab/normality: A critical discourse analysis of the diagnostic criteria for attention deficit hyperactivity disorder and hyperkinetic disorder. *Disability & Society*, 32(4), 565–588.

Freire, E., Williams, C., Messow, C., Cooper, M., Elliott, R., McConnachie, A., et al. (2015). Counselling versus low-intensity cognitive behavioural therapy for persistent sub-threshold and mild depression (CLICD): A pilot/feasibility randomised controlled trial. *BMC Psychiatry*, 15, 11.

French, T. M. (1933). Interrelations between psychoanalysis and the experimental work of Pavlov. *The American Journal of Psychiatry*, 12, 1165–1203.

French, T. M. (1958). *The integrations of behavior*. Chicago, IL: University of Chicago Press.

Freud, S. (1896). *The aetiology of hysteria (The Standard Edition)*. London, England: Hogarth Press.

Freud, S. (1909). Analysis of a phobia in a five-year-old boy. In J. Strachey (Ed.), *Standard edition of the complete psychological works of Sigmund Freud*, Vol. 10 (pp. 3–149). London, England: Hogarth Press.

Freud, S. (1918). *Totem and taboo* (Trans. by A. A. Brill). New York, NY: Moffat, Yard & Co.

Freud, S. (1923). Group psychology and the analysis of the ego. In J. Strachey (Ed.), *Standard edition of the complete psychological works of Sigmund Freud* (Trans. by J. Strachey) (pp. 97–108). London, England: Hogarth Press.

Freud, S. (1948). Some psychical consequences of the anatomical distinction between the sexes. In J. Strachey (Ed.), *The standard edition of the complete works of Sigmund Freud* (Trans. by J. Strachey) (pp. 186–197). London: Hogarth.

Freud, S. (1957). The future prospects of psycho-analytic therapy. In J. Strachey (Ed.), *The standard edition of the complete works of Sigmund Freud* (Trans. by J. Strachey), Vol. 11 (pp. 139–152). London, England: Hogarth Press.

Freud, S. (1958). On the beginning of treatment: Further recommendations on the technique of psychoanalysis. In J. Strachey (Ed.), *Standard edition of the complete psychological works of Sigmund Freud* (Trans. by J. Strachey) (pp. 122–144). London, England: Hogarth Press.

Freud, S. (1961). *Civilization and its discontents* (Trans. by J. Strachey). New York, NY: Norton.

Freud, S. (1963). *Introductory lectures on psycho-analysis* (Trans. by J. Strachey). London, England: Hogarth Press.

Freud, S. (1964). *New introductory lectures on psychoanalysis* (Trans. by J. Strachey). London, England: Hogarth Press.

Frey, L. L. (2013). Relational-cultural therapy: Theory, research, and application to counseling competencies. *Professional Psychology: Research and Practice*, 44(3), 177–185.

Freyer, T., Klöppel, S., Tüscher, O., Kordon, A., Zurowski, B., Kuelz, A., et al. (2011). Frontostriatal activation in patients with obsessive-compulsive disorder before and after cognitive behavioral therapy. *Psychological Medicine*, 41(1), 207–216.

Friedan, B. (1963). *The feminine mystique*. New York, NY: Dell.

Friedberg, R. D., & McClure, J. M. (2015). *Clinical practice of cognitive therapy with children and adolescents: The nuts and bolts* (2nd ed.). New York, NY: Guilford.

Fromm-Reichmann, F. (1948). Notes on the development of treatment of schizophrenic by psychoanalytic psychotherapy. *Psychiatry, 11*, 263–274.

Frost, D. M. (2010). Review of the story of sexual identity: Narrative perspectives on the gay and lesbian life course. *Journal of Gay & Lesbian Mental Health, 14*(1), 88–90.

Fruehwirlh, R. (2013). Christian spirituality and the person-centered approach. In J. H. D. Cornelius-White, R. Motschnig-Pitrik, & M. Lux (Eds.), *Interdisciplinary handbook of the person-centered approach: Research and theory* (pp. 369–380). New York, NY: Springer.

Fry, P. S. (2001). The unique contribution of key existential factors to the prediction of psychological well-being of older adults following spousal loss. *The Gerontologist, 41*(1), 69–81.

Fulkerson, M. (2015). *Treatment planning from a reality therapy perspective*. iUniverse.

Funderburk, J. R., & Fukuyama, M. A. (2001). Feminism, multiculturalism, and spirituality: Convergent and divergent forces in psychotherapy. *Women & Therapy, 24*(3/4), 1–18.

Galante, J., Iribarren, S. J., & Pearce, P. F. (2013). Effects of mindfulness-based cognitive therapy on mental disorders: A systematic review and meta-analysis of randomised controlled trials. *Journal of Research in Nursing, 18*(2), 133–155.

Gardner, W. L., Pickett, C. L., Jefferis, V., & Knowles, M. (2005). On the outside looking in: Loneliness and social monitoring. *Personality and Social Psychology Bulletin, 31*(11), 1549–1560.

Garrett, M. T., & Pichette, E. F. (2000). Red as an apple: Native American acculturation and counseling with or without reservation. *Journal of Counseling & Development, 78*(1), 3–13.

Gaston, L. (1991). Reliability and criterion-related validity of the California Psychotherapy Alliance Scales—patient version. *Psychological Assessment, 3*(1), 68–74.

Gatfield, E. (2017). Augmenting Bowen family of origin work: Using the genogram and therapeutic art-based activity. *Australian and New Zealand Journal of Family Therapy, 38*(2), 272–282.

Gay, P. (1978). *Freud, Jews, and other Germans: Masters and victims in modern culture*. New York, NY: Oxford University Press.

Gay, P. (2006). *Freud: A life for our time*. New York, NY: Norton.

Gedo, J. E. (1979). *Beyond interpretation*. New York, NY: International Universities Press.

Geertz, C. (1973). *The interpretation of cultures*. New York: Basic Books.

Gehart, D. R. (2018). *Mastering competencies in family therapy: A practical approach to theories and clinical case documentation* (3rd ed.). Boston, MA: Cengage.

Geller, J. D. (2003). Self-disclosure in psychoanalytic-existential therapy. *Journal of Clinical Psychology. Special Issue: In Session: Self Disclosure, 59*(5), 541–554.

Gelso, C. J., & Hayes, J. A. (1998). *The psychotherapy relationship: Theory, research, and practice*. New York, NY: Wiley.

Gelso, C. J., & Hayes, J. A. (2007). *Countertransference and the inner world of the psychotherapist: Perils and possibilities*. Mahwah, NJ: Erlbaum.

Gendlin, E. T. (1981). *Focusing* (2nd ed.). New York, NY: Bantam.

Gendlin, E. T. (1996). *Focusing-oriented psychotherapy: A manual of the experiential method*. New York, NY: Guilford Press.

Gere, J., & MacDonald, G. (2010). An update of the empirical case for the need to belong. *The Journal of Individual Psychology, 66*(1), 93–115.

Gergen, K. J. (2009a). *An invitation to social construction* (2nd ed.). Thousand Oaks, CA: Sage.

Gergen, K. J. (2009b). The problem of prejudice in plural worlds. *Journal of Theoretical and Philosophical Psychology, 29*(2), 97–101.

Gergen, K. J. (2011). The self as social construction. *Psychological Studies, 56*(1), 108–116.

Gershoff, E. T. (2002). Corporal punishment by parents and associated child behaviors and experiences: A meta-analytic and theoretical review. *Psychological Bulletin, 128*(4), 539–579.

Gershoff, E. T. (2016). Should parents' physical punishment of children be considered a source of toxic stress that affects brain development? *Family Relations: An Interdisciplinary Journal of Applied Family Studies, 65*(1), 151–162.

Gfroerer, K. P., Kern, R. M., & Curlette, W. L. (2004). Research support for individual psychology's parenting model. *The Journal of Individual Psychology, 60*(4), 379–388.

Ghent, E. (1989). Credo: The dialectics of one-person and two-person psychologies. *Contemporary Psychoanalysis, 25*, 169–209.

Ghezzi, P. M., Wilson, G. R., Tarbox, R. S. F., & MacAleese, K. R. (2009). Guidelines for developing and managing a token economy. In W. T. O'Donohue & J. E. Fisher (Eds.), *General principles and empirically supported techniques of cognitive behavior therapy* (pp. 663–668). Hoboken, NJ: Wiley.

Gibbard, I., & Hanley, T. (2008). A five-year evaluation of the effectiveness of person-centred counselling in routine clinical practice in primary care. *Counselling & Psychotherapy Research, 8*(4), 215–222.

Gil, E. (2010). *Working with children to heal interpersonal trauma*. New York, NY: Guilford Press.

Gil, E., & Shaw, J. A. (2013). *Working with children with sexual behavior problems*. New York, NY: Guilford Press.

Gilbert, L. A. (1980). Feminist therapy. In A. M. Brodsky & R. T. Hare-Mustin (Eds.), *Women and psychotherapy* (pp. 245–266). New York: Guilford.

Gilbert, L. A., & Scher, M. (1999). *Gender and sex in counseling and psychotherapy*. Boston. MA: Allyn & Bacon.

Gilligan, C. (1982). *In a different voice: Psychological theory and women's development*. Cambridge, MA: Harvard University Press.

Gilligan, C. (2003). Hearing the difference: Theorizing connection. *Anuario De Psicología, 34*(2), 155–161.

Gilligan, C., & Attanucci, J. (1988). Two moral orientations: Gender differences and similarities. *Merrill-Palmer Quarterly: Journal of Developmental Psychology, 34*(3), 223–237.

Gingerich, W. J., & Eisengart, S. (2000). Solution-focused brief therapy: A review of the outcome research. *Family Process, 39*(4), 477–498.

Glasser, W. (1965). *Reality therapy: A new approach to psychiatry*. New York, NY: Harper & Row.

Glasser, W. (1989). A clarification of the relationship between the all-we-want world and the basic needs. *Journal of Reality Therapy, 9*, 3–8.

Glasser, W. (1998). *Choice theory: A new psychology of personal freedom*. New York, NY: HarperCollins.

Glasser, W. (2000). *Reality therapy in action*. New York, NY: HarperCollins.

Glasser, W. (2002). *Unhappy teenagers: A way for parents and teachers to reach them*. New York, NY: HarperCollins.

Glasser, W. (2003). *Warning: Psychiatry can be hazardous to your mental health*. New York, NY: HarperCollins.

Glover, E. (1959). Critical notice. *British Journal of Medical Psychology, 32,* 68–74.

Glynn, S. M. (1990). Token economy approaches for psychiatric patients: Progress and pitfalls over 25 years. *Behavior Modification Special Issue: Recent Developments in the Behavioral Treatment of Chronic Psychiatric Illness, 14*(4), 383–407.

Goldenberg, I., & Goldenberg, H. (2008). *Family therapy: An overview* (7th ed.). Belmont, CA: Brooks/Cole.

Goldenberg, I., Stanton, M., & Goldenberg, H. (2017). *Family therapy: An overview* (9th ed.). Boston, MA: Cengage.

Goldfried, M. R., & Davison, G. C. (1976). *Clinical behavior therapy*. New York, NY: Holt, Rinehart and Winston.

Goldfried, M. R., & Davison, G. C. (1994). *Clinical behavior therapy* (Exp. ed.). Oxford, England: Wiley.

Goldman, R., & Greenberg, L. S. (1997). Case formulation in process-experiential therapy. In T. D. Eells (Ed.), *Handbook of psychotherapy case formulation* (pp. 402–429). New York, NY: Guilford Press.

Goldman, R. N., & Greenberg, L. S. (Eds.) (2015). *Case formulation in emotion-focused therapy: Co-creating clinical maps for change*. Washington, DC: American Psychological Association.

Goldman, R. N., Greenberg, L. S., & Angus, L. (2006). The effects of adding emotion-focused interventions to the client-centered relationship conditions in the treatment of depression. *Psychotherapy Research, 16*(5), 536–546.

Goldstein, K. (1939). *The organism: A holistic approach to biology derived from pathological data in man*. Salt Lake City, UT: American Book.

Gonçalves, M. M., Batista, J., & Freitas, S. (2017). Narrative and clinical change in cognitive-behavior therapy: A comparison of two recovered cases. *Journal of Constructivist Psychology, 30*(2), 146–164.

Gonçalves, M. M., Matos, M., & Santos, A. (2009). Narrative therapy and the nature of "innovative moments" in the construction of change. *Journal of Constructivist Psychology, 22*(1), 1–23.

Gonçalves, M. M., Mendes, I., Ribeiro, A. P., Angus, L. E., & Greenberg, L. S. (2010). Innovative moments and change in emotion-focused therapy: The case of Lisa. *Journal of Constructivist Psychology, 23*(4), 267–294.

Gonzalez-Liencres, C., Shamay-Tsoory, S., & Brüne, M. (2013). Towards a neuroscience of empathy: Ontogeny, phylogeny, brain mechanisms, context and psychopathology. *Neuroscience and Biobehavioral Reviews, 37*(8), 1537–1548.

Goodman, D. J. (2011). *Promoting diversity and social justice: Educating people from privileged groups* (2nd ed.). New York, NY: Routledge.

Goodman, E. (2003, January 12). Bush takes sides with the powerful. *The Missoulian*, p. 4.

Gordon, R. M., Gazzillo, F., Blake, A., Bornstein, R. F., Etzi, J., Lingiardi, V., et al. (2016). The relationship between theoretical orientation and countertransference expectations: Implications for ethical dilemmas and risk management. *Clinical Psychology & Psychotherapy, 23*(3), 236–245.

Gornick, V. (2016, December 14). Feeling paranoid. *Boston Review* (July 16, 2017; http://bostonreview.net/politics-gender-sexuality/vivian-gornick-feeling-paranoid).

Gortner, E. T., Gollan, J. K., Dobson, K. S., & Jacobson, N. S. (1998). Cognitive–behavioral treatment for depression: Relapse prevention. *Journal of Consulting and Clinical Psychology, 66*(2), 377–384.

Gottlieb, M. C., & Younggren, J. N. (2009). Is there a slippery slope? Considerations regarding multiple relationships and risk management. *Professional Psychology: Research and Practice, 40*(6), 564–571.

Gould, W. B. (1993). *Viktor E. Frankl: Life with meaning*. Pacific Grove, CA: Brooks/Cole.

Graham, M. A., & Pehrsson, D. (2011). Adlerian theory. In S. Degges-White & N. L. Davis (Eds.), *Integrating the expressive arts into counseling practice: Theory-based interventions* (pp. 7–27). New York, NY: Springer.

Greenberg, L. (2006). Emotion-focused therapy: A synopsis. *Journal of Contemporary Psychotherapy, 36*(2), 87–93.

Greenberg, L. S. (2015). *Emotion-focused therapy* (2nd ed.). Washington, DC: American Psychological Association.

Greenberg, L. S. (2017). Emotion-focused therapy of depression. *Person-Centered and Experiential Psychotherapies, 16*(2), 106–117.

Greenberg, L. S., Elliott, R., & Lietaer, G. (1994). Research on experiential psychotherapy. In A. E. Bergin & S. L. Garfield (Eds.), *Handbook of psychotherapy and behavior change* (4th ed.). New York, NY: Wiley.

Greenberg, L. S., & Foerster, F. S. (1996). Task analysis exemplified: The process of resolving unfinished business. *Journal of Consulting & Clinical Psychology, 64*(3), 439–446.

Greenberg, L. S., & Johnson, S. M. (1988). *Emotionally focused therapy for couples*. New York, NY: Guilford Press.

Greenberg, L. S., Rice, L. N., & Elliot, R. (1993). *Facilitating emotional change: The moment-by-moment process*. New York, NY: Guilford.

Greenberg, L. S., Warwar, S. H., & Malcolm, W. M. (2008). Differential effects of emotion-focused therapy and psychoeducation in facilitating forgiveness and letting go of emotional injuries. *Journal of Counseling Psychology, 55*(2), 185–196.

Greenberg, L. S., & Watson, J. (1998). Experiential therapy of depression: Differential effects of client-centered relationship conditions and process experiential interventions. *Psychotherapy Research, 8*(2), 210–224.

Greenberg, L. S., Watson, J. C., Elliot, R., & Bohart, A. C. (2001). Empathy. *Psychotherapy: Theory, Research, Practice, Training, 38*(4), 380–384.

Greenberger, D., & Padesky, C. A. (2016). *Mind over mood: Change how you feel by changing the way you think* (2nd ed.). New York, NY: Guilford Press.

Greever, K. B., Tseng, M. S., & Friedland, B. U. (1973). Development of the social interest index. *Journal of Consulting and Clinical Psychology, 41*(3), 454–458.

Griner, D., & Smith, T. B. (2006). Culturally adapted mental health intervention: A meta-analytic review. *Psychotherapy: Theory, Research, 43*(4), 531–548.

Grisham, J. R., Brown, T. A., & Campbell, L. A. (2004). *The anxiety disorders interview schedule for DSM-IV (ADIS-IV)*. Hoboken, NJ: Wiley.

Gross, P. R. (1989). Multimodal therapy for generalized and social anxieties: A pilot study. *Behavioural Psychotherapy, 17*(4), 316–322.

Gross, T. J., Duhon, G. J., & Doerksen-Klopp, B. (2014). Enhancing treatment integrity maintenance through fading with indiscriminable contingencies. *Journal of Behavioral Education, 23*(1), 108–131.

Groth-Marnat, G., & Wright, A. J. (2016). *Handbook of psychological assessment* (6th ed.). Hoboken, NJ: Wiley.

Guilford, J. (1956). The structure of intellect. *Psychological Bulletin, 53,* 267–293.

Gushue, G. V., & Constantine, M. G. (2007). Color-blind racial attitudes and white racial identity attitudes in psychology trainees. *Professional Psychology: Research and Practice, 38*(3), 321–328.

Guterman, J. T. (2006). *Mastering the art of solution-focused counseling.* Alexandria, VA: American Counseling Association.

Guterman, J. T. (2013). *Mastering the art of solution-focused counseling* (2nd ed.). Alexandria, VA: American Counseling Association.

Guterman, J. T., & Leite, N. (2006). Solution-focused counseling for clients with religious and spiritual concerns. *Counseling and Values, 51*(1), 39–52.

Guthrie, R. V. (2004). *Even the rat was white: A historical view of psychology* (2nd ed.). Upper Saddle River, NJ: Pearson.

Gwozdziewycz, N., & Mehl-Madrona, L. (2013). Meta-analysis of the use of narrative exposure therapy for the effects of trauma among refugee populations. *The Permanente Journal, 17*(1), 70–76.

Hagen, W. B., Arczynski, A. V., Morrow, S. L., & Hawxhurst, D. M. (2011). Lesbian, bisexual, and queer women's spirituality in feminist multicultural counseling. *Journal of LGBT Issues in Counseling, 5*(3–4), 220–236.

Haley, J. (Ed.). (1967). *Advanced techniques of hypnosis and therapy: Selected papers of Milton H. Erickson, M.D.* New York, NY: Grune & Stratton.

Haley, J. (1973). *Uncommon therapy: The psychiatric techniques of Milton H. Erickson.* New York, NY: Norton.

Haley, J. (1976). *Problem-solving therapy.* San Francisco. CA: Jossey-Bass.

Haley, J. (1977). A quiz for young therapists. *Psychotherapy, 14*(2), 165–168.

Haley, J. (1984). *Ordeal therapy: Unusual ways to change behavior.* San Francisco, CA: Jossey-Bass.

Haley, J. (2015). Explorer in hypnosis. *International Journal of Clinical and Experimental Hypnosis, 63*(4), 380–402.

Hall, C. S., & Lindzey, G. (1970). *Theories of personality* (2nd ed.). New York, NY: Wiley.

Hall, G. C. N. (2001). Psychotherapy research with ethnic minorities: Empirical ethical, and conceptual issues. *Journal of Consulting & Clinical Psychology, 69,* 502–510.

Hall, M. (2012). The honeymoon is over: Narrative sex therapy for long-term lesbian partners. In P. J. Kleinplatz (Ed.), *New directions in sex therapy: Innovations and alternatives* (2nd ed.) (pp. 285–302). New York, NY: Routledge/Taylor & Francis.

Hamilton, J. W. (1995). Some comments on Kohut's "the two analyses of Mr. Z." *Psychoanalytic Psychology, 11,* 525–536.

Hamm, J. S., Carlson, J., & Erguner-Tekinalp, B. (2016). Adlerian-based positive group counseling interventions with emotionally troubled youth. *The Journal of Individual Psychology, 72*(4), 254–272.

Hanna, F. J. (1998). A transcultural view of prejudice, racism, and community feeling: The desire and striving for status. *The Journal of Individual Psychology, 54*(3), 336–345.

Harris, R. (2009). *ACT made simple: An easy-to-read primer on acceptance and commitment therapy.* Oakland, CA: New Harbinger.

Harris, S. E., & Robinson Kurpius, S. E. (2014). Social networking and professional ethics: Client searches, informed consent, and disclosure. *Professional Psychology: Research and Practice, 45*(1), 11–19.

Harris, S. M. (1998). Finding a forest among trees: Spirituality hiding in family therapy theories. *Journal of Family Studies, 4*(1), 77–86.

Hartmann, H. (1958). *Ego psychology and the problem of adaptation.* Madison, CT: International Universities Press.

Hartnett, D., Carr, A., Hamilton, E., & O'Reilly, G. (2017). The effectiveness of functional family therapy for adolescent behavioral and substance misuse problems: A meta-analysis. *Family Process, 56*(3), 607–619.

Hayek, F. A. (1979). *Law, legislation, and liberty: The political order of a free people.* Chicago, IL: University of Chicago Press.

Hayes, J. A., Gelso, C. J., & Hummel, A. M. (2011). Managing countertransference. In J. C. Norcross (Ed.), *Psychotherapy relationships that work: Evidence-based responsiveness* (2nd ed.) (pp. 239–258). New York, NY: Oxford University Press.

Hayes, S. C. (2002). Buddhism and acceptance and commitment therapy. *Cognitive & Behavioral Practice, 9*(1), 58–66.

Hayes, S. C. (2016). Acceptance and commitment therapy, relational frame theory, and the third wave of behavioral and cognitive therapies. *Behavior Therapy, 47*(6), 869–885.

Hayes, S. C., Barnes-Holmes, D., & Roche, B. (Eds.). (2001). *Relational frame theory: A post-Skinnerian account of human language and cognition.* New York: Plenum Press.

Hayes, S. C., Strosahl, K. D., & Wilson, K. G. (1999). *Acceptance and commitment therapy: An experiential approach to behavior change.* New York, NY: Guilford Press.

Hays, P. A. (2013). *Connecting across cultures: The helper's toolkit.* Thousand Oaks, CA: Sage.

Hays, P. A. (2016). *Addressing cultural complexities in practice: Assessment, diagnosis, and therapy* (3rd ed.). Washington, DC: American Psychological Association.

Hazler, R. J. (2016). Person-centered theory. In D. Capuzzi & M. D. Stauffer (Eds.), *Counseling and psychotherapy: Theories and interventions* (6th cd.) (pp. 169–194). Alexandria, VA: American Counseling Association.

Heard, H. L., & Linehan, M. (1994). Dialectical behavior therapy: An integrative approach to the treatment of borderline personality disorder. *Journal of Psychotherapy Integration, 4,* 55–82.

Hearn, J., & Lawrence, M. (1981). Family sculpting: I. Some doubts and some possibilities. *Journal of Family Therapy, 3*(4), 341–352.

Hebb, D. O. (1949). *The organization of behavior: A neuropsychological theory.* New York, NY: Wiley.

Heide, F. J., & Borkovec, T. D. (1984). Relaxation-induced anxiety: Mechanisms and theoretical implications. *Behaviour Research and Therapy, 22,* 1–12.

Helms, J. E. (1994). How multiculturalism obscures racial factors in the therapy process. Comment on Ridley et al. (1994), Sadowski et al. (1994), Ottavi et al. (1994), and Thompson et al. (1994). *Journal of Counseling Psychology, 41,* 162–165.

Henggeler, S. W., & Borduin, C. M. (1990). *Family therapy and beyond: A multisystemic approach to treating the behavior problems of children and adolescents.* Pacific Grove, CA: Brooks/Cole.

Henggeler, S. W., & Schaeffer, C. M. (2016). Multisystemic therapy®: Clinical overview, outcomes, and implementation research. *Family Process, 55*(3), 514–528.

Henggeler, S. W., Schoenwald, S. K., Borduin, C. M., Rowland, M. D., & Cunningham, P. B. (2009). *Multisystemic therapy for antisocial behavior in children and adolescents* (2nd ed.). New York, NY: Guilford Press.

Hepburn, R. (1965). Questions about the meaning of life. *Religious Studies, 1,* 125–140.

Herman, J. L. (1992). *Trauma and recovery: The aftermath of violence—from domestic abuse to political terror.* New York, NY: Basic Books.

Herring, R. D. (1996). Synergetic counseling and Native American Indian students. *Journal of Counseling & Development, 74,* 542–547.

Hettema, J., Steele, J., & Miller, W. R. (2005). Motivational interviewing. *Annual Review of Clinical Psychology, 1,* 91–111.

Higa-McMillan, C., Francis, S. E., Rith-Najarian, L., & Chorpita, B. F. (2016). Evidence base update: 50 years of research on treatment for child and adolescent anxiety. *Journal of Clinical Child and Adolescent Psychology, 45*(2), 91–113.

Hill, C. E. (2014). *Helping skills: Facilitating, exploration, insight, and action* (4th ed.). Washington, DC: American Psychological Association.

Hill, K. A. (1987). Meta-analysis of paradoxical interventions. *Psychotherapy, 24,* 266–270.

Hill, N. L. (2011). Externalizing conversations: Single session narrative group interventions in a partial hospital setting. *Clinical Social Work Journal, 39*(3), 279–287.

Hinsberger, M., Holtzhausen, L., Sommer, J., Kaminer, D., Elbert, T., Seedat, S., et al. (2017). Feasibility and effectiveness of narrative exposure therapy and cognitive behavioral therapy in a context of ongoing violence in South Africa. *Psychological Trauma: Theory, Research, Practice, and Policy, 9*(3), 282–291.

Ho, D. Y. F. (1998). Indigenous psychologies. *Journal of Cross-Cultural Psychology, 29*(1), 88–103.

Hoffman, E. (1994). *The drive for self: Alfred Adler and the founding of individual psychology.* Reading, MA: Addison-Wesley.

Hoffman, L., Stewart, S., Warren, D., & Meek, L. (2009). Toward a sustainable myth of self: An existential response to the postmodern condition. *Journal of Humanistic Psychology, 49*(2), 135–173.

Hofmann, S. G. (2014). President's message: Culture matters. *The Behavior Therapist, 37*(5), 97–99.

Hofmann, S. G., & Barlow, D. H. (2014). Evidence-based psychological interventions and the common factors approach: The beginnings of a rapprochement? *Psychotherapy, 51*(4), 510–513.

Hogan, R. (1975). Theoretical egocentrism and the problem of compliance. *American Psychologist, 30,* 533–540.

Holland, J. M., Neimeyer, R. A., Currier, J. M., & Berman, J. S. (2007). The efficacy of personal construct therapy: A comprehensive review. *Journal of Clinical Psychology, 63*(1), 93–107.

Holmes, J. (2010). *Exploring in security: Towards an attachment-informed psychoanalytic psychotherapy.* New York, NY: Routledge/Taylor & Francis Group.

Holmes, K. Y., White, K. B., Mills, C., & Mickel, E. (2011). Defining the experiences of black women: A choice theory®/reality therapy approach to understanding the strong black woman. *International Journal of Choice Theory and Reality Therapy, 31*(1), 73–83.

Hook, J. N., Davis, D. E., Owen, J., Worthington, E. L., Jr., & Utsey, S. O. (2013). Cultural humility: Measuring openness to culturally diverse clients. *Journal of Counseling Psychology, 60*(3), 353–366.

Hook, J. N., & Watkins, C. E. (2015). Cultural humility: The cornerstone of positive contact with culturally different individuals and groups? *American Psychologist, 70*(7), 661–662.

hooks, b. (2000). *Feminism is for everybody: Passionate politics.* London, England: Pluto Press.

Hopko, D. R., Armento, M. E. A., Cantu, M. S., Chambers, L. L., & Lejuez, C. W. (2003). The use of daily diaries to assess the relations among mood state, overt behavior, and reward value of activities. *Behaviour Research and Therapy, 41*(10), 1137–1148.

Hopko, D. R., Ryba, M. M., McIndoo, C., & File, A. (2015). In C. M. Nezu & A. M. Nezu (Eds.), *The Oxford handbook of cognitive and behavioral therapies* (pp. 229–263). New York, NY: Oxford University Press.

Horner, A. J. (1998). *Working with the core relationship problem in psychotherapy: A handbook for clinicians.* San Francisco, CA: Jossey-Bass.

Horney, K. (1932). The dread of woman. *International Journal of Psychoanalysis, 13,* 348–360.

Horney, K. (1950). *Neurosis and human growth: The struggle toward self-realization.* New York, NY: Norton.

Horney, K. (1967). *Feminine psychology.* New York, NY: Norton.

Horowitz, L. M., Rosenberg, S. E., Baer, B. A., Ureño, G., & Villaseñor, V. S. (1988). Inventory of interpersonal problems: Psychometric properties and clinical applications. *Journal of Consulting and Clinical Psychology, 56*(6), 885–892.

Horowitz, M. J., Marmar, C., Krupnick, J., Wilner, N., Kaltreider, N., & Wallerstein, R. (1984). *Personality styles and brief psychotherapy.* New York, NY: Basic Books.

Horvath, A. O., & Greenberg, L. S. (1989). Development and validation of the working alliance inventory. *Journal of Counseling Psychology, 36*(2), 223–233.

Horvath, A. O., Re, A. C. D., Flückiger, C., & Symonds, D. (2011). Alliance in individual psychotherapy. In J. C. Norcross (Ed.), *Psychotherapy relationships that work: Evidence-based responsiveness* (2nd ed.) (pp. 25–69). New York, NY: Oxford University Press.

Hourani, L., Tueller, S., Kizakevich, P., Lewis, G., Strange, L., Weimer, B., et al. (2016). Toward preventing post-traumatic stress disorder: Development and testing of a pilot predeployment stress inoculation training program. *Military Medicine, 181*(9), 1151–1160.

Hoyt, M. F. (1994). On the importance of keeping it simple and taking the patient seriously: A conversation with Steve de Shazer and John Weakland. In M. F. Hoyt (Ed.), *Constructive therapies* (pp. 11–40). New York, NY: Guilford Press.

Hoyt, M. F. (Ed.). (1998). *The handbook of constructive therapies: Innovative approaches from leading practitioners.* San Francisco, CA: Jossey-Bass/Pfeiffer.

Hoyt, M. F. (2000). Cognitive-behavioural treatment of post-traumatic stress disorder from a narrative constructivist perspective: A conversation with Donald Meichenbaum. In

M. Scott & S. Palmer (Eds.), *Trauma and post-traumatic stress disorder* (pp. 49–69). London, England: Cassell.

Hrdy, S. B. (1999). *Mother nature*. New York, NY: Pantheon Books.

Hubble, M. A., Duncan, B. L., & Miller, S. D. (Eds.). (1999). *The heart and soul of change*. Washington, DC: American Psychological Association.

Hughes, D. (1998). *Building the bonds of attachment: Awakening love in deeply troubled children*. Northvale, NJ: Aronson.

Huguet, A., Rao, S., McGrath, P. J., Wozney, L., Wheaton, M., Conrod, J., & Rozario, S. (2016). A systematic review of cognitive behavioral therapy and behavioral activation apps for depression. *PLoS ONE, 11*(5), 19.

Hunter, P., & Kelso, E. N. (1985). Feminist behavior therapy. *Behavior Therapist, 8*(10), 201–204.

Hwang, W., & Wood, J. J. (2007). Being culturally sensitive is not the same as being culturally competent. *Pragmatic Case Studies in Psychotherapy, 3*, 44–50.

Hycner, R., & Jacobs, L. (Eds.). (2009). *Relational approaches in Gestalt therapy*. Cambridge, MA: GestaltPress Book.

Hyde, J. S. (2005). The gender similarities hypothesis. *American Psychologist, 60*(6), 581–592.

Hymowitz, K. (2011). *Manning up: How the rise of women has turned men into boys*. New York, NY: Basic Books.

Iacovou, S., & Weixel-Dixon, K. (2015). *Existential therapy: 100 key points and techniques*. New York, NY: Routledge.

Iaculo, G., & Frew, J. E. (2004). Relational support in the gay coming-out process. *Gestalt Review, 8*(2), 178–203.

Iliescu, D., Ilie, A., Ispas, D., Dobrean, A., & Clinciu, A. I. (2016). Sex differences in intelligence: A multi-measure approach using nationally representative samples from Romania. *Intelligence, 58*, 54–61.

Ivey, A. E., D'Andrea, M., Ivey, M. B., & Simek-Morgan, L. (2002). *Theories of counseling and psychotherapy: A multicultural perspective* (5th ed.). Boston: Allyn & Bacon.

Jackson, D. D. (1954). Suicide. *Scientific American, 191*, 88–96.

Jackson, D. D., & Weakland, J. H. (1959). Schizophrenic symptoms and family interaction. *Archives of General Psychiatry, 1*, 618–621.

Jacobs, L. (1992). Insights from psychoanalytic self-psychology and intersubjectivity theory for gestalt therapists. *Gestalt Journal, 15*(2), 25–60.

Jacobson, E. (1924). The technic of progressive relaxation. *Journal of Nervous & Mental Disease, 60*(6), 568–578.

Jacobson, E. (1938). *Progressive relaxation*. Chicago, IL: University of Chicago Press.

Jacobson, E. (1978). *You must relax* (5th ed.). New York, NY: McGraw-Hill.

Jacobson, N. S., Dobson, K. S., Truax, P. A., Addis, M. E., Koerner, K., Gollan, J. K., et al. (1996). A component analysis of cognitive-behavioral treatment for depression. *Journal of Consulting and Clinical Psychology, 64*(2), 295–304.

Jacobson, N. S., Martell, C. R., & Dimidjian, S. (2001). Behavioral activation treatment for depression: Returning to contextual roots. *Clinical Psychology: Science and Practice, 8*(3), 255–270.

Jankowski, P. J., & Hooper, L. M. (2012). Differentiation of self: A validation study of the Bowen theory construct. *Couple and Family Psychology: Research and Practice, 1*(3), 226–243.

James, W. (1992). *William James, writings 1878–1899*. New York, NY: Library of America.

Janet, P. (1901). *Fixed ideas*. New York, NY: Putnam.

Jenkins, A. H. (1997). The empathic context in psychotherapy with people of color. In A. C. Bohart & L. S. Greenberg (Eds.), *Empathy reconsidered: New directions in psychology* (pp. 321–342). Washington, DC: American Psychological Association.

Jenkins, W. M., Merzenich, M. M., Ochs, M. T., Allard, T., & Guk-Robles, E. (1990). Functional reorganization of primary somatosensory cortex in adult owl monkeys after behaviorally controlled tactile stimulation. *Journal of Neurophysiology, 63*(1), 82–104.

Jiménez Ruiz, I., Almansa Martínez, P., & Alcón Belchí, C. (2017). Dismantling the man-made myths upholding female genital mutilation. *Health Care for Women International, 38*(5), 478–491.

Johansen, T. (2010). *Religion and spirituality in psychotherapy: An individual psychology perspective*. New York, NY: Springer.

Johnson, R. (2013). *Spirituality in counseling and psychotherapy: An integrative approach that empowers clients*. Hoboken, NJ: Wiley.

Johnson, S. (2010). Emotionally focused couple therapy: It's all about emotion and connection. In M. Kerman (Ed.), *Clinical pearls of insight: 21 leading therapists offer their key insights* (pp. 133–143). New York, NY: Norton.

Johnson, S. M., & Greenberg, L. S. (1985). Differential effects of experiential and problem-solving interventions in resolving marital conflict. *Journal of Consulting and Clinical Psychology, 53*(2), 175–184.

Jones, E. E. (1953). *Sigmund Freud: Life and Work* (Vol 1: *The Young Freud 1856–1900*). London, England: Hogarth Press.

Jones, E. E. (1957). *Sigmund Freud: Life and work* (Vol 3: *The last phase 1919-1939*). London, England: Hogarth Press.

Jones, M. C. (1924a). The elimination of children's fear. *Journal of Experimental Psychology, 8*, 382–390.

Jones, M. C. (1924b). A laboratory study of fear: The case of Peter. *Ped. Sem, 31*, 308–316.

Jones-Smith, E. (2016). *Theories of counseling and psychotherapy: An integrative approach*. Thousand Oaks, CA: Sage.

Jordan, J. V. (2010). *Relational–cultural therapy*. Washington, DC: American Psychological Association.

Jordan, J. V. (2017). Jean Baker Miller, MD, visionary pragmatist. *Women & Therapy, 40*(3–4), 260–274.

Jordan, J. V., Walker, M., & Hartling, L. M. (Eds.). (2004). *The complexity of connection: Writings from the Stone Center's Jean Baker Miller Training Institute*. New York, NY: Guilford Press.

Josephson, J., Einarsdóttir, Þ., & Sigurðardóttir, S. A. (2017). Queering the trans: Gender and sexuality binaries in Icelandic trans, queer, and feminist communities. *European Journal of Women's Studies, 24*(1), 70–84.

Joyce, P., & Sills, C. (2014). *Skills in Gestalt counseling and psychotherapy* (3rd ed.). London, England: Sage.

Jung, C. G. (1953). *Two essays on analytical psychology* (Bollingen series 20). New York, NY: Pantheon Books.

Jusoh, A. J., Mahmud, Z., & Ishak, N. M. (2008). The patterns of reality therapy usage among Malaysian counselors. *International Journal of Reality Therapy, 28*(1), 5–14.

Kabat-Zinn, J. (1990). *Full catastrophe living*. New York, NY: Bantam Books.

Kaplan, D. (2011, July). Changing distorted thinking. *Counseling Today, 54*, 36–38.

Karp, N. A., Mason, J., Beaudet, A. L., Benjamini, Y., Bower, L., Braun, R. E., et al. (2017). Prevalence of sexual dimorphism in mammalian phenotypic traits. *Nature Communications, 8*, 14251.

Kaschak, E. (1992). *Engendered lives*. New York, NY: Harper-Collins.

Kawahara, D. M., & Espín, O. M. (2007). Asian American women in therapy: Feminist reflections on growth and transformations. *Women & Therapy, 30*(3–4), 1–5.

Kazantzis, N., Whittington, C., Zelencich, L., Kyrios, M., Norton, P. J., & Hofmann, S. G. (2016). Quantity and quality of homework compliance: A meta-analysis of relations with outcome in cognitive behavior therapy. *Behavior Therapy, 47*(5), 755–772.

Kazdin, A. E. (2007). Mediators and mechanisms of change in psychotherapy research. *Annual Review of Clinical Psychology, 3*, 1–27.

Kazdin, A. E. (2008). *The Kazdin method for parenting the defiant child: With no pills, no therapy, no contest of wills*. Boston, MA: Houghton Mifflin.

Kazdin, A. E. (2010). Problem-solving skills training and parent management training for oppositional defiant disorder and conduct disorder. In J. R. Weisz & A. E. Kazdin (Eds.), *Evidence-based psychotherapies for children and adolescents* (pp. 211–226). New York, NY: Guilford Press.

Keat, D. B. (1985). Child–adolescent multimodal therapy: Bud the boss. *Journal of Humanistic Counseling, Education & Development, 23*(4), 183–192.

Keillor, G. (Director). (2002, July 25). *The writer's almanac*. [Radio broadcast] Minneapolis, MN: Minnesota Public Radio.

Keith, D. V., & Whitaker, C. A. (1982). Experiential-symbolic family therapy. In A. M. Horne & M. M. Ohlsen (Eds.), *Family counseling and therapy*. Itasca, IL: Peacock.

Kelly, F. D., & Main, F. O. (1978). Idiographic research in Adlerian psychology: Problems and solutions. *Journal of Individual Psychology, 34*(2), 221–231.

Kelly, G. A. (1955). *The psychology of personal constructs*. New York, NY: Norton.

Kelly, G. A. (1969). Ontological acceleration. In B. Maher (Ed.), *Clinical psychology and personality: The selected papers of George Kelly* (pp. 7–45). New York, NY: Wiley.

Kendall, P. C. (Ed.). (2000). *Child and adolescent therapy: Cognitive-behavioral procedures* (2nd ed.). New York, NY: Guilford Press.

Kendall, P. C., Comer, J. S., Marker, C. D., Creed, T. A., Puliafico, A. C., Hughes, A. A., et al. (2009). In-session exposure tasks and therapeutic alliance across the treatment of childhood anxiety disorders. *Journal of Consulting and Clinical Psychology, 77*(3), 517–525.

Keshen, A. (2006). A new look at existential psychotherapy. *American Journal of Psychotherapy, 60*(3), 285–298.

Kim, J. S. (2008). Examining the effectiveness of solution-focused brief therapy: A meta-analysis. *Research on Social Work Practice, 18*(2), 107–116.

Kim, J. S. (2014). *Solution-focused brief therapy: A multicultural approach*. Thousand Oaks, CA: Sage.

Kim, J. S., Franklin, C., Zhang, Y., Liu, X., Qu, Y., & Chen, H. (2015). Solution-focused brief therapy in China: A meta-analysis. *Journal of Ethnic & Cultural Diversity in Social Work: Innovation in Theory, Research & Practice, 24*(3), 187–201.

Kim, K. I., & Hwang, M. G. (2001). The effects of internal control and achievement motivation in group counseling based on reality therapy. *International Journal of Reality Therapy, 20*(3), 11–17.

Kimmel, M. (2010). *Guyland: The perilous world where boys become men*. New York, NY: Harper.

King, J., Trimble, J. E., Morse, G. S., & Thomas, L. R. (2014). *North American Indian and Alaska Native spirituality and psychotherapy*. Washington, DC: American Psychological Association.

Kirkham, J. G., Choi, N., & Seitz, D. P. (2016). Meta-analysis of problem solving therapy for the treatment of major depressive disorder in older adults. *International Journal of Geriatric Psychiatry, 31*(5), 526–535.

Kirschenbaum, H. (1979). *On becoming Carl Rogers*. Oxford, England: Delacorte.

Kirschenbaum, H. (2012). What is "person-centered"? A posthumous conversation with Carl Rogers on the development of the person-centered approach. *Person-Centered and Experiential Psychotherapies, 11*(1), 14–30.

Kirschenbaum, H., & Henderson, V. L. (Eds.). (1989). *Carl Rogers: Dialogues*. Boston, MA: Houghton Mifflin.

Kissane, D. W., Bloch, S., Smith, G. C., Miach, P., Clarke, D. M., Ikin, J., et al. (2003). Cognitive-existential group psychotherapy for women with primary breast cancer: A randomized controlled trial. *Psycho-Oncology, 12*(6), 532–546.

Kivlighan, D. M., Jr. (2002). Transference, interpretation, and insight: A research-practice model. In G. S. Tryon (Ed.), *Counseling based on process research: Applying what we know* (pp. 166–196). Boston, MA: Allyn & Bacon.

Klein, M. H. (1976). Feminist concepts of therapy outcome. *Psychotherapy: Theory, Research & Practice, 13*(1), 89–95.

Klerman, G. L., Weissman, M. M., Rounsaville, B. J., & Chevron, E. S. (1984). *Interpersonal psychotherapy of depression*. New York, NY: Basic Books.

Klerman, G. L., Weissman, M. M., Rounsaville, B., & Chevron, E. S. (1995). Interpersonal psychotherapy for depression. *Journal of Psychotherapy Practice & Research, 4*(4), 342–351.

Knekt, P., Lindfors, O., Härkänen, T., Välikoski, M., Virtala, E., Laaksonen, M. A., et al. (2008). Randomized trial on the effectiveness of long- and short-term psychodynamic psychotherapy and solution-focused therapy on psychiatric symptoms during a 3-year follow-up. *Psychological Medicine, 38*(5), 689–703.

Kocet, M. M. (Ed.). (2014). *Counseling Gay men, adolescents, and boys: A strengths-based guide for helping professionals and educators*. New York, NY: Routledge.

Kocovski, N. L., Fleming, J. E., Hawley, L. L., Ho, M. R., & Antony, M. M. (2015). Mindfulness and acceptance-based group therapy and traditional cognitive behavioral group therapy for social anxiety disorder: Mechanisms of change. *Behaviour Research and Therapy, 70*, 11–22.

Kohler, S., & Hofmann, A. (2015). Can motivational interviewing in emergency care reduce alcohol consumption in young people? A systematic review and meta-analysis. *Alcohol and Alcoholism, 50*(2), 107–117.

Kohn, A. (2005). *Unconditional parenting: Moving from rewards and punishments to love and reason*. New York, NY: Atria.

Kohut, H. H. (1959). Introspection, empathy, and psychoanalysis. *Journal of American Psycholanalysis Association, 7*, 459–483.

Kohut, H. H. (1971). *The analysis of self*. New York, NY: International Universities Press.

Kohut, H. H. (1977). *Restoration of the self*. New York, NY: International Universities Press.

Kohut, H. H. (1984). *How does analysis cure?* Chicago, IL: University of Chicago Press.

Kondas, D. (2008). Existential explosion and gestalt therapy for gay male survivors of domestic violence. *Gestalt Review, 12,* 58–74.

Korchin, S. J. (1976). *Modern clinical psychology: Principles of intervention in the clinic and community.* New York, NY: Basic Books.

Kort, J. (2008). *Gay affirmative therapy for the straight clinician: The essential guide.* New York, NY: Norton.

Kottler, J. A., & Brown, R. W. (2008). *Introduction to therapeutic counseling* (8th ed.). Pacific Grove, CA: Brooks/Cole.

Kottman, T. (1994). Adlerian play therapy. In K. J. O'Connor & C. E. Schaefer (Eds.), *Handbook of play therapy,* Vol. 2: *Advances and innovations* (pp. 3–26). Oxford: Wiley.

Kottman, T. T., & Warlick, J. (1989). Adlerian play therapy: Practical considerations. *Individual Psychology: Journal of Adlerian Theory, Research & Practice, 45*(4), 433–446.

Kovacs, M. (1992). *Children's depression inventory.* Toronto, Ontario: Multi-Health Systems.

Kramer, R. (1995). The birth of client-centered therapy: Carl Rogers, Otto Rank, and "the beyond." *Journal of Humanistic Psychology, 35*(4), 54–110.

Kraus, C. (2015). Classifying intersex in DSM-5: Critical reflections on gender dysphoria. *Archives of Sexual Behavior, 44*(5), 1147–1163.

Kruizinga, R., Hartog, I. D., Jacobs, M., Daams, J. G., Scherer-Rath, M., Schilderman, J. B. A. M., et al. (2016). The effect of spiritual interventions addressing existential themes using a narrative approach on quality of life of cancer patients: A systematic review and meta-analysis. *Psycho-Oncology, 25*(3), 253–265.

Krumboltz, J. D. (1965). Behavioral counseling: Rationale and research. *Personnel and Guidance Journal, 44,* 383–387.

Kupers, T. A., Ross, R., Frances, A., & Widiger, T. A. (2005). Issue 2: Is there gender bias in the DSM-IV? In R. P. Halgin (Ed.), *Taking sides: Abnormal psychology* (pp. 14–40). New York, NY: McGraw-Hill.

Kurtz, M. M., Olfson, R. H., & Rose, J. (2013). Self-efficacy and functional status in schizophrenia: Relationship to insight, cognition and negative symptoms. *Schizophrenia Research, 145,* 69–74.

Kutchins, H., & Kirk, S. A. (1997). *Making us crazy.* New York, NY: The Free Press.

Kuyken, W., Warren, F. C., Taylor, R. S., Whalley, B., Crane, C., Bondolfi, G., et al. (2016). Efficacy of mindfulness-based cognitive therapy in prevention of depressive relapse: An individual patient data meta-analysis from randomized trials. *JAMA Psychiatry, 73*(6), 565–574.

Kwee, M. G., Duivenvoorden, H. J., Trijsburg, R. W., & Thiel, J. H. (1987). Multimodal therapy in an inpatient setting. *Current Psychological Research & Reviews, 5*(4), 344–357.

Lacan, J. (1988). *The seminar of Jacques Lacan, Book I* (Trans. by J. Forrester). Cambridge, England: Cambridge University Press.

Ladinsky, D. (1996). *I heard God laughing: Renderings of Hafiz.* Oakland, CA: Mobius Press.

LaFontaine, L. (1994). Quality schools for gay and lesbian youth: Lifting the cloak of silence. *Journal of Reality Therapy, 14*(1), 26–28.

LaFontaine, L. (1995). Basic needs and sexuality: Is something missing in reality therapy/control theory. *Journal of Reality Therapy, 15*(1), 32–36.

LaFountain, R. (2013). A new, expanded edition of a valuable psychotherapy resource. *The Journal of Individual Psychology, 69*(1), 92–93.

LaFromboise, T. D., Trimble, J. E., & Mohatt, G. V. (1990). Counseling intervention and American Indian tradition: An integrative approach. *The Counseling Psychologist, 18,* 628–654.

Lambert, M. J. (1992). Implications of outcome research for psychotherapy integration. In J. C. Norcross & M. R. Goldstein (Eds.), *Handbook of psychotherapy integration* (pp. 94–129). New York, NY: Basic Books.

Lambert, M. (2007). Presidential address: What we have learned from a decade of research aimed at improving psychotherapy outcome in routine care. *Psychotherapy Research, 17*(1), 1–14.

Lambert, M. J. (2010). *Prevention of treatment failure: The use of measuring, monitoring, and feedback in clinical practice.* Washington, DC: American Psychological Association.

Lambert, M. J. (Ed.). (2013a). *Bergin and Garfield's handbook of psychotherapy and behavior change* (6th ed.). Hoboken, NJ: Wiley.

Lambert, M. J. (2013b). Outcome in psychotherapy: The past and important advances. *Psychotherapy, 50*(1), 42–51.

Lambert, M. J., & Erekson, D. M. (2008). Positive psychology and the humanistic tradition. *Journal of Psychotherapy Integration, 18*(2), 222–232.

Lambert, M. J., Hansen, N. B., Umphress, V., Lunnen, K., Okiishi, J., Burlingame, G. M., & Reisinger, C. W. (1996). *Administration and scoring manual for the OQ-45.2.* East Setauket, NY: American Professional Credentialing Services.

Lambert, M. J., & Lambert, M. J. (2010). *Predicting negative treatment outcome: Methods and estimates of accuracy.* Washington, DC: American Psychological Association.

Lambert, M. J., & Ogles, B. M. (2014). Common factors: Post hoc explanation or empirically based therapy approach? *Psychotherapy, 51*(4), 500–504.

Lang, T., & Hoyer, J. (2007). Massed exposure and fast remission of panic disorder with agoraphobia: A case example. *Behavioural and Cognitive Psychotherapy, 35*(3), 371–375.

Larouche, M., Lorrain, D., Côté, G., & Bélisle, D. (2015). Evaluation of the effectiveness of mindfulness-based cognitive therapy to treat chronic insomnia. *European Review of Applied Psychology/ Revue Européenne De Psychologie Appliquée, 65*(3), 115–123.

Laska, K. M., Gurman, A. S., & Wampold, B. E. (2014). Expanding the lens of evidence-based practice in psychotherapy: A common factors perspective. *Psychotherapy, 51*(4), 467–481.

Laska, K. M., & Wampold, B. E. (2014). Ten things to remember about common factor theory. *Psychotherapy, 51*(4), 519–524.

Lau, M. A., Bishop, S. R., Segal, Z. V., Buis, T., Anderson, N. D., Carlson, L., et al. (2006). The Toronto Mindfulness Scale: Development and validation. *Journal of Clinical Psychology, 62*(12), 1445–1467.

Law, F. M., & Guo, G. J. (2014). Who is in charge of your recovery? The effectiveness of reality therapy for female drug offenders in Taiwan. *International Journal of Offender Therapy and Comparative Criminology, 58*(6), 672–696.

Law, F. M., & Guo, G. J. (2015). The impact of reality therapy on self-efficacy for substance-involved female offenders in Taiwan. *International Journal of Offender Therapy and Comparative Criminology, 59*(6), 631–653.

Law, F. M., & Guo, G. J. (2017). Choice and hope: A preliminary study of the effectiveness of choice-based reality therapy in strengthening hope in recovery for women convicted of drug offences in Taiwan. *International Journal of Offender Therapy and Comparative Criminology, 61*(3), 310–333.

Lazarus, A. A. (1958). New methods in psychotherapy: A case study. *South African Medical Journal, 32*, 660–664.

Lazarus, A. A. (1967). In support of technical eclecticism. *Psychological Reports, 21*, 415–416.

Lazarus, A. A. (1971). *Behavior therapy and beyond.* New York, NY: McGraw-Hill.

Lazarus, A. A. (1973). *Clinical behavior therapy.* New York, NY: Brunner/Mazel.

Lazarus, A. A. (1989). *The practice of multimodal therapy: Systematic, comprehensive, and effective psychotherapy.* Baltimore, MD: Johns Hopkins University Press.

Lazarus, A. A. (1991). A plague on little Hans and little Albert. *Psychotherapy: Theory, Research, Practice, Training, 28*(3), 444–447.

Lazarus, A. A. (1993). Tailoring the therapeutic relationship, or being an authentic chameleon. *Psychotherapy, 30*, 404–407.

Lazarus, A. A. (1997). *Brief but comprehensive psychotherapy: The multimodal way.* New York, NY: Springer (reprinted 2006).

Lazarus, A. A. (2000). Multimodal replenishment. *Professional Psychology: Research & Practice, 31*(1), 93–94.

Lazarus, A. A. (2008). Technical eclecticism and multimodal therapy. In J. L. Lebow (Ed.), *Twenty-first century psychotherapies* (pp. 424–452). Hoboken, NJ: Wiley.

Lazarus, A. A., Beutler, L. E., & Norcross, J. C. (1992). The future of technical eclecticism. *Psychotherapy: Theory, Research, Practice, Training. Special Issue: The Future of Psychotherapy, 29*(1), 11–20.

Lazarus, A. A., & Lazarus, C. N. (1991). *Multimodal life history inventory.* Champaign, IL: Research Press.

Leahy, R. L. (2003). *Cognitive therapy techniques: A practitioner's guide.* New York, NY: Guilford Press.

Leak, G. K. (2006). An empirical assessment of the relationship between social interest and spirituality. *The Journal of Individual Psychology, 62*(1), 59–69.

Leak, G. K., & Leak, K. C. (2006). Adlerian social interest and positive psychology: A conceptual and empirical integration. *The Journal of Individual Psychology, 62*(3), 207–223.

Leber, P. (1991). Is there an alternative to the randomized controlled trial? *Psychopharmacology Bulletin, 27*, 3–8.

Lebow, J. L. (Ed.). (2008). *Twenty-first century psychotherapies: Contemporary approaches to theory and practice.* Hoboken, NJ: Wiley.

Ledley, D. R., Marx, B. P., & Heimberg, R. G. (2010). *Making cognitive-behavioral therapy work: Clinical process for new practitioners* (2nd ed.). New York, NY: Guilford Press.

Lee, C., & Bobko, P. (1994). Self-efficacy beliefs: Comparison of five measures. *Journal of Applied Psychology, 79*(3), 364–369.

Lee, E. B., An, W., Levin, M. E., & Twohig, M. P. (2015). An initial meta-analysis of acceptance and commitment therapy for treating substance use disorders. *Drug and Alcohol Dependence, 155*, 1–7.

Lee, K., Noda, Y., Nakano, Y., Ogawa, S., Kinoshita, Y., Funayama, T., et al. (2006). Interoceptive hypersensitivity and interoceptive exposure in patients with panic disorder: Specificity and effectiveness. *BMC Psychiatry, 6*, 1–9.

Leibert, T. W., Smith, J. B., & Agaskar, V. R. (2011). Relationship between the working alliance and social support on counseling outcome. *Journal of Clinical Psychology, 67*(7), 709–719.

Leichsenring, F., Klein, S., & Salzer, S. (2014). The efficacy of psychodynamic psychotherapy in specific mental disorders: A 2013 update of empirical evidence. *Contemporary Psychoanalysis, 50*(1–2), 89–130.

Lejuez, C. W., Hopko, D. R., Acierno, R., Daughters, S. B., & Pagoto, S. L. (2011). Ten year revision of the brief behavioral activation treatment for depression: Revised treatment manual. *Behavior Modification, 35*(2), 111–161.

Lejuez, C. W., Hopko, D. R., LePage, J. P., Hopko, S. D., & McNeil, D. W. (2001). A brief behavioral activation treatment for depression. *Cognitive and Behavioral Practice, 8*(2), 164–175.

Leong, F. T. L., Kim, H. H. W., & Gupta, A. (2011). Attitudes toward professional counseling among Asian-American college students: Acculturation, conceptions of mental illness, and loss of face. *Asian American Journal of Psychology, 2*(2), 140–153.

Levant, R. F., & Pollack, W. S. (1995). *A new psychology of men.* New York, NY: Basic Books.

Levin, D. E., & Kilbourne, J. (2009). *So sexy so soon: The new sexualized childhood and what parents can do to protect their kids.* New York, NY: Ballantine.

Levine, P. A. (2010). *In an unspoken voice: How the body releases trauma and restores goodness.* Berkeley, CA: North Atlantic Books.

Levy, D. M. (1943). *Maternal overprotection.* New York, NY: Columbia University Press.

Levy, S. T. (1984). *Principles of interpretation.* New York, NY: Aronson.

Lewin, K. (1951). *Field theory in social science: Selected theoretical papers* (edited by DorwinCartwright). Oxford, England: Harpers.

Lewinsohn, P. M. (1974). *A behavioral approach to depression.* Oxford, England: Wiley.

Lewinsohn, P. M., & Libet, J. (1972). Pleasant events, activity schedules, and depressions. *Journal of Abnormal Psychology, 79*(3), 291–295.

Lewinsohn, P. M., Steinmetz, J. L., Antonuccio, D., & Teri, L. (1984). Group therapy for depression: The coping with depression course. *International Journal of Mental Health, 13*(3–4), 8–33.

Lewis, T., Amini, F., & Lannon, R. (2001). *A general theory of love.* New York, NY: Vintage.

Liang, B., Tracy, A. J., Kenny, M. E., Brogan, D., & Gatha, R. (2010). The relational health indices for youth: An examination of reliability and validity aspects. *Measurement and Evaluation in Counseling and Development, 42*(4), 255–274.

Liang, B., Tracy, A., Taylor, C. A., Williams, L. M., Jordan, J. V., & Miller, J. B. (2002). The relational health indices: A study of women's relationships. *Psychology of Women Quarterly, 26*(1), 25–35.

Lichtenthal, W. G., Nilsson, M., Zhang, B., Trice, E. D., Kissane, D. W., Breitbart, W., et al. (2009). Do rates of mental disorders and existential distress among advanced stage cancer patients increase as death approaches? *Psycho-Oncology, 18*(1), 50–61.

Liddle, H. A. (1985). Beyond family therapy: Challenging the boundaries, roles, and mission of a field. *Journal of Strategic & Systemic Therapies, 4*(2), 4–14.

Liddle, H. A. (1995). Conceptual and clinical dimensions of a multidimensional, multisystems engagement strategy in family-based adolescent treatment. *Psychotherapy: Theory, Research, Practice, Training, 32*(1), 39–58.

Liddle, H. A. (2016). Multidimensional family therapy: Evidence base for transdiagnostic treatment outcomes, change mechanisms, and implementation in community settings. *Family Process, 55*(3), 558–576.

Lidz, T., Cornelison, A., Fleck, S., & Terry, D. (1957). Intrafamilial environment of the schizophrenic patient I: The father. *Psychiatry, 20,* 329–342.

Lilienfeld, S. O. (2007). Psychological treatments that cause harm. *Perspectives on Psychological Science, 2*(1), 53–70.

Lilienfeld, S. O., Lynn, S. J., & Lohr, J. M. (2003). *Science and pseudoscience in clinical psychology.* New York, NY: Guilford Press.

Lilienfeld, S. O., Schwartz, S. J., Meca, A., Sauvigné, K. C., & Satel, S. (2015). Neurocentrism: Implications for psychotherapy practice and research. *The Behavior Therapist, 38*(7), 173–181.

Lindfors, O., Knekt, P., Virtala, E., & Laaksonen, M. A. (2012). The effectiveness of solution-focused therapy and short- and long-term psychodynamic psychotherapy on self-concept during a 3-year follow-up. *Journal of Nervous and Mental Disease, 200*(11), 946–953.

Linehan, M. M. (1993). *Cognitive behavioral therapy of borderline personality disorder.* New York, NY: Guilford Press.

Linehan, M. M. (2000). The empirical basis of dialectical behavior therapy: Development of new treatments versus evaluation of existing treatments. *Clinical Psychology: Science & Practice, 7*(1), 113–119.

Linehan, M. M., Comtois, K. A., Murray, A. M., Brown, M. Z., Gallop, R. J., Heard, H. L., et al. (2006). Two-year randomized controlled trial and follow-up of dialectical behavior therapy vs therapy by experts for suicidal behaviors and borderline personality disorder. *Archives of General Psychiatry, 63*(7), 757–766.

Linehan, M., & Schmidt, H. I. (1995). The dialectics of effective treatment of borderline personality disorder. In W. O'Donohue & L. Krasner (Eds.), *Theories of behavior therapy* (pp. 553–584). Washington, DC: American Psychological Association.

Linnenberg, D. M. (2006). Thoughts on reality therapy from a pro-feminist perspective. *International Journal of Reality Therapy, 26,* 23–26.

Lipina, S. J., & Evers, K. (2017). Neuroscience of childhood poverty: Evidence of impacts and mechanisms as vehicles of dialog with ethics. *Frontiers in Psychology, 8*(61), 1–13.

Liu, H., Ting, Y., & Cheng, J. (2010). The effects of a reality therapy group guidance program for underachieving elementary students in regard to their Mandarin learning attitudes and achievements. *Bulletin of Educational Psychology, 42*(1), 53–76.

Lobb, M. S. (2016). Isomorphism: A bridge to connect gestalt therapy, gestalt theory and neurosciences. *Gestalt Theory, 38*(1), 41–56.

Lobb, M. S., & Lichtenberg, P. (2005). *Classical Gestalt therapy theory.* Thousand Oaks, CA: Sage.

Locke, E. A., & Latham, G. P. (2002). Building a practically useful theory of goal setting and task motivation: A 35-year odyssey. *American Psychologist, 57,* 705–717.

Loeschen, S., & Suarez, M. (2008). Human validation process model. In K. Jordan (Ed.), *The quick theory reference guide: A resource for expert and novice mental health professionals* (pp. 311–329). Hauppauge, NY: Nova Science.

Loevinger, J. (1976). *Ego Development.* San Francisco, CA: Jossey-Bass.

Lohr, J. M. (2011). What is (and what is not) the meaning of evidence-based psychosocial intervention? *Clinical Psychology: Science and Practice, 18*(2), 100–104.

London, P. (1964). *The modes and morals of psychotherapy.* New York, NY: Holt, Rinehart, and Winston.

London, P. (1986). Major issues in psychotherapy integration. *Journal of Integrative & Eclectic Psychotherapy, 5*(3), 211–216.

Luborsky, L. (1984). *Principles of psychoanalytic psychotherapy: A manual for supportive-expressive treatment.* New York, NY: Basic Books.

Luborsky, L. (1985). A verification of Freud's grandest clinical hypothesis: The transference. *Clinical Psychology Review, 5,* 231–246.

Luborsky, L., Diguer, L., Seligman, D. A., Rosenthal, R., Krause, E. D., Johnson, S., et al. (1999). The researcher's own therapy allegiances: A "wild card" in comparisons of treatment efficacy. *Clinical Psychology: Science & Practice, 6*(1), 95–106.

Luborsky, L., Singer, B., & Luborsky, L. (1975). Comparative studies of psychotherapies: Is it true that "everybody has won so all shall have prizes?" *Archives of General Psychiatry, 32,* 995–1008.

Luke, C. (2016). *Neuroscience for counselors and therapists: Integrating the sciences of mind and brain.* Thousand Oaks, CA: Sage.

Luria, A. (1961). *The role of speech in the regulation of normal and abnormal behavior.* New York, NY: Liveright.

Ma, Q., Jin, J., Meng, L., & Shen, Q. (2014). The dark side of monetary incentive: How does extrinsic reward crowd out intrinsic motivation. *NeuroReport: For Rapid Communication of Neuroscience Research, 25*(3), 194–198.

Maag, J. W. (2001). Rewarded by punishment: Reflections on the disuse of positive reinforcement in the schools. *Exceptional Children, 67,* 173–186.

Madanes, C., & Haley, J. (1977). Dimensions of family therapy. *The Journal of Nervous and Mental Disease, 165,* 88–98.

Madigan, S. (2011). *Narrative therapy.* Washington, DC: American Psychological Association.

Mahler, M., Pine, F., & Bergman, A. (1975). *The psychological birth of the human infant: Symbiosis and individuation.* New York, NY: Basic Books.

Mahoney, M. (1984). Psychoanalysis and behaviorism: The yin and yang of determinism. In H. Arkowitz & S. B. Messer (Eds.), *Psychoanalysis and behavior therapy: Is integration possible?* (pp. 303–325). New York, NY: Plenum.

Mahoney, M. (1985). Psychotherapy and human change processes. In M. Mahoney & A. Freeman (Eds.), *Cognition and psychotherapy* (pp. 3–48). New York, NY: Plenum.

Mahoney, M. (1991). *Human change processes.* New York, NY: Basic Books.

Main, M., & Solomon J. (1986). Discovery of a new, insecure-disorganized/disoriented attachment pattern. In M. Yogman & T. B. Brazelton (Eds.), *Affective development in infancy* (pp. 95–124). Norwood, NJ: Ablex.

Mairs, L., & Mullan, B. (2015). Self-monitoring vs. implementation intentions: A comparison of behaviour change techniques to improve sleep hygiene and sleep outcomes in students. *International Journal of Behavioral Medicine*, 22(5), 635–644.

Makel, M. C., Wai, J., Peairs, K., & Putallaz, M. (2016). Sex differences in the right tail of cognitive abilities: An update and cross cultural extension. *Intelligence*, 59, 8–15.

Malcolm, W. M., & Greenberg, L. S. (2000). Forgiveness as a process of change in individual psychotherapy. In M. E. McCullough, K. I. Pargament, & C. E. Thoresen (Eds.), *Forgiveness: Theory, research, and practice* (pp. 179–202). New York, NY: Guilford Press.

Malgady, R. G. (2010). Treating Hispanic children and adolescents using narrative therapy. In J. R. Weisz & A. E. Kazdin (Eds.), *Evidence-based psychotherapies for children and adolescents* (2nd ed.) (pp. 391–400). New York, NY: Guilford Press.

Malgady, R. G., & Costantino, G. (2003). Narrative therapy for Hispanic children and adolescents. In A. E. Kazdin & J. R. Weisz (Eds.), *Evidence-based psychotherapies for children and adolescents* (pp. 425–435). New York, NY: Guilford Press.

Malouff, J. M., Thorsteinsson, E. B., & Schutte, N. S. (2007). The efficacy of problem solving therapy in reducing mental and physical health problems: A meta-analysis. *Clinical Psychology Review*, 27(1), 46–57.

Malyon, A. K. (1982). Psychotherapeutic implications of internalized homophobia in gay men. *Journal of Homosexuality. Special Issue: Homosexuality & Psychotherapy*, 7, 59–69. doi: 10.1300/J082v07n02_08

Man Leung, G. S., Ki Leung, T. Y., & Tuen Ng, M. L. (2013). An outcome study of gestalt-oriented growth workshops. *International Journal of Group Psychotherapy*, 63(1), 117–125.

Manaster, G. J., & Corsini, R. J. (1982). *Individual psychology: Theory and practice*. Itasca, IL: F. E. Peacock.

Maniar, S. D., Curry, L. A., Sommers-Flanagan, J., & Walsh, J. A. (2001). Student athlete preferences in seeking help when confronted with sport performance problems. *Sport Psychologist*, 15(2), 205–223.

Mann, D. (2010). *Gestalt therapy: 100 key points & techniques*. New York, NY: Routledge/Taylor & Francis.

Mann, W. E. (1973). *Orgone, Reich and eros: Wilhelm Reich's theory of life energy*. Oxford, England: Simon & Schuster.

Mansager, E. (2008). Affirming lesbian, gay, bisexual, and transgender individuals. *The Journal of Individual Psychology*, 64(2), 124–136.

Marcia, J., & Josselson, R. (2013). Eriksonian personality research and its implications for psychotherapy. *Journal of Personality*, 81(6), 617–629.

Marcus, D. K., O'Connell, D., Norris, A. L., & Sawaqdeh, A. (2014). Is the dodo bird endangered in the 21st century? A meta-analysis of treatment comparison studies. *Clinical Psychology Review*, 34(7), 519–530.

Markowitz, J. C., Lipsitz, J., & Milrod, B. L. (2014). Critical review of outcome research on interpersonal psychotherapy for anxiety disorders. *Depression and Anxiety*, 31(4), 316–325.

Marks-Tarlow, T. (2011). Merging and emerging: A nonlinear portrait of intersubjectivity during psychotherapy. *Psychoanalytic Dialogues*, 21(1), 110–127.

Marlatt, G. A., & Witkiewitz, K. (2010). Update on harm-reduction policy and intervention research. *Annual Review of Clinical Psychology*, 6, 591–606.

Marriott, M., & Kellett, S. (2009). Evaluating a cognitive analytic therapy service; practice-based outcomes and comparisons with person-centred and cognitive-behavioural therapies. *Psychology and Psychotherapy: Theory, Research and Practice*, 82(1), 57–72.

Marterella, M. K., & Brock, L. J. (2008). Religion and spirituality as a resource in marital and family therapy. *Journal of Family Psychotherapy*, 19(4), 330–344.

Marx, J., & Donaldson, N. (2015). Constructing sexualities: A critical overview of articles published in feminism & psychology. *Feminism & Psychology*, 25(2), 165–177.

Mascaro, N., & Rosen, D. H. (2005). Existential meaning's role in the enhancement of hope and prevention of depressive symptoms. *Journal of Personality*, 73(4), 985–1014.

Mascaro, N., & Rosen, D. H. (2006). The role of existential meaning as a buffer against stress. *Journal of Humanistic Psychology*, 46(2), 168–190.

Mascaro, N., & Rosen, D. H. (2008). Assessment of existential meaning and its longitudinal relations with depressive symptoms. *Journal of Social and Clinical Psychology*, 27(6), 576–599.

Mascaro, N., Rosen, D. H., & Morey, L. C. (2004). The development, construct validity, and clinical utility of the spiritual meaning scale. *Personality and Individual Differences*, 37(4), 845–860.

Masnick, A. M., & Zimmerman, C. (2009). Evaluating scientific research in the context of prior belief: Hindsight bias or confirmation bias? *Journal of Psychology of Science and Technology*, 2(1), 29–36.

Masson, J. M. (1984). *The assault on truth: Freud's suppression of the seduction theory*. New York, NY: Farrar, Straus and Giroux.

Master, S. L., Amodio, D. M., Stanton, A. L., Yee, C. M., Hilmert, C. J., & Taylor, S. E. (2009). Neurobiological correlates of coping through emotional approach. *Brain, Behavior, and Immunity*, 23(1), 27–35.

Matthews, J. S. (2014). Multiple pathways to identification: Exploring the multidimensionality of academic identity formation in ethnic minority males. *Cultural Diversity and Ethnic Minority Psychology*, 20(2), 143–155.

May, R. (1953). *Man's search for himself*. Oxford, England: Norton.

May, R. (1962). Introduction. *Existential psychoanalysis* (Trans. by H. E. Barnes) (pp. 1–17). Chicago, IL: Regnery.

May, R. (1969). *Love and will*. New York, NY: Norton.

May, R. (1975). *The courage to create*. Oxford, England: Norton.

May, R. (1977). *The meaning of anxiety* (Rev. ed.). New York, NY: Norton.

May, R. (1981). *Freedom and destiny*. New York, NY: Norton.

May, R. (1982). The problem of evil: An open letter to Carl Rogers. *Journal of Humanistic Psychology*, 22(3), 10–21.

May, R. (1983). *The discovery of being: Writings in existential psychology*. New York, NY: Norton.

May, R., Angel, E., & Ellenberger, H. F. (Eds.). (1958). *Existence: A new dimension in psychiatry and psychology*. New York, NY: Basic Books.

Mays, V. M. (1988). Even the rat was white and male: Teaching the psychology of black women. In P. A. Bronstein &

K. Quina (Eds.), *Teaching a psychology of people: Resources for gender and sociocultural awareness* (pp. 142–146). Washington, DC: American Psychological Association.

McAdams, C. R., I., II, Avadhanam, R., Foster, V. A., Harris, P. N., Javaheri, A., Kim, S., et al. (2016). The viability of structural family therapy in the twenty-first century: An analysis of key indicators. *Contemporary Family Therapy: An International Journal, 38*(3), 255–261.

McCartney, J. (1966). Overt transference. *Journal of Sex Research, 2,* 227–237.

McCleary, R. A., & Lazarus, R. S. (1949). Autonomic discrimination without awareness. *Journal of Personality, 18,* 171–179.

McGoldrick, M., Gerson, R., & Shellenberger, S. (2005). *Genograms: Assessment and intervention* (3rd ed.). New York, NY: Norton.

McGuire, J. K., Doty, J. L., Catalpa, J. M., & Ola, C. (2016). Body image in transgender young people: Findings from a qualitative, community based study. *Body Image, 18,* 96–107.

McIntosh, P. (1998). White privilege: Unpacking the invisible knapsack. In M. McGoldrick (Ed.), *Re-visioning family therapy: Race, gender and culture in clinical practice* (pp. 147–152). New York, NY: Guilford Press.

McIntosh, V. V. W., Carter, F. A., Bulik, C. M., Frampton, C. M. A., & Joyce, P. R. (2011). Five-year outcome of cognitive behavioral therapy and exposure with response prevention for bulimia nervosa. *Psychological Medicine: A Journal of Research in Psychiatry and the Allied Sciences, 41*(5), 1061–1071.

McKay, D. (2011). Methods and mechanisms in the efficacy of psychodynamic psychotherapy. *American Psychologist, 66*(2), 147–148.

McLachlan, N. H., Eastwood, L., & Friedberg, R. D. (2016). Socratic questions with children: Recommendations and cautionary tales. *Journal of Cognitive Psychotherapy, 30*(2), 105–119.

McLean, L. L., La Guardia, A. C., Nelson, J. A., & Watts, R. E. (2016). Incorporating Adlerian and feminist theory to address self-objectification in couples therapy. *The Family Journal, 24*(4), 420–427.

McLean, R., & Marini, I. (2008). Working with gay men from a narrative counseling perspective: A case study. *Journal of LGBT Issues in Counseling, 2*(3), 243–257.

McMillin, R. (1986). *Handbook of cognitive therapy techniques.* New York, NY: Norton.

McNeil, S. N., Pavkov, T. W., Hecker, L. L., & Killmer, J. M. (2012). Marriage and family therapy graduate students' satisfaction with training regarding religion and spirituality. *Contemporary Family Therapy: An International Journal, 34*(4), 468–480.

Meany-Walen, K. K., Bratton, S. C., & Kottman, T. (2014). Effects of Adlerian play therapy on reducing students' disruptive behaviors. *Journal of Counseling & Development, 92*(1), 47–56.

Meany-Walen, K., Bullis, Q., Kottman, T., & Taylor, D. (2015). Group Adlerian play therapy with children with off-task behaviors. *Journal for Specialists in Group Work, 40*(3), 294–314.

Meany-Walen, K. K., Kottman, T., Bullis, Q., & Taylor, D. (2015). Effects of Adlerian play therapy on children's externalizing behavior. *Journal of Counseling & Development, 93*(4), 418–428.

Meany-Walen, K., & Teeling, S. (2016). Adlerian play therapy with students with externalizing behaviors and poor social skills. *International Journal of Play Therapy, 25*(2), 64–77.

Medin, A. C., Astrup, H., Kåsin, B. M., & Andersen, L. F. (2015). Evaluation of a web-based food record for children using direct unobtrusive lunch observations: A validation study. *Journal of Medical Internet Research, 17*(12), 1–14.

Meichenbaum, D. (1969). The effects of instructions and reinforcement on thinking and language behaviors of schizophrenics. *Behaviour Research and Therapy, 7,* 101–114.

Meichenbaum, D. (1977). *Cognitive behavior modification: An integrative approach.* New York, NY: Plenum.

Meichenbaum, D. (1985). *Stress inoculation training.* New York, NY: Pergamon Press.

Meichenbaum, D. (1992). Evolution of cognitive behavior therapy: Origins, tenets, and clinical examples. In J. K. Zeig (Ed.), *The evolution of psychotherapy: The second conference* (pp. 114–128). New York, NY: Brunner/Mazel.

Meichenbaum, D. (1996). Stress inoculation training for coping with stressors. *The Clinical Psychologist, 49,* 4–7.

Meichenbaum, D. (2003). Cognitive-behavior therapy: Folktales and the unexpurgated history. *Cognitive Therapy and Research, 27*(1), 125–129.

Meichenbaum, D., & Cameron, R. (1974). The clinical potential of modifying what clients say to themselves. *Psychotherapy, 11,* 103–117.

Meichenbaum, D., & Goodman, J. (1971). Training impulsive children to talk to themselves. *Journal of Abnormal Psychology, 77,* 115–126.

Meier, S. T. (2015). *Incorporating progress monitoring and outcome assessment into counseling and psychotherapy: A primer.* New York, NY: Oxford University Press.

Meier, S. T., & Davis, S. R. (2011). *The elements of counseling* (7th ed.). Belmont, CA: Thomson Brooks/Cole Publishing Co.

Melnick, J., & Nevis, S. M. (1998). *Diagnosing in the here and now: A Gestalt therapy approach.* New York, NY: Guilford Press.

Merton, T. (1974). *A Thomas Merton reader.* New York, NY: Doubleday.

Metcalf, L. (2008). *Counseling toward solutions: A practical solution-focused program for working with students, teachers, and parents* (2nd ed.). San Francisco, CA: Jossey-Bass.

Metcalfe, C., Winter, D., & Viney, L. (2007). The effectiveness of personal construct psychotherapy in clinical practice: A systematic review and meta-analysis. *Psychotherapy Research, 17*(4), 431–442.

Meyer, T. J., Miller, M. L., Metzger, R. L., & Borkovec, T. D. (1990). Development and validation of the Penn State worry questionnaire. *Behaviour Research & Therapy, 28*(6), 487–495.

Meyer-Bahlburg, H. (2017). Intersex care development: Current priorities. *LGBT Health, 4*(2), 77–80.

Mickel, E., & Sanders, P. (2003). Utilizing CLSI and BNSA to improve outcomes: Perceptions of the relationship between the basic needs and learning styles. *International Journal of Reality Therapy, 22*(2), 44–47.

Millar, B. M., Wang, K., & Pachankis, J. E. (2016). The moderating role of internalized homonegativity on the efficacy of LGB-affirmative psychotherapy: Results from a randomized controlled trial with young adult gay and bisexual men. *Journal of Consulting and Clinical Psychology, 84*(7), 565–570.

Miller, A. (1984). *For your own good: Hidden cruelty in child-rearing and the roots of violence* (2nd ed.). New York, NY: Farrar, Straus, Giroux.

Miller, A. L., Rathus, J. H., & Linehan, M. M. (2007). *Dialectical behavior therapy with suicidal adolescents*. New York, NY: Guilford Press.

Miller, J. B. (Ed.). (1973). *Psychoanalysis and women*. New York, NY: Brunner/Mazel.

Miller, J. B. (1976). *Toward a new psychology of women*. Boston, MA: Beacon.

Miller, P. (1983). *Theories of developmental psychology*. San Francisco, CA: Freeman.

Miller, P. (2010). *Theories of developmental psychology* (5th ed.). New York, NY: Worth.

Miller, S. D., Hubble, M., & Duncan, B. L. (1996). *Handbook of solution-focused brief therapy*. San Francisco, CA: Jossey-Bass.

Miller, W. R. (1978). Behavioral treatment of problem drinkers: A comparative outcome study of three controlled drinking therapies. *Journal of Consulting & Clinical Psychology, 46*(1), 74–86.

Miller, W. R., & Rollnick, S. (2013). *Motivational interviewing: Preparing people for change* (3rd ed.). New York, NY: Guilford Press.

Miller, W. R., & Taylor, C. A. (1980). Relative effectiveness of bibliotherapy, individual and group self-control training in the treatment of problem drinkers. *Addictive Behaviors, 5*(1), 13–24.

Milton, M. (Ed.). (2014). *Sexuality: Existential perspectives*. Ross-on-Wye: PCCS Books.

Minatrea, N. B., & Duba, J. D. (2012). Counseling interfaith couples. In P. A. Robey, R. E. Wubbolding, & J. Carlson (Eds.), *Contemporary issues in couples counseling: A choice theory and reality therapy approach* (pp. 129–141). New York, NY: Routledge.

Minuchin, S. (1974). *Families and family therapy*. Cambridge, MA: Harvard University Press.

Minuchin, S., Reiter, M. D., & Borda, C. (2014). *The craft of family therapy: Challenging certainties*. New York, NY: Taylor & Francis.

Mitchell, J. (1969). *Chelsea morning*. [Recorded by Joni Mitchell]. On Clouds [Phonograph]. Hollywood, CA: A & M Studios. April.

Mitchell, S. A. (1988). *Relational concepts in psychoanalysis: An integration*. Cambridge, MA: Harvard University Press.

Mohr, D. C. (1995). Negative outcome in psychotherapy: A critical review. *Clinical Psychology: Science and Practice, 2*(1), 1–27.

Moncrieff, J. (2015). The myths and realities of drug treatment for mental disorders. *The Behavior Therapist, 38*(7), 214–218.

Monk, G. (1997). How narrative therapy works. In G. Monk, J. Winslade, K. Crocket, & D. Epston (Eds.), *Narrative therapy in practice: The archaeology of hope* (pp. 3–31). San Francisco, CA: Jossey-Bass.

Monk, G., Winslade, J., Crocket, K., & Epston, D. (Eds.). (1997). *Narrative therapy in practice: The archaeology of hope*. San Francisco, CA: Jossey-Bass.

Moos, R. H. (2005). Iatrogenic effects of psychosocial interventions for substance use disorders: Prevalence, predictors, prevention. *Addiction, 100*(5), 595–604.

Moos, R. H. (2012). Iatrogenic effects of psychosocial interventions: Treatment, life context, and personal risk factors. *Substance Use & Misuse, 47*(13–14), 1592–1598.

Moradi, B., & DeBlaere, C. (2010). *Women's experiences of sexist discrimination: Review of research and directions for centralizing race, ethnicity, and culture*. New York, NY: Springer.

Morelli, G. (2015). The evolution of attachment theory and cultures of human attachment in infancy and early childhood. In L. A. Jensen (Ed.), *The Oxford handbook of human development and culture: An interdisciplinary perspective* (pp. 149–164). New York, NY: Oxford University Press.

Morgan, R. (1970). *Sisterhood is powerful*. New York: Vintage.

Morin, C. M., Bootzin, R. R., Buysse, D. J., Edinger, J. D., Espie, C. A., & Lichstein, K. L. (2006). Psychological and behavioral treatment of insomnia: Update of the recent evidence (1998–2004). *SLEEP, 29*(11), 1398–1414.

Mosak, H. H. (1972). Life style assessment: A demonstration focused on family constellation. *Journal of Individual Psychology, 28*(2), 232–247.

Mosak, H. H. (1985). Interrupting a depression: The pushbutton technique. *Individual Psychology, 41*, 210–214.

Mosak, H. H. (1987). Guilt, guilt feelings, regret and repentance. *Individual Psychology, 43*, 288–295.

Mosak, H. H. (1989). Adlerian psychotherapy. In R. Corsini & D. Wedding (Eds.), *Current psychotherapies* (4th ed.) (pp. 65–116). Itasca, IL: Peacock.

Mosak, H. H. (1995). Adlerian psychotherapy. In R. Corsini & D. Wedding (Eds.), *Current psychotherapies*. (5th ed.) (pp. 51–94). Itasca, IL: Peacock.

Mosak, H. H., & Dreikurs, R. (1967). The life tasks III: The fifth life task. *Individual Psychology, 5*, 16–22.

Mosak, H. H., & Maniacci, M. P. (1999). *A primer of Adlerian psychology: The analytic-behavioral-cognitive psychology of Alfred Adler*. Philadelphia, PA: Taylor & Francis.

Mowrer, O. H. (1947). On the dual nature of learning: A reinterpretation of "conditioning" and "problem-solving." *Harvard Education Review, 17*, 102–148.

Mozdzierz, G. J., Greenblatt, R. L., & Murphy, T. J. (1988). Further validation of the Sulliman scale of social interest and the social interest scale. *Individual Psychology: Journal of Adlerian Theory, Research & Practice, 44*(1), 30–34.

Mozdzierz, G. J., Greenblatt, R. L., & Murphy, T. J. (2007). The measurement and clinical use of social interest: Validation of the Sulliman scale of social interest on a sample of hospitalized substance abuse patients. *The Journal of Individual Psychology, 63*(2), 225–234.

Mufson, L., Dorta, K. P., Moreau, D., & Weissman, M. M. (2004). *Interpersonal psychotherapy for depressed adolescents* (2nd ed.). New York, NY: Guilford Press.

Mufson, L., Dorta, K. P., Wickramaratne, P., Nomura, Y., Olfson, M., & Weissman, M. M. (2004). A randomized effectiveness trial of interpersonal psychotherapy for depressed adolescents. *Archives of General Psychiatry, 61*(6), 577–584.

Murphy, J. J. (2015). *Solution-focused counseling in middle and high schools* (3rd ed.). Alexandria, VA: American Counseling.

Mutschler, I., Reinbold, C., Wankerl, J., Seifritz, E., & Ball, T. (2013). Structural basis of empathy and the domain general region in the anterior insular cortex. *Frontiers in Human Neuroscience, 7*, 1–18.

Myers, I. B. (1995). *Gifts differing: Understanding personality types*. Mountain View, CA: Davies-Black.

Nader, K., & Einarsson, E. O. (2010). Memory reconsolidation: An update. *Annals of the New York Academy of Sciences, 1191*, 27–41.

Nanda, J. (2009). Mindfulness: A lived experience of existential-phenomenological themes. *Existential Analysis, 20*(1), 147–162.

Nanda, J. (2010). Embodied integration: Reflections on mindfulness based cognitive therapy (MBCT) and a case for mindfulness based existential therapy (MBET). A single case illustration. *Existential Analysis, 21*(2), 331–350.

Napier, A. Y., & Whitaker, C. A. (1978). *The family crucible*. New York, NY: Harper & Row.

Naranjo, C. (1970). Present-centeredness: Technique, prescription, and ideal. In J. Fagan & I. L. Shepherd (Eds.), *What is Gestalt therapy?* (pp. 63–97). New York, NY: Science and Behavior Books.

Natha, F., & Daiches, A. (2014). The effectiveness of EMDR in reducing psychological distress in survivors of natural disasters: A review. *Journal of EMDR Practice and Research, 8*(3), 157–170.

Neimeyer, R. A., Meichenbaum, D., & Stanley, C. M. (2015). Developing a dialogue: Constructivist convergence in psychotherapy and beyond. *Studies in Meaning, 5*, 182–217.

Newbauer, J. F., & Stone, M. H. (2010). Social interest and self-reported distress in a delinquent sample: Application of the SSSI and MAYSI-2. *The Journal of Individual Psychology, 66*(2), 201–215.

Nezu, A. M., & Nezu, C. M. (2010). Problem-solving therapy for relapse prevention in depression. In C. S. Richards & M. G. Perri (Eds.), *Relapse prevention for depression* (pp. 99–130). Washington, DC: American Psychological Association.

Nezu, A. M., & Nezu, C. M. (2016). Problem solving. In J. C. Norcross, G. R. VandenBos, D. K. Freedheim, & N. Pole (Eds.), *APA handbook of clinical psychology: Psychopathology and health*, Vol. 4 (pp. 449–460). Washington, DC: American Psychological Association.

Nezu, A. M., Nezu, C. M., & D'Zurilla, T. J. (2013). *Problem-solving therapy: A treatment manual*. New York, NY: Springer Publishing Co.

Ng, S. M., Li, A. M., Lou, V. W. Q., Tso, I. F., Wan, P. Y. P., & Chan, D. F. Y. (2008). Incorporating family therapy into asthma group intervention: A randomized waitlist-controlled trial. *Family Process: Special Issue on Families and Asthma, 47*(1), 115–130.

Nichols, M. P., & Schwarts, R. C. (2007). *The essentials of family therapy* (3rd ed.). Boston, MA: Pearson.

Nickerson, R. S. (1998). Confirmation bias: A ubiquitous phenomenon in many guises. *Review of General Psychology, 2*(2), 175–220.

Nielsen, S. L. (2001). Accommodating religion and integrating religious material during rational emotive behavior therapy. *Cognitive and Behavioral Practice, 8*(1), 34–39.

Nielsen, S. L., & Ellis, A. E. (1994). A discussion with Albert Ellis: Reason, emotion and religion. *Journal of Psychology and Christianity, 13*, 327–341.

Nikelly, A. G. (2005). Positive health outcomes of social interest. *The Journal of Individual Psychology, 61*(4), 329–342.

Nobles, W. (2006). *Seeking the Saku: Foundational writings for an African psychology*. Chicago, IL: Third World Press.

Norcross, J. C. (Ed.). (2011). Evidence-based therapy relationships. *Psychotherapy relationships that work: Evidence-based responsiveness* (2nd ed.). New York, NY: Oxford University Press.

Norcross, J. C., Goldfried, M. R., & *Zimmerman, B. E. (2017). Integrative psychotherapies in historical perspective. In A. J. Consoli, L. E. Beutler, & B. Bongar (Eds.), *Comprehensive textbook of psychotherapy: Theory and practice* (2nd ed.). New York, NY: Oxford University Press.

Norcross, J. C., Karg, R. S., & Prochaska, J. O. (1997). Clinical psychologists in the 1990s. *The Clinical Psychologist, 50*, 4–9.

Norcross, J. C., Karpiak, C. P., & Lister, K. (2005). What's an integrationist? A study of self-identified integrative and (occasionally) eclectic psychologists. *Journal of Clinical Psychology, 61*, 1587–1594.

Norcross, J. C., & Lambert, M. J. (2011). Psychotherapy relationships that work II. *Psychotherapy, 48*(1), 4–8.

Norcross, J. C., & Vangarelli, D. J. (1989). The resolution solution: Longitudinal examination of New Year's change attempts. *Journal of Substance Abuse, 1*, 127–134.

Novaco, R. W. (1979). The cognitive regulation of anger. In P. C. Kendall & S. D. Hollon (Eds.), *Cognitive behavioral interventions: Theory, research, and procedures* (pp. 241–285). New York, NY: Academic Press.

Nutt, R. L. (2005). *Feminist and contextual work*. Hoboken, NJ: Wiley.

Oaklander, V. (1978). *Windows to our children*. Moab, UT: Real People Press.

Oaklander, V. (2006). *Hidden treasure: A map of the child's inner self*. London, England: Karnac Books.

Oaklander, V. (2015). Short-term gestalt play therapy for grieving children. In H. G. Kaduson & C. E. Schaefer (Eds.), *Short-term play therapy for children* (3rd ed.) (pp. 124–149). New York, NY: Guilford.

Oakley, M. A., Addison, S. C., Piran, N., Johnston, G. J., Damianakis, M., Curry, J., et al. (2013). Outcome study of brief relational-cultural therapy in a women's mental health center. *Psychotherapy Research, 23*(2), 137–151.

O'Brien, W. H., & Carhart, V. (2011). Functional analysis in behavioral medicine. *European Journal of Psychological Assessment, 27*, 4–16.

O'Hanlon, B. (1988). Solution-oriented therapy: A megatrend in psychotherapy. In J. K. Zeig & S. R. Lankton (Eds.), *Developing Ericksonian therapy: State of the art* (pp. 93–111). Philadelphia, PA: Brunner/Mazel.

O'Hanlon, W. H. (1998). Possibility therapy: An inclusive, collaborative, solution-based model of psychotherapy. In M. F. Hoyt (Ed.), *The handbook of constructive therapies* (pp. 137–158). San Francisco, CA: Jossey-Bass.

O'Hanlon, W. H., & Bertolino, B. (1998). *Even from a broken web: Brief, respectful, solution-oriented therapy for sexual abuse and trauma*. New York, NY: Wiley.

O'Hanlon, W. H., & Weiner-Davis, M. (1989). *In search of solutions: A new direction in psychotherapy*. New York, NY: Norton.

Oliver, M. (1992). *New and selected poems*. Boston, MA: Beacon Press.

Olson, D. H. (2000). Circumplex model of marital and family systems. *Journal of Family Therapy, 22*, 144–167.

Olson, K. (2014). The invisible classroom: Relationships, neuroscience, and mindfulness in school. New York, NY: Norton.

Olver, K. (2012). Multicultural couples: Seeing the world through different lenses. In P. A. Robey, R. E. Wubbolding, & J. Carlson (Eds.), *In Contemporary issues in couples counseling: A choice theory and reality therapy approach* (pp. 33–46). New York, NY: Routledge.

Onedera, J. D. (2006). Functional family therapy: An interview with Dr. James Alexander. *The Family Journal, 14*(3), 306–311.

Onedera, J. D., & Greenwalt, B. C. (2007). Choice theory: An interview with Dr. William Glasser. *The Family Journal, 15*(1), 79–86.

O'Reilly, A. (2011). *The 21st century motherhood movement: Mothers speak out on why we need to change the world and how to do it.* Bradford, ON: Dementer Press.

O'Reilly, A. (2016). *Matricentric feminism: Theory, activism, and practice.* Bradford, ON: Dementer Press.

Orgler, H. (1963). *Alfred Adler: The man and his work.* New York, NY: Mentor Books.

Ortiz, C., & Del Vecchio, T. (2013). Cultural diversity: Do we need a new wake-up call for parent training? *Behavior Therapy, 44*(3), 443–458.

Oryan, S. (2014). The family council: Different styles of family deliberation in two cultures. *The Journal of Individual Psychology, 70*(2), 128–147.

Ost, L., Alm, T., Brandberg, M., & Breitholz, E. (2001). One vs. five sessions of exposure and five sessions of cognitive therapy in the treatment of claustrophobia. *Behaviour Research and Therapy, 39*, 167–183.

Overholser, J. C. (2010). Psychotherapy that strives to encourage social interest: A simulated interview with Alfred Adler. *Journal of Psychotherapy Integration, 20*(4), 347–363.

Pachankis, J. E. (2014). Uncovering clinical principles and techniques to address minority stress, mental health, and related health risks among gay and bisexual men. *Clinical Psychology: Science and Practice, 21*(4), 313–330.

Pachankis, J. E., Hatzenbuehler, M. L., Rendina, H. J., Safren, S. A., & Parsons, J. T. (2015). LGB-affirmative cognitive-behavioral therapy for young adult gay and bisexual men: A randomized controlled trial of a transdiagnostic minority stress approach. *Journal of Consulting and Clinical Psychology, 83*(5), 875–889.

Page, R. C., Weiss, J. F., & Lietaer, G. (2002). *Humanistic group psychotherapy.* Washington, DC: American Psychological Association.

Paivio, S. C., & Greenberg, L. S. (1995). Resolving "unfinished business": Efficacy of experiential therapy using empty-chair dialogue. *Journal of Consulting & Clinical Psychology, 63*(3), 419–425.

Pan, J., Wong, D. F. K., Chan, C. L. W., & Joubert, L. (2008). Meaning of life as a protective factor of positive affect in acculturation: A resilience framework and a cross-cultural comparison. *International Journal of Intercultural Relations, 32*(6), 505–514.

Pan, J., Wong, D. F. K., Joubert, L., & Chan, C. L. W. (2008). The protective function of meaning of life on life satisfaction among Chinese students in Australia and Hong Kong: A cross-cultural comparative study. *Journal of American College Health, 57*(2), 221–231.

Paniagua, F. (2014). *Assessing and treating culturally diverse clients: A practical guide.* Thousand Oaks, CA: Sage.

Panos, P. T., Jackson, J. W., Hasan, O., & Panos, A. (2014). Meta-analysis and systematic review assessing the efficacy of dialectical behavior therapy (DBT). *Research on Social Work Practice, 24*(2), 213–223.

Parlett, M., & Lee, R. G. (2005). *Contemporary Gestalt therapy: Field theory.* Thousand Oaks, CA: Sage.

Parloff, M. B., Waskow, I. E., & Wolfe, B. E. (1978). Research on therapist variables in relation to process and outcome. In S. L. Garfield & A. E. Bergin (Eds.), *Handbook of psychotherapy and behavior change: An empirical analysis* (pp. 233–282). New York, NY: Wiley.

Parrish, T. S. (2017). Introduction to the journal and the editorial board. *International Journal of Choice Theory and Reality Therapy, 36*, 4–5.

Pascual-Leone, A., Bierman, R., Arnold, R., & Stasiak, E. (2011). Emotion-focused therapy for incarcerated offenders of intimate partner violence: A 3-year outcome using a new whole-sample matching method. *Psychotherapy Research, 21*(3), 331–347.

Patterson, C. H. (1973). *Theories of counseling and psychotherapy.* New York, NY: Harper & Row.

Paul, G. L. (1969). Behavior modification research: Design and tactics. In C. M. Franks (Ed.), *Behavior therapy: Appraisal and status* (pp. 29–62). New York, NY: McGraw-Hill.

Paul, R. A. (1991). Freud's anthropology: A reading of the "cultural books." In J. Neu (Ed.), *The Cambridge companion to Freud* (pp. 267–286). New York, NY: Cambridge University Press.

Pavlov, I. P. (1927). *Conditioned reflexes* (Trans. by G. V. Anrep). London, England: Oxford University Press.

Peluso, P. R., Peluso, J. P., Buckner, J. P., Kern, R. M., & Curlette, W. (2009). Measuring lifestyle and attachment: An empirical investigation linking individual psychology and attachment theory. *Journal of Counseling & Development, 87*(4), 394–403.

Penedo, F. J., Traeger, L., Dahn, J., Molton, I., Gonzalez, J. S., Schneiderman, N., et al. (2007). Cognitive behavioral stress management intervention improves quality of life in Spanish monolingual Hispanic men treated for localized prostate cancer: Results of a randomized controlled trial. *International Journal of Behavioral Medicine, 14*(3), 164–172.

Pennebaker, J. W., Zech, E., & Rimé, B. (2001). *Disclosing and sharing emotion: Psychological, social, and health consequences.* Washington, DC: American Psychological Association.

Pérez, D., II. (2017). In pursuit of success: Latino male college students exercising academic determination and community cultural wealth. *Journal of College Student Development, 58*(2), 123–140.

Perls, F. (1945). *Ego, hunger and aggression: A revision of Freud's theory and method* (2nd ed.). Oxford, England: Knox.

Perls, F. (1969a). *Gestalt therapy verbatim.* Moab, UT: Real People Press.

Perls, F. (1969b). *In and out the garbage pail.* Moab, UT: Real People Press.

Perls, F. (1970). Four lectures. In J. Fagan & I. L. Shepherd (Eds.), *What is Gestalt therapy?* (pp. 11–49). New York, NY: Science and Behavior Books.

Perls, F. (1973). *The Gestalt approach and eye witness to therapy.* New York, NY: Science and Behavior Books.

Perls, F., Hefferline, R. F., & Goodman, P. (1951). *Gestalt therapy*. New York, NY: Bantam Books.

Perls, L. (1990). A talk for the 25th anniversary. *Gestalt Journal, 13*(2), 15–22.

Persons, J. B. (1989). *Cognitive therapy in practice: A case formulation approach*. New York, NY: Norton.

Persons, J. B. (2008). *The case formulation approach to cognitive-behavior therapy*. New York, NY: Guilford Press.

Persons, J. B., & Tompkins, M. A. (1997). Cognitive-behavioral case formulation. In T. D. Eells (Ed.), *Handbook of psychotherapy case formulation* (pp. 314–339). New York, NY: Guilford.

Petersen, S. (2005). Reality therapy and individual or Adlerian psychology: A comparison. *International Journal of Reality Therapy, 24*(2), 11–14.

Petroff, E. A. (1986). *Medieval women's visionary literature*. New York, NY: Oxford University Press.

Pezzuti, L., & Orsini, A. (2016). Are there sex differences in the Wechsler Intelligence Scale for Children—Fourth edition? *Learning and Individual Differences, 45*, 307–312.

Pickett, C. L., Gardner, W. L., & Knowles, M. (2004). Getting a cue: The need to belong and enhanced sensitivity to social cues. *Personality and Social Psychology Bulletin, 30*(9), 1095–1107.

Pierce, C. M. (1978). Entitlement dysfunctions. *Australian and New Zealand Journal of Psychiatry, 12*(4), 215–219.

Piet, J., & Hougaard, E. (2011). The effect of mindfulness-based cognitive therapy for prevention of relapse in recurrent major depressive disorder: A systematic review and meta-analysis. *Clinical Psychology Review, 31*(6), 1032–1040.

Pieterse, A. L., & Miller, M. J. (2010). *Current considerations in the assessment of adults: A review and extension of culturally inclusive models*. Thousand Oaks, CA: Sage.

Pina, A. A., Silverman, W. K., Fuentes, R. M., Kurtines, W. M., & Weems, C. F. (2003). Exposure-based cognitive-behavioral treatment for phobic and anxiety disorders: Treatment effects and maintenance for Hispanic/Latino relative to European-American youths. *Journal of the American Academy of Child & Adolescent Psychiatry, 42*(10), 1179–1187.

Pine, F. (1990). *Drive, ego, object, and self: A synthesis for clinical work*. New York, NY: Basic Books.

Pollack, W. S. (2000). *Real boys' voices*. New York, NY: Penguin Books.

Pollet, T. V., Dijkstra, P., Barclds, D. P. H., & Buunk, A. P. (2010). Birth order and the dominance aspect of extraversion: Are firstborns more extraverted, in the sense of being dominant, than laterborns? *Journal of Research in Personality, 44*(6), 742–745.

Polster, E. (1966). A contemporary psychotherapy. *Psychotherapy: Theory, Research & Practice, 3*(1), 1–6.

Polster, E., & Polster, M. (1973). *Gestalt therapy integrated: Contours of theory and practice*. New York, NY: Brunner/Mazel.

Polster, M. (1991). *Eve's daughters: The forbidden heroism of women*. San Francisco, CA: Jossey-Bass.

Pomerantz, A. M., & Handelsman, M. M. (2004). Informed consent revisited: An updated written question format. *Professional Psychology: Research and Practice, 35*(2), 201–205.

Pope, K. S., & Vasquez, M. J. T. (2016). *Ethics in psychotherapy and counseling: A practical guide* (5th ed.). Hoboken, NJ: Wiley.

Pope, L., & Harvey, J. (2015). The impact of incentives on intrinsic and extrinsic motives for fitness-center attendance in college first-year students. *American Journal of Health Promotion, 29*(3), 192–199.

Popkin, M. H. (2014). Active parenting: 30 years of video-based parent education. *The Journal of Individual Psychology, 70*(2), 166–176.

Poston, W. C. (1990). The biracial identity development model: A needed addition. *Journal of Counseling & Development, 69*(2), 152–155.

Powers, M. B., & Emmelkamp, P. M. G. (2008). Virtual reality exposure therapy for anxiety disorders: A meta-analysis. *Journal of Anxiety Disorders, 22*(3), 561–569.

Powers, W. T. (1973). *Behavior: The control of perception*. Chicago, IL: Aldine de Gruyter.

Prochaska, J. O. (1995). An eclectic and integrative approach: Transtheoretical therapy. In A. S. Gurman & S. B. Messer (Eds.), *Essential psychotherapies* (pp. 403–440). New York, NY: Guilford Press.

Prochaska, J. O., & DiClemente, C. C. (1982). Transtheoretical therapy: Toward a more integrative model of change. *Psychotherapy, 19*, 276–278.

Prochaska, J. O., DiClemente, C. C., & Norcross, J. C. (1993). In search of how people change. *American Psychologist, 47*, 1102–1114.

Prochaska, J. O., & Norcross, J. C. (2003). *Systems of psychotherapy: A transtheoretical analysis* (5th ed.). Pacific Grove, CA: Brooks/Cole.

Prochaska, J. O., & Norcross, J. C. (2014). *Systems of psychotherapy: A transtheoretical analysis* (8th ed.). Stamford, CT: Cengage.

Quinn, S. (1987). *A mind of her own: The life of Karen Horney*. New York, NY: Summit Books.

Quirk, G. J., & Mueller, D. (2008). Neural mechanisms of extinction learning and retrieval. *Neuropsychopharmacology, 33*(1), 56–72.

Rachman, S. (1965). Aversion therapy: Chemical or electrical? *Behaviour Research and Therapy, 2*, 289–300.

Rachman, S. (Ed.). (1997). *The best of behaviour research and therapy*. New York, NY: Pergamon.

Rader, J., & Gilbert, L. A. (2005). The egalitarian relationship in feminist therapy. *Psychology of Women Quarterly, 29*(4), 427–435.

Ramey, H. L., Tarulli, D., Frijters, J. C., & Fisher, L. (2009). A sequential analysis of externalizing in narrative therapy with children. *Contemporary Family Therapy: An International Journal, 31*(4), 262–279.

Rapaport, D. (1951). *Organization and pathology of thought*. New York, NY: Columbia University Press.

Raskin, N. J., & Rogers, C. R. (1989). Person-centered therapy. In R. Corsini & D. Wedding (Eds.), *Current psychotherapies* (pp. 154–194). Itasca, IL: Peacock.

Ratts, M. J., Singh, A. A., Nassar-McMillan, S., Butler, S. K., & McCullough, J. R. (2016). Multicultural and social justice counseling competencies: Guidelines for the counseling profession. *Journal of Multicultural Counseling and Development, 44*(1), 28–48.

Rawls, J. (1971). *A theory of justice*. Boston, MA: Harvard University Press.

Redsand, A. (2007). *Viktor Frankl: A life worth living*. New York, NY: Clarion.

Reich, W. (1975). *Early writings: I.* (Trans. by P. Schmitz). Oxford, England: Farrar, Straus & Giroux.

Reich, W., Higgins, M. B., Raphael, C. M., Schmitz, P., & Tompkins, J. (1988). *Passion of youth: An autobiography, 1897–1922.* New York, NY: Farrar, Straus & Giroux.

Reis, E. (2007). Divergence or disorder? The politics of naming intersex. *Perspectives in Biology and Medicine, 50*(4), 535–543.

Reis, E. (2009). *Bodies in doubt: An American history of intersex.* Baltimore, MD: Johns Hopkins University Press.

Reiss, B. K. (1990). *A biography of Mary Cover Jones.* Unpublished doctoral dissertation. Los Angeles, CA: The Wright Institute.

Reiss, N., Warnecke, I., Tolgou, T., Krampen, D., Luka-Krausgrill, U., & Rohrmann, S. (2016). Effects of cognitive behavioral therapy with relaxation vs. imagery rescripting on test anxiety: A randomized controlled trial. *Journal of Affective Disorders, 208*, 483–489.

Reiter, M. D. (2007). The use of expectation in solution-focused formula tasks. *Journal of Family Psychotherapy, 18*(1), 27–37.

Renik, O. (1993). Analytic interaction: Conceptualizing technique in light of the analyst's irreducible subjectivity. *Psychoanalytic Quarterly, 62*, 553–571.

Richardson, B. G. (2016). *Working with challenging youth: Seven guiding principles* (2nd ed.). Philadelphia: Brunner-Routledge.

Richmond, C. J., Jordan, S. S., Bischof, G. H., & Sauer, E. M. (2014). Effects of solution-focused versus problem-focused intake questions on pre-treatment change. *Journal of Systemic Therapies, 33*(1), 33–47.

Richmond, M. E. (1917). *Social diagnosis.* New York, NY: Sage.

Rizzuto, A., & Shafranske, E. P. (2013). Addressing religion and spirituality in treatment from a psychodynamic perspective. In K. I. Pargament, A. Mahoney & E. P. Shafranske (Eds.), *APA handbook of psychology, religion, and spirituality* (Vol 2: *An applied psychology of religion and spirituality*) (pp. 125–146). Washington, DC: American Psychological Association.

Robbins, M. S., Alexander, J. F., Turner, C. W., & Hollimon, A. (2016). Evolution of functional family therapy as an evidence-based practice for adolescents with disruptive behavior problems. *Family Process, 55*(3), 543–557.

Roberts, R. L., Harper, R., Caldwell, R., & Decora, M. (2003). Adlerian lifestyle analysis of Lakota women: Implications for counseling. *The Journal of Individual Psychology, 59*(1), 15–29.

Robertson, D. (2010). *The philosophy of cognitive behavioural therapy: Stoic philosophy as rational and cognitive psychotherapy.* London, England: Karnac.

Robey, P. A. (2011). Reality therapy and choice theory: An interview with Robert Wubbolding. *The Family Journal, 19*(2), 231–237.

Robey, P. A. (2017). Introduction to the special historical edition of the *International Journal of Choice Theory and Reality Therapy, 36*, 6–10.

Robey, P. A., Wubbolding, R. E., & Carlson, J. (2012). *Contemporary issues in couples counseling: A choice theory and reality therapy approach.* New York, NY: Routledge.

Robey, P. A., Wubbolding, R. E., & Malters, M. (2017). A comparison of choice theory/reality therapy to Adlerian individual psychology. *Journal of Individual Psychology, 73*(1).

Robjant, K., & Fazel, M. (2010). The emerging evidence for narrative exposure therapy: A review. *Clinical Psychology Review, 30*, 1030–1039.

Rodenburg, R., Benjamin, A., de Roos, C., Meijer, A. M., & Stams, G. J. (2009). Efficacy of EMDR in children: A meta-analysis. *Clinical Psychology Review, 29*(7), 599–606.

Rogers, A. A., Updegraff, K. A., Santos, C. E., & Martin, C. L. (2017). Masculinity and school adjustment in middle school. *Psychology of Men & Masculinity, 18*(1), 50–61.

Rogers, C. R. (1939). *The clinical treatment of the problem child.* Boston, MA: Houghton Mifflin.

Rogers, C. R. (1942a). *Counseling and psychotherapy.* Boston, MA: Houghton Mifflin.

Rogers, C. R. (1942b). The use of electrically recorded interviews in improving psychotherapeutic techniques. *American Journal of Orthopsychiatry, 12*, 429–434.

Rogers, C. R. (1951). *Client-centered therapy.* Boston, MA: Houghton Mifflin.

Rogers, C. R. (1957). The necessary and sufficient conditions of therapeutic personality change. *Journal of Consulting Psychology, 21*, 95–103.

Rogers, C. R. (1958). The characteristics of a helping relationship. *Personnel and Guidance Journal, 37*, 6–16.

Rogers, C. R. (1959). A theory of therapy, personality, and interpersonal relationships, as developed in the client-centered framework. In S. Koch (Ed.), *Psychology: A study of a science* (pp. 184–256). New York, NY: McGraw-Hill.

Rogers, C. R. (1960). The individual and the design of culture. In Conference on Evolutionary Theory and Human Progress, pp. 15–16.

Rogers, C. R. (1961). *On becoming a person.* Boston, MA: Houghton Mifflin.

Rogers, C. R. (Director). (1963). *Mrs. P.S.* [Video/DVD] Orlando, FL: American Academy of Psychotherapists.

Rogers, C. R. (Director). (1965). *Three approaches to psychotherapy.* [Video/DVD] Corona del Mar, CA: Psychological and Educational Films.

Rogers, C. R. (1967). Autobiography. In E. G. Boring & G. Lindzey (Eds.), *A history of psychology in autobiography* (pp. 341–384). New York, NY: Appleton.

Rogers, C. R. (1969). *Freedom to learn: A view of what education might become.* Columbus, OH: Charles E. Merrill.

Rogers, C. R. (1975). Empathy: An unappreciated way of being. *Counseling Psychologist, 21*, 2–102.

Rogers, C. R. (1977). *Carl Rogers on personal power.* New York, NY: Delacorte Press.

Rogers, C. R. (1980). *A way of being.* Boston, MA: Houghton Mifflin.

Rogers, C. R., Gendlin, E. T., Kiesler, D. J., & Truax, C. B. (1967). *The therapeutic relationship and its impact: A study of psychotherapy with schizophrenics.* Madison, WI: University of Wisconsin Press.

Rogers, C. R., & Haigh, G. (1983). I walk softly through life. *Voices: The Art and Science of Psychotherapy, 18*, 6–14.

Rogers, N. (1996). *The creative connection.* New York, NY: Science and Behavior Books.

Rogers, S. D., & White, S. L. (2017). Experiential reframing: A promising new treatment for psychosocial and existential trauma. *Practice Innovations, 2*(1), 27–38.

Ronen, T. (2003). *Cognitive-constructivist psychotherapy with children and adolescents.* New York, NY: Kluwer Academic/Plenum.

Rose-Inza, K., & Mi Gu, H. (2001). The effect of internal control and achievement motivation in group counseling based on reality therapy. *International Journal of Reality Therapy, 20,* 12–15.

Rosen, G. M., & Davison, G. C. (2003). Psychology should list empirically supported principles of change (ESPs) and not credential trademarked therapies or other treatment packages. *Behavior Modification. Special Issue: Empirically Supported Treatments, 27*(3), 300–312.

Rosenfeld, E. (1978). An oral history of gestalt therapy: I. A conversation with Laura Perls. *Gestalt Journal, 1,* 8–31.

Rosengren, D. B. (2009). *Building motivational interviewing skills: A practitioner workbook.* New York, NY: Guilford Press.

Rosenthal, H. G. (Ed.). (1999). *Favorite counseling and therapy techniques.* Washington, DC: Accelerated Development.

Rosenzweig, S. (1936). Some implicit common factors in diverse methods in psychotherapy. *American Journal of Orthopsychiatry, 6,* 412–415.

Rowling, J. K. (1997). *Harry Potter and the sorcerer's stone.* New York, NY: Scholastic Press.

Roy v. Hartogs, 366 (New York 1975).

Roy, J. (2014). *William Glasser: Champion of Choice.* Phoenix, AZ: Zeig, Tucker, and Theisen.

Roy, J. (2017). From Ventura to Corona: A life that mattered. *International Journal of Choice Theory and Reality Therapy, 36,* 77–82.

Rozsnafsky, J. (1974). The impact of Alfred Adler on three "free-will" therapies of the 1960's. *Journal of Individual Psychology, 30,* 65–80.

Rubin, M., Milanov, M., & Paolini, S. (2016). Uncovering the diverse cultural bases of social identity: Ingroup ties predict self-stereotyping among individualists but not among collectivists. *Asian Journal of Social Psychology, 19*(3), 225–234.

Rüegg, J. C. (2009). Traumagedächtnis und neurobiologie: Konsolidierung, rekonsolidierung, extinktion. Trauma memory and neurobiology: Consolidation, reconsolidation, extinction. *Trauma & Gewalt, 3*(1), 6–17.

Ruggiero, K. J., Morris, T. L., Hopko, D. R., & Lejuez, C. W. (2007). Application of behavioral activation treatment for depression to an adolescent with a history of child maltreatment. *Clinical Case Studies, 6*(1), 64–78.

Rutter, M. (1995). Clinical implications of attachment concepts: Retrospect and prospect. *Journal of Child Psychology and Psychiatry, 36*(4), 549–571.

Ruwaard, J., Broeksteeg, J., Schrieken, B., Emmelkamp, P., & Lange, A. (2010). Web-based therapist-assisted cognitive behavioral treatment of panic symptoms: A randomized controlled trial with a three-year follow-up. *Journal of Anxiety Disorders, 24*(4), 387–396.

Ryan, R. M., Lynch, M. F., Vansteenkiste, M., & Deci, E. L. (2011). Motivation and autonomy in counseling, psychotherapy, and behavior change: A look at theory and practice. *The Counseling Psychologist, 39*(2), 193–260.

Ryan, T. A. (1970). *Intentional behavior.* New York, NY: Ronald Press.

Safran, J. D., & Kraus, J. (2014). Alliance ruptures, impasses, and enactments: A relational perspective. *Psychotherapy, 51*(3), 381–387.

Safran, J. D., Muran, J. C., & Eubanks-Carter, C. (2011). Repairing alliance ruptures. *Psychotherapy, 48*(1), 80–87.

Santiago-Valles, W. F. (2009). Social interest: Context and impact of Raissa Epstein's ideas on Alfred Adler's social imaginary (1897–1935). *The Journal of Individual Psychology, 65,* 360–379.

Santos de Barona, M., & Dutton, M. A. (1997). Feminist perspectives on assessment. In J. Worell & N. G. Johnson (Eds.), *Shaping the future of feminist psychology: Education, research, and practice* (pp. 37–56). Washington, DC: American Psychological Association.

Santucci, L. C., Thomassin, K., Petrovic, L., & Weisz, J. R. (2015). Building evidence-based interventions for the youth, providers, and contexts of real-world mental-health care. *Child Development Perspectives, 9*(2), 67–73.

Sapienza, B. G., & Bugental, J. F. T. (2000). Keeping our instruments finely tuned: An existential–humanistic perspective. *Professional Psychology: Research and Practice, 31*(4), 458–460.

Sartre, J. (1953). *Existential psychoanalysis* (Trans. by H. E. Barnes). Chicago, IL: Regnery.

Sartre, J. (1971). *Being and nothingness.* New York, NY: Bantam Books.

Satel, S., & Lilienfeld, S. O. (2013). *Brainwashed: The seductive appeal of mindless neuroscience.* New York, NY: Basic Books.

Satir, V. M. (1964). *Conjoint family therapy.* Palo Alto, CA: Science and Behavior Books.

Satir, V. M. (1983). *Conjoint family therapy* (3rd ed.). Palo Alto, CA: Science and Behavior Books.

Satir, V., Banmen, J., Gerber, J., & Gomori, M. (1991). *The Satir model: Family therapy and beyond.* Palo Alto, CA: Science and Behavior Books.

Saunders, T., Driskell, J. E., Hall, J., & Salas, E. (1996). The effect of stress inoculation training on anxiety and performance. *Journal of Occupational Health Psychology, 1,* 170–186.

Sayegh, C. S., Huey, S. J., Jr., Zara, E. J., & Jhaveri, K. (2017). Follow-up treatment effects of contingency management and motivational interviewing on substance use: A meta-analysis. *Psychology of Addictive Behaviors, 31*(4), 403–414.

Scharff, J. S., & Scharff, D. E. (2005). *The primer of object relations* (2nd ed.). Lanham, MD: Aronson.

Schauer, M., Neuner, F., & Elbert T. (2011). *Narrative exposure therapy: A short term treatment for traumatic stress disorders* (2nd ed.). Cambridge, MA: Hogrefe Publishing.

Schmit, E. L., Schmit, M. K., & Lenz, A. S. (2016). Meta-analysis of solution-focused brief therapy for treating symptoms of internalizing disorders. *Counseling Outcome Research and Evaluation, 7*(1), 21–39.

Schneider, K. J. (2004). *Rediscovery of awe: Splendor, mystery, and the fluid center of life.* St. Paul, MN: Paragon House.

Schneider, K. J. (Ed.). (2008). *Existential-integrative psychotherapy: Guideposts to the core of practice.* New York, NY: Routledge/Taylor & Francis.

Schneider, K. J. (2010). An existential-integrative approach to experiential liberation. *The Humanistic Psychologist, 38*(1), 1–14.

Schneider, K. J. (2013). *The polarized mind: Why it's killing us and what we can do about it.* Colorado Springs, CO: University Professors Press.

Schneider, K. J., Galvin, J., & Serlin, I. (2009). Rollo May on existential psychotherapy. *Journal of Humanistic Psychology, 49*(4), 419–434.

Schneider, K. J., & Krug, O. T. (2010). *Existential–humanistic therapy*. Washington, DC: American Psychological Association.

Schneider, K. J., & May, R. (1995). *The psychology of existence: An integrative, clinical perspective*. New York, NY: McGraw-Hill.

Schofield, W. (1964). *Psychotherapy: The purchase of friendship*. Englewood Cliffs, NJ: Prentice-Hall.

Schore, A. N. (1994). *Affect regulation and the origin of the self: The neurobiology of emotional development*. Mahwah, NJ: Erlbaum.

Schore, A. N. (2010). The right brain implicit self: A central mechanism of the psychotherapy change process. In J. Petrucelli (Ed.), *Knowing, not-knowing and sort-of-knowing: Psychoanalysis and the experience of uncertainty* (pp. 177–202). London, England: Karnac.

Schore, A. N. (2011a). The right brain implicit self lies at the core of psychoanalysis. *Psychoanalytic Dialogues, 21*, 75–100.

Schore, A. N. (2011b). *The science of the art of psychotherapy*. New York, NY: Norton.

Schumacher, J. E., Milby, J. B., Wallace, D., Meehan, D., Kertesz, S., Vuchinich, R., et al. (2007). Meta-analysis of day treatment and contingency-management dismantling research: Birmingham homeless cocaine studies (1990–2006). *Journal of Consulting and Clinical Psychology, 75*(5), 823–828.

Schur, M. (1972). *Freud: Living and dying*. New York, NY: International Universities Press.

Schwartz, J. M., Gulliford, E. Z., Stier, J., & Thienemann, M. (2005). Mindful awareness and self-directed neuroplasticity: Integrating psychospiritual and biological approaches to mental health with a focus on obsessive-compulsive disorder. In S. G. Mijares & G. S. Khalsa (Eds.), *The psychospiritual clinician's handbook: Alternative methods for understanding and treating mental disorders*. New York, NY: Haworth Press.

Schwartz, R. C. (1995). *Internal family systems therapy*. New York, NY: Guilford.

Segal, Z. V., Williams, J. M. G., & Teasdale, J. D. (2002). *Mindfulness-based cognitive therapy for depression: A new approach to preventing relapse*. New York, NY: Guilford Press.

Segal, Z. V., Williams, J. M. G., & Teasdale, J. D. (2013). *Mindfulness-based cognitive therapy for depression* (2nd ed.). New York, NY: Guilford Press.

Segraves, R. T. (2002). Female sexual disorders: Psychiatric aspects. *Canadian Journal of Psychiatry, 47*(5), 419–425.

Seidler, G. H., & Wagner, F. E. (2006). Comparing the efficacy of EMDR and trauma-focused cognitive-behavioral therapy in the treatment of PTSD: A meta-analytic study. *Psychological Medicine: A Journal of Research in Psychiatry and the Allied Sciences, 36*(11), 1515–1522.

Selekman, M. D. (1993). *Pathways to change: Brief therapy solutions with difficult adolescents*. New York, NY: Guilford Press.

Seligman, M. E. P. (1975). *Helplessness: On depression, development, and death*. San Francisco, CA: Freeman.

Selling, L. S. (1943). *Men against madness*. New York, NY: Garden City Books.

Selvini-Palazzoli, M., Boscolo, L., Cecchin, G., & Prata, G. (1974). The treatment of children through brief therapy of their parents. *Family Process, 13*, 429–442.

Serlin, I. (1999). An interview with Irvin Yalom. *Review of Existential Psychology and Psychiatry, 24*(1, 2, & 3), 142–146.

Sexton, T. L. (2011). *Functional family therapy in clinical practice: An evidence-based treatment model for working with troubled adolescents*. New York, NY: Routledge.

Sexton, T. L., Montgomery, D., Goff, K., & Nugent, W. (1993). Ethical, therapeutic, and legal considerations in the use of paradoxical techniques: The emerging debate. *Journal of Mental Health Counseling, 15*(3), 260–277.

Sexton, T., & Turner, C. W. (2010). The effectiveness of functional family therapy for youth with behavioral problems in a community practice setting. *Journal of Family Psychology, 24*(3), 339–348.

Shadish, W. R., & Baldwin, S. A. (2002). Meta-analysis of MFT interventions. In D. H. Sprenkle (Ed.), *Effectiveness research in marriage and family therapy* (pp. 339–370). Alexandria, VA: American Association for Marriage and Family Therapy.

Shadish, W. R., Ragsdale, K., Glaser, R. R., & Montgomery, L. M. (1995). The efficacy and effectiveness of marital and family therapy: A perspective from meta-analysis. *Journal of Marital and Family Therapy. Special Issue: The Effectiveness of Marital and Family Therapy, 21*(4), 345–360.

Shahar, B., Bar-Kalifa, E., & Alon, E. (2017). Emotion-focused therapy for social anxiety disorder: Results from a multiple-baseline study. *Journal of Consulting and Clinical Psychology, 85*(3), 238–249.

Shapiro, D. H. (1978). Instructions for a training package combining formal and informal Zen meditation with behavioral self-control strategies. *Psychologia: An International Journal of Psychology in the Orient, 21*(2), 70–76.

Shapiro, F. (1989). Eye movement desensitization: A new treatment for post-traumatic stress disorder. *Journal of Behavior Therapy and Experimental Psychiatry, 20*, 211–217.

Shapiro, F. (1995). *Eye movement desensitization and reprocessing: Basic principles, protocols, and procedures*. New York, NY: Guilford Press.

Shapiro, F. (1999). Eye movement desensitization and reprocessing (EMDR) and the anxiety disorders: Clinical and research implications of an integrated psychotherapy treatment. *Journal of Anxiety Disorders, 13*, 35–67.

Shapiro, F. (2001). *Eye movement desensitization and reprocessing: Basic principles, protocols, and procedures* (2nd ed.). New York, NY: Guilford Press.

Shapiro, F. (2002). EMDR treatment: Overview and integration. In F. Shapiro (Ed.), *EMDR as an integrative psychotherapy approach: Experts of diverse orientations explore the paradigm prism* (pp. 27–55). New York, NY: Guilford Press.

Shapiro, J. L. (2016). *Pragmatic existential counseling and psychotherapy*. Thousand Oaks, CA: Sage.

Sharaf, M. (1994). *Fury on earth: A biography of Wilhelm Reich*. New York, NY: Da Capo.

Shaw, B., & Beck, A. T. (1977). The treatment of depression with cognitive therapy. In A. Ellis & R. Grieger (Eds.), *Handbook of rational-emotive therapy* (pp. 309–326). New York, NY: Springer.

Shea, D. (2016). *Cognitive behavioral approaches for counselors*. Thousand Oaks, CA: Sage.

Shedler, J. (2010). The efficacy of psychodynamic psychotherapy. *American Psychologist, 65*(2), 98–109.

Shelley, C. A. (2009). Trans people and social justice. *The Journal of Individual Psychology, 65*(4), 386–396.

Sherman, K. C. (2000). CT/RT in chronic pain management: Using choice theory/reality therapy as a cognitive-behavioral intervention for chronic pain management: A pilot study. *International Journal of Reality Therapy, 19*(2), 10–14.

Shoham-Salomon, V., & Rosenthal, R. (1987). Paradoxical interventions: A meta-analysis. *Journal of Consulting and Clinical Psychology, 55*, 22–28.

Shulman, B. H. (1962). The family constellation in personality diagnosis. *Journal of Individual Psychology, 18*(1), 35–47.

Shulman, B. H. (1965). A comparison of Allport's and Adlerian concepts of life style. *Individual Psychology, 3*, 14–21.

Shulman, G. P., & Hope, D. A. (2016). Putting our multicultural training into practice: Assessing social anxiety disorder in sexual minorities. *The Behavior Therapist, 39*(8), 315–319.

Shure, M. B. (1992). *I can problem solve: An interpersonal cognitive problem-solving program.* Champaign, IL: Research Press.

Sicher, L. (1935). A case of manic-depressive insanity. *International Journal of Individual Psychology, 1*(1), 40–56.

Sicher, L. (1991). A declaration of interdependence. *Individual Psychology, 47*(1), 10–16.

Siegel, D. J. (2010). *The mindful therapist: A clinician's guide to mindsight and neural integration.* New York, NY: Norton.

Siegel, D. J. (2015). *The developing mind: How relationships and the brain interact to shape who we are.* New York, NY: Guilford Publications.

Siegel, D. J., & Bryson, T. P. (2015). *The whole-brain child workbook: Practical exercises, worksheets and activities to nurture developing minds.* Eau Claire, WI: PESI Publishing and Media.

Siegel, D. J., & Hartzell, M. (2003). *Parenting from the inside out.* New York, NY: Penguin.

Silverman, W. H. (1996). Cookbooks, manuals, and paint-by numbers: Psychotherapy in the 90's. *Psychotherapy, 33*, 207–215.

Simblett, G. J. (1997). Leila and the tiger: Narrative approaches to psychiatry. In G. Monk, J. Winslade, K. Crocket, & D. Epston (Eds.), *Narrative therapy in practice: The archaeology of hope* (pp. 121–157). San Francisco, CA: Jossey-Bass.

Simi, N. L., & Mahalik, J. R. (1997). Comparison of feminist versus psychoanalytic/dynamic and other therapists on self-disclosure. *Psychology of Women Quarterly, 21*(3), 465–483.

Singer, J. B., & Greeno, C. M. (2013). When Bambi meets Godzilla: A practitioner's experience adapting and implementing a manualized treatment in a community mental health setting. *Best Practices in Mental Health: An International Journal, 9*(1), 99–115.

Singh, A. A., & Dickey, L. M. (2017). *Affirmative counseling and psychological practice with transgender and gender nonconforming clients.* Washington, DC: American Psychological Association.

Skinner, B. F. (1938). *The behavior of organisms.* New York, NY: Appleton-Century-Crofts.

Skinner, B. F. (1948). *Walden two.* New York, NY: Macmillan.

Skinner, B. F. (1953). *Science and human behavior.* New York, NY: Macmillan.

Skinner, B. F. (1954). A new method for the experimental analysis of the behavior of psychotic patients. *Journal of Nervous and Mental Disease, 120*, 403–406.

Skinner, B. F. (1970). *Walden two* (Rev. ed.). London, England: Macmillan.

Skinner, B. F. (1971). *Beyond freedom and dignity.* New York, NY: Knopf.

Skinner, B. F. (1977). Why I am not a cognitive psychologist. *Behaviorism, 5*, 1–10.

Skinner, B. F., Solomon, H. C., & Lindsley, O. R. (1953). *Studies in behavior therapy: Status report I.* Unpublished report. Waltham, MA: Metropolitan State Hospital.

Sklare, G. B. (2014). *Brief counseling that works: A solution-focused approach for school counselors and administrators* (3rd ed.). Thousand Oaks, CA: Corwin Press.

Smith, B., Kenney, S. R., Sessoms, A. E., & Labrie, J. (2011). Assessing the efficacy of a choice theory-based alcohol harm reduction intervention on college students. *International Journal of Choice Theory and Reality Therapy, 30*(2), 52–60.

Smith, M. L., & Glass, G. V. (1977). Meta-analysis of psychotherapy outcome studies. *American Psychologist, 32*, 752–760.

Smith, M. L., Glass, G. V., & Miller, T. I. (1980). *The benefits of psychotherapy.* Baltimore, MD: Johns Hopkins University Press.

Smith, T. B., Constantine, M. G., Dunn, T. W., Dinehart, J. M., & Montoya, J. A. (2006). Multicultural education in the mental health professions: A meta-analytic review. *Journal of Counseling Psychology, 53*(1), 132–145.

Smith, T. B., Rodríguez, M. D., & Bernal, G. (2011). Culture. *Journal of Clinical Psychology, 67*(2), 166–175.

Smith-Acuña, S. (2011). *Systems theory in action: Applications to individual, couple, and family therapy.* Hoboken, NJ: Wiley.

Smuts, J. (1927). *Holism and evolution.* London: Macmillan.

Snow, M. G., Prochaska, J. O., & Rossi, J. S. (1992). Stages of change for smoking cessation among former problem drinkers. *Journal of Substance Abuse, 4*, 107–116.

Solomon, R. (1964). Punishment. *American Psychologist, 19*, 239–253.

Sommers-Flanagan, J. (2007). The development and evolution of person-centered expressive art therapy: A conversation with Natalie Rogers. *Journal of Counseling & Development, 85*(1), 120–125.

Sommers-Flanagan, J. (2015). Evidence-based relationship practice: Enhancing counselor competence. *Journal of Mental Health Counseling, 37*, 95–108.

Sommers-Flanagan, J., & Campbell, D. G. (2009). Psychotherapy and (or) medications for depression in youth? An evidence-based review with recommendations for treatment. *Journal of Contemporary Psychotherapy, 32*, 111–120.

Sommers-Flanagan, J., Hays, P., Gallardo, M., Poyrazli, S., Sue, D. W., & Sommers-Flanagan, R. (2009, August). In J. Sommers-Flanagan (Chair), *The initial interview: Essential principles and techniques with diverse clients.* Symposium chair at the annual meeting of the American Psychological Association, Toronto, Ontario.

Sommers-Flanagan, J., & Heck, N. (2012). Counseling skills: Building the pillars of professional counseling. In K. MacCluskie & D. Perera (Eds.), *The counselor educator's survival guide* (pp. 149–166). New York, NY: Routledge.

Sommers-Flanagan, J., Richardson, B. G., & Sommers-Flanagan, R. (2011). A multi-theoretical, evidence-based approach for understanding and managing adolescent resistance to psychotherapy. *Journal of Contemporary Psychotherapy, 41*(2), 69–80.

Sommers-Flanagan, J., & Sommers-Flanagan, R. (2001). The three-step emotional change trick. In H. G. Kaduson & C. E. Schaefer (Eds.), *101 more favorite play therapy techniques* (pp. 439–444). New York, NY: Jason Aronson.

Sommers-Flanagan, J., & Sommers-Flanagan, R. (Directors). (2004). *The challenge of counseling teens: Counselor behaviors that reduce resistance and facilitate connection.* [Video/DVD] North Amherst, MA: Microtraining Associates.

Sommers-Flanagan, J., & Sommers-Flanagan, R. (2007a). Our favorite tips for interviewing couples and families. *Psychiatric Clinics of North America, 30*(2), 275–281.

Sommers-Flanagan, J., & Sommers-Flanagan, R. (2007b). *Tough kids, cool counseling: User-friendly approaches with challenging youth* (2nd ed.). Alexandria, VA: American Counseling Association.

Sommers-Flanagan, J., & Sommers-Flanagan, R. (2011). *How to listen so parents will talk and talk so parents will listen.* Hoboken, NJ: Wiley.

Sommers-Flanagan, J., & Sommers-Flanagan, R. (2017). *Clinical interviewing* (6th ed.). Hoboken, NJ: Wiley.

Sommers-Flanagan, R. (2012). Boudaries, multiple roles, and the professional relationship. In S. M. Knapp (Ed.), *APA handbook of ethics in psychology.* Washington, DC: American Psychological Association.

Sommers-Flanagan, R., Elliott, D., & Sommers-Flanagan, J. (1998). Exploring the edges: Boundaries and breaks. *Ethics & Behavior, 8*(1), 37–48.

Sommers-Flanagan, R., & Sommers-Flanagan, J. (2007). *Becoming an ethical helping professional: Cultural and philosophical foundations.* Hoboken, NJ: Wiley.

Sommers-Flanagan, R., Sommers-Flanagan, J., & Welfel, E. R. (2009). The duty to protect and the ethical standards of professional organizations. In J. L. Werth, Jr., E. R. Welfel, & G. A. H. Benjamin (Eds.), *The duty to protect: Ethical, legal, and professional considerations for mental health professionals* (pp. 29–40). Washington, DC: American Psychological Association.

Spence, J. A. (2009). Changes in perception of family environment and self-reported symptom status in adolescents whose parents participate in an Adlerian parent-training intervention (ProQuest Information & Learning). Dissertation Abstracts International: Section B: The Sciences and Engineering, 69 (Electronic; Print).

Sperry, L., & Carlson, J. (2012). The global significance of individual psychology: An introduction and overview. *The Journal of Individual Psychology, 68*(3), 205–209.

Spiegler, M. D., & Guevremont, D. C. (2016). *Contemporary behavior therapy* (6th ed.). Boston, MA: Cengage.

Spivack, G., Platt, J. J., & Shure, M. B. (1976). *The problem-solving approach to adjustment.* San Francisco, CA: Jossey-Bass.

Stams, G. J., Deković, M., Buist, K., & de Vries, L. (2006). Effectiviteit van oplossingsgerichte korte therapie: Een meta-analyse. *Gedragstherapie, 39*(2), 81–94.

Stanton, M. D., & Shadish, W. R. (1997). Outcome, attrition, and family–couples treatment for drug abuse: A meta-analysis and review of the controlled, comparative studies. *Psychological Bulletin, 122*(2), 170–191.

Stark, E., & von der Haar, H. (1977). On the double-bind hypothesis in schizophrenia research. *Psychologische Rundschau, 28*(1), 31–44.

Stern, D. N. (1985). *The interpersonal world of the infant.* New York, NY: Basic Books.

Sternberg, R. J., Roediger, H. L., & Halpern, D. F. (Eds.). (2007). *Critical thinking in psychology.* New York, NY: Cambridge University Press.

Steuwe, C., Rullkötter, N., Ertl, V., Berg, M., Neuner, F., Beblo, T., & Driessen, M. (2016). Effectiveness and feasibility

of narrative exposure therapy (NET) in patients with borderline personality disorder and posttraumatic stress disorder—A pilot study. *BMC Psychiatry, 16*, 11.

Stevens, C., Stringfellow, J., Wakelin, K., & Waring, J. (2011). The UK gestalt psychotherapy CORE research project: The findings. *British Gestalt Journal, 20*, 22–27.

Stewart, S. H., & Watt, M. C. (2008). Introduction to the special issue on interoceptive exposure in the treatment of anxiety and related disorders: Novel applications and mechanisms of action. *Journal of Cognitive Psychotherapy, 22*(4), 291–302.

Stewart-Sicking, J. A. (2015). Cognitive therapy and the punctual self: Using an ascetical framework to critique approaches to psychotherapy. *Pastoral Psychology, 64*, 111–122.

Stiles, W. B., Barkham, M., Mellor-Clark, J., & Connell, J. (2008). Effectiveness of cognitive-behavioural, person-centred, and psychodynamic therapies in UK primary-care routine practice: Replication in a larger sample. *Psychological Medicine: A Journal of Research in Psychiatry and the Allied Sciences, 38*(5), 677–688.

Stoltz, K. B., Wolff, L. A., Monroe, A. E., Farris, H. R., & Mazahreh, L. G. (2013). Adlerian lifestyle, stress coping, and career adaptability: Relationships and dimensions. *The Career Development Quarterly, 61*(3), 194–209.

Story, T. J., & Craske, M. G. (2008). Responses to false physiological feedback in individuals with panic attacks and elevated anxiety sensitivity. *Behaviour Research and Therapy, 46*(9), 1001–1008.

Strang, S., Henoch, I., Danielson, E., Browall, M., & Melin-Johansson, C. (2014). Communication about existential issues with patients close to death—Nurses' reflections on content, process and meaning. *Psycho-Oncology, 23*(5), 562–568.

Strong, T., Pyle, N. R., & Sutherland, O. (2009). Scaling questions: Asking and answering them in counselling. *Counselling Psychology Quarterly, 22*(2), 171–185.

Strupp, H. H., & Binder, J. L. (1984). *Psychotherapy in a new key.* New York, NY: Basic Books.

Strupp, H. H., & Hadley, S. W. (1979). Specific vs nonspecific factors in psychotherapy: A controlled study of outcome. *Archives of General Psychiatry, 36*(10), 1125–1136.

Sturmey, P. (2009). Behavioral activation is an evidence-based treatment for depression. *Behavior Modification, 33*(6), 818–829.

Sue, D., & Sue, D. W. (2008). *Foundations of counseling and psychotherapy: Evidence-based practices for a diverse society.* Hoboken, NJ: Wiley.

Sue, D. W. (2010a). *Microaggressions in everyday life: Race, gender, and sexual orientation.* Hoboken, NJ: Wiley.

Sue, D. W. (2010b). *Microaggressions and marginality.* Hoboken, NJ: Wiley.

Sue, D. W. (2015). *Race talk and the conspiracy of silence: Understanding and facilitating difficult dialogues on race.* Hoboken, NJ: Wiley.

Sue, D. W., Arredondo, P., & McDavis, R. J. (1992). Multicultural counseling competencies and standards: A call to the profession. *Journal of Counseling & Development, 70*(4), 477–486.

Sue, D. W., Bernier, J. E., Durran, A., Feinberg, L., Pedersen, P., Smith, E. J., & Vasquez-Nuttall, E. (1982). Position paper: Cross-cultural counseling competencies. *The Counseling Psychologist, 10*, 45–52.

Sue, D. W., Bingham, R., Porche-Burke, L., & Vasquez, M. J. T. (1999). The diversification of psychology: A multicultural revolution. *American Psychologist, 54,* 1061–1069.

Sue, D. W., Carter, R. T., Casas, J. M., Fouad, N. A., Ivey, A. E., Jensen, M., et al. (1998). *Multicultural counseling competencies: Individual and organizational development.* Thousand Oaks, CA: Sage.

Sue, D. W., Rivera, D. P., Capodilupo, C. M., Lin, A. I., & Torino, G. C. (2010). Racial dialogues and white trainee fears: Implications for education and training. *Cultural Diversity and Ethnic Minority Psychology, 16*(2), 206–214.

Sue, D. W., & Sue, D. (2016). *Counseling the culturally diverse* (7th ed.). Hoboken, NJ: Wiley.

Sue, D. W., & Torino, G. C. (2005). *Racial-cultural competence: Awareness, knowledge, and skills.* Hoboken, NJ: Wiley.

Sue, S. (1977). Community mental health services to minority groups: Some optimism, some pessimism. *American Psychologist, 32,* 616–624.

Sue, S. (1998). In search of cultural competence in psychotherapy and counseling. *American Psychologist, 53*(4), 440–448.

Sue, S., Fujino, D., Takeuchi, D., & Zane, N. (1991). Community mental health services for ethnic minority groups: A test of the cultural responsiveness hypothesis. *Journal of Consulting & Clinical Psychology, 59,* 533–540.

Sue, S., & Zane, N. (2009). The role of culture and cultural techniques in psychotherapy: A critique and reformulation. *Asian American Journal of Psychology, S*(1), 3–14.

Suh, S., & Lee, M. (2006). Group work for Korean expatriate women in the United States: An exploratory study. *Journal for Specialists in Group Work, 31*(4), 353–369.

Sulliman, J. R. (1973). The development of a scale for the measurement of social interest (ProQuest Information & Learning). Dissertation Abstracts International, 34 (6-B) (Electronic; Print).

Sullivan, H. S. (1953). *The interpersonal theory of psychiatry.* New York, NY: Norton.

Sulloway, F. J., & Zweigenhaft, R. L. (2010). Birth order and risk taking in athletics: A meta-analysis and study of major league baseball. *Personality and Social Psychology Review, 14*(4), 402–416.

Swanson, N. M., Vaughan, A. L., & Wilkinson, B. D. (2017). First-year seminars: Supporting male college students' long-term academic success. *Journal of College Student Retention: Research, Theory and Practice, 18*(4), 386–400.

Sweeney, T. J. (2015). *Adlerian counseling and psychotherapy: A practitioner's approach* (5th ed.). New York, NY: Routledge/ Taylor & Francis.

Sweezy, M., & Ziskind, E. L. (2013). *Internal family systems therapy: New dimensions.* New York, NY: Routledge.

Swift, J. K., & Greenberg, R. P. (2015). *Premature termination in psychotherapy: Strategies for engaging clients and improving outcomes.* American Psychological Association, Washington, DC.

Szasz, T. S. (1970). *The manufacture of madness.* New York, NY: McGraw-Hill.

Takeuchi, D., Sue, S., & Yeh, M. (1995). Return rates and outcomes from ethnicity-specific mental health programs in Los Angeles. *American Journal of Public Health, 85,* 638–643.

Tantillo, M., & Sanftner, J. (2003). The relationship between perceived mutuality and bulimic symptoms, depression, and therapeutic change in group. *Eating Behaviors, 3,* 349–364.

Taylor, S., Thordarson, D. S., Maxfield, L., Fedoroff, I. C., Lovell, K., & Ogrodniczuk, J. (2003). Comparative efficacy, speed, and adverse effects of three PTSD treatments: Exposure therapy, EMDR, and relaxation training. *Journal of Consulting and Clinical Psychology, 71*(2), 330–338.

Taylor, S. E., & Gonzaga, G. C. (2007). Affiliative responses to stress: A social neuroscience model. In E. Harmon-Jones & P. Winkielman (Eds.), *Social neuroscience: Integrating biological and psychological explanations of social behavior* (pp. 454–473). New York, NY: Guilford Press.

Taylor, S. E., Klein, L. C., Lewis, B. P., Gruenewald, T. L., Gurung, R. A. R., & Updegraff, J. A. (2000). Biobehavioral responses to stress in females: Tend-and-befriend, not fight-or-flight. *Psychological Review, 107*(3), 411–429.

Taylor, S. E., & Master, S. L. (2011). *Social responses to stress: The tend-and-befriend model.* New York, NY: Springer.

Terman, L. (1916). *The measurement of intelligence.* Boston, MA: Houghton Mifflin.

Thomas, J. J. (1978). *The youniverse: Gestalt therapy, non-Western religions, and the present age.* Oxford, England: Psychology & Consulting.

Thomas, V., & Krum, T. (2015). Experiential approaches to family therapy. In J. L. Wetchler & L. L. Hecker (Eds.). *An introduction to marriage and family therapy* (2nd ed.) (pp. 229–258). New York, NY: Routledge.

Thompson, S. J., Bender, K., Cardoso, J. B., & Flynn, P. M. (2011). Experiential activities in family therapy: Perceptions of caregivers and youth. *Journal of Child and Family Studies, 20*(5), 560–568.

Thompson, S., Bender, K., Windsor, L. C., & Flynn, P. M. (2009). Keeping families engaged: The effects of home-based family therapy enhanced with experiential activities. *Social Work Research, 33*(2), 121–126.

Thorndike, E. L. (1932). *The fundamentals of learning.* New York, NY: Teachers College, Columbia University.

Thorne, B. (1990). Carl Rogers and the doctrine of original sin. *Person-Centered Review, 5*(4), 394–405.

Thorne, B. (1992). *Carl Rogers.* Thousand Oaks, CA: Sage.

Tiefer, L. (2012). The "new view" campaign: A feminist critique of sex therapy and an alternative vision. In P. J. Kleinplatz (Ed.), *New directions in sex therapy: Innovations and alternatives* (2nd ed.) (pp. 21–35). New York, NY: Routledge.

Tillich, P. (1961). Existentialism and psychotherapy. *Review of Existential Psychology & Psychiatry, 1,* 8–16.

Tjeltveit, A. C. (1999). *Ethics and values in psychotherapy.* New York, NY: Routledge.

Tjeltveit, A. C. (2006). To what ends? Psychotherapy goals and outcomes, the good life, and the principle of beneficence. *Psychotherapy: Theory, Research, 43*(2), 186–200.

Tohn, S. L., & Oshlag, J. A. (1996). Solution-focused therapy with mandated clients: Cooperating with the uncooperative. In M. F. Hoyt (Ed.), *Handbook of solution-focused brief therapy* (pp. 152–183). San Francisco, CA: Jossey-Bass.

Tolin, D. F. (2010). Is cognitive–behavioral therapy more effective than other therapies? A meta-analytic review. *Clinical Psychology Review, 30*(6), 710–720.

Tolstoy, L. (1929). *My confession, my religion, the gospel in brief.* New York, NY: Scribner.

Tønnesvang, J., Sommer, U., Hammink, J., & Sonne, M. (2010). Gestalt therapy and cognitive therapy—Contrasts or complementarities? *Psychotherapy: Theory, Research, Practice, Training, 47*(4), 586–602.

Touchette, E., Henegar, A., Godart, N. T., Pryor, L., Falissard, B., Tremblay, R. E., et al. (2011). Subclinical eating disorders and their comorbidity with mood and anxiety disorders in adolescent girls. *Psychiatry Research, 185*(1–2), 185–192.

Tregarthen, J. P., Lock, J., & Darcy, A. M. (2015). Development of a smartphone application for eating disorder self-monitoring. *International Journal of Eating Disorders, 48*(7), 972–982.

Trice-Black, S., & Foster, V. A. (2011). Sexuality of women with young children: A feminist model of mental health counseling. *Journal of Mental Health Counseling, 33*(2), 95–111.

Tryon, G. S., & Winograd, G. (2011). Goal consensus and collaboration. In J. C. Norcross (Ed.), *Psychotherapy relationships that work: Evidence-based responsiveness* (2nd ed.) (pp. 153–167). New York, NY: Oxford University Press.

Tummala-Narra, P. (2016). *Psychoanalytic theory and cultural competence in psychotherapy*. Washington, DC: American Psychological Association.

Turner, E. H., Matthews, A. M., Linardatos, E., Tell, R. A., & Rosenthal, R. (2008). Selective publication of antidepressant trials and its influence on apparent efficacy. *New England Journal of Medicine, 358*(3), 252–260.

Vaihinger, H. (1911). *The psychology of "as if."* New York, NY: Harcourt, Brace and World.

Valentine, S. E., Bankoff, S. M., Poulin, R. M., Reidler, E. B., & Pantalone, D. W. (2015). The use of dialectical behavior therapy skills training as stand-alone treatment: A systematic review of the treatment outcome literature. *Journal of Clinical Psychology, 71*(1), 1–20.

van den Bosch, L. M. C., Verheul, R., Schippers, G. M., & van den Brink, W. (2002). Dialectical behavior therapy of borderline patients with and without substance use problems: Implementation and long-term effects. *Addictive Behaviors. Special Issue: Integration Substance Abuse Treatment and Prevention in the Community, 27*(6), 911–923.

van der Kolk, B. A., Spinazzola, J., Blaustein, M. E., Hopper, J. W., Hopper, E. K., Korn, D. L., et al. (2007). A randomized clinical trial of eye movement desensitization and reprocessing (EMDR), fluoxetine, and pill placebo in the treatment of posttraumatic stress disorder: Treatment effects and long-term maintenance. *Journal of Clinical Psychiatry, 68*(1), 37–46.

van der Pompe, G., Duivenvoorden, H. J., Antoni, M. H., & Visser, A. (1997). Effectiveness of a short-term group psychotherapy program on endocrine and immune function in breast cancer patients: An exploratory study. *Journal of Psychosomatic Research, 42*(5), 453–466.

van Deurzen, E. (2010). *Everyday mysteries: A handbook of existential psychotherapy* (2nd ed.). New York, NY: Routledge/Taylor & Francis.

van Deurzen, E. (2014a). Becoming an existential therapist. *Existential Analysis, 25*(1), 6–16.

van Deurzen, E. (2014b). Structural existential analysis (SEA): A phenomenological research method for counselling psychology. *Counselling Psychology Review, 29*(2), 54–66.

van Deurzen, E. & Adams, M. (2016). *Skills in existential counselling and psychotherapy*. London, England: Sage.

van Deurzen-Smith, E. (1988). *Existential counselling in practice*. Thousand Oaks, CA: Sage Publications, Inc.

VanFleet, R., Sywulak, A. E., & Sniscak, C. C. (2010). Child-centered play therapy. New York, NY: Guilford.

Villares, E., Brigman, G., & Peluso, P. R. (2008). Ready to learn: An evidence-based individual psychology linked curriculum for prekindergarten through first grade. *The Journal of Individual Psychology, 64*(4), 403–415.

von Bertalanffy, L. (1950). An outline of general system theory. *British Journal for the Philosophy of Science, 1,* 134–165.

Vontress, C. E., & Epp, L. R. (2015). Existential cross-cultural counseling: The courage to be an existential counselor. In K. J. Schneider, J. F. Pierson, & J. F. T. Bugental (Eds.), *The handbook of humanistic psychology: Theory, research, and practice* (2nd ed.) (pp. 473–489). Thousand Oaks, CA: Sage.

Vontress, C. E., Johnson, J. A., & Epp, L. R. (1999). *Cross-cultural counseling: A casebook*. Alexandria, VA: American Counseling Association.

Vos, J., Craig, M., & Cooper, M. (2015). Existential therapies: A meta-analysis of their effects on psychological outcomes. *Journal of Consulting and Clinical Psychology, 83*(1), 115–128.

Vromans, L. P., & Schweitzer, R. D. (2011). Narrative therapy for adults with major depressive disorder: Improved symptom and interpersonal outcomes. *Psychotherapy Research, 21*(1), 4–15.

Vygotsky, L. (1962). *Thought and language*. New York, NY: Wiley.

Wachtel, P. L. (1977). *Psychoanalysis and behavior therapy: Toward an integration*. New York, NY: Basic Books.

Wachtel, P. L. (2008). *Relational theory and the practice of psychotherapy*. New York, NY: Guilford Press.

Wachtel, P. L. (2010). One-person and two-person conceptions of attachment and their implications for psychoanalytic thought. *The International Journal of Psychoanalysis, 91*(3), 561–581.

Wachtel, P. L. (2011). *Therapeutic communication, knowing what to say when* (2nd ed.). New York, NY: Guilford Press.

Wagner-Moore, L. E. (2004). Gestalt therapy: Past, present, theory, and research. *Psychotherapy: Theory, Research, 41*(2), 180–189.

Wakefield, J. C. (2008). Is behaviorism becoming a pseudoscience?: Replies to Drs. Wyatt, Midkiff and Wong. *Behavior and Social Issues, 16*(2), 170–189.

Wallen, R. (1970). Gestalt therapy and Gestalt psychology. In J. Fagan & I. L. Shepherd (Eds.), *What is gestalt therapy?* (pp. 1–10). New York, NY: Science and Behavior Books.

Walsh, F. (2009). *Spiritual resources in family therapy* (2nd ed.). New York, NY: Guilford.

Wampold, B. E. (2001). *The great psychotherapy debate: Models, methods, and findings*. Mahwah, NJ: Lawrence Erlbaum Associates.

Wampold, B. E. (2008). Existential-integrative psychotherapy: Coming of age. *PsycCRITIQUES, 53*(6), no pagination.

Wampold, B. E. (2010). *The basics of psychotherapy: An introduction to theory and practice*. Washington, DC: American Psychological Association.

Wampold, B. E., & Imel, Z. E. (2015). *The great psychotherapy debate: The evidence for what makes psychotherapy work* (2nd ed.). New York, NY: Routledge/Taylor & Francis Group.

Wampold, B. E., Mondin, G. W., Moody, M., Stich, F., Benson, K., & Ahn, H. (1997). A meta-analysis of outcome studies comparing bona fide psychotherapies: Empiricially, "all must have prizes." *Psychological Bulletin, 122*(3), 203–215.

Warrington, J. (Ed.). (1956). *Aristotle's metaphysics*. New York, NY: Dutton.

Watkins, C. E. (2012). Race/ethnicity in short-term and long-term psychodynamic psychotherapy treatment research: How "White" are the data? *Psychoanalytic Psychology, 29*(3), 292–307.

Watson, J. B. (1913). Psychology as a behaviorist views it. *Psychological Review, 20,* 158–177.

Watson, J. B. (1924). *Behaviorism*. Chicago, IL: University of Chicago Press.

Watson, J. B., & Rayner, R. (1920). Conditioned emotional reactions. *Journal of Experimental Psychology, 3,* 1–14.

Watson, J. C., Goldman, R. N., & Greenberg, L. S. (2007). *Case studies in emotion-focused treatment of depression: A comparison of good and poor outcome*. Washington, DC: American Psychological Association.

Watson, J. C., Gordon, L. B., Stermac, L., Kalogerakos, F., & Steckley, P. (2003). Comparing the effectiveness of process-experiential with cognitive-behavioral psychotherapy in the treatment of depression. *Journal of Consulting and Clinical Psychology, 71*(4), 773–781.

Watson, J. C., McMullen, E. J., Prosser, M. C., & Bedard, D. L. (2011). An examination of the relationships among clients' affect regulation, in-session emotional processing, the working alliance, and outcome. *Psychotherapy Research, 21*(1), 86–96.

Watson, J. C., Steckley, P. L., & McMullen, E. J. (2014). The role of empathy in promoting change. *Psychotherapy Research, 24,* 286–298.

Watts, R. E. (Ed.). (2003). *Adlerian, cognitive, and constructivist therapies: An integrative perspective*. New York, NY: Springer.

Watts, R. E. (2012). On the origin of the striving for superiority and of social interest. In J. Carlson & M. P. Maniacci (Eds.), *Alfred Adler revisited* (pp. 41–56). New York, NY: Routledge/Taylor & Francis Group.

Watts, R. E. (2013a, April). Reflecting as if. *Counseling Today, 55*(10), 48–53.

Watts, R. E. (2013b). Adlerian counseling. In B. J. Irby, G. Brown, R. Lara-Alecio, & S. Jackson (Eds.), *The handbook of educational theories* (pp. 459–472). Charlotte, NC: IAP Information Age.

Watts, R. E., & Eckstein, D. (2009). Individual psychology. In American Counseling Association (Ed.), *The ACA encyclopedia of counseling* (pp. 281–283). Alexandria, VA: American Counseling Association.

Watts, R. E., & Garza, Y. (2008). Using children's drawings to facilitate the acting "as if" technique. *The Journal of Individual Psychology, 64*(1), 113–118.

Watts, R. E., & Holden, J. M. (1994). Why continue to use "fictional finalism?" *Individual Psychology: Journal of Adlerian Theory, Research & Practice, 50*(2), 161–163.

Watts, R. E., & Peluso, P. R. (2005). Imaginary team members: A couples counseling perspective. *The Family Journal, 13*(3), 332–335.

Watts, R. E., Peluso, P. R., & Lewis, T. F. (2005). Psychological strategies. *The Journal of Individual Psychology, 61,* 380–387.

Watts, R. E., & Pietrzak, D. (2000). Adlerian "encouragement" and the therapeutic process of solution-focused brief therapy. *Journal of Counseling & Development, 78,* 442–447.

Watzlawick, P., Beavin, J. H., & Jackson, D. D. (1967). *Pragmatics of human communication*. New York, NY: Norton.

Weakland, J. (1962). Family therapy as a research arena. *Family Process, 1*(1), 63–68.

Weakland, J. H. (1993). Conversation—but what kind? In S. G. Gilligan & R. Price (Eds.), *Therapeutic conversations* (pp. 136–145). New York, NY: Norton.

Webb, L., Lemberger, M., & Brigman, G. (2008). Student success skills: A review of a school counselor intervention influenced by individual psychology. *The Journal of Individual Psychology, 64,* 339–352.

Weber, M., Colon, M., & Nelson, M. (2008). Pilot study of a cognitive-behavioral group intervention to prevent further weight gain in Hispanic individuals with schizophrenia. *Journal of the American Psychiatric Nurses Association, 13*(6), 353–359.

Weiner-Davis, M. (1993). Pro-constructed realities. In S. G. Gilligan & R. Price (Eds.), *Therapeutic conversations* (pp. 149–157). New York, NY: Norton.

Weishaar, M. E. (1993). *Aaron T. Beck*. London, England: Sage.

Weissman, M. M., Markowitz, J. C., & Klerman, G. L. (2000). *Comprehensive guide to interpersonal psychotherapy*. New York, NY: Basic Books.

Welfel, E. R. (2016). *Ethics in counseling and psychotherapy: Standards, research, and emerging issues* (6th ed.). Boston. MA: Cengage.

Wheeler, G. (2005). Culture, self, and field: A Gestalt guide to the age of complexity. *Gestalt Review, 9*(1), 91–128.

Wheeler, G. (2006). New directions in Gestalt theory and practice: Psychology and psychotherapy in the age of complexity. *International Gestalt Journal, 29*(1), 9–41.

Wheeler, G., & Axelsson, L. (2015). *Gestalt therapy*. Washington, D. C.: American Psychological Association.

Wheeler, M. S., Kern, R. M., & Curlette, W. L. (1991). Lifestyle can be measured. *Individual Psychology: Journal of Adlerian Theory, Research & Practice, 47*(2), 229–240.

Whitaker, C. A. (1958). Psychotherapy with couples. *American Journal of Psychotherapy, 12,* 18–23.

Whitaker, C. S., & Malone, T. P. (1981). *The roots of psychotherapy*. New York, NY: Brunner/Mazel.

Whitaker, R. (2010). *Anatomy of an epidemic: Magic bullets, psychiatric drugs, and the astonishing rise of mental illness in America*. New York, NY: Crown Publishers/Random House.

White, L. (1994). *Stranger at the gate*. New York, NY: Simon & Schuster.

White, M. (1988). The process of questioning: A therapy of literary merit? *Dulwich Centre Newsletter,* 8–14.

White, M. (1993). Commentary: The histories of the present. In S. G. Gilligan & R. Price (Eds.), *Therapeutic conversations* (pp. 121–135). New York, NY: Norton.

White, M. (1995). *Re-authoring lives: Interviews and essays*. Adelaide, South Australia: Dulwich Centre.

White, M. (2007). *Maps of narrative practice*. New York, NY: Norton.

White, M., & Denborough, D. (2011). *Narrative practice: Continuing the conversations*. New York, NY: Norton.

White, M., & Epston, D. (1990). *Narrative means to therapeutic ends*. New York, NY: Norton.

Whitehouse, D. (1984). Adlerian antecedents to reality therapy and control theory. *Journal of Reality Therapy, 3,* 10–14.

Wickman, S. A., & Campbell, C. (2003). An analysis of how Carl Rogers enacted client-centered conversation with Gloria. *Journal of Counseling & Development, 81*, 178–184.

Wiener, N. (1948). Cybernetics. *Scientific American, 170*(5), 14–18.

Wilcocks, R. (1994). *Maelzel's chess player: Sigmund Freud and the rhetoric of deceit.* Lanham, MD, England: Rowman & Littlefield.

Williams, A. M., Diehl, N. S., & Mahoney, M. J. (2002). Mirrortime: Empirical findings and implications for a constructivist psychotherapeutic technique. *Journal of Constructivist Psychology, 15*(1), 21–39.

Williams, J. C., & Jovanovic, J. (2015). Third wave feminism and emerging adult sexuality: Friends with benefits relationships. *Sexuality & Culture: An Interdisciplinary Quarterly, 19*(1), 157–171.

Wilson, E. O. (1999). *Conscilience.* New York, NY: Random House.

Winnicott, D. W. (1965). *The maturational process and the facilitative environment.* New York, NY: International Universities Press.

Winnicott, D. W. (1975). *Through paediatrics to psycho-analysis: Collected papers.* Philadelphia, PA: Brunner/Mazel.

Winslade, J. M., & Monk, G. D. (2007). *Narrative counseling in schools: Powerful & brief* (2nd ed.). Thousand Oaks, CA: Corwin Press.

Wittgenstein, L. (1968). *Philosophical investigations* (3rd ed.). New York, NY: Macmillan.

Wolitzky, D. L., & Eagle, M. N. (1997). Psychoanalytic theories of psychotherapy. In P. L. Wachtel & S. B. Messer (Eds.), *Theories of psychotherapy: Origins and evolution* (pp. 39–96). Washington, DC: American Psychological Association.

Wolpe, J. (1948). *An approach to the problem of neurosis based on the conditioned response.* University of the Witwatersrand.

Wolpe, J. (1954). Reciprocal inhibition as the main basis of psychotherapeutic effects. *Proceedings of the South African Psychological Association, 5*, 14.

Wolpe, J. (1958). *Psychotherapy by reciprocal inhibition.* Stanford, CA: Stanford University Press.

Wolpe, J. (1973). *The practice of behavior therapy* (2nd ed.). Elmsford, NY: Pergamon.

Wolpe, J. (1987). The promotion of scientific psychotherapy: A long voyage. In J. K. Zeig (Ed.), *The evolution of psychotherapy* (pp. 133–148). New York, NY: Brunner/Mazel.

Wolpe, J., & Plaud, J. J. (1997). Pavlov's contributions to behavior therapy: The obvious and the not so obvious. *American Psychologist, 52*(9), 966–972.

Wong, P. T. P. (2008a). Meaning management theory and death acceptance. In A. Tomer, G. T. Eliason, & P. T. P. Wong (Eds.), *Death attitudes: Existential & spiritual issues* (pp. 65–87). Mahwah, NJ: Lawrence Erlbaum.

Wong, P. T. P. (2008b). Transformation of grief through meaning: Meaning-centered counseling for bereavement. In A. Tomer, G. T. Eliason, & P. T. P. Wong (Eds.), *Death attitudes: Existential & spiritual issues* (pp. 375–396). Mahwah, NJ: Erlbaum.

Wong, P. T. P. (2015). Meaning therapy: Assessments and interventions. *Existential Analysis, 26*(1), 154–167.

Wong, P. T. P. (2017). Meaning-centered approach to research and therapy, second wave positive psychology, and the future of humanistic psychology. *The Humanistic Psychologist, 45*, 207–216.

Wood, J. M., Lilienfeld, S. O., Nezworski, M. T., Garb, H. N., Allen, K. H., & Wildermuth, J. L. (2010). Validity of Rorschach inkblot scores for discriminating psychopaths from nonpsychopaths in forensic populations: A meta-analysis. *Psychological Assessment, 22*(2), 336–349.

Wood, J. M., Nezworski, M. T., Lilienfeld, S. O., & Garb, H. N. (2008). *The Rorschach inkblot test, fortune tellers, and cold reading.* Amherst, NY: Prometheus Books.

Woodside, M., Oberman, A. H., Cole, K. G., & Carruth, E. K. (2007). Learning to be a counselor: A prepracticum point of view. *Counselor Education and Supervision, 47*(1), 14–28.

Worell, J., & Chandler, R. (1996). Personal progress scale. Unpublished manuscript.

Worell, J., Chandler, R., & Robinson, D. (1996). Client therapy with women scale. Unpublished manuscript.

Worell, J., & Johnson, D. (2003). Therapy with women: Feminist frameworks. In R. K. Unger (Ed.), *Handbook of the psychology of women and gender* (pp. 317–329). Hoboken, NJ: Wiley.

Worell, J., & Remer, P. (2003). *Feminist perspectives in therapy: Empowering diverse women* (2nd ed.). Hoboken, NJ: Wiley.

World Health Organization. (1992). *International statistical classification of diseases and related health problems*, 10th Revision (ICD-10). Geneva: Author.

Worthington, E. L., Jr., Hook, J. N., Davis, D. E., & McDaniel, M. A. (2011). Religion and spirituality. *Journal of Clinical Psychology, 67*(2), 204–214.

Wozniak, R. H. (Ed.). (1993). *Theoretical roots of early behaviourism: Functionalism, the critique of introspection, and the nature and evolution of consciousness.* London, England: Routledge/Thoemmes Press; Tokyo 156, Japan: Kinokuniya Co.

Wright, L. K. (2002). Book review: Letters to a young feminist. *Women & Therapy, 25*(1), 113–115.

Wubbolding, R. E. (1988). *Using reality therapy.* New York, NY: Harper & Row.

Wubbolding, R. E. (1991). *Understanding reality therapy.* New York: Harper & Row.

Wubbolding, R. E. (1999). Client inner self-evaluation: A necessary prelude to change. In H. G. Rosenthal (Ed.), *Favorite counseling and therapy techniques* (pp. 196–197). Washington, DC: Accelerated Development.

Wubbolding, R. E. (2000). *Reality therapy for the 21st century.* Muncie, IN: Accelerated Development.

Wubbolding, R. E. (2011). *Reality therapy.* Washington, DC: American Psychological Association.

Wubbolding, R. E. (2016a). Reality therapy. In H. E. A. Tinsley, S. H. Lease, & N. S. G. Wiersma (Eds.), *Contemporary therapy and practice in counseling and psychotherapy* (pp. 173–200). Thousand Oaks, CA: Sage.

Wubbolding, R. E. (2016b). Reality therapy/choice theory. In D. Capuzzi & M. D. Stauffer (Eds.), *Counseling and psychotherapy: Theories and interventions* (6th ed.) (pp. 311–338). Alexandria, VA: American Counseling Association.

Wubbolding, R. E. (2017). *Reality therapy and self-evaluation: The key to client change.* Alexandria, VA: American Counseling Association.

Wubbolding, R. E., Al-Rashidi, B., Brickell, J., Kakitani, M., Kim, R. I., Lennon, B., et al. (1998). Multicultural awareness: Implications for reality therapy and choice theory. *International Journal of Reality Therapy, 17*, 4–6.

Wubbolding, R. E., & Brickell, J. (2000). Misconceptions about reality therapy. *International Journal of Reality Therapy, 19*(2), 64–65.

Wubbolding, R. E., & Brickell, J. (2017). *Counselling with reality therapy* (2nd ed.). New York, NY: Routledge.

Wubbolding, R. E., Brickell, J., Burdenski, T., & Robey, P. (2012). Implementing one caring habit: Listening with reality therapy procedures, Part I. *International Journal of Reality Therapy, 32*, 22–26.

Wubbolding, R. E., Brickell, J., Imhof, L., Kim, R. I., Lojk, L., & Al-Rashidi, B. (2004). Reality therapy: A global perspective. *International Journal for the Advancement of Counselling, 26*(3), 219–228.

Wubbolding, R. E., Brickell, J., Loi, I., & Al-Rashidi, B. (2001). The why and how of self-evaluation. *International Journal of Reality Therapy, 21*, 36–37.

Wulfing, N. (2008). Anxiety in existential philosophy and the question of the paradox. *Existential Analysis, 19*(1), 73–80.

Yaholkoski, A., Hurl, K., & Theule, J. (2016). Efficacy of the circle of security intervention: A meta-analysis. *Journal of Infant, Child & Adolescent Psychotherapy, 15*(2), 95–103.

Yakovenko, I., Quigley, L., Hemmelgarn, B. R., Hodgins, D. C., & Ronksley, P. (2015). The efficacy of motivational interviewing for disordered gambling: Systematic review and meta-analysis. *Addictive Behaviors, 43*, 72–82.

Yakushko, O., & Espín, O. M. (2010). *The experience of immigrant and refugee women: Psychological issues*. New York, NY: Springer.

Yalom, I. D. (1980). *Existential psychotherapy*. New York, NY: Basic Books.

Yalom, I. D. (1989). *Love's executioner*. New York, NY: Basic Books.

Yalom, I. D. (1992). *When Nietzsche wept*. New York, NY: HarperCollins.

Yalom, I. D. (1995). *Theory and practice of group psychotherapy*. New York, NY: Basic Books.

Yalom, I. D. (1999). *Momma and the meaning of life: Tales of psychotherapy*. New York, NY: Basic Books.

Yalom, I. D. (2002). *The gift of therapy*. New York, NY: HarperCollins.

Yalom, I. D. (2003). Existential psychotherapy and religious consolation: A short comment. *Tidsskrift for Norsk Psykologforening, 40*(11), 936–936.

Yalom, I. D. (2008). *Staring at the sun*. San Francisco, CA: Jossey-Bass.

Yalom, I. D., & Leszcz, M. (2005). *The theory and practice of group psychotherapy* (5th ed.). New York, NY: Basic Books.

Yektatalab, S., Oskouee, F. S., & Sodani, M. (2017). Efficacy of Bowen theory on marital conflict in the family nursing practice: A randomized controlled trial. *Issues in Mental Health Nursing, 38*(3), 253–260.

Yontef, G. (1988). Assimilating diagnostic and psychoanalytic perspectives into gestalt therapy. *Gestalt Journal, 11*(1), 5–32.

Yontef, G. (2002). The relational attitude in Gestalt therapy theory and practice. *International Gestalt Journal, 25*, 15–35.

Yontef, G. (2005). The relational attitude in Gestalt therapy theory and practice. *Gestalt!, 9*(2).

Yontef, G. (2010). "From the radical center: The heart of Gestalt therapy" Erving and Miriam Polster, person and process. *Gestalt Review, 14*(1), 29–36.

Young, J. F., Mufson, L., & Gallop, R. (2010). Preventing depression: A randomized trial of interpersonal psychotherapy-adolescent skills training. *Depression and Anxiety, 27*(5), 426–433.

Young, K. M., Northern, J. J., Lister, K. M., Drummond, J. A., & O'Brien, W. H. (2007). A meta-analysis of family-behavioral weight-loss treatments for children. *Clinical Psychology Review, 27*(2), 240–249.

Yousefi, N., Etemadi, O., Bahrami, F., Fatehizadeh, M. A., Ahmadi, S. A., Mavarani, A. A., et al. (2009). Efficacy of logo therapy and gestalt therapy in treating anxiety, depression and aggression. *Journal of Iranian Psychologists, 5*(19), 251–259.

Zand, D. H. (2004). Psychoanalytic psychotherapy with lesbians: Has the lavender couch been reconstructed? *Psychology of Women Quarterly, 28*(4), 443.

Zang, Y., Hunt, N., & Cox, T. (2013). A randomised controlled pilot study: The effectiveness of narrative exposure therapy with adult survivors of the Sichuan earthquake. *BMC Psychiatry, 13*, 11.

Zetzel, E. R. (1956). Current concepts of transference. *International Journal of Psychoanalysis, 37*, 369–376.

Zimmer, C. (2016, April 12). Educated guesses: In science, it's never just a theory. *New York Times*, p. D6.

Zwolinski, J. (2008). Biopsychosocial responses to social rejection in targets of relational aggression. *Biological Psychology, 79*(2), 260–267.

Name Index

Abbass, A., 52
Acheson, D. T., 183
Acierno, R., 180
Ackerman, N., 312–313
Adams, M., 89, 90, 98, 99, 100, 101, 102
Adams, N. E., 204
Adegoke, A. A., 250
Adler, A., 25, 35, 36, 38, 39, 55, 59–87, 91, 92,
    101–102, 103–104, 113, 114, 201, 230,
    233, 312, 313, 368, 389, 390
Adler, R. E., 60, 61, 259, 281, 389, 390, 391
Afifi, T. O., 179
Agaskar, V. R., 17
Agishtein, P., 195
Agras, W. S., 183
Agren, T., 182
Ahbel-Rappe, K., 31
Ahmad, Z., 251
Ainsworth, M. D., 38, 40, 41, 50, 374
Alberti, R. E., 173, 184
Alcón Belchi, C., 280
Alegria, S., 109
Aleksandrov, D. S., 85, 86
Alessi, E., 194
Alexander, F., 37, 38, 369
Alexander, J. F., 329, 335
Alexander, S., 299
Alghamdi, M., 306
Ali, A., 269
Ali, S., 307
Alizadeh, H., 62
Allard, T., 21
Allen, B., 373
Allen, J., 199
Allport, G., 117
Alm, T., 182
Almansa Martínez, P., 280
Almond, R., 108
Alon, E., 381
Amendt-Lyon, N., 164
American Counseling Association, 13–14,
    15, 363
American Psychiatric Association, 341, 343
American Psychological Association, 15, 222,
    344, 349, 363
Amini, F., 41
An, W., 386
Andersen, L. F., 175, 300
Anderson, C. M., 317

Anderson, C. N., 263
Anderson, E. M., 52
Anderson, H., 288
Andersson, G., 225
Anestis, J. C., 53
Anestis, M. D., 53
Angel, E., 92
Angus, L. E., 163, 380
Ansbacher, H. L., 61, 63, 64, 66, 68
Ansbacher, R. R., 61, 63, 64, 66, 68
Antonccio, D., 180
Antoni, M. H., 109
Antony, M. M., 183
Arczynski, A. V., 280
Armento, M. E. A., 185
Armfield, J. M, 182
Arnold, R., 381
Arnow, B., 183
Arredondo, P., 343, 344, 348, 353
Arzi, A., 179
Asay, T. P., 9
Askari, S. F., 270
Asmundson, C. J. G., 225
Astrup, H., 175
A-Tjak, J., 386
Atkinson, C., 130, 131
Atkinson, D. R., 137, 194, 352
Attanucci, J., 264
Austin, A., 194
Avicenna, 5
Avis, J. M., 335
Axelson, S. J., 270, 352
Axelsson, L., 163
Azekhueme, K. U., 250

Baca, L., 342
Bacanu, S., 21
Bachelor, A., 49, 123
Bachman, J. G., 136
Badenoch, B., 50
Baer, B. A., 136
Baker, M. J., 12
Baker, T. B., 6, 11
Bakewell, S., 93
Baldwin, L. M., 334
Baldwin, S. A., 334
Balint, E., 38, 40
Balint, M., 38
Ball, T., 21–22

Ballou, M. B., 250, 268
Bance, L. O., 4
Bandura, A., 83, 203, 204, 205
Bañez, L., 300
Bankart, C. P., 4, 26, 30, 31, 60–61, 114, 117,
    155, 168
Bankoff, S. M., 383
Banmen, J., 327
Barber, J. P., 49
Barbrack, C. R., 170
Barclay, S. R., 64
Barelds, D. P. H., 83
Bar-Kalifa, E., 381
Barkham, M., 137
Barlow, D. H., 183
Barlow, H., 12, 190
Barnes-Holmes, D., 385
Barnett, J. E., 14
Baron-Cohen, S., 272
Barrett, S. E., 258
Barrett-Lennard, G. T., 120
Bass, A., 29, 40
Bateson, G., 286, 308, 313, 314
Batista, J., 306
Battista, J., 108
Baumeister, R. F., 66
Baumgardner, P., 156, 159
Bean, O., 142
Beauchamp, T. L., 16
Beauvoir, S. D., 264
Beavin, J. H., 286
Beck, A. T., 49, 59, 102, 136, 180, 185,
    200, 201, 202–203, 206–207, 208,
    209, 211, 214, 215, 218, 226,
    368, 390
Beck, H. P., 169
Beck, J. S., 200–201, 212–213, 215, 369
Beckstead, D. J., 383
Bedard, D. L., 163
Belangee, S., 86
Bell, A. C., 184
Bell, L., 17
Bell, S. M., 40
Bender, K., 327, 334
Benedetti, R., 54
Benishek, L. A., 191
Benjamin, A., 377
Benson, H., 180
Berg, I. K., 287, 292, 297, 299, 389, 390

Counseling and Psychotherapy Theories in Context and Practice: Skills, Strategies, and Techniques, Third Edition. John Sommers-Flanagan
and Rita Sommers-Flanagan. © 2018 John Wiley & Sons, Inc. Published 2018 by John Wiley & Sons, Inc.
Companion website: www.wiley.com/go/sommers-flanagan/theories3e

Subject Index